THE
GLADSTONE
DIARIES

Gladstone aged seventy-three, photographed by Bassano on 10 March 1883

THE
GLADSTONE
DIARIES

WITH
CABINET MINUTES
AND
PRIME-MINISTERIAL
CORRESPONDENCE

VOLUME X
JANUARY 1881–JUNE 1883

Edited by
H. C. G. MATTHEW

CLARENDON PRESS · OXFORD
1990

Oxford University Press, Walton Street, Oxford OX2 6DP

Oxford New York Toronto
Delhi Bombay Calcutta Madras Karachi
Petaling Jaya Singapore Hong Kong Tokyo
Nairobi Dar es Salaam Cape Town
Melbourne Auckland

and associated companies in
Berlin Ibadan

Oxford is a trade mark of Oxford University Press

Published in the United States
by Oxford University Press, New York

British Library Cataloguing in Publication Data
Gladstone, W. E. (William Ewart, 1809–1898)
The Gladstone diaries: with Cabinet minutes and
prime-ministerial correspondence.
Vol. 10: January 1881–June 1883
1. Great Britain. Gladstone, W. E. (William Ewart)
1809–1898
I. Title   II. Matthew, H. C. G. (Henry Colin Gray)
941.081' 092' 4
ISBN 0–19–821137–6

Library of Congress Cataloging-in-Publication Data
(Revised for vol. 10–11)
Gladstone, W. E. (William Ewart), 1809–1898.
The Gladstone diaries.
Vols.   edited by H. C. G. Matthew.
Contents: v. 1. 1825–1832—[etc.]—
v. 10. January 1881–June 1883.—v. 11. July 1883–
December 1886.
1. Gladstone, W. E. (William Ewart), 1809–1898—
Diaries. 2. Prime ministers—Great Britain—Diaries.
3. Great Britain—Politics and government—1837–1901.
I. Foot, M. R. D. (Michael Richard Daniel), 1919–
II. Matthew, H. C. G. (Henry Colin Gray) III. Title.
DA 563.A34   942.081' 092 [B]   68–59613
ISBN 0 19 821137 6

Typeset by Joshua Associates Limited, Oxford
Printed and bound in
Great Britain by Biddles Ltd
Guildford and King's Lynn

PREFACE

Volumes X and XI of Gladstone's diaries continue the pattern established since 1868, that is, in addition to the complete publication of the daily diary text, all of the relevant Cabinet Minutes have been included, together with an extensive selection of Prime-Ministerial correspondence (over 1,400 letters in these two volumes).

Her Majesty the Queen is gratefully to be thanked for permission to include material from the Royal Archives, as is the Archbishop of Canterbury, the owner of the diaries, for permission to publish them. Sir William Gladstone has given permission to publish material written by his great-grandfather and found in the British Library, St. Deiniol's Library, Hawarden, and in many other collections; he is to be thanked for this and for his generous help, in a variety of ways, to the editor and the edition. The editor is also grateful to the following for permission to publish papers in their possession: the Earl of Derby, the Duke of Devonshire, the late Lord Harcourt, the Earl and Countess of Rosebery, Mrs. Maxwell Scott, Mr. A. F. Thompson, the Trustees of Duke University, of Imperial College, London, of the Borthwick Institute, of the Tennyson Research Centre, and the Dean and Governing Body of Christ Church, Oxford.

The following have generously given permission for their illustrations to be reproduced in these volumes: Professor Dudley W. R. Bahlman, Mr. Robin Compton, the Earl of Elgin, Mr. Richard Green, Dr. Agatha Ramm, Bassano and Vandyck of London, the Trustees of the National Portrait Gallery, the Clwyd Record Office, the Gernsheim Collection at the Harry Ransome Humanities Research Center in the University of Texas at Austin, the Dean and Governing Body of Christ Church, Oxford.

The editor continues to be much indebted for support to the *ad hoc* committee which superintends the publication of this edition. Lord Blake continues to be its chairman; its present members are Mr. E. G. W. Bill, Lord Bullock, Dr. J. F. A. Mason, Mr. W. E. S. Thomas, Mr. A. F. Thompson, Dr. J. R. C. Wright, with Dr. I. Asquith of the Oxford University Press as its secretary and Dr. F. Dinshaw of St. Catherine's College (the edition's academic sponsor) as its treasurer.

The research for this volume has been financed by the Archbishop of Canterbury, by the Gladstone Memorial Trust, by Dr. Anthony Henfrey and especially by two Oxford-based trusts: the Rhodes Trust has provided the bulk of the funds needed for research and the Radcliffe Trust, of which Gladstone was chairman for almost thirty years and whose meetings he still occasionally attended in the years of these volumes (see 1 Aug. 83), has enabled the editor to be relieved from his tutorial duties for two years. The Governing Body of St. Hugh's College, Oxford, gave permission to the editor to hold the Radcliffe Fellowship and Dr. John Robertson of St. Hugh's College has most generously made this relief of duties effective.

Christ Church, Gladstone's own college in the University of Oxford, continues to give essential support by accommodating the editor and the research materials of the edition and by renewing the editor in his post of Lecturer in Gladstone Studies.

Two people have been central to the preparation of these two volumes. Mrs. Francis Phillips has continued uncomplainingly to bear the chief burden of bibliographical research—made increasingly perplexing by Gladstone's declining legibility—and of the typing of the notes. Mrs. Jean Gilliland has tirelessly pursued random and awkward queries, transcribed letters in the British Library and by her precision relieved the editor of many time-consuming chores. His thanks goes to both of these for their high standards, commitment, and good cheer.

Many others have assisted in various aspects of the editing of these volumes. Mrs. Fiona Griffiths and Miss Laura Marsland have helped with accurate and astute typing and transcription. Mr. Paul Chilcott assisted with transcription in Liverpool. Dr. John Mason and Mr. Richard Hamer (successively the Librarians at Christ Church), Mr. John Wing (Assistant Librarian there), Mr. Geoffrey Bill of Lambeth Palace Library, and their respective staffs, have all been most helpful. Mr. Christopher Williams of the Clwyd Record Office at Hawarden (which catalogues and produces the Gladstone family papers deposited next door at St. Deiniol's Library) continues to be a major prop of the edition, his extensive knowledge of Gladstone family matters neatly solving many a query. Dr. Allen Warren has kindly read the proofs of the text and notes of these volumes, discreetly spotting several howlers.

Thanks are also due to the staffs of the Bodleian Library, Oxford, the Public Record Office, the National Library of Scotland, the Public Record Office of Northern Ireland, Birmingham University Library, Somerset Record Office, and the Royal Archives where Miss E. Cuthbert has been particularly helpful.

Preparation of the text of the daily diary has continued to use as its starting point Professor H. W. Lawton's transcript (punctuated in places by Professor M. R. D. Foot's helpful marginalia). Professor Lawton's knowledge of French and German meant that his transcription of foreign names and titles is particularly helpful, for the decline in Gladstone's hand in these volumes is marked, as is the accuracy of his memory for the spelling of names and titles. In setting these volumes for the printer, Mrs. Vera Keep has had to deal with a gallimaufry of typescripts as well as the complexities of a variety of type sizes on the page. Her common sense and her exceptional skill have been important factors in presenting this vast mass of material attractively to the reader.

Various scholars have replied with good humour as well as erudition to the editor's 'query-sheets' with their requests for particular items of information. In particular, Professor Peter Parsons has continued to attribute and translate Gladstone's miscellaneous Greek and Latin quotations; Dr. Theo Hoppen and Dr. Allen Warren have helped with information on Ireland, Professor Deryck Schreuder on Southern Africa, Mr. David Hyland on Egypt, Dr. Nicholas Rodger on the navy, Mr. Peter Ghosh on finance and other matters, Dr. Ivor Lunden on Gladstone's Scandinavian trips, Dr. Mark Curthoys on university affairs, Professor George Holmes and Mr. Denis Mack Smith on Italy and Gladstone's Italian, Miss Margaret Jacobs on German literature and theatre. Dr. Agatha Ramm's great knowledge of the period has greatly assisted the progress of the edition both privately and in her matchlessly researched *Political correspondence of Mr. Gladstone and Lord Granville*. The Introduction to these two volumes has been read in whole or in part by Lord Blake, Mr. Peter Ghosh, Dr. Boyd Hilton, Dr. Ross McKibbin, Dr. John Robertson, Mr. A. F. Thompson, and Mrs. Sue Matthew; it has very much benefited from their comments. I am much indebted to them for their encouragement and suggested improvements. Its deficiencies, and mistakes in the edition, are my responsibility.

These two volumes have been a joy to work on. Though they sometimes chronicle disaster as much as triumph and though Gladstone seems more puzzling and remote the nearer he gets to the present, this enhances their interest, together with the extraordinary density of the material; the Liberal governments of the 1880s are among the most curious of the century, perhaps because their direction and Gladstone's contribution to it is ambivalent. It is interesting also to find the diaries coming within direct family memory, with 1886 still remembered, like Suez for my generation, as a significant moment of family dispute.

As I taught an 'A' level Special Subject on Sir Robert Peel to the students of Old Moshi School at the foot of Mount Kilimanjaro, with the Chinese outside the window training freedom fighters for Mozambique, and as I tried to explain to the students while they studied 'imperial' topics as part of the 'English History Outlines' how it was that negotiations between London and Berlin led to the kink in the boundary that placed the mountain and their shambas in Tanzania rather than Kenya, I little thought that it would fall to me twenty-five years later to edit the letter to Dilke (see 14 Dec. 84) in which Gladstone referred to the 'mountain country behind Zanzibar with an unrememberable name' and prevented the arrival of British rule for two generations. We read of it in the recently arrived copy of Robinson and Gallagher's *Africa and the Victorians* and I am sure that anyone who was in that class still remembers the excitement of first reading that remarkable book. A generation later, my children, David, Lucy, and Oliver, are of an age to help with the editing, and, on occasion, they do. They remain good-tempered about an edition which has been with them all their conscious lives. My wife, Sue, also thinks of those pre-Gladstone, Kilimanjaro days; if she resents him, she does not show it; she offers me a constancy of calm advice and support without which that letter to Dilke would never have been reached.

COLIN MATTHEW

Oxford
March 1989

CONTENTS

LIST OF ILLUSTRATIONS

ABBREVIATED CHRISTIAN AND SURNAMES

in text of Volumes X and XI

(*prefixed or suffixed to a name in a footnote indicates an article in the
Dictionary of National Biography)

A.	Agnes Wickham, *daughter,* or the duke of Argyll
A., D. of	duke of Argyll
Agnes	Agnes Wickham, *daughter*
A.K.	A. Kinnaird
A.L.	Alfred Lyttelton
A.M.	A. Morley
Arthur	A. Gordon
Arthur, Lord	Clinton
B., Lord	Lord Beaconsfield
B., Mr.	A. J. Balfour
B., Mrs.	Mrs. Bennett, *cousin*, or Mrs. Birks, *neighbour*
B.C., Mr.	Bertram Currie
C.	Catherine Gladstone, *née* Glynne, *wife*
C., Lord F.	Lord Frederick Cavendish
C., Lucy	Lady Frederick Cavendish, *née* Lucy Lyttelton
C., Mr.	Bertram Currie
C., Sir J.	Sir J. M. Carmichael, *secretary*
C.G.	Catherine Gladstone
C.N.G., Lady	Lady Charlotte Neville Grenville
D.	B. Disraeli *or* Sir C. W. Dilke
D., Lord	Lord Derby
D. of D.	Duke of Devonshire
E.	Elizabeth Honoria Gladstone, *née* Bateson, *sister-in-law*
E.C.	Edward Cardwell *or* Elizabeth Collins *or* Emma Clifton
E.M.P., Lady	Lady Elizabeth M. Pringle
E.T.	Edward Stuart Talbot
E.W.	Edward C. Wickham, *son-in-law*
E.W.H.	E. W. Hamilton, *secretary*
F., Mr.	W. E. Forster
F.C., Lord	Lord Frederick Cavendish
F.E., Lord or Lady	Lord *or* Lady F. Egerton
Ff., Archd.	Archdeacon Ffoulkes
F.H.D.	Sir F. H. Doyle

F.L.	Frank Lawley *or* F. Leveson [Gower]
Frank	Frank Lawley
G.	George Lyttelton, *wife's brother-in-law,* or Lord Granville or Lord Richard Grosvenor, *chief whip*
G., Mr.	J. A. Godley, *secretary*
Gertrude/Gertie	Gertrude Pennant, *née* Glynne, *or* Gertrude Gladstone, *née* Stuart
G.L.	George Lyttelton
G.L.G.	George Leveson-Gower, *secretary*
H.	(Bishop) W. K. Hamilton
H., Lord	Lord Hartington
H., Lady	Lady Herbert of Lea
H., Mr.	E. W. Hamilton, *secretary*
H., Mr. and Mrs.	Mr. and Mrs. Hampton, *the butler and his wife*
Harry	Henry Neville Gladstone, *son*
Helen	Helen Gladstone, *daughter*
Herbert	Herbert John Gladstone, *son*
H.J.G.	*the same*
H.N.G.	Henry Neville Gladstone, *son*
H.P., Sir	Sir Henry Ponsonby, *the Queen's secretary*
H.S.	Horace Seymour, *secretary*
Hs., the two	Harry and Herbert, *sons*
I., Mr.	Henry Irving
J.	John Neilson Gladstone, *brother,* or Johnnie Gladstone, *nephew*
J.L. & co.	Johnson, Longden & Co., *stockbrokers*
J.M., Lord	Lord John Manners
J.M.	John Morley
J.M.G.	James Milnes Gaskell, *or* John Murray Gladstone, *cousin*
J.M.G.(R.)	J. M. G. Robertson, *cousin*
Johnnie	John Gladstone, *nephew*
J.R.	J. M. G. Robertson, *cousin*
J.S.W.	James Stuart-Wortley
K.	A. Kinnaird *or* Lord Kimberley
Kate *or* Katie	Catherine Glynne, *wife's niece,* or Katherine Gladstone, *niece*
L.	Lyttelton *or, occasionally,* Marquis of Lorne
L., Lady	Lady Lonsdale
L., Lord	Lord Lansdowne
Lavinia	Lavinia Glynne, *née* Lyttelton, *wife's sister-in-law*
Lena	Helen Gladstone, *daughter*

L.L.	Lucy Lyttelton
Ln	Lord Lyttelton *or, occasionally,* W. H. Lyttelton
Louey	Louisa Gladstone, *niece*
Louisa	Louisa Gladstone, *née* Fellowes, *sister-in-law*
Lucy	Lady Frederick Cavendish
M.	Meriel Sarah Lyttelton, *wife's niece*
M., Dr.	Dr. Moffatt
M., Mr.	A. *or* J. Morley
Mary	Mary Gladstone, *daughter*
Mary Ellen	Mrs. Robertson Gladstone, *née* Jones, *sister-in-law*
May	Mary Lyttelton, *wife's niece*
Mazie *or* Mary	Mary Gladstone, *daughter, or* Mary Lyttelton, *wife's niece*
M.E.	Mrs. Robertson Gladstone, *sister-in-law*
Meriel	Meriel S. Lyttelton, *wife's niece*
M.G.	Mary Gladstone, *daughter*
Molly	Mary Glynne, *wife's niece*
N., D. of	duke of Newcastle
N.	N. G. Lyttelton, *wife's nephew, or* Sir S. H. Northcote
Neville *or* Nevy	*the same*
Nina	Helen Gladstone, *daughter*
Nora	Honora Glynne, *wife's niece*
P., Col.	Col. Ponsonby
P., Mr.	H. Primrose, *secretary*
R.	Robertson Gladstone, *brother*
R., Lord	Lord Ripon *or* Lord Richard Grosvenor, *chief whip, or* Lord Rosebery
R.G.	Robertson Gladstone, *brother*
Rn (G.)	*the same*
Robn	*the same*
Ronald	Ronald Leveson-Gower
R.P.	Robert Phillimore
R.W., Sir	Sir R. Welby
S.	Lord Spencer
S., Mr.	Horace Seymour, *secretary*
S. of A.	Lord Stanley of Alderley
S.E.G.	Stephen Gladstone, *son*
S.G.	*the same*
Stephy	*the same*
Sybilla	Sybella Lyttelton
T.	(Sir) Thomas Gladstone, *brother*
T., Mrs. *or* Th., Mrs.	Laura Thistlethwayte

T. & B.	Townshend & Barker, *solicitors*
T.G.	Sir Thomas Gladstone, *brother*
Tom	*the same*
V., Mr.	J. S. Vickers, *Hawarden agent*
W.	William Henry Gladstone, *son*
W., Lady	Lady Wolverton
W., Lord	Lord Wolverton
W.H., Sir	Sir William Harcourt
W.H.L.	William Lyttelton
Willy	William Henry Gladstone, *son*
Winny	Lavinia Lyttelton, *wife's niece*
W.L.	William Lyttelton
W.W., Sir	Sir Watkin Williams Wynn
Xt	Christ

ABBREVIATED BOOK TITLES, MSS COLLECTIONS, ETC.

Used in Volumes X and XI

Abbotsford MSS	Papers in Abbotsford House, Melrose
Acland	*Memoir and letters of . . . Sir Thomas Dyke Acland* (privately printed, 1902)
Acland MSS	Papers of Sir T. D. and Sir H. W. Acland in the Bodleian Library
Add MS(S)	*Additional Manuscript(s), British Library*
Africa and the Victorians	R. Robinson and J. A. Gallagher, with A. Denny, *Africa and the Victorians. The official mind of imperialism* (1961)
After thirty years	*After thirty years by the Rt. Hon. the Viscount Gladstone* (1928)
Argyll	Eighth Duke of Argyll, *Autobiography and memoirs*, 2v. (1906)
Armytage	W. H. G. Armytage, *A. J. Mundella* (1951)
Arnstein	W. L. Arnstein, *The Bradlaugh Case* (1965)
Autobiographica	J. Brooke and M. Sorensen, eds., *The prime minister's papers: W. E. Gladstone*. I–IV (1971–81)
Bahlman, *Hamilton*	*The diary of Sir Edward Walter Hamilton 1880–1885*, edited by Dudley W. R. Bahlman, 2v. (1972)
Bannerman	J. A. Spender, *The life of . . . Sir Henry Campbell-Bannerman, G.C.B.*, 2v. (n.d. [1923])
Bassett	A. Tilney Bassett, ed., *Gladstone to his wife* (1936)
Bassett, *Speeches*	A. Tilney Bassett, ed., *Gladstone's speeches: descriptive index and bibliography* (1916)
Bew	P. Bew, *Land and the National Question in Ireland 1858–82* (1978)
BFSP	*British and Foreign State Papers*
Blake	Robert Blake, *Disraeli* (1966)
Blunt, *Secret History*	W. S. Blunt, *Secret history of the English occupation of Egypt* (1907)
Boase, *M.E.B.*	F. Boase, *Modern English Biography*, 6v. (1892–1921)
B.Q.R	*British Quarterly Review*
Brand MSS	Papers of H. B. W. Brand, Lord Hampden, in the House of Lords Record Office
Bradlaugh MSS	Papers of Charles Bradlaugh on film in the Bodleian Library
Brassey	Lady Brassey, 'Mr Gladstone in Norway', *Contemporary Review* (October 1885)
Buckle	W. F. Monypenny and G. E. Buckle, *Life of Benjamin Disraeli*, 6v. (1910–1920)

Buxton, *Finance and Politics*	Sydney Buxton, *Finance and politics: an historical study, 1783–1885*, 2v. (1888)
CAB	Prime Minister's letters to the Queen, on film in the Bodleian Library
Cambridge University Library	Papers of Sir J. D. Acton, first Baron Acton, in the Cambridge University Library
Carlingford MSS	Papers of Lord Carlingford in the Somerset Record Office
Carlingford's diary	Diary of Lord Carlingford in the British Library (1885 published in *Lord Carlingford's Journal ... 1885*, ed. A. B. Cooke and J. R. Vincent (1971))
Chamberlain MSS	Papers of Joseph Chamberlain in Birmingham University Library
Chamberlain, *Political memoir*	*A political memoir 1880–92*, edited by C. H. D. Howard (1953)
Chatsworth MSS	Papers of Lord Hartington and Lady Frederick Cavendish at Chatsworth House
Checkland	S. G. Checkland, *The Gladstones: a family biography, 1764–1851* (1971)
Childers	S. Childers, *The life and correspondence of Hugh C. E. Childers*, 2v. (1901)
Churchill MSS	Papers of Lord Randolph Churchill in Churchill College, Cambridge
Conzemius	*Ignaz von Döllinger: Lord Acton. Briefwechsel 1850–1890*, edited by Victor Conzemius, 3v. (1963–71)
Cowper	*Earl Cowper, K.G. A memoir by his wife* (1913)
C.R.	*Contemporary Review*
Crewe, *Rosebery*	Marquess of Crewe, *Lord Rosebery*, 2v. (1931)
Cromer	*Modern Egypt by the Earl of Cromer*, 2v. (1908)
Dalmeny MSS	Papers and diary of 5th Earl of Rosebery in Dalmeny House
De Vesci MSS	Papers of Lord De Vesci in the Somerset Record Office
Derby MSS	Papers of the 15th Earl of Derby in the Liverpool Record Office
Derby	J. Vincent, ed., *The later Derby diaries* (1981)
DLFC	J. Bailey, ed., *Diary of Lady Frederick Cavendish*, 2v. (1927)
D.N.	*Daily News*
D.N.B.	*Dictionary of National Biography*, 71v. (1885–1957)
D.T.	*Daily Telegraph*
E.H.D.	Unpublished diary of E. W. Hamilton in the British Library
E.H.R.	*English Historical Review* (from 1886)
Elliot	A. R. D. Elliot, *Life of G. J. Goschen*, 2v. (1911)
E.R.	*Edinburgh Review*

F.A.–F.J. *Florence Arnold-Forster's Irish Journal*, edited by T. W. Moody and R. A. J. Hawkins (1988)

Fitzmaurice Lord E. Fitzmaurice, *Life of Earl Granville*, 2v. (1905)

F.J. *Freeman's Journal*

F.O.C.P. Foreign Office Confidential Prints, P.R.O.

F.R. *Fortnightly Review*

Gardiner A. G. Gardiner, *Life of Sir William Harcourt*, 2v. (1923)

Garvin J. L. Garvin, *Life of Joseph Chamberlain*, 4v. (1932–1951)

Gleanings W. E. Gladstone, *Gleanings of past years*, 7v. (1879)

Goodfellow C. F. Goodfellow, *Great Britain and South African Confederation 1870–1881* (1966)

Gopal, *Ripon* S. Gopal, *The Viceroyalty of Lord Ripon, 1880–1884* (1953)

G.P. A. B. Cooke and J. Vincent, *The governing passion. Cabinet government and party politics in Britain 1885–86* (1974)

Guedalla, *Q* P. Guedalla, ed., *The Queen and Mr Gladstone*, 2v. (1933)

Gwynn S. L. Gwynn and G. M. Tuckwell, *Life of Sir Charles Dilke, Bart.*, 2v. (1917)

H *Hansard's Parliamentary Debates*, third series (1830–91)

H.V.B. Hawarden Visitors' Book

Hammond J. L. Hammond, *Gladstone and the Irish Nation* (1938)

Harrison, *Drink and the Victorians* B. H. Harrison, *Drink and the Victorians* (1971)

Hawn P Hawarden Papers (deposited in St Deiniol's Library, Hawarden)

Holland B. Holland, *Life of Spencer Compton, eighth Duke of Devonshire*, 2v. (1911)

Hughenden MSS Library Papers of B. Disraeli in the Bodleian Library

I.H.S. *Irish Historical Studies*

James MSS Papers of Sir Henry James in the Hereford and Worcester Record Office

Jenkins T. A. Jenkins, *Gladstone, Whiggery and the Liberal Party 1874–1886* (1988)

Jones, *1884* A. Jones, *The politics of reform 1884* (1972)

Knaplund, *Imperial Policy* P. Knaplund, *Gladstone and Britain's imperial policy* (1927)

Later gleanings W. E. Gladstone, *Later Gleanings. A new series of Gleanings of Past Years* (2nd ed. 1898)

Lathbury D. C. Lathbury, *Correspondence on church and religion of W. E. Gladstone*, 2v. (1910)

LQV	A. C. Benson, Viscount Esher, and G. E. Buckle, *Letters of Queen Victoria*, 9v. (1907–32) in three series: 1st series: 1837–61; 2nd series 1862–85; 3rd series 1886–1901
Liddon Diary	Diary of H. P. Liddon, in Liddon House, London
Loughlin	J. Loughlin, *Gladstone, Home Rule and the Ulster Question 1882–93* (1986)
Lucy	H. W. Lucy, *A diary of two parliaments* (1886)
MacColl	G. W. E. Russell, *Malcolm MacColl* (1914)
Magnus	Sir Philip Magnus, *Gladstone* (1954)
Magnus, *Edward VII*	Ibid., *King Edward the Seventh* (1964)
Mallet, *Northbrook*	B. Mallet, *Thomas George Earl of Northbrook* (1908)
Mary Gladstone	*Mary Gladstone (Mrs. Drew). Her diaries and letters*, ed. Lucy Masterman (1930)
Masterman	C. F. G. Masterman, ed. and abridged J. Morley, *Life of Gladstone* (1927)
Matthew, *Gladstone*	H. C. G. Matthew, *Gladstone * 1809–1874* (1986)
Matthew, 'Vaticanism'	H. C. G. Matthew, 'Gladstone, Vaticanism and the Question of the East' in D. Baker, ed., *Studies in Church History*, xv (1978)
May MSS	Papers of Sir T. E. May on film in the House of Lords Record Office
Medlicott	W. N. Medlicott, *Bismarck, Gladstone and the Concert of Europe* (1956)
Monk Bretton MSS	Papers of J. G. Dodson, Lord Monk Bretton, in the Bodleian Library
Morgan, *Wales in British Politics*	K. O. Morgan, *Wales in British Politics 1868–1922* (1963)
Morley	J. Morley, *Life of William Ewart Gladstone*, 3v. (1903)
Morley's diary and MSS	Diary and Papers of John Morley in Wadham College, Oxford
Morley, *Recollections*	John Viscount Morley, *Recollections*, 2v. (1917)
Morrell	W. P. Morrell, *Britain in the Pacific Islands* (1960)
Mundella MSS	Papers of A. J. Mundella in Sheffield University Library
N.A.R.	*North American Review*
National Library of Wales	Miscellaneous letters in the National Library of Wales
Newman	*The Letters and Diaries of John Henry Newman*, edited by C. S. Dessain and T. Gornall (1961 ff.)
N.L.S.	National Library of Scotland
N.C.	*Nineteenth Century*
O'Brien, *Parnell*	R. Barry O'Brien, *The Life of Charles Stewart Parnell, 1846–1891*, 2v. (1898)
O'Day, *Parnell*	A. O'Day, *Parnell and the first Home Rule episode 1884–87* (1986)

Ornsby	R. Ornsby, *Memoirs of J. R. Hope-Scott*, 2v. (1884)
O'Shea, *Parnell*	Katharine O'Shea, *Charles Stewart Parnell. His love story and political life*, 2v. (1914)
Phillimore's diary and MSS	Diary and Papers of Sir R. J. Phillimore in Christ Church Library, Oxford
Playfair MSS	Papers of L. Playfair in Imperial College, London
Political speeches, 1884	W. E. Gladstone, *Political Speeches in Scotland in 1884* (1884)
Political speeches, 1885	W. E. Gladstone, *Political Speeches in Scotland November 1885, with the previous Address to the Electors of Midlothian, and letters written during the contest* (1886)
P.M.G.	*Pall Mall Gazette*
Ponsonby	A. Ponsonby, *Henry Ponsonby* (1943)
PP	*Parliamentary Papers*
Purcell	E. S. Purcell, *Life of Cardinal Manning*, 2v. (1962)
Q.R.	*Quarterly Review*
R.A.	Royal Archives, Windsor Castle
RAC	Royal Academy Correspondence
Ramm, II	Agatha Ramm, *Political Correspondence of Mr Gladstone and Lord Granville 1876–1886*, 2v. (1962)
Redlich	J. Redlich, *The procedure of the House of Commons*, 3v. (1908)
Reid, *F*	(Sir) T. Wemyss Reid, *Life of... William Edward Forster*, 2v. (1888)
Reid, *G*	Sir T. Wemyss Reid, ed., *Life of W. E. Gladstone* (1899)
Relief of Gordon	*In relief of Gordon. Lord Wolseley's campaign journal of the Khartoum Relief Expedition 1884–1885*, ed. A. Preston (1970)
Rochdale MSS	Papers of John Bright in the Rochdale Museum, Rochdale
Rosebery MSS	Papers of 5th Earl of Rosebery, in the National Library of Scotland
Rosebery's diary	Diary of 5th Earl of Rosebery, in Dalmeny House
Schreuder	D. M. Schreuder, *Gladstone and Kruger. Liberal Government and Colonial 'Home Rule' 1880–85* (1969)
Selborne MSS	Papers of 1st Earl of Selborne in Lambeth Palace Library
Selborne, II	Earl of Selborne, *Memorials Personal and Political 1865–1895*, 2v. (1898)
Speeches on the Irish question	W. E. Gladstone, *Speeches on the Irish question in 1886* (1886)
Spencer	*The Red Earl. The papers of the fifth Earl Spencer 1835–1910*, ed. P. Gordon, 2v. (1981-6)

Stead, *M.P. for Russia*	W. T. Stead, *The 'M.P. for Russia'. Reminiscences and Correspondence of . . . Olga Novikoff*, 2v. (1909)
Sudan Campaign	H. E. Colvile, *History of the Sudan Campaign*, 2v. (n.d. [1890])
Tait MSS	Papers of A. C. Tait in Lambeth Palace Library
T.A.P.S.	*Transactions of the American Philosophical Society*
Tennyson	*Alfred Lord Tennyson. A memoir, by his son*, 2v. (1897)
Thomas, *Gladstone of Hawarden*	I. Thomas, *Gladstone of Hawarden* (1936)
Thompson, *Australian imperialism*	R. C. Thompson, *Australian imperialism in the Pacific* (1980)
T.T.	*The Times*
Thorold	A. L. Thorold, *The life of Henry Labouchere* (1913)
Walling, *Diaries of Bright*	R. A. J. Walling, *The Diaries of John Bright* (1930)
Ward, *Victorian Oxford*	W. R. Ward, *Victorian Oxford* (1965)
West, *Recollections*	Sir Algernon West, *Recollections 1832 to 1886*, 2v. (1899)
Wilberforce	A. R. Ashwell and R. G. Wilberforce, *Life of the Right Reverend Samuel Wilberforce*, 3v. (1880–2)
Wilberforce MSS	Papers of S. Wilberforce in the Bodleian Library
Wolf, *Ripon*	L. Wolf, *Life of the first Marquess of Ripon*, 2v. (1921)
Wordsworth MSS	Papers of C. Wordsworth, bishop of Lincoln, in Lambeth Palace Library

OTHER ABBREVIATIONS

ab	about
abp.	archbishop
acct.	account
aft(n).	afternoon
agst. or agt	against
amdt.	amendment
appt.	appointment
apptd.	appointed
arr.	arrived
aut.	autograph
b.	book *or* born *or* brother
bart.	baronet
Bd.	board of trade
B.I.R.	board of inland revenue
Bkfst.	breakfast
B.M.	British Museum
B.N.A.	British North America
B. of T.	board of trade
bp.	bishop
B.P.	Book Post *or* Book Parcel
br.	brother
B.S.	Bedford *or* Berkeley Square
B.T.	board of trade
ca.	*circa*
C.G.	Carlton Gardens
Ch.	church *or* Chester
Ch. of Exchr.	Chancellor of the Exchequer
C.H.T.	Carlton House Terrace
C.L.	Civil List
C.O.	colonial office
commee.	committee
commn.	commission
cons.	conservative
cr.	created
ctd.	continued
cttee.	committee
cum	with
d.	died
da.	daughter

deb.	debate
deptn. or dpn.	deputation
dft.	draft
div.	division
do.	ditto
Dowr.	Dowager
Dr.	doctor *or* dowager
E.	Earl
eccl.	ecclesiastical
ed.	edited *or* edition *or* editor *or* educational
E.I.	East Indies *or* East Indian
Ep.	epistle
evg.	evening
f.	father *or* folio
fa.	father
ff.	folios *or* following
F.O.	foreign office
1°R	first reading
G. & co.	Gladstone and company
gd.	granddaughter
gf.	grandfather
Gk.	Greek
gm.	grandmother
govt.	government
gs.	grandson
G.S.	Grosvenor Square (Mrs. Thistlethwayte, usually)
H.C.	holy communion
Hn.	Hawarden
Ho.	house of commons
H.O.	home office
H. of C.	house of commons
H. of L.	house of lords
H.S.	holy scripture *or* Harley Street
I.	Ireland
Ibid.	*ibidem*, in the same place
I.O.	India office
K.	killed
l.	letter
Ld.	lord
lect.	lecture

L.G.B.	Local Government Board
lib.	liberal
L.L.	Lord Lieutenant
Ln.	London
Lord C.J.	Lord Chief Justice
Lpool	Liverpool
L.P.P. Bill/Act	Acronym used by Gladstone for Protection of Person and Property Bill
Ly.	lady
m.	married *or* mother *or, with figures*, mille (a thousand)
ma	*ma* ('but' in Italian)
Mad./Made	Madame
Maharajah, The	Duleep Singh
M.D.R.	Metropolitan and District Railway
mem.	memorandum
mg.	morning
⋒	a million
Nk.	Newark
N.S.	National Society
N.S.W.	New South Wales
nt.	night
n.y.n.	not yet numbered
N.Z.	New Zealand
No. 11	11 Carlton House Terrace
No. 15	15 Grosvenor Square (Mrs. Thistlethwayte)
No. 42 P.P.	42 Portland Place (Lytteltons)
No. 73 H.S.	73 Harley Street
p., pp	page(s)
Par./Para.	paragraph
P.O.	post office
P.P. Bill/Act	Peace Preservation Bill
p.p.c.	*pour prendre congé* (to take leave)
P.P.P. Bill/Act	Protection of Person and Property Bill
pr. or priv.	private
pt.	part
re	concerning
rec(d).	receive(d)
Rector, The	Stephen Gladstone
resp.	respecting
Rev(d)	reverend
R.R.	railway
R.T.	Richmond Terrace

2°R	second reading
s.	son *or* series *or* sister
Sact.	sacrament
Sec. Euch.	Secreta Eucharistica
sd. or shd.	should
S.K.M.	South Kensington Museum
soc.	society
Sol. Gen.	solicitor-general
sp.	speech
S.P.G.	Society for the Propagation of the Gospel
succ.	succeeded
3°R	third reading
T.	Treasury
tel.	telegram
T.P.	Temple of Peace
tr.	translated or translation
Univ.	university
U.P.	United presbyterian
v.	verso *or* very *or* volume
V.C.	vice-chancellor
vol.	volume
vss.	verses
v.v.	*vice versa*
vy.	very
w.	wife
wd.	would
wh.	which
W.I.	West Indies
W.L.	Wine Licences
Xtn	Christian
yesty.	yesterday

Signs used by the diarist

X	rescue work done this day
+	prayer, usually when on a charitable visit *or* plus
m̑	million
ma	'but'
(B.P.)	Book Post or Package

Signs inserted into the text editorially

[R]	follows names of subjects of diarist's rescue work
⟨ ⟩	words written by diarist and then deleted

INTRODUCTION

Let me look a little backward, & around. My position is a strange one. A strong man in me wrestles for retirement: a stronger one stands at the gate of exit, and forbids. Forbids, I hope only for a time. There is a bar to the continuance of my political life fixed as I hope by the life of the present Parliament, and there is good hope that it may not last so long. But for this, I do not know how my poor flesh & blood, or my poor soul and spirit, could face the prolongations of cares & burdens so much beyond my strength at any age, and at this age so cruelly exclusive of the great work of penitential recollection, and lifting of the heart which has lingered so long. I may indeed say that my political or public life is the best part of my life: it is that part in which I am conscious of the greatest effort to do and to avoid as the Lord Christ would have me do and avoid, nay shall I say for this is the true rule as He would Himself in the like case have done. But although so far itself taken up out of the mire, it exhausts and dries up my other and more personal life, and so to speak reduces its tissue, which should be firm and healthy, to a kind of moral pulp. I want so much more of thought on Divine things, of the eye turned inwards & upwards & forwards, of study to know and discern, to expose and to renounce, my own secret sins. And how can this be done, or begun, or tried, or tasted, while the great stream of public cares is ever rushing on me, & covering my head with its floods of unsatisfied demand.

Yet it is a noble form of life which ministers by individual action to the wants of masses of Gods creatures. Man has one neck, not for the headsman, but for the inflow of good. So I abide, and as I trust obey, until He who knows shall find the way to signify to me that I am at length permitted to depart, whether it be from this world, or as I trust first from the storm and fierceness of it into the shade and coolness and calm where the soul may for a while work in freedom before going hence.[1]

I

Again retirement! The theme that punctuated Gladstone's career from the 1830s and permeated it in the 1870s, cries havoc for the first half of the 1880s. The reasons for retirement, the detailed phases of which will be discussed below, are clear and natural enough: old age, a spasmodic but fairly frequent sense of failing powers, a well-established intention to escape from a second-order activity to the 'higher' contemplation of religion and

---

[1] 31 Dec. 83; references to the diary text are in this form.

scholarship. The decisive attempt was made in 1874–5, in considerable measure successfully, when estrangement from the Liberal Party on religious issues was an additional and important factor. Though there were qualifications, Gladstone's political career seemed at an end and one theme of the Introductions to these diaries has been that the retirement of 1874 marked the natural conclusion of that first career. The previous volume of these diaries and its Introduction depicted the start of his second. As was shown there, this was not seen as a career, in the sense of an extended development, but rather in terms of immediate 'exceptional circumstances'.[1] But the return of 1876 was the start of another eighteen years at the forefront of British political life, often complained of, often regretted, and always explained—explained away some would say[2]—in terms of special causes, fresh crises, new, unforeseen and unavoidable commitments. The commitment to these causes was balanced by the intention of beginning a new, non-political life; as Gladstone put it in 1882: 'What I look to is withdrawal, detachment, recollection. So soon as the special calls that chain me to the oar of public duty are sufficiently relaxed, I look to removal not from office only but from London, & to a new or renewed set of employments wholly different from those I now pursue.'[3]

Gladstone's career from the 1830s to the 1870s was in its chief features straightforward and anticipated from his youth: establishment as an M.P., an effective period as a departmental minister, a noted Premiership. Only the change of party was a fundamental surprise to his school friends. But his career after 1875, punctuated though it was by some brilliant moments, was uncertain and tentative in direction. Gladstone was never willing to see himself simply as a political leader. After 1875, the 'great work of penitential recollection' to be undertaken in private was in a series of abatements delayed by political or public activities which formed for Gladstone 'the best part of my life', a part which Christ would, in Gladstone's judgement, 'Himself in the like case have done'. Gladstone had seen political life as a second order matter, necessary and potentially beneficial but not of eschatological significance: those excessively enmeshed in it endangered their souls. In the 1860s he had begun to invest certain courses of action with a higher significance, but not one sufficient to bar his retirement at the end of his first government. Now, in the late 1870s and early 1880s, he found political life, rather as he had found it at the start of his public career as a young M.P. in the 1830s, 'a noble form of life which ministers by individual action to the wants and masses of Gods creatures'. Consequently, two very different dimensions of his personality develop.

On the one hand, he maintained various of the characteristics of retirement and of the 'new employments' he wished to seek: an absence of the full, omnipresent activity of the first government; an insistence at almost all times of a high attention to non-political reading which if not set in the context of this sort of explanation appears at certain moments simply irresponsible; an enthusiasm even at the busiest of political moments for non-political correspondence;

[1] See above, ix. xxiv–xxv for the 'exceptional circumstances' etc.
[2] See Jenkins, ch. 7.
[3] To Mrs. Thistlethwayte, 14 August 1882; this and a selection of Gladstone's letters to her will be included in an Appendix to a later volume.

an interest in reminiscence, early days, dead friends. Even while Prime Minister, Gladstone sometimes behaved as the differently-employed person he hoped to be: not exactly retired, but resolutely involved in non-political matters. This was not at all the same as the enforced semi-retirement of Beaconsfield in the late 1870s or the apparently low-keyed, disengaged behaviour of the later Salisbury; nor was it seen as a wise distancing from the pressure of events (though this was also sometimes intended), for at other times Gladstone acted with intense and explosive political energy, privately investing his public activities with a powerful sense of calling.[1]

That 'call' for which fifty years earlier the undergraduate Gladstone had yearned[2] but had not heard now seemed sufficiently clear, in the rather different context of secular causes, to be noted in the diary as a definite summons, though subject to human error (and Gladstone was careful about this point).[3] In this peculiar situation, it was for 'He who knows' to give the sign that the time had come 'to depart'. Gladstone, to be fair, sought earnestly for that sign, but in the 1880s he never saw it, and those whom he consulted almost unanimously told him not to look for it.

We must at this point be rather careful. Though inwardly driven by a power-ful sense of calling, Gladstone did not publicly assert it. Labouchere's famous jibe, that he did not object to Gladstone always having the ace of trumps up his sleeve, but only to his pretence that God had put it there, was unfair.[4] Glad-stone often claimed to be right, but he did not publicly claim God's support in the manner of some modern politicians. Indeed, the Anglo-Catholic character of his religious views made unity in the Liberal Party more rather than less diffi-cult when God was mentioned, and there was much reason for Gladstone not to express himself on religious issues or in religious language. Moreover, the twin fascination with retirement and calls to action encouraged or imposed a balance, and attempts to see Gladstone solving the undoubted awkwardness of his political position by institutionalizing himself into a system of geriatric control, are simply silly.[5] Gladstone's position was always controlled, carefully and regularly reviewed and discussed with family and friends. As we shall see, his continuing in politics was always strongly encouraged. Indeed, he found that the only Liberal supporter of his retirement was himself. None the less, the dualism of the retired gentleman scholar and the God-summoned statesman was at the least curious, even bizarre, as he himself from time to time sensed. As he wrote to his son, 'the element of old age, incurable as it is, renders all these matters extremely perplexing'.[6] It was Gladstone's complete absence of self-irony that prevented a permanent sense of embarrassment.

Gladstone took office in 1880 with explicitly restorative objectives: the

[1] At the same time, Gladstone believed that, apart from these exceptional circumstances delaying his departure, in general 'mankind is not now principally governed from within the walls of Cabinets and Parliaments'; to Newman, 18 Dec. 81 (reference to letters printed below are in this form).

[2] See Matthew, *Gladstone*, 28, for Gladstone's unanswered hopes in 1830 for a call to the priest-hood.

[3] See above, ix. xxivff.

[4] See Labouchere's entry in *D.N.B.*

[5] See A. McIntyre, *Aging and political leadership* (1988), 285.

[6] To H. N. Gladstone, 16 July 86.

removal of the excrescences of 'Beaconsfieldism',[1] the restoration of proper financial procedures (exemplified by his holding the Exchequer as well as the Premiership), and a general return to the normality of Whig/Liberal government after the restless adventures of Tory jingoism. Unlike the start of his long period at the Exchequer in 1859, and of his first government in 1868, he had in 1880 no personal commitment to innovative legislation. Indeed, the very nature of the campaigns of 1876–80 had tended to direct him away from domestic affairs towards a public debate on Britain's future responsibilities as a world power.

Thus Gladstone in 1880 appears in some respects as a rather conservative figure however radical and even shocking his means, the leader of a popular front of moral outrage at Tory innovations, a front which, in its defence of the mid-century liberal state, to some extent conceded to the Tories on the one hand, and to the Radicals on the other, the role of the initiator. This was a position of some awkwardness for Gladstone, for his earlier strength both as Chancellor of the Exchequer and as Prime Minister had depended first on stimying the Conservatives by pursuing a radical, reforming conservatism which left traditional institutions and status groups stronger and healthier, and second, on outflanking the Radicals by the energetic pursuit of free-trade goals and their accompanying legislation.

Radical conservatism of the Gladstonian sort still had much force, as the Irish question was to show, but free trade had lost its potency to associate Gladstone with radicalism. By the 1880s, the fiscal free-trade programme was completed: the question for the future was not its achievement but its preservation. Fiscal free-trade had been the great programmatic unifying force of the Whig–Peelite–Liberal–Radical coalition of 1852 which became the Liberal Party, and it was to remain the Liberal Party's point of fundamental reference until the 1930s. But its achievement necessarily implied a switch from attack to defence by its promulgators. That the defence was so successful for so long does not diminish the fact that the defensive commitment implied that other areas of policy became the advanced front of liberalism.

Fiscal free-trade meant, of course, much more than simply an absence of protective tariffs. It implied a whole way of conceiving the State as economically neutral with a tax base so small as to give the State no economic responsibility or significance. In the 1860s, little challenge had been offered to this view as both intellectually 'natural' and politically desirable. By the 1880s, however, alternative means of organizing an industrial state were being both widely discussed and, outside the United Kingdom, programmatically achieved. The sharp down-turn in the European economy in the 1870s had produced in most advanced economies save Britain a 'return to protection', marked especially by Bismarck's split with the Liberals, his imposition of protective tariffs in 1879, and the development in the Second Reich of a political economy of cartelization married to harrying the trade unions and suppressing the S.P.D. For those who wished an alternative to the British liberal state, here was one, with all its implications and consequences. Few, of course, advocated out-and-out Germanization, but increasingly Germany was coming to be regarded as the alter-

---

[1] For Gladstone's view of these, see above, ix. lxxi–lxxiii.

native model, the seed-bed for the future. Thus, when the Anglo-French 'Cobden' treaty, due for renewal for the second time in 1880, proved formally unrenewable, Dilke, the minister in charge of the details of negotiations which were spun out until 1882, began to canvass the possibility of 'some day . . . a British Zollverein, raising discriminating duties upon foreign produce as against that of the British Empire'.[1] Such a move would have been not only unacceptable but inconceivable to Gladstone, who showed little interest in the French negotiations, since he regarded the 1860 treaty as 'exceptional and not as being the beginning of a new system of Tariff Treaties'.[2] Gladstone, in other words, embodied the mid-Victorian view that British free trade was economically and morally beneficial regardless of the actions of other states.[3] It was this absence of a sense of comparison—either of comparing relative performance or of discussing alternative fiscal arrangements—that was to prove the most vulnerable point in the free-traders' defences. It explains the rather remarkable absence of any sustained attempt by the British government, and especially the Liberal government of 1880–5, to persuade other major powers of the benefits of maintaining a world free-trade market.

We must be careful not to overstress protectionist feeling in Britain in the 1880s. The Conservatives did not propose tariffs in 1878–80, and as they became an increasingly urban party, so the likelihood of their support for agricultural protection receded. The Redistribution Bill of 1885, by suburbanizing British conservatism, probably ensured that, for all the noise and for all their majorities in both Houses between 1886 and 1906, the Conservatives never formally proposed a peace-time protectionist duty, tempted though they were by increasing pressure from within their own party. None the less, the sense that free trade was under attack began to be a prominent feature of Gladstone's speeches, and this was in itself a considerable success for the fair trade movement.

But if the now relatively small base of English agriculture limited the extent of protectionist demand, and implied that there were more consumer gainers than producer losers from the world-wide fall in commodity prices in the late 1870s and through the 1880s, this was clearly not the case in Ireland. There the assault on free trade in agriculture revived in the form of a ferocious attack on free-market contract as the basis of land tenure, an attack whose extreme form, as represented by the Land League, was only possible because of the general European crisis of agriculture. Whether the Irish crisis (and the much more narrowly based but in some respects similar crisis in the Scottish Highlands and Islands) could be met without disturbing free trade and free contract was a central preoccupation of British politics through the 1880s, and was a central impediment to Gladstone's attempts to maintain the mid-Victorian minimal and neutral state. While events as much as inclination sucked Gladstone deeper and deeper into the quicksands of the Irish crisis, so its sharp contrasts with the norms of mid-Victorian Britain heightened the anomaly of his position.

The Land League, the Irish National League, and the Home Rule Party rejected and set out to frustrate much that the rest of British politics regarded as normative: a free-trade exchequer allied to a centralizing Treasury whose

[1] Gwyn, i. 399–401.   [2] To Dilke, 4 Jan. 82.   [3] See Matthew, *Gladstone*, 122ff.

influence increasingly permeated all sections of the British executive; a Parliament at Westminster with two great parties who between them ordered and co-ordinated domestic and imperial policy and legislation by operating within agreed, largely liberal, parameters; a British nation whose admitted pluralism of church, law, and culture was contained within a sense of acceptance, or at least a fairly easy tolerance; an Anglican, largely Oxford and Cambridge ruling *élite*. That *élite* had seen off the Chartists; it seemed to have incorporated within its political structure the urban and rural working classes (in so far as the franchises of 1867 and 1884 represented them), and it had by adaptation survived urbanization and industrialization much more successfully than any of its European equivalents. But the 'resources of civilization', except those of coercion and incarceration, were exhausted when it came to the Irish, though the demonstration of this even to the 1880–5 government was to be long delayed. What was clear was that, however Ireland was to be dealt with, it would involve a disturbance of mid-Victorian norms, whether financial, constitutional, or libertarian.

Side by side with a growing awareness that the century-long attempt at Irish incorporation was failing, went a sense of rather uncertain changes in foreign and imperial policy. By definition, the Concert system—which as we saw in the previous Volume it was the aim of Gladstone's campaigns of the late 1870s both to preserve and to justify—required general European agreement if it was to function 'in concert'. The Concert could work to cajole or coerce one or perhaps even two recalcitrant members: if all but Britain shared in secret alliances against each other, there could obviously be no meaningful or effective Concert. Equally bad would be a Concert whose chief basis of agreement was the extension of imperial responsibilities, for this implied costs, and more costs.

The premises of the mid-Victorian liberal state were thus increasingly questioned both by other powers and by younger British politicians and were also gradually undermined by the behaviour of the economy. The assumption of a natural equilibrium of the economy at the point of full employment and the capacity of voluntary agencies adequately to supply the welfare services of a modern state were both seriously questioned empirically and systematically in the course of the 1880s, the decade which faced both ways, looking back to the high-noon of mid-century minimalism and forwards to collectivism and imperialism. As the chief executive exponent of that minimal state, Gladstone in the 1880s not surprisingly sometimes seemed beleaguered and felt himself to be so even in his own Cabinet. But it would be quite wrong to see him as despondent. It is perhaps the most striking feature of his political personality in this period that he did not share the political, economic, and cultural pessimism which was beginning to infect many Liberals, particularly the Liberal intelligentsia, and one strain of which was elevated in 1881 to the leadership of the Conservative Party in the person of Lord Salisbury. 'Disintegration' was Salisbury's negative contribution to the mind of the age. Where Salisbury offered warnings, Gladstone offered hope. He strikingly retained the optimism of the Palmerstonian era, while recognizing the difficulties.[1] His constant objective was to place the problems of the 1880s in their historical perspective, and the

[1] For a general comment, see the fine peroration in *Africa and the Victorians*, 472.

theme of the importance of the history of the nineteenth century was of growing importance in his method of analysis. Looked at in this light, the 1880s demanded thanks rather than regret. In concluding a notable survey of the achievements of the century in the light of 'the Prophet' Tennyson's doom-laden reassessment, *Locksley Hall, Sixty Years After*, Gladstone echoed Macaulay's epigraph,[1] that the British

> disposition to lay bare public mischiefs and drag them into the light of day, which, though liable to exaggeration, has perhaps been our best distinction among the nations, has become more resolute than ever. The multiplication and better formation of the institutions of benevolence among us are but symptomatic indications of a wider and deeper change: a silent but more extensive and practical acknowledgment of the great second commandment, of the duties of wealth to poverty, of strength to weak-ness, of knowledge to ignorance, in a word of man to man. And the sum of the matter seems to be that upon the whole, and in a degree, we who lived fifty, sixty, seventy years back, and are living now, have lived into a gentler time; that the public con-science has grown more tender, as indeed was very needful; and that, in matters of practice, at sight of evils formerly regarded with indifference or even connivance, it now not only winces but rebels: that upon the whole the race has been reaping, and not scattering; earning, and not wasting; and that, without its being said that the old Prophet is wrong, it may be said that the young Prophet was unquestionably right.[2]

That this was no mere show of public bravura is seen by Gladstone's private reaction to the assassination of Lord Frederick Cavendish on 6 May 1882, prob-ably the worst moment of Gladstone's public life, a crushing burden personally, and an apparently shattering blow to the Cabinet's new departure in Irish policy. Dining the next evening with his old Oxford and Tractarian friend, Sir Robert Phillimore, Gladstone though 'quite crushed' remained ebullient:

> After the all engrossing topic had been much discussed, G. spoke with a great burst of eloquence upon the subject of the improvements in every department of the State abroad and at home wh. we had witnessed during the last half century.[3]

There was, therefore, the sense of achievement and of the need to preserve that achievement, but also an optimistic sense that, despite the difficulties, the past showed the way to future achievement.

II

The frame of mind which rejected the timid alarms of fainthearted contem-poraries was, of course, highly complex and eclectic, embracing elements both of political conservatism and of political liberalism, and certainly offering no simple categorization. An understanding of it is made more difficult by the fact that Gladstone in these Volumes is in his seventies, an age outside the experi-ence of most of the readers of these diaries and certainly of the author of this

---

[1] Macaulay, *The history of England*, conclusion to ch. iii: 'It is pleasing to reflect that the public mind of England has softened while it has ripened, and that we have, in the course of ages become, not only a wiser, but also a kinder people.'
[2] '"Locksley Hall" and the Jubilee', 16–17; see 15 Dec. 86.
[3] See 7 May 82n.

Introduction. The problem of what new pressures old age brings and what allowance to make for them, adds a further dimension to the already tricky task of penetrating a Victorian mind. It is too easy simply to discount Gladstone's age. On the other hand, it is dangerous to offer it as a simple explanation of his behaviour—'an old man in a hurry', the polite expression of the Tory view that Gladstone was in some way 'mad' or senile—and thus discount considerations of ideology and policy. Gladstone's age is a factor which each reader must bear in mind as he or she reads the text below. Part IX of this Introduction offers some guidelines.

Let us try to see Gladstone as these diaries have presented him. What was distinctive about the man who in 1880, aged seventy, kissed hands as Prime Minister for the second time? The Introductions to these diaries have attempted to describe four great themes as distinctively characteristic of Gladstone's political personality and orientation: the adjustment and development of Church–State relations in a pluralist direction; the construction and maintenance of the free-trade, minimal State; flexible, executive *étatism*; and an innovative form of political communication. In none of these, taken singly, was Gladstone unique, except perhaps in the last. In each he came to lead a powerful movement in British society and politics. On various central aspects of mid-Victorian public life Gladstone's views were thus representative and had a wide appeal. But no other figure of the age attempted so all-embracing an expression of them. Gladstone was thus both characteristic and bizarre. Before examining particular aspects of his third and fourth governments, it may be useful to have a *résumé* of these four themes.

First chronologically and probably personally was the religious pluralism developed from the 1840s onwards. To the extent that the nineteenth-century history of England, Wales, and Ireland represented a shift from an Anglican hegemony to a considerable degree of pluralism, Gladstone, in the development of his political beliefs and in the character of his political achievements, epitomized this fundamental change. The need for the promulgation of the truth in religion rather than religion's Erastian utility placed Gladstone, as it did many Tractarians and High-Churchmen, in the liberal orbit, for it was only such an orbit which permitted the religious pluralism which the Oxford Movement required if it was to survive.[1] There was an unresolved, probably unresolvable, irony here. Although they supported pluralism, Gladstone and the Tractarian High-Churchmen were far removed from moral or religious relativism. Indeed it was their hostility to relativism which, at bottom, caused their suspicion of an establishment which necessarily implied a considerable degree of latitudinarianism. Looking back in 1886 on 'the actual misdeeds of the Legislature during the last half-century', Gladstone found these to be all religious: the Divorce Act of 1857, the Public Worship Act of 1874, and the Ecclesiastical Titles Act of 1851.[2]

---

[1] Gladstone's position, as stated to the Unitarian James Martineau (a strong establishmentarian) in the 1860s, is well summarized in Martineau to Bosworth Smith, 23 December 1885: 'He laid down two positions: 1. The Anglican Church is divine and (except in ecclesiastical machinery) unalterable; and 2. the State must bear itself impartially towards all the religions of its subjects'; *R Bosworth Smith by his daughter* (1909), 208.

[2] '"Locksley Hall" and the Jubilee', 16–17; see 15 Dec. 86.

The first encouraged moral relativism, and to avoid it would have needed a continuance of the confessional state as Gladstone had conceived it in the 1830s;
the second and third restricted or denied religious pluralism. Thus in the 1880s
Gladstone privately regretted Charles Bradlaugh's atheism but permitted his
membership of the House of Commons. The pluralistic arguments used in 1851
against the Ecclesiastical Titles Bill could also embrace Bradlaugh, about whose
case Gladstone had no intellectual difficulties, developing an argument which
was intellectually effective and politically convenient: '*In foro conscientiae* Bradlaugh has committed a gross error by presenting himself to take the oath', but
that was not a matter for the House of Commons, which had acted 'beyond its
powers. . . . B. has fulfilled the law, or he has not. If he has, he should sit. If he
has not, the courts should correct him'; attempts to proceed by 'including
Agnostics and Pantheists and yet excluding Atheists' simply endangered sound
religion by making it look foolish: 'it is best to recognise frankly that religious
differences are not to entail civil disabilities; & in regard to the present controversy that it tends to weaken reverence for religion in the body of the
people', a view inherent in Gladstone's position since the 1840s.[1] Gladstone
stuck to this position tenaciously, 'obeying the inward voice, but defying almost
every outward one!'[2]

With respect to church establishments, however, Gladstone as time passed
rather softened the sharply defined principles laid down in the 1840s and early
1850s. Though always able when required to refer to these principles, Gladstone was careful in the late 1870s and early 1880s not to be drawn into support
for particular disestablishments. Thus he reaches the end of these two volumes
neither pledged to Scottish nor Welsh disestablishment, nor committed to
preventing it, to the irritation of disestablishmentarians and the scepticism of
the establishment lobby.

In principle an acceptor of religious pluralism, in practice Gladstone fought
an effective rearguard action on behalf of the Church of England, and in practice his disagreement with politically conservative Anglicans was usually on the
wisdom of defending what he regarded as untenable outposts, such as preventing
non-Anglicans from using parish churchyards for burials. The last thoroughgoingly Anglican leader of the Liberal Party to head a government, his very
presence in that position helped to maintain a bipartisan political identity for
his Church and in the high noon of political nonconformity to absorb and
deflect the central force of attack.

The confessional state envisaged in the 1830s would thus be replaced with a
society organized largely through voluntary associations (among which the
established church would be important but not unique). These associations
would be of various sorts: the religious, social and educational life of the various
denominations, the self-sustaining friendly societies and charities, the trade
unions and professional organizations, and the vast plethora of other Victorian
associational bodies, self-regulating, but with the discreet legal support of the
state. Though the central state would thus be minimal and neutral, society was
to be not mechanical, but associational, not atomistic and materialistic, but
communitarian.

[1] See to Hubbard, 11 June 81; see also to Tupper, 2 Apr. 83.   [2] 22 Feb. 82.

As we have seen in earlier Introductions, Gladstone was personally active in working such of these institutions as related to his own background, participating energetically in charitable trusts, in the management of various schools, and in a large range of self-help organizations. His support for the Charity Organization Society reflected an awareness that a voluntarist social order needed supervision and co-ordination if it was to achieve equal standards across the nation, but, like the C.O.S. leaders, he certainly did not see the recognition of this as the first step to admitting that voluntarism was in itself generally inadequate. However, in the Elementary Education Act, his first government had denied, in one particular but central area, the capacity of a voluntarist society satisfactorily to supply the needs of an industrial nation. But his second government did not directly attempt further replacement of voluntarism by state action.

Pluralism had thus brought Gladstone from a predominantly conservative confessional Anglicanism into what proved to be the main stream of Victorian thought and Victorian activity. In this development he was characteristic of much of his Oxonian generation.

Second, evolving parallel to religious pluralism and in Gladstone's development causally associated with it,[1] was the free-trade, minimal state. Religious pluralism took the state out of theology; free trade did the same for the economy. The concept of a 'national economy' with its tariffs, bargains, cartels, and economic pressure groups was alien to Gladstone's mind and was not to be allowed to corrupt British public life. A powerful sense of moralism buttressed the fiscal case for free trade, but in a negative way: as the state should no longer point to a particular church or denomination as true, so it no longer selected particular industries as deserving. In Gladstone's view, the Budget was a moral as well as a fiscal engine. It should be regular, balanced and minimal, setting a tone for the nation, and Gladstone saw the pressures of the age increasingly threatening each of these. Consequently, invasion of public revenues, however small, was to be resisted, and this led in the 1880s to delayed decisions in imperial affairs, to loss of initiative over land purchase in Ireland, and to a series of petty disputes with individuals over salary reductions and controls. This absence of a sense of a national economy (and of means of measuring it more sophisticated than income tax returns and the like) meant that the costs and economic implications either of governmental activity or of the absence of such activity simply could not be assessed, except for immediate military and naval costs.

This is not anachronistically to blame Gladstone for an absence of a sense of aggregate demand and supply: such concepts were not available to him and his contemporaries. But it is to point out that strategic decisions about the implications of British imperial expansion—in so far as there were strategic decisions—took place in an economic limbo. Gladstone sensed that such expansions were economically damaging, others that they might be beneficial: neither had any means of calculation.

It was, in Gladstone's view, in considerable measure free-trade legislation which had created the circumstances for the great boom in Victorian living

---

[1] See above, iii. xxxiv–xxxix.

standards, and it was certainly that legislation which was *seen* as the basis of prosperity, an argument powerfully restated in an article on free trade, railways, and the growth of commerce written just before the great election victory of 1880.[1] Thus it was at the end of a paragraph on the economy and 'the condition of England question' that he observed: 'the discord between people and the law is now at an end, and our institutions are again "broad based" upon national conviction and affection'.[2] Empirically based though his free-trade views originally were, and, in his article of 1880 on free trade and railways, continued to be, Gladstone was certainly not prepared to allow in the 1880s any thoroughgoing reassessment of the case against protective tariffs.

Gladstone had reached his position on both of these subjects—religious pluralism and free-trade minimalism—as a result of the experience of government in the 1840s and, less importantly, of acceptance of dogmatic theory. But both *seemed* to ally him with liberal political and economic theories which pointed to absolute positions. If carried through with stringency, they would have produced on the one hand complete disestablishment and absence of a religious requirement in education, and on the other not only free trade but a sharp reduction of Britain's world responsibilities, and a decline in the size and range of the commitments of the navy and the army (which in the years 1881–5 together accounted for 31.3 per cent of gross central government expenditure), and a rigid hostility to colonial expansion.

Gladstone in principle probably favoured such policies, but in practice his executive *étatism*, the third of the themes of these Introductions, curtailed him, as it became interwoven with the first two. It worked at several levels to soften and constrain his tendencies. The Liberal-Tory background from which Gladstone sprang and within which much of his governmental practice continued to be conceived was profoundly ambivalent about the British state, seeing it partly in pragmatic, business-like terms, and partly in the much more eschatological language of moral absolutes.[3] Gladstone through his long executive career reflected this ambiguity: the principles of a mechanistic minimal state were raised but rarely pressed to a conclusion. Indeed executive requirements and particular situations might lead them to quite contrary actions. Gladstone was fully aware of his tendency in this direction. 'In principle', he wrote in 1883, 'perhaps my Coalwhippers Act of 1843 was the most Socialistic measure of the last half century.'[4]

Gladstone believed that individuals worked with the given data of historical situations, not with the abstracts of *a priori* principles, for Christianity was an historical religion, rooting men and women in particular contexts, in national communities placed at a certain point in the evolution of human society. The politician's observation, judgement, and reason, properly used, though 'faint and dim and mutilated' was 'still the best which our capacities can attain', a

---

[1] See W. E. Gladstone, 'Free trade, railways, and the growth of commerce', *N.C.* (February 1880); 16 Dec. 79.

[2] '"Locksley Hall" and the Jubilee', 10.

[3] Boyd Hilton, *Corn, cash, commerce. The economic policies of the tory governments 1815–1830* (1977), ch. vi for pragmatism, conclusion for Chalmers and eschatology.

[4] To Hamilton, 18 May 83; the 1843 Act foreshadowed Edwardian 'new liberal' attempts to tidy up the dock labour market.

vision for his or her time of 'the Divine Will'.[1] Necessarily 'mutilated', this vision could not be complete or perfect. The utopianism of secular liberalism and of an *a priori*, deductivist view of society were thus excluded. The emphasis on time and location gave scope for the politician's art as interpreter, mediator, and leader, however second-best the result of its exercise might be.

In the great divide in the European view of progress, between the deductivist intellectuals and the inductivist practitioners, Gladstone seemed to balance ambivalently, some of his views on pluralism and some of his comments on free trade seeming to place him in the deductivist camp. But his actions and a close scrutiny of his reasoning place him with the inductivists. In the instance of free trade in the 1840s, 'the case was materially altered by events'.[2] It was 'events', and the development of a moral view of the neutral state, not the influence of the deductivist case for Ricardian comparative advantage, which conditioned Gladstone's development into a free trader. Probability as assessed by experience was the guide to conduct.[3] In what was clearly a warning to some of his own side, Gladstone observed in introducing the Representation of the People Bill in 1884:

> We do not aim at ideal perfection, and I hope Gentlemen will not force us upon that line; it would be the 'Road to Ruin' . . . ideal perfection is not the true basis of English legislation. We look at the attainable; we look at the practicable, and we have too much of English sense to be drawn away by those sanguine delineations of what might possibly be attained in Utopia, from a path which promises to enable us to effect great good for the people of England.[4]

At the immediate political level this reflected short-term calculations of prudence and success. But in the context of the various schools of liberalism, such remarks, made at so important a moment in liberal history, had a more general significance.

They also represented a fundamental view of man's knowledge and ignorance of his world. Gladstone's life-time occurred in a period of vast extension of human knowledge and experience, particularly for the British, yet he saw this as merely emphasizing awareness of ignorance and hence of the sense of imperfectibility: progress made cautions about Utopia more rather than less necessary. He commented thus on Joseph Butler's 'Sermon Upon the Ignorance of Man':

> Every extension of our knowledge is an extension, often a far wider extension, of our ignorance. When we knew of only one world we also knew a good deal about its circumstances, its condition, its progress. Now we are surrounded by worlds innumerable, spread over spaces hardly conceivable for their extent; and yet those, who may be rapt in their wonder at the grand discoveries of the spectroscope, may also be the first to admit that as to the condition, purposes, and destinies of all these worlds we are absolutely in the dark. Consider the conditions of our civilization: disease in its multiplied

---

[1] See Matthew, *Gladstone*, 43; the passage was written in 1835, but was characteristic of Gladstone's views throughout his life.

[2] ibid., 78.   [3] See above, ix. xxv.

[4] *H* 285. 122-3 (28 February 1884); the chief items thus excluded were proportional representation and women's suffrage; Gladstone perhaps thought universal male suffrage so Utopian as not to require mention in his list of exclusions.

forms is more rife among us than in savage life, while the problems of the social kind seem to gain upon us continually in the multitude of puzzles which they offer to our bewildered minds. Then, in the moral world, we must be still more conscious of our limitations; for, while we are continually required to pass judgement for practical purposes on actions, every right-minded person will incessantly feel that to form any perfect judgement on any action whatever is a task wholly beyond our power. When Butler pronounced his severe sentence on the claims of the Popes, his horror was not the result of theological bigotry, but, without doubt, he was shocked (with his strong, just, and humble sense of our limitations in capacity) at the daring and presumption of the claims set up by some on their behalf. Yet he keenly saw the obligation that knowledge imposes to act when we know, not less than to abstain when we do not.

On this great and critical subject, he seems never to have let fall a faulty word, and of all the topics he has handled there is not one on which we may more safely accept him as a guide.[1]

The politician therefore retained flexibility and above all cultivated timing, or 'ripeness' as Gladstone sometimes called it, an understanding of the 'golden moments' of history, when political action fused with great, often unseen forces to produce a right and lasting solution. It was the function of the executive politician both to perceive such moments and to provide the capacity, in the form of legislative preparation and party support, for their realization. Thus, although flexibility, attainability, and 'experience' suggested caution, trial and perhaps recognition of error, the notion of the ripe, golden moment, properly grasped, suggested both action and permanence. Here lay the centre of the ambivalence of Gladstone's curious blend of settled solutions and flexible *étatism*, and the secret of his appeal to so wide a spectrum of progressive opinion. Gladstone's famous note on political timing was written at the end of his life in this Butlerian intellectual context: the awareness of ignorance and limitation, the use of reason coupled with the affections to reach conviction on certain central matters, so as 'to act when we know', the careful qualification as to complete certainty:

I am by no means sure, upon a calm review, that Providence has endowed me with anything which can be called a striking gift. But if there be such a thing entrusted to me, it has been shown, at certain political junctures, in what may be termed appreciation of the general situation and its result. To make good the idea, this must not be considered as the simple acceptance of public opinion, founded upon the discernment that it has risen to a certain height needful for a given work, like a tide. It is an insight into the facts of particular eras, and their relations one to another, which generates in the mind a conviction that the materials exist for forming a public opinion, and for directing it to a particular end.

There are four occasions of my life with respect to which I think these considerations may be applicable. They were these:
1. The renewal of the income tax in 1853.
2. The proposal of religious equality for Ireland in 1868.
3. The proposal of Home Rule for Ireland in 1886.
4. The desire for a dissolution of Parliament in the beginning of 1894, and the immediate determination of the issue then raised between the two Houses of Parliament.[2]

---

[1] W. E. Gladstone, *Studies subsidiary to the works of Bishop Butler* (1896), 106–7.

[2] Morley, ii. 240 and *Autobiographica*, i. 136; it is characteristic of Magnus, 190, that he turns Gladstone's uncertainty about 'a striking gift' into an unqualified affirmation.

Read outside the Butlerian context, the passage might, as Morley noted, be labelled 'with the ill-favoured name of opportunist'.[1] Read within it, it represents a political methodology which reduced rather than encouraged dogmatism.[2]

The fourth great theme developed in these Introductions has been Gladstone's integration of the great social forces of his time through the development of a political communication suited to the franchise and media of his day. In part this was a means of control: control of the franchise, influence on the press through the occupation of its columns by great speeches, oratorical leadership of the Liberal Party in the constituencies and of the electorate beyond it. By these means, all interrelated, the British Liberal Party incorporated within itself Anglicans, Nonconformists, Roman Catholics, and secularists, landowners, manufacturers, merchants, bankers, and trade unionists, to an extent only dreamed of by its Continental equivalents.

Not surprisingly, so extensive and complex a coalition of religion and class was difficult to lead, and the consequence of successful integration was acceptance of a pluralism of policies. Each section of the party, however defined, expected to be disappointed as well as cheered, and the Liberal tradition included political collapse and subsequent reconsolidation almost as much as legislative triumph. At the national level, Gladstone's oratory played a central though not, of course, a unique role in the achieving of the great Liberal successes and in the process of regrouping after the disasters. His oratory and his capacity to represent through rhetoric both the aspirations and the difficulties of his party had been the basis of his return to politics in 1876 and of his curious position with respect to his party in the campaign from 1876 to the 1880 general election.[3] His base for power was essentially a rhetorical base: if oratory ceased, the party, conceived as a whole, all but ceased also, for it was through the medium of public meetings nationally reported that the party maintained its national self-awareness. Thus, however much the successful resolution of particular political problems and the apparent clearing of the way to Gladstone's retirement might be achieved, the Liberal coalition's political and rhetorical personality paradoxically depended on Gladstone's continuing political leadership. He remained the keystone of the arch of the Liberal coalition's political identity.

The reception of oratory, through the physical participation of attending meetings and the mental integration encouraged by the day-to-day reading of the speeches in the newspapers, thus provided the means of party deliberation and harmonization of disagreements. In a wider sense, oratory eased the legitimation of the Victorian State, as voters vicariously shared in the ventilation of political debate on a huge and unprecedented scale.[4] But this was no simple mechanism of social control. The rhetorical *élite*—the cadre of speakers who dominated the speech-reporting of the day—was the product of a new medium

---

[1] Morley, ii. 241.

[2] See Boyd Hilton, *The age of atonement. The influence of evangelicalism on social and economic thought* (1988), ch. 9.   [3] See above, ix. li–liii, lxx–lxxi.

[4] See above, ix. lviiff, and H. C. G. Matthew, 'Rhetoric and politics in Great Britain, 1860–1950', in P. J. Waller, ed., *Politics and social change. Essays presented to A. F. Thompson* (1987).

and was shaped by the circumstances of the times just as much as it directed and dictated popular opinion. British political leaders were the beneficiaries of a participatory, representative system whose integrative success constantly astonished them. The great mass of the political press with its uniquely large readership, the participation in local, self-sustaining political debating societies, the high turn-out in elections for Oxford- and Cambridge-led political parties, were largely unanticipated boons, and they knew it. 'The strength of the modern state lies in the Representative system', Gladstone remarked in 1884— it is astonishing that such a remark should as late as the 1880s have given such offence—and a healthy representative system was made possible by spontaneous activity on the part of the electorate, the 'capable citizens' which the system was designed to incorporate.[1] That so many citizens had turned out to be 'capable' was for someone of Gladstone's political origins and generation a matter of constant surprise, delight, and relief. It was also a process to be proud of having shared in; there was no shame in recognizing that his Salisburian prophecies of doom in the 1830s had been proved wrong.

With this enthusiasm for popular politics rationalistically presented in great speeches and public argument to audiences marked by 'singular intelligence & the practical turn of their understanding'[2] went an increasing distress about its dark obverse: Jingoism and the assertion of class interest. The Tories had become the creatures of 'class-preference . . . the central point of what I call the lower & what is now the prevalent, Toryism'.[3] 'Tory democracy . . . is demagoguism . . . applied in the worst way, to put down the pacific, law-respecting, economic elements which ennobled the old Conservatism.'[4] It depended 'largely on inflaming public passion' and was rootlessly unable to 'resist excessive & dangerous innovation'.[5] As he observed the rising opposition to the Irish settlement in 1886, Gladstone concluded: 'More and more this becomes a battle between the nation and the classes.'[6] 'Am I', he wondered, 'warped by the spirit of anti-class? Perhaps—I cannot tell. My dislike of the class feeling gets slowly more & more accentuated: & my case is particularly hard & irksome, because I am a thoroughgoing inequalitarian.'[7]

This was in the first instance a moral, ethical view of class: 'For the fountainhead of my feelings & opinions in the matter I go back to the Gospels.'[8] But behind this view lay a sense not of a simple division of society into crude classes, but a sense that large and influential groups within society—the army, the established clergy, the agricultural interest—were ready to assert class interests in politics and that these were already privileged groups which, in the Peelite tradition, ought to know better. 'The classes' meant the privileged classes, especially in their metropolitan form, and in Gladstone's view they acted as a class in juxtaposition to an as yet non-class nation. Thus he did not in these years have a sense of the working class as separate or separatist; the

---

[1] *H* 285. 107 (28 February 1884).   [2] To Acton, 31 Aug. 84.
[3] To Dilke, 24 Apr. 85. See also to Argyll, 30 Sept. 85. Thus the government's defeat by 8 votes on Chaplin's resolution to restrict foreign cattle importation during a foot-and-mouth outbreak was 'less than we had expected on a class question like this'; 10 July 83.
[4] To Acton, 11 Feb. 85.   [5] 28 Feb. 85.
[6] To Rosebery, 28 Apr. 86.   [7] To R. H. Hutton, 24 May 86.   [8] Ibid.

success of the integrationalist campaigns and of the Liberal Party in 1880 testified to the opposite. It was the growing willingness of already relatively secure groups and institutions—exemplified by the behaviour of the House of Lords—to use political influence immorally and imprudently that was likely to encourage a general sense within the nation of the advantage of asserting separate interests and identities. If the House of Lords gave the example that it did, who could blame other social groups that began to try to use their power to equal effect?

Just as Newman, writing in the centre of a well-established tradition, believed that essential truth is most clearly perceived by the unsophisticated,[1] so Gladstone believed that while the intellect was important it was not a sufficient guide to right decisions on fundamental questions in politics. Indeed, he believed that intellectual training, while in principle encouraging dispassionate judgement, in fact placed the intellectually trained person in a social or professional context in which the self-interest of wealth (intellectual training being a passport to wealth) might well frustrate the exercise of independent judgement: 'the rich too . . . have their mob, as well as their elect and favoured specimens'.[2] Thus, 'the popular judgment on the great achievements of the last half-century, which have made our age (thus far) a praise among the ages, has been more just and true than that of the majority of the higher orders'.[3] Gladstone's own political career had in part been an escape to just this sort of perception of justice and truth, and its validity was confirmed for him in the rapport he felt with the large popular crowds at his public meetings and progresses. This popular judgement was not, of course, uninformed—to keep it informed was the chief function of the Liberal Party in the country—but it was untrammelled by the prejudices encouraged by wealth. This view of popular judgement was first fully stated in Gladstone's dispute with Robert Lowe in 1878 on the franchise and he then, as often later, accompanied it with a litany of reforms passed against the wishes of 'the classes'.[4]

This view of 'the classes' thus had in Gladstone's analysis a long pedigree. It allowed him to assert his claim to have continued the mapping of the high ground of moral progress for so long shared with the Whigs (and still so with some of them). It reached its fullest statement in his conclusion in Liverpool to his election campaign of 1886, in which in a powerful passage, as influential both in the party of progress and historiographically as anything he ever said, he contrasted what he saw as the growing illiberalism of 'the classes' with the hard-won achievements of the nation, and so by implication associated Home Rule with the litany of nineteenth-century progress. 'It is on the weapon of

---

[1] See J. H. Newman, 'Theory of developments in religious doctrine' (1843), Sermon XV in *Fifteen sermons preached before the University of Oxford* (1872), 312ff. The relationship with Gladstone's position is close, because both he and Newman regarded the arguments of Bp. Butler as offering the method by which this fundamental understanding could be argumentatively developed; ibid., 318. The conclusion of Gladstone's 'Postscriptum on the county franchise' (1878), *Gleanings*, i. 200–2, strongly echoes Newman, though without reference.

[2] 'Postscriptum on the county franchise' (1878), *Gleanings*, i. 198.

[3] Ibid.; Gladstone drew Dicey's attention to this passage in 1886; see to Dicey, 12 Nov. 86.

[4] *Gleanings*, i. 198–9.

argument that I rely most', Gladstone told the electors; but against this weapon
was opposed 'a different set of means . . . the long purse . . . the imposing display
of rank and station . . . the power of political organization, and the command of
positions of advantage'. Consequently Liberals

are opposed throughout the country by a compact army, and that army is a combination of the classes against the masses. I am thankful to say that there are among the
classes many happy exceptions still. I am thankful to say that there are men wearing
coronets on their heads who are as good and as sound and as genuine Liberals as any
working man that hears me at this moment. But, as a general rule, it cannot be
pretended that we are supported by the dukes, or by the squires, or by the Established
clergy, or by the officers of the army, or by a number of other bodies of very respectable
people. What I observe is this: wherever a profession is highly privileged, wherever a
profession is publicly endowed, it is there that you will find that almost the whole of
the class and the profession are against us . . . in the main, gentlemen, this is a question,
I am sorry to say, of class against mass, of classes against the nation; and the question
for us is, Will the nation show enough of unity and determination to overbear, constitu-
tionally, at the polls, the resistance of the classes? It is very material that we should
consider which of them is likely to be right. Do not let us look at our forces alone; let us
look at that without which force is worthless, mischievous, and contemptible. Are we
likely to be right? Are the classes ever right when they differ from the nation? ('No.')
Well, wait a moment. I draw this distinction. I am not about to assert that the masses of
the people, who do not and cannot give their leisure to politics, are necessarily, on all
subjects, better judges than the leisured men and the instructed men who have great
advantages for forming political judgments that the others have not; but this I will
venture to say, that upon one great class of subjects, the largest and the most weighty
of them all, where the leading and determining considerations that ought to lead to a
conclusion are truth, justice, and humanity, there, gentlemen, all the world over, I will
back the masses against the classes.
    . . . let me apply a little history to this question, and see whether the proposition I
have just delivered is an idle dream and the invention of an enthusiastic brain, or
whether it is the lesson taught us eminently and indisputably by the history of the last
half century. I will read you rapidly a list of ten subjects,—the greatest subjects of the
last half century. First, abolition of slavery; second, reform of Parliament, lasting from
1831 to 1885, at intervals; third, abolition of the Corn Laws and abolition of twelve
hundred customs and excise duties, which has set your trade free instead of its being
enslaved; fourthly, the navigation laws, which we were always solemnly told were the
absolute condition of maintaining the strength of this country and of this empire;
fifthly, the reform of the most barbarous and shameful criminal code that ever
disgraced a civilized country; sixthly, the reform of the laws of combination and
contract, which compelled the British workmen to work, as I may say, in chains;
seventhly, the change of foreign policy. . . . Mr. Canning, an old representative of Liverpool, . . . emancipated this country from its servitude to the Holy Alliance; and for so
doing he was more detested by the upper classes of this country than any man has
been during the present century. Eighthly—I take another piece of foreign policy—
there was what we call the Jingo policy. That was put down. Who put it down? It was
not put down by the classes; it was put down by the hearty response to an appeal made
to the people. Ninthly, the abolition of religious distinctions; and tenthly, I take the
matter in which I had a hand myself, the disestablishment of the Irish Church. These
ten subjects—many of them are really not single subjects, but groups of subjects—are
the greatest that have formed the staple employment and food of our political life for

the last sixty years. On every one of them, without exception, the masses have been right and the classes have been wrong. Nor will it do, gentlemen, to tell me that I am holding the language of agitation; I am speaking the plain dictates of fact, for nobody can deny that on all these ten subjects the masses were on one side and the classes were on the other, and nobody can deny that the side of the masses, and not the side of the classes, is the one which now the whole nation confesses to have been right.[1]

Whatever the truth of this analysis of class, this was a risky line for the leader of the Liberal Party to take publicly, for it encouraged 'the classes' in the view—with particularly important implications in an era of limited enfranchisement—that they were conservative by temperament and Conservative by party.

These then are the four great themes which previous Introductions have offered as distinctive in Gladstone's career hitherto: none of them unique to him but, when integrated into a single political personality, extraordinary in their force. It might be objected that the locating of these four compass points of Gladstone's political orientation has omitted discussion of foreign and imperial policies, the very issues which brought him again to form a government in 1880,[2] and of Ireland, the issue which was to form the chief focus of the rest of his political life.

Imperial policy had been his first executive concern, in 1834, and had been a natural preoccupation for anyone with a career at the forefront of Victorian politics. But Gladstone's approach to it was notable in so far as he tried to run together two distinct and sometimes contradictory views. On the one hand, his free trade views encouraged a seemly but none the less determined reduction of direct, metropolitan control, and offered no reason for its extension. On the other, his executive itch, his sense of the immediate, of what seemed to be 'practical', encouraged imperial action, eventually as bold as that of any other Victorian. In foreign policy, his High-Church concept of the Concert of Europe, discussed in an earlier Introduction, represented a continuation and extension of the policies of his youth, and brought him into sharp disagreement with 'the Manchester School'.[3] It was, Gladstone felt, an interest forced upon him by events and, important and distinctive though his contribution was, it was not what he would have seen as a positive interest. Ireland, likewise, was something of an intrusion, an unanticipated ulcer on the body politic to be soothed and with time healed. We see in the course of these two volumes Gladstone reluctantly concluding that superficial dressings achieved little, and that major surgery was necessary. In the course of that realization, we also see his growing fascination with the problem and history of Ireland.

III

These intellectual underpinnings to some extent distanced Gladstone from the members of his Cabinet, though there was ample ground for agreement on

---

[1] Speech in Liverpool, 28 June 1886, *Speeches on the Irish question 1886*, 292. The eight points of the litany in 'Last words on the county franchise' (1878), *Gleanings*, i. 178 are exactly the same as the above. On the 'class' question, Gladstone partially exempted lawyers and doctors.

[2] See above, ix. xxxviiiff.

[3] Ibid.

particular policies. So too did his view of his own political position. Gladstone's frequent discussion of imminent retirement did not encourage a consolidation of the Cabinet or the feeling that here was a group working together for at least a Parliament. Despite the large majority in the Commons, there was a sense of the transitory about the Cabinet of 1880–5.

What, then, were Gladstone's plans for and attempts at retirement during his second administration? At the start of the government, his intention was to resign after the remnants of Beaconsfieldism—in particular Afghanistan, the Transvaal, and the frontier question in the Balkans—had been tidied up. By 1881 these matters had been largely dealt with and it was hoped that, once the condition of Ireland had been restored to calm, retirement in 1882 would be possible.

In the autumn of 1881 extensive discussions took place, including—always a telling sign in a politician—consideration of the details of new domestic arrangements. Plans for the preliminary step of separating the chancellorship from the premiership were drawn up. Gladstone's close confidant, Sir Robert Phillimore, concluded: 'I think he will retire in May [1882]'.[1] The month could hardly have been chosen with more retrospective irony. Gladstone in what he hoped in March was 'my last Session as Prime Minister',[2] having in April 1882[3] rented out his London house and thus, as in 1874, planned to have no base but Hawarden, could hardly resign during the Phoenix Park or Egyptian crises.

In the summer of 1882, further plans were adumbrated, and in the autumn of that year, hard on the success of the occupation of Egypt, Gladstone made his most determined effort. Following a visit by Spencer to Hawarden, he sent Spencer a long letter, with copies to Granville and Hartington, setting out the case both political and personal. His return to office had been, as he had always insisted, exceptional; his retirement would 'restore the natural and normal state of things, which existed up to 1880'. Personally, 'it would be of no good to any-one, that I should remain on the stage like a half-exhausted singer, whose notes are flat, & everyone perceives it except himself'.[4] Granville and Hartington both met Gladstone on both counts with clear negatives: no 'young or middle-aged man' exceeded or even equalled him in physical capacity; politically Granville could not 'aid or abet you in striking such a blow on the liberal party'.[5] Harting-ton was 'convinced that there does not at this moment exist in the party any man possessing a fraction of those mental powers which you consider so neces-sary to future constructive legislation'; 'as to the effect of your retirement upon the party, I feel bound to state my own clear and distinct opinion. I think the leadership of the House of Commons, in its present temper, an impossibility for any one but yourself.'[6]

A partial solution was reached by a Cabinet reshuffle in December 1882 by which Gladstone ceded the Exchequer to Childers, and Derby, who had refused office in May 1882, joined as colonial secretary. These negotiations and deci-sions, compounded with the stress of a row about Rosebery's political future, anxiety about an announced visit to Midlothian, and an attack of lumbago led to

[1] See 29 Sept., 6 Oct., 6, 11, 13, 15, 18, 19, 24 Nov., 2, 8, 10, 14, 18, 26, 31 Dec. 81.
[2] To H. N. Gladstone, 3 Mar. 82.   [3] 1 Apr. 82.
[4] To Spencer, 24 Oct. 82.   [5] Ramm II, i. 450.   [6] Holland, i. 378.

a severe bout of insomnia and an extended rest in Cannes.[1] The new Cabinet arrangements in fact diminished the case for retirement. These changes left Gladstone free from departmental duties and indeed free, should he wish it, from anything other than chairing the Cabinet and answering the First Lord's questions in the Commons. In 1883 this was largely what he did: for the first time since 1872 he was not in the forefront of the legislative programme. By the autumn of 1883, as the party gathered itself for franchise reform, Gladstone, despite the warnings of 1866, found himself again in the legislative van. The constitutional imbroglio of 1884, the need to settle Egyptian finance, and the growing crisis in the Sudan and on the Afghan frontier, which taken together produced from October 1884 an equinoctial flood tide of political crisis, carried him through to the resignation of the Cabinet in June 1885. Following that resignation he wrote 'a Minute for circulation on my retirement' proposing 'a bodily not a moral absence' from the front Opposition bench, and anticipating no 'state of facts, which ought to alter my long cherished, and I believe well known, desire and purpose to withdraw, with the expiration of this Parliament, from active participation in politics'.[2] None the less, 'with much difficulty' Gladstone brought himself 'to the conclusion that I ought to offer myself for re-election' in the autumn of 1885.[3]

It is a curious and exasperating catalogue.[4] It is easy to be impatient with Gladstone, and to see him using his retirement and his age as a weapon against his colleagues, rather than making a genuine effort to achieve it, and in effect that was what he ended by doing, presenting himself in May 1885, during the quarrel on Irish policy which effectively brought the government to an end, as merely 'an *amicus curiae*'.[5]

The imminence of retirement had advantages. Gladstone could present himself both as a person above party, called back into politics to settle great moral questions, and, on occasion (as with the franchise demonstrations in 1884), as the leader for the time being of the Liberal Party, the movement essential to the achievement of those settlements. He thus appealed—peculiarly among executive politicians, but together with John Bright—both to the many Liberals who were sceptical about the legitimacy of party organization and to those who were party activists and came together in the Liberal Hundreds. The convenience of this position became increasingly apparent as the second ministry gave way to the third but it can hardly be offered as an explanation of how Gladstone came to find himself in it; it was the consequence of his views about his retirement, not their cause.

What is striking is not Gladstone's behaviour, which was quite consistent both in the short term and in the general sweep of his career, but the reaction of his colleagues to his various attempts to arrange for his retirement. All the

[1] Insomnia set in by 2 Jan. 83, but was clearly threatening before that.
[2] 16 June 85.
[3] To Kimberley, 15 Sept. 85; see also 7 Aug. 85, letters from 22 Aug. 85 and Ramm II, 391ff.
[4] An exasperation exacerbated, perhaps, by his pedantic letters and lists on the length of his public life: 'ought my service in the Ionian Islands, unpaid but strictly official, to be reckoned to my credit?'; to Godley, 1 Jan. 83. See also 19 Feb. 84 for calculations that he was 7th longest-serving Prime Minister out of 31 since the accession of the House of Hanover.
[5] To Chamberlain, 6 May 85.

Liberals whom Gladstone consulted—and while the core was the Whig hierarchy they included men as diverse as Bright and Acton—were uniformly
appalled. Most Prime Ministers who suggested to close colleagues that the time
had come for a successor to emerge would find the proposal rapidly pursued
behind the scenes at the same time as being met by an opposition marked by a
decorous and cautious formality. But in Gladstone's case there were no plots
and few protests. If they thought Gladstone was bluffing, it was a bluff they
dared not call. Nobody replied, 'yes, perhaps the strain is telling, perhaps the
party's long-term interest calls for a regrettable change'.[1]

The fact was that the Whigs could not let him go. They would not let him go
in 1874; they tried to stop him going in 1875;[2] they could not do without him in
1885. For all the rows over Irish property, the Whigs looked to Gladstone for
defence. Gladstone sent the Duke of Bedford, whose duchess he had failed to
prevent resigning as Mistress of the Robes, a copy of Giffen's 'masterly' refutation of 'the well-written but wild book of Mr. George on Progress & Poverty', no
doubt with the implicit reminder that the Prime Minister's Irish Land Act was
in contrast a limited diversion. The Duke replied that he feared 'disturbance
may be at hand. . . . If anyone can save us, it is yourself.'[3] In the fevered atmosphere of the early 1880s, with landowners in a panic unknown since the early
1830s, Gladstone remained the Whigs' last, best hope, unless they were to join
the Tories. Kimberley summed up the Whigs' view:

> no one but yourself could steer the party in an even course between our right and left
> wings, and the future of this country will depend upon the impulse given at the com-
> mencement of the new political era.[4]

Kimberley here identifies two of the bases of Gladstone's indispensability: his
mediation between the groups that made up the Liberal coalition, and his
capacity as an electoral leader. However conservative their policies might be
thought to be becoming, the Whigs were not Tories. The possibility of being
forced out of the Liberal Party with an accommodation with the Tories as their
alternative appalled them more than sitting in Cabinet with Chamberlain and
Dilke. But increasingly it was only the inertia of constituency complications and
political habit that maintained this. Gladstone regretted the 'violent moderation' which seemed more and more the dominant characteristic of the Whigs:

> It is high time that the tones of a decided Liberalism should obtain a somewhat more
> free scope among Peers & Peers sons. I have not the disposition of some Whig Lords to
> reaction on Conservative as much as on Liberal grounds. For more than two centuries

---

[1] Of course, there were frequent discussions as to what would happen if Gladstone did go; his
spasmodic reiteration of intention naturally encouraged these. This is the context of the discussions
in January 1885, which Mr. Cooke and Professor Vincent in the 'Commentary' in Book One of *The
Governing Passion* (1974), 27, call 'the Liberal plot to rid the party of Gladstone and Gladstonianism'.
On that occasion, as on all others, none of those jockeying for speculative positions suggested to
Gladstone that he should do what he said he intended to do, and the moment, like the other such
moments, passed. Curiously, there is no mention of the 'plot' in the 'Diary' in Book Two of *The
Governing Passion*.
[2] See Matthew, *Gladstone*, 226–7 and 7–14 Jan. 75.
[3] To Bedford, 27 Dec. 83 and note. The duchess's resignation, chiefly over Irish land, was delayed
until January 1883; see to Bedford, 28 Aug. 81.
[4] See 15 Sept. 85n.

our Liberal movements have been led by Liberal Lords, and I hold this to have been not only an important but a vital point in our history. . . . I keenly desire the continuance of this feature. . . .[1]

The balance of Gladstone's second government had shown how keen this desire was. That balance, and Gladstone's announcement of relative inactivity, gave the Whigs a further chance to determine the scope of a Liberal government, but, as in 1874, they did not take it. The Whigs were ceasing to be a fertile force in British politics and were becoming predominantly reactive. Whigs, like Spencer and Granville on home rule, could follow resolutely, but they could not lead. The intellectual daring and political initiative of the Russell era was being replaced by the grey conventionality of Hartington: moderately competent, politically respectable, but sterile. Only Ripon in India, and, fitfully, Rosebery, maintained something of the whiggish heritage of bold political solutions to political questions.

The timidity and caution of the leading Whigs added a further complexity to Gladstone's tactical political position: he could not remove himself and expect the other variables to remain constant, because the nature of the government's character as formed in 1880 was determined by his own peculiar position in it. Hartington and Granville could not 'succeed' Gladstone mid-way through a government, when their own attempt at a moulding of the party had been too fragile and too cautious to avoid being so rudely interrupted in 1876. The party as it existed in the early 1880s was not their party. Gladstone's often expressed regret, that he was keeping Hartington and Granville from what was naturally theirs, was beside the point. It was no longer theirs, and they knew it. Moreover, Gladstone made it clear that if a transfer of the Premiership were achieved, he would still retain, as in 1875, a right to and a capacity for ultimate intervention: 'I do not contemplate immediate Parliamentary extinction. A part may yet remain, the part of independent cooperation upon occasion. . . .'[2] The experience of 1876–80 told Granville and Hartington exactly what those sentences meant.

Gladstone was thus boxed in, and so were his colleagues. Derby caught the position exactly in January 1885:

The 'peculiar position' of the Premier, who is always declaring himself to be on the point of retiring, increases the difficulty, for he is very unwilling to do anything that may bind him to stay longer in office, and we cannot act without him.[3]

Gladstone's 'peculiar position' thus unsettled himself and his colleagues. He had formed the Cabinet in 1880 on what he had insisted were clearly seen to be his own terms;[4] yet he had no use for it for the duration of a Parliament.

---

[1] To Lorne, 17 Sept. 85; see also to Argyll, 30 Sept. 85.
[2] To Spencer, 24 Oct. 82.
[3] Derby's diary, 8 January 1885, quoted in Jenkins, 236.
[4] See above, ix. lxx.

IV

This necessarily discursive account of Gladstone's political position and of his relationship to his colleagues prepares us for the curious 'stop-go' quality of his second administration. It is full of great dramas and splendid feats of legislation; it is characterized also by delay, prevarication and incompetence.

The administration depended, of course, on the Liberal Party's majority in the House of Commons, an overall majority of about 47 over Tories and Home Rulers, and a majority of about 112 over the Tories alone. The crusading circumstances of the achievement of power in 1880 might suggest that the party in the Commons would be radical, even truculent in tone, but this did not prove to be the case. Rarely can the party of progress have accepted so many changes of direction and of programme with so little protest. Though the majority sometimes dropped, the government was very rarely defeated,[1] and the party remained firm, if sometimes irritated, until the franchise and redistribution bills had finally gone through in 1885.

Gladstone's practice of keeping the Parliamentary party in line by the provision of 'big bills' for which it could vote and through which it could confront Conservatism in the Commons, in the Lords, and in the country generally, was well-established. Though on his return to power in 1880 he had no particular programme of legislation to offer personally, he soon found himself using the Commons' timetable in the old way. He felt, and on the whole the Cabinet felt also, that the most effective way of maintaining party enthusiasm was for him to lead from the front. Since he was not only First Lord of the Treasury, but also Leader of the House and, until December 1882, Chancellor of the Exchequer as well, Gladstone was necessarily very prominent in the Commons in routine business. But he added to this by continuing his practice of personal responsibility for major measures, which might also be seen as his practice of making some measures major by taking personal responsibility for them. His duties as Prime Minister included, as he saw them, 'the supervision, and often the construction, of weighty legislative measures'.[2] Thus in 1881 he saw the Irish Land Bill through the Commons almost single-handedly on the front bench; in 1882 he took responsibility for the Arrears Bill which with the Crimes Bill delayed the intended business, and he worked the new rules for procedure through the Commons during the special autumn sitting; in 1884 he took the chief responsibility for the Representation of the People Bill and the Redistribution Bill. In addition to this, the Foreign and Colonial Secretaries (Granville, Kimberley, and later Derby) being in the Lords, Gladstone, rather than the relevant undersecretary, often took foremost handling of those subjects in the Commons, particularly at question-time. When, as in 1883, not principally involved in the chief measures planned for the session he reminded Harcourt with respect to the Government of London Bill of the vital connection between legislation and the party: 'The Liberal party as a rule draws its vital breath from great Liberal measures.'[3]

---

[1] See 10 July 83 (defeat on foot-and-mouth).
[2] To Spencer, 24 Oct. 82.
[3] To Harcourt, 18 May 83.

There was, however, a striking difference from the legislation of the first government. Then, the bills on which Gladstone led, with the exception, as it proved, of the Irish Universities Bill, ran with the grain of liberalism. He led the Party against the Conservatives and the Lords. In the second government his lead was needed because several of the bills he sponsored, especially before 1884, frustrated the anticipated Liberal programme and were, though supportable by most Liberals, neither comfortable nor convenient. Gladstone's lead was further needed because his stamina despite his old age could outlast Tory and Irish wreckers, and his 'old parliamentary hand's' resourcefulness could outmanoeuvre them. But the effect of this was that Gladstone spent a good deal of his credit with his party on items and issues seen as marginal to the Liberal cause. He himself recognized the danger. 'It so happens that at present we have many good Bills in hand', he told Harcourt in the letter already quoted, 'but they are not understood as distinctively Liberal Bills.' In the 1868–74 parliament, the opposition to coercion in Ireland had come necessarily from within the Liberal Party; it had consequently been muted. In 1880–5, opposition to coercion was the constant duty of the Home Rule Party that had largely replaced the Liberals as the dominant party in Ireland. Consequently, that opposition was unbridled. Coercion might be necessary, but it was hardly Liberal, and the Liberal Party in the Commons now frequently found itself fighting on two fronts: the Tories baying for more, the Home Rulers ignoring gentlemanly convention to show their distinctiveness—and always with the threat of an unholy combination of the two to throw the government out if its own supporters flagged.

Gladstone's chief whip throughout the 1880–5 administration was Lord Richard Grosvenor, M.P. for Gladstone's own constituency of Flintshire. The appointment of Grosvenor was a clear sign to the Whigs that their interests in party affairs would not be neglected. Despite his only official experience being that of Vice-Chamberlain to the Royal Household in 1872–4, Grosvenor managed the day-to-day business of the government and the party effectively. But he brought to his position no vision beyond that of fixing affairs for the short term. Even there, his usefulness was limited, as his surprising absence from the redistribution discussions in 1884 shows. Gladstone's correspondence with him is rather artificially cheerful, but cautious.[1] For strategic considerations, Gladstone continued to rely on Lord Wolverton, chief whip from 1868–73, and his confidant at all important political moments since. Wolverton, however, also had a very conservative view of the party organization. In terms of structure, the Liberal Party, with the exception of the rather fitfully active National Liberal Federation, remained in the 1880s much as it had been in the 1860s, that is, it hardly had one, for the Central Liberal Association was not much more than a post-box and a publisher of speeches and pamphlets. The National Liberal Club and the Eighty Club were interesting attempts to integrate the

---

[1] Unfortunately, no significant collection of Grosvenor papers has been traced; this means that, apart from A. W. Peel and W. P. Adam (1873–80), there are no Liberal chief whip's papers extant 1868–92. However, it is clear that some of the letters from Gladstone to Grosvenor in the Gladstone Papers are the originals, probably returned to the Gladstone family when Morley was writing his biography.

party with a slightly wider circle of non-Westminster men. The National Liberal Club helped give identity to the growing number of non-Whig Liberals who would have felt uncomfortable at the Reform Club, but it was visited by Gladstone only on the occasional official occasion and never socially; if he used a club, it was the older non-party Grillion's or The Club, and those very rarely.[1] The Eighty Club sponsored the Gladstonian alternative to organization, oratory, and was an important source of speeches cheaply reprinted as pamphlets.

The absence of advance on the organizational front was a striking failure of the Liberal Party in this period. Suppose a Liberal Party with individual membership, a full structure of organization, constitution, and elections, achieving a universal franchise in place of the 1884 bill, how differently might progressive politics in Britain have developed! Yet such a development was outwith the parameters of Liberal thinking about politics. It would have been regarded as profoundly illiberal. To Liberals, to be a citizen was to be a Liberal: nothing more was essentially needed. Many grass-roots Liberals were extremely reluctant to admit the need for party organization at all, for they saw it as corrupting Liberal individualism, a further means of invasion by the Westminster *élite* and another example of the dangers of the centralizing State. Even the caucus-men regarded the caucus as a second-best, a regrettable necessity in the circumstances of an extended electorate.

As it was, the Gladstonian method of rhetorical integration increasingly offered a substitution for or alternative to organization at the national level, with Liberal Associations achieving spasmodic success locally through an *ad hoc* caucus system which rarely proved self-sustaining.[2] As for the franchise, 'a uniform residential, household franchise for the whole country, supplemented by a simple and really effective lodger franchise' was the extent of the demand of Schnadhorst, the doyen of Liberal organizers, to the National Reform Union.[3]

Gladstone stressed the advantages of variety to the party, and positively discouraged a more organized structure for the Parliamentary party:

> Liberalism has ever sought to unite freedom of individual thought and action, to which it largely owes its healthy atmosphere, with corporate efficiency. This aim is noble, but it is difficult. For my own part, although it is not the method best adapted to the personal convenience of those who lead, nothing would induce me to exchange it for the regimental discipline which brings the two minorities, each in a well-fused mass, into the voting lobby. For this valued freedom, and this abundance of variety, cherished in the Liberal party, have not disabled it during the last half-century from efficient action. For more than two-thirds of that period the Liberal party has held power, and fully nine-tenths of our useful legislation has been due to its inspiration and its labours. What modern Britain at this moment is, she has become substantially through the agency of the Liberal party.
>
> Such being the facts, it seems natural to ask—why may not the Liberal party of the future be useful, with the same freedom and the same methods, as in the past?[4]

[1] See below, section VIII.
[2] For the difficulties, see J. Davis, *Reforming London* (1988), 25ff.
[3] F. Schnadhorst, 'The next Reform Bill', speech to the National Reform Union, 23 November 1881, p. 5.
[4] *Political speeches, 1885*, 14.

Striking this balance between 'individual thought' and 'corporate efficiency', gave, Gladstone might have added, a peculiar strength not to the Party but to the Cabinet and to his own position as arbitrator, mediator, and key-stone of the Cabinet-Party arch: 'As the Cabinet is the many-sided buffer on which all the currents of will and opinion in the country spend themselves, so within the Cabinet the Prime Minister . . . is charged with the same passive function.'[1] But with Gladstone a passive function, however cautiously exercised, was likely quickly to become active.

He was not, however, active in directly explaining the predicaments of his government to the electors. The great rhetorical crescendo of 1876–80 left an echo and then a silence. Gladstone made no public speeches, apart from the almost unavoidable Mansion House speeches,[2] until the great meetings at Leeds on 7 and 8 October 1881. This visit, several times delayed, was to thank the electors for electing him in 1880, when he had passed on the seat to his son, Herbert. The Leeds visit, a huge political demonstration with several ancillary speeches, was Gladstone's only direct meeting with the electorate until August 1884,[3] when he spoke in his Midlothian constituency—a meeting postponed regularly since 1881[4]—and made a tour of Scotland defending the administration and increasing pressure on the Conservatives and the House of Lords to settle the constitutional imbroglio over the question of franchise and redistribution.[5] Apart from this 'the People's William' was silent outside Parliament until the election of 1885.[6] 'I have been, I know,' Gladstone told John Cowan, his chairman in Midlothian, 'as scanty in demonstration since the Election of 1880, as I was abundant before it.'[7] Health, the reason given to Cowan, and, in particular, difficulties with his voice in the mid-1880s and especially in 1885, was part of the problem, and certainly Gladstone found exhausting the combination which these visits necessarily involved, of 'a "progress"' combined with 'a Mass Meeting'.[8] But on the other hand he also found them restorative, enormously enjoying the success of his largely spontaneous Scottish speeches in August and September 1884 when public enthusiasm turned every appearance into a Liberal triumph, from a visit to the Forth Bridge in construction (the workmen presenting him with an axe and he them with a library of 'entertaining and improving' volumes), to a visit to the Liberal aristocracy and tenants at Haddo House. Only Tory Preston on the way south, 'vilely managed as usual', where a 'hissing engine . . . effectually silenced me', spoilt the progress.[9]

[1] To Dilke, 28 Sept. 83.

[2] See 9 Nov. 80, 6 Aug. 81.

[3] 30 Aug. 84.

[4] The alternative of a report by letter was tried, and abandoned; see 16 May 82.

[5] 25 Aug. to 26 Sept. 84. This meeting was first anticipated in May 1881 (to Cowan, 30 May 81), delayed by the insomnia of December 1882–January 1883, again anticipated and delayed in December 1883 (To Cowan, 29 Dec. 83).

[6] Of course, there were *ad hoc* speeches when on holiday etc., an interesting appearance at the Garibaldi commemoration in Stafford House (2 June 83), and comments to deputations (e.g. at Knowsley, 27 Oct. 81).

[7] To Cowan, 29 Dec. 83.

[8] To Kitson, 28 Sept., 2 Oct. 81.

[9] 25 Aug.–26 Sept. 84; for the Forth Bridge visit, see 28 Aug., 2 Sept. 84; for Preston, see 26 Sept. 84 and to Grosvenor, 27 Sept. 84.

The limiting of major public appearances had political drawbacks but there were advantages in reticence, not least the avoidance of agitating the Queen and the Whigs. Even without physically appearing, Gladstone was omni-present, his every action the chief focus of the press. The late 1870s and 1880s saw the full flowering of the Gladstonian icon industry. These were the years in which Liberal households came to display their Gladstone statuettes, jugs, plates, and banners in pride of place on the mantel, the Tory country houses answering with chamber pots with his face looking upwards or inwards (a good example is reproduced in the illustrations in Volume XI). Gladstone's age was beginning to give him, amongst his public, something of the status of a relic and, as he knew from his close observations of the display of relics in Naples,[1] the public processing of relics must be carefully and selectively co-ordinated.

There were therefore prudential arguments for avoiding overexposure, already a constant danger from his very frequent speeches in the Commons, and for consequently extracting the maximum excitement from public speeches and appearances when the moment for them came. This sense of the ripeness of the public moment thus existed side by side with other reasons for not making frequent extra-Parliamentary speeches, such as the alarm they gave the Queen and the Whigs, and the misgivings Gladstone felt about appearing as the people's idol when privately he was trying to resign; anxiety about the presenta-tion of his awkward political position was undoubtedly a factor in the crisis of insomnia of January 1883 which led to the cancellation of the Midlothian meet-ing and his departure for Cannes.

The absence of public appearances was balanced by a greater use of party meetings than in 1868–74. To some extent, this reflected the anxieties of the party, but it was also a means of explaining particular policies and setting them in a more general context, which was the usual purpose of the mass meetings. There were party meetings on 27 February 1882, 13 July 1882, 10 July 1884, 1 December 1884, and, in the next parliament, on 27 May 1886. Such meetings were midway between a Commons' speech and a public appearance and to an extent Gladstone used them as substitutes for the latter.

Gladstone had substantial credit with each of the various sections of the party, though each also had substantial reasons for caution about him. Among the radical nonconformists, his opposition to Beaconsfieldism was an impec-cable credential, overlaying at least for the time his dispute with them over reli-gious education in the early 1870s. To the Liberal centre, he offered executive competence, a safe pair of financial hands, and a strong urge for legislative achievement. For the Whigs, he represented especially a guarantee against something worse, and an ability to formulate principles of policy in foreign and imperial affairs which Granville, Kimberley, and Hartington, although cautious about Gladstone's prescriptions, found extremely hard to do themselves.

As it had done since the 1860s, therefore, Gladstone's gallimaufrous political character boxed the compass of the Liberal Party. His Cabinet, however, seemed set upon a predominantly whiggish course, though the notoriety of the second government for whiggish domination is somewhat diminished on close inspection. Of the twenty who served in the Cabinet between 1880 and 1885,

[1] See 5 May 32, 22 Dec. 50.

livTHE GLADSTONE DIARIES

nine can be fairly regarded as Whigs or whiggish (Spencer, Argyll, Granville, Kimberley, Northbrook, Hartington, Carlingford, Derby, Rosebery); as the term was coming by the late nineteenth century to denote more a caste of mind than membership of a particular group of Whig families, it becomes both more flexible and more questionable (Argyll had Peelite origins, Northbrook came from a Liberal banking family, the Barings, and Derby had served in Disraeli's Cabinet as foreign secretary). Gladstone and Selborne were the Peelite remnants. Childers, Dodson, Trevelyan, Harcourt and Forster (despite his Radical origins) represented the work-horse, main-stream Liberals, the group which since the 1860s had formed the sturdy ballast of the party, and Bright (until 1882), Chamberlain, and Dilke (from 1882) the Radicals (together with, in certain respects, Gladstone himself). All of these were English except Argyll, Rosebery and, depending on definitions, Gladstone, and all were nominally Anglicans except Argyll and Rosebery (Church of Scotland, the latter only when inScotland), Bright (Quaker), and Chamberlain (Unitarian).[1] It was striking that the two Nonconformists, Bright and Chamberlain, came from numerically very small sects, and not from the great mass of Methodists and Congregationalists.[2] Despite the fact that most Roman Catholics voted Liberal, Ripon was the only Roman Catholic ever to sit in a Liberal Cabinet, and his claims to office in 1886 on his return from India were based on his Cabinet experience before his conversion in 1874.[3] Apart from Argyll and the three Nonconformists,all had been at Oxford or Cambridge, and most had been either at Christ Church, Oxford or Trinity College, Cambridge (seven each). All of the fourteen members of the Cabinet when it was formed in 1880 had sat in it before, save four: Northbrook, Harcourt, Chamberlain, and Dodson. Of these, Northbrook and, to a lesser extent, Harcourt were experienced men of office, as Viceroy of India and Solicitor General respectively, and Dodson was a long-standing Deputy Speaker.

The Cabinet was thus very clearly a continuation of the previous Liberal administration of 1868–74—rather more so than that had been of the Palmerston/Russell years, and it reflected Gladstone's generally consolidatory mood in 1880. It was, he noted, 'certainly a strong working Government in almost every department'.[4] Only Chamberlain represented a new tone in 1880; his lack of experience in office was for Gladstone—a man reared in a family where rentier money paid for early entry to the Commons—a bar to his swift entry to the Cabinet. It was the inexperience rather than the tone which at this stage bothered Gladstone: he objected to Rosebery on the same grounds (though the objection was dramatically set aside to accommodate Morley as Irish Secretary in 1886). The consolidatory character of the Cabinet was further emphasized in

[1] Forster, a former Quaker, as chief secretary regularly attended Anglican services in Dublin; see F.A.-F.J. passim.

[2] Gladstone defended the number of Nonconformists against Henry Richard's complaints: 'I may however say that Nonconformity was more largely represented in the two Cabinets it has been my duty to form, than in the Parliaments out of which they were formed'; 30 Dec. 82.

[3] Ripon's conversion caused considerable awkwardness in Gladstone's relationship to him and his appointment as Viceroy of India in May 1880 and not the Cabinet place which he could justly have otherwise claimed allowed a correspondence and intimacy which gained greatly from Ripon's physical remoteness.   [4] To H. N. Gladstone, 21 Apr. 81.

its reshuffles. The accessions of Carlingford, Rosebery, and especially Derby implied that the Whig seepage could be stopped and even reversed; in Dilke, Gladstone recognized a man with some of his own executive capacity, and with Trevelyan and Shaw Lefevre he reassured the Liberal intelligentsia.

'Wonderfully harmonious' had been Kimberley's verdict on the first Gladstone Cabinet;[1] he would hardly have written the same of that of 1880–5. As we have seen, uncertainty about Gladstone's position and the succession prevented the Cabinet ever really settling, and the absence of an agreed major legislative measure—the equivalent of Irish Church disestablishment in 1869—prevented a Parliamentary consolidation of the 1880 election result. Nevertheless, the Cabinet coach rumbled along, few passengers actually leaving it. Nor did many threaten to do so before 1885. Despite the malaise, almost paralysis, which at times seemed to affect the Cabinet, despite the drawerful of letters of resignation written in the post-Gordon gloom of the spring of 1885—'Very fair Cabinet today—only three resignations' was Gladstone's laconic note on 16 May 1885[2]— the resignations in fact came to little. The Duke of Argyll resigned in 1881, as he had threatened to do in 1869, over Irish land.[3] W. E. Forster resigned in May 1882, to a considerable extent driven out by the appointment of Spencer as Irish Viceroy (and still, as Lord President, in the Cabinet) and the Cabinet's 'new departure' in Irish policy.[4] John Bright resigned in 1882, as he had done in 1870, over foreign policy, in this case the bombardment of Alexandria.[5] It would be neat, but facile, to say that more trouble was in fact caused by the Minister who, contrary to all convention, refused to resign when asked: Lord Carlingford.[6] Facile, because Bright's loss was serious. In the 1870s he had been persuaded to return; in the 1880s he left as the representatives of radicalism Dilke and Chamberlain—both inexperienced and both, in their very different ways, catastrophic for the future of the radical cause. The end of these volumes, in 1886, finds Gladstone in the same position as in 1880, the most radical Liberal of Cabinet rank. The difference was that the intervening years had led him to a new departure as to radicalism.

Gladstone had good relations with most members of his Cabinet. Although his political *persona* could never be described as whiggish, it is sometimes forgotten how close Gladstone's personal relations with the leading Whigs were. He moved familiarly in Whig society, particularly within the Sutherland and Devonshire connections. Indeed, no one of non-landed origins was more intimately connected with those two great houses. Gladstone was, curiously, much closer socially to the hereditary Whigs than he was to what may be called the

---

[1] See above, vii. xxxvi.

[2] That day he also listed the names of nine cabinet ministers, 'A majority', who had 'appeared to consider resignation' within the last month; 16 May 85.

[3] See to Argyll, 28 Mar. 81.

[4] See 26 Apr. 82ff.; *F.A.-F.J.*, 459ff.; A. Warren, 'Forster, the Liberals and new directions in Irish policy 1880–2', *Parliamentary History*, vi (1987). The term 'new departure' was used at the time to describe the cabinet initiative in April–May 1882.

[5] See to Bright, 12, 13, 14 July 82.

[6] For Gladstone's most exasperated letter, see to Carlingford, 7 Sept. 84. Nervous about the Whigs, Gladstone stopped short of simply demanding Carlingford's resignation; for the protracted negotiations, see the introduction to A. B. Cooke and J. Vincent, *Lord Carlingford's Journal* (1971).

professional Whigs, men such as Northbrook. He married into a Whig family; his eldest son consolidated his links with the Sutherland family by marrying the granddaughter of Harriet, Duchess of Sutherland, his political patron in the Palmerstonian years; his closest political confidant, Granville, was a member of that same family; Granville's nephew, George Leveson Gower, was one of his secretaries (Henry Primrose, Rosebery's cousin, was another); his wife's niece, Lucy Lyttelton, whom he had partly brought up, married Lord Frederick Cavendish, Hartington's brother, whose death was as personal a blow to the Gladstones as it was to the Devonshires. Gladstone might be keeping Hartington from the premiership, but the latter's prominence in executive politics was due to Gladstone's persistence in bullying him into becoming Irish Secretary in 1870,[1] and he offered him the Exchequer in 1882.[2] It was Hartington's nerve, not Gladstone's ambition, that limited his promotion.

Chamberlain sat at the opposite point of the Cabinet compass from the Whigs. Gladstone's letter offering the Cabinet adumbrated the differences: 'Your political opinions may on some points go rather beyond what I may call the general measure of the Government', and Chamberlain was cautioned as to Cabinet secrecy.[3] The second proved more of a difficulty than the first. Chamberlain's legislative proposals in the 1880s were the equivalent of Gladstone's in the 1860s; they seemed alarming, but were not out of the question given the usual political game of give, take, and delay. Much more disturbing to the other members of the Cabinet were Radical Joe's leaks. To a body of men accustomed to intimate conversation, to protecting each other's weaknesses, to prevaricating in secret, and to working towards policy decisions sometimes over a period of months, the Radicals' and particularly, it was thought, Chamberlain's use of contacts with the Press seemed to threaten the viability of Cabinet government, to such an extent that a Cabinet committee on 'leakage from Cabinets' was set up.[4] Of course, this was not the first time there had been leaks from Cabinets—indeed, contact with the Press was in no way unusual for Cabinet ministers—but it seems fairly clear that in 1880–5 the formulation and discussion of policy became awkward in a way not found in 1868–74, the leaks making an already difficult Cabinet worse. Chamberlain and Dilke had a reason: the absence of a party structure and of an agreed programme gave the Cabinet considerable freedom. The party barely had a voice until it was too late: the legislation was drafted and introduced. In that secret process the Radicals often felt excluded and resorted to the leak to embarrass or warn off the Whigs. But this was the consequence of the absence of party structure discussed earlier, not a defect remediable by a method which to some extent spoiled executive government without achieving much in return. Gladstone's practice of avoiding calling Cabinets, and not allowing discussion of certain issues in those called, could be

---

[1] See 30 Dec. 70.

[2] To Hartington, 5 May 82; the Phoenix Park murders next day made an immediate change impossible, but Hartington could have responded later to the offer.

[3] To Chamberlain, 27 Apr. 80.

[4] 6 Jan. 82. The committee curiously recommended an 'additional key' for various persons, the hope presumably being that if there were more keys, the dispatch boxes could be kept closed; 25 Feb. 82.

justified as avoiding leaks,[1] and was thus more tolerated than it would other-wise have been. The upshot of the problem of the 'leaks' was their regulariza-tion in the form of 'the lobby', that peculiar institutionalization of the 'leak' which began in 1884.

Though obviously not drawn to Chamberlain, Gladstone certainly had the basis for an understanding with him. As has been suggested, there were aspects of Radical Joe—his willingness to take on the Prime Minister, his use of the plat-form, his competence in the Commons—reminiscent of Gladstone in his Ex-chequer days in the 1860s, and Gladstone made the flattering comparison during the 1885 election campaign.[2] Moreover, Chamberlain was not unlike the Radicals of the Financial Reform Association of which Robertson, Gladstone's brother and Mayor of Liverpool, had been Chairman and which had backed Gladstone strongly in the 1850s. Robertson Gladstone's marriage had brought Unitarianism into the Gladstone family, easing the way for Gladstone's amicable relationship with the crony of his Penmaenmawr holidays, the promi-nent Unitarian Samuel Darbyshire.[3] But not much was made of this. Glad-stone's visit (not a social call) in 1877 to Southbourne, Chamberlain's house in Birmingham,[4] was not reciprocated until he came to Hawarden as one of a string of ex-Cabinet ministers late in 1885.[5] The cheery invitation to stay, quite a common ending to a Gladstonian letter to a colleague, never concluded one to Chamberlain. Gladstone devoted to Chamberlain none of the cossetting he had bestowed on John Bright. He accurately saw Chamberlain's 'gifts', 'a strong conviction, a masculine understanding, and a great power of clear expression',[6] but he did not nurture them. Their relationship was businesslike, correct, cool, despite the fact that they were often in agreement on policy. But it was to Rosebery that Gladstone increasingly looked as 'the coming man'.

In the toss of business, and the often rather frenetic atmosphere in which the 1880-5 Cabinet existed, Gladstone found little time to encourage the weaker members of the Cabinet, or those with whom he did not naturally have close ties. Lord Carlingford (the Chichester Fortescue of the 1870 Land Act) is the best example. Brought into office when the 1881 Land Bill was at a vital stage in the Lords, and a considerable asset there, Carlingford was still frequently dis-traught as a result of the death of his wife, the former Lady Waldegrave. Rather ineffective in business, but quite shrewd on policy, Carlingford was not im-portant but he could be useful. Gladstone seems simply to have lost patience with him. Carlingford's diary shows him to have been well-intentioned towards Gladstone and the Cabinet, though always a little distanced from it. He visited Ireland for some weeks in March 1882 and thus as a former Chief Secretary met

[1] See to Hartington, 7 Nov. 83, on leaks and the franchise discussions.
[2] *Political speeches 1885*, 107 (21 November 1885). Gladstone was a little sensitive when Rosebery returned to the point a few days later: 'Mr G. in great form this mg. taking a favourable view of the election & absorbed in Greville. . . . He talked much of Ld Palmerston & how he plotted against his finance. Speaking of some part of his character I said "Like Chamberlain?" "Ah but" he replied "I never knew that Chamberlain set up for having my character at all in politics"' (Rosebery's diary, 25 November 1885).
[3] See Matthew, *Gladstone*, 138.
[4] 31 May–1 June 77; to address the National Liberal Federation.
[5] 7–8 Oct. 85.   [6] To Chamberlain, 3 Dec. 85.

the great 'Kilmainham' crisis of April and May exceptionally well-informed. None the less, it was as they entered St. George's Chapel for Prince Leopold's wedding that Gladstone told him of the *fait accompli* of the restructuring of the Irish Offices, including the odd requirement for Carlingford to act as Lord President (*vice* Spencer) without actually being appointed to the office. Carlingford noted: 'This was the first word he had said to me about Irish Govt. or legislation! a characteristic way of acting, wh. is not what I have a right to expect. I said so to Hartington, & he said "I thought you knew everything all along".'[1] It could be lonely outside the inner group of the Cabinet: Gladstone, Granville, Hartington, Harcourt, and perhaps Kimberley. As so often in his career, Gladstone expected his colleagues to be as resilient as he was. In Carlingford's case, the effect was to make a broken man belligerent. Pushed about, Carlingford dug in; made both Lord President and Lord Privy Seal in 1883, he refused in 1884 to take the important and demanding post of Ambassador in Constantinople to allow Rosebery to enter the Cabinet.[2] The cumulative effect of poor management was to produce later a considerable, if minor, irritation. The neglect of Carlingford was the sillier as he and Gladstone sat next to each other in Cabinet. This was because Gladstone had placed Argyll on his left at the Cabinet table and Carlingford had taken his place. The opportunity for a cheery word thus occurred frequently.

How important the Cabinet's seating was could only be known to those present. We do know that Gladstone took some trouble with the placings, as his planning diagram shows. It is reproduced in the illustrations to Volume XI.[3] He himself sat in the middle of the long side of the Cabinet table. Granville, who chaired the Cabinet in the Prime Minister's absence, sat on Gladstone's right—clearly a key placing for the passing of notes as well as a compliment. Most of Gladstone's surviving notes passed in Cabinet are between him and either Granville or Derby (who sat on Granville's right). Granville thus linked up with a little clutch of Whigs, but Hartington was slightly isolated between Trevelyan and Harcourt. Chamberlain and Dilke sat together opposite Gladstone. This might be seen as an attempt to isolate them or keep an eye on them.

[1] Carlingford's diary, 27 April 1882, Add MS 63690. In fact, Carlingford did know a good deal from Spencer from an important talk on 19 April, and Gladstone may have thought this was enough: Spencer 'also told me that Mr G's idea is to make no change in the Cabinet, & for that purpose to leave him, Spencer, President of the Council, although Lord Lt. [of Ireland *vice* Cowper] & to get me to do the work of the Council Office—a strange arrangement wh. I dislike the thought of . . . he alluded to other possible shiftings wh. he did not explain. It does not look well for me. Spencer mentioned the names of Kimberley & Dilke as having to do with arrangements wh. were in Gladstone's mind—& also said that it wd be a good thing to move Forster from the Irish Office, on account of the intense hostility to him of the Parnellites, although it could not be done now, as it wd look like sacrificing him & like a change of policy. I think I see what the plan is—to keep the Council Office for Kimberley (who wd have the lead of the H of Lords, or the F.O., or both before his eyes in the future), make F[orster] Colonial Secretary (his great ambition), and Dilke Chief Sec. [for Ireland] in the Cabinet. Nous verrons.' Carlingford's diary is an important source for this Cabinet; it is now in the British Library, save for 1885 (which is largely in print, ed. Cooke and Vincent).

[2] See above, p. lv. Rather remarkably, Gladstone gave Rosebery a detailed report of the affair; see 10 Oct. 84.

[3] That the Cabinet placings were the same for each meeting can be seen by comparing Gladstone's diagram of 1885/6 in Volume XI (illustrations) with the drawing of the Cabinet in 1883, reproduced in Volume X.

But more likely the opposite was the case: they offered Gladstone a ready echo or even amplifications for views with which the Whigs were likely to disagree. The psychological and physical interplay of those long and often discursive Cabinet meetings cannot be recaptured. Gladstone made little attempt to use his diary for such a purpose, and most of the other members of the Cabinet seem to have taken its procedures for granted, though Rosebery noted on attending his second Cabinet: 'I was more accustomed to the abruptness of manner wh surprised me yesterday.'[1]

The Cabinet usually met weekly on Saturday (or sometimes on Friday) during the Session, i.e. less frequently than Disraeli's Cabinet which usually met twice-weekly in the Session. Gladstone's secretary, E. W. Hamilton, occasionally attended for particular items, but to advise on facts, not to take notes. During the discussions on Commons' procedure and the Bradlaugh affair, the Speaker and Erskine May, the Clerk of the Commons, were sometimes called in. Baring once attended to advise on Egypt. Apart from these rare intrusions, the Cabinet met alone. Its proceedings were essentially conversational. In addition to the required formal letter to the Queen, Gladstone maintained his habit of recording its decisions in brief minutes, sometimes written onto an agenda. This 'hasty noting down, scratching rather than writing' of the 'heads of business as it goes on' was done during the Cabinet 'so that I may not have to rely solely on my memory'.[2] The result was admittedly 'slipshod', though it was much more than any other Victorian Prime Minister attempted.

In 1884, at the height of the pressure of events and particularly concerned that decisions about the proposed Gordon expedition be accurately recorded,[3] Gladstone seems to have considered a return to the formal 'Minutes of Cabinet' of the early nineteenth-century, including the possibility of having them signed by the Cabinet Ministers, presumably so as to tie individual Ministers to unpopular decisions and policies. Nothing came of this. For the change to have been more than an occasional formal recording of particularly important decisions would have implied a secretary—either one of the members of Cabinet acting as such, or an additional person. To give the power of minuting to a colleague would have been dangerous; to alter the informality of Cabinet conversation by introducing a clerk, however dignified, was, as yet, unthinkable and never seems even to have been suggested. Thus Gladstone's recording of Cabinet proceedings remained as it had been in his first ministry, whilst his letters to the Queen became, as relations deteriorated, if anything more arch and, on domestic and party politics, more discreet or silent.[4]

Gladstone called an average of fifty Cabinets a year (forty-eight if allowance is not made for those missed during his absence at Cannes in 1883), the same as in his first government. This surprisingly high average is sustained by the fact that there were special autumn Sessions in both 1882 (procedure) and 1884

[1] Rosebery's diary, 17 February 1885, Dalmeny MSS.
[2] To Grey, 8, 11 June 84.
[3] See Cabinet at 10 June 84.
[4] See Gladstone's comments to Spencer, 24 June 1882, who was, unusually, sent copies (on his request) of Gladstone's letters to the Queen. Spencer was, when Viceroy, in the Cabinet but was rarely able to attend it. Trevelyan, the chief secretary, was, unusually, not in the Cabinet.

(franchise and redistribution), the Cabinet having to meet to discuss the legislative timetable.

It was a well-established convention that the Cabinet met several times in the autumn and sometimes in January to agree to the chief legislative priorities for the next year.[1] The Irish Land Bill cabinets in late 1880 followed almost exactly the pattern for the preparation of the Land Bill in 1869 (though in that year the autumn Cabinets also planned for the Education Bill and a complex structure of other legislation).[2] In 1881, however, only one Cabinet discussed prospective legislation (10 November 1881): a bold plan of 'efficient local Govt. over Ireland & Scotland: London included but not in the van' was adumbrated. But the lack of commitment was immediately shown: the plan was remitted to a Cabinet committee of which Gladstone was not a member. Consequently the Cabinet met Parliament in 1882 with its plans confused and its disputes unresolved. In the autumn of 1882, with the special Session on procedure, the Cabinet met quite frequently. But Gladstone's impending retirement, and the Cabinet reshuffle relieving him of the Exchequer, account in part for the fact that no discussion of prospective legislation is recorded. In 1883, autumn planning Cabinets agreed for 1884 to a County Government Bill (again referred to a committee without Gladstone as a member—as we shall see, a sign of lack of political will) and to a Franchise Bill supervised by Gladstone. Whether redistribution was to be included was left for a time as an open question, which gave Hartington time to come round, as he did. This openness caused some confusion, some of the Cabinet thinking, with some justification, that a decision had been taken.[3] Gladstone's minute at the time is clear enough: 'Redistribution: not to be united with franchise.'[4] The 1884 autumn Cabinets monitored the constitutional crisis but planned nothing of major consequence for 1885. If it was 'big Bills' that kept the Liberal Party in good heart, this sad record shows that the successes of the government and the party came despite the planning of the Cabinet.

The composition of the Cabinet was intended largely to reassure, and in doing so it reflected not only the restorative frame of mind in which Gladstone approached his second premiership, but also a more general hiatus in the development of Liberalism. The decade of the 1880s can be seen both as the last of the old Liberal Party and as the first of the new. It stands poised awkwardly between defending the achievements of the past and building upon those achievements a new structure which would recognize a fresh phase in the evolution of industrial society. The 1880s were, therefore, an awkward moment for the party of progress. The ambivalence of the party's and the government's

[1] i.e. those that were contentious and required particular Cabinet attention; a regular diet of relatively uncontentious matter went undiscussed, or at any rate unrecorded, at these meetings, its place in the timetable decided mainly by the leader of the House (i.e. Gladstone), the Whigs and the relevant ministers; such bills usually came before Cabinet in the form of being dropped at the end of the Session when the timetable became overburdened.

[2] 5, 10 Nov. 69.

[3] e.g. Chamberlain; see to Hartington, 7 Dec. 83. The distinction was that if there was a reform bill, redistribution would follow rather than be included in the franchise bill; technically, the Cabinet was not yet committed to a bill, though one was being drawn up.

[4] 22 Nov. 83.

direction opened both to domination by crises. Any government is, of course, likely suddenly to be affected by an unexpected crisis, but a government, and especially a progressive government, which is uncertain about its own direction is likely to find such crises particularly difficult.

Moreover, we now know that the crises of the 1880s in Ireland, in foreign and imperial affairs, and to some extent in domestic politics also, were in considerable measure affected by a common stimulus whose very existence the Liberals denied: the recession in the world economy. Orthodox political economy could not admit more than a temporary dislocation to the balance of equilibrium, and they believed that the re-establishment of that balance needed only the corrective forces of the free market. Consequently, the Liberal ex-Cabinet refused to sit on the Royal Commission on the Depression of Trade set up by Salisbury in 1885, because to do so would admit the possibility that such a depression could exist and would associate Liberals with an inquiry which would at the least consider protectionist solutions. Because no depression could or did exist, no general explanation of the phenomena of the 1880s could be offered by Liberals. The various crises were thus seen as having discrete and usually political causes. Crises thus reared up unanticipated and to a large extent unexplained,[1] being dealt with in their overt terms. Though developments in imperial policy sometimes reached simultaneous pitches of intensity—Ireland and the Transvaal in December 1881 and the spring of 1882—what is striking is the extent to which, for members of the Cabinet, regional policies remained regional. Though there were obvious similarities between Ireland and the Transvaal, only the odd comment suggests a recognition of this; indeed, in Gladstone's mind and writings, much less so than his analysis of 'conquest' and subsequent 'amalgamation' made in the late 1870s would lead us to expect.[2]

The daily diary, cabinet minutes, and correspondence printed below offer the narrative of Gladstone's involvement in the series of entanglements which prolonged his premiership. It is not the purpose of this Introduction to attempt to repeat that narrative: it is there for the reader to read in all its complexity, detail, and exceptional density. But to analyse this vast range of materials and to discuss the peculiar contribution which Gladstone made to his second government, it will be convenient to retain these discrete categories and to examine them in the following order: colonial, foreign, and defence policy; the domestic legislative programme and the economy; Ireland.

Some have seen Gladstone as governed merely by expediency. He, even in a government of which his membership was intended to be temporary, saw himself primarily as an executant, a defender and, as circumstances required, an originator of policy. Detailed scrutiny reveals a much more coherent and consistent approach to policy than the *ad hoc* character of the second and third Gladstone governments which is suggested by a first glance.

[1] Thus Sir Hercules Robinson, the liberal and perceptive colonial governor, wrote in January 1884: 'How strange it is that the Government which came in on the platform of curtailing Imperial responsibilities should be likely to add more to them than any previous Ministry in the present century—New Guinea, the South Pacific, South Africa—and last, but not least Egypt, in which we are drifting into a protectorate. It is surely the irony of fate'; *Correspondence of J. X. Merriman*, ed. P. Lewsen (1960), 155.

[2] See above, ix. xlvi. For the Cabinet's 'Inter-locking dilemmas' in 1881, see Schreuder, 176ff.

V

Colonial or, as it was increasingly called, Imperial policy and foreign policy were the chief areas in which Gladstone intended to restore right conduct and right principles after the disasters of Beaconsfieldism. Gladstone had seen these disasters as caused by individual failures of 'panic or pride' within what he saw as a systematic perversion of good government: good men with right principles—'the exercise of moral control over ambition and cupidity'—could restore proper conduct and right relations. Though recognizing Britain's inherent capacity for Empire, he explicitly declined to accept that there was any underlying or determinist pattern of causation in recent accessions.[1] On the other hand, he did recognize that certain regional policies, once put in train, were difficult to stop, and he was careful in his criticisms in Midlothian in 1879 and 1880 to avoid absolute commitments and to decline to disavow agreements entered into by the Conservative government. Consequently, despite the apparent differences, British policy in this period was much less oscillating than the French, whose internal political instability was reflected in violent swings in Imperial policy.

In Midlothian in 1879 Gladstone told the electors 'what I think to be the right principles of foreign policy'. These were 1. good government at home, 2. the preservation to the nations of the world, and 'especially to the Christian nations of the world', of the blessings of peace, 3. the cultivation and maintenance of the Concert of Europe, 4. the avoidance of needless and entangling engagements, 5. to acknowledge the equal rights of all nations, 6. the foreign policy of England [*sic*] should always be inspired by the love of freedom.[2]

These famous 'six principles' were cautiously qualified ('avoid needless and entangling engagements') at the same time as bold. But on the fifth principle, the acknowledgement of 'the equal rights of all nations', Gladstone was unequivocal: this was the principle to which he attached the 'greatest value' and to which he returned in his peroration:

> Christendom is formed of a band of nations who are united to one another in the bond of right; . . . they are without distinction of great and small; there is an absolute equality between them . . . he who by act or word brings that principle into peril or disparagement, however honest his intentions may be, places himself in the position of one inflicting . . . injury upon his own country, and endangering the peace and all the most fundamental interests of Christian society.[3]

This passage seemed of world-wide application, but in its context it applied to Europe. The ambivalence haunted Gladstone through the imperial crises of his second government.

Moreover, it is important again to recall that Gladstone was, outside free trade, no Cobdenite. He saw intervention as a natural part of the maintenance of the civilized order of the world. He used military and naval force coolly and without embarrassment. Every Cabinet that he had sat in since 1843 had

---

[1] See above, ix. lxxii–lxxiii.
[2] *Political Speeches* (1879), 115ff. (third Midlothian speech, 27 November 1879).
[3] Ibid., 129.

dispatched a military expedition. On 12 July 1882, the day after the bombardment of Alexandria, Sir Wilfrid Lawson jibed that if a Tory government had
been in office Gladstone would have stopped his train at every station to pro-
claim non-intervention as the duty of the Government. Lawson's jibe produced
this angry retort:

> He seems to think that I am a general apostle of non-intervention. I do not, however,
> see why he should say so; he has quoted nothing that bears out that view. On the con-
> trary, if he will take the trouble to recollect, all my objections to the conduct of the late
> Government for a certain time—in the year 1876 and the year 1877—were, he will find,
> expressly founded on the charge that we had not had intervention enough.[1]

It was where to intervene, and where not to be drawn into intervention, and for
what reasons, that concerned Gladstone. And that was a question of policy and
balance of advantage.[2] A reconciliation between the 'equal rights of all nations'
and the requirements of international order was a highly problematic duty for
the Liberal Prime Minister of an imperial power.

Gladstone sought no expansion of British imperial responsibilities. He was
consequently ready to concede that other powers might expand if they wished
to. He was certainly not, as some Liberals were, hostile to colonization *per se*,
but accepted it, subject to certain provisos, as entirely natural if the relevant
European nation judged it to be in her interest. Thus he twice publicly welcomed German colonial expansion, while sceptical as to whether it was really in
Germany's interest:

> if Germany has the means of expanding herself and sending her children to un-
> occupied places of the earth, with due regard to the previous rights of other nations,
> and with due regard to the rights of the aboriginal inhabitants—subject to those two
> reserves, gentlemen, I tell you I look with satisfaction, sympathy, and joy upon the
> expansion of Germany in these desert places of the earth, upon the extension of civil-
> ization, and upon the blessing to these waste places by the presence of an intelligent,
> industrious community, which will bring forth from the bosom of the land new
> resources for the comfort, advantage, and happiness of mankind. Do not suppose for a
> moment that it is anything but the utmost meanness for us to be jealous of Germany.
> Germany cannot rob this country, even if she desired it, of her colonizing character. It
> is evident—no man can deny it—that it is among the most patent and palpable facts of
> the condition of the world, that God Almighty has given to the people who inhabit
> these islands a great function and a great duty of colonization. And that duty has been
> fulfilled by a pretty liberal appropriation of the country which had not been occupied.
> Come what may, let every other country do what it will,—it is for them to consider how
> far their political strength will be increased by it. Into that question I do not enter.[3]

[1] *H* 272. 174.
[2] Confronted by A. I. Myers, proprietor of the *Jewish Chronicle*, with information about the
Russian pogrom of 1881, Gladstone asked Olga Novikov if there was any satisfactory reply that
could be made to the appalling charges. Novikov dismissed the reports as mere Jewish 'agitation'.
Gladstone fell back on the argument that in 1851 (Naples) and in 1876 (Bulgaria) he had been a
private citizen urging the government to action; it was now for others to do the same—a very weak
argument as the object of his previous actions had been a change in government policy, the sort of
change he was now in a position to make. He also argued that 'the interference of foreign governments in such cases is more likely to do harm than good'. See to Myers (not sent) and to Novikov, 18
Jan. 82 and 25 Jan. 82.
[3] In Edinburgh, 1 Sept. 84, in *Speeches in Scotland, 1884*, 78; see also 12 Mar. 85.

Gladstone looked to balance and stability in the Empire. The essential strength of the Empire sprang, he believed, from the power of the British economy. Anything that diminished that power, such as increased taxation, was undesirable. He was thus a leading exponent of that school which has criticized the extent of Britain's world-wide defence commitment as an important economic incubus and as the imperial epoch in British history recedes, his views have received increasingly powerful historiographical support.[1] During his first government a determined effort was made to force local defence costs on to colonies with responsible government, and the criticism of over-extension was central to his attack on Beaconsfieldism.[2] If there had to be Protectorates, he looked to Selborne's minimalist, and cheap, definition of British responsibility in them.[3] He showed little interest in the anti-slavery cause which made imperial expansion and intervention acceptable to many Liberals.

Strategic concern about the 'route to India' was not one of his principles of foreign policy,[4] and he was 'one of those who think that to the actual, as distinguished from the reported, strength of the Empire, India adds nothing. She immensely adds to the responsibility of Government. . . .' On the other hand, he continued, recognizing the imprisonment of his world vision in the cage of history, 'none of this is to the purpose. We have undertaken a most arduous but a most noble duty. We are pledged to India, I may say to mankind, for its performance and we have no choice. . . .'[5]

This was the position in which Gladstone constantly found himself with respect to Imperial affairs. His executive role countervailed his inclinations and ultimate anticipations. From the failure to hold in balance these two forces sprang many of his difficulties. But the existence of both these forces, and his spasmodic skill in employing them, allowed him considerable manoeuvre in Cabinet, in the Commons, and in his appeal to public support.

The Cabinet faced acute instability at either end of the Islamic area: in Afghanistan, and in Egypt and its satellite, the Sudan. The Conservative government had bought the nest egg of the Suez Canal shares; it had declared, as Gladstone saw it, a 'new Asiatic Empire'[6] through the Anglo-Turkish Convention of June 1878; and it had embarked on a forward policy in central Asia which led to punitive expeditions, the imposition of a new ruler, Abdul Rahman, in Afghanistan, and the possibility of a military presence there for the foreseeable future. This was, in Gladstone's view, primarily inexpedient and imprudent; it was morally wrong only in the execution of the policy.

The British government seemed to extricate itself from Afghanistan, but found itself doing in Egypt what it avoided on the North West frontier of India, and on a far more lavish scale. Militarily overstretched, the government ended with a crisis in each area as the Russians took advantage of the disaster in the

---

[1] See L. E. Davis and R. A. Huttenback, *Mammon and the pursuit of Empire. The political economy of British imperialism 1860–1912* (1986) and P. K. O'Brien, 'The costs and benefits of British imperialism 1846–1914', *Past and Present*, 120 (1988).

[2] See Matthew, *Gladstone*, 188–9 and above, ix. xlii.

[3] 20 Jan. 85 and W. R. Louis, 'The Berlin Congo Conference' in P. Gifford and W. R. Louis, *France and Britain in Africa* (1971), 209–13.

[4] See above ix. xlii.   [5] To Ripon, 4 Nov. 81.   [6] 8 July 78.

Sudan and the consequent instability of the Gladstone government to push forward against the Afghan frontier.

In Central Asia, the subject of the first cabinet of the ministry,[1] Gladstone had his way. Ripon was appointed Viceroy, leaving on 14 May 1880, after Gladstone had worked out for Granville, almost immediately on taking office, the bones of a policy.[2] Salisbury's negotiation with Persia to partition Afghanistan (by Persia's absorbing Herat) was immediately broken off.[3] Gladstone led the Cabinet in the withdrawal from most of Afghanistan, achieved by the spring of 1881, against the advice of the Queen and many others.[4] But the evacuation of troops from Afghanistan was by no means an abandonment of the area, merely of the 'forward policy' method of safeguarding it. A stable *régime* in Afghanistan was a better safeguard than an imposed one, especially if it could give effective British control without direct responsibility. Thus the way continued through 1880 until the defeat at Maiwand was exceeded by the victory at Mazra. Abdur Rahman emerged the victor in the fratricidal struggle for power, his *régime* backed by a British guarantee against unprovoked aggression, in return for British control of Afghanistan's external relations,[5] a guarantee confirmed and extended by Hartington in August 1881 following further Russian activity.[6] Prompted by the Indian government, and strongly supported by Northbrook, the former Viceroy,[7] Hartington, the Secretary for India, then proposed a treaty between Britain and Russia, confirming the Afghan frontier in exchange for tacit acceptance of Russian expansion up to it.[8] This was too bold for Granville, who fell back on the agreement of 1873 and the internal strengthening of Afghanistan.[9] Hartington's enthusiasm for a treaty waned, and Northbrook was subsequently unable to gain Cabinet attention for the proposal.[10]

Gladstone seems to have shown no interest in the idea of a treaty. But Russia was expanding naturally under her own momentum, there being never a serious proposal of a double buffer: a Turkestan buffer to protect the Afghan buffer. When in 1883 Russia demanded from Persia territory which would 'place

[1] 3 May 80.

[2] Ramm II, i. 125.

[3] See F. Kazemzadeh, *Russia and Britain in Persia 1864–1914* (1968), 72.

[4] 7, 10 Jan. 81.

[5] See C. Howard, *Britain and the* Casus Belli *1822–1902* (1974), 116. Abdur Rahman was Lytton's choice as a stable ruler, despite his extensive exile in Russia; he was subsequently backed by Ripon despite the hostility of Stewart, whom the Cabinet had made political adviser as well as military commander at Kabul; 3 May 80 and Gopal, *Ripon*, 8–10; see also 17, 29 May, 19 June 80.

[6] *Ripon*, ii. 60–1; Hartington's statement was not the result of Cabinet discussion.

[7] Northbrook to Ripon, 19 May 1882, Add MS 43572: 'The question of a Treaty with Russia unluckily came before the Cabinet at the only cabinet since the Govt. was formed at which I was not present, having been at Balmoral. I believe the opinion was adverse to taking any steps towards a treaty . . .'; on 9 July 1882, ibid., f. 47: 'You and I are in a minority on the Treaty question.' Northbrook observed Russia's move to Merv with equanimity: 'If we have a conciliatory answer from Russia, we propose to enter into negotiations for laying down the N. Western boundary of Afghanistan by Russian and English officers, and I hope to have this embodied in a Treaty. This is what you & I have long wished for' (Northbrook to Ripon, 22 February 1884, ibid., f. 96).

[8] 10 Nov. 81.

[9] 10 Nov. 81; Gopal, *Ripon*, 35–8.

[10] See Northbrook to Ripon, 11 March, 19 May, 9 July 1882, Add MS 43572, ff. 6, 31, 47.

Russia in contact with Afghan frontier', Gladstone noted 'There can be no objection.'[1] The chance of bargaining an agreed frontier against Russian expansion into Turkestan passed, and Russia, in a British-style manoeuvre, accepted the invitation of the local elders in February 1885 to control of the ancient city of Merv.[2] The moment expected for twenty years had come: Russia was effectively on the Afghan frontier. The logical boundary commission followed, the building of the railway to Quetta was again recommended, and Russian brinkmanship[3] at Pendjeh in March–May 1885 was resolutely blocked.

The sturdy resistance of Gladstone and his Cabinet is sometimes thought of as a ploy to extricate them from the Sudan.[4] But it was in fact wholly in line with their Afghan policy: a friendly, nominally independent and therefore static Afghan state clearly and boldly defended, and with no attempt to meddle with Russia beyond that. What had changed was the need to give precise definition to the frontier. This became necessary once Russia was at Merv; the 'masterly inactivity' school, particularly represented in Cabinet by Northbrook, felt it undesirable to define it earlier. Definition would merely encourage Russia and might force a greater British involvement in Afghanistan's internal affairs. This squared with Gladstone's view: Russian expansion in Central Asia was natural and, with respect to India, benign. There was, in his view, no Russian plan or intention to invade British India; an independent, unified, and guaranteed Afghanistan was therefore a quite sufficient bastion.

Despite constant Conservative charges of negligence and weakness, the Afghan policy was a notable success. In the spring of 1885, without annexation, the Russians were firmly halted at a viable frontier. For the rest of the Imperial period, they never crossed it. 'Surely it must set for a *few* hours' was the apprehensive question of the Bokharan gentry to the traveller Henry Lansdell[5] when he told them in the early 1880s that on the Queen's Empire the sun was unceasingly shining: at least in Central Asia the Liberal Cabinet ensured that there was no British protectorate for Tommy Atkins to defend in the noon-day glare.

Gladstone began and ended his second government resolutely involved in Central Asian affairs. He was not much otherwise directly engaged in the subject because he did not have to be. There was a depth of experience and competence on the Liberal side, deepened by the bonus of Northbrook's presence in the Cabinet. Moreover, there was a general agreement that 'Mervousness' as Argyll dubbed it—panic that Russian extension to the Afghan border implied Russian plans to invade India—was wholly unnecessary. Though the command structure for dealing with the area was complex, involving the Prime Minister, the Foreign Secretary, the Indian Secretary and his Council in London, the Viceroy and his Council in India, the exercise of authority within it was contain-

[1] 5 Mar. 83.

[2] See R. L. Greaves, *Persia and the defence of India 1884–1892* (1959), ch. iv.

[3] That it was such can be seen from D. Geyer, *Russian Imperialism. The interaction of domestic and foreign policy 1860–1914* (1987), 114.

[4] Holland, ii. 31. For a useful comment on this see *Relief of Gordon*, xliii.

[5] H. Lansdell, *Through Central Asia* (1887), 352, quoted in A. P. Thornton, 'Essay and reflection: third thoughts on Empire', *Int. Hist. Rev.*, x. 592 (1988); Lansdell has a useful map and Appendix on the 1885–6 border dispute.

able and worked well. It was clear what the policy, once established, was, and it was clearly executed. The effectiveness of the structure was well illustrated by the majestic display in the spring of 1885 as the Executive, Parliament, and the Empire in the East were swiftly and easily placed on a war footing backed by an £11 million Vote of Credit (i.e. 10 per cent of the annual budget).

Authority with respect to Egypt was, by contrast, at every turn confused and oblique. If Ireland was the great deflector in domestic policy, so was Egypt in foreign and imperial. The Ottoman Empire nominally ruled North Africa. In Egypt the Sultan's authority was rarely effective, though he retained his position as a religious leader and even reformers claimed to act in his service as representative of the realm of Islam.[1] European authority was already asserted by the Anglo-French Dual Control of 1876 and 1879, and de Lesseps retained the 'Concession' of the Canal. Disraeli's purchase of the Suez Canal shares in 1875 had exemplified the extent to which the general interest of safeguarding an international waterway was also a particular British imperial and now also financial interest.

Gladstone's campaigns of the 1870s had given a general impression of hostility to the Ottoman Empire, and the Sultan cannot have welcomed the start of Gladstone's second political career. In fact, however, Gladstone had seen Turkish suzerainty over locally autonomous Christian states as the best way of maintaining stability in the Balkans, and had disliked independence and partition.[2] But his public and private views had hardly been flattering to the Sultan, and in the early months of the government he energetically pursued the Balkan boundary question, being prepared to use British force to coerce the Porte if the Concert failed to act.[3] In 1881 the Sultan lost Tunis to the French. There was never any serious question of British opposition to this move, effectively an extension of Algeria. Gladstone covered the Liberals' position by publishing some of the dispatches on Salisbury's promises in 1878 which seemed to recognize the naturalness of France's expansion, and which had, in Gladstone's view (conveniently?), 'cut away the ground (Italy being out of the question) from under our feet'.[4] This worked for domestic politics; it did not improve British influence with the Sultan. The consequence of all this was that the Liberal government had no capital to draw on as it looked to Constantinople to maintain order in Egypt.

The autochthonous Egyptian reform movement, prompted in part by the British/French attempt to rule Egypt through the imposed Khedive Tewfik (equally disliked by the Sultan) and through the treasury in the form of the Dual Control of 1879 and in part also by the French occupation of Tunis, was at first reported not altogether unsympathetically by Colvin, the British controller of finance, and by Malet, the British consul.[5] Gladstone's reaction to it was to see it

[1] A. Schölch, *Egypt for the Egyptians! The socio-political crisis in Egypt 1878–82* (1981), 284. See also J. S. Galbraith and Afaf Lufti al-Sayyid-Marsot, 'The British occupation of Egypt. Another view', *International Journal of Middle East Studies*, ix (1978).

[2] See above, ix. xxxiv; Gladstone's view was similar to his policy in the 1860s on compulsory church rates: pruning the rotten bough to maintain the tree.

[3] 6 Sept., 1–12 Oct., 10 Nov. 80 and above, ix. lxxiii.

[4] 13 May 81.

[5] Schölch, op. cit., 185–6.

sympathetically through the eyes of Wilfrid Blunt in the sort of terms he had used for Balkan nationalism, a form of analysis which in 1882 he notably did not use with respect to Ireland:

> I suppose we are entitled to hold the present position so far as it is necessary to guarantee the pecuniary interests on behalf of which we have in this somewhat exceptional case been acting in Turkey.
>
> But I should regard with the utmost apprehension a conflict between the 'Controul' and any sentiment truly national, with a persuasion that one way or other we should come to grief in it.
>
> I am not by any means pained, but I am much surprised at this rapid development of a national sentiment and party in Egypt. The very ideas of such a sentiment and the Egyptian people seemed quite incompatible. How it has come up I do not know: most of all is the case strange if the standing army be the nest that has reared it. There however it seems to be, & to claim the respect due to it as a fact, and due also to the capabilities that may be latent in it for the future. 'Egypt for the Egyptians' is the sentiment to which I should wish to give scope: and could it prevail it would I think be the best, the only good solution of the 'Egyptian question'.[1]

When Wilfrid Blunt in December 1881 sent the 'Programme of the National Party of Egypt' written by Arabi and himself, Gladstone felt 'quite sure that unless there be a sad failure of good sense on one or both or as I should say on all sides, we shall be enabled to bring this question to a favourable issue'.[2] But, partly at Granville's urging, Gladstone backed away from this contact.[3]

Blunt was to be no Mrs. O'Shea, and Gladstone's knowledge of Egyptian developments depended subsequently on official reports. The reports of Colvin and Malet from February 1882, increasingly hostile to the reform party and Arabi, prepared the way for European occupation: 'it would . . . be necessary, if it be determined that the present state of things cannot be allowed to continue, that an occupation of the country should precede its reorganization, but it would be wise to allow the experiment to prove itself clearly impracticable before such a measure is resorted to. For very clear grounds can alone justify the suppression by arms of the effort of a country to govern itself.'[4] Moreover, there was always a difficulty for Liberals in seeing constitutional nationalism as worthily embodied in an army, and, however broadly based Arabi's movement may have been, its prospects of success always depended on the army.

As during 1882 the situation in Egypt developed (or deteriorated in the view

[1] To Granville, 4 January 1882, in Ramm II, i. 326.

[2] To Blunt, 20 Jan. 82; see also Blunt, *Secret history*, 202, 559. After the occupation Gladstone, perhaps not surprisingly, found Blunt 'intolerable' but retained some sense—more than Granville—of the possible force of his criticisms; see Ramm II, ii. 97, 101, 104 and Cromer, i. 279–80.

[3] Blunt's subsequent letters were dealt with by E. W. Hamilton; from them Hamilton—already a friend of Blunt—gained the view of a moderate, non-belligerent Arabi now largely held by historians (see Schölch, *passim* and A. G. Hopkins, 'The Victorians and Africa: a reconsideration of the occupation of Egypt, 1882', *Journal of African History*, xxvii. 353 (1986)). But by May 1882 Hamilton had been converted by Malet and Rivers Wilson: 'I am afraid Wilfrid Blunt and all his enthusiasm for the "National" party in Egypt has been shown up'; Bahlman, *Hamilton*, 21 May 1882; none the less he remained in touch with Blunt (see Blunt, *Secret history*, 339).

[4] Malet's despatch of 27 February 1882, PRO FO 78/3435, in Schölch, 220. See also A. Schölch, 'The "Men on the Spot" and the English occupation of Egypt in 1882', *Historical Journal* (1976), xix. 773.

of many Europeans), the following points need to be borne in mind about Gladstone's position. He was not hostile to intervention for the preservation of
order, but this had to be balanced by the claims of local autonomous powers. It
was hard for anyone dependent on the information about Egypt being supplied
by Malet and Colvin in the spring and summer of 1882 to believe other than
that the Arabi movement represented disorder promoted by a small military
clique, and not as Gladstone had thought in January 1882, though with some
uncertainty, a 'sentiment truly national'.[1] Thus when he told Bright that 'the
general situation in Egypt had latterly become one in which everything was
governed by sheer military violence and a situation of *force* had been created,
which could only be met by force', he expressed what was by July 1882 a very
generally held orthodoxy.[2] Gladstone had publicly and stridently warned since
1876 that Britain's acts were entangling, and that British policy had no prudential basis. But he certainly never held that by 1880 Britain was exempt from
involvement in some form. The ends of British policy had been, he told the
Commons, 'most distinctly and repeatedly stated ... they are well known to
consist in the general maintenance of all established rights in Egypt, whether
they be those of the Sultan, those of the Khedive, those of the people of Egypt,
or those of the foreign bondholders'.[3] The Egyptians could work out their destiny only within a tightly defined and controlled framework, externally supervised and consequently, by implication, externally policed.

Hoping that the preferred solution of 'Egypt for the Egyptians'—but with, of
course, their finances still under international direction—would be shown by
events to be a solution which could prevail, Gladstone kept the Cabinet away
from the question as much as possible, and in the spring and summer of 1882,
Ireland by itself supplied a full budget of business. When the Sultan offered
Egypt to the British, reserving only his own suzerainty, Gladstone and Granville
turned him down without consulting the Cabinet.[4] This absence of Cabinet discussion paid a high price, for it encouraged and indeed legitimized independent
action and planning by the Admiralty, the India Office, and the War Office.

As the weight of opinion in London turned against seeing 'Egypt for the
Egyptians' as compatible with 'order', the hope—irony of ironies for Gladstone—was for action by the Porte: 'our first object should be to have the Sultan
committed visibly in Egypt against the unruly'.[5] This failing, and with 'stiff and
difficult' opposition from Hartington, Gladstone and Granville persuaded the
Cabinet to accept the French proposal for a Conference at Constantinople.[6]
With the Porte still prevaricating, the French doubtful (though by now present
with the British fleet in the harbour at Alexandria), and the absence of 'order'

[1] To Granville, 4 January 1882, Ramm II, i. 326.
[2] To Bright, 14 July 82. *The Economist*, 1 July 1882, 802, strongly defending British policy, took just
this view: 'the contingency of anarchy in Egypt, in which event Lord Granville has throughout stipulated for perfect freedom of action, has arrived. Those who were credulous enough to imagine that
Arabi was the sincere exponent of a genuine and innocent popular movement must be rudely
deceived by the facts disclosed in the papers recently presented to Parliament.'
[3] *H* 270. 1146 (14 June 1882).
[4] Exchange of letters on 25 June 1882, Ramm II, i. 381–2.
[5] To Granville, 29 May 1882, Ramm II, i. 376.
[6] 31 May 82.

apparently confirmed by the riots in Alexandria on 11 June,[1] contingency plans for a separate British expedition were authorized on 15 June at a 'Quasi Cabinet' (i.e. a semi-formal meeting). The difference between Hartington and the rest of the Cabinet was merely that a public announcement of this at the Conference would be 'premature'.[2] By 21 June Gladstone had drawn up the sequence for military involvement. It was clear that troops were to go: the only question was, whose? The answer was 'to ask the Powers to provide for or sanction a military intervention other than Turkish under their authority'.[3] Given the preponderance of British interest and influence in Egypt, this was all but a British, or an Anglo-French force. When the French suggested negotiation with Arabi, they were quickly reprimanded.[4] Thus Arabi's strengthening of the forts of Alexandria—the occasion for the bombardment by the British navy on 11 July—was merely an incident after the strategic decisions had been taken.

Certainly Gladstone was very sceptical about aspects of those decisions. He did not associate himself with the India Office argument about the security of the route to India, a factor in play in Cabinet from 21 June. He very strongly opposed independent British seizure of the Canal—proposed by Hartington, the Secretary for India—as Arabi was unlikely to tamper with it unless provoked and as 'an act full of menace to the future peace of the world', supplying 'dangerous arguments' which might be used against Britain in Panama, the Dardanelles and the Bosphorus.[5] His article, 'Aggression on Egypt and Freedom in the East', written in 1877, had spelt out his general objections. He referred Blunt to this article in 1882, as containing his 'opinions about Egypt ... I am not aware as yet of having seen any reasons to change them'.[6] In 1884 he republished the pamphlet almost unchanged (and clearly intended as a warning, to some of his colleagues as well as the public, of the dangers of further involvement in the Sudan).[7] His concern was for order, engineered, he hoped, through the Concert. He told his son Harry, then in India: 'In Egypt the embarrassments have been extreme. But the Conference has gone to work and this is of itself a considerable fact; a bulwark against precipitate follies.'[8]

But if, for Gladstone, strategic arguments were not convincing and indeed were even dangerous, what was it that made 'order' in Egypt a question on which Britain was to act singlehandedly, in the face of the reluctance of France (her most likely partner) and of the Conference sitting in Constantinople? Why was Gladstone ready, however reluctantly, to agree, despite his better judgement, to the demand of the India Office, the War Office, and the Admiralty for a decision to which he could be 'no party'?[9]

[1] For these and the Cabinet's misunderstanding of their nature, see M. E. Chamberlain, 'The Alexandrian massacre of 11 June 1882 and the British occupation of Egypt', *Middle Eastern Studies*, xiii (1977).
[2] 19 June 82.
[3] 21 June 82; at this meeting, the security of the Canal came to the fore, as a rather late concern.
[4] 3 July 82.
[5] Mem. for Granville, 5 July 1882, in Ramm II, i. 385.
[6] To Blunt, 20 Jan. 82.
[7] 12 June 84.
[8] To H. N. Gladstone, 23 June 82.
[9] To Granville, 4 July 1882, Ramm II, i. 384.

The most obvious reason was that, by the end of June 1882, Gladstone was simply outnumbered and outflanked in his Cabinet and was anyway physically and mentally exhausted by his constant work in the Commons on the Irish Crimes and Arrears Bills: on 1 July, 'My share of the sitting I take at nineteen hours. Anxious Cabinet on Egypt behind the [Speaker's] Chair 4–5'; by 5 July, 'My brain is *very* weary.' But Gladstone did not take, even in principle, John Bright's view of intervention as simply wrong. As we have seen, he was not a non-interventionist in international affairs. 'Disorder' in Egypt threatened various interests and raised several spectres. One of them was the question of the Egyptian debt and the possibility of the failure of the Dual Control to extract payments and of the Khedive being prevented from paying the Tribute to the Porte. In 1880, 66 per cent of the revenue of Egypt went to servicing the debt and the Tribute:[1] was it likely that a government representing 'Egypt for the Egyptians' could honour so enormous an obligation? 'Order' meant civilian and strategic order, but it also meant financial security. Money was tied in with power and imperial strategy in an unusually direct and explicit form in Egypt, however careful the attempts to keep the foreign bondholders a legally separate international entity, different from the interests of their respective national governments.

The interest of the bondholders was real, and the Prime Minister was in a sense one of them—a bondholder at second hand. He was a substantial holder of the two Egyptian Tribute Loans, Turkish loans guaranteed by the Egyptian Tribute paid annually to the Porte by the Khedive out of Egyptian revenues. In December 1875 Gladstone owned £25,000 of the 1871 Tribute Loan at 42, worth £10,500; by 1878 this had risen to £30,000, worth £15,900; in 1879 he added £15,000 of the 1854 loan, worth £12,000. Thus by December 1881, as the Egyptian crisis began to break, Gladstone owned in all £51,500 of Egyptian Tribute Loan Stock, worth £40,567. The Egyptian Tribute Loan Stock 1871, bought at 42, was worth 62 in 1881 and had fallen to 57 in the summer of 1882; but by December 1882 it was worth 82.[2] At his annual reckoning of his assets in December 1882 (drawn up, as always, in his own hand), Gladstone's holdings of

---

[1] A. Milner, *England in Egypt* (1894 ed.), vii.

[2] Figures taken from the 'Approximate Annual Sketch of Property' prepared by Gladstone at the end of each calendar year; Hawn P. What Gladstone noted in his accounts as 'Egyptian Loans' were in fact the Turkish government loans of 1854 and 1871 raised on the international market by Messrs. Dent, Palmer & Co.; the loans were guaranteed by the 'Egyptian Tribute' paid to the Sultan by the Khedive as the first call on Egyptian revenues not assigned to the debt. *The Times*, 5 September 1871, 5a, explained their working: 'The first hypothecation of the Egyptian tribute was to its entire extent of £282,872, but in 1866 the sum payable by the Khedive was raised to £705,000 and it is this extra amount of £422,128 that is now pledged, and of which His Highness has engaged to remit direct to the Bank of England the sum of £399,000 per annum.' When the 1871 loan was launched, *The Economist* (9 September 1871, 1089) warned: 'the security of the tribute is not a firm one—no firmer than the credit of Egypt, which is better than Turkish, but is not of the best'; after 1876 Egyptian credit was, of course, much less secure than Turkish. The price of the Tribute Loan stock rose not on the bombardment of Alexandria, but on Wolseley's expedition in August with its implication of at least a short-run occupation; *T.T.*, 21 August 1882, 8a, noted 'There was a strong demand for those Turkish loans which are secured on the Egyptian loan' and on 16 September 1882 *The Economist*, 1157, recorded 'the fresh great rise in Egyptian and in the Turkish Tribute Loans'. The Egyptian Tribute Loan was not part of the Egyptian debt subject to the Law of Liquidation and to the International Conference which met in 1884.

Egyptian Tribute Loan accounted for about 37 per cent of his portfolio. To have over a third of his portfolio invested in stock dependent on the credit of a *régime* whose deceit, untrustworthiness, and immorality he had so frequently denounced was hardly rational, unless he presupposed that external action would in the last resort require the Sultan and the Khedive (or whoever was ruling Egypt) to honour the loan.

Gladstone clearly saw no conflict of interest in his holding of this stock, nor was there a code of practice or even a convention to which he might have referred. It would no doubt be crude and simplistic to infer any personal corruption, or even a conscious awareness of an association between personal investments and 'order' in Egypt. Certainly there is no evidence of such an awareness. But the absence of any sense of peculiarity or incongruity simply heightens the naturalness of the British occupation and of the inherent, almost unselfconscious relationship of capital and imperial policy. Almost unselfconscious, because, as we have seen, before occupation was decided upon Gladstone mentioned the rights 'of the foreign bondholders' as on a par with those of the Sultan, the Khedive, and the people of Egypt. After the bombardment he told the Commons 'that undoubtedly it is not for the exclusive or special interest of the bondholders of Egypt—and indeed it is almost wholly without reference to them—that the proceeding of yesterday was taken'.[1] In the context of the bombardment, this was true. But the careful Gladstonian qualifications are revealing: if not in the 'exclusive or special' interest of the bondholders, it was in their general interest as part of the clutch of 'established rights' in Egypt which Gladstone had earlier defined as subject to the British government's guardianship and which it was now moving to guard directly. The means had changed, not the end.

It can now only be a matter of speculation as to what part, if any, the Prime Minister's personal stake in the stability of Egyptian affairs played in his eventual agreement to go along with the change from indirect to armed intervention in Egypt by Britain alone.[2] His behaviour suggests that it was at most an underlying factor encouraging private accommodation: Gladstone certainly cannot be presented as a proponent of the change nor was he, once their major objective of a European presence had been gained, a friend of the bondholders of the Egyptian debt in the long negotiations after 1882. When trying to settle this question in 1884, he was ready to leave the bondholders exposed and almost defenceless, by reducing the rate of interest on all Egyptian debts.[3]

Gladstone's candid preservation of his financial archives, and their unusual public availability, gives a peculiar insight into the financial interests of a man of power. His holdings were probably not unusual for a person of his class and scale of assets; almost anyone with a substantial portfolio would have held one

[1] *H* 272. 173; 12 July 1882.
[2] It should be noted that Arabi's movement was loyal to the Sultan (and may actually have been in league with him against the Khedive), and was therefore less likely to forswear the Tribute than to repudiate the debt; it should also be noted that the constitutionalists' stated aim was only to control that part of the budget not needed for servicing the debt and the Tribute (Schölch, op. cit., 203, 213, 246, 310–3). On the other hand, Gladstone's complete discounting of Arabi's stated constitutional objectives would imply a discounting of this assurance also.
[3] 21 June 84.

or other issue of 'Egyptians'.[1] Indeed, it was probably in his reluctance to invade Egypt that Gladstone was unusual. Even so, his holding of Egyptian Tribute Loan is a fact that, once known, is hard to forget.

Though Gladstone 'did not feel the necessity',[2] he agreed to the bombardment of Alexandria on 11 July 1882 with no comment on its morality and without an expression of regret as Britain began the imposition of 'order' on behalf of the international community. When John Bright resigned, Gladstone rightly placed the Alexandrian forts and the bombardment as a 'bye-question' to the general issue of order.[3] He told Musurus, the Sultan's ambassador, that the bombardment 'was a supreme moment for the Ottoman Empire', but when the Porte refused to act, he planned the Wolseley expedition with enthusiasm. No expression of regret or reluctance qualified Gladstone's determination that once the decision to intervene militarily in Egypt was taken it should be done comprehensively: 'Instructions to Wolseley; Put down Arabi & establish Khedive's power.'[4] Wolseley departed for Egypt, and Gladstone for a short holiday. On 15 September 1882 the relevant ministers met in London to hear the news: 'Conclave on Egypt $12\frac{1}{2}$–$2\frac{1}{2}$. Another flood of good news. No more blood I hope. Wolseley in Cairo: Arabi a prisoner: God be praised.' Gladstone asked the Archbishop of York and the Bishop of London (the Archbishop of Canterbury being ill) to have the church bells rung and the Secretary for War to have the guns fired in the London parks: 'I hope the guns will crash all the windows.'[5] These were no mere public gestures, though they were that also: a decisive answer to the long years of Tory baiting. Gladstone read Macaulay's patriotic *Lays of Ancient Rome* and Campbell's *Battle of the Baltic* during the crisis and he welcomed the troops home with obvious enthusiasm. The Liberal, Cardwellian army had performed with efficiency: 'We certainly ought to be in good humour, for we are pleased with our army, our navy, our admirals, our Generals, and our organization. Matters were not so conducted in the days of the Crimea. . . .'[6] Moreover, unlike the Crimea, a good proportion of the military expenses were charged to the Indian government, even though it had not been consulted about the expedition.[7] Gladstone was even able to score a point off the Queen who could hardly refuse to Wolseley the peerage she had for the two years previously so energetically prevented.[8]

If there was to be an expedition, it could hardly have gone better. On 10th

---

[1] When in 1884 Gladstone had time to survey his portfolio, he made no comment on his 'Egyptians', concentrating on his 'one heavy mistake', his Metropolitan District Railway holdings (see 3 Oct. 84). However, in 1884, though it certainly could not be regarded as a mistake, he sold his Egyptian Tribute Loan (1854) stock and invested the money in New Zealand 4%s and in Canadian and Scottish railways stocks, thus reducing the 'Egyptians' to about 22% of his portfolio, clearly a much more prudent distribution. He retained the 1871 Egyptian Tribute Loan stock until the late 1880s.

[2] To Granville, 9 July 1882, Ramm II, i. 388.

[3] To Bright, 14 July 82.

[4] 31 July 82.

[5] To Bishop of London, 16 September 1882, Tait MSS 100, f. 160 and to Childers, 15, 16 Sept. 82.

[6] To Madame Novikov, 15 Sept. 82; see also to Cardwell the same day.

[7] A long wrangle about this ensued; see to Hartington, 28 Aug. 82, to Ripon, 6 Sept., 1 Dec. 82. See also 24 Oct., 27 Nov., 1 Dec. 82.

[8] To Wolseley, 15 Sept. 82.

July 1882, Britain's involvement in Egypt had been oblique and without immediate responsibility. By 14 September she was the effective power in the land. It
was a spectacular exhibition of British supremacy, and a marked contrast with
the earlier French imbroglio in Algeria. It was also, however unintended, the
chief step towards the fulfilment of the prophecy issued by Gladstone himself in
1877 like a latter-day Isaiah (the prophet who warned against foreign entanglements):

> our first site in Egypt, be it by larceny or be it by emption, will be the almost certain egg
> of a North African Empire, that will grow and grow until another Victoria and another
> Albert, titles of the Lake-sources of the White Nile, come within our borders; and till
> we finally join hands across the Equator with Natal and Cape Town, to say nothing of
> the Transvaal and the Orange River on the south, or of Abyssinia or Zanzibar to be
> swallowed by way of *viaticum* on our journey.[1]

In 1877, the prophecy was intended as a warning against taking that first 'site'.
In 1882, the prophet himself ordered the church bells to be rung. The hope was
for a limited stay and a swift restoration of 'order', but the prophecy suggested
otherwise; moreover, it had continued with respect to Egypt: 'it is vain to disguise that we shall have the entire responsibility of the government, if we have
any of it at all'.

The Cabinet was no more agreed as to what to do with Egypt than it would
have been if the Canal had been captured in 1956. But the range of options was,
unlike 1956, considerable, from withdrawal through protectorate to annexation. India offered many precedents of informal advice backed by force. The day
Wolseley entered Cairo, Gladstone tried to narrow the possibilities by writing a
long memorandum for the Cabinet, 'The settlement of Egypt',[2] emphasizing
the need for neutrality, the support of the Khedive by a minimum force, and the
effective ending of Turkish authority in Egypt, using the model of 'the Balkan
and Rouman Suzerainties' (though Gladstone was careful to retain for the
Sultan 'the continuance of the tribute', by which the Turkish Egyptian loans
were guaranteed). He looked in fact for the sort of solution he had advocated
for the Balkans in the 1870s. He gained support for much of this in Cabinet.[3]
The first of what were to be at least sixty-six protestations of the temporary
nature of the British presence in Egypt were made,[4] and Gladstone was sufficiently confident of calm in Egypt to make in October 1882 the most determined of his efforts at retirement.[5]

There were two difficulties. Withdrawal of the army was to be 'regulated
exclusively and from point to point, by the consideration of security for life and
property', which included the Canal. But the Canal would never be as secure
without British troops as with them, and thus a presence would be needed as
long as Britain held India. The Indian argument may not have weighed much
with Gladstone, but it certainly did with others.[6] Second, political settlement

[1] 'Aggression on Egypt', *N.C.*, ii. 149 (August 1877); *Gleanings*, iv. 358.
[2] 15 Sept. 82.   [3] 21 Oct. 82.
[4] 15 Sept. 82. See Hopkins, art. cit., 388.   [5] To Spencer, 24 Oct. 82.
[6] Northbrook told Ripon, who had doubts at least about the bombardment: 'my own opinion is
that India might fairly be asked to pay the whole cost of the contingent, for the interest she has in
the canal ... is undoubtedly great—greater indeed than England's—for if we had not India why

depended, in Gladstone's view, on replacing Turkish sovereignty with a Khedive supported by a law of succession and 'the reasonable development of self-governing institutions'.[1] But Wolseley's army had smashed the Egyptian constitutional movement, the only possible basis for such institutions, and Gladstone, influenced by his Tractarian friend Phillimore, at first backed the execution of Arabi, its leader.[2] As Gladstone pointed out, the 're-establishment of orderly Government . . . has been accomplished not by the Proclamation of the Sultan but by the victory at Tel-el-Kebir'.[3] As in India, 'order' in Egypt now rested ultimately on British force. That force might be small and 'fixed as a minimum' and Gladstone might be successful in combating the Queen's arguments, 'almost as unconstitutional as they are irrational', that it should be large.[4] But a force it had to be. Egypt had become like the income tax, disliked, 'temporary', but indispensable.

On the other hand, even if desirable (and it is unlikely that even a Tory cabinet would have found it so in 1882), formal rule—a Protectorate or annexation—would have been diplomatically explosive, financially expensive as Britain would have taken over direct responsibility for Egyptian affairs, and an even more dramatic blow to the stability of the Ottoman Empire than 'temporary' military occupation. Thus it came about that Britain as the representative of the international interest maintained local 'order', but by disclaiming sole responsibility left open the door to other members of the Concert to exercise theirs. From this sprang long and complex series of negotiations on the succession to the Dual Control and the settlement of Egyptian finances. It was one of the many ironies of the Egyptian diplomatic imbroglio that it was the Liberals, for so long the party of non-entanglement, who should, by the occupation of Egypt and the consequent management of Egyptian finances, give the Continental powers and especially Germany the general lever of purchase on British diplomacy which they had for so long lacked. That same imbroglio, as Gladstone had foreseen in 1877, brought to an end the *rapprochement* with France which the Gladstone/Cobden Treaty of 1860 had exemplified a generation earlier.

Regularization of Egyptian affairs, the situation complicated by Lesseps' concession, went on through 1883 into 1884. A second canal, getting round the difficulty of the concession and of the narrowness of the original, and backed by a British government loan of £8,000,000, was negotiated with Lesseps in 1883 only to be shouted down by the British shipping interest as too favourable to the Canal Company.[5] The financial settlement of Egypt was highly contentious, for it involved some definition of Britain's governmental relationship to the

should we be meddling in Egypt at all?' (25 August 1882, Add MS 43572, f. 70); Kimberley told him the same: 'But for India, I feel certain that no Egyptian expedition would ever have taken place' (11 January 1883, Add MS 43523, f. 12).

[1] 15 Sept. 82.
[2] To Granville, 22 September 1882; Ramm II, i. 429. Arabi was made to plead guilty, and was then imprisoned in Ceylon; see 16 Nov. 82.
[3] 15 Sept. 82.
[4] To Hartington, 4 Oct. 82.
[5] 10, 12, 13, 19, 23 July 82 and D. A. Farnie, *East and West of Suez* (1969), ch. xvii.

area which with the defeat of Hicks in the Sudan had from November 1883 a further strategic dimension[1] which will be examined shortly.

Gladstone saw the resolution of the confusions of Egyptian finances as the essential preliminary to British withdrawal. It was, he thought, a 'holy subject'.[2] It was also politically a very dangerous subject, for even his own Cabinet included the spectrum from immediate withdrawal and a declaration of Egyptian bankruptcy to long-term, sole British occupation.[3] With considerable labour, a Conference of the Powers was convened in London in June 1884 to settle the finances of Egypt and the position of the bondholders. Gladstone was

> much oppressed beforehand with the responsibility of my statement upon Egypt: but much pleased with the reception of it. . . . God is good: & I feel strong in the belief that we have the interests of justice, peace, & freedom in our hands.[4]

As the pressure mounted in Cabinet for a Sudan expedition to rescue Gordon and as the Lords prepared to reject the Franchise Bill, the Conference failed to agree. The British proposals were rejected by France, despite an advance private agreement, and the Conference was abandoned in early August 1884. Gladstone wrote later that 'we broke up the Conference because it would not consent to dock the dividends [of the bondholders]'.[5] This was partly true, but the financial details were only one aspect of the question. France, encouraged by Germany, had Britain on the rack and energetically exploited the opportunity. Britain's dependence on international agreement opened a door at which Bismarck pushed. The Egyptian negotiations involved Britian in the complex balance of French domestic politics and of Franco-German relations: when that balance altered, as it did at the end of 1884, the way for a negotiated solution quickly appeared.

The failure of the Conference was a major setback for Gladstone: withdrawal from Egypt moved into the middle distance at best and at home the failure implied a further bruising series of Cabinet and Parliamentary struggles. 'Egypt. Egypt. Egypt. Egypt.' read the heads of one Cabinet's agenda in July 1884.[6] For the next ten months Egypt in its various manifestations threatened to break up the Cabinet and bring about the fall of the Government. 'The Egyptian flood comes on us again and again, like the sea on the host of Pharaoh, which had just as much business to pursue the Israelites as we have to meddle in Egypt.'[7] Still, meddling they were, and with more effect than the host of Pharaoh had had on the Israelites.

Faced with the failure of the Conference in July 1884, Gladstone and Granville led the Cabinet—perhaps with a rapidity which they later came to regret—quickly to persuade Northbrook to go on a mission to Cairo to report and to advise.[8] His appointment was announced on 5 August 1884, moments before Gladstone moved the Vote of Credit for the Gordon relief expedition. Northbrook's instructions were as hurriedly drawn up as Gordon's had been and led

---

[1] See to Hartington, 28 June 84.   [2] 8 June 84.
[3] See *Africa and the Victorians*, 132ff.   [4] 23 June 84.
[5] To Northbrook, 20 Nov. 84.   [6] 16 July 84.
[7] To Northbrook, 6 Jan. 85.
[8] 2, 5 Aug. 84. For the report, see 15 Nov. 84n.; there is a copy in MS Harcourt dep. 313, f. 232.

to a rather similar difficulty. Northbrook's report in November 1884 proposed
sole British financial control and a more favourable treatment of the bondholders; it simply discounted the objections of other Powers. The report was a
considerable victory for the Hartington wing of the Cabinet and was quite
unacceptable to Gladstone[1] and many Liberals. A '*réchauffée* of the proposals
put before the Conference'[2] was quickly prepared as an alternative. But Northbrook (a Baring and a relative of Evelyn Baring, the British agent and consul-
general in Egypt) represented powerful interests: the government faced
dangers from the radical wing of the party and other Liberals for going too far
and from a potential Tory–Liberal/Whig combination for not going far enough.
On 20 January 1885 the Cabinet voted 8:4 to accept that 'French proposals
form a reasonable basis for friendly communications with a view to a settlement
of Egyptian finances'.[3] On the basis of these proposals, with Northbrook and
Hartington just kept in tow (the Gordon crisis may have helped here), a settlement was reached in March 1885 expressed in a Declaration, a Convention, and
a Decree by the Egyptian Government, agreed to by the Powers and by the
Porte, the latter under threat of losing Egypt altogether.[4] The settlement
included a two year breathing space for Egypt to put her finances into order
and decide whether or not taxation levels could reasonably support the whole
of the payments to the bondholders who in the *interim* would suffer a half per
cent reduction on their receipts. The settlement was backed by an internationally guaranteed loan of £9 millions. After the two years there would be, if necessary, an International Commission of inquiry.

An international dimension was thus maintained, as Gladstone wished, but,
as he also wished, it was not an international control.[5] The ending of all control
in Egypt remained his objective and there was, he argued, even after 1882 no *de
jure* interference in the government of Egypt: even Britain had 'no determinate
or legal right of interference'. But there were, however, 'rights which are indeterminate, that are frequently as real as those which are more defined, and
there are moral rights', and these Britain did have. Moreover, Britain had the
function of the 'natural adviser': 'In the present circumstances, and especially
until some more permanent arrangement can be made by general consent, we
are the natural advisers of the Egyptian Government for the time.'[6]

Like the Princely states of India—though Gladstone did not make an analogy
which would have suggested a long-term stay—Egypt was to enjoy the advice of
the British Government and to have the privilege of paying for an army of
occupation. The position of Egypt was thus regularized by the Gladstone

---

[1] 15, 19, 20 Nov. 84; see also Bahlman, *Hamilton*, ii. 729, 735. Northbrook, the First Lord of the
Admiralty, returned from Egypt to find the navy crisis at its height; his position in Cabinet to press
for his report was thus much weakened and the Gordon crisis, with troops in action, made it very
difficult for Hartington, the war secretary, to resign. Sir James Carmichael was sent to Egypt to make
further inquiries about increasing Egyptian revenues. He recommended extra taxation on the rich, a
course which Gladstone thought 'more equitable' than taxing the bondholders or placing the
burden 'on the shoulders of the British people', but Northbrook thought this impracticable; see 2,
18–19 Dec. 84.

[2] Hamilton's phrase, 20 November 1884; Bahlman, *Hamilton*, ii. 737.
[3] 20 Jan. 85.
[4] 24 Mar. 85.
[5] *H* 296. 687 (26 March 1885).
[6] Ibid., 688.

Government, shortly before its resignation, but with options remaining open: no permanent, direct imperial responsibility had been accepted and the possibility, indeed the stated intention of withdrawal remained. On the other hand, the Hartingtonians knew that the longer *de facto* occupation continued, the more entrenched British control of Egypt became, whatever the legal fiction. What Milner called 'the veiled Protectorate' was firmly in place.[1]

The settlement within Egypt was hardly what Gladstone had intended in 1882, though it was what he had feared: the 'nest egg' was hatching. Would it prove to be a double-yolker? What was to be the fate of the Sudan, that territory to the south whose order was the responsibility of the Khedive acting for the Sultan?

Gladstone showed little interest in the impact of his Cabinet's actions on North Africa generally. He did, however, note in his memorandum on settlement in September 1882 that the defence of 'the territory especially in the direction of the Soudan' was a prime military responsibility.[2] But while advice backed by British force worked conveniently within Egypt, it was an extremely complex device when applied to Egypt's peripheral territories. In these, the Porte and the Khedive both exercised responsibility; moreover, there was great reluctance to commit British troops to the extreme conditions and extended lines of supply of the upper Nile. The Cabinet decided to have the 'Southern Army separate, paid from Soudan revenues'.[3] The control of this army was left to the Khedive. Thus it was that in September 1883 William Hicks (in the Khedive's employment) led the southern Egyptian army into the Sudan to suppress the Mahdi, who had been declared a 'False Prophet' but who represented in an extreme form that militancy which Britian thought she had seen in Arabi.

As with Arabi and his movement, Gladstone initially had considerable sympathy for the Mahdists; it was of them that he coined one of his most famous phrases: 'Yes; these people are struggling to be free; and they are struggling rightly to be free.'[4] Moreover, unlike Egypt, the Sudan in the early 1880s was not thought of immediate importance by even the most ardent imperialist.

The first miscalculation was a lack of understanding of Egypt's interest in the area, of the tensions within different schools of Mohammetanism, and of Egypt's willingness to take risks. Though successful earlier in the year at Berber, Hicks was killed and the Khedive's army ambushed in November 1883 just as the Cabinet was preparing the further reduction of the Egyptian garrison and its withdrawal from Cairo to Alexandria. The failure to prevent the Khedive's sending of Hicks into the Sudan was, Cromer later thought, 'the sum total of the charge which can be brought against Mr. Gladstone's Government'.[5]

The Cabinet heard the news of the Hicks disaster in November 1883,[6] but no further Cabinets were held that year so as to prevent the issue of redistribution causing Hartington's resignation. That tactic was successful, but meant that Sudanese policy was arranged by letter. Even so, agreement was reached: the

[1] A. Milner, *England in Egypt* (1894 ed.), title of ch. iii.
[2] 15 Sept. 82.   [3] 3 Nov. 82.
[4] *H* 288. 55 (12 May 1884).   [5] Cromer, i. 385.
[6] 20, 22 Nov. 83.

Sudan was to be evacuated, a decision confirmed at the Cabinet of 3 January 1884. The consequent resignation of the Egyptian ministry was successfully surmounted.[1] Gladstone returned to Hawarden and left the small print to the relevant ministries.

In retrospect, this seems casual. At the time, it was not an unusual proceeding, though Gladstone must often have regretted it later. Granville, Hartington, and Northbrook (respectively the Foreign and War Offices and the Admiralty) were hardly inexperienced and the policy was a simple withdrawal: a policy of occupation would have warranted greater Prime-Ministerial superintendence. To Northbrook, accustomed as a retired Viceroy of India to rapid and complete obedience, the operation seemed straightforward:

> I have been spending a good part of the day in arranging for the mission of Chinese Gordon to Suakin [on the Red Sea] to arrange for the evacuation of the Soudan.[2] I was very glad to find that he readily & even cordially accepted our policy that the Egyptians should give up the administration only holding to the sea coast. He is not at all alarmed at the situation; & does not believe in the immense power some think this Mahdi has, either spiritual or physical.[3]

Of course, it was not so simple. Gladstone had an acute sense of political trouble which operated well with respect to others, less effectively with himself. Perhaps remembering his own restless activity as High Commissioner in the Ionian Islands 1858-9, he warned Granville about Gordon when his appointment was in the air but not settled, that 'while his opinion on the Soudan may be of great value, must we not be very careful ... that he does not shift the centre of gravity as to political and military responsibility for that country'.[4] However, Gladstone did not countervail an appointment he knew was about to be made. Thus the Prime Minister and Baring, the 'man on the spot', were both sceptical:[5] but it was left to the ministries. These, undoubtedly, failed in their technical assessment of the situation. 'Withdrawal' was not a simple matter: many civilians were involved, Egyptian troops were scattered in pockets about the Sudan, the logistics of movement were complex, some sort of alternative authority was needed, Gordon was in the employment of the Khedive, not of the British government (this, indeed, had been part of the attractiveness of sending him, for he had held similar employment before, with conspicuous success). No-one in Britain was directly responsible for assessing the situation

[1] 3 Jan. 84 and Cromer, i. 376-84.
[2] Even here, there is muddle: Gordon was to *report* on the means of evacuation, not to 'arrange' for it.
[3] Northbrook to Ripon, 18 January 1884, Add MS 43572, f. 72; Northbrook gave a slightly different account to Baring (Cromer i. 429); he told Ripon, 25 January 1884, Add MS 43572, f. 78: 'Gordon has gone out heartily to carry out our policy of withdrawal from the Soudan. He is quite against reconquering it for Egypt.'
[4] To Granville, 16 January 1884, Ramm II, ii. 150.
[5] See Cromer, i. 423-6. Gordon's appointment was urged from 1882; the campaign led by the *Pall Mall Gazette* and the *Morning Advertiser* merely gave the last push to a move widely welcomed by the army. Stephenson, the commander in Egypt, wrote on 21 January 1884: 'Gordon ... is, I think, by far the best man the Government really could have sent out, and if anyone can get the Egyptian Government out of their Soudan difficulties, he will'; F. C. A. Stephenson, *At home and on the battlefield* (1915), 313. See also M. Shibeika, *British policy in the Sudan 1882-1902* (1952), 146-60.

militarily: the Foreign Office got information from Baring, the Admiralty from the Red Sea ports, the War Office rather indirectly from British officers trapped in the Sudan. As Gladstone noted on the plans for the Nile route for rescue, 'although this may not properly be Admiralty business, it is I suppose still less within the view of the War Office'.[1]

Gladstone appreciated that the problems of ignorance in London about the details of the situation in the Sudan implied giving Gordon what amounted to a free hand. Thus he did not require, nor did his departmental ministers offer, categorical advice. His political instincts told him things might go wrong; his rather legalistic sense of 'rightness' told him that it was not the Government's fault. Nor was it technically, for Gordon effectively disobeyed the orders which he had been given in London and which had been reinforced in Cairo by Baring, though also crucially restated. But the popular excitement which had been a part of Gordon's appointment, the penetration of the telegraph a good way up the Nile and the consequent frequent bulletins in the London press, either from Gordon or, after his isolation, from the advancing rescue force, meant that the Gordon drama was played out morning by morning at the breakfast tables of Britain. Even after March 1884 when he was out of direct telegraphic contact (the government suspected deliberately), he continued to be heard from indirectly 'in so many odd ways'.[2]

Livingstone had disappeared in Africa for years at a time; Gordon's was a death almost on stage. And since the flow of information was largely one way—from North Africa outwards, whether from Gordon or Wolseley—it was a flow that they could control, and which they did control with skill. The Sudanese journals of Gordon and Wolseley vie with each other in contempt for their governmental superiors, Wolseley's also reflecting an almost pathological hatred of representative government which would have amazed and appalled the Liberal politicians whose patronage he apparently so gratefully received.[3] It is curious that Gladstone, of all the Victorians usually the most hypersensitively aware of the possibilities of political presentation, seems to have failed to sense this central dimension of the Gordon mission.

It was Gordon as symbol, as an icon of his age, that was important, a point grasped by Gordon himself and by W. T. Stead, the leading liberal journalist of the day. Stead's championing of the appointment of Gordon was partly intended to show that the patriotic card was one that Liberals could play: Palmerstonianism was not necessarily lost to the Tories. Whatever the details of the rights and wrongs of the Gordon affair, the Cabinet bungled this hand. They did so partly because they, and Gladstone in particular, refused to look beyond the complexities of Egyptian and Sudanese policy. They took their stand on details, and on these they had a much better case than is often allowed, when what was really at issue was presentation and image.

Once off the leash and officially the employee of the Khedive and made Governor General of the Sudan by him, Gordon acted as Gladstone had warned. His position as Governor General and the restatement of his orders

[1] To Northbrook, 24 Apr. 84.
[2] To Northbrook, 14 Aug. 84.
[3] See *Relief of Gordon, passim.*

approved by Baring when he was in Cairo suggested an executive role markedly different from his original instruction to 'report' on withdrawal from the Sudan.[1] Quickly, these executive functions predominated. By the start of February 1884 the Cabinet realized the 'Soudan business' was adrift, and began the long series of meetings that continued almost to the end of the ministry; Gladstone was incensed to find Gordon had effectively rewritten his orders:[2] 'the times are stiff & try the mettle of men. What shd *we* have done, with the Mutiny at the Nore.'[3] By the middle of February 1884, the possibility of having to 'rescue' Gordon—or in effect to arrest him—was becoming a possibility, perhaps a necessity. But with Gordon in post and on the Nile, the hope was still that all would be well. Once on the Nile, Gordon was never given a simple, direct instruction by the Government to withdraw with his immediate force to Cairo, or even to Berber.[4] Gladstone and Granville considered such an instruction in September 1884, but did not nerve themselves to send it. Gladstone supported Gordon's request that Zobeir, the notorious slaver, be made Governor of Khartoum as the most effective person to maintain order, but the Cabinet took fright at the anti-slavery lobby (which wanted, moreover, occupation rather than withdrawal from the Sudan).[5]

The spring and summer of 1884 were spent debating various possibilities: whether to relieve at all, a large *versus* a small force, the Nile route *versus* the route west from the Red Sea port of Suakin. Even a rescue via the south (i.e. Uganda and down the Nile) was considered, a solution that would have had spectacular consequences for East Africa.[6] Gladstone dreaded that the rescue expedition would—as it nearly did—become effectually an occupation. Thus he especially disliked a railway from Suakin, with its implication of permanence, 'the substitution of an Egyptian domination there of an English domination over the whole or a part', and he therefore favoured a small, fleeting force, 'leaving no trace behind it'.[7] The military advice was self-contradictory.[8] Costs were drawn up anticipating a Red Sea expedition,[9] but 'nothing to be done now beyond preliminary proceedings'.[10] By July 1884 when the Cabinet agenda read 'Egypt. Egypt. Egypt. Egypt', two of those 'Egypts' meant the Sudan.[11] Slowly the balance, pushed energetically by the Whigs, tilted towards action[12] and a Vote of Credit, and in September 1884 Wolseley was on his way up the Nile, the route chosen chiefly by Wolseley on the basis of his Red River experience in Canada a generation earlier,[13] and forced through by the 'Wolseley Ring' in flagrant disregard of the warnings about its difficulties offered by the Admiralty and Stephenson, whom Wolseley replaced as commander at the last moment.[14]

[1] Cromer, i. 440–52.　　　　　　　　　　　　　　　　　[2] 9, 10 Feb. 84.
[3] 11 Feb. 84.　　　　　　　　　　　　　　　　　　　　[4] Ramm II, ii. 259–62.
[5] 15 Mar. 84.　　　　　　　　　　　　　　　　　　　　[6] 16 July 84.
[7] To Northbrook, 28 May 84; to Dilke, 30 May 84.
[8] To Northbrook, 24 Apr., 28 May, 2, 4 June 84; to Hartington, 13 Apr., 13, 16 May, 19, 21, 23 Aug., 13 Sept. 84; to Childers, 30 May, 6 June, 23 Sept. 84; to Dilke, 30 May 84; to Selborne, 30 July 84.
[9] 24 May 84.　　　　　　　　　　　　　　　　　　　　[10] 27 May 84.
[11] 16 July 84.　　　　　　　　　　　　　　　　　　　　[12] Ibid. and 2 Aug. 84.
[13] See to Hartington, 23 Aug. 84; to Rosebery, 23 Aug. 84.
[14] To Hartington, 23 Aug. 84 and *Relief of Gordon*, xxxi.

The news came on 5 February 1885 when Gladstone was staying at Holker Hall with Hartington:

> After 11 AM I heard the sad news of the fall or betrayal of Khartoum: H. & I, with C. went off by the first train and reached D. Street soon after 8.15. The circumstances are sad & trying: it is one of the least points about them, that they may put an end to this Govt.[1]

Gordon probably dead, though it was briefly hoped that he might not be,[2] the Cabinet moved with a rapidity and apparent decision it had never shown when he was alive: within two days it had instructed Wolseley to crush the power of the Mahdi at Khartoum (probably in the autumn), had begun the railway inland to Berber from the Red Sea, and prepared to crush the revolt of Osman Digna in the eastern Sudan with a substantial body of force.[3] This might be thought to imply a dramatic reversal in the Government's Sudanese policy which if it had been capped—as it very nearly was—by the appointment of Wolseley as Governor-General would have amounted to accepting for the Sudan at least the same responsibility as Britain now had in Egypt. Gladstone told the Sultan's envoys that the 'original policy . . . has undergone no change . . . the recent decisions are military decisions'.[4] Technically this was true: the Governor General-ship, though approved in draft, was withheld.

Was this a change of policy, or merely the armoury necessary for the survival of the Government? The instruction that the 'power of the Mahdi at Khartoum must be overthrown' maintained a degree of ambivalence, and Gladstone avoided an immediate Vote of Credit for a Sudan war.[5] Certainly, nothing could happen quickly, except perhaps a further disaster: the loss of Wolseley's army, for, Khartoum fallen, Wolseley was in an extremely exposed position and had consistently underrated his opponent's strength.[6] The death of Gordon was a blow in terms of policy and prestige but, like Majuba, was militarily insignificant. The defeat of Wolseley, representing, as he was seen to do, the liberal ideal of merit, reform, and efficiency, would have been a real disaster. The Mahdi sat tight in Khartoum and let Wolseley and the Government off the hook. The Cabinet, whose discussions after the death of Gordon were 'difficult but harmonious',[7] was afforced in the Lords by Rosebery,[8] and rode out the votes of censure. Gladstone lobbied Bright, who voted with the Government,

[1] 5 Feb. 85.

[2] Wolseley's telegrams (see 6–7 Feb. 85n) encouraged the view that Gordon had been captured.

[3] 5–7, 10 Feb. 85. Gladstone offered no explanation to the Queen for this, but merely referred her to the enclosed telegram; Guedalla, *Q*, ii. 330. He told Hamilton, who protested mildly at the change, that 'the decision had been determined by the regard which they felt bound to have for the effect which the triumph of the Mahdi might have on our Mahometan subjects'; Bahlman, *Hamilton*, ii. 790.

[4] 10 Feb. 85.

[5] To Childers, 16 Feb. 85. The suggestion in *G.P.*, 196–7, that Gladstone hoped for an 'innocuous and early success on the Suakin front' which he could trade against Wolseley's autumn campaign is intriguing, but it is unlikely that in the hot season a successful assault on Osman Digna could have been quickly enough mounted to have such an effect. It is more likely that Gladstone's concern over the command of the Suakin expedition was one further round in the battle with the Court (see 9, 11 Feb. 85).

[6] *Relief of Gordon*, 137–40.

[7] 6 Feb. 85.   [8] To Rosebery, 8 Feb. 85.

and Goschen, who voted for the censure motion.[1] It was, Gladstone noted, 'an extreme case of the irony of Fortune' that he should receive 'a telegram from the Sultan expressly to congratulate the Govt. & me personally on the defeat of the Opposition & on our continuance in office'.[2]

Gladstone's reaction to the events of February 1885 did not at first display his usual resource. Despite his secretary's advice, he greatly and wilfully offended by going in the Dalhousies' party to 'The Candidate' at the Criterion Theatre ('capitally acted') on the night Gordon's death was confirmed.[3] The crisis made him physically ill, and he took to his bed, 'the disturbance, wh has had so many forms, having at last taken the form of overaction of the bowels', and anxiety produced a skin disease on his hands.[4] His initial Commons statement was brusque. Gladstone admitted to himself his 'reception could not be warm',[5] but he went out of his way to make it cold, deliberately omitting any compliment to Gordon, the troops or the colonies for their offers of help.[6] It was, as he said, 'a serious crisis in the face of the world'.[7] Rarely can a Prime Minister have faced the Commons in more embarrassing circumstances—embarrassing, because the Gordon affair handed to the Tories a jack (G.O.M. = M.O.G.: Grand Old Man = Murderer of Gordon), if not an ace, to be played for the rest of Gladstone's career. When Northcote loyally did not play this card in opening the censure debate, Tory contempt for him reached its height. Gladstone was clearly within a whisker of resigning. He discussed Commons' contingencies 'on the possible resignations' with the Speaker. When the Government's majority fell to 14 on the censure motion, he noted: 'the final decision in my mind turned the scale, so nicely was it balanced'.[8] Next day, he persuaded the Cabinet to continue; within a week, he felt 'wonderfully better'.[9] The Queen's notorious telegram *en clair*[10] sent to Granville, Hartington, and Gladstone as a public rebuke was the most personal of several reasons which made a resignation dishonourable (a dissolution with the Redistribution Bill not yet passed was impossible).

The same day as deciding to carry on, the Cabinet considered developments on the Afghan frontier, where, as we have seen, the long wave of Russian expansion was finally breaking on the Penjdeh breakwater.[11] Two Cabinets later, Wolseley was warned that because of the military dangers in Central Asia 'we are unwilling to take any step in the nature of a further general declaration of policy'.[12] The government thus faced simultaneous crises in Egyptian finance, as the negotiations reached their final phases, the Sudan, and Afghanistan. Estimates for a Vote of Credit went quickly from £7½ millions to £11 millions: 'The pressure of affairs, especially Soudan, Egypt, & Afghan, is now from day to day extreme.'[13] The Vote of Credit for £11 millions, the largest ever raised for military purposes, studiously did not distinguish between Central Asian and North African needs.[14] By May, with the

---

[1] 26 Feb. 85.   [2] 6 Mar. 85.
[3] 10 Feb. 85 and Bahlman, *Hamilton*, ii. 794.
[4] 12, 18 Feb. 85.   [5] 19 Feb. 85.
[6] Bahlman, *Hamilton*, ii. 798.   [7] H 294. 1099.
[8] 24, 26 Feb. 85.   [9] 3 Mar. 85.
[10] 5, 9 Feb. 85.   [11] 28 Feb. 85.   [12] 12 Mar. 85.
[13] 16 Mar. 85; see also to Hartington, 1 Apr. 85.   [14] 20, 21 Apr. 85.

financial affairs of Egypt at last internationally agreed,[1] the evacuation policy for the Sudan was confirmed.[2] The Sudan was put on ice—a return to what had been the Cabinet's consistent policy save for the flurry in February 1885. Wolseley withdrew and, for all the noise, the Tories did not send him back. The Liberal policy had been sensible: unless another European power threatened occupation, Britain had no interest in the Sudan. It was a simple enough policy which had not been simply enough stated or pursued.

North Africa was thus within three years the scene of the most successful of all the Victorian military expeditions and, in political terms, of the greatest fiasco before the 1899 South African War. But it was the 1882 success which set the tone. In the 'grab' for colonial possessions which followed, others would niggle at but would not directly confront British power. On the other hand, the Gladstone Cabinet showed little interest in exploiting this advantage, for the existing difficulties in North and South Africa sufficiently absorbed its energies, and even these fought often unsuccessfully for Cabinet time with Ireland and domestic legislation. Although it was clear that the Cabinet was overburdened, little was done to make it a more effective institution and few lessons about the co-ordination of policy seem to have been learned. From time to time a Cabinet committee was used, as with considerable effect in the case of West Africa,[3] a committee renewed when the Cabinet agreed to the West African Berlin Conference in 1884,[4] but there was no system of Standing Committees of Cabinet even for problems such as Egyptian finance which were obviously enduring, nor does one ever seem to have been considered: it would no doubt have been thought inimicable to Cabinet solidarity. It would also have been regarded by Gladstone as likely to produce activist and therefore expensive policies. Thus it was that there was little overall superintendence or co-ordination of policy save at the highest level and, in so far as this was possible, within individual ministries.

At the highest level, Gladstone's attention to foreign and imperial affairs in all their dimensions was, as we have seen, spasmodic. Granville's decline made the situation worse; his colleagues were agreed in 1885 not to allow him back to the Foreign Office.[5] Derby at the Colonial Office had a reputation for a lacadaisical attention to policy and at first glance it would seem that Cabinet decisions on the New Guinea protectorate were simply not implemented. A second glance shows, however, that the maintenance of a coherent policy on New Guinea was extremely difficult, for it was at the centre of the awkward attempts of the British government to come to terms with German colonial aspirations.[6]

The difficulties of both Granville and Derby were not merely personal. They were caught in the centre of a Cabinet which represented most, if not all, of the various British political responses to the imperial tide. Thus, as other European nations capitalized on Britain's bondage in Egypt and the Sudan to increase colonial activity in 1883 and 1884, Britain was particularly awkwardly placed to respond. The alienation of France, the contempt of Bismarck for Gladstone and

[1] 7 Mar. 85 (Cabinet); the London Convention was signed on 17 March 1885.
[2] 7 May 85.   [3] 25 Oct., 22 Nov. 83.   [4] 8 Oct. 84.
[5] Gladstone was distressed at having to exclude him from the Foreign Office; see 30 Jan. 86.
[6] See 6, 9 Aug., 6 Oct. 84, 21 Jan. 85.

the British Cabinet generally, the absence of agreement in the Government about an overall policy for Africa, and the need for foreign support to achieve a financial settlement in Egypt all encouraged other Powers to action, not in the form of a major assault on a central British interest, but in the form of a series of initiatives in places of apparently marginal significance.

A flurry of darts blew from Continental blow-pipes: West Africa, Madagascar, Angra Pequeña, Zanzibar and East Africa, New Guinea, islands in the Pacific. Each had its complex case history involving local interests and, in the British case, the sub-imperial interests of the various white colonies, but each also related to the other in the sense that the decisive agents were Britain, France, and, *tertius gaudens*, Germany. By pressing forward these questions in 1884–5, the Continental Powers forced Britain towards a coherent, active imperial policy in response. This Gladstone was determined to avoid.

Gladstone's view was that while Britain had certain historic interests, she had no manifest destiny in tropical Africa and that local accommodations would be sufficient: Britain could hardly expect to exclude other major powers should they be determined on activity. Thus no plan co-ordinated Zanzibar with Nigeria, Egypt with Angra Pequeña: Britain had no unique and not many particular interests. Distinctively among British statesmen confronted imperially by Germany, Gladstone's policy was not the maintenance of the *status quo* (i.e. a British hegemony either formal or informal which excluded Germany), but rather an accommodation of German ambitions. As he wrote in 1884 to Derby on German activity on the East African coast: 'Is it dignified, or is it required by any real interest, to make extensions of British authority without any view of occupying but simply to keep them out?'[1]

Gladstone recognized that in the temper of the 1880s this was an 'old fashioned' view.[2] 'Colonial alarmism',[3] as he called it in 1884, was making the running and was hard to prevent. Yet from the perspective of the late 1980s his view has a curiously modern ring, certainly more so than the Cape-to-Cairo enthusiasms of the Imperial Federation League, also of 1884, so quickly has the British experience in tropical Africa begun to seem remote, strange, and, from the British point of view, almost comic in its presumption.

The incorporation of Germany in the imperial brethren was simply done. Bismarck, assuming British deviousness to equal his own and supposing the British Cabinet to regard all deserts with maximum jealousy, involved himself in extraordinary contortions with respect to Angra Pequeña (on the S.W. African coast), not revealing his own plans and despatches to Münster, his ambassador in London, or, consequently, to Granville. But once it was clear what Bismarck wanted, he got it immediately. The Cabinet of 14 June 1884, baffled by a rising German antagonism whose basis was, to the British Cabinet, quite obscure, agreed to ask *via* Herbert Bismarck, then in London, 'what it is the German Govt. want'; the Cabinet of 21 June ('Important') gave it to him:

---

[1] To Derby, 30 Dec. 84.   [2] Ibid.
[3] To Derby, 24 Dec. 84. John Bramston, assistant under-secretary at the Colonial Office, told Robert Meade, the C.O.'s representative at the Berlin Conference, 'clearly the G.O.M. alone stops the way' (this with respect to securing the whole S.E. African coast); 31 December 1884, Clanwilliam/Meade MSS D.3044/J/17/54.

'Angra Pequeña: No objection could be taken to the claim, or intention, of the German Government to provide means of protection for German subjects.'

Not only this: a German presence in Southern Africa and in the Pacific could in Gladstone's view be a useful device for keeping the increasingly truculent white colonies in order. The first Gladstone government had been alarmed to find that responsible government led to irresponsible tariff policies by Canada and Australia.[1] The second found a complex international situation further confused by 'sub-imperialism' (expansionist policies urged on Britain by her colonies, or even carried out by them—particularly Australian expansionism in the Pacific).

Gladstone was in 'absolute sympathy' with Derby in regarding the proposals of the Australian Convention for a 'Monroe doctrine laid down for the whole South Pacific' as 'mere raving'; he went further than Derby in also proposing again to reject Australian claims for a protectorate in New Guinea (already once refused),[2] but he went out of his way to accommodate Germany's claims there, conceding Bismarck's case while disliking his tone and method. The advantage was clear: 'German colonisation will strengthen and not weaken our hold upon our Colonies: and will make it very difficult for them to maintain the domineering tone to which their public organs are too much inclined.'[3]

The same was the case in Southern Africa: 'I should be extremely glad to see the Germans become our neighbours in South Africa, or even the neighbours of the Transvaal. We have to remember Chatham's conquest of Canada, so infinitely lauded, which killed dead as mutton our best security for keeping the British Provinces.'[4] Far from being a threat, therefore, Germany could be seen as a means both of reducing the amount of vacant territory into which Britain might be drawn, and of bringing the existing colonies to heel. This view implied a sense of Germany as a rival in that region, with an implication of future local defence costs which Gladstone does not seem to have anticipated, or which perhaps he thought would be borne by the colonists; but it also recognized the extent to which German colonization unsupported by a fleet was always ultimately subject to British permission. The further corollary, that encouraging German colonialism would ultimately encourage such a fleet, was not considered.

The notion of Germany as a *deus ex machina* in South Africa showed the extent to which the difficulties in that area remained intractable: 'To piece together *anything* in South Africa is an attractive prospect rather than otherwise.'[5] The high-profile problem was the Transvaal, but the long-running difficulty was Zululand. At the start of the ministry, the Cabinet, despite the expectations raised by Gladstone's Midlothian speeches, returned to the policy

[1] Matthew, *Gladstone*, 189.

[2] To Derby, 8 Dec. 83. See 13 June 83 for the rejection of the 'so-called annexation'.

[3] To Granville, 29 January 1885, Ramm II, ii. 329.

[4] i.e. by eliminating France as a threat; to Derby, 21 Dec. 84. This letter was widely circulated in the Colonial Office; Fairfield, the clerk with particular responsibility for Southern African affairs, told Robert Meade, then representing the Colonial Office at the Berlin Conference: 'We have been plying Lord Derby with annexation pills, but it is no good up to now, as the G.O.M. objects' (Fairfield to Meade, 31 December 1884, Clanwilliam/Meade MSS D. 3044/J/17/47 in P.R.O.N.I.)

[5] To Derby, 2 Sept. 83.

of voluntary Confederation which it had introduced in 1871.[1] In 1880, as in the early 1870s, the hope was that the Cape would relieve Britain of her direct South African responsibilities by leading, as Ontario had done in Canada, an autochthonous movement for confederation; hence, for the time being, the Transvaal, and Sir Bartle Frere (Governor of the Cape and High Commissioner of South Africa) must be retained.[2] In June 1880 the Cape declined to act; confederation was dead; Frere was recalled; but no solution to the position of the Transvaal was offered. On 19 December 1880 the news came that the Transvaal had proclaimed its own solution; on 20 December at Bronkhorstspruit occurred the first of several Boer victories in small skirmishes. These culminated in the death of Colley and ninety-two British soldiers on Majuba Hill on 27 February: 'Sad Sad news from South Africa: is it the Hand of Judgment?'[3]

The news found Gladstone wounded ('slipt off my heels in the powdered snow by the garden door, fell backwards, & struck my head most violently . . .' 'with very uncomfortable feelings *inside* the skull'),[4] battling with the Queen over a peerage for Wolseley, and in the final stages of preparation of the Irish Land Bill. None the less, he handled the crisis consummately. Majuba sprang largely from a failure of commonsense and co-ordination on the veldt. The Cabinet had already offered a Royal Commission to the Boers which was almost certain to recommend an end to annexation.[5] Colley both bungled the timing for the acceptance of an armistice (Kruger being out of touch), and had unnecessarily brought his troops forward to Majuba. Gladstone protected Kimberley, the colonial secretary, from both Whigs and Radicals, gained time for the details of the muddle on the veldt to clarify themselves, and maintained the existing policy of conciliation of the Transvaal and an agreed solution with the Boers.[6] This could only mean an ending of annexation and some recognition by the Boers of Britain's general supremacy in the area. The negotiations were handled with considerable good sense by Colley's successor, Sir Evelyn Wood, and the settlement was set down in the Convention of Pretoria, signed on 3 August 1881. It was, Gladstone recalled, 'the best, perhaps the only feasible, expedient in a critical situation'.[7] The 'native' interest was safeguarded by a British Resident at Pretoria, the imperial interest by the Transvaal's acceptance of 'suzerainty' and British control of foreign policy. 'Suzerainty' was the solution Gladstone had advocated for an Ottoman Empire unable to retain control in the Christian Balkans.[8] It was used, therefore, in the context of weakness.[9] Gladstone's advocacy of it for South Africa represented an acknowledgement that any long-term solution must recognize Dutch obduracy, the cost of permanent military subjugation of the Transvaal and perhaps the Orange Free State, and

[1] 6 Nov. 71; 3, 12 May 80.
[2] See the excellent analysis in Goodfellow, 188–9.
[3] 28 Feb. 81.   [4] 23 Feb. 81.   [5] 15 Feb. 81.
[6] See cabinet and letters to Kimberley, 27 Feb.–8 Mar. 81 and Schreuder, 134–46.
[7] To Derby, 25 Apr. 83.   [8] See above, ix. xliv–xlvii.
[9] As a legal title for intervention, the word was vague; Kimberley prepared a memorandum on its meaning, using quotations supplied by James Murray, the lexicographer, who had recently become friendly with Gladstone; Murray's quotations included several from Gladstone's classical articles, but none from his articles on the Balkans; 29 April 1881, Add MS 44627, f. 1.

the danger of Dutch revolt at the Cape.[1] Moreover, had not the South African Dutch done what the British had wanted, and that rather well?

> Is it unreasonable to think that as the Dutch have Africa for their country, as they went out from the Cape greatly to our relief, as they have solved the native question within their own borders, they are perhaps better qualified to solve the Zulu question outside the Reserve, than we can in dealing with it from Downing Street?[2]

This regard for the Dutch character allied to a general irritation with the various parties in Southern Africa and a feeling that British interests there were already adequately safeguarded, allowed Gladstone to watch without dismay the Transvaal's demands of 1883 for a renegotiation of the Pretoria Convention. He did not discourage the renegotiation, which implied the dismantling of the Convention, but he did dislike this being done by a Transvaal deputation in London.[3] Even an accommodation between the deposed Zulu chief, Cetewayo, and the Transvaalers—one of the great nightmares of the Cape and of the Colonial Office—did not alarm him: 'It does not appear to me certain that it would be a very bad thing if he [Cetewayo] and the Boers were, in the old phrase, to put their horses together.'[4]

Gladstone set up the Cabinet discussion on the renegotiation with a series of questions to Derby which implied regarding the Transvaal as being in the same relationship to Britain as the Orange Free State.[5] Consequently, in Cabinet the suggestion, 'shall we reserve a *veto* over any engagements they may make with foreign countries', and the answer 'Cabinet inclined to make this demand', seemed like a positive move from no safeguards to limited safeguards, rather than the dilution of the 1881 Pretoria Convention that in fact it was. Probably the minimalist retention of control of treaties in the 1884 London Convention represented what Gladstone had wanted all along. Even the 'native' question did not bother him, as he argued that the popularity of 'native' immigration into the Transvaal showed there was no need 'for retaining any power of interference within their frontier'.[6] His reading of Olive Schreiner's *Story of an African Farm* (1883) in 1885, 'a most remarkable, painful, book', came too late to affect this view.[7] Nor did he show concern when the Transvaal immediately broke the new convention by expanding across the agreed frontier into Bechuanaland. Given all this—the readiness to accept Germany, the satisfaction with the Transvaal, the absence of strategic concern—the Cabinet's decision in November 1884 to send Sir Charles Warren to declare a Protectorate over Bechuanaland[8] (in effect restricting German expansion inland eastwards and Transvaal expansion westwards) was a considerable defeat for Gladstone, though he does not seem to have fought very hard against it. Probably he recognized that the combination of the 'forward' group in the Cabinet with the demands for protection by the Cape politicians would be too strong to defeat. When Warren wrote of the danger of German interference in the Transvaal, Gladstone commented,

[1] To Derby, 28 Jan. 85.   [2] To Derby, 11 June 84.
[3] To Derby, 20 June 83.   [4] To Derby, 2 Sept. 83.
[5] 16 Nov. 83.
[6] 20 Nov. 83; see also 13, 20 Nov. 83.   [7] 26 Apr. 85.
[8] Discussed since 1882 *pari passu* with the Transvaal question and hitherto avoided.

'such a letter makes me as much afraid, at least, of Sir C. Warren as of the Germans'.[1]

Gladstone had his best success in East Africa, the only area where in this administration he successfully stopped the expansionists. German activity in the Zanzibar hinterland increased in 1884 as it did in South West Africa; the British countered by reasserting their traditional influence over the Sultan of Zanzibar. Early in December 1884 Gladstone spotted in the papers circulating in the despatch boxes a plan for a forward policy in the East African hinterland. He expostulated memorably to Dilke, one of a group of Cabinet ministers advocating, successfully in the Bechuana instance, sustained blocking or prevention of German colonial expansion:

> Terribly have I been puzzled & perplexed on finding a group of the soberest men among us to have concocted a scheme as that touching the mountain country behind Zanzibar with an unrememberable name [i.e. Kilimanjaro]. There *must* somewhere or other be reasons for it, which have not come before me. I have asked Granville whether it may not stand over for a while.[2]

Stand over it did until the end of the government. The 'forward' group on the East African question had no equivalent of the Cape ministry with which to coalesce against the Prime Minister. The key was Egypt. There, with the break-up of the Conference on finance, the need for the approval of the powers for British proposals for resolving the financial deadlock, and the Wolseley expedition heading for the Sudan, German help against France seemed essential. Gladstone told Derby a week after challenging the East African initiative:

> No doubt we must be most cautious here as to Colonial alarmism: but any language at Berlin [i.e. at the West African Conference] appearing to convey sympathy with it might at this moment do extraordinary mischief to us at our one really vulnerable point, Egypt.[3]

If this was so with respect to West Africa, where Britain already had significant commercial interests, it was *a fortiori* the case in East Africa where she had none of much importance. Thus Gladstone successfully avoided balancing concessions to Germany in West and South West Africa by resistance in East Africa.[4] The German protectorate of Tanganyika was declared in March 1885, and it lay as a *bloc* across the Cape to Cairo route, preventing in the twentieth century the consolidation of a settler-dominated British Empire in Central

---

[1] To Derby, 17 Nov. 84.   [2] To Dilke, 14 Dec. 84.

[3] To Derby, 24 Dec. 84. Meade, negotiating with Bismarck and Busch in Berlin, and caught in the difficult position of both making concessions to the Germans and resisting them, considered (ironically?) the full implications of Gladstone's position, though without referring to East Africa: 'If however the Government really share Mr. Gladstone's view that he "should be extremely glad to see the Germans become our neighbours in South Africa, or even the neighbours of the Transvaal", why do we annex the Kalahari desert in order to cut the Germans off from reaching Bechuanaland and the Transvaal from Angra Pequeña on the west, and why hoist the flag at St. Lucia Bay to cut them off on the south east? Surely it would be better to go to the Germans with such an offer, which would enable us to make almost any terms we pleased about Egypt, New Guinea and the South Seas. . . . But, I submit, it is bad policy to do neither one thing nor the other. We are now neither making terms with Germany nor stopping the gap' (Meade to Herbert, 3 January 1885, Clanwilliam/Meade MSS D.3044/J/17/56; P.R.O.N.I.)

[4] See *Africa and the Victorians*, 189–93.

Africa.[1] Gladstone's view that German colonies would act to curb the wilder excesses of British colonialism received a powerful posthumous vindication.

This survey of Gladstone's involvement in imperial affairs in his second administration has necessarily focused on those subjects with which he allowed himself to be particularly associated. With some, for example the Berlin Conference of 1884–5, he was hardly involved, despite the interest he might have been expected to take in one of the chief constructs of the Concert in that decade.[2] His interests bear out his own view that he was carried forward in office by difficulties. The means of squaring the circle between local nationalism and European expansionism had not been found, nor in certain cases, as the Egyptian instance showed, could it be. Gladstone's case was not that such expansionism was wrong, indeed he saw it as natural, but that in the British case it was imprudent, particularly as exemplified by cost, actual and prospective. Unfortunately for him, prudence, a reasonably effective criterion in his first administration, was hardly such in his second. With Bright gone and the Cabinet Radicals Chamberlain and Dilke fast turning into Radical Imperialists, Gladstone increasingly fought his corner alone. That corner was not anti-Empire, but it was anti-imperialist. Unfortunately for Gladstone, the distinction was by the 1880s becoming politically unsustainable. Peel's colonial secretary had no difficulty with the Empire as such, but he disliked its marginal expansion, and in the 1880s the margins were becoming very wide.

These extra-European developments were the context for Britain's relations with foreign states during the second Gladstone government. This was a dramatic change from the first government, which was dominated by the Eurocentric Franco-Prussian war and its aftermath. As Bismarck used his new German Empire to develop a series of entangling alliances, fundamentally ruinous to Gladstone's concept of the Concert of Europe, there was little that the Liberal Government could do. Though it was common ground (to all but Bright) that Britain might intervene in some major crisis, such as an imminent occupation of Belgium, and that she might intervene *via* the Concert on behalf of worthy causes, it was inconceivable to the Cabinet that she should become involved on a regular basis in an alliance with a European power of Concert-level, a point recognized by Bismarck, who did not continue with the Liberal government the suggestion of an Anglo-German alliance made with some success to Disraeli.[3] Moreover, the considerable number of Conferences in these years, dealing with Turkish, Egyptian, and imperial questions, disguised the extent to which the alliance system would in the long-run undermine the concept of the Concert.

The transition of the Concert system from the club of monarchies which it had been since the eighteenth century to a wider base of popular legitimacy of

---

[1] Even once in British hands, after 1918, Tanganyika, as a League of Nations Mandate, could not be part of Sidney Webb's dream (as Colonial Secretary) of a single white-settler colonial unit stretching from Kenya to the South African border; fulfilment of this would surely have given Britain the Algerian imbroglio only just avoided in Southern Rhodesia in the 1960s and 1970s.

[2] It is interesting, in view of the recent stress placed on the limited objectives of the Conference, to note that Gladstone records it in Cabinet as 'a conference on colonising Africa & application of principles of Treaty of Vienna to Congo & Niger' (8 Oct. 84).

[3] See P. Kennedy, *The rise of the Anglo-German antagonism 1860–1914* (1980), 34–6.

the sort attempted by Gladstone in the campaigns of the 1870s was given no further encouragement.[1] The moderate interventionism of the Gladstonian liberals in fact took for granted a good deal of Cobdenite international harmony promoted by international trade. The rapid introduction of protection in many countries in the late 1870s might have suggested that as the Cobdenite basis eroded, so the Concert system needed codification and institutionalization, but Gladstone was entirely at one with those who thought like him in making no effort to counter protectionism and the continental system of secret alliances by the advocacy of a refurbished, modernized Concert system. The old system limped on in decline, but there was little attempt at invigorating or strengthening it until the First World War had shown its impotence.

As the Cabinet simply took for granted the efficient working of the British economy, so it presupposed an harmonious international order. In this sense, the second Gladstone government in general, and Gladstone in particular, remained thoroughly mid-Victorian, the last ministry and the last Prime Minister to be so.[2] There would always be minor dislocations to be corrected, but fundamentally Britain had no enemies and sought no enemies. Bismarck's wild rages against Gladstonian Liberalism were met with an indifference,[3] wrongly interpreted by Bismarck as contempt, which made him wilder still. Bismarck's duplicity which broadened from muddle about the disclosure of his aims in 1884 to open contempt for agreed procedures in 1885, did not deflect Gladstone. As he told the Queen, 'there is no great objection to the acts of Germany in themselves, but only to the careless impropriety, which attaches to the manner of them'.[4] The chief difficulty in foreign policy was the fluctuation of French politics, especially in 1882; but this was an imperial difficulty with no real European consequences. France might seem a rival, but it was still a country where the British Prime Minister would, quite naturally, spend weeks by the sea-side convalescing.[5]

Behind this sense of security lay the fleet: the strength of Britain was 'not to be found in alliances with great military powers, but is to be found henceforth, in the sufficiency and supremacy of her navy—a navy as powerful now as the navies of all Europe'. The 1868–74 government had devoted considerable effort to a reconstruction of the army, Gladstone being only partially successful in achieving the full scope of his plans.[6] Apart from the final abolition of flogging and minor adjustments to the Cardwellian system, there was little military reform in 1880–5.[7] Despite the implications of increased colonial rivalry in the 1880s, the Admiralty was left to itself to expand and refurbish the fleet. When, after eighteen months of work, Northbrook sent his memorandum comparing the deficiencies of the British fleet, as left by the Disraeli government, with the condition of the French, Gladstone sent the briefest of notes, accepting it

[1] See above, ix. xxxviiiff.

[2] Hamilton caught the mood well: 'Stead taunted me with our having no allies. . . . He was a little surprised when I held that we did not want to make allies'; Bahlman, *Hamilton*, ii. 763.

[3] See Kennedy, op. cit., 157ff. for Bismarck's 'Ideological war against Gladstonism', a war of which Gladstone seems to have been oblivious.

[4] To the Queen, 5 January 1885, in *L.Q.V.*, 2nd series, iii. 592.

[5] See Jan.–Feb. 83.   [6] Matthew, *Gladstone*, 208–9.

[7] See Childers, ii, ch. xi; Hartington at the war office seems to have promoted no reforms.

'freely'.[1] The secret Royal Commission on Colonial Defences, set up by the Disraeli government under Carnarvon's chairmanship, received even less attention. To Carnarvon's fury, its report, which had important recommendations on coaling stations and the navy, was effectively shelved.[2]

None the less, as with the foreign policy which it buttressed, the ability of the mid-Victorian fleet to defend British interests was being questioned. The bluff of 'a gigantic deception, perpetrated by all and believed by all'[3] was being called, and the first really loud shout was in 1884. Carnarvon then had his revenge. As the Egyptian and Sudanese crisis worsened, he supplied W. T. Stead with encouragement and information for the *Pall Mall Gazette*'s 'navy scare' in September 1884,[4] which broke just after Northbrook, the First Lord, had been appointed to go on his special mission to Egypt to report on the financial deadlock.

The moment was well-chosen: Gladstone was caught in a pincer-movement of Tories, Whigs, and 'blue-water' Radicals[5] (the same combination as had convinced the Cabinet that to go forward with plans for a Channel tunnel was pointless).[6] He did not try to escape, but, after deferring the expected statement, succeeded on 2 December at the last minute—the statement in the Commons being due that day—in persuading the Cabinet to reduce the extra sum for naval expenditure from £10,725,000 to £5,525,000. He declined to be seen supporting the programme, telling his Cabinet colleagues: 'As one resolved on retirement when the "situation" is cleared, I do not feel justified in using pressure with reference to a prospective plan reaching over a term of years, although it has not my sympathy.'[7] Coming on top of extra estimates from the Sudan and Bechuanaland less than a month earlier,[8] with a penny on income tax to pay for them, it was an important moment in the gradual crumbling of the edifice of Gladstonian finance, and, as we shall see, played an important part in the fall of the government five months later. The 'scare' also marked an alliance repeated in each subsequent Liberal government, which each of those governments, like that of 1884, found irresistible. Never was the Admiralty happier, than with the Liberals in office and the Tories free to combine with 'blue water' Liberals to agitate for the fleets they found too expensive to build when themselves in office.

[1] Gladstone to Northbrook, 27 January 1882, Add MS 44545, f. 96 and Mallet, *Northbrook*, 202. There was a real substance to Northbrook's concern; to make adequate dispositions for the bombardment of Alexandria, the Admiralty was forced to assemble almost all its effective ships; see C. S. White, 'The bombardment of Alexandria 1882', *The Mariner's Mirror*, lxvi. 35 (1980).

[2] See to Kimberley, 12 June 80 and n.; Sir A. Hardinge, *Carnarvon* (1925), iii. 38ff.; *H* 278. 1831 (4 May 1883).

[3] The view of N. A. M. Rodger in 'The dark ages of the Admiralty, 1869–85' in *The Mariner's Mirror*, lxi–lxiii (1975–7).

[4] See Stead–Carnarvon correspondence, July–September 1884, in Carnarvon MSS, Add MS 60777. It would be wrong to see Carnarvon as instigator of the scare; Stead later credited this role to H. O. Arnold-Forster; see F. Whyte, *Life of W. T. Stead* (1925), i. 146ff.

[5] Radical support was thought to be quite extensive; see Bahlman, *Hamilton* ii. 687, 690, 699.

[6] 18 Feb. 82, 31 Mar. 82, 19 July 83; a further attempt was made in the third government, see 13 Mar. 86. For Gladstone's visit to the tunnel's works, about which he was enthusiastic, see 11 Mar. 82.

[7] 2 Dec. 84. The episode remains rather obscure: were there expansionists in the Admiralty keen to take advantage of Northbrook's absence?

[8] 11 Nov. 84.

VI

Gladstone supervised the domestic and legislative policy of his second government from four perspectives. As Prime Minister he had an overall responsibility for balance and content. As Chancellor of the Exchequer (until December 1882) he was responsible, at the least, for raising revenue and controlling expenditure. As Leader of the House of Commons, he was in charge of the strategic and tactical conduct of the legislative programme and of the proper working of the Commons, involving daily and usually lengthy attendance there. Lastly, as the chief force behind several of the Government's major bills, he was responsible for arguing their case at second reading and for seeing them through the Committee stage. Any one of these responsibilities would normally be regarded as an adequate load. Taken together, with foreign and imperial affairs added, it is surprising that Gladstone, in his early seventies, was not more often ill and out of action.

It was, in fact, an extraordinary, excessive burden, which overpersonalized the government, held back able men, and encouraged attention to the particular rather than the general. Yet it was a load which did not break its bearer's back and which remained more or less in balance until towards the end of the government. It was inherent in the antecedents to the Government's formation that Gladstone should bear a load of this sort. It was exactly the range of responsibilities he had had in the last months of his first Government and it was, as we have seen, his intention to shed all of it after a year or so by resigning from political office. As we know, only the Chancellorship was discarded.

Gladstone took the Exchequer personally in 1880 to mark a return to proper financial procedures. Using the traditional Peelite method of a short-term increase in income-tax to cover a temporary deficit caused by a beneficial commercial reform, he commuted the malt tax into a beer duty;[1] and in 1881 he carried further and reformulated Northcote's reforms of the various death duties[2] in order, in part, as we shall see, to prepare the way for a reform of local government finance. Both of these were quite formidable technical achievements, the first an objective of Chancellors for half a century, and they were accompanied by declarations of superlatives: they were questions 'the largest and most difficult still remaining to be effectively dealt with by Parliament'.[3]

Gladstone deliberately set out by such hyperbole to maintain the narrow horizon of expectations of the Exchequer. For him, the government's relationship to the British (perhaps not the Irish) economy was what it had been since the days of Peel: minimal. The Cabinet had no view of 'the economy' as such: economic policy simply did not exist as an item on its agenda. Whereas it had extensive data on the performance of the Egyptian economy and the productivity of the fellaheen, the Cabinet had none on the British economy, save the odd comment on the buoyancy or otherwise of indirect taxes. The 'Great Depression', so prominent a feature of the literature of and on the period, went unrecognized.

---

[1] 4, 7 May 80.   [2] 2 Oct. 80.
[3] See Buxton, *Finance and politics*, ii. 288–296, which gives a good *résumé* of the malt and death duties reforms.

The Cabinet never, between 1880 and 1885, discussed the consequence for Britain of the sharp rise in the price of gold nor did it discuss 'unemployment', the intellectual discovery of the decade. It was, of course, to be a long time before Cabinets could usefully discuss macro-economic prescriptions for 'unemployment', but it is remarkable, in the light of the exceptional dependence of the British economy on overseas trade and on world banking—both backed by the gold standard—that no attention at all should have been given by the Cabinet to the problem of gold supply and the implications of changes in the price of gold.[1]

It was not, of course, that individual Cabinet members were ignorant of either industry or banking. Though few were still involved directly in firms or banks, most were men of affairs with extensive financial interests especially in agriculture, railways, banks, and the debts of various governments. Land owners such as Gladstone and Granville were also coal mine owners. None knew better than Gladstone the personal consequences of a fiscal crisis for local industry and estate finances.[2] He also had a general sense of the direction of the economy and was aware of its difficulties, but he never in these years either as Chancellor or as Prime Minister suggested that the Cabinet should discuss these. The absence of such discussion showed how the mid-century view of government as parallel to and completely distinct from economic activity was, for a Liberal Cabinet, now thoroughly entrenched and instinctive.

When the minority Salisbury government of 1885 set up a Royal Commission on depression of trade and industry under the chairmanship of Northcote (by then Iddesleigh), thus effectively guaranteeing a majority free-trade report despite the nod to fair trade that the appointment of the Commission represented, the Gladstonians refused to nominate any members of it. They felt that the Commission would not only give a platform to anti-free traders, but that it dignified a nonsense: 'depression of trade', other than short-term dislocation which was self-corrective, was intellectually and practicably impossible. When in 1882, in his last Budget Speech, rather skimpily prepared in the midst of the 'Kilmainham' discussions, Gladstone considered this question he looked in classic Peelite terms to a 'natural' return to equilibrium disturbed by 'unhealthy' fiscal dislocation. There was no significant comment to be made on wider questions:

> the position of the Expenditure is that it is a somewhat growing Expenditure, and with respect to the Revenue is that it is a sluggish Revenue. . . . It is very remarkable that although employment is generally active, and although the condition of trade cannot be said to be generally unsatisfactory, yet the recovery of the country from the point of

[1] The cabinet once (25 June 81) discussed bimetallism, surprisingly not with complete hostility: 'WEG stated his willingness to apply to the Bank on cause shown, but not to take the initiative'; this may simply have been a ploy: when Hartington tried to take the matter further, Gladstone sent his letter on to the Treasury Secretary (i.e. Cavendish, Hartington's brother) and nothing further came of the matter, the Treasury being systematically opposed to bimetallism; see to Hartington, 27 June 81 and, for the Treasury, E. H. H. Green, 'Rentiers versus Producers? The political economy of the bimetallic controversy *c.* 1880–1898', *E.H.R.*, ciii. 611 (1988).

[2] W. H. Gladstone did not stand for re-election in 1885 partly to have more time for the Hawarden estate, 'to a certain extent checked by the double pressure of corn and coal distress, those being its two props'; to Grosvenor, 23 Sept. 85.

extreme depression has been a slow and languid recovery, especially as regards the action of that recovery upon the Revenue of the country. No doubt, there is a natural explanation of the circumstances in the extreme excitement—the unnatural and the unhealthy excitement—of prices which existed during the period of prosperity which preceded the time of depression; and it is to that cause that we must look for the slackness of the recovery to which I have referred, and not to any diminution whatsoever in the resources of the country, or any deterioration in its industrial prospects.[1]

The consequences of the heavy-handed corrective mechanism of the market were very much with the government, but they were dealt with departmentally. For example, Chamberlain's famous Board of Trade circular on public works in 1886 was not discussed by the Cabinet and went unmentioned by the Prime Minister.[2] As we have seen, fiscal unorthodoxy was very occasionally mentioned in Cabinet but apart from the subject of non-protectionist commercial treaties there was never any recorded discussion either of Britain's trade deficit or of her enormous export of capital in this period. Nor was there any attempt in the Treasury at a general appraisal of the costs and economic benefits of imperial expansion. Since the Treasury did not think in terms of the 'economy' as such, but only of the revenue potential of sections of it, an appraisal of that sort was intellectually inconceivable. Any reform which implied the recognition of a national economy and consequently of some governmental responsibility for it was strongly resisted. Thus Gladstone rejected Chamberlain's suggestion of a Ministry of Commerce[3] and downgraded the equivalent proposal for a Ministry of Agriculture, ensuring that it took the form of a Committee of Council, a mechanism already known for ineffectiveness from the example of the education committee. Moreover, by putting Carlingford in charge of the committee, he made inaction certain.[4]

After the Trafalgar Square 'riots' of February 1886, Gladstone pointed out that the fall in commodity prices had made the 'bulk of the working classes . . . (comparatively) not ill but better off' and that it was 'dangerous in principle' to make 'the State minister to the poor of London at the expence of the nation'.[5] In recognizing the untypicality of the London labour market as a basis for generalization about national conditions, he was well ahead of most of the social commentators and his observations on living standards were correct with respect to most of those in employment, but he used his denial of the 'great depression' and of the primacy of London as a reason for a mere reliance on existing voluntarist and poor law mechanisms.

Gladstone resisted new ministries which might be active, but he hankered, as he had since the 1850s, after a Ministry of Finance, which would be negative in its influence, keeping down government expenditure by further extending Treasury control over other government departments and generally preserving the minimal State. Rising expenditure was often thought of as a chief and growing concern, and Gladstone often presented it as such. The Budget of 1873

[1] *H* 268. 1273–4; 24 Apr. 82.
[2] Though see to Ponsonby, 16 Feb. 86.
[3] Garvin, i. 412.
[4] See 15, 17 Mar., 17 Apr. 83.
[5] To Ponsonby, 16 Feb. 86.

had estimated expenditure of £73 millions; that of 1881, of nearly £85 millions, in the interval prices having fallen significantly. Gladstone declared that he had 'great doubts' as to whether the system by which the estimates were prepared 'upon the exclusive responsibility of the Government' was a good system: the Commons ought to be involved also.[1] This was a return to the view expressed in 1862, that posthumous scrutiny by the Public Accounts Committee was insufficient,[2] but, as in the 1860s, he was unwilling to make proposals which significantly diminished the executive's freedom and flexibility. The furthest he would go was the suggestion—not in fact carried out—that there be a Select Committee on Expenditure to scrutinize the estimates, and expenditure generally.[3]

Executive prerogative was one reason for inaction. Another was that, despite Gladstone's lamentations that the era of economic reform was passed, and despite his complaints about the costs of military expeditions and the 'contagion' of foreign countries which 'necessarily affects us',[4] in fact central government expenditure remained remarkably low in relationship to the size of the economy, given that Britain found herself still the only world power. The increases of the 1870s and the first £100 million Budget in 1885 seemed large, but in that year central government expenditure bore the same relationship to G.N.P. as in 1865: 7.9 per cent.[5] When the Radicals in 1883 moved a Resolution to reduce government expenditure consistent with the efficiency of the public service, Gladstone, speaking for the government, was rather caught. He accepted the Resolution, partly on the grounds that there were no significant reductions to be made. He calculated that if grants-in-aid and payments to reduce the debt were taken out of the figures, a central government expenditure of £47 million in 1840 had only risen to £62 million in 1882—an increase of about 34 per cent, in a period when the population had increased by 65 per cent and the taxable revenue of the country (the nearest contemporary concept to G.N.P.) by 115 per cent,[6] a remarkable absence of government growth and an exceptional success for Peel–Gladstone finance, though with serious if unrecognized consequences for the 'national economy' which existed despite the Cabinet and the Treasury.

The household suffrage in the towns had not led to the surge of expenditure financed by direct taxation feared by its opponents. Indeed what is striking in the 1880s is the absence of sustained or systematic political challenge to the Gladstonian minimal central state. Of course there were individual claims from particular interest groups—more money for education, for the navy, for imperial ventures—but there was no general argument for the government to answer for a positive move away from the minimal state to a new plateau of public expenditure. Though Imperialists, New Liberals, and Socialists were in the 1880s each in their different ways challenging the presuppositions of the

[1] H 268. 1297–8.
[2] See Matthew, *Gladstone*, 117.
[3] Speech on Rylands' motion on national expenditure, 6 April 1883; H 277. 1669–70.
[4] H 268. 1298.
[5] See table in Matthew, *Gladstone*, 115.
[6] H 277. 1673–4.

mid-nineteenth century minimal state, their challenges were surprisingly slow
to take on a programmatic form. Only in Ireland was there significant demand
for central government money for social purposes, and land purchase was as
much a cry of the landed class as it was of the peasantry (which as yet of course
had no vote).

Expenditure was thus low. Marginal increases, or potential increases, were to
be sternly resisted so as to keep it low. Gladstone fought these at every level.
The difficulty was the classic one. Large expenditures tended to go relatively
unsupervised. To gain a policy objective once agreed upon, Gladstone was
ready to allocate whatever sum was necessary; hence his combativeness up to
the point of decision. Thus expeditions were well-financed and well-manned.
To gain the objective of an effective second Suez Canal, the Cabinet was ready
to give Lesseps an £8 million loan at minimal interest, in effect, Gladstone told
the Commons, 'a great pecuniary gift to the Canal Company'.[1] On the other
hand, small expenditures were curtailed in ways that sometimes seemed petty
and vindictive. This was particularly so in the area of official salaries, where
Gladstone hoped to save money by abolishing the Privy Seal[2] and by a series of
minor money-saving measures, the most notorious of which was his attempt to
reduce by £300 the salaries of Jesse Collings and Henry Broadhurst when they
took office in 1886.[3]

Large, exceptional items of expenditure such as naval expansion and the 1884–
5 Votes of Credit drove budgetary planning into a corner. By 1885 the Cabinet
faced the need to raise revenue to cover expenditure of over £100,000,000 if all of
the Vote of Credit for the Sudan and Russia were spent, and this in the face of an
imminent General Election on the new franchise. Even before the need for the
Vote of Credit, Gladstone had been alarmed that some increase in indirect as
well as direct taxation would be necessary, and 'such a proceeding, esp. in the
last year of a Parlt., would raise a political question of the first order'.[4] With the
Vote of Credit adding an extra £11,000,000, some increase in indirect taxation
was hardly avoidable. The Budget in its first form, presented on 30 April, largely
met a deficit of £15,000,000 by increasing income tax from 5d. to 8d. (producing £5,400,000 extra), by increasing indirect taxes on drink (producing
£1,650,000), by extra succession duties, and by adjustments to the debt. Despite
the fact that direct taxation bore much the larger share of the increase, and
indeed reminded voters that the Liberals were the party of direct taxation,
Chamberlain and Dilke made a strong pitch, almost to the point of resigning,
against the increase in indirect taxation.[5]

A revised version of the indirect tax proposals was prepared—embarrassing
in itself given Gladstone's complaints in the late 1870s about irregular Tory
budgeting—but on this occasion the revisions were downwards as £2,000,000 of

---

[1] *H* 282. 145.

[2] This controversial suggestion was discussed throughout the 1880–5 ministry; in 1886, Gladstone took the post himself (Disraeli had done the same 1876–8), getting cabinet agreement to its
being merged with the First Lordship (16 Feb. 86); but Salisbury revived it as a separate office.

[3] See correspondence in early Feb. 86 and in Garvin, ii. 176–8.

[4] To Childers, 2 Feb. 85.

[5] See 20, 21 Apr. 85 and to Dilke, 21 Apr. 85.

the Vote of Credit were not needed (that £9,000,000 were needed was odd in view of the fact that neither the Sudanese campaign nor the Russian war, for which the Vote had been jointly raised, had occurred). The revisions were announced on 5 June.[1] On 8 June Beach's amendment on indirect taxation was the occasion of the defeat and resignation of the Government, the victorious majority being, in Gladstone's view, wholly unprincipled, made up of '1. The Irish who are opposed to indirect taxation generally: 2. The Tories who are even more friendly to it than we are.'[2] In the light of the financial and 'economical' elements of the attack on 'Beaconsfieldism' in the Midlothian Campaigns of 1879 and 1880, it was a striking irony that it was on finance that the Liberal majority of 1880 withered away in 1885. This was a posthumous revenge for Disraeli, the more so as 1852 was the previous occasion on which a defeat on its budget had led to the resignation of the Government.

Gladstone's argument in 1883 that government expenditure had not relatively increased greatly depended in part on deducting grants-in-aid—the 'doles', as he called them—paid by central to local government. Awareness of the importance of this deduction in fact lay behind what was intended to be one of the chief legislative achievements of the Liberal government: the creation of a nation-wide series of elected county and district councils to supplement the limited system of elected municipal corporations. Related to this was to be the long-demanded reform of the rates, by early 1881[3] threatening to be as much of a nuisance as it had been 1868–74.[4]

Gladstone had sketched his position in January 1874,[5] and he returned to it in 1881 as the ministry worked towards a County Government Bill. His position was this: elected local authorities should take over 'certain taxes or parts of taxes' allocated to local authorities by central government, thus abolishing grants-in-aid and decentralizing powers presently exercised by the Local Government Board; these local authorities would be subject to 'general rules and conditions to limit their discretion where necessary', though it was hoped such control would be minimal; there would thus be 'not only a great Local Government Bill, but a great decentralisation Bill' in which local initiative would be linked to local financial responsibility, though education would have to continue to be centrally supervised.[6] Much of the money to replace the grants-in-aid (which Gladstone saw as being unfairly paid by 'a fund of which one half (more or less) is contributed by labour') and to reduce the rates, would come from taxes on personalty, in particular 'the abolition or diminution of the remarkable preferences now allowed to land under the Death-duties'.[7] Gladstone's idea was thus to end the oblique method of grants-in-aid and replace it by taxation which local electors would relate directly to local expenditure, and register their approval or disapproval through local elections. This was too bold for Dodson, despite a reminder.[8] His draft bill was, in the view of Sir Henry

[1] After considerable delay; see to Childers, 7, 31 May 85; to Hartington, 11 May 85; and 15, 16 May, 5 June 85.
[2] To Hartington, 10 June 85.
[3] To Dodson, 19 Jan. 81.
[4] See Matthew, *Gladstone*, 215–17.
[5] To Lambert, 2 Jan. 74.
[6] To Dodson, 4 Nov. 81, 10 Jan. 82.
[7] To Dodson, 10 Jan. 82.
[8] To Dodson, 21 Nov. 81.

Thring, the parliamentary draftsman, 'in no respect a decentralising Bill';[1] its proposals were based on the continuance of the existing county rate with some reform, plus grants-in-aid.[2]

Gladstone's financial interest in county government associated him with a much wider movement in the Liberal Party which favoured a plurality of representation at every level, exemplified by the fact that the draft County Boards Bill of December 1881 became the draft County Council Bill of 1882 which, under Dilke, became a draft Local Government Bill (i.e. County and District Councils) for 1884.[3] Yet the government failed to pass a single one of the various English, Scottish, and Irish county and local government bills discussed and in some cases introduced in the 1880–5 Parliament. The County Government and the London Government Bills planned for 1882 and the Provincial Councils (Ireland Bill) drafted by Gladstone in April 1882 came to nothing in that year, nor again in 1883; in 1884 there was an attempt to give a London Government Bill a run, but it did not get beyond Second Reading; in 1885 Irish local government brought the Cabinet to the edge of disintegration. The resignation of June 1885 was the consequence of these two elements coming together. The rift in the Cabinet over Chamberlain's Central Board proposal for Ireland was almost irreconcilable; the failure to reform the rates despite all the attempts in the first government and between 1880 and 1885 was an important ingredient in the success of Hicks Beach's amendment to the Budget in 1885, the occasion of the resignation.

Undoubtedly, the clogged parliamentary timetable was partly to blame for the failure to pass a Bill: local government needed to be the priority bill of the session. It had its best chance in 1882, but this was spoilt by the unforeseeable crisis in Ireland, as the 1881 Land Act turned out to be the first step, not, as Gladstone had hoped, the last. Moreover, Dodson, the minister responsible, was a man of worth but not of power, unable to provide the force needed to drive a bill of this sort through (Gladstone recognized this in pushing him aside in the 1882 reshuffle).[4] As early as March 1882, Gladstone told him that, as the result of 'the obstructionists of the two Oppositions', 'no confident expectations can be formed as to any Bill of magnitude & complexity like this until we see our way in some degree as to Procedure & Devolution to which we must give all our disposable energies'.[5]

An important dimension of the Home Rule Bill of 1886 was its attempt to bypass this deadlock by removing Irish business and all or most of the Irish

[1] See Thring's mem., 17 November 1882, Monk Bretton 55.

[2] Dodson's mem., for Cabinet of November 1881, allowed for 'the levying of some local tax or taxes other than rates' but this is not explicitly mentioned in his drafts of a County Council Bill, January and March 1882 (Monk Bretton 55); the Queen's Speech for 1882 promised 'financial changes' and Gladstone, when announcing no bill could be introduced in 1882, mentioned that 'an important financial re-adjustment' would have accompanied it; *H* 268. 1301 (see also *H* 266. 1307); Thring's mem. of 17 November 1882, looking to a bill in 1883, stated 'it is important to recollect that the Government associate with the scheme of county government a proposal to pay to the county authority, in a lump, the large subventions now contributed by the Treasury for local purposes and to entrust the expenditure of those sums to the County Council, free from all central control'; but he made no mention of a tax or rate reform; Monk Bretton 55.

[3] See Dilke's draft bill, 21 November 1883; Monk Bretton 55.

[4] To Dodson, 23 Dec. 82.

[5] To Dodson, 14 Mar. 82.

M.P.s from Westminster. But the difficulties went beyond obstruction and the timetable. The Liberals had not brought local government into coherence. Like Egypt in foreign affairs, it was the concern of a variety of ministries: the Local Government Board, the Home Office, Dublin Castle, the Lord Advocate, or the Scottish Office (if the Government could agree to have one: a bill establishing administrative devolution for Scotland was one of the various measures introduced each year too late in the Session to be passed, the Tories putting it through in 1885). Thus Dodson and Dilke at the Local Government Board with their County and Local Government Bills jockeyed with Harcourt at the Home Office with his London Government Bills. Gladstone moved in and out of the question, directing Dodson on finance, trying and failing to persuade Harcourt that the police in London should be subject to the elected body,[1] spasmodically encouraging Forster and then Spencer to action on local government in Ireland, and himself drafting a Provincial Councils (Ireland) Bill to go with land purchase in 1882. Sidetracked by Bradlaugh, Ireland, and the aftermath of the murders in 1882, exhausted and absent from the planning cabinets in 1883, Gladstone failed to assert a strategic command over the plurality of local government measures considered by his Cabinet.

Beyond this hung the difficulty that the question of the county franchise had not been resolved: by the 1880s, it seemed odd to give voters a local while denying them a parliamentary vote, and, alternatively, the achievement of local government might be used as an effective argument against resolving the parliamentary franchise question. Yet here was a paradox: conventionally, a new parliamentary franchise led quickly to a general election. If the county franchise were to enable new voters to shape local government, the achievement of the first might put at risk the Liberal parliament which would deal with the second. Moreover, the exercise of that parliamentary franchise would very probably result in Irish local government—in whatever form—becoming a very strongly asserted priority. If the Liberals got local government and franchise reform the wrong way round, there were strong reasons why that was the case.

To two of the questions related to local government reform, Gladstone did however give full attention: 'Procedure and Devolution', and parliamentary reform.

'Procedure and Devolution' meant devolving Commons' business to Grand Committees and introducing the mechanism of the closure to enable government business to be expedited. 'Devolution' in minutes and correspondence in the early 1880s thus usually has this technical meaning, rather than the usual one of Home Rule or extensive local government. As Leader of the House, Gladstone necessarily played a central part in formulating and carrying the various measures. The clogged Parliamentary timetable was a long-standing problem, especially for Liberal governments with their habit of starting government bills in the knowledge that many of them would have to be axed by the July Cabinets.[2] The introduction of *clôture* (the term emphasised the foreignness of the concept to the habits of the Commons) was considered in the

[1] To Harcourt, 19 Dec. 81, 27 Feb., 20, 24, 26, 30 Mar., 4, 5 Apr. 83.
[2] See above, vii. lxvi–lxvii and A. Ramm, 'The parliamentary context of Cabinet government 1868–1874', *E.H.R.*, xcix. 739 (1984).

first government but never to the point of a proposal. The general context for a change in the Commons' Standing Orders thus existed as the large majority of 1880 made slow progress with its legislation, but the particular context for change was created by the Irish crisis of the early 1880s.

Irish 'obstruction' took two forms: first, out-and-out filibustering, points-of-order, motions that Gladstone be not heard, etc.; second, and much more common, there was what to non-Irish M.P.s seemed an overconscientious attention by Home Rule M.P.s to the improvement of proposed legislation, usually that affecting Ireland, of which there was, between 1880 and 1882, a vast amount. The first form, already tried in the latter phases of the Beaconsfield government,[1] was rare, but it reached its culmination in the famous $41\frac{1}{2}$ hours sitting of 31 January to 2 February 1881, when Speaker Brand, 'worthy of his place' in Gladstone's view,[2] adjourned the House on his own responsibility. The Cabinet plans for *clôture* were already in preparation[3] but Northcote, 'weaker than water',[4] withdrew his support. On 3 February there was

An extraordinary evening. The crass infatuation of the Parnell members caused the House to be cleared of them before nine. I then proposed my Resolution for a quasi Dictatorship. Before two it was adjusted in all points, and carried without division.[5]

Next day, on the Protection Bill, 'What a change!'[6]

In the sense of provoking the House to the extent of passing the 'urgency' Standing Order, Parnell had blundered, and the Protection Bill passed under its aegis. But, of course, in the sense of promoting his own position in Ireland and of making a draconian Bill be seen to be being passed draconianly, Parnell had lost nothing. This was the difficulty for a Liberal Cabinet: the Irish crisis might be responsible for corrupting the conventions of the Commons, but the result was a considerable increase in the power of the executive, however much it might be disguised by making it the Speaker's job to superintend business during the period of 'urgency'. This was confirmed when the Speaker laid on the Table a further sixteen rules to apply during 'urgency', one of which was the *clôture* agreed with the Cabinet before the Irish *fracas*,[7] and another what became the *guillotine*.[8]

The 'quasi Dictatorship' of 'urgency' was unpopular and undignified: it suggested panic in the heart of the Mother of Parliaments. Moreover, the constructive, devolutionary dimension was lost, as indeed it had been on a greater scale in 1880 when Gladstone's ambitious 'Obstruction and Devolution' proposals had been pushed aside by the Irish emergency.[9] In 1882, therefore, the Cabinet with the Speaker and Erskine May, the Clerk of the Commons, in attendance tried to normalize procedures by expediting business without a declaration of 'urgency', and by creating Grand Committees for Law and Trade to relieve the Commons' time-table. Ireland and Egypt and the Cabinet's indecision about the Conservatives' amendment that a two-thirds majority for closure be needed,[10] meant deferral of 'procedure and devolution' to a special Session in

[1] Redlich, i. 142–51. [2] 2 Feb. 81. [3] 22, 29 Jan. 81.
[4] 1 Feb. 81. [5] 3 Feb. 81. [6] 4 Feb. 81. [7] 22 Jan. 81.
[8] Redlich, i. 165 ff. [9] See 23 Oct. 80 and above, ix. lxxvii–lxxviii.
[10] See 18 Feb., 29 July, 3, 12 Aug., 20 Oct., 2 Nov. 82 and to Hartington, 9 Oct. 82.

the autumn of 1882 when, with the '2/3 amendment' defeated by 84 votes,[1] the new Standing Orders passed after 34 nights of debate: 'A great day, as I think, for the House of Commons itself.'[2]

So might Gladstone think, but it was really a great day for executive government. Many Liberals were uneasy. Despite the success of the Grand Committee in dealing with Chamberlain's Bankruptcy Bill in 1883, the devolutionary side of the system lapsed at the end of 1883 and was not renewed.[3] The details of the Standing Orders were unpopular and not brought into play.[4] Despite all the time spent on procedure and devolution, little more progress was in practice made than was made legislatively on local government. And as with local government, the solution pointed one way: remove the Irish from the House.

Parliamentary reform was the great liberal legislative triumph of Gladstone's second ministry, going far to redeem the promise of the majority of 1880 and to obliterate for many Liberals the disappointments and failures of the government. 1831–2 and 1866–7 had created a pattern and a warning: 'reform' meant a clutch of measures and a political crisis. There was no such thing as a straightforward reform bill, for it involved that most complex of all political manoeuvres: a political system transforming its nature by changing its own rules. The new dispensation of franchise and redistributed constituency boundaries had to be constituted by the members of Parliament (in both Houses) who owed their power and presence to the old. Gladstone's aim was to simplify the clutch of measures and thus, he hoped, contain the crisis. This would be achieved by keeping franchise and redistribution separate, with various other measures, such as a new registration bill for each country, to follow. It would also permit Gladstone to pass a simple franchise bill and then retire, leaving the details of redistribution to others.

Gladstone was committed to franchise reform by his pledge of 1873 that he believed 'the extension of the Household Suffrage to counties to be one which is just and politic in itself, & which cannot long be avoided'.[5] The reform of the county franchise—despite Gladstone's wishes—linked parliamentary reform to the land campaign in Britain as well as in Ireland and was urged in Cabinet by Chamberlain from an early stage in 1880. Chamberlain ran up against Gladstone's argument that 'this subject, entailing as it would a new dissolution, ought to be deferred till towards the close of the new Parliament just elected',[6] i.e. deferred till 1884 or 1885, the latter being probably the latest year for a bill

---

[1] 2 Nov. 82.   [2] 1 Dec. 82.

[3] The Standing Orders for Grand Committees were for 1883 only; the failure to continue them is something of a mystery; asked about them on 31 July 1883, Gladstone replied that despite their 'increased importance' the government did not 'think the time or the circumstances convenient for making a proposal'; *H* 282. 1156.

[4] Redlich, i. 174–5: 'the House tacitly abandoned many parts of the new procedure and it never was really put into force'. It seems the closure was never used in 1882–5, for in the one case noted by Redlich, i. 177n., that of 20 February 1885, the Resolution for precedence for the Redistribution Bill was not in fact moved under the Standing Order and was not a closure but a precedence motion, of a sort that could have been moved at any time.

[5] See 23 July 73.

[6] Chamberlain, *Political memoir*, 4 and Jones, *1884*, 3; Gladstone did not record Chamberlain's proposal. Chamberlain raised the question again in 1881, proposing the sequence followed by Gladstone in 1883, a franchise bill alone, with redistribution 'postponed'; see 10 Nov. 81n.

or bills on which a dissolution on a new register and with new boundaries could be held in early 1887 (the latest time allowed by the Septennial Act and the financial timetable of the year). It was most unusual for a Parliament to run its full course, and thus the Cabinet's move in the autumn of 1883 to plan a bill or bills for 1884 was a choice for the earlier of the two options. In that sense it reflected the disappointment of the Liberal Party in the absence of achievement by its majority in 1880–3, but not too much should be made of this. Indeed, in 1882 Gladstone had seen the Session of 1884 as the latest year in which to tackle the question, keeping 'a year to spare in case of accidents'[1]—as it turned out, a very prudent safeguard. The Cabinet's movement towards parliamentary reform in the autumn of 1883 was thus anticipated and was not haphazard.

Gladstone initiated matters on his return from a cruise to Scandinavia with Tennyson by asking Sir Henry James, the Attorney General, to consider the possibility of drafting a single Bill for all three 'Kingdoms'[2] (Scotland, Ireland, England-and-Wales); hitherto there had been a separate bill for each, the Irish franchises being almost unrelated in character or chronology to those of the mainland. Thus Gladstone's strategy was clear from the start. Remembering the disastrous set-back of 1866, when the Gladstone/Russell bill led to the fall of the ministry—though ignoring the importance of the absence of a redistribution proposal in causing that set-back—he was determined to keep the legislation as simple as possible: 'form is of the utmost political importance. And by form I mean brevity. . . . Every needless word will be a new danger', because 'the endeavour will be to beat us by and upon entangling details'.[3] A single bill for the three Kingdoms would trump the opposition to franchise extension in Ireland, assuming Ireland were to be included at all, as well as shortening the amount of parliamentary time needed. With luck, only half a Session would be needed, leaving room for a local government bill.[4] Ireland, in Gladstone's view, had to be included in both the franchise and the redistribution bills: 'It would I think be impolitic and inequitable to exclude Ireland from both [sc. either of] these great subjects: I believe too that the exclusion would ensure failure.'[5]

In Gladstone's mind, therefore, the question was not whether to include Ireland, but on what basis: a harmonization of the existing Irish borough and county franchises on the £4 borough standard, or, what might be in fact though not in appearance 'more conservative', the assimilation of the Irish franchise with 'the pure British franchise', i.e. a household suffrage for the three kingdoms.[6] The view of Dublin Castle, as expressed by G. O. Trevelyan, the Irish Secretary, was that it was 'impossible to propose a different franchise for Great Britain and Ireland' and that household suffrage, in reducing the influence of farmers, would encourage in the latter 'some sense of political responsibility'.[7] By early November 1883, a harmonization of the United Kingdom's franchises, on the basis of household suffrage in the boroughs and counties of the three kingdoms, was the basis of the bill, if there were to be one.[8] Gladstone coaxed the bill through the autumn Cabinets with considerable skill: its 'provisional'

---

[1] To Goschen, 1 June 82. [2] To James, 3 Oct. 83.
[3] To James, 5 Nov. 83. [4] To Hartington, 22 Oct. 83.
[5] Ibid. [6] To Trevelyan, 23 Oct. 83.
[7] Ibid., n. [8] To James, 5 Nov. 83.

nature technically allowing dissidents to hang back; *if* there were to be a bill 'it shall be with the franchise *alone*',[1] i.e. redistribution to be taken separately. This was partly a means of keeping open the possibility of retirement in the foreseeable future: Gladstone argued that he could manage a franchise bill but not a redistribution bill. But there were wider considerations also. The chief whip thought the Cabinet 'never made a more sensible decision' than 'the Franchise *alone*'.[2] This way of proceeding Gladstone required, despite the precedent of 1866 when the failure to deal with redistribution had been a chief cause of disaster, as part of his strategy of ensuring safe passage through the Commons.

In one way this was a fair point: the attempt to deal with franchise reform in one bill only was a novelty and, given the history of legislation in 1880–3, the assumption of delays and difficulties was not unreasonable. But the separation of franchise and redistribution admitted another point: the Liberals generally agreed, as with local government, that reform was a natural use of their large majority, but also, again as with local government, there was little agreement about how the redistribution should be carried out, and there was no mechanism for arriving at a party view on the matter. The distinction between town and country, so carefully preserved in 1832 and 1867, the accommodation of extensive demographic changes, the possibility of proportional representation: all these were disputed areas which could reasonably be seen as jeopardizing the harmony of Liberal agreement on a simple franchise extension, if they were dealt with in the same bill. Moreover, there was the obvious point, characteristically not made in the rather decorous style of Liberal letter-writing, that redistribution in 1885 would keep the government's supporters (who on this issue included, unusually, the Parnellites) in line for another Session, thus delaying the dissolution which would naturally follow the passing of the various reform bills. This indeed proved to be the case, though not in the circumstances Gladstone had expected.

Gladstone carried his approach; Hartington's price for agreeing to it was that Gladstone should therefore be seen to be responsible by taking charge of the Bills in the Commons (including redistribution), an arrangement patched up in a flurry of letters and meetings in the week after Christmas 1883.[3] Gladstone carried the Franchise Bill in the Commons by the end of June 1884, largely through the self-restraint of the Liberal Party which on the whole obeyed Gladstone's entreaty 'not to endanger the Bill by additions',[4] and of the Home Rule M.P.s who sensed from the start the advantage they would gain from the bill.

Conceptually, the 'Bill to amend the Law relating to the Representation of the People in the United Kingdom', whose motion for introduction Gladstone moved on 28 February 1884 was, as we would expect from him, extremely conservative. In this, belief merged happily with prudence. Radical issues such as proportional representation and the enfranchisement of women were ruthlessly thrust aside. The Bill followed the 1832 and 1867 models in adding to the existing franchises a household franchise for county voters, together with two

---

[1] 22 Nov. 83 and to Grosvenor, 23 Nov. 83.
[2] To Grosvenor, 23 Nov. 83n.
[3] See 25–31 Dec. 83.
[4] *H* 285. 132.

'enlargements' of the household franchise, the lodger and service franchises. There was no attempt at 'reform upon a system', and the vote was no more a right than it had ever been: it was a privilege granted by statute to certain adult men.[1] The purpose of the Bill was 'the enfranchisement of capable citizens', and the criterion of capability had become, through weight of numbers and the absence of the expansion of other forms of franchise, the occupation of property: 'occupation will inevitably be, under the new system, the ground and main foundation of our electoral system'.[2] The man who did not occupy property, as a householder, as a lodger (narrowly defined and hard to register),[3] or as the living-in servant of a householder or as owner of business premises, could not expect a vote. Gladstone admitted no category of persons as deserving but still excluded from the franchise,[4] with the possible exception of women. Gladstone argued that concern for the passing of the bill meant that 'to nail onto the Extension of the Franchise, founded on principles already known & in use, a vast social question, which is surely entitled to be considered as such, appears to me in principle very doubtful'; if passed in the Commons, a women's suffrage amendment would give the Lords just the excuse they sought to reject the bill.[5] Gladstone's own position on whether women were admittable to the franchise thus remained studiously undisclosed.

Retrospectively, the 1884 bill seems conservative, an important step in the long process by which the British ruling class created the illusion of democracy while carefully limiting its reality. To contemporaries, however, the bill seemed dramatic and, in the context of the politics of the 1880s, several of its consequences were so. The bill seemed to enfranchise both the Liberal land campaign and the residue of the Land League. The distinction drawn between a Franchise Bill in 1884 and a Redistribution Bill in the near but unspecified

[1] Ideas of abolishing ancient right franchises (see to Lambert, 22 Dec. 83) were dropped: 'we leave the "ancient right" franchise alone' (*H* 285. 120); the Bill did abolish the £50 Chandos clause of 1832, as no longer necessary; ibid., 113.

[2] *H* 285. 116. For the consequences of this, see N. Blewett, 'The franchise in the United Kingdom, 1885–1918', *Past and Present*, xxxii (December 1965) and H. C. G. Matthew, R. I. McKibbin and J. A. Kay, 'The franchise factor in the rise of the Labour Party', *E.H.R.*, xci. 723 (1976). E. Gibson, the Irish Tory, though strongly opposed to the bill, sharply picked up Gladstone's skilful elision of the criteria of capability and occupation: 'The argument of the Prime Minister prove[d] infinitely too much. It proved that it was right to give the franchise to every man with a house; but every man without a house, although fully qualified in other respects, was not said to be capable of the franchise'; *H* 285. 152.

[3] Gladstone maintained the especial restrictiveness of the register with respect to lodgers (whose small representation on the register he had correctly and approvingly anticipated in 1867) by suggesting to Lambert that it would continue to be desirable that 'lodger-votes, and property votes of all kinds, must come there by claim', i.e. must be claimed in person each year; to Lambert, 22 Dec. 83.

[4] Of the various other possible changes (chiefly reducing existing property franchises) mentioned by Gladstone as necessarily omitted—'we are determined . . . not to deck-load our Franchise Bill'—only the enfranchisement of women would have extended the franchise to those without it; *H* 285. 123.

[5] To Dilke, 13 May 84; see also 24 May 84 and to Woodall (who moved the women's suffrage amendment on 11 June 1884), 10 June 84. On Mason's motion in 1883, Hamilton noted: 'Mr. G. and the preponderance of the Government did not support it. The balance of his mind seems to be against such a proposal, but he would not equally object to the extension of the franchise to women on the Italian plan which is, I believe, that they vote by male proxy'; Bahlman, *Hamilton*, ii. 458.

future opened, despite Liberal disclaimers, the possibility of a dissolution on the new franchise but on the old distribution of seats.

In 1866 the bill had failed in the Commons largely because of the redistribution question; in 1884 it passed the Commons despite it. Accordingly, on 8 July the Lords rejected the Second Reading of the bill: 'What a suicidal act of the Lords!', Gladstone noted,[1] as Salisbury played the first card of a long-drawn out poker game. It was a game Gladstone manifestly enjoyed. In the short term, Salisbury seemed to have given him a considerable advantage. That the Lords would reject the bill (except, *via* Cairns' amendment, as part of 'an entire scheme') was certainly not part of Gladstone's initial calculations. As the possibility arose, he went to considerable lengths to mobilize the bishops and peers of Liberal appointment or creation, including Tennyson.[2]

Gladstone was certainly seen to have tried to get the bill through, but failure to have done so was not necessarily a tactical disadvantage. Privately, Gladstone could point out to the Queen the folly, irresponsibility, and riskiness to the monarchy of the Tories' position in making 'organic change in the House of Lords' an issue which, if the Franchise Bill were not passed, the Liberal Party, however reluctantly, would be bound to take up, an issue which, once taken up, would eventually be taken to a conclusion.[3] With the Queen, it was for once Gladstone who was the calming man of caution, and he encouraged her mediation with a long, skilfully-angled memorandum pointing out the dangers to the hereditary principle (and consequently to the monarchy) if the Tory peers were not brought to reason.[4] Publicly, Gladstone could reap the advantage of the Lords' action by the hugely enthusiastic reception he was given during his tour of the agricultural constituencies of central and east Scotland in the late summer of 1884, 'a tour of utmost interest: which grew into an importance far beyond anything I had dreamt of'.[5] The party of progress was given the opportunity for a really hearty cheer, its last for almost twenty years. Gladstone denounced the specific action of the Lords, while defending the principle of an hereditary second chamber.[6]

But if the Lords' action posed problems for the Conservatives in their appeal to the new democracy, it also created considerable difficulties for the Liberals. Gladstone needed the bill: he it was who had persuaded the Cabinet and the Commons that a Franchise Bill first, with redistribution second, would expedite and simplify. The Cabinet had already lost the business of one Session; it could not be seen to be subservient to the dictates of the Lords. Although Gladstone 'considered the points of a Manifesto speech', he persuaded the Cabinet not to dissolve on the Franchise Bill, but to hold an autumn Session:[7] 'To allow Lords to force a dissolution would be precedent worse than anything since beginning of the reign of Geo. III.'[8] Moreover, the crises over Egyptian finance and over

---

[1] 8 July 84.
[2] To Benson, 2 July 84; to L. Tennyson, 3 July 84; to Tennyson, 6 July 84.
[3] To the Queen, 19 Aug. 84.
[4] Ibid. and 25 Aug. 84.
[5] 26 Sept. 84.
[6] To the Queen, 19 Aug. 84.
[7] 9 July 84.
[8] Monk Bretton's note of Gladstone's remarks; 9 July 84n.

the rescue of Gordon in themselves made a dissolution in July 1884 almost impossible: 'This day for the first time in my recollection there were *three* crises for us running high tide at once: Egypt, Gordon, & franchise.'[1] The creation of peers as a means of curtailing the Lords would have gone against all Gladstone's personal constitutional instincts, and would anyway have been unacceptable to the considerable Whig/Liberal group led by Hartington which had argued all along that the bill should deal with redistribution and franchise together, let alone would it have been acceptable to the Queen.

A coming to terms was thus called for: the issue was, on what terms and on whose? By his cool playing of the Lords' card, Salisbury had gained a considerable advantage: he had blocked the Liberal majority in the Commons and, since the Liberals had continued to play within the existing constitutional conventions (while complaining that Salisbury was flouting them), he had gained the point that the Tory majority in the Lords counted. Put crudely, the Liberals were to gain on the franchise, the Tories on the redistribution. This was the effect of the agreement by which Gladstone, Dilke, and Hartington met Salisbury and Northcote as 'Legates of the opposite party'[2] in a series of meetings in November 1884[3] which settled the political geography of the United Kingdom until 1918.

The Cabinet had moved towards preparation for an accommodation of some sort by appointing a Committee, of which Gladstone was not a member, on 9 August 1884 'to prepare materials for Redistribution and give directions as to Boundaries'.[4] Gladstone had laid out his own position during the initial arguments the previous winter:

> While looking to a comparatively large arrangement, I am not friendly to Electoral districts, am ready to consider some limitation on the representation of the largest town populations, & am desirous to keep alive within fair limits the individuality of towns with moderate population.[5]

He had little enthusiasm for Hartington's demand for the representation of 'minorities' (i.e. Protestants) in Ireland, and insisted that if there were to be such representation it would have to be accepted that 'we cannot have a minority plan *for Ireland only*'.[6] Apart from the question of minorities—brushed aside in the rush in November 1884—Gladstone found himself on the defensive. The energetic radicalism of Dilke, who effectively controlled the Cabinet committee, and the—as Gladstone saw it—thoroughgoingly unconservative opportunism of Salisbury left little space for Gladstone's Peelite notion of the continued

---

[1] 2 Aug. 84. For the process leading up to this see Aug.-Nov. 84, Jones, *1884*, ch. 7 and Appendix and M. E. J. Chadwick, 'The role of redistribution in the making of the Third Reform Act', *Historical Journal* (1976).

[2] To Dilke, 26 Nov. 84.

[3] 19-28 Nov. 84. Gladstone had hoped to get away with a compromise which did not involve bargaining with the Tories, by meeting Northcote (once his private secretary) in Algernon West's house (see 13 Nov. 84), but (see 15 Nov. 84) Salisbury would have none of it.

[4] 9 Aug. 84. As it was agreed that redistribution would follow franchise reform, it is perhaps surprising that the cabinet had not made this move earlier; this was probably because the disagreements in cabinet on redistribution were likely to be much sharper than those on the franchise. According to Dilke, he and Gladstone had already 'hatched the Bill' in July; see 14 July 84n.

[5] To Hartington, 29 Dec. 83.   [6] To Spencer, 6 Dec. 84.

harmony of town and country separately represented according to the criteria of communities rather than that of numbers. A rearguard action to keep seats for boroughs of 10,000 population yielded to Dilke's 15,000 (Dilke and Gladstone subsequently successfully defending this against Salisbury's demand for 20,000), as did the attempt to confine single-member seats to the boroughs.[1] But Gladstone did not press his views very hard. Surrounded by difficulties in foreign and imperial affairs, he was relieved to find in Dilke an energy and competence as to detail rare in his ministry, and was consequently willing to make concessions 'if we could thereby effectually promote peace & get the Franchise Bill passed'.[2] Gladstone was an effective broker with the Tories partly because of his innate command of detail which redistribution required, and partly because he was working to the Cabinet's brief, not his own. Thus was the bargain struck: the Franchise Bill 'to pass forthwith' in exchange for a radical redistribution, the ending of double-member constituencies save in cities between 50,000 and 150,000 and the absorption of existing borough seats of under 15,000 into the surrounding counties.[3]

This was not perceived as a bad bargain. In that it dismantled a distribution of seats in which the Liberals usually won, it was clearly risky. But Liberals do not seem to have seen the extent of the advantage to the Tories of single member constituencies and absorption of small borough seats into the counties. Liberals counted on their gains in the rural seats through the enfranchisement of the agricultural labourers at least balancing Tory advantages in the redistribution. Dilke, generally acknowledged as an expert, at one point contemplated a much more widespread absorption of boroughs into the counties.[4] Gladstone's attempt to defend the small borough seats was not based on Liberal advantage but on historic principles and a communitarian theory of representative government, 'a tenderness for individuality of communities in boroughs & counties' rather than their disintegration into areas of class or sectional interest.[5] Indeed, the absence of party calculation by the Liberals on the redistribution question is rather striking. They relied too simply on the advantage of franchise extension, and even there what calculation there was spelt largely difficulty: the assumption was that the 'so-called National Party in Ireland' would increase its number of M.P.s from 'a little over forty to near eighty', about twenty-five of these being taken from the Liberals.[6] Despite this acceptance of the disappearance of Liberalism in Ireland, a reduction of the number of seats in over-represented Ireland was strongly resisted. The chief consequence of the reform acts for the mainland—the enabling of villa Tory suburban voters to escape to single member seats, 'high and dry on islands of their own', and thus found the modern Conservative Party[7]—was far less anticipated by Liberals than it was by Tories. The Liberals rightly anticipated gains in the counties; they did not anticipate that they would soon in England be predominantly the party of the countryside.

[1] To Dilke, 26 Oct. 84.
[2] To Dilke, 29 Sept. 84.
[3] Memorandum of agreement, 28 Nov. 84.
[4] Gwynn, ii. 67.
[5] To Dilke, 29 Sept. 84.
[6] 19 Aug. 84.
[7] J. Cornford, 'The transformation of conservatism in the late nineteenth century', *Victorian Studies*, vii. 58 (1963).

For Liberals generally, this was because they did not have and could not have a developed sense of class: to do so would cut straight across the nature of the Liberal mind and the view that votes were won by policies, not contained by class-affiliation. In Gladstone's case, though he shared that view, there was a further reason. In the long haul of the reform process—from September 1883 to the passing of the final bills in the summer of 1885—Gladstone conducted himself effectively, and in marked contrast to his impassioned behaviour in 1866-7. The 'smash without example' was not repeated. But in 1866-7 Gladstone was so impassioned because his reform proposals had a close, direct and organic relationship to his more general plan of public finance and political economy. His deliberately limited proposals of 1866 had precise intentions, and the household suffrage of 1867, the creation of the curious alliance of Radicalism and what Gladstone regarded as Conservative opportunism, had created a political world not of his making.[1] Ironically, he and Salisbury, who had resigned over household suffrage in 1867, both danced in 1884 to the dead Disraeli's tune. They both, however, danced happily. Salisbury was able to exploit any advantage which the system gave him: if that system had little legitimacy, so then was his activity liberated and Conservatism was free to take what it could. Gladstone had found the household suffrage in fact enfranchising very much the sort of electorate for which he had been seeking in 1866: the campaigns of the 1870s had shown its capacity for capable citizenship. Even so, there is a certain sense of distance between Gladstone and the reform measures in 1883-5. He saw his role in them as an executive rather than a creator, and with respect to them his tactics were as sharp as his strategy was disastrous.

The Redistribution Bill cleared the Commons on 11 May 1885, and the three Registration Bills received Royal Assent on 21 May 1885; the new dispensation was all but in place, and the need for extreme self-control in the Commons by the Liberals ended, and so did the need for Parnellite support for their reform measures: the doubling of the Home Rule Party now lay before it. On 8 June a combination of Tories and Parnellites carried Hicks Beach's amendment to the budget with many Liberal M.P.s absent: 'Beaten by 264:252. Adjourned the House. This is a considerable event.'[2]

The defeat of the Budget in 1885 conformed to type: in every Liberal government between Grey in 1832 and Campbell-Bannerman in 1905 the parliamentary majority eventually disintegrated and led to a dissolution or, more usually, a minority Tory government. In 1885 dissolution was impossible, the Redistribution Bill being still in the Lords and the registers of the new constituencies and new voters not yet drawn up. Gladstone therefore did as he had done in 1873 on the Irish University Bill and resigned, on this occasion with the positive encouragement of a Cabinet exhausted by crisis and crushed yet again in the Irish forceps of coercion and conciliation. Salisbury then followed precedent (Peel in 1834, Derby in 1852, 1858, and 1866) and, ignoring Disraeli's reticence in 1873, accepted office after considerable haggling. Thus one Christ Church man ceded the premiership to another, so small was the nexus of the Victorian ruling class.[3] Salisbury's behaviour moved Gladstone to a rare note of

---

[1] See Matthew, *Gladstone*, ch. 5.   [2] 8 June 85.
[3] Christ Church held the premiership from 1880 to 1902.

personal criticism in his diary: 'He has been ill to deal with, requiring incessant watching.'[1] So the second ministry ended: 'At 11.45 cleared out of my official room & had a moment to fall down and give thanks for the labours done & the strength vouchsafed me there: and to pray for the Christlike mind.'[2]

If precedent were to be followed, the Liberals would regroup and return to office invigorated by a spell in opposition and reunited in some fresh cause: 'It is in opposition, & not in Govt., that the Liberal party tends to draw together.'[3] It was clear from the circumstances of the resignation of the Cabinet that effective reunion would in large measure depend on Irish policy, either by replacing the dispute on Ireland by some quite different issue, or by resolving it in favour of an agreed initiative.

It is therefore time to turn to the second ministry's handling of Irish affairs, of all the travails of the government the least rewarding and still today the most contentious.

VII

In 1921 the British government, sustained by a Conservative-dominated coalition, signed a treaty with the Irish Free State, already a *de facto* republic, thus effectively admitting the end of union between the United Kingdom and most of Ireland. Such an outcome would have been regarded by any member of any British cabinet of the 1880s, and certainly by Gladstone, as an utter failure for British policy. That this was less than forty years after the 'Kilmainham Treaty' and that one participant in the events of the 1880s, A. J. Balfour, was still in the Cabinet and another, T. M. Healy, was the first Governor-General of the Irish Free State, are reminders of how misleading it is to dissociate the developments of the 1880s from their results, by setting them merely in a short-term, tactical context. For those concerned to maintain the United Kingdom as an entity, it is also a reminder of a lesson learnt too late. 'What fools we were,' George V told Ramsay MacDonald in 1930, 'not to have accepted Gladstone's Home Rule Bill. The Empire now would not have had the Irish Free State giving us so much trouble and pulling us to pieces.'[4]

In his first government, Gladstone had set out to show the Irish that 'there is nothing that Ireland has asked and which this country and this Parliament have refused. . . . I have looked in vain for the setting forth of any practical scheme of policy which the Imperial Parliament is not equal to deal with, or which it refuses to deal with, and which is to be brought about by Home Rule.'[5] Disestablishment of the Irish Church in 1869 and the Land Act in 1870 sought to demonstrate this point and hence to encourage constitutionalism as against Fenianism, as did, less probably, the abortive Irish University Bill of 1873, a bill which, however, seemed to show that Gladstone's notion of the virtual

---

[1] 24 June 85.   [2] 25 June 85.   [3] 12 July 86.
[4] MacDonald's diary, 6 July 1930, quoted in K. Rose, *George V* (1983), 240. George V was twenty-one in 1886, so the events of that year were part of his adult political experience. In 1882, the Prince of Wales had taken him and his brother on a visit to Gladstone in Downing Street; see 15 Aug. 82.
[5] Matthew, *Gladstone*, 201.

representation of Home Rule interests by the Westminster Parliament was increasingly difficult to sustain.

His position, self-evidently, implied that if the Westminster Parliament could not by its various 'boons' give the Irish what they believed they needed then some form of 'Home Rule' or more would, eventually, be the natural consequence. The objective of the first government, of attempting to remove the Protestant ascendancy, would, if achieved, pacify Ireland by leaving no major grievance. The problem of this strategy was that its measures, dramatic though they seemed at the time, were too modest and too slow. They did not prevent and perhaps even encouraged the emergence of a more organized Home Rule movement in the mid-1870s. To Gladstone's surprise, Irish questions were the chief parliamentary business of his administrations in the 1880s.

In the 1860s, Gladstone had hoped to make the Irish choose between constitutionalism and Fenianism and to express their choice by support for the Liberal Party which then held most of the Irish seats. Now, by 1880, Liberal seats were turning into Home Rule seats and the choice was between liberal constitutionalism and a rapidly growing Home Rule movement, constitutional in objective but linked, through the Land League, to aspects of Fenianism. Quite quickly, Ireland had become from the metropolitan point of view much more problematic. Irish demands were becoming systematized in a call for constitutional reform and institutionalized in a Home Rule party which was assimilable within the ideology of British politics. Indeed, like the Indian National Congress of 1885, they appealed to what was best in the British liberal tradition. British politics had been bound to reject Fenianism in the same way that it had rejected Chartism: the demands made were simply not compatible with other assumptions about the nature of the political system. But an effective Home Rule Party was bound to put the Liberals on the spot. Home Rule was the equivalent of the Reform League for franchise reform in the 1860s: the demands might be disliked but they were not instantly incompatible with the assumptions of contemporary policy makers, unless, that is, 'Home Rule' came to be seen as an aspect of Fenianism rather than as the means to its defeat. Judgement of this balance was to be a central question for the 1880s. In its Land League phase, constitutionalism was, at least superficially, severely compromised.

As we have seen,[1] the consequence of agricultural depression in Ireland in the later 1870s, in the form of the rapid spread of the Land League, took Gladstone aback. Only with reluctance did he accept the need for another land bill. His instinct, after reading about the history of the imposition of the Union in 1800, was to introduce 'remedial legislation' as described in his long paper on 'Obstruction and Devolution', but the immediate crisis of the prosecution of Parnell in 1880, 'the sheer panic' in Ireland, the demand for coercion and the need to counter the land campaign by some direct response in the form of a land bill, meant that the treatment of 'what is called (*in bonam partem*) Local Government and (*in malam*) Home Rule' had to be set aside.

The Land League campaign was as near a revolutionary movement as anything seen in the United Kingdom between 1800 and 1914. Though having

---

[1] See above, ix. lxxiv–lxxix, of which the rest of this paragraph is a brief summary.

important regional variations in its support and in its techniques, the Land League was, none the less, in the circumstances, a fairly cohesive organization in the sense of having an institutional presence in most of Ireland.[1] But its thrust came not from its structure or from its central committee, but from the tenant farmers who were its motor, afforced by agricultural labourers and small-town shop-keepers.[2] Innovative on the British political scene though the Land League was, the essentially conservative objectives of its tenant farmer supporters gave the government the opportunity to leave its more politically motivated high command stranded. Making this distinction between the motives of the supporters of the Land League and those of its leadership, and, even more, acting on it, required at the time considerable boldness on the part of Liberal Cabinet members.

The Land League had no ideology of modernization or efficiency; it faced the government with no call for a fundamental recasting of the Irish economy. For its primary objective it did not look beyond the consolidation of the position of the tenant farmer as less of a tenant and more of a proprietor, a fixed figure on the social scene absolved from the obligations of a tenant but without the fixed-cost burdens of the landowner. Some, notably Davitt, saw that this could only be a short-term settlement, and that the success of the rent-strike and of the legal recognition of 'fair rent' must imply the end of the landowning classes.[3]

The debate within the Liberal Cabinet in 1880–1 took place largely on these terms: however violent some of its methods, the Land League called for stability in the Irish countryside: how should the Cabinet answer this call? Its first response was to attempt the destruction of the League's organization through coercion and the prevention, as far as possible, of physical violence in the localities (the Protection of Person and Property Bill and the Peace Preservation Bill). These dealt with the methods of the League: its aims would be dealt with by a land bill which would consolidate order in the Irish countryside. The Land Act of 1870—dictated by similar political considerations of stability and order[4]—had contained two approaches: a strengthening of the tenant's position, and, through the clause introduced by John Bright, a very limited provision for tenants to turn themselves into owners by purchasing their farms with a government grant.

The Land League was predominantly a tenant-right organization, though a peasant proprietary was the objective of the more politically conscious central committee.[5] Tenant-right implied a legal readjustment of social and financial relationships: no State money was involved. It also meant that tenants continued to be tenants, however secure; thus landlordism continued also, however weak. The alternative solution, peasant proprietorship, through the wholesale removal of the landowning class and the creation through a land purchase scheme—financed directly or indirectly by the State—of a large class of small landowners in hock to the government for their properties, raised very large questions of finance and, Gladstone always argued, of the creation of a repre-

---

[1] S. Clark, *Social origins of the Irish land war* (1979), ch. 8.

[2] Ibid. and K. T. Hoppen, *Elections, politics and society in Ireland 1832–1884* (1984), 473ff.   [3] See B. L. Solow, *The land question and the Irish economy 1870–1903* (1971), 166–7.

[4] Matthew, *Gladstone*, 195–6.   [5] Clark, op. cit., 302–3.

sentative local government structure of some sort to make it work. All Gladstone's notions of social hierarchy, finance and debt predisposed him to the first of these, though he had always, even in moving his Irish Church Resolutions in 1868, recognized the potential importance of the second.[1]

The absence of a significant scheme of land purchase had important consequences.[2] It implied a sequence of governmental involvement: the continuance of the overwhelmingly Protestant landowning class meant that there would be more land agitation, which in turn would mean more coercion. The landowning class was, in Gladstone's view, maintained so as to keep order in Ireland, but the opposite was really the case: it was the landowners that were the cause of the disorder. The landowner was, Gladstone wrote in 1886, 'the salient point of friction'.[3] His maintenance simply intensified metropolitan rule through coercion bills passed against the votes of an ever-increasing body of Irish Home Rule M.P.s. Maintaining coercion so as to maintain the landowner guaranteed the demise of Liberalism in Ireland. This was the treadmill on which the Liberal Party ran from 1880 to 1885.

In the novel context of quasi-revolutionary Irish politics the 'Three F.s'—fixity of tenure, fair rent, freedom of sale—once so bold a demand, quickly became a modest request advocated by Dublin Castle, by the Bessborough Royal Commission, appointed by the Liberals, and by the Liberals' minority report to the Richmond Royal Commission, appointed by the Conservatives. To both of these Commissions Gladstone had looked for caution: 'Read Reports of Commn—(Confusion worse confounded).'[4] Gladstone only reluctantly agreed with W. E. Forster, the Irish Secretary, 'that the Cabinet ought to understand that while there is a great body of Irish opinion for something called the 3 F.s, & another body as I suppose for Parnell's plan & that of the Land League, there is no such body in favour of anything short of these, though intelligent & weighty *individuals* may be cited in some strength who are for amending the [1870] Land Act'.[5] Gladstone's position of 1880, that all that was needed was a modest amendment of the 1870 Act, was thus admitted to be quite insubstantial: if he tried to sustain it he would find himself cornered with Whigs such as Argyll.

There was therefore a strong prudential element in Gladstone's thinking as in December 1880 and January 1881 he came to terms with the scale of change which would be necessary if the land bill was to balance the various measures of coercion. What was needed from Forster was an assessment of exactly at what point on the scale of Irish demands 'a definitive settlement'[6] of the land question could be made. This shows the extent to which the Bill of 1881 was a political operation. Only in its emigration clauses was the wider question of the creation of a more prosperous Irish economy directly touched, and then only negatively.

Gladstone's attitude to the various options was complex. Ultimately, he saw the occupation of property as a fulfilment of a God-given privilege, property

---

[1] See H. Shearman, 'State-aided land purchase under the disestablishment act of 1869', *Irish Historical Studies*, iv. 58 (1944); also Matthew, *Gladstone*, 193.

[2] There were spasmodic but never very determined attempts at a government scheme; see, e.g., 28 Apr. 84.   [3] 23 Mar. 86.

[4] 11 Jan. 81.   [5] To Forster, 10 Jan. 81.   [6] Ibid.

having duties attached to it, but no absolute rights. The land-owner or occupier was thus the executor of 'a kind of sacred trust',[1] and of course it was, and is, the case that there is no absolute ownership of property in the United Kingdom save by the Crown. However, in his acceptance in the 1840s and 1850s of much of the intellectual framework of liberal political economy as the most suitable available mechanism for the proper organization of a modern society, Gladstone had placed himself, particularly in his view of the fiscal state, in the camp of political economists for whom fiscal, and consequently social, relationships were essentially a-temporal, predicated on general, universal rules and not on inductive enquiry into particular historical traditions.

It would, however, be wrong to see Gladstone as in every respect a supporter of that view. His sense of the fiscal state did have that a-temporal dimension; but his understanding of community and particularly of religious communities and national churches as being particularist, local examples, each with subtle variations, of the 'institution called in the Creed the Holy Catholic Church',[2] also gave him a historical and localist perspective. As this religious analysis was the starting point for Gladstone's analysis of any society, there was therefore an inherent historical dimension to his approach which cut across his political–economic universalism.

In the Irish case, Gladstone had doubly incorporated this historical dimension: disestablishment in 1869, and his proposal in 1869 that the Land Bill be built on a generalization of Ulster tenant right, a proposal limited by the Cabinet to tenant-right in Ulster, compensation for disturbance for the rest. The tenant-right solution had several attractions, not least that as it could be presented as thoroughly Irish it could not obviously be used as a precedent for England[3] nor, probably, for Scotland (though the historicist argument would have more force there). Compensation for disturbance could, however, be so used, and so could several aspects of the 'Three F.s'.

Gladstone's initial view of Irish land in 1880–1 was to keep reform as much as possible within the precepts of the free market. Thus, if there had, for political reasons, to be fixity of tenure, could there not be a provision for 'a future return to free contract'?[4] Explaining the bill to Carlingford, his colleague in drafting the 1870 Act, Gladstone 'seemed very averse to interference with "freedom of contract"'.[5] As the coercion bills were forced through between January and March 1881, Gladstone sought to keep this in the forefront of the drafting of the Land Bill. The consequence was that the bill only equivocally granted the 'Three F.s' and, so as to incorporate this equivocation, was in its drafting tortuous, wordy and sometimes obscure. Gladstone's position was reflected in the distinction the bill made between 'present tenancies' and 'future tenancies' (those created after 1 January 1883), to which the Act would not apply. For

---

[1] Matthew, *Gladstone*, 26; letter to W. G. C. Gladstone, 6 June 1897; Magnus, 434.

[2] To Morley, 27 Oct. 80. This seems to me an important further dimension to the interesting approach in C. Dewey, 'Celtic agrarian legislation and the Celtic Revival: historicist implications of Gladstone's Irish and Scottish Land Acts 1870–1886', *Past and Present*, no. 64 (1974).

[3] Matthew, *Gladstone*, 194–6.

[4] To Forster, 10 Jan. 81, repeated to him, 5 Mar. 81.

[5] Carlingford's diary, 25 March 1881, Add MS 63689; 25 Mar. 81n.

'present tenants' the Act would apply for a period of fifteen years, renewable after review by the Court.[1]

In introducing the Bill on 7 April 1881, Gladstone's ambivalence between historicism and economic deductivism was clearly stated. On the one hand, 'the old law of the country, corresponding, I believe, with the general law of Europe, recognizes the tenant right, and therefore recognizes, if you choose to call it, joint proprietorship'. On the other hand, 'there is no country in the world which, when her social relations come to permit of it, will derive more benefit than Ireland from perfect freedom of contract in land. Unhappily she is not in a state to permit of it; but I will not abandon the hope that the period may arrive.'[2] Not surprisingly, therefore, given the discrepancy of the economic need for larger farms as against the bill's consolidation of the division of Irish land into smallholdings, Gladstone told the Commons 'I decline to enter into the economical part of the subject'.[3]

The immediate context of the bill was the Land League Campaign, and the nature of the bill was squarely in line with the Gladstonian tradition of a big bill and a long passage in the Commons to enable its public, political effect to be established and dramatized. Thus: 'Again worked hard on Irish Land: and introduced the big Bill (for such it is in purpose more than bulk) 5¼–8.'[4] The Bill was intended to castrate the Land League by attracting the Irish tenants into Courts and a Land Commission appointed by the Westminster Parliament, local agencies of the State to which the Irish tenantry would voluntarily apply and which would reduce their rents. Thus the Irish tenantry would voluntarily associate itself with a mechanism provided by Westminster for the creation of social order in the Irish countryside. The metropolitan parliament would thus be seen to be offering a boon which the Land League could not match. Thus the Land Bill (and not Forster's Coercion Bills) 'seems to constitute nearly the whole of our substantial resources for confronting & breaking the Land League'.[5] Hence for Gladstone it was the provision of the Court which was 'the salient point and the cardinal principle of the Bill'—a legal authority, voluntarily used, reaching into the far recesses of the confusions of Irish social relationships, an orderly presence creating stability and reconciliation in exactly those places which state coercion could never reach. This was a 'right and needful measure', but it

---

[1] Leaseholders and tenants in arrears were excluded from the Act, though there was provision for arrears to be wiped out by a loan from the Land Commission financed by money from the Church Temporalities Commissioners. For the Act and a detailed commentary, see R. R. Cherry, *The Irish Land Law and Land Purchase Acts 1860 to 1901* (3rd ed. 1903). On the making of the Act and its political consequences, see A. Warren, 'Forster, the Liberals and new directions in Irish policy 1880–1882', *Parliamentary History*, vi (1987) and, for the general context of Gladstone's views on Irish land, his 'Gladstone, land and social reconstruction in Ireland 1881–87', *Parliamentary History*, ii (1983) which forcefully demonstrates Gladstone's insistence that land purchase must be linked to Irish local government of some sort and also shows the significant relationship of the events and decisions of 1882 to those of 1885-6.

[2] *H* 260. 902.   [3] *H* 260. 918.   [4] 7 Apr. 81.

[5] To Lorne, 1 June 81. Given this objective, Gladstone could hardly have consulted Parnell, the leader of the Land League, on the drafting of the bill, as Hammond, 220, thought he should have done. Dillon's remark on 13 April 1881 was fair enough: 'I very much fear that this Act was drawn by a man who was set to study the whole history of our organisation and was told to draw an Act that would kill the Land League'; F. S. L. Lyons, *John Dillon* (1968), 49.

was one that admitted existing chaos, for it was a 'form of centralization, referring to public authority what ought to be transacted by a private individual';
Gladstone advised the Irish not to 'stereotype and stamp [it] with the seal of
perpetuity',[1] but he made no provision for its review.

Presenting the bill both as a 'definitive solution' and as containing an ultimate escape back to free contract, Gladstone was able to offer it, ultimately
unsuccessfully, to Argyll as the latter,[2] and to the Irish as the former. In this
sense, it has the ambivalence of all the great Gladstonian initiatives from the
1853 budget onwards. Because of it, Gladstone never admitted that the bill
granted 'the Three F.s', but he was certainly not going publicly to deny that it
did: 'the controversy as to whether or not the "three F's." are in this Bill is
one into which I have not entered', he told the Commons, continuing in a
passage of classic obscurity: 'the "three F's" I have always seen printed have
been three capital F's; but the "three F's" in this Bill, if they are there at all,
are three little f's.'[3]

The long battle over the bill in Committee through the summer of 1881 was
a formidable physical effort for Gladstone, and he found it absorbing to the
point of difficulty: 'Spoke on Transvaal & voted in 314:205. But I am too full of
Ireland to be *free* in anything else.'[4] But the prolonged debate had political
advantages. It worked the Liberal majority towards a positive end approved of
by much of the party, and it split the Land League. As Gladstone intended, the
introduction of the bill recaptured the initiative from the League, already puta-
tively split over the abstention *versus* constitutionalist debate about the proper
reaction to the suspension of Irish members following their obstruction of the
Protection Bill.[5] The League was confronted with an Irish agricultural community eager to take advantage of the new Court and Commission and it thus
faced a dilemma. To obstruct the Bill in the Commons and the Act in the
countryside was to do down its own supporters; to make the bill better by
amendment and to encourage the use of the Court and the Commission was to
prove the Government's point that Westminster legislation could still give
Ireland valued boons.

Gladstone determinedly drove home his advantage against the League. On
29 April his casting vote in Cabinet (having already voted once in the tie)[6]
imprisoned Dillon despite his ill health, one of the most intransigent opponents
of the Bill. In October, prompted by Forster, he goaded Parnell into attacking
him. Gladstone believed Parnell to be weak, vulnerable, and dangerous. Parnell
was 'by his *acts* (not motives) ... an enemy of the Empire'.[7] Gladstone drew a
distinction between the twelve or so M.P.s who with Parnell adhered to the
League, and whom he regarded as intent on wrecking the Act, and the wider
movement of the League in the localities, largely intent on using it. It was for
the latter that the attraction of the voluntary use of the Court was provided by

[1] *H* 260. 908.   [2] To Argyll, 9 Mar. 81.
[3] *H* 263. 1419; 20 July 81. See also to Argyll, 28 Apr. 81. The concept of a 'fair rent' which the bill
attempted to define proved legislatively, if not practically, extremely perplexing, and was unresolved
well after the bill was already in Committee; see 28 May 81 and to Forster, 6 June 81.
[4] 25 July 81.   [5] See Lyons, *Dillon*, 44ff.
[6] 29 Apr. 81.   [7] To Forster, 21 Sept. 81.

the Westminster Parliament. He thus had to maintain an awkward balance between defusing the passion of the Land League's rank and file through the release of some suspects, while at the same time preparing to break up its leadership by incarceration. Gladstone attached a quite misguided importance to a speech by Dillon (released from gaol in August 1881) which seemed to advocate a free run for the Land Act, and he contrasted it with 'the almost frantic denunciations of Parnell (not to mention Miss Anna [Parnell's sister]) the violence of which I take to be the measure of his apprehensions lest the Land Act should take the bread out of his mouth, as a speculator on public confusion, by tranquillising the mind of the Irish people'.[1]

Liberal success in the Tyrone by-election—'a great event as a defeat of Toryism in a strong hold but far greater as a defeat of Parnell'—encouraged the tactic of splitting the League further by releasing suspects such as Father Sheehy, the Land League priest.[2] Dublin Castle counselled waiting until after the Land League conference of 16 September.[3] Forster was at Hawarden that day, and a programme for the release of suspects seems to have been agreed upon.[4] Gladstone determined at the same time on preventing 'Parnell & Co', whom he thought had a monopoly of speaking in Ireland, from making further headway. He was especially angered by Parnell's proposal to arrange test cases for the Land Act, and in interpreting this as a hostile approach he was influenced by Forster, and probably also by Cowper, the Irish Viceroy, who was also visiting Hawarden: 'It is quite clear as you said that P. means to present cases which the commission must refuse, and then to treat their refusal as showing that they cannot be trusted, & that the Bill has failed.'[5] Of course, if that were the outcome, the whole spring and summer of 1881 would have been squandered.

In his speech at the great meeting at Leeds in October 1881, Gladstone repeated the contrast already drawn privately between Dillon (by now 'an opponent whom I am glad to honour') and the malicious Parnell in what has been called 'a classic instance of English incomprehension of Irish realities'.[6] Gladstone provoked Parnell with the famous phrase, 'the resources of civilization against its enemies are not yet exhausted'. He noted in the diary: 'Voice lasted well. It was a great relief when the anxious effort about Ireland had been made.'[7] Parnell gave no ground, and was incarcerated in Kilmainham Gaol in the first of a series of arrests ratified by the Cabinet, on Forster's recommendation, on 12 October:

[1] To Portarlington, 2 Sept. 81.
[2] To Cowper, 9 Sept. 81, to Forster, 8 Sept. 81.
[3] See to Cowper, 5 Sept. 81n.
[4] 16 Sept. 81 and to Forster, 21 Sept. 81.
[5] To Forster, 21 Sept. 81. Gladstone later said that 'the Land Act . . . created the crisis [in October 1881] by compelling the promoters of the Land League to take choice between a good course and a bad one. It compelled them either to advance or recede, and they chose to advance; but by that advance they created for us a completely new state of circumstances. That new state of circumstances led to the arrests . . .'; he then explained that the demand for lower rent was 'an important factor' and that the series of test cases was 'an important fact in the history of the whole transaction', but that the arrests under the P.P.P. Act were for reasonable suspicion of some crime punishable by law; 'we did not believe, up to that time, that we could allege any case to Parliament that we had this suspicion of such persons individually. We then had belief, and upon that belief we have acted'; *H* 266. 874, 16 February 1882.
[6] Lyons, *Dillon*, 56.   [7] 7 Oct. 81.

'arrests to be made also in the provinces progressively for speeches pointing to ⟨an Irish Republic⟩ treason or treasonable practice . . . Land League meetings to be prohibited when dangerous to the public peace or tending to intimidation'.[1] On 20 October, after declaring an ineffective 'No Rent' strike in response to Parnell's arrest, the Land League was proscribed.

Gladstone may have misunderstood Irish realities. Parnell may not have been trying to bring down the Land Act, Dillon was certainly not trying to give it a fair chance. But Gladstone was right in his central perception. The Land Act had had the intended effect. He had the Land League on the run. Usually cautious about coercion, and particularly indiscriminate coercion, Gladstone was as ruthless a wielder of power as any contemporary when he saw a necessity or a benefit, as Parnell found in 1881, and Arabi in Egypt in a more violent form in 1882. The benefit was the working of the Land Act and the weakening of the League, and in this Gladstone was successful: as Parnell wrote to Mrs. O'Shea on the day of his arrest, 'the movement is breaking fast'.[2] By December 1881 'the difficulty is now that we cannot open [Land] Courts enough for them'[3] and the Land League was broken. Whether the arrest of Parnell was necessary for this is not-proven. The arrest or flight abroad of the other members of the League's high-command probably did prevent its capitalizing further on the continuing agrarian crisis and thus preserving its formal structure; it would have been odd to exempt Parnell from a programme of mass-arrests (and, incidentally, disastrous to Parnell's own standing in Ireland). Parnell's imprisonment was advantageous to him,[4] and his arrest encouraged the constitutionalist 'new departure' of 1882.

The Land Act and its *démarche* was a high-risk strategy which had considerable political success in the medium-term.[5] But it opened a number of awkward questions. The Act was explicitly a Liberal assessment of Irish needs, a further 'boon' bestowed. For all Gladstone's qualifications and expressions of hope for a return to free contract, it went a considerable distance towards social immobility, while simultaneously declining to give the Irish M.P.s who tried to amend it what they wanted, that is, at the least, an explicit recognition of the 'Three F.s'.[6] It left the Irish landowning class with a diminished role, and diminished expectations. Gladstone frequently complained of the failure of the landlords to act effectively against the League. He no longer looked to them as a reliable support for the government; the Land Act presaged their economic eclipse while retaining their nominal presence. To whom, then, was the government to turn in Ireland? Would it be possible to build a stable political society in collaboration with a political movement whose objective was Home Rule, without

---

[1] 12 Oct. 81.

[2] O'Shea, *Parnell*, i. 207.

[3] To H. N. Gladstone, 2 Dec. 81.

[4] See Lyons, *Dillon*, 55–6.

[5] Historians of Ireland are unwontedly harmonious in their agreement that the Land Act combined with arrests successfully undercut the Land League; see Clark, op. cit., 334ff., Bew, chs. 8 and 9, O'Brien, *Parnell*, 65ff., J. S. Donnelly, *The land and the people of nineteenth-century Cork* (1975), 288ff.

[6] See e.g. Healy: 'The Prime Minister said that the measure did not give all three "F"s", and that was certainly true. The tenants of Ireland could not exercize free sale . . .'; *H* 261. 1469; 27 May 1881.

admitting the validity of that objective? This was, of course, an even more awkward question for the Conservatives, as in 1881-2 they began to advocate land
purchase (i.e. buying out the landlord class) as the next necessary step in Ireland.

In the winter of 1881-2, Gladstone began to consider these questions. The
ability of the landlords to act effectively as a separate class was gone but he
hoped that they would reassert their influence through an alliance with the
tenantry, 'call meetings of their tenants, propose to them united action on
behalf of law & personal freedom'. If some such union of property was not
developed, then the options offered by the existing constitution were
exhausted:

> If Ireland is still divided between Orangemen & law-haters, then our task is hopeless:
> but our belief & contention always is that a more intelligent & less impassioned body
> has gradually come to exist in Ireland. It is on this body, its precepts & examples, that
> our hopes depend, for if we are at war with a nation we cannot win.[1]

Such a body would have to be able to express itself not merely by its orderly
presence at the local level, but institutionally. What form that institutional
representation should take was a central preoccupation of British politics until
the mass of Ireland was lost in 1921. In the autumn of 1881, Gladstone toyed
with the Home Rule solution, telling Granville: 'I am rather advanced as to
Home or local rule, not wishing to stipulate excepting for the supremacy of
Parliament, and for not excluding Scotland in principle from anything offered or
done for Ireland',[2] and he continued to think along these lines through the
winter.

When P. J. Smyth moved a home rule amendment to the Queen's Speech in
February 1882, Gladstone's reply concentrated, after a statement on the need
to maintain ultimate Imperial authority, on the difficulty of defining the distinction between Imperial and Irish affairs. He told those who wished for change
that 'they cannot take the first, the most preliminary step, until they have
produced a plan and set forth the machinery by which they mean to decide
between Imperial and local questions'.[3] As we shall see, this call for the Irish to
offer a plan took on considerable importance for Gladstone in 1885. The day
after his speech on Smyth's amendment, Gladstone noted a talk with his son
Herbert: 'Conversation with H.J.G. on "Home Rule" & my speech: for the subject has probably a future.'[4] But Gladstone in the winter of 1881-2 was also
planning retirement. An Irish local government bill was thus a more practicable
objective, which, 1881 having been largely devoted to Irish affairs, would follow
the English and Scottish local government bills intended for 1882. Irish local
government might be risky, but it was an important means of consolidating the
success of the Land Act:

> [If] your [Forster's] excellent plans for obtaining local aid towards the execution of the
> law break down, it will be on account of this miserable & almost total want of the sense

[1] To Forster, 13 Oct. 81.
[2] To Granville, 13 September 1881, in Ramm II, i. 291.
[3] H 276. 260; 9 Feb. 82. See also to Roundell, 26 Oct. 83.
[4] 10 Feb. 82.

of responsibility for the public good & public peace in Ireland; & this responsibility we cannot create except through local self government.

If we say we must postpone the question till the state of the country is more fit for it, I should answer that the least danger is in going forward at once. It is liberty alone, which fits men for liberty. This proposition like every other in politics has its bounds; but it is far safer than the counter-doctrine, wait till they are fit.

In truth I should say (differing perhaps from many) that, for the Ireland of today, the first question is the rectification of the relations betwen landlord & tenant, which happily is going on; the next is to relieve Great Britain from the enormous weight of the Government of Ireland unaided by the people, & from the hopeless contradiction in which we stand while we give a Parliamentary representation hardly effective for anything but mischief, without the local institutions of self-government which it presupposes, & on which alone it can have a sound & healthy basis.[1]

This classic statement of the primacy of politics and political institutions melded with several very different preoccupations: the Conservative plan for a land purchase bill, supported by Irish M.P.s generally, including Home Rulers; the apparent acceptance of the Land Act by those Home Rule M.P.s not in gaol, in the form of a bill to amend it; the renewal, partial renewal or nonrenewal, of coercion in Ireland as the bills of 1881 determined, and the replacement of Cowper, the Viceroy, probably by Spencer, a move 'long delayed'.[2] W. H. Smith's land purchase plans (combined with a call for the release of Parnell) were known to Gladstone from an early stage because they were, most unusually, prepared with the help of the Treasury.[3] In response, Lord Frederick Cavendish and Childers prepared a liberal scheme.[4] Gladstone was not enthusiastic about land purchase, but he met it not by a negative but by raising questions about the difficulty of its integration into the political process, and the need for its proponents to accompany it with Irish local government, which, as we have seen, he already favoured on other grounds. It was to a Provincial Councils Bill, which would provide the local framework which Gladstone believed essential to land purchase, that he gave attention, drafting a Bill in early April 1882.[5] Certainly, it was already common ground for all parties in early 1882 that the Land Act did not represent a 'definitive settlement'. The development of its limited land purchase clauses, or of its arrears clause, or both, was widely canvassed. When Gladstone introduced the Arrears Bill in May 1882, he was able to offer it as a limited, rather restricted measure compared with other land reforms in the air.

The events of 1881 thus led, on several simultaneous fronts, to the developments of 1882. With the breaking of the Land League, the use of the Protection of Person and Property Act became less necessary, and Herbert Gladstone's view that outrages were now 'committed to prove the government wrong in coercing' received a sympathetic hearing from his father, who favoured replacing direct coercion with a supplementing of the ordinary law.[6] Forster's

[1] To Forster, 12 Apr. 82.
[2] See Warren, loc. cit., 112–16 and to Spencer, 3 Apr. 82.
[3] To Welby, 17, 27 Mar. 82.   [4] To Cavendish, 12 Apr. 82.
[5] 3 Apr. 82 and Hammond, 259.
[6] Herbert Gladstone's diary, 23 March, 6 April 1882, ed. A. B. Cooke and J. Vincent, *Irish Historical Studies*, xviii. 75, 77 (1973).

advocacy of further coercion through a renewal of the full-blooded P.P.P. Act for a year came as a shock.[1] It seemed to suggest that all the travails of 1881 had been to no effect. Gladstone reminded Forster of his plan in 1880 for an alternative to the P.P.P. Bill, namely, proscription of named societies in the United Kingdom as a whole, thus avoiding particularist legislation for Ireland and indiscriminate coercion there.[2] He admitted that the P.P.P. Act 'has served a most important purpose during a great crisis, which without it we should not have had the means of adequately meeting'.[3] But that great crisis was now over. Gladstone's approach was to build on what he saw to be the constitutionalism inherent in the Healy/Redmond bill to bring tenants in arrears and some leaseholders within the scope of the 1881 Act.

It was in this context that the various discussions at second-hand with Parnell (already let out on parole for his nephew's funeral by Forster and Cowper) began in late April 1882,[4] some conducted by Herbert Gladstone with F. H. O'Donnell, but mostly, and more famously, by Chamberlain with Captain O'Shea with Cabinet knowledge and approval. The decision for the release of Parnell, Dillon, and O'Kelly was finally made on 2 May 1882, that for Davitt on 4 May.

Gladstone was very careful to keep his hands clean. Commenting on Chamberlain's report to the Cabinet on 1 May 1882, he noted, *inter alia*, his own position:

> W.E.G. Not for arrangement or for compromise or for referring to the present assurances. There has been *no* negotiation. But we have obtained information. The moment is golden.[5]

The 'information' was that Parnell and his immediate colleagues intended to promote law and order *via* the land legislation: 'Arrest was for intentions wh. placed us in the midst of a social revolution. We believe the intentions now are to promote law & order. . . . *Had Parnell (the No Rent Party) declared in October what they declare now, we could not have arrested him*.'[6]

This was quite true. The release of Parnell and the other 'suspects' (under the P.P.P. Act they had not had to be indicted) reflected strength rather than weakness on the part of the Government. Parnell's position, as understood through O'Shea, represented an admission that the quasi-revolutionary phase of Irish politics had passed.[7] The League in disarray, local government in the offing, the support of Parnellite M.P.s for the Land Act acknowledged through an Arrears Bill in preparation which would greatly increase the number of tenants who could be incorporated in the Act: Gladstone saw in this 'golden moment' a chance worth taking: 'the future, not the past'.[8] Spencer had already replaced Cowper as Viceroy,[9] Cowper having proved both negative and rather feeble,

---

[1] Bew, 201ff.

[2] See Carlingford's diary of his Dublin visit, quoted in to Forster, 5 Apr. 82n.

[3] 30 Apr. 82.   [4] To O'Shea and to Forster, 15 Apr. 82.

[5] 1 May 82.   [6] Gladstone's italics; 4 May 82.

[7] O'Brien, *Parnell*, 76–9.

[8] 4 May 82.

[9] At least in principle; Cowper was still technically Viceroy, and thus had to sign the papers for Parnell's release; see to Cowper, 2 May 82.

and the resignation of Forster as Irish Secretary allowed a second fresh appointment: Lord Frederick Cavendish, the brother of Hartington (and a member of one of the largest of the Irish landowning families), a man closely associated with the movement within the Liberal Party for land purchase. Had Cavendish lived, it is hard to believe that a development of the 1881 land purchase clauses would not have been an important part of the legislative programme for 1883 or that the land purchase plan of 1884—the nearest the government got to a serious proposal—would not have been more thoroughly prepared and supported by a stronger political will.[1]

The murder of Cavendish and Burke in Phoenix Park on 6 May 1882 was the Cabinet's Majuba in Irish policy: a disaster, but one essentially irrelevant to the flow of policy. Gladstone, however personally shaken, was not politically deflected, and the Arrears Bill was introduced on 15 May, outstripping in significance the Crimes Bill into which the coercion measures, already in preparation though not yet agreed, necessarily developed. He was both confident and unrepentant about his position with respect to the discussions with Parnell, and refused ever to admit that there had been a 'Kilmainham Treaty'. It was only with difficulty that the Cabinet dissuaded him from deciding to second Northcote's motion for a select committee of inquiry into the Kilmainham negotiations, and from offering to appear before such a Committee.[2] That the Arrears Bill followed almost exactly what Carlingford noted as the Irish 'condition' (in the sense of requirement),[3] Gladstone of course did not allude to.[4]

There was some elision of view in all this. If Parnell now represented the encouragement of legality and constitutionalism, then there was no more objection to an arrangement with him than to any other political pact. If he did not represent these forces, then he might be released in due course through an absence of any reason to restrain him, but not on the ground of positive advantage. Of course, nothing was so clear cut. The simple juxtaposition of moral force and physical force in Ireland was always a gross oversimplification.[5] What is curious and important about Gladstone's attitude to Parnell at this time was

---

[1] See to Spencer, 13 May 84; cabinet of 17 May 84; this was far too late for a determined effort in 1884, especially as the Prime Minister and Viceroy were on different sides in an important Cabinet vote (see 17 May 84n.).

[2] 22, 23 May 82.

[3] 25 Apr. 82n.

[4] If he had, his explanation would doubtless have been that the making of the Arrears Bill, which gave a gift to tenants-in-arrears from the Consolidated Fund Commissioners *via* the Church Temporalities Commissioners, was a good deal more complex than a simple recognition of Parnellite expectations or 'conditions'; for Gladstone's statement on the Healy/Redmond Bill, and the content of the Arrears Bill, significantly narrowed the area of further land reform by cutting out land purchase which, according to Carlingford, was in the early stages of cabinet discussion of Healy's bill very much in play: 'the idea of a Bill was dropped, *except as to Arrears & Purchase*' (22 April 1882, Add MS 63690). On 5 April Hamilton had noted: coercion of some sort, plus measures 'to extend the purchase clauses of the Land Act and to deal with arrears (both of which questions must be taken in hand) will absorb all the remaining legislative time of the session'; Bahlman, *Hamilton*, i. 250. There were certainly many more forces in play in April/May 1882 than Parnell. In this sense the Arrears Bill, meeting the most immediate but also the most short-term of Parnell's conditions, was an opportunity for Gladstone to set aside an embryonic Tory–Whig–Irish collaboration on land purchase.

[5] See, e.g. Bew, 121–6 on the sophisticated ambivalence of the 'rent at the point of the bayonet' tactic.

the Prime Minister's transformation of the rather isolated leader with his little band of twelve or so M.P.s—Gladstone's view of him in the autumn of 1881—into the central figure in the calculations about the future of Irish politics. If the Land League was broken, why bother about Parnell, who was hardly in any position to make 'conditions'? No comment by Gladstone on this in early 1882 seems to have survived. The answer is probably to be found at least in part in the absence of alternatives. There was something of an attempt in March 1882 to revive William Shaw, the previous Irish leader who had seceded from the Home Rule group in January 1881, as a significant political figure, but Shaw came to nothing.[1] Further, the prospects for a Liberal revival in Ireland were quite unrealistic. If Irish politics were to remain incorporated within British politics, the Parnellite position was unavoidable. That position, of course, sought to use British politics to achieve 'Home Rule'. Given the Liberals' decline in Ireland, seeing Parnell as the focal point of Irish political development was only undesirable to the extent that Home Rule was undesirable. Such was the implication of Gladstone's position in the summer of 1882, and also, it might be thought, of Joseph Chamberlain's, the chief negotiator with Parnell *via* O'Shea and also the chief proponent in the Cabinet of the franchise reform which would turn Parnell's influence in Ireland into seats at Westminster.

In 1883 Gladstone agreed, at the request of Hartington, to delay his retirement so as to see through the franchise and redistribution bills, a process uncompleted by the fall of the government in 1885. The intention was that the Franchise Bill would be immediately followed by 'a heap of Local Government',[2] and thus both the representative and the constitutional structures of the United Kingdom would have received legislative completion. Gladstone, however, expected to play no part in the second part of this process: 'I am glad the time has not come when new points of departure in Irish legislation have to be considered, and that good old Time ... will probably plant me before that day comes outside "the range of practical politics".'[3] In the winter of 1883–4 imperial policy and parliamentary reform thus formed his horizon of personal commitment.

Parliamentary reform was likely considerably to increase Irish difficulties. As we have seen, household franchise in Ireland might be construed as more 'conservative' than a lesser extension, but the likelihood was never strong that the Irish National League which succeeded the Land League could be stranded as a tenant movement with a limited electoral base. Gladtone might assure Hartington in December 1883 that 'according to all the authorities you greatly overestimate the effect of an altered franchise in augmenting the power of Parnellism',[4] but he told the Queen in 1884 that the Liberals would lose about twenty-five seats in Ireland, with the Home Rulers returning nearly eighty M.P.s.[5] The essential Cabinet decision had been whether to allow the situation in Ireland to frustrate franchise reform generally. The decision had been, to take the consequences.

---

[1] To Forster, 24 Mar. 82.
[2] To Rosebery, 15 Nov. 83.
[3] To Harcourt, 29 Dec. 83.
[4] To Hartington, 29 Dec. 83.
[5] 19 Aug. 84.

Those consequences were considerable, but they became fully apparent only in a context of increasing and unanticipated complexity. The absence of Liberal agreement about the form of local government applied *a fortiori* in Ireland, where the question was compounded by complications of order and imperial power. In early 1885 all the factors were still in play: land reform (in the form of land purchase, already an abortive government proposal in 1884), local government, and coercion (the Crimes Act of 1882 expired in September 1885). Over this hung the question of the accommodation of the Irish representatives after the elections to be held once the reform bills were all passed. As dispute within the Cabinet rose to a point of irreconcilability far greater than any reached hitherto on Ireland and as the Sudan and Afghan questions reached at least partial solution, Gladstone made a further effort at retiring in the spring of 1885.

The new element in early 1885 was the Chamberlain–Dilke attempt at an Irish settlement based on a 'Central Board' solution (i.e. elected County Councils sending representatives to a central board which would have control of various Irish government departments). Not surprisingly, Dublin Castle, accustomed to an almost Indian-style autocracy, had reservations about the viability of such an arrangement which, if seen as a settlement of the constitutional future of Ireland, still left the role of the Irish M.P.s uncertain. Parnell promoted the idea *via* O'Shea to Chamberlain because it would give Ireland greater domestic control without harming the case for an Irish legislature; Chamberlain saw it as a solution which would remove the case for such a legislature. Misunderstandings led to ructions between Chamberlain and Parnell.[1] The Radicals built up the case for a central board in the Cabinet until on 9 May 1885 it was narrowly rejected.

Gladstone's position with respect to the proposal and to the negotiations was oblique: he was associated with the central board scheme, but not fully committed to it. Partly this was because the Gordon crisis in the Sudan, the solution of the Afghan frontier crisis, and the complexities of the Redistribution Bill, coincided with the Chamberlain–Dilke initiative: 'The pressure of affairs, especially Soudan, Egypt, & Afghan, is now from day to day extreme.'[2] There was no agreed plan of legislation beyond the Franchise Bill and, since December 1884, the Redistribution Bill: the Queen's Speech which began the Session lasting through the summer of 1885 was that of August 1884, mentioning only the Franchise Bill.[3] This absence of even a nominal framework of legislation beyond a Franchise Bill reflected the extent to which imperial affairs and the reform crisis dominated politics. It also perhaps reflected Gladstone's intention not to be shackled to some further round of legislation which would again prevent his retirement. As it became clear that the special autumn Session of 1884 was in fact likely to last through to the summer of 1885, so the need for legislation other than redistribution, registration, etc. became clear. There was an understanding that local government would be prominent, but there was no attempt to draw up a programme.

[1] See Garvin, i. 581ff.   [2] 16 Mar. 85.
[3] This was because the autumn session was intended—at least in theory—to be short, with the Franchise Bill being passed in both houses.

It was in this rather vacuous context that Chamberlain and Dilke made their moves. Without Gladstone's close involvement, there was never much likelihood of the Radical plan succeeding. The Chamberlain–Dilke base in Cabinet was too narrow to take on Spencer, Campbell-Bannerman (by now Irish Secretary), and Dublin Castle on such a central question of Irish politics. An Irish local government measure would have to come publicly either from the Prime Minister or from the Irish ministers. Gladstone gave the central board plan a general support, but there was none of the curiosity about detail, the craftiness of Cabinet presentation, the gradual build-up of correspondence and the careful integration of potential Cabinet opponents, which were the hallmarks of a serious Gladstonian initiative.

The absence of interest in detail is reflected in the diary and in the cabinet minutes. Several of the meetings with Chamberlain and Dilke are not recorded by Gladstone. It is curious that one noted by Chamberlain as having taken place on 18 January—his initial report of his meeting with O'Shea and Gladstone's encouragement to continue the communications—could not have taken place that day, Gladstone then being at Hawarden. When Cardinal Manning intervened to support the central board plan, Gladstone left contact with him entirely to Chamberlain; Gladstone's poor personal relations with Manning in the aftermath of the *Vatican Decrees* no doubt largely accounts for this, but if he had been fully committed to seeing the central board solution as a successful bill, he would have found a way round.[2] Gladstone's behaviour over the central board affair testifies to the genuineness of the attempt at retirement which was then his objective.

When the central board plan was narrowly defeated in Cabinet, Gladstone declared it 'dead as mutton for the present, though as I believe for the present only. It will quickly rise again & as I think perhaps in larger dimensions.'[3] Gladstone had, humiliatingly, to announce that despite expectations, no measure of local government for Ireland could be proposed that Session.[4] Privately, he mixed warnings about the future of Ireland with statements about his own imminent retirement. His self-presentation as only an '*amicus curiae*' in Cabinet—his work on redistribution nearly completed, and the Sudan and Afghan frontier no longer points of immediate conflict—contributed to the Cabinet's malaise.

On 8 June 1885, Gladstone began the Cabinet by announcing that defeat on the Budget that evening was a possibility.[5] The Cabinet that day continued to be deadlocked on the renewal of coercion. That evening the government was defeated on Hicks Beach's amendment to the Budget. Much was made then and since of the Tory-Irish alliance which contributed to the defeat of the government. But the government could only lose its overall majority through abstention or absence on its own side. Despite a speech on the amendment by Gladstone, seventy Liberals were unpaired and absent from the lobby. It is hard

[1] Chamberlain, *Political memoir*, 141.
[2] For the central board episode, see C. H. D. Howard, 'Joseph Chamberlain, Parnell and the Irish "central board" scheme, 1884-5', *I.H.S.*, viii. 324 (1953).
[3] To Spencer, 9 May 85.
[4] 15 May 85.   [5] Rosebery's diary, quoted at 8 June 85n.

to avoid the conclusion that Grosvenor, the chief whip, had given up. Gladstone noted that there was no Tory–Irish harmony on the immediate issue of
indirect/direct taxation, the Liberals being a buffer between the Irish 'opposed
to indirect taxation generally' and the Tories 'even more friendly to it than we
are'.[1] Next day ministers agreed to offer their resignations;[2] and, after declining
a peerage,[3] Gladstone on 24 June 1885 kissed hands to mark the end of his
second premiership.

The end of the government thus left Gladstone curiously uncommitted as to
the future of Ireland. He was associated with the central board plan, a 'posthumous bequest' he told the Queen's secretary,[4] but not as its protagonist. He
had announced, separately, both a modest renewal of the Crimes Act and a land
purchase bill,[5] but viewed neither with enthusiasm. The end of the government
also imposed upon Gladstone the release so often claimed. But even before the
government was defeated, the usual forces for retention were operating. Gladstone had openly talked of retirement in May 1885[6] and discussed it with his
son at Hawarden.[7] Predictably, Wolverton appeared, as he had at most
moments of importance since his days as chief whip in Gladstone's first government. His previous interventions had all been against retirement, and it therefore seems likely that, when Gladstone and Wolverton 'opened rather a new
view as to my retirement',[8] it involved some arrangement for further delay.
Wolverton remained on the scene during the aftermath of the Cabinet's resignation and on 16 June Gladstone circularized his ex-Cabinet colleagues with a
minute stating that he would take his seat 'in the usual manner on the front
Opposition Bench' but because of his loss of voice would take 'the first proper
opportunity ... of absenting myself from actual attendance ... a bodily not a
moral absence'. He did not 'perceive, or confidently anticipate, any state of
facts' to prevent his withdrawal from active participation at the end of the Parliament.[9] Elsewhere, though not in this minute, the usual qualifications about
future usefulness and need were made.[10]

Within thirteen months, Gladstone had fought two elections, had proposed a
gigantic settlement of the Irish question which dominated Liberal politics for
the rest of their significant existence, and had split his party. We now, therefore,
turn our attention to that 'mighty heave in the body politic', 'the idea of constituting a Legislature for Ireland'.[11] *History of an Idea* was the title of the first
half of the apologia on Home Rule which Gladstone wrote in 1886 after his
electoral defeat.[12] The phraseology and the format of a public, historical explanation take us back to *A Chapter of Autobiography* (1868), Gladstone's other
public apologia. There are obvious parallels between his handling of Irish

[1] To Hartington, 10 June 85.   [2] 9 June 85.
[3] See to Sir T. Gladstone, 19 June 85.   [4] To Ponsonby, 29 May 85.
[5] 15, 20 May 85.   [6] See, e.g., to Chamberlain, 6 May 85, to Spencer, 9 May 85.
[7] 25 May 85.   [8] 30 May 85.   [9] 16 June 85.
[10] To Sir T. Gladstone, 19 June 85.   [11] To Rosebery, 13 Nov. 85.
[12] *The Irish Question. I.—History of an Idea. II.—Lessons of the Election* (1886); see 26 July 86.

disestablishment and Home Rule. But it is important to note that Gladstone denied that Home Rule involved a change of mind, even as it is sometimes phrased a 'conversion',[1] of the sort that undoubtedly did occur over disestablishment. In the case of the Irish Church, 'change of opinion' required public explanation; in the case of Home Rule, 'I have no such change to vindicate'.[2]

The diary bears this out, albeit in a negative way. In the 1840s, Gladstone went to great lengths to chronicle for himself and for posterity the process by which his view of the confessional state came to be seen as practically untenable. The reason for his careful records of the public and private crises of the 1840s is clear enough; the process of change, and Gladstone's need to understand it, was fundamental to his ecclesiastical and political identity. In the 1880s, the path to Home Rule receives only glancing mentions. This may irritate the historian, but it reflects two important aspects of the process by which the Home Rule policy evolved.

First, the evolution involved for Gladstone no inward struggle, no resolution of contending tensions. Second, he saw the policy as political in the narrow sense of the word, evolving not from an inference from some cosmic, *a priori* interpretation of the nature of man and his world, but from the experience of government and the consideration of alternatives. He had stated his view of the ideal state in *The State in its Relations with the Church*, and he had been forced from it by experience and by a painful public and private process to a liberal, pluralistic view of citizenship. But this was always a second order principle. The secular state and political life were matters of temporary arrangements not of eternal verities. Gladstone did not share that potent Imperial-State worship which for many Unionists in the late-Victorian period became a substitute for the Church-and-State Toryism of the past, and his underestimation of its strength was probably of considerable importance in 1886. He realized Home Rule was a 'mighty heave'; but he probably did not realize quite how mighty a heave it would in fact turn out to be.

The process of evolution of Home Rule for Gladstone was thus similar to the process of the gradual disclosure of his disestablishmentarianism in the years 1845–68, an assessment of opportunity and 'ripeness', but it lacked the public and private crises of the 1840s and also 'the ideal' from whose abandonment those crises sprang. Rather, it was a further development or consequence of the crises and reappraisals which had led to the 'conversion' to disestablishmentarianism and the abandonment of the notion of Ireland as part of a British confessional state. In 1839, Gladstone had been struck 'ineffaceably' by a remark in the House of Commons by Lord John Russell, then his political opponent. Gladstone recalled it to Russell during the Irish land debates in 1870 and he recalled it to the House of Commons during the Home Rule debate in 1886:[3] 'You said, "The true key to our Irish debates was this: that it was not properly borne in mind that as England is inhabited by Englishmen, and

---

[1] e.g. Jenkins, 248 and Loughlin, 34.
[2] *The Irish Question*, 3–4.
[3] *Speeches on the Irish question*, 63–4 (13 April 1886).

Scotland by Scotchmen, so Ireland is inhabited by Irishmen".[1] In the sense that the Government of Ireland Bill was Gladstone's ultimate comment on the implications of this simple nostrum, there was a clear relationship to his youthful political reorientation. But it was a relationship mediated through the attempt in the 1868–74 government to end the Protestant ascendancy by disestablishment, the land bill and the university bill. Whether that ascendancy could be ended without the process of ending it in itself promoting Home Rule or something like it, was an obvious question which faced Gladstone in the 1870s and early 1880s, and whose answer was never clearly stated.

The context of Gladstone's way of thinking was thus in 1885 very different from that of those who were by then his contemporaries and for whom his curious political odyssey since the 1830s, by which whiggish political positions were reached by non-whiggish paths, was part of a history of which they had perhaps read but had not shared. This in part explains Gladstone's isolation.

Home Rule also related closely to Gladstone's theoretical disestablishmentarianism in another way. Disestablishment, especially in Scotland, was a major cry in 1885, and had been for some time. Unlike several of the ingredients of the 'Radical Programme' of that year, it was in principle clearly acceptable to Gladstone and we know that privately he did not expect the Church of Scotland to remain established for long.[2] Though during his second government he dampened down Free Church enthusiasm on the grounds of the already clogged legislative timetable,[3] the position he took was of considerable importance for Home Rule for it set up a framework of proof: Disestablishment in Scotland on fair terms was not impossible: 'It is a Scotch question and ought to be decided by the people of Scotland, i.e. Parliament ought to accept their sense.'[4] The Scots would have to show that the proposal was 'the genuine offspring of Scottish sentiment and Scottish conviction'.[5] Thus, if Scotland spoke clearly and specifically, in terms not of an abstract resolution but of a viable legislative proposal, there could be no reason in principle to decline her case. Gladstone was not personally prepared to play any part in enabling Scottish opinion to express itself. He did not see himself as the progenitor of a bill. During the 1885 election campaign, in a speech intended, for tactical reasons of Liberal party unity, to play down the disestablishment question both in Scotland and England—a speech clearly delivered with considerable private embarrassment on Gladstone's part[6]—he told the Scots that, following his usual

[1] To Russell, 12 Apr. 70; see Matthew, *Gladstone*, 44.   [2] See above, ix. lv and 18 June 78.
[3] See to Rainy and G. C. Hutton, 29 Nov. 81, to McLaren, 22 Dec. 81; see also 29 Aug. 84 and to Rosebery, 16 Aug. 84.
[4] To G. C. Hutton, 28 July 85; the letter was released to the press, as Gladstone must have expected. See also to Rainy, 3 Nov. 85.
[5] *Political speeches (1885)*, 66.
[6] 11 Nov. 85. For this speech and the tactical context see A. Simon, 'Church disestablishment as a factor in the general election of 1885', *Historical Journal*, xviii. 791 (1975). The tactical difficulty was well stated to Rainy (3 Nov. 85): '... the one case is the inverse of the other. In Scotland Disestablishment is I believe pressed largely as a test by the Liberals. In England Establishment is keenly pressed as a test by the Tories: & the request is coolly made that no Liberal shall vote for a candidate favourable to disestablishment. This we entirely resist, but the resistance appears to be incompatible with a forward movement in Scotland.' See also to Chamberlain, 6 Nov. 85, to Rosebery, 7 Nov. 85.

practice, he would not vote for an abstract resolution on Scottish disestablishment: it would have to be seen 'in a long vista', that is, not in the next Parliament.[1] Even so, Gladstone had set the Scots a target on a question of organic
constitutional and national importance.

In the second half of 1885, therefore, Gladstone approached the differing
sorts of claims from Scotland and Ireland in a rather similar manner. The difference was that he knew that the Scots, whom he publicly instructed on the
means to success, would not speak with sufficient unanimity, whereas the great
majority of the Irish, to whom he refrained from giving quite such explicit
instruction, would. In both cases, the one public, the other largely private, there
was a willingness, unprecedented and rarely repeated, to make metropolitan
politics available to the claims of the numerically inferior constituent national-
ities of the United Kingdom. In this sense, the Scots had played an important
though clearly subordinate part through their disestablishment campaign since
the 1870s in setting up the context for Home Rule.

The idea of 'Home Rule' did not, of course, spring up fully formed in an
instant, nor was there a single moment of decision. Since it was for Gladstone
not a deductive construct resulting from a general constitutional hypothesis,
but rather the product of experience and the recognition of particular contingencies, its emergence was a complex process integrating long-, medium-, and
short-term influences. In attempting to understand Gladstone's mind in 1885
and 1886, a wide variety of factors must therefore be taken into consideration
which may for convenience be discussed as the general context of nineteenth-
century liberalism, the immediate context of the mid-1880s, the process of
1885-6, and the policy. As Gladstone saw the policy as inherently related to the
process, a consequence of evolution by 'stages', the reader will find that discussion of the process merges seamlessly into the discussion of the policy.

Liberalism in the nineteenth century had sought and seen the achievement
of the grouping of small, often princely, states into large units roughly defined
by nationality. Gladstone had, with reservations, favoured this development in
both Italy and Germany. But liberalism with its stress on representation and
minimum central government had also favoured decentralization within these
large units in the form of various types of local government to counteract the
centralization inherent in its imposition of national standards. The *Essai sur les
formes de gouvernement dans les sociétés modernes* (1872) by Gladstone's friend Emile
de Laveleye is a good statement of this sort of constitutional modernization.

In the British case, a development of the Whigs' Municipal Corporations Act
of 1835 into a general system of local government had been several times
attempted by the second Gladstone government without legislative success,
though ironically Ripon achieved by Resolution in India in 1882[2] what the
Liberal Cabinet failed to achieve for Britain by legislation. At the larger level of
imperial affairs British policy had, since the 1830s, been one of general devolution whenever possible, with the British North America Act of 1867, passed by

---

[1] *Political speeches (1885)*, 70. He consequently spoke but did not vote on Cameron's disestablishment and disendowment motion (or on Currie's amendment) in March 1886; see 30 March 86.
[2] See S. R. Mehrotra, *The emergence of the Indian National Congress* (1971), ch. 6.

a Conservative government but largely prepared by the Liberals with Gladstone handling the financial settlement, as the chief triumph. It is important to remember that, for a man of Gladstone's generation, this was the main drift of imperial development, not the creation of the autocratic structure of district officers on the Indian model which was the consequence of the tropical acquisitions of the 1870s and 1880s. This was the way to achieve both order and loyalty and consequently, from the metropolitan point of view, strategic safety. Advocacy of responsible and representative government in the settled colonies, with particular attention to the demarcation between Imperial and colonial responsibility, had been an important aspect of Gladstone's developing liberalism in the late 1840s and early 1850s.[1]

It is, therefore, not surprising that as Gladstone began to turn 'Home Rule' into a legislative proposal, he asked Grosvenor, the chief whip, to send him copies of 'the Canada Union & Government Act *1840* ⟨or *close* to that year⟩ and Canada Government (Dominion) Act 1867'.[2] Clause 2 of the Government of Ireland Bill empowered the Queen 'by and with the advice of the Irish Legislative Body, to make laws for the peace, order and good government of Ireland'; Gladstone noted next to these words in his early draft for the Cabinet 'The words proceeding are *mutatis mutandis* from "The British North America Act, 1867".'[3] Representative decentralization was thus a common policy for the United Kingdom and its overseas possessions and it is in this rather than in European precedents that the groundings of 'Home Rule' are to be found.

Ireland, with her peculiar combination of M.P.s at Westminster and Viceroy in Dublin Castle, fitted neither the colonial nor the simply localist model exactly. As Grattan's famous metaphor ran, quoted by Gladstone when introducing the Government of Ireland Bill:[4] Ireland 'hears the ocean protesting against separation, but she hears the sea protesting against union. She follows therefore her physical destination when she protests against the two situations, both equally unnatural, separation and union.'[5] Grattan used this metaphor to argue that the union of the Parliaments was unnecessary as Britain and Ireland were thus inherently related. Gladstone regarded the Act of Union of 1800 as a gigantic, though excusable, mistake,[6] the product of the war against France which he regarded as an even greater mistake, but he never seems to have seriously considered its repeal, partly because he saw no serious demand for it, and partly because the Irish parliament in its historic form had not existed for eighty-five years.

Self-evidently, any settlement of the Irish question short of Irish independence was bound to reflect the complications of Ireland's curious relationship to the rest of the United Kingdom. Even those who advocated the *status quo* advocated what was already a form of pluralist constitution created by the

[1] See above iii. xxxivff. and Knaplund, *Imperial policy*, ch. ii.
[2] To Grosvenor, 9 Oct. 85; i.e. before the dissolution was announced. It was a little unusual to ask Grosvenor for documents of this sort, and was probably also intended as a hint.
[3] Add MS 44632, f. 194; 31 March 1886.
[4] Gladstone quoted it in the form 'The Channel forbids union, the ocean forbids separation'; *Speeches on the Irish question 1886*, 50.
[5] S. Gwynn, *Henry Grattan and his times* (1939), 337.
[6] 19 Sept. 85.

process of historical change, a pluralism that existed despite, and parallel to, the 'absolute supremacy of Parliament' identified by A. V. Dicey in his *Law of the Constitution*, a book read and strongly approved by Gladstone as the decision to commit himself publicly to Home Rule evolved in November and December 1885.[1]

In those months, Gladstone reminded himself of Burke's historicist and prudential case for magnanimity and an empire whose cohesion came from decentralized power. This gave him a distinguished pedigree of conservative whiggery which he might have more acutely exploited against the dissentient Whigs in 1886. At the same time, Dicey's analysis had a strong appeal for Gladstone, whose instinct was always to think in terms of executive action and progress through statute; he never showed much interest in common law, the bar to Dicey's universal sovereign.

Gladstone strikingly quoted Dicey when introducing the Government of Ireland Bill:

> No work that I have ever read brings out in a more distinct and emphatic manner the peculiarity of the British Constitution in one point to which, perhaps, we seldom have occasion to refer, namely, the absolute supremacy of Parliament. We have a Parliament to the power of which there are no limits whatever, except such as human nature, in a Divinely-ordained condition of things, imposes. We are faced by no co-ordinate legislatures, and are bound by no statutory conditions. There is nothing that controls us, except our convictions of law, of right, and of justice.[2]

Here in fact lay the intellectual key to Gladstonian Home Rule: the creation of a new form of pluralism, recognizing historical forces and traditions, but contained within the a-temporal casket of Dicey's parliamentary absolutism: a combination of historicism and deductivism which would reflect the peculiarities of the British and Irish predicaments. Common-sense and self-interest would harmonize to create a natural balance. Gladstone criticized Dicey in 1886 for his absence of historical awareness[3] and, certainly, Dicey's argument in *England's case against Home Rule*[4] was deliberately abstract, a theoretical dissection of the inconsistencies of the Government of Ireland Bill. But as every British statesman knew, the constitution was already riddled with inconsistencies: the function of statesmanship was to make it work and adapt by observing custom, convention and compromise. Within this context of living by experience rather than by abstract principles, the Home Rulers argued, Home Rule could be accommodated. On the other hand, Gladstone relied on Dicey's systematic and deliberately non-historical formulation of the absolute supremacy of the Crown in Parliament for part of the intellectual force of his argument that Home Rule in no wise impaired, but rather strengthened, 'the supreme statutory authority of the Imperial Parliament'.[5] With Dicey on the

---

[1] Begun 2 Nov. 85, resumed 3 Dec., finished 29 Dec. 85. Gladstone had thus started to take Dicey on board—and the central theme of the book is immediately obvious to the reader—before the sketch of the Government of Ireland Bill made on 14 Nov. 85; his rereading of Burke followed on from this.

[2] *Speeches on the Irish question 1886*, 13-4.

[3] To Dicey, 12 Nov. 86. Gladstone criticized Dicey on this from the first; see to MacColl, 4 June 83.   [4] See 10 Nov. 86.

[5] *Speeches on the Irish question 1886*, 15.

reference shelf, the imperial veto was secure. Dicey was turned against himself. The Unionists' most famous apologist had shown the essential intellectual harmlessness of Home Rule,[1] because a Government of Ireland Act could always be repealed by the same process as created it, the Crown in Parliament. In practical terms, however, experience was the guide: 'The case of the Veto cannot be solved by any theory, but has been practically solved by a Colonial policy now nearly half a century old which combines the judicious use of it with the free action of responsible Government.[2]

A further dimension and one closely associated with Liberal enthusiasm for decentralization, was the corruption of the British liberal state which the constant presence of the Irish question in British politics involved: the normal processes of the 1880–5 Parliament had been perverted by the introduction of closure and guillotine (needed in turn to impose coercion and to give yet more power to a Viceroy responsible only to the executive); a Liberal Cabinet had found itself returning to the *ancien régime* in the use of secret service money for surveillance and the establishment of what became the Special Branch; the Prime Minister needed an armed bodyguard for the first time since the 1840s or earlier. Gladstone hated all of these, and saw them as examples of the gradual corrosion of a liberal society. He left the Cabinet room rather than attend a discussion of the use of secret service money, and he gave his police bodyguard the slip whenever possible, complaining of its imposition and its cost. The Fenian bombing campaign in Britain (especially London), at its height in 1883–5, corroded the liberalism of domestic legislation, with the Home Office's reluctance to allow local control of the Metropolitan police scuppering the London Local Government Bill.[3]

Gladstone was prepared, reluctantly, to meet violent disorder in Ireland with coercion, but the more he had to do so, the more he sought a long-term political solution which would pacify the Irish, achieve social order, and restore the norms of liberal civil society. Pacification and the absence of the forces which made coercion necessary were the goals Gladstone sought through the 'Trilogy' of social order, a complete land settlement and Irish autonomy in Irish affairs which made up the proposed Irish settlement of 1886:[4] land and the Irish legislature were the means, 'social order' was the goal. Only with the achievement of this 'Trilogy' would there exist the prerequisite for liberty for the Irish, peace for the Empire and the clearing of the way at Westminster. Gladstone never thought, as many Victorians did think, that the Irish were inherently violent or that violence there was chronic and endemic; he always believed that a proper social and political relationship between Britain and Ireland would rather quickly lead to pacification. Political action and, particularly, dramatic legislation could therefore be quickly and directly effective. Thus the 'Trilogy' of 1886 replaced the 'Upas Tree' of 1868: the means had changed but the mission of pacification, and the assumptions about the way of achieving it, remained.

[1] See to Stead, 18 Dec. 85.
[2] To R. W. Dale, 29 Apr. 86.
[3] B. Porter, *The origins of the vigilant state* (1987), 36 and *passim* for an interesting discussion of this subject.
[4] To Morley, 2 Feb. 86.

In the development of Gladstone's views on Ireland, the precise context of 1885 and early 1886 was also of great importance. Though he did not attempt, in his diary or elsewhere, to maintain a self-justifying record, this immediate context is fairly well defined. There was a clear deadlock on Ireland in Cabinet in the spring of 1885. The government's timetable in 1880, 1881, and 1882 had been ruined by unexpected Irish legislation. If the usual pattern of Liberal con-solidation during a Tory minority government was followed by the accustomed Liberal victory at the polls,[1] the next Liberal government would find on taking office that little had changed. As in 1868–70 and 1880–2, it would spend its early years attempting to pacify Ireland, with the additional difficulty that with each round of quasi-pacification, the Liberal Cabinet found it more difficult to agree on measures, as 1885 had shown. Unless there was an alternative initi-ative, coercion, eschewed by the Tory minority government but by the end of 1885 felt to be unavoidable, would be the first business of the session. Directly related to this, there would be the additional difficulty of a greatly increased number of Home Rule M.P.s, an obvious development since 1884, but one focused upon particularly by Gladstone after the fall of his government in June 1885:

> The greatest incident of the coming election is to be the Parnell or Nationalist majority. And such a majority is a very great fact indeed. It will at once shift the centre of gravity in the relations between the two countries.[2]

These two factors—Liberal fissiparousness and Irish Home-Rulers' imminent strength—especially conditioned Gladstone's views in the summer of 1885. Not surprisingly, therefore, as he considered future Liberal policy for Ireland, Glad-stone started from a rather negative position: as Derby noted, 'One thing he saw plainly, that parliament could not go on as it had done.'[3] From the liberal point of view, all the alternatives had been tried and had produced neither last-ing social order nor an Ireland politically integrated into the United Kingdom: despite all efforts the integration was the other way, towards an Ireland largely integrated by a demand for Home Rule. This tone continued through to the introduction of the Government of Ireland Bill on 8 April 1886. Concluding his speech, Gladstone observed, 'Well, sir, I have argued the matter as if it were a choice of evils'; even when he then came towards his peroration, the mood was significant: 'I cherish the hope that this is not merely the choice of the lesser evil, but may prove to be rather a good in itself.'[4]

The process of working through the choice of evils to the point of regarding as the least of them the settlement publicly proposed in April 1886 was complex. It began during the hiatus following the Liberal Cabinet's resignation in June 1885: 'Prepared a sketch on Irish Contingency.'[5] This sketch has unfortunately not been

[1] A generally expected result, see Jenkins, 244.

[2] To Spencer, 30 June 85; see also 14 July 85 and n. and Sir T. D. Acland's notes below XI, Appendix I.

[3] *Derby*, 32 (1 October 1885).

[4] *Speeches on the Irish question 1886*, 51.

[5] 12 June 85. The circular of 16 June 85 was probably a reduced version of this; Gladstone told Granville that the mem. circulated was an 'amended' version 'in the mildest form available' (Ramm II ii. 386).

found. It must partly have involved the considerable possibility that Salisbury would decline or be unable to take office at that time, leaving the Liberals again immediately face to face with coercion, land purchase, and the central board; but it may also have reflected conversations with Wolverton, whose comments on Gladstone's secret circular of qualified resignation (sent round on 16–17 June) referred to 'your proposed Irish policy', and to Wolverton's hope that 'reading between the lines of your memorandum, I see your patriotic inclination upon a defined and great policy to forgo for the sake of all, your strong claim for immediate release'.[1] Wolverton had thus extracted from Gladstone an agreement which confirmed his by now well-established position, that is, as Gladstone put it to his brother: 'My profound desire is retirement, and nothing has prevented or will prevent my giving effect to that desire, unless there should appear to be something in which there may be a prospect of my doing what could not be as well done without me.'[2]

Gladstone at once combined this 'doing' with the Irish consequences of the 1884 Franchise Bill:

> Nothing can withhold or suspend my retirement except the presentation of some great and critical problem in the national life, and the hope, if such a hope shall be, of making some special contribution towards a solution of it.
>
> No one I think can doubt that, according to all present appearances, the greatest incident of the coming election is to be the Parnell or Nationalist majority. And such a majority is a very great fact indeed. It will at once shift the centre of gravity in the relations between the two countries.
>
> How is it and how are its probable proposals, to be met?
>
> If the heads of the Liberal party shall be prepared to unite in rendering an *adequate* answer to this question, and if they unitedly desire me to keep my present place for the purpose of giving to that answer legislative effect, such a state of things may impose upon me a formidable obligation for the time of the crisis. I cannot conceive any other form in which my resolution could be unsettled.[3]

This position therefore involved Gladstone in two very different and perhaps conflicting activities: helping the Liberal Party and solving the Irish crisis. 'An Irish crisis, a solid party': these meant for Morley a course between 'two impossibilities'.[4]

The first step, as Gladstone saw it, was to establish what the 'Parnell or Nationalist majority' would want. Thus immediately after his formal resignation and the day after moving out of Downing Street, he asked for Parnell's paper of January 1885 on the central board which Gladstone had on receipt sent on to Spencer, 'that I may (for the first time) peruse it'[5] (even given the press of events in January 1885, it is astonishing that the Prime Minister should not have found time to read such a proposal from such a source). Having got the paper, he asked Grosvenor to discover through Mrs. O'Shea if the proposal

---

[1] Jenkins, 241. Gladstone's letter to Wolverton (see 17 June 85) clearly establishes that the circular of 16 June is the 'secret draft' to which Wolverton's letter refers. The 'sketch' of 12 June does not seem to have been sent to anyone, and is not referred to by Hamilton.

[2] To Sir T. Gladstone, 19 June 85.

[3] To Spencer, 30 June 85; see Hammond, 390.

[4] Morley, iii. 220.

[5] To Spencer, 27 June 85.

'stands good as when it was written'.[1] Parnell made no definite answer. Thus, though there was a presumption that the central board scheme was dead,[2] by the start of August 1885 Gladstone had 'entirely failed to extract any independent information on the question whether the Central Board scheme is dead or not'.[3]

In the meantime, 'the high biddings of Lord Randolph'[4] and the unprecedented attacks by the Tory ministers on Spencer's record as Viceroy in his handling of the Maamtrasna murder case made it likely that Parnell's confidence would grow as the increase of his parliamentary party became imminent. On the Liberal side, Chamberlain and the Radicals proposed a plan of national councils and Gladstone, vocally out of action, failed to persuade Childers, in his role as ex-Chancellor, to oppose Ashbourne's land purchase bill,[5] which was, in Gladstone's view, 'a real subsidy to the Irish landlords'.[6]

Gladstone then wrote directly to Mrs O'Shea on 4 August about the absence of a definite reply on the central board question.[7] She replied that the approach *via* the development of county councils would be 'putting the cart before the horse . . . it is now felt that leaders of English opinion may fairly be asked to consider the question of granting to Ireland a Constitution of similar nature to that of one of the larger Colonies', while taking account of 'guarantees for the Crown, for landowners, and for freedom of conscience and fair treatment of the minority'. 'Mr Parnell', wrote Mrs O'Shea, 'would like me to send you a draft of detailed propositions.'[8] But Parnell's 'Proposed Constitution for Ireland' was not sent to Gladstone until early November.[9] Mrs O'Shea's letter of 5 August had been written just after Parnell's secret meeting with Carnarvon, and it may well be that the delay was caused by the need to see the fruits of that remarkable discussion. In early August, therefore, Gladstone knew that Irish expectations as expressed through the Home Rule party were moving well beyond the central board proposal regarded by it in the early months of 1885 as the immediate goal. The cart and the horse had changed positions.

As far as can be ascertained—the absence of the private papers of Parnell and Mrs. O'Shea makes detailed checking obviously difficult—Gladstone was accurately informed. Mrs. O'Shea's role as go-between was a rather satisfactory solution to a tricky problem. 'Kitty O'Shea' has the smack of a colleen, but she was in fact a very suitable person for her role. The daughter of the Rev. Sir John Page Wood, the niece of Lord Hatherley (Gladstone's first Lord Chancellor), the sister of Sir Evelyn Wood whom we have seen handling the negotiations with the Boers after Majuba so sensibly, Katharine O'Shea was a member of a distinguished Liberal family. In marrying Captain O'Shea she had married beneath herself. Gladstone had some sympathy for her and her husband and tried, perhaps inadvisedly, to help him to a post in Dublin Castle; Grosvenor, the chief whip, replied with the retort that '*every* Irishman, without a single exception, always jobs'[10] and the attempt came to nothing.

[1] To Grosvenor, 6 July 85.   [2] To Derby, 17 July 85.
[3] To Chamberlain, 1 Aug. 85.   [4] To Derby, 17 July 85.
[5] To Childers, 23, 25 July 85.   [6] To Chamberlain, 1 Aug. 85 and to Carmichael, 23 Apr. 86.
[7] To Mrs. O'Shea, 4 Aug. 85.   [8] To Mrs. O'Shea, 4 Aug. 85 and note.
[9] To Mrs. O'Shea, 24 Oct., 3 Nov. 85.
[10] To Grosvenor, 29 Aug. 82n. For Gladstone's attempt to assist Capt. O'Shea in the 1885 election, see to Grosvenor, 18 Nov. 85.

Mrs. O'Shea was an unexpected bonus. She played her part confidentially and with some skill.[1] Gladstone and Parnell were enabled to establish a fairly close vicarious relationship which, had it been direct, would have been very impolitic, probably indeed impossible, on both sides. On the Liberal side there was no secrecy in the sense that the letters were all shown to the chief whip and usually to the Irish ministers. Undoubtedly, the Katharine O'Shea connection carried matters forward. It was an important factor in encouraging Gladstone to conclude in 1883: 'though Parnell is a Sphinx, the most probable reading of him is that he works for & with the law as far as he dare. I have even doubt whether he hates the Government.'[2] There is no record of what Gladstone knew or thought at this time of the private relationship between Mrs. O'Shea and Parnell.[3] Probably he felt that the less known, the better. He paid Katharine O'Shea, as he did Olga Novikov, the rather modern compliment of treating her as a political figure rather than a woman.

At the same time as exploring Parnellite intentions, Gladstone had been involved in a series of discussions on Ireland with members of the inner circle of his party. A special dinner had been set up with Goschen,[4] but it had not been a success. Despite the embargo on using his voice, Gladstone 'had to speak more than was desirable: the occasion was important; it was the coming Irish question'.[5] After disagreeing with Goschen, who objected to the idea of a National Council because it was '*elective*', Gladstone spoke to Sir Thomas Acland, the only one of his undergraduate friends still in politics. Acland noted: 'he beckoned me to sit on the sofa by him—& said the Lib. party wd. break up— he should have no more to do with leading still less with combinations of moderate Lib's & conservs. The only thing that would call him out wd. be the need of seeing some great ansr[?] to the Council question.'[6] Conversations such as these showed Gladstone that his view that 'there *is* an emergency at hand'[7] might be shared, but that there was little agreement about the means of dealing with it.

It might be thought that during the summer of 1885 Gladstone dragged his feet. But it must be remembered that a serious throat condition prevented him from any public and most private speaking, and that he was going through an arduous series of twenty-one daily treatments.[8] Good progress seems to have

---

[1] Herbert Gladstone went to considerable pains to discredit parts of O'Shea, *Parnell* (see *After thirty years*, 295ff.); curiously, he does not mention Mrs. O'Shea's major factual error, her muddling of the date of Parnell's 'proposed Constitution for Ireland'; her book is an odd mixture of exaggeration and accuracy; though written *ca.* 1913, the dates of her meetings with Gladstone in 1882 are correct, as are various other details checked against Gladstone's diary; clearly, when she wrote, she had quite an extensive archive available to her.

[2] To Spencer, 29 June 83.

[3] According to Dilke's 'Memoir' (Gwynn, i. 445), Harcourt told the cabinet on 17 May 1882 that 'Captain O'Shea [was] "the husband of Parnell's mistress"'. But there was no cabinet that day; it seems likely, however, that Harcourt made an announcement of that sort during the post-Kilmainham cabinets. See also Sir R. Ensor, *England, 1870–1914* (1936), Appendix B.

[4] To Goschen, 11 July 85.

[5] 14 July 85.   [6] See Appendix I.

[7] To Goschen, 11 July 85.

[8] For discussion of the illness, see below, section IX.

been made, and on 8 August Gladstone left for a voyage to the Norwegian fiords on Thomas Brassey's yacht *Sunbeam*. He was away until 1 September. Before leaving he brought together the Irish and the party elements of his thoughts and conversations since the fall of his government by a conversation with Hartington, at which Gladstone read a memorandum, in fact the basis for his election address. This reviewed the spectrum of Liberal problems and possibilities with a view to the general election, but it was Ireland that Gladstone particularly emphasized ('Ireland. An epoch: possibly a crisis . . .').[1] He does not seem to have told Hartington of his recent sounding of Parnell *via* Mrs. O'Shea,[2] but he made it clear that the basis for agreement on a limited 'Central Board scheme' had gone. Gladstone remained puzzled both as to his personal position and as to an appropriate Irish policy: 'What to say publicly' about the 'considerable changes' that may be desired 'must be most carefully considered on my return'.[3]

On board the *Sunbeam* Gladstone developed the memorandum into a draft address, to take the form of a 'small pamphlet';[4] its unusual length partly reflected the fact that it was not yet clear that he would be able to resume public speaking. It attempted to bridge the gap between the 'left' and the 'right' liberals by emphasizing four topics on which the party was agreed for action: parliamentary procedure, land reform, electoral registration reform, and 'local govt (liquor laws)'. On his return, he solicited and received general support for his continued leadership which was to be based on his role as consolidator and co-ordinator and which was to be pursued by consulting Hartington and Chamberlain 'who may be considered to be our two poles', only Hartington's unsuccessful request for a meeting of the ex-Cabinet indicating unease.[5] At the same time Gladstone let it be known that he remained 'perplexed' about Ireland.[6] Meanwhile, Hartington's speeches in reply to Parnell's demands showed how difficult it was to move Hartington and 'our friends' towards what Gladstone regarded as a recognition of the consequences of the development of British and Irish history since the 1830s.[7]

The position was made more complex by uncertainty about Parnell. The document which Mrs. O'Shea had promised in early August was still not available. Gladstone, while on ship, had asked Grosvenor to enquire further about it so that the Irish section of the Address could take it into account, but the Address was written without Parnell having replied.[8] As published, that section, placed at the end, could be read as offering either the maximum or the minimum. It was a masterpiece of short-term political integration. This was deliberate. Parnell's recent declarations oscillated between demands for 'national independence' and for Ireland being treated like 'one of the larger

---

[1] 7 Aug. 85.

[2] He had told Granville 'It would not surprise me if he [Parnell] were to formulate something on the subject' (6 August 1885, Ramm II, ii. 390).

[3] 7 Aug. 85.   [4] To Grosvenor, 22 Aug. 85.

[5] To Hartington, 8, 13 Sept. 85; to Chamberlain, 9, 11 Sept. 85; to Derby, 14 Sept. 85.

[6] To Hartington, 3 Sept. 85.

[7] To Hartington, 8 Sept. 85.

[8] To Grosvenor, 22 Aug. 85.

colonies'.[1] Gladstone was 'astonished at the rather virulent badness of what he [Parnell] has uttered with respect to Irish Government'.[2] Because any successful settlement had to involve, in Gladstone's view, some accommodation with the Home Rule party, no step could be taken until Gladstone could be reasonably satisfied that demands for 'Home Rule' were exactly that.

This then was Gladstone's position by the end of September 1885: his address, the 'small pamphlet' drafted on the *Sunbeam* and now carefully entitled 'On the Liberal Party',[3] was published, offering a programme of the lowest common denominator, designed to maintain the moderates within the party at the risk of estranging Radicals who had nowhere else to go. The intention in issuing so extensive an address well before the date of the dissolution was known was clearly to try to give the Liberal Party a unifying reference point in the face of the Radical Programme, the disestablishment issue, and the Irish question. The address thus admitted policy weakness and called for the party to fall back on its inherent strength in the mainland constituencies. It was thus the obverse of Gladstone's calls to legislative action during the previous period of Liberal regrouping during a Tory minority government when in 1868 Irish disestablishment had provided a rallying point of spectacular constitutional innovation. The address of September 1885 was the only moment in Gladstone's career when he acted as a party leader in the normal modern mould, integrative, cautious, holding the centre ground.

Privately, encouragement was given in various directions to think of the consequences of an eighty-strong Home Rule party and of the need to see the Irish question in other than a short-term perspective. Here lay the paradox of Gladstone's position. On the one hand, he shortened the political horizon, seeing no further than ensuring a reasonably united party at the time of the dissolution: Hartington and Chamberlain were wrong to 'write as if they were fixing the platform of a new Liberal Government, whereas I am solely endeavouring to help, not to embarrass, Liberal candidates for the Election. The question of a Government may have its place later on, not now.'[4] On the other hand, he anticipated an Irish crisis 'open, after the Dissolution, like a chasm under our feet' in which a brief moment, ripe for action, would embody the consequences of great historical forces and changes: Pitt's Act of Union, Gladstone concluded in mid-September, had been 'a gigantic though excusable mistake'.[5] But out of this situation he still could not 'pretend to see my way'.[6]

During October 1885, Gladstone read and reread works on Ireland in the eighteenth and nineteenth centuries and began thinking of a measure based on the Canada Acts of 1840 and 1867.[7] His main reading and writing, however, was for his article 'Dawn of creation and of worship'[8] (whose long perspective doubtless helped set the Irish question in context) and an extensive reading of

---

[1] See to Hartington, 3 Sept. 85n.
[2] To Dilke, 18 Sept. 85.
[3] To P. W. Campbell, 29 Sept. 85.
[4] To Harcourt, 12 Sept. 85.
[5] 15 Sept. 85.
[6] To Spencer, 15 Sept. 85.
[7] To Grosvenor, 9 Oct. 85.
[8] See 6 Oct. 85.

the French religious sociologist, Le Play. He also, on 11 October, drafted for Herbert Gladstone, whose home rule views were pronounced and well-known, a letter for Herbert to send to Henry Labouchere, who was in touch with Parnell, explaining 'my own [i.e. Herbert Gladstone's] impressions as to my Father's view', namely that he stood by his Address on Ireland, and that 'he, as I think, in no way disapproves of the efforts of the nationalists to get the Tory party to take up their question . . . it might be the shortest way to a settlement'; Gladstone regarded the launching of a specific plan as 'gratuitous': Ireland must speak through her representatives 'plainly and publicly'.[1] This was to be his position through the general election: no plan should be announced pending Ireland's statement through the ballot box, with the hope that the Tories would take the lead in legislating for a settlement.

At the same time, reading and reflection were producing consolidation of view:

> I am trying to familiarise my mind with the subject and to look at it all round, but it still requires a good deal more looking at before I could ask myself to adhere to anything I had conceived. I adhere however to this one belief that there is great advantage in a constructive measure (which would be subject to change or recall) as compared with the repeal of the Union.[2]

The spectrum was thus between 'a constructive measure' and repeal of the Union, the former being preferred since the continuing supremacy of the West-minster Parliament—this was the period of Gladstone's study of Dicey—could always, in the last resort, 'change or recall'.

But what was 'a constructive measure'? On 1 November, Gladstone received Parnell's 'proposed Constitution for Ireland'.[3] If this had been sent in August, when it, or something like it, was first mentioned by Mrs. O'Shea, the effects on Gladstone's election Address might have been dramatic. As it was, the process was under way and the narrow, unifying terms for the Liberal Party were set for the general election. Gladstone refused to be drawn by Parnell into a public auction for the Irish vote, and his reply, sent in the name of Grosvenor, was non-committal. More interesting is the unsent letter to Mrs. O'Shea (i.e. to Parnell) which set out his thinking at some length, repeating the message sent to Labouchere and emphasizing the importance of Conservative settlements of 'sharply controverted matters' in 1829, 1845, 1846, and 1867.[4]

Publicly, therefore, as the election campaign in November proceeded, Parnell probed and Gladstone parried. Privately Parnell believed he knew that he had a degree of Tory support for Home Rule. He did not know that, whereas the various Liberal ministers who had conducted discussions with him in 1885 had kept their Cabinet informed of details, his conversation with Carnarvon on Home Rule was not reported to the Tory Cabinet by Salisbury. In November and December 1885 both Gladstone and Parnell underestimated the narrow cynicism of Salisbury, the leader of the 'patriotic' party whose conception of the

---

[1] 11 Oct. 85.
[2] To Granville, 22 October 1885, Ramm II, ii. 411.
[3] 1 Nov. 85 and to Mrs. O'Shea, 24 Oct. 85; see O'Shea, *Parnell*, ii. 18 and Hammond, 422.
[4] To Mrs O'Shea, 3 Nov. 85.

national interest was to equate it with the short-term advantage of the Conservatives.[1] Gladstone hoped Salisbury would be a Peel, but he turned out a Castlereagh, though longer-lived.

Parnell's 'proposed Constitution' must have pleased Gladstone for it showed Parnell, and committed him on paper, as a rather moderate constitutionalist, flexible as to detail (Irish M.P.s at Westminster might be in or out) and well within the framework of colonial precedent which Gladstone was looking at in the Canada Act of 1867. At Dalmeny for the Midlothian election campaign, Gladstone was asked by Rosebery why he did not respond specifically to Parnell's public request for a Liberal plan. He explained his reasons to Rosebery in a letter on 13 November (even though they were staying in the same house) in a series of points drawing together those made in the previous weeks, with the 'final and paramount reason ... that the production of a plan by me would not only be injurious, but would destroy all reasonable hope of its adoption'. Abstinence from stating a plan presupposed that 'such a plan can be framed'. As yet there was no such plan. Thus the next day Gladstone 'wrote on Ireland', jotting down the headings of a Home Rule measure and telling his son Herbert the gist of them in a letter.[2] These headings related to Parnell's 'proposed Constitution' quite closely. The private need for knowledge of Irish intentions having been satisfied by Parnell, the sketch of Gladstone's measure followed quickly and naturally.

This is the point at which we may say that the process of considering various possible policies and of taking into account the complex changes of British politics hardened into a policy. Gladstone's 'Sir Robert Peelian horror of *abstract* resolutions' and his training in the practical, down-to-earth school of the British Cabinet made him suspicious of propositions in politics (however attractive they might be in principle) until he could see his way to a legislative enactment, that is, the statement of concepts and aspirations in the clear, hard clauses of a bill which could be put to Parliament. Moreover, as the point of 'Home Rule' was in part to meet Irish demands, the development of a policy had to be in part a response to a clear and in Gladstone's view practical statement of those demands. This he now had.

Gladstone's commitment to Home Rule involved the Peelite view that government should, through legislation, redress an established grievance, and he saw the 1885 election as the moment at which that establishment of grievance would be publicly confirmed. But 'Home Rule' was a notoriously empty casket, as Gladstone himself had several times remarked. As soon as it began to be filled by Parnell's 'proposed Constitution', Gladstone conceived a measure to which the Irish would necessarily be attached in detail as well as in principle. In this sense, he began a process of imposing Home Rule upon the Irish, turning a slogan into the fine print of legislation bold in conception but regarded by its framer as essentially within the confines of the Imperial constitution. There was also, in the accompanying proposals for a land settlement, an element of retribution, as the Home Rule party was put in charge of rent and

---

[1] For Salisbury's single-minded pursuit of party advantage in 1885-6, see P. T. Marsh, *The discipline of popular government. Lord Salisbury's domestic statecraft 1881-1902* (1978), ch. 3.
[2] 13-14 Nov. 85.

repayment collection in Ireland. Gladstone cannot but have enjoyed the thought of the ex-Land Leaguers running the government in Ireland which would collect the monies for the Receiver General.

Gladstone does not seem to have shown Rosebery, his host in Midlothian, either Parnell's 'proposed Constitution' or his own sketch despite their frequent conversations on Ireland during the campaign.[1] But from this point, his argument to his close colleagues was that no plan should be publicly produced, not, as hitherto, that he did not have one.

The argument that a settlement should be introduced by the Salisbury government was thus formulated before the general election. As it was associated with expectations of a political crisis in three months' time, that is, at the start of the Session, it suggests that Gladstone may have been less confident about a Liberal majority than many others.[2] It would have been an extraordinary manoeuvre that a Tory government should, whatever the grounds, remain in office if the Liberals had a working majority over them and the Irish (that is, if there was a repeat of the 1880 result in 1885, as many Liberals at first expected).

The Irish National League's directive just before polling began that Irish voters should vote to frustrate Liberal success, the Liberals being 'perfidious, treacherous, and incompetent'[3] and the electoral result, a dead heat if it were supposed that the Tory–Home Rule 'alliance' continued, intensified the case for Gladstone's view that all must wait until government policy was clarified. Thus during December 1885 he made no significant change to his position. He began to codify the tests needed for judging action, and to encourage his senior colleagues to accept 'a healthful slow fermentation in many minds, working towards the final product',[4] while at the same time discussing the situation with visits to Hawarden from Granville ('we are already in promising harmony'), Spencer (the key man if a Home Rule policy was to be seriously advanced), Rosebery, Wolverton, Chamberlain, and Sir Thomas Acland.[5]

There were two main difficulties about this position. Gladstone wanted to give the Conservatives a chance at a Home Rule bill, and he was no doubt correct in thinking that support, or at least lack of fundamental opposition, on the part of the political right was, if not an essential, at the least a highly desirable part of a Home-Rule settlement. Yet his contempt for the Conservative Party, which 'leans now upon its lame leg, the leg of Class interest',[6] grew by the month. Gladstone knew by December of the strong Home-Rule influence among the senior civil servants in Dublin Castle,[7] and believed 'Salisbury &

---

[1] Rosebery would surely have recorded in his diary sight of so historic a document; he does record receiving Gladstone's letter 'composed yesterday' as to 'why (rightly) he will not put a plan before the public. We talked over this letter after luncheon' (Rosebery's diary, 14 November 1885, Dalmeny MSS).

[2] See Jenkins, 244.   [3] 21 Nov. 85n.

[4] To Granville, 9 Dec. 85; several letters to Granville in 1885–6 not available to Dr. Ramm (or only partially available in Morley) have come to light and are printed below.

[5] 6–12 Dec. 85; for Acland's notes of these home rule discussions, see below, xi, Appendix I, and for Rosebery's diary, see 8 Dec. 85n.

[6] 10 Dec. 85.

[7] See 12, 13, 15 Dec. 85.

Carnarvon are rather with Randolph' (then thought to be canvassing a Home-Rule solution), though they 'are afraid of their colleagues and their party'. He approved more of Salisbury than he had in the summer, no doubt recalling the spirit of 'equity and candour' which Salisbury had shown in the redistribution conferences in 1884,[1] the best recent precedent, though clearly only a partial one, for the sort of agreed settlement which Gladstone sought. He had mitigated his anger at Balfour whose 'almost raving licence of an unbridled tongue' in 1882 had grieved Gladstone to the point of a vicarious rebuke.[2] Yet he despaired of the party which would be their instrument.

The second difficulty was that Gladstone's desire to encourage discussion, reading and thought on Ireland could only be done privately and without a clear public lead from him. He had devised a public position which protected his party from division and the Irish question from partisanship, but at the price of putting public discussion of Liberal Irish policy on ice. The election result lowered the temperature even further, with Gladstone even more determined not to be seen bidding for the Irish vote and not to make any move until the Irish had publicly ended their alliance with the Tories. Without this, any move would look like a bid or a bribe. Thus the fruit of party support for Home Rule had to ripen without the attentions of the chief gardener.

Gladstone made a move implicit in his position since early October: on 15 December at Eaton Hall, the Westminsters' house in Cheshire, he 'saw ... A. Balfour to whom I said what he will probably repeat in London'. Next day, a 'day of anxious & very important correspondence', he drafted a letter to Balfour confirming the 'urgency of the matter' and going further by emphasizing the 'public calamity if this great subject should fall into the lines of party conflict', and promising his support if a Tory government proposed a complete settlement. But the letter was not sent until 20 December. Meanwhile:

> Matters of today required meditation. After dealing with the knottiest point, I resumed Huxley. We felled a good ash. Read Burke, Dicey. Suspended the Balfour letter.[3]

Gladstone's initative, curiously half-hearted and delayed considering its importance to his position—he told Granville later that he had met Balfour 'accidentally'[4]—was too late in every sense. The Cabinets on 14 and 15 December had decided that the Conservative government had no Irish policy. Carnarvon, the Viceroy, who had tried to move the ministry towards some sort of Home Rule solution and whose resignation was being held back at Salisbury's request, noted in his diary:

> 14 December ... discussion on Ireland—the result of wh. was that the Cabinet would do nothing & announce no policy—but they wd. not debar themselves from proceeding later by Committee if circumstances sd. favour this.
>
> 15 December. A long talk again on Ireland. The Cabinet will do nothing & they only say that if & when a gt. change comes it must be done by other hands.[5]

---

[1] To Salisbury, 5 Dec. 84.

[2] To Hartington, 15 Dec. 85 and to Helen Gladstone, 17 May 82.

[3] 16 Dec. 85. For the Balfour letters, see 20, 23 Dec. 85; Balfour's report to his uncle was wholly tactical; see Balfour to Salisbury, 23 December 1885 in *The Salisbury-Balfour correspondence 1869-1892*, ed. R. Harcourt Williams (1988), 127.

[4] To Granville, 22 Dec. 85.   [5] Add MS 60925.

The delay meant that the letter to Balfour was not sent until after Herbert Gladstone had inadvertently flown the 'Hawarden Kite', the culmination of a series of newspaper speculations and supposed disclosures, the news of which was published in the press on 17 December.[1] Herbert, a pronounced Home Ruler, was privy to his father's views in general, and, having had considerable experience in Ireland, probably influenced their development. He also knew a good deal about the particulars. He had made a copy of Gladstone's note of 12 December that amounted to a brief restatement of his Home Rule sketch of 14 November (of which Herbert had been sent the gist), and he had at the time of the drafting of that sketch unsuccessfully encouraged his father to a public declaration.[2] Gladstone had spoken through him before,[3] but there is no evidence that he incited or encouraged Herbert's visit to London on 14 December. Given that that was the day before the private initiative to Balfour (of which Herbert could not have known as it occurred 'accidentally'), it was exactly the wrong moment for what was widely interpreted as a public bid for Irish support. On the other hand, Gladstone's response was calm and unalarmed: 'Wrote . . . Telegrams to Press Assn., C. News & other quarters on the Irish rumours about me.'[4] Herbert noted in his diary the same day, 'Father quite *compos*.'[5]

The 'Kite' lessened the likelihood of a Tory-led, nonpartisan settlement, and it coincided with a gathering awareness that it would be the Liberals who would have to face up to home rule: such indeed was the immediate reaction to the 'Kite' in the metropolitan Liberal newspapers, the *Daily News* and *The Pall Mall Gazette*. Gladstone maintained his position that only a government was equipped to prepare a plan, but in December he also toyed with the tactic of 1868 of proceeding by resolution as a preliminary to removing the Tory Government.[6] Though renewing contact with Parnell through Mrs. O'Shea, he was extremely careful to make no commitment while making clear the general drift of his thinking: 'My fear is that to open myself on this subject before the Govt. have answered or had full opportunity of answering, would probably be fatal to any attempt to carry with me the Liberal party.'[7] The notion of 'carrying' the Liberal Party could only suggest to Parnell one direction of movement.

During the course of December 1885, Gladstone was coming to see the Liberal Party in some sort of association with the Home Rulers as the providers of a settlement for Ireland. This represented a shift of view. Before the election, he had thought: 'Nothing but a sheer and clear majority in Parlt. could enable Liberals in Government to carry a plan. Personally I shake myself free of any other idea.'[8] But Gladstone did not shake himself free of other ideas, nor could he, given the electoral arithmetic. If Home Rule was workable, as he knew it was, if it was acceptable to the Irish M.P.s, as he knew it was, and if it was not

[1] For the 'Kite', see below, xi, Appendix I and Jenkins, 263–4. Herbert Gladstone had during the election urged his father to make a clear public statement; see to H. J. Gladstone, 14 Nov. 85. See also Gladstone's comments to Hamilton, 31 Dec. 85, exculpating his son.
[2] See to H. J. Gladstone, 14 Nov. 85 and 12 Dec. 85.
[3] See 11 Oct. 85.   [4] See 17 Dec. 85.   [5] See below, xi, Appendix I.
[6] See Rosebery's note of his visit to Hawarden, 8 Dec. 85.
[7] To Mrs. O'Shea, 19 Dec. 85.
[8] To H. J. Gladstone, 18 Oct. 85.

acceptable to the Tory government, as he was almost certain by the end of December it was not, then only one course was open to him.

The general constitutional crisis of Ireland, under consideration at least since July 1885, took on a particular urgency. Gladstone knew in December from men as various as James Bryce, Sir Robert Hamilton of Dublin Castle and E. G. Jenkinson,[1] head of the Special Branch in Ireland, that the political and social calm there was very fragile, and in the view of all three that the fragility pointed to a Home Rule initiative to defuse a further rent crisis and to incorporate the Parnellite M.P.s in the Westminster process. Otherwise there was thought to be a real chance of their withdrawing to Dublin and setting up their own Assembly.[2] This would make an orderly Liberal compromise on devolution impossible. The Gladstonian case rested on an Irish legislature being inaugurated by the Westminster parliament, as a result of a legislative proposal from a British government responding to a respectably stated case. Though intended to deal with an abnormal situation, a political settlement of Ireland would have to be seen to be done by the book.

Given his premises, Gladstone played his cards well in December 1885 and January 1886. He gave the Tories the maximum chance to take the initiative, and they stood aside. He flushed them out as the party of coercion, the policy which they had rejected in June 1885 as the price of removing his previous government. He avoided any public or private pledges to the Home Rulers and he sought no assurances from them. He insisted on waiting until it was publicly established that the Tory–Irish alliance was at an end. He bided his time during a series of tactical discussions about how the government might be removed without the Liberals being compromised on Home Rule, and he took the opportunity of Jesse Collings' amendment on English agricultural policy for the felling of the Tories, thus defeating the Government before the item on Ireland in the Address to the Queen was reached (it was the item next after agriculture) and avoiding public display of the variety of Liberal views on Ireland.[3] 'I spoke on J. Collings's motion & we were driven by events to act at once. We beat the Government, I think wisely, by 329:250 so the crisis is come. . . .'[4] Just after midnight on the night of 29–30 January, 'in came Sir H. Ponsonby with verbal communication from H.M. which I at once accepted'. There was less prevarication by the Queen than in 1880, and fewer conditions about men than in 1868.[5]

Gladstone thus formed his third government without publicly going further than the pre-election Address which had been designed to hold the Liberal Party together. The outline of his approach given to John Morley in January 1886 was consistent with his behaviour generally: 'He had "expressed opinion,

---

[1] For Bryce and Hamilton, see Loughlin, op. cit., 39–42 and to Bryce, 2 Dec. 85 and Bryce MS 11, f. 99; for Jenkinson, see 12 Dec. 85. On 2 July 1884, Jenkinson, at dinner at Harcourt's, had told John Morley that he 'saw necessity for Home Rule' (Morley diary).

[2] To Grosvenor, 7 Jan. 86. This is Gladstone's only known reference to this possibility; it seems to me to be an important but not a determining factor.

[3] Not to have put Ireland earlier in the Speech and the consequent Address was clearly a tactical error on the part of the Conservative cabinet.   [4] 26 Jan. 86.

[5] Victoria started overtures to Goschen, who rapidly shut them off; these were not made public, though Gladstone probably had wind of them (see 29 Jan. 86n.); she blackballed Granville and Kimberley for the Foreign Office and Dilke for any office; *LQV*, 3rd series, i. 22–34.

but not plans or intention". We must advance by stages: consider each stage as it arises: next stage is the Address [on the Queen's Speech].'[1] This approach continued after the formation of the Cabinet. The first step to be taken by the Cabinet with respect to Ireland—and the basis on which its members were invited to join it—would be an examination of the practicability of 'the establishment, by Statute, of a Legislative body, to sit in Dublin'.[2]

In this sense he followed a thoroughly Peelite interpretation of the right and duty of government to propose legislation and policy unencumbered by mandate. With its many echoes of Peel's handling of protection in 1840-6—and with its similar *dénouement*—Gladstone's handling of Home Rule in 1885-6 was a return to the constitutional orthodoxy of his youth and a marked contrast to the prophetic Irish programme endorsed by the 1868 general election. This is yet another example of the way in which Gladstone saw Home Rule as essentially a conservative rather than a radical measure.

So ended the process of opposition. Gladstone had aimed at consistency and sequence, and on the whole he had found both. Not asking to see the distant scene, he found 'one step enough for me'. Reading the diary and correspondence below, it is hard not to see in their record a series of steps in the same direction.

It is interesting that, at the same time, Gladstone was involved in a controversy on evolution and Genesis, in which he defended the tradition of Christian evolutionism. He linked it to that sense of a 'series' which had since the 1840s formed so important a part of his Butlerian conception of politics:[3]

Evolution is, to me, series with development. And like series in mathematics, whether arithmetical or geometrical, it establishes in things an unbroken progression; it places each thing (if only it stand the test of ability to live) in a distinct relation to every other thing, and makes each a witness to all that preceded it, a prophecy of all that are to follow it.[4]

He hoped 'to make a Butlerian argument upon a general and probable correspondence'.[5]

In hindsight, what is perhaps most striking about this process are the lacunae: the House of Lords, the problem of Ulster, and the problem of the Liberal Party. The Lords, thought Gladstone, simply 'would not dare': presupposing a land purchase settlement, the Lords would back down on a plan 'carried by a sheer Liberal majority', though it might take a governmental resignation to achieve this.[6] It is important to note that Gladstone formed this view in October 1885; he does not seem to have considered the implications for the Lords of a bill carried in the Commons by Irish as well as British votes. It was Gladstone's view throughout that the Irish representatives were exactly that: representatives of Irish opinion whose views had to be taken at face value

[1] Morley's diary, 15 January 1886.
[2] 30 Jan. 86.
[3] See e.g., 20 Dec. 45.
[4] 'Proem to Genesis', *Later gleanings*, 69–70; see 8 Dec. 85.
[5] To H. W. Acland, 16 Dec. 85.
[6] To Rosebery, 13 Nov. 85, to H. J. Gladstone, 18 Oct. 85.

and that what they valued was 'Home Rule'. He paid Parnell the compliment of treating him like any other party leader and treating his 'proposed Constitution' as the objective of those M.P.s who followed him. Sir Thomas Acland noted after an important conversation with Gladstone in December 1885: 'any ideas of going behind the constitutional voice of the present Irish M.P.s is brushed aside as out of the question'.[1]

These two presuppositions, that parliamentary representation and its expression through votes on legislative measures was the determining feature of the British constitution, and that the Home Rulers were not separatists, were the two 'essentially contested concepts'[2] of the next generation of British politics, and therefore, by definition, the dispute admits of no resolution.[3] Gladstone did not anticipate, perhaps understandably, the development of the Unionist view that Irish votes did not count and that though Unionism by definition regarded the United Kingdom as requiring a single representative assembly, within that assembly only English votes counted on questions of organic change.

Gladstone paid little heed to Ulster. He had attempted to allow the Province an important voice in Irish government on Forster's resignation of the Irish Secretaryship in 1882 by offering it to Andrew Porter, M.P. for Londonderry and a Presbyterian, but Porter declined it.[4] In 1883 he considered the electoral chances of the Ulster Liberal M.P.s to be poor, and seems to have discounted them.[5] When planning Home Rule in November 1885 it was the position of landowners not of Protestants in Ulster that he thought needed particular attention: 'I do not quite see what protection the Protestants of Ulster want, apart from the Land of the four provinces.'[6] The collapse of the Liberal Party in Ulster might even be seen as an advantage: 'Perhaps had we large and cordial Ulster support, it might have abridged our freedom more than it would have enlarged our Votes.'[7] He included provision for 'the minority' in his early plans, and his Government of Ireland Bill speech in April 1886 seemed to encourage amendment of the bill on this point. But in general his view was that Ulster could not be allowed to dictate the future of Ireland: 'I cannot allow it to be said that a Protestant minority in Ulster, or elsewhere, is to rule the question at large for Ireland.'[8]

[1] See Acland's notes of 12–20 December 1885, below, xi, Appendix I.

[2] W. B. Gallie, 'Essentially contested concepts', *Proceedings of the Aristotelian Society* (1955–6); 'Home Rule' is an exceptionally good example of such a concept.

[3] The contemporary Unionist concern was that 'Home Rule' was not a settlement but a significant and irreversible step towards Irish separation; the Unionist fear was that the Parnellites meant more than they said. Recently, it has been argued that they meant less, and were not really serious or committed to home rule; see A. O'Day, *The English face of Irish nationalism: Parnellite involvement in British politics, 1880–86* (1977). K. T. Hoppen, *Elections, politics, and society in Ireland 1832–1885* (1984) sees Irish politics as characteristically localist, but punctuated by periodic 'peculiar moments' of nationalism.   [4] 3 May 82.

[5] See to Spencer, 2 Oct. 83 on the probable 'almost entire extinction' of 'Moderate Liberals' in Ireland at the next election, presumably including Ulster, as the letter discusses comments from an M.P. for Tyrone.

[6] To Hartington, 18 Nov. 85; a consistently held view, see to Childers, 28 Sept. 85, to H. J. Gladstone, 18 Oct. 85.   [7] To Bryce, 2 Dec. 85.

[8] The secret draft on Irish government of 20 March 1886 (see below, xi, Appendix II) provided for the consideration during the progress of the bill of the exception from it of 'any particular portion of Ireland' (Gladstone noting that if Ulster was omitted, it was hard to see how she could

On both these questions—the Lords and Ulster—Gladstone's view was that a quick, clean passing of a definitive settlement would avoid constitutional blocking and would not be seriously challenged within Ireland.[1]

The Liberal Party was a much more immediate difficulty.

> It will be as difficult to carry the Liberal party, and the two British nations, in favour of a legislature for Ireland, as it was easy to carry them in the case of Irish Disestablishment: I think it can be done but only by the full use of a great leverage. That leverage can only be found in the equitable and mature consideration of what is due to the fixed desire of a nation, clearly and constitutionally expressed.[2]

But a lever requires an operator to pull it. Gladstone's tactics, successful though they were in bringing about his third government, themselves frustrated his role as operator and educator. And his position once in government, of preparing his Irish settlement in much the sort of purdah in which he was accustomed to prepare his budgets—the Irish bills of 1886 received far less Cabinet discussion than any of his previous Irish measures—compounded party confusion.

The tactics were clear enough. The Cabinet, formed on a tentative basis to 'examine', was never given an opportunity thoroughly to do so. Gladstone hoped to trump Cabinet doubts and party unease by the production of a great bill. This, surely, is the chief explanation of the pace of preparation in the spring of 1886. 'Action at a stroke', Gladstone told Hartington before the elections in November 1885, 'will be more honourable, less unsafe, less uneasy, than the jolting process of a series of partial measures.'[3]

Such a proceeding was completely in line with Gladstone's usual approach to the handling of the party in the Commons. There was considerable force behind his view that the preparation of a measure was quite different from its discussion in opposition, that many centrifugal forces operate on those in office and on those sustaining a government from the backbenches which a skilled operator could manipulate. Gladstone's experience in preventing resignations, however often threatened, during the 1880–5 government had shown how effective could be the 'one step at a time' tactic with its series of reasons for remaining in office. No one should resign on a possibility: wait until a formal proposal is made: once the proposal is made, then the intending resigner is responsible in part for the Cabinet that has made it: even then, wait until the Commons vote upon it, there being no point in resigning unnecessarily: once the Commons has approved the principle on the Second Reading, there is always the possibility of amending unsatisfactory details. . . . Many a member of a Gladstone Cabinet, however stern his intentions at the start, had found himself sucked in by these arguments and carried, as by a rip-tide, almost unawares into voting for a Third Reading.

Gladstone's step-by-step handling of Ireland since June 1885 was intended to

enjoy the benefits of the land purchase bill); his speech on 8 April 1886 adumbrated this possibility; *Speeches on the Irish question, 1886*, 19–20.

[1] i.e. seriously in the sense of rebellious resistance; see J. Loughlin, *Gladstone, home rule and the Ulster question 1882–93* (1986) for the view that 'while Ulster Protestant opposition to Home Rule was certainly intense, there is nevertheless little evidence to support the view—still widespread— that they were prepared to resist violently the implementation of Home Rule in this period'.

[2] To Rosebery, 13 Nov. 85.   [3] To Hartington, 10 Nov. 85.

facilitate just such a series of developments, and Hartington, caught so often before, was equally intent on avoiding the trap. It was sprung with full force on Chamberlain and Trevelyan and various courtiers in March 1886 but with limited success, at least briefly achieving the postponement of the Chamberlain–Trevelyan resignation.[1] This sensitivity to the process of politics, this Machiavellian awareness of the eventual primacy of *virtù* in the context of an acute sense of timing, of 'ripeness' and of political control, had its limitations. With the resignations of Chamberlain and Trevelyan already in but deferred, Gladstone tried a last twist, and switched to a general Resolution which might get round or diminish the importance attached to the difficulties of the details and refocus Cabinet attention on the general problem of Irish government. But this came to nothing.[2]

The greatest limitation to this method of proceeding by stages and 'series' had, as we have seen, already been stated by Gladstone himself. The Cabinet, or most of it, might be drawn into the process, but the party was not.

The sensational production of the Government of Ireland Bill on 8 April 1886, the greatest of all the Gladstonian 'big bills', was also, self-evidently, the riskiest: the lever was to be pulled in one stroke. Consequently, the education of the party could not begin until the examination was almost at hand and it was necessarily unaccompanied by any Gladstonian extra-parliamentary speech-making.

Gladstone had sensed this difficulty all along, and had been alarmed in the autumn of 1885 that close colleagues did not view what seemed to him to be a self-evidently grave situation with the same alarm or historical perspective. He had, as early as August 1885, encouraged discussion of the future of Ireland in Knowles' *Nineteenth Century*;[3] from this sprang Barry O'Brien's notable articles.[4] This was quite in line with the usual liberal expectation of the primacy of rationality and exposition, but it hardly amounted to an adequate public discussion. Gladstone's own publications in these months were articles defending, from a moderate evolutionist position, Genesis against Réville and Huxley.[5] These to some extent recovered the ground that he had lost during the election, when his ambivalent handling of the disestablishment question had left the party just united but his own position defensive. His Christian evolutionism was well and widely received,[6] but it was, even so, a strange production on which to spend considerable time when personal and public education on Irish history was essential. The real drive to win the argument through pamphlet warfare did not come until *after* the defeat of the Government of Ireland Bill, when, using the secret service money as part of the finance, Gladstone, as we shall see, encouraged a series of publications.[7] Neat though was the paradox of

---

[1] To Chamberlain and Trevelyan, 15, 27 Mar. 86; to Heneage, 9 Apr. 86; to Lord Morley, 10 Apr. 86; to Sydney, 17 Apr. 86.

[2] 18, 22, 23, 26 Mar. 86.

[3] See to Knowles, 5 Aug. 85.

[4] See 1 Nov., 31 Dec. 85.

[5] See 6 Oct., 8 and 26 Dec. 85.

[6] See, e.g. *The Christian Million*, 7 January 1886, 172.

[7] To Bryce, 17, 26 July 86; an idea anticipated in a small way in April (see to Carmichael, 27 Apr. 86).

the secret service money funding liberal rationalism, it was a classic case of bolting the stable door with the horse already gone. The Liberal Party faced Home Rule with remarkably few intellectual points of reference. 'The people do not *know* the case'; this was an appalling admission (in July 1886) for the leading exponent of government by argument to have to make.[1]

Even before the exhausting work of forming the ministry was completed, Gladstone withdrew to Mentmore, Rosebery's vast house, and 'worked for some hours in drawing my ideas on Ireland into the form of a plan'.[2] Thus at the earliest moment, Gladstone as Prime Minister began his work on the 'definitive settlement' of Ireland, and the diary shows him working daily on Ireland through February and early March 1886, particularly assisted by Welby and Hamilton of the Treasury and Sir Robert Hamilton, the Permanent Under-Secretary at Dublin Castle, who had urged on Carnarvon the need for Home Rule.

During this period, the Cabinet was in as much difficulty over finance as it had been at the same time in 1885, Gladstone placing Harcourt in the embarrassing position of having Childers brought in to supervise his work at the Exchequer on the army and navy estimates.[3] Time for the preparation of the Irish bills was gained by introducing the Crofters Bill, which also had the advantage of working the Liberal M.P.s together on a 'Celtic fringe' question. Gladstone had been initially as cautious about the bold recommendations of the Napier report in 1884 on the condition of crofters and cottars in the Highlands and Islands as he had been about those of the Bessborough report in 1881 on Irish land.[4] In 1884–5 he had worked hard on Harcourt, then Home Secretary, to limit the terms of the Crofters Bill which followed from the Napier report. But having established that the bill would apply to the Highlands and Islands only and would have no general implications, Gladstone showed himself a powerful historicist. Initially, his solution had been 'compensation for disturbance' on the model of the 1870 Irish Land Act, that is a solution generally applicable to any case of social tension caused by land.[5] By 1885 he was arguing in a classically historicist way:

> no one intends to change at this moment the Land Law in general for the sake of the Crofter parishes ... the new law should take effect in Parishes where it should have been proved to the satisfaction of some proper judicial authority ... that within the last hundred years the hill lands of the parish ... had been held and used in common pasturage? For it is, after all, this historical fact that constitutes the Crofters' title to demand the interference of Parliament. It is not because they are poor, or because there are too many of them, or because they want more land to support their families; but because those whom they represent had rights of which they have been surreptitiously deprived to the injury of the community.[6]

[1] To Bryce, 8 July 86.   [2] 8 Feb. 86.

[3] 15, 22 Feb. 86 and to Harcourt, 16, 19, 20 Feb. 86 and to Childers, 20 Feb. 86; Harcourt's was thus the first 'resignation' letter of the third government (see 19 Feb. 86n.).

[4] To W. H. Gladstone, 14 Sept. 84.

[5] Ibid. The 1885 bill was effectively lost by the govt.'s resignation.

[6] To Harcourt, 19 Jan. 85. This was despite critical comments on Blackie's strongly historicist *The Scottish Highlanders and the land laws* (1885); see 26 Dec. 84 and to Harcourt, 15 Jan. 85. See also C. Dewey, 'Celtic agrarian legislation and the Celtic Revival: historicist implications of Gladstone's Irish and Scottish Land Acts 1870–1886', *Past and Present* (1974). For the 1886 bill, see to Trevelyan, 12 Mar. 86.

The Crofters Bill thus went further than either of Gladstone's Irish Land Acts in an explicit acceptance of historicist criteria. It squeezed through in June 1886, just before the dissolution.

On 13 March, the land purchase part of the Irish settlement plan was explained to the Cabinet. Members of the Cabinet, particularly Chamberlain and Kimberley, then 'opened the subject of Home Rule', that is, were reluctant to discuss the land purchase proposals without knowledge of the political settlement of which land purchase was the corollary.

Gladstone consequently 'stated his view that there be an Irish authority one & legislative'.[1] Next day he prepared a circular stating that in view of the 'closeness of the connections between the two subjects of Irish Land and Irish Government, which the Cabinet have justly felt', he would press forward 'the drawing into a Bill of the first option [i.e. land purchase]' while at the same time endeavouring 'to set into better shape materials which I have prepared on the subject of Irish Government' (presumably the notes on an Irish legislature prepared on 14 November 1885 and subsequent memoranda) so that the Cabinet would then 'have the whole matter in view at once'.[2]

Let us turn then to what Gladstone regarded as the constituent elements of 'the whole matter'. These were, he told the public on seeking re-election for Midlothian, 'social order, the settlement of the land question, and a widely prevalent desire for self-government'.[3] The problem of social order was to be solved by the resolution of the other two issues.

Gladstone had been consistently cautious about land purchase, but, from disestablishment in 1869 onwards, he had never excluded it. The idea of a peasant proprietary, especially favoured by Bright, had run as a quiet counterpoint to the dominant theme in 1870 and 1881 of tenants' security. From 1882, Gladstone had begun to accept the future primacy of purchase, but he strongly disliked the expensive form of the Conservatives' Ashbourne Act of 1885. None the less, he saw land purchase, from the start of serious consideration of Home Rule in 1885, as an essential element of a settlement, but only within the context of a general settlement.[4] There were two reasons for this: the strategic argument that an orderly Ireland now could not be so without a considerable degree of peasant proprietary, and the tactical argument that without the opportunity for escape which land purchase gave to the landlord class, the bill would have no chance of passing.

Both reasons presupposed that a political settlement was not achievable without a large measure of social engineering—the British solution to the settler problem from the West Indies in the 1830s to the Kenyan highlands in the 1960s. The euthanasia of the landlord through his transfiguration into a rentier was the price paid for decolonization by governments across the political spectrum, but it was not a price Chamberlain was willing to pay in 1886. Though

---

[1] 13 Mar. 86.

[2] 14 Mar. 86; Granville and Spencer advised against disclosing 'our whole plan' to Chamberlain in this circular, but the version finally sent was more assertive ('I cannot see my own way to any satisfactory measure except . . . a Statutory Legislative Chamber in Dublin'; ibid.).

[3] To de Vesci, 12 Feb. 86 with extracts.

[4] The land settlement was at first referred to in the context of the 'protection of the minority'; it is explicitly referred to as 'Land Purchase' in the mem. at 23 Dec. 85, though with reluctance.

largely forgotten as an aspect of the legislation proposed in 1886,[1] land purchase preparation took up much more time than the political settlement. The Land Puchase Bill was to have been the third of Gladstone's Irish Land Acts, but, in distinction to the others, it was integrally linked to a political settlement.

Unlike the first two Land Acts, which had sought to alter legal relationships, it was based on the employment of the credit of the British state. Gladstone told his Chancellor of the Exchequer:

I am the last to desire any unnecessary extension of demands on our financial strength. But I am morally certain that it is only by exerting *to the uttermost* our financial strength (not mainly by expenditure but as credit) on behalf of Ireland, that we can hope to sustain the burden of an adequate Land measure; while, without an adequate Land measure, we cannot either establish social order, or face the question of Irish Government.[2]

The detail of such a scheme was extremely complex, and it therefore took priority of preparation: 'I have framed a plan for the land and for the finance of what must be a very large transaction. It is necessary to see our way a little in these at the outset, for, unless these portions of any thing we attempt are sound and well constructed, we cannot hope to succeed.'[3]

The precedent was the buying out of the black apprentices from their owners in the West Indies in the 1830s,[4] the settlement in which Gladstone had effectively been the spokesman for the owners in their negotiations with the Whig government. The precedent, with its implication that some Irish landlords were little better than slave-owners, was a nice reply to Salisbury's much more explicit implication that the Irish were like Hottentots.[5] The land purchase scheme, unlike the West Indies settlement, was to be voluntary, that is, landowners did not have to sell unless they wished to. Gladstone personally still hoped landowners would stay on in Ireland. He recognized that 'there is something most grave in the idea of bringing about a wholesale emigration of the resident proprietors and depriving society of those who should be its natural heads and leaders'.[6] But the 'object of this bill is to give all Irish landowners the option of being bought out'.[7] The bill was thus a cushion for a nervous class, in England as well as in Ireland. The Irish would have to pay a double price. First, to ensure the escape of landowners unwilling to live with an Irish legislature, the tenants of a landowner wishing to sell would be compelled to buy (with the exception of very small tenants). Second, the security of the Imperial loan would be that all the 'rents and other Irish revenues whatsoever' must go in the first instance to a Receiver General under British authority, though he would not be responsible for levying or assessing.

This raised two obvious difficulties: first, the whole point of the agrarian crisis in Ireland was that many tenants could not pay their rents; second, that,

[1] See Loughlin, op. cit., ch. 3.   [2] To Harcourt, 12 Feb. 86.
[3] To H. N. Gladstone, 12 Feb. 86.   [4] *Speeches on the Irish question 1886*, 76: 16 April 1886.
[5] The precedent was to the fore in both the 1881 and 1886 land bills, in 1886 for its financial dimension, in 1881 as an interference in contract; in the 1881 instance Gladstone was more careful than in 1886 to deny the correlation of Irish landowners and the slave owners; *H* 290. 893–4 (7 April 1881).
[6] 23 Dec. 85.   [7] *Speeches on the Irish question 1886*, 101.

even if the rents were paid, Gladstone calculated privately, 'for a time, seventy or 60%, in round numbers, of the gross revenues & (public) rents of Ireland may be due to us', chiefly in the form of payments through the Receiver General on the credit advanced for land purchase.[1] The political tensions in such a situation were obvious, and widely expressed.[2] Gladstone's reply was that 'a measure quite out of the common way' necessitated this, and, less moralistically, that the Irish would be anxious to build up a credit market of their own. In the circumstances of world financial markets, this would effectively mean raising money in London. Thus 'Ireland, towards us, must be Caesar's wife',[3] that is, her reputation for credit-worthiness must be above suspicion.

Because the scheme was voluntary, it was difficult to cost. The first settled estimate was that an issue of £120 millions of three per cent stock would be needed for purchase to be available until 1890. Faced with the objection of Chamberlain and others that this was an 'enormous and unprecedented use of British credit',[4] Gladstone reduced this to £60 millions on 20 March and to £50 millions in the Bill, while privately noting, for a meeting with his Irish ministers and Harcourt as Chancellor, that the reasons for this were presentational, and that, if the Act worked well, Parliament could enlarge the sum,[5] a point made publicly though briefly by Gladstone in his speech introducing the Bill.[6] Privately, Gladstone continued to anticipate '2 or 3 years hence, another 50 may be required' (was his shorthand sign for million).[7]

There was a curious ambivalence about the land purchase proposal, reflected in the fact that it was strongly pressed on Gladstone by both Spencer and Parnell. In one sense it sought to allay the fears of the propertied classes in Ireland and in the United Kingdom. But its financing alarmed the monied as much as its social objective pacified the landowners. In another sense, it sought to respond to the Irish National League's call for a peasant proprietary to ease the question of social order in Ireland for the Home-Rule dispensation.[8] Yet it expected a high level of economic performance and political steadfastness from these peasants. The large tenant farmers would no doubt respond to calls for the need for Irish creditworthiness but the small tenant turned peasant proprietor might well have more immediate and personal criteria. In both cases, Gladstone probably underestimated the cross-currents within classes and probably overestimated the integrative effect of his two huge bills.

For Gladstone, it is clear that it was the first of these—the convenience of the landowners to go or to stay—that was foremost: 'the great object of the measure

[1] To Morley, 19 Apr. 86.

[2] Loughlin, op. cit., 85ff.

[3] To Morley, 19 Apr. 86 and *Speeches on the Irish question 1886*, 104. This is a defence of some force, which Dr. Loughlin does not address.

[4] Chamberlain's letter, 15 March 1886, Garvin, ii. 187.

[5] 20 Mar. 86.

[6] *Speeches on the Irish question 1886*, 101.

[7] To J. Morley, 19 Apr. 86.

[8] Rhetorically, Gladstone tried to square his circle by calling as his chief witness J. A. Froude, a man by this time notoriously hostile to him and particularly to his Irish policy; see *H* 304. 1782ff. and 25 Mar. 86. It should be noted that Gladstone's re-reading of Froude occurred well after the main decisions on the Land Bill of 1886 had been taken.

is not to dispose of the entire subject of Irish land, but to afford to the Irish land-lord refuge and defence from a possible mode of government in Ireland which he regards as fatal to him'.[1] The land bill was regarded by some, Gladstone noted after the election in *The Irish Question*, as a 'gigantic bribe' to the land-owners and he did not disavow this. The bill was a 'daring attempt we made to carry to the very uttermost our service to the men whom we knew to be as a class the bitterest and most implacable of our political adversaries'.[2]

Certainly the sums involved were large, but they need to be kept in per-spective, and they were very much less than would have been the case if the Ashbourne Act of 1885 had been expanded and used as the mechanism for the 1886 proposal.[3] If we presuppose the maximum, that the measure had been very popular with the tenants and the £50 millions had to be extended to £120 millions over the period 1886–90, the issue of stock would have meant an increase of about 4.5 per cent in the national debt in each of its four years (1.9 per cent if the £50 millions in the Bill were not increased). The interest on the money advanced for land puchase was to be the first charge to be paid out of the receipts to the Irish Receiver General, and would thus cost the British tax-payer virtually nothing. Even if those receipts were zero, that is, even if the Irish legislature completely reneged on all its financial obligations under the Land Purchase Bill and was permitted to do so by the Imperial government and par-liament—an extremely improbable outcome—the increment to the British budget would be about 4.0 per cent (1.7 per cent if the £50 millions was not increased). The export of British capital was reaching its height in the later 1880s, with interest rates remaining low and the price of Consols rising. It could hardly be argued that the stock to finance the land purchase scheme would have been difficult to issue, expensive, or prejudicial to the British economy. Indeed, by retaining the capital within the United Kingdom's economy, albeit for a rather unproductive purpose, it could have been beneficial both in itself and as a precedent.

This guarantee for the propertied class in Ireland was incorporated into the Government of Ireland Bill.[4] Similarly, the Land Purchase Bill could not become an Act without the passing of the Government of Ireland Bill.[5] There was, therefore, a 'Siamese twinship' of the bills, as Gladstone put it. It may well be that the greatest tactical error of 1886 was not to include both purchase and government in a single bill. This was Lloyd George's successful solution in 1911 to outflanking the various opponents of unemployment and health insurance. Certainly the political formula for mutual self-contradiction was there: the land-owning classes disliked Home Rule: many Home Rulers in England, Wales and Scotland, disliked land purchase.

At first, work on land and on the 'Irish Authority' proceeded *pari passu*, papers on them being circulated to some Cabinet members as 'different

[1] Paper for cabinet, 10 March 1886, Add MS 44632, f. 165.
[2] *The Irish question*, 44.
[3] See to Carmichael, 23 Apr. 86.
[4] Clause 12.3.
[5] Clause 35; see also to Thring (who drafted both bills), 2 Apr. 86 and n. Thring advised making the division between land and government starker than hitherto expected by confining land to the land bill, but with the 'proviso' linking clause. See also Loughlin, op. cit., 80–4.

Chapters'.[1] Early in March, partly for manageability and partly for tactical reasons, separate bills were envisaged.[2] But considerable movement of content between the bills seems to have existed up to almost the last moment in early April.[3] 'The question of precedence between the two plans seems to be one of policy', Gladstone told Spencer.[4]

The need to lead with Home Rule was the need to set the Liberal Party behind it, Gladstone never having much doubt that the landowners would swallow the land purchase bribe. But to alarm the Liberals with land purchase first, when they were already uncertain about Home Rule—anxieties confirmed by the resignations of Chamberlain and Trevelyan—would be obviously foolish. Delaying land until after Home Rule also to some extent silenced Chamberlain, who knew most of the details of the land purchase proposals but was not allowed to mention them until the bill was introduced, whereas he had left the Cabinet before the Home Rule details were disclosed.[5]

The second 'Chapter' or 'plan', but the first to be introduced to parliament, was the Government of Ireland Bill. Sketched earlier, but finalized later than land purchase, the Irish Government Bill was less problematic than land. Initially, it was, like Gladstone's great budgets, almost literally sketched on the back of an envelope.[6] The relative simplicity of Victorian central government and the bold decisiveness of the Victorian statesman made this possible. Though land purchase was unavoidable, it was the Irish Government Bill which was essential. The object of the bill was 'social order',[7] and it was thus the culmination of that series of constitutional measures proposed by Gladstone to solve the Irish question. His mission was still to pacify Ireland, not to liberate it.

In this sense, the bill was a great metropolitan, imperial measure. Pacification meant social, political, and civil order, and consequently, as with Canada, imperial security. Gladstone's experience had eventually taught him that only through liberation could pacification be achieved, but the latter remained the objective. Hence there was no recognition of Irish nationalism in any absolute sense, but only in so far as the Irish were perceived as a distinct but component part of the United Kingdom. Nothing could be done for Ireland that could not also be done for Scotland: this was one of the earliest tests devised by Gladstone for any political settlement. That was why, when returning from his convalescent cruise to Norway early in September 1885, he was 'embarrassed' to find Parnell claiming the Scots had lost their nationality.[8] This view of Irish nationality as, at bottom, centrifugal rather than centripetal, or as at least

---

[1] To Spencer, 20, 24 Feb. 86.

[2] 5 Mar. 86 and Loughlin, op. cit., 83–4.

[3] To Thring, 2 Apr. 86 and n.

[4] To Spencer, 18 Mar. 86.

[5] See to Chamberlain, 4, 11 Apr. 86. The text below for February to April 1886 certainly supports Loughlin's view, op. cit., 80ff., that throughout this period Gladstone saw Irish government and land purchase as linked and with a combined priority. For a different view, see J. Vincent, 'Gladstone and Ireland', *Proc. Brit. Acad.*, lxiii. 226 (1977), and *G.P.*, 52, 55; but the 'Diary' in Part 3 of *G.P.* (especially 377ff.) gives a very useful narrative of these events.

[6] 14 Nov. 85; one side of a small sheet of Dalmeny Park writing paper.

[7] See the opening of his speech introducing the bill on 8 April; *Speeches on the Irish question 1886*, 1.

[8] 2 Sept. 85.

neutral as between those forces, was fundamental to the central concept of the bill.

The Government of Ireland Bill set out to devolve the authority of the Westminster parliament to what in the first instance was called 'An Irish Chamber for Irish affairs', then an 'Irish Authority', then 'a Legislative Chamber or Parliament',[1] then, in the bill, 'a Legislative Body'. Much was in a name, because it mirrored the conceptual difficulty. The British constitution—a series of acts historically cumulative recognizing conquests and bargains, ancient pre-parliamentary Crown powers balanced by the common law, vital institutions such as the Cabinet and political parties unmentioned in law—worked by convention. Attempts at codification had always been resisted. Thus its only abstract definition was likely to be of the sort that Dicey advanced in his *Law of the Constitution*. Any attempt at devolution was therefore bound to be a messy business, for it was very hard to devise an intellectually systematic plan when the constitution whose powers were to be devolved was not systematically stated in law.

Gladstone's solution raised all the problems which still face devolution a hundred years later. There were two possible models, once the idea of a 'co-ordinate Legislature' (i.e. a return to a separate Irish parliament) had been set aside—and this possibility never seems to have been seriously canvassed in 1885–6. Gladstone examined the Norway/Sweden parallel legislatures during his cruise in August 1885, but those, and the rather similar dual monarchy in the despised Hapsburg Empire, were merely used as an end of a spectrum which highlighted the Irish Government Bill's moderation.

The real models were the Canadian[2] and the federal.[3] The Canadian was clearly dominant. Intellectually, it had the merit of simplicity and precedence. Gladstone's first paper for the Cabinet on Irish government followed it in devolving to the Irish Body legislative powers, except in certain reserved areas, most importantly, defence, foreign and colonial relations, and trade and navigation to the extent of preventing protectionist duties (a characteristic touch, recalling Gladstone's irritation at Canadian and Australian protectionism)[4] but not non-protective indirect taxes. This at once highlighted the difficulty. Ireland was to remain part of the United Kingdom fiscal system, her defence was to be integrated, and she was to pay an annual sum. Thus Canada was the precedent at first glance, but not in the details.

The alternative, federal solution, was hinted at in 1886 in Gladstone's criterion that nothing be done for Ireland that could not be done for Scotland. But it was no more than hinted at, for there was no basis of support for federalism in England, and very little in Scotland, where the cry, led by Rosebery, was, until the Government of Ireland Bill, for administrative not legislative devolution.[5]

---

[1] 14 Nov. 85; to Spencer, 24 Feb. 86; paper of 20 March 1886, below, xi, Appendix II.

[2] Used in the sense of power devolved from the Westminster parliament to another legislature; the constitution devolved to Canada was, of course, federal in form in the way that it worked in Canada, but this is irrelevant to the concept of devolution from Westminster.

[3] For a useful analysis of these, and of the developing internal inconsistencies of the 1886 bill, see V. Bogdanor, *Devolution* (1979), ch. 2.

[4] See Matthew, *Gladstone*, 189.

[5] For the practical problems inherent in the intellectually more rigorous federal solution, see Bogdanor, op. cit., 35ff.

Wales, Gladstone simply ignored. The Government of Ireland Bill, if passed unamended, would in fact have made a subsequent federal solution very awkward, since it proposed there be no Irish M.P.s at Westminster. Such a provision would also have made subsequent Scottish devolution on the Irish precedent almost impossible, because the two devolutions would have had the effect of leaving an 'Imperial Parliament' composed of English and Welsh M.P.s only.

What was offered, therefore, was a diluted version of the Canadian precedent, designed for the peculiarities of the Irish case. The dilution strapped the Irish firmly to the United Kingdom, as did the complex composition of the Legislative Body. Gladstone seems at first to have thought of simply constituting it from the 103 Irish M.P.s plus another 103 elected by the same constituencies.[1] But this was thought too simple with respect to minorities and too open to control by a 'single influence'.[2] So it was to include two 'Orders' normally debating and voting together, but with each able to call for a separate vote, thus giving each 'Order' a veto (though only for a limited time). The 'First Order' would be made up of twenty-eight Irish Peers (Gladstone hoped that most of the Irish Representative Peers at Westminster would sit) plus seventy-five members elected for a ten year term on a £25 occupier franchise, with candidates having to be men of substantial property. The 'Second Order' was to consist of 202 county and borough members, 101 of whom would in the first instance be the existing Irish M.P.s (plus two seats for Dublin University and provision for two for the Royal University). These would stand for election at least every five years. From the two 'Orders' an executive would gradually emerge *via* Privy Councillors as the Viceroy became like the Canadian Governor-General. The narrow franchise and slow turn-over of the 'First Order', and the provision for a veto for each 'Order', made this body powerfully conservative in constitution. Though allowing the unpromising parallel with the States General in 1789, Gladstone did not think there would be a deadlock through the First Order being simply Home Rulers and the Second, simply Tories.[3]

As Gladstone had anticipated from the moment he received Parnell's 'proposed Constitution for Ireland',[4] it was the financial arrangements that posed the chief difficulty between the Government and the Home Rule M.P.s. Under pressure from the Cabinet, which thought the Irish would pay too little, and from Parnell who thought they would pay too much, Gladstone began negotiating. The negotiations revolved round the financial settlement, but also raised the question of the future place of the Irish M.P.s. The bargain was this: all customs and excise duties would be managed by Westminster, and the Irish would only have to pay one-fifteenth of Imperial costs rather than one-fourteenth as hitherto envisaged (or one-thirteenth in the first Cabinet paper).[5] So keen to

[1] See mem. at 28 Dec. 85; this explains the pasage introducing the 'Legislative Body' in his speech on 8 April 1886 (*Speeches on the Irish question, 1886*, 32); but his mem. of 28 Dec. 86 may also imply a second chamber.
[2] *Speeches on the Irish question, 1886*, 32; see ibid. and pp. 317–19 for the following details.
[3] To Morley, 22 Mar. 86.
[4] See the first draft (not sent) of reply to Mrs. O'Shea, 3 Nov. 85.
[5] See below, vol. xi, Appendix II; initially (see mem. at 28 Dec. 85) Gladstone had considered the much larger proportion of $\frac{1}{9}$.

gain this reduction was Parnell that he agreed to Westminster control of indirect taxation without Irish M.P.s in the Commons, that is, he agreed to taxation without representation.[1]

Though the size of the Irish contribution was calculated during the discussions as a proportion and is commonly discussed as such by historians, in the bill it was expressed as a fixed sum of money, unalterable (except downwards) for thirty years. This showed a touching faith in the stability of money values not uncharacteristic of the Victorians, though Gladstone knew well enough how inflation had after 1832 eroded the excluding force of the £10 criterion for the householder vote. In the 1880s the value of gold rose and the Irish would thus have paid rather more than they had expected, but from the later 1890s deflation turned to inflation and thus the Irish in the later part of the thirty years would have had an extraordinary bargain, even supposing British defence costs remained constant. That the Treasury, in the person of Harcourt, should have agreed to a money rather than a proportionately expressed contribution is perhaps the most remarkable of all the Cabinet's concessions to Gladstone. For it reflected a view of the minimalism of the British fiscal state which Gladstone wished was true, but which the experience of recent decades of British finance overall hardly warranted.

Gladstone's argument was that though overall central government expenditure had risen (£71.8 millions in 1868, £92.2 millions in 1886), on the two chief items of the Irish contribution—the national debt and defence—costs had not risen much over the previous fifteen years. Gladstone required the Irish to be provident in domestic government costs in a way that the British were failing to be and in which he thought the Irish administrations of the past had been particularly profligate. It would also be the case that if Home Rule was successful in ending Irish disorder, the traditionally high expenditure on the Irish police would fall. In requiring Home Rule Ireland to be, like Britain, both low-spending and non-protectionist, Gladstone was discounting the peculiar character of the Irish economy vis-à-vis the British, exactly that factor which had been one of the chief stimulants to the Irish sense of distinctiveness.

But if we look at the way the settlement would have worked over its first thirty years, we shall see a spectacular boon to the Irish. On the debt charges, they would have been entitled to a small rebate, as provided by the bill (debt charges falling from £23.5 millions in 1886 to £20.8 millions in 1910). But on defence, the Irish contribution would have fallen from one-fifteenth to one-thirtyfourth by 1910.[2] Overall—the exact figures are uncertain because of definitions of Imperial civil charges—the Irish contribution, because it was expressed in fixed money terms, would by 1910 have fallen from one-fifteenth to about one-twentyfifth. The financial clauses of the 1886 Bill are sometimes seen as a source of subsequent friction because of Irish difficulty in paying the

---

[1] 1-6 Apr. 86.
[2] The bill provided for a rebate if United Kingdom expenditure fell, but expressly forbade an increase, except in time of war 'for the prosecution of the war and defence of the realm'. By excluding 'what strictly ought to be called war charges', i.e. votes of credit for imperial campaigns of the sort the Parnellites usually opposed, the bill avoided a potentially very serious irritant; British imperialism was to be financed from British taxation; *Speeches on the Irish question 1886*, 43.

contribution. More likely, had the Bill become an Act, would have been a British demand for an amendment to the 'thirty year rule'. It would have been a further irony of Irish history if 1916 (the year for review) had in fact been the occasion of a desperate attempt by an Irish Legislative Body to preserve the financial bargain struck in 1886. Unsatisfactory to Britain though Gladstone's settlement would have been in its financial terms, they could have turned out to be the most powerful of all reasons for Irish enthusiasm against separation and for the settlement. It is obvious that the financial settlement would not have been definitive, but it is unlikely it would have produced more than the sort of second-order revisions with which we have been familiar in the European Economic Community since 1972.

The inclusion or exclusion of the M.P.s of the devolved area has been a central point of controversy in all attempts at devolution in Britain. In his 'proposed Constitution', Parnell was unemphatic: the Irish M.P.s 'might be retained or might be given up'; if retained, the Speaker could rule on what were the Imperial questions in which they should take part.[1] Gladstone's sketch of 14 November 1885 kept them in, 'question to be decided by the House or the Speaker', with a 'Schedule' of Imperial questions as a guide, and Irish M.P.s to be involved in votes on 'Ministerial responsibility which touch the reserved subjects only'.[2] This was a position difficult to sustain, for such votes also affected the continuance or fall of the ministry, with many implications for non-Irish affairs. By the time of the introduction of the Government of Ireland Bill, and as a result of pressure especially from John Morley, the Irish Secretary, the Irish M.P.s were to be out altogether, a provision widely felt to encourage subsequent separatism.

This uncertainty on such a central question reflected the English stranglehold on the United Kingdom constitution. The English would not alter the Imperial parliament, because it was their domestic parliament also: the Acts of Union of 1707 and 1800 had simply brought Scottish and Irish M.P.s to Westminster. But the unitary parliament offered non-unitary legislation, thus maintaining legal as well as sentimental nationalism within the United Kingdom. When such nationalism wished to regain, short of repeal of the Union, some control of the legislation lost, effectively to England, by the Act of Union, then the absence of a genuinely Imperial Parliament, to which all such areas (including England) could relate was bound to produce an intellectually untidy result with respect to the constitution of the Parliament at Westminster. Such untidy results could of course be lived with: from 1920 to 1972 there was a devolved parliament in Ulster with Ulster M.P.s at Westminster. Probably the solution envisaged by both Parnell and Gladstone in November 1885—a Speaker's ruling on Irish inclusion—offered the characteristically British way out, as it did to the question of finance bills and the House of Lords a generation later.

The Irish settlement proposed in 1886 would have required tolerance on both sides for it to work: 'the determining condition will I think be found to be the temper in which men approach the question'.[3] Gladstone's calculation was

---

[1] O'Shea, *Parnell*, ii. 20.
[2] 14 Nov. 85. See also to Selborne, 30 Jan. 86, to J. Morley, 2 Feb. 86.
[3] To R. W. Dale, 29 Apr. 86.

that the Home Rule party which would take power in Ireland would act as men of 'common sense', anxious to gain credit in the financial markets, and with no reason to distance themselves further from the United Kingdom. Indeed, the opposite would be the case: 'Home Rule is ... a source not of danger but of strength—the danger, if any, lies in refusing it.'[1] The Dissentient Liberals were the real 'Separatists'.[2] Gladstone's 'work and purpose' was, he said, 'in the highest sense Conservative'.[3] The proposed settlement of 1886 thus fitted exactly into the approach to Ireland pursued since 1868 even, perhaps, since the *bouleversement* on Maynooth in 1845. It was the boldest of all possible attempts to save Ireland for constitutionalism and from Fenianism.

Gladstone had, since the autumn of 1885, recognized the likelihood of failure in the Commons. Characteristically, he had not done much to prevent it. As in 1866, during the Reform Bill *débâcle*, there was an off-hand, 'take-it-or-leave-it' quality about his approach, which relied largely on public rhetoric for its success. Even press contacts, so assiduously nurtured in 1866, were not exploited. The Liberal Party, perceived from the start as the weak link, was only reluctantly courted. Gladstone tried to use the Irish government and land purchase bills as measures so large and so important that, like the Lords, the Liberal Party 'would not dare'. Proposed legislation could, perhaps would, integrate in a way that generalized resolutions could not do.[4]

It was clear that the Liberal Party was at best only likely to be sufficiently integrated for a bare pass on second reading. Various possibilities were considered—the Irish M.P.s back in, the financial settlement rearranged[5]—but Gladstone refused any basic change either in the bill or in the parliamentary strategy. When he spoke on the Second Reading of the Government of Ireland Bill, he felt 'the reception decidedly inferior to that of the Introduction'. Next day, 'Prospects much clouded for 2 R'.[6] In the face of this, he agreed to tell the party that if the bill was given a second reading, it would be withdrawn, the clauses on Irish representation reconstructed (largely in fact in line with Gladstone's original plan of November 1885), and the bill reintroduced at an autumn Session.[7] On 31 May there was 'great dismay in our camp on the report of Chamberlain's meeting', i.e. the decision, on Bright's lead, to vote against the second reading of the bill rather than abstain.[8]

Barring a spectacular last-minute shift of opinion among Liberal M.P.s, defeat was probable. But Gladstone, whatever situation he found himself in politically, always believed he could win. Never was there a less pessimistic political

[1] Public letter to *Daily Chronicle*, 24 Apr. 86.

[2] To Argyll, 20 Apr. 86; 'Separatist' is here used punningly, the dissentient liberals being separatists from their party and also promoting Irish separation by opposing Home Rule.

[3] To Tennyson, 26 Apr. 86.

[4] The suggestion of proceeding by resolution, considered in December 1885, fell away, to be revived by Pease when the bill was in serious danger (see to Pease, 15, 21 May 86). No comment by Gladstone on this switch has been found. The precedent of the 1868 Irish Church Resolutions, it is sometimes forgotten, was a precedent of resolutions moved in opposition; between July 1885 and Salisbury's resignation in January 1886 there was only the opportunity of the Queen's Speech, and by then Gladstone was committed to his tactic that only the government was in a position to judge.

[5] 5 May 86.   [6] 10, 11 May 86.

[7] 26, 27 May 86.   [8] 31 May 86.

tactician. Only an astonishingly bold, robust, and self-confident politician could have forced the pace the way Gladstone did between January and June 1886. What others saw as wilfulness was Gladstone's armour: the obverse of self-confidence was the absence of self-doubt.

The vote on the second reading was taken on 7 June 1886:

> Worked on Irish question & speech through the forenoon at Dollis [Hill] in quiet ... H. of C. 4–8½ and 9–2¼. We were heavily beaten on the 2d Reading, by 341 to 311. A scene of some excitement followed the declaration of the numbers: one or two Irishmen lost their balance. Upon the whole we have more ground to be satisfied with the progress made, than to be disappointed at the failure. But it is a serious mischief. Spoke very long: my poor voice came in a wonderful manner.

Gladstone presented his Government of Ireland Bill in words which still haunt Anglo-Irish relations:

> This, if I understand it, is one of those golden moments of our history; one of those opportunities which may come and may go, but which rarely return, or, if they return, return at long intervals, and under circumstances which no man can forecast.[1]

This was the second 'golden moment'; the first had been the start of the confirmation of constitutionalism through the release of Parnell in 1882.[2] Whether the settlement would have worked, of course we cannot know. As the Kilbrandon Royal Commission on the Constitution remarked in 1973, the 1920 Act was the only Home Rule bill 'that ever came into effect, and then in the one part of Ireland that had said it would fight rather than accept home rule. Northern Ireland, by one of history's choicest ironies, is the one place where liberal home rule ideas were ever put into practice—and by a solidly Unionist government. It can be truly said to have been given a constitution that it did not want and that was designed for another place.'[3]

The Irish settlement of 1886 was forged, as were all the great initiatives of Victorian Britain, by a politician working with the given circumstances of the moment. Like those other initiatives, it was not an *a priori*, systematic dispensation drafted, as a Utilitarian would have liked, by politically neutral experts, but a proposal hammered out in the heat of the political sun. It was not 'reform upon a system', in Lord John Russell's phrase, but reform within the conventions of British political behaviour. A majority of M.P.s felt Gladstone was trying to stretch those conventions too far and too quickly.[4]

Gladstone asserted the individual's capacity to change the political climate at a stroke with a dramatic innovation larger in scope than any of the other participants in political life had anticipated. In this he fulfilled just the sort of Liberal role which men such as Acton expected of him, while also satisfying his own criteria of continuity, development, and growth. He worked thoroughly within the British political tradition by advancing the view that the British constitution already contained all the necessary ingredients of a just political

[1] *Speeches on the Irish question 1886*, 165.
[2] 1 May 82.
[3] *Royal Commission on the Constitution* (1973), i. 376.
[4] For the view that M.P.s voted on the Government of Ireland Bill on the basis of policy (rather than class), see W. C. Lubenow, *Parliamentary politics and the home rule crisis* (1988), especially ch. 6.

society, needing only a little modification and assistance to achieve a new balance. Gladstone was never a Whig in a party political sense, close though his ties with leading Whigs were, but never was there conceived a more classically whiggish measure than Home Rule.

1884–6—the parliamentary reform settlement and the consequential Irish settlement—was the last great Victorian political initiative. It represented a belief in the primacy of constitutionalism, both as the chief activity of parliament and as the ultimate means of solution to questions of social, economic, and political order. The first part of the settlement passed with difficulty. The second was rejected on principle. The way was not, however, clear for a simple switch from the politics of constitutionalism to those of welfare, for the cause of the delay in 1884 (the House of Lords) and a cause of the promotion of the Irish settlement (the 85 home-rule M.P.s) were each by the experience of these years both emboldened and entrenched. It was to take Britain a generation to pass those two issues through her political digestion[1]—exactly that generation when a bold new form of the British State was, by the development of relative economic decline, most needed.

The delay was, from the viewpoint of the twentieth century, disastrous. The chief irony is that of all those involved in the crisis of 1884–6, Gladstone most dreaded the onset of the politics of welfare, that 'leaning of both parties to Socialism which I radically disapprove'.[2] Yet it was his failure, not his success, that delayed them. The settlement of Ireland in 1886, if achieved, would have both shown that the Lords 'did not dare', and would have cleared the way for the development of the Liberal Party as a party of positive social welfare. The defeat of the Irish settlement in 1886 meant that the political parties of Great Britain were tied into an extraordinary knot. The Unionist coalition, supposedly dedicated to the burial of Home Rule, had no greater political interest than that Home Rule should continue to be the leading question of the day. Nothing relieved the Unionists more than another Home Rule speech by Gladstone. The Liberals, dedicated to clearing the way, found themselves unable, save in 1905–10, again to form a government without the support of the Irish they wished to remove. Thus both British parties found themselves still sweating on the Irish treadmill, the Unionists fearing the disappearance of Home Rule, the Liberals toiling for a success whose achievement would mean their political eclipse. The gold of the moment of 1886 indeed turned to lead.

VIII

We have thus far looked at the high ground occupied by Gladstone in this period, a ground marked out by the 'special causes' which retained him in political life. His own view was that those special causes were external to himself, causes objectively given by the process of politics. Yet in the 1880s that process was so dominated by his own political personality and so shaped by his

[1] The metaphor is Gladstone's; he thought Ireland brought into political life 'what I may perhaps call constipation'; to McLaren, 22 Dec. 81.
[2] To Argyll, 30 Sept. 85; see also to Southesk, 27 Oct. 85 and to Acton, 11 Feb. 85.

distinctive style of rhetorical leadership that it is hard and probably unhistorical
to try to separate the personality and the process. Gladstone seems to have
underrated the extent to which the force of his political personality in itself
shaped those causes, and it is in that underestimation that we find the key to
what otherwise can seem like a disingenuous series of excuses for not keeping
his word about retiring.

We must be careful here: parliamentary and local government reform,
Ireland, a correct financial, imperial, and foreign policy, these would have been
obvious Liberal concerns in the 1880s even if Gladstone had died before the
1880 general election. Yet each of them as actually shaped by the British
government in the 1880s bears a distinct Gladstonian stamp. Though 'counter-
factuals' stimulate the historical imagination and are a natural consequence of
the advantage that hindsight gives the historian, they are particularly difficult to
apply to questions of political judgement: political leadership is the most
unquantifiable of phenomena. So the answer to the question, what form would
British handling of the Irish question in the 1880s have taken without Gladstone? can hardly rise above speculation. But equally tricky, then, is the distribution of blame. The historian can point to failure or inconsistency within the
terms and goals set by his or her subject. We have seen that there is such in
Gladstone's handling of Egypt and of Ireland, particularly in his estimations of
the parliamentary success of Home Rule. Yet complaint and blame over details
are not to much constructive purpose: the fascination of the period lies in the
understanding of a remarkable, and in some ways remarkably distant, liberal
mind and its consequential actions. The consequences can be assessed, but
there is not much point in expecting Gladstone to have been different from
what he was.

Gladstone's extended political career, though dedicated to 'special causes',
led also to his involvement as Prime Minister, as Leader of the Commons (and
as *de facto* Leader of the Liberal Party though the fiction of a mere temporary
hiatus was maintained) in a wide range of more ordinary activities. Even these,
partly because of Gladstone's involvement in them, sometimes took on extraordinary dimensions. Let us now look at these more routine aspects of his
Premierships in the 1880s.

As Prime Minister, Gladstone spent more time dealing with the Queen than
with any other person. Victoria was not a model Bagehotian constitutional
monarch; indeed she did not see her role in Bagehot's terms. The history of
Liberal governments in late Victorian Britain does not suggest the successful
evolution of a non-executive constitutional monarchy with its prerogative
powers in commission to the Cabinet. Victoria saw herself as an integral part of
the making of policy, with the right to instruct, to abuse, and to hector. She
corresponded about Liberal government policy and the content of the Queen's
Speech with Conservative opposition leaders (but not *vice versa*); she continued
to exclude certain Liberal M.P.s from Cabinet, and to object to lower-level
appointments on grounds of policy; she expected revenge for Majuba; she
opposed the Cabinet's withdrawal or reduction of British troops from Afghanistan and Egypt; she abused her ministers privately and, in the notorious episode
of the '*en clair* telegram', publicly over their handling of Sudanese policy; she

objected to Cabinet ministers' speeches; she opposed Home Rule; and she did all these in her official capacity as Queen and Empress.[1]

As in his first government, Gladstone shielded the Queen from the consequences of her actions.[2] As far as possible, her railings were kept from the Radical and even the Liberal members of the Cabinet. Gladstone and Granville, especially the former, bore the brunt of the royal onslaught with discretion and, on the whole, remarkable patience. Gladstone personally wrote to the Queen after each Cabinet and, as Leader of the House, each evening when the Commons was sitting, reporting its proceedings. These were routine letters, expected of any Prime Minister who was in the Commons (though Gladstone was the only such in Victoria's reign after 1878). But there were many extra letters to be written as replies to the Queen's frequent letters and telegrams, particularly at times of political crisis. Sometimes these amounted to six in a day.

Gladstone was painstaking about these replies, and about his handling of the Court generally. The conservative side of his political personality gave a high religious and constitutional role to monarchy. In his conception of hierarchy and order, the monarchy was a natural point of focus. Nor does he seem to have been hostile to the notion of the monarchy as a functioning part of the constitution.[3] His objection to Victoria's behaviour was to its tone, its omnipresence, and its partiality, not to its reasonable activity. He saw, probably correctly, Victoria's behaviour as *sui generis*, unlikely to be repeated. His friendship with the Prince of Wales, marked in these volumes by frequent meetings of an amiable sort, told him that the Crown would pass, eventually, to a much more liberal spirit, who had to be restrained from voting in the House of Lords for the Franchise Bill in 1884.[4]

---

[1] The Court tried to have it both ways, letting the Queen have her head when alive, but once dead not being ready to accept responsibility for her actions while at the same time trying to prevent some of these from being disclosed. There was little discernible attempt to moderate the Queen's partisan behaviour during her life-time. Between 1926 and 1932 there appeared G. E. Buckle's edition of the second and third series of the *Letters of Queen Victoria*, designed to show, in Buckle's words (themselves highlighting the ambivalence) that 'the approach of old age did not lessen her steady, day-by-day application to her duties as a Constitutional Monarch; while the maturity of her judgment and the wider range of her experience gave increased weight and authority to her *decisions*' (my italics). In *After Thirty Years* (1928) Herbert Gladstone tried, by disputing particular incidents, to contest what he saw as Buckle's 'definite scheme of attack on Mr. Gladstone'. The Gladstone family then decided rather shrewdly that the best way to correct the record and answer Buckle was simply to publish the Gladstone–Victoria correspondence. H. N. Gladstone commissioned Philip Guedalla to edit an extensive selection from it. When Guedalla in 1933 sent George V the proofs of his edition of *The Queen and Mr. Gladstone*—an edition prepared not under the scrutiny of Windsor Castle but from the Queen's letters to Gladstone (many of which were sent without copies being made) and Gladstone's copies of his letters to her—the Court was clearly alarmed to find just how immoderate her behaviour had been. Letters written in the authority of the Crown (including comments on South Africa and an attempt to exclude L. H. Courtney from appointment as colonial undersecretary) were proposed for excision (including some already printed in Buckle's *Letters of Queen Victoria*!). Clive Wigram, George V's secretary, concluded one letter: 'one feels that, as it were, she needs a little "protection from herself". I am sure you will know what I mean' (Wigram to Guedalla, 30 August 1933, Bodleian Library, Guedalla MSS Box 3).

[2] Whether the Queen was 'right' in some of her demands is irrelevant to the fact of their existence.

[3] See comments to Chamberlain, 2 July 83.

[4] Magnus, *Edward VII*, 182; for the Prince of Wales's liberalism, see 4 Mar. 82.

There was also a prudential consideration to Gladstone's reticence about the Queen's behaviour. The monarchy and the House of Lords stood together at the apex of the constitution, an extraordinary hierarchical *bloc* in an increasingly egalitarian political culture. Each knew that they might also fall together, or, at least, that each was unsustainable without the other. Any criticism of the monarchy within the Liberal Party instantly raised whiggish alarms, for as the Whigs felt increasingly threatened so their whiggery became less whiggish in the traditional sense,[1] more defensive and less cautious about the Court. Gladstone could in 1884 use this to advantage. His long memoranda to the Queen argued that the Lords' action in rejecting the Franchise Bill raised the question of 'organic change' in the constitution; that if the Liberal Party were forced to make that change a political objective it would, like all other major Liberal reforms, eventually be carried; that 'organic change of this kind in the House of Lords may strip and lay bare, and in laying bare may weaken, the foundations even of the Throne'.[2] But, for Gladstone, this was an unusual position of strength.

The Queen, in the end, rarely got her way, though she did sometimes (for example, in 1882 preventing Derby from becoming Secretary of State for India and Dilke from becoming Chancellor of the Duchy of Lancaster, thus affecting the Cabinet reshuffle generally). It would not be possible to argue that she imposed a royal imperial policy, much though she would like to have in 1880–5. But if her aim was to drive Gladstone from office by attrition, she had some success: 'Position relatively to the Queen' was high on his list of reasons for trying to leave.[3] More generally, she was undoubtedly successful in contributing to the creation of what was for Liberals an atmosphere of caution and restriction, with the telegram from Windsor, and the wearisome explanations it required, being the first consequence of the expression of many a political intention.

These telegrams, letters, and visits from Sir Henry Ponsonby, Victoria's secretary, could not be set aside. They related, and were known to relate, to a body of opinion of considerable importance, particularly in the army where royal obstruction supported what Gladstone called, in the context of the Wolseley peerage dispute, 'the great conspiracy against the nation, in respect both to change and to reforms, which lives and moves among the heads of the military class, and which enjoys in the House of Lords its chief arena for development and exercise',[4] a view interestingly echoed by Sir William Butler, one of the Wolseley 'ring' but a much more committed Liberal than his chief. Butler accounted for the Gordon imbroglio, in which he was involved, not only by emphasizing the extent of opposition to evacuation of the Sudan by 'the official world of Cairo—English and Egyptian', but also by distinguishing between the 'permanent' government of Britain which was conservative and entrenched in the army and the navy, and 'the passing Liberal Executive Administration' which was thus doomed to frustration.[5]

---

[1] Traditional whiggery had had something of a final fling in the opposition to the Royal Titles Bill in 1876.

[2] 19 Aug. 84; see also 25 Aug. 84.

[3] To Bright, 29 Sept. 81.   [4] To Hartington, 21 May 81.

[5] Sir W. F. Butler, *Charles George Gordon* (1889), 213–14.

Gladstone's championing of Wolseley's peerage—'a nasty pill for Her' he told Hamilton[1]—was a deliberate assault on this sort of royal obstruction. The Court view related also to opinion in parts of the foreign and colonial services, certainly in the Tory Party and in parts of the Liberal Party. The Court was by no means a negligible force in the development of the climate of imperial expansion which was, however reluctant in tone, such a central feature of the political culture of the governing class in the 1880s. Indeed, to some extent the Queen did the Whigs' work for them. She was able to disagree with the Prime Minister with a stridency and tenacity which in a Cabinet minister would have implied resignation.

'It is innocence itself' was Gladstone's comment on reading *More Leaves from the Journal of a Life in the Highlands*.[2] The innocence in this instance was his. The Queen's second book was an important stimulus to the public perception of her as a non-political person, interested chiefly in worthy rural pursuits.[3] It confirmed exactly that view of the monarchy which made Liberal protests against her political partisanship impossible unless they were to be part of a planned attempt at a reconstruction of the monarchy.

Gladstone's position was particularly awkward, for in shielding the Queen from the Liberals and Radicals in his Cabinet, he isolated himself from those who were on many issues his natural Cabinet allies against the Court. His discretion meant that there was no basis for public comment, and his discretion was necessary unless he was prepared to lead a crusade which would be immensely divisive for his party, which would play into the hands of the 'patriotic' lobby in the Conservative Party—always on the look-out for a closer identification of Crown, Church, and Party—and which would go against all his instincts. There was little Gladstone could do but write the letters and remain polite. It was a considerable strain. A characteristic entry is that for 30 November 1881: 'Off at 11¾ for Windsor. Received with much civility, & had a long audience: but I am always outside an iron ring: and without any desire, had I the power, to break it through.' The absence of such a desire on Gladstone's part no doubt made a bad situation worse, but the reason for the absence was a partisanship on the part of the monarch which by 1881 had on her part become instinctive. Very different was a meeting with the Queen's daughter and her husband, heir to the German throne: 'He was as always delightful: she talked abundant Liberalism of a deep-rooted kind.'[4]

Closely related to dealings with the Crown was Prime-Ministerial patronage. Despite the increasingly partisan character of the House of Lords, and Gladstone's perception of it as a major political problem, his creation of peers remained orthodox. That is to say, he accepted the usual criteria of land, wealth, and status, and appointed peers within those lines of guidance. Gladstone was quite aware of the increasing tendency of property and privilege to fuse with

---

[1] Bahlman, *Hamilton*, i. 112.   [2] 2 Feb. 84.

[3] See e.g. Max O'Rell [L. P. Blouett], *John Bull's Womankind* (n.d. [1884]), 113: 'In the second volume of the Queen's *Life in the Highlands* ... you will look in vain for the slightest allusion to politics; it is the journal of a country gentleman's wife, who takes but small interest in anything outside the family circle. It is the diary of a queen that gives her people but one subject of complaint, which is that they do not see enough of her.'

[4] 16 July 81.

Conservatism. In analysing the 'causes tending to help the Conservative party' he included 'the concentration of the higher and social influences . . . and their ready & immediate influence from day to day on the action of the legislature through the different forms of social organization used by the wealthy & leisure class'.[1] Of these forms, the peerage was obviously the political and institutional seal. Yet Gladstone, despite this analysis, made no attempt to break that seal. Indeed his approach, if anything, set it more firmly. He did not try to refurbish the peerage. Indeed, as his table, drawn up in 1892, shows, he was in the 1880s a good deal less lavish with his use of honours than Lord Salisbury, who fulsomely rewarded his supporters, especially during his minority government of 1885–6, with a shower of every sort of status promotion. Though the Liberals were in a clear minority in the Lords, considerably fewer Liberal peers (84) were created in the eleven years of Liberal governments between 1868 and 1892 than were Conservative peers (101) in the twelve years of Conservative rule between 1874 and 1892.

	Peers	Privy Councillors	Baronets	Knights[2]
Gladstone 1868–74	42	56	31	117
Disraeli 1874–80	37	56	32	82
Gladstone 1880–5	33	39	34	97
Salisbury 1885–6	14	25	16	24
Gladstone 1886	9	17	4	25
Salisbury 1886–92	50	54	63	193

Gladstone, always a stickler for form, was cautious in these matters and would not create peers except when a peerage was clearly deserved and strongly supported. Acton in 1869 was perhaps his only idiosyncratic creation. Even the eighty-four creations are a little misleading, for of the thirty-three peers created in 1880–5, twelve were promotions within the peerage and one was a royal duke. But there were, of course, restrictions of a less personal character. Since Gladstone accepted that the conventions were not to be set aside, there were by the mid-1880s fewer suitable Liberal candidates than Conservatives for these positions. It was difficult to find Liberals for the peerage who passed the usual tests and who would remain loyal Liberals, and whose children were likely to be loyal Liberals: there was no point in increasing the Tory peerage a generation into the future. It was the job of Godley and Hamilton to make discreet inquiries about such matters. Moreover, the dignity of the peerage and the absorption of the new Peer into a political culture suffused if not dominated by what was now on most issues an intensely partisan Court at Windsor, if not at Sandringham, encouraged conservatism in newly created Liberal peers. The Lords did not have to vote on the Government of Ireland Bill of 1886, but the split in the Liberal Party in that House was at least as serious as that in the Commons.

This failure to build a Liberal peerage was exemplified in an angry public

[1] 14 Aug. 82.
[2] Secretary's tables made in 1892, at Add MS 44775, f. 278.

exchange between Gladstone and Westminster, whom he had created a duke in 1874 and who campaigned energetically against the Liberal government in 1886.[1] The Duke of Westminster was not aberrant. Of the thirty-three peers created during the government of 1880–5, at least 20 were Unionists after 1886 (and four others were dead).[2] Of those 33, at most eight were active Liberals after 1886. Whereas for a Conservative a peerage was an additional bond with his party, for many a Liberal it was a solvent.

Two of Gladstone's creations in the 1880s rose above the usual routine of political worth, and both of them were his holiday companions on sea voyages to Scandinavia. Thomas Brassey, son of the railway magnate, and founder of the *Naval Annual* and a social commentator, took Gladstone on a cruise to Norway on his famous yacht, *Sunbeam*, in 1885.[3] In 1886, though he had not risen above the rank of parliamentary undersecretary, he was created baron, his wealth, increasingly deployed in land and leisure, enabling him to leap-frog most of his official colleagues.

The Brassey voyage, during which Gladstone wrote his manifesto for the 1885 election, was less dramatic than the Tennyson voyage two years earlier. In 1883 Tennyson was part of the company on the cruise to Norway on Donald Currie's *Pembroke Castle*.[4] Indeed Tennyson got Gladstone into a 'scrape' with the Queen, for it was at the former's request that the steamer made an unplanned visit to Copenhagen, pitching Gladstone, without permission from the Queen, into a huge gathering of Eastern European royalty. Angry rebukes from Windsor followed. In the course of the voyage, Tennyson raised the question of the baronetcy which he had previously declined, indicating that this time he would accept. Alerted to this by Arthur Gordon, Gladstone was agreeable. Gordon recorded

I then asked him whether he did not think he might go a step further and offer Mr. Tennyson a peerage. His first answer was characteristic: 'Ah! Could I be accessory to introducing *that hat* into the House of Lords?'[5]

Inquiries were made about Tennyson's financial position and as to whether he would vote in the Lords 'if an urgent question of state-policy required it'; the offer of a barony was formally made and accepted with protestations of reluctance.[6] Some delay of the announcement was felt suitable 'to dissociate the peerage from the trip'.[7] In a letter characteristically analysing the precedents, Gladstone arranged with the Treasury for Tennyson's patent fee, about £500,

[1] See 14 July 86. Westminster had been annoyed in 1881 at not being made volunteer *aide de camp* at Court; Rosebery noted: 'he has been made a Duke, a K.G., & Ld. Lieut & his brother patronage secretary for no service that I can make out except the one for leading the other for whipping the party that turned WEG out in 1866. The fact is that Westminster is a very good noble fellow, but a spoilt child' (Rosebery's diary, 28 June 1881).

[2] I am much obliged to Dr. Andrew Adonis for this information and for his comments on the peerage generally.

[3] See 8–29 Aug. 85.

[4] For the voyage, see 8–21 Sept. 83.

[5] *The Gladstone Papers* (1930), 80–1.

[6] See R. B. Martin, *Tennyson. The unquiet heart* (1980), 539ff.

[7] To Tennyson, 25 Sept. 83.

to be waived: 'I propose to let Tennyson off. Macaulay appears to have paid; but he was a confirmed bachelor & there was no succession.'[1] Gladstone discreetly forbore to mention that Macaulay had made so much money from his *History* that £500 was of no account, whereas Tennyson's profitable earnings—never very large—were in 1883 long in the past, a point on which Tennyson almost morbidly dwelt. Despite attempts to link Tennyson to Liberalism, he sat on the crossbenches and during the autumn session of 1884 issued his sonnet, 'Compromise', with its admonitory opening, 'Steersman, be not precipitate in thine act'—lines, Gladstone may have felt, better addressed to the House of Lords than to himself.

Gladstone had hoped to anticipate the peerage for Tennyson with a knighthood for Henry Irving, many of whose famous productions with Ellen Terry he attended. Objections to Irving's lack of respectability—his estrangement from his wife and his friendship for Terry—prevented this plan going forward.[2] Gladstone's view of these objections may be judged from his invitation to Irving, shortly after this episode, to visit Hawarden; unfortunately, the dates did not coincide, but they met instead at Knowsley.[3]

Gladstone also wished to reward the pre-Raphaelite artists, a school with which he had been associated since the 1850s, and with which additional links, particularly with Burne-Jones, were made by his daughter Mary. A crop of artists, their lack of respectability now sufficiently in the past to be ignored (Ellen Terry again being involved as Watts' divorced wife), was to be given baronetcies. This plan led to considerable rancour. Gladstone wanted to baronet G. F. Watts, who had painted him twice, the second time unsuccessfully,[4] J. E. Millais, whose second and best of three portraits was then in the process of being painted, and Frederic Leighton. Gladstone tentatively mentioned the three names, while feeling that the Queen 'would (*justly*) think the number too large'. She did. Leighton was dropped, to the Queen's irritation. So two baronetcies were offered, to Watts and Millais. Despite prior indication that he would accept, Watts declined. Leighton already knew of the offers to the other two and in such circumstances could not be offered the title which Watts had declined. Gladstone anyway had ceased to be Prime Minister and was thus 'out of court'. Robert Browning interceded on Leighton's behalf; Gladstone told Ponsonby of the muddle, and Leighton got a baronetcy in February 1886.[5]

Millais was delighted with his baronetcy, the more so, perhaps, as his behaviour towards Gladstone had been rather odd. The episode merits discussion. Gladstone's college, Christ Church, Oxford, wanted a portrait of its distinguished member. G. F. Watts and W. B. Richmond had in turn been commissioned to paint one and Gladstone had sat for each, the portraits being rejected in turn by the College. [6] Millais was commissioned in 1884, sittings began and a

[1] To Childers, 25 Sept. 83.
[2] Bahlman, *Hamilton*, ii. 450, 453 (June 1883).   [3] 2, 9 Oct. 83.
[4] See Introduction above, ix. xcii.   [5] See 24 June–2 July 85.
[6] See Introduction above, ix. xcii and Christ Church Governing Body Minutes, i. 298, 301; the commission to W. B. Richmond was confirmed at the G.B. meeting of 25 Jan. 1882 at which it was announced that Watts had paid back the fee given him in 1878; a marginal note on the Richmond portrait reads: 'shewn in Grosvenor Gallery, & condemned' (the chronology of the account in

reference photograph for Millais to work from was taken by Rupert Potter, father of Beatrix Potter the writer and illustrator. Millais was excited: 'Only a moment to write, so hard at work. I have Gladstone better than the first time ... I never did so fine a portrait.'[1] All was thus set fair for a triumph for Christ Church and a great satisfaction for Gladstone, devoted as he was to Oxford. In November 1884, Rosebery visited Millais' studio to see his daughter's portrait, also in preparation. He noted in his diary:

> To Millais' studio where Peggy's portrait finished. Gladstone's half finished. M. very pleased & straightforward. Peggy will cost 2000£—he will paint a kitcat for Ch.Ch. of Gladstone & let me have this for 1000£.[2]

Rosebery, in other words, was to have Millais' finest portrait, while the body that had commissioned it was to have a half-length copy. When Gladstone heard that this was happening, he refused to let Christ Church be fobbed off with a copy and offered to sit again. In the summer of 1885 there were three more sittings[3] and the portrait now in Christ Church Hall was hung in October 1885. It and Rupert Potter's contrasting photograph are reproduced in Volume XI. Rosebery, another Christ Church man, may not have known that the picture was commissioned by the college. Millais certainly did know and his treatment both of his patron and of his subject made his baronetcy the more generous.

Church patronage was equally problematic, but overall rather more satisfactory, even though it involved a further series of tussles with the Queen. By the 1880s, Gladstone saw the clergy, together with the army and the law, as part of the 'existence of powerful professional classes more or less sustained by privilege or by artfully constructed monopoly';[4] these classes he saw as increasingly deliberate buttresses of the Conservative Party: an 'Established Clergy will always be a tory Corps d'Armée'.[5] He deplored 'the unmitigated Toryism of the bulk of the clerical body'.[6] This view of the clergy encouraged him to make Liberal appointments, ceteris paribus. He was distanced from the Queen in this area by G. V. Wellesley, Dean of Windsor, who had the confidence of both and acted as mediator. Even so, on A. P. Stanley's death, Gladstone lost the filling of the Deanery of Westminster, the Queen's candidate, G. G. Bradley being appointed. This was a difference about personalities rather than politics, for Bradley was a Liberal. 'Does she really think the two positions of Sovereign & Minister are to be inverted?' Gladstone expostulated to Wellesley.[7] In the Westminster case, they were.

A. M. W. Stirling, *The Richmond Papers* (1926), 236 is hopelessly muddled, confusing Richmond's portraits of 1867 and 1882). For sittings to Richmond, see 16 Jan. 82ff.

[1] J. G. Millais, *Life and letters of Sir J. E. Millais* (1899), ii. 166. For 1884 sittings, see 7 July–4 Aug. 84.   [2] Rosebery's diary, 14 November 1884.
[3] See 15, 25 June, 13 July 85. Christ Church Governing Body Index to Minutes (Po); pencil note: 'Millais undertook to paint Mr. Gladstone's Portrait for Ch. Ch. This portrait Millais sold to Lord Rosebery for (on dit) 1000£, & was then going to send us a Replica; but Mr. Gladstone sat again, & the result is the Portrait now in Hall.' See also Sir J. Mowbray, *Seventy years at Westminster* (1900), 341–3. A good replica by C. H. Thompson was presented by Lord Gladstone to Lambeth Palace in 1925. Rosebery's version—a three-quarter length portrait—is now in the Hall of Eton College.
[4] 14 Aug. 82.   [5] To Harcourt, 3 July 85.
[6] To Bp. Goodwin, 8 Sept. 81.   [7] To Wellesley, 11 Aug. 81; see also 17 Aug. 81.

Wellesley's death in September 1882 seemed a sharp blow to Gladstone as it removed a buffer between the Queen and himself on what was—at least for him—the tenderest of subjects: 'with few of my colleagues have I taken as much personal counsel as with him [Wellesley] during the last 14 years. . . . I reckoned his life the most precious in the Church of England',[1] a noteworthy assessment made two days after the death of E. B. Pusey. As it happened, after the difficulty of appointing E. W. Benson to Canterbury was got round—Gladstone prevailing over the Queen with a candidate about whom he had some reservations—there were few contentious church appointments until a flurry of sees early in 1885. In the meantime Benson, an underestimated figure, gave what was in the circumstances rather a brave support to the Liberal government over the reform crisis in 1884[2] and provided something of a balance to the disciplinarian, conservative ethos of Tait's last years.[3]

Political allegiance in clerical appointments was thus of importance, but it should not be overstressed. Gladstone was probably more exercised over the church party affiliation of candidates for preferment. Challenged by the Queen for appointing too many High-Churchmen, he made a devastating statistical response: only eleven out of thirty places had gone to High-Churchmen in the early years of his second administration; his main fault was that, of the residue, the Broad Church was disproportionately higher in representation than the Low.[4] Suitable Evangelical candidates for bishoprics were hard to find with 'the Evang. party now so barren'. Gladstone rose at 5.00 a.m. one morning at Hawarden to telegraph Ponsonby not to put to the Queen his recommendation of James Moorhouse for the see of Southwell; he had been troubled in the night by thinking about a report that Moorhouse had allowed a presbyterian to preach in his cathedral in Melbourne.[5]

Gladstone spent a great deal of time over these appointments aided by E. W. Hamilton, his secretary and the son of a bishop, and his daughter Mary. The Prime Minister's peculiar position as the fulcrum of clerical patronage made him central to the effective discharge of what Gladstone called 'the working energy of the Church'.[6] The search for suitable appointees had a peculiar

---

[1] To Anson, 19 Sept. 82; and see 18 Sept. 82. Wellesley's death in the middle of Tait's fatal illness made the filling of the archbishopric of Canterbury, eventually by Benson against the Queen's wishes, even more problematic; see to Wellesley, 26, 27 Aug., 3 Sept. 82. After recommending Benson (see 9 Dec. 82), Gladstone thought he might not prevail and covered himself by consulting Jacobson, bishop of Chester, about Benson and E. H. Browne (Gladstone's original preference); see 11 Dec. 82. The dispute about Benson coincided with the Queen's obstruction of aspects of the government reshuffle.

[2] See to Benson, 2, 9 July 84 and notes.

[3] Gladstone tried to secure the release of S. F. Green, the rector of Miles Platting imprisoned for ritualism under the Public Worship Regulation Act, whose passing in 1874 Gladstone had vigorously opposed; his tactic was to release Green for ill-health; Harcourt, a strong supporter of the Act, disliked this, as did Green, who did not want release on a compromise; see to Harcourt, 6, 13, 23 Sept. 81, to Selborne, 16 Aug. 82. On the other hand, having failed to secure a compromise, Gladstone was careful not to be drawn into the agitation for the release of Green, treating his case with a certain caution ('Ecce aeternum Greene'). For Gladstone's sharp reaction to the disestablishmentarian remarks of W. J. Knox-Little, a canon of St. Paul's, see to Wellesley, 12, 13 Oct. 81.

[4] To Ponsonby, 14 June 83; see also to J. A. Godley, 16 Apr. 83.

[5] 15 Jan. 84; see also to Benson, 20 Apr. 84.

[6] To Ponsonby, 14 June 83.

fascination for Gladstone. He enjoyed mentally filing away potential candidates and could recall strengths and weaknesses years after hearing a sermon. His ingenuity was always stretched by Welsh sees. He was particularly concerned to show the Welshness of the Anglican Church in Wales, as he believed Nonconformity was a recent deviation, Wales during the Civil War having been 'a great stronghold of the Church: so says Mr Hallam. . . . Puritanism struck there but small and feeble roots.'[1]

> A vacancy in a Welsh see costs me more trouble than six English vacancies. I feel it my duty to ascertain if possible by a process of exhaustion whether there is any completely fit person to be had among men of Welsh mother tongue. In the main it is a business of constantly examining likely or plausible cases & finding they break down. The Welsh are to be got at through the pulpit: & yet here is a special danger, for among the more stirring Welsh clergy there is as much wordy & windy preaching as among the Irish.[2]

In the case of the see of Llandaff, the process was literally exhausting, as it contributed to the insomnia which drove Gladstone to recuperate in Cannes in January 1883.

Less arduous, indeed almost off-hand, was Gladstone's treatment of the vacancy in the Regius Chair of Modern History at Oxford which he created by sending William Stubbs to the see of Chester in 1884. As was his usual practice with Oxford appointments, Gladstone wrote for advice to H. G. Liddell, the moderately Liberal Dean of Christ Church. Gladstone mentioned S. R. Gardiner and Mandell Creighton as possibilities, but thought E. A. Freeman, the medievalist and Liberal campaigner, as 'the first Oxford man by far', perhaps even unjustly treated when Stubbs was appointed in 1866: a remarkable judgement. Gladstone noted that Freeman 'is a strong Liberal. I fear he makes enemies and I am told he is little versed in manuscripts . . . [but] he would give a powerful impulsion to historical study at Oxford.'[3] How the Dean responded to this is unknown, but his reply, if made, was probably redundant. The same day, Freeman wrote to the Prime Minister proposing himself for the chair, very possibly the only occasion on which a Regius Chair has been applied for. Gladstone told Freeman next day that he had submitted his name to the Queen, and concluded: 'I anticipate with lively satisfaction the introduction into academical life of a fresh and solid piece of not less stout than healthy Liberalism, as well as the great impulse which your depth, range and vigour will impart, in our beloved Oxford, to a study so vital to all the best interests of man.'[4] It is unlikely that Gladstone would have used so political a tone in his first government; it reflects the stronger concern for a liberal historicism which he had developed during the campaigns of the late 1870s, as well as the increasingly partisan temper of the times.

A more successful use of patronage in academic matters was the award of a Civil List pension to James Murray to aid him in his work on his dictionary.[5] The

---

[1] To Bevan, 13 May 83.
[2] To Lightfoot, 28 Dec. 82.
[3] To Liddell, 13 Feb. 84.
[4] To Freeman, 14 Feb. 84.
[5] 1 Oct. 81 and K. M. E. Murray, *Caught in the web of words* (1977), 236.

pension meant that the State effectively bore a third of the editor's salary and also encouraged Oxford University in its support for that remarkable work. The pension for Murray was an exception to Gladstone's usual rule, that the ancient universities had large endowments to enable them rather than the State to fund institutions such as the new British School in Athens. Gladstone was happy to speak in support of the School as a private person, but he refused a request for government money for it.[1] In the case of the dictionary, he had a high opinion of Murray, whom he first met in 1879 and with whom he corresponded on lexicography, and he probably recognized the unique importance of the dictionary. He was also, in Murray's case, supporting an individual rather than an institution.

Leadership of the House of Commons was another routine call on Prime-Ministerial time, and a very considerable call it was. As with church services, Gladstone always noted attendance at the Commons and the time spent there. When he was piloting a bill as well as leading the House, this could be lengthy. In July 1882—the month of the Egyptian crisis—he spent 148 hours on the Treasury bench, an average of nearly seven hours per day and night (he frequently sat on the bench until after 1.00 a.m.). In that month, he was not only answering frequent questions and guiding the passage of the Arrears Bill, but he had to take over the Egyptian Vote of Credit as well: 'spoke (40m) in winding up at Hartington's request, who was to have done the work'.[2] In a very easy month, and leading on no bill, as, for example, June 1883, he still attended the House every day it sat except four, and averaged almost six hours on those days that he attended.

Gladstone usually broke from the Commons for dinner at 8.15 for about an hour. Sometimes he dined at home at Downing Street, sometimes with one of his secretaries, sometimes with a friend (almost always one like Sir Charles Forster, not of the first or even of the second political rank: rarely with another Cabinet minister), occasionally at The Club or Grillion's,[3] and very occasionally at a political club as a guest.[4] At Grillion's he once dined alone, noting in the club's minute book this couplet from *Paradise Lost*:

> The mind is its own place, and in itself
> Can make a heaven of hell, a hell of heaven.[5]

This solitary occasion in 1885 was commemorated by Lord Houghton, Poet Laureate to the club, in some sharp verses:

> Trace we the workings of that wondrous brain,
> Warmed by one bottle of our dry champagne;
> Guess down what streams those active fancies wander,
> Nile or Ilissus? Oxus or Scamander?
> Sees he, as lonely knife and fork he plies,
> Muscovite lances—Arab assegais?
> Or patient till the food and feuds shall cease,
> Waits his des(s)ert—the blessed fruits of peace?

[1] To Jebb, 6 Feb. 83 and 18 May, 25 June 83. [2] 27 July 82.
[3] See, e.g., 28 Feb. 82, 2 Apr. 83. [4] 21 Nov. 84, 11 Feb. 85.
[5] *Grillion's Club. A chronicle 1812–1913* (1914), 96.

Yes, for while penning this impetuous verse,
We know that when (as mortals must) he errs,
'Tis not from motive of imperious mind,
But from a nature which will last till death,
Of love-born faith that grows to over-faith,
Till reason and experience both grow blind
To th'evil and unreason of mankind.[1]

Houghton's tone, moving from the genial to the acerbic, shows why it was that during the sessions of the 1880s Gladstone was rather careful about the extent to which he offered himself to a London society which he regarded as increasingly illiberal, corrupt, 'ploutocratic', and isolated from the Liberalism of non-metropolitan Britain. But beyond this, Gladstone probably had enough of exclusively male political society in the House of Commons. He enjoyed the company of women. Having resigned from the Reform Club on resigning as Prime Minister in 1874 (he had only joined on the chief whip's insistence), he did not rejoin in 1880; though President of the new National Liberal Club, he did not use it as a club and only went there when required to make a speech.

The great procedural reforms of 1882 did not lead to a reform of Gladstone's parliamentary habits. He reduced the burden in one minor but significant way: questions to the Prime Minister, hitherto indiscriminately intermingled with the other questions, themselves in no particular order, were on Gladstone's suggestion to the Speaker[2] gathered into batches as were those of other ministers, thus beginning what later became 'Prime Minister's Question Time'.

There was little complaint about these hours spent listening and speaking. Gladstone enjoyed the House and enjoyed being an 'old Parliamentary hand'. 'Peel', he recalled, 'once said to me when I was going to speak officially "don't be short".'[3] Gladstone could certainly never be accused of neglecting that advice. He relished the procedures of the House and their manipulation, and he respected those who used them as resourcefully as himself. Apart from their spasms of obvious obstruction, he admired the way the Home Rulers used the House in Committee: their mastery of the details of legislation and of procedure. He saw in this the essential constitutionality of their politics, a broad-minded view considering that it was often at him that their tactics were directed. Gladstone disliked the tone of the 'Fourth Party', complaining to his daughter that Balfour's comments on Kilmainham were 'the almost raving licence of an unbridled tongue'[4] (he especially resented the violent personal comments of Balfour, a friend and a frequent guest), and noting on reading Churchill's anonymous article 'Elijah's Mantle': 'very cleverly *written*, but a sad moral bathos'.[5] But he respected the 'Fourth Party's' toughness and resource, and was easily drawn into verbal scrapping with its members. Despite his complaints about Balfour, the latter continued to be a family friend and a visitor to Hawarden.[6] It was Northcote's supposed lack of back-bone in his role in the

---

[1] Ibid.

[2] See to Brand, 3 July 81; Gladstone at the same time suggested that his questions should come last, but this did not happen.

[3] To Kimberley, 8 May 83.   [4] To Helen Gladstone, 17 May 82.

[5] 14 May 83.   [6] 20 Oct. 83.

House that Gladstone despised, the only person in the whole of these two large volumes to receive repeated censure.[1]

This brief survey of two areas of routine Prime Ministerial activity show that, while great causes were the stated reason for Gladstone's continuation in office and while on occasion he might act the part of a retired person, he was certainly not idle in routine matters. Indeed, his attention to Court and parliamentary detail was, if anything, overdone. For a man in his seventies, his vigour was exceptional. Even so, it is hardly surprising that the pace of the 1880 government caused strains and breakdowns. We now turn, therefore, to the private Gladstone.

IX

Gladstone rather haphazardly protected himself from the consequences of old age and overstrain and was in his turn rather more systematically protected by the Gladstonian circle, by the 1880s a well-defined body.

First, his relaxation. Gladstone read prolifically. Though he kept very well up to date with the questions of the day, as a glance at the diary will show, his reading is, taken as a whole, less policy-orientated in his second and third governments than in his first. He particularly enjoyed memoirs of court life and read extensively on the French eighteenth-century court, for example Touchard-Lafosse's *Chronique de l'oeil-de boeuf*, a large work on the *petits apartements* of the Louvre.[2] The records of the French monarchy of the *ancien régime* may have encouraged him in his tussles with the Queen. He read the novels of the day, Shorthouse's *John Inglesant*[3] being of particular interest to him, with Henry James's *Madonna of the Future* and *Daisy Miller*,[4] Olive Schreiner's *The Story of an African Farm*,[5] and many lesser works which made an impact in their time, such as Annie S. Swan's *Aldersyde*[6] and General Wallace's *Ben-Hur*.[7] He reread much of Cervantes, Defoe, Dickens, George Eliot, and, as always, Walter Scott, and partially caught up with Disraeli, reading *Sybil* for the first time in 1884.[8] He made no comment on the latter, but sometimes his telegraphic diary notation of his reading conveys a paragraph in a phrase: 'Silas Marner, finished—noble, though with spots';[9] 'Finished S. African Farm. A most remarkable, painful, book';[10] 'Read through Kidnapped [at a sitting]: a book to be recommended.'[11]

---

[1] 'Really weaker than water', 1 Feb. 81, a recurring simile; see also to Halifax, 2 Aug. 83, to Argyll, 31 Aug. 84, 13 Jan. 85. Harcourt on the Liberal side drove Gladstone to irritated entries—echoing the other cabinet diarists of the time—during the crisis of preparation of the Irish bills in 1886; see 1, 6 Apr. 86 and Morley's diary at 14 Apr. 86.

[2] 19 Apr. 82; see also, among many, 5 Aug. 83 (a Sunday!), 10 Nov. 83.

[3] 14 July 81 and to Doyle, 22 Oct. 81.

[4] 23 Aug. 81, 14 Apr. 84.

[5] 17, 26 Apr. 85.

[6] 10, 16 Apr. 83.

[7] 23 Sept. 83.

[8] 20 Feb. 84.

[9] 24 Apr. 84.

[10] 26 Apr. 85.

[11] 30 July 86 (out of office); he also read Stevenson's *Dr Jekyll and Mr Hyde* (13 Feb. 86), *Treasure Island* (14 Apr. 84), and *The New Arabian Nights* (16 Apr. 84), the last two perhaps at the suggestion of Henry James, whom he met at Rosebery's house, The Durdans (14–15 Apr. 84).

Outside fiction, he ranged eclectically from 'Muggletonian Hymns!!'[1] through Olga Janina's *Souvenirs d'un Pianiste*, 'an almost incredible book',[2] to the *Kama Sutra*,[3] no comment recorded. He was also capable of letters of a high order of literary criticism, as for example his observations on Mary Wollstonecraft in whom he became considerably interested.[4] The reader who follows Gladstone's non-political reading and writing through these years of office would think he or she was pursuing a rather well-occupied *littérateur*.

A particular pleasure was helping in the preparation of biographies of his former contemporaries in many of which he was a principal character. He continued to supply letters for and read the proofs of the *Life of Samuel Wilberforce*;[5] he prepared materials, helped with research, and read all the proofs of the *Life of James Hope-Scott*,[6] and he much enjoyed reading Milnes Gaskell's *Records of an Eton schoolboy* (1883).[7] He had a high estimate of John Morley's *Life of Cobden*—'it is one more added to the not very long list of our real biographies'[8]—in whose preparation he had, as a correspondent and as a trustee of Cobden's MSS, been considerably involved. Out of office, he made papers and his library available to C. S. Parker, the Liberal M.P., for the preparation of his *Papers of Sir Robert Peel*.[9] He read enthusiastically about his own past in these and various other works, complaining to John Murray in December 1884 about the index to the *Croker Papers*: 'the Index is rather *thin*. I find in it two references following my own name. I have noted in the text at least twelve. What is more important, such a point as the authorship of the Waverley Novels p. 351 is not noticed except under Croker, where it might not be looked for.'[10] He also read widely in the other biographies of the day, taking a particular interest in the 'Life of Miss Evans' (as he archly called J. W. Cross's life of George Eliot (often spelt 'Elliot' by Gladstone));[11] he found time in the midst of the Gordon crisis to regret that his daughter Mary and Acton had 'lifted her above Walter Scott . . . yet I freely own she was a great woman. I have not yet got to the bottom of her ethical history.'[12]

Gladstone was also quite a regular theatre-goer, and moved enthusiastically among the Irving–Terry set as well as frequently visiting performances of drawing-room comedies and dramas. He saw Irving's notable series of Shakespeare productions at the Lyceum,[13] often going backstage after the

[1] 13 Dec. 81. He followed this up, trying to buy a Muggletonian hymnbook ('uncut') from a bookseller's catalogue; 14 Jan. 82n. This interest is an unusual confirmation of the continued presence in the public mind of the seventeenth-century sect; see N. Lamont, 'The Muggletonians 1652–1979: a "vertical" approach', *Past and Present*, xcix. 739 (1983).
[2] 10 Oct. 84.   [3] 3 May 84.
[4] To Kegan Paul, 29 Nov. 83.
[5] To R. G. Wilberforce, 6 July 82. For help with Martin's *Lyndhurst*, of which Gladstone did not think much, see 31 Aug., 4 Dec. 83, and to Coleridge, 2 Jan. 84.
[6] To Mrs. Maxwell Scott, 27 July 83 and see 31 Oct., 24 Nov., 10, 16 Dec. 83, etc.
[7] To Milnes Gaskell, 23 Oct. 83.
[8] To Morley, 24 Oct. 81.
[9] 4 Dec. 86; see also to Reid, 16 Oct. 83 (Sydney Smith).
[10] Gladstone to Murray, 24 December 1884, Add MS 44547, f. 154.
[11] 10, 13 Feb. 85.   [12] To Acton, 11 Feb. 85.
[13] See, e.g., 25 Oct. 82; see also 9 Oct. 83. For Irving's production of W. G. Wills' version of 'Faust', see 10 Apr. 86 and to Irving, 11 Apr. 86.

performance: 'Saw Miss Terry behind' as he unfortunately put it. This was the context of his well-blazoned friendship with Lillie Langtry, whom he first notes meeting in January 1882, soon afterwards going to see her in Robinson's 'Ours' at the Haymarket.[1] The friendship, from Gladstone's point of view, was much less important than contemporary rumour suggested, though such rumours were not surprising, given Lillie Langtry's reputation and the gossip about Gladstone's nocturnal activities circulating in the clubs. He noted: 'I hardly know what estimate to make of her. Her manners are very pleasing, & she has a working spirit in her.'[2] In February 1885 he noted: 'saw Mrs Langtry: probably for the last time'.[3]

Gladstone took a considerable interest in foreigners playing in London. He attended a performance of 'The Winter's Tale' in German, presented by the visiting Saxe-Meiningen Court Theatre;[4] when the American actress Mary Anderson played Juliet at the Lyceum he saw the performance and later arranged a large breakfast at 10 Downing Street, a notable recognition of a famous production but also an important step in the growing respectability of the theatre.[5]

A new development for Gladstone was an interest in operas and musicals: he may have been encouraged in this by E. W. Hamilton, a knowledgeable and regular opera-goer. Gladstone went to 'The Phantom of the Ship of Wagner' and was seen clapping enthusiastically;[6] he saw MacKenzie's 'Colomba' and the Carl Rosa Company in 'Carmen'.[7] He went with Granville—rather a suitable choice—to 'Iolanthe'; he later, out of office, went to 'The Mikado', and heard George Grossmith, the D'Oyly Carte's patter-singer, at a private cabaret ('very entertaining but less than on the stage').[8]

For all the cares of office and of the Commons, Gladstone had rather a jovial time in the 1880s; his general boisterousness is confirmed by the various accounts of his dancing with his wife and frequently singing songs at dinner such as 'My 'art is true to Poll'.[9] This persistent good cheer, most frequently exemplified by a stream of miscellaneous but erudite conversation, at first almost always charmed. It reflected the natural confidence, curiosity, and ebullience of his character. But it probably had a purpose also. Gladstone knew the significance of the actor's craft, directly comparing his own with it,[10] and he knew, as he said with respect to public speaking, how to 'put on the steam'.[11] In this period, he knew that even every private dinner party was a performance for the record: it was almost certain that one of the guests would note his conversation and mood in a letter or diary. He knew that between E. W.Hamilton and his daughter Mary most of what he did or said, and particularly every sign of frailty, went into their diaries. When he went to Norway on the *Sunbeam* in

---

[1] 26 Jan., 4 Feb. 82.   [2] 3 Apr. 82.
[3] 16 Feb. 85.   [4] 17 June 81.
[5] 8 Nov. 84, 23 Apr. 85 (on which day he also saw her in a double bill at The Lyceum, 'Pygmalion' and 'Comedy and Tragedy').
[6] 10 Mar. 82.   [7] 12 Apr. 83, 3 May 84.
[8] 4 Dec. 82; 29 July 85; 10 Aug. 86.
[9] *Mary Gladstone*, 313 (1 May 1884).
[10] See to Mrs. Tennyson, 14 Nov. 82.
[11] A recurring metaphor, see 30 July 78, 3 Apr. 84.

August 1885, at least four of the company were keeping diaries; that of his hostess, Lady Brassey, was immediately published in the *Contemporary Review*.[1] He must have been when in company as constantly on his guard as an actor on the stage.

Margot Tennant, later Asquith, who became a friend of the family in these years, thought Gladstone had 'a tiger smile'.[2] Derby, when exposed at some length to Gladstone's conversation, was at first captivated, but then had second thoughts: 'For the first time, a suspicion crossed my mind that there is something beyond what is quite healthy in this perpetual flow of words—a beginning perhaps of old age.'[3] It was more likely that it was not old age in the sense of senility but a calculated attempt to keep old age at bay which in the case of the Knowsley visit was taken too far. The flow of words produced entertainment and offered flattery; it suggested intimacy across the generations while at the same time preserving distance. For a man whose close friends were all dead— Sir Robert Phillimore, the last friend who was an old crony rather than being in some way politically involved or obliged, died in 1885[4]—such an emphasis on this aspect of his personality was advantageous. It allowed Gladstone to present himself in an engaging character, which by its nature allowed him to keep a little apart from those who were now his contemporaries. Much is made of Gladstone's lack of self-consciousness. But Margot Tennant thought that 'this curious lack of self-consciousness, though flattering, was deceptive'.[5] It may well be that, by the 1880s, Gladstone's lack of self-consciousness was being consciously cultivated.

Gladstone began his second government aged 70; he was 76 when he introduced the Government of Ireland Bill. A generation, or two generations, older than many of his colleagues, the 'Grand Old Man', as Labouchere dubbed him,[6] needed carefully orchestrated support behind the scenes to a much greater extent than in his first government. The family circle and the 'Private Secretariat'[7]—the two quite often tending to merge—were thus additional and increasingly important props. The Gladstone family was an integral part of a Gladstone administration. Catherine Gladstone always opposed her husband's attempts to resign. In October 1885, on the question of whether Gladstone should attempt to form another government after the election, Rosebery noted: 'his family has settled the question for him'.[8] Though Mrs. Gladstone continued her charitable work and her assistance to sick relatives, her attention was much more than hitherto focused on her husband, and she was much less away from him than in his previous periods of office. She even helped at critical moments as secretary, her arthritic hand painfully adorning the copies of the letters, and she undertook a political mission to Rosebery, though without success, during

---

[1] *C.R.*, xlviii. 480 (October 1885).

[2] Countess of Oxford and Asquith, *Off the Record* (1943), 47.

[3] Derby's account of Gladstone's visit to Knowsley, October 1883, quoted below, vol. xi, Appendix I.

[4] Gladstone baronetted him in 1881; Phillimore was '"over the moon" with a most innocent delight'; to Mrs. Gladstone, 2 Dec. 81 (see also to Grosvenor, 14 Nov. 81). Phillimore was perhaps the only confidant to encourage Gladstone to retire; see 10 Dec. 82.

[5] Countess of Oxford and Asquith, op. cit., 46.   [6] Thorold, 144.

[7] The term used by Gladstone; see 8 July 85.   [8] 27 Oct. 85n.

the confusions about his position in January 1883.[1] As in other volumes of these diaries, her support is taken for granted by her husband and largely unmentioned, though from time to time there is an admiring comment. When apart, Gladstone wrote a short note or letter to her each day; the tone of these shows the extent to which a considerable level of political discussion was a part of their life when together. The letters almost always begin 'My own C.' and usually conclude 'Ever your afft. WEG' (occasionally 'Your most afft. WEG'). They show a Gladstonian style much more relaxed than the rather rigid correctness of most of his correspondence. Added to the rather formal subscription he used for letters to his wife, the effect is sometimes curious: 'I must however knock off, & am your ever afft. WEG'.[2]

When the Gladstones were at Hawarden, the two oldest sons, Willy and Stephen, now respectively the squire and the rector (and aged 43 and 39 in 1883), helped out, putting up the parents, helping the tree-cutting, ferrying the guests. The strain told. Willy's political career languished. He did not stand in the 1885 election, partly because of the need to tend the Hawarden estates, and he opposed his father on Home Rule. He was with difficulty encouraged into editing the 1886 Irish speeches.[3] He may well already have been affected by the brain tumour which killed him in 1891. The birth of his three children, Evelyn in 1882, Constance in 1883, and William Glynne Charles Gladstone, heir to Hawarden and killed in action in 1915, cheered his rather forlorn life as he worked to mitigate the consequences of the agricultural depression on the Hawarden estates. Stephen suffered a crisis of self-confidence as a result of holding the family rectory, one of the wealthiest in the land. He wished to go to India as a missionary because of a failed engagement and because at Hawarden he felt, as Rector, 'too closely related to what may be called the "temporal power" or the ruling family of the place'.[4] Nothing came of this and he was, after his marriage in January 1885, much more settled at the Rectory.

Henry, the businessman, was in India for much of this time, the recipient of some of his father's most interesting letters.[5] When at home he helped secretarially and gradually established himself as the determining future influence on the family's fortunes and, within the family, as the most effective guardian of his father's reputation. Herbert was given the seat his father won in Leeds in 1880 and began to make his own political career in the form of an advanced version of aspects of his father's. Several visits to Ireland—he was unsuccessfully urged on Spencer as an assistant by the Prime Minister after the Phoenix Park murders[6]—made him an important conduit of Home Rule opinion into the household. He, like the others, helped as secretary and as an important link with the Party. He managed with considerable tact both to work with his father and to develop his own position—though the attempt to do both simultaneously broke down spectacularly in December 1885 with the 'Hawarden Kite'.[7]

---

[1] 10 Jan. 83.   [2] 25 Mar. 83.
[3] 9 Apr. 81, 2 Aug., 14 Sept. 84, 3 July 86. See also 18 Apr. 81 and 24, 30 June 86.
[4] 10 Sept. 82 and n.
[5] See particularly those of 21 Apr., 2 Dec. 81, 12 Feb., 16 July 86.
[6] To Spencer, 9 May 82.
[7] See above, section VII and below, vol. XI, Appendix I.

More important in the household than any of the sons was the second living daughter, Mary—known as 'Von Moltke' outside the circle. Much of the day-to-day organization of her parents—by the 1885 election aged 75 and 73—fell to her, especially out of Session. She discreetly organized the household at Hawarden and her obvious intelligence placed her on something like a par with visitors such as Acton.[1] There is some indication that she screened Gladstone's fiction for him but probably not too much should be made of this.[2] In February 1886 she married Harry Drew; as he was curate at Hawarden this marriage made much less difference to the working of the Gladstonian *ménage* than had that of the first daughter, Agnes, whose marriage in 1873 had taken her outside immediate contact with her parents. Helen, the youngest daughter, was outside such contact because of her Fellowship at Newnham, Cambridge. She turned down the offer of the headship of Royal Holloway College in 1886 as, unlike Newnham, it would prevent her being at Hawarden in the vacations to assist and sometimes relieve Mary's secretarial work.[3] On the fringes of the family circle was the tragic figure of Lucy Cavendish, Mrs Gladstone's niece, widow of the murdered Lord Frederick Cavendish whom Gladstone had from an early stage groomed for high office, much more than he had his sons. Lucy Cavendish—'altogether one of us'[4]—was often at Hawarden; she was politically shrewd, was a committed Liberal, and acted as an additional link with her brother-in-law Hartington.[5] The Gladstones stayed with her at 21 Carlton House Terrace in January and February 1886, while the Home Rule Cabinet was being formed, and again after the defeat of the Government.

With the partial exception of Willy, the Gladstone children were all strong political supporters of their father. Taken together, they offered a powerful political and domestic support to their parents, who expected one or other of them to be on hand as needed. With the exception of Agnes and her children at Wellington College, and H. N. Gladstone when in India, the Gladstones remained a very locally based family with the parents, whether in Downing Street or at one of the various houses at Hawarden, very much the focal point, an arrangement which seems to have been regarded as natural on both sides. Willy, Stephen, Herbert, Mary and, in the vacations, Helen, were each in their different ways powerful buttresses of a Gladstonian premiership, and Catherine Gladstone was its emotional and physical bedrock.

The secretariat overlapped with this.[6] As we have seen, several of the family helped with the secretarial work, even at the most confidential level. One of the official secretaries, Spencer Lyttelton, was Mrs Gladstone's nephew. The other secretaries also had close connections with Gladstone or other members of the Cabinet. Horace Seymour was Lord Spencer's brother-in-law; Henry Primrose, later the most dogmatic Gladstonian in the Edwardian Treasury, was Rosebery's cousin; George Leveson-Gower was Granville's nephew. J. A. Godley was

---

[1] P. Jalland, 'Mr. Gladstone's daughters' in B. L. Kinzer, ed., *The Gladstonian turn of mind* (1985).

[2] See to Rosebery, 15 Nov. 83.

[3] See 1, 24 July 86. It was characteristic of her relationship with her father that she only took charge of North Hall of Newnham College after he 'freely assented' to her so doing; 13 Jan. 82.

[4] 24 Dec. 83.

[5] 28 Dec. 83 (on this occasion on the franchise/seats bill wrangle).

[6] For a good discussion of the secretariat, see Bahlman, *Hamilton*, i. xviiiff.

the son of J. R. Godley, the colonial reformer with whom Gladstone had worked in the 1850s on the Canterbury Association for settlement in New Zealand; Godley further related to the Gladstonian past by marrying the daughter of W. C. James, Lord Northbourne, once a Peelite M.P. and now one of Gladstone's oldest political friends. E. W. Hamilton, who succeeded Godley as principal private secretary in August 1882, was the son of W. K. Hamilton, one of Gladstone's closest undergraduate friends and with him at one of the most important moments of his life, the vocational crisis of 1830;[1] Gladstone had helped to secure his bishopric against Broad and Low Church opposition. Sir James Carmichael, bart., on the secretarial staff in 1885 and again in 1886, had been Childers' secretary and was an authority on Egyptian land and finance; as such he was useful on Ireland in 1886. Unusually among Gladstone's Prime Ministerial secretaries, he went on to a political rather than a civil service career.

Many of the functions of the secretaries were routine. Gladstone continued to write all important and many less important letters in his own hand. The secretaries copied these into the letter book when Gladstone marked the letter ✔ in the bottom left-hand corner, or when he marked it ✔✔, onto a separate piece of paper.[2] They answered low-level non-official correspondence in his name and as these letters were often immediately published in the press considerable tact was required. Gladstone's confidence in them was well-justified. The secretaries also had a more complex role, liaising with the Queen's secretary, with Cabinet ministers and with M.P.s on points of policy. Here the emollient and cheerful Godley and Hamilton were rather effective, compensating to some extent for Gladstone's notorious absence from the lobbies and the tea-room, an absence the more remarkable considering the amount of time we have seen him spending in the House but on the front bench. Most of the secretaries—Seymour was the exception—formed strong personal bonds with Gladstone, who in most cases saw that they went on to influential posts in the civil service. But their relationships to the Cabinet Whigs meant that they also represented something of a watching brief for the whiggish section of the Cabinet on the innermost activities of the Premier.

The secretaries also delayed business or restrained Gladstone when they—particularly Hamilton—thought he was acting precipitately. Because they read the papers and letters going in and out, they were very well-informed. But the creative side of Downing Street policy-making came from Gladstone. The secretaries were not a *cabinet* in the sense of generating policy proposals or position papers. Hamilton played something of such a role in the preparation of the Irish land legislation in 1886, but by that time he was seconded by the

[1] See Matthew, *Gladstone*, 22.

[2] When combined, these copies almost always provided a fuller record of Gladstone's out-going correspondence (when in office) than the collection of holograph letters kept by the recipient; this may be in part because ministers often forwarded his letters to colleagues or civil servants for comment and they were not returned. Gladstone's own papers have curious gaps in the incoming correspondence—a surprisingly high number of his letters printed below have no recorded reply, even when one was obviously called for. This may be because the reply was forwarded and not returned or because the reply was given verbally: not all ministers had Gladstone's appetite for writing or his enthusiasm for being 'on the record'.

Treasury and was not part of the Downing Street staff. To a remarkable extent, Downing Street's influence on politics was Gladstone's own. For all the support of family and secretaries, Gladstone remained, as he always had been, a rather solitary figure, usually at least one step ahead of those around him.

A government which depended so much on the Prime Minister's leadership also much depended on his health. Gladstone suffered from bad eyesight, bouts of diarrhoea, of lumbago, and of neuralgia in his face, chronically poor teeth, spells of insomnia and, in 1885, a loss of voice. His oculist, T. Henri, was not successful in preventing a marked decline in his eyesight; it may be that the '"Pure Periscopic" pebbles' which he fitted to Gladstone's pince-nez were not quite what was required.[1] His doctor, Andrew Clark, and his dentist, Edwin Saunders, whom he respectively baronetted and knighted in 1883, kept him on the whole up to the mark with the assistance of Catherine Gladstone, who sent him to bed early when possible, administered quinine and chloroform[2] and prepared the small bottles of sherry and egg to go by the despatch box in the Commons—one for an important speech, two for an exceptionally long one, such as the introduction of the Government of Ireland Bill.[3]

Despite their efforts, Gladstone was from time to time unwell, sometimes missing Cabinets at important moments, such as the wrangle over Gordon's request for the help of the slaver Zobeir Pasha.[4] Sometimes he was ill simply from political pressure, as in the stress he felt as a result of the death of Beaconsfield in April 1881:

> At 8 a.m. I was much shocked on opening a Telegram to find it announced the death of Ld Beaconsfield, 3½ hours before. The accounts 24 hours ago were so good. It is a telling, touching event. There is no more extraordinary man surviving him in England, perhaps none in Europe. I must not say much, in presence as it were of his Urn.
>
> I immediately sent to tender a public funeral. The event will entail on me *one* great difficulty; but God who sends all, sends this also.[5]

This '*one* great difficulty' was that it fell to Gladstone, both as Prime Minister and as Leader of the House, to propose in the Commons a public memorial to the man whose premiership he believed had been a moral and a practical disgrace. The offer of the public funeral was declined; Gladstone was invited to the private one at Hughenden but told Rothschild that heavy engagements would prevent his attending.[6] The next piece of Disraeliana was the Royal Academy dinner: 'Made my speech: this year especially difficult.'[7] This was because in the ante-room to the dining hall was prominently placed Millais' portrait of Beaconsfield—the pair to his portrait of 1879 of Gladstone. Comparison and comment was thus unavoidable; Gladstone turned the moment with a classical quotation. Next day he became ill with diarrhoea and remained inconvenienced or worse until the speech proposing the public monument was made six days

---

[1] See 17 Jan. 86.   [2] 28 May 83, 13 Sept. 85.
[3] *Illustrated London News*, 17 April 1886, 397–8, 400.
[4] 9–18 Mar. 84; a heavy cold affecting the chest, larynx, and voice. The Cabinet met at Coombe Warren (Bertram Currie's house) where Gladstone was convalescing, but only after the decision to appoint Zobeir had been reversed; 29 Mar. 84.
[5] 19 Apr. 81.   [6] To Rothschild, 24 Apr. 81.
[7] 30 Apr. 81.

later. As usually happens with such situations, the contemplation was worse than the action: 'Meditated over my very difficult task a little before the House; & I commit myself to God, who has ever helped me. . . . As to the Monument all went better than I could have hoped. . . .'[1] This was, obviously, a unique moment, the death of the only person in British politics with whom Gladstone had been able to strike no personal *rapport*. Gladstone comforted himself that there was at least a bond in their respective devotion to their wives.

Two longer illnesses are of particular note. December 1882 started badly with diarrhoea spoiling the end of the procedure debates.[2] By the end of the month Gladstone—usually a sturdy sleeper even before a big parliamentary occasion—began to suffer from severe insomnia,[3] that most curious of conditions, which the exercise of the will compounds rather than alleviates. There was a clutch of causes: his wife's insomnia, a problem since the summer; the failure of his plans to resign; the anxieties and arguments with colleagues and with the Queen over the reshuffle; concern about the see of Llandaff; irritation at Rosebery's refusal to come easily into line; and anxiety about what to say at the meeting arranged for January 1883 in Midlothian. In these fraught circumstances, the husband's insomnia encouraged the wife's, and *vice versa*.[4] Clark, summoned to Hawarden, prescribed rest, and Wolverton, intervening discreetly as always at a time of crisis, arranged for the Gladstones to stay at Château Scott, his villa in Cannes, a stay that was extended until after the session had begun in London.[5] Gladstone's sleeping quickly revived but Catherine Gladstone's insomnia, deeper seated than her husband's, was much slower to improve. She kept a little diary of the visit, a rather desolate document with a hint of desperation in the scrawled hand. She noted the sleeping each night, usually referring to William Gladstone as 'he' or 'Husband': 'Not a good night but Husband sleeps very well *every night*!!!'[6]

Gladstone missed Westminster: 'I feel dual—I am at Cannes & in D. St at my [eve of session] dinner.'[7] But he revelled in the break, enjoyed long walks and conversations with Acton, 'a most satisfactory mind',[8] meeting the young Clemenceau—the conversation was overheard and reported in the *Daily News*[9]—having lunch with the Comte de Paris, and inspecting the French ironclads.[10] He commented on two old men whom he saw: 'Count Pahlen: aged 93. Suggestive of many thoughts' and Edward Cardwell, now senile, 'a sad spectacle, monitory of our lot'.[11]

The insomnia episode was a warning. Gladstone got over it quickly, and the relative inactivity of the 1883 session (partly the result of his absence from the January cabinets which effectively ducked the issue of Irish local government) helped to settle and relax him. There was a recurrence of insomnia in December 1884–January 1885, following the Seats Bill negotiations and a painful

---

[1] 9 May 81.   [2] 28 Nov.–1 Dec. 82.
[3] First noted on 2 Jan. 83, but clearly earlier ('my sleep was further cut down . . .').
[4] 16 Jan. 83.   [5] For Cannes, see 18 Jan.–26 Feb. 83.
[6] Catherine Gladstone's diary, written on loose sheets of paper, is in Mary Gladstone's papers, Add MS 46269, ff. 1–14.
[7] 14 Feb. 83.   [8] 12 Feb. 83.
[9] 8–10 Feb. 83.   [10] 9, 12, 16 Feb. 83.
[11] 23 Jan., 22 Feb. 83.

dispute within the Cabinet on Egyptian finance and, with sleep on one night down to an hour and a half,[1] there was again talk of a retreat to Cannes. This time, however, the lack of sleep did not become chronic and rest at Hawarden proved a sufficient cure.[2] Sometimes he read Scott in bed to compose himself for sleep, and sometimes he 'took up a good supply of strawberries'.[3]

Loss of voice in 1885 was the second of Gladstone's illnesses which seriously affected the pattern of his political behaviour. By the time of the resignation of the government in June 1885 he was seriously concerned about his speaking powers, referring in his memorandum on his future position to his need to restore them 'to something like a natural condition'.[4] Obviously enough, a Gladstone silenced would be a Samson shorn. In early July he visited Oxford, staying with the Talbots at Keble College. As usual there was a round of visits to town and gown—Christ Church, New College, a tour of Headington, a visit to 'the "Puseum" so called [Pusey House, commemorating E. B. Pusey]: dis-appointed: in the House and Library'.[5] Something, perhaps the dampness of the air in that city of sore throats, markedly worsened his condition and medical assistance was summoned. Next day he foolishly spoke for nearly an hour in the Commons despite having seen Saunders, his dentist and throat specialist, in the morning. Once a proper examination was made by Saunders and Clark, 'silence rather rigidly enjoined [as] a condition of fairly probable recovery. *No* House of Commons.'[6] Soon after, 'immediate "treatment" of the throat decided on'.[7] Mr. Thistlethwayte presented him with an 'aureoniophone'—presumably an ampli-fication device of some sort, possibly a hearing trumpet used as a loud speaker—but Gladstone told Mrs. Thistlethwayte that his needs went much beyond its powers.[8]

Gladstone was suffering from acute vocal strain, nowadays called 'myaes-thenia laryngis', a condition common enough among elderly actors, less so today among politicians as their calling no longer requires such prodigious or regular feats of vocal projection.[9] Felix Semon, to whom Saunders and Clark referred their patient, was the leading expert of the day on cancer of the larynx. He diagnosed Gladstone's condition as 'chronic laryngeal catarrh'.[10] In a series of twenty-one daily treatments between 18 July and 8 August 1885, Semon applied 'daily treatment by medicine & by interior applications to the vocal chords as well as by galvanism outside'.[11] It may be that this treatment included cauterization of the polyps which are sometimes part of this condition. Whether it was Semon's treatment or simply rest which caused improvement

---

[1] 31 Dec. 84. [2] See 1–10 Jan. 85.

[3] To Mrs. Gladstone, 1 July 86.

[4] 16 June 85. The condition was noticed in 1881; to Kitson, 2 Oct. 81. For a previous period of enforced silence (occasioned by a cough), see 18–22 Apr. 82.

[5] For the Oxford visit, see 3–6 July 85.

[6] 14 July 85. [7] 16 July 85.

[8] To Mrs Thistlethwayte, 21 July 1885; see also 21 Mar. 86; the transcription is not quite certain; no appropriate device has been identified.

[9] I am obliged to Professor Henry Harris and Mr. B. H. Colman for their comments on Glad-stone's condition.

[10] 20 July 85.

[11] To Mrs. Thistlethwayte, 21 July 1885.

cannot now be known. Gladstone was uncertain whether the voyage to Norway on the Brasseys' yacht *Sunbeam*,[1] planned from the start as a part of the treatment, was in fact beneficial, for the 'soft air is against my throat'.[2] Clark accompanied him on the cruise and continued 'applications'. However, during the Midlothian Campaign of November 1885 Gladstone was able to make a series of speeches of over an hour each. Clearly he was not up to full power and his performance on 28 November disheartened Rosebery and Hamilton.[3] But to manage six major speeches, several of them to audiences of over 2000 without, of course, any form of amplification, was in the circumstances at the least satisfactory. There was a return of the condition just before the speech introducing the Government of Ireland Bill in 1886, but Clark was able to maintain the voice by administering three 'inhalations'.[4]

His recovery was characteristic. It reminds us of the underlying toughness and resilience of Gladstone's physique and of the danger of generalizing from a particular episode. Clearly his health in his seventies needed watching and could obtrude, and on occasion could be used to obtrude, dislocating political life. It contributed to his uncertainty about his political future, his doctor, Clark, often being consulted when retirement was in the air.[5] But Gladstone remained fit and hard, the illnesses usually being understandable reactions after periods of intense strain. During such periods he mostly performed as well or better than his colleagues, still on his feet in the Commons when men half his age had collapsed. Staying at Balmoral in 1884, he climbed Ben Macdhui, the highest point in the Grampians, in a walk from Derry Lodge of 20 miles in 7 hours and 40 minutes 'with some effort' on what is even today a little used route.[6] He compared it with his previous ascent by a longer route in September 1836 and noticed 'A change!'[7] But it was by any standards a creditable performance and rather more than that for someone aged seventy-four.

Weekending was an important part of Gladstone's relaxation throughout the 1880–5 government.[8] Hawarden was too far from London to be convenient for a weekend and was only used out of session or during the Easter and Whitsun breaks. There was no 'Chequers' in those days and the Gladstones were thus always guests for their weekend breaks. Even with the most amiable of hosts this must have been less relaxing than if they had been in their own house. Rosebery provided in The Durdans at Epsom (just off the race course) a house which was convenient and an atmosphere which was congenial: bookish but not demanding, though some of the guests, for example the novelist, Henry James, sometimes were so.[9] Some of the misunderstanding about Rosebery's expectations about his political promotion may have arisen from a confusion of roles. As Gladstone's frequent host, Rosebery—also of course his patron in Midlothian—gained a familiarity which he expected to see reflected in a rapid rise

[1] For the voyage, see 8 Aug.–1 Sept. 85.
[2] See 19 Aug. 85 and to Grosvenor, 22 Aug. 85.
[3] See 28 Nov. 85 and Rhodes James, *Rosebery*, 174.
[4] See 7 Apr. 86.   [5] See, e.g., 26 Nov. 82, 1 June 86.
[6] 11 Sept. 84.   [7] 9 Sept. 36, 26 Sept. 84.
[8] Gladstone's pattern of week-ending can most easily be seen in 'Where was He?' at the end of each volume.
[9] 14–15 Apr. 84.

to the Cabinet. Gladstone was perhaps unwise to allow the confusion of roles to develop.

The other houses were those of persons often with political interests but without strong political ambitions. Dollis Hill, the Aberdeens' Villa then north of London, was an attractive and very close refuge, much used from 1882; Gladstone's connection with the area was commemorated when the exchange system of telephone numbers was introduced, the exchange for that area being GLAdstone, and is still marked by Gladstone Park. Littleburys at Mill Hill, also Lord Aberdeen's, was a similar sort of place; Gladstone became fascinated by its connection with Nell Gwyn, and it was when staying there that he struck up a friendship with James Murray, a pronounced Liberal, then begining his dictionary while teaching at the nearby school.[1] The other houses generally used were Wolverton's Combe Warren and Combe Hurst, owned by Mrs. Vyner, a distant relation of Lord Ripon whom he met at Cannes.[2]

These were all secluded retreats. The Gladstones' company was also sought by less reticent hosts. Gladstone was sometimes displayed as an icon or more often paraded as a 'turn' and held up as a 'catch' by one of the predators hovering on the fringe of the Gladstonian court, such as Sir Donald Currie (knighted in 1881) whose shares stood to benefit at least as much as Gladstone's health from one of his trips on the Castle Line steamers.[3] A cruise on one of Currie's steamers was as public a holiday as a trip to Brighton.

The usual out-of-session break was, as in the first government, a long spell at Hawarden: sometimes staying in the Castle with Willy and his family (until his house in the Park was finished),[4] sometimes with Stephen at the Rectory,[5] sometimes moving from one to the other in the hope of better sleep.[6] Even at Hawarden, therefore, there was a degree to which the Gladstones were guests. Their own home, 73 Harley Street, was rented out from 1882,[7] an emblem, not willingly shared by his wife, of William Gladstone's intention to retire and leave the London scene.[8] The Gladstones' curiously nomadic life, with a series of borrowed houses in 1885 and 1886 and no house of their own in London, reflected the uncertainty of his political position.[9] Undoubtedly, Gladstone felt most at home in Hawarden Castle, sorting his books in his study, 'the Temple of Peace', or chopping trees in the Park with one of his sons. Volume XI contains a fine photograph of him among his books in the 'Temple of Peace' taken by J. P. Mayall for his series *Artists at Home*. Gladstone qualified for the series on the

----

[1] 29 Apr. 81n., 31 July, 1 Oct. 81.

[2] 30 Jan., 23 June 83.

[3] Currie's K.C.M.G. was described by *Vanity Fair* as 'Knight of the Cruise of Mr. Gladstone'; for this, and for the value to Currie of the Gladstonian connection, see A. Porter, *Victorian shipping, business and Imperial policy* (1986), 76, 108, 226.

[4] See 27 Sept., 20 Oct. 84.

[5] e.g. the stay from 9–24 April 1881 seems to have been entirely at the Rectory.

[6] 11–13, 27 Dec. 84.   [7] See 1 Apr. 82n.

[8] See 18, 21 Nov. 81.

[9] On moving out of Downing Street, the Gladstones camped with Bertram Currie, a partner in Glyn's bank and thus a further dimension of the Wolverton connection (see 24 June 85). In July 1885, they stayed with the Aberdeens at Dollis Hill, leaving their possessions with Currie; in 1886, before and after the third government, they stayed with Lucy Cavendish (see above).

rather curious grounds that he was Professor of Ancient History at the Royal Academy throughout this period.

There were political gatherings at Hawarden, but not often. The flurry of visits in the autumn of 1885—Bright, Chamberlain, Granville, Rosebery, Spencer[1]—was distinctly unusual (as was the Gladstones' stay at Chatsworth in February 1885 and his two visits to Derby at Knowsley).[2] For a good deal of the parliamentary vacation, Gladstone's links with his Cabinet colleagues were by letter. This allowed him to some extent to control the speed and distribution of his views. Gladstone's absences from London helped his own and his colleagues' recuperation from what were usually very tiring sessions, but they had the result that there was often an absence of force behind the build-up to the pre-Christmas planning Cabinets, and, as we have seen earlier in this Introduction, this lack of force had a high cost in the absence of a coherent plan for the various initiatives in local government legislation which constituted both the chief ambition and the chief failure of the ministry.

Very different from the family evenings and early-to-bed life at Hawarden, though in its own way also a relaxation from the strain of politics, was the 'rescue work' which Gladstone pursued when in London. Though not as intense an experience as it had been in his early middle age, it remained regular. Quite often on two evenings a week during the session he would record a conversation with a prostitute (often with more comment than he would make on political conversations). Few of the encounters were highly charged, though Mrs. Bolton, eventually saved from prostitution and herself involved in rescue activity, encouraged something of the fascination he had experienced with other cases in earlier times[3] and in an encounter with 'Cooper (& another) [Gladstone] was carried into dreamland, with disappointment X'.[4] He encountered prostitutes of all ages, including 'Hunter (12)',[5] but this did not encourage him to a favourable view of W. T. Stead's 'Maiden Tribute' campaign in the *Pall Mall Gazette* against child prostitution. At Mrs. Meynell Ingram's request he read 'the first of the too famous P.M.G.s. Am not well satisfied with the mode in which this mass of horrors has been collected, or as to the moral effect of its general dispersion by sale in the streets.'[6] 'Rescue work' for Gladstone had always been a private matter coming under the Tractarian doctrine of 'reserve'. He disliked sensationalism and also the politicization of the question whether in the form of the campaign against the Contagious Diseases Acts or for the raising of the age of consent and he remained as apart as he could from pressure groups.

The absence of interest in the role of the State in such matters may have reflected political prudence, but this is unlikely, for Gladstone's behaviour night

---

[1] These visitors were: Chamberlain (7 Oct. 85), Bright (15 Oct. 85), Harcourt, Whitbread (22 Oct. 85), Rosebery (27 Oct., 8 Dec. 85), A. Morley (28 Oct. 85), Granville (31 Oct., 5 Dec. 85), Spencer (8 Dec. 85), T. Acland and Wolverton (10 Dec. 85), and several visits from Grosvenor who lived nearby. Henry James, the attorney-general, was summoned for an important discussion on franchise; see 19 Oct. 83. See also 19 Dec. 83.

[2] 30 Jan.–5 Feb. 85. For Gladstone at Knowsley, see 26–9 Oct. 81, 8–12 Oct. 83, and below, vol. xi, Appendix I.

[3] For her, see 4 Apr. 82, 3 Jan. 84, 19 Oct. 86.

[4] 9 Jan. 82.   [5] 22 July 81.   [6] 15 July 85.

by night was not prudent. On at least four occasions he was warned about the supposed political dangers, first by Rosebery (after nervously losing the toss of a coin to Granville) in February 1882, and three times by E. W. Hamilton in May 1882, February 1884, and July 1886.[1] On each occasion Gladstone noted the conversation but without comment. Rescue work by this time seemed an inherent part of his London life, nor was Rosebery quite the sort of person to persuade him to give it up. Hamilton had a much better chance. In February 1884 he warned that the reticence of the policemen responsible for guarding Gladstone could not be relied on: 'For the simple affidavit of one of them there are many malicious and unscrupulous persons who would give large sums. There is no saying to what account these persons might not turn such information.'[2]

Gladstone ignored this warning. In July 1886, at the height of the divorce scandal involving Sir Charles Dilke, Hamilton tried again. This time, responding to warnings from Canon MacColl and Stead, he emphasized the effect which rumours were already having in the metropolitan constituencies and the extent to which Liberal friends were bewildered as to what they should say when challenged with stories of Gladstone's activities. He told Gladstone that there was 'a conspiracy on foot . . . to set spies on you to watch your movements'.[3] The implication that 'rescue work' endangered victory in the Home Rule campaign did the trick. Gladstone replied to Hamilton: 'As I fear there *does* exist in the world the baseness you describe, I believe on the whole that what you say is true and wise, and I give you my promise accordingly.'[4] For the rest of 1886 and for all of 1887, though considerable time was spent in London, rescue work ceased—a remarkable achievement for Hamilton.

Soon after this Gladstone burned the letters of one of the most striking of the courtesans with whom he had had dealings in the 1850s:

> Today I burned a number of old letters, kept apart, which might in parts have suggested doubt & uneasiness: two of the writers were Mrs Dale and Mrs Davidson: cases of great interest, in qualities as well as attractions certainly belonging to the flower of their sex. I am concerned to have lost sight of them.[5]

Mrs. Dale was the courtesan whose portrait Gladstone had commissioned from William Dyce, and which is reproduced in Volume V. It is very unlikely that the destruction of these letters was the elimination of a political risk, for the letters kept in the 'Octagon' at Hawarden were completely safe. It is more probable that this was part of that preparation for death and for posterity which culminated in the declaration about his rescue work made in 1896 to his son Stephen.[6] Gladstone was well aware that his diary and his papers contained material that would astonish his children and perhaps even his wife.

Mrs. Thistlethwayte[7] was not a political risk: her salon in Grosvenor Square

[1] 10 Feb., 9 May 82, 14–16 July 86. For these incidents see Bahlman, *Hamilton*, i. 222, 269, E.H.D., 14–16 July 1886, Magnus, 108–9, and Hamilton to Gladstone, 6 February 1884, 14 July 1886, Lambeth MS 2760, ff. 188, 192.

[2] Hamilton to Gladstone, 6 February 1884, Lambeth MS 2760, f. 188.

[3] Hamilton to Gladstone, 14 July 1886, Lambeth MS 2760, f. 192 and 26 July 86n.

[4] To Hamilton, 26 July 86.

[5] 16 Oct. 86.   [6] See above, iii. xlvi.

[7] For Gladstone's letters to her up to 1870, see above, viii, Appendix. A selection of his letters to her from 1871 until her death in 1894 will be included in a later volume.

was by the 1880s quite respectable, more regularly attended by various political figures such as C. P. Villiers, the veteran M.P. for Wolverhampton, than by Gladstone. 'Mrs. Th.' was by now no longer a temptation and had in fact become something of a burden: her frequent little gifts and invitations to lunch, tea, or dinner needed acknowledgements (quite how her letters were to be processed in the office led to irritating muddles); Gladstone quite often accepted invitations only to cancel at the last minute. Even allowing for the calls on his time in these years, duty rather than pleasure seems to predominate in his visits. On the other hand, in 1883, with Catherine Gladstone at Hawarden, he visited her two days running, and he visited her in her cottage in Hampstead immediately after the resignation Cabinet on 20 July 1886.[1] Mrs. Thistlethwayte's financial rows with her husband—leading in 1882 to a new law case reported in the newspapers—occasioned his sympathy and support. He was also grateful for her help to the wretched Lady Susan Opdebeck (divorced widow of his former colleague the Duke of Newcastle) now almost penniless.

It was through Newcastle in the mid-1860s that Gladstone had first come in contact with Laura Thistlethwayte, then a notorious and only recently, perhaps only partly, retired courtesan.[2] Gladstone delayed his retirement in 1881 as a Trustee of the Newcastle Estates so as to try to obtain a better settlement for Lady Susan which, with Mrs. Thistlethwayte mediating with the Newcastle children, he seems to have succeeded in doing. The episode must have brought back both the high noon of his relationship with Laura Thistlethwayte and his bizarre expedition to Italy in 1849 shadowing the beautiful Lady Susan,[3] 'once the dream of dreams', and her lover: 'I cannot dismiss the recollection of her as she was 50 years back one of the brightest among stars of youthful grace & beauty.'[4]

Gladstone did not visit Laura Thistlethwayte often but he found her *salon*, if not Laura herself, attractive when he did. It was perhaps at dinner in her house in Grosvenor Square on 8 October 1884 that he became drawn into the spiritualist movement, then fashionable in certain sections of society[5] (though in June 1884 he had, together with some fifty other M.P.s, attended a 'Thought-reading' at the House of Commons).[6] Certainly, Laura Thistlethwayte's religion—deistic post-evangelicalism—was a common feature of the spiritualists of the 1880s.

Whether or not Laura Thistlethwayte was the link, Gladstone attended a *séance* on 29 October 1884 at 34 Grosvenor Square, a house rented by Mrs. Emma Hartmann, no doubt the wife of Eduard von Hartmann, a well-known writer on spiritualism. The *séance* was conducted by William Eglinton and mainly took the form of 'slate writing', Gladstone participating by writing two

[1] 25–6 Oct. 83; 20 July 86.
[2] See above, iv. lxii. Laura Thistlethwayte maintained her connection with the Newcastle family through the 5th duke's children, and one of them was the beneficiary of her will.
[3] 5 Aug. 49; see also 20 July–4 Aug. 49.
[4] To Mrs. Thistlethwayte, 3 August 1885; a further attempt at raising money for Lady Susan.
[5] Mrs. Thistlethwayte's agency is my supposition; spiritualism is not discussed in Gladstone's letters to her. However, it is clear that she was acquainted with Lady Sandhurst who organized the second *séance* attended by Gladstone.
[6] See 19 June 84.

questions, first: 'Which year do you remember to have been more dry than the present one'; second, 'Is the Pope well or ill', to which the medium replied (supposedly without seeing the questions): 'In the year 1857' and 'He is ill in mind, not in body'.[1] In reply to another question, the medium was unwilling to tip the winner of the Cesarewitch.

Gladstone was intrigued but cautious: 'For the first time I was present at his operations of spiritualism: quite inexplicable: not the smallest sign of imposture.'[2] He was unfortunate in the choice of medium. Eglinton was, in the view of a number of spiritualists, a society fraud. He was denounced as such by Mrs. Sidgwick, A. J. Balfour's sister and Helen Gladstone's superior at Newnham College, Cambridge, in what became a bitter controversy in the pages of the *Journal of the Society for Psychical Research* in 1886.[3] Shortly after the *séance*, mention of it appeared in the London evening papers. Eglinton blamed one of Mrs. Hartmann's servants and promised a 'correct version of the whole affair in next week's *Light*',[4] an account also printed in the *Morning Post* of 7 November 1884, in the midst of the parliamentary crisis over the reintroduced Franchise Bill. Recourse to blaming the servants was the last refuge of many a Victorian scoundrel and, given his record elsewhere, the likelihood must be that Eglinton could not resist creating the excuse to write a public account of the proceedings (in the *Morning Post* report, Gladstone and Eglinton were the only named members of the company).

Despite this publicity, Gladstone tried again, attending a *séance*, this time with guaranteed privacy, at Lady Sandhurst's on 18 November, the day before the first conference with Salisbury on redistribution. The medium, Mrs. Duncan, was clearly much more satisfactory, falling into a trance and offering religious and moral exhortation, as well as advice about his throat. Gladstone did not contribute actively to the proceedings: 'I declined all active part hearing & noting it *ad referendum*. To mix myself in these things would baffle & perplex: but good advice is to be remembered come how it may.'[5]

Such were Gladstone's direct dealings with the spiritualists, though he agreed to be elected as an honorary member of the Society for Psychical Research in 1885[6] and occasionally read its journal.[7] In general terms, involvement with spiritualism in the 1880s was common enough in the professional classes and the aristocracy. As traditional beliefs about heaven, hell, and sacramental religion declined among the intelligentsia and 'agnostic' became a common self-description, attempts to communicate beyond immediate consciousness were seen as a natural form of progress, rather as the eugenics movement a little later sought for physical progress. This may explain why the detailed report in the *Morning Post*, irritating though it was for the Prime

---

[1] *Morning Post*, 7 November 1884, 3f.

[2] 29 Oct. 84.

[3] *Journal of the Society for Psychical Research*, ii. 282 (June 1886). For the Sidgwicks' successful visit to Hawarden, see 24–5 Sept. 85.

[4] See Eglinton to Mrs. Hartmann and Mrs. Hartmann to Gladstone, neither dated, the latter docketed 1 November 1884, Add MS 44488, f. 4.

[5] 18 Nov. 84.

[6] *Journal of the Society for Psychical Research*, ii. 449 (July 1885).

[7] 22 Aug. 85.

Minister, seems to have had little ongoing effect in the press. The Society for Psychical Research, led by Cambridge intellectuals such as the Sidgwicks and F. W. H. Myers, Fellow of Trinity, had several clergy on its Council including two bishops: Goodwin of Carlisle and Boyd Carpenter of Ripon, both Gladstonian appointments.[1] The Society offered a meeting ground for Christians and agnostics.

Even so, it is surprising to find Gladstone involved in this circle. In most respects he was an orthodox sacramentalist with what was by the 1880s an old-fashioned view of heaven; an anglo-catholic was the least likely sort of Anglican to be drawn to the Society. The lingering evangelicalism of his youth was certainly not of the post-Christian, 'other world' character of some of the members of the Society for Psychical Research. On the other hand, Gladstone was always curious and we have often seen in these Introductions the extent to which he was, rather despite himself, attracted to certain Broad Church views, as when he defended Seeley's *Ecce Homo*.[2] He believed that all phenomena were explicable within the Christian experience. Thus, if contact with the 'other world' existed, it would be so explained. He attended the *séances* in this spirit of investigation. Annoyed by Eglinton and fundamentally unimpressed by Mrs. Duncan, he seems to have taken no further active part in psychical research.[3]

This brief survey of some aspects of the private Gladstone indicates the richness of the material printed below. The daily diary gives a spine to this material. Individual entries remain uninviting. Gladstone did not find writing his diary a literary relaxation, nor did he use it as a means of scoring points in the debates of posterity. The alternative model of Greville came before him in 1883[4] but he made no change of format even when out of office. For the most part, the diary continues to be an accumulation of recorded facts, of letters written, church services and political debates attended, books, pamphlets, and articles read. Used for individual entries, it will disappoint; used cumulatively it will illuminate.

A good example and one of central interest to this period is the diary's record of Gladstone's Irish reading. This was always thorough. It shows that there were few works of substance that did not catch his eye. He was particularly interested in all aspects of Irish history and read at a variety of levels. He twice read O'Connor's *Chronicles of Eri*,[5] he had read J. A. Froude, Lecky,[6] and the various works of Barry O'Brien as they came out.[7] He read extensively in the seventeenth-century history of Ireland especially through the large pamphlet collection made by J. T. Gilbert in his *History of the Irish Confederation and the War in Ireland*, the chief research collection for Irish history published in these years.[8] Not surprisingly,

---

[1] For the movement, see J. Oppenheim, *The other world. Spiritualism and psychical research in England, 1850–1914* (1985), especially ch. 3, 'Spiritualism and Christianity'. Lady Sandhurst told Gladstone that 'the spirit and purpose' of her *séance* was 'wholly Christian and biblical'; 18 Nov. 84.

[2] See Matthew, *Gladstone*, 154–5.

[3] Though some reading followed; see 21 Dec. 84, 11, 18 Jan. 85.

[4] 14 July 83.

[5] 15 Jan. 83, 20 Apr. 86.

[6] See e.g. for Lecky, 6 Feb. 72; for Froude, 25 Nov. 72, 25 Mar. 86.

[7] For O'Brien's *Parliamentary history* (1880), see 4 Nov. 80; *Irish land question* (1881), 11 May 81; *Fifty years of concessions* (1883–5), 9 Oct. 83, 12 Oct. 85.

[8] 11 Jan. 82 etc.

there was a particular emphasis on eighteenth- and nineteenth-century Ireland and the constitutional developments of the Pitt–Grattan years. However, it is important to note that though this reading intensified in the autumn of 1885, especially at the time of the important entry on the Union ('I have always suspected the Union of 1800 . . .'),[1] this was mostly a checking of well-known sources.[2]

What was systematically engaging Gladstone's attention at the time was P. G. F. Le Play's *La réforme sociale en France*, 2v. (1864) (an important work of conservative religious sociology emphasizing the need for parental authority in the factory as well as the home)[3] and, a little later, his controversy with Huxley. Gladstone was a life-long student of Burke and he turned again to that 'magazine of wisdom'[4] in December 1885 as Home Rule became a political probability. Thus Burke on America and Dicey on *The Law of the Constitution* constituted a neat pairing—the old historicism and the new deductivism—for systematic study in the important months of November and December 1885.[5] Gladstone had always had a general interest in Irish history and he continued, as always, to read the literature, including many pamphlets and articles, as it was published. But what is striking about Gladstone's historicist reading is that the period of really intense reading on Ireland *per se*—general interest there had always been—was after the strategic decisions for Home Rule had been taken. It is in the spring and summer of 1886 (from March 1886 onwards) that we find the full emphasis on the need for historical understanding; the extensive 'inquiry' and note-taking[6] date mainly from that time.

Just as organization of propaganda paradoxically followed the Home Rule defeat, so detailed work on the history of the Union followed rather than anticipated the decision for Home Rule. The second paradox is not as great as the first: as we have seen, Gladstone was well-informed, at least *via* the medium of reading, about Irish history and Irish affairs, and that general understanding was clearly important to him in his sensing in 1885 that a turning point had been reached. Even so, the relative absence of Irish historical reading in the summer and autumn of 1885 and the relative dominance of it in 1886 are striking features of these diaries.

The domination of Ireland increased as Gladstone's ability to control events decreased. The frenetic election campaign of June–July 1886 saw Gladstone at bay, attempting to hold the Home Rule line and to defend Home Rule candidates with a flurry of endorsing and sometimes injudicious letters and telegrams. The absence of a proper party structure, despite the securing of the National Liberal Federation for the Gladstonian cause, was never more marked.

---

[1] See 19 Sept. 85.

[2] See, e.g. 18 Oct. 80 for Grattan's *Speeches . . . comprising a brief review of the most important political events in the history of Ireland* (1811), and Pitt's speeches on the Union; 10 Apr. 82 for consultation of the *Annual Register*'s recording of the Union debates.

[3] Read 29 July 85–19 Sept. 85; the book was sent to him by Olga Novikov; see 1 July 85. On 20 Sept. 85 Gladstone began Le Play's *La constitution de l'Angleterre*, 2v. (1875).

[4] 18 Dec. 85.

[5] See 18, 19 Nov. 85, 1, 8, 17, 22, 23, 29, 31 Dec. 85.

[6] See Add MS 44770 for Gladstone's extensive notes on his Irish reading.

Characteristically, Gladstone saw the election defeat as welcome retribution and relief:

> The defeat is a smash. I accept the will of God for my poor country or the English part of it. To me personally it is a great relief: including in this cessation of my painful relations with the Queen, who will have a like feeling.[1]

A mood of stoic optimism followed. He wrote *The Irish question*[2] and, with Acton, visited Döllinger in Bavaria: Döllinger 'gratified me much by his view of my pamphlet'.[3] He restarted work on the Olympian religion, the work planned in the 1860s as the successor to *Studies on Homer and the Homeric Age*, 3 vols. (1858). But he found it hard to concentrate. In bed with a cold, he noted

> There is a disposition to grudge as wasted these days. But they afford great opportunities of review. Especially as to politics, and my politics are now summed up in the word Ireland, for probing inwardly the intention, to see whether all is truly given over to the Divine will.[4]

For all the difficulties, Gladstone was fundamentally optimistic. At home he planned for the future, discussing the 'meditated Nucleus-Building' and making the first steps towards what became St. Deiniol's Library, the residential library at Hawarden that is his national memorial.[5] At large, he wrote the defence of nineteenth-century optimism, '"Locksley Hall" and the Jubilee',[6] with which we began this Introduction; he looked with delight at the 'varied and far-reaching consequences'[7]—the possible disintegration of the Salisbury administration—which he anticipated from Randolph Churchill's resignation; he looked with caution at the implications of a return of the 'dissentient Liberals';[8] and he found in his own political position a cause for fundamental calm and reassurance which set the tone for the remainder of his life:

> O for a birthday of recollections! It is long since I have had one. There is so much to say on the soul's history: but *bracing* is necessary to say it, as it is for reading Dante. It has been a year of shock and strain: I think a year of some progress: but of greater absorption in interests which though profoundly human are quite off the line of an old man's direct preparation for passing the River of Death. I have not had a chance given me of escaping from this whirlpool, for I cannot abandon a cause which is so evidently that of my fellowmen *and* in which a particular part seems to be assigned to me. Therefore am I not disturbed 'Though the hills be carried into the midst of the sea'.[9]

---

[1] 8 July 86.   [2] 26 July 86n.
[3] 30 Aug. 86.   [4] 12 Oct. 86.   [5] 12 July 86.
[6] 15 Dec. 86.   [7] 23 Dec. 86.
[8] See the flurry of correspondence resulting from Churchill's resignation and Chamberlain's 'eirenicon', 24–30 Dec. 86.
[9] 29 Dec. 86.

Sat. Jan. 1. 1881. Circumcision. London.

St. And. Wells St. 5 P.M. Wrote to Ld Hartington—Sir H. Ponsonby—Sir C. Dilke—and minutes. Went through the [land] Purchase question with Bright. Saw Consul Kirby Green[1]—Mr Forster—Mr Bright—Ld Granville—Mr Wortley—Mrs Th. Read on Irish Land—Austin's letter[2] and other Tracts. Saw Macgregor: who goes to Australia on the 5th [R].

To Sir C. W. DILKE, foreign undersecretary, 1 January 1881.   Add MS 43875, f. 42.

It is not possible for me at this time to anticipate what may be our financial position in March. Events like those in South Africa, of the latest occurrence, are affecting it unfavourably. But without saying anything positive I think I ought to say the outlook is not very promising as to our having a spare half million to bestow upon the Wine Duties. You will please to take this as a perfectly indeterminate announcement, but it is a reason, as far as it goes, for a great coolness of attitude towards these High & Mighty Powers of the Peninsula.

To W. E. FORSTER, Irish secretary, 1 January 1881.   Add MS 44544, f. 125.

1. I send for perusal my report to the Queen on yesterday's Cabinet.[3]
2. With ref. to the enclosed letter from Argyll on assignment, would you let me know from some one (not you) how the Land Act *de facto* stands as to assignment?
3. I have had a pleasant & pretty full conversation with Bright as to his clauses[4] & an attempt at rude reduction of them which I have made.
4. Will Monck be the proper person for any Com. relating to them? If so, he will be an excellent adviser as to getting them into shape.
5. I have worked on the thorniest part of the Speech, & have read my rough attempt to Granville & Bright, but will ponder it a little more before troubling you.

2. 2. S. Xmas

Chapel Royal mg (with H.C.) and aft. Visited Caroline & Miss Cary. Read on Irish Land—Read Claude on the Eucharist[5]—ONeill on Darwin[6]—Gaussen on Inspiration[7]—Hubbard on Religious Census.[8] Saw Mr Heywood.

3. M.

Wrote to Ld Kimberley—Mr Lefevre MP.—Mrs Th—D. of Westminster—Mr Reid—Ld Northbrook—Ld Hartington & minutes. Worked on the Queen's

---

[1] (Sir) William Kirby Green, 1836–91; chargé in Montenegro and consul at Scutari 1879–86; minister in Tangier from 1886; kt. 1887.
[2] Perhaps W. Austin, *Letters from London* (1804).
[3] In *L.Q.V.*, 2nd series, iii. 170, dated 31 December 1881.
[4] i.e. the Bright land purchase clauses of the 1870 Act.
[5] By J. Claude, probably *The Catholic doctrine of the Eucharist in all ages* (1684).
[6] T. W. O'Neill, *The refutation of Darwinism* (1880).
[7] S. R. L. Gaussen, *Théopneustie ou inspiration plénière des Saintes Ecritures* (1842).
[8] In *N.C.*, ix. 131 (January 1881).

Speech. Saw the Mover & Seconder, 12–1¼[1]–Ld Northbrook 1¼–2¼–Ld Chancellor–Do cum Archbishop of Canterbury 3–4–Ld Wolverton–Ld Granville. Saw also Lady Susan: after some 32 or 33 years! I felt something & could say much.[2] To unbend after the strain, we went to the Lyceum & saw the Cup & Corsican Brothers:[3] with a kind of interlude which Mr Knowles & I had behind the scenes. The Cup had some very fine passages with a beautiful *mise en scéne*: I cannot quite estimate it as a drama until after reading it. Read Arabian Poetry.

4. *Tu.*

Wrote to Mrs Goulburn–Ld Hartington–Sir R. Lingen–Ld Kimberley–The Queen–and minutes. [Queen's] Speech Cabinet 2½–5½. Saw Lord R. Grosvenor–Mr Forster–Ld F. Cavendish–Mr P. Ralli–Ld Kimberley–Mr Childers. Read Capper on Boden See.[4] Dined at Lord F.C.s.

Cabinet. Jan. 4 1881. 2 P.M.[5]
1. Speech considered & agreed on
2. Determined to push forward Protective enactments if possible *de die in diem.*
3. Short Bill for Suspension of *Habeas Corpus*: to be presented alone. To be shortened to the uttermost.
4. Arms Bill to follow.

To LORD KIMBERLEY, colonial secretary, 4 January 1881.   Add MS 44544, f. 126.

Please to examine critically. I think direct *praise* of the colonists might raise adverse criticism.[6] Perhaps you may agree.

5. *Wed.*

Wrote to W.H.G.–The Queen Tel.–Marq. of Huntley–Sir T.E. May–Sir H. Ponsonby Tel. & minutes. Dinner to the official Corps. Final & formal revision of Speech. Saw Mr Rendel cum Slagg–Lord A. Grosvenor–Ld Granville cum Ld Hartington–Sir W. Harcourt–The Speaker–Musurus Pacha–Sir T. May–Sir R. Blennerhassett and others. Read Capper on the Boden See. Putting papers a little into order: and paying bills.

6. *Th. Epiph. & C.G.s birthday.*

May the Lord crown her with every blessing. Wrote to Ld Granville–Mr Forster–Mr Darwin–Mr Ouvry–The Queen–Mr Otway & minutes. H. of C. 4½–8¾ and 10–12¼. Spoke 50 m. in answer to Northcote. Not self-defence but the Land

[1] Of the Queen's Speech: S. Rendel (see 20 Dec. 80) and John Slagg, 1841–89; liberal M.P. Manchester 1880–5, Burnley 1887–9.
[2] i.e. Lady Susan Opdebeck, formerly Lady Lincoln. For Gladstone's pursuit across Italy, on Lincoln's behalf, of her and her lover, see 25 July–8 Aug. 49; in 1881 he successfully obtained some increase in her allowance from the Newcastle estate (though see 11 Nov. 81).
[3] Tennyson's new play, *The Cup*, staged in a double bill with Boucicault's *The Corsican Brothers* (1848), with Irving and Terry.
[4] S. J. Capper, *The shores and cities of the Boden See* (1881).
[5] Add MS 44642, f. 129.
[6] Draft of the Queen's speech; the final version omitted any reference to the colonists.

Bill is our difficulty.[1] Saw Ld R. Grosvenor—Sir S. Northcote—Sir T.E. May—Mr Forster. Read Capper's Boden See—Irish Land Pamphlets.

7. Fr.

Herbert's birthday. God bless & guide him. Wrote to Ed. Daily News—Ld Hartington—Mr Maciver—Lord Granville—Mrs Hope—Lady Susan O[pdebeck]—Mrs Th.—Ld Kimberley—Mr Ouvry—The Queen 1.2.—Mr Ken—and minutes. Saw Mr Ouvry—Ld R. Grosvenor—Lady Susan O—Ld F.C.—Ld Bessborough—Mr Goschen—Mr Childers—Sir C. Herries. H. of C. $4\frac{1}{2}$–$8\frac{3}{4}$ & 10–$12\frac{3}{4}$.[2] Read Capper Boden See.

I have little doubt that the Cabinet will authorise me at once to convey to the Queen the assurance she desires.[3]

It is plain that a declaration of intention is almost as a matter of course subject to the condition which H.M. specifies. W.E.G. Jan. 7. 81[4]

To LORD HARTINGTON, Indian secretary, 7 January 1881　　Chatsworth MSS 340.1055.

Another point occurs to me with reference to military vote of thanks—the point of *time.* As we knew of this victory before the prorogation, should not the thanks if any have been *then*? Would there again be any precedent for thanks so long after the time? The proceeding of the late Government I apprehend was *absurd*, & could only have been carried in a Parliament of abject servility: but it makes a precedent as all bad precedents do.

I told Forster that I thought it probable you would be ready to speak tonight if needful.

To F. H. HILL, Editor of the *Daily News*, 7 January 1881.[5]　　Add MS 44468, f. 10
'*Private*'.

You will not be sorry to receive from me a remark on one of the points in your very fair though regretful article of today on my intimation about the Land Bill we are likely to introduce. Some expression of mine may have misled your Journal: but there is really no foundation for the supposition that my reference to assignment had in view proposals in favour of the landlord:[6] while I think I stated that this point went to the root of the whole matter.

It is one of those on which the House of Lords in 1870 brought about an unfavourable change in the Bill we had introduced.

---

[1] Defending the non-recall of Parliament in December and mildly anticipating the 1881 Bill; *H* 257. 104.

[2] Ireland, Basutoland, Queen's Speech; *H* 257. 190.

[3] The Queen refused consent to the Queen's Speech unless the cabinet agreed that 'should circumstances arise rendering the retention of Candahar desirable, the Government will not hesitate to continue to hold that position'; *L.Q.V.*, 2nd series, iii. 180.

[4] Holograph circulated to Granville, Hartington, Argyll, Selborne, Northbrook, Chamberlain, Childers, and initialled by them concurring; Add MS 44765, p. 79.

[5] Holograph.

[6] *D.N.*, 7 January 1881, 5b: 'the protection of landlords by making new provisions respecting the assignment by the tenant of his interest in the holding'.

To LORD KIMBERLEY, colonial secretary, 7 January 1881.   Add MS 44544, f. 127.

I quite agree as to the answer to be made to the request of Mr. Mills.[1] From one point of view its acceptance would involve us in an infringement of the constitutional rights of the Cape Government; while from another, namely from our own side, I should certainly say that the principle of Guarantee, which has a great tendency to blossom into subsidy, is the most exceptionable mode of taking part, and is certainly a mode of taking part, in a war.

8. Sat.

Wrote to Ld Huntly—Mr Broadhurst MP—Ld Camperdown and minutes. Old Master's Exhibition at 3.30. Saw Miss Farrar—Ld Granville—Lady Derby (a long conversation)—Ld R. Grosvenor—The Speaker—Mr M. Brooks MP. and others. Dined at Spencer House. Conversation with Lady Sydney on the Theatre. Worked most of the day on Irish Land, remodelling the plan.[2]

To H. BROADHURST, M.P., 8 January 1881.   Add MS 44544, f. 127.

I have to acknowledge with thanks your letter of yesterday, and I am much gratified, as my colleagues will be, to receive an expression of confidence from your Committee with regard to our declared intention of asking Parliament to amend the Land Laws of Ireland.[3]

It would be altogether premature and inconvenient to state the nature of our proposals before the day arrives (and that day will not be delayed by any gratuitous act of ours), when we can explain them fully and clearly to Parliament.

For the present, it has only been practicable to point in general terms to the most serious deficiencies of the law as it stands. Among these I have mentioned the subject about which your Committee expresses so just an anxiety.[4] On this particular point, our opinions are in conformity with their language; and I hope we shall be able to propose on this and all the other portions of the subject effective remedies for the evils which now exist.

To Sir W. V. HARCOURT, home secretary, 8 January   MS Harcourt dep. 8, f. 62.
1881.

I send you herewith a memorandum from Sir R. Lingen:[5] from this paper you will see that the concession in principle which you desired will (not without effort) be made, and if any particulars require to be further considered I will ask F. Cavendish to be ready to speak to you.

9. 1. S. Epiph.

Chapel Royal mg & aft. Saw Ld Granville—Mr Ouvry—Mrs Th.—Ld Acton, who dined with us. Wrote to The Queen & minutes. Read Certainty in Religion[6]—

[1] Letter of Capt. Mills (untraced), 'Spriggs' agent here . . . shows that the Cape Govt. is beginning to feel the pressure of its reckless policy'; sent by Kimberley, 6 January, Add MS 44226, f. 1.
[2] Draft Bill, dated 10 January, in Add MS 44626, ff. 13–15; jottings at Add MS 44765, ff. 1–8.
[3] Letter forwarding a resolution from the T.U.C. Parliamentary cttee.; published with this reply in T.T., 10 January 1881, 10c.
[4] 'the unjust operation of the present law has destroyed the interest of the peasantry in the soil'.
[5] Grudgingly conceding that men of the 'working class' might be appointed factory inspectors; MS Harcourt dep. 8, f. 64.
[6] Perhaps H. E. Manning, 'The objective certainty of the immaterial world' (1879).

The Supernatural in Nature (Reynolds)—What Church X Bullock.[1] Read Land Tenure Bill.

10. M.

Wrote to Sir H. Ponsonby—Mr Forster—Mr Shaw MP.—Mr Childers—Viceroy Dublin—Att. General—The Queen tel. and minutes. Further worked up the Irish Land Plan and sent it to be struck off.[2] Saw Ld Monck—Ld R.G.—Ld Kimberley—Mr Forster—Priv. Secs as usual.—Mr Bright. H. of C. $4\frac{1}{2}$-$8\frac{3}{4}$ & $9\frac{3}{4}$-$12\frac{1}{2}$.[3] Saw two [R].

To W. E. FORSTER, Irish secretary, 10 January 1881.   Add MS 44544, f. 128.

There is one question as to the three F.s, which I think ought to be considered[?] in placing before the Cabinet the great amount of demand for them.[4]

These F.s I think mean in the mouths of different persons different things—
(1) F.s with a future return to free contract.
(2) F.s with periodical revaluation
(3) F.s with a rent fixed once for all—
seem to me to be very different; but whether that be so or not, it seems essential to know whether the great tide of Irish opinion in favour of the F.s is an opinion which will accept, as a definitive settlement, any incorporation of the 3 F.s such as No 1, or such as No 2; or whether it is an opinion for No 3 only.

Subject to this explanation, I quite agree with you that the Cabinet ought to understand that while there is a great body of Irish opinion for something called the 3 F.s, & another body as I suppose for Parnell's plan & that of the Land League, there is no such body in favour of anything short of these, though intelligent & weighty *individuals* may be cited in some strength who are for amending the Land Act.

To Sir H. PONSONBY, the Queen's secretary, 10 January 1881.   Add MS 45724, f. 94.

Many thanks. I am glad that the business has ended well.[5] Hartington's frank & straightforward ways are sure in such a case to please a person of corresponding character. I hope the Queen did not hear of one absurd misreport which made me say that if there was a complaint of (a certain matter) it was owing to an inadvertence on the part of the Queen!! for Queen was to be read 'complainer'.

11. Tu.

Kept my bed (with Tonsils slightly relaxed) for a few hours. Wrote to Sir H. Ponsonby—Mr Ouvry 1.2.—The Queen 1.2. & minutes. H. of C. $4\frac{1}{2}$-$8\frac{3}{4}$.[6] To

[1] [J. W. Reynolds], *The supernatural in nature* (1878); C. Bullock, *What church?* (1868).
[2] i.e. printed for Cabinet; CAB 37/5/2.
[3] Question on licensing; Queen's speech; *H* 257. 330.
[4] See Forster's letter this day (Add MS 44158, f. 121): 'I can not help telling you that I believe the feeling for the 3Fs in Ireland prevails even more than I had supposed. If there was an election, I believe there would not be ten Irish Members returned who would not go for that or something stronger. Does not this fact make your warning to the Queen really a warning to the Cabinet? . . .'
[5] The Queen's worries about Kandahar; Guedalla, *Q*, ii. 135.
[6] Questions; spoke on public business; *H* 258. 448.

bed soon after ten. Read Reports of Commn—(Confusion worse confounded)[1]—Trevelyan's Fox.[2]

To Sir H. PONSONBY, the Queen's secretary, 11 January 1881.   Add MS 44544, f. 128.
(1) In the probable event of the acquittal of the Traversers[3] we should I apprehend take the advice of our legal authorities: and they, I presume, would hardly give such advice, until they were aware of the views taken by the Judges, and of all the circumstances of the acquittal.
(2) We have considered the contingency of obstruction: but it does not seem possible to make a further provision against it as yet than we have already proposed by the motion to put aside all other business. Some powers the new rules already supply. An attempt to obtain new ones, if made too early, might lose more time than it could serve. I am exceedingly sensible of the kindness of the Queen's intimation. I have already communicated with Sir S. Northcote as to my Notice: and there has been no difficulty.
(3) I will make known to my colleagues Her Majesty's desire for information, to which I am sure they will carefully attend.

12. Wed.

Kept my bed till 2 P.M. Wrote to Lady Susan, Poverina![4]—The Queen—& minutes. Rose for a deputation of 18 M.P.s 3–5. Stiff conversation on Irish Land question in all its branches. It was useful politically but it did exhaust me.[5] Saw Mr Godley—Ld Granville—Mr Forster—Ld R.G. Read Trevelyan—Stubbs's Myth[6]—Healy on Irish Land.[7]

13. Th.

Wrote to Ld Hartington—Ld Kimberley & Minutes. Read Trevelyan's Fox. Kept my bed all day with energetic measures. Saw Dr Clark—Mr Godley. Much & I hope not unfruitful rumination on Irish Land. Meantime I heard the debate by ambassadors.

14. Fr.

Better thank God. Wrote to Lady Susan—Lord Spencer—Mr Ouvry—Mr Richards MP and minutes. Read Trevelyan's Fox and [blank.] Wrote on Irish Land—wrote plan against obstruction. Saw Mr Godley—Ld R. Grosvenor—Dr

---

[1] Majority and minority reports of the Richmond Royal Commission on agricultural distress, which reported separately on Ireland, Carlingford's minority report recommending the '3 Fs'; *PP* 1881, xv.
[2] See 18 Nov. 80.
[3] i.e. the prosecution in Dublin of Parnell and others; on 23 January, the jury failed to reach a verdict; the Queen had 'commanded' information on the Cabinet's intentions on this and on obstruction; Guedalla, *Q*, i. 135.
[4] 'poor woman'.
[5] Deputation led by Shaw, including Ulster M.P.s but no Parnellites, presented a memorial requesting the 'three F.s'; Gladstone 'declined for the present to enter upon the question of weak or strong measures'; *T.T.*, 13 January 1881, 7b.
[6] C. W. Stubbs, *The mythe of life* (1880).
[7] T. M. Healy, *Why there is an Irish land question and an Irish Land League* (1881).

Clark—Ld Granville—Mr Bright.[1] Much discussion about going to H. of C. ended in my stopping at home, rather ignobly by reason of the cold.

To LORD HARTINGTON, Indian secretary, 14 January 1881.   Add MS 44544, f. 129.

I think the development of obstruction this week renders it expedient that we should a little consider the matter at the Cabinet to-morrow. In the meantime it might be well if you circulated these papers[2] with the mark 'immediate'.

My own opinion is, as far as I have formed one, that the Speaker's office would not bear the weight likely to be laid upon it if he were called upon to secure the House against the various forms of an obstruction organized by a considerable body of members; & I will try to suggest, perhaps to-morrow, an alternative mode of proceeding.

I am waiting for Andrew Clark and hope to send you the result of his visit by Lord Richard.

To H. RICHARD, M.P., 14 January 1881.   Add MS 44544, f. 129.

I think that your letter[3] supplies so excellent a medium, it will be best that I should answer the Peace Society of Holland through you.

Pray assure the Society of my cordial respect and of my appreciation of the spirit in which they write.

The matter, which is one of some anxiety, will have the careful attention of the Government, & I cherish the hope that both the Society & you yourself may not find cause to be dissatisfied with the temper in which we shall endeavour to approach it.

15. Sat.

Cabinet 2–5¼. and Cabinet dinner 8–11¼: but three colleagues begged off as being invalided. Saw Ld R. Grosvenor—Mr Godley—Mr Childers—Mr Bright. Wrote to The Queen and minutes. Read Q.R. on Ritualists[4]—On Ireland— Trevelyans Fox.

Cabinet. Jan. 15. 1881. 2 P M[5]
1. Part VI of W.E.Gs draft on Irish Land to be put into clauses of a Bill.
2. Order in Council giving effect to the opinion of the Judges to be supported.
3. F.O. has nothing to submit: Giers's[6] scheme sanctioned.—Greek papers to be delayed.
4. Forster to prepare Clause on Emigration.

16. 2 S. Epiph

Saw Dr Clark. Strictly inhibited from going to Church: reduced to private reading &c. Saw Sir R. Phillimore. Read Q.R. on Endymion[7]—British Q.R.[8] Divers

---

[1] Discussing obstruction and land; Walling, *Diaries of Bright*, 453.

[2] Probably letters from Thorold Rogers and Lord E. Fitzmaurice sent by Hartington this day; Add MS 44145, f. 175.

[3] Of 13 January, Add MS 44468, f. 31; forwarding a memorial of the Peace Society of Holland, ibid., f. 33, on the Transvaal, requesting peace, but conciliatory in tone.

[4] *Q.R.*, cli. 201 (January 1881).   [5] Add MS 44642, f. 130.

[6] Nikolai Karlovich Giers, 1820–95; Russian assistant foreign affairs minister 1875–82, minister 1882–95 (Ramm II, ii. 481).

[7] [A. Austin], *Q.R.*, cli. 115 (January 1881).

[8] *British Quarterly Review*, lxxiii. 1 (January 1881).

Articles. Dr Rupp on prayer: also Memoir[1]—Stubbs, Myth of Life. Wrote to Granville—Mr Miller—Scotts.

17. M.

Wrote to Sir W. Harcourt—Watsons—Scotts—The Queen & minutes. Worked on Irish Land—Anti-obstruction scheme.[2] Saw Ld F. Cavendish ($\frac{1}{2}$h)—Ld R. Grosvenor—Mr Godley—Herbert J.G.—Mr Morley—Ld Rosebery—Ld Granville—Ld Hartington—The Speaker. Read Trevelyan's Fox.

18. Tu.

Wrote to Duke of Argyll—The Queen & minutes. Saw Ld Granville—Ld R.G.— Mr Godley—The Speaker—Mr Forster. Worked on Irish Land scheme. Read Irish Land reports. Montgomery on Irish Land[3]—Land & Skilled Industry.[4] Trevelyans Fox. H. of C 12$\frac{3}{4}$.[5]

To the DUKE OF ARGYLL, lord privy seal, 18 January 1881.   Add MS 44544, f. 129. '*Private*'.

You will be interested in reading the Reports of the Richmond Commission herewith sent in the rough—please to return them.

I am struck with the length to which Carlingford, a chief author of the Land Act, has gone: but the assent of the majority to legislative interference with rent is a weightier fact.[6]

19. Wed.

Wrote to Lady Susan O.—Abp of Canterbury—Mr Dodson—Mr Childers—The Speaker—The Queen 1.2.—Watsons and minutes. Dined at the Speaker's. Saw Ld F. Cavendish 1.2.—Ld R. Grosvenor—Dr Clark—Ld Granville—Mr Godley— Ald. Lawrence—The Speaker—Mr Agnew MP.—H of C. 4$\frac{1}{2}$-6.[7] Read Trevelyan's Fox—Montgomery on Irish Land.

To J. G. DODSON, president of local government board,   Add MS 44544, f. 129. 19 January 1881.

I see no reason for questioning your suggestion as to a commutation of Grant in aid.[8]

Most assuredly I hope to see grants in aid *largely* dealt with; but for this year our extinguisher is put almost upon everything.

It is very desirable to get rid of Mr. Duckham's proposal.[9]

[1] J. Rupp, *Reason and religion . . . with a biographical sketch of the author* (1881).
[2] And attended the Commons: questions, answered McCarthy; *H* 257. 868.
[3] H. de F. Montgomery, *Irish land and Irish rights* (1881).
[4] See, perhaps, 22 Dec. 80.
[5] The end of the debate; *H* 257. 994.
[6] Argyll replied next day criticising Carlingford and reminding Gladstone of the latter's resistance to differentiation in 1853: Add MS 44105, f. 1.
[7] Dawson's amndt. to Queen's Speech on Irish borough franchise; *H* 257. 1004.
[8] Requested on 18 January, Add MS 44252, f. 106.
[9] For a select cttee. on local taxation; ibid.

20. Th.

Wrote to Mr A.E. West—Ld Kimberley—Sir Thos G.—Col Colthurst[1]—The Speaker—Sir H. Ponsonby—The Queen—Ld Hartington—and minutes. The same weather still holds: but I had a short walk. Saw Ld R.G.—Mr Godley— H.J.G.—Ld Kimberley—H.N.G. on the Burmah case.[2] The Speaker, and colleagues on the course of business, & remedy for obstruction—Sir T. Acland. H. of C. $4\frac{1}{2}$–$9\frac{1}{4}$.[3] Read Trevelyan's Fox—Tracts on Irish Land.

To H. B. W. BRAND, the Speaker, 20 January 1881.   Brand MSS 232.

There is nothing to complain of in the tone of Sir S. Northcote's note.[4]

Difficulty lies I fear at the very root of the case. I can see no method of proceeding which will be effectual without placing the minority, I mean the regular minority, of the House, at the mercy of the Speaker—to which if it stood alone they might readily consent—and also to some extent at the mercy of the Government.

It would probably have to be a matter of honourable understanding, and of personal reliance.

I would rather plod on a little longer, suffering as we now are, to have a clear case & a decisive measure, rather than take an indecisive measure a few days sooner.

Meantime I need only say 1. That if possible it would be very desirable for us to decide on our course *tomorrow* evening & then to give the proper notices. 2. If we are thus prepared, probably we ought to force through the Report tomorrow night by a continuous sitting.

To D. LA TOUCHE COLTHURST, M.P., 20 January 1881.   Add MS 44544, f. 130.

I thank you for sending me the Bishop of Cloyne's letter.[5] I am afraid he is not exempt from error in his over-estimating the practical power of a Government as to the degree in which it can charge itself with the works which a society ordinarily performs itself. I should be obliged however if you could learn in what way it is that he thinks the Government should make provision for labourers.

To Sir S. H. NORTHCOTE, M.P., 20 January 1881.   Add MS 50014, f. 233.

I thank you very much for your note[6] and I am sorry you are a semi-invalid. Every fair minded man must feel that the gravest question which arises on a clôture of any kind is that of protection for the minority and this it is your special duty to consider though we I hope do not undervalue it.

I do not think it at all likely that we shall make a proposal or even come to a resolution until after adequate communication with you. We should like to come to a decision tomorrow evening if possible. The plan we are now in the first place considering is that which the Speaker sent you. Through the kindness of Sir R. Cross I have been put in possession of his opinions through the Lord Chancellor.

[1] Col. David La Touche Colthurst; liberal M.P. Co. Cork 1879–85.
[2] Significance unclear; H. N. Gladstone advising on basis of his Indian experience?
[3] Series of Irish amndts. to Queen's Speech; *H* 257. 1042.
[4] On closure, sent by Brand, Add MS 44195, f. 6.
[5] Not found.
[6] This day, Add MS 44217, f. 167: happy to consider confidentially a proposal for closure.

21. Fr.

Wrote to Ld Kimberley—Ld Hartington—The Queen and minutes. Wrote Preface to my Irish Land Project, now nearly mature, after much thought. Saw Ld Kimberley—Ld Granville cum do.—Ld R.G.—Ld F.C.—Mr Godley—Mr Grant Duff—Colleagues on Obstruction—H. of C. $4\frac{1}{2}$-$8\frac{1}{2}$. Spoke on Transvaal.[1] Harry had a respite of 14 days granted him: a real boon to us. Read Trevelyan's Fox—Divers Tracts on Irish Land.

To LORD HARTINGTON, Indian secretary, 21 January 1881.   Add MS 44544, f. 130.

I had in my own ruminations arrived at the conclusion that Parnell's very clear change of front last night would require a change on our part. I had also yesterday told Northcote that it was most unlikely that we should arrive at any conclusion until after adequate communication with him. Thus I was quite prepared for your note.[2] I think we had better gather for a few minutes behind the Speaker's chair after questions today to consider the position.

To LORD KIMBERLEY, colonial secretary, 21 January 1881.   Add MS 44226, f. 11.

You have seen and justly described the objection to my Part V.[3] It complicates the measure. Yet I submit that the argument in favour of something of the kind greatly preponderates. 1. The minority of the Richmond Commission and Kavanagh in the Bessborough by no means recommended cutting loose from the Act of 1870. 2. We have rather formally announced that we mean to work from that starting point. 3. Part V is the only part which saves the *status quo*, which enables all persons in Ireland who may be so disposed to go on as they are, without taking any new step of a positive kind, only with increased guarantees. 4. It is adopted to save the Ulster Custom from extinction, with which it is otherwise menaced, and which may prove not to be universally or even generally desired. 5. This system of Court management, though perhaps we cannot shut it out, is really a great burden and in the long run a special burden to the weaker party. But unless we keep Part V we almost drive people under the Court (as leases are under suspicion and by no means generally desired), whereas Part V offers what is meant to be a scheme of increased security with little or no litigation. 6. Its retention is far more favourable to the general underlying purpose of saving freedom of contract as the ultimate system for Irish agriculture.

I shall hope to see you as soon as you can come.

[P.S.] 7. I am disposed to add that Part V will tend to give unity and fixity to the law, by supplying general standards of guidance for the Court.

22. Sat.

Wrote to Ld Granville—U.S. Minister—The Queen 1. & Tel and minutes. Cabinet 2-5. 12 to dinner: music afterwards. Saw Mrs Hamilton[4]—Ld R. Grosvenor—Mr Godley—Mr Ratcliffe. Read Trevelyan's Fox—Tracts on Irish Land and [blank]

---

[1] 'To disapprove the annexation of a country is one thing; to abandon that annexation is another'; *H* 257. 1141.

[2] Of 20 January, Add MS 44145, f. 183, on need to consult Northcote.

[3] Kimberley objected, 20 January, Add MS 44226, f. 9, to Part V as unnecessary, its substance already given by clauses I–III; 'on the other hand you would lose the continuity between the Act of 1870, and the new Law'. This Part V, on 'passing out' of the Act (i.e. return to free contract), later absorbed into other Parts.   [4] Eddie Hamilton's mother; see 24 Nov. 44.

Cabinet. Sat. Jan. 22. 2 P M.[1]
1. Ld Granville mentioned Memorial of Irish Members to the Empress of Austria about state of Ireland. Declined by Karolyi.
   To say the channel shd. be English.
2. Mr Smyth's question—What answer shall WEG give? 'Dilatory'.[2]
3. Form of clôture. Speaker's draft provisionally adopted subject to a modification Whitbreads suggestion of previous question on Clôture resolution only to be adopted after fair opportunity has been allowed.
4. H[abeas] C[orpus] Bill to last until Sept. 1882. Shall Davitt be arrested? (WEG). Opinion.
5. Abp of Canterbury's inquiry as to Commn.—Yes.[3]
6. Order of Home Office respecting bequest. D. of Richmond not to be opposed.
7. Childers's plan as to numbers & ranks of officers reducing numbers in the aggregation & duplicating the highest ranks [:] mentioned & approved.
8. To resist tacking ⟨compensation for disturbance⟩ restraint upon eviction in case of non pay[men]t of rent to Habeas Corpus Bill.

1. That the ordinary rule in the case of great & difficult measures is to make no partial disclosures on account of their tendency to mislead. Applies with special force in this instance. Whatever is made known must be authentic.
2. Procedure by Resolutions—inapplicable. Must proceed by *Bill.*
   Protection & Land Reform really independent. Question is how far can we go, consistently with duty to meet a desire which we respect but which we cannot recognise as founded on strict principle.
   We must dispose in substance of the most important protective proposals.
   We hope then to introduce the Land Bill before any protective measure leaves this House.[4]

23. 3 S. Epiph.

Chapel Royal mg & evg. Dined at Phillimores. A Church Conversation and long retrospect.[5] Read Dean Church on Ch & State in 1850.[6] Ch. Quarterly Review—Neale—Williams on Patriarchate of Antioch.[7]

24. M.

Wrote to Ld Clifton—Mr Smyth MP—Ld Spencer—The Queen 1.2.3.—Mrs Th—Mr Maclaren[8] and minutes. H. of C. 4¾–8½ and 9½–12.[9] Read Virchow on

[1] Add MS 44642, f. 131. [2] See 24 Jan. 81.
[3] Ecclesiastical Courts Commission, chaired by Benson, *PP* 1883 xxiv. See 23 Jan. 81n.
[4] Undated holograph; Add MS 44642, f. 134.
[5] Phillimore noted: 'G.s dined here.... He reviewed at length (as is now his wont) the last 50 years & the general identity of (his & mine) opinions on Ch. & State matters. Govt. have assented to the proposal of the Abp. to issue a Royal commission to inquire into the existing Eccl. courts & the discipline of the Clergy. G. was amazed & pleased at the tone of the Abp., so wholly different from what it was 2 or 3 years ago'; Phillimore's diary.
[6] R. W. Church, *On the relations between church and state* (1881); reprint of 1850 article on Gorham.
[7] J. M. Neale, *A history of the Holy Eastern Church. Part I* (1850), appendix includes G. Williams, tr., *Memoirs of the Patriarchs of Antioch.*
[8] On his retirement from the Commons, in J. B. Mackie, *Life... of Duncan McLaren* (1888), ii. 229.
[9] Protection of Person and Property (Ireland) Bill, motion for leave to introduce; stalled on date of the Land Bill; *H* 257. 1201, 1209.

Ilios[1]—Finished Trevelyan's Fox. Saw Ld R.G.—Ld. F.C.—Mr Godley—Ld Granville—The Speaker—Mr Forster—Sir S. Northcote—Ld Hartington.

25. Tu. Conv. St P.

Wrote to Sir Th.E. May—Mr Forster—The Queen & Minutes. H. of C. $4\frac{1}{2}$-$2\frac{1}{4}$: on
my motion for taking all days.[2] Then home. Saw Mr G.—Ld R.G.—Mr Forster—
The Speaker—Sir T. May—Sir S. Northcote—Mr Childers—Sol. Gen. Ireland.
Read Miss Misanthrope.[3]

26. Wed.

Wrote to Sir Thos G.—The Queen 1.2.—Mr Forster—Mrs Wortley—Mr
Lefevre—Lord Hartington—and minutes. H. of C. $10\frac{1}{2}$-$2\frac{1}{2}$: satisfactory result of
the all night sitting: resolution carried.[4] Saw Ld Kimberley—Ld Granville—Mr
Childers—Mr G.—Lord R.G.—Mr F.L. Gower—Mr Th. Rogers—Sir S. Northcote. Read Miss Misanthrope. Dined at Mr Hankeys—Conversation with Gov.
of Bank.—Mr Goschen—Mr Wollaston Blake.[5]

To LORD HARTINGTON, Indian secretary, 26 January   Chatsworth MSS 340. 1059.
1881.

I entirely agree with you[6] that we ought not to have either 1. a general and aimless
inquiry into Indian affairs, or 2. an inquiry intended to serve the indirect purpose of incul-
pating the late Government. But I hope that if you refuse inquiry altogether you will do it
upon the ground that the engagements and responsibilities of the present Session have
already reached such a point that we cannot venture on making the serious addition to
them of an Indian inquiry.

I must say that my impression is that an absolute refusal except on the ground of time
could not be justified, and also that if issue were joined in the House the ground of refusal
would be one difficult to hold and even dangerous.

The restraints imposed by the Act on the use of Indian forces were entirely nullified by
the doctrine and practice of the late Government and surely must undergo a further consideration though I think we ought to make this as little controversial as was the original
introduction of the Clauses. I am also led to suppose that the relations of the Sec. of State
to the Council of India, and the constitution and composition of the Council, are matters
proper to be examined: but upon this I speak with little direct means of forming a judgment.

27. Th.

Wrote to Mr Shaw—Mr Wollaston Blake—The Queen & minutes. H. of C. $4\frac{3}{4}$-$8\frac{1}{4}$
& $9\frac{1}{2}$-$12\frac{1}{4}$.[7] Saw Sir S. Northcote—Ld Granville—Ld R.G.—Ld F.C.—Mr Godley

[1] R. L. C. Virchow, *Preface to H. Schliemann's Ilios* (1880).
[2] i.e. Precedence for Irish Protection of the Person and Peace Preservation Bills; *H* 257. 1313.
[3] J. MacCarthy, *Miss Misanthrope*, 2v. (1878).
[4] After a sitting of 22 hours; *H* 257. 1487.
[5] Henry Wollaston Blake, 1815–99; director of the Bank of England.
[6] Letter of 26 January, Add MS 44145, f. 185, on Fowler's question on a Select Cttee. or Royal
Commission on Indian affairs.
[7] Protection Bill: *H* 257. 1573.

—Herbert J.G.—Mr Bright[1]—Mr Childers—Ld Hartington. Read Miss Misan-thrope.

To W. SHAW, M.P., 27 January 1881.   Add MS 44544, f. 132.

On one point of great importance you will have been reassured by Mr Forster's state-ment.[2] With regard to the Land Bill, I am afraid there can be no safe or satisfactory expo-sition without *production*. I will, however, make known your wishes & see that they are considered when the Cabinet next meets, though I fear I can pledge myself no further than to assure you we are most anxious to bring our proposals relating to Land under the public eye.

28. *Fr.*

Wrote to Mr Ouvry 1.2.—Messrs Watson—Ld E. Clinton—Messrs Herries—Dr Bennett—Sir C. Ibbetson[3]—The Queen & minutes. H. of C. $4\frac{1}{2}$-$8\frac{1}{2}$, and $9\frac{1}{4}$-1. Spent most of the available day time on the facts and figures of the Irish ques-tion. Saw Mr Godley—Lord R.G.—Mr Forster. Spoke $1\frac{1}{2}$ hours on the Close: rather an effort.[4]

To F. OUVRY, solicitor to the Newcastle Trust, 28 January   Add MS 44544, f. 132.
1881.

Referring to the various communications between us, and to my former retirement jointly with Lord De Tabley from the late Newcastle Trust, I think the time has now come when I may, not only without detriment but with great advantage to the affairs of the family, retire from the Trust which, after the death of the late Duke, devolved solely upon me.

In those affairs my interest will always continue, and some positive duty may yet have to be done in relation to the papers, or what remains of them. But it is I think greatly to be desired that Ld. E. Clinton should now assume the place and duties for which he is so evidently marked out and I am glad to think that Lord Lyttelton will act as his coadjutor.

I would therefore beg that the arrangements for the change may, if as I believe all parties are agreed, go forward with all practicable expedition.

29. *Sat.*

Wrote to Duke of Argyll—Sir W. Barttelot—The Queen—Sir C. Du Cane and minutes. Saw Mr Godley—Ld R.G.—Ld F.C.—Ld Northbrook. Cabinet 2-$6\frac{1}{4}$. Much tired. Dined at Sir H. Verney's. Saw Sir B. Frere. Read Miss Misanthrope.

Cabinet. Sat. Jan. 29. 1881.[5]
1. Clôture. WEG wanted communications. Finish on Monday by Continuous sitting.
2. Intermediate evictions. Mr Litton's new form of amendment[6] considered—legal con-sideration to be undertaken—to aid the Cabinet.

[1] Persuading him to speak; Walling, *Diaries of Bright*, 455.
[2] No letter from Shaw found.
[3] None thus; probably Sir Henry John Selwin-Ibbetson, 1826-1902; 7th bart.; tory M.P. Essex 1865—92; cr. Baron Rookwood 1892.
[4] Harassed by Parnell and Healy; *H* 257. 1692.
[5] Add MS 44642, f. 136.
[6] Perhaps an alternative to Lyons' amndt., but not moved.

3. Preliminary explanation of Land Bill. No amendment to be made [?]. 2d R. H. of [blank]
4. Drafting of Land Bill. Direct Thring to draw Bill on the basis of the paper circulated.
5. Ansr. to Transvaal question approved.[1]
6. Ld Herries's letter[2]—approve his objections to the meeting
7. Case of Davitt. To be watched & arrested *sharp* upon any new offence.
8. Ld Granville recited what has taken place with respect to Greek frontier: & the suggestion for Goschen's action at Athens in case of an opening. Goschen to return by Berlin, starting on Wed[nesda]y.

To the DUKE OF ARGYLL, lord privy seal, 29 January 1881.   Add MS 44544, f. 132.

Several of the points which you have raised[3] will I think stand for consideration as open questions in settling the draft of our Bill.

Of some form of 'free sale' I am certain we cannot get rid if we do anything beyond merely strengthening the scales for disturbance. I cannot but remain persuaded that the power to raise the rent will be an effectual guard to the landlords' proprietary right. I am not sure that in some extreme cases the tenant's improvements will be *as* well guarded.

Where shall I find Mr. Hamilton's Evidence?[4]

30. 4. S. Epiph.

Ch. Royal mg & aft. To bed at 7: slept 12 or 13 hours. Read 19 Cent Ritualism—Jews[5]—Bp Wordsworth's Letter—Q.R. on Edict[6]—& some Tracts.

31. M.

Wrote to Ld Elcho—Ld Fitzwilliam—Mr Childers—Mr Bayley Potter—The Queen—Viceroy of Ireland 1.2. and minutes. H. of C. $4\frac{1}{2}$-$7\frac{3}{4}$ and $10\frac{1}{4}$-2. Left the House sitting *through*.[7] Saw Sir H. Thring—Sir E. Henderson—Dr Clark—Ld R. Grosvenor—Mr Godley—Ld F. Cavendish—The Speaker—Mr Walpole—Ld Derby. Read Drapier's Letters.[8] Saw the Liberal MP.s of Scotland.

To H. C. E. CHILDERS, war secretary, 31 January 1881.   Add MS 44544, f. 133.

I do not like the notion of giving prominence to the telegrams as if the matter had been theretofore neglected. I should say that we never had the smallest idea that any General in his senses would treat Boers as rebels, & that the telegram had simply been sent to satisfy the doubts of others.

---

[1] Absence of horses, answered by Childers, *H* 257. 1736.
[2] Not found.
[3] On 28 January commenting on the Land Bill proposals and especially objecting to free sale and interference with contract; Argyll, ii. 363.
[4] Agent on the Leinster estates who had, Argyll argued, disproved evidence in the Bessborough Commission's report.
[5] *N.C.*, ix. 201, 338 (February 1881).
[6] Perhaps the article on ritualism; *Q.R.*, cli. 201 (January 1881).
[7] i.e. through the night; *H* 257. 1745.
[8] By Swift (1724); see 7 Nov. 61.

To LORD ELCHO, M.P., 31 January 1881.   Add MS 44544, f. 133.

I thank you for your kind expressions and I much value your approval of my speech because I know it is sincere, and given without respect of persons.

I think with you that the present Land *Laws* of Ireland are amidst the prevailing excitement frequently described in terms of great exaggeration: and that as an important part of the case it would be well to have some regard to the Land Laws existing in other countries.

Whether it would be practicable now to undertake abstracting the volume you refer to I do not know but I will speak to Mr. Forster. Meantime I have written to Mr. Bayley Potter suggesting that the Volume published by the Cobden Club on the same subject should if not now in print be reprinted.[1]

London. Tues. Feb. One. 1881.

Wrote to Mr Bayley Potter—Ld Ailesbury—Mr Childers—Att. Gen. Irel.—Mrs Th.—The Queen & minutes. Informal Cabinet on plans for meeting obstruction. H. of C. $4\frac{1}{2}$-$8\frac{1}{2}$ & $9\frac{1}{4}$-$11\frac{1}{4}$.[2] The weary strain continues: it is the sameness of the tug which makes it tell upon the brain. Communications with the Speaker—and with Northcote who is really weaker than water.[3] Read Miss Misanthrope—at night.

To H. C. E. CHILDERS, war secretary, 1 February 1881.   Add MS 44544, f. 134.

Your estimates have come in presenting the figures which you described to me and I beg you to accept my thanks for the labour you have bestowed upon them in cutting down the ordinary charge so as not to let it stray beyond the figure of last year.

From what you have said as to the shape in which matters were handed over to you my hopes are rather buoyant for next year: and I am sure you will allow me to request on the part of the Treasury, that, so long as its nominal responsibility as a Department continues, great effort may be hereafter made to allow it an opportunity of considering the Votes not directly connected with the amount of force before they are finally & formally fixed.[4] But I end as I began by thanking you for your great and useful labours.

2. Wed.

Wrote to The Speaker—Lady Verney—Mr Leake MP—The Queen Tel & 1.—Sir Thos G.—Ld Hartington—& minutes. H. of C. $8\frac{1}{2}$-$9\frac{1}{2}$, 12-3 and $3\frac{1}{2}$-5.[5] The Speaker showed himself worthy of his place. But the Hydra has many heads. Royalty dinner came off. They were all very kind—But with the Duchess of Edinburgh I was simply delighted. Saw Ld Derby—Sir T. May—Bp of Ely—Mr Vivian—C. Carolyi—C. Münster—Mr Forster—Mr Bright and others. Read Miss

---

[1] *Systems of land tenure* (1870), published by the Cobden Club; new ed. 1881.

[2] Speakers frequently called to order for irrelevance; *H* 257. 1296.

[3] Northcote rescinded his support for the clôture; Bahlman, *Hamilton*, i. 103.

[4] Childers replied next day: 'the reduction ... will be large, but the process is slow'; Add MS 44129, f. 154.

[5] Sitting of $41\frac{1}{2}$ hours eventually adjourned, controversially on the Speaker's initiative, after Protection Bill 1°R and Gladstone read out his Resolutions on procedure; *H* 257, 2035 and Redlich, i. 164; later in the day, he took part in prolonged procedural wrangles with the Irish M.P.s and Lord R. Churchill who sent notice of his question; *H* 258. 6; Add MS 44468, f. 69.

Misanthrope. Lay awake till four. Walked to see the absurd monument at Temple Bar.[1]

3. Th.

Wrote to Ld Granville—Mr Anderson MP.—The Speaker—The Queen & minutes. Saw Ld Granville—Mr G.—Lord R.G.—Mr Whithead. (Informal) Cabinet at 3: much debate on the Resolution & Amendments: prospect not bright. H[artingto]n very stiff. H. of C. $4\frac{1}{2}$–$9\frac{1}{2}$ and $10\frac{1}{4}$–2. An extraordinary evening. The crass infatuation of the Parnell members caused the House to be cleared of them before nine. I then proposed my Resolution for a quasi Dictatorship. Before two it was adjusted in all points, and carried without division.[2]

4. Fr.

Wrote to Ld Granville—Prince of Wales—Ld Hartington—Dr Stack—Ld F. Cavendish—The Queen and minutes. Dined with the Jameses. H. of C. $4\frac{1}{2}$–$8\frac{1}{4}$ and 10–$11\frac{1}{4}$.[3] What a change! Saw Mr G.—Ld R.G.—Ld F.C.—The Speaker—Mr Vincent—Ld Granville—Herbert J.G.—Sir W. Harcourt. Read Miss Misanthrope—Contemp. Rev. on Transvaal.[4]

To LORD F. C. CAVENDISH, M.P., financial secretary,   Add MS 44544, f. 134.
4 February 1881.

With reference to our floating notions as to devolution of Local Vote monies to local bodies, would it be quite impossible to begin this year by doing something in that way for Scotland? I do not know whether you could strike out a spark of light on this subject or whether we have anybody whom you could consult—possibly C. Bannerman. *If* there is anything in the idea, it would be worth while to say a word to Childers.

5. Sat. [*High Elms, Farnborough*][5]

Wrote to Sir W. Harcourt—Ld Kimberley—The Speaker—Mrs Heywood and minutes. Off at four to High Elms. Saw Ld Granville—Mr Forster—Sir J. Lubbock—Mr Borlase—Mr Craik MP.[6] Read De Bowe's Review[7]—Loris [blank] (Gennadios).[8]

---

[1] Temple Bar was removed in 1878; a model of the Bar with marble statues by Boehm was placed at 227 Strand in 1880, probably the object of Gladstone's visit.
[2] First Dillon, then Parnell, then 33 other Irish M.P.s (some of them in a batch) were named by the Speaker and suspended on Gladstone's motion; the resolution for the expedition of business in cases of urgency was then agreed to, with slight amendment, and it was agreed to regard the Protection Bill as urgent; *H* 258. 156, Redlich, i. 164, iii. 247.
[3] Protection Bill 2°R; *H* 258. 170.
[4] *C.R*, xxxix. 220 (February 1881).
[5] Sir J. Lubbock's house.
[6] William Young Craig, 1827–?; liberal M.P. N. Staffs. 1880–5.
[7] *De Bow's Southern and Western Review*; American journal of trade; from 1866 published in Nashville.
[8] D. Bikelas, *Loukis Laras*, tr. J. Gennadios (1881); on the Greek war of independence.

To Sir W. V. HARCOURT, home secretary, 5 February   MS Harcourt dep. 8, f. 74.
1881.

I understand, and it may be well to report to you, that there is a feeling in the House
favourable to your giving Davitt a treatment as mild & with as much comfort as can be
fairly given. In this I have no doubt you will concur. Having put him out of the way of mischief, any allowable consideration for him will be so much to the good.[1]
[P.S.] Do not think of replying. I saw Mr Vincent.

To LORD KIMBERLEY, colonial secretary, 5 February 1881.   Add MS 44544, f. 134.

Colley with a vengeance counts his eggs before they are hatched,[2] & his curious letter
throws some light backward on the proceedings in India. His line is singularly wide of
ours. I entirely agree with your telegram as proposed. I also agree about Martial Law. Ere
long I hope Colley will find you are able to work, & at work, on safer lines than his.

6. 5 S. *Epiph.*

Farnborough Ch mg & H.C. Walk in aft. Wrote to Ld Kimberley 1.2. Read Lid-
den on Troubles &c.[3]—Quinet on Religion in France & Pref.—Stone's God's
Acre.[4]

7. *M.* [*London*]

Wrote to Sir Thos G.—Viceroy of Ireland—Ld Hartington—The Queen and
minutes. Saw The Prince of Wales—Sir H. Thring—Mr Forster—Ld Kimberley—
The Speaker—Lady de Vesci—Mr Bright. H. of C. $4\frac{1}{2}$-8 and 10–$11\frac{3}{4}$.[5] Read Louris
Loukas—Mr Gladstone & the three F.s.[6] Wrote Memn of H.J.G.s Will.[7]

8. *Tu.*

Wrote to Ld Hartington—Sir W. Harcourt—Mr Childers—Mr Chamberlain—Mr
Fenwick—The Queen 1.2.—Ld Spencer—and minutes. H. of C. $4\frac{1}{2}$-$8\frac{1}{2}$ and $9\frac{1}{2}$-$1\frac{1}{2}$.[8]
Read Louris Loukas. Drive with C. (short) & walk. Saw Mr G.—Ld R.G.—
H.J.G.—Sir T.E. May—The Speaker—Ld F.C. cum Mr Welby.

To LORD HARTINGTON, Indian secretary, 8 February   Chatsworth MSS 340. 1078.
1881.

I have now looked into the state of our cash affairs and prospects and I am ready, if you
approve, to propose to the Cabinet as follows:
1. To remit the annual repayment from India, in all two millions, & spread I think over
some six or seven years.

[1] Davitt arrested in Dublin 3 February, imprisoned in Portland gaol this day.
[2] Kimberley enclosed a private letter from Colley of 21 January on means of restoring order in
Transvaal, including 'a heavy war tax' to reward 'the loyals, and the townspeople'; Add MS 44226,
f. 18.
[3] H. P. Liddon, 'Thoughts on present Church troubles' (1881).
[4] E. Quinet, probably *La Révolution religieuse au dixneuvième siècle* (1857); E. Stone, *God's acre*
(1858); on churchyards.
[5] Questioned on timing of introduction of the Land Bill; *H* 258. 266.
[6] By Lord de Vesci in *C.R.*, ix. 53 (January 1881).
[7] i.e. on his sister Helen's will; Hawn P.   [8] Spoke on adjournment; *H* 258. 420, 430.

2. To propose that there shall be, on account of the Afghan War, annual payments of half a million for each of the next six years, making three millions. Five millions in all.

3. If the first payment of half a million is to be laid on the year 1880-1, it will require a vote in supply before March 31 and before the Budget. If on 1881-2 it would be stated in the Budget, probably early in April, and voted afterwards. I am ready to take *either* of these courses as you may prefer.[1]

9. *Wed.*

Wrote to Ld Spencer—Ld Kimberley—Mr Morley—Sir H. Thring—The Queen and minutes. Read on Irish Land—Loukis Laras. Saw Mr G.—Ld R.G.—Sir T.E. May—Ld Young—The Speaker—Mr Morley—Ld Granville. Saw Western [R]. Dined at Lady Stanley's. Speakers Levee afterwards.[2]

To LORD HALIFAX, 9 February 1881.   Add MS 44544, f. 136.

It is a great pleasure to receive the expression of your approval although accompanied with an acc[ount] of your health which I sincerely trust when I next hear of or from you may be improved.

We have in front of us a more difficult subject & a greater anxiety than the Hab. Corp. Bill, I mean the measure or probably measures relating to land. I hope we may in this also approve ourselves to your judgment; but it is the most difficult matter, I think, to which I have ever had to apply myself.

You will have observed the crowd of witch [*sic*] ideas which are afloat.

The Speaker has been acting admirably. He has submitted his rules today.

To LORD KIMBERLEY, colonial secretary, 9 February 1881.   Add MS 44544, f. 136.

Colley's plan is all wrong; I entirely agree with your draft answer to his telegram.[3] I am very glad H.M. has approved the previous tel.

10. *Th.*

Wrote to Bp of Nova Scotia[4]—Ld Hartington—The Queen—Ld Moncreiff & minutes—Mr Maskelyn. H. of C. $4\frac{1}{2}$-$8\frac{1}{4}$ and $8\frac{3}{4}$-$1\frac{1}{4}$.[5] Read Miss Misanthrope. Saw Sir H. Thring 12-2—Mr Forster—Mr Childers—Att. General—Mr Richards M.P.—Mr G.—Ld R.G.

To LORD HARTINGTON, Indian secretary, 10 February   Chatsworth MSS 340. 1080 1881.

Separating the two questions[6] 1. of amount, 2. of mode of payment, I will give you first my reasons for proposing an annual subvention.

They are two. 1. If we pay in a lump, we must borrow to pay, which is in every way open to objection. If we pay in two lumps we should probably have to do the same. I wish to

---

[1] Hartington's reply, 9 February, Add MS 44145, f. 200, requested £6.5 million in a lump sum or in not more than two instalments. See 5 Mar. 81.

[2] And questioned on Central Asia; *H* 258. 434.

[3] Add MS 44226, f. 25. Colley, looking to complete military victory, ignored Boer peace overtures; Schreuder, 114.

[4] H. Binney; see 8 Apr. 52.

[5] Spoke on privilege (*The World* newspaper): *H* 258. 515.   [6] See 8 Feb. 81n.

avoid this financial derangement. 2. What I feel yet more is that after borrowing we, or Parliament and the Country, would *forget*; & the lesson, & moral check on policy would be lost. These I certainly wish to keep alive by the form of annual payment.

As regards the amount, I thought my five millions not illiberal, and I do not feel sure what Parliament may say: the Tories will I should think probably oppose[.] At the same time, if the Cabinet generally think the sum niggardly, I would not resist the addition of another million.

Lastly: the first instalment would in any case be forthcoming before November 30, and in case we proceed before March 31, the second also.

11. Fr.

Wrote to Lady Stratford de R.—Dean of Windsor—D. of Argyll—The Queen 1.2. and minutes. Read Adams Ch & Law.—Ld Stratford on E.Q.[1] Saw Mr G.—Ld R.G.—Ld F.C.—Canon Farrar. H. of C. $4\frac{1}{2}$–$8\frac{1}{4}$ & $9\frac{1}{4}$–1.[2] Dined at Sir W. James's.

To the DUKE OF ARGYLL, lord privy seal, 11 February 1881.   Add MS 44544, f. 137.

It is a pure figment![3] I am struggling hard, with Thring, to get the draft into shape: but the plan of alternatives, though the only one I think that the case admits with justice, involves difficulties of drafting, and his work is not yet finished.

I fear it is hardly possible to *conjecture* an earlier day for the introduction of the Land Bill than March 3. But Thring's draft will be ready, I think some day next week, perhaps before the last days.

12. Sat.

Wrote to Sir H. Thring—Sir R. Phillimore—The Queen—Mr Max Müller—Sir H. Ponsonby—Demarch of Athens—Sir G. Campbell MP and minutes. Cabinet 2–$5\frac{1}{2}$. Saw Mr G.—Ld R.G.—Ld F.C.—Jas. Wortley—Lady Cork. Dinner at Ld Cork's. Saw Grove, Edwards & another [R].

Cabinet. Sat. F. 12. 81. 2 P M[4]
1. State of business in H of C. a. Finish H.C. Bill b. Arms Bill. c. Introduce Land bill?) d. Supply.
2. Arms Bill Ireland. Resolved to introduce one forthwith, *contra* WEG, Bright, Chamberlain, Northbrook, & perhaps Argyll & Spencer.
    Provisions to be reviewed, to see whether any ought to be extended to U.K. Also Gun Licence Act to be examined.
(WEG esply objected to bringing in Land[5] Bill at a time when we cd. not at once proceed with it.)
3. Fortune Bay: proposal for a reference on the U.S. fishermen's claims.
    Newf[oun]d[lan]d demurs to liability & wishes to make a counter claim—really meaning that they will not pay.

This is an international question. Must be decided by methods of international law. i.e. either by communication between the parties which we can secure [?] for them[,] or by a reference ultimately to a third & impartial party.

[1] S. Canning, Lord Stratford de Redcliffe, ed. A. P. Stanley, *The Eastern question* (1881); sent by his widow.   [2] Protection Bill cttee.; *H* 258. 635.
[3] Argyll's complaint untraced.   [4] Add MS 44642, f. 138.
[5] Could read 'Law Bill'; but this passage in brackets may refer to item 1c.

Again ask the Govt. to bind itself to the proposed mode, or to propose another measure. Presuming you ⟨will⟩ have any opportunity of presenting [blank][1]

Alternative I. No Arms Act.[2]
Say:
P.P. Bill passes H of C., 21st; Land Bill introd[uced], 24th Feb.; Monday Rule, 25th; Army Number of men, 28th; Supply Thursday, 3d [March]; ditto, 7th; Land Bill 2R, 10th to 14th; Supply urgent, say, 15th to 18th; Finish Land Bill 2r., 21st; Begin Land Bill Committee before Easter.

Alternative II
Supply without urgency, 3 weeks; Arms Act with urgency, 2 weeks from F. 22 to Mch 29; Introduce Land Act, say, Mch 28; Budget after Easter 2r., Ap 4. M. or 7 Th.

To F. Max MÜLLER, 12 February 1881.   Max Müller MS dep 170, f. 199.

I have to thank you very sincerely for your kind remembrance of me in a copy of your Selected Essays.[3]

My hope to examine them with great interest is not the less lively because it is, unhappily, directed towards a not immediate future: at least as regards the kind and degree of examination which alone would satisfy me.

I never see you now: but I hope that when my after Easter breakfasts come round (on Thursdays at ten) you will kindly find some opportunities of promising, & giving me, your company.
[P.S.] The appointment to the Provostship of Trinity College [Dublin] was with the Viceroy. I am very sensible of Mr. Mahaffy's[4] merits in the important line you mention.

13. *Septua S.*

Chapel Royal mg & Guards Chapel evg: Dined with the Phillimore's: conversation with him on Ch matters.[5] Wrote to Dean of Windsor—The Queen Tel—Dr Pusey. Read Dr Pusey's Unlaw[6]—Life of Sister Augustine[7]—Spicer on Ch & Stage.[8]

14. *M.*

Wrote to Dean of Windsor—Rev. Mr Butler—The Queen 1 & Tel.—Ld Kimberley—& minutes. H. of C. $4\frac{1}{2}$-$8\frac{1}{2}$ and 10-$12\frac{1}{2}$.[9] Read Ch Association Report and Poems. Sir W. Harcourt. Do *cum* Mr Fawcett—Mr G.—Ld R.G.—Ld F.C.—Mr Fenter[10]—Ld Kimberley—Mr West—Mr Childers—The Speaker.

[1] Undated holograph note, presumably on Newfoundland fishery dispute; Add MS 44642, f. 139.
[2] Add MS 44642, f. 141.
[3] *Selected essays on language, mythology and religion*, 2v. (1881).
[4] Mahaffy (see 26 Oct. 77) was appointed, but not until 1914.
[5] 'Gs dined here—very well—in good spirits, though he sd money was pouring into the Land League from America. I impressed on him the great importance of fairly composing [?] the Royal Commission on the Eccl. Courts'; Phillimore diary.
[6] E. B. Pusey, 'Unlaw in judgements of the Judicial Committee and its remedies' (1881).
[7] *Sister Augustine, Superior of the Sisters of Charity* (1880).
[8] H. Spicer, *Church and stage* (1881).
[9] Protection Bill cttee.; *H* 258. 774.
[10] Probably W. H. Fenton of the statistical office.

To LORD KIMBERLEY, colonial secretary, 14 February 1881.   Add MS 44544, f. 138.

As far as my memory serves me I never *received* the Transvaal address.[1] But for the extraordinary pressure and confusion of last April, I would say positively I did not receive it.

I will however say pretty positively that I never answered it; and most certainly I never made any communication to any one on the subject which conveyed any encouragement to resistance or expectation respecting our withdrawal from the territory.[2]

Thoroughly disapproving of the annexation in principle & in policy, I had no means of forming a judgment that it could be revoked. Had I been prepared to work in that sense I should have done it first in Parliament.

15. *Tu*

Wrote to Ld Dufferin—Lady Lovelace[3]—Sir H. Tufton—Ld Kimberley—The Queen 1.2. & Tel. Cabinet 12½-3: on the Transvaal. Saw Sir W. Harcourt & conclave—Mr G.—Ld R.G.—Ld F.C.—Ld Granville—Mr MacColl—The Speaker—Scotts. H. of C. 4¾-9 and 9½-12¼.[4] Read Land Report[5]—Poems.

Cabinet. Tues. Feb. 15. 81. 12.30 PM.[6]
Ld Kimberley stated communications of yester[da]y on the Telegram of 13th from Colley.[7]
1. Telegram agreed to with offer to the Boers of a Commission duly empowered to develop scheme & otherwise.
2. Separate Tel. from Childers to Colley respecting the interval before ansr. from Boers.
3. WEG telegraphs in cypher to H.M.
4. Ld K. sends H.M. (1).

16. *Wed.*

Wrote to Mr Ogilvy—Ld Dufferin—Ld Kimberley—The Queen—The Speaker & minutes. Walk. Saw Fernand—Graham [R]. Saw Mr G.—Ld R.G.—Ld F.C.—Sir H. Thring—12-2.—Ld Kimberley—The Speaker—Att. Gen. Ireland—Mr Forster—Ld Fitzwilliam. Dined at Ld Fitzwilliam's. Lady Harcourt's afterwards. H. of C. 2¾-5¾.[8] Read Sister Augustine—Land Reports.

---

[1] Selborne, Granville, Argyll and Spencer reported by Kimberley this day as demurring 'to so large a concession to the Boers at this moment', and request a cabinet; Kimberley's letter does not mention this Address; Add MS 44226, f. 26.
[2] Though technically true, this simply sets aside the condemnation of annexation in Midlothian; *Speeches in Scotland* (1879), 48.
[3] Jane, wife of 1st Earl of Lovelace, had complained about railways; Add MS 44544, f. 138.
[4] Protection Bill cttee.; *H* 258. 893.
[5] See 11 Jan. 81.
[6] Add MS 44642, f. 144.
[7] Colley's telegram of 13 February announced Kruger's proposal of a Royal Commission coupled with a warning that if annexation were upheld, the Boers would 'fight to the end'; Gladstone at this Cabinet agreed to end annexation, but Selborne, Granville, Argyll and Spencer refused; the wire sent on 16 February offered a Commission and authorised Colley to agree to a truce if the proposal was accepted; Goodfellow, 200 and *PP* 1881 lxvii. 9–11.
[8] Protection Bill cttee.; *H* 258. 996.

17. Th.

Wrote to Sir H. Thring—Mr Richard M.P.—Mr Firth MP—Mr Morley MP—Consul Gould[1]—D. of Westmr—Mr Warburton—The Queen and minutes. Saw The Speaker—Sir H. Thring—Mr Joy—Mr G.—Ld R.G.—Mr Errington—Ld Hartn—Mr Whitbread. H. of C. $4\frac{1}{2}$-$8\frac{1}{2}$ and $9\frac{1}{2}$-$2\frac{1}{2}$.[2] Read [blank.]

To H. RICHARD, M.P., 17 February 1881.   Add MS 44544, f. 139.

I have not failed to read the interesting letter you have sent me relating to the unhappy business of the Transvaal.[3]

I will only express my hope that you may very soon know exactly what we are about, & my belief that you will *not* be dissatisfied with it.

18. Fr.

Wrote to The Queen 1.2. and minutes. 10.35-3.45. To Windsor—Audience: The Queen copious & gracious. Saw the Dean of Windsor—Sir H. Ponsonby—Sir D. Wolff—Ld Kimberley—Sir H. Thring—Irish Sol. Gen.—The Speaker—Ld Sandhurst. Read Taming of the Shrew—Sister Augustine. H. of C. $4\frac{1}{2}$-$8\frac{1}{4}$ and $8\frac{3}{4}$-1.[4]

19. Sat. [Brighton]

Wrote to The Speaker—Mrs J.S. Wortley—Mrs Th.—The Queen 1.2. and minutes. Cabinet 12-$3\frac{1}{4}$. Saw Mr G.—Ld. R.G.—Sir G. Wolseley—Ld Spencer. Off at 4 to Brighton. Most kindly received & entertained in the Huntingtower house.[5] Read Report on Boers—Longfield on Tenures.[6]

Cabinet. Sat. Feb. 19. Noon.[7]
1. Parl. situation. Shall we proceed at once with the Arms Bill?—No.[8]
2. Provisions of Land Bill considered—open meeting Tues[day]. Noon. appointed.[9]
3. Telegram from Colley requesting interpretation. Telegram in reply agreed on: *Status quo* the military basis, conditioned by the first step on the part of the Boers.

To Sir H. THRING, 19 February 1881.   Add MS 44544, f. 137.

I have had doubts about my suggestion of a division of the Land Bill into Temporary Provisions and Permanent Provisions; and an impression, that it might be simpler in form, and more just in principle, to divide between present tenancies and future tenancies, or rather to except *present* tenancies from *all* tenancies, for certain purposes; i.e. to

[1] Louis Eugene Gould, consul in Belgrade; business untraced.
[2] Spoke on progress of Protection Bill cttee.; *H* 258. 1094.
[3] Richard sent a further appeal from Holland to end the war; Add MS 44468, f. 132. See 14 Jan. 81.
[4] Questioned on Transvaal; Protection Bill cttee.; *H* 258. 1223.
[5] Lady Huntingtower's house, 24 Brunswick Terrace, Brighton; Wolseley was of the party.
[6] Longfield's important article; see 7 Nov., 14 Dec. 80.
[7] Add MS 44642, f. 147.
[8] Holograph note on a separate sheet, ibid. f. 148; '*Sketch*: Thurs 24: 3°H.C. Bill, 25: Arms Bill; 28: Supply? Tues. Mch 1.2.3: 2 R Arms Bill; 4: Committee; 10. Thurs 11—18: Supply.'
[9] Holograph note, ibid., f. 150: 'Considering what rough waters we are in, I am not ill satisfied with this *first* conversation on the Land Bill.'

say *present* tenancies may, within a fixed time, 1. pass under fixity, 2. pass under supervision, 3. go into Court to fix rent *pro hac vice*; all tenancies, except as above, shall 1. fall under the new Part I (*olim V*). 2. have power to cut out of the Act by leases. By present tenancies, I understand agricultural tenancies from year to year (or under leases not taking them out of the Land Act) which shall not have determined.

If this note, instead of simplifying, confuses, pray consider it unwritten.

20. *Sexa S.*

—St Patrick mg—St Paul's evg. Walk with C. Also with Mrs Roundell,[1] whom I much like. Read Bossuet & Claude[2]—Impar Congressus[3]—Sister Augustine—Foxton on Christianity.[4]

21. *M.* [*London*]

Wrote to Rev. Dr Barry—Ld Brougham—Ld Cowper—D. of Devonshire—The Ld Chancellor—Sir H. Ponsonby—The Queen 1.2.—Ld Granville. Walk in Brighton. Return to town $1\frac{1}{2}$-$3\frac{1}{2}$. Read Longfield—Schliemann. Saw Mr G.—Mr H.—Ld R.G.—Mr Forster—Ld Kimberley—Lord F.C. cum Mr Welby.—Lord Bath. H. of C. $4\frac{1}{2}$-$8\frac{1}{2}$. $9\frac{1}{2}$-1.[5]

To Sir H. PONSONBY, the Queen's secretary, 21 February   Add MS 44544, f. 139.
1881.

(1) I hope to have the honour of availing myself of Her Majesty's gracious invitation for Monday.[6] In the present confused state of business, I doubt not Her Majesty will excuse my coming if there be an imperative call in Parliament. We have no idea that the proceedings on the H.C. Bill can be prolonged beyond this week—even after all that has happened.

(2) I feel confident that from the effect of this Bill we have a position in Ireland such that no misapprehensions of a serious kind can be caused by the postponement of an Arms Bill.

(3) I entertain the same hope & belief as to South Africa, though the grounds are of necessity less definite.

(4) I inclose a note from Lord Hartington, which will inform Her Majesty as to the reasons that have led me to desire a Baronetcy for Sir D. Stewart simultaneously with the Baronetcy for Sir H. [*sc.* F. S.] Roberts.

22. *Tu.*

Wrote to Sir Thos G.—Ld Granville—Lord Fife—The Queen and minutes. Informal Cabinet 12-$3\frac{1}{2}$. Ill spent time, the progress was so small, the conversation circular. H. of C. $4\frac{1}{2}$-$8\frac{1}{4}$ and 9-$12\frac{1}{4}$.[7] Read Schliemann.[8] Saw Mr G.—Ld R.G.—Ld F.C.—The Speaker—Mr Forster—Sir R. Blennerhassett—The Ld Advocate.

---

[1] Probably Julia, *née* Tollemache, wife of C. S. Roundell (see 13 June 68), who had a place in Sussex.
[2] J. B. Bossuet, *Conférence avec M. Claude ... sur la matière de l'Eglise* (1682).
[3] Untraced.
[4] See 15 Apr. 60.
[5] Questions, Protection Bill cttee.; *H* 258. 1376.
[6] Responding to Ponsonby's two letters of 20 February; Guedalla, *Q*, ii. 140.
[7] Questions, Protection Bill; *H* 258. 1529.
[8] H. Schliemann, *Ilios, Stadt und Land der Trojaner* (1881).

Cabinet. Tues. Feb. 22. 1881. Noon[1]
Called to consider informally the Land Bill. Much conversation[.] Little progress.
Mr Forster submitted Parnell's case, as to his recommen[datio]n to plough up evicted lands.[2]
Postpone bill Thursday declar[atio]n as to course of business.

23. *Wed.*

Wrote to The Queen 1.2.—Sir S. Northcote 1.2.—Master of Univy—The Queen and minutes. H. of C. most of the afternoon.[3] Saw Dean of St Paul's—Mr Hamilton—Ld R.G.—Mr Banter[4]—The Speaker—Ld Granville—Ld Rosebery—Sir W. Harcourt—Musurus Pacha. Dined at Marlborough House: conversation with the Royalties. On my way home slipt off my heels in the powdered snow by the garden door, fell backwards, & struck my head most violently (I was hatless) against the edge of the stone step. A wound of $1\frac{3}{4}$ inch was cut open, which bled profusely. All the household were soon most kindly busy: a neighbouring doctor came & bound it up perfectly well, C.G. arrived, & soon Dr Clarke. I got to bed with very uncomfortable feelings *inside* the skull, as it appeared to me, and some difficulty in placing the head: but thank God had an excellent night.

24. *Thurs.*

A day of absolute rest from reading, writing, business & interviews: except a short note to Granville. Sir Jas. Paget & Dr Clark attended.

25. *Fr.*

Wrote to Hartington—also saw him. Even this was more than was good for me of business. Read some of Dead Mens Shoes[5] by way of trial. And C.G. read some of Sister Augustine. Asleep 10-12 hours out of the 24! How good is God to me, how ill am I to Him.

To LORD HARTINGTON, Indian secretary, 25 February   Chatsworth MSS 340. 1087. 1881.

As time is valuable I write a line in anticipation of your visit.
1. On your answer as proposed for tonight I have no criticism to make except that as we do not I think look to abandonment, at least as involved in any present decision, I would leave that out of the answer.
2. As regards proceeding with the Arms Bill at once you know the leaning of my mind, and I have not altered it but I hope the Cabinet will decide freely on what it deems to be for the best and I shall adhere loyally to the decision.
If however they return to the idea of going on with the Arms Bill at once, let them reckon carefully the bearing of the Case in connection with 1. Supply &c March 31. 2. The position of independent members. 3. The Land Bill. 4. The Budget—*after* March

[1] Add MS 44642, f. 151.
[2] Parnell had publicly retracted his advice to evicted tenants to plough their land to prevent its use for grazing, finding the act illegal; see *F. A.-F. J.*, 77.
[3] Spoke on procedure; *H* 258. 1607.
[4] Perhaps W. Banton of the accountant general of India's staff.
[5] [M. E. Braddon], *Dead Men's Shoes*, 3v. (1876).

31. Of these, (1) is imperative at a certain time—the others are open in various degrees. Budget & Land Bill ought to be kept separate as far as may be.

The paucity of ejectment notices in Ireland makes rapid introduction of the Land Bill less urgent.

Paget as well as Clarke is greatly pleased with my progress, & I imagine the outside of my head is better than the in. But I am sorry to say that whereas I was reckoning on appearing in the House on Monday, his answer to my pleas was 'most unlikely'. There is no doubt that yesterday's repose has paid wonderfully well and except as to a short visit from you I am still to keep on the same lines.

[P.S.] I am so sorry to give you all so much trouble.

26. Sat.

Wrote to Granville. Read Dead Mens Shoes more freely. Saw Sir R. Phillimore. C.G. read Sister Augustine to me. Clark & Paget most kind: meet daily. Yesterday they were surprised at the rapid closing of the wound. *That* however I have not regarded as the main thing. The huge capacity of sleep continues.

27. Quinqua S.

Left my room but not allowed to go out. Service for & by myself. Saw Sir R. Phillimore. Read Foxton's Xty—Crampton on the Heavens (what wonders)[1]—Sister Augustine finished.

28. M.

Left my room yesterday & today after luncheon. Saw Godley—& did much business with him. Saw Ld R.G.—Ld F.C.—Ld Hartington—Herbert J.G.—also C.G. about him & Miss T.[2]

Sad Sad news from South Africa: is it the Hand of Judgment?[3]

Read Contemp. Rev. on Tuscan Land[4]—Guizot[5]—Jews in Germany—Hopkins on Ch & State[6]—Longman on Copyright[7]—Dead Mens Shoes.

Tues. Mch One. 81.

Up & out of my room in aftn. Daily visits from the medical men continue. Saw Mr G.—Ld R.G.—Ld F.C. and others Read N.C. on Ireland[8]—Dead Mens Shoes.

---

[1] J. Crampton, *The three heavens* (3rd ed. 1878).

[2] Either Octavia Laura Tennant, 1862–86, who m. Alfred Lyttelton 1885, or her sister, Emma Alice Margaret (Margot), 1864–1928, who m. H. H. Asquith 1894; Margot's diary (September 1883) notes: 'I took Herbert Gladstone from Laura'; but Laura wrote in January 1883: 'H. Gladstone is such a bearfighter—the constant locking of bedroom doors, blowing out of candles, booby traps, water jugs upset etc. etc. has a very small charm for me.'

[3] News of the disastrous skirmish on 26–7 February at Majuba Hill, in which Colley and 95 other British troops were killed, reached London at 11.45 p.m. on 27 February; Schreuder, 134–5, *PP* 1881, lxvii. 17.

[4] *C.R.*, xxxix. 440.

[5] Probably Mme. de Witt, *M. Guizot in private life* (1881).

[6] Not found.

[7] C. J. Longman, in *Fraser's Magazine*, ciii. 372 (March 1881).

[8] *Nineteenth Century*, ix. 397 (March 1881).

2. Ash Wed.

Service alone. Wrote to The Queen—Ld Kimberley 1.2. and minutes. $2\frac{1}{2}$–$4\frac{1}{2}$. Conclave with Inl. Revenue on Death Duties.[1] Saw Mr G.—Ld F.C.—Mr Childers. Read Merimée[2]—Dead Mens Shoes (finished)—Lady A. Blunt's Arabia.[3]

To LORD KIMBERLEY, colonial secretary, 2 March 1881.   Add MS 44226, f. 37.

I quite concur in your general remark;[4] & in the spirit, & indeed the letter of your instructions. I suggest however for consideration one short insertion if not two. It seems to me that the last political telegram to Colley should be accompanied, probably, with the short military telegram which referred to the conduct he might pursue while awaiting a reply from the Boer Government so to call it. The other point is one which much [*sc* must] reach its settlement long before Roberts gets to Africa & I am not sure that it has properly any place in your Instructions, though it is important. Suppose, for argument's sake, that at the moment when Colley made the unhappy attack on the Majuba Hill, there shall turn out to have been decided on, & possibly even on its way, a satisfactory or friendly reply from the Boer Government to your Telegram?[5] I fear the chances may be against this: but if it prove to be the case, we could not because we had failed on Sunday last insist on shedding more blood.

3. Th.

Wrote to Ld Rosebery—Abp of Canterbury—Ld Hartington & minutes. H. of C. $4\frac{1}{2}$–8.[6] Read Ireland's True Daughter[7]—Foreign Land Tenures[8]—Merimée. Saw Mr G.—Ld R.G.—Ld F.C.—Mr Bright (2)—Herbert J.G.—Ld Kimberley—Sir G. Wolseley—Conclave on Public Buildings—Mr Chamberlain—Deputn of Members on the Transvaal.[9] Read Merimée—Ireland's True Daughter—Bagehot on Tenures.[10]

4. Fr.

Wrote to The Speaker—Mr Monk MP—The Queen—Ld Kimberley and minutes. Saw Mr G.—Ld R.G.—Ld F.C.—Ld Kimberley[11]—Ld Granville cum Mr Childers—Mr C. Russell MP.—Ld Hartington—H. of C. $4\frac{1}{2}$–$7\frac{1}{2}$.[12] Read Merimée

[1] Eleven questions, with answers, in preparation for the meeting, dated 1 March 1881, at Add MS 44765, f. 88.

[2] P. Merimée, *Lettres à M. Panizzi, 1850-70* (1880).

[3] Lady A. Blunt, *A pilgrimage to Nejd, the cradle of the Arab race*, 2v. (1881).

[4] No relevant letter found. Kimberley was under intense pressure to reverse his pacific policy; he had already asked Wood (1 March, *PP* 1881 lxxvii. 18) for details of the timing of the peace offer.

[5] Gladstone's query gained time, see Schreuder, 138; Wood replied on 4 March, *PP* 1881 lxxvii. 20. Kruger was 4 days off and could not answer in the 48 hours stipulated by Colley; on receipt of the message, Kruger answered promptly and positively; see 8 Mar. 81.

[6] Questioned on Transvaal negotiations; *H* 259. 147.

[7] *Ireland's true daughter*, 3v. (1881); romantic novel by 'Marcellina', dedicated to Gladstone.

[8] See 31 Jan. 81n.   [9] No account found.

[10] Probably a confusion with *Foreign land tenures*, though Bagehot not a contributor.

[11] Important lunch on the Transvaal; Schreuder, 140.

[12] Questioned on Transvaal and Basutoland and on date of introduction of the Land Bill; *H* 259. 335.

—Sir G. Wolseley on Short Service[1]—Ireland's True Daughter, hardly readable from slightness. Tracts on Ireland & Irish Land. The controversy with the Queen is serious.[2]

5. Sat. [St George's Hill]

Wrote to Ld Granville—Robertson & N.—Sir C. Herries—The Queen 1.2.—Mr Forster and minutes.—Rev. Mr Rose—Mr Cobbe. Cabinet 2-4¾. Off to St Georges Hill at 5.5.[3] Saw Mr H.—Mr G.—Ld R.G.—Ld F.C.—Ld Granville—Mr Childers. Read Lady A. Blunt, Nejd—Mr Gott's Orlando &c.[4]

Cabinet. March 5. 81. 2 P.M[5]

Transvaal. See over.[6] Message agreed on. Lawson's question.[7]

Treatment of combatants other than Boers, if taken. Roberts will not inquire who they are.

Land Bill—Tuesday. as to general basis. Open Cabinet 12.

W.E.G. stated his three conditions. a. [blank] b. return to free trade open[?]. c. against *fixity*. Sir W. H[arcourt] differs but will accept. Gr[anville] agrees. D. of A & Chancellor agree to principles, not to all the applications. Bright wants more strength in the Bill. Chamb[erlai]n ditto but hopes it may be found right in detail.

Indian Subvention: To be 5m̃ viz. 2m̃ remission, 3m̃ in six equal yearly pay[men]ts beginning 80-1.[8]

[South African business: item I continued:]

[February] 13 Colley's message. Feb. 19: Explained Telegram sent off by Cabinet. 27: Battle [of Majuba Hill]. 27-8: News.

Mch 1: Wood asked when & what Colley had done: & whether an a[nswer] was to be expected.

3 Further Tel. Bok[9] explains to Wood there can be no answer from Krüger for 4 days.

5. Wood's Tel. of 4. Colley wrote Feb 21 to *Joubert*: Offering suspension if answer came within 48 hours. (Had probably written to Krüger before K)—Woods of 4th rec[eive]d today: will not be ready for a week.—Also his message to Brand. Offers to wait till March 10.[10]

---

[1] Wolseley in dispute with the duke of Cambridge in *N.C.*, ix. 558 (March 1881).

[2] She successfully resisted, until after the Egyptian campaign, Gladstone's proposal to ennoble Wolseley; the row leaked, see Bahlman, *Hamilton*, i. 113.

[3] Seat near Byfleet of Sir F. Egerton, sailor and liberal M.P.; see 15 Jan. 70.

[4] Possibly Clementina Black, *Orlando* (1879).

[5] Add MS 44642, f. 152.

[6] See later in this day's cabinet notes.

[7] On 7 March 1881.

[8] See 8 Feb. 81.

[9] W. E. Bok, 1846–1904, Transvaal politician.

[10] The assembling of this information gave Gladstone time to see off the radicals' pursuit of Kimberley, and to allow development of Wood's mediation; Schreuder, 136–41, *PP* lxvii. 17–21. Sir (Henry) Evelyn* Wood, 1838–1919; 2nd in command to Colley 1881; commissioner in Transvaal 1881; with Wolseley in Egypt 1882; commanded Egyptian army 1882.

To W. E. FORSTER, Irish secretary, 5 March 1881.   Add MS 44544, f. 142.

Your paper reached me a moment before the Cabinet,[1] & a moment after it I came down here, when I have only a few minutes before post time to write to you with only the guidance your letter affords me; mainly to mention what happened in the Cabinet of today, on the subject of Irish Land, though it was not much.

I am sorry we have not, apparently quite the same point of view; though I have certainly moved further in your direction, since the publication of the Reports,[2] than I expected to have done.

It is however a great advantage to me to have my proposals criticised & dissected from every quarter, especially by you. I am not vain or enamoured of them, & I have neither seen nor heard of any plan that makes any tolerable approach to perfection. To me personally it would be a great comfort & relief if the Cabinet saw its way to any other scheme which, though too far from my ideas to be placed in my hands, I might loyally support in Parliament.

I have not however observed even amidst the thickest rain of objections from the four quarters of the sky any kind of relative preference in the Cabinet at large for any other plan.

Today there was a partial conversation only, in anticipation of a meeting to begin anew the details on Tuesday at 12.

I named to the Cabinet 8 points of detail which seemed to me to demand much consideration,—some of them rather cardinal. I send a rough note of them within.

As to the prescribed period I think there are great objections to fixing a long time for it, but I also think it might perhaps be parted with altogether which would very much simplify the Bill.

I stated to the Cabinet some of what I may call 'limiting conditions' which affect my own action; not to transfer the kernel of the property to the tenant from the landlord, to leave open the way for an eventual return to free contract as far as possible, & to reduce to a minimum the disturbance of existing relations, not compelling people to do things on the passing of the Act, but only empowering them.

I will only say before closing that in my belief either the Dowse or the Shaw plan, especially the former, would be torn to shivers by argument in debate.

The 'supervision' if we remove the prescribed period might be brought on at any time upon a 'present tenancy', a phrase, you will remember of very large meaning.

I am afraid you must have had very hard work in Dublin.

The opposition to the Bill has thus far been less formidable than I think most of us anticipated. Their only chance is in Committee & we shall see what this comes to.

Points for consideration.[3]
1. Joining the Bills.
2. Prescribed period (a) any? (b) for what purpose (c) how long $7\frac{1}{2}$ yrs?
3. Court. Grounds of disallowing & evicting.
4. Definition of fair rents.
5. Minimum leave by which to get out of it.
6. Mode of treating custom lands.
7. As to demanding reductions.
8. Improvements.

---

[1] Forster's letter of 4 March, Add MS 44158, f. 138: 'I have sent a mem. for circulation on the Land Bill. I can not say with what reluctance I have written it. I do so dislike not agreeing with you....'   [2] i.e. the two Royal Commission reports.

[3] Another version, holograph, is at Add MS 44765, f. 14; it includes: '9, Remedies' (see to Forster next day).

To Sir C. HERRIES, chairman of board of inland revenue,   Add MS 44544, f. 141.
5 March 1881.

Please to let it be cons[idere]d in your Dept. whether in any measure on the Death
Duties we can include some annual Tax in lieu of Death Duty on Charities large & small.

6. 1. S. Lent

Byfleet Ch mg. & H.C. Wrote to Sir W. Harcourt—Mr Forster—Sir H. Thring—
Mr Stansfeld—Ld Kimberley. Walk in aft. Read Southey's Wesley[1]—Life of
Chaloner.[2]

To W. E. FORSTER, Irish secretary, 6 March 1881.   Add MS 44544, f. 142.

Besides the 8 points of the Land Bill named in my last, there is a ninth—the state of law
as to landlord's remedies in Ireland. This cannot be overlooked, though it should perhaps
if undertaken now be dealt with in a separate Bill, & by the lawyers.

To Sir W. V. HARCOURT, home secretary, 6 March 1881.   MS Harcourt dep. 8, f. 76.

One point occurs to me as to the proposal that the Govt. should purchase the Arms
taken under the Bill in Ireland. I conclude our measure is drawn according to the precedents in like cases. If this is doubtful, would it not be well to have them looked up.[3]

To LORD KIMBERLEY, colonial secretary, 6 March 1881.[4]   Add MS 44226, f. 43.

It appears that 200000 rounds of ammunition have been ordered by the Free State
Government upon requisition as opposed to permit: a quantity made in excess of its ordinary demands. It is plain from the accompanying correspondence that the Free State
Govt. must on a former date have requisitioned for ammunition not intended for its own
use. That Govt. does not now say that the 200000 rounds are required for its own use.
Under the Treaty it does not appear entitled to make any claim except for Government
purposes. The question appears to be thrown back upon us for decision.

I doubt if it be enough to rely upon the President *ex post facto*. He has a good will but
may not have the power. I should recommend informing the President that permission
would be immediately given for so much of the ammunition as he shall certify to be for
Government use. That any further supply would only be allowed for some other purpose
described by him in the quantity required for that purpose & upon his guarantee for its
exclusive application thereto.[5]

[P.S.] I do not understand Childers' reference to another Telegram. I suppose you have
not made any discovery in regard to the tantalizing document mentioned yesterday by
Chamberlain.

7. M. [London]

Wrote to Mr Grant Duff—Att. Gen. for Ireland—Sir C. Herries—The Queen and
minutes. H. of C. $4\frac{1}{2}$-$8\frac{1}{4}$, $9\frac{3}{4}$-12.[6] Saw Sir Gilbert Lewis—Sir H. Ponsonby—Ld

---

[1] See 25 Mar. 49.   [2] Perhaps J. Barnard, *Life of Richard Challoner* (1784).
[3] Harcourt replied that there was no precedent; Add MS 44196, f. 146.
[4] Copy by Mrs. Gladstone.
[5] Kimberley thought the 'more prudent course will be to allow the ammunition to go on', but no
further supplies to go; Add MS 44226, f. 45. See 29 Mar. 81.
[6] Questioned by Lawson on instructions to Colley; Wood's armistice with Joubert announced; *H*
259. 429.

Granville—Ld Kimberley—Mr G.—Ld R.G.—Ld F.C.—Mr Stansfield [*sic*]—Sol. Gen. for Ireland. Read Irish Land Reports—Vivian's conv. with Napoleon.[1]

8. *Tu.*

Wrote to Ld Hartington—Sir C. Herries—The Queen 1.2.3.—Mr Errington— Lady Susan Opdebeck and minutes. H. of C. $4\frac{1}{2}$–$8\frac{1}{4}$ & $9\frac{1}{4}$–11.[2] Cabinet 12–$3\frac{1}{2}$. Saw Mr G.—Ld R.G.—Ld F.C.—Mr Stansfeld—Mr Law—Duke of Argyll—Sir H. Thring—Mr Forster cum Sir W. Harcourt and others. Read Merimée.

Cabinet. Tues. Mch 8. 1881.[3]
1. Answers to questions on the Transvaal considered & agreed on.
2. Series of Telegrams not to be yet presented [to parliament].
3. Answer to Wood's Tel. of 7th Mch conveying Kruger's ans. dated Heidelberg Feb. 28 considered & agreed on.[4] Also Tel. to Robinson respecting the Commission[5] [on the peace in South Africa].
4. Kandahar. First disposable day to be placed at the command of Stanhope.[6]
5. Ld Granville stated failure of the 15 m[ille] proposal & falling back on the arbitration.[7]
6. Reported on the Greek frontier.
7. Mr Forster d[itto] on the state of Ireland.

In reply to a communication from Krüger certain ⟨proposals⟩ announcements with a view to a settlement were made to the Boers and Sir Geo. Colley was directed to allow a reasonable time for the transmission, & for the receipt of an answer.

The instructions given for his conduct before the receipt of answer have already been made known to the House.

If the proposal of H.M. Govt. were accepted, he was in that case authorised to agree to a suspension of hostilities. ⟨There was no instruction to obtain an armistice.⟩ We never directed our Commander to ask for or obtain an armistice, but we entirely approve of the conduct of General Wood.[8]

9. *Wed.*

Wrote to The Queen—Sir H. Ponsonby—Mr Geo Leeman—and minutes. Saw Capt. Trotter[9]—C. Karolyi—Sir Geo Young—Sir H. Thring—Ld Dalhousie.

---

[1] Untraced.

[2] Questioned on the armistice: 'we have never directed our Commanders to ask for or obtain an armistice; but we entirely approve of the conduct of ... Wood'; *H* 259. 551; see cabinet notes for this day.

[3] Add MS 44642, f. 154. Note by Hartington reads: 'A communication having been rcd. from Kruger certain proposals were made to the Boers. Directions were given to Colley to allow a reasonable time for receipt of an answer; & he was authorised if our proposals were accepted to agree to a suspension of hostilities. We never directed our commander to ask for or to obtain an armistice, but we entirely approve of the conduct of Wood'; ibid., f. 156; see Gladstone's answer in Commons this day.

[4] i.e. Kruger's favourable answer to the proposal of a Royal Commission, thus vindicating Gladstone and Kimberley's decision not to avenge Colley; Schreuder, 144, *PP* lxvii. 23.

[5] Possible names; see Schreuder, 144 and 12 Mar. 81.

[6] Stanhope moved his resolution on 24 March.

[7] Newfoundland fishery dispute.

[8] Draft for answer to a question; Add MS 44642, f. 155.

[9] Perhaps Major Henry Trotter, consul for Kurdistan 1879–82.

Dined at the Duke of Edinburgh's. Conversation with the Duchess (by whom I was irregularly placed): & with the G. Duke Alexis[1] who is very intelligent. H. of C. $12\frac{1}{4}$-2 and 3-$4\frac{1}{2}$.[2] Saw Phillips [R]. Read Campbell's Journal.[3]

To the DUKE OF ARGYLL, lord privy seal, 9 March 1881.   Add MS 44544, f. 149.
'*Secret*'.

Thanks for your letter.[4] I hope you comprehend the *limited* purpose of mine. Pray *observe* its terms.

When I said 'free sale' had been settled, I meant, and I think I added immediately afterwards, 'provisionally', or 'for the purpose of our present revision'.

Pray remember our 'free sale' will not be 'free' except in not being under the absolute veto of the landlord.

And on the other hand that judicial rent may be balanced, in law, by judicial restraint upon sale, in the interest of the incoming tenant.

I do really think Forster has given up a great deal. He now seems to like and incline to the provisions for saving contract as much as we can.

10. Th.

Wrote to Ld Chancellor—Ld Granville—Mr Baxter—Sir H. Ponsonby—The Queen 1.2.—Ld Hartington—Mr Kenyon and minutes. H. of C. $4\frac{1}{2}$-8 and 10-$11\frac{3}{4}$.[5] Conclave of Ministers on Procedure. Saw Sir S. Northcote—The Speaker—Sir T.E. May—Scotts—Mrs Th.—Mr Forster—Sir H.H. Allan—Mr G.—Ld R.G.—Ld F.C. Dined at Ld Dalhousie's.

To LORD HARTINGTON, Indian secretary, 10 March   Chatsworth MSS 340. 1092.
1881.

1. I think the Cabinet should know as early as possible i.e. on Saturday what is meditated about Kandahar, now that the possibility of staying beyond April is opened.
2. I agree with your letter of the 4th of March,[6] but the Telegram I think hardly comes up to it. It seems to me that the postponement could hardly be justified by the prospect of giving Abdur Rahman a better chance: but only by our seeing that *in all likelihood* with a departure in April he would not succeed, & with a departure in August he would. In such a case I would also at once put the maximum of pressure upon him for the earlier measure, & let him have no inkling of the latter.[7]

11. Fr.

Wrote to Sir C. Herries—Ld Breadalbane—Mr Bryce—The Queen 1.2.3. (Tel)—Mr Gennadios—Sir S. Northcote—& minutes. Conclave in H. of C. 4.15.[8] Saw

[1] Son of Alexander II; especially active in naval affairs.
[2] Peace Preservation Bill cttee.; *H* 259. 659.
[3] *Life of John, Lord Campbell*, ed. Mrs Hardcastle, 2v. (1881), includes his diary.
[4] Untraced.
[5] Questioned on International Monetary Conference, on Transvaal; *H* 259. 715, 733.
[6] Not found.
[7] See Hartington to the Queen, 13 March, Chatsworth MSS 340. 1096: govt.'s policy is to give govt. of India 'the fullest discretion as to the time and mode of terminating the occupation'.
[8] On the estimates; jottings at Add MS 44765, f. 95.

Mr G.—Ld R.G.—Ld Kimberley—Mr Rathbone—Mr Whitehead—Sir W. James—& others. Read Carlyles Reminiscences I.[1] H. of C. 4½–8¼ and 9½–1¼.[2]

To Sir C. HERRIES, chairman of the board of inland revenue,   Add MS 44544, f. 143.
11 March 1881.

I feel some difficulty in understanding the 'detailed statement'[3] you have sent me & should be glad if you would again come here to-morrow at twelve.

(1) I do not see why the 1 per Cent Legatees should be relieved one farthing at the expence of the Exchequer and I wish a *full* equivalent for the 1 per Cent duty to be laid upon Probate.

The relief from Law Charges will be quite enough for them.

(2) I see from paper sent me the percentage of Probate on each rate but I wish to know what it is as shown by the whole yield on the whole property taxed.

(3) Surely there will be an additional gain from the tax on Estates left wholly to widows.

(4) Also we ought to estimate the average annual increment of property liable to Probate say for 20 years and then take either this or part of this as an addition for 1881–2 to the dutiable property of 1878–9?

(5) I cannot help thinking there must be a further gain connected with the present postponement of reversions to children after the widow—I will try to explain myself on this tomorrow.

To Sir S. H. NORTHCOTE, M.P., 11 March 1881.   Add MS 44544, f. 144.

Your note has just reached me.[4] It is serious. If I have anything further to communicate I will do it at 4.30 when questions begin.

12. Sat.

Wrote to The Queen—Sir H. Ponsonby—Mr Waddy—The Maharajah[5]—Mr Holyoake—Sir G. Campbell & minutes. Cabinet 2–6. Dined at Ld Granville's. Royalty, brandy, merriment. We know not what a day would bring forth! Saw Count Münster. Read Carlyle's Reminiscences.

Cabinet. Mch 12. 81. 2 PM[6]
1. Northampton writ motion. Oppose if pressed.[7] Chiltern Hundreds? No.
2. Northcote's question about getting fresh information from Wood on the Armistice.[8] Ld K. Telegraphs to inquire.
3. Transvaal—names of Commissioners: Sir H. Robinson—Gen Wood—Mr De Villiers. Mr Brand. {assume an amicus curiae

---

[1] T. Carlyle, ed. J. A. Froude, *Reminiscences*, 2v. (1881).
[2] Made a statement on public business; *H* 259. 815.
[3] Add MS 44468, f. 162.
[4] Tories cannot support Supply being made urgent on Monday; Add MS 44217, f. 174.
[5] i.e. Duleep Singh (see 4 Oct. 73) on Transvaal; see Bahlman, *Hamilton*, i. 114.
[6] Add MS 44642, f. 158. Names in pencil at top left hand corner: 'Sir H.P., Sir G. Campb[ell], Holyoake, Waddy'.
[7] Opposed by James on 14 March; *H* 259. 894; the intention was to delay a by-election until Bradlaugh's appeal in the case of Clarke *v.* Bradlaugh had been heard; Arnstein, 94–5. See 1 Apr. 81n.
[8] Asked on 11 March; Gladstone gave fresh details on 14 March; *H* 259. 905.

4. Transvaal—Terms of settlement.
'Suzerainty.' Telegram[1] drawn in detail with much conversation. Armistice to 18th for Boer answer if desired.
5. Terms of Commission to Boers.
Embodied in our message with the names of the Commissioners.
6. Candahar; practical withdrawal of troops. Telegram or possible postponement of departure considered. Viewed with much mislike.
7. Granville reported on Greek frontier. We cannot promise to urge Greece to accept line without Larissa.

Transvaal[2]

1. a. military submission. b. plebiscite.
2. Substitute Protectorate ⎫
             Suzerainty ⎬
                    for Annexation
Commission to Boers, with time for reply; Amnesty; Names of Commissioners; Basis of Arrangement.
Suzerainty. Powers to sever within certain limits in the East.
Self Govt. except a) Foreign relations b) Native affairs
Boers discretion [?] ⟨Garrisons.⟩ British Resident.

[3]Self Govt. under British Suzerainty.
British Resident at Praetoria. ⟨Assent of the Crown necessary to laws affecting natives.⟩
Provisions for protection of interests of natives & as to frontier affairs.
    Limited severance of country on the Eastward to divide Transvaal from Zulus & Swazis, and exclude the great native districts to the E. & NE. Controul of foreign relations reserved.

[Granville:] Suzerainty: Fullest self Govt. *Complete* amnesty subject to necessary condition as to lands & natives.
[Gladstone:] Will the word *suzerainty* be of any use in South Africa?
[Granville:] Yes—But I am rather afraid in the other direction, of how a stipendiary officer is to provide efficiently for land & native questions.[4]

To S. D. WADDY, M.P., 12 March 1881.   Add MS 44544, f. 144.
    The work and pressure of Parliament have nearly reduced me to inanition.
    Do not let me seem ungrateful, though I must seem timid.
    I should like much to dine with you & your friends: but does not a dinner of fifty mean toasts? toasts mean speeches? speeches mean if not reporters yet reports?
    All these things daunt me: perhaps I am impertinent in asking, but I did not like summarily to decline.

---

[1] Naming commissioners 'to consider following points: complete self-government under British suzerainty, with British Resident at Pretoria, and provisions for protection of Native interests and as to frontier matters'; *PP* lxvii. 25 and Schreuder, 149. Full instructions to Commissioners sent 31 March, *PP* lxvii. 291.
[2] Undated holograph; Add MS 44642, f. 159.
[3] Ibid., f. 160.
[4] Add MS 44642, ff. 161–2.

13. 2 S. Lent

Chapel Royal mg (Bp of P.) and evg. Saw Granville—Sydney & others. The dreadful news of the assassination at St Petersburgh reached.[1] Read Carlyles Irving[2]—Illingworth's Sermons[3]—Geogr. of Ocean.[4]

14. M.

Wrote to Ld Advocate—The Queen—Mr Sykes—and minutes. Read Carlyles Irving finished—Mr G. & Mr G.s Commn. H. of C. 4½–8¼ and 9¼–12¼.[5] Saw Mr G.—Ld R.G. Conclave on Urgency situation—Ld Wolverton—Sir H. Thring—Sir H.H. Allan—Sir Thos G.

15. Tu.

Wrote to Ld Reay—Ld Granville—Mr Morley—The Queen & minutes. H. of C. 4½–8¼ & 9½–12. The calm continues: but calm in H. of C. means progress. Saw Mr G.—Ld R.G.—Ld F.C.—Mr Welby on urgency—Sir R. Blennerhasset. Proposed the address on the assassination.[6] Read Carlyle's Reminiscences and re-read Mad. Novikoff's Article.[7]

16. Wed.

Wrote to The Queen—Dean of Salisbury—Mr Law—Archdn Kaye & minutes. H. of C. 12¼–2 & 2½–5. Proposed Indian Subvention:[8] satisfactory debate. No Div. Saw Mr G—Ld R.G.—Mr Childers—Ld Rosebery. Dined with Sybella [Lyttelton]. Read Carlyle Reminiscences.

17. Th.

Wrote to Mr Childers—Ld Kimberley—The Queen 1.2.—Sir W. Harcourt—Ld Granville—Sir H. Ponsonby (2) & minutes. Saw Mr G.—Ld R.G.—Sir H. Thring—Mr Childers—Mr West. H. of C. 4½–8.[9] Dined with Mr West. Read Eastern Question—Carlyle's Reminiscences. Cabinet 2–4¼.

Cabinet. Mch 17. 1881. 2 PM.[10]
Sir E. Woods two Telegrams of March 16 considered.[11]

[1] Of Tsar Alexander II.
[2] i.e. Edward Irving, in the *Reminiscences.*
[3] By J. R. Illingworth (1881).
[4] Perhaps W. L. Jourdan, *The ocean, its tides and currents* (1873).
[5] Gladstone declared the supply votes 'urgent' under the new rules, but the motion, though carried by 84, did not get the required 3:1 majority; *H* 259. 926.
[6] *H* 259. 1062, 1066.
[7] Probably her article on the Alexandrine reforms, *Fraser's Magazine*, ciii. 30 (January 1881).
[8] *H* 259. 1148.
[9] Supply; *H* 259. 1252.
[10] Add MS 44642, f. 163.
[11] Boer acceptance in general terms, but demand for representation on Commission in proportion of two to three, and govt. 'would deal with interior native affairs'; Kimberley's reply this day: 'we could not agree to mixed Commission', but Boer representatives would attend; the Commission would consider 'securities . . . as to future treatment of natives'; *PP* lxvii. 27.

To Sir W. V. HARCOURT, home secretary, 17 March 1881. MS Harcourt dep. 8, f. 77.

The Queen writes to me 'should not any manufacture or rather even any sale of bombs of this horrible nature be prohibited or put under control like the sale of poisons she believes are'?[1] Could you direct a short mem. to be sent me shewing the state of the law as to the sale of materials of destruction? (For H.M.).[2] Bombs or other such things I conclude are never sold?

To LORD KIMBERLEY, colonial secretary, 17 March 1881.   Add MS 44226, f. 55.

I have summoned Cabinet at two.[3] There is certainly difficulty ahead but in my opinion the concession made by the Boers in agreeing to the principle and the main business of dispersion is enormous and it will be a sad pity if after this we cannot work things out—with the agreement to disperse I join the *acceptance of the Suzerainty* and I think that out of the two we ought to be able to extract and adjust materials of a peace.
Now I go to the particulars as you give them. 1. The Commission is not a tribunal of arbitration but is intended to advise with great moral authority the British Government. Its proceedings will be open—let the Boers appoint their agents who shall have cognisance of everything and if the Boer agents differ we shall wish to be let know. 2. Our troops must remain, with the function of a friendly police force and it will be an essential part of their duty to prevent loyal English from using the situation to the prejudice of the Boers. 3. Difficult but not a *sine qua non* according to the last Cabinet—and the terms of our message. 4. Depends a good deal upon the former. If there is no severance, interior native affairs would be of enormously wide scope. Resident ought to concur under any circs. which affect or deal with natives *as such.* I should incline to stiffness on this point. 5. Concession to us most important—because privilege and freedom are octroyés from the Suzerain. 6. I would grant a stipulated amount of force to cooperate in maintaining order as a police force until final adjustment when we should withdraw. (Remember the case of the old American colonies.)
Thus my first views are a little more rosy than yours but not I think in conflict with them. On your No 7[4] I do not touch.

18. Fr.

Whitehall Chapel at noon. (Mr Boyd Carpenter)[5]—Wrote to Abp. of Canterbury—Sir Ch. Herries—Ld Dufferin (2)—Sir H. Ponsonby—Mr Neville—The Queen & minutes. Saw Mr Godley—Mr Forster—Ld R.G.—Sir H. Thring. H. of C. $4\frac{1}{2}$–8 and 9–$11\frac{1}{2}$.[6] Read Carlyle.

To LORD DUFFERIN, 18 March 1881.   Add MS 44544, f. 145.

In reply to your letter of the 10th inst. I have no hesitation in saying that, unless my

---

[1] Guedalla, *Q*, ii. 147; on the Tsar's assassination.
[2] Harcourt promised a mem., untraced; Add MS 44196, f. 150.
[3] Kimberley this day sent two telegrams, whose upshot was, *inter alia*: two Boers on the commission, British troops to be withdrawn from the Transvaal; 'Govt. to deal with native affairs'; Boers accepted suzerainty, but some troops not to be dispersed; Kimberley commented: 'the demands of the Boers appear to me to be inadmissible'; Add MS 44226, f. 53.
[4] 'Sir E. Wood thinks considering our disasters it is better to fight &c.'; ibid.
[5] William Boyd *Carpenter, 1841–1918; royal chaplain 1879; canon of Windsor 1882; bp. of Ripon 1884–1911.
[6] Questions on Transvaal; *H* 259. 1363.

memory totally deceives me,[1] I had no communication whatever with you respecting the Irish Land Question before the introduction of the Bill dealing with that subject in 1870.

(No. 2) I cannot but write another line to say how sorry I am that you should have been assailed by acrimony and untruth after all you have done and striven to do in Ireland: and that I should have been in any way the channel through which it had to be transmitted. I thought it, however, impossible to proceed upon the paper without making an intimation to you.

To Sir H. PONSONBY, the Queen's secretary, 18 March 1881.   Add MS 44544, f. 145.

While considering, as I intended, the letter received from you last night[2] I observe that Her Majesty is under the impression that Sir Garnet Wolseley if raised to the House of Lords would be a political officer.

I can give the most positive assurance that he would in no sense, and in no degree be a political officer.

The test of a political officer is that he comes in and goes out with the Government. Sir Garnet Wolseley has not come in & would not go out with it.

The Commander in Chief is not a political officer, and yet he has a certain approach to the character because he speaks for the Government in matters of Army discipline. Sir Garnet Wolseley would not have this office in any way belonging to him, and thus would not have any semblance of being a political officer.

But further, if he were to be a political officer, I certainly could not recommend his elevation to the House of Lords. Her Majesty graciously offers a Peerage for Sir John Adye. This would give to the military system now prevailing able and professional support. But the object which is aimed at by my recommendation is to obtain support which shall be not only able and professional, but independent. This of course could not be gained by the elevation of Sir John Adye: for whom we greatly desire a seat in the House of Commons.

I would hope that this explanation may like some former ones be graciously received by Her Majesty.

I apprehend that, if it be thought needful, there could be no difficulty in defining, by a note or memorandum for clearer understanding, the exact relation to the Commander in Chief in the H. of Lords.

19. [*The Durdans, Epsom*][3]

Wrote to Ld Granville—The Queen—Ld Chancellor—Ld Spencer—Ld Granville—Mr Arnold MP & minutes. Cabinet 2–4. Off at 4.30 to the Durdans, a breezy drive. Late evg. & much conversation. Finished Carlyle's Reminiscences: they do not raise him.

Cabinet Mch 19. 81. 2 PM.[4]
1. Candahar motion.
Arnold's letter. Take a direct negative. Dilke to begin.[5]

---

[1] It did; for quite extensive communications, see 13 Oct., 3 and 13 Nov. 69.
[2] Together with this reply and other letters on the Wolseley affair, in Guedalla, *Q*, ii. 148.
[3] Rosebery's house.
[4] Add MS 44642, f. 164.
[5] On 24 March; Dilke replied for the govt. directly opposing Stanhope's resolution, rather than supporting Arnold's sympathetic amndt.; *H* 259. 414, 1852.

2. Chaplin & Acland Bills.
Support 2 R of each. reserve as ⟨to⟩ Maskelyne: leave it to the House.[1]
3. Procedure—order of subjects: Land Bill—7th [April], 2R 25th; Budget—4th; Easter Vacation—8th to 25th; Candahar Thurs. & Fri.; Transvaal 20th; Mutiny Bill—next week.
4. Candahar—Telegrams from Ripon read.
5. Transvaal. No intelligence: indispos[itio]n of Chiefs on one side or both. Last Telegram read *in extenso.*
6. Land Bill. W.E.G. commenced.

Cabinet. Sat. Mch. 19. 81.[2]
1. Queen's Birthday. Wish of Queen to keep her birthday made known last year to Ld Kenmare. This year *Tues* (May 24).

20. 3 S. Lent.

Ch mg & evg. Walk in aft. Much conversation with Mr M'Coll on the Palmer republication.[3] Read Stoughton Ch & State[4]—Illingworth Sermons.

21. M. [London]

Back home at 1.2. Wrote to Sir H. Ponsonby 1.2.—Sir C. Herries—Mr Dallas—The Queen 1.2. and minutes. Photographed at the Durdans. Saw Mr G—Ld R.G.—Ld Granville 1.2.—Herbert J.G.—The Speaker—Mr Labouchere—Sir T. May—Mr Plunkett—Mr Playfair. Saw Harris—Rands and another [R]. Read Ld Campbell's Journals.[5]

22. Tu.

Wrote to Ld Kimberley—Resident Sister Soho Square[6]—The Queen l & tel.—Mr [blank.] Saw Rands; an interesting case [R]. Saw Mr G.—Ld R.G.—Ld F.C. Spent much time happily with Lord Kimberley on the Transvaal arrangements. A tumultuary cabinet at 2.30.[7] H. of C. $4\frac{1}{2}$-6 and 10-1.[8] Saw Dean S. & The Thynne House. Read Merimée, Letters to Panizzi.

To LORD KIMBERLEY, colonial secretary, 22 March 1881.   Add MS 44226, f. 57.
    Thank God.
    I have read with a critical eye as well as I could the long Telegram;[9] and I do not detect

---

[1] Both got 2°R for their Tenants Compensation Bills on 23 March; *H* 259. 1731; Maskelyne supported the Acland bill.
[2] Add MS 44642, f. 166.
[3] The unsuccessful attempt at a revised ed. of W. Palmer, *Treatise on the Church of Christ*, 2v. (1838); see to MacColl, 27 Mar. 81.
[4] J. Stoughton, *Church and state two hundred years ago* (1862).
[5] See 9 Mar. 81.
[6] i.e. of the House of Mercy on the corner of Rose Street and Soho Square.
[7] On the Transvaal; no notes found. The Queen objected to Wood's agreement with the Boers; see Guedalla, *Q,* ii. 151 and *L.Q.V.,* 2nd series, iii. 203.
[8] Misc. business; *H* 259, 1638.
[9] From Wood: Boers accept British suzerainty, Resident and control of foreign relations if self-govt. instituted within six months; *PP* lxvii. 29, Schreuder, 155.

any reason for hesitation. If I am right in this, we two agreeing, it is of the utmost import-ance to proceed without losing an hour that we can save. I suggest sending a Messenger *instantly* to Windsor, acquainting H.M. that you are obtaining the judgment of the Cabinet—that you and I have no doubt they will at once approve, that it is of importance to communicate today our reply—that you hope if H.M. agrees She will graciously at once telegraph her approval. In the meantime by circulation you can get the opinion of the Cabinet.

Of course all this *depends* upon the preliminary question on whether we can approve. In my view the Telegram is as a whole rather better than we had any right to expect. I assume it to be an authentic document, acknowledged as to all the material parts by the Boers. If we approve, Wood ought to receive emphatic praise—and query whether we can hereafter do anything complimentary for Brand.

23. Wed.

Wrote to The Queen 1.—Ld Carlingford—Mr Mackie MP[1]—Rev. S.E.G. tel.—Sir W. F. Williams—Ld Chancellor (2)—Mr Childers—Ld R. Grosvenor and minutes. Tea, & the White Cat, at Walter Phillimore's. [Read] Rogers on Horne Tooke.[2] Saw Mr G. Ld R.G.—Ld F.C.—Sir H. Thring—Sir R. Phillimore—Ld Granville—Mr Hubbard—Gov. of Bank. Dined with Gov. of Bank—Ld Tenter-den's afterwards.

To LORD CARLINGFORD, 23 March 1881.   Carlingford MSS CP1/196.

I have much wished to see you about the Irish Land Bill on the subject of which there is certainly in my judgment no higher living authority. I have postponed writing partly from the great pressure, partly from not knowing whether or when you were in town.

If you can come without inconvenience on any early day I should much prize the opportunity of conversing with you.[3]

24. Th.

Wrote to Sir C. Herries—Sir R. Phillimore—Mr Forster—Sir H. Ponsonby—Mrs Th.—The Queen & minutes. Saw Mr G.—Ld R.G.—Sir H. Thring 12½-2½—Ld Gr.—Ld H. & Mr Childers on the Wolseley Peerage. H. of C. Candahar 4½-8¼ and 9-12.[4] R. Grosvenor absolved me from speaking. Read Th. Rogers on H. Tooke.

25. Fr. Annunc.

Wrote to Ld Granville 1.2.—Ld Selborne—The Queen and minutes. Saw Ld Granville 1. on Greek Frontier 2. on Wolseley Peerage. 12-2. Inland Revenue—Conclave on Death Duties &c.[5] 2½-4, Ld Carlingford.[6] Dined at Lord North-

---

[1] Robert Bownas Mackie, 1820-85; liberal M.P. Wakefield from 1880.
[2] See 26 Aug. 78n.   [3] See 25 Mar. 81.
[4] *H* 259. 1831.
[5] Budgetary preparations; see Bahlman, *Hamilton*, i. 117, 122.
[6] 'Gladstone . . . began by talking of the tremendous & formidable difficulties of the Land Bill & gave me an outline of its provisions—which I found very hard to understand. He seemed very averse to interference with "freedom of contract". His views seemed to me confused & I was unfavourably impressed': Carlingford's diary, 25 March 1881.

brooks. H. of C. $4\frac{1}{2}$–$7\frac{1}{2}$ and $9\frac{3}{4}$–2. Voted in 336: 216. Hartington's speech even better than the division.[1]

26. Sat.

Wrote to The Queen—Bp of Manchester 1.2.—Mr E. Arnold—Mr C. Reed—Ld Aberdeen—Princess of Wales—Archbishop of Canterbury and minutes. Cabinet 2-6. Irish Land Bill made real progress. Saw Ld Granville—Mr E. Arnold—Mr Welby—Mr G—Ld R.G.—Ld F.C.—Lord Chancellor. Dined at Tennyson's— Mrs T. is delightful. He read to us the passing of Arthur.

Cabinet. Mch 26. 1881. 2 PM.[2]
1. Ld Advocates Bill for reducing the Scotch Judges by 2.—Adjourn: & inquire as to Sheriffs.[3]
2. Greek frontier. Ld Granville's Telegram to Goschen authorising him to join the other Ambassadors in accepting the last Turkish line rather than contemplate sole material action on behalf of Greece: after recording his view on behalf of a better.[4]
3. Article in the Freiheit. Query whether to prosecute? Ld Granville stated (on Munster's authority) German Govt. wd. prosecute if advised that the law warranted it. Decided to prosecute.[5]
4. Harcourt—motion on highways:[6] mode of meeting by plan or Plans extended.
5. Irish Land Bill: revision of clauses begun.

27. 4 S. Lent.

Chapel Royal mg & aft. Saw E. Hamilton—Mrs Th.—Lord Spencer. Wrote to Mr M'Coll—Mr Beresford Hope. Wrote 'dots' on Irish Land. Read Stoughton's Ch & State—Illingworth's Sermons—T. Brown, Dryden's Conversi[7]—Marriage Law of Scripture[8]—Letters on Rabelais & autres.[9]

To Rev. M. MacCOLL, 27 March 1881.   Add MS 44544, f. 148.

You will have conceived and represented the idea I tried to convey to you on Sunday last better than I can explain it on paper; yet I am not easy without writing a few words to help in making the record.

What I want to have, on the basis of Palmer's work,[10] is a setting forth, according to the methods which theological science provides, of the Civitas Dei, the City set on a hill, the pillar and ground of truth, the Catholic and Apostolic Church, the *Fortsetzung der Fleischwirkung*, exhibited, not as against Nonconformists, nor even principally as against the Jesuit aggressive Church of Rome, but as a positive dispensation, a form divinely given to

[1] Notable govt. success on the Kandahar motion; *H* 259. 2033.
[2] Add MS 44642, f. 167.
[3] See 2 June 81.   [4] See Ramm II, i. 249.
[5] The article rejoiced in the Tsar's assassination; the editor was arrested on 30 March; see Harcourt's answers to questions, *H* 260. 345, 464 and *T.T.*, 1 April 1881, 4d.
[6] Motion to defray part of costs of highways by other than county rates moved on 28 March by Col. Edward William Harcourt, 1825–91; tory M.P. Oxon. 1878–86.
[7] Perhaps T. Brown, *The works of M. Voiture... made English by John Dryden* (1705).
[8] Perhaps J. P. Bishop, *Commentary on the law of marriage and divorce*, many eds.
[9] [Voltaire], *Lettres à son Altesse... sur Rabelais et sur d'autres* (1768).
[10] i.e. Palmer's *Treatise on the Church of Christ*, see 20 Mar. 81.

the religious idea, which challenges with authority, but agreeably to reason, the assent of
the rational and right-minded man, in competition with all the other claimants on that
assent. I want some solid scientific work which shall set up historical or institutional
Christianity to take its chance in the mêlée of systems dogmatic and undogmatic,
revealed and unrevealed, particularist, pagan, secular, antitheistic or other, which marks
the age.

Having spent fifty years of adult life in this mêlée, I find the method I describe the most
rational of all, and I wish that there should be a textbook of it for the help of doubtful or
uninstructed minds.

Also that this textbook, founded on the principle I have described, should apply the
principle, for the benefit of Englishmen, to the case of the English Church, under the
shadow of which our lot is providentially cast.[1]

28. M.

Wrote to Rev. Dr Allon—Mrs Tennyson—The Queen 1.2.—Duke of Argyll—Sir
Thos. G.—Abp of Canterbury—Mr Fawcett—Ld Granville—Mr Wills MP—Mr
Jarvis & minutes. H. of C. $4\frac{1}{2}$-$5\frac{3}{4}$ and 9–1. Spoke on Col. Harcourt's motion.[2] Saw
Mr G.—Ld R.G.—Ld F.C.—Sir H. Ponsonby—Mr Bright—Sir T. M'Clure—Mr
Rathbone. Dined with the Jameses. read Ld Campbell. Saw Rand [R].

Cabinet. Mch 28. 81. 12 o'clock[3]
1. Telegram to Goschen *approving* line etc. approved.[4]
2. Irish Land Bill. Further revision of Clauses.

[5]It is curious to see how minds are unconsciously acted on by pressure. Bright was
satisfied with my original draft. It has been *much* strengthened. He finds it now utterly
too weak.

To Rev. H. ALLON, 28 March 1881.   Add MS 44544, f. 149.

I have a wish, to which I seek to give effect, and I do not quite know how. Perhaps you
can help me. For the present, I only commend it to your thoughts.

This wish is to find some mode in which I can, consistently with my general rules, and
appropriately in reference to the subject in hand, offer in some suitable quarter some
token that would serve to record my sense of the invaluable service done by the Nonconformists during the Easter Controversy of recent years to the cause of liberty and justice.

Would the Memorial Hall and its library afford a central and representative point at
which some presentation might be made: or is there any other suggestion which would
be more available?

Perhaps you will kindly come & breakfast with us on some of our Thursdays after
Easter (at 10. a.m.) and the interval may allow you, if you are kindly so disposed, to turn
over the matter in your thoughts.

I shall try to contrive something analogous for Scotland.

[1] Part in Lathbury, ii. 318. MacColl replied, 28 March, Add MS 44244, f. 273, that he had 'not
altogether succeeded ... in conveying to Palmer's mind an exact copy of the plan which you suggested ...'.
[2] See 26 Mar. 81n.
[3] Add MS 44642, f. 168.
[4] Accepting Turkish proposal to give Greece all Thessaly without Crete; Ramm II, i. 249.
[5] Undated holograph; ibid., f. 169.

To the DUKE OF ARGYLL, lord privy seal, 28 March 1881.   Add MS 44544, f. 148.
'Private'

As far as I have been able to gather, your main point of difficulty in the matter of Irish Land is the right of sale.

You do not I think 'stumble' at the interference of 'the Court' with rent; which in my mind is a far more advanced proposition.

As to this right of sale I think it quite an open question in principle whether when the Court limits rent it should also limit the price of the tenant right.

It stood so in my original draft.

But, apart from this, I earnestly beseech you not to arrive at any hasty conclusion adverse to the right of sale.

I have gone through this part of the subject fully in my mind; I must deal with it at great length (in the coming monster speech) & I am convinced that the argument is *overwhelming*.[1]

[P.S.] Some things please me much; among others (so far as I understand it) Forster's present attitude.

To H. FAWCETT, postmaster general, 28 March 1881.   Add MS 44544, f. 149.

I do not doubt the advantage of your plan[2] for reducing the price of Telegrams & improving the mode of charge, but it has to be compared with other demands for reduction of taxation and there is I am sorry to say no present chance of our being able to afford 167m[ille] for this purpose.

To W. H. WILLS, M.P., 28 March 1881.   Add MS 44544, f. 149.

The upshot of my reference to the Revenue Departments on the Tobacco Duties is, that I am absolutely precluded from entertaining at the present time any proposal for the repeal of the Tobacco Duty lately imposed under the Government of Lord Beaconsfield. The immediate loss of revenue would be such as I have no means of meeting in the present state of our revenues and expenditure. The estimate of this loss is, you are aware, one which in the main I must accept from the Customs Department: and if it is contested, argument would best be addressed to that Department on this particular point. Should you desire any explanation of this note, I shall be happy to afford it you orally in the House of Commons: & I am sure you will comprehend the distinction between approving an impost & being unable at a given time to remove it.

29. Tu.

Wrote to Mr Murray—Lord Chancellor—Mr E. Arnold—Sir C. Herries—Sir R. Malins—Ld Granville—D. of Argyll—Abp of Canterbury—Mr Welby—Ld Kimberley—The Queen & minutes. Saw Mr G. Ld R.G.—Mr Welby 12-1½. H. of C. 4½-6 and 9-1. Read Ld Campbell's Memoirs. Went up to enquire for Lord B.[3]— Ld Barrington reported him better. May the Almighty be near his pillow.

[1] In Argyll, ii. 370. Argyll replied next day, Add MS 44105, f. 16: no further comment until he has seen the final bill; he wrote resigning on 31 March, correspondence following on time of disclosure, with further attempts by Gladstone to retain him; ibid., ff. 21-60.
[2] Sent 27 March, Add MS 44156, f. 71: use the surplus to reduce telegram prices.
[3] Beaconsfield died on 19 April.

To W. E. FORSTER, Irish secretary, 29 March 1881.   Add MS 44158, f. 140.

I find many are under the impression that your speech of yesterday announced, if not an intention of the Govt. to apply for 'further' in the sense of 'stronger' powers in Ireland, yet that they had it in contemplation more or less.

I am sure you had no intention of this kind inasmuch as the Govt. have nothing in contemplation on a matter which they have not considered and which the time has not come for considering.

I know the difficulty of judging a speech from report, and I will not fall into that error, but I fear your words have produced an impression they were not intended to convey, and which may even materially affect the number in the division of Thursday unless the House understands the true state of the case.[1]

To Sir C. J. HERRIES, chairman of the board of inland revenue,   Add MS 44544, f. 149.
29 March 1881.

(1) As to the [£] 75000, I grieve to say I positively cannot afford it! Please therefore to see how far we can get rid of it. And here I have to say

a. If you *can* contrive to make an ad valorem charge it will enable us to sail closer to the wind.

b. We are going to confer an immense boon on the 14050 Estates from £300 to 1m[ille] by the deduction of debts—and there is not the slightest occasion to *give* them anything more.

c. Even as to the Estates under *£300 gross*, the relief we are about to give otherwise than by remission of tax is so great, that I think we may a little increase the charge on them if necessary.

(2) As to settled personalty. It is most desirable to frame a plan if you can: setting a commuted charge on the settlement, in lieu of the Probate Duty: without touching for the present either realty or charges laid upon realty.

Could we in settled personalty abolish also the 1 per Cent Duty and put this into the charge on the settlement? either compulsorily or optionally?

Any money you can get me, honestly & decently, from this source, will be thankfully received. I am devoured by the Transvaal.

(3). I should like *now* to bring to a head my transactions with you for the Budget of Monday. Shall you be ready for this *on Thursday at 12?* If not, say Friday. Please to bring Mr Young[2] as an addition to your party for I want to know exactly what I shall say about the Beer Duty.

To LORD KIMBERLEY, colonial secretary, 29 March 1881.   Add MS 44544, f. 150.

As the peace is now made with the Boers, I think we cannot enforce war measures. So I rat, & go over from Childers to you, in favour of letting the ammunition go.[3]

It was a strong measure before to stop it. Nothing but the critical nature of the case would warrant it. That has now disappeared. We must take care not to make Brand's[4] position impossible.

---

[1] No reply found.
[2] Adam Young, the deputy chairman.
[3] See 6 Mar. 81.
[4] (Sir) Johannes Henricus Brand, 1823–88; president of Orange Free State from 1863; hon. G.C.M.G. 1882.

30. *Wed.*

Wrote to Mr Summers MP[1]—Att. Gen. for Ireland—The Queen—& minutes. Cabinet 1-5:[2] with an interval of 1 hour to see the Queen at Buckingham Palace; frank & kind as usual; avoiding all sore & tender places. Went up again to enquire for Lord B.—Saw Ld B[arrington] & Dr Kidd.[3] The better account confirmed. Saw Mr G.—Ld R.G.—Mr West—Sir H. Ponsonby. Ld Kimberley on the Instructions. Went early to bed in the shadow of a cold: giving up the Play. Read Taming of the Shrew, finished—Memoirs of Wilberforce—Campbell.

31. *Th.*

Wrote to Lord Chancellor—Bp of Tuam—Ld Granville—D. of Argyll—Sir C. Herries 1.2.—The Queen—Attorney General and minutes. Saw Mr G.—Ld R.G.—Ld F.C. Conclave on B.I.R. questions 12-3. Mr Wills MP—Mr West—Mr Hamilton—Mr Latham. H. of C. $4\frac{1}{2}$-$6\frac{1}{2}$.[4] Read Ld Campbell—19th Cent England's Impressor—Burt on Coercion.[5]

To LORD SELBORNE, lord chancellor, 31 March 1881.   Add MS 44544, f. 150.

By the Queen's desire I send you a paper on the rule at Court as to ladies divorced.[6]

The question is, if there be a departure, can a safe limit of departure be found? If it can the Queen would I think like it: and this I promised should be carefully examined. It might be right to consult the Att. General.

But there is great force in the argument of Lds. Sydney & Kenmare.[7]

Frid. Ap. 1. 1881

Wrote to Ld Halifax—Pres. Edinb. Philos. Assocn.[8]—D. of Argyll 2—Sir C. Herries—Mr West—The Queen and minutes. H. of C. $4\frac{3}{4}$-$7\frac{1}{2}$.[9] Read Ld Campbell—Lady Martin's Ophelia.[10] Saw Mr Welby 12-$3\frac{3}{4}$. Sir R. Wilson—Mr West—Mr Hamilton—Sir C. Ducane—Mr G.—Ld R.G.—Mr Stanhope cum Mr Talbot—Mr Earp MP.

2. *Sat.*

Wrote to Mr Bryce MP—Duke of Argyll—Sir R. Cross—The Queen—Mr West and minutes. Cabinet 2-$6\frac{3}{4}$: with an interval in D. St. Hard at work on Budget.

[1] On the beer duty; *T.T.*, 4 April 1881, 7e.

[2] No minutes found; on the Land Bill, according to Hamilton; Bahlman, *Hamilton*, i. 122.

[3] Beaconsfield's doctor, a homeopathist.

[4] Questioned on the Canal shares; *H* 260. 348.

[5] *N.C.*, ix. 577, 611 (April 1881).

[6] Selborne replied this day: only viable distinction: 'ladies who *have divorced*, and those who *have been divorced by*, their husbands'; Add MS 44297, f. 148.

[7] Mem. forwarded to Ponsonby, 5 April, Add MS 45724, f. 105, with note: 'the Court can only act I fear on broad distinctions: this dealing with individual cases would be like endeavouring to divide the colours of the rainbow'.

[8] Declining hon. membership if it causes dispute within the Association; Add MS 44469.

[9] Bradlaugh's appeal having failed, Labouchere, with Gladstone's approval, moved the writ; *H* 260. 490.

[10] Lady H. Martin, *On Ophelia and Portia* (1880).

Saw Mr West—Mr G.—Ld R.G. Haymarket Theatre; Masks & Faces: admirably acted.[1] Read Life of Wilberforce.[2]

Cabinet at Ld Granville's. Sat. Ap. 2. 2 P.M.[3]
1. Budget. Settled.[4]
2. Land Bill considered (without the Chancellor) especially on fixing a limit for tenant right.[5]
3. Vote of thanks to Sir F. Roberts.

3. 5 S.L.

Chapel Royal mg (with H.C.) & aft. Wrote to Mr West 1.2. and [blank.] $2\frac{1}{2}$–$4\frac{1}{2}$. With Mr West & Mr Welby on the Budget. Saw Arthur Lyttelton. Read Life of Selwyn[6]—Stoughton on Restoration Period.[7]

4. M.

Wrote to The Queen—Mr Forster 1.2.—D. of Argyll—and minutes. Dined interstitially with Sir T. May. Worked all day on Budget figures. Saw Sir C. Herries—Mr Welby—Ld F. Cavendish—Mr Forster—Mr West & others.[8] H. of C. $4\frac{1}{2}$–2. Spoke Financial Statement: 2h.10m.[9] Spoke also after 1 a.m. on Mutiny Bill. Read Bp Wilberforce.

To W. E. FORSTER, Irish secretary, 4 April 1881.　　　　　Add MS 44544, f. 151.

You will remember that we discovered a flaw in the Land Bill on Saturday. It *appeared* that the Landlord's pre-emption, devised with quite a different view, would *accidentally* create a future tenancy. I cannot doubt that I shall be allowed to rectify this? Do you think there would be any objection & could you settle the matter for me?[10]

5. Tu.

Wrote to The Queen 1.2.—Mr Williamson MP—Bp of London—Ld Granville—Sir H. Ponsonby and minutes. Saw Mr G.—Ld R.G.—Ld F.C.—Mr Welby—D. of Argyll—Sir H. Thring 3 h. on Irish Land.—Sol General for Ireland—Mr Forster—Ld Rosebery—Danish Minister (Gk. Frontier)—Dean of St Paul's.—Ld Chancellor—Ld Tenterden. Attended Levee. Ten to dinner:[11] evg. Party afterwards.

---

[1] No author given; *T.T.*, 2 April 1881, 10f.
[2] The 2nd vol. of the *Life of Samuel Wilberforce*; see 22 Nov. 80.　　　[3] Add MS 44642, f. 170.
[4] Notes on it, ibid., ff. 171-3. According to Hamilton, Gladstone's 'financial proposals were not accepted', the death duties proposals being altered, and income tax being reduced by 1*d.* rather than 1½*d.*; Bahlman, *Hamilton*, i. 124.　　　　　　　　　　　　[5] See 4 Apr. 81.
[6] See 22 Mar. 79.　　　　　　　　　　　　　　　　　　　　　　　　[7] See 20 Mar. 81.
[8] Including Florence Arnold-Forster, W. E. Forster's adopted da., who sat next him at dinner; *F.A.-F.J.*, 112.
[9] *H* 260. 586, 676; his 11th budget, 'probably the last time'; 'I fully admit I have no brilliant picture to present to the Committee'.
[10] No reply found.
[11] R. W. Church to Blachford, 6 April 1881 (*Life and letters of Dean Church* (1895), 290): 'I dined with Gladstone yesterday, and I am bound to contradict the suggestion that, outwardly, he shows the smallest sign of impaired strength ... there he was at dinner, as full of talk on every subject, trade, agricultural depression, down to handwriting. . . .'

6. *Wed.*

Wrote to The Queen—Ld Carlingford—D of Argyll—Ld Granville 1.2.—Sir H. Ponsonby and minutes. A tough day on Irish Land. Pleasant dinner party at Ld Bath's. Saw Mr G.—Ld R.G.—Ld Granville—Ld Spencer—Sir H. Thring. Saw Rands [R]. Read Life of Bp W. A tough day on Irish Land.[1]

To LORD CARLINGFORD, 6 April 1881.   Carlingford MSS CP1/197.

I am only now able to send you a print of the Bill. One or two minor amendments may yet be made. I hope you will not arrive at the conclusion that the intervention of the Court ought to be made universal & compulsory.

7. *Th.*

Wrote to Ld Granville—Ld Hartington—The Queen—and minutes. Read Stoughton Ch. & State. Saw Mr G.—Ld R.G.—Prince Woronzow[2]—Mr Ford—Mr Lecky. Again worked hard on Irish Land: and introduced the big Bill (for such it is in purpose more than bulk) $5\frac{1}{4}$–8.[3] Dined with Sir E. May. Off home at $11\frac{1}{4}$.

To LORD HARTINGTON, Indian secretary, 7 April 1881. Chatsworth MSS 340. 1100.

I thank you for your very frank note, and have no difficulty in acceding to your general plea for exemption.[4] I would only make one special qualification. I have no doubt about our having done what we best could to define fair rent: and I am heartily in favour of giving this a very substantial meaning. Nor have I any doubt about the justice of our allowing the Court, which is to fix rent, also to interfere with the price for tenant right. I cannot say as much for the manner in which at your instance that interference is to be shaped. I may not be master of the whole case, but so far as I can see I shall find this hard or impossible to defend in debate, & I am doubtful whether many members of the Cabinet are more confident. I commend this point, therefore, to your reflection.

8. *Fr.*

Wrote to D. of Argyll—The Queen 1.2. & minutes. Conclave on disclosure in Standard.—Finished Stoughton—Cabinet $12\frac{1}{4}$–2. H. of C. $2\frac{1}{4}$–$5\frac{1}{4}$.[5] Saw Mr G.—Ld R.G.—Ld Houghton. Dined at 15 G.S. Saw Rands[R].

Cabinet. Friday Ap 8. 81. Noon[6]
1. Argyll's resignation. Carlingford's success[ion] mentioned. Much approval. Union with L.S. Commission[7] considered. Thought doubtful.

---

[1] Repeated phrase added in the margin. Some notes, marked 'Cancelled. Ap. 6.', on application to the Court, at Add MS 44765, f. 15.
[2] Count J. J. Woronzov-Dachekow, aide-de-camp of Alexander III, with a message from him; see Ramm II, i. 252.   [3] Land Law (Ireland) Bill introduced and 1°R; *H* 260. 890.
[4] Commenting on the Argyll/Gladstone letters on resignation sent by Gladstone on 5 April, Hartington asked (6 April, Add MS 44145, f. 236), first, that the Land Bill should adhere in the main to the agreed principles, second, that he should 'not be asked to take part in its defence more than can be helped'.
[5] Moved adjournment for the Easter Recess; *H* 260. 1036.   [6] Add MS 44642, f. 174.
[7] Apparently *sic*; the idea was for the lord privy seal to oversee agriculture.

2. Forster mentioned state of Ireland, now worse again. More arrests likely.
3. Article in Standard.[1] It being ascertained that the article is based upon No 14, inquiry is to be made as to the copies of that No. circulated, & what has become of them.
4. Ld Kimberley stated the difficulties which might arise in the Potchefstrom case if the case should prove to be of a certain character. Was the surrender due to bad faith—was it a valid transaction.[2]
5. Greek frontier question. Much left in the hands of Ld G. & Mr. G. for the recess.
6. Mr Childers paper on the Militia.[3] A limited number after a vote of the men & money may be called out without Proclamation of national danger.

To LORD CARLINGFORD, 8 April 1881.					Add MS 44544, f. 152.

You will have learned from the newspapers the sad loss we have experienced in the resignation of the Duke of Argyll. I am desirous to repair the mischief which has thus befallen us: and there is no way in which I can so hopefully set about it as by asking you to give me the benefit of your aid at this serious juncture by assuming his office.

This I sincerely hope you may do: and there will be on our part a double satisfaction and advantage, first in a great accession to our strength for the purposes of a vital measure, and secondly in welcoming the return of a valued and able colleague to his proper place as a minister of the Crown.[4]

9. Sat. [Hawarden]

Wrote to Mr Peake—Mr Armitage—Sir R. Cross—Rev. Dr. Simpson—The Queen—Mr Fawcett & minutes. A good stiff morning bringing papers &c into a little order. Saw Mr G.—Ld R.G.—Ld Granville—Freshfields—Ld Hartington—Mr Sanders—Ld Carlingford—Mr Wortley. Off at 4.45 from Paddington—At the Rectory 220 miles by 10.10. Read Brenon's Poems[5]—Noel's Poems.[6]

To Rev. W. S. SIMPSON, 9 April 1881.					Add MS 44544, f. 153.

I thank you very much for your courtesy in presenting me with a copy of your work on St. Paul's. Both the subject & the apparent mode of execution (for I have only as yet given it a glance) will render the perusal of it most attractive to me.[7]

The Cathedrals of the country are not only great architectural constructions, but they form a constituent element of the nation's life, & there is every sign amidst the manifold activities of the present day that they are strengthening rather than losing their hold on the general sympathy & love. To this end I trust your work may materially contribute.

[1] Details of the Land Bill revisions leaked; Hamilton thought Chamberlain responsible, Chamberlain thought it was Forster; Bahlman, Hamilton, i. 125.
[2] British garrison there surrendered after the end of the war, the Boer besiegers maintaining the siege; there was a demand for compensation; Schreuder, 183.
[3] Introducing the territorial system; see Childers, ii, ch. xi.
[4] Carlingford accepted this day, Add MS 44123, f. 96. The circumstances of his appt. led to considerable rancour, see 7, 11 Sept. 84.
[5] Edward St. John Brenon sent his The tribune reflects and other poems (1881), dedicated to Gladstone.
[6] R. B. W. Noel (see 20 July 74) sent his A little child's monument (1881).
[7] W. S. Simpson, Chapters in the history of Old St. Paul's (1881).

10. *Palm S.*

Ch mg & evg. Wrote to Prince of Wales—Ld Granville—Mr Hamilton[1]—Mr Saunders—Mr Macmillan—Rev. Mr Skinner and minutes. Read Account of the Opium Trade[2]—Skinner's Devotional Work[3]—Rowland Williams Devotions[4]—B. Denison agt the Sceptics.[5]

11. *M.*

Ch 8½ a.m. & 7 P.M. Wrote to Ld Granville Tel 1. 2.—Mrs Walker—D. of Argyll—Mr Roden Noel and minutes. Saw Miss Waters. Read The Old Church Clock[6]—History of Gypsies[7]—Lecky's Rationalism.[8] Walk with S.E.G.

To the DUKE OF ARGYLL, 11 April 1881.   Add MS 44544, f. 153.

My reluctance to touch a sad subject is the only qualification to the pleasure with which I thank you for your indifferently deserved but most touching reference to me in your farewell words on Friday evening.

I look anxiously for the first door open, by which I may escape from office & bid it a final farewell. Of all occupations there is none which so much as the political one, in my case especially, demands a space between the arena & the grave. As I can never take office again, our official parting is I fear final; you have done everything to make it bear that character which unhappily it so often misses.

The completion of the Land legislation for Ireland now lies before me as the chief remaining demand upon me. Every remnant of energy that I possess, & the whole determination of the Government, will be addressed to its prompt settlement. I am sure you will feel with me that the matter is one too critical by much for hanging over from year to year.

I have been agreeably surprised at its reception on both sides so far as the Landlord & Tenant part is concerned. Have you been amused at the Conservative fears about the public advances? You know that on that subject, I was a little afraid of you.[9]

12. *Tu.*

Ch 8½ a.m. & 7 P.M. Wrote to Abp of Canterbury—Ld Chancellor—The Speaker—E. Hamilton 1. & Tel.—J. Clare Tel—Mr Walpole—Ld Granville—Pr. Leopold—Mr Tomlinson[10]—Mr Cameron and minutes. Walk with W. (daily calls on one or more). Read The Old Church Clock—History of the Gypsies—Wylie's Carlyle.[11]

---

[1] Inquiring about public funerals since 1827, with Beaconsfield in mind; Add MS 48607, bundle 2.
[2] Perhaps the manifesto of the society for suppressing the opium trade, est. Jan. 1881.
[3] J. Skinner, *An act of spiritual communion* (1880).
[4] R. Williams, probably *Psalms and litanies* (1872).
[5] Probably one of E. B. Denison's polemics.   [6] Untraced.
[7] Perhaps F. H. Groome, *In gypsy tents* (1881).
[8] See 3 June 65.
[9] For reply, see 14 Apr. 81n.
[10] James Tomlinson, 1840-1910; banker and liberal; contested the Wirral April 1881 and other constituencies; liberal M.P. 1900-10. This letter, on the Transvaal, led to questions in the Lords on 10 May; *H* 261. 136.
[11] W. H. Wylie, *Thomas Carlyle. The man and his books* (1881).

13. *Wed.*

Ch 8½ a.m. & 7 P.M. Wrote to Sir W. Harcourt—Mr Justice Lawson—Mr Brenan & minutes. Walk with W. & stiff conversation on Irish Land.[1] Read Edinb. Rev., Oxford School—do Herries Memoirs[2]—Arnold Preface to Poems[3]—Bagehot Biogr. Papers[4]—Wylie's Irving.[5] Saw Fairbrother: probably on his deathbed.[6]

Sir W. V. HARCOURT, home secretary, 13 April, 1881.　　　MS Harcourt dep. 8, f. 78.

No one can be better qualified than you to choose a successor to Dr Bateson: and on the other hand few worse qualified than I am, from want of general knowledge of the resident body: I at once accept Mr Blore.[7]

The reception of the Land Bill has been beyond my expectation: and I am not ill pleased that Conservative jealousy should seem to be directed to the part about public advances, for the disposition of the Irish, almost to a man, to pull at the central purse is perilous.

Salisbury will certainly have to say or do something in the Tunis affair. He has I fear sensibly suffered in character within the last three years. One needs to regard his good fame as part of the national Estate.

You will find Sandringham agreeable & healthy. I do not remember ever, until today, to have seen the daisies, buttercups, and primroses, come before the snowdrops had gone.

14. *Th.*

Church 8½ a.m. with H.C. and P.M. Conversation with Mr MacColl. Wrote to Mr Tomlinson—Ld Chancellor—Scotts—Mr Whithead—Ld Coleridge—Ld Kimberley—H.N.G.—D. of Argyll—Mr West—Mr Hamilton 1 & Tel—Ld Granville Tel—and minutes. Tea party at the Coffee-house: very satisfactory. Read Pocock Recovery[8]—Edinb. Rev. on Pellagra—On Carlyle's Reminiscences[9]—Wylie's Carlisle [*sic*].

To the DUKE OF ARGYLL, 14 April 1881.　　　　　Add MS 44105, f. 66.

There is no doubt that my personality is pledged over head and ears to the Irish Land Bill, and to passing it this Session. But I did not so pledge it; it pledged itself.

With a country under coercion, and only just escaped from anarchy, after such an antecedent history with men like the Land Leaguers, and an institution like the Land League, to confront and overcome, it is a question of the peace of Ireland, and perhaps of

---

[1] W. H. Gladstone was increasingly cautious about liberal policy towards Ireland; his retirement from the Commons in 1885 partly reflected a desire not to have openly to oppose his father. See 3 July 86.

[2] *E.R.*, cliii. 304, 390 (April 1881).

[3] Matthew Arnold, new complete ed. of his *Poems*, 2v. (1881), sent by Macmillan.

[4] W. Bagehot, *Biographical Studies*, ed. R. H. Hutton (1881); includes Bagehot's essay on Gladstone. See to Mrs Bagehot, 25 Apr. 81.

[5] Probably W. Wilks, *Edward Irving* (1854), see 17 Feb. 56; or part of Wylie's *Carlyle*.

[6] See 5 Feb. 57.

[7] Harcourt recommended Edward William Blore (1828-85, cricketer and vice-master of Trinity, Cambridge) as a liberal for the Cambridge University Commission; Add MS 44196, f. 152.

[8] N. Pocock, *The recovery from the principles of the Reformation* (1877).

[9] *E.R.*, cliii. 448, 469 (April 1881).

the union of the Three Kingdoms; and were I the greatest poltroon on the face of the earth I should for one be driven forward by forces such as the motives thus supplied, & must reckon as comparatively dust in the balance any Parliamentary opposition we may meet with. But I do not quite know how to read together two passages in your letter[1] 1. where you speak of what you can submit to (you used to say I think *accept*) as a Peer, as distinct from what you could be responsible for proposing. That is a sound principle. But if 'on the other hand' you must 'speak out in defence' of the opinion on which you have resigned, what meaning remains in the passage I have just quoted? In what material way can you refuse acceptance or submission, *except* by 'speaking out'? In what way accept, except by forbearing to oppose?

As to the Cabinet, it stood thus. Of twelve (besides you and me) six distinctly wished to go further: and the one who in all the later stages most sympathised with you, had at the earlier stage proposed a plan *far* more radical than the Bill. There is but one more of them more 'conservative' than myself [*sic*].

As to the opinion you cite from Kimberley pray remember he said at the very beginning he thought landlordism was doomed in Ireland (which I by no means admit); and if you ask him now whether he thinks the Bill goes too far all circumstances considered I am confident he will reply *No.*

Here we have had snowdrops on the ground together with daisies, buttercups and primroses. I never saw it before: whether because I did not look or not may be uncertain.

To LORD KIMBERLEY, colonial secretary, 14 April 1881.   Add MS 44544, f. 155.

[First Letter]   1. I agree with what you have said to Wood.[2]

2. No doubt there is danger, but could it be otherwise? If the leaders & older men stand true, must we not look to them to control the younger, & is not this all we can expect.

3. As to the 50m. I am aware of no answer to what you justly urge but on a question of this kind I always communicate with the Department & I will cause an answer to be sent to you.

4. Thus far, my letters on the Land Bill are good beyond expectation or hope.

[Second letter]   I will answer the Cyprus Telegrams in your language, with the addition of a few words of kindness.[3]

The *first* one, on which I founded the reference to you was veiled & said nothing of annexation to Greece.

Now that the transfer from the F.O. to you is completed[4] (which I had not before clearly understood) has not the time come for considering whether we should give the island something in the nature of free institutions?[5]

---

[1] Argyll's letter, 13 April, Add MS 44105, f. 62, regrets govt. took up Irish land: 'It was no part of yr. *programme.* It was an accident . . . I have all along felt that as a Member of Parliament I cd *submit* to many proposals which I could not be responsible for proposing. On the Land I must speak out in defence . . . Kimberley declared that, after the Bill passed, he cd not conceive any land lord spending a shilling on Improvements.'

[2] Proposal of 13 April to allow Wood £50,000 for 'carrying on Transvaal Govt.'; Add MS 44226, f. 66.

[3] Draft sent by Kimberley on 13 April in reply to wire on rumour that Britain has offered Cyprus to Greece: Britain holds Cyprus through the Convention as part of the Ottoman Empire and cannot violate its terms; Add MS 44226, f. 72.

[4] Kimberley's letter is docketed: 'Ld G. thought C.O. ought to advice, not F.O.'

[5] Kimberley replied, 16 April, ibid., f. 93, that this was already in hand, but Biddulph would have to be removed first.

The population is I imagine mainly European & Greek? If so hardly one for us, especially for a Liberal Government to rule despotically.

15. *Good Friday*

Ch 10½–11¾. 2–3½: part of Station Service: again 7 P.M. Wrote to Granville 1 & Tel—Ld Kimberley—Ld Spencer—Rev. Mr Knox Little and minutes. Read Skinner's Spiritualism—The Old Church Clock—Life of Bp Wilberforce.

To LORD SPENCER, lord president, 15 April 1881.   Add MS 44544, f. 156.

I thank you for sending me Bessborough's letter.[1] Considering how far we are from moving on the lines he has recommended, I think it does him great honour.

And *thus far* I am greatly pleased, and even agreeably disappointed, with the reception of the Bill; but, taught by experience, I bear in mind that *thus far* does not mean everything.

I doubt if it will have great alterations, and think that except in a few points people will have to like it or lump it. This I say especially in view of the House of Lords, where as I fear, Argyll if he continue in his present mind, will prove a formidable part.

He is a man of loyal and warm affections and of very remarkable powers in several directions, but he has never thoroughly given himself to politics and has *learnt* I think less, since he became a Minister nearly thirty years back, than many men inferior to him would have done.

16. *Easter Eve.*

(It ought to be nearly the most profitable day in Lent) Sat. Ch 8½ a.m. and 8 P.M. Wrote to Abp of Canterbury—Mr Milbank M.P.—Ld Devon—Ld Kimberley L & Tel—Mr Cotes MP.—Mr Kavanaugh[2]—Mr Forster—Ld Granville Tel and minutes. Walk with Mr MacColl. Tea at Mrs Burnett's. Read Ed. Rev. on Schliemann[3]—Old Church Clock (finished)—Life of Bp Wilberforce—Wylie's Carlyle.

17. *Easter Day.*

8–9 H.C.—11.–12½. Morning service: a great crowd, very heartening. Again in evg. at 6.30 crowded. Read the lessons. Wrote to Mayor of Nottm.—Sir H. Ponsonby—Ld Granville—Ld Kimberley—& minutes. Read Life of Wilberforce[4] ... on 2d. Resurrection. Ch Q.R. on Religion in Oxford—too pessimistic.[5] Life of Buckle.[6] Walk with the party

18. *Easter M.*

Ch 8½ A.M. & 7 P.M. Wrote to Ld Hartington—Ld Kimberley—Mrs Morrison—Ld Granville—The Queen 1.2.—Ld Queensberry—Mr Walpole—Rev. Knox

[1] Not found; sent by Spencer on 14 April, Add MS 44308, f. 125.
[2] i.e. A. M. Kavanagh, M.P.; Add MS 44469, f. 75.
[3] *E.R.*, cliii. 514 (April 1881).
[4] From here to start of 20 Apr. 81 in facsimile in Masterman, 256.
[5] 'Recent fortunes of the Church in Oxford'; *Church Quarterly Review*, xii. 201 (April 1881); gloomy review of the effect of the 1871 Tests Act on the clerical presence in Oxford.
[6] A. H. Huth, *The life and writings of H. T. Buckle* (1880); Kimberley, *inter alia*, thanked in preface.

Little, Tel 1.2.—Ld Houghton—Mr Borlase MP—Mr Phipps Eyre—Mr Farsey—
Sir W. Harcourt—Mr Pease MP—The Speaker—Watsons and minutes. W. went
off to political service. I had an interesting & weighty conversation with his wife
about him. Read Bagehot—Bp Wilberforce—Buckle.

To Sir W. V. HARCOURT, home secretary, 18 April   MS Harcourt dep. 8, f. 80.
1881. '*Private*'.

I am extremely concerned at what you report of Rosebery,[1] and, hoping against hope, I
cling to the shadow even of a notion that he may have misled you, or if not that there is a
temporary emotion which will pass away. I assure you with confidence that the notion of
a title to be consulted on the succession to a Cabinet office is absurd. It is a title which
Cabinet ministers do not possess. During 38 years since I first entered the Cabinet, I have
never known more than a friendly announcement before publicity, & very partial consultation perhaps with one or two, especially the leader in the second House.

I believe Rosebery to have a very modest estimate of himself & trust he has not fallen
into so gross an error.

Meantime I am consulting Granville, & have only to thank you very much for making
known the circumstances. Also for Powerscourt's letter;[2] one I am happy to say of many
which please me much.

Let me here do justice to your own wisely & kindly conciliatory spirit when we handled
this most difficult, this most crucial matter in the Cabinet. Could Argyll but have looked
at the matter with a like disposition to abate somewhat of his ideas!

To LORD KIMBERLEY, colonial secretary, 18 April 1881.   Add MS 44544, f. 156.

I was able to answer by Telegraph your very clear & full letter as to the position in the
Transvaal.[3]

Should matters continue as they are, I incline to think we shall have to deprecate for
the time a debate on the motion of Hicks Beach.[4]

Apologetic defence in the H. of Commons, on a motion of this kind is mischievous—
almost ruinous. On the other hand, all that we should have to say would at such a juncture be mischievous. It was quite a different affair when we could hope that our
settlement was really settled. And it may be so again. This of course will keep till we meet.

About Cyprus I need only express satisfaction & thanks.

I never knew till yesterday that you knew Buckle & must have seen a good deal of him.
I shall be curious to get your account of him.

To LORD QUEENSBERRY, 18 April 1881.   Add MS 44544, f. 157.

I had not failed to notice, at the period of the Election, the sacrifice which you have
been called upon to make to your opinions; and I am not called upon to defend what I
suppose to be the rather peculiar state of the law as to Scotch Peers. But I own I had
always regarded the transaction as one taking place within the precinct of the Conservative party, & had not considered that the change of convictions, on which you had

---

[1] Harcourt reported him 'in a very great state of disappointment & irritation' about the privy seal;
had expected to be consulted; 15 April, Add MS 44196, f. 157.

[2] Supporting the Land Bill in the Lords; ibid.

[3] Of 16 April, Add MS 44226, f. 84, on the Potchefstrom affair.

[4] Eventually held on 25 July.

(of course in my view most unhappily) been called to act, constituted a ground for your being now named to the Queen for a British peerage.[1]

We have found it our duty in the H. of Commons to incur some odium in an endeavour to do justice, where the motives at work were in some degree kindred. But there our difficulty thrust itself in our way & was not gratuitously invited.

To S. H. WALPOLE, 18 April 1881.   Bodley Eng. lett. e 30, f. 17.
'*Private.*'

Houghton had, as you probably know, very long and ardently desired to be a Trustee of the Museum.[2]

He had I think many claims: but his relations with Panizzi, and something like a hostile fanaticism possessing him, offered a fatal obstacle.

I find his anxious desire continues. Do you think as I incline to do that it ought to be gratified on a proper occasion?

The probabilities opened in connection with the present vacancy exclude him. But I, who at one time did my duty in the Trust, have for a long time been smitten with barrenness, and must always so continue. The employments of my life, after I escape from office, have been long ago carved out, and the Museum can by no possibility be included among them. It has long been my wish to resign. If you agree with me about Houghton, why should I not resign now, and get leave to propose him?[3]

I could give him a little Sermon on his entry into the Trust which might tend to prevent any small ruffling of relations.

19. *Easter Tu.*

Ch 8½ AM with H.C.: and 7 P.M. Wrote to Prince of Wales—Mr Knox Little—Ly Derby—Bp of Durham—M Gopcevic—Ld Rowton Tel & l and minutes.

At 8 a.m. I was much shocked on opening a Telegram to find it announced the death of Ld Beaconsfield, 3½ hours before. The accounts 24 hours ago were so good. It is a telling, touching event. There is no more extraordinary man surviving him in England, perhaps none in Europe. I must not say much, in presence as it were of his Urn.

I immediately sent to tender a public funeral. The event will entail upon me *one* great difficulty: but God who sends all, sends this also.

Mr Forster and his party came. Conversation of two hours with him. Also walk. Conversation with Mr MacColl. Tea at Miss Scotts. Read Buckle—Wilberforce—Bagehot.

To S. GOPČEVIĆ, 19 April 1881.   Add MS 44544, f. 159.

I respectfully accept, and highly value, the gift of the new work,[4] which you have been so good as to send me.

---

[1] Queensberry's letter untraced; hitherto a Scottish representative peer, he supported Bradlaugh and in 1880 was not re-elected to the Lords 'on account of his agnostic opinions' (*G.E.C.*, x. 706); his letter had, clearly, requested a U.K. Peerage; Rosebery later gave one to his eldest son.

[2] i.e. Beaconsfield's; Houghton had reminded Gladstone of his wish, see T. W. Reid, *Life of Houghton* (1890), ii. 404.

[3] Though a trustee *ex officio*, Gladstone was also an elected trustee, and succeeded in getting Houghton elected, but *vice* Beaconsfield; see 4 May 81.

[4] *Oberalbanien und seine Liga* (1881), sent from Vienna; Add MS 44469, f. 65.

So nearly as I have arrived at the close of my public life, I cannot again expect to be concerned in diplomatic affairs touching upon the fortunes of Montenegro. Yet I cannot regard the tie of sympathy as broken, or dropped to the ground. In 1879 I made provisional arrangements for one of my sons[1] to visit the Principality in 1880. But before the time arrived he had entered the field of politics and was with his elder brother and myself busily engaged as a member of the House of Commons. Perhaps this or some similar plan may be devised. In any case, I have a desire to send to Montenegro some small memorial of the real interest I have felt in its welfare, and I hope that either my own thoughts, or a friendly aid from others, may supply me with some appropriate suggestion.

To LORD ROWTON, 19 April 1881.   Add MS 44544, f. 158.

It was with a sad surprise, after the more favourable accounts of successive days down to yesterday morning, that I learned this day at an early hour the decease of Ld. Beaconsfield, which will be regarded with so much mournful interest throughout the country & beyond its limits.

In conformity with the message I have already sent, I desire at once to inform you & his Executors that, if it should be agreeable to their wishes, I shall be prepared to give the necessary directions for a public funeral.

In tendering this honour on the part of the Government, I feel assured that I am acting in conformity with the general expectation & desire.

[P.S.] Should the proposal be accepted, I beg you at once to convey the intimation to my Private Secretary E. W. Hamilton now in Downing Street.[2]

20. Wed.

Ch 8½ a.m: also attended our neighbour Fairbrother's funeral. At night C.G. gave me some good news hardly hoped. Not quite sure.[3] Wrote to Mr Chamberlain—The Queen 1 & Tel—Mr West Tel—Sir D. Marjoribanks—Mrs Bennett—Mr Wilberforce & minutes. A little woodcraft with my sons. Read Wilberforce (finished)—Bagehot—Buckle, & Pocock's 2nd. Tract, 'The Principles of the Resurrection.'[4]

21. Th.

Ch 8½ a.m. Wrote to Ld Granville 1 & Tel.—Ld F. Cavendish—H.N.G.—Ld Chancellor—Mr Godley—Ld Hartington & minutes. Saw Mr Salisbury jun. on his and his father's matters. Read Buckle—Wylie's Carlyle—Bagehot—M. Seeley's Biographies.[5]

To H. N. GLADSTONE, 21 April 1881.[6]   Hawarden MSS.

I have 25 minutes available before I start by the Great Western to spend my Easter holidays at Hawarden, and I dedicate them to beginning a letter to you. It is sad to me that I am so seldom able either to perform this duty, or to give myself this pleasure.

[1] i.e. Herbert.
[2] Rothschild and Rose declined the offer by wire and letter next day; Add MS 44469, f. 122.
[3] See 23 Apr. 81?
[4] N. Pocock, *The principles of the Reformation shown to be in contradiction to the Book of Common Prayer* (1875).
[5] M. Seeley, *The later evangelical fathers* (1879).
[6] Begun 9 April, finished this day.

First let me say that none of the limitations, or of the absorbing calls, upon my thoughts, in the slightest degree mar the interest or the satisfaction with which I hear of you in the several arrivals of letters from India. We have indeed much to thank God for, in your safely traversing the globe through regions so wide apart & in the manner in which your health has adapted itself to the severe trial of hard work in a climate like that of Calcutta.

I am much pleased at the choice of our cousin your partner[1] to be a Director of the Bank of England. It is a tribute at once to his personal merit, & to the standing and character of his and your house; which, I am well assured, will never suffer in your hands. Glad shall I be if when you marry & are blessed with children, some one of them, long after I am gone, may in his turn be raised up to maintain the commercial traditions of the family, which have now lasted for a century, & which I hope never will be lost.

I hope that 'ere long the name of Gladstone may be introduced into your firm,[2] which has three Gladstones among the partners (if not more): the name having now elsewhere become no better than a cipher.

Now I would if I could turn to the further purpose of my letter & tell you what I have been about and how public matters stand: but my time is up, & the Brougham ready to take me to the rail.

Ap. 21. I resume at Hawarden. And my first words must be upon the sad event which has sounded out throughout England & beyond it this week, the death of Lord Beaconsfield, whose rival some call me, much against my will, for I am not and never was his rival, so far as it depended on my will or intention.

I will not tell you any thing of what you have had from the papers, but will only say first there is something very touching in his determination to be buried by the side of his wife. His devoted and grateful attachment to her was I think the brightest spot in his whole life.

People speculate upon the succession to his place as leader of the Tory party. I think it will be the Duke of Richmond. Cairns is an interloper. Cranbrook has no temper for it. Northcote no backbone. Salisbury might have had it, but he has unhappily clouded his reputation with suspicions (to say the least) as to his truth; which I very deeply regret. No one can say what the effect of his death on the party may be. They may commit imprudences of the moment from which he would have saved them, but *a longue vue* I do *not* think they will suffer.

I have been most widely and sharply severed from him but by something totally different from personal hatred; and I am bound to say I do not think he felt any hatred towards me.

Before the holidays I had severe work in the preparation of the Budget and of the Land Bill. The former effects little but it does something in the way of relief for people who want it and something to strengthen the foundations of our finance. The Irish Land Bill was so difficult that I almost despaired of it. The reception of it has been so favourable as to astonish me. Still the carrying of it will be a most arduous affair. We cannot allow the Lords to tamper with it. If it passes it will have to pass without alteration so far as its general principles are concerned.

We have an election in West Cheshire tomorrow which we are not expected to win: we were beaten by 600 at the General Election. The general position of the Government is certainly not weakened in the country since we came in: and the party is more consolidated in the House of Commons & more hearty than I have almost ever known it. The pressure and arrear of work constitute a tremendous difficulty and there is no early prospect of its mitigation.

---

[1] Samuel Steuart Gladstone of Capenoch, 1837–1909; merchant and banker.
[2] Ogilvy, Gillanders & co.

As for myself, I am ever brooding upon the desire, scarcely yet a hope, of escaping from office, and spending my last days in that retirement & recollection which ought to precede the grave. But I know not when or how God will open the door for me. Last year I used to say it would be this year, and this year I am beginning to say it will be next year. It cannot be too soon for my inclinations but it must be fixed by my duties and we begin to see the questions which stood for discussion when we came in one by one disappearing. The evacuation of Afghanistan is nearly complete. The relations with the Transvaal are under a momentary cloud owing to the bad conduct of a handful of Boers at Potchefstroom: but we have made in substance the best settlement the case admits of. The Montenegrin frontier is settled. The Greek frontier question has undoubtedly made a greater progress than I could have expected considering the halfheartedness of several of the Powers. In domestic policy we have not been able to grapple with the greater questions which appeared to confront us but a good deal of work has been done both this year and last. It is certainly a strong working Government in almost every department.

We were all delighted with Herbert's *debût* as a speaker and I hope soon to have him regularly installed at the Treasury. All here are well. We have much enjoyed a happy and domestic Easter recess under Stephy's hospitable roof. Indeed it is a lively pleasure, were there no other, to witness the admirable way in which he bears the arduous charge of this parish. So is it, dearest Harry, to hear regularly and well of you, under your now very considerable responsibilities, which I feel confident you will bear with honour and advantage. God be with you day & night & in all you think say & do. Your afft. Father WE Gladstone

To LORD HARTINGTON, Indian secretary, 21 April 1881.   Add MS 44544, f. 159.

1. I send you a communication from the Speaker about Bradlaugh. I agree generally in his view.

It will be difficult in my case, I think, for the objectors to Bradlaugh so to manage the case as to exclude Pease's motion.

2. What I *understood* R. Grosvenor to say was not that we should have a bad division, i.e. a small majority, but that we should probably be beaten. This would be a moral as well as a Parliamentary calamity. I do not gather clearly what you propose to do. But if we are to have a fight I should wish two things. (1) to be supplied with information for arguing the question whether the disconnection of the Government from the growth would practically do good or harm. I agree with you in your (apparent) opinion that we should not be guided mainly by regard to the theoretical question of complicity. (2) to have likewise the information which may shew that we do not by what I may call treaty compulsion prevent the Chinese from increasing their duties if they are so inclined.[1]

If the proof of this is rather doubtful, shall we not have to accede to the general proposition that we ought not to exercise such a compulsion.

3. I have had some correspondence with Argyll which does not tend to show rose coloured prospects for the Land Bill in the Lords.

22. Fr.

Ch 8½ a.m. Wrote to Mr Godley 1.2.3.—Ld Granville Tel 1.2.—Sir H. Ponsonby—Mr Walpole—Sir S.H. Northcote—Rev. Mr Melvill—Mr Forster—Duke of Argyll & minutes. Tea with Edith D[umaresq] in the Church House. Read Buckle—Bagehot—L. Bloomfield in Ireland.[2] Walk and full talk with Herbert: he was most satisfactory.

---

[1] Growth of opium trade; see *H* 260. 1451.   [2] Not found.

To the DUKE OF ARGYLL, 22 April 1881. Add MS 44544, f. 161.

I am not eager to prolong correspondence on our present subject:[1] but you did not say to the Cabinet 'you should submit to the inevitable' (and even if you had said this it would by fair moral implication somewhat, perhaps, abridge your liberty) but that you could accept what you could not propose. I think if you reflect on the meaning and force of words like these, and by a colleague to colleagues in the very act of opening his differences, you will see that they constitute rather a grave fact. Such as they are, I commend them to your reflections; and I will not again return to the subject. On one, however, of the points raised by your letter I must say a word. The Duke of Wellington's argument, which you appear to assign to me, I altogether (to use the northern phrase) repel.[2] I have never used it in writing to you, or in Cabinet, or in Parliament, or in my own mind. On the contrary, in my speech I put it aside. But I do not put it aside as a reason *de plus* for firmly standing by the Bill in its essence and virtue, where I think it is in place.

Our purely official severance I lament less than I should have done at a former time, because only a short time can elapse before my following you.

This sad event in London dwells much upon my mind. The persistancy of his conjugal affection is very touching. There above all things he was human. Taking the thing as a whole it is very mournful. Should it prove to be my duty to propose a public monument for him, what an irony of fortune! But if it prove to be duty it must be done: and yet must be done truthfully.

I am sorry to hear of the loss of your silver firs. I think 135 feet is the greatest height I ever heard of in this country.

Have you any 'scientific' Trustee to suggest for the Museum? I think the P. of Wales (private this) will probably fill B's vacancy.

To W. E. FORSTER, Irish secretary, 22 April 1881. Add MS 44544, f. 160.

I return Young's interesting letter.[3] I should be most glad to have the reference to show that I was wrong about the Commission on the 'optional' character of the tribunal. Certainly I believe myself only too right, & I am not yet undeceived. If again I was wrong about the 'fair rent' where my memory may have deceived me, it will be easy to find an opening for doing justice.

On the 'fair rent' clause, I think we must sift Cullinan's objection[4] to the bottom, and clearly it ought to be met. The argument of the Times[5] was I think grossly wrong. It is the very point of the case of Ireland that 'the solvent tenant' test alone would produce a rent eating up the tenant right and far in excess of what it would produce in England. In my opinion the main substantive elements of legitimate tenant-right in *Ireland* are in the main 1. the improvements, in which he is to be presumed generally to have an interest. 2. The good will & price of livelihood, an element known, though but slightly known, here, but in Ireland swollen into a powerful factor through abnormal circumstances. Neither of these items of value ought to pass into the rent and I conceive it to be the simple object of our words (which of course may be amendable) to keep them out.

I expect to be in the House about five, if not *sooner*. There can hardly be anything said *there* of Beaconsfield, I think: but I anticipate as probable a more regular opportunity.

---

[1] Argyll's long letter of 20 April in Argyll, ii. 372.
[2] 'Wellington, in recommending Catholic Emancipation, once said, "I'm afraid of Ireland". This seems to me the only argument in favour of *parts* of the Bill'; ibid.
[3] Sent on 21 April and returned; Add MS 44158, f. 145.
[4] William Fitzpatrick Cullinan, parliamentary draftsman in the Irish Office.
[5] See Forster's second letter of 21 April on leaders in *T.T.* on fair rent; ibid., f. 148.

I inclose a letter from Argyll for your perusal. It portends a storm, and he is the petrel. I have done all I could with him: but his keenness about land is something fearful, and the raven croaking from Howick will help the brother bird. We only regretted the shortness of your visit which I hope will be renewed.

To Sir S. H. NORTHCOTE, M.P., 22 April 1881.   Add MS 50014, f. 236.

The first inclination of my mind is rather unfavourable to the idea of adjournment over Tuesday.[1] As the step would be unusual, motives would probably be suggested in connection with the nature of the business of the day. Had the funeral been on Wednesday, the matter would have been simpler. I will, however, think carefully over the whole subject: and in the meantime I have no doubt that in any case arrangements can be made to provide that any objections to be made to Mr. Bradlaugh's taking the Oath should not be shut out by the attendance of a large or important body of members at Lord Beaconsfield's funeral.

The whole circumstances of his death are extremely touching: and perhaps most of all this that the devoted affection to his wife should be as it were the last gleam of light over his sepulchre.

23. Sat.

Ch 8½ a.m. Heavy post. Dispatch certainly over 100. Wrote to Ld Kimberley Tel.—The Speaker Tel—Mr Godley T. 1.2.—Mr Forster Tel.—Ld Granville Tel.—Ld Tenterden Tel—Mr Tomkinson—Ld R. Grosvenor Tel. and minutes. Walk with Willy: a full and satisfactory talk as to his future career and as to the arrangements for Herbert. Read Buckle—Bagehot (finished).

24. Low S.

Ch 8 a.m. H.C.—11 a.m.–3 P.M. (past)—6½ P.M. Wrote to Ld Granville l & Tel— Queen Tel—Sir S. Northcote—Ld Chancellor—Sir N. Rothschild—Mr Godley— G.W.R. Manager and minutes. The delightful visit to this dear son ends tomorrow! Read Buckle's life (finished), a saddening book—Robertson on O.T.[2]—Illingworth's Sermons.[3]

To Sir N. M. de ROTHSCHILD, M.P., 24 April 1881.   Add MS 44544, f. 162.

I thank you for the invitation to the funeral[4] on Tuesday, and for your very considerate words to Godley in relation to it.

You were right in anticipating that my engagements, which are very heavy, will preclude my attending. I will not trouble you with any more formal answer.

It would please me much to be allowed on some *future* day, if it is not asking too much, to visit the spot in a private manner.

We think of proposing tomorrow that the House shall meet at eight on Tuesday, which I hope will meet the convenience of all who go to Hughenden.

[1] Northcote proposed no public funeral, but an adjournment to enable M.P.s to go to Hughenden; Add MS 44217, f. 179.
[2] W. Robertson *Smith, *The Old Testament in the Jewish church* (1881); his higher criticism lost him his chair this year.
[3] See 13 Mar. 81.
[4] Printed invitation card (number 37) received on 21 April, at Add MS 44469, f. 175.

Notice will also be given on my behalf, at half past four, of a motion tomorrow fort-night for a monument to Lord Beaconsfield.

Do not think for a moment about the publication of the correspondence earlier than as you had announced. I perfectly understand how in the confusion and pressure of such a time the order of business may occasionally be a little disturbed.

25. M. St Mark [London]

Ch. 8½ a.m. Wrote to Mr Godley 1 & Tel—Mr Weld Blundell—Mrs Bagehot & minutes. Worked on my Testamentary paper & left it ready.[1] 11¾–5¾. To London by G.W.R. Saw Mr Forster—Ld Hartington—Mr Knox Little—Mr G.—Ld R.G. Read Boers, Blacks & British.[2]

To Mrs BAGEHOT, 25 April 1881.   Add MS 44544, f. 162.

Having now perused the volume[3] which you have been so very kind as to send me, I am in a condition to return to you less unworthy thanks than those which are conveyed upon receipt of such a gift.

Some of the articles are not new to me. I remember, & I still feel, how true the article on myself is in the parts least favourable to my vanity; & also with respect to the article on Sir Geo. Lewis, written without much personal acquaintance, how superior a production it is to the Essay by Sir E. Head,[4] a very able man, who enjoyed in the execution of his task all the advantages of a life long friendship.

Undoubtedly your lamented husband was a man of most remarkable gifts, & among them comes a singular discernment as to public characters, & a not less excellent faculty for embodying the results in literary form.

I think that as to Ld. Althorp his materials were too slender, & that he has not quite done justice to that admirable man.

26. Tu.

Wrote to The Queen L. & Tel—Ld Granville—The Speaker—Rev. Mr Barker (Tel) and minutes. Dined with Dr Acland—& the Medical Council. Put up to speak in mid-dinner![5] Saw Mr Ouvry—Dr Acland—Sir A. Paget. Conclave on the Bradlaugh case. Deputation of silver-smiths. Deputation of silver-smiths' work-men.[6] Mr G.—Ld R.G.—Mr West. After a hard day, H. of C. 9–2½. A bad night: bad acrid intolerant feeling, & unseemly squabbles. Beaten by 33.[7] Quite upset in the night for once.

[1] Various additions dated this day, printed with the main memorandum at 1 Jan. 79.
[2] F. R. Statham, *Blacks, Boers and British, a three-cornered problem* (1881); Francis Reginald Statham, journalist, formerly in Natal, sent a long letter on 8 April suggesting a Commission sent from Britain; Add MS 44469, f. 47.   [3] See 13 Apr. 81.
[4] [E. Head] in *E.R.*, cxviii. 138 (July 1863); this remark confirms the attribution of the *Wellesley Index*, i. 512.   [5] No report found.
[6] As a result of these dpns. Gladstone next day announced that the budget's proposals on the silver duties would be dropped; *H* 260. 1269; *T.T.*, 28 April 1881, 4b.
[7] On Northcote's motion that Bradlaugh be not permitted to take the oath; Gladstone declined to move that Bradlaugh should withdraw; *H* 260. 1241. The Liberals had no whip for the division; Arnstein, 110.

27. Wed.

Wrote to The Queen—Dean of St Pauls—Mr Saunders—& minutes. Saw Sir C. Dilke—Sir R. Wilson—Mr G.—Ld R.G. Ld Carlingford cum Mr Forster (Fair Rents &c)—Messrs Garrard—Mr Morley—Ld Reay—The Speaker. H. of C. $12\frac{1}{4}$-5. Spoke on the Bradlaugh case.[1] Dined at Ld Reays. Saw Graham, & H. who renounces [R]. Read Blacks, Boers, & British.

28. Th.

Wrote to Ld Caithness—Ld Granville 1.2.—D. of Argyll—Mr O'Donnell MP & minutes. Read Blacks Boers &c. Nine to breakfast $10-11\frac{1}{2}$. Saw Ld G.—Lord R.G.—Dr Allon—Mr R. Noel—Sir R. Phillimore—Mr Forster—Mr Lecky. Visited Mr Saunders. H. of C. $4\frac{1}{2}$-$8\frac{1}{4}$ & $9\frac{1}{2}$-$12\frac{3}{4}$. Debate all with us.[2]

To the DUKE OF ARGYLL, 28 April 1881.   Add MS 44544, f. 163.

The temptation to enter again on the subject is effectually counteracted by the demands upon my time.[3]

I *must* however say that your report of what I said on an occasion in a Cabinet [*sic*]. I said there might be forms of the Bill which I could support as P.M. but would decline actually proposing which implies the very highest & closest identification: but I never said, and never thought, that the three F's were one of them. To these I am now opposed, as in 1870, and as in last Decr. since which time I have made one serious change and one only, under the recommendation (as I conceive it) of the Richmond Commission: a change which you also seem in principle to adopt.

29. Fr.

Wrote to R.C.—Abp of Canterbury—Abp of Armagh—Sir J. Hogg—The Queen 1.2.—Mr Grantham—Ld Granville—Ld Rosebery—Mr O'Donnell & minutes. Read Q. Review. Cabinet 3-$4\frac{1}{4}$ (Dillon &c). Saw Mr G.—Ld R.G.—Sir C. Dilke. Visited Royal Academy. H. of C. $4\frac{3}{4}$-$8\frac{1}{4}$ (Spoke on motion of Mr Richard) and $9\frac{3}{4}$-$12\frac{3}{4}$.[4]

Cabinet Friday Ap. 29. 81. 3 PM[5]
　　1. Mr Dillon.[6] See over [i.e. item 6]
　　2. ⟨Irish Bishops⟩
　　3. Transvaal.[7]

---

[1] Agreeing now to proceed by a bill on certain procedural conditions; *H* 260. 1268.
[2] Questions; Land Bill 2°R; *H* 260. 1322.
[3] Further letters from Argyll, 25, 26 April, Add MS 44105, ff. 76, 80.
[4] Resolution to limit powers of British representatives abroad; *H* 260. 1434.
[5] Add MS 44642, f. 176.
[6] Arrested at Portarlington on 2 May and released on grounds of ill-health in August (see 6 Aug. 81), again arrested in October. John *Dillon, 1851-1927; home rule M.P. Tipperary 1879-83, E. Mayo 1885-1918; unsuccessfully prosecuted 1880-1 (see above ix. lxxvii); frequently imprisoned.
[7] Kimberley reported that the Commission had begun its work; Schreuder, 191. See also Kimberley's mem. of this day on 'suzerainty', with lexicographical note by James *Murray (see 1 Oct. 81); Add MS 44627, f. 1.

✓ 4. Oaths.[1] Mode of procedure. A[ttorney] G[eneral]'s proposal agreed to. Bill to apply to the H. of Lords.

✓ 5. Knaresborough writ.[2] agreed to move the writ.

✓ 6. *For arrest*: Hartington; Forster; Harcourt; Kimberley; Chancellor; WEG. *Against*: Dodson; Bright; Chamberlain; + Carlingford; Northbrook; Childers. It was referred to me and I said *aye.*

To D. MacGETTIGAN, Archbishop of Armagh, 29 April 1881. Add MS 44544, f. 165.[3]

I have to acknowledge the receipt of your letter,[4] which incloses the resolutions of the Roman Catholic Bishops of Ireland on the Land Bill now under discussion in the House of Commons.

I need not say that, together with my colleagues, I am sensible of the weight attaching to any representation on a great Irish question from a body so intimately associated with the history, the feelings, and the interests of the people. I am thankful for the acknowledgment given in this document of the intention with which it admits the measure to have been framed: and I can say without fear that, if it be recognised, as it appears to be, by the representatives and the people of Ireland as a valuable Bill, there shall be no reason to complain of any slackness or indecision, on the part of the Government, in putting it forward until it becomes law.

At the same time I must frankly add, after reviewing the list of the numerous and important changes advised by the Bishops, that Her Majesty's Government while they will welcome any amendment from whatever quarter that may tend to improve the Bill, cannot hold out the expectation of their acceding to any changes which would give it a new character.

To LORD ROSEBERY, 29 April 1881. '*Private.*'   N.L.S. 10022, f. 70.

Will you have the kindness to look at a question put to me last night by Mr Barclay, and at my answer,[5] in the morning's paper.

It relates to a subject of very great importance, in its first aspect Scotch, but leading on into a field which embraces the three kingdoms.

If we could contrive to meet at a snatch-dinner here when you come up, I could explain to you my meaning about County Government in Scotland.

But the practical upshot for the moment is this. Although the *squeeze* & *cram* of business is worse this year than ever, yet when the Scotch members agree upon a measure for Scotland, they can carry it without much interference from the rest of the House or taking up much of the time of the House.

And if a measure of County Govt. is needed for Scotland & the Scotch members could agree upon it, this would be an excellent stroke of work first for Scotland but also for the country.

I think you will see that the subject is not a slight one.

The Irish Land Bill looms larger & larger. In the Amendment of [Lord] J. Manners, I see the first effect of the death of Beaconsfield, and it certainly is a very bad effect. Not at all

---

[1] Parliamentary Oaths Bill introduced by James on 2 May; *H* 260. 1618.

[2] Seat vacant after petition; the Liberals lost the subsequent by-election.

[3] Published in *T.T.*, 2 May 1881, 12c.

[4] Add MS 44469, f. 185; Daniel MacGettigan, d. 1887; archbishop of Armagh (R.C.) from 1870.

[5] Questioned by J. W. Barclay on a county board for Scotland; Gladstone answered that if the Scottish M.P.s wanted one, he would try to find Parliamentary time. Rosebery suggested, 30 April, Add MS 44288, that the Lord Advocate call a conference.

so for us in a party sense but for the country. There is no crisis, short of a revolution, into which this question may not lead us.

Argyll's resignation has I do not doubt helped to lead them astray.

30. Sat.

Wrote to Mr Darwin—The Queen and minutes. Saw Mr G.—Ld R.G.—Ld F.C.—Ld Chancellor—Ld Kimberley—Ld Dufferin. Grosvenor Exhibition $12\frac{1}{4}$–$1\frac{1}{4}$.—R. Academy do 3.–$5\frac{1}{4}$. R. Acad. dinner $6\frac{1}{2}$–$10\frac{1}{2}$. Made my speech: this year especially difficult.[1] Read Quarterly Review.

To C. R. DARWIN, 30 April 1881.   Add MS 44544, f. 165.

I take the liberty of informing you that there is a vacancy created in the Trust of the British Museum by the death of Lord Beaconsfield: and to say that I shall be very happy, if it be agreeable to your views, to suggest your name for the purpose of filling that vacancy.

The electing Trustees will meet next week: and if you permit me to place your name before them I do not doubt that they will consider it an advantageous opportunity for doing honour not more to you than to the Museum.[2]

2. S.E. SS. Phil. & J. May One.

Chapel Royal noon with H.C. and afternoon. Saw Ld Sydney—Ld Spencer—Mr Walpole—Edw. Lyttelton—Lady Sydney. Read Robertson on O.T.—Q.R. on Speakers New Test[ament]—do on Ch. Engl. Endowments[3]—Ch. Q.R. on Apocr. Gospels and Notices.[4]

2. M.

Wrote to Duke of Argyll—Ld Rosebery—Dr Quain[5]—Sir F. Leighton—Dean of Ch.Ch.—Princ. Librarian B. Museum—The Queen 1.2. & minutes. H. of C. $4\frac{1}{2}$–$8\frac{1}{4}$ and $9\frac{1}{2}$–1. More signs of wish to throw on us the dirt of Atheism.[6] Saw Ld Granville—Mr G.—Ld R.G.—Ld F.C. Read Quarterly Review.

To E. A. BOND, Librarian of the British Museum, 2 May 1881.   Add MS 44544, f. 165.

I beg to convey through you to the Trustees of the British Museum my resignation of office as a personal Trustee of that institution.

My motive is that seeing no likelihood of my being able, even when out of office, to resume the performance of active duty, not long intermitted, I desire to make way for some new Trustee who may give better service.

[1] The speakers preceding Gladstone all referred to Millais's portrait of Beaconsfield, exhibited in the ante-room; Gladstone briefly discussed this and Millais's portrait of himself, remarking of the former: 'It is, indeed, an unfinished work. In this sense it was a premature death (Cheers). "Abstulit atra dies, ac funere mersit acerbo"'; *T.T.*, 2 May 1881, 13c.

[2] Letter from Darwin, declining, on 2 May: unable regularly to attend meetings from want of strength; Add MS 44469, f. 218. See to Liddell, 2 May 81.

[3] *Q.R.*, cli. 352, 502 (April 1881).   [4] *Church Quarterly Review*, xii. 84 (April 1881).

[5] Richard Quain, M.D., 1800–87; London surgeon.

[6] Gladstone's resolution to make time for the Oaths Bill opposed by Lord R. Churchill; *H* 260. 1556.

I hope there is no reason why the electing Trustees may not at their approaching meeting fill up this together with the other two vacancies.

To H. G. LIDDELL, dean of Christ Church, 2 May 1881.   Add MS 44544, f. 166.

I wish to be allowed to propose your name, at a meeting to be held on Friday next, as a Trustee of the British Museum.[1] Personal regard would not & ought not to have led me to make this proposal except with the conviction that your qualifications for the office were alike eminent and diversified.

The duties however of Trustee, as such, would make but rare calls upon you, on the occasion of the General Meetings. The ordinary government of the Museum is in the hands of a select body of Trustees termed the Standing Committee. You do not succeed a working Trustee, and if you are asked to join the Committee, you will be quite free to say Aye or No.

Pray therefore give me the permission which I seek.

3. *Tu.*

Confined to bed with diarrhoea. But rose at $9\frac{1}{2}$ p.m. Saw Mr G.—Ld R.G.—Dr Quain—Lady M. Alford—Mr Doyle—Herbert J.G. Read Quarterly Review (finishing nearly all the No)—Tylor's Anthropology[2]—Statham's S. Africa (finished).

4. *Wed.*

Wrote to Abp of Canterbury—Ld Houghton—The Queen 1.2. and minutes. Dined at Ld Airlies: evg party. Walk. Saw two [R]. Cabinet 12–2. House $2\frac{1}{4}$–$3\frac{1}{2}$.[3] Saw Mr G.—Ld R.G.—Duchess of St A.—Sir W. Harcourt—Mr Bright. Read Rogers on Laud:[4] thin. Tea with Lady Derby: & long private conversation.

Cabinet. Wed. May 4. 1881. Noon.[5]
1. Sunday Closing. Support from Harcourt, perhaps me. Not a Cabinet question.[6]
2. Conference on Nihilism having been declined, the question arose whether we should modify our law.[7]

To LORD HOUGHTON, 4 May 1881.   Add MS 44544, f. 166.

I am very glad to have been *at length* enabled to effect an arrangement, under which (with the approval of the Principal Trustees) I am in a condition to propose you on Friday to the Electing Trustees as a Trustee of the Museum.

I hope it will be agreeable to you that I should take this step.[8]

5. *Th.*

Wrote to Abp of Canterbury—Earl Granville—The Queen & minutes. Framed the difficult motion for the Beaconsfield Monument on Monday. Saw Mr G.—

---

[1] Liddell accepted and was elected *vice* Gladstone.
[2] E. B. Tylor, *Anthropology* (1881).
[3] Spoke on Welsh Sunday drinking; *H* 260. 1770.   [4] J. E. T. Rogers, *Historical gleanings* (1881).
[5] Add MS 44642, f. 178.   [6] See this day's deb.
[7] Britain declined to take part in a conference on nihilism; Ramm II, i. 256ff.
[8] In *Life... of Lord Houghton* (1890), ii. 405; see 18 Apr. 81; Houghton was elected *vice* Beaconsfield.

Ld R.G.—Mr H.—Servian Minister (+)—Sir C. Pressly—Dean Church—Mr Oxenham—Mr E. Talbot—Dr Clark: not too soon. Ten to breakfast. H. of C. 4½–8½: and 12–1.[1] This latter visit thoroughly upset me again after my three days struggle. The Opposition are not unkind to me personally, as they might fairly enough have been: but very factious I think towards the Govt as such. Read Dun on Irish Land[2]—Cooper's Autobiogr.[3]

6. Fr.

Bed all day. In the evg. I began to get quiet. Clark came twice. He is quite perfect in the thoroughness of his work. Saw Mr G.—Ld R.G.—Ld Granville—Ld Rosebery. Read Cooper's Autobiography (It is in books of this order that we find what is truly noble. I place him morally far above Carlyle.) Dun on Irish Land—Rogers on Wiclif.

7. Sat. [The Durdans, Epsom]

Wrote to Ld Lyttelton—Ld Granville—Sir R. Cross—Bp of Winchester and minutes. Saw Clark (also Mr G.—Mr H. & Lord Granville:) Off to the Durdans at 11.15. The country was heavenly. Much conversation with Rosebery. Read Virgil Æn.VI.VII.[4] —T. Cooper Autobiography—Daumas, Horses of the Sahara.[5]

8.

Only allowed afternoon service: at the (gimcrack) Old Church—Read 'Salem Chapel'[6]—Cooper Autobiography finished. Robertson on Old Testament—'Physician' on the Pentateuch.[7] Wrote to Bp of Manchester. Saw Ld Granville—Ld Rosebery.

9. M. [London]

Wrote to Major Baring—The Queen—and minutes. Read Edgar Quinet[8]—Salem Chapel. Saw Ld Granville—Mr G.—Ld R.G. Back to town D. St 1½. Meditated over my very difficult task a little before the House: & I commit myself to God, who has ever helped me. H. of C. 4¾–8¼: and 10½–1¾.[9] As to the Monument all went better than I could have hoped, & the discussion was kept within about an hour. Northcote was more than handsome in acknowledgment: as he would always be when free.

[1] Wrangles at the end of the evening about the ending of the Land Bill 2°R; *H* 260. 1912.
[2] See 4 Dec. 80n.
[3] *The life of Thomas Cooper, written by himself* (1872), quoted in his speech on 9 May on the Beaconsfield monument.
[4] 'Aspice, ut insignis spoliis Marcellus optimis ingreditur, victorque viros supereminet omnes'; quoted in his speech on Beaconsfield after consultation with Granville; Ramm II, i. 273.
[5] M. J. E. Daumas, *The horses of the Sahara* (1863).
[6] By Mrs. Oliphant, 2v. (1863).
[7] [R. Willis], *The Pentateuch . . . by a Physician* (1875).
[8] R. Heath, *Edgar Quinet* (1881).
[9] The motion passed without a division after Labouchere's amndt. was defeated in 54:380; in addition to commenting on his personal qualities, Gladstone emphasised the constitutional right of Beaconsfield to act as he did; *H* 261. 38.

10. Tu.

Wrote to Pr. of Wales—Mr Forster—Mr Williamson—The Queen & minutes.
Sculptor came mg. Then two sittings in aft. to Mr Böhm and Mr Joy at their
studios.[1] Saw Mr G—Ld R.G.—Mr West—Lady Sherbrook—Ld Granville—Mr
Knowles—Ld Sherbrook. Read Modern Review[2]—Coopers Poems.[3]

11. Wed.

Wrote to Ld Carnarvon—Lady Cowell Stepney—Sir W. Harcourt—Ld R. Gros-
venor & minutes. Read Modern Review. Read also The Irish Problem[4]—OBrien
Irish Land Question.[5] Saw Mr G—Mr H—Ld RG—Ld Granville—Bp of Ely—Mr
& Mrs Th—Ld F.C.—Mlle d'Houne.[6] Dined at Bp of Ely's.

12. Th.

Wrote to The Queen—Sir H. Ponsonby & minutes. H. of C. $4\frac{3}{4}$–$8\frac{1}{2}$ & $9\frac{3}{4}$–$12\frac{1}{4}$.[7]
Visited Christies. Eleven to breakfast. Saw Mr Herbert Spencer—Mr R. Brown—
Mr Knowles—Dr Fairbairn—Mr Myers—Mr Gurdon—Mr G.—Ld R.G. Read
Tracts on Ireland—Modern Review on Elam.[8]

To Sir H. PONSONBY, the Queen's secretary, 12 May 1881.   Add MS 44544, f. 168.

I had not noticed the omissions from the Division list, which you have been instructed
to name:[9] not indeed having referred to the list at all.

As regards members of the Government not in the Cabinet, I think a single case of
absence, in circumstances where individual votes were unimportant, would not according
to usual practice be taken account of. In *strictness*, however, leave ought to be asked.

Undoubtedly members of the Cabinet are bound to vote in every case—apart from
accidental absences.

I think it likely that the two ministers you name may have deemed themselves too
sharply committed, by declarations touching Lord Beaconsfield as contradistinguished
from his policy, to make it suitable for them to vote.

There is no doubt that the case was a peculiar one without any precedent covering the
whole breadth of it.

It was also one in which circumstances made it proper for me to arrive at a decision
without waiting for the re-assembling of my Colleagues: and the rule I have stated as to
the obligations of Cabinet Ministers has for its correlation the supposition that they have
been parties to the discussion of the subject in the Cabinet.

---

[1] Plaster model of Boehm's bust is in Victoria and Albert museum; marble untraced, exhibited at
Royal Academy 1881. Henry G. Joy, British sculptor.
[2] *Modern Review*, ii. 1 (April 1881).
[3] By Thomas Cooper, the chartist (1877).
[4] *The Irish problem and how to solve it* (1881).
[5] R. B. O'Brien, *The Irish land question* (1881).
[6] Unidentified.
[7] Spoke on progress of the Land Bill; *H* 261. 286.
[8] *Modern Review*, ii. 368 (April 1881).
[9] Bright, Chamberlain and Dilke; Guedalla, *Q*, ii. 156.

13. Fr.

Wrote to Mr West—Mr Ridgway—The Queen 1.2. and minutes. H. of C. $4\frac{3}{4}$–$8\frac{1}{2}$ and 10–$11\frac{1}{4}$.[1] Saw Mr G.—Ld R.G.—Ld Granville—Ld Northbrook. Read Cooper's Poems. Cabinet 2–$4\frac{1}{4}$.

Cabinet Friday May 13. 81. 2 PM.[2]
1. Bradlaugh   } We can do nothing till the
   Sir Wilfred Lawson } Land Bill is virtually disposed of
2. Answer about Tunis[3]—Terms discussed. As to notice about not fortifying Biserta, *prendre acte.*[4]
3. Land Bill. Mode of procedure in Committee. Propose morning sittings.
4. Treaty of Commerce with France.[5] Negotiations to be at Paris. Persons considered: without conclusion.
5. Famagosta. Spend nothing.

14. Sat. [*Windsor*]

Wrote to Ld Rosebery—Mr Yates Thompson—Ld Advocate—Sir F. Doyle—Ld Granville—& minutes. Royal Acad. & Exhibitions. Saw Mr G. (& spoke on his prospects)—H.J.G.—Ld F. Cavendish—Ld Rosebery[6]—Pres. Wesl. Conference[7]—Dr Moulton. Read Doyle on the Horse[8]—and Eternal Purpose.[9] Dined (it was semi-public) with Mr Waddy at the Devonshire. At 10 PM. after my speech off to Windsor.

15. 4 S.E.

St Georges 11 Palace Chapel 12. St Geo. 5 P.M. Wrote to Ld Granville 1.2.—Mr Forster 1 & Tel.—Mr Kimberley. Queen gave me long & kind audience. Saw Dean of Windsor—Sir H. Ponsonby. Read Eternal Purpose—Consols in Job[10]—Robn Smith O.T.[11]—Miss [blank] Science & Belief.[12]

To W. E. FORSTER, Irish secretary, 15 May 1881.   Add MS 44544, f. 169.

You will either have heard from Hartington or have gathered from my telegram that notice had been taken here of the account in the Standard about the pelting affair, and a credence given to it which was premature. Mr Jephson sent me a very prompt answer which enabled me speedily to disabuse Her Majesty.

[1] Spoke on Bradlaugh; *H* 261. 423.
[2] Add MS 44642, f. 179.
[3] French treaty signed with Tunis, effectively giving France control, 12 May 1881.
[4] Holograph note reads: 'I am of opinion that Salisbury's proceedings have entirely cut away the ground (Italy being out of the case) from under our feet. How can they be kept secret if debate arise?'; a row ensued over the publication of papers on Salisbury's supposed offer of Tunis to France in 1878; Ramm II, i. 247n, A. Marsden, *British diplomacy and Tunis 1875-1902* (1971), 59–75.
[5] Details in *PP* 1881 xcii; see 20 Aug. 81.
[6] Rosebery again (see 10 July 80) turned down the Under-Secretaryship at the India Office; *Rosebery*, 121.
[7] Ecumenical methodist conference shortly convened in London.
[8] In *F.R.*, xxxv. 572 (May 1881).   [9] [W. R. Hart], *Eternal purpose* (1881).
[10] Perhaps S. Cox, *A commentary on the book of Job* (1880).
[11] See 24 Apr. 81.   [12] Untraced.

Taken at best, however, the business looks an unpleasant one; and it may form an inconvenient example.

Perhaps you may soon receive accounts which may give one a fuller and clearer view.[1]

I do not know whether you are now in full possession of the history of those three days, during which the arrest of Dillon was delayed. It is a matter certainly worth sifting to the bottom. Neither you nor any man can sit in London for your extensive and worrying Parliamentary business, and at the same time work efficiently those executive duties in Ireland which at the present moment are of such peculiar difficulty: and if your administrative organization there is weak at any point you must not let your kindliness of disposition prevent you from entering fully upon the question.

I am disposed to speak tomorrow. The Solicitor General I suppose will not take above one hour: otherwise we should be accused of too great encroachment if both speak. R.G. agrees with me that I had better not delay longer.

To LORD KIMBERLEY, colonial secretary, 15 May 1881.   Add MS 44544, f. 169.

Upon the whole I gathered from your note today[2] that you meant me to send in the Telegrams to & from Wood to the Queen, and to judge whether to delay your reply to him. I did not think delay necessary, the Queen having gone out, and I sent them in with the mem. enclosed:

The accompanying Telegrams from the Cape reached Mr. G. after he had quitted Y.M.'s presence. The liberty of detail accorded by Lord K. did not appear to require any delay in the instruction.

16. M. [London]

Upset in the night. But went to London at 10.30. Saw Clark, & determined on speaking at 5 this evg. as a choice of difficulties. This I did for $1\frac{1}{2}$ hour, with some effort; and after awkward preliminary business.[3] Wrote to the Queen. Saw Mr G.—Ld R.G.—Mr Childers. Read Robertson Smith—Life of Edgar Quinet. H. of C. $4\frac{3}{4}$–$8\frac{1}{2}$. Went home to bed—relieved of a weight.

17. Tu.

Wrote to The Queen—Ld Kimberley—Mr Forster—Ld Hartington—Ld Rosebery—Bp of Gloucester—Sir W. Harcourt & minutes. Saw Mr G.—Ld R.G.—Ld Granville—Rev. S.E.G.—Mr Clark mg & evg.—Mr F.L. Gower—Mr Prescott Hewett. Read Robertson Smith—Life of Quinet—Duc d'Aumale's Discours.[4] Better, not well. The fund of vital force is large for my time of life: but not large enough for the very heavy calls upon it. So Nature murmurs and resents from time to time.

---

[1] Forster replied, 16 May, Add MS 44158, f. 154: 'I am glad Jephson's telegram relieved H.M. . . . orders have been sent to the Police to try to identify the stone-throwers, but clearly the newspaper report was a sensational exaggeration. I return O'Shea's letter. I do not think you can do more in reply *to him* than tell him his letter will be considered, but there is no doubt that the state of matters is very anxious. . . . What we want is to stop the unreasonable evictions while making the fraudulent men pay . . . viz. stop all evictions whether by Superior or other courts for arrears done before last November.'

[2] Not found.

[3] Regaining initiative on the Land Bill 2°R, after questions on Tunis and Transvaal; *H* 261. 585.

[4] H. E. P. L. d'Orléans, duc d'Aumale, 'Séance de l'Académie Française du 7 Avril 1881' (1881).

To W. E. FORSTER, Irish secretary, 17 May 1881.   Add MS 44544, f. 170.

I will answer O'Shea as you propose.[1] The question of the arrears will have to be considered I think by the Cabinet, & I advise your getting your ideas into order so as to give them full information upon it.

I am not quite sure whether the suggestion in your letter is intended as a complete suggestion. If so, does it not appear that the landlord might complain.

I am as yet much in the dark upon the subject, sensible only of difficulty on the one side, urgency on the other.

As to Irish Government, I am convinced that Spencer would do anything which patriotism recommended, but I presume you do not mean an exchange.

Let us talk of this, when you think it needful: even today should you desire it.

To LORD KIMBERLEY, colonial secretary, 17 May 1881.   Add MS 44544, f. 170.

1. The Queen was quite satisfied about the telegram to Sir E. Wood. She likes & esteems him, but thinks him a man of many words. She agreed however when I pointed out that he appeared also to be a man of action, indeed of considerable civil talents.
2. Have the goodness to look back to what happened in 1843 about the Ashburton Treaty. Palmerston moved a vote of censure on it, & called it the Ashburton Capitulation.[2] Hume, though in opposition, moved a counter-motion of praise, which was carried.

It occurs to me in relation to the motion of Hicks Beach[3] that we might take or favour the taking of a similar course. I have mentioned it this morning to Granville & R. Grosvenor—both of whom highly approve. I inclose for your consideration a very rough note of the sort of amendment that might possibly be moved. It has two parts: the amendment might include both, or might be confined to the second. Please to consider it when convenient.

I have to keep my bed today but hope to be right tomorrow.

To LORD ROSEBERY, 17 May 1881.   N.L.S. 10022, f. 78.

Thinking over our rather *pressed* i.e. compressed conversation of Saturday I write a line to say that on some future day I should like, in Scotch phrase, to supplement it.

The account I gave of the relation of a seat in the H. of Lords to the Official order was true but not the whole truth indeed it was only one side of the truth and the other side was one of rather more general colouring.

I am out of sorts but hope to be well tomorrow.

18. *Wed.*

Wrote to The Queen 1.2.—Duke of Argyll—Dr Moulton—Ld E. Fitzmaurice—Mr O'Shea—Mr Hamilton—Le Duc d'Aumale—and minutes. Saw Mr G—Ld RG—Ld Rosebery—Dr Clark 1.2.—Sir R. Phillimore—Deputn Sugar Refining Workmen—Deputation Licenced Victuallers[4]—Ld Granville. Read E. Quinet—Robertson Smith on O.T.—Salem Chapel.

---

[1] See 15 May 81n. Gladstone's answer untraced.
[2] Settling American-Canadian differences; for Palmerston's attack, which Gladstone heard, see 21 Mar. 43. Kimberley promised to look it up; Add MS 44226, f. 109.
[3] Hicks Beach's motion on the Transvaal, eventually moved on 25 July.
[4] Reports on both in *T.T.*, 19 May 1881, 11b.

To the DUKE OF ARGYLL, 18 May 1881.   Add MS 44544, f. 171.

I thank you for your letter.[1] We are not really at variance about the Act of 1870. I spoke entirely of the effect, not of the intent. I do not think I was myself aware, at the time, of the mode in which, & the force with which, compensation for disturbance would engender tenant right and even to some extent form a measure of it.

19. Th.

Wrote to Sir W. Dunbar—Sir R. Phillimore—Mr Rymer—The Queen—& minutes. Wrote & circulated draft probably final on the Wolseley affair.[2] Saw Mr G—Ld RG—Mr Forster—Mr Hutton—Mr Fitzgerald—Mr D. Currie—Mr Chamberlain—Mr Hastings *cum* Mr Tracey. Twelve to breakfast 10–11½. H. of C. 5–8½ and 10½–2½. Voted in 352:176 for 2 R. of Irish Land Bill.[3] Read Salem Chapel—Aldis Departed.[4] Drive with C. Admitted Fellow of the Royal Society.[5]

20. Fr.

Wrote to The Queen 1.2.—Ld Kimberley and minutes. Cabinet 12–3½. Saw Mr G—Ld R.G.—W.H.G.—Ld Granville—Mr Ouvry—Ld Spencer—Mr Forster—Mr Bond—Mr B. Price. H. of C. 4¾–8¼ and 9–11¾.[6] Read Salem Chapel.

Cabinet. Friday May 20. 81. 12 Noon.[7]
1. Tunis. Ld Granville's draft to the French Ambassador read amended & approved.[8]
5. Transvaal motion. An independent counter motion may be promoted.
4. Fair Rent considered.[9]
3. Procedure on Land Bill. Morning sittings—Yes
2. Labanoff's application for an extradition Treaty. (Rather to recommend delay).
6. H. of L. motion for a Scotch Department. Outline of reply agreed on.[10]

[1] Of 17 May, Add MS 44105, f. 87, protesting at Gladstone's objections to the Lords' amndts. in 1870, which were not intended to sanction sale in all cases.
[2] Add MS 44765, f. 116; draft to the Queen renewing recommendation of peerage for Wolseley.
[3] Hartington concluded for the govt.; *H* 261. 928.
[4] Not traced.
[5] Under the Statute for election of Privy Councillors; Prime Ministers were normally elected, though Gladstone had not been in his first term.
[6] Answered Rogers' charge that declining number of firsts at Christ Church was due to its links with Westminster School; spoke on arrests in Ireland; *H* 261. 960, 974.
[7] Add MS 44642, f. 181. Gladstone wrote out the headings in advance, and then numbered them in the order of discussion.
[8] British subjects' rights under 1875 treaty reaffirmed; Marsden, op. cit., 74–5.
[9] Carlingford's diary, 20 May 1881: 'The Land Bill mainly clause 7 "fair rent". Law and Johnson the Irish law officers present. I took a principal part—my memm. seemed to have made an impression on Gladstone. No decision arrived at—but most of the Cabinet, & Mr G. inclined to my solution to leave out both the "competition rent" and the "tenant's interest".... Forster at the end said he thought we should have to stick to the clause as it stands! He does not at all understand the question.' See 28 May 81.
[10] Fife raised this on 13 June, Granville promising the govt.'s 'fullest consideration': *H* 262. 323.

21. *Sat.* [*Pembroke Lodge*]

Wrote to Mr Childers—Ld Hartington 1.2.—Sir B. Leighton and to the Queen: putting my draft of Thursday into a letter: rather heavily charged.[1] Sent Tel. to Ld Granville 1.2. and minutes. Saw Mr G.—Ld R.G.—Charles Lyttelton—Mr Childers—Ly Russell—Baron A. Rothschild—Read Salem Chapel. In aft. drove to Gunnersbury & saw Baroness Lionel [de Rothschild]. Then on to Pembroke Lodge[2] to stay Sunday.

To LORD HARTINGTON, Indian secretary, 21 May 1881.   Add MS 44145, f. 252.

[First letter]   It is, I need not say, matter of great concern to me that you should have seen cause to change your mind[3] at this stage in the important matter of the Wolseley Peerage.

At the same time I fully admit that the worst thing any of us can do is to persevere in what he believes to be wrong. I am not aware of any fresh arguments used by the Duke of Cambridge to which you refer. Childers' report of the conversation did not specify them, nor do you. At the previous stages of the correspondence we have been made acquainted pretty fully with his views; and I do not gather from you that he produced anything new.

It appears to me that the arguments in my draft are strong (in which I may be wrong): but they form a very faint indication of what I think of the great conspiracy against the nation, in respect both to change and to reforms, which lives and works among the heads of the military class, and which enjoys in the House of Lords its chief arena for development and exercise.

With this view, I cannot recede; and I send you a copy of a Telegram, which I have despatched to Granville, after seeing Childers and showing him the memorandum I had received.

[Second letter]   Many thanks for your letter. I cannot say that I am moved by the arguments of the Duke which you have kindly taken the pains to set out. Every one of them smells strongly of what I conceive to be the standing plot of the class against the nation.

I would certainly have awaited, though time now presses, another conversation with Granville, had he altered his mind. But you will observe that he still gives the proposal a support though a weakened support by (expressly) not withdrawing anything he had previously said. The letter will go.
[P.S.] I do not know that I am influenced by it as an argument, but I could not look Wolseley in the face if I receded.[4]

22. 5 S.E.

Ch (Petersham) mg. Aft. Prayers at home. Saw Mr Leckie—Mr Trevelyan—Read Robn Smith (finished)—Consols in Job—Eternal Purpose—Salem Chapel. A good deal of rest: shirking the afternoon gathering here.

[1] On Wolseley; part in Guedalla, *Q*, 158.

[2] Lady Russell and her grandsons, John Francis Stanley, 1865-1931, 2d Earl Russell, and Bertrand* (see 20 Apr. 78n.).

[3] Hartington was now reluctant to press Wolseley's peerage on the Court; note this day, Add MS 44145, f. 251.

[4] This day, Add MS 44145, f. 253: Wolseley would be attacked in the Lords and Cambridge might reply when Wolseley 'professes opinions in his hearing from which he altogether dissents'.

23. M. [London]

Wrote to Mr Trevelyan—Mr Forster—The Queen 1.2. and minutes. Back to town at 11.45. H. of C. 4¾–8. and 8½–2¾. Working the Finance Bill.[1] Saw Mr G.—Ld R.G.—Ld F.C.—Ld Granville—Ld Kimberley. Read Salem Chapel—Mutiny at the Nore.[2] Attended the Levee.

24. Tu.

Wrote to The Queen 1.2.—Sir C. Dilke—Att. Gen. Ireland—Ld F. Cavendish and minutes. H. of C. 2¾-3¼ & 4¾-7.[3] Saw Mr G.—Ld F.C.—Sir W. Dunbar—Sir C. Trevelyan—Ld Granville cum Ld Hartington—Mr [blank] U.S.—Ld Dufferin—Mr Ogilvy. Read mutiny at the Nore—Salem Chapel. Evening party here.

25. Wed.

Wrote to the Queen Tel—Ld Carlingford—Mr Lefevre—Ld F. Cavendish—Ld Kimberley & minutes. Read Life of Dodds[4]—Meeting at the Nore—Salem Chapel. Saw Mr G.—Ld R.G.—Mr Childers—Ld Spencer. Do cum Ld Gr. & Ld H. 2½-4 on the Wolseley matter. It stands over to make some prior communications. Saw Mad. Neillson. Dined at Mr Flowers. Mr Yorke's recitations. Saw one X.

To LORD CARLINGFORD, lord privy seal, 25 May 1881.   Carlingford MSS CP1/198.

We propose to have a small Committee to review the enormous list of amendments to the Irish Land Bill and note them according to their several characters as slight or serious, and as good or bad, reserving for other notice everything except what may safely be passed by. Forster acts as far as he is able: the Irish Law Officers, English Solicitor, Lefevre, Sir H. Thring: Playfair we hope will be there, in another character. Will it be agreeable to you to give your aid?
[P.S.] If your answer is affirmative, as I hope, please to communicate at once with the Irish A.G.[5]

To LORD KIMBERLEY, colonial secretary, 25 May 1881.   Add MS 44544, f. 172.

I have seen Childers & heard from him that you & he agree with the military Council in siding with Robinson & de Villiers against Wood & taking strong powers for the Resident. I agree.
We mentioned it to Granville & he agreed with us it need not go to the Cabinet particularly as Forster (who might take a special interest) is in Dublin.

To G. J. SHAW LEFEVRE, first commissioner of works,   Add MS 44544, f. 172.
25 May 1881.

One word on your coming article:[6] I am sure you will not in any way dally with the proposition that the State is to buy the estates in Ireland of all Landlords desiring to sell.

---

[1] Local taxation; H 261. 1094.
[2] [W. J. Neale], History of the mutiny at Spithead and the Nore (1842).
[3] Defended the Irish executive briefly; H 261. 1261.
[4] T. Dodd, Memoirs of Thomas Dodd, William Upcott and George Stubbs (1879).
[5] Carlingford replied, 'happy & anxious to act'; Add MS 44123, f. 103.
[6] 'The Duke of Argyll and the Irish Land bill', Nineteenth Century, ix. 1044 (June 1881).

It is only the immense mischief of any countenance, express or implied, to such a proposition from any quarter connected with the Government that leads me to write & make security doubly sure, lest there should be any line or phrase liable to misconstruction on this head.

26. Th. Ascension Day.

Chapel Royal 11 a.m. with H.C. Wrote to Sir B. Leighton—Sir G. Young—Mr Fawcett—Mons. Zancoff—The Queen 1.2.—King of Sweden[1]—Ld Granville—Col. Stewart—Mr G.—Ld R.G. Nine to breakfast. Conclave at $3\frac{1}{2}$ on the Wolseley matter.[2] I adhered to my recommendation: but adopted suggestions altering the form of letter to H.M. & admitting postponement. Dined at Spencer House. H. of C. 5–8 (Taxing Bill) and $10\frac{1}{2}$–1 (Land Bill).[3] Read Salem Chapel.

To D. K. ZANKOF, prime minister of Bulgaria, 26 May 1881.   Add MS 44544, f. 172.

I have the honour to acknowledge your letter of the 9th current.[4] I have a pleasant recollection of our conversation on Bulgarian affairs in 1876:[5] &, retaining as I do all my interest in the country and the people, I am truly sorry that you should address me under an apprehension of danger.

The desires of the British Government can only act within the limits of its ability, but they will always be found on the side of legality and liberty. It is in this light that they will seek to examine every question.

I am not yet sufficiently acquainted with the nature of the propositions which the Prince of Bulgaria may contemplate, to be able to pronounce or form any opinion upon them.

27. Fr.

Wrote to Mr Shaw MP.—The Queen—and minutes. H. of C. $2\frac{1}{4}$–7. and $9\frac{3}{4}$–$11\frac{1}{2}$. With Land Bill, in Committee.[6] Saw Mr G.—Ld R.G.—Ld F.C.—Mr Hamilton—Sir G. Wolseley—S.E.G. (who goes on well). Read Salem Chapel. Dined with the Jameses.

28. Sat.

Wrote to Ld Granville—Mr Forster—Lady Matheson—Sir H. Peek—A.G. for Ireland—Mr Bryce MP—The Queen—Mr Forster and minutes. Read Waller's Afghanistan[7]—Life of Dodd & Upcott. Cabinet 2–5. Saw Ld Kenmare[?]—

[1] Informing him that the deb. in the Commons he was planning to attend had ended; Add MS 44470, f. 16.
[2] Selborne, Granville, Hartington, Bright, Childers summoned; Add MS 48607, bundle 2. For Gladstone's letter, dated 25 May, adhering to his recommendation but 'in deference' withholding it until 'the business of the year is further advanced', see Guedalla, *Q*, ii. 160.
[3] *H.* 261. 1336.
[4] Reply to Zankof's letter of 9 May, requesting help against the Prince's attempt to revise the constitution, delayed until details checked by the F.O. (see to Dilke 24 May, Add MS 44544, f. 172). Prince Alexander suspended the constitution and summoned a national assembly, Zankof being later arrested for his election address.
[5] See 10 Oct. 76.   [6] *H* 261. 1464.
[7] i.e. P. F. Walker, *Afghanistan: a short account . . .* (1881).

Mr G.—Ld R.G.—Ly Gladstone. [Queen's] Birthday dinner party. Prince of Wales most kind & conversible. I told D. of Devonshire what I thought of his contribution to his country in his two sons. The King of Sweden[1] came. F.O. afterwards. Saw Musurus—Mrs Hardcastle—G. Strahan.

Cabinet May 28. 81. 2 PM.[2]
1. Transvaal. Ld Kimberley submitted the Telegrams on severance of Transvaal by retention of territory.[3]
2. Disfranchisement Bill.[4] WEG to see Attorney General. General view to persevere in what we have already before Parlt.
3. Land Bill. Fair Rent & tenant right: definition if possible.
4. Leopard affair[5]—French captain wrong: claim for damages if any to be reserved.
5. Turkish protest about Tunis: commend reserved character of Paris proceedings. We do not intend formally to protest.
6. Pender—Tweeddale—H. Vivian. Only to secure them fair play.[6]

By a fair rent we mean such a rent as, apart from any improvements made by the tenant or his predecessors in title, ['*a solvent and responsible tenant could afford to pay* fairly and without collusion'][7] would be obtained in a market ⟨for farms⟩ when the supply ⟨and demand were⟩ of farms is ordinarily equal to demand.

The tenant right is a right to occupy at a fair rent: i.e. such a rent as leaves to the tenant 1) the benefit of ⟨his⟩ improvements made by him or his predecessors in title, 2) the full profit which a solvent and responsible tenant would obtain in an ordinary market. In the circumstances of Ireland, 2) is abated by the excessive bidding for farms. Bidders can be found, beyond the mere value of tenants' improvements, for the right to occupy a farm at what in England would be a full rent.[8]

29. S. aft Ascn.

Chapel Royal mg & aft. Dined at Mrs Heywoods. Read Contemp. Rev. on Carlyle & on Beaconsfield[9]—Minerva on Carlyle[10]—Gospel for the 19th Century[11]—Colenso on the Romans—Revised version—The Pentateuch[12]—Life of Christ.

---

[1] Oscar II.

[2] Add MS 44642, f. 182.

[3] '. . . no part of the Transvaal should be retained as British territory against the will of the Boers, powers being reserved to British Resident . . .'; instructions to the commissioners (who were in disagreement), pushed through despite Victoria's objections; *L.Q.V.* 2nd series, iii. 220 and Schreuder, 195; see 25 May 81.

[4] Corrupt Practices (Suspension of Elections) Bill passed this session.

[5] French warship *Léopard* intercepted the *Nova Stella* on 23 May; see Dilke in *H* 261. 1644.

[6] Details obscure.

[7] Gladstone's brackets.

[8] Undated holograph at Add MS 44765, f. 22. The 1898 Royal Commission found (*PP* 1898, xxv. 16): 'even after the Act of 1881 has been in operation for 16 years, there is, so far as we can learn, no judicial exposition of the two weightiest words in the whole statute—"fair rent"'. See also Hammond, 232ff.

[9] *C.R.*, cxl. 904, 991 (June 1881).

[10] Not found.

[11] See 1 Feb. 80.

[12] All works by J. W. Colenso.

30. M.

Wrote to Mr Cowan—Lord Cowper—The Queen 1.2.—and minutes. Prepared draft of letter to Transvaal Memorial.[1] Saw Mr G.—Ld R.G.—Ld F.C.—Sir Thos Gladstone—Mr Knowles (& went with him to the Millais and other pictures)[2]— Mr Chamberlain—Sir W. Harcourt. H. of C. $4\frac{3}{4}$-$8\frac{1}{2}$ and $9\frac{1}{4}$-1. (Parnell row: Irish Land).[3] Read Salem Chapel.

To J. COWAN, 30 May 1881.   Hawarden MSS.

I have read with pleasure & with gratitude the report of the Executive Committee of the Midlothian Liberal Association.

It is with much interest, and with hope, that I look forward to rendering at a future date in person an account of the manner in which I have thus far striven to act upon the principle declared by me before the Electors of Midlothian, and to discharge the trust conferred upon me as their representative.

A combination of affairs in Ireland, so novel and dangerous as was hardly to be expected, has seriously interfered with other domestic affairs; and I grieve to think that Scotland has suffered a full share of disadvantages from this unhappy cause.

Her representatives have, however, in overwhelming proportion, laboured steadily at the work of rendering whatever yet remains to be rendered of full justice to Ireland.

Beyond sea, in Europe, Asia, and Africa, we have carefully and constantly striven to fulfil the expectations I may have led you to entertain. And although all the clouds have not yet disappeared, I am thankful to say that the horizon has been greatly cleared and a progress made in the sense of liberty, justice, and humanity, at least as great as in a time so limited it would have been reasonable to expect.[4]

31. Tu.

Wrote to Sir W. Harcourt—The Queen 1.2.—Mr Fawcett—Ld Kimberley—Mr Forster and minutes. H. of C. $2\frac{1}{4}$-7 (Land Bill).[5] Conclave on Govt of Ireland 1-2.[6] Saw Mr. G—Ld R.G.—Herbert G.—Dean of Durham—Mr Pyke—Persian Minister—Evarts—Mr Burne Jones and others. Eight to dinner: and evening party. Read Salem Chapel—Miss Nadin's Poems.[7]

To W. E. FORSTER, Irish secretary, 31 May 1881.   Add MS 44544, f. 174.

1. I postponed answering your interesting letter of the 29[8] yesterday when it arrived, in order that I might consult some of our colleagues upon it. (Carlingford is in Scotland).

---

[1] Petition from Transvaal 'loyalists' requesting govt. not to 'abandon' them to Boer rule; reply sent on 1 June; Schreuder, 197.
[2] See 30 Apr. 81n.?
[3] Row about letter of P. Egan in the *Freeman's Journal*; H 261. 1675.
[4] Read to annual general meeting of Midlothian liberal association; *T.T.*, 2 June 1881, 6c.
[5] H 261. 1795.   [6] See today's letter to Forster.
[7] C. C. W. Naden, *Songs and sonnets* (1881).
[8] Add MS 44158, f. 167: '. . . Cowper must be replaced by Spencer which could hardly I think be managed without giving great pain & also without the awkwardness of an apparent acknowledgement of failure—O'Hagan must be replaced by an efficient Chancellor. If we had Sullivan in his place I think we could get on. . . . O'Hagan is rich, tired of work & in poor health, & above all he is shy of responsibility. . . . Would you think it desirable to consult Spencer, Hartington & Carlingford on this matter. . . .' Forster again urged on 2 June that he could not leave Ireland 'unless Spencer replaces him [Cowper], or Sullivan replaces O'Hagan', ibid., f. 174.

2. We at once accept the declaration of your intention to remain in Ireland until after the short Whitsuntide recess, & we shall be glad to think that the initiative in these difficult circumstances will be in the hands best qualified to administer it. I may say that Law has answered his questions very well, in a manner impassive & slightly professional, thus far with very good effect.

3. The evening of Friday is to be given to the further prosecution of the MacCarthy debate, if as is expected, the paper can be virtually cleared for the purpose. As I had the opportunity of saying a few words last week, I should perhaps allow myself to be silent, after having worked the morning sitting on the Land Bill.

4. We were all of opinion that it would be most desirable to effect a change in the Chancellorship, such as you describe. There was however a disposition to doubt whether your proposed method of proceeding is a safe one, & whether it might not possibly, if the alternative of daily attendance & advice were accepted, make the situation worse than it is now. On the other hand, compulsory removal is a strong measure, & without any exact precedent available for it. Please to think over the matter & give me the result of your further reflections. The consequential questions as to Law & otherwise can stand over for a while. Remember however that he would have to be *passed* through the Supreme Court in order to qualify, & that it would be dangerous, at a critical time, to revive the recollection of the Collier precedent,[1] extravagantly & mischievously exaggerated though it was.

5. A further opinion I think prevailed, which can hardly be discussed with effect except when you are here. It is to the effect that a change in the Chancellorship does not of itself dispose of the whole question, that the true initiative of government in difficult times cannot lie with the Chancellor but must be either with the Lord Lieutenant, or with a Chief Secretary who though a Cabinet Minister is on the spot.

6. It was recommended that I should write to Cowper & ask him to send for the information of the Cabinet a statement of his views on the present condition of Ireland & the mode of dealing with the difficulties which lie so thick on the daily path of the Executive.

7. Ground has thus far been broken on the Land Bill without the occurrence of any sinister circumstances. Last night Brand behaved well; Fitzmaurice's criticisms were very acrid.

To Sir W. V. HARCOURT, home secretary, 31 May 1881.   MS Harcourt dep. 8, f. 84.

I send you two communications on the Scotch Teinds Bill:[2] & I hope that the Lord Advocate will take much care in the matter. The difficulty of time even if it stood alone cannot be put out of consideration. Witness the Pulman Cars!

Do you think it would be well for the Lord Advocate to consult with Rosebery, who could give an impartial opinion—please ascertain what Lord G. thinks, in virtue of your supervisory authority as Sec. of State.

Wed. June 1881.

Wrote to Marquis of Lorne—Ld Kimberley—D. of Argyll—Ld F. Cavendish—Sir Thos G.—Ld Hartington—and minutes. Saw Rands [R]. Saw Mr G.—Mr H.—Mr Dalby[3]—Mr & Mrs Th.—Sir F. Leighton—Mr Millais. Dined with Mr Millais. Read N.C. Arnold on Land Bill[4]—Lefevre on do[5]—N.C. on [blank.]

---

[1] See 16 Oct. 71.

[2] See Lord Advocate's mem., April 1881, Add MS 44196, f. 161, on Scottish support for it; opposition largely ecclesiastical.

[3] Perhaps W. B. Dalby, surgeon in Savile Row.   [4] *N.C.*, ix. 1026 (June 1881).

[5] Ibid., 1044; see to Lefevre, 25 May 81.

To the MARQUIS OF LORNE, Governor General of Canada,   Add MS 44544, f. 174.
1 June 1881.

Many thanks for your letter.[1]

The question of Emigration from Ireland is one of *extreme* delicacy: and on this account I would rather not multiply communication for myself on it beyond what is necessary. So that I could do little more than refer Sir J. Macdonald to Mr. Forster.

You will I daresay understand at once why it is that great jealousy prevails on this subject. The Tory party will press it and their pressing it will additionally tend to create suspicion among the Irish members & in the priesthood. I daresay an opportunity will arise for my speaking to Sir John Macdonald & I will do it carefully.

It gives me much pleasure to find you cheerful as to the prospects of Canada with regard to the attractions she can offer to emigrants.

We all deeply feel the loss of the Duke your Father & his cooperation alike in a personal & in a political sense.

Only about eight Irish members voted against the second reading of the Land Bill.

In truth that Bill seems to constitute nearly the whole of our substantial resources for confronting & beating the Land League.

I witness with much pleasure your peaceful & prosperous career.

2. Th.

Wrote to Ld Granville—General Badeau—Mr Forster—The Queen 1.2.3. and minutes. Finished Salem Chapel. $11\frac{1}{4}$–$1\frac{1}{4}$ To the Lake marriage at St Paul's Kn.[2] and the breakfast afterwards at Sir Thos G.s. Saw Mr G.—Ld R.G.—Ld Granville—Att. Gen. for Ireland—Mr Childers—Mr Chamberlain. Dined at Sir C. Forsters. H. of C. $4\frac{1}{2}$–$8\frac{1}{4}$ & $9\frac{1}{2}$–$1\frac{1}{4}$. Working Irish Land Bill.[3]

Cabinet. Thurs June 2. 2 PM. (1881)[4]
1. Conversation on evictions & resistance in Ireland.
2. Queen's dissatisfaction with Telegram on the strip of territory reported. Ld K. 'A smaller matter than she supposes'.[5]
3. Scotch Judges & Sheriffs Bills. Chancellor recommended two Bills. Harcourt with the Ld Adv. to see the Scotch Members after the recess.
4. Discussion with the Attorney General on the admission of free contract for:
   purchased   tenant-right lands
     ditto   Landlord-right lands
   (when the interests are now united they need not be severed)
   All lands not within the Act at its passing to be under the contracting-out Clause tho' they become agricultural holdings—
   and on the tenant right Court will strike out
5. Minute by Sir Thos Steele on the position of the military in executing evictions.[6]

3. Fr. [*The Durdans, Epsom*]

Willy's birthday: God bless him. Wrote to Ld Portarlington—Ld Kimberley—Mr Forster—Mr Goschen—The Queen—Sir Th. Bagley—M. Zancoff (Tel) &

---

[1] Not found; the emigration clauses in the Land Bill were among the most contentious.
[2] Katharine, da. of J. N. Gladstone, m. Dean W. C. *Lake (see 4 Mar. 40).
[3] And spoke on the Land League, and Transvaal; *H* 261. 1882, 1885.   [4] Add MS 44642, f. 184.
[5] In the Transvaal; see 28 May 81.   [6] Not found.

minutes. H. of C. $2\frac{1}{4}$–$6\frac{1}{4}$: Irish Land Bill, & rows.[1] Saw Ld R.G.—Mr G.—Ld Granville—Mr Goschen—Ld Dufferin—Ld Rosebery. To the Durdans at 6.30. A small party of men there. Read Nadin's poems—Meeting at the Nore.

To LORD KIMBERLEY, colonial secretary, 3 June 1881.   Add MS 44544, f. 176.

I see that Chamberlain is announced to address his constituents next week.[2]

Would it not be well to ask him to speak fully on the Transvaal? I am told that the constant inflammatory telegrams & speeches with our silence are working mischief in the constituencies.

If you think with me, pray communicate with Chamberlain accordingly.

4. Sat.

Wrote to Ld Kimberley—Ld Granville—Mr Forster—Sir H. Ponsonby—Viceroy of Ireland 1.2.—Mr Hamilton & minutes. Drive to Betchworth Clump: & reminiscence. Read Nadin's Poems (finished)—Fitzgerald's Geo. IV.[3]—Bose, Hindoos as they are[4]—Herries's Reply.[5]

To LORD COWPER, Viceroy of Ireland, 4 June 1881.   Add MS 44544, f. 176.

I am afraid I have not clearly indicated my thoughts respecting the present form of the charter for a Presbyterian University.[6] Two points occur to me which I hope you will consider fully with Law.

1. No doubt there are precedents, if I remember rightly, for the establishment of Universities limited (either literally? or) virtually to a single faculty. But in the Academical history & idea of this country it would be a poor innovation: I am by no means sure that it is desirable; nor yet that it is called for by any need. Why cannot the powers to grant theological degrees be given without dubbing the granting body an University? Such degrees are given by the Archbp. of Canterbury (inheriting I rather think from the Pope).

2. I am very doubtful whether it should be in the discretion of the proposed body, without conditions or control, to determine what literary or other qualifications should be required from candidates for Theological degrees. The question is important; similar powers may be asked by other communions; & we are now making a precedent. Would it be well to insert in the Charter a condition that degrees in Theology should only be granted 1. as Hope proposed to Graduates in arts. 2. to others under Rules to be approved from time to time by the Government. These are only tentative suggestions; there may be better modes of proceeding.

To LORD KIMBERLEY, colonial secretary, 4 June 1881.   Add MS 44544, f. 177.

[First letter] I have read the reports of representations from native chiefs sent to us from Pretoria on April 11; & it occurs to me that they require rather more of consolatory reply than they have received.

---

[1] J. M'Carthy's motion of censure of Irish executive; *H* 262. 58.

[2] On 7 June; see 8 June 81; on 4 June, Gladstone reminded Kimberley (who quite agreed 'as to Chamberlain speaking on the Transvaal', Add MS 44226, f. 135) to encourage Chamberlain; Add MS 44544, f. 176.   [3] P. H. Fitzgerald, *The life of George the Fourth*, 2v. (1881).

[4] S. C. Bose, *The Hindoos as they are* (1881).

[5] E. Herries, 'A letter to the Editor of the *Edinburgh Review*' (1881); defence of J. C. Herries.

[6] Gladstone had written to Cowper on 30 May, sympathising with Beresford Hope's question that day; see *H* 261. 1660; Add MS 44470, f. 19.

Could they not be put in the hands of the Boer leaders, in a friendly way, & could not direct assurances be had from the Boer leaders themselves, which might be as it were countersigned by us?

I cannot but think something joint would be more satisfactory *both there & here*, than the mere statement from us, who are in one sense about to leave the country.

If you concur, please do what can be done in the matter.

[Second letter]   Cetywayo has I fear been vilely used, & I do not see what you can write better than this draft.[1]

Should not Granville & Hartington see it, as they took their line at the time of the Zulu War.

5.

Ch mg with H.C. & parish Ch. aft. Read Revised Version—Life of Law[2]—Ross Lewin, Continuity[3]—Gospel for 19th Century. Wrote to Mr Standen.

6. M.

Wrote to Mr Forster—Sir G. Airy—Mr Fowler M.P.—Sir R. Dease—Mr Fawcett—The Queen—Mr Howell—J. Hynn & minutes. Drive to Norbury Park: & walk of $1\frac{1}{2}$ hr: singularly beautiful. Read Heptalogia[4]—Fitzgerald's Geo. IV.— Mutiny at the Nore (finished). Saw Mr Whitwell Reid.

To W. E. FORSTER, Irish secretary, 6 June 1881.   Add MS 44544, f. 177.

But for Tottenham's notice about the Irish executive & the Land League,[5] you might I think have had *carte blanche*; but I am afraid difficulty might arise on that subject if you were not in your place next Thursday.

On the other hand I do not know why you should not afterwards return to Ireland if so inclined; for we are well supported by Shaw & others in the discussion on the Irish Land Bill, & we experience little difficulty.

Of course when we have the question of arrears or of evictions in view your presence would be urgently required.

I feel the force of all you say about evictions & do not see my way to interference.

As to fair rent what we should like best would be if possible to use very general words in the Bill. But it would still be material to consider what language to use about it in debate, as explanatory of our own ideas.

Now my idea of a fair rent might be given roughly in any or all of the following ways. It is such a rent

1. as is actually taken on the well managed estate in Ireland

---

[1] Kimberley, 3 June, Add MS 44226, f. 133, sent an untraced letter from Cetewayo and commented that the Zulu war had been 'unjust and unnecessary. But we could not replace him in Zululand without a gross breach of faith to the Chiefs.'

[2] J. H. Overton, *William Law, non-juror and mystic* (1881).

[3] C. H. Ross Lewin, *The continuity of the English church* (1880).

[4] [A. C. Swinburne], *The Heptalogia; or, the seven against sense* (1881).

[5] On 3 June, Tottenham gave notice of a resolution on the Land League for 9 June, never in fact moved; *H* 262. 23. Arthur Loftus Tottenham, 1838-87; tory M.P. Leitrim 1880-5, Winchester 1885-7; spied on Gladstone rescuing a prostitute and dined out on it 1882 (Bahlman, *Hamilton*, i. 269).

2. as would be got in a market for farms where nothing had occurred to disturb the natural or healthful or ordinary proportion between supply & demand.

3. As leaves to the tenant a fair living or trading profit.[1]

If you wish for a Cabinet on Thursday (at 2) please telegraph to Godley.

7. Tu.

Wrote to Mr Hutton—The Speaker—Mr Forster Tel—Sir R. Cross—Mr Hamilton & minutes. Walk with R[osebery]. Read Hunter, 'Englands work in India'[2]—Mrs Grey Man & Woman[3]—Tiberius[4]—Miss Broughton's 'Second Thoughts'[5]—Overton's Law.

To H. B. W. BRAND, the Speaker, 7 June 1881.   Brand MSS 266.

I feel embarrassed as to the subject of your letter.[6] Not in the least as to your ruling or the support the House is likely to give to it. About this I cannot entertain a doubt. The only point which occurred to me as *possibly* open to question was your declaration that you would have expurgated Tottenham's question[7] had you seen it in print: & this is quite in the other sense.

I fully allow the force of your observation that challenges against the Speaker's ruling ought not to remain long undisposed of on the notice paper.

It is both an inconvenience and an indecency. Yet I do not clearly see my way whether we shall have to bear it for a season together with other inconveniences, and indecencies.

Parnell is looking for every opportunity to impede business for the sake of impeding the Land Bill without appearing to impede the Land Bill. I am desperately afraid, now that rulings from the Chair are necessarily so frequent, of giving him an opportunity of covert obstruction by a pretended challenge of them. If the Government, when he chooses to deliver such a challenge, is to bestir itself to clear the [order] paper for him—a thing only done with great difficulty & by appearing to incur obligations—does not this mean that such matters ought by right to be treated as matters of privilege?

Should Tottenham's motion against the Land League come on, I think we might perhaps introduce into the debate some stout declaration adverse to Parnell's view.

On the whole I do not feel well able to decide anything, and I propose to let the matter stand until I come up on Thursday forenoon. All these difficulties tend to inspire the hope, but it is no more than a hope, that the House may at length awake to the necessity of large & not merely formal measures to uphold or restore its dignity by securing its efficiency.

[P.S.] If you should call about one on Thursday, there is another matter on which I should like to say a very brief word to you.

8. Wed.

Wrote to Ld Young—A.G. for Ireland—Mr Hamilton—Mr Chamberlain—Mr

[1] See also Thring's mem. on 'Fair Rent', 23 May 1881. Add MS 44627, f. 28.
[2] W. W. Hunter, *England's work in India* (1881).
[3] Perhaps Mrs T. Grey, *Idols of society; or gentility and femininity* (1874).
[4] A. W. T. Stahr, *Tiberius* (1873).
[5] R. Broughton, *Second Thoughts*, 2v. (1880).
[6] Of 6 June, Add MS 44195, f. 44, on means of dealing with Irish tactics.
[7] Tottenham's question of 3 June attributed a murder to the Land League which led to the suspension of O'Kelly and the question's rewording: *H* 262. 17.

Pierrepoint[1] & minutes. Read Stahr's Tiberius—Swinburne's Ballad[2]—Bose on Hindoos—Second Thoughts—Hunter, Engl. work in India. Walk with Rosebery & Sir C. Dilke. Saw Mr Morley & Mr Smalley in evg.

To J. CHAMBERLAIN, president of the board of trade,   Chamberlain MSS 5/34/5. 8 June 1881.

I have read with pleasure what you say of the Transvaal: yet am not prepared, for myself, to concede that we made a mistake in not advising a revocation of the annexation when we came in.[3] My purpose however in writing is to know whether you have any plan, or any suggestion to make, about your Bankruptcy Bill.

In any circumstances if that Bill went to a Committee, the Committee would be a large one say 23 or 25. But this would not save discussion in the House. Is it practicable, and if so would it be politic, to organise something in the nature of a Grand Committee for it? and so to put it through. I am *inclined* to some course of this kind. If adopted, the experiment might serve as a pilot-balloon. The grievous block of business inside, and the strong desire of the commercial classes outside, seem to offer a favourable occasion. Pray speak to the Speaker on the subject, provisionally, or to Sir T. May: if you think fit.[4]

9. *Th.* [*London*]

Wrote to Mr Forster—Mr J. Collings MP.[5]—Mr W.C. James—Ld Kimberley—Mr Chambers—The Queen—C.G. and minutes. Dined at Ld F. Cavendish's. Read Second Thoughts—Stahr's Tiberius. Saw Mr G.—Ld R.G.—Ld F.C.—Mr Morley—Ld Lyttelton: and others—Mr Bright. H. of C. $4\frac{1}{2}$–8 and 10–$12\frac{1}{2}$.[6]

To LORD KIMBERLEY, colonial secretary, 9 June 1881.   Add MS 44544, f. 179.

I am glad Wood only suggests retirement.[7] Such a step, apart from the embarrassment it would produce, would be so far as I know without precedent, and very damaging to him as well as us. He accepted the Commission under the terms of March 17 and how can he have a title to retire upon a decision which lies evidently and strictly *within* the options given by them. I hope your answer to him will accompany his Telegrams when they go to Balmoral. Herewith I return your draft Telegram about the native chiefs, which doubtless you will forward without delay.

10. *Fr.* [*The Durdans*]

Wrote to Ld Kimberley 1.2.—Rev. Mr Jowett—The Queen—Ld Cowper—Mr Godley—Ld R.G.—Ld F.C.—The Speaker—Mr O'Shea—A.G. for Ireland—Mr Forster & minutes. H. of C. $2\frac{1}{2}$–$6\frac{3}{4}$ and 9–$11\frac{1}{2}$.[8] Dined with W. James. Our

---

[1] Edwards Pierrepont, 1817–92, bimetallist; American jurist; minister in London 1876–7; in New York from 1878.

[2] See 6 June 81n.

[3] At Birmingham on 7 June Chamberlain said: 'I frankly admit that we made a mistake ...'; Garvin, i. 441. See 3 June 81.

[4] This year's bill was withdrawn without a Grand Cttee.; the Bankruptcy Bill passed in 1883, *via* two Grand Cttees.; Garvin i. 416–18, Add MS 44125, f. 71.

[5] Jesse *Collings, 1831–1920; liberal (unionist) M.P. Ipswich 1880–6, Bordesley 1886–1918; Chamberlain's henchman.   [6] Estimates; *H* 262. 146.

[7] Telegram sent by Kimberley on 7 June, Add MS 44226, f. 139.

[8] Estimates; *H* 262. 242.

coachman died today to our great concern. Back to the Durdans by midnight train. Read Stahr—Jowett's preface &c, Naville[1] & other tracts—Follies & Fancies.[2]

To B. JOWETT, Master of Balliol College, Oxford, 10 June 1881. Add MS 44544, f. 180.

I thank you very much for your Thucydides:[3] a gift ill deserved, but let me assure you, not ill appreciated.

Since it came to me this forenoon I have looked into the translation, sufficiently to appreciate its ease, care, and good English: and have read the Dedication in which Truth and Mercy have happily harmonised their claims, and the very interesting and suggestive Preface.

I well remember that in my undergraduate days I was wont to resist & resent the treatment of Thucydidean solecisms as blunders—like manners in Tennyson, they are not 'idle'—perhaps not wholly unlike the exordium of some of Fox's speeches, in which, as contemporaries report, he was wont to be overdone by the abundance of his matter, struggling to clothe itself in form.

You will soon I hope be free to run up to town, and I put in a humble plea for your company to breakfast some Thursday at ten, which I hope you will graciously accord. Only a notice is required, not a proposal.

11. Sat.

Wrote to Mr Hubbard—Ld Northbrook—Mr Pusey—Sir F. Leighton and minutes. Drive to Tadworthy Court. Read Stahr's Tiberius—Second Thoughts (finished)—Woodruff on the Trotter[4]—Life of Law.

To J. G. HUBBARD, M.P., 11 June 1881.   Add MS 44544, f. 180.

Your note[5] is very kind: like all that comes from you to me. In one point I am agreed with you. I think that *in foro conscientiae* Bradlaugh has committed a gross error by presenting himself to take the oath. He has no moral right to bisect it into a significant & an unmeaning part. The law prescribes it not merely as a promise but as an oath: and as an oath he does not take it. So I think that unhappy woman Baroness B. Coutts has committed a still grosser error in her marriage.[6] But *I* could not on that account interfere to prevent it; nor can I deny her legal right to do this deplorable moral wrong. I fear that here we part company. The H. of C. has acted, in my view, beyond its powers: has acted, as I should say in ignorant & lay phraseology, illegally. Can any good come of this? B. has fulfilled the law, or he has not. If he has, he should sit. If he has not, the courts should correct him. In contending that Atheists have no conscience, no doubt you have great predecessors. Locke, I think, argued this when he denied them toleration. Or it may have been that his philosophy did not allow of any conscience at all, & that he only thought that atheists had not the fear which serves the purpose of one.[7] But I cannot hold this

---

[1] E. Naville, probably *The Christ* (1880).   [2] [H. Lennard], *Follies and fancies* (1881).
[3] Jowett's translation, 2v. (1881), with preface and suffuse dedication to Sherbrooke.
[4] H. W. Woodruff, *The trotting horse of America* (1868).
[5] Of 10 June, Add MS 44095, f. 290, enclosing his speech, 'Parliamentary oaths and affiliations', 25 May 1881; conscience without God impossible.   [6] See 6 Sept. 80.
[7] Gladstone was right first time; see R. Klibansky and J. Gough, eds., J. Locke, *Epistola de Toleran-tia. A letter on toleration* (1968), 134: 'those who deny the existence of the Deity are not to be tolerated at all. Promises, covenants and oaths, which are the bonds of human society, can have no hold upon . . . an atheist'.

proposition in the face of such facts as Holyoake: such as (at one time) John S. Mill. And I am very doubtful of the proposition as a proposition of philosophy. God may have been pleased to impress upon our nature enough of himself to imply the rudimentary obliga- tion & faculty which may suffice for some natures, though not for the common run. What I think as to any further legislation is that no good is to be drawn (sic)[1] by including Agnostics & Pantheists and yet excluding Atheists: that it is best to recognise frankly that religious differences are not to entail civil disabilities: & in regard to the present con- troversy that it tends to weaken reverence for religion in the body of the people.

12. *Trin. S.*

Kew Ch 11 a.m. and H.C.–Parish Ch at 3. Wrote to Ld Kimberley–Sir T. Chambers–Ld Granville–Mr Godley 1.2. & minutes. Read Life of Law– Sermons and Tracts–Gospel for 19th Century. Royal party aft. & till midnight. I did not show all the time. Conversation with P. of Wales–Princess of Wales– Count Redern–Mr Chaplin.

To LORD KIMBERLEY, colonial secretary, 12 June 1881.   Add MS 44544, f. 181.

I am sorry to say I have not enough of personal knowledge or geographical information duly to advise upon these papers[2] without further explanations, though I have suggested an alteration of a phrase in the Telegram which does not touch the substance.

I conjecture that they bear materially 1. upon the question of the powers to be reserved to the Resident, 2. upon the expediency of full & direct assurances from the Boer leaders themselves with a view of giving confidence to the natives. As regards the former of these, it may be that there will be difficulty in the exercise of large powers by the Resident, but our stipulating for these reserves our rights in ulterior contingencies. It is upon the ques- tion of protection for the natives that we shall justly be subjected to the sharpest scrutiny. I expect to be in D. St. between 11 & 12 tomorrow.

13. *M.* [*London*]

Wrote to Ld Castletown–The Queen 1.2. and minutes. Cabinet 2–4¼. H. of C. 4½–8½ & 9–1. Irish Land Bill.[3] Back to D. St at 12. Read Hodder Westropp on Development[4]–Life of Law. Saw Mr G.–Ld R.G.–Ld Granville–Mr Forster.

Cabinet. Monday June 13. 81. 2 PM.[5]
1. Local option. Resolution will not be supported by members of the Govt.[6]
3. Assassination literature: read: United Irishman. Doteul[?]: P. of Wales: sentence of death on Gladstone. Also the World. Statement to be submitted to the Govt.
3. Mr O'Shea's note & letter[7]
2. Relations with Govt. of Tunis: M. Roostan being Foreign Minister there—a. It has no bearing upon our treaty rights & affords no cause for alteration in our relations.[8]

---

[1] Secretary's comment.
[2] 'important despatch as to the natives in the Transvaal' sent by Kimberley on 11 June; Add MS 44226, f. 153.   [3] Working the bill; *H* 262. 361.
[4] H. M. Westropp, *The cycle of development* (1881).   [5] Add MS 44642, f. 186.
[6] Bright, for the govt., made the vote on Lawson's resolution free; *H* 262. 562.
[7] See next day.
[8] Théodore Roustan, French minister at Tunis, acted as 'intermediary' or foreign minister of the Bey; see Marsden, *British diplomacy and Tunis*, 76.

4. Considered whether to suppress the circulation in this country of the World & U. Irishman. State of the law to be ascertained.[1]

5. Harcourt's draft letter to Mayor of Liverpool:[2] suspended till we see our way as to measures.

6. Mr Forster explained the state of affairs in Ireland. Land League cannot be put down directly & absolutely without a new Law.[3]

14. Tu.

Wrote to The Queen—Mr O'Shea MP—Mr Forster—Signor Mancini and minutes. Ten to dinner: and evening party. Attended the Northcote marriage: the prettiest I ever saw.[4] H. of C. 2¼–7 and 10¾–12¾.[5] Saw Mr G.—Ld R.G.—Ld Granville—Sir Thos G. Read Scenes of Clerical Life.[6]

To W. H. O'SHEA, M.P., 14 June 1881.   Add MS 44544, f. 181.
'Private'.[7]

I have not failed to submit to my colleagues the letter and proposal which you have done me the honour to bring before me,[8] and which was of too much importance for me to enter upon except in concert with them.

We feel indebted to you for the earnest and just desire you feel to promote a prompt settlement of the Land question in Ireland, and for the zeal with which you have undertaken a difficult operation, in that view. But we do not see our way to any form of action on the basis you propose without raising difficulties, which might prove to be greater than any of those which we have at present to encounter. Some of these have reference to passing any proposal of this kind through Parliament; some to its effect upon those who may think themselves, or may be, over-rented in England or Scotland. I need not enter on the grave character of the financial drain, which would be added to the liabilities, possibly very large, already entailed by the measure upon the Treasury. In these are yet more serious considerations, which we cannot undertake to face, connected with the moral and political effect such as we think to be produced in Ireland by such a plan, particularly as regards the Land League and the new place (as I may say) which would be given to it, as the evident direction of Governmental action, in the estimation of the people. Glad as we should be to extend to all parties in Ireland that favourable temper with which the Bill has so largely [been] received, we must be careful not to forfeit or compromise the position which it actually holds; and must trust for its successful progress to the good sense of those who desire more, or desire less, and to the general convictions of the people of the three Kingdoms on which we think we can rely.

[1] Matter apparently not further discussed in cabinet.
[2] Probably on powder magazines anchored in the Mersey; matter passed to defence depts.; see *H* 262. 1822.
[3] Carlingford's diary, 14 June 1881: 'Spencer told me that while I was away, there was a discussion between Mr G. & a few members of the Cabinet about the personal questions of the Irish Government—& that the removal of both Cowper & OHagan was talked of—the latter useless to the executive—& the former, though a man of good judgment, would not act.'
[4] J. S. Northcote, Gladstone's godson (see 2 Feb. 50), m. Hilda Farrar.
[5] Land Bill and Lawson's resolution (see 13 June 81); *H* 262. 494.
[6] George Eliot, *Scenes of Clerical Life*, 2v. (1858).
[7] In Hammond, 223.
[8] Letter of 10 June, Add MS 44269, f. 5., enclosing mem., already read to Parnell, on amndt. of the Land Bill to compensate, by an Exchequer grant, landlords who reach rent agreements with tenants; Parnellites would then let the Bill through. O'Shea's mem. is docketed 'circulate to Cabinet'.

15. Wed.

Wrote to Ld Advocate—Ly Huntley—Ld Granville 1.2.—Mr Chittenden (U.S.)—
The Queen & minutes. Cabinet 2–4¾. Saw Mr Morley & Bristol Depn[1]—Mr G.—
Ld R.G.—Ld F.C.—Mr Forster—Mr Booth—Mr Irving. Lyceum Theatre 8–11¼:
saw Othello. Booth's performance highly wrought: but I should think him
better fitted for Iago.[2] Read Scenes of Clerical Life.

Cabinet. Wed June 15. 2 PM.[3]
1. Business in H of C: Transvaal debate: WEG's answer considered; Army Discussion
   25th Ju?; Comm[ittee] Land Bill.
2. Terms of Transvaal counter-motion. agreed on.[4]
3. Land Bill. Fair Rent. May be stated in general terms.[5]
4. Letter to Consul at Tunis on communication with Roostan approved:[6] also a representation to be made respecting the protection of Tunisian subjects in Egypt. It wd. not be
   eo nomine.
5. Italian settlement on the Red Sea. English ship to accompany Italian as requested.
6. Forster mentioned the subject of arrears in Ireland: which he will touch more fully at
   the next Cabinet. Character of the current evictions in Ireland.
7. Nolan's bill—will not support.[7]

To G. R. CHITTENDEN of Illinois, 15 June 1881.   Add MS 44544, f. 182.

I have had the honour to receive your letter of May 28,[8] and I am much gratified by the
feeling which has been shown towards me by the inhabitants of the settlement which
they have been pleased to term Gladstone.[9]
   The sympathy between our two countries is of ever growing strength, and is maintained through a thousand channels: it is always a matter of pleasure to me when one is
added to the number.
   With every wish for the prosperity of the local community, and of the great nation to
which it belongs . . .

16. Th.

Wrote to Ld Chancellor—Ld Granville—Mr Monk—Mr Price—Ld Ailesbury—
Mr Williams—The Queen & minutes. Nine to breakfast. Conversation on

[1] Presenting on behalf of the Bristol Operatives' Liberal Association a silver claret service; letter
of thanks in *T.T.*, 24 June 1881, 9f.
[2] Edwin Booth, 1833–93, American actor and brother of Lincoln's assassin; alternated Othello
and Iago with Irving.
[3] Add MS 44642, f. 189.
[4] Undated holograph note reads (ibid., f. 192): 'Transvaal answer: 1. Potchefstroom. 2. questn. not
whether in abstract desirable. 3. Commission on Land Bill.' The amndt. to the tory resolution on 25
July was moved by Rathbone, a liberal back-bencher; *H* 263. 1784.
[5] Undated holograph note reads (ibid., f. 191): 'Judicial tenant right under pre-emption. It is
agreed that, when the landlord wishes to take a sum less than the fair rent which the Court has fixed
or would fix, the tenant is not entitled to have the margin between that sum & the fair rent reckoned
as part of the basis of his tenant right.'
[6] See Marsden, op. cit., 76.
[7] Nolan's Suspension of Evictions (Ireland) Bill had been 1°R on 14 June; *H* 262. 564.
[8] Not found.
[9] i.e. Gladstone, Illinois.

Revised Version—Robertson Smith[1]—*inter alia.* Saw Mr G.—Ld R.G.—Mr Bryce—Mr Th. . . . H. of C. $4\frac{1}{4}$-$8\frac{1}{4}$ & 9-1: Irish Land Bill.[2]

17. *Fr.*

Wrote to Mr Playfair—Mr Biddell MP—Ld Granville—M. Zancoff—C.G.—The Queen and minutes. H. of C. 2-7. I. Land Bill.[3] Saw Mr G.—Ld R.G.—A.G. for Ireland—Mr Welby. German play 8-10.[4] Read Scenes from Cler. Life—Germ. Tr. Winter's Tale & Othello.

18. *Sat.* [*Windsor*]

Wrote to C.G.—Ld Chancellor—Mr Hughes—Ld Hartington—Ld Kimberley & minutes. Found Jim Wortley old & weak. Saw Mr G.—Ld Granville—The Wortleys—Mrs Walker. Reached Windsor at 5. Two hours drive & 1 hour walk with the Dean gave ample scope for confidential conversation. Read Winter's Tale—Ellenborough's Diary.[5]

To LORD KIMBERLEY, colonial secretary, 18 June 1881.   Add MS 44544, f. 183.

In view of a Transvaal debate a fortnight or 3 weeks hence, it is very desirable that when it comes it should find *main* points already settled in S. Africa and beyond the risk of disturbance.

In this I have no doubt you will agree;[6] and it occurs to me to suggest whether it would be well for you to convey a hint to Robinson or Wood on this subject.

19. *1. S. Trin.*

Garrison Church mg. by order of the Prince of Wales. Luncheon afterwards, & survey of the barracks which was tiring but instructive. Saw Col. Hume[7]—Mr Chaplin—Captain Finch—Lady Spencer. St Georges Chapel aft. Saw Princess Christian—Mr Pearson. Walk with the Dean & a quiet evening. Lady Ponsonby yesterday 'Betty' today. Wrote to Mrs Wortley—Ld Granville—Mr Lowell and minutes.

20. *M.* [*London*]

Wrote to Ld Granard—Ld Granville—Lady M. Alford—Mr Spottiswood—The Queen—Ld Chancellor—Mr Bradlaugh—& minutes. H. of C. $4\frac{1}{4}$-$8\frac{1}{4}$ and 9-$1\frac{1}{2}$. (Irish Land Bill).[8] Back to London 11.30. Saw Mr G.—Ld R.G.—Mr Seymour—Ld Granville—Mr Forster. Read Scenes from Clerical Life Chamberlain's Speech.[9]

[1] See 24 Apr. 81.
[2] Spoke on Tunis; *H* 262. 652.
[3] *H* 262. 773.
[4] 'Wintermarchen' ('The Winter's Tale') at the Theatre Royal by the visiting Saxe-Meiningen company; *T.T.*, 17 June 1881, 8f.
[5] E. Law, *Lord Ellenborough. A political diary 1828-1830*, 2v. (1881).
[6] Kimberley did agree, and wired to Wood; Add MS 44226, f. 155.
[7] Colonel Henry Hume of the Queen's bodyguard.   [8] *H* 262. 867.
[9] Of 7 June, reprinted as a pamphlet; see 8 June 81.

To C. BRADLAUGH, M.P., 20 June 1881.   Bradlaugh MS 858.

I have the honour to acknowledge the receipt of your letter, in which you desire to have an interview with me on the subject of your seat for Northampton and your exclusion from the House of Commons.

On reflection, I am of opinion that it will be far better if our communications are carried on by writing on this particular subject. You are aware to how considerable an extent Liberal and public interests have been brought into prejudice by untrue suppositions as to communication between you and the Government. Now there is no change whatever in the spirit in which we should desire to approach the question, much as we may be hampered by its difficulties. But whether the difficulties be great or otherwise, I am sure it is expedient that there should be no room for misrepresentation as to what may pass between us, and that with reference to the interests of justice in the case there should be a record of what we say and do.

I rely upon your candour with the utmost confidence to interpret aright the purport of this letter.[1]

21. Tu.

Wrote to Ld Shaftesbury—Ld Rosebery—Ld Chamberlain—The Queen—Ld Granville—Lady M. Alford and minutes. Read Speech of Mr Evarts[2]—Scenes from Clerical Life. Saw Mr G.—Ld R.G.—Ld F.C.—Gov. of Bank—Ld Granville— Mr Morier—Danish Minister. H. of C. 2–7. Irish Land.[3]

22. Wed.

Wrote to Ld Granville—Mr Thorold Rogers—The Queen—Ld F. Cavendish—Ld Rosebery and minutes. Dined at Ld Breadalbane's: Devonshire House afterwards. Saw Mr G. Ld R.G.—Ld F.C.—The Greek Minister. Tea at Holland House. Saw Ld & Lady Lytton. Saw two: one case good [R]. Read Tiberius— Scenes from Clerical Life (dft).

To LORD F. C. CAVENDISH, financial secretary,   Bodley MS Eng. Lett. e. 141, f. 39.
22 June 1881. '*Early*'.

See Mr. Fawcett within.[4] The subject is too stiff and too large to be dealt with on an Irish Land day; so I would propose Wed. next at 2.30 if it suit you.

As far as I have looked into the matter, my attention is drawn to several points. 1. I am not quite satisfied with the expectation of 'no loss' as a basis for an operation of this extent and risk. It seems to me that when the Government undertakes (which it should of course only do on special grounds) a business, that business ought to offer the expectation of a reasonable profit. 2. I feel the greatest difficulty in acceding to a proposition that the Companies may in the great towns, or at such points as they may select, compute with us in carriage and delivery while we pay them half our gross receipt at a fixed and profitable rate for the simple act of conveyance. In the case of the Telegraphs we absolutely refused the purchase except on condition of monopoly. Is it now proposed that we

---

[1] Further letter, of 24 [*recte* 23?] June, in *T.T.*, 7 July 1881, 10f.
[2] W. M. Evarts, 'Speech at the International Monetary Conference' on 19 May (1881).
[3] *H* 262. 994. And the Gladstones had a party: 'Mrs G's evening party. . . . Curious and interesting to see G. commenting on his own picture (by Millais) on an easel in the room, simply as a work of art. G. looked much happier than his picture'; Phillimore's diary.
[4] On the parcel post: not traced.

shall in this traffic pay one half of a hard and fast sum to the Companies for all the business we do at the profitable points, and at the same time leave them to carry at lower rates and so put us out of business at those points, and console ourselves by the privilege of relieving the Companies from the business of the country parcel post which they have shown themselves totally incompetent to perform. 3. I am desirous to know whether we are *free* to fall back upon the proposal to deal with the Companies as agents. 4. I wish also to be exactly informed as to the present power of the P[ost] M[aster] G[eneral]. Is there any thing to prevent his extending as he may think fit his present parcels Post, except that the Companies may in new contracts make a higher charge for conveyance? If there is not, he has a vantage ground which ought not, it would seem, to be lightly surrendered. All these points I will mention to the P.M.G.

23. *Th.*

Wrote to Mr Bradlaugh MP.—Ld Carrington—Mr Lea MP—Archim. Duchich[1]—Mr Synan MP—Ld Shaftesbury—The Queen—The Prince of Wales and minutes. Dined at Sir C. Forsters. Thirteen to breakfast. Saw Mr Evarts—Ld Wolverton—Mrs Craven—Mr Blake—Ld Kenmare—Mr G—Ld R.G.—Mr H[amilto]n—Mrs J.S. Wortley. H. of C. $4\frac{1}{2}$–$8\frac{1}{4}$ & $9\frac{3}{4}$–2. Irish Land Bill.[2] Read Scenes from Clerical Life—India past & present.[3]

24. *Fr.*

Wrote to Ld Hartington—Mr Forster 1.2.—Sir R. Blennerhassett—Mr Chamberlain—Ld Kimberley—Sir Thos G.—The Queen and minutes. Saw Rions (Beresford) [R]. Saw Mr G.—Ld R.G.—Ld Granville. Pictures & drawings (Agnew). H. of C. 9–$1\frac{1}{2}$ (Foreign Policy).[4] Read Scenes from Cl. Life.

To LORD KIMBERLEY, colonial secretary, 24 June 1881.   Add MS 44544, f. 186.

As to Consuls for the Transvaal I entirely concur.[5] The case is stronger than that of the Ionian Islands, if there be a difference. *There*, our controul of the foreign relations was I think an inferential abridgment of a sovereignty which was admitted to remain in the Septinsular Republic. Here, it is a portion of Sovereignty expressly reserved by us, as a portion of the Suzerainty, at the time when the Suzerainty is constituted.

25. *Sat.* [*Littlebury's, Mill Hill*]

Wrote to The Queen—Ld Granville—Mr Godley—Duke of Bedford—Sir Thos Bateman—Sir Thos McClure and minutes. Cabinet 12–$2\frac{1}{2}$. Saw Mr G.—Ld R.G.—Ld Houghton—Mr Plunkett—Stephen Lawley—Grillion's to breakfast

[1] Nicephore Duchich, Serbian writer and patriot; described by Hamilton as 'a great Serbian "swell", half soldier, half priest', in mem. on him at Add MS 44470, f. 102.
[2] *H* 262. 1125.
[3] Possibly early version of J. Samuelson, *India past and present* (1889).
[4] Spirited defence of the Concert in deb. on the 1878 Anglo-Turkish Convention; *H* 262. 1320.
[5] Kimberley reported, 23 June, Add MS 44226, f. 157, that rumours were probably false that the Boers were intending to appoint Consuls, but, to be sure, it was best to restate the Ionian precedent that 'Transvaalers abroad should be under the care of our Ministers and Consuls'.

10 a.m. Wortley Marriage $11\frac{1}{2}$.[1] Off at $3\frac{1}{2}$ to Littleburies.[2] Read Monaco[3]—Tiberius.

Cabinet June 25. 1881. Noon.[4]
1. As to taking days for Land Bill. To move on Tuesday [28 June] at 2 PM.
2. Levees. 1st Lords Private Secretary to look to having a quorum.[5]
3. Bradlaugh. Recital of communications.
4. Amendments in Clause 7 of Land Bill—see over [i.e. items at the end]
5. Lord Mayor's dinner. Sat. Aug 6.
6. Bimetallism. WEG stated his willingness to apply to the Bank on cause shown, but not to take the initiative.

1. Sir G. Campbell on admission of the landlord to the Court approved. 2. Law's amendment upon fair rent approved. 3. As to *rent* or valuation as the test in clause 5. Keep to rent.

26. 2. S. Trin.

Ch mg & aft. Wrote to Mr Hamilton—Bp of Lincoln. Read Life of Law (finished)—Revised Version—Gospel for 19 Cent—Macfarlanes Sermons (unsatisfactory).[6]

27. M. [London]

Wrote to Dalrymple—Mr Grant Duff—Bp of Lincoln—Ld Hartington—Sir R. Cross—Mr Parker M.P.—Mr Cain[e] MP.—Duc d'Aumale—The Queen and minutes. H. of C. $5\frac{1}{4}$-$8\frac{1}{4}$ and 9-1. (I. Land).[7] Saw Mr G.—Ld F.C.—Ld Sydney—Mr Welby—Sir H. Ponsonby—Sir S. Northcote. Went off to town at 10. Then to Windsor for an audience: cheerful & gracious. Read Scenes from Clerical Life—Stahr's Tiberius.

To LORD HARTINGTON, Indian secretary, 27 June 1881.   Add MS 44544, f. 187.

1. I have sent your letter on bimetallism to F.C.[8] I rather suppose it was written before you had seen the Treasury letter of Saturday—which I suppose went on that day, when it passed (after Cabinet) through my hands.
2. I should think it pretty clear that there may be cases for promotion to G. Duff's place[9]—a representative Under Sec's position is rather a high one. No doubt Kimberley will have his say on this subject.

---

[1] Caroline Susan Theodora, da. of J. A. Stuart-Wortley, m. this day Norman de l'Aigle Grosvenor, 1845-98, s. of Lord Ebury.
[2] Aberdeen's house at Mill Hill.
[3] A tract on Monaco with 'both curious and painful particulars' which he sent to the Queen; Guedalla, *Q*, ii. 164; very probably J. Polson, *Monaco, and its gaming tables* (4 eds. in 1881).
[4] Add MS 44642, f. 193.
[5] The Prince of Wales had complained at ministers' poor attendance; Lee, *Edward VII*, i. 516.
[6] J. Macfarlane, probably *Pulpit echoes* (1868).
[7] *H* 262. 1381.
[8] Letter of 25 June, and Gladstone's docket, Add MS 44145, f. 265; on need to consider working with Germany to support the value of silver.
[9] See 30 June, 27 July 81.

28. Tu.

Wrote to Ld Kimberley—Bishop of Truro—Mrs Adam—Williams & Co—Mr Bradlaugh—Mr Forster—Mr Welby—Ld Mayor—Rev. Mr Ouvry—The Queen and minutes. H. of C. 2½–7. I Land Bill.[1] Dined at the Club: evening party. Saw Mr G.—Ld R.G.—Ld F.C.—Duc d'Aumale. Home arrangements with C. Read Scenes from Clerical Life. The change to daily work (say from 24 hours to 36 per week in H. of C. on Land Bill) will be trying for my poor brain: but onwards and upwards must be my motto.

To LORD SPENCER, lord president, 28 June 1881.   Add MS 44544, f. 187.

I think you are right in supposing that the practical consideration of the question respecting Agriculture & Trade must stand over until the recess.[2] I think however that there is much force in what you say. With regard to printing & circulating, might not that stand over until the time for practical action arrives?

29. Wed. St Peter.

Wrote to Duc d'Aumale—The Queen—A.G. for Ireland—Sir T. Bateson—Ld E. Clinton—Mr Howe—Mr Goschen and minutes. Saw Mr G.—Ld R.G. Conclave on Parcels Post.[3] Read Scenes from Cler. Life. Dined at Sir J. Goldsmids. Conversation with many Ladies: with Mr Lowell on the assassination[4]—Literature. Saw Four [R]. H. of C. 12¼–6. I Land Bill.[5]

30. Th.

Wrote to Sir R. Wilson—Messrs Farrer—The Queen—Ld Craven—Mr P.J. Smythe—Ld Norreys & Mr Bustic.[6] Captain Aylmer and minutes. H. of C. 4¾–8¼ & 9¼–1. Irish Land Bill. A good day.[7] Conclave on succession to Grant Duff.[8] Saw Mr G.—Ld R.G.—Ld F.C.—Ld Kimberley—Ld Granville—Mr Howe—Dr Weymouth—Mr Rodwell—Mr Morley MP. Read Scenes from Cler. Life. Nine to breakfast.

To Sir C. RIVERS WILSON, comptroller-general of the   Add MS 44544, f. 189.
national debt office, 30 June 1881.

I do not think after receiving your kind message that I need trouble you to call, & I have the fear that I might accidentally say something to traverse or hamper the proceedings of Sir C. Dilke in whom we have perfect confidence.

My general position is that of one who looked on the Treaty of 1860 as purely excep-

[1] Successfully moved that the Land Bill take precedence; *H* 262. 1490.
[2] Untraced enclosure sent by Spencer on 25 June; Add MS 44308, f. 134.
[3] See to Cavendish, 22 June 81.
[4] Presumably of Lincoln; Garfield was assassinated on 2 July 1881 and d. 19 September; see 21, 26 July 81.
[5] Sixteenth day in cttee.; *H* 262. 1546.
[6] *Sic*; unidentified.
[7] *H* 262. 1660.
[8] Who had been offered Madras; he was eventually succeeded at the colonial office by Courtney, Rosebery becoming undersecretary at the home office.

tional, who has little faith in Tariff Treaties & much sense of the false position into which the negotiators are often thrown; and who believes the English nation to be strong enough in its commercial position to let 'the world wag' and take its own course; relying upon this that every country which adopts protection thereby so far disables itself from effectually competing with us in the markets of the rest of the world.

But I do not venture on any rigid or hasty application of these rules to particular cases where our countrymen may not be agreed.

Friday Jul. One. 1881.

Wrote to Cardinal Newman—Ld Edw. Clinton—Govr of Bank—Mr F. Leveson—The Queen and minutes. Read Lettres d'une Bourgeoise.[1] Saw Mr G.—Ld R.G.—Mr Fowler—Mr Sullivan—Mr Maguire—Mr Laing. H. of C. $2\frac{1}{2}$–7 & $9\frac{1}{2}$–1. I. Land Bill. Good & bad.[2]

To A. E. WEST, 1 July 1881.   Add MS 44544, f. 190.

Mr. Laing would like to put a question as to the falling off in the Excise, if I *could give him a reassuring answer.* I told him I was rather doubtful about this, though I knew no very desponding view was taken at Somerset House. Please to consult, & advise me what should be done.[3]

2. Sat. [*Littlebury's, Mill Hill*]

Wrote to Card. Newman—Mr de Coverley—Mr Bradlaugh—Mr Chamberlain—Mr Smith MP—The Queen and minutes. Saw Mr G.—Ld R.G.—Mr Welby—Ld Spencer—Ld Kimberley cum Mr Childers—Mr Farrar. Cabinet 12–2$\frac{1}{4}$. Off to Littleburys at 4. The place becomes on each visit more curious & interesting.[4] Read Contempt. Rev. on Bence Jones[5]—Lettres d'une Bourgeoise.

Cabinet. Sat. Jul 2. 81. Noon.[6]
1. Bills. See Separate Mem.—result of conversation.
2. Ld Granville. The trial at Constantinople. Wait for the report of Ld Dufferin.
3. Bulgaria. Labanoff's note: new proposal, for pressure on the Bulgarian assembly. Adhere to our first answer.[7]
4. Plan for dealing with arrears—
   a. condition to be payment by tenant of the two last half years b. charge on Church Fund c. arrears of two years, not three, to be dealt with.

For July 4. 81 [sc. *2. 81*][8]
0 1. Parliamentary Oaths; 0 2. Corrupt Practices; 3. Bankruptcy; 0 4. Ballot amendments; 5. Alkali; 6. Rivers Conservancy; 7. Educ. Endowments Scotland; 8. Naval Discipline

---

[1] Not found.   [2] *H* 262. 1835.
[3] Laing put the question on 5 July; Gladstone explained the decrease as resulting from 'the different distribution of the Malt Duty and the Beer Duty' over the year; *H* 263. 32.
[4] Nell Gwynn had lived there, see 19 June 80.   [5] *C.R.*, xl. 127 (July 1881).
[6] Add MS 44642, f. 195.
[7] Also agreed to await Dufferin's report on the situation; C.A.B. 41/15/30.
[8] Add MS 44642, f. 196. Gladstone's list is extracted from a longer list supplied in another hand; ibid., f. 198. '0' before an item indicates its abandonment; see 4 July 81n.

Amendment; 9. Regulation of the Forces; 10. Ballot continuance; 11. Corrupt Places suspension of writs; 12. Judicature Amendment; 0 13. Irish County Government; 14. National Debt & Local Loans; 0 15. Thames River; 0 16. Merchant Shipping Amendment; 17. Bill Charging Irish University on the Church Fund.

To C. BRADLAUGH, M.P., 2 July 1881.   Add MS 44544, f. 190.

In conformity with a previous intimation I have to inform you that the Cabinet have this day considered their position with reference to the demands of the Irish Land Bill on the time of Parliament, and the effect of those demands on our means of proceeding with other subjects. Among them the Parliamentary Oaths Bill holds a prominent place; especially inasmuch as the expectations of its easy progress, which prevailed on the first suggestion of the Bill, and materially influenced the decision of the Government, have declined or disappeared.

It has been found that it will not be possible for us to proceed with the greater part of the measures mentioned in the Speech from the Throne, and under these circumstances you will not be surprised at my adding that we do not intend to proceed further with the motion for leave to bring in a Bill for the purpose of dealing with Parliamentary Oaths.

I lose no time in making known to you, as I promised, the decision at which we have arrived. I shall announce it on Monday in Parliament.

To J. CHAMBERLAIN, president of the board of trade,   Add MS 44544, f. 190.
2 July 1881.

I return your inclosures[1] which have only reached me after the Cabinet. They could not I think have altered the decision. They show that we may have awkward days ahead; but one trouble to a certain extent shuts out another.

3. 2 S. Trin.

Ch mg. (with H.C.) and evg. Friends came in aft: the Spencers, as inquirers. Wrote to Attorney General—The Speaker. Read Science & the Bible[2]—Gospel for the 19th Cent. finished—Lectures on the Ch. of Scotland[3]—Dean of Peterb. on Revised Version.[4]

To H. B. W. BRAND, the Speaker, 3 July 1881.   Brand MSS 267.

It appeared to me on Friday or Thursday, when I was questioned about the absence of Ministers at question-time, & the suggestion fell from me on the moment that the questions might be arranged so as to bring together those to each Minister severally, that the House liked the idea of it. I do not know whether it is worth while to attempt a piecemeal reform where much more is evidently required. But if they were to be so arranged, I would ask, by the privilege of my office, to have my questions last.

To Sir H. JAMES, attorney general, 3 July 1881.   Add MS 44544, f. 190.

I think you should see a letter which Chamberlain has had from Labouchere inclosing one from Bradlaugh to himself.[5] And I shall be desirous to know whether you think that

[1] Letters from Labouchere and Bradlaugh; see next day and Add MS 44125, f. 81.
[2] Probably T. L. Brunton, *The bible and science* (1881).
[3] Perhaps J. Anderson, *Scotland in early Christian times* (1881).
[4] J. J. S. Perowne, perhaps *The study of holy scripture* (1879).
[5] See 2 July 81.

there is any likelihood of serious embarrassment. I wrote to Bradlaugh yesterday to tell him that the Government could do nothing more with the Parliamentary Oaths Bill during the session. If B. resorts to physical force, & mischief results, it will be very difficult to carry on the resistance to him by physical force only. I wish it were possible for him to get an appeal to a court of Law.

4. M. [London]

Back to D. St at 12.30. Wrote to Mr Chamberlain—Lady Huntingtower—Duke of Bedford—Mr Laing MP—U.S. Minister—Sir T. Sinclair—Ld Carlingford—The Queen and minutes. H. of C. $4\frac{1}{2}$–$8\frac{1}{2}$ & $9\frac{1}{4}$–1. Irish Land Bill.[1] Read Tiberius. Scenes from Cler. Life. Saw Mr G.—Ld R.G.—and others.

To S. LAING, M.P., 4 July 1881.   Add MS 44544, f. 191.

I think, after inquiry,[2] I can undertake to answer a question about the revenue in such a manner as to have a composing effect—and of this I lose no time in informing you.

5. Tu.

Wrote to The Queen—Mr Welby & minutes. Saw Mr G.—Ld R.G.—Ld F.C.—Mr Trevelyan—Mr Forster. H. of C. $2\frac{1}{4}$–7 and $9\frac{1}{2}$–$12\frac{1}{4}$ Irish Land Bill. 289 to 157 on Clause VII: a very decisive division.[3] Read Tiberius. Scenes from Cler. Life.

6. Wed.

Wrote to Dean of Carlisle—The Queen & minutes. Read Tiberius—Gerard Gunpowder plot[4]—Scenes from Cler. Lif. Saw Mr Hine—Mr Cundall[5]—D. of Bedford—Count Menabrea. Saw Scott. X. H. of C. 12–3 and $8\frac{3}{4}$–6.[6] Mr Pennington's reading at $3\frac{1}{4}$. Princess Louise & a party of 22 to dinner.

7. Th.

Wrote to Lady James—Rev. Dr Allon—Professor Adams[7]—Ld Kimberley 1.2.— The Queen & minutes. Read Scenes from Cler. Life. Conclave on peerages $2\frac{1}{2}$– $3\frac{1}{2}$.[8] Nine to breakfast. Saw Mr G.—Ld R.G.—Mr Welby—Ld Granville—Mr D. Corrie. H. of C. $4\frac{3}{4}$–$8\frac{1}{2}$ & $9\frac{1}{2}$–1. Irish Land Bill.[9]

[1] Also making statement on abandoning of bills; H 262. 1967.

[2] See to West, 1 July 81n.

[3] The clause dealt with the determination by the Court of rent of present tenancies; he also spoke on the new French tariff; H 263. 37, 52. Phillimore dined with the Gladstones this evening, with 'Lord & Lady Aberdeen & A. Wood. . . . G. radiant with his last victory on the Irish Bill. "It is either the Govt. bill or the Land League now (he said to me). My bill is really a landlord's bill". G wonderful, quite fresh & except in outward appearance quite young'; Phillimore's diary.

[4] J. Gerard, ed. J. Morris, Condition of Catholics under James I (1871).

[5] Probably Joseph H. Cundall, 1818–95; superintendent of publications at S. Kensington museum 1866–90.

[6] Land Bill; H 263. 140.

[7] Offering the post of astronomer-royal (which he declined) to John Couch *Adams, 1819–92; professor of astronomy in Cambridge from 1858; discovered 'Neptune'.

[8] Decided to postpone creations till the Land Bill had passed; Bahlman, Hamilton, i. 150.

[9] And questioned on bimetallism; H 263. 255.

To LORD KIMBERLEY, colonial secretary, 7 July 1881.   Add MS 44544, f. 191.

The point raised by me is only touched in the first lines of your letter on 'British subjects'.[1] It is not quite the same question whether the severance ought to be so sharply
exhibited as it will be by the use of the phrase 'British subjects' for their neighbours or
residents among them in documents where they also are named. On this account L[?]
suggested 'persons under the sovereignty of H.M.' which touches the exact point of distinction. There may be a better phrase—or there may be no Alternative but the one I
rather regret.[2]

8. Fr.

Wrote to Ld Chancellor—Mr J.A. Bright—Mr A. Pease MP—Mr M. Arnold—Mr
Hunter—Ld Kimberley—The Queen and minutes. Read Tiberius. Saw Mr G.—
Ld R.G.—Ld F.C.—Mr Forster—Ld Thurlow. H. of C. 2¼-7 and 9–1. Irish Land
Bill.[3]

To MATTHEW ARNOLD, 8 July 1881.   Add MS 44544, f. 192.

The volume which Mr. Macmillan has sent me has only reached me simultaneously
with the later volume which I owe to your kindness.[4]

The interest of a book of extracts from Byron, such as you with sympathetic insight are
sure to have made, can well bear any competition. Yet Burke must always be a real
competitor. Even when he is (I think) largely wrong, as on the French Revolution, he
does not lose his charm. Being as he is on other political subjects splendidly right, the
brilliancy of his genius shines out without a cloud; & no surfeit or nausea of Irish business
in the House of Commons can ever mar the pleasure with which I ever recur to Burke's
writings upon Ireland.

But I hope that no long time will elapse before I am in a condition to appreciate by
actual experience both these most acceptable presents.

I thank you for affording me your valuable testimony to the merit of Mr. O'Conor.[5] The
time of year has now just arrived, when the Fund for the year becomes available; & I hope
soon to be able to consider the several & commonly numerous claims upon its limited
account.

9. Sat. [York Lodge, Twickenham]

Wrote to Sir H. Thring—Mr di Cesnola—The Queen and minutes. 4–5½. Drove
to York Lodge.[6] Cabinet 12–2¾. Saw Mr G.—Ld R.G.—Ld Kimberley—Ld
Spencer—Ld Northbrook—Mr C. Russell—Mr Walpole jun. Read Life of Sir R.
Peel by Barnett Smith.[7]

---

[1] Of 6 July, Add MS 44226, f. 172: great difficulties 'if we treat citizens of the Transvaal State as
"British subjects", because they are under the Suzerainty of the Queen', because it will also be used
to describe Britons resident in the Transvaal.

[2] Kimberley replied, 8 July, ibid., f. 178 with further reasons, including fear of Natal gravitating
towards Transvaal: important to maintain two tiers of status.

[3] *H* 263. 365.

[4] *The poetry of Byron, chosen and arranged by Matthew Arnold* (1881); *The letters, speeches and tracts of
Edmund Burke on Irish affairs, collected and arranged by Matthew Arnold* (1881).

[5] Gladstone gave a £50 pension to Charles Patrick O'Conor, b. 1837?, recommended by Arnold as
'a poor Irishman . . . he has a small vein, but it is a genuine one'; Add MS 44470, f. 182.

[6] Grant Duff's house in Twickenham.   [7] G. Barnett Smith, *Sir Robert Peel* (1881).

Cabinet. Sat. Jul. 9 (Noon) 1881.[1]
Irish Land Bill. a. Commissioners to be appointed. b. Finance. Mr Smith. authority to act for the best. c. Court. d. Lease. e. Arrears. NB Prelim Committee to limit. f. Emigration. g. Registry.
(Naval Discipline Act Amendment Bill. Conversation with Northbrook).

10. 3 S. Trin

Twickenham Ch mg & evg. Music extremely good. Read Life of Bp Seabury[2]— Bp Abraham Sermon on Job.[3] Stephens, Xty & Islam.[4] Saw Ld Ampthill—Mr Grant Duff.

11. M. [*London*]

Wrote to Rev. Dr Allon—Rev. S.E.G. Tel.—H.M. Tel. and l & minutes. Read Sir R. Peel—G. Elliot [*sic*]. Back to D. St at 11.15. Saw Mr G.—Ld R.G.—Ld F.C.—Sir J. Goldsmid—Ld Kimberley—Mr D. Grant—Rivingtons. Luncheon at Ld Granville's to meet King of the Sandwich Islands.[5] H. of C. $4\frac{1}{2}$-$8\frac{1}{2}$ and 9-$1\frac{1}{2}$. Irish Land Bill: &c.[6]

12. Tu.

Wrote to Ld Granville—The Queen—and minutes. H. of C. $2\frac{1}{4}$-7 and $10\frac{1}{2}$-$12\frac{3}{4}$. Irish Land Bill.[7] Saw Mr G.—Ld R.G.—Mr Forster—Count Münster and others. Read Scenes from Clerical Life (finished)—Life of Peel. Dined at German Embassy to meet Prince & Princess of Prussia.

13. Wed.

Wrote to Ld Lyttelton—Sig. Francesco[8]—Ld Spencer—Ld Chancellor—The Queen—Mr Heneage & minutes. Read Life of Landor[9]—Life of Stubbs.[10] Saw Mr G.—Ld R.G.—The Speaker—Mr Forster—D. of Buckingham—W.H.G. H. of C. $12\frac{1}{4}$-$5\frac{3}{4}$.[11] Dined with Ld S. at S. Kensington.

14. Th.

Wrote to The Queen 1.2.3.—Sir W. Harcourt and minutes. Read Inglesant Romance[12]—Life of Landor. H. of C. $4\frac{3}{4}$-$8\frac{3}{4}$ and $9\frac{1}{2}$-$1\frac{1}{4}$. Irish Land: an outbreak.[13] Nine to breakfast. Saw Mr. G.—Ld R.G.—Mr Freeman—Ld Monck—Mr Ramsay—Mr Shaw?

---

[1] Add MS 44642, f. 201.
[2] E. E. Beardsley, *Life . . . of Samuel Seabury* (1881).
[3] C. J. Abraham; not found published.
[4] W. R. W. Stephens, *Christianity and Islam* (1877).
[5] King David KalaKana, 1836–91; elected king 1875; visited Europe 1881; crowned 1883.
[6] And spoke on the working of the Protection Act; *H* 263. 522, 542.
[7] *H* 263. 657.   [8] Thanking F. Francesco of Naples for a portrait; Hawn P.
[9] By S. Colvin (1881).
[10] E. T. Stubbs, *In Memoriam. H.M.M.S*[*tubbs*] (1877).   [11] *H* 263. 762.
[12] [J. H. Shorthouse], *John Inglesant; a romance* (1881); this tale of 17th-century Roman catholicism much impressed Gladstone, see to Doyle, 22 Oct. 81.
[13] Of opposition from Home Rulers on the emigration clause; *H* 263. 865.

15. *Fr.*

Wrote to Ld Granville—Rev. D. Smith—Sir J. Ramsden—The Queen—and minutes. A day of extraordinary heat: registering in the shade 92° up to 98°! H. of C. $2\frac{1}{4}$-7 and $9\frac{3}{4}$-12. I.L.B.[1] Saw Mr G.—Ld R.G.—Mr Forster—Mr Vernon—H.J.G. on Mr Currie's offer.[2] Dined with Lady James. Read John Inglesant.

16. *Sat.* [*Windsor*]

Wrote to The Queen—Mr Rathbone—Mr Maguire—Sir M.H. Beach—Ld Kimberley—Mr D. Currie—Mr Chamberlain and minutes. Read Lettres d'une Bourgeoise—Tiberius. Saw Mr G.—Ld R.G.—Mr Forster—Mr Welby. In the afternoon we had a tea party for the Prince & Princess [of Germany]. He was as always delightful: she talked abundant Liberalism of a deep-rooted kind. We went at 6.40 to Windsor: dined with the Queen.

17. *4 S. Trin.*

Eton Chapel mg: St Georges evg. Saw the Provost & the Master on the Revised Version: which none approve. Walk with the Dean: also with Ld Spencer. Wrote to Mr Forster. Read Life of Seabury—Stephen's Xty & Islam (finished).

18. *M.* [*London*]

Off at 10.30. Wrote to Ld Shaftesbury—Sir C.R. Wilson—Mr Picton—Ld Powerscourt—The Queen and minutes. H. of C. $4\frac{3}{4}$-$8\frac{3}{4}$ and $9\frac{1}{4}$-$1\frac{1}{4}$. Irish Land Bill.[3] Saw Rands [R]. Saw Mr G.—Ld R.G.—Mr G. Richmond—Mr Law—Mr W.H. Smith. Left Windsor 10.30 am. Read Lettres d'une Bourgeoise.

19. *Tu.*

Wrote to Mr Ingram—Sir Geo. Bowyer—The Queen 1.2.3. & minutes. Read Lettres &c. Q. Rev. on Walpole's Hist.[4] H. of C. $2\frac{1}{4}$-7 and $9\frac{1}{2}$-1.[5] Irish Land Bill. A sharp & long continued labour, full of interest and κίκυς:[6] the heaviest I have ever had: it will I think be followed by a severe fit of lassitude. Ten to dinner: open air. Saw Mr G.—Ld R.G.—Ld F.C.—Sir J. Lacaita. Cabinet 1.-2 P.M.

Cabinet. July 19. 1881. 1 A.M. [sc. *P.M.*][7]
I. Mr Healy's 2 year amendment. Accept.[8]
II. (1) To use every effort to finish Committee this week—Sitting on Saturday if necessary.

---

[1] *H* 263. 1014.
[2] Invitation for a cruise; declined next day; Add MS 44544, f. 194.
[3] *H* 263. 1139.
[4] *Q.R*, clii. 239 (July 1881).
[5] *H* 263. 1273.
[6] An Homeric term: 'strength' or 'vigour'.
[7] Add MS 44642, f. 202.
[8] Presumably the amndt. moved as a govt. amndt. this day to deem lessees as yearly tenants to gain the bill's benefits: *H* 263. 1302. See also 27 July 81.

(2) Monday unconditionally offered a. to Hicks Beach b. to Rathbone[1]
(3) Drop Charitable Trusts Bill.
(4) Shall probably ask after Land Bill is read a third time for the remaining days.
(5) With the intention of devoting the principal hours of each evening to Supply until it is finished, or nearly finished, setting aside imperative calls of public duty.
III. Bradlaugh. See L. to H.M.[2]

20. *Wed.*

Wrote to Mr Welby—The Queen—Mrs Th.—and minutes. H. of C. $12\frac{1}{4}$-$4\frac{1}{4}$ & $5\frac{1}{4}$-8. Irish Land Bill.[3] The residue is now chiefly for Forster—thank God for all His goodness. Saw Mr G.—Ld R.G.—Ld F.C.—Pr. of Wales—Princess of Wales— Ld Spencer. Dined at Ld Granville's. Saw Mrs Craven—Ld Stafford—Mr Leveson Gower & others. Read Lettres &c. Saw three [R].

21. *Th.*

Wrote to Mr G. Leeman—Mr Jordan MP.—Mr Farrar—Sir W. Dunbar—Mrs Garfield[4]—The Queen—Dean of Windsor—Ld E. Clinton—U.S. Minister—Ld Granville and minutes. Nine to breakfast. Saw Lady S. Opdebeeck—Mrs Th.— Mr Fraser—Sir R. Phillimore. Read Lettres &c. H. of C. $4\frac{3}{4}$-$8\frac{1}{4}$ and $9\frac{1}{2}$-$12\frac{3}{4}$.[5] 12 to dinner.

To Mrs GARFIELD, 21 July 1881.   Add MS 44544, f. 195.

You will I am sure excuse me, though a personal stranger, for addressing you by letter, to convey to you the assurance of my own feelings and those of my countrymen on the occasion of the late horrible attempt to murder the President of the United States, in a form more palpable at least than those of messages conveyed by Telegraph.

Those feelings have been feelings in the first instance of sympathy and afterwards of joy and thankfulness, almost comparable, and I venture to say only second to the strong emotions of the great nation of which he is the appointed head.

Individually I have, let me beg you to believe, had my full share in the sentiments which have possessed the British nation.

They have been prompted and quickened largely by what I venture to think is the ever growing sense of harmony and mutual respect and affection between the two countries, and of a relationship which from year to year becomes more and more a practical bond of union between us.

But they have also drawn much of their strength from a cordial admiration of the simple heroism which has marked the personal conduct of the President, for we have not yet wholly lost the capacity of appreciating such an example of Christian faith and manly fortitude.

This exemplary picture has been made complete by your own contribution to its noble and touching features, on which I only forbear to dwell because I am directly addressing you.

I beg to have my respectful compliments and congratulations conveyed to the President.[6]

[1] For the long-delayed Transvaal deb.; see 25 July 81.
[2] C.A.B. 41/15/32; legitimate for the executive to aid the Speaker.
[3] Deb. on the Commissioners; also spoke on the Transvaal; *H* 263. 1370, 1391.
[4] Lucretia, wife of J. A. Garfield, 1831-19 Sept. 1881; president of U.S.A. 1881: shot 2 July, expected to recover.   [5] Land Bill, and questioned on Potchefstroom; *H* 263. 1470, 1478.
[6] The letter was at once made public, a copy being sent to J. R. Lowell; see 26 July 81.

22. Fr.

Wrote to Messrs Farrer—Lady S. Opdebeck—Mr Dodson—Bp of Exeter—The
Queen and minutes. H. of C. $2\frac{1}{4}$-7 and 10-$1\frac{1}{2}$. We finished amidst hearty cheer-
ing the committee on the Irish Land Bill after 32 nights work. God be thanked.[1]
Dined at Ld Dalhousies. Saw Mr G.—Ld R.G.—Ld F.C.—Mr Hill—Sir C. Dilke.
Saw Hunter (12) [R]. Read Lettres d'une Bourgeoise.

23. Sat. [Littlebury's]

Wrote to The Queen—Lord Advocate—C.G.—Lady S. Opdebeeck—Ld Kimber-
ley—Dean of Windsor—Ld Granville—D of Argyll and minutes. Cabinet 12-2.
To Littleburys at 4. Saw Mr G.—Mr H.—Ld R.G.—Mr Forster—Ld E. Clinton.
Read Ld Ellenborough's Journal[2]—Lettres d'une Bourgeoise.

Cabinet. Saturday July 23. 81. 12 noon.[3]
2. Transvaal Debate. Discussed: Chamberlain to speak.
3. Rivers Conservancy. Agency to be prolonged.
4. Order of votes in Supply. Outline of plan.
5. Proposal to move Treaty negotiations to Paris. Minute sent in reply.
1. Transvaal Telegram:[4] enumerating the points on which the Boer leaders make or
anticipate difficulty.
(1) Controul of foreign affairs. Hold our ground. (2) Compensation for property taken
by Boers for loan purposes. Ditto. (3) Payment of gratuities to officers unwilling to
serve. Agree with Boers. (4) N[ative] L[ocation] Commission not to be Trustee for
Native Lands: but *Native Secretary.* (In former Tr. Republic, natives cd. *hold no land.*)
(Allegation that the natives have come into the country since Boers came). We see
great objections. (5) Native location Commission (districts where the Boers are not to
have land). Pres[ident] + Res[ident] + 3rd man agreed on by both. *Hold our ground.*
(6) Burgers & Hamilton pensions.—Disposed of. (7) Payment of Resident—We undertake it.
(8) Suzerainty. Questions on 'British Subjects'—? query distinguish. Outside Transvaal all
are British citizens. Inside Transvaal: a. Transvaal citizens. b. Other than Transvaal
citizens. Persons so registering before a certain date shall not be subject to military
service. Committee of Cabinet appointed[5]
Appointment of Resident: 1. De Coty. 2. Hudson: *preferred.*[6]

[1] *H* 263. 1722. 'At half-past one o'clock this morning Mr Gladstone shut up his papers, pulled
down his cuffs, tugged violently at the back of his coat, and walked out of the House amid loud
cheering from the Ministerialists'; Gladstone was much discomforted by a new coat worn for dinner
with the Prince of Wales at Dalhousie's; Lucy, 190.
[2] See 18 June 81.
[3] Add MS 44642, f. 203.
[4] Telegram from Robinson in Pretoria on progress of the Commission; this Cabinet discussion
left the settlement very close to the Convention as announced on 3 August, only the definition of
suzerainty being outstanding; Schreuder, 208.
[5] 'Committee of Cabinet on Transvaal Citizenship & other than Transvaal Citizenship: Kimberley; Chancellor; Harcourt; Chamberlain; Att. General?'; Add MS 44642, f. 205.
[6] T. Hudson was British Resident in Pretoria until 1883, leaving in disgrace after a land scandal;
Schreuder, 209.

To Mrs GLADSTONE, 23 July 1881.[1]   Hawarden MSS.

I do hope the sea air is doing you good and I am only sorry that your visit has been so shortly before the Transvaal debate which may tempt you back—I should be glad if I learned that you had determined to stay notwithstanding. But, be your visit short or long, may it do good. Yesterday was another long and stiff day but it afforded an interval 8–10 a.m. [*sic*] for a pleasant small dinner with the kind and pleasant Dalhousies.

At half past one we actually closed (after 32 days work) the Committee on the Land Bill, and it was reported to the House in a tumult of cheers. Just afterwards I came out & they kindly gave me another ringing cheer.

The Transvaal debate is expected to close on Monday.

The strange arrangement of Dean Stanley's funeral, which is to begin at 4 & last until 6 entirely shuts me out from the power of attending.

The affair of Emily Clinton sounds even worse than I had supposed for it seems that on Friday last the Master of the Rolls, I suppose in despair, agreed to the arrangement for her living with her mother and Mr Holer![2] I have seen E. Clinton who is sad enough about it all—Ever your afft WEG

[P.S.] Cabinet 12–2. Off to Littlebury I hope before 4.

To G. V. WELLESLEY, dean of Windsor, 23 July 1881.   Add MS 44544, f. 196.

I have thought much about the appointment & its various demands. Two cases of *transplantation* have been brought before me: Dean Liddell & Bishop Fraser. Both are good men; but my information about the latter is more direct & is to this point—that he desires escape from the burden of Manchester & would almost certainly take it.[3]

If so I think him better than any other man of those we have talked about as on the lines of promotion.

He would maintain generally all that is best in the tradition of Dean Stanley, & would carry on with great efficiency the work of this great metropolitan position, being at the same time an excellent preacher & head of a chapter.

Just escaped from the heavy work of the Land Bill. I *must* give Monday to picking up a little of the Transvaal case, on which, that very evening, we are to be tried for our lives.

They have contrived an hour for the funeral which to my great concern makes my attendance impossible.

I wish you could have slept—or could sleep—here, & on Tuesday morning we might talk at large.

24. 5. S. Trin.

Ch mg & evg. Wrote to Ld Kimberley. Read Scottish Church Lectures—Life of Bp Seabury—Harrison's Charge[4]—Dr Flint's & other Sermons.[5]

[1] Part in Bassett, 235.

[2] Newcastle's grand-da.; in June 1882 she m. Prince Alfonso Pamphilji, duc d'Avigliano.

[3] The deanery of Westminster was offered to Bp. J. Fraser, who declined it: 'it did not require ten minutes' thought to put it aside' (T. Hughes, *James Fraser* (1887), 317); see also to Acland, 2 Aug. 81 etc. Notes on later candidates (G. G. Bradley appt.) at 17 Aug. 81n.

[4] B. Harrison, 'The Church's work and wants at the present time' (1881).

[5] R. Flint, 'A sermon preached in St Giles' Edinburgh' (1881).

25. M. [London]

Wrote to Mr V. Stuart MP.[1]—The Queen—C.G.—Sir Thos G and minutes. H. of C. 4½–8½ & 9½–2¼. Spoke 1h. on Transvaal & voted in 314:205.[2] But I am too full of Ireland to be *free* in anything else. Saw Ld Kimberley—Mr G.—Ld R.G.—Ld F.C.—Sir H. Ponsonby—Sir R. Phillimore. Attended the *fino* portion of the lamented Dean Stanley's funeral service.

26. Tu.

Wrote to Mr Pease—Bp of Manchester—The Queen—Ld Hartington—Ld F.C.—U.S. Minister—Mr Oscar Wilde[3] & minutes. H. of C. 2½–7 and 10–12¾. Irish Land Bill. & a dangerous 'friendly' amendment, only beaten by 241–205; after a 'stout' speech from me.[4] Read Lettres d'une Bourgeoise. 10 to dinner. Saw Dean of Windsor—Ld Granville.

To J. R. LOWELL, American minister in London, 26 July 1881.   Add MS 44545, f. 2.

The heavy pressure of business has prevented me from acknowledging your very obliging & interesting letter of the 22nd current[5] until this day, when I have received your further letter of yesterday.

My letter to Mrs Garfield has acquired a celebrity which was in no way within my expectation, for my request to you was in the main an apology to you for adopting another channel for the expression of my sentiments instead of transmitting my congratulations to you as the representative of your country.

Although I really was innocent of courting the fame which you have given to my letter, yet when I consider that the effect, far beyond its own claims, which it appears to have produced is one of the kind which both you & I must desire, I must offer my cordial thanks both to you & your Government for the unmerited honour you & they have done me on this occasion.

I sincerely hope that the recent check in the course of the President's recovery has been purely temporary & without inconvenient consequences.

[P.S.] Though I have not mixed the questions, I am not the less obliged by what you have said of the Land Bill; the subject to me alike of earnest labour, lively hope, & I now almost venture to say commencing joy.

27. Wed.

Wrote to The Queen—Mr Childers—Ld Granville—Sir W. Harcourt—Mr Gorst MP—Mr O. Wilde—Ld Kimberley and minutes. Dined with the Leightons.

---

[1] Henry Villiers-Stuart, 1827–95; historian of Egypt, Irish land lord and liberal M.P. Co. Waterford 1873–4, 1880–5. See 12 July 72.

[2] Hicks-Beach's resolution criticising govt. policy in South Africa, with Rathbone's amndt. which was carried; *H* 263. 1847.

[3] Who had sent his *Poems* (1881); Add MSS 44470, f. 239, 44545, f. 1. See 1, 3 Aug. 81 and R. Hart-Davis, *The letters of Oscar Wilde* (1982), 79.

[4] Lord E. Fitzmaurice's amndt. to exempt from the judicial rent clause tenancies of more than £100, i.e. the large tenant farmers; *H* 263. 1942.

[5] Add MS 44470, f. 241: Lowell will telegraph the letter to Mrs Garfield of 21 July and include it in despatches; he also sent congratulations on the progress of the Land Bill: 'it will be a better monument than any in the Abbey'. Secretary Blaine's acknowledgement of the letter to Mrs Garfield, sent on 23 July, is at Add MS 44470, f. 250.

H. of C. 12¼-6. Irish Land: the port is in view.[1] Read Lettres d'une B. Saw Sir W. Harcourt—Mr G.—Ld R.G.—Sir R. Cross. Saw Murphy [R].

To Sir W. V. HARCOURT, home secretary, 27 July 1881.   MS Harcourt dep. 8, f. 89.
'*Private*'.

The time seems to have come when the vacant office[2] ought to be filled up. May I sound Rosebery, provided Kimberley is willing to take Courtney? I am persuaded 1. that under such an arrangement as we have talked of you will have no difficulty in the recess; 2. that any needful help on particular Bills can be afforded you—possibly through new arrangements upon next Session, *but at any rate* by the existing staff; notably by Hibbert whom I am sure Dodson could possibly spare.

But I do not think you as Home Secretary can escape the rather disagreeable duty of working the Wednesday Bills on behalf of the Government, and of doing this personally, whether you have an U. Sec. in the House or not.

[P.S.] I find both Granville and R. Grosvenor think on the whole Courtney is the right man.[3]

28. Th.

Wrote to Ld Carlingford—Duke of Argyll—Mr Dodson—Sir C. Dilke—Ld Garvagh—Sir W. Harcourt—Ly Sandhurst—Dean of Windsor—The Queen and minutes. Read Lettres d'une Bourgeoise. Saw French Ambassador—Mr Dodson—Mr Smith—Mr G.—Ld R.G. H. of C. 4¾-8¼ & 9¼-11¾.[4]

To LORD CARLINGFORD, lord privy seal, 28 July 1881.   Add MS 44545, f. 3.

Our long fight in the Commons is nearly over, and I write a line to beg that you will undertake the charge of the Land Bill in the House of Lords.[5]

It is now I think firmly compacted in all its main parts, and though the wisdom of the hereditary legislators may give trouble and do mischief the foundation stones are really so welded together that they cannot be touched.

You will find Law a perfect master of every path through the labyrinth of details.

To Sir C. W. DILKE, foreign undersecretary, 28 July 1881.   Add MS 43875, f. 56.

I have today seen the French ambassador at his request.

He is considerably disturbed by our letter on the transportation of the negotiations to Paris.

I told him I was less in a condition to discuss the matter with him than I should have been, had not accidental circumstances prevented your laying before the Cabinet on Saturday last your account of the exact situation of affairs.

[1] Accepted the spirit of Healy's amndt. to cl. 7 (8 in the Act), which Law then proposed in stronger form: the 'Healy clause', providing that a tenant's improvements be discounted when assessing a fair rent; *H* 263. 1981.

[2] Colonial undersecretaryship vacated by Grant Duff; see 27 June 81.

[3] Harcourt's reply this day urged the need for the home undersecretary to be '*in the House of Commons & trained & experienced in business*'; Add MS 44196, f. 176. Courtney went to the colonial, Rosebery to the home office.

[4] Questions and Irish land; *H* 264. 34.

[5] Carlingford agreed this day, already 'deep in the Bill with Law, when your note came'; Add MS 44123, f. 114.

He stated (this is by the way) that when the proposal to change to Paris was made, it was welcomed and approved on the English side.

He said the French Govt. was prepared to make concessions with regard to our principal industries—that probably we should also abate our demands—but they could not state their ultimatum; it depended in part on discussion, & discussion could be best carried on in Paris.

I referred to the Vote in the H. of Commons, & the very susceptible state of opinion in this country; and I expressed it as my own opinion that the choice on our side lay between no Treaty, or no Tariff Treaty, and a Treaty which as a whole should, in so far as it varies from the Treaty of 1860, vary from it, as a whole, in the sense of improvement, of greater & not less favour to liberty of commerce.

I said the removal to Paris was open in principle to no objection; but, in the actual state of affairs, it would be considered here a new measure (démarche) & one of importance, & it would be necessary, if we became parties to it, that we should be in a condition to assure our public that the state of the negotiations warranted favourable anticipations of the final result.

I told him I would communicate with you and hoped you might soon see the Cabinet: & he might thereupon expect a further communication.

He on his side described the *present* situation as one far from satisfactory, & I on my part referred to French ideas as the cause of difficulty. I thought it plain that they are most anxious not to break off, and this may be turned, one would hope, to some account.

29. Fr.

Wrote to The Queen—Ld Kimberley—C.G. and minutes. Read Ed. Rev. on H. IV & Phil. III[1]—Life of Voltaire (Parton)[2] Lettres d'une Bourgeoise (finished). Saw Mr G.—Ld R.G.—Mr Hn. Saw Dean of Windsor—Mr Dodson—Mr Callan—Sir Ch. Dilke—Saw Hunter X. H. of C. 2¼–7 and 9–10¾. Irish Land Bill passed, after vexatious delays, but amidst great enthusiasm. I spoke briefly on the Third Reading.[3] The Members of Parlt. & the whole world have behaved to me on the occasion of this bill with extravagant generosity. God grant modesty to me, and His blessing to the measure.

To Mrs GLADSTONE, 29 July 1881.[4]   Hawarden MSS.

I write on the forty-sixth and last day of the debates on the Irish Land Bill. The Opposition have exhibited the most ludicrous divisions. Lord Randolph Church [*sic*], with violent personalities, and Elcho without them, went vehemently against the Bill, and resolutely forced a division. Gibson made an elaborate and vehement speech against the Bill but thought prudence the better part of valour, and went off with most of his friends. Upon the whole it was an edifying spectacle. Russell MP for Aylesbury chastised R. Churchill with much severity. I was very short with him, & not over civil. The numbers were For the Bill .   .
Against it   .   .
Dean Wellesley has been with me again about the Deanery of Westminster. The Bishop of Manchester has, I am sorry to say, flatly i.e. positively declined. Liddell is not

[1] *E.R.*, cliv. 224 (July 1881).

[2] J. Parton, *Life of Voltaire* (1881).

[3] The deb. ended with a row about Irish MPs being denied a place on a deputation to Gladstone; the 3°R was carried in 220:14; *H* 264. 192.

[4] Part in Bassett, 235.

yet wholly out of the question: if so E.T. would probably follow him.[1] Another plan is Barry, to be followed in his Canonry by Holland. I hope to hear more about the Bishop of Oxford.

I must not forget to say that Shaw delivered a most glowing and touching eulogy on my conduct.

I am not surprised at the soothing impressions of your arrival at Bettishanger[2] that nest of peace and home of purity and excellence: and I trust these were followed by a thoroughly good night.

It is now post time and I must close. Ever your Afft WEG

To LORD KIMBERLEY, colonial secretary, 29 July 1881.   Add MS 44545, f. 4.

I have had some correspondence with Childers about the Cape Garrison & I understand from him that you wish an increase, & that new barracks are contemplated, on account of the state of feeling which prevails among the Dutch population.

I can quite understand this as a temporary necessity. We may have rough times in S. Africa if our arrangement fails either now or at the ratification. But surely it may be otherwise. If our plans succeed we are justified I think in anticipating not a bad but a good state of feeling.

I would therefore propose that the augmentation be at present sanctioned, as a temporary measure, for a certain number of months, whatever be the proper number. The question of permanent increase can then be raised afresh if it should seem necessary.

30. Sat. [*Littlebury's*]

Wrote to Ld Rosebery—Sir R.G. Price—C.G.—Ld Kimberley—Sir W. Harcourt—Maharajah Dhuleep Singh and minutes. Saw Mr G.—Ld R.G.—Ld Kimberley—Mr Forster—Sir W. Harcourt—Mrs Th.—Mr Butterfield—Mr Wortley. Reached Littlebury's 4.45. Read Coneybeare's Iceland[3]—O'Connors Disraeli Vol II[4]—Tiberius.

To Mrs GLADSTONE, 30 July 1881.[5]   Hawarden MSS.

A hasty line on a busy day—for Mill Hill, & an early hour, make it busy & much pressed.

I am so sorry for the indifferent night: but the absence of the noise is a great & good fact.

The Bill passed last night as you will see. There were circumstances of annoyance to the House rather than the Government. We indeed had every reason to be gratified: and I in particular have been enormously overpraised. I do not remember such a case. I believe that many prayers from many hearts have upheld me: and I have been helped by the hope that it would be my last labour of the kind.

Not a single Irish member voted against us. A few Leaguers walked out.

I have just written to *sound* Rosebery. God bless you Ever Yours WEG

To LORD ROSEBERY, 30 July 1881. '*Private*'.   N.L.S. 10022, f. 82.

It has been reported to me that you would be disposed to take the U. Secretaryship of the Home Department, with the Scotch business in particular, & to represent the Department in the H. of Lords.

---

[1] i.e. E. Talbot would become Dean of Christ Church.   [2] Lord Northbourne's.
[3] C. A. V. Coneybeare, *The place of Iceland in the history of European institutions* (1877).
[4] T. P. O'Connor, *Benjamin Disraeli, Earl of Beaconsfield*, 2v. (1879–81); vol. ii in fact by A. Foggo.
[5] Part in Bassett, 236.

If so, the office is entirely at your disposal: and such a disposal I need hardly say would give me great pleasure. For my hour-glass is running out, and I should be grieved not to see you brought into closer relation with the Government of your country, & with your natural & destined career.

I have three things to say:

1. I do not write on the ground of a mere rumour on the one hand nor of a breach of faith on the other. It is something between knowledge and report, and the way to verify it is I think by the question direct.

2. I do not think the arrangements would last very long in the present form. There *must* be within the next six months further manipulation of political offices: and with this there is the likelihood of development, uncertain as to time, but certain, & so more than a likelihood, except as to that element.

3. This should be more than unusually private, as your acceptance will entail a new arrangement for Home Office business in the H. of Lords.[1]

[P.S.] With the U.Sec.ship would be naturally combined P.C.ship & the Scotch Commn. of Education.

31. 7 S. Trin.

Ch mg & evg. Much conversation with Mr Butterfield on Church matters. Also on this very curious house. Saw Dr Murray.[2] Read Life of Seabury—Humphry's on Revised Version.[3]—Lay Sermon[4]—New Englander (Maryland R.C.s[5]

Mond. Aug. One. 1881 [London]

Wrote to Archdn Jones—Mr Monk MP—The Queen 1.2.3.—Sir W. Harcourt—C.G.—Dean of Windsor Tel, and minutes. Saw Mr G.—Ld R.G.—Ld Rosebery—Mr Mills—Mr Forster. Dined at Grillion's. H. of C. $4\frac{1}{2}$–$7\frac{3}{4}$ & $10\frac{1}{2}$–11.[6] Read Life of Seabury—Oscar Wilde's Poems[7]—Tiberius—Ellenborough's Diary. Back from L. at 12.

To Mrs GLADSTONE, 1 August 1881.   Hawarden MSS.

I am well satisfied and pleased with your account of yourself today.

Butterfield[8] went down to Littleburies and is interested even far beyond what I had anticipated.

Rosebery has been here to say he accepts thankfully, if assured—which he now is—that his doing it will entail no inconvenience. I inclose his note: please to return it.

After full conversation with Dean Wellesley, upon the refusal of Bp Fraser & impossibility of Bp Mackarness I have recommended Barry for Deanery of Westmr. and Holland to succeed him in his stall. Inclosed is Wellesleys last letter: see what he says of Bp of Oxford, & please return.[9]

---

[1] Rosebery accepted on 1 August, noting 'the shifting of offices it involves may cause you inconvenience'; Add MS 44288, f. 73.

[2] i.e. the lexicographer, who lived at Mill Hill; see 1 Oct. 81n.

[3] An early version of W. G. Humphry, *A commentary on the Revised Version* (1882).

[4] J. S. Blackie, *Lay sermons* (1881).   [5] Untraced.

[6] Spoke on progress of public business; *H* 264. 373.

[7] See 26 July 81n.

[8] The architect; see 23 Feb. 45n.

[9] A. Barry declined the offer.

The Bradlaugh business at present stands for Wednesday, & I am very doubtful whether I can move, on this account.

Accounts of the prospects of Irish Land Bill in the Lords are favourable. Ever your Afft WEG

To Sir W. V. HARCOURT, home secretary, 1 August 1881.   Brand MSS 269.

I think the Speaker is right in proposing to debar Bradlaugh from the precincts. If you agree, will you send the paper[1] on to him, with our joint consent, to sanction.

I feel no difficulty in supporting what the Executive may think proper to do. When the House is solicited for further forms of action against the law, then the puzzle begins anew.

2. Tu.

Wrote to The Queen Tel–1.1.1.–Dr Acland–C.G.–and minutes. H. of C. 4½– 8¾. A Bradlaugh crowd.[2] Read Tiberius–Highland Sketches.[3] Saw Dashwood: (149 Keppel St) [R]. Saw Mr G.–Ld R.G.–Dean of Windsor–Herbert J.G. Conclave on French Treaty.

To Dr. H. W. ACLAND, 2 August 1881.   Add MS 44545, f. 5.

A rumour has reached me which I think you may be able to verify or contradict; it is that the Dean is desirous or disposed to quit Ch.Ch. when [?sc. where] he has reigned so long. Can you tell me if it be so?[4]

If it be, I am able to offer to submit his name to the Queen for the Deanery of Westminster.

Even if you are not in possession of the Dean's mind upon the subject, I would beg you to ascertain it for me. Perhaps it may be well that you should not mention me in the matter (but this I leave to your discretion) before probing his mind. But if you see cause, you may say all I have said.

I need hardly add that the sooner it can be done the better.

The difference of income as I daresay you know is against Westminster.

3. Wed.

Wrote to Mr Richards MP–Ld Advocate–Hon. C.L. Wood–The Queen– C.G.–and minutes. Dined with the Sydneys. Saw Mr G.–Ld R.G.–Lady Holker–Sir W. Harcourt. Conclave on Land Bill Amendments. H. of C. 12–5¼.[5]

---

[1] Not found (returned by Harcourt to Brand, Add MS 44196, f. 185); memorial of 14 July by Bradlaugh stating his intention of presenting himself at the Table 'on or before' 3 August; Brand MSS 268.

[2] Supply; *H* 264. 569. Bradlaugh's well-advertised intention to take his seat on 3 August produced a huge crowd on 2 August; Gladstone did not succeed in leaving Westminster unrecognised; Arnstein, 119.

[3] Probably Sir T. D. Lauder, *Highland legends* (sundry eds.).

[4] Acland replied, 6 August, Add MS 44091, f. 113, that Liddell was in Scotland, and unlikely to accept.

[5] Questioned on the Transvaal; during his answer, Bradlaugh was forcibly expelled from the Palace, after attempting to enter the Commons' Chamber; Labouchere's motion that the serjeant-at-arms had exceeded his powers was defeated in 191:7, Gladstone supporting the officers' action, Bright speaking in general terms in favour of Bradlaugh; *H* 264. 698.

Slipped unawares into a Bradlaugh crowd ovation on my walk home. Drove with M. to Mr Burn Jones's Studio: met Mr O. Wilde.[1] Saw Monty X, Ricardo, Herrings &c [R]. Read Tiberius.

4. Th.

Wrote to Ld Selborne—Dr Plumtre—Ld Aberdeen—Mr Murray—Sir H. Ponsonby—The Queen and minutes. H. of C. $4\frac{1}{2}$–9 and $9\frac{3}{4}$–$11\frac{1}{4}$.[2] Eight to breakfast. Saw Mr G.—Ld R.G.—Dean of Windsor—Mr Sprigg—Sir R. Biddulph—Mr Forster. C.G. returned: better thank God. Read Stronbuy.[3]

5. Fr.

Wrote to Mr Bright—Ld Advocate—Mr Lowell—Ld Moncreiff—Mr C.L. Wood—Sir W. Harcourt—The Queen—Sir H. Ponsonby tel and minutes. H. of C. $4\frac{1}{4}$–$5\frac{1}{4}$ & 10–$11\frac{1}{4}$. Very much tired.[4] Saw Mr G.—Mr H.—Ld R.G.—Ld F.C.—Sir R. Phillimore—Mr Forster—Mr Macarthur. Saw Ricardo: a singular character [R]. Read Tiberius. Q.R. on Protection.[5]

To Sir W. V. HARCOURT, home secretary, 5 August 1881.   MS Harcourt dep. 8, f. 93.

In sending you the letters my sole object was to keep you informed. I have asked Bright to consult some dispassionate member of the Govt. if he regards you as a party in the matter, & have not given him or the L.A. any expectation of our receding.[6]

6. Sat. [Littlebury's]

Wrote to The Queen—Sir H. Ponsonby Tel.—Mr Murray—Sir W. Harcourt. (2).—Ld Northbrook & minutes. Cabinet 12-4. Saw Mr H.—Ld R.G.—Ld Granville—Ld Rosebery—Attended the Ld Mayor's dinner & returned thanks for Ministers in a general outline of over 15 months.[7] Drove to Littleburies afterwards, arriving at one [a.m.]. Read Tiberius and [blank.]

Cabinet. Aug. 6. 1881. Noon.[8]
2. Bradlaugh. Labouchere's Motion. *Ascertain* that Resolution is sessional & that the previous question would settle the matter: & thereupon to give the assurance as in the Paragraph within.[9]
1. French Treaty. Decide to put the best construction on Lacour's letter of 4th.

[1] Mary Gladstone noted: 'Carried Papa off to B.-J.'s studio, not a perfect succedge [*sic*]'; *Mary Gladstone*, 230.
[2] Questions; spoke on suspension of O'Kelly; *H* 264. 850, 866.
[3] *Stronbuy: Highland yarn, by the author of Tobermory* (1881).
[4] Questions, public business; *H* 264. 993, 998.
[5] [L.J.Jennings], 'English trade and foreign competition'; *Q.R.*, clii. 141 (July 1881); strongly anti-free-trade.
[6] Harcourt reported the department 'in despair' without an undersecretary in the Commons; Add MS 44196, f. 187.
[7] *T.T.*, 8 August 1881, 6b; he was 'received enthusiastically'.
[8] Add MS 44642, f. 206.
[9] Not found; moving the 'previous question' was the tactic reaffirmed and followed in 1882; see 7 Feb. 82.

3. Irish Land Bill Amendments: Went through the Amendments.
4. Release of Dillon.[1]

7. 8. S. Trin.

Ch mg (with H.C.) and evg. Saw E. Lyttelton—Mr Burne Jones, with whom much conversation. Wrote to Dean of Windsor—Rev. E. Wickham. Read John Inglesant—Life of Seabury.

8. M. [London]

Wrote to Mr Forster—Ld Advocate—The Queen 1.1.—Dean of Windsor—Sir Thos G.—Mr Childers—and minutes. Read John Inglesant—Capefigue's Dss of Portsmouth.[2] Saw Mr H.—Ld R.G.—Ld Granville—do *cum* Mr Forster. Dined at Grillions: conversation with Houghton, Kimberley, Sherbrooke (whom I think much softened). Saw three [R]. H. of C. $4\frac{1}{2}$–$7\frac{1}{2}$.[3]

To G. V. WELLESLEY, dean of Windsor, 8 August 1881.   Add MS 44545, f. 6.

The Dean's *No*[4] has arrived. Under the circumstances I do not know that I can do better than recommend Hornby? As poor Barry has gone to the wall, & H. in some respects is certainly better. I presume he is not much of a politician.

I have written to Dr. Plumptre for more copies of his verses.

9. Tu.

Wrote to Mr C.L. Wood—Dean of Windsor—The Queen—Bp of Winchester and minutes. H. of C. $4\frac{1}{4}$–$1\frac{1}{2}$. Nearly all the time on I.L. Bill.[5] 20 minutes. for dinner. Saw Mr G.—Mr H.—Ld R.G.—A.G. for Ireland—Do *cum* Mr Forster. Read J. Inglesant.

To G. V. WELLESLEY, dean of Windsor, 9 August 1881.   Add MS 44545, f. 6.

1. I should have thought Bradley,[6] as *gentleman*, was much on the footing of Barry. Hornby very much higher in that point.
2. When the Commission on Eccl. Courts was framed, the Abp of Canterbury thought it right that on it should be, as representative men, one of the two Deans who wish to drive the Ritualists out of the Ch. of England. Perowne was put there accordingly. But I do not know why I should go out of my own political line to take a man of that kind for Westminster. If a disorganizer is to be admitted, [H. M.] Butler's claim revives & is higher. Bp Thirlwall had been a great man, but there were signs that in his latest years his judgment went greatly down hill.
3. Edwin Palmer the Chancellor's brother has been suggested to me.
4. You were the first suggester of Hornby, who I think stands well.
5. I agree that Hannah is not the best man for this post.

---

[1] Instruction for release on grounds of ill-health sent next day and read to the Commons by Forster on 8 August; *H* 264. 1205. See 29 Apr. 81.

[2] J. B. H. R. Capefigue, *La Duchesse de Portsmouth et la cour galante des Stuarts* (1861).

[3] Questions; *H* 264, 1204.

[4] i.e. Liddell's; see 2 Aug. 81.

[5] Lords' amndts. to the Land Bill; *H* 264. 1388.

[6] Wellesley had stated the Queen's enthusiasm for G. G. Bradley; Add MS 44340, f. 106.

You are most kind in offering to come up. *If* you think it needful & are disposed to take the trouble, which may not be necessary, I am at your service on any day after tomorrow at four o'clock.

11. [sc. *10*] *Wed.*

Wrote to The Queen 1.2.—Dean of Windsor Tel. and others. Twelve to dinner. Saw Dhuleep Singh[1]—Sir C. Dilke—Sir J. Paget—Ld Stafford—Mr Brand—Mr G.—Ld R.G. Read J. Inglesant.[2]

12. [sc. *11*] *Th.*

Wrote to Mayor of Rochester—The Queen Tel & l.—Dean of Windsor Tel & minutes. H. of C. $4\frac{1}{2}$-$8\frac{3}{4}$ & $9\frac{1}{2}$-$1\frac{1}{2}$: am 6° on Land Bill disposed of, but later.[3] Saw Mr G.—Ld R.G.—H.J.G.—Rev. E. Wickham—Sir H. Elliot. Dined at Sir C. Forsters. Walk with C. Read John Inglesant—Memoirs of Duchess of Portsmouth.

To G. V. WELLESLEY, dean of Windsor, 11 August 1881.   Add MS 44545, f. 7.

I have inquired a good deal about various men—and the upshot is that I have little doubt Edwin Palmer,[4] the Chancellor's brother, is the best man at our command.

Edw. Talbot, a high Churchman & Edw. Wickham, a broad Churchman are at one in this belief. I send you E. Talbot's account and I have seen Wickham today.

The Queen has just sent me a telegram[5] of which I inclose a copy. Does she think the two positions of Sovereign & Minister are to be inverted? This really cannot go on long, with me at least, but mind the most awkward things that have happened in this province are not yet known to you.

What can she mean about Butler? Surely not that I am to say to him, *Do* this & I will do the other?

[J.] Perceval is a stronger man than Bradley, of the same school—& very good in any matter save one, that he is not a good manager of those under him.

Bradley is an excellent person & a very distinguished schoolmaster; but he has the mark of the Schoolmaster too much upon him. As regards manners & representation, I should say he is not above Barry, but a little below him; nor do I know anything in which he is superior.

Upon full consideration, I think Hornby is an unexceptionable man, in the strict sense of the word, but certainly without great merits or recommendations.

This is all I think that I have to say today.

Except this, as to E. Palmer, that he has been the man who did a principal part of the work at Balliol, which has raised that college to so very high a position. His Oxford career was one of extraordinary distinction, I send you the list. And he is *not* very well placed as Archdeacon, whereas Bradley is thoroughly well placed as Head & Canon.

[1] Who embarrassed Gladstone by presenting 'a massive silver inkstand'; see Ramm II, i. 290.
[2] And spoke in the Commons on the Land Bill; *H* 264. 1471.
[3] Lords' amndts. completed and cttee. elected to give reasons for disagreement with their amndts.; *H* 264. 1634.
[4] In 1881, archdeacon of Oxford; see 28 Jan. 53.
[5] 'Butler is so far the best, and greatly wished for by the late Dean'; Gladstone should see him; 'if not, Bradley is best'; *L.Q.V.*, 2nd series, iii. 231. The Queen eventually prevailed, Bradley being appointed.

13. [sc. 12] Fr.

Wrote to Ld Granville—Mr Dillwyn—Mrs W. Johnson-Robertson[1]—The Queen—Mr Cross MP and minutes. Read J. Inglesant. Nine to dinner. H. of C. $4\frac{1}{2}$-$8\frac{1}{2}$ and $9\frac{1}{2}$-1.[2] Saw Mr G.—Ld R.G.—Dean of Windsor: long & anxious conversation.

13. Sat. [Mentmore, Leighton Buzzard]

Wrote to The Queen 1.2.3. Disturbed in the night: kept my bed till 11.30. H. of C. at 12:[3] all safe then: Cabinet until 3.30. Then to Mentmore.[4] Saw Mr G.—Ld R.G.—Sir W. Harcourt—Mr Evarts—Dr Donaldson.[5] Read John Inglesant.

Cabinet. Sat 13. Aug. 81. 12 Noon.[6]
Lords Re-amt. to Irish Land Bill considered & decided.
Parnell amendment left open: to drop *unless* we see our way clearly to amending.[7]

14. 9 S. Trin.

Ch mg & evg. C. went off to London to catch Clark: having a touch of erysipelas. Drive with Ld R. to send off Telegrams. Read Life of Seabury—John Inglesant. Wrote to E. Hamilton—Ld Hartington—Mr Forster—A.G. for Ireland. Conversation with Mr Evarts—Ld R.—Dr Donaldson.

15. M. [London]

Off to London at 10. Wrote to Ld Carlingford—Sir B. Frere—The Queen l & Tel and minutes. H. of C. $4\frac{3}{4}$-$8\frac{1}{4}$ and 9-2. Working Irish Land Bill, I hope for the last time.[8] Saw Sir W. Harcourt—Mr Archer—Mr Balfour—Mr G.—Ld R.G. Conclave on Irish Land Bill, substance & technicalities.[9] [Saw] Sir H. Ponsonby—Dr Clark —Mr J. Collings MP. Excellent progress of C.G. Finished John Inglesant.

To Sir BARTLE FRERE, 15 August 1881.   Add MS 44545, f. 8.

I write briefly in reply to your recent letter,[10] with no controversial intention, to say that I *think* you have unintentionally fallen into some error of fact.

---

[1] Thanking her, a relative on his mother's side, for 'a portrait of my maternal great grandfather, which I prize very much'; Add MS 44545, f. 7.

[2] Questions, French treaty; *H* 264. 1718, 1733.   [3] Questions; *H* 264. 1816.

[4] The Roseberys' great house. Henry James was also a guest; *Mary Gladstone*, 231; see 23 Aug. 81n.

[5] Probably Principal Donaldson, a friend of the Roseberys; see 4 July 79.

[6] Add MS 44642, f. 210.

[7] Probably Parnell's amndt. on compensation moved on 15 August, agreed with by Gladstone, but rejected as unnecessary; *H* 264. 1975.

[8] Lord's amndts. finished for the second time, and reasons for disagreement agreed; *H* 264. 2009.   [9] Notes on Lords' amndts. at Add MS 44765, f. 127.

[10] Of 'July 1881', Add MS 44470, f. 268, replying to Gladstone's charges against him in Midlothian in 1879 and mentioning his imminent pamphlet; Gladstone's letter went astray, Frere replying, 17 September, Add MS 44471, f. 247, reiterating his lack of association with Lytton and complaining that Gladstone implied such an association.

The mode in which I connected your name with the recent Affghan war is fully explained in p. 205 of Vol: I of my Midlothian Speeches. It was simply treating you as an advocate of the 'policy of advance'. With the actual proceedings of Lord Lytton I never directly or indirectly connected you—of those proceedings you are quite right in supposing that I have spoken in the House of Commons and elsewhere in the strongest terms— but I have never thought or said that the forward policy involved of itself a moral error or reproach.

You will I think agree with me that the lengthened passage in p. 205 explains the short one in p. 49. Had I been myself the corrector of my speeches, I should probably have inserted the word 'cited' after 'authority'.

If I am wrong in my statement or in any statement of a declaration of yours respecting Africa I shall be most ready to make my apology for the error.

I have certainly differed from you widely on grave matters much affecting the public interests, but I am not conscious of having been led at any time into the use of any expression concerning you which was not consistent with the fullest respect and regard.

16. Tu.

Wrote to Watson & Smith—Sir W. Harcourt—The Queen—Mr O'Sullivan—Ld Spencer—Ld Powerscourt—Ld Kimberley & minutes. Saw Mr G.—Ld R.G.—The Speaker—Mr Stead—Mr Collings—Mr Macmillan. Read Tiberius—Life of Quinet.[1] Saw Ricardo [R]. H. of C. 4¼-5 & after dinner.[2] A long night in bed.

To Sir W. V. HARCOURT, home secretary, 16 August 1881. MS Harcourt dep. 8, f. 95.

Pray look at the note of Galleys[3] antecedents which I have obtained from your office. Unless that can be shaken[?] I would propose for your cons[ideratio]n my plan
1. To ask no vote from Parlt so that any Galley-Slave who may wish to interfere will have nothing for it but an 'interpellation' which I readily undertake to meet.
2. I propose that I from the Special Service Fund should pay you whatever you may want for bringing him home, and should purchase for him an annuity of £1 per week for life.

Pray consider this favourably. I am quite certain that a lump sum of £1000 will be the ruin of this excellent man & send him to the bad, just as did Strzelechi's angelic butler who had stood the temptations of his position through 30 years service but got a legacy of this amount & was ruined by it.

To W. H. O'SULLIVAN, M.P., 16 August 1881.   Add MS 44545, f. 8.

I thank you for your kind note; and for the inclosure.[4] It expresses feelings very naturally excited and alarmed. I earnestly hope that those feelings may be allayed by what has since taken place, and that the House of Lords may not further prolong a conflict which its well wishers, more than other persons, should view with misgiving and alarm. I take the liberty of expressing my own sense of your manly and independent conduct on important occasions during the discussions on the Bill.

[1] See 9 May 81.
[2] Questioned on Land Bill Commissioners; H 265. 34. The Lords this day accepted the Commons' amndts.
[3] Case of Edmund Galley, erroneously convicted of murder and transported 1839; Add MS 44196, f. 196.
[4] Untraced Resolution on the Lords and the Land Bill.

17. Wed.

Wrote to Watson Tel.—Mr M'Laren—Lord Chamberlain—The Queen 2—Dean of Windsor 2—and minutes. Saw Mr G.—Ld R.G. Conclave on the Maltsters 3–5.[1] Saw Mr West. Saw The Speaker—The Solicitor General—Ld Granville—Sir C. Dilke—Herbert J.G. H. of C. 12¼–2.[2] Attended the Fish dinner and spoke. Presentation of a chair and a short speech before it. Crowds and much enthusiasm.[3] Saw Percy X.

To LORD SELBORNE, lord chancellor, 17 August 1881.   Selborne MS 2498, f. 75.

I am much concerned to see that you were unwell in the House of Lords last night and were obliged to go home. I trust that now there may be nothing to interfere with your giving careful and unbroken attention to your health, which, to judge by visible signs, has for some time really required it. The bearer of this note will ask how you are at your door.

But this preamble is not the only or main purpose of my note; which, having waited until the Land Bill was settled, I was about to write when I read the disagreeable paragraph in the newspaper. I cannot let the occasion go by without offering you my emphatic thanks for the constant and signal service you have rendered us in our long, anxious deliberations upon the most difficult measure I have ever known to come under the detailed consideration of a Cabinet—I feel a scruple as a layman in praising a sermon to the preacher. So I now feel a scruple in paying a compliment to a Judge. I will say nothing therefore about the qualities you have displayed in themselves; but, speaking only of my own impressions I will say that I have felt you, all along, to be a tower of strength, and I am most grateful to a friend in need who has been a friend indeed.[4]

To G. V. WELLESLEY, dean of Windsor, 17 August 1881.   RA VIC d/7/88.

Not having heard anything more from you, I write to give the result of my inquiry & consideration with respect to the Deanery of Westminster.[5]

1.2. Mr. Bradley as a man is entirely free from any objection. His personal character is high, he is a very good scholar, and a very successful schoolmaster. His sermons are good, but he is not an effective preacher & would I believe be lost in the Abbey. There is no reason to believe he would be very effective outside the Abbey in all those matters in which a Dean of Westminster is called upon, or very well suited, to take part. His training has been exclusively that of schoolmaster and head of a College. But it is also desirable in a high degree that the Dean of Westminster should be a person of a certain station, manner, and bearing: in a word as high a gentleman as can be had for the place. In this particular I must say that Mr. Bradley falls rather short of any & every other person who has been named. Mrs. Bradley, no unimportant incident, the same & rather more decidedly. In a word Mr. Bradley is Dr. *Barry over again but rather worse* (not that either is *bad* in any particular) while Dr. Barry has been much more in the eye of the Church and of the world. Both these gentlemen are well placed in their present offices & work.

---

[1] No record found.

[2] Irish executive; *H* 265. 157.

[3] *T.T.*, 18 August 1881, 3e.

[4] Printed in Selborne II, ii. 27; Selborne noted this 'the most demonstrative letter which I ever received from him', and replied this day, charmed; Add MS 44297, f. 184.

[5] Wellesley had stated the Queen's enthusiasm for G. G. Bradley, Add MS 44340, f. 106. Gladstone discusses the qualities of G. G. Bradley (see 13 Nov. 72); J. J. Hornby (14 Nov. 69); John Percival, 1834–1918, president of Trinity, Oxford; E. Palmer (28 Jan. 53); W. Boyd Carpenter (18 Mar. 81); W. Cadman (3 June 76).

On the point of preaching I may say that when Mr. Bradley preaches at St. Mary's the gallery is *one third* full—you will know what this means.

3. Dr. Hornby's appointment would fall rather short of the mark in some points: as gentleman I believe he would do very well: as to his energy in the outer circle of the duties of the office, I do not feel very certain.

4. Perceval is excellent except in the one, certainly important point, that his relations with those near him have not been happy. In opinion and learning he may be described as of the same school with Bradley.

5. Archdeacon Palmer is evidently superior to Bradley & Barry in the points in which they are lacking. He is brother to the Lord Chancellor, which gives him an advantage in the point of station, and is of the same colour in his capacity as Churchman, while he is beyond doubt a wise and eminently considerable man. I think indeed that he is one of the best men who could now be available for a Bishopric. He has been one of the main agents in elevating Balliol.

6. Mr. Boyd Carpenter might be worth further inquiry but that I am sorry to say he would be inaudible in the Abbey. This I found in Eton Chapel. The blame might be laid on my years. But Spencer had the utmost difficulty in following him.

7. Cadman of Trinity Church Marylebone is an excellent specimen of the Low Church School without strong party spirit, and a very respectable preacher: but I am afraid he would not have the distinctive qualities required for this Deanery.

Bishop Fraser & Dean Liddell being now out of the question (to my great regret) I will not lengthen my catalogue.

My judgment, and I think my impartial judgment is that Palmer is the best man: he is also insufficiently placed where he is. If I am, in the view of the Constitution, the person responsible for the appointment, it requires strong & exceptional considerations to justify me in not sustaining this opinion by a corresponding recommendation.

Still I feel that the Queen has a peculiar feeling in this case founded on strength of personal attachment: and on every ground I should in such a case go as far as possible out of my way to gratify it, if after a full consideration of the case, upon the best evidence attainable, she entertains a strong view upon the matter before us.

In conclusion I hope that on some suitable occasion, & *not* with a view to any particular preferment, Dr. Butler may be led by wise friends to disconnect himself from that very unwise association, which seems to have no better apology to plead than that its formally announced 'principles' do not enter into the field of its action. As the busy Master of Harrow, he probably has had little time to consider the formal statements of the body.[1]

18. *Th.*

Wrote to Mr C. Russell—The Queen 1.1.—Sir Thos G—Sir W. Harcourt—Sir H. Thring and minutes. Read Tiberius. H. of C. $4\frac{1}{2}$-$8\frac{1}{4}$ & $9\frac{1}{2}$-$12\frac{3}{4}$. Spoke on Irish Govt.[2] Saw Mr G.—Ld R.G.—Ld Rosebery—Mr West—Sir W. Harcourt—Mr Kitson—Mr Beresford Hope—H.J.G.

[1] Sent with accompanying note that this could be shown in whole or part to the Queen; RA VIC D 7/87.

[2] Defending govt. policy, on Parnell's resolution on the working of the Protection Act; *H* 265. 289.

To Sir W. V. HARCOURT, home secretary, 18 August 1881. MS Harcourt dep. 8, f. 98.

Many thanks for your memm.[1] which I will make full use of. Is it the fact that the Lord Advocate has in Scotland an office and business of his own, apart from the Home Office? If so and if this embraces a principal part of his functions it would be well for me to say so? Another method would be to answer more generally but perhaps this would lead to a request for the production of any minute you may make.

To Sir H. THRING, 18 August 1881.   Add MS 44545, f. 10.

As it is now a certainty that your Irish Land Bill will be added to the Statute Book, the time has come when I may express my strong sense of the public service you have rendered in encountering and overcoming the difficulties of the complex plan which the circumstances of Ireland required us to place in your hands for skilful manipulation.

The Act will perhaps yet cost some head-aches to Irish Judges, Lawyers and last but not least Commissioners: yet I think these inflictions would have been far more numerous and severe had the drafting been intrusted to less able and practised hands. Pray accept the thanks which I tender on behalf of the Government.

19. Fr.

Wrote to Ld Houghton—Ld Provost Edinb.[2]—Ld Halifax—Dean of Windsor Tel—Prince of Wales—W.H.G.—The Queen 1.1. and minutes. H. of C. $4\frac{1}{2}$-8 and 10-12$\frac{3}{4}$.[3] Read Tiberius—Hist de la Relig. Unitaire.[4] Saw Mr G.—Ld R.G.—Conclave on H. of C. procedure. Sir W. Harcourt—Mr Balfour. Eight to dinner. Worked further on draft for Queen's Speech.

20. Sat.

Wrote to Sir H. Ponsonby—The Queen 1.1.1.1.—Sir W. Harcourt—Italian Ambassr & minutes. Finished work on draft. Cabinet 2-3$\frac{1}{2}$ for the Speech &c. Saw Mr G.—Ld R.G.—Mr Childers—Ld Spencer. House sat 12-11$\frac{1}{2}$: I went to & fro all the time.[5] Saw Scarsdale [R]. Read Tiberius (finished)—Hist du Xtme Unitaire.

Cabinet Sat. Aug. 20. 81.[6]
1. Queen's Speech read 1° and 2° amended & approved.
2. Plan for the public offices.[7] Demarcation of the ground approved so far as W.O. & Admiralty are concerned.
3. France. If Tariff Treaty fail try for m[ost] f[avoured] n[ation] Clause Treaty.[8]

[1] On duties of the Lord Advocate; Harcourt dep. 8, f. 100.
[2] Offering a knighthood to Thomas Jamieson Boyd, 1818–1902; lord provost of Edinburgh 1877–82.
[3] Questioned on public business; *H* 265. 366.
[4] G. Bonet-Maury, *Des origines du Christianisme unitaire chez les Anglais* (1881).
[5] Davitt; Irish estimates; spoke on drink in Wales; *H* 265. 601.
[6] Add MS 44642, f. 211.
[7] Secretary's note that Lefevre wants the Cabinet to deal with this before the recess; ibid., f. 216.
[8] Declaration signed in Paris, 21 Sept., prolonging Anglo-French trade treaties; *PP* 1882 lxxx. 299.

21. 10 S. Trin.

Chapel Royal mg. Whitehall aft. Wrote to Dean of Windsor—C.G.—Miss Talbot—Rivingtons. Read Quinet's Life—Seabury's Life (finished)—Hist. du Xtme Unitaire—Hawkins Sermons.[1] Saw Mrs Th. A most quiet day.

22. M.

Wrote to Ld Spencer (2)—Dean of Llandaff.—C.G.—Viceroy of Ireland—Ld Reay—A.L. Gladstone—Ld Howth—Sir H. Johnstone—The Queen—Sir D. Marjoribanks—Ld Tweeddale—Dean of W. Tel—Sir H. Tufton Bt[2]—Mr Forster & minutes. Saw Scarsdale, with much interest: Graham [R]. Saw Mr H.—Ld R.G.—Mr A.J.B. Hope—Scotts. H. of C. 3-3¾ and 5-8.[3] Sat to Walker Photographer. Went to the Herbert Exhibn. Read Life of Quinet and Kossovo.[4] Lecture on Vivisection.

To LORD COWPER, Viceroy of Ireland, 22 August 1881.   Add MS 44545, f. 11.

Your recommendation[5] will be carefully considered should the time arise for a distribution of medical honours; we could hardly take them separately for Ireland.

We have now indeed come to a very critical moment, that of the real battle between the Land League & the Land *Act* as I am happy to think it may now be called. The question of release of prisoners—a thing devoutly to be wished for if it where [*sic*] or when it is safe—should I apprehend be looked upon exclusively with reference to its bearing on the tremendous competition which means the tranquillity or non-tranquillity of Ireland.

23. Tu.

Wrote to The Speaker (2)—Ld R. Grosvenor—Mr Bradley[6]—Sir G. Wolseley—Mr Childers—Ld Bessborough—Mr J.C. Trench—The Queen 1.1.1.—Mr Heneage—C.G. & minutes. Mrs Scarsdale (H.J.G. Tel.) Packing books, making feeble attempts to set my things in order, & preparing for departure tomorrow. Read The Madonna of the Future.[7] Saw Mr H.—Ld Kensington—Mr Childers[8]—Sir C. Dilke—The Speaker. H. of C. 3-9¼ with intervals: a short half-hour's absence for dinner. Bantering reply 15 min. to Ashmead Bartlett.[9] Saw Scarsdale: heard singing there [R].

To LORD BESSBOROUGH, 23 August 1881.   Add MS 44545, f. 12.

I thank you very much for your kind letter.[10]

Your favourable view of the Land Bill, at a stage when it had not yet acquired all the

---

[1] Probably E. Hawkins, *Sermons on the Church* (1847).

[2] Offers of peerages to Johnstone, Reay, Tweeddale, Marjoribanks and to William Ulrick Tristram St. Lawrence, 1837–1909; 4th earl of Howth; liberal M.P. Galway 1868–74; 1st Baron Howth (U.K.) 1881, and Sir Henry James Tufton, 1844–1926; 1st Baron Hothfield 1881.

[3] Questions; Indian finance; *H* 265. 613.

[4] *Kossovo: Serbian national song about the fall of the Empire* (1881).

[5] Untraced.

[6] Offering G.G. Bradley the deanery of Westminster, which he accepted.

[7] H. James, *The Madonna of the Future*, 2v. (1879); see 13 Aug. 81n.

[8] See to Childers, 6 Sept. 81.

[9] Replying to his comments on foreign policy; *H* 265. 792.   [10] Not found.

public favour which (I think) eventually crowned it, was most comforting to me; and, while I much regret the cause[?] which deprived us of the benefit of your support in the most authoritative form,[1] I never could for a moment suppose this loss of ours was owing to any defect of will on your part.

The next few weeks & months will be of immense importance in their bearing on the future of Ireland.

To H. B. W. BRAND, the Speaker, 23 August 1881.   Add MS 44545, f. 12.

I send herewith, for you & Sir T. May, two copies of a paper printed.

I sent it in MS to certain members of the Cabinet, whose notes are appended. It was then printed with these notes for the Cabinet at large. But at that stage I found the state of Irish affairs so pressing, that it never came before the Cabinet for practical consideration & this will account for its never having been sent to you or Sir T. May.[2]

The difficulties of the subject are very great, & as I earnestly involve your aid, *ab initio* & as if you had never received this paper; as also that of Sir T. May.

To LORD R. GROSVENOR, chief whip, 23 August 1881.   Add MS 44315, f. 40.
'*Private*'.[3]

I send you herewith the list of 'intending' Baronets.[4] Unfortunately I feel very little able to contribute from my own resources towards the final selection. But please to put it in hand, consulting Wolverton & any one else you think proper. There is no *hurry*: but the consideration may *begin*, for H.M. herself has reminded me of the matter a-propos of the P. of Wales' men: rather 'an awkward squad' for us. We must however make *one* of them if we can.

To J. COOKE TRENCH, 23 August 1881.   Add MS 44545, f. 12.

Your letter makes known to me the death in a ripe old age of one of the best men I ever knew.[5]

He was also a man gifted with talents which, but for his retiring disposition and his modest estimate of himself, would probably have given him a much more advanced position in the party to which he belongs; unless indeed some feeling or conviction of his own had hindered it.

You speak of his having been ripened for death by his long illness; and doubtless there are many degrees and stages of ripening, and his illness may probably have led him from a stage that was high to others which were higher still. But to me he always appeared unusually collected and ripe for death, and all intercourse with him was a privilege and a lesson.

I much lamented the severance of our political opinions, or rather his objections and difficulties about mine; and I please myself with thinking that a recent growth in his difficulties, which I fear took place, may have been owing in some degree to the advances of age and to his withdrawal from the responsibilities of active life.

---

[1] Bessborough was unable to speak on the Land Bill.
[2] i.e. 'Obstruction and devolution', see 23 Oct. 80 (secretary's marginal note, Add MS 44545, f. 12).
[3] Holograph.
[4] Lists of candidates in Add MS 44765, ff. 122, 129, but not including the Prince of Wales's 'squad'.
[5] Sir W. Heathcote, M.P. for Oxford University (with Gladstone until 1865), see 3 May 38; Trench's fa.-in-law; Add MS 44471, f. 81.

However that may be, nothing did change or could change my feelings of regard & affection towards this admirable man now gone to rest and light, which I heartily hope may increase more and more upon him until the final day.

I beg you to convey to his family the assurance of my sympathy.

24. Wed. [The Castle, Deal][1]

Wrote to Ld Monson—C.G. Tel—Rev. Mr Spurgeon—Sec. Distr. R.R. Co—E. Hamilton—Lady C. Kerrison—Mrs Stuart Wortley—C.G. Tel—Ly Sydney do. and minutes. Saw Mr H.—Ld Kensington—Sir W. Harcourt—H.J.G.—H. of C. 12–1. and goodbye.[2] NB I had a curious conversation on Monday with the old OGorman Mahon who will have it that I ought to go to the Lords. He spoke quite affectionately. But indeed I have been overwhelmed with undeserved interest and kindness. Reached Deal 7.30: received with immense kindness by the Sydneys. Read Kate Trevelyan[3]—History of St Kilda.[4]

25. Th.

Wrote to E. Hamilton—Ld R. Grosvenor—Ld Kensington & minutes. Went to Walmer & had long conversation with Granville. Read Kate Trevelyan—Macaulay's St Kilda—Curci's Nuova Italia.[5] Saw Mr Rowsell—Ld Sydney on the Duckworth case.[6]

To LORD R. GROSVENOR, chief whip, 25 August 1881.[7]   Add MS 44315, f. 42.

So glad to receive your good news of the ménage. But I contend that you are having not one but *many* additions to your family just now e.g. 1. Herbert J.G. 2. Buchanan, and a lot more.

Many thanks also for your explanation. I had *before* receiving your letter determined that it would not do for me personally to meddle. But I wrote out a draft[8] which I inclose of what might be truly said against Parnell if it were useful to say it. If you can make any use of it through any body, well and good: and if not, well and good also.

Weather here is deplorable. Yesterday the West Kent crops looked to me thin in quantity and woebegone in colour, but those of East Kent plentiful & of healthy hue. But this is I imagine the worst day yet, with a heavy south-wester. Granville gives a good account of himself. The Sydneys are as host and hostess quite perfect. My wife profiting greatly. We are all but *in* the sea. Brabourne (as you may conceive) not in the best odour here. Again & again let me acknowledge, though I cannot pay, my debt of thanks to you.

---

[1] Sydney's castle, one of Henry VIII's Cinque Ports.

[2] Parliament eventually prorogued on 27 August.

[3] Not traced; clearly a work of substance; possibly some confusion with the Macaulay of the next note?

[4] Kenneth Macaulay, *Voyage to St. Kilda* (1763).

[5] C. M. Curci, *La Nuova Italia ed i vecchi zelanti* (1881); on political parties.

[6] Complications *re* the position of R. Duckworth, vicar of Marylebone; see Bahlman, *Hamilton*, i. 146.

[7] Holograph. Grosvenor's letter untraced.

[8] Draft of public letter *re* Parnell and N. Durham by-election; Add MS 44315, f. 44.

26. Fr.

Wrote to H.J.G.—Mr Hamilton Tel—Count Menabrea—Mr Macknight & minutes. Saw The Mayor of Deal. Read Kate Trevelyan—Life of Erasmus[1]—Herbert's Speeches[2]—Æneid—Macaulay's St Kilda (finished). Saw Granville—Ld Carlingford.

27. Sat.

Wrote to Ld F.C.—Bp of Carlisle—Mr Childers—Dean of W (Tel)—Mr Rowsell—Mr Hamilton—The Queen tel—Mr Forster. Saw Ld Sydney—Ld Carlingford—Mr Young—Mr Godley—Ld Granville—Sir W. James on Church affairs. Visit to Bettishanger—Dined at Walmer. Read Kate Trevelyan—Life of Erasmus.

To W. E. FORSTER, Irish secretary, 27 August 1881.   Add MS 44545, f. 14.

1. I have now before me ten excellent candidates for K.C.B. & 2 vacancies. Of the 10 four are not C.B. I have considered carefully & repeatedly the question of breaking down my rule as to the preliminary step, broken by the late Government without any cause & against the will of Sir A. Liddell. And it is really so reasonable that I cannot depart from it.
   The four are Herbert, Farrer, Burke, C. Gore, the last case the strongest of all.
2. I am very sorry that Sir T. Buxton's name did not come up sooner for consideration. I am now under pledge to the Queen to submit no more for some time; & indeed it is agreeable to the reason of the case that these Peerages on *general* grounds should only be considered after certain intervals.
3. Herbert will hold himself ready to obey your commands, when you shall have returned, I hope with benefit, from your short trip.
4. I should like to be kept informed of the comparative state of agrarian crime in Ireland during the critical time through which we have now to pass. Were I younger I should like to try a visit to Ireland myself; but this must not now be thought of.
Thanks for the letter of the Friends.

28. 11 S. Trin.

Garrison Chapel mg. Parish Ch aft. Saw Mr Rowsell—Ld Granville. So much pleased with young Mr Paget.[3] Wrote to Duke of Bedford—Helen G.—Ld Granville. Read Links & Clues[4]—Kate Trevelyan—Birks on Pentateuch.[5]

To the DUKE OF BEDFORD, 28 August 1881.   Add MS 44545, f. 14.

   You must long ago have found out that you have to deal, in me, with an obstinate impracticable old man, & you will therefore I am sure excuse me for the infirmity of my nature, if, until otherwise instructed, I construe your letter just received as the expression of a high-minded scruple rather than of a real difficulty.[6] All these difficulties (to treat the

---

[1] R. B. Drummond, *Erasmus*, 2v. (1873).
[2] i.e. H. J. Gladstone's various speeches at Leeds.
[3] Probably Francis *Paget, 1851-1911; student of Christ Church 1876; professor of pastoral theology 1885-92; dean of Christ Church from 1892.
[4] [V. S. Wortley], *Links and clues* (1881).
[5] T. R. Birks, *The Pentateuch and its anatomists* (1869).
[6] Again asking Gladstone to 'lay before the Queen the resignation of the Duchess'; Add MS 44471, f. 107.

question exhaustively) are in the past, the present or the future. It is not the past, for the Land Act is a by-gone, & there is nothing to do for or against it. Not the present, for the recess now beginning makes no Bills good or bad. And surely not the future. If (which I hardly suppose) you are apprehensive of some Irish Land Bill for Great Britain, that can never be under the present Government. If of some other Land measure, & some such must come at some time under any Government, you would I think agree that the time to judge them would be when they had come into practical existence. You will however be wearied out with this argumentation & I will end it by expressing my hope that I need not before we come to some new real dilemma, say anything to the Queen on the subject of your note. Every dissociation of a family like yours from what is obviously the national tone is the true public misfortune.[1]

29. M.

Wrote to The Queen 1.1.—Dean of Windsor—Mr C. Gore—Mr Bayley Potter. . . . Miss de Lisle—Mr F.C. Gower—Ld Kimberley—Mr Leveson [Gower]—Viscount Gort & minutes. Went to the Life Boat launch. Tea party: introduced to many Dealians. Read Kate Trevelyan—Rev. 2 Mondes on French Finance[2]—Life of Erasmus.

To LORD KIMBERLEY, colonial secretary, 29 August 1881.   Add MS 44545, f. 14.

I have read the letters of Cetewayo with extreme pain,[3] and a considerable sense of Cairns' blushing humour. You may be right about Colenso but in the main they seem to be such as a man of some mother-wit in his position ought to write, & would write. Can we do nothing to pour a little oil into his wounds? Is he without *any* of his (polygamous) family, and if he is must he continue so? If the present arrangement in Zululand is likely to break down, cannot we temporize and give him some gleam of national hope, and is it wholly out of the question to do this by letting him visit England? He was villaneously used & we owe him all that the nature of the case will allow or enable us to pay.[4]

To T. B. POTTER, M.P., 29 August 1881.[5]   Add MS 44545, f. 14.

I think much of the pamphlet you inclose is good but some of the arguments are such as the Cobden Club, fountainhead of pure doctrine, ought hardly to be committed to. See e.g. p. 16. With best wishes for your holidays.

[1] She eventually resigned as Mistress of the Robes in January 1883.
[2] *Revue des deux Mondes*, xlvi. 562 (August 1881).
[3] Cetewayo's petition to the Queen for restitution had been declined in July; he wrote to Gladstone on 15 July, forwarded by Kimberley on 26 August, Add MS 44226, f. 241, asking him to 'put me back with some good and discreet men'. Kimberley thought the letter 'betrays European inspiration', 'Bp Colenso and his friends in S. Africa, and Mr Chesson and the Aborigines Protection Society at home'.
[4] Kimberley then set in motion procedures resulting in Cetewayo's visit in August 1882: 'I believe we shall ultimately have to let him go back to Zululand' (2 September 1881, ibid., f. 253).
[5] Potter had sent a Cobden Club tract 'on reciprocity' (secretary's note); perhaps A. Mongredien, 'Free trade and English commerce' (1879 and reprints) of which p. 16 is ch. 4: 'If protection be beneficial as between country and country, it must be beneficial as between province and province'.

30. Tu.

Wrote to Watson & Smith—Ld Granville—W.H.G.—and minutes. Walk to Kingsdown.[1] Saw Sir John Mellor. Read Virg. Æn. Finished I.—Hist. du Xtme Unitaire—Life of Erasmus. Saw Mr Rowsell.

31. Wed.

Wrote to The Queen—Rev. Mr Rowsell—Mr Childers—Rev. Mr Knox Little—Mr Roundell and minutes. Full conversation with Ld Granville on 1. the Wolseley affair 2. the Assab Bay.[2] Read Hist. Xtme Unitaire—Contemp. Rev., three articles—The Æneid—Drummond's Erasmus. Walk to Sandown: fast disappearing.

To H. C. E. CHILDERS, war secretary, 31 August 1881.   Childers MS 5/41.

All things taken together the Wolseley question has become one of the most entangled I have ever known in the region of personal matters.[3]

One new fact comes out on these papers: new I mean to me. I had supposed the A.M.G.ship to be a great working office. Wolseley says, & you do not contradict, it is a sinecure. If this be so, I am much taken with the idea of holding it unfilled, which I suppose would be preferable to formal abolition.

I stated to you last week a serious difficulty about the peerage, which grows out of my own position, and my firm expectation of finding a comparatively early opportunity of retiring finally from Office.

I am inclined to think on the whole that Wolseley's proposal about Gibraltar is not inadmissable.

Your plan of making him Adjutant General would probably be better for the public service in the Dept.: but then this is a proposal, is it not, to solve difficulty by cumulating it.

I have had an opportunity of seeing Granville today, and showing him the letters. He agrees in this view. It is certainly an advantage, if the thing is to be done, that the first suggestion of it should have come from Wolseley himself. I return his letter.

[P.S.] Wind gone to the N. today and some hope of fair weather.

Thurs. Sept. One. 1881.

Wrote to Mr Hamilton (Tel)—Viceroy of Ireland—Ld Garvagh & minutes. Read Drummond's Erasmus—Virg. Æneid—Xtme Unitaire—Taylor in Nineteenth Cent.[4] Walk with C. Whist in evg. Explained to Ld Hardinge the whole affair of Littleberries as well as I could.

To LORD COWPER, Viceroy of Ireland, 1 September 1881.   Add MS 44545, f. 15.

I am not aware whether there are any means of communicating with your Chief Sec. during his short absence, or whether there are any circumstances which would justify your acting upon the suggestion of the Rev. M. Mooney. But the spirit of his letters

---

[1] Seat near Dover of Sir J. Mellor, retired judge.

[2] The Wolseley peerage affair and the Bay on the Red Sea owned by Egypt under Turkey but now claimed by Italy. Gladstone rejected Egypt's requests for British support; Ramm II, i. 288n.

[3] Childers forwarded Wolseley's letter requesting the governorship of Gibraltar and suggesting making him adjutant general; Add MS 44129, f. 238.

[4] N.C., x. 317 (September 1881).

makes me feel it my duty to bring them under your notice, & I own that I should look
with much desire to any suitable opportunity of doing any act of clemency which would
not weaken the authority of the law, & would tend to attract & conciliate the milder
spirits among the misled. Such an act would tend to counteract Parnell's desperate game,
& it would remove barriers out of the way of those genial influences which after the
recent & remarkable speech of Dillon[1] I presume that we are more than ever justified in
expecting from the Land Act.
I inclose Mr. Mooney's letters.[2]

2. Fr.

Wrote to Mr Knowles—Mr Hamilton 2 Tel. & letter—Rev. Dr Stock—Mr
Litton—Herbert J.G.—Ld Chancellor—Ld Portarlington—Viceroy of Ireland Tel.
and minutes. Walk with F.L. Gower & long conversation on my political situation and intentions. Read Virg. Æn. Drummond's Erasmus—Harrison on block
in H. of C.[3] Articles in Fortnightly. Whist in evg.

To J. R. KNOWLES, editor of the *Nineteenth Century*,   Add MS 44545, f. 16.
2 September 1881.

I thank you for your letter received this morning and though I have not yet read the
whole of Mr. Harrison's paper[4] I have read enough to be able to welcome it as one of
much value & to put down the following opinions on it.
1. He is by far too good to me.
2. He is right about the Irish Land Bill, by no means a very great bill, but undoubtedly (I
think) a most difficult one; quite another affair.
3. It took by far too much time. The whole work might as well have been done in 20
nights as in 50.
4. I heartily agree that the required reform must be partly restrictive, but must partly consist of means other than penal for giving more free[?] action to the House. Both are essential but the second I place first in importance.
5. It is I fear too probable that the question of internal reform which with[5] a Leader of
Opposition such as Peel could easily have been kept out of the vortex of party, will by the
weakness of Northcote be let slip into it.
I will not forget your other suggestion.

To LORD PORTARLINGTON, 2 September 1881.   Add MS 44545, f. 16.

I have to thank you for your kind note.[6] I must add my thanks for the encouragement
which was supplied to me by your opinions and your conduct in the performance of an
arduous task.
The case is too difficult to allow of confident anticipation as to the result. But I am able
to find favourable signs not only in friendly opinions such as yours, but in events such as
the remarkable speech which Dillon has delivered & as the almost frantic denunciations

---

[1] On 29 August, suspicious of the Irish parliamentary party and advocating a free run for the
Land Act; see 7 Oct. 81n. and F. S. L. Lyons, *John Dillon* (1968), 54.
[2] Evidently on the release of Fr. Sheehy; Cowper replied that he would look into his condition,
though Mooney had little direct knowledge of it; 3 September Add MS 44471, f. 145. Probably
Maurice Mooney, Roman catholic incumbent in Clare.
[3] F. Harrison, 'The deadlock in the House of Commons', *N.C.*, x. 317 (September 1881).
[4] See this day and Add MS 44232, f. 1.
[5] MS reads 'will' but this is probably a mistranscription by the copyist.   [6] Not found.

of Parnell (not to mention Miss Anna) the violence of which I take to be the measure of his apprehensions lest the Land Act should take the bread out of his mouth, as a speculator on public confusion, by tranquillising the mind of the Irish people.

To LORD SELBORNE, lord chancellor, 2 September 1881.   Selborne MS 1867, f. 186.

I read with sincere pleasure your improved account of yourself[1] and I sincerely hope you will keep yourself by care in a position to make more such reports to your friends until you can make the announcement that you are entirely well.

I am sad and sore in divers respects about the universities but I agree with you in declining leading strings of the State. On such lines I was able to keep the Aberdeen Government in 1854 and from them I am not disposed to depart; unless indeed it were possible to bring in with utility some negative and prohibitory powers.

My own (ignorant) opinion of Holker[2] as a lawyer has always been very high and I am glad to infer from your letter that you think he should have the place in the Court of Appeal offered to him. Until now I had not clearly taken in that it belonged to me to fill these offices. In dealing with them however I should act on what has been hitherto my uniform rule; not merely to consult the Chancellor, but to be guided in the last resort by his opinion. I shall not fail to write to Coleridge as you recommend.

What singular provisions are those named in the P.M. Gazette from Stanley's will.[3] With and under all his kind and all his fine qualities he seems to have had a kind of negative fanaticism.

[P.S.] Thanks for your intimation about W. Chitty.

3. Sat. [*Walmer Castle*][4]

Wrote to Herbert J.G.—Mr Hamilton Tel—Ld R. Grosvenor—Duke of Bedford & minutes. Bid goodbye to our kind hosts: & went to Walmer. Walk with F.L. Gower. Saw Ld Granville—Count Menabrea—Lady G. Fullerton[5]—Mr Finnis. Whist in evg. Read Æneid—Erasmus—Harcourt Papers.[6]

4. S.

Walmer Ch mg (with H.C.) and aft. Wrote to Ld Kimberley—Ld Brougham— Mr Hamilton—Ld Northbrook & minutes. Conversation with Ld G.—Lady G. Fullerton. Read Life of Erasmus—Hist du Xtme Unitaire.

5. M.

Wrote to Mrs Hitchman—Mr Knox Little Tel.—Ld Cowper—Mr A.G. Symonds—The Queen—Ld Waveney—Mr Forster—H. Seymour—Mr C. Gore and minutes. Conversation with Granville—Lady G. Fullerton. Drove to the

---

[1] 25 August, Add MS 44297, f. 186.

[2] Sir John Holker, 1828–82; tory M.P. Preston 1872–82; Disraeli's attorney general 1875–80; lord justice of appeal Jan. 1882.

[3] A. P. Stanley's will included legacies to those of Lady L. Grant's da.s not in convents; *P.M.G.*, 1 September 1881, 7.

[4] Granville's residence as Warden of the Cinque Ports.

[5] Lady Georgiana Fullerton (see 29 Mar. 45), Granville's sister, and her husband were both Roman Catholics. Gladstone had anon. reviewed her *Ellen Middleton* in 1844; see 8, 13, 24 May 44.

[6] E. W. Harcourt, ed., *The Harcourt papers*, 14v. (privately printed, 1876–91).

model house at St Albans.[1] Read Paradise Lost—Æneid—Xme Unitaire—Drummond's Erasmus—Whist in evg.

To LORD COWPER, Viceroy of Ireland, 5 September 1881.   Add MS 44545, f. 17.

It would be awkward to do anything in Forster's absence even with his assent, since it would certainly be construed as due to the removal of the pressure of his influence.[2]

Also I admit that the meeting of the 16th, as you describe it, may form an epoch in the case. But I do not regard it as decisive. The official Land League may, as Mr. Parnell unquestionably will, do every thing it can to disparage, obstruct and neutralise the Land Act. All will do this with whom the League has only been a means for ends lying far beyond the scope of the Land Act, & this class may govern the proceedings in Dublin. On the other hand if the country is quiet or moving visibly towards quietness, it *may* be right, in defiance of turbulence within the precinct of the Land League, nay it may be eminently wise by reason of such turbulence, to meet the good feeling of the country, & to resist the acts of the turbulent by some release of prisoners.

I am very doubtful as to the expediency of asking them to sign undertakings.

I return to town tomorrow or Wednesday. Granville is much better.

To W. E. FORSTER, Irish secretary, 5 September 1881.   Add MS 44545, f. 18.

I send you herewith copy of a letter I have had from Cowper & of my reply dated today. I have some scruple in interfering even thus far with your little holiday, but it will probably be near the time for your turning your face homewards when this reaches you.

We have before us in administration a problem not less delicate & arduous than the problems of legislation with which we have lately had to deal in Parliament. Of the leaders, the officials, the skeleton of the Land League I have no hope whatever. The better the prospects of the Land Act with their adherents outside the circle of wirepullers, & with the Irish people, the more bitter will be their hatred, & the more sure they will be to go as far as fear of the people will allow them in keeping up the agitation which they cannot afford to part with on account of their ulterior ends. All we can do is to thin more & more the masses of their followers, to fine them down by good laws & good government, and it is in this view that the question of judicious releases from prison, should improving statistics of crime encourage it, may become one of early importance.

In this view generally I think Granville concurs, while neither of us lean to precipitate or wholesale measures.

Dillon's speech is eminently encouraging & Parnell's utterances not less instructive.

I am awaiting anxiously information about the state of crime in Ireland.

On Wednesday I go to town, & to Hawarden I hope by the end of the week.

To A. G. SYMONDS, Secretary of the National Reform Union,   Add MS 44545, f. 18.
5 September 1881.

I have received your letter[3] with interest and will make it known to Lord R. Grosvenor. I remember to have heard it from Lord Wolverton as a tradition of the party that it suffered in bye elections, and I also remember that even during the Reform agitation of 1830-2 the Tories won one or two remarkable bye elections, though when the general

---

[1] Near Wingham, seat of William Oxenden Hammond, 1817-1903; soldier and tory.
[2] Cowper argued on 2 September that the release of suspects 'would be most disastrous' and on 3 September drew attention to the Land League's Convention of 16 September, opposing release until after it; Add MS 44471, ff. 143, 145.   [3] Not found.

election came in 1832 they were reduced from 270 to 140, mainly by the extinction of close Boroughs.

6. Tu.

Wrote to E. Hamilton—Bp of Carlisle—Mr Herbert R.A.—Mr Childers—Dean of St Paul's—The Queen—Sir W. Harcourt—Mr Jerningham—Mr Knox Little & minutes. Saw Ld Gr.—Mr Fullerton—Ly G.F.—Ld Sydney. Walk to Villa Vita. Read Æneid—Fortnightly Rev. on Bulgaria[1]—Lady G.F.'s Novel & appx.[2]—Drummond's Erasmus.

To H. C. E. CHILDERS, war secretary, 6 September 1881.   Add MS 44545, f. 19.

Your letter is I think thoroughly correct in form & substance & I this day forward the recommendation to the Queen.[3]

It is hard[er] to see further into the thick perplexities of the coming winter than into the proverbial millstone; but I shall be very glad to have, when an opportunity offers, the chance of resuming the conversation I had with you just before the Prorogation in regard to my own position. There is no change in my desire & hope to execute the *whole* movement I then described, but I am not quite as sure whether it will be practicable to divide it into halves.

To Sir W. V. HARCOURT, home secretary, 6 September 1881.   MS Harcourt dep. 8, f. 102.

I forwarded to you in due course Dr Belcher's application & certificate relating to the Rev. Mr Green. I now transmit his reply to my inquiry founded on his first letter, and I have no doubt you will deal with these as the case may require.

Here in strictness I ought to close but there is one point which, if I am correct in my facts, will undoubtedly crop out at least in retrospect with reference to a rather strange chapter of Ecclesiastical History. I am under the impression that Mr Green's imprisonment grows out of disobedience to a judgment of the Privy Council touching clerical vestments. But unless I am grossly mistaken, that same judgment is disobeyed systematically & with impunity every day in the year by every Clergyman who wears what is called a stole, that is I imagine by far more than ninetynine in every hundred of the whole Clergy of the country. I fully admit that this observation has but a slight connection with the health of Mr Green.[4]

I wish you heartily a pleasant vacation & we should be very pleased if you and Lady Harcourt could contrive to visit us at Hawarden on your way southwards.

7. Wed. [London]

Wrote to Scarsdale—Mr W.O. Hammond—Dr Bradley—Ld Selborne—C.G.—Ld Bridport—Col. Romilly and minutes. Saw Scarsdale: with good hopes [R]. Saw

[1] *F.R.*, xxxvi. 284 (September 1881).

[2] Lady G. Fullerton, *A will and a way*, 3v. (1881).

[3] Of 4 September, Add MS 44129, f. 241: reasons against making Wolseley governor of Gibraltar; adjutant general or undersecretary possible.

[4] Harcourt replied from the Hebrides, 10 September, Add MS 44196, f. 216, that Sidney Faithhorn Green (1841–1916, rector of Miles Platting 1869–82), imprisoned March 1881 (effectively for ritualism, technically for contempt) was not ill and that there was no 'decent excuse' to release him; Gardiner, i. 385. Negotiations eventually gained his release in November 1882.

Mr Hamilton—Ld Rosebery—Ld Granville—Mr & Lady G.F.—May Hardy—Mr
Knowles. Read Erasmus—Æneid—Life of Voltaire. Dined with Mr H. at Reform
Club.[1]

8. *Th.*

Wrote to Mr Roundell—Dean of Windsor—Mr Forster—Dean of St Paul's—Abp
of York—Bishop of Carlisle. Mrs Scarsdale & minutes. Saw L. Hope (singular
narrative) [R]. Mr Hamilton—Mrs Th. (& Ld A. Clinton)—Scotts. Read Shakespeare—The Priests Blessing[2]—Erasmus.

To W. E. FORSTER, Irish secretary, 8 September 1881.[3]   Add MS 44545, f. 20.

The unexpected victory in Tyrone[4] is an event of importance & I own it much increases
my desire to meet this remarkable *Irish* manifestation & discomfiture both of Parnell &
Tories with some initial act of clemency—in view especially of the coming election for
Monaghan.

I do not know whether the release of the priest[5] would be a seasonable beginning but I
shall be very sorry if we cannot do something to meet the various friendly & hopeful
indications of which this Ulster election is the most remarkable.

To reduce the following of Parnell by drawing away from him all well inclined men
seems to me the key of Irish politics for the moment.

Though I felt reluctant that anything should be done in your absence yet I think the
impendency of the Monaghan election is a fact of commanding importance in the case
before us.[6]

[P.S.] I go to Hawarden on Saturday. I have asked Granville's opinion on the point put in
the letter. Possibly a reply to this in words of *reference* may be suitable for telegraphing.

To H. GOODWIN, bishop of Carlisle, 8 September 1881.   Add MS 44545, f. 21.

I admit that with what I hear of the Carlisle Deanery there may be physical objections
to Mr. Grey.[7] The chief objection to Dr. Hannah I think is that it seems so very uncertain
whether he would take the Deanery.

With regard to Mr. Oakley I had not heard of the published document you referred to
& as he is a liberal in politics I am surprised at his belonging to the Church Defence
Society which I look upon as a piece of Tory machinery. The excuse for the others I suppose is that it is a body which exists not to persecute others but to resist persecution. I
will try to inquire further about Mr. O. Meanwhile your Lordship's reference to Dr. Gott
reminds me of the excellent Mr. Wood who would have been Vicar had not Dr Gott been
chosen & whose admirable qualifications made it a matter of difficulty to decide between
them. I do not know if your Lordship has much information about him. I ought to add
that on this occasion I am desirous to propose a clergyman of liberal opinions in politics.

---

[1] With Hamilton; lively account in Bahlman, *Hamilton*, i. 166.

[2] H. Jay, *The priest's blessing* (1881).

[3] Copy of this letter forwarded next day to Cowper.

[4] Success at a by-election of Thomas Alexander Dickson, 1833–1909, standing as a liberal; the
Home Ruler a wretched third (Dickson, 3168; Knox (tory) 3084; Rylett (H.R.), 907).

[5] Father Eugene Sheehy, soon released and active with Parnell.

[6] See to Givan, 10 Sept. 81. Forster was at Hawarden 15–16 September.

[7] Bp. Goodwin had written on possible appointees; Add MS 44471, f. 179.

The unmitigated Toryism of the bulk of the clerical body obliges me to have some, though not an uniform regard to this qualification.[1]

9. Fr.

Wrote to Mrs L. Hope—Mr Childers (2)—L. Dashwood—Sir W. Harcourt—Mrs Th.—Mr Fergusson MP[2]—C.G.—Mr Thorold Rogers—Viceroy of Ireland. Saw Mr Hamilton—Mr H. Seymour—Mr Knowles. L. Hope 1.1. & there is hope—Scarsdale: change arranged. Dashwood 149 [Keppel Street?] hopeful. Phillips: a case for pity & others [R]. Read The Priests' Blessing. Dined at Mr Montgomery's.[3] Met Ld Orford.[4] Mr Law[5] brother of Rev. T.G.L.—Duchess of Montrose—Mr Mitford & others. Worked on arranging papers &c.

To LORD COWPER, Viceroy of Ireland, 9 September 1881.   Add MS 44545, f. 21.

I send you copy of my recent communications to Forster.

The Tyrone election[6] is a great event as a defeat of Toryism in a stronghold but far greater as a defeat of Parnell.

It makes me more desirous of some early act of clemency which might be as it were an acknowledgement of the disposition of the Irish people as shewn in the election.

If it be true, as I saw it stated, that ¼ of the voting power is R.C. then Parnell has been in a *minority*, as I reckon, among the R.Cs. themselves.

What the act of clemency should be, what is most politic and safe, I do not know. At first sight the release of the Priest [i.e. Sheehy] recommends itself.

I left Granville on Wednesday. We talked over the subject and I have since learned that he agrees in my view of the Tyrone election. I go to Hawarden tomorrow.[7]

10. Sat. [Hawarden]

Wrote to Mr Childers—Sir D. Marjoribanks—Mr Givan[8]—Ld R. Grosvenor—and minutes. A long busy morning of arranging & packing. Saw Mr Hamilton—Ld Granville. Read The Priest's Blessing—Drummond's Erasmus—The Gospel of the Divine Life.[9]

To J. GIVAN, M.P., 10 September 1881. '*Private*'.   Add MS 44545, f. 22.

My first and most obvious duty on receiving your letter is to thank you for the offer it contains, and the high public spirit with which you are acting in a matter certainly of great importance.

[1] John Oakley (see 20 Feb. 67) was appt. dean, after Frederick John Wood, perpetual curate in Leeds, declined; see Add MS 44545, f. 30.
[2] Robert Ferguson, 1817–98; manufacturer and liberal M.P. Carlisle, 1874–86.
[3] Probably H. de F. Montgomery of Berkeley Square; an Irish landowner; later in dispute with Gladstone on Ireland, see 9 Nov. 86.
[4] Horatio William Walpole, 1813–94; 4th earl of Orford 1858; a tory.
[5] T.G. (see 17 Dec. 78) had several brs.; this is probably Francis Towry Adeane Law, 1835–1901; soldier; served in the 1st Boer war.
[6] See 8 Sept. 81n.
[7] Cowper's reply on 10 September expected further releases; Cowper, 520.
[8] John Givan, b. 1837; Irish lawyer; liberal M.P. Monaghan 1880–3, when appt. Crown Solicitor.
[9] T. Griffith, *The gospel of the divine life* (1881).

Next I think it plain that a final decision can hardly be taken in Mr. Forster's absence; and as he expects to return in the middle of next week, I hope there can be no difficulty in the short postponement which is required. Meantime I will communicate with Lord R. Grosvenor.

I observe that you dwell upon the want of a first class candidate. Am I to understand that if such a person were forthcoming the County of Monaghan might be safely fought? And, if this is so, it seems desirable to look far and near for such a candidate though perhaps none can be found.

After the terrible blow which you have been able to inflict on Parnell and Parnellism in Tyrone, Mr. P. might think thrice before playing his game in Monaghan unless it were there subject to little doubt as to the issue.

[P.S.] Perhaps I ought to have said more explicitly that in my opinion, as you generously permit it, the question of the state of the County and of general policy *ought* to enter into the subject of your finally accepting or not.[1] I go to Hawarden today.

11. S. Trin

Ch mg & evg. Wrote to Ld Cowper—Ld Granville Tel—Rev. S.E.G.—Archdn Blunt.[2]—Hope and minutes. Read The Great Dilemma[3]—Nevins on Development[4]—White, Discipline of Suffering.[5]

12. M.

Ch $8\frac{1}{2}$ a.m. Wrote to Sir C. Dilke—Tel—Dr Schliemann—Ld Dufferin—Ld Granville—Rev. Mr Simeon Lea—Bp of Tasmania—Mr Forster—Scotts—Mr Hamilton—W.H.G. and minutes. Worked on Bank Book & account of property. arranging letters. Walk with E. Wickham. Read K. Trevelyan (finished)—Reflections of M. Antoninus.[6]

13. Tu.

Ch $8\frac{1}{2}$ a.m. Wrote to Ld Granville 1 & Tel—Mr Hamilton Tel. 1.2.—Sir H. Ponsonby 1. & Tel—Messrs Pears—Mrs Th.—Mr Downing—Mr Holland MP—Sir W. Harcourt and minutes. Worked on Books: a heavy task is before me for my shelves are threatening to burst. Walk with A. Lyttelton. Photographed for Leeds. Read M. Aurelius—Serbian Folk Lore.[7]

To Sir W. V. HARCOURT, home secretary, 13 September   MS Harcourt dep. 8, f. 105.
1881.

Your letter appears to be from Paradise;[8] but you have not put any date of [*sic*] place—except the Home office. I quite agree that you can do nothing about Green unless it were

---

[1] Givan, one of the few remaining Liberal M.P.s in Ireland, did not accept this post; when he resigned in 1883, Healy won the seat, the liberal coming third with 5% of the votes.

[2] Richard Lefevre Blunt, 1833-1910; archdeacon of the E. Riding 1873-92.

[3] By H. Ottley (1881).

[4] W. P. Nevins, *Development versus fossilised Christianity* (1881).

[5] G. C. White, *The discipline of suffering . . . readings on the history of Job* (1880).

[6] Many eds.; perhaps that of 1874 by G. Long.

[7] See 22 Aug. 81.

[8] See 6 Sept. 81n.

to make sure that the Doctor is aware of the reference to the state of his mind. It will be right to inform Belcher but I would not, in so doing, make any reference to the power of self-liberation, as this might induce controversial matter.

This is a *bad* business in Egypt.

[P.S.] I go to Leeds in the first week of October, but do not contemplate any other act of absenteeism before the time for Cabinets.

14. *Wed.*

Ch 8½ a.m. Wrote to Mr Forster Tel—Bp of Ripon—Mr Childers—Mr Hughes—Scotts and minutes. Worked long & laboriously on books. Read Serbian Folk Lore—Physiologie du Mariage[1] and [blank]. Company gathering.[2]

To H. C. E. CHILDERS, home secretary, 14 September 1881. Childers MS 5/49.
'*Private*'.

In the matter of Wolseley it is easier, I admit, to point out the difficulties than to suggest expedients. For example, I do not see a way of escape through the Under Secretaryship. 1. It requires a difficult and rather far-fetched condition[3] previous. 2. It gives up the essential point so long maintained. 3. It diminishes very decidedly the authority with which W. would speak in the H. of Lords. 4. It gives him a lower position in the eyes of the world. I own I much prefer Gibraltar were it open.

You might I think put your proposed question to him in such a way as to leave you perfectly free. But in the great difficulties of the case it would I think be a mistake wholly to shut out the Gibraltar notion.

The state of facts disclosed by the language of H.R.H. is indeed extraordinary and highly embarrassing.[4]

15. *Th.*

Ch 8½ a.m. Wrote to Dean of Windsor—Ld Kimberley and minutes. Worked 10–2 on arranging books & at last got something like order. But pamphlets! Saw Mr Forster—Bp of Winchester. Twelve to dinner. Read Serbian Folk Lore—Armenian's Letters on Ireland.[5]

16. *Fr.*

Church 8½ a.m. Wrote to The Queen (2)—Sir H. Ponsonby (Tel)—Ld Granville l & Tel—Mr Leatham MP—Viceroy of Ireland—Mr Wortley & minutes. Eleven to dinner. Spent the morning with Mr Forster on Irish & other affairs. Saw Bp of Winchester—Folk Lore of Serbia—Royaume de Roumanie[6]and [blank.]

To E. A. LEATHAM, M.P., 16 September 1881. Add MS 44545, f. 23.

I am truly sorry to be unable to comply with the wish expressed in your kind note.[7] But my day for making political circuits has gone by. I visit Leeds entirely for the purpose of

---

[1] *Nouvelle physiologie du mariage, ou De l'ignorance du mari et des déceptions de l'épouse* (1866).
[2] Including Forster and E. H. Browne; later Cowper; H.V.B.
[3] Reading uncertain.
[4] Cambridge's objections to Wolseley's 'professional views'; Add MS 44129, f. 254.
[5] See 5 Aug. 79. [6] Not found.
[7] Invitation untraced.

paying, or at least of acknowledging a debt. I have been obliged already to decline many other invitations, which if accepted would give quite a different character to the proceedings, & you will at once see that the negative answer must, if it were only to avoid offence, be uniform.

17. Sat.

Ch 8½ a.m. Wrote to Mr Bechopoulos[1]—Rev. Dr Nevin—Mr Pease MP—Sir R. Blennerhassett—Mr Richardson MP[2]—Bp of Lincoln—Ld R. Grosvenor and minutes. The Bp of W. & his party went. He is excellent. Walk with E.T. & A.L. Read Serbian Folk Lore—Royaume de Roumanie—Poems of Marino.[3]

To Sir R. BLENNERHASSETT, M.P., 17 September 1881.   Add MS 44545, f. 24.

I am going to put to you an abrupt & bold question. Do you think you could do anything to move Dr. Döllinger to come to this country next month?[4]

The Bp. of Winchester, one of our most learned & wisest Prelates, who has just been here, tells me that Bp. Reinkens & some other of the most learned German Divines of his communion are at that time to pay a visit to Cambridge.

It would in my opinion be *a* great service done to religion generally if he would come.

Religion still, in the words of Burke, lifts her united front in courts & palaces among us, but she lifts it less than heretofore in the halls devoted to the training (especially) of the human intellect. Wherever Döllinger goes, he goes not merely as a professed theologian but as a great intellectual light; recalling in a measure Dante's noble line.

Di cherubica luce uno splendore.[5]

If you take this matter in hand, & if he will listen, the proper way will I think be to send some person well up to the ways of travelling to bring him, so that he should have no trouble at all but only obey orders.

I should hardly have written this letter, but for a conversation which I had with you early in the year.

I have just been reading the letter of Campello;[6] & I shall try to get more information about him. It seems like the production of a man of some mark.

To LORD R. GROSVENOR, chief whip, 17 September 1881.   Add MS 44315, f. 47.

I see it stated in the newspapers that Childers has accepted an invitation to meet me at Leeds; & I am told the Cabinet generally have been invited. It appears to me that any such acceptance is a mistake, simply as a *waste.*

We shall have lots of liberal meetings during the autumn & the people at all of them will want Cabinet Ministers if possible to attend them, & there will be as there always is great difficulty in getting them. I do not know whether *you* can do anything to check this useless cumulation, but it appears to me worth considering whether you would write to

---

[1] Of Smyrna, sent regards and some of his sister's needlework; Add MS 44471, f. 65.

[2] James Nicholson Richardson, b. 1846; merchant and liberal M.P. Armagh 1880-5.

[3] See 21 Sept. 78, 23 July 80 (f.l.).

[4] Blennerhassett did not get this letter until 23 September, replying that Döllinger was 'staying with the Actons at Tegernsee. I have written to him ... but I fear there is little chance'; Add MS 44471, f. 216.

[5] Dante, *Paradiso*, xi. 39.

[6] Count Enrico di Campello resigned his canonry of St. Peter's, Rome, on 13 September, subsequently founding the Reformed Italian Catholic Church; see 29 Oct. 81.

Childers & tell him you will certainly have to invite him to do duty this autumn at one or more than one place.

The Tories are developing a portentous activity in speechifying. Northcote will I fear be worked off his legs; it is well there is no demand upon his back bone.

Forster went on from us to Ireland yesterday, anxious & I think justly anxious to release suspects as fast as the state of the country in its several districts will permit.
[P.S.] My day at Leeds is the 6th.

18. 14 S. Trin.

Ch mg & evg. Wrote to Sir R. Wilson—Ld Halifax—Mrs Forster and minutes. Read A New Analogy[1]—Hist. du Xme Unitaire (finished)—Bate on Ritualism & Liturgy[2]—Bp of Tasmania on The Crisis[3] and other tracts. Walk with Alfred & E. Talbot.

To LORD HALIFAX, 18 September 1881.   Halifax MSS A 4/88.

Many thanks for your very considerate & kind note.[4] We shall not enjoy your hospitality on our brief visit to Leeds, but we shall I hope have the benefit of the next best thing to it, as we are to go direct from Leeds to Mrs Meynell Ingram. I hope you and Lady Halifax are both well.

The Egyptian business caused us anxiety a few days ago but we are much relieved by the favourable turn it has taken with a fair prospect of continuance.

The bloodless emancipation of Thessaly is a subject of unmixed satisfaction. The Sultan has been cherishing notions of getting back his power in Egypt but I do not think he will kick over the traces.

With what surprise and disgust you must regard the 'Fair Trade' imposture and the use made of it by the Tories to repair some portion of their defects. My inclination is to denounce it out and out at Leeds, but I shall weigh the matter well.

Parnell too seems a proper object for a just and strong description. He has not above a dozen Irish members really with him and even these he rules with a rod of iron.

19. M.

Ch 8½ a.m. Wrote to Viceroy of Ireland Tel and minutes. Read Rousseau, Verses[5]—Vie de l'Abbé Dubois[6]—Royaume de Roumanie—Lettre à son Altesse &c.[7] Walk & much conversation with E. Talbot: what a fine fellow:—his wife.

20. Tu.

Ch 8½ a.m. Wrote to Watsons—E. Talbot—Mr Beet—Dean of Windsor—Mr

---

[1] *A new analogy between religion and nature* (1881).

[2] J. Bate, *The perils of ritualism* (1881).

[3] C. H. Bromby; probably an untraced article.

[4] Unable to invite him: scarlet fever in the village; Add MS 44186, f. 171. Halifax's reply, 20 September, ibid., f. 173, encouraged speaking out 'as to Parnell'.

[5] J. J. Rousseau, *Oeuvres poétiques*, 2v. (1823 ed.).

[6] V. de Seilhac, *L'Abbé Dubois*, 2v. (1862).

[7] Voltaire; see 27 Mar. 81.

Chant Tel[1]—Lady Portsmouth—Dr Warren[2]—Bp of Manchester—S.R. Lawley—
Sir H. Johnstone—and minutes. Worked on accounts: & framed a plan in
preparation for the endowment of St Thomas Toxteth. Saw Edw. Talbot—Earl
Cowper. The Cowpers came in afternoon. Drive & walk with them. Read
Dialogue of Egalité and the Regent.[3]

To G. V. WELLESLEY, dean of Windsor, 20 September 1881.   Add MS 44545, f. 25.

I am greatly obliged for all the trouble you have taken and I think, indeed I feel certain,
I can satisfy you about Oakley[4] and Disestablishment. First by assuring you that I would
not on any account recommend to the Queen a Clergyman favourable to Disestablishment; not because there need be guilt or folly in it, nor alone because of what she thinks
or wishes, but on account of what I conceive to be the office of the Crown in regard to
Church Patronage, namely to promote men who will work loyally with & for the existing
system of Church Law & Connection between Church and State. Secondly I am certain
(& am strongly confirmed in this by E. Talbot) that what my son refers to [is?] disestablishment rather than surrender truth of doctrine, not the disestablishment of Mr.
Maconochie, which is I think what you mean. Thirdly any man prepared for disestablishment would really be a fool if he joined as Oakley has done the Church Defence Association: a measure certainly in advance of me. But fourthly I think you will agree with me the
Archbishop never would have offered Ramsgate to a disestablisher: and on that subject I
conceive that the Archbishop's nose (for even an Archbishop has a nose) is infallible.

I await the answer from Balmoral, to make the offer to Wood.[5] Oakley I may add is
reported to me to have begun as a Broad Churchman but to have moved gently upwards.

Now pray do crown your grace and goodness by coming here from Aberystwith: we are
really *all but* on your way.

In my letter O. is not *abreast* of W. but only comes up if W. declines.

21. Wed. St Matthew

Ch 8½ a.m. & H.C. A day of conversation. Wrote to Ld Granville Tel—Ld Hardinge—Mr Scharf—Mr Forster—Rev. Mr Wood and minutes. Wrote Mem. on
Mill Hill.[6] Finished the Egalité Dialogue. Read Don Quixote[7]—Royaume de
Roumanie—Tracts. Conversation with Cowper. They went off: so kind. Drive
with C. & walk.

To W. E. FORSTER, Irish secretary, 21 September 1881.   Add MS 44545, f. 26.

I need hardly say that your letter[8] and the accompanying papers received today afford
much and disagreeable matter for reflexion.

---

[1] Possibly Thomas Beet of Clarendon Road, London, and Thomas Chant of Adelaide Road,
Hampstead, but business untraced for both. Or, for Beet, see 8 Mar. 82.
[2] William Fairfield Warren of Boston University had sent his article on cosmology; Add MS
44471, f. 127.
[3] Untraced.
[4] For the deanery of Carlisle; Wellesley reported he knew nothing of Oakley (see 8 Sept. 81); Add
MS 44340, f. 130.
[5] Who declined it, see 8 Sept. 81n.
[6] Not found.   [7] See 5 Apr. 27.
[8] Of 20 September, Add MS 44159, f. 13, enclosing an exchange between Forster and Ulster
Tenant-Right Associations which requested wholesale release of suspects.

Gladstone and his secretaries *ca.* 1883
(left to right: Horace Seymour, Spencer Lyttelton, George Leveson Gower, Edward Hamilton)

Gladstone in the Temple of Peace at Hawarden, photographed as the
Royal Academy's Professor of Ancient History on 6 June 1884 by J. P. Mayall for *Artists at Home*

Family Group at Hawarden in the early 1880s
(Back row: Mrs W.H.G., W.H.G., Mary G., W.E.G. Middle row: H.N.G., Mrs. G., S.E.G.
Front row: H.J.G., Agnes Wickham, E. C. Wickham, Helen G.)

The Cabinet in July 1883
(Clockwise from Gladstone: Carlingford, Childers, Northbrook, Spencer, Chamberlain, Dilke, Selborne,
Harcourt, Hartington, Dodson, Kimberley, Derby, Granville)

Lord Granville

Lord Spencer

Lord Frederick Cavendish

Lord Hartington

(1) I observe that you make no reference to the process of piecemeal release of the suspects which we considered fully: but I take for granted it will go on. This I gathered also from Cowper's conversation.

(2) It certainly seems hard that so far as speaking is concerned Parnell & Co have a monopoly in Ireland. Pray consider, & if need be consult R. Grosvenor on the question whether anything can be done in this matter.

(3) And it is a grave point for me to consider whether I should (at Leeds) describe him by his *acts* (not motives) as what he is an enemy of the Empire.

(4) The circumstances embrace so much that is ugly that I wish you could have some Mem. drawn for the information of the Cabinet: especially considering how possible it is that in a few weeks you *may* be compelled to consult them.[1]

(5) It is quite clear as you said that P. means to present cases which the Commission must refuse, and then to treat their refusal as showing that they cannot be trusted, & that the Bill has failed.

(6) I return your *letter*—inclosures—not very certain how much opportunity Mr. Robinson has for passing a judgment.

The Cowpers went on this morning.

22. Th.

Ch 8½ a.m. Wrote to Lady Selborne—Ld Coleridge—Ld Granville—Watsons—Sir B. Frere and minutes. Read Marcus Aurelius—Biogr. of Damiens[2]—M. Aurelius —Nineteenth Cent on Free Trade[3]—Don Quixote—Eichthal's Socrate.[4] Ventured on a little woodcutting—But I am no longer equal to the true woodmans work. Made some examinations on the subject of trade.[5]

23. Fr.

Ch 8½ a.m. Wrote to Bp of Manchester—Ld Mayor of L.—Mrs Th.—Sir W. Harcourt—Lady Hutt—Sir H. Moncreiff—Mr Cent—Dean of Windsor Tel.—Ld Rosebery—Mr Hamilton Tel and minutes. Woodcutting: in small. Read L'Apoteosi (Casti)[6]—Eichthal's Socrate—M. Aurelius—Don Quixote—Puschkin.[7]

To Sir W. V. HARCOURT, home secretary, 23 September   MS Harcourt dep. 8, f. 109. 1881.

Ecce eternum Mr Greene [*sic*]. I inclose to you 1. A letter from Dr Walter Phillimore cut out of the P.M. Gazette of yesterday. I do not know of the value of his precedents but I presume that they could be looked at, & I deem it possible you may not have seen the letter. 2. A letter just received from the Bishop of Manchester, with copies of the letters he inclosed, & with my reply, which last contains the little I have to say upon the subject.[8]

---

[1] See Forster's mem. on the condition of Ireland, 9 October; PRO CAB 37/5/22.
[2] Perhaps W. H. Dilworth, *The royal assassins, containing the trial and execution of R. F. Damiens* (1759).
[3] G. Potter on fair trade in *N.C.*, x. 430 (September 1881).
[4] G. d'Eichthal, *Socrate et nôtre temps* (1881).
[5] Preparing for the Leeds speech.
[6] By G. Casti in his *Novelle* (1801), vi. 133.
[7] A. S. Pushkin, *Eugene Onéguine*, sent by the translator, Lt.-Col. Spalding (1881).
[8] This coordinated attempt to release Green failed as he declined the compromise, remaining in gaol until December 1882; Gladstone's letter and others in T. Hughes, *James Fraser* (1887), 268.

Had I when I began remembered that I might spare you needless repetition I need not have committed my small and short letter to this dignified sheet of paper.

24. Sat.

Ch 8½ a.m. Wrote to the Queen Tel—Ld Granville—Mr Forster—Dean of Windsor—Mr Hamilton—A.L. Gladstone and minutes. Wood-cutting: mildly. Read M. Aurelius (bad style: then translations, more accurate)—Rousseau, Origine des Langues (which has curious matter)[1]—Puschkin's Poem—Diderot's Fils Naturel[2]—a Catholic's Rules.[3]

The sea ever weltering on our coasts from time to time gains here and loses there. And even so it might seem as though the restless human intellect, moving onwards at periods so much and widely [?] and in many things was nevertheless insensibly and simultaneously losing ground in others on which it had released its hold: and as if this mixture of progress and recession was for our wayward race almost a law.[4]

Rousseau observes that there are sonorous tongues favourable to liberty, but that *les nôtres sont faites pour le bourdonnement des divans.*[5]
It may seem remarkable that the English tongue should so largely have formed itself under Elizabeth and James the First, when Government was but little free. But the first of these reigns was all along the grand struggle for national freedom. And individual freedom followed in its wake. That *corollarian* struggle took form under the first Stuart and reached a climax under the second.[6]

25. 15 S. Trin.

Ch mg & [blank.] Wrote to Ld Hartington + A lengthened statement[7]—Mr Childers—Mr Barran MP—Mr Salkeld & minutes. Read Eichthal's Socrate—Medd's Sermons[8]—Rev. North, Blackburn, Philip.[9]

26. M.

Ch 8½ a.m. Wrote to Ld Kimberley—Mr Godley l & Tel.—Rev. Mr Leeman—Mr G. Howard MP—L. Lady Waterford and minutes. Woodcraft with W. Worked on books. Read M. Aurelius—Eichthal's Socrates—Diderot Fils Naturel (finished)—Don Quixote.

The dangers of our age are great: but the greater they are the more animating they should be. They are each one of them a source of life unto life for all those, who shall

---

[1] See following mem.   [2] By D. Diderot (1758).   [3] Untraced tract.
[4] Holograph dated 24 September 1881; Add MS 44765, f. 132.
[5] In ch. xx of Rousseau's *Essai sur l'origine des langues* (1781): there are some languages which promote liberty; these are the sonorous, heavy languages whose speeches can be heard from a great distance. Ours are made for the hum of the drawing room.
[6] Holograph dated 24 September 1881; Add MS 44765, f. 131.
[7] On the Wolseley peerage affair.
[8] P. G. Medd, probably *Diligence in prayer* (1878).
[9] J. H. North, 'Two Sermons' (1877).

finally be numbered among the saints of God. The excess in these dangers is the measure of their privilege. And that privilege which itself is in degree will be high and higher still in proportion as to their promptitude in discerning this part of their vocation, and their energy in acting upon what they have discerned.

Every stroke of the battering ram of scepticism and sceptical criticism against miracle, against inspiration, against revelation, against sacred books, against the Church of God, against the Christian religion, against the Divine perfections, against the very existence of God, will be to the servants of God a new minister for good, if the end of the searching and struggling inquiries on which these shocks may launch them [is] to make them more careful than heretofore in bringing into an absolute parallelism the whole body of theological and ecclesiastical tradition in all its forms with the unbending requisitions of the moral law.

Here then is the upshot. Upon the mixed and fluctuating scene of human destiny, so far as bad men are embraced in it (and bad men there are, tremble my soul lest thou be found among them) the curtain falls, and rises not again. These wicked are shown to us in the condition of suffering which befits and accompanies a state of persistent hardened sin: and they are shown to us no more. The consolation which Faith withholds, reason does not supply, for the philosophy of human nature exhibits on its way to moral fixity, teaches that its final state is determined by practice, that the doctrine of habits overhangs and embraces all the laws and facts of our condition, that we pass gradually beyond the reach of change, be it into continued life or into nothingness. The formation of all theories which go to show that our probation here is in no case a probation, and that life on earth is but a vestibule of moral discipline, may serve to show to what expedients men are driven when in desperate straits, but the history of the operations of the human mind affords no purer example of the practice which is called building castles in the air.[1]

To LORD KIMBERLEY, colonial secretary, 26 September   Add MS 44545, f. 28.
1881.

The telegram in the Standard on Saturday made me uneasy although its correspondent in S. Africa has always seemed to me to be in the highest degree a sensationalist. The non-conformation reassured me in part & for the time but I now observe that his bad report is a day later than the more favourable anticipation in the Times.[2] I hope to hear from you tomorrow as you can by this time hardly be without official news. And in the meantime I write to say 1. we must have no scruple in calling a hasty Cabinet if need be, though it might not be attended by all our colleagues: 2. I hope Sir E. Wood is in the way for military questions may turn up. The Speech of Joubert reads ill; but this may turn on niceties in the translation.[3]

27. Tu.

Ch 8½ a.m. Wrote to Mr Godley 1 & Tel.—Bp of Winchester—The Queen—Ld Midleton—Mr Forster—Ld Granville—Dr Reichel[4] and minutes. Woodcraft with W.H.G. Read Eichthal finished—M. Aurelius—Don Quixote—Reichel's

[1] Holograph dated 26 September 1881; Add MS 44765, f. 133; illegible added phrases omitted.
[2] Volksraad unlikely to ratify the convention; Imperial govt. likely to have to modify terms; *Standard*, 24 September 1881, 5f and *T.T.*, 24, 26 September 1881, 5b, 5d.
[3] Kimberley replied, 27 Sept., Add MS 44226, f. 265: 'I have strange to say no official news as to the Volksraad', which is clearly reluctant to ratify, but 3 months allowed from 3 August, and 'our military position is good'.
[4] C. P. Reichel (see 19 Oct. 74) had sent his 'Irish Church Methodist Society address' (1881).

Portsdown Address. Saw Mr . . . . Much conversation, Mr Sidgwick—& Mr [H. Scott] Holland.

To W. E. FORSTER, Irish secretary, 27 September 1881.   Add MS 44159, f. 27.

Unquestionably I would mete out to Sexton,[1] and (if possible yet more decidedly) to Parnell the same measure as I should award or have awarded to less conspicuous offenders.

Only it is requisite, for the sake of the public cause, to be still more scrupulous in examining the grounds upon which, by its own discretion, the Executive is to bring such persons within the scope of a protective law, and within the walls of a prison.

If you are deliberately advised by your lawyers that Parnell has by his speech been guilty of treasonable practices, I not only say that if he does the like in the provinces he should be arrested but I do not at present see your reason for considering his speech of Sunday not to form a proper ground for action at once upon the general principle to which you appear justly to incline. Sexton, though hotter still, seems wrapt up in the cloak of metaphor.

[P.S.] I will send you a letter from Ld Midleton, with my reply.

Is Mr M. Arnold about to leave you? We receive friends until next Saturday when there is a break up, and we should be so happy to see him. He could probably come to Broughton Hall station.

To LORD MIDLETON, 27 September 1881.   Add MS 44545, f. 29.

I have received your painfully interesting letter, and I will at once communicate with Mr. Forster upon it.[2]

The circumstances of Ireland generally are grave and critical, but the district of which you write exhibits them in a form happily less exaggerated elsewhere.

As I think your letter is a kind of appeal to me, I will not waste words in expressions of sympathy with your case which might have the appearance of hollowness, but will go to the point at once.

I am not certain that I know the meaning of your reference to a vigilance Committee. Does it signify that there are legal acts which could (?'good')[3] citizens might do for the maintenance of public order and the just rights of property, but which by some agency you do not name they are prevented from performing?

Neither do I fully understand the meaning of your statement that 'the Government can take effectual action', and will be responsible for not taking it. You probably have unfolded all this in your communications with the Irish department, but your letter does not unfold it. With boycotting as such I apprehend the Government cannot deal. You do not state that, where there is intimidation, the Government have withheld protection. The main remaining question is whether you consider the individuals, whom you have named to Mr Forster, to come within the terms of the Protection Act, so that we have reasonable ground for supposing them to be parties to proceedings subversive of peace and order. *If* this is so the question is one of which you are clearly entitled to demand the consideration.[4]

[1] Forster to Gladstone, 26 September, Add MS 44159, f. 24: Law regards Sexton's speech as bringing him within the Act.
[2] Presumably not returned by Forster.   [3] Copyist's query.
[4] Midleton replied, 29 September, Add MS 44472, f. 16, explaining: 'the action of the law is paralysed. The Land League have permeated the whole social fabric, evidence cannot be obtained, juries will not convict, even magistrates, in some cases will not act. . . .'

28. *Wed.*

Ch 8½ a.m. Wrote to Mr Kitson jun.—Ld Kimberley 1 & Tel. and minutes.
Worked on arranging papers. Much conversation again. Read Marcus Aurelius
—Don Quixote: Mr Bulmer on Persius.[1] Much conversation with Mr S. & Dr
[Henry] A[cland]—also W.H.G.—Woodcraft.

To LORD KIMBERLEY, colonial secretary, 28 September 1881.   Add MS 44545, f. 29.

I have received this afternoon your letter[2] and your Telegram. The first explains the
last. As they leave so much time for pranks, it is not improbable they may be seeking to
intimidate. This is a very hazardous game for them. We could not have carried our Transvaal policy under the circumstances existing in South Africa, unless we had here a strong
Government, and we spent some, if not much, of our strength in carrying it.

This ample margin of time removes the likelihood of present pressure, so far as the
main upshot is concerned. But I should like to know whether you think it likely the Boers
will hold intermediate communications with Wood, and whether you are well assured
that he knows what language he ought to hold in such communications. He ought I think
to found himself on these ideas; first, that it was the unshorn strength of our Administration which enabled us, rather to the surprise of the world, to spare them the sufferings of
a war, secondly that many who followed us in our proceedings will altogether decline to
assume a new standing-point in the same direction; thirdly that if they do more than
represent & *appeal* in respect of what they may have to say, i.e. if on whatever grounds
they refuse to ratify the views such a course will alarm & throw the whole responsibility
on those who advise it.

It *will* in truth be an outrageous course. A people in revolt declining to be bound by, or
rather to ratify the engagements contracted by those to whom were intrusted their whole
civil and military destinies, strains violently the principles of good faith. A little extension
of the strain, and we might have the constituency declining to accept the judgment of the
Volksraad, which is only acting, as the Triumvirate were, on a commission received from
the mass.

To J. KITSON, 28 September 1881.   Add MS 44545, f. 30.

I thank you for the very clear and careful account of the proposed proceedings at
Leeds.

It lacks as yet that *rough* statement of numbers at each meeting which is requisite to
enable me to understand what I shall have to do: this will be fixed by the scale of the
meeting.

I see no difficulty but one. A procession through principal thoroughfares is one of the
most exhausting processes I know *as a preliminary* to addressing a Mass Meeting. A Mass
Meeting requires the physical powers to be in their best and freshest state, so far as any
thing can be fresh in a man near seventy two: and I have on one or more former occasions
felt them wofully contracted. In Midlothian I never had anything of the kind *before* a great
physical effort in speaking: and the lapse even of a couple of years is something. It would
certainly be most desirable to have the mass meeting first, and then I have not any fear at

---

[1] J. Bulmer, *Elegiacs* (1881).

[2] See 26 Sept. 81. Kimberley replied, 30 September, Add MS 44226, f. 269, that he agreed, but
nonetheless the Boers are 'ungovernable, excessively ignorant, and now elated by their successes';
but hopes of ratification remain.

all of the procession through whatever thoroughfare you think fit. I hope you may be able to arrange this and, with much regret to give you trouble in the common interest. [P.S.] I return the paper provisionally.[1]

29. *Th. St Michael & all Angels*

Ch 8½ a.m. Wrote to Ld Kimberley—Mr J. Talbot MP—Mr Bright—Sir John Adye—Mr Godley—Messrs Leeman & minutes. Walk with Sidgwick & Acland. Also much late conversation. Free Trade Facts. Read M. Aurelius—Don Quixote—Bourinot's Canada.[2]

To J. BRIGHT, chancellor of the duchy, 29 September 1881.   Add MS 43385, f. 298.

The indications in Ireland, and in South Africa, [are such] as may develop into a very disagreeable state of things, and secure for us as uneasy a recess as that which we passed last year. On all accounts we shall unite in saying God forbid. In the meantime I write about other matters.

On Thursday next week, I must go to Leeds, and I shall have divers speeches to make there. My inclination is to denounce outright Parnell (not the Irish Party, nor even the Land League) and his works and ways. Also to denounce, not less unsparingly, the mischievous imposture which is now stalking abroad under the name of Fair Trade. It is I think one of the advantages of the last stage of public life that one may use it to say things which, though true and needful in themselves, could not properly be said by any man with twenty or even ten years of his career before him.

Please tell me how this matter strikes you. And now I go to a longer outlook into the future.

You will I daresay remember my giving you reasons, in conversation at this place, and during the reign of the great Jingo deity, why I should not return to office. They were I *think* much as follows.

1. Age and probable failure of faculties
2. Probable exasperation of the tone of party strife.
3. Position relatively to the Queen.
4. The just claims of Granville and Hartington.
5. A disinclination founded upon views which to myself, at least, appear serious, and which under any *ordinary* circumstances would quite justify my refusal.

Now I wish to 'take stock' of these reasons.

As regards the two first, I need not at this date say any thing except to admit that I do not feel at all certain that party strife has been specially embittered by my being at the head of the Government. This, as far as it goes, is a relief and satisfaction.

No 3 has certainly been upon the whole worse, and now greatly worse, than I had anticipated.

No 4 I continue to feel with increasing strength. I accepted my mission in April of last year as a special and temporary mission. I never hoped to get over it, so regarded, sooner than in the autumn of the present year; and in most parts of it, e.g. India, the Eastern question, and perhaps finance, as much progress has been made as I anticipated, or more. Ireland, however, came upon us unawares, looming very large. This question, and the question of the Transvaal, still hang in the balance. From neither of them can I run away. I must, health and strength continuing, remain chained to the oar until each of them has reached what, in our way of speech, we call a settlement. But when it pleases God that

---

[1] Partly printed in Morley, iii. 59; no reply found, but see 2 Oct. 81.
[2] J. G. Bourinot, *The intellectual development of the Canadian people. An historical review* (1881).

that point is arrived at, then I think will be the suitable and becoming time for me to retire. It may perhaps be my duty to take my share in an endeavour, if we can make one, to put into good working order the organisation of the House of Commons, but this, if done at all, will most probably fall within the next six months, so I do not reckon it as an extension of the time.

You were so considerate and tolerant in the reception of what I had to say, that I have been all the more tempted now that it has to be done in writing to trouble you with this exhibition of the forms under which the old ideas still abide in my mind. They need not press upon you for any early reply, but I certainly long for the time when I may make over to the fit and proper leaders of the party the office which unusual circumstances have kept for a time out of their hands.[1]

To LORD KIMBERLEY, colonial secretary, 29 September 1881.   Add MS 44545, f. 30.

The successive telegrams as they come in are not very reassuring. It is however probable as you say that any occasion which may first come & which may require consultation will be one requiring nothing less than the Cabinet. But it may also happen that something of great pressure as to time, & yet capable of being dealt with by a smaller authority, may come & it is worth remembering that you and I can if need be meet in town at shorter notice than the Cabinet, for which an interval of 24 hours or upwards is necessary.[2]

I beg you also to understand that I have an engagement at Leeds which I must not fail on any account to keep from Thursday afternoon next to the Saturday evening afterwards.

Upon the subject itself, which may cause us much trouble, I should like to know the exact military position with reference to command of practicable ways of access to the Transvaal country. I gathered from Wood's telegrams early in the year that he had in view a road altogether apart from Laing's Neck. However that may be I think it is evidently an important point in the case that we should be sure of this access whether by Laing's Neck or otherwise: and it *may* very speedily become a question for consideration whether we ought not if need be to give ourselves this command. But of all if we have it already (?)[3]—and this I should much like to know as speedily as may be. I will send a line to Sir John Adye on the subject.

So much has been said by the Tories about our cowardly conduct in South Africa, that the Boers may have been tempted unduly to believe in it.

30. Fr.

Ch 8½ a.m. Wrote to Abp of Canterbury—Mr Childers—Messrs Leeman—Rev. Mr Wood—The Queen—Dean of Windsor l & Tel—Mr Forster & minutes. Walk with Sir J. Lacaita. Read M. Aurelius—Don Quixote—Gennadios &c on H. Eucharist—Bourinot's Canada. Lacaita examined some old books & bindings of mine. Conversation with him & Welby.

---

[1] Bright replied, 4 October, Add MS 44113, f. 160, cautious about Gladstone building up Parnell by denouncing him 'from your eminent position', but certain of his immorality and mendacity: 'his main object is a break-up of the United Kingdom, for he hates us & England even more than he loves Ireland'. On retirement: 'I do not see how you can desert—neither can I see how your great responsibilities are to be borne.'

[2] Kimberley replied, 1 October, Add MS 44227, f. 1, that personal consultation unnecessary, 'the Boers are proverbially slow . . .'; he proposed to wire Wood to be ready 'to seize passes into Transvaal'; Gladstone (docket on Kimberley's letter) required 'communication with London before message in these terms'.   [3] Secretary's query.

Sat. Oct. One. 1881.

Ch 8½ a.m. Wrote to Ld Hartington—Ld Granville Tel—Sir John Adye—Scotts—Dr Murray[1] & minutes. Saw Mr Welby. Saw Dr Nevin—Walk with him. Read Don Quixote—Ld Derby, Mr G. Smith & Mr Ecroyd, in 19th Century[2]—Marcus Aurelius.

2. 16 S. Trin.

Ch 11 a.m. with H.C. and [blank.] Wrote to Mr Kitson jun—Ld Kimberley tel & l.—Ld Rosebery—Sir C. Dilke—The Queen l & Tel—Ld Granville & minutes. Read Haughton's Sermon[3]—Gennadios on H. Eucharist and various sermons & tracts. Saw F. Cavendish.

To LORD KIMBERLEY, colonial secretary, 2 October 1881.   Add MS 44545, f. 31.

I hope, and make no doubt, that my telegram of today will reach you.

I am not quite convinced by your argument that a further message to Wood would not be useful were he at present our official agent and representative dealing with the Boers. But as Hudson is on the ground and reports to Robinson who again reports to you, the case is altered as regards Wood, and it has also got rid of *probable* urgency as to time.[4]

But it will be a deplorable predicament, if the Boers attempt any broad reopening of the negotiations.

I am glad to find from London that our military position is so good.

Two or three more days are likely I presume to bring us some significant intelligence.

To J. KITSON, 2 October 1881.   Add MS 44472, f. 55.

I should be very sorry to put aside any of the opportunities of vision at Leeds which the public may care to use: but what I had hoped was that these might come *after* my speeches of considerable effort made not *before* them [*sic*].

To understand what a physical drain, and what a reaction from tension of the senses is caused by a 'progress' before addressing a great audience, a person must probably have gone through it, and gone through it at my time of life.

When I went to Midlothian, I begged that this might never happen; and it was avoided throughout. *Since* that time I have myself been sensible for the first time of a diminished power of voice in the House of Commons, and others, also for the first time, have remarked it.

But I am not in the least afraid of any progress after the speaking: it is then only common fatigue, which rest will not remove.

I hope therefore that the hours may be so arranged as to reverse the order. Otherwise I shall have to begin half-exhausted.

[1] On the pronunciation of 'anthropophicism'; (Sir) James Augustus Henry *Murray, 1837–1915; lexicographer; a staunch liberal; Gladstone met him when a master at Mill Hill (see 11 June 79), securing him a pension in 1884; see K. M. E. Murray, *Caught in the web of words* (1977), 185–6, 236; Add MS 44545, f. 31.
[2] In the October number of *N.C.*, x; Derby's article is on the Land Act; Gladstone replied to Farrer Ecroyd's article 'Fair Trade' in his Leeds speech.
[3] S. M. Haughton, 'The precious name' (1881), sent by Reichel at Gladstone's request.
[4] Kimberley dealt through Hudson and Robinson, rather than Wood (see 29 Sept. 81); Add MS 44227, f. 13.

Your offer of Sunday hospitality is most kind: but all our arrangements have been made for going on Saturday to Mrs. Meynell-Ingram.[1]

3. M.

Ch 8½ a.m. Wrote to Ld Kimberley l & Tel—Mr Hamilton Tel—Mr Kitson Tel.—Macmillans—Murrays—Ld Granville—The Queen—Mr Forster (2)—Ld Coleridge and minutes. Felled a beech with Willy. But *non sum qualis eram.* Read Cambridge M.A. on Future Punishment[2]—Marcus Aurelius—Don Quixote—Arkite Worship[3]—Eugene Onéguine. Quiet family evening.

To W. E. FORSTER, Irish secretary, 3 October 1881.   Add MS 44159, f. 39.

[First letter]   Your sad and saddening letter[4] supplies material for the most serious reflection, but I need not reply at great length, mainly because in the points most urgently practical, I very much agree with you. I almost take for granted, and I shall assume until you correct me, that your meaning about 'ruin to property' is as follows—you do not mean the ruin to property which may directly result from exclusive dealing, but you mean ruin to property by violence, e.g. burning of a man's haystack because he had let his cars on hire to the Constabulary. On this assumption I feel quite prepared politically to concur with you in acting upon legal advice to this effect.

Nor do I dissent, under the circumstances, from the series of propositions by which you seek to connect Parnell and Co. with the prevalent intimidation.

But I hardly think that so novel an application of the Protection Act should be undertaken without the Cabinet. I anticipate their concurrence, and their preference of this mode of proceeding to an Autumn Session for the purpose of putting down the League (my old fancy). But the Cabinet, besides being strong in itself, has four members who have Irish experience, three of them in the House of Lords. Here is a force the use of which I am disposed to think the occasion calls for.

As for the time, I do not know whether you see advantage in waiting for the Commission to act: I presume its action could not be felt and understood, so as to operate upon the case before us, until after days, perhaps weeks, from its meeting.

If you agree in this, what would you say to Wednesday in next week. Reply by telegraph or post, as may be convenient. You may wish for an earlier day.

I send your letter, and copy of this reply, to Granville, asking him to send it on to Hartington.

The Queen desires reports from Ireland. (These I think it falls to the Viceroy to supply: making a provision during his absence).

I presume that, if there is a Cabinet, you will move him to return. No observation is needed on what you say of Father Sheehy & of Parnell.

I hope that you will find adequate support under your labours and anxieties. I am sure you will continue with unabated manfulness to look them in the face.

[Second letter]   I expect to see Herbert at Leeds & hope to recollect your messages.

He has a good courage and will not I think be dismayed. Of what use he may be to you remains to be proved; but I do believe he will be a pleasant & cheering presence.

---

[1] Part in Morley, iii. 60.   [2] Untraced, probably an article.
[3] R. Balgarnie, *Arkite worship* (1881).
[4] Of 2 October, with this reply in Reid, *F*, ii. 340: need for 'simultaneous arrest' of central and local Land League leaders, or a special session to legislate to suppress the League.

Should you be unable to manage a Cabinet you might try a memorandum. Your letter to me would supply it. However I think it would lead to a Cabinet.

I lament Lord Derby's article.[1] He has carefully spared the Government but I think the paper tends to damage the public interests.

To J. G. TALBOT, M.P., 3 October 1881.   Add MS 44472, f. 57.

The memorial[2] you have forwarded to me is signed by persons of great weight; and the purpose of securing adequate and sound instruction in religion is one with which few will fail to sympathise; but I do not well see how it could at present with advantage be made the subject of discussion between a deputation and myself.

The Legislature, on the proposal of the late Government, referred the subject of provision for the Government of the Colleges of Oxford to a Commission, and arranged the mode in which the results of its deliberations were to take effect. But the Statutes, on which it has determined, have not yet received a final sanction, and I do not see how the Executive Government can entertain the question of further legislation until the work of the Commissioners is finally disposed of.

I may add that, when the Tests Act [of 1871] was passed, it was not anticipated that the execution of the Act in the Colleges would be entrusted exclusively to the hands of persons in Holy Orders, or of members of the Church of England: but the obligation was imposed upon the Governing Bodies to do certain things, irrespectively of any such anticipation, which it was evidently believed they would competently perform. I do not therefore see the immediate connection between the first and the following paragraphs of the Memorial.

By the competency of the Governing Bodies, which I think the Legislature presumed, I mean a competency, not personally for each or any man to give religious instruction whatever his religious profession or position, but collectively to make the arrangements which the Act enjoins.

The terms of the new Statutes on this subject may be deemed either sufficient or insufficient for insuring the fulfilment of the Act. But to the contents of these Statutes I do not see any allusion in the Memorial: nor do we yet know how the Statutes themselves may be disposed of. Upon the whole, I do not conceive that this important subject is ripe for the communication you propose.

4. Tu.

Ch 8½ a.m. Wrote to Ld Kimberley Tel & l.—Dean of Windsor l & Tel—Ld Granville l & Tel—The Queen Tel—Mr Chamberlain—Scotts—Ld Chancellor—Ly Selborne—Mr Forster—Mr Scharf—Mr Hamilton—Mrs Hope and minutes. Saw Mr J. Griffiths—Mrs Potter. Read Don Quixote—M. Aurelius—Eugene Onéguine.

To J. CHAMBERLAIN, president of the board of trade,   Chamberlain MSS 5/34/6.
4 October 1881.

I entirely agree with your opinion on the question of a Treaty with France:[3] while I

[1] See 2 Oct. 81.
[2] Memorial that religious instruction in Oxford University be given by Anglicans, preferably ordained; Add MS 44472, f. 15.
[3] No resumption of negotiations without an understanding with France *re* textiles; Add MS 44125, f. 98.

regret that Protectionism in that country may prevent a work eminently desirable in a political sense at the present juncture.

The question of course remains for consideration whether I ought to give any degree of indication in this sense at Leeds. I will try to avoid anything rash.

The news from Ireland is generally bad.

To W. E. FORSTER, Irish secretary, 4 October 1881.   Add MS 44545, f. 32.

These answers to your searching questions are sufficiently discouraging.

There is one other enquiry, which I should like to put. Can a mode of proceeding be suggested under which *in case of necessity* the government, going beyond the law, could make an appeal to Parliament for an Act of Indemnity, before any disparaging incident could occur in Ireland, & without any fear of seeing its measures rendered ineffectual by the failure of intermediate agency?

Such a reference would probably be better made by conversation than in any other way.

To LORD KIMBERLEY, colonial secretary, 4 October 1881.   Add MS 44545, f. 32.

I agree with your reservation of powers in the Cyprus Constitution—with your argument for including official members in the Civil List—& generally with your letter & draft despatch subject to the following observations.[1]

1. In draft page 1 is the word 'new' appropriate—have they now what can be called a Constitution. 2. I admit that if the Mahometan minority are equally interspersed with the majority over the surface of the Island you will require a provision such as you propose. 3. It will be awkward to make a provision for the subjects of the Sultan—e.g. are Tunisians or Egyptians his subjects? This is a practical—i.e. a legal difficulty. But I do not see the strength of the argument for including all Turkish subjects, & I think this requires further consideration? I do not think you mean it in the same sense as Mr. Herbert's doctrine or equation: Officials & Mahometans = Christians, which I must own as a principle I entirely renounce. It was the old principle of our Colonial Government under the famous 'Her (?) Mother Country' i.e. the Downing Street of other days. 4. I hope there will be a proper provision about language whether in the Constitution or not. 5. Would it be right to say anything against forced labour? The old bad land ordinance I believe is gone? Now as to that still worse one which raised the detestable High Police of the Ionian Islands. I am glad Sir R. Biddulph will have an opportunity of commenting before we act.

5. *Wed.*

Ch 8½ a.m. Wrote to Mr Hamilton—Tel & 1—Mr Forster 1 & Tel—The Queen Tel—Ld Granville—Mr Kitson—Duke of Leinster—Ld Dalhousie—Mr Jas. Howard and minutes. Kibbling with W.H.G: who worked for me as Priv. Sec. Read Don Quixote—Eugene Onéguine (finished). Worked on Facts & Figures for Leeds: but under[?] too much pressure.

To W. E. FORSTER, Irish secretary, 5 October 1881.   Add MS 44159, f. 49.

If the lawyers think that exclusive dealing of itself, carried to the point of ruin, amounts to criminal intimidation under certain circs., it is the more satisfactory that we are to have a Cabinet on Wedy.

---

[1] Of 2 October, Add MS 44227, f. 5.

But a new embarrassment arises in the state of the Ld Chancellor's health. It is *improb-able* that he will be able to attend: & I lose no time in mentioning that, in order that you may get any points of law wh. are to be raised brought under his notice beforehand.

I cannot blame you seeing the Press under such circs. With Gray[1] we have a real power on our side, in the Bishops, & some *little* in his own inclinations [*sic*]: but of course the very greatest caution here will be requisite.

For purposes of public impression, I fear the prolonged absence of Cowper at such a time will be very unfortunate.

On the case of Patrick Eary[2] I am anxious to know something wh. I ask by telegraph.

Also I am sorry that the Constabulary should have had no inkling of an armed party going round to a variety of farms. Is it wholly impossible to enlist the action of loyal men as Special constables or otherwise in support of law & order, e.g. for day work in relief of the Constabulary, in some parts of Ireland at any rate if not in all, so as to relieve an over-worked force, and increase the total of our available means? I feel anxious, but I cannot bring myself to despair, about this.

At Leeds I shall do my best. I must avoid the use of words which wld. rouse the suspi-cions of Parnell. I do not like to bind myself now: for it is in near & close consideration that *balance* is best determined on. But I think there is a double challenge in the passage of Ld Derby to wh. you refer, & in Northcote's 'Hands off': & this double challenge must be frankly & fully accepted. I mean to treat Parnell as an irreconcileable: & to take for my prospective basis this—that no force, or fear of force, shall, so far as the Govt. can decide the question, prevent the people of Ireland from having the full benefit of the Land Act.

Thanks for information supplied—& God be with you in all your duties.

[P.S.] I advise your writing to the Ld Chancellor. He might like us to have in case of need one or both the English Law Officers at hand.

I earnestly urge your having things in such a state in Ireland if next Wednesday the Cabinet determine on arrests, the one great arrest at any rate may be affected with (I was going to say) lightening speed. Every moment will be of the utmost value.

To the DUKE OF LEINSTER, 5 October 1881.   Add MS 44545, f. 33.

The painful representation you have forwarded to me forms part of an aggregate of painful circumstance. Ireland is indeed in a great & sore crisis, & I have directed a Cabinet to be summoned with a view to its consideration. In the meantime I shall have occasion to make pointed reference to the subject at Leeds.

I return your inclosure. Without doubt the circumstances will have been made known to the Irish Government. Am I right in my recollection that Kildare has, or had 5 years ago, a priest of the old O'Connell School? As if so the case is all the worse. I can hardly feel surprised that Mr. Hamilton in his call for 'doing something' gives no indication what that something is to be.

[P.S.] I rejoice to see some signs in Ireland of legitimate spontaneous action of self-defence—which has been so much wanting.

6. *Th.* [*Spring Bank, Headingley, Leeds*]

Ch 8½ a.m. Wrote to Ld Kimberley Tel—l—Mr Hamilton Tel—Dean of St Paul's—Lt Col. Spardeling [*sc.* Spalding] & minutes. 2¼–5¾. Hawarden Castle to

---

[1] i.e. Sir J. Gray of the *Freeman's Journal*; see Forster's letter of 4 October, Add MS 44159, f. 45 and Reid, *F*, ii. 346.

[2] Shot by armed men on 3 October; Gladstone's telegram untraced.

Leeds.[1] Some gathering, of great warmth, on the way: & a processional reception. Large party & preparation for tomorrows proceedings. But unhappily I was caught with a little lumbago from exposure. Worked on Statistics. Read Don Quixote.

To LORD KIMBERLEY, colonial secretary, 6 October 1881.   Add MS 44545, f. 33.

The telegrams received today are very grave: the worst that could have been expected.[2] I telegraph to you to convey this, that I shall be ready to call the Cabinet as soon as you may think the intelligence sufficiently developed. The Queen has communicated also with me. I told her of your Monday's telegram. I return your inclosure & think we are quite in harmony.[3]

7. Fr.

Wrote to The Queen Tel—Dean of St Pauls. Off at 11. Three speeches & four processions: ending at 11.30 P.M. Lumbago just manageable. Kindness & enthusiasm on all sides unbounded. Voice lasted well. It was a great relief when the anxious effort about Ireland had been made.[4] The torchlight procession with (I should say) 250–300 m[ille] the most remarkable I ever witnessed. Saw Mr Wood. Read Don Quixote. Saw Mr Teal the Surgeon[5] who pleased me well.

8. Sat. [Hoar Cross]

Photographer at 10.30: then off. Three more speeches: two processions: The Speeches were on Free Trade: luncheon compliments, & a general review in the Cloth Hall for an hour, with political declarations respecting the Transvaal.[6] The effort of the voice, before 25m people for so long a time was the greatest I ever made: & it was completely exhausted. Nothing delighted me so keenly as the reception of Herbert by the huge mass of working men. Dined at Mr Barran's[7] pleasant residence: & off by train a little after nine. Reached Hoar

[1] By special train provided by L.N.E.R., which was cheered as it passed through stations on the way, especially at Huddersfield. Gladstone stayed with J. Kitson; he had been returned for Leeds in 1880 without visiting the constituency; Herbert Gladstone had been returned unopposed in the subsequent by-election. See T.T., 7 October 1881, 6b.

[2] Boer claim that the Convention was contrary to the Sand River treaty of 1852, and demand for extensive renegotiation; Schreuder, 240–1.

[3] Kimberley replied this day, Add MS 44227, f. 20, that the cabinet arranged for Wednesday was soon enough: 'we should avoid the appearance of haste'; though ready for war, he hoped a 'firm stand now as Robinson advises' would suffice.

[4] Huge crowds filled the city centre, there being 'a general suspension of business ... no political squibs or posters of an adverse character appear to have been issued, with the exception of one facetious *menu* for the banquet'; touts sold 6d tickets for 5/- or 6/-. The first major speech dealt chiefly with free and fair trade, the second, Ireland, Gladstone distinguishing O'Connell from the new departure, praising Dillon as a man of honour for giving the Land Act a chance, and making a sustained appeal to Parnell, ending with the famous peroration: 'if the law, purged from defect and from any taint of injustice, is still to be refused and the first condition of political society to remain unfulfilled, then I say, gentlemen, without hesitation, that the resources of civilization are not yet exhausted'; T.T., 8 October 1881, 7c.

[5] Thomas Pridgin Teale, F.R.C.S.

[6] T.T., 10 October 1881. 7a.

[7] John Barran (see 13 June 77) the other liberal M.P. for Leeds.

Cross[1] at a quarter after midnight: with the greatest cause for thankfulness. It has been probably my *last* serious effort of the kind.

9. 16 S. Trin.

At the beautiful Ch mg: in evg, lumbago forbade me. Wrote to Dean of St Paul's—Dean of Windsor—Bp of Lichfield—The Queen 2—Sir Thos Acland—Mr Forster—Ld Granville—Mr Godley—Ld Kimberley—Ld Dufferin (Tel) and minutes. Read Blackburns Sermons[2]—Contemp. on Brahmo Somaj[3]—Rae on Ornaments Rubric.[4] Conversation with Mr McColl—Bp Abraham—Ld Devon—Ld Halifax—Mr Acland—Mr Spottiswoode & others.

To W. E. FORSTER, Irish secretary, 9 October 1881.   Add MS 44545, f. 34.

The reception of your name at Leeds in both the Cloth Hall meetings was everything that could be desired.

There is no time for details. But in one word—it is a *wonderful* community. I expected much & found much more. I was delighted with the hold which Herbert has really taken upon the working men. You will see that I dealt with the Irish case at length & made much more of it in order to lay the ground hard & broad for any measures however strong that may become necessary. I hope you will be fortified with this: perhaps you may even think I went too far. My speeches have been many & long, but there was in truth a good deal of *business* to do by them.

I send you Hartington's comments. He a little misses my point where the illegible word comes: but it is immaterial.

I gave Herbert your message.[5] Finding that you are to be in London on Wednesday, he fixes Thursday for crossing to Ireland & he is now at Hawarden. Barran & Illingworth gave support about Ireland in a very marked manner.

10. M.

Wrote to Ld Granville—Mr Forster Tel—Mr Vickers—Rev. C.A. Row—Mr Rathbone—Baron Malorti—Ly G. Fullerton—Mrs Hope & minutes. Lady A. Wood drove me to Bagot Park, where we examined the trees & measured. Most pleasant party. Conversation with Ld Halifax: Sir G. Wolseley: Mr Acland: Mr Holland and others. Read Don Quixote—Mr M'Coll on Tractm & Ritualism.[6]

11. Tu. [London]

Wrote to Mr Godley Tel—Mr Forster Tel—Sir E. Malet—The Speaker & minutes. $2\frac{1}{4}$-$6\frac{3}{4}$. By Rugeley to D. St—a gathering of folk of Rugeley. Saw Ld Kimberley—Mr Godley—Ld Halifax—Saw Hope, with disappointment—Ricardo [R]. Read Don Quixote—'Mind' on the Homeric words for soul[7]—Sister Rose.[8]

---

[1] Elizabethan house, seat of Mrs Meynell Ingram, seven miles W. of Burton-upon-Trent.
[2] T. Blackburn, *Visions of the King* (1881).
[3] *C.R.*, xl. 570 (October 1881).
[4] M. J. Rae, 'The ornaments rubric' (1881).
[5] H. J. Gladstone to telegraph about Forster's communications with Selborne; Add MS 44159, f. 55.   [6] See 11 Apr. 75.
[7] C. F. Keary, 'The Homeric words for "Soul"', *Mind*, vi. 471 (1881).
[8] E. S. Holt, *Sister Rose* (1870).

12. Wed.

Wrote to The Queen 3 letters & Tel—Dean of Windsor—Ld Powerscourt—Ld Blandford[1] & minutes. Saw Dean of St Paul's—Ld Granville—Mr Forster[2]—Mr Childers—N. & R. Lyttelton—Mr Godley. Read Don Quixote—Mad. de Remusat Letters.[3] Cabinet 2-6.

Cabinet. Thurs. Oct 12. 81. 2 PM.[4]
1. State of Ireland. Mr Forster recommended
   a. arrest of Parnell and the leaders of the L[and] L[eague] at the centre:
   b. arrests to be made also in the provinces progressively for speeches pointing to ⟨an Irish Republic⟩ treason or treasonable practice
   c. Land League meetings to be prohibited when dangerous to the public peace or tending to intimidation at the discretion of the Irish Govt.
   The leading spirits. Parnell. Sexton? Quin. Healy. O'Brien (United Ireland). Egan.[5]
   Swearing in of special constables: tentatively: or some offer of that kind. Discussed. W.E.G. favourable. Some inquiry to be made. W.E.G. to write to Forster.
2. Transvaal. Ld Kimberley stated the case & went over the articles. Sir H. Robinson's 17545 down to 'tested' adopted i.e. no change before ratification & experience.[6]
3. Commission on Treaty with France to meet without preliminary conditions: but we hold our ground as to cottons & woollens.
4. Egypt. Cabinet disposed to promote cooperation with France, & cooperation of Turkey with both, in keeping the *status quo.*
5. Commission authorised (Small, under Dodson, to collect facts bearing upon Grants in aid.[7]
6. Channel Tunnel. Watkins's proposal declined.[8]

To G. V. WELLESLEY, dean of Windsor, 12 October 1881.   Add MS 44545, f. 35.

Thanks for your kind note.[9] Pray keep the copies. I had already, with a good deal of reflection, made up my mind that under all the circumstances of the case, it would be well to let Oakley stand over.

I am inclined to recommend Mr. Curtis, Canon of Lichfield, Bampton Lecturer & late

---

[1] George Charles Spencer-Churchill, 1844–92; styled marquis of Blandford; 8th duke of Marlborough 1883; had sent Gladstone his article on Ireland in the *Nouvelle Revue*; Add MS 44472, f. 81.
[2] A meeting before the Cabinet to arrange Irish business; Reid, *F*, ii. 354.
[3] F. C. Hoey and J. Lillie, *A selection from the letters of Mme. de Rémusat* (1881).
[4] Add MS 44642, f. 217.
[5] Parnell was arrested in Dublin next day; Thomas Sexton (1848–1932, Home Rule M.P. Sligo 1880-6, Belfast 1886–92, Kerry 1892-6) and J. P. Quinn, secretary of the Land League, on 14 October; O'Brien, O'Kelly and Dillon on 15 October with Timothy Michael *Healy; 1855–1931, home rule M.P. Wexford 1880–3, Co. Monaghan 1883–5, sundry constituencies 1886–1918; brilliant critic of the Land Bill; 1st Governor of the Irish Free State 1922–8. A 'No Rent' manifesto was issued by the League on 18 October, signed by the imprisoned leaders. Egan went abroad with the League's funds.
[6] 'They decided, after a short conversation, which hardly amounted to a discussion, not to entertain any question of change in the Convention [of Pretoria] by instituting a new negotiation, but to await its ratification until the 3rd of November, when the time allowed for it expires'; to the Queen this day, *L.Q.V.*, 2nd series, iii. 243.
[7] See to Dodson, 4 Nov. 81.
[8] Though preliminary excavations were made, see 11 Mar. 82.
[9] Of 11 October, Add MS 44340, f. 149: 'this is a crisis ... Put aside Oakely'.

Principal of the Training College. He must be known to you as a very able learned man & sound Churchman with sympathies of mind High & Broad. You will remember that he was strongly recommended by Dean Liddell & others for Dr. King's[1] Professorship, and was the one rival seriously weighed against that Divine.

About Knox Little I am very seriously disquieted.[2] The Dean of St. Paul's who has been here this morning expects him in London tonight and will talk over the whole matter with him. The Dean is I think altogether judicious and right-minded about the question involved. I confine myself to this proposition; Mr. Green being engaged in that resistance to the law, which is known as Contumacy, it is really nothing less than a monstrous indecency that the Crown should through its Church patronage be placed in association with that resistance. He agrees: I told him I was afraid it would be my duty to dissociate myself from the art & language of Mr. Knox Little; and in this I think he also agrees. He says that Mr. K.L. feels how exceedingly indiscreet he has been, but the question is can he express his regret in such terms as properly to close up the matter?

Taking your advice I have suggested nothing and indeed I do not quite know what to suggest. I do not know whether you can at all see your way.

13. Th.

Wrote to Earl of Dysart—Mr Vickers—Mrs Th—Mr Forster—Mr Bright—Dean of Windsor—Mr Hyam[3]—The Queen—Mr Westell and minutes. $11\frac{3}{4}$-$3\frac{1}{4}$. Received an address in the City: 3000 persons in Guildhall.[4] Spoke about 50m. on political but now party matters.[5] Then luncheon & speeches. After which the Turnery Exhibition.[6] It was out of doors a good popular reception: but the Jingo hooters, $\frac{1}{500}$ in Leeds or Midlothian were perhaps $\frac{1}{10}$ here. The arrest of Parnell created a *furore*. Dined with the Lytteltons. Examining book parcels and preparing for *exit*. Conversation with Lady Mayoress.

To W. E. FORSTER, Irish secretary, 13 October 1881.   Add MS 44545, f. 35.

At Leeds, as you are aware, I read a passage from the letter of a friend (it was Bright) which deplored the prevailing want in Ireland of aid to the Law, & the Government, from the sound part of society at this great crisis. This passage referred chiefly to the field of discussion, of which the Land Leaguers may be said to have a monopoly. At the same time, I feel a strong anxiety, which as you know is in a certain degree shared by ⟨some of our⟩ colleagues, that no stone should be left unturned, at a period of such grave

---

[1] i.e. E. King, professor of pastoral theology at Oxford.

[2] Knox-Little had visited the imprisoned Green; it was felt he should offer resignation though it would not be accepted; Gladstone to Church, 9 October 1881, Add MS 44545, f. 34.

[3] Of the household, see 18 Nov. 81.

[4] Gladstone announced: '. . . even within these few moments I have been informed that towards the vindication of law, of order, and the rights of property, of the freedom of the land, of the first elements of political life and civilization, the first step has been taken in the arrest of the man (loud and prolonged cheering, accompanied by the waving of hats and handkerchiefs)—in the arrest of the man who, unhappily, from motives which I do not challenge, which I cannot examine, and with which I have nothing to do, has made himself, beyond all others, prominent in the attempt to destroy the authority of the law (cheers), and to substitute what would end in being nothing more nor less than anarchical oppression exercised upon the people of Ireland'; *T.T.*, 14 October 1881, 8b.

[5] In the margin: 'They say only 40 min.'.

[6] He was a member of the liberally inclined Turners' Company; see 16 Feb. 76.

uncertainties & such possible dangers, & in this view the question arises whether it might not perhaps be found practicable to obtain physical aid from the same quarter.

I feel the serious difficulties which attend this question in Ireland when all partisans must as far as possible be kept in check but there are three things to be remembered. 1. The necessity never was so great. 2. I assume that any persons acting in aid of the Government would act with & under its regular agents. 3. That any effort to be made would in the first instance be tentative, in carefully selected districts, probably not those where Orange feeling was high, & where there are persons of influence who can speak for others & whose discretion & public spirit can be relied on. 4. That the labour imposed on the Constabulary is immense & that numerous as they are in proportion to the population their duties are at such a time imperfectly performed. 5. That if the lighter parts of these duties are taken over the force might thus be to some extent set free for the heavier. 6. Wheresoever there has been an anti-boycotting centre, there might be found a hopeful spot for some nucleus of action against lawlessness, & when a nucleus has once been formed it will probably spread. 7. It is difficult to understand why landlords of the best class might not call meetings of their tenants, propose to them united action on behalf of law & personal freedom, & then hold communication with the authorities as to the means. 8. Although the mind first turns to the familiar notion of Special Constables, I always suppose the powers of the executive in time of public danger to be large, & such a time has arrived, so that one of the points to be considered would be whether there are other forms of action lawful under the circumstances. 9. Finally: if Ireland is still divided between Orangemen & law-haters, then our task is hopeless: but our belief & contention always is that a more intelligent & less impassioned body has gradually come to exist in Ireland. It is on this body, its precepts & examples, that our hopes depend, for if we are at war with a nation we cannot win. If such a body exist, I would call upon it in places, even if single parishes where it is strong: just as under the new Poor Law England was divided legally into Unions, but no Unions were actually exacted except in the more prosperous & disciplined districts, from which they were gradually extended over the whole country. I cannot conceive it possible that *you* could add to your other overwhelming cares & occupations the task of thoroughly examining this question, which would require much time for conference with the boldest and wisest men who might be consulted first as to making a beginning; then as to extension; but the beginning would probably in this case be more than half the whole.[1] The conversation in the Cabinet yesterday throws some light upon the question who the proper man or kind of man would be. The City, assembled in Guildhall today, was enthusiastic about Ireland generally, & in raptures on hearing the arrest of the ringleader.

To G. V. WELLESLEY, dean of Windsor, 13 October 1881.   Add MS 44545, f. 35.

I go down to Hawarden tomorrow starting at 11.30.

Canon [F. K.] Leighton I am told is dead. I must think over the possible men of whom perhaps the two having the most urgent claims are Rowsell & Holland (Quebec—there is another Holland, Christ Church, of very great merit, but a much younger man.)[2] I continue horribly puzzled about Knox Little. I think he will very probably offer to resign but I wish some form of regret could be devised that would avoid that extreme resort.

---

[1] No reply found.
[2] T. J. Rowsell was appointed.

14. Fr. [Hawarden]

Wrote to The Queen—Mrs Leighton—L. Hope—Ld R. Grosvenor—Watsons—Dean of Windsor—Warden of Keble & minutes. Saw Dean of St Paul's—Mr Godley—Mr Westell—J. Fidd. 11½-5¾. Journey to Hn. Read Don Quixote—Ellis on Aryan Language[1]—[blank] on Sleep & Death. Packing &c: a busy morning.

15. Sat.

Ch 8½ a.m. Wrote to A.L. Gladstone—London Ed. N.Y. Herald—Herbert J.G.—Mr Childers—Dean of Windsor—Scotts—Ld Dalhousie—Mr Hole—M. Jules Ferry—Mr Godley—Mr J. Dodson & minutes. Went with W.H.G. to examine the damage done by the storm yesterday. Axe-work. Relaxed sore throadt [sic] in evg: a suite I think from last Saturday. Read Don Quixote.

To H. C. E. CHILDERS, war secretary, 15 October 1881.   Childers MS 5/79.

Surely Roberts' personal convenience might bend a little as to date.[2]

What I do not feel clear about is this: are we to be prepared for H.R.H.s resignation, and, if we are, can it be quite certain that you and I are competent not only to stand this (for which I am quite ready) but to bring it about without consulting any one else, I mean particularly Granville and Hartington.

It seems to me, & this I indicated in my letter to the Queen, that you will require to ascertain beyond all doubt *in a producible form* that the Duke has no ground of complaint to stand upon, and means to condemn Wolseley on Dr Fell's ground, the real motive being the old system against the new. This point seems to me the key to the whole position and I would not allow Roberts' date in any way to interfere with it.[3]

[P.S.] I suppose no military step can or ought to be taken respecting the Transvaal until after date for ratification. I mean *new* step in the way of extended or visible preparations for action? I am not quite sure, however, how this stands.

To the LONDON EDITOR of the *New York Herald*,   Add MS 44472, f. 102.
15 October 1881. [*Not sent*][4]

I heartily appreciate the spirit of the communication with which you have favoured me this day by Telegraph, on the part of the New York Herald. At the same time I hope you will excuse my entering into oral communication with the representative of any journal in particular with regard to a subject on which my opinions, such as they are, may be said to be the property of the whole body of my fellow countrymen.

On various occasions both in and out of Parliament during past years I have referred to

---

[1] One of the many articles by the philologist A. J. Ellis.

[2] Sir Frederick Sleigh *Roberts, 1832–1914; in England (after succeeding Colley in S. Africa) before becoming c. in c. Madras; demanded appt. there by 20th.

[3] By 28 October Childers had planned a compromise: Adye to be adjutant general, Wolseley to succeed him as S.G.O. with peerage; Add MS 44129, f. 281.

[4] Holograph draft, marked 'Copy on signed sheet, and send *unless* I am wrong in thinking N.Y.H. is a respectable print.' Marked on the verso in Gladstone's hand: 'O.15 Cancelled draft. to corresp. N.Y. Herald'.

the extension of local and subordinate self government generally as an object of just and warm desire; ⟨the claims of Ireland are in some respects particularly strong; and, but for the tenacious opposition offered to the Bills of the Government during the last Session I see no reason to doubt that we should have been able to carry a valuable measure for the Irish Counties⟩ as I did at the Guildhall and have pointed out that I do not in principle offer any limit to its extension except that the supremacy of the Imperial Legislature must for Imperial purposes be steadily maintained. I am well satisfied that these opinions should be submitted to the intelligent appreciation of your countrymen.

16.

Spent the day in bed, using my prayer book. Read Ottley's Dilemma[1]—Bp of Ontario's very able charge[2]—Langen, Geschichte.[3] Wrote to [blank.]

To J. MORLEY, editor of the *Pall Mall Gazette*, 16 October 1881.   Morley MSS.

With reference to Sir G. Elliot & the Durham triumph, *if* you agree with me in the fact, perhaps you would point out in the P.M.G. that his vindication completely establishes my charge. I appear to [have] said that he undertook to vote for the unconditional release of the suspects. That might mean their release whether they entered into engagements or not. It might also mean whether the Government approved it or not. I had the latter sense in my mind: but by his stupid letter he proves that he meant both.[4] I hope you enjoyed your vacation but I beg you not to be at the pains to notice this benevolent wish, or my note generally.[5]

17. M.

Rose at midday. Saw W.H.G.—Ld R. Grosvenor. Cold migrated from throat to head; & at night to chest. Read Langen's Geschichte—Don Quixote and [blank.] Wrote to [blank.]

To Rev. W. J. KNOX-LITTLE, 17 October 1881.   Add MS 44472, f. 110.

You have written me a very full & kind letter, but I am afraid you have not seen the matter of the declarations relative to Mr. Green in the light in which it strikes me. It is, be assured, no question of personal trouble or anxiety with me, but only a question of public duty.

You are stated to have supported a resolution declaring that the authority of the Judicial Committee, or of any Court under it, could not be acknowledged by obedience in any matter of ritual as well as of faith.[6] Now I do not enter into the merits of this proposition, but I hold that it is one with which the authority of the Crown cannot be becomingly associated: for the Crown is bound to see to the execution of the law, & to

[1] H. B. Ottley, *The great dilemma: Christ his own witness or his own accuser* (1881).
[2] J. T. Lewis, 'The holy eucharist' (1881).
[3] The 1st v. of J. Langen, *Geschichte der römischen Kirche bis zum Pontifikate Leo's I*, 4v. (1881–93).
[4] Elliot reneged on his promise to vote for release of suspects; see *P.M.G.*, 14 October 1881, 4.
[5] Morley next day thanked Gladstone for his note, declared his desire 'to place myself at the point of view of the Government' but observed: 'The crisis for Liberalism seems to me very sharp in every way'; Add MS 44255.
[6] Press cuttings of speeches in this vein by Knox Little, and his letter of 14 October, at Add MS 44472, ff. 68, 98; see to Wellesley 13 Oct. 81. Gladstone had appt. him canon earlier in 1881.

use all its rights & powers with a due regard to it. As the adviser of the Crown in regard to ecclesiastical preferments, I should act most culpably, were I knowingly to associate myself with the announcement of such a doctrine. It would be *on my part* a breach of honour & of trust. But if a gentleman who has just accepted the nomination of the Crown to a Stall, declares that no sentence of the Courts called ecclesiastical is to be obeyed, I put it to you whether a fair inference does not arise that I am not disposed to use the influence of the Crown in support of that opinion, & whether the Crown, the supreme minister of the law, is not thus presumably placed in conflict with the law. Please to consider, & if necessary to consult upon, this issue of the question.

18. *Tu.*

A day of short rations & severe measures to produce strong perspiration. Wrote to Ld de Vesci—Ld Granville—A.R. Gladstone—H.J. Gladstone—Mr Childers Tel.—Ld Derby—Mr Holt—N.Y. Herald Tel.—& minutes. Read Don Quixote.

To R. D. HOLT, 18 October 1881.   Add MS 44545, f. 38.

For more reasons than one I feel that at the present time I ought not to appear publicly in Liverpool. But if you are averse to my being in the neighbourhood without a note of communion I see no objection, & I find Lord Derby sees none, to the reception at Knowsley of a party (which in my opinion should not go beyond ten or a dozen at the outside) through whom might be said or read anything that is desired. It would be a little like our meeting here on a former occasion, and you probably would arrange about reporting in the manner then used. My nephews would readily give Courthey for the purpose, but as the visit is to Knowsley it seems that this would be going out of the way. I should not think of a lengthened speech but it is needful to keep the public attention alive on the subject of Ireland: & though I could not with propriety invite you to pay me a compliment I should be glad of your giving me an opportunity.[1]

19. *Wed.*

Measures of yesterday broke my cough more speedily I think than heretofore. Rose at one. Wrote to Ld Kimberley—Dean of Windsor—Herbert J.G.—Dean of St Paul's—Mr Lowe—Mr Godley Tel & minutes. Read Don Quixote. Kept my sittingroom, but conversed a good deal with Mr Furse[2] who came to dine.

To LORD KIMBERLEY, colonial secretary, 19 October 1881.   Add MS 44545, f. 38.

Robinson's last has come to me in cipher, the last four figures not clear. But I had already learned that the Boers (a dirty lot!) had now taken their stand on £.s.d., and I think with Robinson we need only hold our ground.[3]

If any point will bear postponement for the advantage of fresh experience, and on the other hand affords much too narrow a ground for postponing a great political settlement, it is this. I write this by post to London from whence if need be the substance can be tele-

---

[1] Holt's letter untraced; he received a dpn.; see 27 Oct. 81.
[2] Perhaps C. W. Furse, see 12 Dec. 79.
[3] The Boers reduced their objections to the financial clauses of the Convention; Schreuder, 248. Kimberley replied on 21 October, Add MS 44227, f. 29, 'very glad we are so entirely agreed' on the Volksraad.

graphed to you if in the country. I entertain no doubt as to the concurrence of the Cabinet.

20. *Th.*

Went out in evg to Church for the Sermon. A most crowded congregation. Wrote to Ld Kimberley—Watsons—Bp of Durham—Ld O'Hagan—Sir W. Harcourt—Mr Justice Lindley—Mr Forster 1 & Tel & minutes. Treatment of cough has been very successful. Read Don Quixote & ?.

21. *Fr.*

Rose at 9.30. Wrote to The Dean of Windsor—Mr Forster (2)—Ld Granville—Mr Godley (2)—Mr A. Black—L. Hope—Herbert J.G.—Mr Brand—Mr Cyrus Field—Ct Münster—Mr Mackie MP & minutes. Read Henry IV p.1.—Don Quixote—Labitte Catalogue[1]—Emerson's Life of W.E.G.[2] Off the sick list I hope.

To W. E. FORSTER, Irish secretary, 21 October 1881.   Add MS 44159, f. 78.

I have telegraphed my satisfaction as regards the substance of this morning's intelligence that you have with adequate legal support proclaimed the Land League illegal.[3]

As regards the form, it has been considered by persons more competent than myself: but from the political side I should have been more completely satisfied had the language been such as to make it stand out more broadly & clearly that it could not have been done before.

It cannot be, I apprehend, the difference between no rent & Griffith's valuation on which the illegality can be said to rest.

Next week at Knowsley I shall probably receive a deputation of 10 or 12 gentlemen from Liverpool, & this will give me an opportunity of again presenting our case & bringing it down to the then present moment.

It is in no way to qualify the pleasure I express if I add that your Proclamation seems to bring into view the possibility of an early or special meeting of Parliament, since I presume it will come before juries sooner or later: perhaps however late enough to be capable of being dealt with at the usual time.

Croke's letter is a great fact & I hope it will be followed up.

As regards aid from the community, I remain unconvinced, & I think the adverse opinion a new proof how deep the old & bad tradition has eaten in. But I take thankfully what I can get—an inch where I want an ell. All anti-boycotting association, & all self-defending union seem to be good as far as they go.[4]

Kindly let Herbert see my letters when convenient.

[P.S.] Surely after these rowdy mobs in Dublin *something* will be said or done in a voluntary way by order & property, or they will sink into universal contempt.

---

[1] Perhaps J. Labitte, *Le renversement temporel de la Papauté* (1861).

[2] G. R. Emerson, *William Ewart Gladstone. Prime Minister of England. A political and literary biography* (1881), well researched, with some interesting, unattributed interviews of contemporaries.

[3] On 19 Oct. the Land League began a 'No Rent' campaign; on 20 Oct. the Land Court opened and the Land League was proscribed.

[4] Forster replied, 22 October, Add MS 44159, f. 79: 'I am not surprised at your seeing political objections to the wording of the circular: but what we had to consider was order in Ireland, rather than the debate on the Address'.

22. Sat

Rose at 9.30. Wrote to Dean of Windsor l & Tel—Bp of B. & Wells—Dr A. Clark—Ld Granville Tel—Mr Forster—Mr Knox Little—Mr T. Hughes—Messrs Ward & Lock[1]—Sir F. Doyle—Lord Lyons—Mr Bright—Dr Liddon & minutes. A wild wet day. Read Q.R. on Revision & Dean Stanley,[2] part—Don Quixote.

To J. BRIGHT, chancellor of the duchy, 22 October 1881.   Add MS 43385, f. 301.

A propos of your trip to Llandudno, I write to say that we expect the F. Cavendishes to be here through the week after next; and if it suited you then to pay us a visit, we should be most happy to see you. There may be others: but the party will not be large.

The quotation I made from you at Leeds[3] has caused me to be bespattered from the law and order side while I have it plentifully on the other. No such declaration does or can mete out exactly equal justice to all. But it was needful that something should be said and I think it has done good.

There seems to be a kind of collapse of the League: but we are not yet out of the wood. The submission to the Proclamation is however a great thing. For if perchance life had been lost in stopping a meeting, there would infallibly have been a verdict of wilful murder against Forster, Cowper, and me. Which indeed there may yet be. I shall probably say a few more words on Ireland to a Liverpool deputation at Knowsley.

To Dr. A. CLARK, physician, 22 October 1881.   Add MS 44545, f. 39.

I feel that I have no right to get well without your leave, or at least without reporting to you; under my strict prescription that you are not to answer.

I think it was an enormous exertion of throat & voice in the Cloth Hall at Leeds which came out in a relaxed throat: then the evil travelled through the head to the usual form in the chest. Spec. wine, barley-water &c. freely taken, with masses of covering, caused most profuse perspiration, & the cough which was hard and sore for one day broke I think more quickly than ever before. I only remained rather weak.

My wife has made very great progress in the recovery of sleep, & she does not lose the ground gained.

I want you to read a remarkable book called John Inglesant, just of the kind that will suit you. Mary has an idea that you have it already. Unless in two or three days I receive a cover and the words written 'I have John Inglesant' I shall send it you.

I had thought to get off coming up for Nov. 9 but find I cannot. Granville is suffering heavily from an ill-natured cold.

To Sir F. H. C. DOYLE, 22 October 1881.   Add MS 44545, f. 41.

I cannot resist the desire, impertinent though it may be, to know whether Rumour for once tells truth in reporting that the death of an aged relative has made a material addition to your fortune.

[1] Thanking the publishers of Emerson's life for sending a copy: 'If a reprint comes I should like it not to be repeated that at Oxford I "voted" against the Roman Catholic claims. My early sentiments were always in their favour, & the reverse of the statement is recorded in the proceedings of the Oxford union'; Add MS 44545, f. 40. The error, on p. 22 of the 1881 ed., was corrected on p. 16 of the popular, 1/- ed., n.d., 1882(?).
[2] *Q.R*, clii. 307, 414 (October 1881).
[3] See to Forster, 13 Oct. 81.

You will I am sure forgive the question, whatever the answer may be.[1] Is there any chance of your coming northwards this year? If so, do not forget us.

I wonder whether you have read John Inglesant, & what you think of it? It is certainly no common book.[2]

To W. E. FORSTER, Irish secretary, 22 October 1881.   Add MS 44545, f. 40.

I return your inclosure (M.S.)[3] with thanks & not without the wish that it had been possible to give the defence people a little pat on the back.

I also return Monck's letter. But I find in all the Irish opinions given in that sense, a strong sense of the bad tradition of the country with regard to self help, from which they have not yet I think escaped.

Monck's arguments as against wholesale proceedings I admit to be good: not as against tentative and selected effort.

The abandonment of meetings by the Land League is the greatest step yet made, I suppose, and a very great one, so that I heartily congratulate you upon it—whatever else there may lie ahead.

I should like to be in possession of the case of illegality about the Land League. I understood it to turn upon intimidation of people to prevent their doing what they have a right and duty to do.

But if this be so, *is not the League illegal in England*, & should it be allowed to meet?

I am glad to see A. M. Sullivan's declarations. Sadly bored by the police hanging about this house. This shall go round by London; out of respect to your Sunday—if you have what that name means.

23. S. Trin.

Ch 11 & 6½. Wrote to Ld Kimberley—Herbert J.G.—Mr Forster—Abp of Canty—Mr Macfie—Sir B. Frere—Sir Thos G.—Mr Godley 2 Tel. & minutes. Worked till 5 P.M. Read Q.R. on Revision (finished)—Brown on Unicorn Symbolism.[4]

24. M.

Ch 8½ a.m.—in the old groove; delightful. Wrote to Mr Godley 1 & Tel—Dean of Windsor—Mr Morley—Mr Knox Little—Miss Cobden—A.G. for Ireland and minutes. Woodcraft with S.E.G. Read Morley's Cobden[5]—Don. Quixote.

To H. LAW, Irish attorney general, 24 October 1881.   Add MS 44472, f. 166.

Would you kindly inform me—or cause me to be informed which will be just as well—and either exactly or approximately. 1. *Who* were the persons indicted or proceeded against by the late Government in connection with Irish Land Agitation. 2. Which of them could be considered significant. 3. *When* the first proceedings were taken. 4. *When* they would have come to issue in the regular course. 5. Was any evidence given you on taking office that the late Government intended to *proceed*?

[1] Doyle replied that he had succeeded to about £800 p.a.; Add MS 44150, f. 242.
[2] See 14 July 81.   [3] Not found.
[4] R. Brown, *The unicorn* (1881).
[5] J. Morley, *The life of Richard Cobden*, 2v. (1881), sent by Miss Cobden. Gladstone had been involved in its preparation both as a correspondent and as a trustee of Cobden's MSS; see 20 June 77, 29 Jan. 78n; to Morley this day.

I may add my recollection is that Parnell was *then* a person to proceed against, for his declarations about rent—and that they did not dare to touch him.[1]

To J. MORLEY, editor of the *Pall Mall Gazette*, 24 October   Add MS 44545, f. 42.
1881.[2]   The Life came yesterday & today. I am obliged to say that if not, like Socrates, a corruptor of youth, you are at any rate a corruptor of old age, for you seduce greybeards into a neglect of duty. I have spent my morning in your second volume; and after what you tell me of rapid work I am astonished, not at the freshness of the work, but at the care & exactitude with which it has been executed. It is one more added to the not very long list of our real biographies. The climax of Cobden's illustrious life was that which brought him into the closest connection with me, & I have naturally turned to the Treaty period. It was the most laborious time of his life, the most searching & trying of mine. In p. 235 you have glanced at my position, in terms most considerate, & wonderfully true, considering that you had no hieroscope with which to examine the interior of the Cabinet. Evelyn Ashley has, with much tact, trodden this ground almost in silence.[3] But I have a great deal to say on the subject; it would take 2 hours in talk, or a *long* chapter. The complications of the position were such that I do not think even you can have any idea of them. I do not think Cobden was wrong in refusing. I am confident I was right in accepting & remaining. One thing, however, I effected which Cobden did not know, & as to which Theodore Martin has done me serious wrong.[4] The fortification scheme, which I reluctantly accepted, was not 12, or 10, or 9 millions: it was cut down, I think to 5, as you will find in the Act of Parliament if I remember right: though Lord Palmerston misrepresented it in his speech, I believe through forgetfulness. In p. 116 [of Morley's *Life*] Cobden speaks of me with others as having in 1852 more affinity with the Tories than the Liberals. This is true of my sympathies at that time (& after), not of my opinions. I desired, however, the advent of the Protectionists to office; not from sympathy, but as being in my view the only mode of exploding, and that with safety, a mischievous imposture. I will not now touch upon Ireland further than to say that I fully appreciate your desire & effort to agree with us as much as may be, & I rejoice to think there is so much on which we are agreed entirely.[5]

25. *Tu.*

Ch 8½ a.m. Wrote to Mr Godley 1 & Tel—Mr Forster Tel—Mr Holt Tel—Sir W. Harcourt—Mr Childers—Bp of B. & Wells—Mr Guest—Att. Gen. for Ireland and minutes. Woodcraft. Saw Mr Townshend—Mr Vickers—Mr Johnstone and others. Read Don Quixote—Morley's Life of Cobden.

[1] Law sent press cuttings, but his letter avoided discussion of tory actions or intentions, save for stating that until the 1881 Land Bill was passed 'it was practically impossible to "suppress" the League "manu forti"'; Add MS 44472, f. 167.

[2] Morley wrote this day: 'I am afraid the narrative will seem very thin and shadowy to a prominent actor . . . I should have liked to be free to use some of Cobden's letters to you, but your monition on that point in your letter to Mrs Cobden was so express that I dared not transgress it'; Add MS 44255, f. 29.

[3] E. Ashley, *Life . . . of Viscount Palmerston* (1879), ii ch. xiv; Cobden declined the Board of Trade in 1859. Morley wrote that Palmerston would have resisted even Gladstone afforced by Cobden, and that the latter would have resigned; Morley, *Cobden*, ii. 235.

[4] T. Martin, *Life of the Prince Consort* (1880), v. 341–2.

[5] Morley replied, 29 October, Add MS 44255, f. 31, that Gladstone was 'a lenient critic' and that 'Cobden was sometimes almost reckless in his aversion to Lord Palmerston'.

To Sir W. V. HARCOURT, home secretary, 25 October　　MS Harcourt dep. 8, f. 113.
1881. '*Secret*'.[1]

The Childers–Wolseley–Cambridge imbroglio is indeed serious, and H.M. I fear will not mend it by multiplying channels of communication; but it is not unnatural that she should, by herself & her belongings, feel for a soft place in the heart of the successive Ministers who may appear at Balmoral. You have been I think very constitutional. I am surprised that the temperature should now be high, because so far as I know Childers has given time, leaving the 'enemy' so to speak in full possession of the field for the moment. No doubt his resignation would be an awkward fact for us but to him damning. I will send your letter to Childers & probably more light may be thrown upon the matter when we meet in town.

I hope to hear in your next that you are coming here.

26. *Wed.* [*Knowsley Park, Prescot*]

Ch 8½ a.m. Wrote to Herbert J.G. Tel—Mr Forster—Dr Earlson—Mr Godley—Ld Monson . . . & minutes. Read Morley's Cobden—Mad. du Hausset.[2] 3.30–6. To Knowsley by Runcorn & Edgehill:[3] where we were received with the utmost kindness. Conversation with W.H.G.—Mr Baring—Ld D.—Lady Galloway[4] & others.

27. *Th.*

Walk with Ld D. morning. Drive with Lady D. aft. Much pleased with this spacious house. Wrote to Ld Kimberley—Rev. Mr Young—Mr Childers . . . & minutes. Read Mad. du Hausset. Conversations, with Lady D.—Ld D.—Ld Halifax—Mr Knowles—the gentlemen from Liverpool. Worked up Irish information & spoke 40m? in answer to Address.[5]

To LORD SPENCER, lord president, 27 October 1881.　　Add MS 44545, f. 43.

I return Cowper's letter with thanks.[6] Probably there would be no advantage in my trying to press the question farther. But I think had I been in the Irish Government I could have managed a little more than perhaps the Castle traditions have allowed to be done. Cowper does not seem to have observed that it is one thing to recommend general action & another to make tentative effort in carefully selected places. However there seems, thank God, to be fair hope that the League is now getting undermost with such means as we have actually employed.

I have been holding forth today in Derby's dining room to a very hearty Liverpool deputation—with a view of stamping in the proper public impression. He seems much in earnest & is very kind. I do grudge you your long journey for so little.

---

[1] In Gardiner, i. 416.

[2] *The private memoirs of Madame du Hausset, lady's maid to Madame de Pompadour* (1825).

[3] 'As we drove we talked of Ld. Derby's being Lib. P.M. Papa expects it more than I do'; *Mary Gladstone*, 234. For Derby's account of the visit, see below, xi, Appendix i.

[4] Mary Arabella Stewart, 1835–1903, wife of 10th earl of Galloway; she was Salisbury's sister and Derby's stepdaughter.

[5] *T.T.*, 28 October 1881, 8a; on the Land League, and O'Connell's respect for property.

[6] Sent by Spencer on 24 October, Add MS 44308, f. 163; Gladstone had on 16 October urged Spencer to write to Cowper on encouraging active support of govt. by the Irish propertied classes; ibid., f. 161 and see *Spencer*, i. 174.

28. Fr.

Longer walk with Ld D. mg.—with Lady D. to Croxeth & Courthey aftn. Wrote to Mr Herbert l & Tel—Mr Childers Tel—Mr E. Arnold—Mr Morley—Mr Forster Tel—Bp of Durham—Sec. Mersey Co.—Mr Jerningham[1] and minutes. Read Du Hausset (finished)—Carpenter on Germ Theory.[2] Saw Lady D—Ld D.—Mr Knowles—Mr Bilston—Mr Rathbone—& others.

29. Sat. [Hawarden]

Wrote to Lady Derby—Mr Childers (2)—Mr Godley—The Speaker—The Queen (2)—Lady Mount Temple—& minutes. Conversation with Ld Halifax—Ld Derby: who had been most kind and satisfactory. More lionising in the house. Off at 12.30. Reached Hawarden at 3. Read Fraser on Privateering[3]—Campello's Cenni Autobiogr.[4]—& Tracts. Ten to dinner.

30. 19 S. Trin.

Ch mg & evg. Wrote to Ld Kimberley—Ld Mayor—Dr Lyons MP.—Bp of Chester—& minutes. Read Farrar Future Pun.[5]—Cenni Autob. di Campello—Bernard Bampton Lect[6]—Langen Geschichte.

To LORD KIMBERLEY, colonial secretary, 30 October 1881.   Add MS 44545, f. 45.

I suppose that Robinson's telegram of the 27th[7] will require some notice, but that as nothing remains to be done, and as the notice could not be of simple gratulation, the delay of answering by post might perhaps be convenient?[8]

It appears to me that ratification is a simple and formal *Aye* to the Treaty and that the sense of it cannot be affected nor the force of it impaired by any preamble.

Such preamble might be taken for an endeavour by one of the parties to a Convention to alter its sense by attaching to it an interpretation to which the other is no party. Such one-handed interpretations are contrary to the nature and law of Treaties.

We, I suppose, shall take the explanations in the best sense of which they are susceptible but shall maintain the full force of the Treaty which is not in any sense provisional though open to change like all other instruments by mutual consent.

31. M.

Ch. 8½ AM. Wrote to Ld Kimberley Tel.—Ld R. Grosvenor—Herbert J.G.—Dean of Windsor—Mr M'Kie[9]—Ld Granville—Mr Scharf—Col. Colthurst—Ld

---

[1] Congratulating H. E. H. Jerningham (see 24 June 66) on his return for Berwick; Add MS 44545, f. 44.   [2] W. B. Carpenter, *The truth about vaccination and small-pox* (1881).

[3] *Fraser's Magazine*, civ. 589 (November 1881).

[4] E. di Campello, *Cenni autobiografici che rendono ragione dell' uscita di lui dalla Chiesa Papale* (1881).   [5] See 3 Mar. 78?

[6] T. D. Bernard, *The progress of doctrine in the New Testament* (1864).

[7] The Boers had ratified the Convention while adding their own Preamble stating their dissatisfaction with it; Schreuder, 249.

[8] Kimberley thought this 'decidedly the best mode of proceeding. I entirely agree with your view of the ratification' and the importance of not adding further conditions; 1 November, Add MS 44227, f.44.

[9] Thanking T. M'Kie for sending his 'The politics of the future'; Add MS 44545, f. 45.

Chancr—Mr Knox Little—Bp of Durham—and minutes. The Lubbocks came. Ten to dinner. Read Cobden's Life. Saw F. Cavendish long on Treasury affairs[1]—WHG & S.E.G. on Buckley.

Tues. Nov. 1. 81. All S.

Ch. 8½ with H.C. Wrote to Central News Tel.—Mr Forster Tel.—Mr Billson—Ld Tweedmouth—Mr A. Arnold—Mr W.H. Thornber[2]—Mr Godley Tel.—& minutes. Stephey surprised me with an important disclosure, the. . . .[3] But all he said was thoroughly worthy of him, and I was not obliged to offer any impediment to the free course of his feelings. Nor did his mother with whom I afterwards discussed it.[4] This led me to remain at Ch. for H.C. Read 19th Cent on Cathedral for Liverpool—Order of Corporate Reunion[5]—Also read Cobden's Life Vol I. Nine to dinner. Walk with Sir J. Lubbock & the party. Saw F.C. Received C.Q.R.R. Party.[6]

2. Wed.

Ch. 8½ A.M. Wrote to Mr Chamberlain—The Queen Tel.—Ld Kimberley—Ld Halifax—Ld Granville—Viceroy of I.—Sir C. Dilke—Mad O. Novikoff—and minutes. Saw Ld F. Cavendish—Sir J. Lubbock. Woodcraft with WHG. Read Cobden Vol I.—19th Cent on Naseby and Yorktown[7]—Hincks on G. Smith[8]—Mulhall on Trade[9]—Don Quixote.

To Sir C. W. DILKE, foreign undersecretary, 2 November 1881.   Add MS 43875, f. 76.

I thank you very much for your letter of the 29th[10] and I see the difficulties and risks of the position. As to mode and form I am satisfied the best will be done: as to substance we cannot take worse terms than before on the two great staples, but no doubt it will [be] made clear that the objection to specific duties is not abstract but practical.

For my part, if we fail to make a Treaty, I shall regret it most on political grounds; and yet in regard to those grounds we with our insular position can afford the loss infinitely better than France can.

In a commercial sense I am certainly of opinion that we are so strong in our command of the general market of the world—although we sometimes get a little frightened about it—as to be independent of all huckstering, a matter much more

---

[1] The first of several talks between Gladstone and Cavendish on Gladstone's plans and reasons for retirement; notes of Cavendish's comments recorded by Lady F. Cavendish on 4 November in *D.L.F.C.*, ii. 295.

[2] Regretting his inability to attend celebrations in Rochdale marking Bright's connection; Add MS 44545, f. 45. See 3 Nov. 81.

[3] Space of about two lines here, once with writing but so faded as to be completely illegible.

[4] An abortive love affair; see to H.N. Gladstone, 2 Dec. 81.

[5] *N.C.*, x. 735 (November 1881).

[6] Expansion of the Conah's Quay railway.

[7] In fact Goldwin Smith in *C.R.*, xl. 683 (November 1881).

[8] Ibid., x. 825.

[9] M. G. Mulhall, *Balance sheet of the world 1870–80* (1881).

[10] Add MS 44149, f. 45, from Paris: 'it will be difficult for M. Gambetta to make a Treaty with us that we will accept', with difficulty of *ad valorem* duties.

suitable for those who have not yet extricated themselves from the arid labyrinths of Protection.[1]

[P.S.] I hope you are deriving physical benefit even from a leisureless recess.

3. Th.

Wrote to Ld Kimberley—Mr Thornber Tel—Mr Billson—Sir H. Ponsonby—The Queen (2). Saw Rochdale Deputation, who came despite me.[2] Woodcraft with W.H.G. Read Pref. to Savonarola[3]—Morley's Cobden—Don Quixote. Nine to dinner. Conversation with Sir W. Harcourt—Mr Goldwin Smith.

To LORD KIMBERLEY, colonial secretary, 3 November 1881.   Add MS 44545, f. 47.

I agree with you very decidedly that the Volksraad should not be hindered from making the proper communication to Foreign Powers. I should say that, although moribund (in one particular), they were alive until the ratification was in our hands. Therefore any act done by them anterior to that juncture of time would be valid although the power to do it ceased with the ratification.[4] In principle then, & not only for policy, (if I understand the order of facts aright) I allow the act.

For once, I do not like the form suggested by Robinson in [telegram] 18,874. It is to accept '*as* a ratification' and thereby to import doubt into the proceeding, what is categorically a ratification. The 'Considerances' which precede it have no more effect on the ratification than any rigmarole which you or I might prefix to a cheque giving a man £100. I take it that the ratification of any Treaty is a defined act, admitting of no addition, and no deduction.

I would even have preferred your Telegram without 'we consider' but this as between Robinson and Wood matters little.

4. Fr.

Ch. 8½ AM. Wrote to Rev. Mr Russell—Mr Forster Tel.—Watsons—Rev. Mr Oakley—Mr Dodson—Mr Childers—Mr Godley—Mr Jas Wilson—& minutes. Walk with the party. Fourteen to dinner. Saw Sir W. Harcourt—Bp of Durham—Lord F.C.[5]—Mr Johnson *cum* Mr Frost. Read Morley's Cobden.

To J. G. DODSON, president of the local government board,   Add MS 44545, f. 48.
4 November 1881.

I fear that a laziness which has a deep root, and is more likely to increase than diminish, has retarded unduly the fulfilment of my pledge to write to you on a subject which was partially and roughly opened at the last Cabinet.

[1] Dilke replied, 4 November, ibid., f. 47: 'We shall not insist on ad valorem duties'.
[2] See 1 Nov. 81n.
[3] Perhaps E. Warren, *Savonarola* (1880).
[4] i.e. the Volksraad had the power up to the moment of ratification to communicate directly with foreign powers, and so should be allowed to announce the ratification directly; Courtney, Herbert, Granville and the Queen objecting, permission was given; Schreuder, 250–1 and Add MS 44227, f. 44.
[5] See *D.L.F.C.*, ii. 295, according to which Cavendish urged that a peerage was his only possible course if he was bent on retiring; Lucy Cavendish thought retirement improbable unless forced by physical decline. Her entry may be *recte* 6 November; the form of the MS at Chatsworth suggests it was written up later.

There are a group of questions which, either from their intrinsic claims, or from the amount of force which they can array, will probably, or perhaps, be found to stand in the very first rank when Parliament is enabled to resume the work of general legislation, from which it has this year been in the main excluded. These are, in my view,

1. Local Government, in the three kingdoms.
2. Amount and incidence of local taxation.
3. Extent and form of assistance to it from Central funds.
4. The first and third of these stand in close association with the alleviation of the burdens on the time of Parliament, and the more effective dispatch of its business.
5. If local taxation on real property is to be relieved at the expense of the Exchequer, there ought I think undoubtedly to follow a full examination of the questions whether real property, as distinguished from the occupiers of it, is at present unduly taxed, and whether, if that portion of the taxes on it which is paid through the occupiers be diminished, this change ought to entail any other readjustment in a different sense.

It would be difficult, and is not needful, to specify now all the different questions which may be raised under the heads I have enumerated. But I think it is plain that we ought to put ourselves in a condition of capacity to judge between two modes of proceeding, either of which seem open to the Government, while one or the other we may find it quite necessary to adopt. The one is the continuance and further extension of the system of grants in aid; or Parliamentary rates for local purposes; the other is the abolition of these grants, & the allocation of certain taxes or parts of taxes to local authorities instead of them.

The latter of these alternatives seems to require

a. the existence everywhere of local government, or local authorities, so constituted that they may safely and properly take over the administration of these funds.

b. the establishment of general rules and conditions to limit their discretion where necessary, and to establish the relations between them and the central authority, the direct intervention of which it is I presume most desirable to reduce to the minimum defined by the necessity of the case.

I have spoken in general terms, but I presume that the Education Vote would remain; nor do I know whether any other exemption or exceptions might be found requisite, in the event of the adoption of a new system. It would also I suppose be very difficult to include Ireland, at the first start, within the scope of any plans such as I glance at.

The immediate question is the collection of all the facts necessary to enable the Government to deal with the considerations of policy involved.

Among these I would specify

1. The actual grants for England and Scotland: and the exact channels through which they are distributed.

2. The comparative position of the two countries, in the adaptation of the grants respectively to their population and wealth.

3. The existence or non-existence in each local circumscription or in connection with each purpose to which grants are applied, of bodies competent to administer them: and the reforms or provisions necessary for procuring such competency.

4. The general rules necessary to guide or limit such administration, and the means of securing their observance.

5. The proceeds of taxes, (or powers of taxation, or both, but these modes appear doubtful,) which might conveniently be made over to local authorities in lieu of the monies now received from the Exchequer.

For the examination of these and all the kindred facts, as I understand, it is decided that a working Commission shall be appointed. I presume that it would be mainly official;

but the presence upon it of men such as Mr. Rathbone of Liverpool might be of great value. I presume however that its numbers should be limited, not over seven or nine, and that you as head of the Local Government Board would undertake to conduct it.

I do not know whether the new plans, if they proceed, ought to embrace all the points which Goschen handled some years back with such conspicuous ability: but, according to the ideas I have set forth, they would go much farther in fiscal change.

This is undoubtedly opening a formidable chapter of public labours: but one the really dangerous part of which is pretty sure, and that without a year's delay, to be forced upon the Government, unless they meet it with a scheme which will neutralise the dangers, and secure great and various advantages. Such would be

1. A relief to occupiers generally admitted to be equitable and needful.
2. The close of a long & irritating controversy between classes.
3. The extension of the salutary principles & practice of local government.
4. The decentralisation of administrative work.
5. The restored action of motives for economy in local expenditure, which suffer so much from the present method of grants in aid.
6. The diminution of *central* expenditure, and therewith of any political discontent or agitation connected with raising the taxes applied to meeting it.
7. The relief of Parliament from an incessant and vicious pressure greatly productive of extravagance, and from a very considerable demand upon its time.

You and those who may be associated with you will undertake a considerable work but in accomplishing it will achieve a great public service.[1]

5. Sat.

Ch. 8½ A.M. Wrote to Dean of Windsor 2 Tell.—Bp of Manchester—The Queen—Bp of Bath & Wells—Mr Forster Tel.—and minutes. Saw Sir W. Harcourt—Bp of Durham—Sir R. Lingen—Mr Goldw. Smith—Lord F.C. Walk with the Bp. A quiet evg. Read Morley's Cobden & Don Quixote.

6. 21 S. Trin.

Ch mg with H.C. and evg. Wrote to Abp of Canterbury—Sir H. Ponsonby—The Queen—Bp of Carlisle—Ld Granville—Ld Nelson—& minutes. Walk with F.C. Explained to him fully my personal position and desires. He was beyond anything kind & considerate: yet did not give in.[2] Read Life of Dr Harper[3]—Life of Luisa de Carvahal.[4]

7. M.

Ch. 8½ A.M. Wrote to Station Master Chester (2)—Mr Forster Tel—The Speaker—Mr Hamilton Tel.—Sir T.E. May—The Prince of Wales—Duke of Bedford[5]—Sir T. Acland—Dean of Windsor—Mr E. Jones—Lady Derby[6]—& minutes.

---

[1] Dodson replied, 7 November, Add MS 44252, agreeing to need for reform in grants in aid and introduction of County Councils; Goschen's plan had been too ambitious.
[2] See 4 Nov. 81.   [3] A. Thomson, *Life of Principal Harper* (1881).
[4] Lady G. Fullerton, *Life of Luisa de Carvajal* (1873, 2nd ed. 1881); on English catholics and the reformation.
[5] Delighted that the duchess has withdrawn resignation as Mistress of the Robes; Add MS 44545, f. 50.
[6] Informing her that the duchess is not resigning; Add MS 44545, f. 50.

Woodcraft with WHG. Treasury business with F.C. Read Morley's Cobden. Finished Don Quixote. My estimate of it is below the highest. Sancho is very nearly perfect. There is too much of it: especially in the Second Part.

8. Tu. [London]

Ch. 8½ A.M. Wrote to Earl of Rosse—The Queen—& minutes. 10¾-4. Journey to London. Saw Rev. S.E.G.—Ld Granville—Mr Thistleth.—Mr Hamilton. Saw Rands [R]. Read Brehm's Bird Life[1]—Burke on Ireland.[2] Dined at F.C.s.

9 Wed.

Wrote to Mrs Th.—Mr Shorthouse—Mr Childers—Dr Plumptre—& minutes. Conclave on military appointments 3-4¼.[3] Saw Mr Godley—Mr Hn—Mr Forster—Ld Granville—Lord F.C.—Sir C. Herries—Mad. Novikoff—The Speaker. Dined at Guildhall: & spoke (over 20 m) for H.M. Ministers.[4] We were very well received. Read Webster's Duchess of Malfy.[5]

10. Th.

Wrote to The Queen—Lady S. Opdebeeck—Mad. Novikoff—& minutes. Cabinet 2-5¾. Saw Mr Godley—Mr Hamilton—Ld R. Grosvenor—Mr Chamberlain—Ld K. cum Mr C. 11-12½. Conclave on Customhouse Removal.[6] Read Burke on Penal Laws—Fortnightly on the Month.[7] Dined at Sir W. Harcourt's. Saw Miss Ponsonby—Sir C. Dilke—Ld F.C.—Mr Chamberlain. Saw Scarsdale (alas)— Ricardo—& two more [R].

Cabinet. Thurs. Nov. 10. 1881.[8]
1. Shall the subjects comprehended in Sir T. E. May's memorandum under the title of Procedure and Discipline, with any other kindred topics, form the first proposals of the Govt. in the coming Session? Yes.[9]
2. That we shall meet Parliament with plans for an efficient local Govt. over Ireland & Scotland: London included but not in the van.[10]
3. Examination of question referred to Committee of Cabinet: Kimberley; Spencer; Dodson; Chamberlain; Childers; Harcourt.[11]
4. Maintaining troops in South Africa. Propose to reduce gradually: bring the force down to 4700: further proceedings hereafter according to circumstances. Substantial force.

[1] A. E. Brehm, *Bird-life*, tr. H. M. Labouchere and W. Jesse (1874).
[2] See 8 July 81n.
[3] Further difficulties with Wolseley, etc.
[4] *T.T.*, 10 November 1881, 6c.
[5] Webster's play (*ca.* 1614) was probably read in Hazlitt's ed. (1856).
[6] See 12 Nov. 81.
[7] Morley's monthly comment, *F.R.*, xxxv. 660 (November 1881).
[8] Add MS 44642, f. 220.
[9] Carlingford's diary, 10 November 1881: 'Chamberlain pressed for County Franchise, postponing Redistribution, & Bright supported him, but no one else'.
[10] *The Standard*, 14 Nov. 1881, announced 'County Boards' as the next Session's business. Gladstone by circulation asked the cabinet to 'throw light' on the leak; 13 noted comments, none admitting responsibility, Add MS 44765, f. 139.
[11] See Dodson's mem. *ca.* 15 Nov. 1881, Monk Bretton 55.

2 Cavalry Reg. Ld Kimberley stated that affairs in Zululand had not yet assumed a settled aspect.[1]

5. Parliament to be proclaimed on 30 Nov. to meet for disp. of business on Tues. Feb. 7.
6. Mr Forster reported on state of Ireland.
7. Ld Hartington referred to the papers on an arrangement between G. Britain & Russia respecting Central Asia.[2]

11. Frid.

Wrote to The Queen—Mr A. West—Mr W. Rathbone—Mr Young[3]—& minutes. 5-6. Saw Ld Granville on my tenure of office. He protested against any resignation unless on failure of health. I claimed the privilege of 50 years, subject to the condition that the calls of special exigency should cease. We discussed many persons, & many contingencies.

Saw Lady Susan O.[4]—Sir Rivers Wilson—Ld Spencer—Mr Godley—Mr Hn— Ld F.C.—Ld Hartington—Mr Knowles. Luncheon at 15 G. Square. Much conversation with C. on the breakdown of dear S's expectations. Dined at Lady Herberts. Saw Ld Herries. Read Burke on Ireland.

12. Sat.

Wrote to The Queen—Mr A. Young—Canon Stubbs—Rev. Mr West—Rev. S.E.G.—Lady Phillimore—Watson & S.—Mrs Meynell Ingram—Mr A. Montgomery—& minutes. $11\frac{1}{4}$-$1\frac{1}{2}$. Went with F.C. & Sir R. Lingen to see the Customhouse & Billingsgate etc. Got much interesting knowledge. Saw Mr Godley—Sir W. Harcourt—Mr Pringle—Ld Granville—Mr Forster—Ld F. Cavendish—Mr West—Mr A. Montgomery. Dined at Mr West's: curious rencontre with a crying boy & the person in charge. Read Lucy Phillimore's Life of Wren.[5]

13. 23 S. Trin.

Chapel Royal mg. Mel. Chapel Evg. Saw Mrs Birks (luncheon)—Mrs Wortley— Mr Thistl.—Sir R. Phillimore—*Lady P.* Dined with Sir R. Phillimore.[6] Read Life of Wren—Bp Ryle's Charge,[7] part—Faber's Provincial Letters.[8] Wrote to M.G.— Rev Mr Yonge.

[1] Information from Wood, received 7 Nov.; PP 1881 xlvii. 549.

[2] Hartington's proposal for talks with Russia for a treaty: Russia 'not to interfere with Afghanistan—& we, without saying so sh. leave her to do what she like with Turkestan & Merv. Granville was agst it'; agreed to ask Russia to renew the understanding of 1871 [*sc.* 1873]; Carlingford diary, Add MS 63689, f. 246 and CAB 41/15/42.

[3] West became Chairman of the Board of Inland Revenue, with Adam Young, 1817-97, his deputy.   [4] i.e. Lady Susan Opdebeck, formerly Lady Lincoln.

[5] L. Phillimore, *Sir Christopher Wren* (1881).

[6] 'G. Dined here. He ... was going to buy Lucy's Wren. He gave her advice about authorship generally. Much Church talk, all in his old strain—politics apart (?). I think he will retire in May. No idea of being Earl of Liverpool as the papers say'; Phillimore's diary.

[7] J. C. Ryle, 'The charges delivered at his primary visitation' (1881).

[8] Untraced work, probably article, by F. W. Faber, probably on Pascal.

14. M. [*Hawarden*]

Wrote to Rev. Mr Oakley—Sir J. Stanhope—Mayor of Leeds—Mr Forster—Lady Hutt[1]—Sir H. Ponsonby—Mr Knowles—The Queen (2)—Ld R. Grosvenor—Bp of Lincoln—Lady Dudley—and minutes. Saw Mr Godley—Mr Howell. Went by the 2.45 Train & reached Hawarden at 8¼. Saw S.E.G. Read Bp Ryle X.—Dean Goulburns Tract.[2]—Life of Cobden.

To LORD R. GROSVENOR, chief whip, 14 November 1881.   Add MS 44315, f. 51.

I find that it would be agreeable to Sir R. Phillimore and his family if he were made a Baronet. It does not seem to me an unreasonable idea: but I may be biased, as in every vicissitude for fifty years, in Parliament & out, he has been one of my fastest friends. The family promises to connect its name honourably with jurisprudence. His father was a lawyer of some note, Chancellor of York (I think) and his son is making an income almost unknown among stuff gowns of his age.

Considered as a Judge, he is P.C. and might be content: but besides being rather a notable example of a self made man—for I think he began from £0. 0. 0—he has been a constant and distinguished labourer in the field of international law and is quoted in Europe & America, I believe, as the first English authority of his day.

Forster is inclined to recommend Sullivan for the same honour.[3] They would in no way clash with the Baronetcies on *general* grounds. Please write, or telegraph, reply to Hawarden.

15. Tu.

Ch. 8¼ A.M. Wrote a Secret letter to Ld G. & reserved it for consn.[4] Wrote also to Rev. E. Wickham—Bp of Bedford—Rev. R. Yonge—Bp of B. & Wells—Mr Pringle—Mr Godley—Scotts—Mr Hamilton Tel & letter—The Queen 2 Tell.—and minutes. Persevered on S.s matter with Mary—& with WHG.[5] Read Life of Cobden—Uncle Zed.[6] Woodcraft with W.H.G. On Monday I dispatched near 200 letters.

16. Wed.

Ch. 8½ A.M. Wrote to Earl of Listowel—Mr Hamilton 2 Tell.—Sir H. Ponsonby—Mr Childers—Mr G. Pringle (2)—Ld F.C.—Ld Hartington—Mr Newton—and minutes. Princess Louise with Lorne and party came over from Eaton to luncheon. The day was unkind & they saw but little of the place. Woodcraft with W. & S. Read Morley's Cobden—Holyoake's Stephens[7]—Uncle Zed.

17. Th.

Ch. 8¼ AM. Wrote to Lord Chancellor—The Queen—Mr Childers—Mr Richmond—Mr Forster—Mr Welby—Mr Downing[8]—and minutes. We brought down

[1] Fanny Anna, wife of Sir W. Hutt (see 24 Feb. 42), on her husband's illness.
[2] E. M. Goulburn, 'Confession of a reticent Dean' (1881).
[3] Phillimore and Sullivan were both cr. bart. December 1881.
[4] Plans for the reconstruction of the cabinet; sent to Granville on 21 November.
[5] See 1 Nov. 81.   [6] G. Phillimore, *Uncle Z* (1881).
[7] G. J. Holyoake, *Life of Joseph Rayner Stephens* (1881).   [8] Unidentified.

a large elm, mutilated by the storm. Read Uncle Zed—Holyoake's Stephens—Morley's Cobden (finished).

To R. E. WELBY, assistant financial secretary of the treasury,   Add MS 44545, f. 56.
17 November 1881.

I follow your observations[1] in detail with great concurrence but on two points of a general character I am a shade more hopeful.

(1) I have not yet heard anything to make me suppose the Defence Estimates will show an increase and I feed myself with a hope of the contrary, which I admit may be rudely dispelled.

(2) There has been now for a twelve-month (say) that sort of on-the-whole revival of trade, which Lord Beaconsfield rather prematurely announced in November 1879 and I think the *next* financial year ought to show the result of it upon revenue.

(3) I think also that we need not at present assume any further relief to local taxation by means of grants in aid.

On the whole therefore I think you might tell Sir R. Wilson that we do not interpose an absolute preliminary bar, but that the broad distinction should be maintained in speeches between *fiscal* and *protective* remissions, and a large price in the latter exacted if we are to touch the former.

18. Fr.

Ch. 8½ AM. Wrote to Bp of Lincoln—Mr Childers Tel—Sir Ar. Gordon—Mr Rathbone MP.—Ld Spencer—Ld Kimberley—Miss de Lisle—Ld Mounttemple—Ld F. Cavendish—& minutes. Conversation with C.G. on the gap in the household wh Hyam's Managership has created. I am, more than she, desirous of keeping in view facilities for comparative retirement on going out of office. Finished Uncle Zed—Life of Stephens—De Caux on the Herring[2]—Egypt & Modern Thought[3]—Gibson's Poems (U.S.).[4]

To LORD F. C. CAVENDISH, financial secretary, 18 November   Add MS 44545, f. 57.
1881.

Many thanks for the reference to Caird. It has been a formidable effort for my eyesight, but is very well worth it; a most interesting paper.[5]

I am not sure however that it contributes much to the solution of the question of legislation for the tenant. He appears to contemplate the introduction of 'compensation for disturbance'. But in the first place how could a scale for it be framed in *this* country by Parliament? In the second, it only secures the tenant's interest when the landlord puts him out but does not provide for his wishing to go out. I think also that an arbitration *required by statute* is in principle the same as a reference to a Court of Justice. On the other hand I admit that there are grave difficulties attending the sale of the tenant's interest, though this rests on the old land-law of Europe, though for personal interest I should not be sorry if it actually existed. As to the landlord's making the improvements I do not go so

[1] Not found.
[2] J. W. de Caux, *The herring and herring fishery* (1881).
[3] See 14 July 78.
[4] W. Gibson, *Poems of many places* (Boston, 1881).
[5] J. Caird's address on 15 November to the Royal Statistical Society, 'The English land question' (*Transactions*, xliv. 629), reprinted as 'The British land question' (1881).

far as Caird: for I do not value it when it is done with borrowed money, as is so often the case.

19. Sat.

Ch. 8½ A.M. Wrote to Mr Knowles (cancelled)[1]—Rev. Dr Nevin—Rev. Mr Bonset[2]—& minutes. Forenoon conversation with Ld Rosebery: walk in aftn. We went over the ground of possible resignation. Walter Gladstone came. Read Hershon's Talmud[3]—Curci, Nuova Italia[4]—Arthur, Introd. to Campello[5]—Miss Pfeiffer's Drama.[6] Walter Gladstone came with 'Louise'.

To Dr. R. J. NEVIN, 19 November 1881.   Bodley MS Eng. Lett. e. 123, f. 101.

I am much obliged to you for the pains you have taken to inform me about the interesting case of Count Campello.[7] But I have no answer from Mr. Knowles[8] yet, and I have written to say that unless I hear in three or four days I shall consider my letter as withdrawn. You are quite right in your purpose: and if the 19th C. be not open to you, probably you will try the Contemporary.

I have been reading at least some of Curci's *La Nuova Italia*, and it impresses me very much. Favourably, in the first place, as to him personally. In the second place if he is right the Latin Church in Italy is losing (p. 17) a portion of its life-blood—and it has not got too much—through the Protestant Propaganda. It seems to show that Italy has the same material which exists in Germany and Switzerland, but of which France has exhibited so little. It seems further to show that Count Campello was right in his endeavour to promise the establishment of an organisation based upon that material.

The 'Autobiography' has the appearance of proceeding *in part* from a distinct pen, and one that uses more of a scoffing or at least polemical tone than Campello himself.

In an introduction to an English translation of it, W. Arthur (English Wesleyan) says he has himself known thirty seceded Italian priests, and that at least forty he believes are now labouring as 'Ministers of the Gospel'.

[P.S.] Since I began this letter I have received from Mr Knowles the inclosed satisfactory reply.

20. Preadv. Sunday.

Ch. mg & evg. Wrote to Ld Tenterden—Mr Forster—& minutes. Read Luisa de Carvahal[9]—Bassett on Ep. St James[10]—Boyce 'Nigh unto the End'[11]—Life of Smart[12]—Macmillan on Revised Version.[13] Walk with Rosebery.

---

[1] Not copied by the secretaries.
[2] Probably James Armitage Bonser, vicar of Shillington.
[3] P. I. Hershon, *Treasures of the Talmud* (1881).   [4] See 25 Aug. 81.
[5] W. Arthur, tr., *Count Campello. An autobiography, giving his reasons for leaving the papal church* (1881); see 29 Oct. 81.
[6] E. J. Pfeiffer, *Under the aspens* (1881).
[7] Letter from Rome of 5 November, Add MS 44472, f. 230.
[8] Written to on 14 November on the possibility of an article by Nevin on Campello (see 17 Sept. 81); Add MS 44545, f. 56. Nevin's article is in *N.C.*, ix. 606 (April 1882).
[9] See 6 Nov. 81.
[10] F. T. Bassett, *The catholic epistle of St James* (1876).
[11] J. C. Boyce, *Nigh unto the end* (1880).
[12] Probably *The poems of . . . Christopher Smart*, 2v. (1791), with a life.
[13] *Macmillan's Magazine*, xliv. 436 (October 1881).

21. M.

Ch. 8½ AM. Wrote to Sir K. M'Kenzie[1]—Mr Forster—Mr Frith R.A.[2]—Mr Dodson—The Queen (Tel)—Sec. Servian Scientific Soc.[3]—and minutes. Read Amn Rev. on Religion—Savarese's noteworthy Introduction[4]—Life of Sir C. Wren—Miss Pfeiffer's Drama. Woodcraft with W. & S. Conversation with C. on prospective social or household arrangements. At present we do not regard them from quite the same point of view. The question is raised by the choice of a new Butler. I lean strongly to the desire that my next retirement from office may be an adieu not only to ministerial life but to general society.

To J. G. DODSON, president of the local government board,   Add MS 44545, f. 58.
21 November 1881.

Thanks for your paper[5] which appears to me generally sound & hopeful. I am glad you take to direct election and I hope that when the financial side is considered the decentralising spirit will be strong and efficacious.

To W. P. FRITH, 21 November 1881.   Add MS 44545, f. 58.

Although my occupations are, and I fear must continue to be, very pressing, yet, bearing in mind the honour which the Academy has done me in electing me to be one of its Honorary Members, I cannot refuse the compliment you are pleased to offer me, and I hope to find an opportunity for the sitting you have proposed.[6] As it is uncertain when I may go to London, I beg you to let me know within what dates the sitting may be given, and also to mention how far your residence is from the Great Western Station at Paddington.

22. Tu.

Ch. 8½ A. M. Wrote to Ld Granville l. & Tel.—Sir Thos E. May—Sir H. Ponsonby—Sir Jas Paget—Ld Spencer—Mr Heneage MP—Lady Airlie—and minutes. Woodcraft with W.H.G. Worked on my Library. Read Life of Sir C. Wren—Life of Rev. Dr Conant[7]—The Devil in Oxford.[8] The Hamiltons came.[9] 'Nurse', from Courthey, had tea with us. A character!

---

[1] Offering Sir Kenneth Smith Mackenzie (1832–1900; 6th bart. 1843) the lord lieutenancy of Ross-shire; he accepted; he stood as a liberal candidate for Inverness-shire 1880 and 1885.
[2] William Powell Frith, 1819–1909; chiefly known for his subject paintings. Gladstone sat for 'The Private View', which included many celebrities; begun in 1881, it was exhibited in 1883: 'Mr Gladstone was one of the first to come, but his first sitting was cruelly short, as he was obliged to attend another appointment. How agreeable he can make himself goes without saying'; see W. P. Frith, *My autobiography* (1887), ii. 257.
[3] Accepting hon. membership; Add MS 44470, f. 109.
[4] G. B. Savarese, *Introduzione alla storia critica della filosofia dei sancti padri* (1856).
[5] On County Councils, printed for cabinet; Add MS 44252, f. 122.
[6] Frith's letter of 14 November asked him to sit for his 'Private View' (later known as 'Varnishing day at the R.A.'), and for his exact height; Add MS 44473, f. 57. See 2 Dec. 81, 25 Mar. 82.
[7] *The Life of the Rev. John Conant, written by his son, John Conant* (1823).
[8] Probably *The Devil at Oxford* (1847); satirical verses.
[9] E. W. Hamilton and his mother, the bp.'s widow.

23. Wed.

Ch. 8½ A.M. Wrote to Mad. Novikoff—Prince Leopold—Lady Hutt—Ld F. Cavendish Tel.—Ld Kimberley Tel.—The Queen Tel.—& minutes. Woodcraft with W. & E.H. Worked on my Library. Read Life of Sir C. Wren—Freeman's Venetia[1]—Reresby's Memoirs[2]—'The wickedness of God',[3] sad & terrible words to write!—The Devil in Oxford.

24. Th.

Ch. 8½ A.M. Wrote to Mrs Kirkpatrick Tel.[4]—Ld Kimberley—Ld Ripon—Ld Granville—Mr Forster—Bp of Liverpool—Messrs Pears—Messrs Watson—Mr Dodson—Mr Heneage—& minutes. Woodcraft with W.H.G. Church conversation with Mrs H[amilton] who went off. Read Life of Wren—Life of Sir J. Reresby—The Devil in Oxford.

To J. G. DODSON, president of the local government board,   Add MS 44545, f. 60.
24 November 1881.

In the general ideas of your letter of yesterday I very much concur.[5] I would not ask you to make known all particulars to me when in embryo or in growth, but as you may find it expedient or may desire to consult me.

What I am most anxious about is free and large decentralisation, and this on very many grounds.

Prima facie I think it absurd that we should rest content with controul in the case of poverty, and make over administration to local authorities, but should think prisoners entitled to the higher position of being directly under the central authority.

I do not say that what has been done can be revoked, but I say it ought if it can, and if it cannot I should at the proper time like to know why.

In the same *spirit* I should go through all the local grants, were I dealing with them.

I quite agree that *as towards the rate*, we ought on various grounds to deal liberally in making over taxes. There is a separate question as to the claim of landed *property* for relief from traditional burdens: but that should I think be separately looked at.

[P.S.] The Irish case certainly moves at present rather in the wrong than the right direction.

To LORD RIPON, Viceroy of India, 24 November 1881.   Add MS 43515, f. 5.

I have read with the utmost interest your full explicit and able exposition of the acts of your Indian administration:[6] with a satisfaction too, not less than the interest, and with a concurrence I think absolutely unbroken. I need hardly say that if the confidence, which we reposed in you at the time when you assumed your arduous office, was capable of increase, that increase it has acquired.

Under these circumstances it is not necessary, indeed it would be hardly rational, for me to go over the ground of your letter only repeating in varied forms the cuckoo cry, 'ditto to Mr. Burke.'

[1] E. A. Freeman, *Sketches from subject and neighbour lands of Venice* (1881).
[2] Sir J. Reresby, *Memoirs* (1734), notes at Add MS 44765, f. 162.
[3] Untraced.
[4] Unidentified.
[5] Add MS 44252, f. 125; local govt. proposals.
[6] Long letter of 22 October, Add MS 44286, f. 238.

I am one of those who think that to the actual, as distinguished from the reported, strength of the Empire, India adds nothing. She immensely adds to the responsibility of Government; and I am rather moving towards the belief that by our army arrangements we (at home) have made her the means of fastening upon us large military expenditure which might well have been avoided. But none of this is to the purpose. We have undertaken a most arduous but a most noble duty. We are pledged to India, I may say to mankind, for its performance and we have no choice but to apply ourselves to the accomplishment of the work, the redemption of the pledge, with every faculty we possess.

There is that little corner of the Afghan question, relating to Pishin; on which for the present I reserve my judgment.[1] I follow with imperfect knowledge, but with sympathy, what you say upon Education. I agree strongly with you that administrative perfection is not always and at all costs to be pursued, when the alternative is local self-government. Your Land question I dare not touch: but I embrace with all my soul your doctrine that in all matters, financial and other, India is to be governed for herself, and not for England. That monstrous Vernacular Press Act of Lytton or Salisbury or both I am content to leave in your hands. The financial problem immediately depending had been opened to me in conversation by Hartington a few days before the arrival of your letter: and he has since written to me, after perusing all you had written, in terms the most considerate, of which I am certain you would not disapprove. As the matter stands, I think I had better leave it wholly in his hands; waiting at any rate for a time until it is ripe for final discussion. I may say however that my own prepossessions have all along been somewhat adverse to an Indian Income Tax.

In a former letter[2] you mentioned to me the case of Mr. Pollen, and I brought it under the special notice of Lord Spencer. I am afraid he does not see his way to any backward step: but I am sure that you will believe that whatever he decides will be decided in a spirit of the most perfect fairness.

And now one moment for our house affairs and the general position of the Government. Almost the whole of the work, which confronted us in April 1880 as of immediate urgency, thanks to you in one most important division of it, has been accomplished. I, who only came back to office with what I thought a special mission, ought, on this showing to be packing up my portmanteau and preparing for a final retirement. But two formidable obstacles have since come up: the alarming state of Ireland, and the incapacity of the House of Commons, under present circumstances, to discharge its duties with even a tolerable degree of adequacy. The present mind of the Cabinet is to devote the early part of the Session to dealing with the last-named and intolerable mischief. I am sorry to say that present appearances indicate factious opposition from the Tories, under their weakest of all leaders: and they perhaps are willing to purchase, by the sacrifice of legislation generally, the defeat of the legislation which they dislike and fear. As to Ireland we are still in conflict with the last and basest result of the *delicta majorum*; in the shape of a most immoral, most wicked assault not only on law and order but on private rights, and not only upon private property, but yet more upon personal liberty, the direct offspring of the abominable teaching of Parnell and his friends. Much has been done by putting down the external and visible action of the Land League; but much more remains to be done—God grant that we may have wisdom and strength given us to do it. Our great object I hope has been effectually, and all but universally, secured: that is the free access of the Irish people to the Land Court, which six weeks ago appeared to be placed in the greatest jeopardy.

---

[1] Ripon's view that Pishin be retained prevailed; *Ripon*, ii. 44.
[2] Of 28 February, ibid., f. 231: virtues of J. H. Pollen, formerly his secretary, dismissed from his post at S. Kensington museum without pension; docketed by Gladstone for inquiry.

And now I must break off this hasty epistle, written at the end of a rather long day's work. In so doing let me send to you and Lady Ripon our united and fervent good wishes.

25. Fr.

Ch. 8½ A.M. Wrote to Mr A. Gustavsen[1]—D. of Argyll—Mr Godley Tel.—Earl of Fife—Sir H. Ponsonby—Mr G. Harris—Mr A. Sullivan MP.—& minutes. Cutting a great oak with W. Read Sir John Reresby—Anderson 'Latest of questions'[2]— Life of Wren—Devil in Oxford. Worked on Library.

26. Sat.

Ch. 8¼ A.M. Wrote to Ld C.J. of England—The Queen (2)—Mr Godley—Ld Granville—Mr Frith—Messrs Watson—& minutes. Walk with W. & S. Saw Mr Spencer. Read Reresby's Memoirs—Life of Sir C. Wren (finished)—Devil in Oxford (finished).

27. Advent S.

Ch. mg & evg. Wrote to Dean of Westminster—Dowager Viscountess Milton— Rivingtons—Wms & Norgate—& minutes. Read Luisa de Carvahal—Anderson's Latest of Questions—Bassett Messianic Texts—Bp Ryle's Charges finished— Sermons by Spurgeon, Eyton, Ellis, Hiron.[3]

28. M.

Ch. 8½ A.M. Wrote to Sir H. Ponsonby—Ld Granville Tel.—The Queen—Dean of Westmr—Mr Childers—Dean of Windsor—Mad. Novikoff—& minutes. Worked on Library. Saw WHG on accounts. Read Reresby's Memoirs—Paris en Mini- ature.[4] We brought down a fine (mutilated) Oak.

29. Tu.

Ch. 8½ A.M. Wrote to Ld Kimberley—Mr Godley l. & Tel.—Rev. Dr Rainy—Rev. Dr Hutton—Rev. Dr Nevin—Mr L. Serjeant—Mr Dease—The Queen—Wat- sons—Mrs Th.—Mr Courtney—W. Hyam—Sir R. Phillimore—M. of Rolls (Ire- land)—Mr D. Currie MP—and minutes. Walk with Ld Rosebery. Read Reresby (finished).

To Rev. G. C. HUTTON, 29 November 1881.   Add MS 44545, f. 63.

I attach due importance to the full and explicit representation you have laid before me on the case of Disestablishment in Scotland.[5] But your candour will I am sure perceive

[1] Axel Carl Johan Gustafson, author, had written on Sir B. Frere; Gladstone declined to be drawn into attacking Frere's record; Add MSS 44473, f. 79, 44545, f. 61.
[2] W. Anderson, *The latest of questions answered in the earliest of books* (1881).
[3] C. H. Spurgeon, 'Be of good cheer' (1881); R. Eyton, 'The Kingdom of Christ' (1877); R. Ellis, 'Some aspects of a woman's life. Five Lenten addresses' (1881); S. F. Hiron, 'Things old and new' (1881).   [4] Perhaps C. Monselet, *Le petit Paris* (1879).
[5] See Add MS 44469, f. 82. George Clark *Hutton, 1825-1908; convenor of the United Presby- terian cttee. on disestablishment 1872; U.P. Moderator 1884; principal of U.P. college 1892-1900. See 1 Apr. 75.

how little it is open to any Government, supposing it to be prepared in principle, to consider this question as a question of today. The discussions which preceded the general election did not I think tend to give it that character; while there was a heavy mass of legislative arrear, in many departments of public and national interest, waiting to be dealt with. But since that epoch, I grieve to say, we have, for the gain of no one and the loss of all, been thrown back a good two years partly by the affairs of Ireland, partly by the organisation of obstruction and the necessity for a great effort to reform Parliamentary procedure. So that really it is not so much at this moment a question on what we shall legislate, as when we shall proceed to legislate at all.

The lesson of patience is not the pleasantest in the world but I am afraid all will have to learn it, even in cases which have been well ripened by discussion or which, as you believe to be the case with Scottish Disestablishment, have the support of decisive majorities of the population.

On the merits of the question I do not seek to enter as our position at this moment is precisely that which was assumed at and before the Dissolution.

To R. RAINY, principal of the Edinburgh Free Church College,   Add MS 44545, f. 64.
29 November 1881.

I have reflected and taken counsel upon your letter of the 22nd.[1] I had gathered from your previous communication that there was no desire in your communion to stir at the present juncture the question of Disestablishment in Scotland—and I still presume that I am not to consider this request as modifying the effect of that former communication.

But if this be so I cannot help representing to you that my receiving a Deputation on the subject from the Free Church would draw much attention on various grounds, and among these because it is contrary to my usual practice, indeed the pressure of business hardly permits me, to enter into oral discussion on matters not intended to be pressed at the time in the way of action.

It would have a distinctly disturbing effect on the public mind. I have been holding forth on the absolute necessity of dealing with Parliamentary proceeding, and have been treating legislation on subjects on which it has been fully discussed & expected as thrown more or less into the background. Were I now to receive the proposed deputation it would raise enquiries which I fear it would be impossible to allay and give rise to the charge of a conspiracy between the Government and you without so far as I can see any compensating benefit. Perhaps therefore you would allow me on some ground not discourteous to request that the meeting may for the present be waived.

30. Wed. [Windsor]

Ch. 8½ A.M. Wrote to Mr Childers Tel.—The Queen. Conversation with Ld R. Off at 11¾ for Windsor. Received with much civility, & had a long audience: but I am always outside an iron ring: and without any desire, had I the power, to break it through.

To THE DUKE OF ARGYLL, 30 November 1881.   Add MS 44545, f. 64.

(1) I do not learn from the Bishop of Durham that the Newcastle Bishopric Fund is as far advanced as Mr. Burns supposes, but in any case, when the time comes, the name of Archdeacon Prest will be duly considered with those of others.

---

[1] Not found; Gladstone successfully delayed meeting the dpn., replying to Rainy's letters *via* his secretary; see to Rosebery, 11 Dec. 81 and P.C. Simpson, *Life of Principal Rainy* (1909), ii. 13.

(2) Nothing can be more kind than the tone of your letter[1] but surely some of the assertions require a little further consideration, especially that which declares, if I understand it right, that the Commissioners appointed to act as Judges are not acting judicially while they pretend so to do. If this be true every man of them should be impeached, and probably those who appointed them.

With regard to the barbarism of the Act and the Country I will only observe as I always do that the main provision of the Act which is of a violent character, the interference with rents, rested on the recommendation of a mainly Tory Commission, as well as of every other Tory and nonTory member of the two Commissions. You may call it barbarous, and I for one have never thought or called it highly civilised, but I am afraid every reproach of barbarism against Ireland recoils in the main upon the British Legislature which so oppressed and so mismanaged it. Although you are unhappily out of office, I am afraid you and all members of either House may hear more of these painful subjects and find that they still have duty and responsibility in regard to them.

I write in haste and am just off to Windsor but I may say I was much struck with your figures in a published letter on the application of tenant right on this side of the water i.e. in the case of Farms such as you described. But I do not remember what you said as to the current proposal about compulsory valuation of improvements under the (English) Land Act. I am not sure that a landlord might not often be disposed to permit his tenant to sell, rather than be bound by this compulsory valuation.

I have read only a little of that Life of Voltaire but I hope to return to it.

[P.S.] I am afraid the letters you refer to ill reward your pains in keeping them.

[No entry for 1 and 2 December: half a page blank]

To Mrs GLADSTONE, 2 December 1881.[2]   Hawarden MSS.

Sir Erskine May very kindly came up to see me today—I therefore shall press on matters with a view to coming down by the 10 am GWR train tomorrow and shall expect to be met at Saltney *at 4.10 PM.* I think it will be rather too late in the day for you to come. Today I dine with Ld Coleridge.

I have sat to Frith today at an infinite distance in Bayswater and found Lady Lonsdale sitting also. Woolner has been chosen by the City Committee to do the bust for the Guildhall.

I saw Grogan today: he was glad Mrs Hampton was coming up about No 73 [Harley Street].

There has been no time to go to the Bank or do other matters that I wanted to do: not even to call on Lucy. But if any one writes pray let her be told why I used her so basely last night—it was to dine with the Phillimores, the occasion of the Baronetcy being so very special, & they more than 'over the moon' with a most innocent delight—

I write to Harry by the post. Hoping to meet so soon, I am your afft WE Gladstone

To H. N. GLADSTONE, 2 December 1881.   Hawarden MSS.

For once I take up my pen to write to you. You well know that, although this is so rare an occurrence, on no day are you absent from my thoughts, & every notice we receive of your active and progressive life stirs my heart. I am vexed and even ashamed at not writing but the cause is simple. The incessant repetition of demands which I mislike but cannot escape perfectly sickens and exhaust me and while I hardly ever send a letter written otherwise than from necessity nearly all the letters that I should like to write remain unwritten.

---

[1] Of 29 November, in Argyll, ii. 382, on the Land Act.   [2] Fragment in Bassett, 237.

As to public affairs, we have the utmost cause to be thankful in regard to the difficult and painful matters which had for some time confronted us before the present Gov.^t was formed. Montenegro & Greece have got in the main what they were entitled to—Afghanistan is in the main evacuated—the Transvaal is restored. Also we have at home I hope re-established the proper balance between Income & Charge which is the essential condition of all good finance. But two other subjects have sprung up, even more urgent in their character: the condition of Ireland, and the loss of capacity in the House of Commons under its present rules to discharge its legislative duties. I came into office with the view & intention of retiring from it, so soon as the questions I have named were disposed of; That would have been in the autumn of the present year. But my hopes are dashed to the ground by the appearance of these two new subjects on the stage, and I am chained to the oar I fear for another session. Next year will be the fiftieth of my public life: and beyond that very round figure I trust that, at all events in office, I shall not be called upon to go: as to the Cabinet it has worked extremely well and the Government outside the Cabinet is singularly well manned with strong & able workers. On the other hand the leading men of the Opposition are incessant & most violent in their attacks, which I do not believe have done us the smallest harm though one Tory has taken a County seat from us by promising or supporting a 5/- duty on corn, and another has performed the still more amazing feat of engaging himself to vote for the release of the suspects in Ireland with us or against' us, and has thereby gained in Durham the Irish vote. We have lost three seats this year—there is no great meaning in it, and singularly few of *their* seats have been opened by death or otherwise: still a little gloss has been rubbed off from us, & we should like very well to gain a seat or two. In Ireland, agrarian crime still abounds: but we have gained the one vital and indispensable point of securing the free access of the Irish people to the Land Courts & the difficulty now is that we cannot open Courts enough for them. There will be rough work when the Session opens both as to the suspects whom we are obliged to keep in prison, and as to the proposals we shall probably have to make for enabling Parliament to get through its work.

Now let me turn to family matters. We are all looking forward with the utmost interest to the fulfilment of Willy's hopes in the birth of a child towards the close of next month—God grant all may go well, a prospect in which I am sure you will have joined. You have heard of the manner in which the Archer-God as he used to be called transfixed poor Stephy's heart without any sort of notice of what was coming. His character is so firmly balanced that we have no apprehension of any serious disturbance from this untoward incident. The dear fellow clings to the hope that the thing will come to pass. I do not think it will. But Mama believes that some other attachment will in due time be formed, though of course *he* has not the remotest idea at present of such a thing. Herbert has been working hard in Ireland and is now making a tour under as much of an *incognito* as he can manage, which I have no doubt will be most useful to him. Mary makes herself of great value at home & constantly pursues the cultivation of her mind. Helen seems to have found a home for her mind & heart at Cambridge which in no degree steals her away from domestic affections. We understand that the headship of the Hall will be offered her shortly when Mrs Sidgwick retires from it.

We have had a long visit from 'Nurse' of Courthey, a decided 'character', & this has been the means of bringing over Walter to bring her & Richard to take her away. His whistling to the pianoforte is truly delightful: & he is so modest about it. Meanwhile I am sorry to say that Louey remained, when I last heard, very ill at Fasque. In childhood & youth she was most lovely: but the winter of life seems to have come soon upon her.

Here you see is rather a long story from Downing Street—I end by few but fervent words, God bless you, prosper you, keep you in your going out and your coming hence[?], & give you more & more a heart true to Him and whole with Him. Ever your afft Father WE Gladstone.

To LORD ROSEBERY, home undersecretary, 2 December 1881.   N.L.S. 10022, f. 90.

Many thanks. A most interesting book as far as Bishop Thirlwall is concerned, but badly indexed, edited with gross neglect & carelessness, & stuffed out into the bulk of a volume by audacious bookmaking expedients.[1]

3. Sat. [Hawarden]

Wrote to Watsons—Sir S. Scott & Co. . . . & minutes. Saw Mr Hamilton—The Lord Mayor—Dean Church. 9½-4½. To Hn by G.W.R. Read Sir T. May on Procedure—Mr Torrens M'Cullagh on do[2]—Dr Adler's Reply to G. Smith.[3]

Dec. 4. 2 S. Adv.

Ch. 11 A.M. & 6½ P.M: read all the Lessons. Wrote to Ld Kimberley—D. of Argyll—Ld Granville—Ld Spencer—Mr E. Wilberforce—Bp of N. Scotia—and minutes. Read Life of L. de Carvajah—Congreg. Mag.—Graham, Religion & Science[4]—Spurgeon's Sermon—Powell's Four Addresses.[5] Walk with C.

5. M.

Ch. 8½ A.M. Wrote to Mr A. Mitchell[6]—Mr Forster (2)—Mr Shorthouse—Mr H.G. Reid—Mr Hamilton (Tel.)—Mr Gresham—Mr Godley—& minutes. Saw W.H.G. *cum* Mr Vickers. Began kibbling the great Oak. Read Graham's Creed of Science—Steel on Probability[7]—Doris Barugh[8]—Two Years in the Pontif. Zouxon.[9] Worked on accounts of St Thomas Toxteth. C.G. threaded a needle 1¼ inch long by candlelight without spectacles.

To W. GRAHAM, 5 December 1881.   Add MS 44545, f. 67.

I beg to offer my best thanks for the volume you have kindly sent me.

I have read the introduction and some portion of the work beyond it; and, although weariness of brain from other indispensable employment greatly hinders, it will go hard with me if I do not read it through; attracted as I am by its singular lucidity and the complete mastery of its subject which it displays.

Grateful for the wealth of knowledge accumulated by observers of nature, and now habitually called science as if there were no other science in the world, I am a determined rebel against (what seems to me) the dogmatism of many among those who pursue it; and I rejoice to observe the broad distinction which you draw in from introduction[?]

[1] Probably C. Thirlwall, *Letters, literary and theological*, ed. with annotations and memoranda by J. J. S. Perowne and L. Stokes (1881).
[2] W. T. MacCullagh, *Reform of procedure in parliament* (1881).
[3] *N.C.*, x. 813 (December 1881).
[4] W. Graham, *The creed of science, religious, moral and social* (1881).
[5] F. G. M. Powell, *Four addresses to the clergy of Coventry* (1881).
[6] To Dalkeith liberals; *T.T.*, 14 December 1881, 6f.
[7] Untraced.
[8] K. S. MacQuoid, *Doris Barugh. A Yorkshire story*, 3v. (1878).
[9] Untraced.

between the facts established and the theories which are founded by reasoners or specu-
lators upon them.

I am also a believer in the harmony between science & religion, and I expect to carry
that belief with me to my grave & beyond it, although I am also sensible that some of the
forms of thought, which religionists have invented, and have taken for parts of religion,
have been and will be roughly handled in the light of modern research.

To J. H. SHORTHOUSE, 5 December 1881.   Add MS 44545, f. 66.

I thank you very much for your interesting paper upon Wordsworth's Platonism.[1]

You say that the effect of his teaching is a sacred peace. Your words remind me of words
used to me by Sir James Stephen in the C.O. nearly 50 years ago. He said 'Wordsworth is the
most sabbatical book I know.' With both sentiments or both forms of the one sentiment, I
strongly sympathise. He has been a great teacher & a great blessing to mankind.

I am glad to see from the form of your tract that the spirit of Baskerville is not wholly
expelled from its convenient haunts.

6. Tu.

Ch. 8½ A.M. Wrote to Ld Granville l. & Tel.—Mr Forster—Mr Jas Wilson—Ld
Spencer—Mr Sassoon—Mr Francis—Sir W. Harcourt—Lord Mayor (Tel.).[2]
Luncheon at Rectory & conversation with Bp of St Asaph. Read Creed of
Science—Jennings's Newman[3]—Life of Blakey.[4] Worked on Library.

Theol. A Grammar of Assent.
1. Belief in God is required by reason. 2. If so, belief in Revelation is required by reason.
3. If so, belief that the Scriptures convey a Revelation, is required by reason. 4. If so, belief
in an historical Church or Polity, founded by Christ, and to endure throughout all time, is
required by reason. 5. If so, belief in the Communion of the Anglican Church to represent
that polity within this Kingdom, is required by reason.

All which does not shut out important admissions: 1. The problems of the Universe
and of human life, are unsolved, and apparently incapable of solution by human wit.
2. The whole of these propositions rest on probable evidence only; probable in various
degrees, but in all of them sufficient to oblige. 3. The polity, which is indefestible [*sic*], is
not therefore infallible. 4. Nay, were it infallible, its existence would pass wholly beyond
those prevailing laws of analogy which mark throughout the Divine work on earth for
man: so that the effort to procure a greater ease in our position would introduce a new
element destructive of its basis.[5]

7. Wed.

Ch. 8½ AM & Sermon at 7.30 P.M. (Mr Smithwick).[6] Wrote to Mr Godley (2)—
Mr R. Brown jun.—Solr General for Ireland—Mrs Johnson—and minutes.

[1] Read to the Wordsworth Society, July 1881; printed in *Literary remains of J. H. Shorthouse* (1905),
233.
[2] First of series declining govt. aid for the 'justifiable' Mansion House Fund for Defence of Irish
Property; *T.T.*, 23 December 1881, 8b.
[3] H. J. Jennings, *Cardinal Newman. The story of his life* (1882); Gladstone's note of approbation (8
December) was published in *T.T.*, 10 December 1881, 9f. See to Newman, 12 and 17 Dec. 81.
[4] *Memoirs of R. Blakey*, ed. H. Miller (1879).
[5] Holograph dated 4 and 6 December 1881; Add MS 44765, f. 166.
[6] Robert Fitzgerald Smithwick, De Tabley's chaplain at Tabley.

Kibbling with S.E.G. Read Blakey's Life—The Creed of Science—Life of Newman—Austin's Savonarola.[1] Worked on Library.

8. Th.

Ch. 8½ A.M. Wrote to H.N.G.—Lord Kimberley—Baron Hengelmuller—Sir Geo.
Bramwell—Lord Mayor of Ln (Tel)—Mr Jennings—and minutes. Saw Rev. Mr
Smithwick. Worked on Library. Woodcraft with S.E.G. Read Blakey's Life—
Newman's Life (finished)—Contemp. Rev. on Brick Wealth & Austro-Italian
alliance[2]—Miserrimus.[3]

9. Fr.

Ch. 8½ A.M. Wrote to Ld Granville—Mr Childers—Mr Forster—Mr Winthrop—
Ld Cork—Dean of Westmr—Mr Milbank—Mr Salisbury—Mr Hamilton—Ld R.
Grosvenor—and minutes. Woodcraft with S.E.G. Read Blakey's Life (finished)—
Liddell's Hist. Rome[4]—Miserrimus (finished)—Graham's Creed of Science—
Winthrop's Address.[5]

10. Sat.

Ch. 8½ A.M. Wrote to Professor Blackie—Ld Kimberley l. & Tel.—Mr E. Lyne-
ham—Ld Rosebery—& minutes. Woodcraft with S.E.G. Saw Mr MacColl. Read
Account of F. Spira[6]—Case of Bp Atherton[7]—Pim on Free Trade[8]—Blackie's Lay
Sermons[9]—Caricature Hist. of the Georges.[10]

To LORD KIMBERLEY, colonial secretary, 10 December   Add MS 44545, f. 69.
1881.

I return the draft for South Africa on the ratification of the Convention.[11] Please look
to my proposed amendments: I attach most importance to that on the paragraph touching the word provisionally as I wish to keep even a little farther than you do from any
admission that the carping Preamble can have any [*sic* ?even][12] the smallest effect on the
Ratification.[13]

The contents of it would have been more seemly, and just as effective, in a separate
Dispatch.

---

[1] A. Austin, *Savonarola; a tragedy* (1881).
[2] *Contemporary Review*, xl. 877, 921 (December 1881).
[3] [F. M. Reynolds], *'Miserrimus'. On a Gravestone in Worcester Cathedral* (1833).
[4] H. G. Liddell, *A history of Rome*, 2v. (1855).
[5] R. C. Winthrop, 'Address at the unveiling of the statue of Col. W. Prescott' (1881).
[6] Perhaps N. Bacon, *A relation of the fearefull Estate of Francis Spira in the year 1548* (1637).
[7] *The case of John Atherton [bp. of Waterford and Lismore]* (1710).
[8] Untraced; an article?
[9] See 31 July 81.
[10] By T. Wright (1867?).
[11] Sent on 6 December, Add MS 44227, f. 85.
[12] Secretary's note.
[13] See 30 Oct. 81.

To LORD ROSEBERY, home undersecretary, 10 December 1881.   N.L.S. 10022, f. 92.

1 and 4.[1] I am glad of the negative and the pause respectively.

2. I do not understand whether this is information only or a reference to me. If the latter, it would have to go to the Cabinet. The question of incidence of the rate, and representation of owners and occupiers respectively, are part of the matter referred to the Committee of Cabinet to consider and they constitute a difficulty, not I hope insurmountable both in England and in Scotland.

3. This would of course be for the Cabinet. On the question of existing leases, I would observe that we did not in the Irish Land Bill interfere with them, excepting where there had been undue proceedings on the part of the lessor. And as regards the abolition of entail, to which I am thoroughly friendly, there is this difficulty. It is a stiff resolution for a Cabinet to take: and some might not like to be driven to a decision involving the three Kingdoms on the occasion of a Bill affecting Scotland only.

5. My good relative's announcement at Glasgow was, all things considered, rather strong. I do not however wish him even the chastisement of its being punished in some London paper.

11. 3 S. Adv.

Ch. 11 AM & 6.P.M. Read all the Lessons. Wrote to Ld Hartington—Chester Registrar—Mr Moss—Bp of Chester—Ld Rosebery—Mrs Bramwell[2]—and minutes. Tea at Mary Glynne's. Read Bp of Ely's Charge—Bp of Rochester's Charge[3]—Dr Luccock on the Prayer Book.[4]

To LORD ROSEBERY, home undersecretary, 11 December 1881.   N.L.S. 10022, f. 96.

You see Rainy sticks to his point.[5] I am inclined to write that I shall be happy to make an appointment before the question comes on for discussion in Parliament: but that I hope they will excuse my asking that it may stand over until that time, as it would be very difficult for me under the pressure of necessary business to receive deputations for oral discussion of subjects except in view of pending legislation or other proceeding. (The fact is I am to be used as a means of demonstrations or advertisement. They are excellent people, but this I think is a mistake.)

[P.S.] I inclose the note of the Prayer books which seems cheap.

12. M.

Ch. 8½ A.M. Wrote to Messrs Leeman—Sir H. Verney—Mr Godley—Herbert J.G.—Mr Forster—Cardinal Newman—Mr A. Montgomery—Ld F. Cavendish—& minutes—Mr Hamilton Tel.—Bank of England. Saw Ld Mayor's Secretary—Rev. Mr MacColl. 12½-5. To Chester. Saw the Bp.—Mr Moss

---

[1] Rosebery's letter of 9 December, Add MS 44288, f. 83; 1. a payment by his agent not to be made; 2. the 'very serious difficulty' in local government of a ratepayers' council; 3. proposal for an Entail Bill; 4. has an offer of Lansdowne House for 3 years, no sudden decision; 5. Sir T. Gladstone at a tory meeting in Glasgow hoped Midlothian's verdict would be reversed.

[2] Mrs C. E. Bramwell, the rescue case, see 23 May 55; assistance now unnecessary as she is in New York; Add MS 44545, f. 70.

[3] By J. R. Woodford and A. W. Thorold (both 1881).

[4] H. M. Luccock, *Studies in the history of the Book of Common Prayer* (1881).

[5] See 29 Nov. 81.

(Commr)—The Registrar—& examined & made notes from the Deeds affecting St Thomas Toxteth. Read Creed of Science—Thirlwall's Letters Vol. I.[1]

To CARDINAL NEWMAN, 12 December 1881.   Add MS 44473, f. 154.

I must write to your Eminence a brief line of apology for my note on your Life by Mr. Jennings, which he has put in the newspapers.[2]

It would have been an impertinence in me to have written such a note for publication: and I should not have written it to Mr. Jennings had I known he was a *journalist* for 'tis their nature to'. This is my excuse, which I hope you will accept.

And I trust that your Eminence is enjoying this mild and beneficent season; as I, now fairly within the precinct of old age, day by day rejoice in it.

13. Tu.

Ch. 8½ A.M. Wrote to Ld Mayor Tel. 2—Ld Hartington Tel & l.—Ld Granville Tel. & l.—Mr Hamilton Tel.—Ld F. Cavendish Tel.—Sir H. Ponsonby—Hon J.K. Howard—Sir W. Harcourt—Hon. C. Gore—Ld Kimberley—Sir J. Lambert—and minutes. Kibbling the fallen ash. Read Creed of Science—Thirlwall's Letters— Muggletonian Hymns!![3]—Barboni on Homer.[4] Worked on Library.

To LORD HARTINGTON, Indian secretary,   Chatsworth MSS 340.1130.
13 December 1881.

You would get early this forenoon my Telegram on the Property Defence affair.[5] Your personally subscribing, especially in your position as important proprietor in Ireland, would not I think attract sinister interpretation from candid persons. As to other members of the Cabinet generally, I am not so clear. But I do not think the neutrality of the Govt. need abridge their freedom of personal action. I hope it will not be forgotten that the question is twofold, and that the Ladies Aid branch of it seems simple.

2. In view of your opinion I have further considered the question of approving v. standing aloof, and I remain strongly of Forster's & my own opinion. Your description of my answer to the Lord Mayor is not mine, and I modify my own a little now that I have the reply before me, for I think it as accurately balanced as such a thing can be. This seems to me right. We have no hold over the Property Defence Association. There is a question of *confidence* involved. For all I know it may be under the influence of men like Tottenham M.P.—I suppose you would hardly say that Lawson & Fitzgerald could properly subscribe. But *we* have, under the Protection Act, functions to perform that are judicial though private, and much more delicate & responsible even than those of Judges, although from the necessity of the case the Cabinet as a whole cannot be cognisant of them from day to day.

---

[1] See 2 Dec. 81; and *Letters to a friend*, ed. A. P. Stanley (1881); the 1st v. contains comments on Gladstone but no letters by or to him.

[2] For Gladstone's note of praise for Jennings' biography (see 6 Dec. 81) and for Newman's amiable reply of 13 December, see *Newman*, xxx. 31–2. See also 17 Dec. 81.

[3] The Muggletonian sect, then still active, published various volumes for its use.

[4] Untraced work by L. Barboni.

[5] Irish Property Defence Association now supplemented by Lord Mayor's cttee. in London; Hartington's speech on 17 Dec. praised 'the most legitimate' Irish-based fund; see *P.M.G.* 17 December 1881, 1 and 16 Dec. 81n.

14. Wed.

Ch. 8¼ AM. Wrote to E. of Kingston Tel.—Ld Granville—Mr Chadwick[1]—Ld Hartington—Bp of Ely—Ld F. Cavendish—Mr Forster—Ld Kimberley Tel.—Ld Acton-Ld Spencer—& minutes. Saw Mr Morris & Mr Turner,[2] & walked them in Park. Also Mr J. Griffiths. Read The Creed of Science—Thirlwall's Letters—Blackie's Lay Sermons.

To LORD ACTON, 14 December 1881.   Cambridge University Library.

The prospect of seeing you floats attractively before me & I am exceedingly anxious not to lose it, while the calls upon me in London, uncertain as to date, are rather imperative when they come. The week beginning Jan. 1 is that on which I could most satisfactorily count i.e. from Dec. 31 onwards. But give us any chance you can, in that or any week; and be not, I pray, too niggardly in dealing out your days.

One only assault am I prepared to make upon you, that is upon your doctrine that I am chained to the oar for as long as my fingers can clutch it. Against this I set up that 'when the hurly-burly's done' I shall be entitled if it please God to set up my fifty years of service as I [sc. a] reason why I should run, or walk, out to grass, instead of being driven until I am fit only for the knacker.

Very often have I wished to write to you, most at the moment of sadness—but my usual state of exhaustion, as to letter writing, at the end of the day, is hardly to be told; unless I can convey an idea of it by saying that once in six months is my average to my *son* in Calcutta![3]

15. Th.

Ch 8½ A.M. Wrote to Mr Hamilton Tel. 2.—The Maharajah [Duleep Singh]—Sir M. Smith—Attorney General—Messrs Pears—Bp of Rochester—Messrs Scott—Mr Chamberlain—Mr Godley—and minutes. Woodcraft with S. Saw Mr Vickers—The Pundit[4]—Herbert—on his return. Read Creed of Science—Thirlwall's Letters—Divine Justice & Divine Vengeance.[5]

To J. CHAMBERLAIN, president of the board of trade,   Chamberlain MSS 5/34/7.
15 December 1881.

From Mr. Plunkett's speech I learn that you are a very dangerous person; but I have little else to do than say *ditto* to your letter[6] on the Irish question & the tone to be adopted. As far as my present knowledge goes, I see no case for compensation, and no case for coercion; and the abolition of trial by jury would appear to be sheer folly. My son Herbert who has been travelling about Ireland desires a provision in the law for fining

---

[1] David Chadwick, solicitor, in correspondence on a charter for (Royal) Holloway College for Women, buildings begun 1879; Add MS 44473, ff. 144, 168.

[2] Not further identified.

[3] Acton replied from Cannes on 20 December telling Gladstone he must stay on to win the next General Election: 'if you have provided for the succession you have not tied up the estate', i.e. passed 'the remaining measure of Reform which will establish Democracy for good'; Figgis and Laurence, i. 236. Acton visited Hawarden on 31 Dec. 81.

[4] Probably H. J. Gladstone, just back from a tour of Ireland; no alternative name in H.V.B.

[5] Not found.

[6] Of 14 December, on dislike of compensation to landlords and of a further measure of coercion; Garvin, i. 346.

districts; but, if he is right, this is not what is meant by coercion. I do not feel that I am possessed of complete knowledge about the case of Ireland, though I am in constant communication with Forster: but I have no expectation of hearing anything fresh about present facts which would modify what I have said. The face of Ireland is like the harvest in England, singularly various. From some parts come good & sanguine accents, from others the accents of despair. Two Irish Bishops have actually gone to Rome & are reporting there that peace & order prevail: but without doubt there is great & formidable mischief to deal with, & the Government will act free & boldly in support of the law as it is now doing, & with any additional improvement of means which experience may suggest.

16. Fr.

Ch. 8½ A.M. Wrote to Ld Granville Tel.—Mr Forster Tel.—Sir Thos G.—Mrs Tennyson—Ld R. Grosvenor—Sir W. Harcourt—Sec. Hawarden Institute—and minutes. Long conversation with Herbert, who speaks at Manchester tonight.[1] Worked on Library. Wrote Phil. Mema. Read Thirlwall's Letters—Creed of Science.

To Sir W. V. HARCOURT, home secretary, 16 December   MS Harcourt dep. Adds 10.
1881.

1. I have your memm. on the Govt of London[2] & will give it very early perusal. Heartily do I wish I could relieve you from your difficulties as to that question, but of one thing I am sure that no part of these arises from the postponement of Cabinets. That postponement took place because it appeared that the first work of the Session (and that one probably occupying many weeks) ought to be Procedure, and that Procedure would be more advantageously considered in January than in November. It was also thought that County Govt. would be best considered by a Committee which went to work at once. Bankruptcy and Corrupt Practices with Ballot are to be considered I suppose as indispensable legacies from the last Session & we have the Bills ready made. If we succeed in disposing of the matters I have named, with the usual proportion of secondary measures, it will be a fair Session. But the London Govt. is so important that (as I understood) you & the Cabinet were desirous to be prepared for all favourable chances and to have the measure ready to go forward with. At that time I think I estimated the burden of the details higher than you did. At any rate I am not surprised at what you say of them: but I am afraid that Fate is stronger than the good man, & that though the Cabinet may come to a resolution now, no resolution can really make it certain when, or even whether, you can legislate for London next year. I presume that in the Committee you will consider the points of contact between County Government and the Metropolis.

It may be that there are points of principle, governing the structure of your Bills, on which you may desire to have the judgment of the Cabinet, and if this is so it will be quite proper that the Cabinet should meet at once for the purpose. If this *be so*, as we are nearing Xmas, you probably had better let me know by telegraph tomorrow.

2. With respect to your Commission, as you deem the matter urgent, I do not think you

---

[1] H. J. Gladstone's speech, partly on the Property Defence Association, argued that his father distinguished between an Irish-funded cttee. ('justified') and one receiving aid from England; *P.M.G.*, 17 December 1881, 7.

[2] Of 13 December, MS Harcourt dep. 110/25: new corporation with common council of 240 members, incorporating, as a county, most existing authorities; see J. Davis, *Reforming London* (1988), 74.

need wait, but I would suggest your consulting Spencer and Dodson. Spencer will be here, I suspect, tomorrow night or Sunday morning.
3. Not knowing the details, I hope to stand by you in the matter of the Bribery sentences: at least I think the limit should only be what public opinion will endure without reaction.
4. I hope you observe that Irish juries are beginning to return verdicts against agrarian crime.

17. Sat.

Ch. 8½ A.M. & Holy Commn. Wrote to Cardinal Newman—Mr Forster 1. & 2 Tell.—Ld F. Cavendish—Sir C. Dilke—Father Nolan—Mr Pringle—Hon C. Wood—With Memm on St Thos Toxteth—Watson & Smith—and minutes. Saw The Pundit—Walk with J. G[ladstone] of Bowden. Wrote Phil. Memm. Read Creed of Science—Thirlwall's Letters. Ld & Ly A. Russell came.[1]

Ph. Heredity. Is it not far from the truth & nearer the reverse of truth to say that excellence once attained maintains & propagates itself? Among the lower animals (as they are called) is not the excellence of breeds maintained from without by constant superintending care? Among men why did not the descendants of Homer improve upon Homer? (and by Homer I mean a class). On the contrary
> Rade volte risurge per gli rami
> L'umana probitade.[2]

Nature seems to be fatigued as it were by the production of what is exceptionally good and to compensate herself at once or after a time by relaxed endeavours. So that nothing is more rare than to find male descendants in the world of great men who lived many generations back. No doubt excellence brings many improving tendencies into force: but of them a large part are pro-airetic: and a tendency to abate, derogate or lapse from the standard attained, is shown by a large experience.

In the matter of the senses. Along with a forward movement say in the sense of hearing with which we now appreciate much that the savage knew not of, we have had actual loss & retrogression. His sense of hearing in the gross was far stronger than is ours. Ours recognises & practises in detail particulars we have gradually learned. But note how that our gain has been pro-airetic, the effect of will and study: one loss has been against or without our will, the fault of nature, by failure in 'heredity'.[3]

Darwinism.
It is attempted by means of the Darwinian doctrines of selection and heredity to overthrow the argument of design.
But it may be held 1. That there is great exaggeration in the Statement of the doctrine which goes beyond experience & contradicts it. 2. That if they be allowed in their extremest form they have no adverse bearing whatever on the argument of design but rather tend to enhance design by showing it to be more complex, comprehensive, elaborate.
As to 1. The doctrine is that by natural selection there is a continual upward movement in all the orders of being brought about in this way that of all things new that are engendered by evolution whatever is below the standard is dropped, whatever tends to raise it is preserved. Or if we put it somewhat lower than this the average in each genera-

---

[1] i.e. Lord Arthur and Lady Laura Russell; see 18 Dec. 73.
[2] 'Rarely does human integrity rise through the branches'; Dante, *Purgatorio*, vii. 121–2.
[3] Holographs dated 17 December 1881, Add MS 44766, f. 191.

tion of each order is at every step improved. And whatever has once been improved by selection is maintained by heredity. These are the laws under which the Universe moves on.

But who made the laws: that is to say who impressed upon them different orders of being the upward tendency of selection and the conserving tendency of heredity? The more persistent and widespread these 'laws', the more wonderful the Design which made them. In truth Design so presented opens a new door to a fresh kind of wonder. The old argument of design resting only on the thing produced claimed at once for it a produce without any intermediate wonder. But now the method of production even apart from the thing produced is a thing so constructed as to supply a new chapter of argument to prove the existence of its Maker.[1]

To CARDINAL NEWMAN, 17 December 1881.   Add MS 44545, f. 74.[2]

I hope you will not think that I abuse the kindness shown even beyond former example, in your delightful & moving letter,[3] when I write to you on a public matter. So you see that 'Your Eminence' is a title with a tail behind it.

But I will begin with defining *strictly* the limits of this appeal. I ask you to read the inclosed papers; and to *consider* whether you will write anything to Rome upon them. I do not *ask* you to write, nor to tell me whether you write, nor to make any reply to this letter, beyond returning the inclosures in an envelope to me in Downing Street. I will state briefly the grounds of my request, thus limited.

In 1844, when I was young as a Cabinet Minister, & the Government of Sir Robert Peel was troubled with the O'Connell manifestations, they made what I think was an appeal to Pope Gregory XVI for his intervention to discourage agitation in Ireland. I should be very loathe now to tender such a request at Rome.

But now a difficult case arises. Some members of the Roman Catholic priesthood in Ireland deliver certain sermons & otherwise express themselves in the way which my inclosures exhibit. I doubt whether if they were laymen we should not have settled their cases by putting them into gaol. I need not describe the sentiments uttered. Your Eminence will feel them & judge them as strongly as I do.

But now as to the Supreme Pontiff. You will hardly be surprised when I say that I regard him, if apprised of the facts, as responsible for the conduct of these priests. For I know perfectly well that he has the means of silencing them; and that, if any one of them were in public to dispute the decrees of the Council of 1870 as plainly as he has denounced law & order, he would be silenced.

Mr. Errington, who is at Rome, will I believe have seen these papers, & will I hope have brought the facts as far as he is able to the knowledge of His Holiness. But I do not know how far he is able; nor how he may use his discretion; he is not our official servant, but an independent Roman Catholic gentleman & a volunteer.

My wish is as regards Ireland, in this hour of her peril & her hope; to leave nothing undone by which to give heart & strength to this hope & to abate the peril. But my wish as regards the Pope is that he should have the means of bringing these, for whom he is responsible, to fulfil the elementary duties of citizenship. I say of citizenship; of Christianity, of Priesthood, it is not for me to speak.

The papers are in their nature confidential; but may be used confidentially as far as the purpose I have described requires. They are in the nature of depositions, as they are

---

[1] Holograph dated 17 December 1881; Add MS 44766, f. 189.
[2] Also copy at Add MS 44473, f. 184. Letter sent on 18 December.
[3] See 12 Dec. 81n.

reports taken by responsible persons, & such as, the case arising, we should produce & use in a Court of Justice.[1]

To FATHER NOLAN, 17 December 1881.   Add MS 44545, f. 75.

I read with much interest your letter[2] on behalf of one of the younger suspects. I wrote to Mr. Forster on the subject; and it is now under careful examination in Ireland. I may in the meantime say that I rely entirely on your assurance, and so I am [convinced with?][3] my colleagues at Dublin Castle. But I am bound to recollect that they *may* know of things unknown to you. I hope this may not be the case and that we may have the double pleasure of meeting your wish and of diminishing by one the number of persons now imprisoned on suspicion.

Your anticipation of a favourable course of events in Ireland gives me much pleasure. I am certain that you have promoted, and still promote it, in your personal sphere. There are some of your brethren, I trust very few, who work in an opposite sense, and share the delusion which has done so much mischief.

Finally let me thank you for the concluding part of your letter, and assure you that I set much value on your prayers. May you be yet spared to add other years to the many you have passed in honour and may your end when it comes be peace.

18. *4 S. Adv.*

Ch. 11 AM 6 PM. Read all the lessons. Wrote to Sir W. Harcourt—Cardinal Newman. Read Geikie on Genesis[4]—Creed of Science (finished)—Luccock [*sic*] on Common Prayer. Walk with the A. Russells. Saw The Pundit.

To Sir W. V. HARCOURT, home secretary, 18 December   MS Harcourt dep. Adds 10. 1881.

I have a certain amount of recollection to the effect that the Cabinet agreed, at least provisionally, to the plan of dealing with London as a whole & creating a central body with subordinate organs for the parts. This is what I understand you now to mean.

To CARDINAL NEWMAN, 18 December 1881.   Add MS 44473, f. 185.

Together with this innocent looking note, you will receive a more formidable cover,[5] and what I now write is in truth a sigh of regret for troubling you with the other packet.

My intrusion would not have taken place, had I not been emboldened to it by your kindness, but I fear it will seem a perverse use of that kindness.

The present state of Ireland, critical and even menacing in some parts, is not without favourable features.

But in all its darker parts, it is the main impediment to my fulfilling the only dear [clear?] earthly wish I entertain for myself that of bidding adieu, after half a century, to the arena of political contention, which I have always felt to be ill suited to the closing stages of life.

---

[1] Partly printed in Morley, iii. 62; Newman's reply of 23 December (*Newman*, xxx. 36) declined action: 'I think you overrate the Pope's power in political and social matters . . . local power and influence is often more than a match for Roman might.'

[2] Untraced; Nolan not further identified.

[3] Passage in [ ] so marked by E. W. Hamilton, the copyist.

[4] J. C. Geikie, *Hours with the Bible* (1881).

[5] See previous day.

With this desire for rest, I have a feeling that mankind is not now principally governed from within the walls of Cabinets and Parliaments—higher issues are broadly revived, and higher interests are in question, than those with which Ministers and Opposition mainly deal; and it is by subtler and less obtrusive instruments that the supreme wisdom acts upon them.

We have lived through a great period; the next half century may perhaps be greater still: I think it looks more alarming.

19. M.

Ch. 8½ A.M: goodbye to the Pundit. Wrote to Sir W. Harcourt—Sol. General—W.H.G.—Mr Hamilton l. & Tel.—& minutes. Worked on Library. Woodcraft with S.E.G. Read Poems of Brodrick[1]—Heygate[2]—V. Vita[3]—Thirlwall's Letters—Austin's Savonarola. Saw Ld Spencer (from Ireland) & much conversation.

Th. Idola Templi. 1. Excommunication of all beyond the pale of the visible election.
2. Assumption of a title to rule the decision of questions lying within the domain of natural science.
3. Importation into theology of metaphysical opinions such as the natural immortality of the soul and the *substantio* in matter.
4. The persecution and proscription of opinion.
5. Exaggerations man-wards, prompted by the desire to fortify a polemical position: e.g. Infallibility of the Pope, or of an Oecumenical Council, *ipso facto*; Absolute inspiration of all that is contained in the volume of Holy Scripture; Ascription of spiritual right or function to Crown or State; Vindication of bad actions by elect men, or falliations of the same; Ascriptions to God of such a nature as are dishonouring to the Divine Character, e.g. (a) denial of free will, (b) 'sovereign' or undiscriminating grace, (c) grant of pardon conditional upon absolute knowledge of pardon, (d) severance of pardon from spiritual renovation, (f) exaggeration of the doctrine of future punishment.

It is idle to say we have ceased all these things. For first, we have not: and second if we had it is not enough for a criminal to leave off—the shadow if not the taint of his criminality remains: it is like England saying to Ireland I no longer misrule you.

There is another chapter of attenuations to make good: indeed I must add 6) Misreadings of history. Theological partisanship causes us to treat historic crises and controversies as if all the right lay on one side. But it does not, and it cannot, even in the cases where blame is unequally divided, which does not always happen.[4]

To Sir W. V. HARCOURT, home secretary, 19 December   MS Harcourt dep. 8, f. 115.
1881.

I have now read your very able paper[5] on the London Municipal Reform and it pleases me much. It well deserves good fortune and I hope you may be able to found on it a memorable piece of legislation. I have no cause, on perusing it, to qualify in any way the short note which I addressed to you yesterday.

I agree I think in everything that has the aspect of a principle, and such points as do not at once commend themselves are I think all of them below that rank.

---

[1] A. Brodrick, *Forest poems* (1869).
[2] W. E. Heygate, *Sudden death* (1880).
[3] See 5 Mar. 79.
[4] Initialled and dated 19 December 1881; Add MS 44765, f. 170.
[5] See 16 Dec. 81.

1. I am a little startled at the number of 240: but no doubt, it must be a large number.
2. Is it expedient that all the members should retire at the same time.
3. Is it necessary to extinguish all unpaid magistracy. Is the paid magistracy more necessary in all parts of the Metropolitan District than in Liverpool & Manchester. Should the parish Magistrates be appointed by the Crown? Are they so in the great towns?
4. May we not put into the Bill some enactment to show that we do not contemplate retaining for ever the controul of the Police by the Executive for 4 millions of people. The argument for it seems chiefly applicable to Westminster the region of the Court and Parliament. Could we take it for a few years and then let the question come up again.
5. I embrace the principle of letting old *personnel* into the new body, but of course the proportion must be limited, and I do not know whether you can wholly exclude the vestries from the privilege.
6. The idea of the District Councils seems to have many recommendations but to raise a good deal of difficulty: they seem to carry a slight savour of dualism.

Such are my first thoughts, probably not much worth. They in no way qualify my general liking of the paper. Perhaps I should specify one point more: I do not feel sure about the Recorder & Common Sergeant.
[P.S.] I need perhaps hardly add that these suggestions to you are not in any sense inquiries or meant to give you the trouble of present reply.

20. Tu.

Ch. 8½ A.M. Wrote to Mr Forster l. & Tel.—Mr Hamilton Tel—Ld Rosebery—& minutes. Conversation with Ld S. who went at 11. Worked on Library. Examining Vols of Poems: verdicts of Guilty preponderate.[1] Read Thirlwall's Letters—Rawle on Land Legislation[2]—Woolner's Pygmalion.[3]

21. Wed. St Thomas.

Ch. 8½ A.M. Wrote to Mr Hamilton—Sir W. Harcourt—Mr J. Talbot—U.S. Minister—Ld Chancr—Ld Kimberley—and minutes. Woodcraft with Herbert. Read Woolner—Thirlwall finished (there is much to say on this noteworthy book)—Collingwood on Genesis.[4] Poems on trial—I feel like a Land Commr in Ireland trying Rents: it is a Rhadamanthine business. Read Wilkie's Poems[5]—Darvak's do[6]—and others. Otium Norvicense.

22. Th.

Ch. 8½ A.M. Wrote to Mr Hamilton 2 Tell.—Baron Tauchnitz—Ld Coleridge—Mr D. Maclaren—Mr Hankey—Mr G. Pringle—The Queen—Walter Gladstone—Mr Woolner—Mr Street and minutes. Read Woolner's Pygmalion—Abergeroyle

[1] Gladstone made various lists of contemporary clerical poets, finding two-thirds of them 'in express or general sympathy with the great theological & religious movement of the time [i.e. the Oxford movement]. Three only can be quoted as antipathetic to it: Dean Milman, Alford, and Stanley'; Add MS 44765, ff. 172-5.
[2] Pamphlet on land sent by J. R. Lowell; Add MS 44545, f. 76.
[3] T. Woolner, *Pygmalion* (1881).
[4] C. Collingwood, 'A vision of creation' (1872).
[5] W. Wilkie, *Poetical works* (1794).
[6] Author's name scrawled.

Papers[1]—Morley on Engl. Literature[2]—Further trial of Poems—Reisehiep eines Diplomaten.[3] Woodcraft with Herbert. Worked in Library.

To D. McLAREN, 22 December 1881.   Add MS 44545, f. 77.

The report of your speech[4] I think fully and clearly expresses the view which an impartial observer may take of the position of the Government with regard to the question of Disestablishment in Scotland.

I am tempted however to go a little beyond this recognition and to say a word in the same character (as far as I may) of an impartial observer.

Since the Election & Election speeches, the affairs of Ireland have as you know introduced into the business of the State a new and potent element of obstruction and arrear, of what I may perhaps call constipation.

Were the cause of Disestablishment sufficiently powerful and mature to force its way to the front in defiance of all competition, its friends need not be deterred from bringing it into activity & prominence at head quarters.

But if it has not reached that very advanced stage, my opinion is that the measure is much more likely to be thrown back than pushed forward by endeavours to bring the Government or Parliament prematurely to entertain it: just as the cause of Parliamentary Reform was (you will recollect) greatly thrown back by the unfortunate Bill of 1860,[5] thrust on the notice of Parliament when the public interest ran in other directions.

My observation has no reference to any proceedings taken in Scotland.

To T. WOOLNER, 22 December 1881.   Add MS 44545, f. 77.

I am extremely obliged to Mr. Frith if as you say he made the suggestion which has procured for me an early sight of your (to my mind) very beautiful Poem,[6] which I am reading with much enjoyment.

It shows how close you sit to the centre of your art, and how you have drunk in its soul.

This making of Hebe is full of interest for me: as I believe myself to have done one and only one good thing in my life for Art, i.e. to have been the first to teach and preach that the secret of excellence in the Art of Greece lay in the anthropomorphism, or as I commonly call it, the anthropism, of the Olympian religion.

Do I understand you to have the City Commission for a bust of me?[7] If so I shall be sincerely glad, and ready to hear from you at any time about your preparations & plans.

23. Fr.

Ch 8½ a.m. Wrote to Mr Hamilton Tel—Mr Forster 1 & Tel—Ld Chancellor (minutes)—Ld Granville—Mr O. Simm—Ld F. Cavendish—J. Taylor—Ld Houghton—Mr Rathbone P.S. and minutes. Woodcraft with the party. Prosecuted the

[1] Reading uncertain; untraced.
[2] The start of John Morley's long series of *English men of letters* (1878-1919), sent by Tauchnitz.
[3] Reading uncertain; untraced.
[4] Brief report in *D.T.*, 21 December 1881, 3h; full report in *The Scotsman*, 21 December 1881, 8.
[5] See 1 Dec. 59, 16 Jan. 60.
[6] See 20 Dec. 81, sent by Woolner that day, Add MS 44473, f. 198.
[7] Not mentioned by Woolner in his letter of 20 December; see 29 Dec. 81.

examination of many Vols of Poems: Outram's[1] were a prize. Read Outram (also) aloud—The Astrologer of Leeds.[2]

24. Sat. Xmas Eve.

Ch 8½ a.m. Wrote to Ld Mayor of L. 1 & Tel—Sir J. Lambert—Ld Sydney—Ld R. Grosvenor—Mrs Raleigh—Mr S. Morley MP—and minutes. We brought down large elder. Finished reviewing Poetry and excisions. Read Pygmalion—Finished Astrologer of Leeds.

25. Xmas Day.

Ch 11 a.m. with H.C. & 6½ P.M. Visited the Hall dinner. Wrote to Ld Granville—Ld Chancellor—Mr Hamilton and minutes. Read Hatch, Bn Lectures[3]—Geikie Hours with the Bible—Luccock [sic] on Prayer Book.[4]

26. M. S. Stephen

Ch 8½ a.m. Wrote to Mr Forster (2)—Mr Childers—Dr A. Clark—Mr L. Morris—Ld Acton—Mr T. Archer[5]—Mr Whitaker—Mr Lyon Playfair—Mr Jolly—Mr G. Pringle—Sir Thos G. and minutes. Made out the accounts as well as I could for my plans at St Thomas Toxteth. Read Pygmalion (finished)—Savonarola—E. Wickham on Scr. Critm[6]—Watts 'The Newer Criticism'.[7] Walk & much conversation with E. Wickham.

To LORD ACTON, 26 December 1881.   Cambridge University Library.

We have just telegraphed to pray you to come on Saturday if you can.[8] This is an act of avarice perhaps, but of an avarice pardonable in its kind. Since I last wrote,[9] I have been moved to appoint a Cabinet in London for the 6th—and if you do not come till the 2nd this will give us so short a time, for I must go up to town on the evening of the 5th. I hope it may be in your power to deal equitably and compassionately with my request.

Not only am I not moved by your argument in enforcement of my perpetual servitude, but I hope—a daring word—to shake you and bring you round to my way of thinking which is that when the great specialities are disposed of I am outwardly free and inwardly bound to ask for my dismissal.

Thank God, the aspect of the speciality in Ireland somewhat improves: the reports and impressions of intelligent men become less unfavourable: the outrages tend to diminish: the Land League does not get its head lifted from the ground.

[1] G. Outram, *Lyrics, legal and miscellaneous* (1874).

[2] J. Howard, *The astrologer of Leeds . . . a romance of the twelfth century* (1881).

[3] E. Hatch, *The organization of the early Christian churches* (1880).

[4] See 11 Dec. 81.

[5] Thomas Archer, 1830-93; novelist and historian; had sent the first part of his *William Ewart Gladstone and his contemporaries: fifty years of social and political progress*; the parts were published together in 4v. (1883).

[6] An unpublished work by his son-in-law.

[7] R. Watts, *The newer criticism and the analogy of the faith* (1881).

[8] See 31 Dec. 81.

[9] See 14 Dec. 81.

To H. C. E. CHILDERS, war secretary, 26 December 1881.   Childers MS 5/137.

The *special* object of the Cabinet on Friday next and any following days will be to consider the subject of Parliamentary procedure & after a short time given to steady work
upon it we may again have an interval before the final gathering.

It might I thought be convenient to you to have this general indication, with reference
to the preparation of your Estimates.

I had for some time hoped that you would have to look specially at these Estimates
from my present position and not from yours. I still hope that such may be your point of
view before they come out at the close of the coming financial year as expenditure.

In any case, you will I am sure do your best to ensure their bearing the mark of tendencies, in connection with which you have earned *ab antiquo* an honourable reputation.
You will have noticed the taunts on the subject of expenditure to which during the recess
we have been unjustly, yet plausibly, subjected. We have now a starting point more
favourable than last year: and, without any extravagant expectations, I hope you will be
able to turn it to account for the silencing of cavillers. These must in all likelihood be the
last estimates with which I can have to do: and I hope to be able to look at them with
some kindly feeling.[1]

27. Tu. St John.

Ch 8½ a.m. Wrote to Ld Kimberley—Ld Normanton—Sir F. Doyle—Lady S.
Opdebeeck—Sir H. Loch and minutes. 2¾-5½ to Buckley Church. Fair & Con-
juror with S.E.G. Very grave conversation on the walk home. 7¾-10½ To the
Hawarden Play. We were well entertained. Read Molesworth's Hist.[2]—W.E.G.
& his Contemporaries[3]—Wilson's Lect. on Water[4]—Savonarola.

28. Wed. Innocents.

Ch. 8½ a.m. With H.C. Wrote to Sir H. Ponsonby—Mr E. Harcourt—Ld Gran-
ville—W.L. Gladstone—Sir Thos G.—Earl Cowper—Mr Forster and minutes.
Read Austin Savonarola (finished)—Chadwick on the Man Christ[5]—Lady
Verney French Tour.[6] Woodcraft with S.E.G.

29. Th.

Ch 8½ a.m. Wrote to Duke of Westminster—Mr Hamilton l & Tel—Mr Woolner—Mayor of Denbigh—Sir H. Ponsonby—Ld Carlingford—D. of Devonshire—
Mr Thorold Rogers & minutes. Ly A. Tollemache[7] came over with her party.
Walk with S.E.G. & party. Tea at Mrs Best's. Dinner at the Rectory. What a
series of gaieties! In truth I am overwhelmed from all quarters with kindness
and good will. The Telegrams came in all day. It ought to have been

[1] Childers, 27 December, Add MS 44129, f. 320, hoped for 'wise economy' but stressed strong
pressures for extra expenditure, e.g. Cambridge's planned additions to the infantry.
[2] W. N. Molesworth, *History of the Church of England from 1660* (1882).
[3] See 26 Dec. 81.
[4] Perhaps W. S. Wilson, *The ocean as a health-resort* (1880).
[5] J. W. Chadwick, *The man Jesus* (1881).
[6] Article by Lady Verney, reprinted in her *Cottier owners... and peasant properties* (1885).
[7] Apparently *sic*; probably Mary, wife of 2nd Lord Tollemache of Peckforton.

a day of recollection. Read Stubbs's Sermons[1]—Dean Plumptre's Sermon[2]—Ly Verney's Article, finished—Coke's Letter to Bp of B. & Wells[3]—Pfeiffer's Poems.

I have never closed a year more abounding in signs of what is termed prosperity, and what are certainly causes of thankfulness: but neither have I ever touched a birthday with such eagerness for a change of position, such a hope that my political work is all but done, such a dread of reaching the term of another of the very few years that can remain to me without being free from the great *fardel* now upon me. In any & in every case let me give thanks always & for all things.

To T. WOOLNER, 29 December 1881.   Add MS 44545, f. 81.

I must, on receiving your letter,[4] go straight to business. My difficulties as to sittings are hardly to be coped with. In the first place I may say with nearly literal truth that though I sometimes have an hour free, I hardly ever have two hours at my free disposal. Then (1) I am in the hands of Mr. Frith but that is a small matter. (2) The City Liberal Club has given a Commission for a Statue. (3) Most of all Mr. Watts has now (after I will not say what of time spent) thrown up the picture he was painting for Christ Church Hall & they want to start me again for W. Richmond. Under these circumstances you will not be surprised at my asking what plan you can throw out & what expectations you can give. After all I am the man I was when you took me before,[5] but a little more wrinkled, & with my head a little whiter, a little barer, and a little bigger.

30. Fr.

Ch 8¼ a.m. Wrote to Mrs Meynell Ingram—Ld Chancellor—Ld de Tabley—Prince of Wales—D. of Argyll—Mr A. Acland—Sir F. Doyle—Mr Hamilton—Sir S. Waterlow—Dr Buchholz & minutes. Walk & conversation with E. Wickham. Read Brodrick on Land act[6]—'Fraser' Polit. Outlook, Weak![7]—N.A. Review on Monroe Doctrine[8]—G. Government in Ireland—Contemp. Rev.[9]—Macmillan (i.e. Pigott) on Irish Land Act.[10]

To Eduard BUCHHOLZ, 30 December 1881.   Add MS 44545, f. 82.

I have had the high honour to receive the gift of your new and important treatise presented by yourself: and I rejoice to find that you are actively engaged in the prosecution of your great work, which will in my opinion be the most fruitful boon ever conferred by a student of Homer on his fellows and his followers.[11]

[1] C. W. Stubbs, 'Christianity and democracy' (1881).
[2] E. H. Plumptre, 'The ideal of cathedral life' (1882).
[3] Untraced correspondence with Lord A. C. Hervey.
[4] Of 26 December, Add MS 44473, f. 229: 'I have the commission to do your bust for the Guildhall whenever you can give me the sitting. . . .'
[5] Large bust and Homeric plinth presented by his constituents to Oxford University; illustrated above, vi. 360.
[6] G. C. Brodrick, *The Irish land question: past and present* (1881).
[7] *Fraser's Magazine*, civ. 800 (December 1881).
[8] *North American Review*, cxxxiii. 523 (December 1881).
[9] J. P. Mahaffy in *C.R.*, xli. 160 (January 1882).
[10] *Macmillan's Magazine*, xlv. 165 (December 1881).
[11] The 2nd v. of his *Die Homerischen Realien*, 3v. (1871–85), dedicated to Gladstone, 'dem eifrigen Pfleger und föderer der Homerischen Forschung'.

It is by your composition far more than by any other that this study will be drawn out of the vicious arbitrary form of speculation about Homer, and placed upon its true lines, where Homer will be judged by and out of himself.

Though not in merit or performance, I am one with you in spirit, and long for a day which I know may never come to one so advanced in life, the day of return to honest work on the text of the Poems.

31. Sat.

Ch 8½ a.m. Wrote to Messrs Williams—Ld Egerton of Tatton and minutes. Ld Acton came. Long walk with him & set out as well as I could my case for retirement on a fair opportunity.[1] Doyles, Clarks, Lytteltons came. Went over many pamphlets & papers in the forenoon. Also read 19th Cent. Rev. on Procedure—Agnostics at Church—the Verses on Stanley.[2] Made out the annual account of property. I ought to recast my testamentary arrangements: but I cannot find the time *with* the brain-force.

I might & ought to say much on closing the year: a year of much burden, much support, much suspense. Better in some respects than some that preceded: probably not in all. But aspiration for repose looks boldly into the future and refuses to be denied. May God's will decree it.

[1] Which Acton opposed; see to Acton, 14 Dec. 81.
[2] F. Harrison, Goldwin Smith, and L. Greg, with Matthew Arnold's verses on A. P. Stanley in *N.C.*, xi. 1 (January 1882).

Hawarden Jan 1. 82. Sunday. (Circumcision.)

Ch. 11 A.M. with H.C. and 6½ P.M. Wrote to Mr Max Müller—& minutes. Read Lady C. Elliot's beautiful Poems[1]—and divers Tracts. Walk & conversation with Ld Acton—Dr A. Clark—Sir F. Doyle.

To Sir C. W. DILKE, foreign undersecretary, 1 January 1882.   Add MS 43875, f. 80.

You have had an anxious and arduous work, now I hope near its close.[2] The French Government must know I suppose that a Treaty is of far greater consequence to them than to us. We cannot afford indeed to make one unless it is a manifest or certain, though I do not say it need be a large advance on 1860.

I am glad that Gambetta sees that he is in the same boat with us as to Panama. Our safety there will be in acting as charged with the interests of the world *minus* America.

2. M.

Ch. 8½ A.M. Wrote to Mr Forster l. & Tel.—Ld Kenmare Tel.—Mr Pears—The Queen 2.—W.H.G.—Ld Hartington—H.J.G.—Mr MacCarthy—K. of the Belgians—The Chancellor Tel.—and minutes. Walk with Acton & a party. Gave up some of my morning: hard driven after in consequence. Read Hitchens The Penalty[3]—The New Ceylon:[4] & tracts. Saw Mr Ward's party. Ld Kenmare[5] came: to discuss Irish matters, & the meeting tomorrow.[6]

3. Tu.

Ch. 8½ A. M. Wrote to Ld Chancellor Tel.—Ld Granville—The Queen—Mr Meldon MP.[7]—Messrs Pears—Ld Kimberley—Mr Spurgeon—and minutes. Walk with Ld Acton. Saw Mr Vickers. Read 'The New Ceylon'—Ashy Pyee (U. Burmah)[8]—Prescott on Methodism[9]—Hamilton Smith on the Horse[10] (much horse & Homeric conversation with Doyle in evg)—Theolog. Tracts.

To LORD KIMBERLEY, colonial secretary, 3 January 1882.   Add MS 44545, f. 83.

I agree with you that Robinson's Telegram is not quite the thing and also that it will be well to let the Cabinet have its say [on Basutoland].[11]

---

[1] Lady C. Elliot, *Mary Magdalene, and other poems* (1880).
[2] Letters of 28 and 31 December from Paris, Add MS 44149, ff. 61–4 on poor progress of negotiations.
[3] J. H. Hitchins, *The penalty* (1878); on future retribution.
[4] J. Hatton, *The new Ceylon, being a sketch of British North Borneo or Sabah* (1881); see Ramm II, i. 326.
[5] See 10 Dec. 68; he was lord chamberlain 1880–5.
[6] Huge meeting of landlords in Dublin, which led to the Lords cttee. on the Land Act.
[7] Charles Henry Meldon, d. 1892; liberal M.P. Kildare 1847–85.
[8] W. F. B. Laurie, *Ashee Pyee, the superior country* (1882).
[9] P. Prescott, 'Methodism in relation to popery' (1880).
[10] C. Hamilton Smith, *The natural history of the horse* (1841).
[11] Kimberley, 1 January, Add MS 44227, f. 106: 'We must remember that the present Colonial

My own personal inclination, subject always to correction, would be to send a rather brief reply consisting virtually of or based upon these two propositions—(1) that if they the Colonial authorities think it needful on their responsibility to enforce the award we *shall not question* their discretion in the measures they may take for that purpose; (2) that if they deem it requisite to impose new terms we shall not interfere unless impelled to it by Imperial considerations (in substantial correspondence with your language about measures beyond the competence of the local government.) Please to consider whether this goes too far—it is a little, & not much, on the Colonial side of your draft.

To Rev. C. H. SPURGEON, 3 January 1882.   Add MS 44545, f. 83.

Some time ago you were good enough to promise me a safe seat at one of your services: and if it consist with your convenience to do me this favour on Sunday evening next, when I hope to be in London, I shall hope to be present myself at the exact time and place which you may kindly name.

Should you desire to postpone your compliance with my request, I shall hope for another opportunity of preferring it three or four Sundays hence.[1]

4. *Wed.*

Ch. 8¼ A.M. Wrote to Sir H. Ponsonby—Mr Broadhurst—Sir C. Dilke—Mr Forster Tel.—Ld Granville—Mr Rathbone MP—W.H.G.—The Queen—Mrs Th.—Sir Thos G.—& minutes. Walk with Ld Acton. More Hom. talk with Doyle. Read Purcell on St Petersburgh[2]—London Quarterly on Defoe—Curci—Darwinism.[3]

To H. BROADHURST, M.P., 4 January 1882.   Add MS 44545, f. 84.

I have read your letter[4] with much pleasure and you are right in supposing that I had perused Mr. Harrison's timely and very useful article. I take the letter, I hope rightly, as a sample of the impressions which the present state of the arrangements for business in the House of Commons, when duly set forth, can hardly fail to make upon the minds of intelligent and impartial men.

To Sir C. W. DILKE, foreign undersecretary, 4 January 1882.   Add MS 43875, f. 81.

I have this morning received your letter of the 2nd.;[5] and, as I hope to see Granville either tomorrow evening or on Friday, I will defer replying to it.

One thing, a step removed into the future, occurs to me as important. It is the Treaty of 60 which as a consequence has involved us in the present negotiations with France. Now that treaty was always vindicated as exceptional and not as the beginning of a new system of Tariff Treaties. This being so, if we fail with France, I think it will require careful

Ministry is opposed to the policy which brought on these difficulties, and that Masupha and his followers are now utterly in the wrong.'

[1] See 8 Jan. 82; Spurgeon sent a letter and a map, later apologising that a reporter was present at the service; Add MS 44474, f. 14.
[2] Not found; article by E. S. Purcell?
[3] *London Quarterly Review*, lvii. 345 (January 1882).
[4] On Harrison's article, 3 January, Add MS 44474, f. 11; see 31 Dec. 81.
[5] Add MS 44149, f. 65: Gambetta wants a joint British/French representation to the Sultan about Egypt; Dilke cautious about this (see 7 Jan. 82n.); should we ask the French for 1 year's m.f.n. treatment in the Treaty?

consideration whether we should attempt a Tariff Treaty with Spain or anybody else. I should not on this account be averse to encouraging or meeting Spain on the path of liberal legislation by mending the wine duties, if our finance, which is fair but not brilliant, will permit.

5. Th. [London]

Ch. 8½ A.M. Farewell to Acton & Doyle. Wrote to Sir W. Harcourt—Sir H. Ponsonby—Mr Godley Tel.—Ld Granville—Sir Thos G (2)—Walter L. Gladstone—Mr M. Bernard—Mr Vickers—and minutes. 1–6¾. To Downing Street. Meeting Willy at Euston was a great delight. We dined with him & saw the Baby.[1] Then I went to F. Leveson's & saw Granville 9½–11½. Read Memoirs of the Duchess of Kingston.[2]

6. Fr. Epiphany

This day C.G. in marvellous health & vigour touches 70. 'True yet incredible'. God be with her evermore. Wrote to Ld F. Cavendish—Sir John Holker—The Queen (3)—Mr Collings MP—Mr Childers—H.N.G.—& minutes. Cabinet 2–5¼. Saw Ld Chancr *cum* Ld Granville—Ld R. Grosvenor—Mr Ford—Ld F. Cavendish—Mr Godley—Mr Burn Jones. Dined at Sir B. Leighton's. Read Duchess of Kingston (finished)—Heine Translation & Preface.[3]

Cabinet. Jan. 6. 1882.[4]
1. Queen & opening Parliament. Simply express regret[—]no more.[5]
2. Time of Pr. Leop[old's] Marriage proposal. Explain that we *cannot* get in before party subjects: without every effort to avoid any delay of the marriage: reserve awhile [?] on the time of the proposal.
3. Bradlaugh. No Bill. Leave to previous question.[6]
4. Procedure: Sir G. Grey; Queen's offer; Sir T. E. May; Speaker.
5. French Treaty. Cabinet approve the attitude assumed. They are to ask for m[ost] f[avoured] n[ation] Claim in the *last resort.*
6. Basuto Telegram. Read & approved.
7. Leakage from Cabinets: Committee.[7]
8. London Govt.[8] Committee of Cabinet.[9]

[1] Evelyn Catherine, 1st child of W. H. Gladstone, b. 2 Jan. 1882, d. unmarried 1958.
[2] See 4 Aug. 72.
[3] H. Heine, *Poems and ballads*, tr. E. Lazarus (1881).
[4] Add MS 44643, f. 1.
[5] Gladstone's note reads: 'Please to see whether *annually* since marriage of Princess Royal & including it, the Queen has opened Parlt. on all occasions when a grant was to be asked for one of the Royal Family'; Godley replied '... she did *not* open it 1) when grant was to be asked for the Princess Royal 2) when grant was to be asked for the Prince of Wales; we looked no further'; ibid., f. 3.
[6] i.e. move the 'previous question', the Commons thus opting out of taking a view, the tactic followed on 7 February; Arnstein, 127.
[7] 'To inquire into Printing—& use of Keys'; members: Granville, Carlingford, Kimberley, Spencer, Add MS 44643, f. 6; see 25 Feb. 82.
[8] Illegible abbreviation here.
[9] Mem. by Harcourt, with Chamberlain's criticisms, on London municipal govt., Add MS 44628, f. 1.

7. Sat.

Wrote Sir H. Ponsonby—The Queen & minutes. Cabinet 12–4½ on Procedure.
Saw Ld Granville—Ld Northbrook—Mr Forster—Mr Childers—Mr Godley—Ld
Rosebery. Dined at Ld Rosebery's. Saw Read—with promise [R]. Read Lay
Monastery[1]—Account of Society for Reformation of Mariners.[2]

Cabinet. Saturday Jan 7. 82. Noon.[3]
1. Hinde Palmer's suggestion mentioned by Bright.[4]
2. '*American Previous question*': to be ⟨preferred⟩ adopted.
    1. By Speaker? 2. Under previous vote of urgency? 3. Mode of adopting it. Resolution
    drawn by Childers & given to Sir E. May to reconsider the terms—providing *major*
    form except for Clauses of Bills, then the minor.

1. To adopt in some form & under some conditions the American Previous question.
2. To place that proposal in the Van. 3. Proposal to be made by the Leader of the House.[5]

8. 1 S. Epiph.

Ch. Royal at noon. In the Evg went with Willy to Mr Spurgeon's Tabernacle.
Saw him before and after. There would be much to say upon it. Read Account
of Societies—Beckett Dennison on Revised Version[6]—Rev. Banerjea on the
Vedas.[7] Luncheon at Ld Blantyres. Dined with the F.C.s.

9. M.

Wrote to Mr Playfair—Mr Goschen—Mr Burne Jones—The Queen—Mr Chil-
ders—and minutes. Saw F. Cavendish—Mr Shaw Stewart—Ld Blantyre—W.H.G.
Saw Cooper (& another) & was carried into dreamland, with disappointment X.
Read Tallain's Preface[8]—Account of Societies (finished). Dined at Ld Blantyre's.
Saw dear Gerty looking wonderfully: & her beautiful infant.[9] Cabinet 12–6.

Cabinet. Monday Jan. 9. Noon[10] *Procedure.*
1. Draft Resolution of Sat. considered & amended.
2. Nine Resolutions more considered & adopted.
3. Sir Erskine May will consider & arrange the formal drafting.
4. Question of Devolution considered in conversation.
    Hartington's ⎫
    Childers   ⎭ plans to be printed.[11]
5. Enquiries from Forster about Ireland.

---

[1] *The lay monastery. Consisting of essays* (1714).
[2] Various publications on it *ca.* 1719.
[3] Add MS 44643, f. 10. This cabinet also approved the Anglo-French joint note supporting the
Khedive; Chamberlain, *Political memoir*, 70.
[4] Perhaps Palmer's suggestion that the Speaker propose procedural changes; *H* 266. 1168.
[5] Undated holograph; Add MS 44643, f. 12.
[6] E. B. Denison, 'A reply to Dr. Farrar' (1882); on the revised authorised version.
[7] K. M. Banerjea, *Rig-Veda Sanhita* (1875).
[8] Reading uncertain; untraced.
[9] See 5 Jan. 82.
[10] Add MS 44643, f. 13.   [11] Not found printed.

6. Cabinet to meet about 25th.
7. Contention between Indian Govt. & War Office about a cavalry regiment. Decided (in a thin Cabinet—Bright went away in the middle!) for Childers.

To E. C. BURNE-JONES, 9 January 1882.   Add MS 44545, f. 85.

Even if I were so wrong-headed as to object to an appeal to public opinion in Europe by or on behalf of persons who suffer unjustly, my objection ought not to be considered by them as of the smallest weight.[1]

But so far am I from objecting, that it is the course I myself have adopted and followed upon various occasions.

And in my opinion it is the proper course as contradistinguished from a reliance upon a Government to interfere in the internal affairs of another country.

In making such an appeal great care ought to be taken to avoid injustice and if the case be one of perverted popular feeling which the Government desires and endeavours to controul then not to cast upon such a Government more than a due share of responsibility, and to endeavour rather to strengthen its hands.

In the case of these afflicting and harrowing details I am inclined to believe the chance of doing good will depend a good deal upon the care taken in these respects so that the offending population may know that a true popular & human sympathy has been awakened, and may not suppose it to be an affair of national prejudice or political intrigue.

10. Tu. [Hawarden]

Wrote to Mr Childers—Lady Rosebery—Mr Hayward—Lady Holker—Mr Dodson—Mr Chamberlain—Ld R. Grosvenor—and minutes. Saw Mr Godley—Ld Granville—Scotts—Ld F. Cavendish—Mr Lefevre—W.H.G. Sat 1½ hour to Woolner.[2] Off at 4½: reached Hawarden 10.15.

To J. CHAMBERLAIN, president of the board of trade,   Chamberlain MSS 5/34/8.
10 January 1882.

The point you raise with regard to certain cases of eviction of tenants in arrear is one of much delicacy and I will refer your letter[3] to Forster. To amend the Land Act at any point at this moment would be hazardous.

To H. C. E. CHILDERS, war secretary, 10 January 1882.   Add MS 44545, f. 86.

I understand that there has been a little apprehension at the Treasury about your expenditure for the current year & that you, having heard of it, have examined & been satisfied. For my part I am satisfied with your satisfaction, as I rely upon it. But the truth is, our revenue is not good; at the best it is middling only, & this makes us sensitive. If you would like to see a memorandum which Welby has just written on the state of the revenue, send to Godley for it.

---

[1] See Burne-Jones' letter of 7 January, Add MS 44474, f. 18, on persecution of Jews in Russia. Gladstone sent a copy of this letter to Lady Rosebery, also active in this campaign; Add MS 44545, f. 86.
[2] See 22, 29 Dec. 81.
[3] Chamberlain's docket on this letter: 'Letter from Gray M.P. arrears'.

To J. G. DODSON, president of the local government board,   Monk Bretton 52.
10 January 1882.

If we meet again, as is probable, on the 25th, and your Local Government Bill is then ready, you will have I hope an early hearing.

I was much pleased with the outline of the Bill as one really corresponding with the spirit of its title.

There is, however, one point on which I have so strong a feeling and opinion, and one which might so greatly influence my personal action, that I am desirous to mention it. It is that your measure, with which I hope your name will be honourably associated, should not only be a great Local Government Bill, but a great decentralisation Bill: that to the utmost possible extent administration by the local authority, subject to fixed rules and conditions, of money raised for it by the Imperial authority, and handed over to it subject to those rules and conditions, should be the principle of our local expenditure and should replace the principle of administration from the centre which has of late been forcing itself into our system. Also that those rules and conditions should be carefully revised, and not such as some absurd rules under which we now bribe the local authority to keep more police than it wants.

It has been my duty heretofore to show, very ineffectually, a rather stern front in Parliament against the extension of grants in aid partly on account of the manner in which it has been worked in the interest of Rents, but partly also because it saps the root of the principle of local responsibility and true popular government in the secondary organs of public authority.

There is a strong feeling that personalty now become the greater part of our wealth, should bear some considerable or sensible share of local burdens, and also that the case of the rate-payers in the towns is a hard one. The second of these propositions is undeniable, and the first quite admissible: as indeed one huge lump of our personalty, Railway property, pays already to the rates. The operation of carrying over this burden to personalty is a critical one. By the vicious system of grants in aid it is carried over not to personalty but to a fund of which one half (more or less) is contributed by labour, namely the general taxation of the country. It will be an advantage when such arrangements are made that the relief to property shall come from property, and not as to one half of it from labour, which has hitherto been the case; and which has been in my eyes an odious arrangement, taking into view the fact that the relief of rates on land is an eventual and permanent boon to the landlord.

If Parliament is to be first, a great special relief to land will have to be attended or followed by the abolition or diminution of the remarkable preferences now allowed to land under the Death-duties.

About the pecuniary part of the question, however, I do not feel so much anxiety: what I feel strongly is that now or never is the time to decentralise and though I admit it may be impracticable to apply this rule to Education, yet it will I hope when your measure is past become our general rule.

My own position with regard to these matters is peculiar. The special matters which gave me so to speak a commission at the period of the Election, are in the main disposed of. The circumstances of Ireland have been improving, and they may, though I dare not say they will, very soon attain a point at which they would cease to constitute a call upon me. The operations we contemplate for restoring the efficiency of the great legislative instrument will almost certainly be concluded, if we succeed in them, before Easter. When these matters are out of the way a time would have arrived suitable in many points of view for the release of an old stager, in the 73rd year of his age and the 50th of his public service. It may be however that a change of this kind in the middle of the Session would be attended with much inconvenience, and I should if this were so be prepared to hold it over until the quiet season (by comparison) of the year. But I could not undertake to face or to be responsible for any settlement of the questions of Local Government and Grants in Aid which did not include and apply, on an extended scale, the principle of decentralisation.

In our estimate of this principle I sincerely hope we are agreed. But I only write to commend to you for consideration the matter of this letter, and by no means to obtain or ask any immediate reply.[1]

11. Wed.

Ch. 8½ A.M. Wrote to Prince of Wales—Ld Granville Tel.—Mr Godley—Ld Hartington—Mr Hughes—Sec. Customs—Sir T.E. May—Archdeacon Jones—W.L. Gladstone—Mr Downing—and minutes. Read Goody Two Shoes[2]—Introduction to Irish Confederate War[3]—Moon on Revised Version.[4] Long walk & conversation with S.E.G. Saw Mr Turner—Mr Taylor.

12. Wed. [sc. Thursday]

Ch. 8½ A.M. Wrote to Bp of Liverpool—Rev. W. Dunkerley[5]—H.J.G.—Sir H. Ponsonby—Ld Monson—Ld Chancellor—Ld Granville—Mr Godley Tel.—Mr Vickers (cancelled)—and minutes. Saw Mr Vickers—Mr Jones (Cross Tree). Read Westmr Review on British in India—Origines of Christianity—George Elliot [sic][6]—History of Liverpool.[7] 3.30.–6. Attended Rent dinner & spoke a good while on Agricultural matters.[8]

13. Fr.

Ch. 8½ A.M. Wrote to Ld Granville 2 Tell.—Mr A. Hayward—The Speaker—Mr Jas Wilson—Sir T. Acland—Ld F. Cavendish—Mr Childers—Ld Tenterden—E. Cooper—& minutes. Saw Helen on her views at Cambridge and freely assented to her taking charge of the Hall.[9] Called at Dutton & Lees Farms with C. Read Hist of Liverpool—Goody Two Shoes (finished)—Huxley, Place of Man.[10]

To Sir T. D. ACLAND, M.P., 13 January 1882.[11]   Add MS 44545, f. 88.

If the Welsh enter into a Land League, they have an awkward model in their recollection, that of Rebecca.[12] But it is well to hear that generally they look to no more than

---

[1] Dodson replied, 14 January, Add MS 44252, f. 145, that local govt. and grants in aid measures were in hand.   [2] Goody Two Shoes, Introduced by C. Welsh (many eds.).
    [3] 1st 2v. of J. T. Gilbert, ed., History of the Irish confederation and the war in Ireland, 7v. (1882–91); reprints of 17th-c. MSS, pamphlets, etc.
    [4] G. W. Moon, The Revisers' English, 2v. (1882–6).
    [5] William Dunkerley, vicar of Hoar Cross (8 Oct. 81); became vicar of Gladstone's living of Toxteth 1882; rector of Sigglesthorne 1886.
    [6] All in Westminster Review, lxi (January 1882).
    [7] A. Hume, Ecclesiastical history of Liverpool (1881); Gladstone was much exercised by Hume's statistics on class and religion in inner Liverpool.
    [8] Opposing protection for agriculture: 'the evils from which you have suffered are due to bad seasons and bad trade'; T.T., 13 January 1882, 6a.
    [9] i.e. of North hall, Newnham college; see 26 Oct. 78n.
    [10] T. H. Huxley, Evidence as to man's place in nature (1863).   [11] In Acland, 343.
    [12] The Rebecca riots, allied to Chartism, of 1839–43.

publicity & fair discussion: your advice will I hope do good. We are here as to agriculture completely in the English circle, but I heard the other day from an English friend who lives upon a border really Welsh, that in his neighbourhood the farms vacated by English tenants were commonly taken up by Welshmen—which seems to indicate pressure further in.

The severance in religion and language added to that in politics makes the gaps rather too wide between many Welsh landlords and their tenants.

England undoubtedly stands best of the *four* countries in that respect.

14. Sat

Ch. 8½ A.M. Wrote to Abp of Canterbury—Mr Forster—Mr Salkeld[1]—Mr Craw-furd—Mr Godley Tel.—Cardinal Manning—Sir E. Perry—Mr Vickers—Scotts—Bp of Chester—and minutes. Read West Rev. on Cobden[2]—Abelard & Heloise (Burlesque)[3]—Preface to Belliss, & Belliss[4]—Memoirs of Mad. d'Epinay[5]—Walk with SEG. Saw Mr Fox.

To CARDINAL MANNING, 14 January 1882.[6]   Add MS 44250, f. 190.

I have duly received the Resolution of the Bermondsey meeting for local option.[7] There is some hope I think that by a plan which we now have in preparation *some* real progress may be made in this difficult question: but nothing can as yet be said in a public or a binding way.

15. 2 S. Epiph.

Ch mg & evg. Wrote to Sir W. Harcourt—Mr Childers—Sir R. Wilson—Mr Pease—Mrs Irons—and minute. Read Brown Rel. Medici[8]—Bp Goodwin, Pastoral Letter[9]—Moon on Revised Version finished—Wild on do[10]—Beckett Denison on do—Willis's E.I. Papers (most interesting)[11]—& tracts. Walk with C. Saw S.E.G.

To H. C. E. CHILDERS, war secretary, 15 January 1882.   Add MS 44545, f. 89.

I return your memorandum.[12] By all means circulate it: please look to two marginal marks of mine.

I am a decided opponent of the Minority Vote in the constituencies. But I think there is

---

[1] Bookseller; inquiring about a 'Muggletonian Hymn Book, uncut'; Add MS 44545, f. 89.

[2] *Westminster Review*, lxi. 98 (January 1882).

[3] *Histoire des amours . . . d'Abelard et d'Éloise, mise en vers satiricomi-burlesque par M. [Armand]*, 2v. (1724).

[4] Probably *sic*, but perhaps Bellows: perhaps *The Channing centenary*, ed. R. N. Bellows (1881).

[5] See 14 Oct. 58.

[6] Holograph draft.

[7] Sent by Manning, 13 January, Add MS 44250, f. 190.

[8] First published in 1642.

[9] H. Goodwin, 'My second year. A pastoral letter . . .' (1871).

[10] G. J. Wild, *The Revised Version* (1879).

[11] Probably one of the publications of Edward Francis Willis, Oxford university's missionary to India; perhaps 'Difficulties of Indian conversion, and the Oxford mission to Calcutta' (1880).

[12] Probably that on composition of Grand Cttees., printed version dated 17 January 1882, circulated again on 4 August; Add MS 44130, ff. 8, 65.

very much to be said for it with regard to our present purpose, by reason of the extreme difficulty of other methods. The cumulative form is less invidious than the other I think.

To Sir W. V. HARCOURT, home secretary, 15 January   MS Harcourt dep. Adds 10.
1882.

No inclosure in your letter.

About distress[1] I come rather behind the world, having an idea that it is not intended to abolish *all* preferential creditorship. But I must admit that the opinion of the party & the farmers seemed to be pretty fully forward and I think you cannot be asked to hold your tongue.

There are *particulars* in our law of distress which no one I think could defend but the desire for change seems to go beyond them.

I am not well acquainted with the perjury case. But is there no way of getting reparation from the offenders? It would seem a hard case on the public, unless public authority be in fault. Whatever happens I hope we shall not come to a Parliamentary vote. The mischief of them in such cases is very great.

16. M.

Ch 8½ AM. For once I was knocked up in the night: I am not so well up to this now. Wrote to Ld Granville 2 letters & 2 Tell.—Rev. Mr Smethwick—Duke of Abercorn—Watsons—Mr Spurgeon—Sir W. Harcourt—Ld F. Cavendish—Mr Godley Tel.—& minutes. Read Belliss's History—Mad. d'Epinay's Memoirs—The World Round & Over[2]—She Stoops to Conquer.[3] Mr Richmond came: to repeat the hard task of painting me.[4]

To Sir W. V. HARCOURT, home secretary, 16 January   MS Harcourt dep. 8, f. 120.
1882.

Having enlarged my inquiries in the case of the two farmers I find the perjurer is dead. What I would suggest (perhaps after the fact) is that you should ascertain the condition character & prospects of the men, generally & as affected by the imprisonment & that we should consider quietly whether anything is right to be done and what, without waiting till the wind rises.

To Rev. C. H. SPURGEON, 16 January 1882.   Add MS 44545, f. 91.

I was not at all surprised at what happened and had not the smallest disposition or cause to suspect you.[5] My life is passed in a glass bee-hive: with this particularity that I fear many see in it what is not there, by which I am unjustly a gainer.

I thank you very much for the interesting book of photographs which you have been so good as to send with an inscription. I am very far from deserving. I wish I had a better return to make than the inclosed: but these are the best I can lay my hand on.

---

[1] Harcourt suggested a short bill to alter the law of distress, requesting advice for a speech, also raising the plight of 'respectable farmers' imprisoned for perjury under the Act; Add MS 44197, f. 1.

[2] Perhaps C. C. Coffin, *Our new way round the world* (1882).

[3] By Goldsmith (1773); Langtry's performance as Kate was the success of the season, just finished; see 26 Jan. 82.

[4] For W. B. Richmond's first effort, see 30 Oct. 67; this second portrait was commissioned by Christ Church, Oxford, following the rejection of Watts's portrait (see above, ix. xcii), and was similarly found unacceptable.   [5] See 3 Jan. 82n., and 8 Jan. 82.

When you were so good as to see me before and after your service[1] I felt ashamed of speaking to you lest I should increase your fatigue: but before very long I hope to find a better opportunity.

17. Tues.

Ch. 8½ AM. Wrote to Lady Stanley—Ld Granville—Mr Forster—Dean of St Paul's—Mr Hayward—and minutes. Saw Mr Ottley. Preliminary sitting to Mr Richmond. Took him to see the Rowley bevy. Walk, & much conversation. Read Mad. d'Epinay—She Stoops to Conquer (finished)—Huxley, Place of Man.—Shallcross on Sabbath.[2]

18. Wed.

Ch. 8½ A.M. Wrote to Mad. Novikoff—The Speaker—Sir Thos G.—Ld Spencer—Mr A. Myers[3]—Mr Godley—& minutes. Woodcraft with Willy: who came in the night. Sat 2½ h. to Mr Richmond. He lost however some time with the lights. Read Persecution of the Jews in Russia[4]—Mad d'Epinay—Fortnightly on Peasant Proprietors.[5]

To H. B. W. BRAND, the Speaker, 18 January 1882.   Add MS 44545, f. 91.

I thank you for your letter[6] which I will at once make known to my colleagues. It will help to enlarge our horizon in the rather blind work in which we are engaged.

In the meantime I make the following notes. (1) Your contract [*sic*] & you enlarge our No. 1—and both the contradiction and the enlargement are considerable. I take it for granted that the limitation of 'closure' to obstruction would have a soothing effect while no doubt the provision for stopping debate on pending amendments will help to excite opposition. (2) Of the obstruction offered to Government proposals I should say that enormously the larger part takes effect not by the outrageous prolongation of some particular debate—which alone the Speaker could touch by closure—but by the multiplication of questions. (3) Certainly we ought to have a rule for Supply. *À propos* to this would it not be well to provide that on Supply nights (with a special view to the Fridays) amendments should be taken in their order and should drop like Notices. (4) Do you think the House would consent to part universally with the Debate on the Speaker's (first) leaving the Chair for Committee?

[P.S.] We go up, for *bad*, on Tuesday.

[To A. I. MYERS, 18 January 1882.   Add MS 44475, f. 282.

I have received your letter of the 11th;[7] and, since the receipt of it, an account of the most shocking nature has come under my eyes entitled 'Persecution of the Jews in Russia 1881'.

[1] See n. 5, p. 196.
[2] Author uncertain; word scrawled.
[3] Asher Isaac Myers, 1848-1902; active in Anglo-Jewish affairs; journalist and proprietor of the *Jewish Chronicle* from 1878.
[4] *The persecution of the Jews in Russia* (1881), reprinted from *The Times*; see 25 Jan. 82.
[5] *F.R.*, xxxvii. 1 (January 1882).
[6] Of this day, approving cabinet's view of May's draft rules, but with comments on (1) procedure for closing debate, (2) amndts. to be put by the Chair on a deb.'s closing; Add MS 44195, f. 77.
[7] Not found.

The spirit of your appeal to me commands my respect and sympathy. I am not sure however whether I am to understand that you think I ought to take as a Minister the same course which I took in 1851 with respect to Naples, and in 1876 with respect to Bulgaria, as a private individual: that is, to make an appeal not to Governments, not even to my own countrymen specially or alone, but to the civilised nations of Christendom through the press. I carefully abstained on those occasions from promoting the interference of any one Government with the proceedings of another in its internal affairs, not because I think such interference under all circumstances unwarrantable, but on the very different grounds 1. that it is certain to be misunderstood, 2. that it is commonly quite ineffectual. But appeals, on the other hand, to the opinion of civilised mankind, apart from political motive and diplomatic action, supply a natural and a safe mode of action, and have, when well based upon facts, been attended with considerable results.

I give no present opinion on the allegations as to their truth; for I have had no opportunity of examining into the grounds on which they rest. But their subject is undoubtedly of the very gravest kind, and should be sifted to the bottom. I have pointed out what appears to me the safest mode of promoting the establishment of the truth upon this sad and revolting subject.[1]]

To Madame O. NOVIKOV, 18 January 1882.   Add MS 44545, f. 91.

I remember making a suggestion to you about replying to certain accusations which proved to be barren or ill-timed. Nevertheless, the freedom you kindly permit me to use, and my really good intention, induce me to lay before you the opinion that a pamphlet lately printed by Spottiswoode's and entitled 'Persecution of the Jews in Russia in 1881' calls for attention.

It would give me the utmost pleasure to see a satisfactory reply: for the statements are of the grossest kind.

You may have observed in Opposition papers vilifying appeals to me: 'why does not he show up the atrocities in Russia as he showed up or pretended to show up those in Bulgaria.'

My answer, were I to make one, would be that I appealed to public opinion not to governments, and that as a Minister I find it wise to leave these subjects to public opinion now. But I am not the less aware what a powerful hold these statements may make if the terrible facts they embrace remain unassailed and unconfuted.[2]

I hope to be in London (hope is an odd word to apply) next week.

19. Th.

Ch. 8½ A.M. Wrote to Ld Granville—Ld F. Cavendish—Sir T. May—Parl. Circular Letter[3]—Mr Godley Tel. Woodcraft with WHG. Three hours of sitting to Mr Richmond. An awful gash in my poor day. Read Mad. D'Epinay—Swinburne on Mary Q. of Scots.[4]

---

[1] Holograph; docketed 'To Mr. Myers. (Cancelled)'. See 25 Jan. 82.

[2] Novikov pointed out her article in this day's *T.T.*, and urged Gladstone to delay comment: 'not even in the "Black Book of Russia" has the credulity of the English public been more grossly misled & deceived than in this last agitation originated & supported by the Jews. It is simply monstrous'; Add MS 44168, f. 258.

[3] Letters of summons.

[4] *F.R.*, xxxvii. 13 (January 1882).

20. Fr.

Ch. 8½ A.M. Wrote to Mr Marjoribanks MP—Ld Granville—Mr Firth MP.[1]—Mr Wilfrid Blunt[2]—D. Frenchly—Messrs Watson—& minutes. Sat to Richmond (& Photogr) 1¾ hours. Walk with party—called at Roberts & Bowers Farms. Read Mad. d'Epinay: what a sad but touching picture!—Keane on Meccah.[3]

To W. S. BLUNT, 20 January 1882.   Add MS 44545, f. 92.

You will I am sure appreciate the reasons which disable me from offering anything like a becoming reply to your very interesting letter[4] on Egyptian affairs; which occupy I am sorry to say no insignificant share of my daily attention.

But I am sensible of the advantage of having such a letter from such an authority, & I feel quite sure that unless there be a sad failure of good sense on one or both or as I should say on all sides, we shall be enabled to bring this question to a favourable issue.

My own opinions about Egypt were set forth in the '19th century' a short time before we took office;[5] & I am not aware as yet of having seen any reason to change them.

21. Sat.

Ch. 8½ A. M. Wrote to Ld Granville l. & Tel.—Ld F. Cavendish—Sir C. Dilke—Mr Hershaw—Sir C. Ducane—Mr Hamilton Tel.—and minutes. Calls: & saw Mrs Bevington—Miss Scott. Sat 2 h. to Richmond. Read Mad. d'Epinay—Pfeiffer's Poems.[6]

To LORD F.C. CAVENDISH, financial secretary, 21 January   Add MS 44545, f. 93.
1882.

1, The Spaniards have put in a suggestion on the Wine Duties, which seems more practicable, or nearer our limits, than they have usually been. It is within; & underneath I have written a supposed scale.[7]

2. France also seems to be coming nearer to the Treaty, & if she does this she will probably import the wine into the negotiations.

3. I have written a minute on the Kenmare application. It was not new to me; he had been down here on the subject.

4. As to deficiency Bills & the surplus revenue of 1880–1, I shall not hold out against you & Welby if you both have a strong opinion, but otherwise I should prefer applying half at any rate of that surplus to the reduction of debt. The elements of the case which lead me in this direction are a. not expecting *early* calls from Ireland. b. hopes depending

---

[1] Asking Joseph Firth Bottomley Firth (1842–89; liberal M.P. Chelsea 1880–5, Dundee 1888–9) to second the Address.

[2] Wilfred Scawen *Blunt, 1840–1922; poet, horseman, traveller and anti-imperialist.

[3] J. F. T. Keane, *Six months in Meccah* (1881).

[4] Sent in December but not found; it enclosed the 'Programme of the National Party of Egypt' written by Arabi helped by Blunt (see A. Schölch, *Egypt for the Egyptians!* (1981), 187–8). Blunt replied on 17 February from Cairo on the increasingly national character of the Egyptian movement, based especially in Ayhan University and the army; Gladstone docketed the reply: 'Ld Granville. I suppose I shd. ansr. in a few words. WEG 28 F.'; Granville's docket: 'please', and Gladstone's note for secretary (the means of answering subsequent letters), Add MS 44110, f. 9.

[5] Presumably 'Aggression on Egypt'; see 21 July 77 and above, ix. xlii.

[6] See 19 Nov. 81.

[7] Scale not printed.

on the Smith Scheme. c. a disposition not wholly to exclude from view some moderate improvement in revenue which always after an interval follows an *established* improvement in trade such as we may be said now to have.

22. 2 S. Epiph.

Ch mg & evg. Wrote to Mr Hamilton—Ld Granville—Messrs Watson—Mr Forster—Mr Pringle—Sir W. Harcourt—Mad. Novikoff—& minutes. Read through the astonishing work of the Escaped Nun[1]—Life of L. de Carvahal (to me most unsatisfactory)[2]—B. Denison on Revised Version—and. . . .

To Madame O. NOVIKOV, 22 January 1882.   Add MS 44545, f. 94.

Like all that you write your letter[3] is full of talent: & it also contains matter of much weight. But I do not think that when you wrote it you had read the Tract of which I sent you the title, & with which if you have it not, I can easily cause you to be supplied. It contains specific statements which seem to require notice. I am coming up on Tuesday.

23. M.

Ch. 8½ A.M. Wrote to Ld F. Cavendish—Sir C. Dilke—Sir Thos G.—Miss Scott—Mr Murray—Mr Downing—Mrs Pfeiffer[4]—and minutes. Sat 1½ h. to Richmond. Woodcraft with W.H.G. Read Wynn of Wynn-havod (finished)[5] and Hist Confed.[6] Began my manifold attempts to establish some order before going in my books & papers.

To J. MURRAY, 23 January 1882, '*Private*'.   Add MS 44545, f. 94.

I must not omit to send you more than formal thanks for the gift of Mr. Beckett's able book.[7] The calamity (I cannot use a weaker word) which it was written to avert is I trust no longer impending; undoubtedly he has given us an additional security against it. The English nation, while they retain their senses, never can assent to such a substitution as this.

The revised version cannot be *corrected*; the work will have to be begun anew on other principles; & the good work will have to be picked up out of the mass of trashy alterations. Such is my surmise.

24. Tu. [London]

Ch. 8½ AM. Saw Mrs Burnett. Sat to Richmond for a short half hour. Wrote to Sir Thos G.—Mr Lefevre—& minutes. 10¾-4¼. To D. St by LNW. Read Ed. Rev. on Whigs—Irish Discontent—Life of Cobden[8]—and Autobiogr. of Pomo.[9] Saw

[1] Josephine M. Bunkley, *The escaped nun* (1857).
[2] See 6 Nov. 81.
[3] See 18 Jan. 82n. Gladstone's secretary sent the pamphlet, denounced in reply by Novikov on 25 January, Add MS 44168, f. 265: 'I did not find any name, any authority . . . [it] is nothing more than a Jewish compilation, concocted to excite bad feelings against my country'.
[4] Had sent the poems; see 21 Jan. 82.
[5] Probably J. A. Roberts, *Wynnstay and the Wynns* (1876).
[6] See 11 Jan. 82.   [7] See 8 Jan. 82.
[8] *E.R.*, clv. 60, 155, 279 (January 1882).
[9] P. Pomo, *Percy Pomo; or the autobiography of a South Sea Islander* (1881).

Ld Granville—Do *cum* Sir R. Wilson—Mr Godley—Ld Northbrook—U.S. Minister. Dined at French Embassy.

25. *Wed. Conv. St P.*

No Church! Wrote to W.H.G.—Ld Kimberley—Sir G. Grey—Mr J. Talbot—Mr Woolner—Mr Spurgeon—The Queen—& minutes. Cabinet 2-5½. Saw Mr Godley—Mr Seymour—Mr Dodson—Mr Myers—Ld Granville—Ld Spencer—Ld Rosebery. Saw Phillips [R]. Dined at Ld Roseberys. Read 'Through Siberia'.[1]

Cabinet. 25 Jan. 82. 2 P.M.[2]
Ld R. G[rosvenor] attended[3]
1. Procedure—resumption of subject on a further day
2. Bradlaugh—Govt. not to attempt to regulate the time of its coming on.
3. Prince Leopold—as at present advised, take procedure first—but reserve *final decision.*
4. Foreign—Egypt.
Comm[unicated] to Party respecting the joint notes read by Ld G[ranville]. Cabt. concurred.
Alternative of concert (1) joint occupation (2) and the Turk (3) discussed at much length.[4] Granville to ask Ch. Lacour to put his views in writing.
5. Kimberley's drafts: Zululand; Natal responsible Government; *his views approved.*[5]

I saw the Jew[6] today to whom I wrote a letter afterwards & cancelled at your [Granville?] insistance. I authorised him to quote me as having said to him that in my opinion the interference of foreign Governments in such cases is more likely to do harm than good. Jan 25.[7]

26. *Th.*

Wrote to Ld Kimberley—Rev. E. Coleridge—Ld Granville—Mr Forster—WHG—and minutes. Sat 1½ hour to Woolner. Dined with Mr M'Coll. Saw Mr Godley—Mr Hunt—Attorney General—Dr Coxe—long conversation on Christian matters. At M'Coll's dinner, with a company most variously composed, the Revised Version came into view & was scouted on all hands *as a rival* to the Authorised Version. Saw Mrs Th—Mr Th—Miss Ponsonby—Mrs Langtry[8]—Also saw 3 including one sad case of much interest & hope [R]. Read Ed. Rev. on Italian Poets—Through Siberia.

[1] H. Lansdell, *Through Siberia* (1882).
[2] Add MS 44643, f. 16.
[3] As chief whip.
[4] Carlingford diary, 25 Jan. 1882: 'all preferred a Turkish to an AngloFrench occupation, wh. France wd. very much like'.
[5] Despatch sent to Bulwer, 2 February: restoration of responsible govt. subject to local approval; *PP* 1882 xlvii. 385.
[6] i.e. A. Myers, see 18 Jan. 82.
[7] Holograph note; Add MS 44643, f. 17.
[8] Emilie ('Lillie') Charlotte Langtry, *née* Le Breton, 1853–1929; actress and personality; see 4 Feb. 82. She had met Gladstone earlier, casually, at Millais's studio; see L. Langtry, *The days I knew* (1925), 175-7.

To LORD KIMBERLEY, colonial secretary, 26 January 1882.   Add MS 44545, f. 95.

We are rather alarmed at the possible effects of the Bill for extending the jurisdiction of Courts over the Pacific Islands in the liabilities which it may entail administrative & pecuniary. I should like at any rate to know whether it has had full legal consideration from the Chancellor, the Law Officers, or both? I am told that the late Law Officers were strongly against it.[1]

27. Fr.

Wrote to Mr MacColl—The Speaker—Mr Myers—Mr Mavrocordato—The Queen—Ld Northbrook—Ld R Grosvenor. Saw Mr Godley—Ld R.G.—Ld F.C.—Mr West—Mr Goschen. Cabinet 2-6¼. Dined with E. Hamilton & West at Brookes's.[2] Saw Swanhill (good prospects) and also Cooper [R]. Read Through Siberia.

Cabinet. Friday Jan 27. 82. 2 PM[3]

1. *County Councils Bill. Election* of the whole Council to be *direct.* By ballot—single vote—(as owner and separate as occupier)—in one Union only. Leave out proposal of Committee[4] as to altering the mode of electing Guardians.

Could it be feasible or expedient, on the first Election, to enact that ⟨Ratepa⟩ Electors should choose a certain proportion from among the magistrates.[5]

28. Sat.

Wrote to The Queen—Mrs O'Connell[6]—The Speaker—Ld Kimberley—Mr Hunt—Mr Repington—and minutes. Sat to Woolner 1½ hour. Eleven to dinner at home. Saw Mr Godley—Ld R.G.—Ld F.C.—Sir B. Leighton—Mr Bryce—Mr Hayward. Read Duke of Argyll on Agriculture[7]—Fair Athens &c.[8]

29. 4 S. Epiph.

Chapel Royal mg. St Paul's afternoon in Dr Stainer's Organ Loft. Tea at his house afterwards.[9] Walk & conversation with WHG. Read G. Smith on Morals[10]—Conformity of Science & HS.[11]—Ross on Primitive Religion[12]—

---

[1] Kimberley replied, 27 January, Add MS 44227, f. 111, that he would send the bill to the Chancellor and the law officers, and that its purpose was 'restraining and punishing outrages by natives instead of the present system (or no system) of shooting and hanging them without trial'.

[2] *Sic.* See Bahlman, *Hamilton*, i. 215.   [3] Add MS 44643, f. 19.

[4] For the cttee. see J. P. D. Dunbabin, 'The politics of the establishment of county councils', *Historical Journal*, vi. 229.

[5] To the Queen this day, CAB/41/16/3: 'these councils should be elected by a rate-paying constituency voting directly, secretly, and singly; but each owner having a vote in that capacity as well as in the character of an occupier'.

[6] Ellen Mary O'Connell, wife of Daniel O'Connell *fils*; see Add MS 44474, f. 97.

[7] Argyll on 'Agricultural depression', *C.R.*, xli. 177 (February 1882).

[8] E. M. Edmonds, *Fair Athens* (1881).

[9] J. Stainer; see 9 May 77.

[10] G. Smith, 'Has science yet found a new basis for morality', *C.R.*, xli. 335 (February 1882).

[11] Perhaps A. Winchell, *Science and religion* (1882).

[12] J. L. Ross, *Traces of primitive truth* (1858).

Divers on Materialism &c.—Lilly on Libres Penseurs. Wrote to Mr Lilly—Mr Arnold MP.

To W. S. LILLY, 29 January 1882.   Add MS 44545, f. 96.

Your interesting article in the Contemporary Review for February[1] has a passage, marked by courtesy and evident sincerity, in which you have, I am sure unwittingly fallen into error concerning an opinion of mine, to which you do me the honour to refer.

I have never laid it down, or believed, that a religion of authority is incompatible with freedom of thought. Forty three years ago I was severely criticised by Lord Macaulay in the Edinburgh Review for having maintained the exact contrary, which I have at all times held, and have variously endeavoured to set forth, as for example within the last few years, in articles published in the Nineteenth Century respecting Sir George Lewis's work on the influence of authority in matters of opinion.

30. M.

Wrote to Mr Dodson—Ld Hartington—Mr J. Talbot—Ld F. Cavendish—Ld Rosebery—Sir W. Anderson—Miss Marsh—The O'Donoghue—Sir H. Ponsonby Tel—Sir W. Harcourt—The Queen—& minutes. Saw Mr Godley—Mr Forster— Dean of Westmr—Sir W. Harcourt. Cabinet 2-6. Read Keane on Medinah[2]— and. . . . Worked on Queen's Speech. Dined with the A. Russells. Saw Montague X: a ray here.

Cabinet. Monday Jan 30. 82. 2 PM.[3] *Procedure.*
a. Speaker's amendments on first Resolution adopted. Speaker & Sir T. May introduced.[4]
b. The Eight other Resolutions further considered & amended.
c. Other ⟨Resolutions⟩ decisions added.
d. Communications with Speaker to be averred but without any shifting of responsibility.

To J. G. DODSON, president of the local government board,   Add MS 44545, f. 96.
30 January 1882.

I fully appreciated as did others the reasons which led the Committee of Cabinet to abstain from recommending any change in the general incidence of rates on the occupier: but did you examine separately the question whether *new* rates should be divided, which seems to be a different one?[5] It was I think very hard upon the farmer to have to meet the whole burden of the Education and Highway Rates.

To Sir W. V. HARCOURT, home secretary, 30 January   MS Harcourt dep. 8, f. 121.
1882.

I am sorry to find that there is a rather polemical correspondence between the Home Office and the Treasury on the occasion of a proposal you have made to insert in the Estimates a provision for a new London Police Court and two new Police Magistrates.

---

[1] William Samuel Lilly, 1840-1919; journalist and secretary to the Catholic Union from 1874; wrote 'Free thought—French and English', *C.R.*, xli. 223 (February 1882). Lilly replied, offering to make amends; Add MS 44474, f. 119.
[2] J. F. T. Keane, *My journey to Medinah* (1881).
[3] Add MS 44643, f. 22.
[4] i.e. they attended the Cabinet. Final copy of Resolutions in CAB 41/16/6.
[5] Dodson replied, 30 January, Add MS 44252, f. 161, that '*future* rates' had not been considered, but arguments against dividing existing rates would not apply to future rates.

Out of this demand seems to have arisen an affirmation and negation of certain general principles. I do not know how much exactly is meant to be denied, but it seems to me that the application of the principles in question can only be settled in detail and it has not yet I think been touched by the Cabinet. In my letter to you of 19th Decr. I suggested to you by query, what is really my opinion, that there is no reason for making a difference between the Metropolis generally and the great towns in regard to the appointment of paid Magistrates & the source from which they are to be paid. I certainly am not willing to be committed to the opinion that new Courts & Magistrates should be established in the Metropolis at the public expence. I do not know whether you hold absolutely an opposite opinion. If you do, would not the best course be to let the matter stand over *without prejudice.*

[P.S.] Rosebery & F. Cavendish might meet to consider whether this should be done by cancelling the correspondence, or by a mild letter from the Treasury in terms agreed on beforehand.

To LORD ROSEBERY, home undersecretary, 30 January 1882.   N.L.S. 10022, f. 102.

1. Under the circumstances you describe as to Local Government,[1] I suppose the proper course may be to frame our County Councils Bill & the accompanying or consequent financial scheme for England, & *then* to see what shall be done or left undone in the same department for Scotland.

2. I do not know whether to understand from your letter that the proprietors under £100 p.a. are taxed, & administered for, by those over it—nor do I know the position of the feuar under the present law as to Local Government. But these points do not press.

3. It will be very unfortunate indeed if we do not mention Scotland in the Speech.

4. The question of the Entail Bill & the mention of it will I have no doubt be carefully dealt with. I am not sure that I quite understand your view. Cairns's Bills as I understood modified the conditions of entail but left the principle in full general operation. Do I understand you to say (1) That this is what should be done for Scotland (2) That by doing *this* for Scotland we should in no degree prejudge the case of England?[2]

[P.S.] 8th I am sorry is blocked by an engagement. 21st A Parliamentary night—I would gladly accept but it could only be subject to the chances.

31. Tu.

Wrote to The Speaker—Ld Kimberley—Mr Hunt?—& minutes. 12–1½ Deputn on Local Taxation.[3] Saw Mr Godley—Ld R.G.—Ld F.C. *cum* Mr Dodson. R. Academy with C.G: such splendid English pictures! Saw Ricardo—Hume—Swanham—all with more or less good [R]. Evening at home. Read Keane's Medinah—Ed. Rev. on Procedure.[4] Worked on Speech.

To H. B. W. BRAND, the Speaker, 31 January 1882. '*Private*'.   Add MS 44545, f. 98.

I meant to have mentioned yesterday a minor point which escaped me amidst the number of subjects before us. It is the inconvenience & loss of time now sustained from

---

[1] Rosebery's letter, 29 January, Add MS 44288, f. 85, argued the impossibility of legislation for Scottish local govt., but stressed an Entail Bill most wanted.

[2] Rosebery replied, 1 February, ibid., f. 89, affirmatively to both questions.

[3] Dpn. from the Central and Assoc. Chambers of Agriculture requesting what Gladstone called 'an augmentation of State aid'; *T.T.*, 1 February 1882, 10a.

[4] *E.R*, clv. 205 (January 1882).

what I may call interlocutory or consequential questions, so frequent especially in the practice of Irish members of a certain type.

These questions are I think a novel and a rapidly growing impediment to public business. A member putting a question and receiving what he thinks an insufficient answer cannot I suppose be deprived of the title to ask there and then that the answer be completed. But ought not this right to be confined to him, at least at that time? Especially ought not other members to be prevented from tacking to the answers all manner of questions going beyond the scope of the original question, and interrupting the regular course of business on the question paper? Might it not be provided by a new rule, or else adopted in practice as a rule really required by elementary considerations, that only the member putting a question might rise after the answer to require an explanation or addition within the limits of the question, and that any other inquiry must be reserved until the list of printed questions has been disposed of.

As you are out of town today I will ask Sir Erskine May to look at this on its way to you.

Wed. Feb. One. 1882.

Wrote to Mad. Novikoff—Ld Kimberley—The Queen—& minutes. Saw Mr G—Ld RG—Ld Northbrook—Ld Spencer—Mr Bright. Cabinet 2–7: & Cabinet Dinner 8–12. All politics: & most of it regular discussion. Read Keane's Medinah.

Cabinet. Wed. Feb. One. 1882. 2 PM.[1]
1. Private Bills—Subject to stand over for a future occasion.
2. (Speaker & Sir T. May introduced).[2]
'Evident' in Res. 1. Inserted before 'sense'.
3. Further discussion on penal Resolution. No change.
5. Egyptian Telegrams read & considered. ⟨Determined⟩ Suggested to propose by Telegraph: send French & English Commn. with a Turkish Commn.
withdrawn: but recent draft agreed to with modification.
ag[ains]t joint interference bringing into view a. The Turk b. The Concert.
4. Question of Delegation to Grand Committees discussed at large: of Bills; of Supply.
Committee to be parts [?] of the House (Ld. Hn.) making up the whole.
Committees to be chosen by Panels of the House: local included. Childers—WEG.
Committees to be chosen by a new Committee of Selection.
Determined to propose an experimental scheme for Grand Committee in Two Clauses (a) Trade &c (b) Law &c. to be chosen not exceedin[g] 80 by *present* Committee of Selection (with whom *some* consultation to be held). Sir T. May to draft Resolution.[3]

Cabinet Dinner. Feb. 1. 1882.[4]
1. Egypt. Granville reported his execution of the instruction of the Cabinet. Approved.
2. Basutoland. Question of confiscation. Message with amendments approved.[5]

[1] Add MS 44643, f. 26.   [2] i.e. again attending the Cabinet.
[3] Gladstone's mem. on Grand cttees. at Add MS 44766, f. 18.
[4] Add MS 44643, f. 30; Gladstone kept these notes in pencil, later superscribed in ink, probably by Hamilton.
[5] 'The Cabinet considered the terms of a telegram in which Lord Kimberley proposes to inform the Cape Government how far it would be proper for the British Government to avoid any interference with the Colonial Legislature in the measures it might desire to take for the settlement of Basutoland'; CAB 41/16/8.

0 Bills for the Speech.
0 Bradlaugh. On what ground to move the previous [question].[1] Conversation with
 Bright.
3. Clarendon Granville agreement with Russia. Draft to Thornton for demarcation of
 Persian Frontier down to Afghanistan (with Russia (done [?]) + Turcoman country +
 Afghanistan). Agreed to.[2]
4. Queen's absence during Session—discussed. Papers to be circulated.[3]

2. Th. Purifn.

Wrote to Ld Granville—Ld Rosebery—Mr Lilly—The Queen—Ld Hartington—
Sir W. Harcourt—& minutes. Sat 1 h. to Woolner. 5. P.M. St Andr. Wells St. Saw
Mr G—Ld RG—Ld FC—Ld Granville—Mr Newman Hunt[4]—Mr Wollaston
Blake—Govr of Bank—Ld F.C. *cum* Mr Welby. Saw Lefevre—Rands: hopeful
[R]. Dined with Mr Hankey.

3. Fr.

Wrote to Lord Mayor[5]—Ld Spencer—Serj. Simon[6]—Sir T. May (2)—The Queen
(2)—Sir S. Northcote—and minutes. Cabinet 2–6. Speech agreed on. Saw Mr
G—Ld RG—Ld Spencer—Mr Knowles—Mr Smalley—Ld Granville. Saw Wade—
Seymour [R]. Read Keane's Medinah. Dined at Mr Ralli's. Escorted by police
through the fog homewards!

Cabinet. Friday Feb 3. 1882. 2 P.M[7]
1. Queen's Speech. Settled for H.M.'s approval.
2. Sir E. May's Draft. Additions suggested.
3. Communication with Opposition on Procedure a. Not to use H.M.[8] b. See paper.
4. Granville read Tel. on Egypt—Freycinet's conversation with Lyons.[9]

To Sir S. H. NORTHCOTE, M.P., 3 February 1882.   Add MS 50014, f. 240.
'*Private & Confidential*'.

   On the part of the Cabinet, I have to convey to you the inclosed Resolutions[10] relating
to Parliamentary Procedure.

---

   [1] See 6 Jan. 82.
   [2] Granville to Thornton, 2 February, F.O.C.P. 4797: Granville suggested to Lobanov, who
showed little interest, a British/Russian/Persian agreement with possibility of a British/Russian
agreement on the Afghan frontier to follow, a development of the 1869–73 agreement.
   [3] Note circulated by Spencer on 2 February proposed not appointing Lords Justices, so as not to
call attention to the Queen's absence; most of the cabinet agreed; Add MS 44643, f. 34.
   [4] Thomas Newman Hunt, 1806–84; banker and chairman of public works loan commission.
   [5] Who had sent Resolutions on the treatment of Russian Jews; Add MS 44474, f. 108.
   [6] (Sir) John Simon, 1818–97; barrister and liberal M.P. Dewsbury 1868–88; questioned Gladstone
on fate of Jews in Russia on 9 Feb.; *H* 266. 244.
   [7] Add MS 44643, f. 35. Undated holograph note reads: 'You have observed R. Grosvenor's taking
the Chair at Channel-Tunnel Co.s meeting?'; Grosvenor was a leading proponent of the tunnel.
   [8] The Queen had offered to negotiate with the opposition on the Resolutions; Bahlman, *Hamilton*, i. 218.
   [9] New French govt. agreed that immediate action in Egypt unnecessary; hostile to Sultan sending
troops; *Africa and the Victorians*, 100.   [10] Add MS 50014, ff. 242–52.

Together with them, we intend to propose a few other Resolutions, of which the drafting is incomplete, but the effect of which will be to authorise the appointment by the Committee of Selection of large Standing Committees, two in number, to which would be referred on committal Bills (a) relating to Trade & Shipping, (b) relating to Law & Courts of Justice: unless in any case or cases the House should think fit to order otherwise. The numbers of the Committee to be between 60 & 80. Their Reports to be received in lieu of Reports from Committees of the whole House. What I have roughly described (for the moment) would be proposed by us strictly as a tentative & experimental measure, in relief of the burdens of the House.

With regard to the whole proposal, I am induced to send it to you, in order to take advantage of whatever hope previous & confidential communication may afford either of a concurrence among leading members of both parties in a subject of deep common interest, or of narrowing as much as possible, at the very least, the field of any subject matter in which there may be differences of opinion.

The proposals are in our view moderate, while adapted to the circumstances; but the details are numerous, and I do not say that on every particular they already exhibit a final determination.

Should you desire to make them the subject of personal communication, I should propose to meet you in company with Lord Hartington, who has given a good deal of attention to the subject, & of course we should be happy to see any friend whom you might see it fit to associate with yourself. This might be on Monday; or Tuesday early.

I think I need only add that these Resolutions have been kept most strictly secret, & that we rely implicitly on your so using them that no inkling of their character shall reach the press or public in consequence of this communication before the time comes for giving notice of them in the House, which I hope may be on Tuesday next.

4. Sat.

Wrote to Sir C. Russell—Mr Fawcett—Mr Dodson—Mr Larkins—& minutes. Finished Medinah: read Mecca. Saw Mr Godley—Ld F.C. cum Mr Welby—Ld F.C.—Ld R.G.—Mr Forster—Ld Granville—The movers & seconders [of the Queen's Speech] *cum* Lord G. 11-12¼.—Ld Monck. To the play[1] at 8 in most dense fog, walking. Music at 5 O'clock tea.

5. Septua S.

Chapel Royal mg and aft. Wrote to Mr MacColl—Sir H. Ponsonby. Saw Mr Hamilton (& H.J.G.) on corrections of speech, *verbal*—Ld Spencer—Mr Bright—Sir W. & Lady Farquhar. Read Q.R. on Revised Version (dead as mutton, quâ rival)[2]—Refutation of Darwin[3]—Watkins's Charge[4]—and tracts.

6. M.

Wrote to Ld Halifax—Prince of Wales—Sir C. Russell—Mayor of Manchr—Ld Chancr of Ireland—Dean of Windsor Tel—and minutes. Saw Ld Granville—Ld Wenlock—do *cum* Sir C. Dilke—Mr Godley—Mr Hamn—Lord F. Cavendish

---

[1] T. Robinson's *Ours*, with Langtry, at the Haymarket; see 26 Jan. 82.
[2] *Q.R.*, cliii. 1 (January 1882).
[3] See 2 Jan. 81.
[4] H. W. Watkins, 'The church in Northumbria' (1881).

cum Mr Welby 3–4¼. Meeting of Trustees of N.P. Gallery. Saw Wade—not hopeless [R]. Saw Mrs G. Malcolm.

At 7 PM this day I record the sad ungovernable nausea with which I return to the performance of the offices which this life of contention imposes upon me as duties. It is not anything particular in the life, it is the life itself.

Dinner to forty for the Speech. Evening party after. Saw The Speaker—Greek Minr—Turkish & Austrian Ambassadors—Count H. Bismarck.[1] Read Keane's Meccah.

7. *Tu.*

Wrote to The Queen (3)—Ld Carlingford—and minutes. Read Keane's Mecca. Cabinet 12–2. Saw Mr G—Ld R.G—H. of C. 4½–12 save ½ h for dinner. Spoke on Bradlaugh & arrests Committee.[2] Weary, weary!

Cabinet. Tues. Feb. 7. Noon.[3]
1. Shall motion be made to question Bradlaugh?[4] No. W.E.G. to move previous question.
2. Drafting of Resolutions for Devolution. Approved.
3. Shall Resolution on Clôture come first. Northcote's letter. Order to remain as agreed.
04. Question of Lords Justices.[5]
5. Corrupt boroughs. Postponed to Saturday.
6. Greeks ask for English Officers to organise army. Precedents to be examined.
7. Pamphlet published in Ireland by the Commission. Part taken by Solr. and Sec[retar]y respectively.[6]

8. *Wed.*

Wrote to The Queen (2)—and minutes. H. of C. 12¼–5½. Spoke 1¼ hour on the Speech especially Ireland.[7] Saw Mr G.—Ld R.G.—Count Münster—Mr Goschen—Ld Derby—Lady Derby—and others. Saw Montague [R]. Read Keane's Mecca—Last night the H. of C. was dull & adverse: & I vaguely hoped they might say of me 'he is done up'.

9. *Th.*

Wrote to The Queen—V.C. Cambridge—and minutes. H. of C. 4½–8¼ & 9–12½. Spoke on repeal of the Union with Ireland.[8] Saw Mr G—Ld RG—Ld F.C—do

---

[1] Count Herbert von Bismarck, 1849–1904, s. of the chancellor; spent much time in Britain; a friend of Rosebery; at the London embassy 1882–4.
[2] In Gladstone's absence, Harcourt, following cabinet policy on the Bradlaugh affair, moved the previous question, which was defeated in 286:228 after Gladstone's speech summing up; he then spoke on the arrest of Parnell & co.; *H* 266. 81, 110.   [3] Add MS 44643, f. 40.
[4] Bright's suggestion: Speaker ask Bradlaugh if he felt morally bound by the oath; the cabinet maintained the policy of August 1881; Arnstein, 127.   [5] See 1 Feb. 82n.
[6] Salisbury questioned the govt.'s printing in Dublin a pamphlet 'How to become the owner of your farm'; *H* 266. 221.
[7] *H* 266. 160; 'you will never hear anything better from me', he told H. J. Gladstone; Bahlman, *Hamilton*, i. 220.
[8] On P. J. Smyth's amndt. to repeal the Act of Union: defended maintenance of Imperial authority, and drew attention to difficulties of definition of non-Imperial purposes; *H* 266. 260.

cum Mr C. Gower—Mr Childers (on the Army Estimates 12–1)—Ld Granville.
Read Keane's Meccah (finished)—History of the Heavens.[1]

10. Fr.

Wrote to Ld Shaftesbury—Sir Jas Paget—Mr W. Pears—Sir W. Farquhar—Mr
Chamberlain—The Queen—and minutes. H. of C. $4\frac{1}{2}$–8 and 10–$12\frac{1}{4}$.[2] Dined at
Sir C. Forster's. Saw Mr G—Ld RG—Dean of St Pauls—Ld Granville—Ld Wol-
verton—Ld Rosebery.[3] Conversation with H.J.G. on 'Home Rule' & my speech:
for the subject has probably a future. Read. . . .

To J. CHAMBERLAIN, president of the board of trade,   Add MS 44545, f. 100.
10 February 1882.

I daresay you are aware that various references have been made in Debating the
Address to public declarations of yours. These you will I am sure be able to meet without
difficulty. But I think it would be well, if it meets your convenience, that it should be done
in the Debate tonight and I hope you will either speak in it, or arrange with Bright for
him to take a part should you prefer a later occasion.[4]

11. Sat.

Wrote to Dean of St Paul's—The Queen . . .—and minutes. Cabinet 2–6. Dined
at Ld Spencer's: an evening party there. Saw Mr G—Ld RG—Ld Chancellor—
Mrs Baring—Mr Childers—Mr M'Coll. Read. . . .

Cabinet. Sat. Feb. 11. 2 PM.[5]
1. Procedure *a.* Res. I. No amendment to be proposed by us now. *b.* Ashton Dilke. Not to
   commit Cabinet in introductory speech.
2. Corrupt Boroughs. Disfranchise 3: Boston for 2 Parlts, three others for one. Wigan: no
   writ this Session. See within [i.e. below].
0 Lords Justices. (WEG asked powers to be ascertained).[6]
3. Channel Tunnel. see over.
4. Sexton's Bill—to repeal L & P Protection Act. Block continues (i.e. notice) for the
   present.
5. Irish Boro' Franchise. Support 2nd Reading.
6. Tel. to Cape agreed to instructing Hudson to remind Transvaal of obligation to
   neutrality.
7. Question respecting Errington. He had not any diplomatic communication to make

---

[1] See 27 Feb. 81.
[2] Ireland; *H* 266. 389. Phillimore noted in his diary: 'I took G. in carriage to H of C. Tho' in high
spirits he sd he was weary of the strife & conflict & intimated pretty plainly that he wd not be in
office long'.
[3] Rosebery, after tossing a coin with Granville, raised the question of the political propriety of
Gladstone's rescue work; Bahlman, *Hamilton*, i. 222.
[4] Prevented by a cold from speaking this day, Chamberlain defended himself pugnaciously on
13 Feb.; *H* 266. 523 and Add MS 44125, f. 121.
[5] Add MS 44643, f. 41.
[6] Notes read: 'I suppose you will be inclined to agree with those of the Cabinet who have written
as to the Lord Justices. G[ranville]'; 'Will you tell the Queen so' [Gladstone]: ibid., f. 45. See 1 Feb.
82n.

but conveyed information personally collected by him & the cousin's official correspondence. O'Hagan did the same.[1]
8. Donoughmore moves for a Committee on the Irish Land Act. Resist it on the score of
time.[2]
9. Mr Forster stated Solr. Fottrell's resignation had been accepted by Land Commission.

Channel Tunnel. Leanings.
Against: Selborne, Kimberley, Harcourt, Granville?, Hartington, Carlingford, Chamber-
lain?, Forster?
For: Childers, W.E.G., Bright, Northbrook.
Silent: Dodson, Spencer.
Papers now with the Depts. to be sent round to the Govt.

[Gladstone:] Queen has a decided opinion on the Tunnel. I am not told what. I suppose
wrong.
[Granville:] I have not a decided opinion but my inclination is *wrong.*

[*Corrupt Boroughs*:][3] Within 7 days of commencement of Session
Class A: Total disfranchisement; Macclesfield, Sandwich   *Yes*
Class B: Suspended during this Parliament: Canterbury, Chester, Oxford   *Yes*
Eligible for either A or B: Boston   *Reprieve*; to revive next Parlt. but one
                           Gloucester   *Death*

12. *Sexa S.*

Chapel Royal mg, Whitehall aft. Dined with the Phillimores. Saw Mr Hamilton—Sir R.P.—Ld Cork—Baron A. de Rothschild—Mrs Hunter. Read Par. Lost—
Life of Christ—Père Didon, Science without God[4]—Mrs Collins's Poems[5]—&
alia.

13. *M.*

Wrote to Mr Hill MP.—Ld Blandford—The Queen (2)—Ld Granville (2)—Mr
West—and minutes. Read Wolfern Chase.[6] H. of C. 4½-8¼ and 9-12¾.[7] Saw Mr
G—Ld RG—Musurus Pacha—Mr Rowley Hill—and minutes.

14. *Tu.*

Wrote to Mr Maclure MP.—Archbp of Canterbury—The Queen—Dean of Can-
terbury—Mr C.—and minutes. H. of C. 4½-8¼.[8] Saw Mr Westell—Mr G—Ld
RG—The Speaker *cum* Ld R.G.—Ld Granville. Read Whewell's Life[9]—Green's
Making of the English people.[10]

---

[1] Errington's unofficial communications with the Vatican to produce pressure from the Pope on
the Irish clergy.
[2] Unsuccessfully resisted, to the govt.'s irritation; see 18 Feb. 82.
[3] Add MS 44643, f. 43; the list is in Godley's hand; the decisions on the right are in Gladstone's.
[4] H. L. Didon, *Science without God* (1882).
[5] Perhaps E. Collins, *Metrical translations from the works of Lamartine* [*with*] *original poems* (1850).
[6] Untraced.   [7] Queen's speech: Ireland; *H* 266. 504.
[8] Queen's speech: Ireland; *H* 266. 680.   [9] J. M. Douglas, *The life of William Whewell* (1882).
[10] J. R. Green, *The making of England* (1882); an expansion of Green's *History*.

15. *Wed.*

Wrote to Mr Pears—Sir R. Wilson—The Queen—and minutes. Dined at Sir W. Harcourt's. Conversation with Mrs Laurence Oliphant.[1] Began the stewing process for a cold but was obliged to break it & rise for the H. of C. at noon: where I spent most of the day.[2] Read Whewell's Life—Green's Making &c. Saw Mr G—Ld RG.

16. *Th.*

Further stewing to dislodge my little cold: got up in the evening to go down to the H of C. 9-1. Spoke an hour in reply.[3] Saw Mr G—Ld RG—Ld G. Wrote to the Queen. Read Whewell's Life—Greens Making &c.

17. *Fr.*

Wrote to Ld Lyttelton—Sir H. Verney—Ld Granville—and minutes. Kept the House & my bed till evg when I dined with Sir W. James to talk over the subject of the Newcastle Bpric.[4] Saw Mr G—Ld RG. Read Whewell's Life—Pattisson on Fair Rent[5]—Greens Making &c.

18. *Sat.*

Wrote to The Queen—Mr Bradlaugh—Sir T. May—and minutes. Cabinet 2-6. Sixteen to dinner. Saw Mr G—Ld RG—Ld Northbrook—Ld F.C. Read (W. Collins) Jezebel's Daughter[6]—and Day Census of the City.[7]

Cabinet. Sat. Feb. 18. 82. 2 PM.[8]
2. Procedure. Bare majority. Amendment on the forty ⟨meeting of party⟩ Chairmanship of Standing Committees by Committee of Selection or by ⟨H of⟩ C Committee of Selection.
   Resolutions: to be made if H[ouse] shall approve before the close of the Session. Speaker advises standing orders. WEG to review [?] ascertain liberty.
3. Lords Justices: will not advise appt.[9] on the present occasion.
1. Lords Committee & course to be taken. Notice to be given on Monday by [   ] for [   ] of motion within[10]—against Parliamentary inquiry at the present moment.

[1] Alice Oliphant, d. 1887; an occultist like her husband (see 17 June 80); active with him in 1882 in colonizing Palestine with Jewish settlement.
[2] Queen's speech: Egypt: *H* 266. 692.
[3] Queen's speech: on six of his declarations (1872, 1874, 1879-80, 1881) on local govt. and Home Rule for Ireland, again asking 'what are the provisions which you propose to make for the supremacy of Parliament?'; *H* 266. 860.
[4] Created by order of council on 17 May 1882; E. R. Wilberforce was the first bp.
[5] Possibly untraced article by R. H. Patterson, economist.
[6] W. Collins, *Jezebel's daughter*, 3v. (1880).
[7] Attempts by the City to count its users rather than residents to frustrate liberals' case for reform; see J. F. B. Firth, *London government* (1882), 116.   [8] Add MS 44643, f. 46.
[9] i.e. no appointments to be made during the Queen's absence; notes on precedents, requested by Gladstone, ibid., f. 53.
[10] Lords committee (on Donoughmore's motion) set up to inquire in the Land Act; Commons' Resolution of its inopportuneness drafted by Harcourt, with Forster's alterations, at Add MS 44643, f. 48; moved by Gladstone on 3 March.

4. Ld Ripon. Govt. will defend
5. Native Envoy to Cabul: Afqul Khan—approved.
6. Engineering Committee to ascertain the course as to destruction where needful of Channel Tunnel. Approved.
(On the matter of Lords Justices,[1] I dissented & gave my grounds. I did not perceive that any one agreed, except Hartington & Childers)
(Principle of simple majority. Why not universally applied? Because our quorum of the House is so small. Therefore we take provision that this form shall not be exercised except in a House of a certain magnitude)

To C. BRADLAUGH, M.P., 18 February 1882.   Bradlaugh MS 945.

I have to acknowledge the receipt of your letter of the 17th[2] and to thank you for referring to my words on the 8th of last August in relation to the question of your taking your seat.

When the words were used, I had in view as the probable means of giving them effect the moving of the previous question, which I thought to be the most regular and Parliamentary method by which the House of Commons might have declined to exercise any jurisdiction in your case, and have left you to act on your own responsibility.

Exactly this course has been pursued, and as you are aware the House has determined by a considerable majority to take into its own hands the exercise of this jurisdiction.

Thus the measure which I contemplated has failed, and I may say in reply to your inquiry that I am not prepared with any other to propose.

19. *Quinqua S.*

Chapel Royal mg (Dr Butler preached a striking Sermon) & aft. Wrote to Ld Hartington. Read Laroche's Life[3]—Monro's Parish (hasty composition)[4]—Holland's Sermons.[5] Saw Mr Hamilton—Mr Paget—Lady Gladstone & L.

20. *M.*

Wrote to Ld Granville—Sir W. Harcourt—Sir C. Dilke—Sir H. Ponsonby—The Speaker—H.H. Dhuleep Singh—The Queen—Prince of Wales—Bp of St Albans—& minutes. Worked up as well as I could the subject & the facts of the Resolutions on procedure. Read Jezebel's Daughter. Saw Mr G—Ld RG—Abp of Canterbury—do *cum* Sir W. Harcourt. Dined at Ld Dalhousie's. H of C. $4\frac{3}{4}$-$8\frac{1}{2}$ and $10\frac{1}{4}$-$12\frac{1}{2}$. Spoke $1\frac{3}{4}$ h on Procedure: besides other matter.[6] A sustaining power seemed to come down upon me.

[1] See 1, 11 Feb. 82.
[2] Add MS 44111, f. 126, asking Gladstone as Leader of the House 'whether or not you are prepared to take any steps to have the Law obeyed in relation to the representation of the Borough of Northampton'; docketed by Gladstone: 'Attorney General. Please to advise the terms of an answer. Obviously we *can* do nothing. I think. WEG F.18'.
[3] Perhaps M. de La Roche, *Mémoires littéraires*, many vols. (1720-4).
[4] E. Monro, *The parish: a poem* (1853).
[5] H. G. Holland, *Logic and life* (1882).
[6] *H* 266. 1124.

To Sir W. V. HARCOURT, home secretary, 20 February   MS Harcourt dep. Adds 10.
1882.

I sent your new Edition[1] to Forster and Granville, who have not quite the same view of it, and taking all circumstances together, time especially, I think we must stay where we are as to the terms of the motion and I will give notice accordingly.

21. Tu.

Wrote to Mrs Halkett—Lady S. Opdebeeck—Watson & S.—Sir R. Temple—The Queen—and minutes. Attended Ld Rosebery's Christening dinner:[2] conversation with P of Wales. Saw Mr G—Ld RG—Ld F.C.—Maharajah Duleep Singh (a painful interview)[3]—Town Clerk of City—Bp of London—Ld Granville—Mr Th. Rogers—Mr Whitbread. H of C. $4\frac{1}{2}$-$8\frac{1}{4}$ and $10\frac{1}{2}$-1.[4] Read Jezebel's Daughter— and. . . .

22. Ash Wed.

Chapel Royal 11-$12\frac{1}{2}$. Wrote to The Queen (2)—and minutes. Saw Mr G—Ld R.G—W.H.G.—Herbert G—The Speaker. Cabinet 1-2. Went into the House obeying the inward voice, but defying almost every outward one! H of C. 2-5. Spoke on Bradlaugh and stuck to 'abstention'.[5] Read Jezebel's Daughter—Life of Father Lowder.[6] Saw Lady Stepney.

Quasi-Cabinet. Room at H of C. 1 PM. Feb. 22. 82.[7]
Bradlaugh Question. Shall Govt. interfere?
In attendance: Att. General; Sol. General; Ld R. Grosvenor.
Members: Granville; Spencer; Northbrook; Carlingford; Kimberley; Hartington; Childers;
         Dodson; Chamberlain; Harcourt; W.E.G.
All for our taking the initiative, except Chamberlain; Bright (absent); W.E.G.
But initiative to *suspend* only: Harcourt; Childers; Dodson; & perhaps some Peers.

That expulsion is a consistent and warrantable course for the majority in a case of disobedience (which is in this case flagrant); that as this measure would be consequential on what has been already done, it ought not to be opposed by the Government; the Government have opposed the Resolution of the House: have acquiesced in the consequential proceedings: & when the question has threatened to become one of police, but it is not so now. They will continue to defer according to the usual practice of minorities.[8]

[1] Proposed rewording of the Resolution on the 1881 Irish Land Act; Add MS 44197, f. 21.
[2] Of Albert E. H. M. A. Primrose, 1882-1974; Lord Dalmeny; 6th earl of Rosebery 1929.
[3] The Maharajah was requesting govt. help for his financial difficulties.
[4] Labouchere's attempt to move the writ for Northampton led to a wrangle; Bradlaugh then administered the oath to himself and took his seat; Gladstone moved the adjournment; *H* 266. 1259.
[5] i.e. Gladstone, despite a majority against him in cabinet, maintained his view that the Commons was acting *ultra vires* in the main question; he thus declined to advocate Bradlaugh's expulsion, which was achieved by a tory motion; *H* 266. 1315.
[6] Probably C. F. Lowder, *Twenty-one years at St. George's mission* (1881).
[7] Add MS 44643, f. 54; under 'Members', Gladstone bracketed respectively the members of the Lords and the Commons.
[8] Undated holograph; Add MS 44643, f. 55. Form of words largely followed by Gladstone in declining to oppose Northcote's consequent motion; *H* 266. 1344.

23. Th.

Wrote to Mr J.R. Hill[1]—Ld Granville (2)—The Queen—and minutes. H of C.
$4\frac{1}{2}$–8 and $10\frac{1}{2}$–$1\frac{1}{4}$.[2] Dined with the Wests. Read Jezebel's Daughter. Saw Mr G—
Ld RG—Ld Granville—Mr Forster—Mr Chamberlain—Ld F.C. *cum* Mr Welby.
Sat to Mr Woolner $2\frac{1}{2}$–4. Attended the Levée.

24. Fr.

I failed for once to make out my sleep. These apparently lost hours ought to be
most profitable hours.

> 'Beneath the shades of night,
> And with the morning light,
>   And setting sun
> In great things and in small
> In each thing and in all
>   Thy will be done.'

Conversation with Herbert on the present Irish Government. Wrote to Mr A.
Morris (Sydney)[3]—Ld R. Grosvenor—Ld Granville—The Queen—& minutes.
Saw Mr G—Ld R.G—Ld Granville—Ld Shaftesbury—Bath—Kenmare—Cork—&
others, on the Lords Comm[ittee] question: also with Forster, Hartington, Har-
court: finally, a conversation with Gibson in wh I explained clearly our position.[4]
H. of C. & H of L. $4\frac{3}{4}$–8 and 10–12.[5] Read Whewell's Life—Jezebel's Daughter.

To LORD R. GROSVENOR, chief whip, 24 February 1882.   Add MS 44315, f. 63.
'*Private*'.

   With reference to Col Harcourt's motion tonight, I intend to say, and probably to say
when moving that the Speaker leave the Chair that it is the place and intention of the
Government to make a proposal in conjunction with the financial scheme of the year,
which will be conformable to the terms of the motion. I should therefore appeal to all
parties to save the time of the House and waive the division, entering into Supply at once.
   As regards our own friends the matter has another aspect. I must suppose that they
believe an unequivocal promise given by me on behalf of the Government. If *they* vote for
the motion after such a promise (instead of the virtual previous question offered by
Supply) such a vote is from them simply a declaration that I am not to be believed; and I
need not say must be taken as intended to put an end to all relations of confidence
between any of them, who might think it necessary so to act, and myself. It is only fair to
you, and to such gentlemen, that you should have the means of letting them know the
state of the facts.

---

[1] J. Rowley Hill, on the living of Suckley; Add MS 44545, f. 103.
[2] Supply; *H* 266. 1375.
[3] Secretary of the 1879 Sydney International Exhibition, sent its *Official Record*; Hawn P.
[4] Lords select cttee. on Irish land law nominated this day, despite exceptional govt. reluctance;
H 266. 1522.
[5] Commented on E. W. Harcourt's motion on local taxation; Gladstone's motion for the Speaker
to leave the chair carried without division; *H* 266. 1539.

25. Sat.

Wrote to Mr Roundell—Rev. Mr Wigner[1]—The Queen—Abp of Canterbury—Sir S. Northcote—Ld F. Cavendish—Mrs Langtry—& minutes. Dined at Ld Spencers. Cabinet 2–4½. Saw Mr G—Ld RG—Ld Granville—Mr Childers—Rev Mr Holland—Count Karolyi. Read Jezebel's Daughter.

Cabinet. Saturday Feb. 25. 82. 2 PM[2]
1. Cathedral Commission. Assent to principle of Bill?
2. Debate on Land Acts Committee. Granville's recital of communications. 1. W.E.G. to write to Northcote as within.[3] 2. Meeting the party on Monday at 3. (Ld R. Grosvenor called in.)
3. Dodsons points on local Govt. Bill. 1. agreed to. 2. [blank]
4. Granville reported that Committee of Cabinet recommended an additional *Key*[4] for members of the Cabinet; P. Sec of two leaders; Queen, & her first Secretary.

26. 1 S. Lent.

Chapel Royal mg. Whitehall aft. Wrote to Ld Shaftesbury—Dean of Windsor—Mr Leeman MP.—Sir H. Ponsonby. Dined with Sir R. Phillimore: legal & other conversation with him. Read Baptist Hymns—Father Lowder—Noel's Philos. of Immortality[5]—RC.N.A. Review divers Articles.

27. M.

Wrote to Mr Forster—The Speaker—The Queen—and minutes. H of C. 4¾–8¼ and 10¼–12: much speaking. A good night.[6] 11¾–2½ To Windsor, for Council & Audience, & back. Also saw Dean of Windsor—Sir H. Ponsonby—The Speaker—Sir W. Harcourt—Mr S. Samuel—Mr Hayward. Dined at Sir C. Forster's. Read Jezebel's Daughter.

To W. E. FORSTER, Irish secretary, 27 February 1882.   Add MS 44545, f. 104.

It must evidently be kept clear in the debate that, our overture having been rejected, we are under no pledge whatever. The question whether you if called should decline to be examined[7] is a very nice one on which I think there would be no advantage in arriving *now* at a decision, since we have not the whole case before us. The objections are great and obvious yet refusal is serious as well as assent. It may be very doubtful whether you will be asked.

28. Tu.

Wrote to Mr Pringle (2)—Rev. Mr Dunkerley—Watson & Smith—Mr Forster—and minutes. P. of Wales's meeting for Musical Institute 12–1½.[8] Saw Mr G—Ld

---

[1] J. T. Wigner had sent a nonconformist hymn book; Add MS 44545, f. 103.
[2] Add MS 44643, f. 61.   [3] Various drafts; ibid. f. 62 ff.
[4] See 6 Jan. 82; i.e. additional key to despatch boxes.
[5] R. B. W. Noel, *A philosophy of immortality* (1882).
[6] Moved Resolution that parliamentary inquiry was, at present, injurious; *H* 266. 1729. He also attended at 3 p.m. a meeting of the parliamentary Liberal Party where he denied that dissolution or resignation was imminent; *T.T.*, 28 February 1882, 10c.
[7] i.e. by the Lords Committee on the Land Act; Forster did not appear; see 1 Mar. 82.
[8] Meeting to inaugurate fund for Royal College of Music; *T.T.*, 1 March 1882, 6a.

RG—Ld F.C—Ld Granville—Sir W. Harcourt. Extempore Cabinet at 4 PM. H of C. 4½-8.[1] Dined at the Club.[2] Conversation with Ld Derby—Dr Smith—Mr H. Reeve. Read Jezebel's Daughter—Whewell's Correspondence.

Wed. Mch One. 1882.

Wrote to Ld Chancellor—The Speaker—Mr C. Gore—The Queen—& minutes. Dined with the Speaker. Saw Mr G—Ld R.G (2)—Ld Granville—The Speaker— Herbert J.G. (conversation on Sunday observance)—Mr Murray—Conclave of Cabinet Ministers after dinner on the answer to be given by Forster to Cairns. Read Fraser & Contemp. Rev. on Land[3]—Finished Jezebel's Daughter. Tea at Lady Derby's.

Urgent. I have seen Harcourt, Childers, Chamberlain, Dodson, and have *heard* of Bright. I have endeavoured to embody their views and mine in the enclosed Telegram which I hope our other colleagues will approve. The Tories now talk of prolonging considerably the Debate. It seems as if they are waiting for Forster's refusal to throw up the cards. W.E.G. March 1. 82. 11 P.M.
cipher: Gladstone to Forster, Dublin Castle: we have consulted on the proposal of Cairns and we think if you approve you should tell him by Telegraph at once that having learned views of colleagues you cannot consent to attend committee.[4]

2. Th.

Wrote to Mr Forster Tel & L.—A.G. for Ireland—Ld Granville—Ld Tenterden— Mr Rathbone MP.—Sir H. Ponsonby—The Queen 2. Saw Mr G—Mr H—Ld RG—Attorney General. Watts Exhibition at 3.30.[5] Royal Society at 4.15 to introduce the Prince of Wales.[6] Saw Mr Huxley—Mr Bowman[7]—and other Fellows. H. of C. 5-8½ and 9¼-12½.[8] Read Whewell's Life—Dickinson on Legislatures.[9]

3. Fr.

Wrote to Sir H. Ponsonby Tel. & l.—Messrs Scribner—H.N.G.—Ld Kimberley— The Queen—Sir S. Northcote—Ld Granville—and minutes. Saw Mr G—Ld R.G.—The Speaker—Ld Granville—Mr Callan—Sir W. Harcourt—Att. General— Mr Rathbone MP. H. of C. 4¾-8½ & 9¼-1. Spoke on Jews.[10] Read Whewell's Life.

---

[1] Meath election; *H* 266. 1842.
[2] i.e. the club founded by Dr. Johnson, of which he had been a member since 1857, but recently very rarely attended.
[3] *Fraser's Magazine*, cv. 385 (March 1882); *C.R.*, xli. 462 (March 1882).
[4] Add MS 44766, f. 29. Note of colleagues agreeing, ibid., f. 32. Forster did not attend.
[5] At the Grosvenor Gallery.
[6] On his admission as F.R.S.; *T.T.*, 3 March 1882, 9f.
[7] (Sir) William *Bowman, 1816-92; ophthalmic surgeon; F.R.S. 1841; cr. bart. 1884.
[8] Irish Resolution; *H* 266. 1950.
[9] R. Dickinson, *Summary of the rules and procedure of foreign parliaments* (1882).
[10] In Russia: the British govt. had no title, as distinct from the Bulgarian atrocities, to attempt to intervene; *H* 267. 45.

To H. N. GLADSTONE, 3 March 1882. Hawarden MSS.

You are (shall I say) very indulgent to me about writing, for after all that can be said I feel there is something horrid in my long silences, though true it is that in this case 'out of sight' and 'out of sound' is not 'out of mind'.

All you say about money is what I had expected from you. The sum of four thousand pounds shall be at your credit with Messrs. O[gilvy], G[illanders] & Co on Ap. 1., and *after* that date your quarterly £50 will disappear at Scotts. I have told Herbert about his extra £5000: he only expressed a scruple lest it should be unfair to others but I have told him they do not suffer. Whenever you with his assent are ready to make an investment for him not exceeding this amount, or otherwise to make profitable use of the money, of course it will be forthcoming. It will of course be understood in all these cases that my payment of any sums in this way is final, and that I have no further responsibility in regard to them; but I really believe they are safer in your hands than in mine. And now I have done with business for the present.

In family matters we have much to be thankful for. The birth of Willy's child & the good recovery of his wife has been followed by Agnes's apparently rapid & easy confinement, & that fine little fellow, whom I call William of Wykeham, has now got a little brother. Mama had a threatening a few days ago of what looked like erysipelas but she has thrown it off with great vigour. I am rejoiced to hear from Gurdon the good account of your health, and from you that you are going, at length, to have a bit of holiday. Also it is a great pleasure to feel that your return home is now coming within a more measurable distance. When once we get you here, I hope we shall keep you a long time.

The state of the Govt. & public affairs may be roughly given in two or three sentences. Abroad, matters have on the whole gone exceedingly well since we came into office. Ireland has been our sad and terrible drawback: but it is, if not rapidly, yet sensibly improving, and we have good & growing hopes that the Land Act, in spite of Parnellites and Tories, will beat the Land League. This however and the block of business in the H of C. are our main difficulties. Before the Session began, the Tories were supposed to be in great spirits, and the Bradlaugh business of course was in their favour. But they now do not seem to be very sanguine, though they are active enough, and, although we may either gain or lose credit by the experience of the Session I do not see that our existence is beset by any great perils. It will I hope be my last Session as Prime Minister—I have now held that office over 7 years. In the last century, only three have held it longer: Ld Palmerston, Ld Liverpool, Mr Pitt.

We have a poor Revenue but it must improve more or less with trade. For this year I cannot hope to do much more than make ends meet. God bless you in all things dearest Harry. Ever your afft Father WE Gladstone.

To Sir S. H. NORTHCOTE, M.P., 3 March 1882. Add MS 44545, f. 105.

I think it most likely that, following the precedents from July 1842 onwards we shall move no Address to the Queen;[1] & in that case I hope you will with me think it best that nothing should be said of one in public.

The man was dismissed last July from Wells Lunatic Asylum.

4. Sat.

Wrote to The Queen—Mr M. Henry MP.—Sir S. Northcote—Mr Dillwyn MP—

[1] Shot at by R. Maclean when leaving Windsor station; see 4 Mar. 82. Northcote's letter this day reported some tory dissatisfaction at the absence of an Address; Add MS 44217, f. 197.

and minutes. Read Coutts Memoirs[1]—Memoirs of Whewell. Saw Mr G—Ld RG—Count H. Bismarck. Dined at Marlborough House: beautiful music in evening. The Princess of W[ales] on coming up to see me said 'You have been giving it them well.' Unmistakeable Liberalism, I fear! Cabinet 2–5.

Cabinet. Sat. Mch 4. 82. 2. PM.[2]
1. Mr Bradlaugh's Election.[3] Ld R. Grosvenor, Attorney General attended. Various alternatives discussed: Bill; Instructing A.G. to revise[?] a Suit; Committee (Hn). Decided that if Resolution of Feb. 7 be renewed we again move the previous question.
2. Childers. Patronage of Colonels. P. of W. demands as to patronage of Brigade of Household Cavalry that on expiry of vested interests patronage shd. pass to him. Give to the P. of Wales while continuing P. of Wales.
3. Duke of Abercorn's petition of Irish landowners. H.M. Govt. having considered do not feel able to advise any action thereupon.
4. Address to H.M. To be moved—Joint.[4]

Ritchie's motion—to be opposed.[5]
Channel Tunnel: Shall we stop operations below low water Mark until Parlt. has decided. Postponed.
Basuto Land Memorial.
Egyptian affairs. Ld Granville sketched what had occurred. Conversation.

To Sir S. H. NORTHCOTE, M.P., 4 March 1882.   Add MS 44545, f. 106.
    Many thanks for your note. Circumstances have assumed something of a new form since my note of yesterday, and we have decided that upon the whole we had better renew the proceeding of 1840 & 1842. This we shall desire to do as simply and quietly as possible to a Joint Address on Monday. I cannot dismiss from my mind, as one element in the case, the impression that every addition to the stir, however natural & proper in itself, has some tendency to attract morbid minds towards a repetition of these shocking and perilous attempts. But this rather remote consideration must give way.
[P.S.] I shall move to concur with the Lords and I inclose a copy of what will be moved there.

5. 2 S. Lent.

Chapel Royal mg. St Geo. H. Square aftn. Saw Ld Kenmare—Mr Hamilton. Read Father Lowder—King on Disestablishment[6]—Rainoldes & Hart 1584.[7]

6. M.

Wrote to The Queen—Sir W. Harcourt—Mr Goschen—Ld Hartington—Sir H. Ponsonby Tel.—& minutes. H. of C. 4–8¼ and 9–12.[8] Finished Father Lowder +.

---

[1] C. Rogers, *Genealogical memoirs of the families of Colt and Coutts* (1879).   [2] Add MS 44643, f. 66.
[3] Bradlaugh was this day again returned for Northampton.
[4] Joint address moved on 6 March.
[5] Moved on 24 March by C. T. Ritchie for a select cttee. on effect of foreign tariffs on British commerce.   [6] Untraced; perhaps an article by E. *King.
[7] *The summe of the Conferences betwene John Rainoldes and John Hart; touching the Head and the Faith of the Church* (1584).
[8] Irish Resolution; row with Lord C. Hamilton; *H* 267. 227.

Saw Mr G—Mr H—Ld RG—The Speaker—Ld Granville—Mr Goschen—Mr Roundell—Sir W. Harcourt.

7. *Tu.*

Wrote to W. Phillimore—Rev. G. Butler—Sir H. Loch—The Queen—& minutes. Worked on books. Dined with the Jameses. H. of C. $5\frac{3}{4}$-$8\frac{1}{4}$.[1] Saw Mr G—Ld RG—Sir W. James—Mr Wills MP. Read Whewell's Life—Donnelly's Atlantis.[2]

To W. H. WILLS, M.P., 7 March 1882. '*Private*'.   Add MS 44545, f. 107.

With reference to your letter of the 13 ult.[3] I think I ought to say that the probable esti-mates of revenue and charge for the coming financial year are such as to preclude any rational expectation of remission of duty involving an appreciable loss to the revenue, such as would follow upon the surrender of the increment of duty enacted a few years back. In these circumstances, I think you will agree with me that it is better for me to avoid any discussion with representatives of the trade, as such discussion would tend to interfere with the regular course of deliveries, besides tending to excite expectations which could not be fulfilled.

In saying this you will I am sure understand that I convey no opinion as to the compar-ative claim of any particular duty for remission in case of the existence of an available surplus. And I venture to recommend that you should accept as my official answer to your letter the simple statement that the application for remission cannot be entertained.

8. *Wed.* [*Windsor*]

Wrote to Ld Derby—Dean of Windsor—Ld Northbrook—Dean of Norwich—Ld Granville—Attorney General—Mr Beet[4]—Sir W. Harcourt—Ld Chancr—Bp of Durham—& minutes. Calls. Saw Harris [R]. Read Mahaffy on Preaching[5]—Moreau Hist. Nat. de la Femme[6]—19th Cent. on Tunnel—Manning on Brad-laugh.[7] Off at 5 P.M. to Windsor. Saw the Queen (twice)—Princess Beatrice—Sir H. Ponsonby.

9. *Th.* [*London*]

After Prayers, saw Dean of Windsor. Wrote to Sir H. Ponsonby—Sir W. Har-court—Mr Brooks MP.—Ld E. Fitzmaurice. Wrote also to D. of Argyll—Mr Pringle—Sir T. May—The Queen tel. & 2 l.—and minutes. Attended Levée. Returned to town 10.30. Saw Mr G—Ld RG—Mr Childers—Sir W. Harcourt with the Law Officers on the Queen's case. Read Mahaffy on Preaching.

[1] Misc. business; *H* 267. 320.
[2] I. Donnelly, *Atlantis: the antediluvian world* (1882); see 11 Mar. 82.
[3] Wills' letter, and interview this day, requested reduction of tobacco duty; *T.T.*, 11 March 1882, 9f.
[4] A bookseller, to complain about the defective Moreau; Add MS 44545, f. 107.
[5] J. P. Mahaffy, *The decay of modern preaching* (1882); see 20 Mar. 82.
[6] J. L. Moreau, *Histoire naturelle de la femme*, 2v. (1803).
[7] *N.C.*, xi. 305, 458 (March 1882).

10 Fr.

Wrote to Dean of Windsor—Bp of Durham—The Queen—Mr Chamberlain—and minutes. H. of C. 5-7¼ and 10¾-12.[1] Read Mahaffy. 11¾-3¾. To Windsor for Council & Audience of H.M. Saw Ld Northbrook—Ld Spencer—Sir H. Ponsonby—Mr. Challemel Lacour (PPC)—Mr Childers. Went by invitation to the Opera to see the Phantom Ship of Wagner.[2]

To J. CHAMBERLAIN, president of the board of trade,   Add MS 44545, f. 108.
10 March 1882.

Will you kindly arrange for dealing by yourself or Ashley with the Blennerhassett motion[3] tonight which belongs to your department. The report of the Duke of Devonshire's Commission furnishes I think material for easy dealing with the motion.
[P.S.] I was inclined to look kindly on the principle of the motion: but the Report seemed to bar the way effectually.

11. Sat.

Up at 7¾ to go to (near) Dover (8½-1½). We saw the Channel Tunnel Driftroad (with the beautiful Electric Light).[4] It was most interesting. Saw Mr Godley—Mr Childers—Mr Forster—Mr Vivian—Mr Welby—Miss Swanwick—Lady Stanley (Ald.)—Mrs Tennyson—Mr Tennyson—Mrs Goldsmid. Dined at Mr Tennysons: a very interesting party. Wrote to Mr Donnelly (U.S.)[5]—Ld Spencer—Mr Dodson—and minutes. Read Atlantis—How John Bull lost London—and Whewell.

To J. G. DODSON, president of the local government board,   Add MS 44545, f. 108.
11 March 1882.

As we have not had a Cabinet today I write a line to express a hope that, in concert with the Cabinet Committee—which I trust has worked well—you are getting on with the Local Government Bill so that it may be in a condition to be introduced before Easter, should circumstances happily permit it.[6]
Our prospects as to business were dark at the beginning of the Session & the loss of a fortnight through the folly of the Lords has made them darker still. But we must still endeavour to get ready the material needed for the fulfilment of our promise, and I hope you are in a condition to go forward, with the Committee, towards perfecting the work.

---

[1] Spoke on Blennerhassett's observations proposing State ownership of Irish railways; *H* 267. 652.
[2] 'The Flying Dutchman' (replacing 'Tannhauser': the tenor ill) by the Carl Rosa company at Her Majesty's; Gladstone's attendance postponed from Wednesday; sitting in the Royal Box, he 'frequently applauded the singers'; *D.N.*, 11 March 1882, 5c.
[3] In fact 'observations' rather than a motion; Ashley spoke for the govt.
[4] But the Cabinet halted digging for the time being; see 31 Mar. 82.
[5] Ignatius Donnelly, 1831-1901; American populist, politician and author, had sent his 'Atlantis'; Add MS 44474, f. 189.
[6] Dodson replied, 13 March, Add MS 44252, f. 168, that the bill was being circulated this day to cabinet; timetabling difficulties in the Commons.

To I. DONNELLY, 11 March 1882.   Add MS 44545, f. 108.

I thank you very much for your Atlantis, a copy of which you have been so kind as to present to me.[1] Though much pressed by public affairs, I have contrived to read already an appreciable portion of it with an interest which makes me very desirous to go through the whole. I may not be able to accept all your propositions, but I am much disposed to believe in an Atlantis: and I think I can supply you with another case in which traditions have come down into the historic age from periods of time lying far away in the background of preceding ages.

Homer unquestionably (I do not fear to say) believed in a sea exit from the northern Adriatic, and imagined the north of Europe to be an expanse of water. And this geology I believe assures us that it was, but not within what we have heretofore viewed as the limit of the memory of man. Three or four years ago the Duke of Argyll was at Venice and saw in some fish-stall a fish which he was familiar with on the West Coast of Scotland, but which is unknown in the Mediterranean generally. And on further examination he found that the corner of the Adriatic corresponded as to local fish in a high degree with the Atlantic. This is a curious and perhaps a significant fact.

12. S.

Chapel Royal mg & Evg. Saw Ld Spencer—Mr Hamilton—Sir Thos G.—Mrs Bennett. Read Howards Life—how noble![2]—Col. Gardiner's Life[3]—N.A. R.C. Review on Man's Destiny—& on Homerics[4] . . . on 'The Evil & Evil one'

13 M.

Wrote to Mr Forster—Viceroy of India—Mr West—Ld Kimberley—The Queen (2)—Lucy Cavendish & minutes. H. of C. 5–7¾ and 10–4: the Block is worse & worse.[5] Read N.A.R.C. Review on Westmr Abbey—Count Jos. de Maistre—Whewell's Correspondence & L. Saw Mr G.—Scotts—Calls.

To LORD RIPON, Viceroy of India, 13 March 1882.   Add MS 43515, f. 9.

I am truly sorry you should have had the trouble of writing a lengthened explanation with a view to your defence against a possible attack on the ground of your munificent but thoroughly warrantable subscription to the North Riding Election.[6] Very shabby things have been and are being done in the present Parliament but shabbiness must go beyond all previous precedent if any serious attack is to be made upon you. In any case you will be defended with a good heart. And I cannot but hope you will not be further troubled in the matter.

Your administration in India is a standing source of comfort and justification. I am delighted at your success about that disgraceful Press Act. It is one of the last steps in the great undoing process which the late Government bequeathed to us.

At home, our *one* difficulty (and it is a very grave one) is the deadlock of business in the

[1] See 7 Mar. 82. Sent on 18 February, Add MS 44474, f. 189.
[2] Perhaps W. A. Guy, *John Howard's writer's journey* (1882).
[3] P. Doddridge, *Life of Col. James Gardiner* (1832).
[4] *American Catholic Quarterley Review*, 7 (1882).
[5] Redmond's Resolution on the Protection Bill; supply only reached after midnight; *H* 267. 785.
[6] Ripon wrote, 19 February, Add MS 44286, f. 262, regretting his announcement of financial support in the N. Riding by-election had led to embarrassment: 'it is of course a piece of pure hypocrisy to single me out for attack'; notoriously tory peers give 'far larger' subscriptions.

House of Commons which a large number of the Tories steadily labour to aggravate & the mass of them appear to contemplate with more or less excusable satisfaction.

Please to give my kindest regards to Lady Ripon.

To A. E. WEST, chairman of the inland revenue commission,   Add MS 44545, f. 109.
13 March 1882.

(1) You may remember my expressing an opinion last year, or at least a surmise, that the compensation which we took in Probate Duty for our surrender of Legacy Duty was not quite sufficient. How does this stand on the returns?

(2) I sometimes think whether it would be desirable to abolish the consanguinity scale prospectively, and substitute a commuted duty which should be uniform & added to Probate: 1. On all future wills; 2. On all intestacies accruing [six months] after the date of the Act. But this could not at present be applied to land. I only throw this out for criticism.[1]

14. *Tu.*

Wrote to Mr Dodson—Mr Sidgwick—Ld Granville—Ld Percy—The Queen and minutes. Saw Mr G.—Ld R.G.—Ld F.C.—Mr Welby—Mr Smith MP—Lady C. Clive—C.G. & R. Gower. H. of C. $4\frac{1}{2}$–$7\frac{1}{2}$.[2] Saw three [R]. Read Bell on Atlantis.[3] Dined at Ld F.C.s.

To J. G. DODSON, president of the local government board,   Add MS 44545, f. 109.
14 March 1882.

I agree with you that the Local Government Bill should not be introduced until there is a prospect of proceeding to the second Reading. But further, the loss of a fortnight through the folly of the Lords has infinitely improved the position of the obstructionists of the two Oppositions & no confident expectations can be formed as to any Bill of magnitude & complexity like this until we see our way in some degree as to Procedure & Devolution to which we must give all our disposable energies & which now form the key to the position.

[P.S.] I agree very much with you as to the alternative mode of operation.[4]

15. *Wed.*

Wrote to Mr Childers—Mr Welby—Mary G.—Mrs Th.—Scotts—Sir A. Gordon— R. Wilberforce and minutes. Saw Mr G.—Ld R.G.—Hon. B. Lawley—Lucy G. H. of C. $3\frac{1}{2}$–6.[5] Dined with Duke of Cambridge. Conversation with him— Hartington—Carlingford. Read Ellis's Blundell (Crosby papers)[6]—Whewell's Life & Letters. Saw Two [R].

---

[1] No reply found.
[2] Questions; *H* 267. 890.
[3] Perhaps by Nancy Bell, who tr. J. Verne.
[4] i.e. as a last resort, deal with aids separately from the budget, and if County Bill fails, drop both and reintroduce in 1883; Add MS 44252, f. 169.
[5] Irish franchise; *H* 267. 917.
[6] T. Ellison Gibson, ed., *Crosby records; a cavalier's note-book: being notes... of William Blundell* (1880).

16. Th.

Wrote to Mr Gray MP—Ld Granville—Sir G. Balfour—Mr Pender—The
Queen—Mr Courtney (2) and minutes. H. of C. 5–9 and 10–11¾.[1] Saw Courtney
respecting E. Cornwall. What a curious specimen of humanity![2] There ought to
be no will in the world but his. Saw Mr G.—Ld R.G.—The Speaker—Ld Granville—Mr Goldwin Smith. Read Crosby Records . . . on Foreign Parlts.[3] I tried to
begin a Letter to my Constituents after the fashion of Burke to Bristol & especially Ld J. Russell to Stroud:[4] but my brain became a cloud: I have not sufficient
force.

[Gentlemen: Nearly two years, crowded with events, have passed, since it was your
pleasure to elect me as your representative in Parliament.

Charged during that period with duties over, and even beyond the ordinary measure of
the offices I have held, I have found myself unable to render to you a personal account of
the manner in which, conjointly with my colleagues, I have endeavoured to redeem the
pledges I had given you.

The generous confidence, which you reposed in me at the Election, has been accompanied with an indulgence not less generous; and, aware that I was doing my best to serve
you here you have called for no account of the particulars and manner of my service.

I feel however that the time has arrived when I ought spontaneously to render such an
account in the only form now open to me, and I have determined to address to you this
letter especially for the two following reasons.

First the Commission which I virtually received from you as a member of Parliament,
and which the existing Government undertook to execute was a special one. Its peculiarity was that it related in most, and in the most important, of its particulars, to questions
over-seas, in no less than three of the quarters of the globe, which required immediate
handling and which if rightly handled promised early results. Our proceedings in these
great matters are now in some cases virtually all complete; in all they have reached a
stage which will in some degree supply you with the means of judging how far we have
been faithful to our engagements.

The last year before the accession of the Beaconsfield Government to office was
1873–4. The expenditure for that year, including £3197000 for the Alabama Claims
which were no legitimate charge on the year for the purpose of the present argument,
was £76,466,000. In 1878–9 this was raised to £85,407,000, and in 1879–80, the last year
of that Government, it was reduced with the Dissolution in near view, but only reduced
to £84,105,000. This apparent augmentation of more than seven and a half millions in six
years. If we deduct in each case the costs of collection the increase will still remain at
seven and a quarter millions or more than a million per annum.

In addition to questions of policy abroad, I called your attention to matters of finance:
to the growth of the public expenditure, to the many burdens entailed on India and the
menacing condition of its finance, and to the series of deficits in the balance of revenue
and charge at home, which threatened according to appearances to become habitual.][5]

---

[1] Statement on public business; *H* 267. 1021.
[2] By-election in E. Cornwall on peerage for Robartes; Courtney sat for Liskeard; Gladstone next
day successfully pressed Sir T. D. Acland to get his s. C. T. D. Acland to stand; Add MS 44545, f. 110.
[3] See 2 Mar. 82n.
[4] i.e. E. Burke, 'Two letters . . . to gentlemen in the city of Bristol' (1778), the famous defence of
the M.P. as representative, and Lord J. Russell, 'Letter to the electors of Stroud' (1839), side-stepping
the 'finality' of the 1832 Reform Act.
[5] Not sent. The last two paras. on separate sheets; undated holograph; Add MS 44766, ff. 41–4.

17. Fr.

Wrote to Sir T. Acland—Plymouth Advr (Tel)[1]—Mr Welby—Dean of Windsor—Mr Hubbard—Mr Macfarlane—The Queen and minutes. Read Whewell's Life & Letters. Saw Mr G—Ld R.G.—Ld Granville—Ld G. & R.G. with Ld Hartington on list of Baronets—Mr Forster: on the *core* of the Irish question. Mr Acland *cum* Sir T.A. & Mr Borlase[2]—Mr O'Shaughnessy. H. of C. $4\frac{3}{4}$–$8\frac{3}{4}$ & $9\frac{1}{2}$–$12\frac{1}{4}$. Spoke on N. Borneo Charter.[3]

To R. E. WELBY, assistant financial secretary, 17 March 1882.   Add MS 44545, f. 111.

I think that when you see Mr Smith[4] you will probably be able to ascertain whether he still adheres to his doctrine that the Land operation in Ireland should be based upon 'an Irish fund'. This is the vital point; almost all turns upon it.

18. Sat.

Wrote to Bp of London—Ld Granville—Mr Cooper—Mr C. Russell—Mr Monk—Mr Fawcett—Mr Tuer—The Queen & minutes. Cabinet 2–$4\frac{1}{2}$. Saw Mr G.—Ld R.G.—Ld Rosebery—Ld Fife—Sir Cooper Key—Sir D. Currie. Saw St George—Backler [R]. Dinner at Ld Rosebery's. Read Blundell's Note Book (Crosby Records)—Whewells Life, & Letters.

Cabinet. Sat. Mch 18. 82.[5]
1. Closing-power. Hartington to speak on Monday before dinner. Course of the debate. Shall the Resolutions be standing Orders? Yes. Notice on Monday.
2. Prince Leopold. Thursday next *if* we find debate must last over next week.
3. Easter Holidays. Tues 4th to Monday 17
4. Budget. After Easter: fix day for it before Easter.
5. Devolution: stand till next Saturday.
6. Motion of Thorold Rogers—for Select Committee on Univ. Commissioners report. Object: but favour a discussion in the sense of disapproving the facilities for marriage.[6]
7. Landowner Debate in H. of Lords next week on Purchase Clauses. To minimise.
8. Endowed Schools; Welsh Education. Prepare Bills *dually*.

19. 4 S. Lent.

Ch. Royal mg—St Georges aft. Saw Bp of Bath & Wells whom I brought to luncheon.—Lady Stapylton—Read Rainolde's & Hart[7]—Madeline (poor)[8]—Deane on Book of Wisdom[9]—Macnaught on *Coena Domini.*[10]

---

[1] Not found published; probably on the E. Cornwall by-election.
[2] The other member for E. Cornwall.
[3] Defending the charter as non-interventionist; *H* 267. 1188.
[4] W. H. Smith, returned from an Irish visit determined 'with regret, to make the tenant the owner', was being given some treasury help in preparing a land purchase plan; see 27 Mar. 82 and Sir H. Maxwell, *Life of W. H. Smith* (1893), ii. 68ff.
[5] Add MS 44643, f. 69.
[6] Rogers's motion not moved; he questioned Gladstone on 1 May on the new Statutes.
[7] See 5 Mar. 82.
[8] Perhaps *Madelaine; a story of French love* (1880).
[9] W. J. Deane, *Ecclesiastes* (1880).
[10] J. Macnaught, *Cæna Domini* (1878).

20. M.

Wrote to Mr Mahaffy—Mr Lefevre—W. H. Smith—The Queen & minutes. Saw Mr G.—Ld R.G.—Ld F.C.—Ld Bessborough—Mr Forster. H. of C. $5\frac{1}{4}$–$7\frac{1}{4}$ and $10\frac{3}{4}$–$12\frac{1}{2}$.[1] In the interval went with Mr Penders party to the Crystal Palace to see the Electric Lights, amidst vast crowds. Explanations were given: but I want the rudiments. Read Crosby Records.

To J. P. MAHAFFY, 20 March 1882.   Add MS 44545, f. 111.

I have read the treatise on preaching,[2] which you have been so good as to send me, with much interest & advantage. It says much & it suggests much. I am very glad you have given so much thought to a subject so well worthy of all the thought that can be given to it.

Bishop Lloyd of Oxford, a most able man (Peel's tutor & friend) told me about 55 years ago his recommendation to his clergy was not to preach a second sermon but to expound in the afternoon some part of the Scriptures appointed for the day. I do think some advantage might be gained by a larger adoption of the expository method.

21. Tu.

Wrote to Ld Stair—The Queen and minutes. 3–4 P.M. Scarlatina Convalescents meeting. Spoke briefly.[3] Saw Mr G.—Ld F.C.—Ld R.G.—Ld F.C. *cum* Sir C. Ducane—Mr Forster. H. of C. $4\frac{3}{4}$–$8\frac{1}{4}$ and $9\frac{1}{2}$–$1\frac{1}{4}$. Spoke on County Franchise.[4] Read Crosby Records.

22. Wed.

Wrote to Mr W. Brown—Rev. Sir G. Prevost—The Queen and minutes. Dined at Ld Reay's—Speakers—Levee & German Embassy after. Conversation with Herbert on tone of parties, the Beaconsfield influence. Saw Mr G.—Ld R.G.—Ld F.C.—Ld F.C. cum Mr Welby—Ld Granville—Mr Childers—Mr Blunt (Egypt)— The Speaker—Ld Derby—Mr Robertson—Mrs Howard—Dr A. Clark—Ld Spencer. Read Whewell L & L—La Questione del Papa—Crosby Records (finished).

23. Th.

Wrote to Ld Granville—Mr Raikes—Mr West—The Queen & minutes. H. of C. $4\frac{1}{2}$–$8\frac{1}{4}$ and $9\frac{3}{4}$–$1\frac{1}{4}$. Proposal as to Prince Leopold: Saw Mr G.—Ld R.G.—Ld F.C.—Sir C. Dilke.[5] Read Whewell—Atlantis—Ward's Reformation.[6] The first day of Spring was the only winterday we have had for months. The weather has quickly mended.

[1] Procedure; *H* 267. 1301.   [2] See 8 Mar. 82.
[3] Mrs Gladstone's meeting, chaired by the bp. of London, to raise funds for a Scarlet Fever Convalescent Home; *T.T.*, 22 March 1882, 5e.
[4] Supporting Arnold's Resolution for extending the county franchise, though warning of the dangers of an 'abstract Resolution'; *H* 267. 1468.
[5] Leopold's marriage settlement, which Labouchere opposed; *H* 267. 1671.
[6] Possibly W. Ward, 'The reformation from popery commemorated' (1817).

24. Fr.

Wrote to Mr Forster 1 & Tel—Mr Miller (Tel & L)—The Queen and minutes. H. of C. 4¾-8¼ and 9¼-2. Spoke on Foreign Trade Committee.[1] Saw Mr G.—Ld R.G.—Ld Granville—Mrs Clark?—Mr Childers—Mr Th. Read Whewell—Miss Fox Memoirs & Journal.[2]

To W. E. FORSTER, Irish secretary, 24 March 1882. '*Secret*'.   Add MS 44545, f. 112.

The movement of feeling in the House of Commons has become less favourable to us for the division of next Thursday. Irish friends, and semi-friends, are giving way under pressure. Such (with other matters) are R. Grosvenor's reports *today.*

The motive presented to, & forced upon, them, is that by stopping the closing power they will prevent the renewal of the Coercion i.e. Protection Act.

The only mode of rallying them, which occurs to me, is that Shaw should come over and declare in the debate that in his opinion it is impossible, the state of Ireland continuing as it is now, that this Act should be renewed by any Government, with or without a closing power.

Can he be put in motion for this purpose? You know more than I do of his relation to things and persons. You are more entitled than I am to form a judgment whether anything can be done. I certainly have an opinion that with the Land Act working briskly, resistance to process disappearing, and rents increasingly and even generally though not uniformly paid, a renewal of so odious a power, as that which we now hold, *is* impossible, and that whatever may be needed by way of supplement to the ordinary law must be found in other forms. But to make this opinion known to Shaw would be a serious matter.

Upon the whole case, the occasion being grave, I hope that if you see your way through any channel to the doing of good, you will get him up, and will act, for this end, without loss of time.[3]

[P.S.] Ld Red[esdale?] understands that it will require real pressure to bring Shaw over.[4]

25. Sat. Annuncn

Wrote to Duke of Leinster—Abp Sophronius (Cyprus)[5] Tel & minutes. Off at 12 to Kensington Palace & thence with Princess Louise to Harrow for a function, inspection & luncheon with Dr Butler, a great schoolmaster, very interesting: but they made me speak.[6] Back at 4¾. Sat 1¼ h. to Mr Frith.[7] Dined at Sir [A.] Hayters. Saw Mr G.—Ld R.G.

26. 5 S. Lent

Chapel Royal mg. Wrote to Mr Forster 1 & Tel.—Ld Hartington—Att. Gen. for Ireland. Saw Ld Spencer—Mr Hamilton. Read Christ our Ideal[8]—Onesimus by

---

[1] Ritchie's motion; *H* 267. 1909; see 4 Mar. 82.

[2] *Memories of old friends, being extracts from the journals and letters of Caroline Fox*, ed. H. N. Pym, 2v. (1882).

[3] Forster replied next day: 'It would be very difficult, if not impossible, to keep the suspects in prison, if we let it be supposed that we shall not ask for renewal'; Reid, *F*, ii. 407.

[4] Shaw did not speak on 30 March. Forster's 'mind was at once made up *not* to speak' to Shaw about Gladstone's letter; *F.A.-F.J.*, 418.

[5] New constitution for Cyprus published previous day.   [6] *T.T.*, 27 March 1882, 6f.

[7] See 21 Nov. 81.   [8] *Christ our Ideal. An Argument from analogy* (1882).

Dr Abbott[1]—Cellarius, New Analogy[2]—Linton on New Version[3]—Tracts. Dined with the Phillimores. That excellent man has rapidly and greatly aged.

27. M.

Wrote to Ld Breadalbane—Dean of Westminster—Mr Welby—The Queen (2) & minutes. The Belmores dined. Saw Mr G.—Lord R.G.—Ld F.C.—Mr A. Arnold—Ld Belmore—Sir W. Harcourt. H. of C. 5-8$\frac{1}{4}$ and 9$\frac{1}{2}$-1.[4] Read Whewell—Miss Fox's Journal.

To R. E. WELBY, assistant financial secretary, 27 March 1882.[5]   Add MS 44545, f. 113.

I think that if Mr Smith desires to communicate with Mr Murray[6] he must also retain his intention to communicate with you respecting the funds which are to support the working of the Bright Clauses. If this be so I have no objection. It is another question whether if he does not choose to communicate with you, the head of finance and my immediate adviser, he ought to communicate with other officers of Govt. who work subordinate to the Dept., & on this I must suspend my opinion.

28. Tu.

Wrote to The Queen—Ld Hartington—Sir T. Acland and minutes. H. of C. 2$\frac{1}{4}$-4$\frac{1}{2}$ Spoke on the three suspects.[7] Saw Mr G.—Ld R.G.—Maharajah Dhuleep Singh—Adm. Wilson. 5-6$\frac{1}{4}$ at Sir F. Leightons to see his beautiful works. Conversation with Princess of Wales—Mr Watts—Sir F.L. Read Atlantis—Miss Fox's Journal.

To Sir T. D. ACLAND, M.P., 28 March 1882.[8]   Add MS 44545, f. 113.

I am sorely ashamed when I read what you have said of me. But I do not write to say or dwell on this. I write only to remind you of what I think is the safest, as well as eminently true, ground for your son as to Bradlaugh (who I learn is being worked with some effect against him).[9] It is this: *we do not say Bradlaugh ought to sit*: but simply that his right or non-right to sit should be determined by law; by a dispassionate Court of Law, instead of by a House of Commons, of which the majority have in dealing with this question exhibited a degree of unfavourable excitement rare even in the struggles of party; struggles from which this question of pure law ought to be kept immeasurably remote.

29. Wed.

Wrote to E. Hamilton—Ld Granville (2)—Mr Forster—Mr Childers—The Queen (2)—Mr Westell and minutes. Saw Mr Ouvry Library at Sotheby's. Dined

[1] E. A. Abbott, *Onesimus* (1882).

[2] Cellarius [T. W. Fowle], *A new analogy* (1881).

[3] C. R. Linton, 'The Revised Version of the New Testament' (1881).

[4] Procedure; *H* 268. 35.

[5] See 17 Mar. 82.

[6] (Sir) George Herbert *Murray, 1849-1936; treasury clerk; succ. Welby as its head 1903; Gladstone's secretary 1892-4.

[7] Refusing them parole to vote on the procedure Resolution; *H* 268. 169.

[8] In Acland, 344.

[9] By-election in E. Cornwall; C. T. D. Acland just held the seat.

at Ld Tweedmouths. Saw Mr H.—Mr G.—Ld R.G.—Ld Granville—Mr Forster—Mr Shaw MP—Mr Welby *cum* Lord F.C.—Duke of Argyll—Ld Carlingford *cum* Lord Blandford. Saw Gresham X.

30. Th.

Wrote to The Speaker—Mr Walpole—Lord Portsmouth—The Queen—Ld E. Cavendish and minutes. H. of C. $4\frac{3}{4}$–$8\frac{1}{2}$ and $9\frac{1}{2}$–$2\frac{1}{2}$. Spoke 50m at the close as prudentially as I could: voted in 318:279.[1] Saw Mr G.—Ld R.G.—Mr Hn—Ld Granville—Mr Forster—Mr Samuelson. Saw Mr Herkommer's pictures.[2] Read Whewell—& Miss Fox.

31. Fr.

Wrote to Sir S. Scott & Co.—Ogilvy Gillanders & Co—Ld Granville—Mr Childers—Mrs Amos—The Queen and minutes. Dined at Ld Sherbrook's. Saw Mr G.—Ld R.G.—Ld F.C.—The U.S. Minister (2)—Sir H. Parks. Cabinet 2–$4\frac{1}{4}$. H. of C. $4\frac{1}{4}$–$7\frac{3}{4}$. Spoke on the Eccl. Commission.[3] Read Whewell's Life.

Cabinet. Friday Mch. 31. 2 PM[4]

1. Revenue for 1881–2, 1882–3: submitted.
2. Ecclesiastical Commission Inquiry. Decline Commission at present but without any disapproval.[5]
3. Procedure Resolution. Hold the same language as heretofore without pushing our pledges any further.
4. Order of business: Navy Estimates 20th; Budget 24th; Procedure 27th (April); Monday, Mutiny [Bill]: Monday next 1st Order.
5. American suspects:[6] application of U.S. Govt.
   a. we may offer to examine with a view to release on condition of their leaving the country: with assurance from U.S. Minister: each case to be examined. *Formula* drawn by Chancellor.
   b. general dispatch in preparation.
   c. make known that we have been willing to let some out who would be willing to go.
6. Question to Carlingford from Ld Lansdowne (Juries). Answer to leave the future open.[7]
7. Mr Chamberlain to warn [Channel] Tunnel S.E. Co against proceeding beyond low water mark in the present state of the proceedings.

---

[1] Defeating Marriot's amndt. to the procedure Resolution; *H* 268. 314; 16 homerulers voted with the govt., 37 against.

[2] See 11 Oct. 79.

[3] *H* 268. 507.

[4] Add MS 44643, f. 70.

[5] A. Arnold's proposal for select cttee. withdrawn this day; *H* 268. 495.

[6] 'an urgent but very friendly representation ... in the interest of such of the suspects as are citizens of the United States. ... [We] are of opinion that it may be practicable ... to allow these suspects to quit the country'; CAB/41/16/16.

[7] Irish jury laws; *H* 268. 444.

Sat. Ap. One 1882 [*The Durdans*].

Wrote to Messrs Grogan & Boyd[1]—The Speaker—Mr Cowan—Mr A.E. West—
The Queen—The Maharajah and minutes. Saw Mr G.—Ld Granville—The
Speaker. Off to Durdans 4.30. Evg. & much conversation with Ld Rosebery.
Read Whewell (finished)—Polson's Monaco[2]—Experience of Police Magistrate.[3]

To H. W. B. BRAND, the Speaker, 1 April 1882. '*Secret*'.　　　Brand MSS 286.

We considered our position as to Procedure yesterday in the Cabinet up to a certain
point.

1. We thought it well to have a little time after the recess before returning to the contest, & we hope then to get on with something more like continuity. 2. We went a good
deal into the *merits* of the two thirds plan: & we think it on its merits (shall I say) detestable.[4] 3. We have considerable faith in the Parliamentary argument to be made against it.
4. We believe that a large part of our friends are vehemently opposed to it. 4. [*sic*] At the
same time we have not—at the moment—arrived at any positive resolution as to our
course if we fight & the House rides over us.

To A. E. WEST, chairman of the inland revenue commission,　　Add MS 44545, f. 114.
1 April 1882.

At the close of the Easter recess I shall be glad to hear more particularly what we are
now to think of the practical working of the Beer duty. Also of any effects produced by
the Temperance movement on the Revenue. You will I have no doubt be ready with all
facts relating to the House Tax—including the figures of its earlier forms when it was
graduated.

I should also like to have an answer to the following question. Supposing the final estimates of Revenue from yours & the other Departments give us no prospect of an *adequate*
surplus; and supposing that we want a sum of £250 m[ille] or £300 m. in temporary relief
of the Highway Rate, how would you recommend getting the money? Would the
Assessed Tax Licences afford the best means? Quaere as to an increase in the carriage
licences for this purpose.

2. *Palm S.*

Ch. mg (with H.C.) and evg. Wrote to Mr Forster l. & Tel. Read C. Wesley's
Sermons[5]—19th Cent. on Agnostics and on Campello[6]—Contemp. on Lamen-
nais and Kingsley[7]—Froude's Carlyle Vol. II: *the* Chapter.[8] Trash? Rosebery & I
were quite agreed.

[1] Arranging for 73 Harley Street to be let on lease to W. H. H. Jessop, who paid rent until at least
1888; it is unclear when Gladstone sold the lease.
[2] J. Polson, *Monaco, and its gaming tables* (1881). See 25 June 81n.
[3] *Metropolitan Police Court Jottings. By a Magistrate* (1882).
[4] Gibson's proposal that closure should need a ⅔ majority. Brand thought 'detestable' too strong
but otherwise agreed; Add MS 44195, f. 101..
[5] By C. Wesley (1816).　　　　　　　　　　　　[6] *N.C.*, x. 650, 606 (April 1882).
[7] *C.R.*, xli. 627 (April 1882).
[8] Probably Ch. xvii, a *résumé* of Carlyle's unfeeling behaviour towards his wife at Craigenputtock,
in J. A. Froude, *Thomas Carlyle: a history of the first forty years of his life*, 2v. (1882); bitterly contested by
some of Carlyle's family and friends.

3. M. [London]

After inspecting the great elm blown down, & stated at 135 feet high, off to London at 11.12 AM. Wrote to Ld Granville (2)—Mr Lowell—Sir H. Ponsonby—Ld Spencer—Miss Eggleton—The Queen—& minutes. Read Dr Prompt on Le Jeu.[1] Mr Forster—Conclave on Irish Local Govt 2-3½.[2] H of C. 5-6 & 7-8½, 9¾-12.[3] Saw Mrs Langtry: I hardly know what estimate to form of her. Her manners are very pleasing, & she has a working spirit in her.

To J. R. LOWELL, American minister, 3 April 1882.   Add MS 44545, f. 115.

I have received your letter & will give due attention to its contents.[4] But I do not see how any general rule of release upon parole can be adopted in the case of foreigners, without being extended to British subjects. The question of such an extended parole must it is evident be dealt with upon domestic considerations and can hardly be disposed of by the interchange of telegraphic messages.

Allow me again to remind you that we have never yet seen the international case on which your Government takes its stand. The regular presentation of the argument is not a form but enlarges our means of judgment & seems little short of an essential condition of the satisfactory transaction of this kind of business.

To LORD SPENCER, lord president, 3 April 1882. '*Private*'.   Add MS 44545, f. 115.

Matters in Ireland do not improve so far as outrage is concerned though the Land Act works increasingly & rents are paid. Forster goes off tonight, unhappy about coercion. He thinks that change in the Executive has become a necessity: & it has indeed been long delayed. One of his plans for a change is his becoming Lord [Lieutenant] Deputy (& remaining in the Cabinet) which I do not think will do. He greatly hopes something may be arranged with you. You will I suppose come back this week[5] & I should be very glad if you could talk the possibilities of the case over with Granville who will I assume have got to Walmer before your return.

[P.S.] I am bound for Hawarden tomorrow afternoon.

4. Tu. [Hawarden]

Wrote to Mrs Bolton BP.—The Speaker—Ld Granard—Mr Baxter—Mr Welby—Mr Shaw—The Queen—and minutes. Saw Mr G—Ld RG. Saw Mrs Bolton who was introduced it seems years ago. Can I do her any good?[6] H of C. 2-4¼. Spoke on state of Ireland.[7] Then off to Hawarden: arrived 10½ at the hospitable Rectory. Read 'Le jeu'. A threatened diarrhoea from chill in the morning all but stopped our movements.

---

[1] P. I. Prompt, *Le jeu public et Monaco* (1882).
[2] Draft bill for Provincial Councils; Hammond, 259.
[3] Misc. business; *H* 268. 641.
[4] Not found; on release of U.S. suspects; see 31 Mar. 82.
[5] Spencer was on duty with the Queen in France; *Spencer*, i. 182; he had already discussed Cowper's replacement with Carlingford; Spencer thought Cowper should be replaced but he feared being asked to succeed him; 'when he [Spencer] was in Ireland in Jany he brought back Cowper's offer to resign ... Gladstone had his resignation in his pocket now & could act upon it at any moment' (Carlingford's diary, 3 March, Add MS 63690).
[6] A rescue case, not mentioned earlier; resident for a time in a hostel in Leicester; later herself involved in rescue work.   [7] *H* 268. 689.

To W. SHAW, M.P., 4 April 1882.   Add MS 44545, f. 115.

I receive with much regret & sympathy the memorials you have sent me setting forth the distress of the labourers in certain districts of the County of Cork.[1]

The Land Act generally dealt with a definite relation between known parties which it sought to improve. The memorialists will I am sure be sensible how difficult it is for Parliament to act in cases where no such definite relation subsists, otherwise than by framing the laws in such a way as to encourage the outlay of capital, which raises the wages of labour. We are nevertheless anxious to give every consideration in our power to all practical suggestions which may be made for improving these provisions of the Land Act which touch the case of labourers.

5. *Wed.*

Ch. 8½ A.M. & 7 P.M. Wrote to Mr Forster (2) and Memm & Tel.—Gerty G.—Ld Granville—Mr Welby—Dean of Ch. Ch.—Rev. J. Kelly—Mr M. Arnold—Mr Godley—and minutes. Read Prompt, Le Jeu—Ch. Quart. on Text of N.T.[2]—Arnold's Essay on Ireland[3]—Green's Making of England.

To MATTHEW ARNOLD, 5 April 1882.   Add MS 44545, f. 116.

I thank you very much for your book.[4]

At present I will only say a word on Copyright—a subject which from time to time I have considered.

I was an old & zealous supporter of Talfourd,[5] but I am shaken in my first opinions without having positively settled down upon others. Using the negative form of speech, as in this case the most convenient, I am *not* sure that the present form of law is the best for them [*sic*] any more than for the public; *not* sure that authors would *not* be better remunerated (also publishers who by contract take the place of authors) were it enacted, as a general rule, that after a *start* of a few months for the first publication, open publication should be permitted subject to Royalty. There is of course much in this that would require consideration. But I think there is much in your point; & I am quite open to the idea that on a basis of this kind a longer term after death might be granted.

I wish I could get you to a Thursday breakfast, but I know you are difficult to be had.

To W. E. FORSTER, Irish secretary, 5 April 1882.   Add MS 44545, f. 116.

My intention had been, before sending you any inclosure on the mode of dealing with the Irish case, to have asked the English and the Irish Law Officers to meet me, that I might fully inform myself as to the actual condition of the law. For want of this, any written suggestion of a plan at this moment must be much at fault: but I send it in answer to your request. You have heard it from me before, and I *rather think* have had it from me in writing, eighteen months ago, when I placed it before you, and other members of the Cabinet, among whom I remember Kimberley and Bright, but found an apparently universal preference for another method of proceeding.[6] There are other

---

[1] Shaw's letter and enclosures untraced.

[2] *Church Quarterly Review*, xiv. 37 (April 1882).

[3] M. Arnold, *Irish essays and others* (1882).

[4] See this day; sent with a letter drawing special attention to his essay on copyright, and his 'Speech at Eton'; Add MS 44475, f. 5.

[5] Sir T. M. *Talfourd's copyright bill eventually passed 1842; for diarist's involvement, see 1 May 39.

[6] Apparently again sending the mem. at 10 Nov. 80 (proscription of the Land League rather than indiscriminate coercion). Carlingford, shown this letter when in Dublin, noted: 'He [Forster]

aspects of the question apart from this: such as the fining of districts and the Jury Laws.

J. Morley is a clever fellow but I do not see that in his special article of Monday[1] he has done much to mend the matter.

In the former Government, Coleridge tried to mend the absurd requisition of unanimity in Juries, but failed. I suppose this reform, is now much missed: it would have the advantage of being general. I assume however that the Irish Jury laws also require special handling. Of course it will be a great object that our legislation whatever it may be should be concise.

When Gorst gave his notice on Monday I had no opportunity of communicating with you, & probably arrangements already made tied you by the leg. In your absence, & with many gaps in my information I made the best statement I could—& left the House just before half past four: after a poor, small, shabby speech from Northcote. I should like to say to him what Peel said to the far better educated Conservatives of that day, on his Income Tax in 1842, 'elevate your vision'.

It is certainly strange that both Gorst and Northcote, I suppose studiously? framed their speeches so as not to speak a word that should tend to injure their harmonious relations with their No-Rent allies in the House of Commons. Can it be all blundering & blindness, that they seem to see nothing, except a parcel of criminals, and a feeble Government, in the Irish case.

I return O'Hagan's note—with thanks & pleasure.[2]

6. *Th.*

Ch. 8½ AM with HC. and [blank]. Wrote to The Queen (2)—Sir H. Ponsonby (2)—Ld Carlingford—Mr Lefevre—Ld Granville—Mr Anderson—Mr Knollys—Mr Godley—Mr Hamilton (Tel)—Mr Welby—and minutes. Visited the Roberts family: a child has been drowned. Read Arnold on Ireland—Le jeu a Monaco—Hubbard, Relig. Census[3]—and Canning's Macaulay.[4]

To R. E. WELBY, assistant financial secretary, 6 April 1882.   Add MS 44545, f. 119.

I suppose it is possible & even probable that our estimate of revenue for the year may improve a little before I have to consider the Budget in the week after next. But I do not dare to hope for such an improvement as would give me the balance that I want, namely a surplus of 600 or 750 m[ille] to meet any charge we may undertake for the roads, with a fair margin for possible increase of expenses in Ireland.

Please to think over the following & any other suggestions & let Lord F. [Cavendish] see this. I premise only this that we ought to find the money we may want on this occasion from property & not from labour.

showed me a plan, in G's writing, for putting down the Land League, *and* all mischievious bodies by a general enactment to be permanent & not confined to Ireland—a vain attempt to avoid specially Irish & coercive legislation—also a draft Bill, drawn at G's desire, for creating in Ireland four "Provincial Councils'"; Carlingford diary, 12 April 1882, Add MS 63690. Bahlman, *Hamilton*, i. 250 (12 Apr. 82) confirms this: 'Mr G.'s suggestion . . . is to have a law applicable to the U.K. to enable the proclamation in a district of a combination intended to conduce to illegal acts'.

[1] *P.M.G.*, 3 April; leader on 'New policy for Ireland', proposing clearing arrears, releasing Parnell, ending coercion, administrative reform, replacement of Forster.
[2] Forster replied, 7 April, Add MS 44160, f. 77, proposing renewal of P.P.P. Act for one year with release of suspects.   [3] See 2 Jan. 81, reprinted 1882.
[4] A. S. G. Canning, *Lord Macaulay, essayist and historian* (1882).

1. We might increase the duty on carriages: but would this yield enough?[1]

2. We might reconstruct the House Tax, but this ought to yield more than we want; & also they would say it was laying rates on in another form.

3. After long consideration, I think the principle of the consanguinity scale hard to defend on any economic or financial grounds. It is for the State to take an equal tax, & for testators to adjust their gifts accordingly. But I think a principle like that of Mr Dodds[2] could only be adopted on wills made after the date of the proposal, & with a notice say of 5 or 6 months for intestacies. Something might be made out of this for the year. I have mentioned the subject to West.

I send a copy of this to Lord F. Cavendish.

7. *Good Friday.*

Church at 10.30.—$2\frac{3}{4}$ (end of the Station Service) and [blank] P.M. Wrote to Mr Broadhurst MP.—Mr J.S. Bankes—Mrs Bolton—D. of Westm.—and minutes. Read Arnold's Essays—Fuller, Speaker's Commentary[3]—Life of Locke[4]—Christ our Ideal. Walk with S.E.G.

To J. S. BANKES,[5] 7 April 1882. '*Private*'.   Add MS 44545, f. 118.

I see that there has been trouble on the subject of payment to the police in this county for guarding me. On my return hither the guard has been removed. Nothing can be more considerate than the members of the force, of all ranks, have been with reference to our privacy & comfort. Still there is a consciousness which they cannot charm away.

On the other hand, in my belief, there is not a shadow of a shade of danger, indeed I should not fear in the least to walk from one end of Ireland to the other. I think the question [which] had been raised has only been due to the very great sensitiveness due to present circumstances about all charges upon the rates.

But might they not be relieved by putting a stop in a quiet way to the service? Do not take the trouble to reply.

To H. BROADHURST, M.P., 7 April 1882.   Add MS 44475, f. 25.

I thank you for your letter and I can set your mind at rest on the subject to which it refers.[6]

It is quite true that we have attached strong safeguards to the exercise of the closing-power, which greatly limit its working, and may to some extent interfere with its purpose. Our reward is that opponents shut their eyes to them, and indulge in fears, such as in kind they have experienced on the approach of all the great and beneficial changes in our laws which have made the century illustrious: but, when considered with reference to the magnitude of the object which excites them, even more strange is their exaggeration. We have however proposed that when the closing-power is to be applied, it shall be applied

---

[1] Duty proposed in budget, but later abandoned.

[2] Joseph Dodds (1819–91, liberal M.P. 1868–88 (disgraced by embezzlement)), proponent of uniform death duty on all property, and irrespective of consanguinity; see, e.g., *H* 268. 1317 regretting this budget's failure to develop the 1881 duties.

[3] J. M. Fuller, *The Speaker's commentary* (1879).

[4] Probably H. R. F. Browne, *The life of John Locke*, 2v. (1876).

[5] John Scott Bankes, 1826–94; chaired Flints. Quarter Sessions from 1863; sheriff of Flints. 1869; stood unsuccessfully as a tory for Flints. C.C. 1889.

[6] Of 5 April 1882, Add MS 44475, f. 15, urging steadfastness on the closure.

by a simple majority: and this proposal we shall to the best of our ability press upon the House.

I earnestly hope that if there be among our friends any one who has a leaning towards the adoption of what is called a proportionate majority, he will at any rate reserve his judgment until we come to the debate.

[P.S.] *Private.* Pray use your discretion as to publishing this letter.[1]

8. *Easter Eve.*

Ch. 8½ A.M. and 8 P.M. Wrote to Mr Hamilton—Mr Forster (2)—The Queen—Ld Granville—Mr Russell—Ld Rosebery—and minutes. Read Russell's Letter[2]—Ld Brougham & Miss Wellmett[3]—Truth about the L. League[4]—Life of Locke—and [blank.]

To C. A. RUSSELL, M.P., 8 April 1882.   Add MS 44545, f. 119.

I thank you for your pamphlet received this morning. We missed your support sorely in the division on Closure but the tone of your letter leads me to hope we may have it on further stages. It is impossible to give a better description of the measure than you have drawn in pages 3–5: I would only add that we have safeguarded it almost up to the point of throttling it. The association of such a measure with a coercion Bill is really preposterous.

Given the wretched supposition of a Coercion Bill, with an obstructive opposition, and we must have something as different from our Resolutions in order to pass it, as chalk from cheese. Surely there can be no doubt that the desire of the No Rent party to put out the Government was a main & justifying reason for their vote. The Government is identified with the Land Act. The Land Act is the one powerful instrument against No Rent. The premiss may be bad, but the conclusion is surely good as from that premiss. It is this, I think, which gives us our claim upon Irish members, who are not for No Rent, in this very matter of procedure.

I do not enter on the other, & most important, matters which you have touched with such force and clearness: for I should much like to converse with you upon them when Parliament re-assembles.

9. *Easter Day.*[5]

H.C. at 8 A.M. Mg prayer 11 & Evg at 6.30. Wrote to Ld Spencer—and minutes. Read Life of Locke—Christ our Ideal—Maidstone Pulpit—and [blank.]

I close this Volume under a heavy mental burden, with intense anxiety for escape, but with much to cheer me: among sustaining causes is this blessed and benignant spring which seems as if sent to heal our sores.

The scarlet rhododendron is well out, the wild hyacinth beginning, horse

[1] Hamilton 'kept back' this letter, as Broadhurst was sure to publish it; 'may the letter not be committing yourself somewhat too positively against recession?'; note by Hamilton, 8 April 1882; ibid., f. 27.

[2] C. A. Russell, 'Letter to the electors of Dundalk on the condition of Ireland' (1882); see this day's letter.

[3] Obscure; a squib?

[4] H. O. [Arnold-Forster], *The truth about the Land League* (1882); see 12 Apr. 82.

[5] This day Forster decided to release Parnell on ten days' parole to attend his nephew's funeral in Paris; he returned to Kilmainham gaol on 25 April.

chestnuts and thorns in good leaf, sycamores and larches following. All creation seems to mingle in one hymn of joy.

[Inside back cover contains, in pencil:—]

S. Hill 7 Bridport St Blandford Square.
G. Harris 94 Highbury New Park N.
A. Thorndike Rice 551 Broadway
Suffield 60 South St Reading
Morris J 1 Upper Spring Street
Blundt Harris 13 122 164. 167. 19 B. Squ
Mrs Sim Axford Marlborough
Shaw
Read 45/
C. Gower 51. 9
11 PM 14 Jan G Squ S. side.

[End of Volume XXXIV]

[VOLUME XXXV][1]

[The inside front cover contains:—]

ἀγωνίζεται γὰρ ὥσπερ ἀθλήτης κατὰ
τὸν βίον, ὅταν δὲ διαγωνίσηται, τότε
τυγχάνει τῶν προσηκόντων.[2]

Private.

No 35

Ap 10. 82–Dec. 31. 83.

Considerate la vostra semenza:
   Non foste nati a viver come brutti
     Ma per seguir virtude, e conoscenza.[3]

ἐπάμεροι· τί δέ τις; τί δ'οὔτις;
σκιᾶς ὄναρ ἄνθρωποι . ἀλλ'ὅταν αἴγλα
Διόσδοτος ἔλθῃ,
λαμπρὸν ἔπεστι φέγγος ἀνδρῶν,
καὶ μείλιχος ἀιων.
              Pyth. VIII. 135.[4]

      θανεῖν δ'οἷσιν ἀνάγκα,
τί κέ τις ἀνώνυμον γῆρας ἐν σκότῳ
καθήμενος ἕψοι μάταν;
              Ol. I. 131.[5]

---

[1] Lambeth MS 1449.

[2] 'For he contends like an athlete in his life; and when he has finished the contest, then he obtains his due reward'; Plutarch, *Moralia*, 561A (*de sera numinis vindicta* 18).

[3] 'Think of what seed you are come: you were born, not to live as the beasts, but to seek after virtue and wisdom'; version of Dante, *Inferno*, xxvi. 118–20.

[4] 'We are creatures of a day. What is a man? What is he not? Human kind is a dream of a shadow. But when god-given glory comes, a shining light dwells on men, and a sweet life'; Pindar, *Pythians*, 8. 95–7.

[5] 'Since we must die, why should a man sit idle in darkness and nurse to no purpose an old age without renown?'; Pindar, *Olympians*, 1. 82–3.

Hawarden April 1882.

10. M.

Ch. $8\frac{1}{2}$ A.M. and 6 P.M. Wrote to Mr I. Donnelly—Mr Forster—The Queen—and minutes. Read Life of Locke—Armstrong's Poems[1]—Erskine on the War (1797)[2]—⟨The Making of England⟩—Hist. of Irish Union in Ann. Reg.[3]

11. Tu.

Ch $8\frac{1}{2}$ AM with H.C. and 6 P.M. Wrote to Mr Hamilton Tel.—Mr Forster l. & Tel.—Ld Granville—Mr O'Shea—and minutes. Read Wilkes on Shakespeare[4]—Erskine on the War (finished)—D'Arduory Cour d'Angleterre[5]—Nathan der Weise.[6] Walk with S.E.G.—At 6 he had blood spitting: Burlingham & then Doby came.[7]

To W. H. O'SHEA, M.P., 11 April 1882.   Add MS 62114A, f. 1.

Upon receiving the note of April 8[8] with which you have favoured me, I have reverted to our correspondence of last June.

I do not see any mode of proceeding upon the lines which you have drawn, but the finance of Irish Land must be dealt with during the present year & I hope that the plan will be such as to suit itself to whatever may be the scale of any possible operations.

12. Wed.

Wrote to Ld Spencer—Abp of Canterbury—Mr Forster l. & Tel.—Ld F. Cavendish—Prof. Sbarbaro—L. Eggleton—Ld Chancellor—& minutes. The Rector going on well. Read Wilkes on Shakespeare—on Indian Missions—Nathan der Weise. Tea with Mary Glynne—Ch. $8\frac{1}{2}$ AM.

To LORD F. C. CAVENDISH, financial secretary,   Add MS 44124, f. 161.
12 April 1882.

I think there is much constructive skill exhibited in your paper on the Purchase Sections of the Land Act.[9] I send it on to Childers for his comments.

He may perhaps borrow from you as you have appropriated from him, and make his Capital Fund (which ought not to be large) a separate fund guaranteed upon a Parliamentary Grant.

The difficulties that strike me are
1. Whether the Board of Guardians is a body strong enough for this function (but Mr C. Russell recommends employing them). What would the remaining Landlords say?

---

[1] Perhaps J. Armstrong, *Poetical works* (1781); see 28 Dec. 65.

[2] T. Erskine, Lord Erskine, *A view of the causes and consequences of the present war with France* (1797).

[3] Ch. xv of *Annual Register* (1800) on popular and parliamentary debs. on the passing of the Act of Union.

[4] G. Wilkes, *Shakespeare, from an American point of view* (1877).

[5] May read D'Ardnory; not found under either.   [6] Play by Lessing (1779).

[7] The Hawarden doctor (see 15 Aug. 78n) and William Murray Dobie, physician in Chester.

[8] Add MS 44269, f. 15: in the compromise he proposed last year, 'my estimate of the forces was proved right, and the bargain offered wonderfully easy . . . terms might still be possible, although of course Sibylline . . .'. See 14 June 81, 15 Apr. 82.

[9] See Add MS 44124, f. 159.

2. Whether your lien upon grants in aid is to be on such grants in aid only as touch matter now within the province of the Guardians. If so, is it not a very limited fund which you provide?

It would be a great advantage if we could lay foundations which could carry, on one & the same basis, whatever it may be right to do as to purchase clauses, as to arrears, and even as to labourers if there be anything more that can safely be done. But *this* is most dangerous ground. It could more safely be trodden by a body really representative and really Irish. I ought perhaps to add a third difficulty: I am not yet satisfied that an advance for the entire purchase money can be safe.

Pray come here on your way back should you find it convenient. We might all go up together on Monday by train due at Euston 3.45 (I believe).

To W. E. FORSTER, Irish secretary, 12 April 1882.[1]   Add MS 44545, f. 120.

1. About Local Government for Ireland, the ideas which more & more establish themselves in my mind are such as these.

(1) Until we have seriously responsible bodies to deal with us in Ireland, every plan we frame comes to Irishmen, say what we may, as an English plan. As such it is probably condemned. At best it is a one-sided bargain, which binds us, not them.

(2) F. Cavendish has framed a plan of finance for the purchase clauses, which has many excellent points. But he has no body to place between the purchasing tenant & the Treasury, except the Boards of Guardians—are they strong enough for this purpose?

(3) [If] Your excellent plans for obtaining local aid towards the execution of the law break down, it will be on account of this miserable & almost total want of the sense of responsibility for the public good & public peace in Ireland; & this responsibility we cannot create except through local self government.

(4) If we say we must postpone the question till the state of the country is more fit for it, I should answer that the least danger is in going forward at once. It is liberty alone, which fits men for liberty. This proposition like every other in politics has its bounds; but it is far safer than the counter-doctrine, wait till they are fit.

(5) In truth I should say (differing perhaps from many) that, for the Ireland of today, the first question is the rectification of the relations between landlord & tenant, which happily is going on; the next is to relieve Great Britain from the enormous weight of the Government of Ireland unaided by the people, & from the hopeless contradiction in which we stand while we give a Parliamentary representation hardly effective for anything but mischief, without the local institutions of self-government which it presupposes, & on which alone it can have a sound & healthy basis.

2. I quite agree that you had no choice but to let out Parnell on *parole*. The only misfortune was, that from the nature of the case the explanation could not precede the act.

3. As to Parliamentary business I should think Thursday 20th would do quite well for your return. I look to you for information about Healy's question on the Hartington clause as it might be called; I mean as to what has recently taken place. I cannot undertake to get up Kenmare's case in detail but will of course attend to the debate should it promise to be serious. By the time of Smith's motion we ought to be ready with our plan; & I own [*sc.* owe?] it to local self-government by which I look to stopping the party move for landlords' compensation, which is too likely to lie at the heart of his scheme.

4. I am very glad to hear of the movement for emigration as being one local & spontaneous, most of all as coming presumably with the good will of the clergy.

---

[1] Reply to Forster's letter of 10 April, sending a draft bill for Provincial Councils, in Reid, *F*, ii. 421; unsigned printed draft, dated 7 April 1882, at Add MS 44628, f. 76.

5. It would be a grand thing if we could put upon one & the same basis, & that a truly Irish one, all the machinery for working the money clauses of the Land Act.

6. As to Irish Government I quite agree that after you reach London there should be no delay in decision or in action.

7. As to the pamphlet I think it does much credit to the author.[1] Moreover it is in my view of great importance, & much use should be made of it. For these reasons I hold all the more to my point that a chapter on the initiation of the Land League & its progress before we came in, should be added. The materials for this would be public. I see also it is defective at various points in verifying references, which are most valuable, even if they can only be given in an approximate form.

13. Th.

Ch. 8½ A.M. Wrote to Mr Hamilton Tel.—Ld Granville l. & Tel—Mr West—Mr Forster l. & Tel.—Miss Lonsdale—Rev. F. Burnett—Dean of Wells ... and minutes. Read Arnold's Essays—Nathan der Weise—Wilkes on Shakesp.— Indian Missions. Mrs Heywood visited us: but saw not much. Rector makes progress.

14. Fr.

Ch. 8¼ A.M. Wrote to Sir H. Ponsonby—Dean of Ch Ch—The Queen (3) & Tel.—Mrs Th.—Scotts—and minutes. Read Nathan der Weise—Arnold's Essays—Ind. Missions. 12-1½. River Dee Trust Meeting. Went with C. over the new Garden Works.

15. Sat.

Ch. 8¼ A.M. Wrote to Sir W. Harcourt—Ld Rosebery—Ld Selborne—Mr Goschen—Mr Heneage—Ld Spencer—Sir C. du Cane—Ly Galloway—Sir T.E. May—Mr O'Shea—Mr Forster—and minutes: also Tel. to Dean of Windsor. Finished Arnold's Essays—Also Nathan der Weise. Read Nihilisme[2]—Wilkes on Shakespeare. Joined W. & H. in cutting down a hard ash. Visited the workhouse with C.

To W. H. O'SHEA, M.P., 15 April 1882. 'Private'.[3]   Add MS 62114A, f. 3.

I have this day received your letter of 13th[4] and I will communicate with Mr Forster on the important and varied matter which it contains.

I will not enter upon any portion of that matter but will simply say that no apology can be required either for the length or for the freedom of your letter. On the contrary both demand my acknowledgments. I am very sensible of the spirit in which you write,

---

[1] 'The pamphlet I sent you was by my son'; Forster, 10 April, Add MS 44160, f. 196. See 8 Apr. 82. Hugh Oakeley *Arnold-Forster, 1855-1909; Forster's adopted s. and p. sec.; later a liberal unionist M.P. and minister.

[2] Perhaps Kropotkin's article in *F.R.*, xxxi. 654 (April 1882).

[3] Letter read to the Commons by O'Shea, 15 May 1882, *H* 269. 784.

[4] Add MS 44269, f. 18; a fresh offer to mediate: Parnellite support for procedure if govt. dealt with arrears, perhaps a land bank, and judicial rents back-dated to the gale. Gladstone commented, *H* 269. 800, 15 May 1882: 'that letter I took to represent the sentiments of the Hon. Member himself, and not those of any other Member'.

and I think you assume the existence of a spirit on my part with which you can sympathize.

Whether there can be agreement upon means or not, the end in view is of vast moment and your letter is not the first favourable sign I have observed. Assuredly no resentment or personal prejudice, or false shame, or other impediment extraneous to the matter itself, will prevent the Government from treading whatever path may most safely and shortly lead to the pacification of Ireland, I should rather say of the districts to which that term, strong as it is, may be thought applicable.

To W. E. FORSTER, Irish secretary, 15 April 1882.   Add MS 44545, f. 123.

I send you herewith a letter from O'Shea containing important matter. I may observe that last year he did not I believe name or allude to Parnell in his communications.

I regard the Amending Bill[1] as a good & pacific sign; a new presumption, I will *not* say proof that the No Rent agitation is defeated.

In a correspondence of this kind, very much depends on the personality of the correspondent, & I have very little knowledge on this matter. You will have more, or can easily get it.

[P.S.] I have thought it right to reply in the sense of not shutting the door—if indeed it be open.

16. 1 S.E.

Ch. 11 A.M. and 6½ P.M. Wrote to Sir H. Ponsonby—Prince of Wales—Ld Granville—Ld Kimberley—Mr Fawcett—Dean of Windsor—Scotts—and minutes. Read Life of Raleigh[2]—Memoirs of Cloyne Cath.[3]—and several tracts. Conversation with Mr M'Coll.

To LORD KIMBERLEY, colonial secretary, 16 April 1882.   Add MS 44545, f. 123.

1. Shall I endeavour to meet Gorst's motion about Cetewayo tomorrow with a few soothing words, or shall I leave the matter in Courtney's hands.[4]

2. It is really of importance that we should get in the Cyprus tribute to meet the default of the Porte. Parliament will be sufficiently vexed to find that in a year when we escape from the expenses of the Transvaal War we have no surplus & must (in all likelihood) ask for fresh ways & means. That vexed temper will easily pass into indignation, if the Treasury shows any remissness in calling in such funds as we possess. I hardly can justify the delays that have already occurred.

17. M. [London]

Ch. 8½ A.M. Wrote to Sir H. Ponsonby—Duke of Westmr—The Queen (2) & minutes. Preparations for departure: & journey to London 10¾-4¼. H of C. 4½-8 and 12¼-1¼.[5] Saw W.H.G. & told him of my intention to convey to him the fee simple of my estate—Ld R. Grosvenor—Sir W. Harcourt. Dined with Mr

---

[1] See 22 Apr. 82.

[2] M. Raleigh, *Alexander Raleigh* (1881).

[3] R. Caulfield, *Annals of the cathedral of St. Coleman, Cloyne* (1882).

[4] No reply found; Kimberley on 18 April, Add MS 44227, f. 146, complimented Gladstone on his 'intervention'.

[5] Spoke on Cetewayo; *H* 268. 769.

Macarthur to meet Sir H. Parkes: arrived after long wanderings.[1] Read Irish Agitation of 1879: a telling history.[2]

18. Tu.

Wrote to Sir J. Hogg—Mr Samuelson—Mr O'Shea—The Queen—& minutes. Saw Mr G—Ld RG—Sir W. Harcourt—Ld Spencer—Mr Welby & conclave on finance. H of C. $4\frac{1}{2}$-$8\frac{1}{4}$.[3] Read Ireland in 1879 finished—Gostwick on German Literature[4]—Miss Fox's Journal.[5] Cough worse: bed early & saw Dr Clark. Saw Mrs Bolton [R].

To W. H. O'SHEA, M.P., 18 April 1882.   Add MS 44269, f. 31.

I thank you for your obliging note[6] and I only reply to ask you *not* to expect to hear from me by the end of this week. It is for me the financial week of the year, and any serious progress with complicated constructive schemes outside that province will absolutely require a little further law [*sic*].
[P.S.] I shall not be able to consult the Cabinet earlier than Saturday, perhaps not so soon, and the work may be such as they cannot dispose of at a moment's notice.

19. Wed.

Wrote to Mr Chamberlain—Mr Forster—Ld Hartington—Ld Kimberley—& minutes. Kept my bed till 2.30 under appliances. Saw Mrs Bolton [R]. Saw Mr G—Ld R.G—Dr Clark—Mr Welby 3-4. H of C. 4-$8\frac{1}{4}$. Spoke on the Errington affair.[7] Read L'Œil du Boeuf[8]—Fox's Journal.

To J. CHAMBERLAIN, president of the board of trade,   Chamberlain MSS 5/34/9.
19 April 1882.

I will send your letter[9] to Forster. With you I attach importance to the fact that the extreme men are introducing a Bill to amend the Land Act. It may be a question whether they could go farther except upon some movement from us towards meeting their overture.

20. Th.

Wrote to The Queen (2) & Tel.—Sir H. Ponsonby—Ld Granville—Ld Spencer— Mr Welby—Mr Dodson—Mr Forster—and minutes. Cabinet 2-4.[10] Bed (mostly)

[1] Sir Henry Parkes, 1815-96; freetrader and colonial sec. N.S.W.; in U.K. 1882. Macarthur championed British/Australian Pacific imperialism.
[2] Possibly R. Staples, 'Agitation in Ireland from a landlord's point of view' (1880, reprinted from 1879 articles).
[3] Questioned on Ireland; *H* 268. 881.
[4] J. Gostwick, *German culture and Christianity* (1882).
[5] See 24 Mar. 82.   [6] See 15 Apr. 82n.
[7] i.e. on relations with the Vatican; *H* 268. 894.
[8] G. Touchard-Lafosse, *Chronique de l'oeil-de-boeuf, des petits appartements de la cour du Louvre sous Louis XIV, Louis XV, Louis XVI*, 8v. (1829-33), 4th ed. in 2v. (1878-80).
[9] Of 18 April, proposing negotiations with Parnell (out of prison on parole) and proposing himself as communicator; Garvin, i. 352.
[10] No notes found; details of the budget were given, see CAB 14/16/17.

before and after. Half an hour in the garden: Clark prescribes air, proscribes speech. Conclave on Finance. Bar Deputation 1–2.[1] Saw Mr G. Read L'Œil du Boeuf—Fox's Journal.

21. Frid.

Wrote to The Queen—Mrs Bramwell—Mr Vivian—A. Matheson—M.T. Bass—Mr Richardson—Earl Cowper—Mr Milbank—Mrs Th.—C.E. Adam—Mr Pease—Mr Bright—Mr Freake—Mr Lawes. 2–3 Conclave on the Viceroyalty of Ireland. Saw Ld H. & Ld G. on possibility (H.) of a party accommodation.[2] Saw Mr G.—Ld R.G.—Read L'Œil du Boeuf—Miss Fox's Journal. Worked on Budget.

To LORD COWPER, Viceroy of Ireland, 21 April 1882.   Add MS 44545, f. 126.
'*Private & Confidential*'.

I have this morning received your letter,[3] and I assure you it is with much concern that I contemplate a possible close of my official relations with you.

You have I believe clearly understood from Forster what is the point, namely that the idea he threw out in conversation with you was purely and exclusively his own.

At the same time I feel that the task of the Executive Government in Ireland has assumed proportions altogether unusual. Forster's presence will be required in Parliament, as a general rule, during the remaining months of the Session; whereas last year, arduous as the circumstances then were, the work here was of a kind that I with others could do.

Under these circumstances I cannot deny that if the Executive business in Ireland could be placed in the hands of one who could discharge it with the authority of a Cabinet Minister, especially if uniting to that authority former Irish experience, there would be public advantage in such an arrangement, and the public would at once understand that a change imputed no disparagement to yourself. Indeed I must say that the opinion which I had long ago formed of your highly cultivated faculties has only been confirmed by observing the discernment, and judicial balance of mind, with which on more than one occasion you have during the last two years expressed to me your views on Irish problems of no small difficulty.

One or two colleagues, with whom I have communicated in strict confidence, share the view of the Irish case which I have above expressed: and after a post or two I hope to write further on the subject.[4]

22. Sat. [The Durdans]

Wrote to The Queen—Rev. W.B. Carpenter and minutes. Worked on Budget. Cabinet 12¼–4. Saw Mr G.—Ld R.G.—Ld Spencer—Lady Spencer. Off at 4.30 to The Durdans—Early to bed: rest for the voice being Cl[ark]'s extra prescription. Read L'Œil du Boeuf—Miss Fox's Journal.

---

[1] No account found.
[2] See this day's letter.
[3] Of 20 April, *Cowper*, 566, relating Forster's proposal to him that he should 'take a long leave', Spencer acting for him.
[4] Printed in *Cowper*, 567.

Cabinet. Sat. Ap. 22. 1882. Noon.[1]

1. Main Clauses of Mr Healy's Bill.[2]

yes. a. Judicial rent may date from application provided rent due in the interval has been paid in due course. To be deducted from next payment of rent and v.v. for the landlord.

no. b. Stay all proceedings for levying rent while the rent is before the Court.
   c. Town parks.
   d. Tenants' improvements. Conversation.

It was informally arranged that Mr Chamberlain should carry on his communication with Mr O Shea[3] and Herbert G.s mem. of conversation with [F. H.] O'Donnell was read.[4] Granville explained on Egypt.

1. Mr Parnell's participation is essential.
2. The doctrine of no-rent, and all opposition to the attempt to interfere with the free action of the people under the Land Act[.]
   An attitude thoroughly favourable to the free action of all Irishmen individually: especially in relation to Land Tenure.[5]

23. 2 S.E.

Kept my bed till luncheon time. Went to evening Church. Worked on Budget figures. Wrote to Mr Hamilton—l. & Tel. Read Gostwick on the German movement[6]—Carlisle on Evil Spirits.[7] Saw Ld Spencer—Dr Donaldson.

24. M. [*London*]

Wrote to Mrs Bolton—The Queen—& minutes—Bp of London. Back to D. St before twelve. Worked on Budget (chiefly) till 5.—Financial statement (my 13th) two hours. Saw Mr G—Mr H—Ld RG—Ld F.C.—Mr Welby—Sir T. May—Sir F.L. Gower. H of C. 5-12¼:[8] but dined at Sir T. May's. Read L'Œil du Boeuf.

25. Tu.

Wrote to The Queen (2)—Sir F. Leighton—Mr Dodson—Sir H. Ponsonby—Att. General—Mayor of Gloucester—and minutes. Read Fox's Journal—L'Œil du Boeuf. Saw Mr G—Ld RG—Mr Goschen—

Mr Chamberlain ⎫
Mr Forster (2) ⎬ on Ireland
Ld Spencer ⎭

Informal Cabinet 3-5 on ditto. H of C. 2-3½.[9] Sir Thos G. dined.

---

[1] Add MS 44643, f. 71.

[2] Redmond-Healy bill to amend 1881 Land Act (implicitly accepting its usefulness) to include tenants-in-arrears and pre-1870 leases. See 26 Apr. 82.

[3] Chamberlain saw O'Shea this day offering a plan to deal with arrears on understanding of cessation of outrages, Boycotting etc. Undated note by Forster reads: 'How would it do for me to see Justin McCarthy privately. He is their estimable leader'; Add MS 44643, f. 73.

[4] An alternative means of mediation which came to nothing; see Malet, 93; mem. in *I.H.S.*, xviii. 87.   [5] Undated holograph; Add MS 44643, f. 72.

[6] See 18 Apr. 82.   [7] W. Carlisle, *An essay on evil spirits* (1825).

[8] Presented his financial statement; *H* 268. 1273.

[9] Misc. business; *H* 268. 1412.

Informal Cabinet. (at H. of C) 2½ *P.M. Ap 25. 82.*[1]
Arrears considered. (Irish Govt. stands over). Wednesday's Debate—W.E.G. to speak. Business on Thursday: not Procedure. Procedure: ⅔: Conversation on amendments. Mr Chamberlain detailed his conversations since Saturday with Mr O'Shea, Mr Healy; and Mr J. MacCarthy who had volunteered for a conversation.[2]

26. *Wed.* [*Windsor*]

Wrote to The Queen (2)—Mr Martin M.P.[3]—Mr Childers— and minutes. Off to Windsor at 5. Grand dinner in the Waterloo Gallery: & soirée after.[4] H. of C. 12¼-2½. Spoke on Land Bill amendment: a crisis, perhaps a turning point.[5] Saw Mr G—Ld RG—Mr Forster—Mr Shaw—Commns, Judge O'Hagan & Mr Vernon—Sir H. Ponsonby. Read Q.R. on Miss Fox's Journal[6]—L'Œil du Boeuf.

To LORD COWPER, Viceroy of Ireland, 26 April 1882.   Add MS 44545, f. 127.

Since I wrote to you last week, the matter has reached its ripeness; and not without many regrets on our part it has been decided to advise the Queen to give Lord Spencer the Viceroyalty of Ireland: regrets I need hardly say, not at the appointment but at the withdrawal which it entails.

I think I cannot better supply you with a record of the motives which have prompted this measure than by sending you in confidence a letter in which I have submitted it to the Queen.[7]

Spencer will himself write to you on the subject; in the meantime I will venture to assure you that the closing words of the letter are not utterances of mere form.[8]

[P.S.] I quite enter into the explanations kindly supplied in your last letter.

27.

Breakf. at 9: but all prayers are suspended at present here & in St Georges. At 11½ We went to St George's. The wedding,[9] a brilliant and touching spectacle

---

[1] Add MS 44643, f. 75; Harcourt and Selborne noted absent.

[2] See Chamberlain, *Political memoir*, 38ff.; on 24 April O'Shea, hoping for a govt. statement, sent a list of requirements, including settlement of arrears, land puchase, ending coercion, royal commission on labourers. Chamberlain replied this day, presumably after this cabinet: 'It would be impossible, however, to make so extended and definite a statement as is suggested in your note. . . .'

Carlingford noted: 'Chamberlain gave us a most interesting and able report of his pourparlers with O'Shea (representing Parnell), Healy (who assured him of his undying hatred of the English Govt.), & Justin MacCarthy. The main thing they require as a condition of giving up the Land agitation & their sine quâ non, is a settlement of the *arrears*, not by loan but by gift & compulsorily—much discussion of this—Mr G is willing to make the relief a gift—compulsion is a great difficulty (the Chancellor is agst it)'; Add MS 63690.

[3] (Sir) Ralph Biddulph Martin, 1838–1916; liberal (unionist) M.P. Tewkesbury 1880–5, Droitwich 1892–1906; bart. 1905.

[4] Visit of King and Queen of the Netherlands.

[5] Welcoming the spirit of the Redmond-Healy bill (see 22 Apr. 82), and accepting in general terms the case on arrears and allowing for amndt. to the tenure but not to the purchase clauses, but unable to agree to 2°R as the bill also attempted general revision of the 1881 Act; *H* 268. 1488.

[6] *Q.R.*, cliii. 530 (April 1882).

[7] On the Irish changes, and Cowper's potential; *Cowper*, 573.

[8] i.e. Gladstone's closing words to the Queen on desirability of reemploying Cowper; this letter in *Cowper*, 573, probably despatched next day; Cowper accepted retirement meekly, ibid., 575.

[9] Of Prince Leopold, duke of Albany (see 7 Apr. 53) to Princess Hélène of Waldeck and Pyrmont.

was over at half past one. Then we managed a short Cabinet at which I announced Spencer's going to Ireland: all were pleased. Then came a grand luncheon: rest: a short walk with that excellent man Dalhousie & much conversation. Saw Mrs Wellesley—Ld Spencer—Mr Forster—Lady Morton—& others. Grand dinner in St George's Hall, with good neighbours today, as I had yesterday. Long soirée: royalties as plenty as blackberries. At the wedding, the most striking point was the responding of the bride: next, I think, the Queen's walk. Read same as yesterday. Wrote to Viceroy of Ireland—The Queen (2)—Mr Godley—& minutes.

28. Fr. [London]

Off at 10.20. Wrote to Sir J. St Aubyn—Mr Mostyn Williams—The Queen—and minutes. R. Academy 1-2 much pleased. Saw Ld Sydney—Ld Granville—Ld Spencer—Mr Forster—Mr G—Ld F.C.—Ld Kensington—Mrs Bolton: not without hope of good [R]. Dined at Marlborough House. More tired after these three days of ceremonial than at the close of any. Yet it was pleasant, & everybody kind. Much pleased with Mrs Monson, & with the C. Prince. The explanation is simple: *anno aetatis suae 73.* Read Fox's Journal—L'Œil du Boeuf, finished Vol I.

29. Sat. [St. George's Hill]

Wrote to Mr Forster—Dean of St Paul's—Ld Spencer—Sir H. Ponsonby Tel.— Mr Forster—Lord Monck—The Queen—& minutes. Saw Mr G—Ld Kensington—Mr Woolner—Mrs Th.—Lady Lindsay—Lady Enfield. To St George's Hill in aftn.[1] The hosts, as ever, most kind. Saw Grosvenor Gallery—Royal Academy Exhibn—Both very interesting. Read Fox's Journal—L'Œil du Boeuf—Lord Moreland, Edited by J. Wesley: for the sake of the Editor[2]—Fraser's Mag. on J. Inglesant.[3]

To W. E. FORSTER, Irish secretary, 29 April 1882.   Add MS 44545, f. 127.

1. I send you a note from Cowper[4] which is all we could desire. 2. I make no doubt you will take care that on Monday we have (a) the April outrages, distinguishing the two halves of the month, (b) all that O'Shea (or anyone else) can tell us about Parnell & the interview of today. 3. On the Viceroyalty I have nothing from the Queen & here are these disastrous paragraphs again—I think you will have observed that this leakage happens specially in Irish matters?[5]
[P.S.] I am afraid that as to Richardson any present step would be 'too late'.

---

[1] Francis Egerton's place; see 6 Aug. 70.
[2] H. Brooke, *The history of a reprobate as given in . . . 'Henry, Earl of Moreland' abridged by J. Wesley* (1784).
[3] *Fraser's Magazine*, cv. 599 (May 1882).
[4] See 26 Apr. 82n.
[5] Forster's letter this day, Add MS 44160, f. 152, stated that short of a 'public declaration' from Parnell, he could not be 'a party to his release'.

30. *3 S. Easter.*

Ch. at 11 AM: some prayer with C. in aftn. Wrote to Ld Granville (2)—Mr Forster—E. Hamilton—Sir H. Ponsonby. Messenger with very important papers from London in aft.[1] Great trouble, but greater & absorbing cause for thanksgiving. Walk with D of D. and Adm. E[gerton]—conversation on Ireland. Read Gostwick: & much of the Ch. of E. Quarterly.

1. No final judgment can at present be arrived at on the paramount question, to which every other must give way, what legislative provisions may be required in Ireland with a view to public security, on the termination of the period in which the L[ife] and P[roperty] Protection Act is in force.
2. All that can now be done is to say what is probable, or what the Government would propose were that expiry already so near, as to make this the proper moment for proposing legislation.
3. We do not agree with those who hold that the L. & P. Protection Act has failed, for we think that it has served a most important purpose during a great crisis, which without it we should not have had the means of adequately meeting.
4. We do not at present contemplate asking Parliament to renew this power of arrest which the Act contains at any rate in its present basis.
5. But, should it appear that the peace and security of the country are placed in jeopardy by Secret Societies, we shall propose, as against their members, the continuance of the power of the present Act, or the enactment of any other powers which the case may require.
6. We think (subject to No. 2) that it will be necessary to strengthen the ordinary law by provisions applicable under certain circumstances to districts requiring them: which will tend to obviate such difficulties as have been experienced in the administration of justice and in securing private rights.
7. We shall continue anxiously to look for the earliest opportunity which may be available for confirming and extending the principles of local Government in Ireland as well as in Great Britain.[2]

To W. E. FORSTER, Irish secretary, 30 April 1882. '*Secret*'.   Add MS 44160, f. 160.

You have certainly used a laudable self-denial, altogether worthy of you, in giving no intimation of your own first impression to O'Shea, or in the circulation-box.

Your short note[3] made me begin Parnell's letter to O'Shea with an unfavourable expectation—I may almost say with a heavy heart. But I came to this sentence in the third page:—'If the arrears question be settled upon the lines indicated by us, I have every confidence, a confidence shared by my colleagues, that the exertions, which we should be able to make strenuously and unremittingly, would be effective in stopping outrage and intimidation of all kinds'.

I own myself at a loss to gather your meaning when you say, 'the result of his visit to Parnell is less even than I expected'.

With great sagacity, Parnell goes on to state his other aims under the amendment of

---

[1] The 'leak' of Cowper's resignation; first drafts for statement dated this day, Add MS 44766, f. 53.
[2] Marked 'Draft'; initialled and dated 30 April 1882, Add MS 44766, f. 53. Further drafts and final, shorter version of 2 May, at ibid., ff. 57—62.
[3] This day, enclosing mem. of Forster's conversation with O'Shea on 30 April, Add MS 44160, f. 156, with Parnell's letter to O'Shea, 28 April, ibid., f. 168 (see 15 May 82n.).

the Land Act. But he carefully abstains from importing any of them as conditions of the former remarkable statement. He then proceeds to throw in his indication or promise of future co-operation with the Liberal Party. This is a *hors d'oeuvre* which we had no right to expect, and, I think, have at present no right to accept.
[1][I may be far wide of the mark, but I can scarcely wonder at O'Shea's saying 'the thing is done'. Not that I see the whole way smooth. I am in no agreement with the Tories as to the Purchase clauses, if they mean to establish the Irish tenant under a scheme of vast width as the debtor of the British Exchequer. But Childers I think offers a way of escape from a plan in which the last state would be worse than the first.]
I return your two papers with thanks, but please let me have them again as soon as convenient, for a short time, to make and keep copies of them.[2] On the whole, Parnell's letter is, I think, the most extraordinary I have ever read. I cannot help feeling indebted to O'Shea.

Monday May One 1882. SS. Phil. & J. [London]

Wrote to The Queen 2 & Tel—Ld Chancellor—Ld Cowper—Ld Houghton—Mr Forster—Dr Lyons—Mr Hutton—and minutes. Back to D. St 11.15. Cabinet 2–4. The intermediate time occupied in anxious conferences with Granville—with him & Hartington—with Forster: from whom no fruit. H. of C. 4.30–12.30 on Procedure: with ½ hour for dinner.[3] Read Fox's Jnal. Saw Forster late at night.[4] A most anxious day.

Cabinet. Monday May 1. 82. 2 PM.[5]
Release of suspects.
Declaration of intentions as to legislative measures—discussed 2–4.
Decision in view: but absolute close of the conversation suspended till tomorrow at 12.

Chamberlain. May 1. 82.[6]
Must it be a public assurance? It can be had. Is it politic? It treats them as the Govt. of I. better refer only to private assurances.

Kimberley—against bargain—or declaration. 'We are the strong people'.

W.E.G. Not for arrangement or for compromise or for referring to the present assurances. There has been *no* negotiation. But we have obtained information. The moment is golden.

---

[1] Passage in [ ] marked as such in Mrs Gladstone's copy of this letter, and presumably omitted in version sent to Forster; omitted in second copy at Add MS 44160, f. 164.
[2] In fact, Gladstone kept the originals, Forster already having copies; Add MS 44160, f. 166.
[3] *H* 268. 1853.
[4] 'We heard from Mother that he [Forster] had practically resigned, but things were not positively settled—there was to be another Cabinet tomorrow'; *F.A.–F.J.*, 469.
[5] Add MS 44643, f. 79. Granville's note: 'It is important that Hartington should have his say early.' Exchange of notes reads: [Forster:] 'I must I fear tell you the fact. They cannot be released without the signature of the L.L. or Chief Secretary'; [Gladstone:] 'But Cowper is Lord Lieut?'; [Forster:] 'Can you tell him he must do it? I know he did agree with me.' See next day's wire.
[6] Gladstone's holograph notes at Add MS 44643, ff. 81–2.

To LORD COWPER, Viceroy of Ireland, 1 May 1882. '*Secret*'.   Add MS 44545, f. 128.

In consequence of the altered position of the No-Rent party, further attested to us by important information which (without any covenant) we have obtained, the Cabinet has this day discussed anxiously the question whether the three Members of Parliament now in prison should be released; with a view to further progressive release of those not believed to be implicated in crime upon careful examination of their cases.

No decision has been actually taken: but the Cabinet meets again tomorrow at twelve, and it is probable that a telegram may then be sent to you requesting you to give directions for an immediate liberation of the three.

The information we have had is in the briefest words shortly this. We know authentically that Parnell and his friends are ready to abandon No Rent formally, and to declare against outrage energetically, intimidation included, if & when the Government announce a satisfactory plan for dealing with arrears. We had already as good as resolved upon a plan & we do not know any absolute reason why the form of it should not be 'satisfactory'.[1]

[P.S.] Very many thanks for your last note.

2. Tu.

Wrote to Ld Granville—Mr Forster—The Queen (2)—Sir H. Ponsonby Tel.—Ld Cowper 2 Tel—Ld R.G.—and minutes. Cabinet 12–2. House 2–7.[2] Saw Ld Granville—Ld Spencer—Mr Forster—Sir J. Hay—Mr Chamberlain. Wrote Cabinet Mem. & careful words in detail for Ministerial explanation. Saw Mr G—Mr Eyton—Ld Halifax—Ld Derby—Ly M. Beaumont—Archbp of York. Dined at Mrs Meynell Ingram's. Saw Scoresdale—Badeler [R]. Read Fox's Journal.

Cabinet. May 2. 82. Noon[3]
1. Release.[4]
2. Measures as to police.
3. Measures as to land. a. Arrears. b. Purchase Clauses.

Committee on new Law of peace & order: Chancellor, Spencer, Carlingford, Harcourt, Bright, Hartington.[5]

The Cabinet are of opinion that the time has now arrived when with a view to the interests of law and order in Ireland the three members of Parliament who have been imprisoned on suspicion since last October should be immediately released: and that the list of suspects should be examined with a view to the release of all persons not believed to be associated with crimes.

They propose at once to announce to Parliament their intention to introduce, as soon as necessary business will permit, a bill to strengthen the ordinary law in Ireland for the

---

[1] Printed in *Cowper*, 577, with reply of 2 May protesting.
[2] Ministerial statement on resignations of Cowper and Forster, on release of suspects 'on our own responsibility alone', and on nonrenewal of the P.P.P. Act (to be replaced by a bill strengthening the 'ordinary law'); *H* 268. 1965; final draft of statement, Add MS 44766, f. 61.
[3] Add MS 44643, f. 85.
[4] Cowper, after objecting, later this day signed the order of release for Parnell, Dillon and O'Kelly.
[5] Note ibid., f. 86. Note by Forster asking for clarification of the procedure for resigning, ibid., f. 87.

security of life and property, while reserving their discretion with regard to the Life and Property Protection Act, which however they do not at present think it will be possible to renew if a favourable state of affairs shall prevail in Ireland.[1]

To LORD COWPER, Viceroy of Ireland, 2 May 1881.   Add MS 44475, f. 82.
Cypher telegram.

Matter being settled here for immediate action and on a footing in last named telegram to sign and give necessary directions for the three forthwith.[2]

3. Wed.

Wrote to Mr Chamberlain—Ld Chancellor—Ld R. Grosvenor (2)—Ld Northbrook—Ld Spencer Tel.—The Queen (3)—Sir W. Harcourt—F. Cavendish—and minutes. 11–12¼. Conclave on the Irish Secship Gr.[3] Sp[encer] & H[artington]. Saw Mr Porter[4]—Lord F. Cavendish 1.1.—Ld Granville—Ld Spencer—Mr OConnor Power—Ld OHagan—Prince of Wales—Ld Northbrook—Sir W. Harcourt. Saw Bolton [R]. Read Fox's Journal. This anxious day closed with a large dinner to the Cr. Prince of Denmark & the P. of Wales. The Princess had to excuse herself at the last moment. They remained until after midnight. Mr Shorthouse[5] came. On this day I had to be thankful for escape unharmed from serious injury, possibly even death, from a brickbat which a workman let fall or threw from a housetop in Regent Street. It smashed and splintered the flags within I think 12 inches of my foot in front of me.

New appointments
Ld G. Here is Porters note—I had expected a second call from him. Have you any further lights or shall I at once see F.C. W.E.G. My. 3.
[Granville:] I have no further lights—I regret Porter, but we are all agreed that Freddy Cavendish stood next. I have heard several individuals today objecting to Chamberlain.[6]

[1] Memorandum sent to the Queen, 2 May 1882, the accompanying letter noting that Forster 'dissents from this Memorandum, and is not willing to share the responsibility of the Cabinet'; CAB 41/16/21 and *L.Q.V.*, 2nd series, iii. 275.
[2] Cowper objected, Gladstone pointing out in a further telegram that 'your signature, if required, as it would be after resignation, would be merely ministerial and without political responsibility'; Add MS 44475, f. 83 and O'Brien, *Parnell*, i. 348.
[3] Granville, though read by Hammond, 281, as Grosvenor (see this day's mem. and Bahlman, *Hamilton*, i. 263); Lord F. Cavendish was this day appointed.
[4] (Sir) Andrew M. Porter, 1837–1919; presbyterian and liberal M.P. Londonderry 1881–3; Irish solicitor general 1881–3; briefly attorney general 1883; Irish master of rolls 1883. This day he declined the secretaryship 'chiefly on personal grounds' (Bahlman, *Hamilton*, i. 263).
[5] Joseph Henry *Shorthouse, 1834–1903; author of *John Inglesant* (see 14 July 81); see his *Life and letters* (1905), i. 112–14, 149.
[6] Add MS 44766, f. 66.

To J. CHAMBERLAIN, president of the board of trade,   Add MS 44545, f. 129.
3 May 1882.

I have been anxiously considering & consulting about the vacancy & I thank you much
for your note.[1] I will tell you when we meet what I think are the obstacles in the way of a
suggestion which has so much to recommend it as that you have sent me; but I cling a
good deal to the Irish idea.

I am highly gratified by your good opinion of yesterday's recital.

To LORD COWPER, Viceroy of Ireland, 3 May 1882.   Add MS 44475, f. 87.

When do you come to London? I quite understand your letter as it shows me *to my
surprise that you have had no previous information which I think will alter your view as it* ⟨*altered
ours*⟩ *acted upon ours.*

To LORD R. GROSVENOR, M.P., chief whip, 3 May 1882.   Add MS 44315, ff. 70, 75.
'*Private & Imm[ediate]*'.[2]

[First letter:]   It may be that F. C[avendish] will succeed Forster. I take it for granted
that his seat is safe? Who would be the best man to succeed him? There must be a patient
power of hard work with tact & temper.
[P.S.] Among the candidates for *entry* into office, who is the best? What of young Brand?

[Second letter:]   East wind & wet here given way to west wind & dry: so I hope you are
better. And so I hope you will be better about Ireland when you know what has taken
place. Of 'new departure' we know nothing: but of new hopes and prospects much. If we
are wrong in this belief we are very wrong & must soon go to the rightabout.

To Sir W. V. HARCOURT, home secretary, 3 May 1882.   MS Harcourt dep. 8, f. 129.
'*Secret*'.

Your suggestion[3] has been most carefully considered, & much may be said in its favour:
but a less aspiring course, and no seat in the Cabinet, seem on the whole to have
preponderating recommendations. It will, I think be F. Cavendish but not a word can be
said. I can explain more fully when we meet, should there be a moment.

To LORD NORTHBROOK, first lord of the admiralty,   Add MS 44266, f. 124.
3 May 1882. '*Secret*'.

If it should happen as is not unlikely that F. Cavendish should follow Forster, Trevelyan
comes among the names for this post; which post is always of very great importance and
at present is lifted beyond its usual mark by my being Chancellor of the Exchequer for the
time, an arrangement which must very soon end, so that it does not much enter into the

---

[1] Of 2 May, Add MS 44125, f. 136: need for an Irishman, perhaps Shaw, as chief secretary.
[2] Both letters holograph; Gladstone the previous day had asked his opinion for the Irish
secretaryship, Grosvenor preferring Hartington, failing him, Trevelyan, but deploring Chamberlain
and Lefevre; he believed 'agitation in Ireland will *never* cease now'. This day he reported
Cavendish's seat 'absolutely safe', and recommended Trevelyan for the Treasury and Brand and
Fitzmaurice for promotion; Add MS 44315, ff. 69–72.
[3] Not found.

question. Would Trevelyan be the man for the mass of work requiring constant toil and patience, in F.C.'s office? Pray give your opinion.
[P.S.] I do not feel sure that T. would take it. What do you think?[1]

4. Th.

Night a little disturbed. Nine to breakfast, including Mr Shorthouse. Wrote to Earl Granville—Mr Marling[2]—The Queen l.l.l.—Ld Chancellor—Ld Spencer—& minutes. Read Fox's Journal. Saw Mr G—Ld R.G.—Ld Rosebery—Mr Hutton— Ld F. Cavendish—Conclave on Offices at 3.45—Mr OShea MP. H of C. $4\frac{1}{2}$-$8\frac{1}{4}$ and $9\frac{1}{4}$-$12\frac{1}{4}$. Spoke on Forster's explanation.[3]

Cabinet. Thurs. May 4. 1882. 3 PM.[4]
Smith[5] & Bright clauses cannot be tomorrow.
Arrears
M. Davitt shd. be released.[6]
Treasonable practices: how to be understood.
Spencer asked as to the *line* to be drawn in releases.

Prevention, not punishment. The future, not the past. Arrest was on suspicion of opposition to the law and to contracts for rent and especially to the Land Act.
   What was the Land Act? Our instrument for giving contentment to Ireland. The L. & P. Act was an expedient to defend its operation agt. violence.
   Arrest was for intentions wh. placed us in the midst of a social revolution. We believe the intentions now are to promote law & order. How could we keep those in prison who [we] believe seek to ally with us in our first duty. Act is for prevention—*what are we to prevent?*
   But how do we know it. By information tendered to us. Shall *we* give the particulars? We leave[?] it.
   Had Parnell (the No Rent Party) declared in October what they declare now, we could not have imprisoned him. What *is* the change charged upon us?[7]

5. Fr.

Wrote to Ld Hartington—Ld Granville—Dean of Windsor—Mr Givan MP—The Queen 1.1.1.1. & Tel.—E. Hamilton—& minutes. H. of C. $4\frac{1}{2}$-$8\frac{1}{4}$ & 10-$12\frac{1}{4}$.[8] Saw Mrs Bolton [R]. Saw Mr G.—Ld RG—Sir W. Harcourt (2)—Ld Cowper—Mr Childers jun.—Scotts—Mr Givan—Mr Playfair—Mr O'Shea—Mr Goschen—Mr

---

[1] Trevelyan very well suited for the financial secretaryship if his health bore up, thought Northbrook, 4 May, Add MS 44266, f. 125.
[2] Baronetcy for Samuel Stephens Marling, 1810-83; liberal M.P. Stroud 1875-80.
[3] Denying any arrangement between the govt. and Parnell, who then confirmed Gladstone had not 'either in writing or verbally, referred to my release'; *H* 269. 121, 128.
[4] Add MS 44643, f. 90.
[5] W. H. Smith's clause to extend the land purchase clauses of the 1870 Act; withdrawn this day; see *L.Q.V.*, 2nd series, iii. 280.
[6] Davitt was released on 6 May.
[7] Dated (later?) '4 May'; perhaps notes for this day's reply to Forster, but only loosely related to it, though docketed 'Statement in H. of C.' by secretary; Add MS 44766, f. 69.
[8] Questioned on Ireland; *H* 269. 234.

Bright—Ld Granville *cum* Ld Hartington—Sir C. Dilke—Ld Spencer. Read Fox's Journal—Waugh's Besom Ben.[1]

I saw Mr. O'Shea at his request at about six o'clock this evening. He had been up all night, and had long and in his opinion most satisfactory conversation with Parnell who he is confident will carry through what he has intended.

Parnell does not object to the announcement of strong measures in Ireland but is most anxious that they should not be precipitated.

He is confident that the state of Ireland will have greatly improved in a short time. Among the instruments on whose aid he reckons, are Egan and Sheridan.[2] In perfect keeping with what he had reported to Forster he told me that Sheridan was the man who organised the anti-legal agitation throughout Connaught, and who would now be an effectual agent for putting down.

He speaks with the same confidence of Egan.

Mr. O'Shea himself detests and denounces the previous action with regard to outrage.

Parnell much regretted the declarations of Dillon and O'Kelly yesterday during his absence. He also regretted that he had misunderstood my reference to him in consequence of inaccurate information with which *Cowen* supplied him before his actually entering the House.

He considers that he has now got his hand upon Dillon who is difficult to manage and intensely ambitious.

He states that there are great jealousies around him in Parliament: and some men are alarmed at the prospect of losing their livelihood. I am not sure whether this proceeded from O'Shea or from Parnell but I think it seemed as if derived from Parnell, perhaps not as a message.

It is already made known in Ireland that the No Rent manifesto is 'void' and Parnell is anxiously considering what further practical steps he can take with regard to getting formally rid of it.

Parnell *had* communicated with his fellow prisoners before writing his letter to O'Shea.

As nothing can be more clear than that he has used lawlessness for his ends, so O'Shea's statements tend to impress the belief that he is now entirely in earnest about putting it down; but that he feels himself in some danger of being supplanted by more violent men.

O'Shea is to send me the names of some men whom he recommends for early liberation that they may work under Parnell in repressing outrage: I promised to send them to Lord Spencer.

He said he had been up all night: and I do not doubt he has worked hard. W.E.G. May 5. 82.[3]

To LORD HARTINGTON, Indian secretary,   Chatsworth MSS 340. 1145.
5 May 1882.

Putting all things together I see plainly we have no one who can really fill Freddy's place, such as it has been in his hands. An additional provision therefore ought to be made: and I feel that the time has now come, marked out by this change, when I ought to

---

[1] E. Waugh, *Besom Ben* (1865).

[2] For Egan, see 12 Oct. 81; Patrick J. Sheridan, Land Leaguer associated with the 'Invincibles', using disguise of 'Fr. Murphy'; fled to U.S.A. after the murders; T. Corfe, *The Phoenix Park murders* (1968), 141.

[3] Holograph dated 5 May 1882, Add MS 44766, f. 71; in *Autobiographica*, iv. 58.

press the appointment of a Chancellor of the Exchequer; for I am well aware and I feel increasingly from physical signs that I have no additional stock to draw upon.

I am sure you will kindly and carefully consider the question whether in view of the future you should take the office.[1]

6. Sat.

Wrote to The Queen (2)—Ld Northbrook—Mr D. Grant—Mr Chamberlain—Mr Monk—Lucy Cavendish—Mr Leake—Sir W. Harcourt—Mr O'Shea—Dean of Windsor—Ld Spencer—Mr M. Henry—H.J.G.—Bp of London—Mr ...—Bp of Durham—& minutes. Cabinet 12-2. Saw Mr. G.—Mr H—Ld Kensington—Ld Hartington—C. Karolyi—Countess Karolyi. Saw Beckler—May—Scarsdale— French [R]. Read Sister Dora 2°.[2]

Dined at Austrian Ambassador's: walked home: met by the frightful news from Dublin of the assassination of dear F. Cavendish and Burke.[3] We went over to see Lucy, already informed by Lady L. Egerton. It was an awful scene but enlightened by her faith and love. We saw likewise Granville and Harting-ton: and we got to bed before two, Meriel staying with her sister.

Cabinet. Sat May 6. 82. Noon.[4]
1. Amt. to Sir M. H. Beach[5]
2. To be moved by Ld H.
3. Conciliatory offer to be made.[6]
4. Notice to Northcote forthwith.
5. Militia to Aldershot for coming inspection—*no.*

To J. CHAMBERLAIN, president of the board of trade,   Chamberlain MSS 5/34/10.
6 May 1882.

I am truly concerned that you, as well as Spencer & Harcourt were absent from a Cabinet which the notices of last night made it necessary to call.

We have decided to accept Gibson's amendment (so to speak) on probation, provided we find that we can thereby effectually accelerate action on procedure. This offer will be public, but Northcote has notice of it.

We think it will do good, *whether* accepted or rejected: taking into account certain vital conditions of the case: a. that the opposition, however beaten, will obstruct, & will land us in most formidable difficulties, so that probably we shall be obliged to break off procedure whatever we do. b. that our friends will much desire a clear stage for Ireland at an early

[1] No reply found.
[2] See 15 Feb. 80.
[3] Murdered at 7.17 p.m. in Phoenix Park by the 'Invincibles', five of whom were hanged in May 1883 in Kilmainham; see T. Corfe, *The Phoenix Park murders* (1968).
[4] Add MS 44643, f. 93. Gladstone's note to Granville reads 'I had a long & pleasant conversation with Dilke yesterday on his matter about the [royal] grants. He thanked me'; ibid., f. 97 (see *L.Q.V.* 2nd series, iii. 290).
Undated holograph reads: 'Mr Bright—*ultro. "I do not call myself a radical but I have run a little lie with them"'*; Add MS 44643, f. 100.
[5] Beach's Resolution for papers on the Kilmainham affair was never moved; *H* 269. 235. See 23 May 82.
[6] On procedure; see to Chamberlain this day.

date. c. that the deadlock upon procedure will be a heavy discredit to the House of Commons itself.
[P.S.] Bright kindly undertook to write to you.

To Sir W. V. HARCOURT, home secretary, 6 May 1882.   MS Harcourt dep. 8, f. 131.

After considering your objections[1] or difficulties to which they attach much weight, the Cabinet took into view other elements of the case, which they think turn the scale the other way. Hartington undertook to write to you. Meantime I send you copy of a note I have written to Chamberlain.

To Sir S. H. NORTHCOTE, M.P., 6 May 1882. '*Private*'.   Add MS 44217, f. 201.

I thank you for your note of yesterday. We intend to move an amendment upon Sir M. H. Beach's Resolution in the terms which I inclose.

But before the debate, I propose to offer a short statement founded upon this basis; that, while we do not think the actual moment for Irish legislation has arrived, we are firmly convinced that it ought not to be long delayed.

With a view to this end, and adverting to the fact that you are now acting together as a party, and also to the character and especially the length of the debates, thus far, on the first Resolution, of Procedure, we are prepared, without having modified our own views, to accept the amendment of which notice has been given by Mr Gibson, with the intention of allowing the Resolution, thus altered, to be fairly tested by experience; provided we are assured (in the House for I do not ask from you any undertaking, or any reply to this note beyond acknowledgement) that you and the heads of your party will on that basis use exertions to expedite the action of the House on Procedure, and will enter on the consideration of the remaining Resolutions in what I may term a spirit of co-operation. I think I need not here trouble you with any statement of the motives which have led us to adopt this course but the suggestion is tendered with a conciliatory aim.[2]

To W. H. O'SHEA, M.P., 6 May 1882. '*Private*'.   Add MS 44545, f. 131.

1. Your note about suspects[3] when it arrives shall go at once to Lord Spencer.

2. You may as well know at once that, in view of the state of Ireland & of the importance of being free to propose legislation of the proper kind at an early date, we have made known our willingness to accept Mr. Gibson's amendment (which retains all such protection as is proposed for small minorities) on *probation*, if we are assured that we can thereby effectually accelerate the action of the House on Procedure. This whether accepted or rejected will I think do good.

To LORD SPENCER, Viceroy of Ireland, 6 May 1882.   Althorp MSS K5.

1. I send you a copy of a Memorandum I have made of a conversation held yesterday evening with O'Shea, at his request. 2. He wished to send a list of suspects whose release is desired *in order* that Parnell, who relies upon them, may *actively employ* them in the restoration of obedience to the law. I at once promised to send to you their names with a view to the examination of their cases. 3. As far as I can judge Parnell is running true.

---

[1] Harcourt's objections to accepting Gibson's ⅔ amendment. See 1 Apr. 82n.

[2] Holograph draft; Northcote's reply turned into a note of condolence by the Irish news; Add MS 44217, f. 205.

[3] Letter this day, Add MS 44269, f. 36, regretting his 'list of suspects' not yet ready; list probably not sent.

7. *4 S.E.*

Chapel Royal at noon with H.C.: and in evening. Wrote to Lucy Cavendish—The Queen—Sir S. Northcote—Pr. of Wales—Mr O'Shea—Ld Granville—The Speaker—Ld Spencer Tel.—Mayor of Cork—and minutes.

I rose early to write to L.C. This grief lay heavy & stunning upon us but with much to do & think of as to Parliament, Ireland, & many things & persons.

Saw Mr H—Mr G—Mr H S[eymour]—Ld Kensington—Ld Cowper—Ld Granville—Mr Forster[1]—Sir R. Phillimore—W.H.G.—N. Lyttelton—Lady Spencer—and Lucy—who was marvellous in the armour of a Christian heroism. Dined with the Phillimores.[2] Read Prophets of Israel.[3]

Pro-Cabinet. Sunday May 7. 82.[4]
Present:
W.E.G.; Dodson; Harcourt; Bright; Granville; Chancr; Carlingford; Northbrook; Kimb. Conversation on question as to Irish legislation on *order*. a. substance. b. time. Resume tomorrow.

To H. B. W. BRAND, the Speaker, 7 May 1882.   Add MS 44545, f. 132.

I thank you much for coming & calling. We all think that on this unexampled event there should be an adjournment of both houses either instantly or before public business. Please consider this.

I never thought to have lived into the events of the last 10 days. But even in this black crime & terrible calamity, there may I hope be a seed of good—this may be a turning point in the history of Parliament—the pure & noble life may be a great peace-offering.

You will see a circular tomorrow (only *described* to me) with the names of Parnell, Dillon & Davitt;[5] that is itself an event, denouncing the assassins, & fervently exhorting the Irish people to detect & give them up. My colleagues will be here tomorrow at two.

To W. H. O'SHEA, M.P., 7 May 1882.   Add MS 44545, f. 132.

My duty does not permit me for a moment to entertain Mr. Parnell's proposal,[6] just conveyed to me by you, that he should if I think it needful resign his seat; but I am deeply sensible of the honourable motives by which it has been prompted.

---

[1] Offering to return as chief secretary, Spencer turning him down; *F.A.-F.J.*, 482, 485.

[2] 'May 7. Lord F. Cavendish & Mr Burke. Saw Mr G. at Carlton House quite crushed. The Gs came to dinner to wh. they had been engaged some time. Nobody but ourselves & I persuaded them for both their sakes to come. . . . After the all engrossing topic had been much discussed, G. spoke with a great burst of eloquence upon the subject of the improvements in every department of the State abroad & at home wh. we had witnessed during the last half century'; Phillimore's diary.

[3] By W. R. Smith (1882).

[4] Add MS 44643, f. 101. Undated note from Godley records Shaw Lefevre's offer to become Secretary to the Treasury; ibid., f. 103.

[5] Written by Davitt; in O'Brien, *Parnell*, i. 358.

[6] O'Shea's note this day Add MS 44269, f. 42: 'I am authorised by Mr Parnell to state that if Mr Gladstone considers it necessary for the maintenance of his (Mr G's) position and for carrying out his views, that Mr Parnell should resign his seat, Mr Parnell is prepared to do so immediately'. See also O'Brien, *Parnell*, i. 357.

8. *M.*

A day of constant pressure. Wrote to Ld Ripon Tel.—The Queen l.l.l.l.—The Speaker—Ld Granville l.l—Mr Childers—Ld Spencer l.l. & Tel.—Sir S. North-cote—Mrs Bolton—Ld Hartington. Also Mem. on Sir C. Dilke's case & other Mema[1]—and minutes. Saw Mr Trevelyan—The Speaker—Mr O'Shea—Mr Chamberlain—Mr Ross. Cabinet 2-4¼ and 5-5¾. Went reluctantly to the House & by the help of God forced out what was needful on the question of the Adjournment.[2] Evg at home. Read Q.R. on Revised Text—N.T.—Swift—Ireland.[3]

Cabinet. May 8. 82. 2 P.M.[4]
1. Executive appointments: Successor to Col. Hillier—Col. Brackenbury.[5]
                    Burke—Mr Hamilton.
    Temporary appt. against Secret Societies—Col. Bradford.[6]
2. Irish Secretaryship. Sir C. Dilke to succeed without Cabinet if agreeable to Spencer.[7]
3. Adjournment. Yes—& *who attends*: W.E.G.
4. Promise ⟨statement tomorrow⟩ Bill on Thursday.
5. Gibson (Mr Goschen) intention to vote urgency. Conversation & stands over.

To LORD HARTINGTON, Indian secretary, 8 May 1882.   Chatsworth MSS 340. 1149.
'*Secret*'.

I trust the Duke continues to bear up against the terrible affliction.

The Cabinet today sanctioned (all in concert with Spencer) appointments *vice* Burke and Hillier—also Col. Bradford to look after Secret Societies.

They put Dilke 1. for the Chief Secretaryship but he refuses obstinately, on account of non-admission to the Cabinet. This is bad.

Trevelyan accepts and I am just sending the recommendation of him to the Queen.

We see nothing sufficient but Courtney for the Treasury—no other back quite strong enough. I shall tell him that a separate C[hancellor] of E[xchequer] will probably be appointed.

I think you will like this. If not please to telegraph forthwith. *He* will run a certain risk, perhaps learn a lesson.

A prevention of Crime Bill on Thursday. Arrears as soon afterwards as may be. Procedure goes overboard.

Parnell regretted the first announcement but could understand its being unavoidable.

I was reluctant to go to the House for fear I should give way and make a scene: but it was thought requisite. No difficulty about adjournment.

I expressed confidence that our measures would be duly expedited in all quarters.

To LORD SPENCER, Viceroy of Ireland, 8 May 1882.   Althorp MSS K5.

[First letter:] Amidst all this grief & confusion, and with efforts little less than diabolical made in the Times of today to fasten this hellish crime upon the Irish nation, it is a great

---

[1] See *L.Q.V.*, 2nd series, iii. 290.   [2] *H* 269. 320.
[3] *Q.R*, cliii. 309 (April 1882).   [4] Add MS 44643;, f. 106.
[5] Brackenbury replaced Hillier, becoming assistant undersecretary for police and crime pending reform of the police structure; (Sir) Robert *Hamilton, 1836–95, previously a Westminster civil servant, replaced Burke.
[6] John Fowler Bradford, 1805–89; formerly in Indian army.
[7] Spencer agreed, but Dilke refused to serve without the cabinet. See also next note.

comfort to me to thank you for your admirable letter, and to think that such a man as you are is on the spot and in supreme command. May the Almighty guide and carry you well through your arduous labour.

The matters most pressing upon us are: 1. The Executive appointments instead of *Burke & Hillier.* 2. The succession to our dear dear Freddy.[1] 3. Peace & order Legislation—substance. 4. Legislation—time. I am struck by your demand for an English eye to aid the Police. I have repeatedly pressed this on Forster—but in vain. Indeed I do not remember that he ever accepted an executive suggestion from me.[2]

[Second letter:] Various motives, which I think you would have appreciated, inclined the Cabinet (whom under all the circs. I consulted) to Dilke, but he has refused, plump & positively, on account of the non-admission to the Cabinet. Very wrong indeed I think. The notions of rights, as between party & person, have greatly changed since I was young.

So Trevelyan has been recommended to the Queen. Tomorrow I hope to make known to you her answer.

Captain Ross,[3] whom you recommended as the last & best witness to the exterior facts of the terrible catastrophe has been understood by Her Majesty to have a confidential mission to explain the state of Ireland! His opinion is that the whole population are members or tools of secret societies.

9. *Tu.*

Wrote to Ld Chancellor—Ld Spencer l. & Tel.—Ld Granville—Mr Childers (2)—Att. General—Pall Mall Gazette—The Queen l.l.l.—Mrs Th.—Duchess of Sutherland—Sir H. Ponsonby—Lucy—Miss De Lisle—& minutes. Saw Mr G—Mr H—Ld RG—Ld Northbrook—Mr O'Shea—Ld Granville—Mr Welby—Mr Trevelyan—H.J.G.—Sir W. James. Dined with the James's, shirking the House. A short drive: & shopping. Read Dicey's Egypt[4]—Burhill's Reminiscences[5]—Q.R. on Lecky's Hist.[6]

To LORD SELBORNE, lord chancellor, 9 May 1882.   Add MS 44545, f. 133.

O'Shea made an observation to me last night which I think worth reporting to you. It was that where a jury failed to convict there might be a power of ordering a new trial without one. Considering that one latent Fenian may baffle eleven sound men I thought this worth *considering.* What I hope is that we shall strike strongly at secret societies of whatever kind, but shall not legislate in view of this murder against the *people* of Ireland.

To LORD SPENCER, Viceroy of Ireland, 9 May 1882.   Althorp MSS K5.

[First letter:] I have made known to you Trevelyan's acceptance and approval. He is a good fellow. Dilke made a horrible mistake.

What you say of the police with knowledge is the expression of my own feeling on more distant observation, to which Forster never would attend.

I have willingly consented to take the question of crime in Ireland at once for Parliamentary handling and I am also quite ready for strong legislation against all capital

---

[1] A. M. Porter again considered, but no offer made; *I.H.S.*, xviii. 81.
[2] Version printed in *Spencer*, i. 194 with Spencer's letter this day on police incompetence.
[3] F. J. Ross, Spencer's aide, sent to report to the Queen; Guedalla, *Q*, ii. 192.
[4] E. Dicey, *England and Egypt* (1881).
[5] Could read Burkill; untraced for both readings.   [6] *Q.R.*, cliii. 489 (April 1882).

offences reasonably believed by the Executive to spring out of treasonable or other secret societies.

What I desire to avoid is special legislation, on this occasion against the people of Ireland. The tide of their feelings is now running in the right directions and we must try not to repress it.

Upon this horrible crime I hope that (probably through the car) you will get evidence, and I have a rather sanguine belief that if you get evidence you will get a conviction; unless some concealed Fenian insinuates himself in the body.

We have dangers to avoid on the right & on the left; & all of them pressing.

I hope the evidence will *stand* from which it appears (*Daily News*) that the man who spoke on meeting the dray did not speak with an *Irish* accent.[1]

We have certainly an opportunity *for* taking hold of Irishmen on their good side such as has never before offered itself to an English Government.

[P.S.] I have telegraphed to you about more help. I thought of Nevy [Lyttelton]—or perhaps my son Herbert; as capable of being useful.

[Second letter] '*Immediate*'. In my postscript today I named conjecturally Nevy and my son Herbert. Herbert is a member of the Government—has worked much with, i.e. under, Forster last autumn—has a subordinate charge of Irish business—and could go down with Trevelyan tomorrow night. I think he has pluck steadiness and judgment without any egotism: & he might be very useful as an intelligent & faithful instrument, in police-work under you. He could well be spared here I think for a moment.

[P.S.] If you wish him to come, telegraph the word *come* to him at Wellington College, Wokingham.[2]

10. Wed.

Wrote to The Queen 1.1.1.—Viceroy of Ireland—Mr O'Shea—Dean of Windsor—Mr L. Courtney—Mr Campbell Bannerman—Mr E. Ashley—Sir R. Lingen—Ld Hartington—Ld Granville—Ld Kimberley—Mr Shaw MP.—Duke of Buckingham—Mr Chamberlain—Mr L. Stanley—Sir A. Otway—and minutes. Cabinet 12-4 mostly on the repression of Crime Bill. Saw Ld Granville—Ld Kimberley—D. of Argyll—Mr G—Mr H—Ld R.G. (2)—Mr Childers *cum* Mr Welby on arrears. Drive with C. Read Q.R. on Cobden[3]—Miss Fox—Swift. Dinner party put off.

Cabinet. May 10. 1882. Noon.[4]
1. Title of Bill. Prevention of Crime Bill.
2. House to meet tomorrow at *nine.*
3. Harcourt to bring in Bill.
4. Question of *now* asking U.S. whether they mean to answer respecting the Assassination Literature. Yes.[5]
5. Provisions of Crime Bill considered at great length.

[1] *D.N.*, 9 May 1882, 5f: 'the man who called out to the draymen spoke with an English accent'.
[2] Spencer replied, 10 May, Add MS 44308, that he did not need more help.
[3] *Q.R.*, cliii. 552 (April 1882).
[4] Add MS 44643, f. 110.
[5] i.e. to ask for American action on the U.S. Irish press; Ramm II, i. 367.

Provisional sketch of Arrears Bill.

1. Limit of £30 [£25] valuation. 2. Compulsion: on ⟨the landlord⟩ application of either party. 3. Tenant to pay rent Nov. 80–81. 4. Land Commission to act on being satisfied through subcommissioner or County C. Judge of inability of tenant to pay. 5. Grant as against advance. 6. Grant not to exceed an moiety of arrears or one year's rent. 7. Arrears thereupon to be absolutely released. 8. Rateable distributions when arrears due to person other than landlord. 9. Court may assign to the year 80–1 any payment made during the year preceding Act. 10. Limit of Act June 30. ⟨82⟩ 83. ⟨11. Tenant able to pay in part, but not without injury to his means of cultivation, may receive loan to the extent of such part, without prejudice to other privilege under this Act—repayable in not more than 10 years, & payments to be collected with County Cess?⟩[1]

To W. SHAW, M.P., 10 May 1882. '*Private*'.   Add MS 44545, f. 134.

I take a great liberty in asking your advice as to the answer I should give to this letter—if you can give it. I shall quite understand if you cannot. My only reason is that while I have a high respect for Mr Smyth[2] I have not the advantage of personal acquaintance with him or means of appreciating his judgment.

In my view from the moment of becoming satisfied that *prospectively* we had no 'reasonable suspicion' of Mr. Parnell's inciting to crime by his action, we had (I speak in rough & general terms) no legal title whatever to keep the prison doors closed upon him.

To LORD SPENCER, Viceroy of Ireland, 10 May 1882.   Althorp MSS K5.

We have had a long and necessarily from the nature of the case a stiff Cabinet of four hours on the Prevention of Crime Bill—a good spirit on all sides has carried us through. I am rather afflicted at the quantity of matter in the Bill; but I presume this cannot be helped. The sense of hurry under which we are acting is a serious misfortune.

I send you herewith a *private* note sent me by O'Shea in regard to the Resident Magistrates and the Special Residents.

Arrangements will I hope be made to send you tonight the conclusions of the Cabinet as they stand that, should it be essentially necessary, you may have the opportunity of communicating with Harcourt by Telegraph.[3]

To E. L. STANLEY, M.P., 10 May 1882.   Add MS 44545, f. 136.

I thank you for the new encouragement which your letter affords.[4] It is a sharp edge at a dizzy height along which we have now to walk but I place undiminished and indeed enhanced reliance on that thorough comprehension of the situation by our great party which has been all along so remarkable, and of which your letter affords me a fresh proof.

11. Th. [Chatsworth]

Wrote to Mr Hamilton—Mr Marum MP.[5]—& minutes. Read American R.C. Q.R. on England's Retreat—Government for Ireland—Pope's temporal dominions[6]—

---

[1] Initialled and dated 10 May 1882; docketed: 'After Cabinet as amended, show to Mr. Welby. WEG May 13'; see 13 May 82.

[2] Letter untraced; possibly from W. R. Smythe of Killnean, whose sister was murdered in April; see *Cowper*, 559, 585.

[3] Spencer replied, 11 May, Add MS 44308, f. 242, that he had wired Harcourt but 'had no criticism to make upon the draft Bill'.   [4] Untraced.

[5] Edward Purcell Mulhallen Marum, 1827–90; nationalist M.P. Kilkenny 1880–90.

[6] *American Catholic Quarterly Review*, 11 (1882).

Gostwick on Germn Literature. 9.20–1.2. To Chatsworth by special train. Saw Ld Granville on Egypt—Ld Hartington—Edw. Talbot—Lady Emma C.—Lucy, & the Duke [of Devonshire]—Both wonderful under their several great griefs. At 2 we walked in sad & slow procession to the Church. E. Talbot officiated, admirably. The crowds may have reached 20,000. Their conduct was most touching. I drove back to avoid excitement: numbers rushed & ran with us. It is a great occasion: another tie snapped; and 'reversed our nature's kindlier doom'.

12. Fr. [London]

Lines forced their way into my head: I wrote down some at an early hour. After seeing the Duke & Lucy as well as Ld Hartington, we went off at 10.30 & reached D. St at 3 P.M. Audience of the Queen at 3.30. H of C. $4\frac{1}{4}$–5 & 9–12.[1] Saw The Speaker—W.H.G.—Mr Bright—Mr Chamberlain—Mr G—Mr H—Ld R.G. Read Gostwick on German Culture. Wrote to Mr M. Brooks MP—Mr Douglas—Mr Shaw MP—Ld Mayor of Dublin—Sec. Belgian Royal Acad.[2]—Ld Spencer—The Queen 1.1.—Mr Holmes MP.—and minutes.

To W. SHAW, M.P., 12 May 1882.   Add MS 44545, f. 136.

I think that perhaps conversation would more easily than writing convey as between us the character of our respective views.[3] I understand you to say that Mr. Parnell should have been released but that there should have been no new departure. But to release him without any fresh information as to his intentions would have been on *our* part a new departure of the gravest kind. Whether he is as far from us as ever at this moment I cannot say but he is as far as ever in regard to us, and I am not aware of the slightest limitation of our freedom in regard to him.

To LORD SPENCER, Viceroy of Ireland, 12 May 1882. '*Secret*'.   Althorp MSS K5.

I spent yesterday and also passed the night at Chatsworth where we left both Lucy & the Duke better than we could have hoped. Once in particular at the funeral he had to make great efforts. He was greatly soothed by the wonderful manifestation of feeling on the part of the vast crowds assembled.

I thank you for your great consideration about Herbert, and I am glad you begin to feel well manned, but your work seems to me immeasurable if I only consider three questions so large, so urgent, and requiring so much personal and responsible attention, as 1. Constabulary, 2. R[esident] Magistrates, 3. List of suspects—all being urgent, and the last not the least so. Herbert himself is most ready to take his place as one of your staff if you see cause.

I did not, of course, hear the introductory debate last night. It is a Bill of strong provisions, with strong safeguards. Some tell me the last were not put forward in perfect proportion to the first. Some say that the speeches of Forster & Goschen blew the coals as well as that of Chaplin, whose business it was.

I fear you are not able to take much care of yourself but I hope your strength will hold. Should you see cause to think your work cannot be so rapid and so soon wound up as we hoped at first, I reckon on your letting me know, as it might affect manipulation in the Cabinet.

---

[1] Business of the House; *H* 269. 558.   [2] Business untraced.
[3] No letter from Shaw found.

13. Sat.

Wrote to The Queen—Mr Chamberlain—Ld Spencer 1.1. & Tel.—Ld Houghton—Dean of Windsor—Mr A.C. Brown[1]—Mr Weaver—Scotts—Sir W. Harcourt—Miss Burke[2]—Prince of Wales—Duchess of Edinburgh. Cabinet 2–4½.
Saw Mr G—Ld R.G.—Mr Welby—Ld Carlingford—Ld Granville *cum* Ld Hartington. Drive & walk with [blank.] Saw Mrs Bolton [R]. Read Contemp. Rev.
on Ireland (2)—Samothrace—Scotch Disestablishment.[3]

Cabinet. Sat May 13. 82. 2. P.M.[4]
(d) 1. Arrears a. when? b. what? c. alone?
(a) 2. Egypt. agreed on a draft.[5] ask French to make known.[6]
(c) 3. Sunday opening. Open question.
(b) 4. Spencers Telegram. course approved.[7]
(c) 5. Jury Clauses to be inserted in Crime Prevention Bill in Committee.
     6. Extradition. Russia asks what has been given to the other Governments. Yes.

To J. CHAMBERLAIN, president of the board of trade,   Chamberlain MSS 5/34/11.
13 May 1882. '*Secret*'.

Referring to our conversation last night, I think there are some things we can & some
things we cannot expect from men who however strong their opinions on the Land question & Home Rule yet abhor outrage, & have no wish (like the murderers) to exasperate
the relations of Great Britain & Ireland.
    We cannot expect, if they think the Bill excessive that they should forbear to say so, or
should not try to amend it.
    What I think we may in reason expect is that they should renounce all idea of obstruc-
tion & consequently should take all detailed objections in the *Committee* where I am confident they might expect fair play after having given it.
    When I speak so seriously of obstruction, I am not thinking of the loss of time it causes:
at this moment it would lead to a resistless cry for a very severe urgency, & would
seriously embitter the entire situation & damage the prospect whatever it be of peace.
    If you see O'Shea before Thursday, please to thank him for his note to me, & I advise
your speaking to him in this sense so far as you agree.
[P.S.] Since I wrote this, I have had the inclosed from O'Shea. Please return it.

To LORD SPENCER, Viceroy of Ireland, 13 May 1882.   Althorp MSS K5.

1. I cannot think your speech open to any charge. It seems to me admirable alike in
respect of feeling & of judgment. Indeed I can only desire that with God's help you may
go on as you have begun.

[1] Alexander Crum Brown, 1838–1922; professor of chemistry, Edinburgh, 1869–1908; see Add
MS 44475, f. 145.
[2] Civil list pension for the sister of the murdered undersecretary.
[3] All in *C.R.*, xli (May 1882).   [4] Add MS 44643, f. 112.
[5] Freycinet on 12 May agreed to Anglo-French naval demonstration at Alexandria and that, if a
landing was necessary, Turkish troops under Ango-French control should pacify Egypt; Britain
hoped for a naval demonstration by the Concert; *Africa and the Victorians*, 102.
[6] Anglo-French demonstration announced on 15 May.
[7] 'In reply to a Telegram in which Lord Spencer proposes to deal gradually with the cases of such
suspects as can safely be released, the Cabinet expressed their concurrence and left the matter with
confidence in his hands'; CAB 41/16/25.

2. As to the Bill I feel confident of its general justness and appropriateness, & I think the feelings of the better men among those few who are alarmed at it will be modified when they see it in print and observe the careful safeguards. It certainly imposes very great responsibilities on the Lord Lieutenant at least while it continues to be an operative measure. I do not feel certain about the necessity of caution money for a newspaper, nor am I perfectly clear as to the reason why we take power to suppress *un*lawful meetings, which I should have thought we had: this is a point legal more than political; it is plain that unlawful meetings ought to be liable to suppression.

3. It is clear that we must override the Judges, & that their reluctance cannot avail them: unless indeed they produce reasons stronger than we have yet heard.

4. I am able to give Miss Burke a Civil List Pension of £300 a year.

5. The matter of Trevelyan had I think better stand over for decision. As I understand you, he might take his seat on the 18th. If so, there are 4 sitting days before Whitsuntide. They might be all Irish days. We cannot tell yet. The arrangements for his coming are that I think he ought, as an introduction to his work, to be associated in the face of Ireland with the Arrears Bill as a measure of conciliation; and secondly that his hand, which would not be a hard one, might be useful in the Committee on the Crime Prevention Bill. It *may* therefore be worth his while to make a run over, but this need not yet be decided.

6. I think you were quite right under the circumstances in letting Law continue his meeting. To stop it after the summons would have been a snub *in limine.*[1]

14. 5 S.E.

Chapel Royal mg, and [blank.] Read Gostwick on German Culture & Xty—Scrimgeour, Christ Crucified[2]—The Revisers of the Greek Text.[3] Dined with Mrs Heywood. Wrote to Lord Spencer—Lady Spencer—and minutes.

15. M.

Wrote to Ld Spencer—Sir H. Ponsonby—Ld Cowper—Ld Kimberley—Mr Hunter—Ld Rosebery—The Queen—Mr Beresford Hope—& minutes. H of C. 4½-8¼ and 9½-2: Introduced the Arrears Bill.[4] Saw Mr G—Ld RG—Ld Granville 1.1.—Sol. Gen Ireland—Mr Welby—Sir H. Thring—Mr Stewart MP—Mr Onslow Ford (Sculptor)[5]—Mr Chamberlain—Mr Mundella. Read A Demure Man on Channel Tunnel[6]—Waugh Lanc. Sketches.[7]

To A. J. B. BERESFORD-HOPE, M.P., 15 May 1882.   Add MS 44545, f. 139.

I thank you warmly for your kind note:[8] and indeed I rejoice, with cause, at the multiplying testimonies which every day produces to the excellence of the man whom we have lost.

[1] Partly printed in *Spencer*, i. 196.

[2] E. P. Scrymgour, *The doctrine of the Cross* (1882).

[3] *The Greek testament, with the readings adopted by the Revisers* (1881).

[4] *H* 269. 767. In questions, Parnell read his letter to O'Shea of 28 April, Forster demanding then supplying the final para. (though see Hammond, 289n.); Gladstone then stated that Parnell 'asked nothing from us, and he got nothing from us. On our side, we asked nothing and got nothing from him.' See *I.H.S.*, xviii. 86 and to Forster, 30 Apr. 82.

[5] Edward Onslow *Ford, 1852-1901; sculptor; this bust unveiled at the National Liberal Club, 1884; *T.T.*, 10 January 1884, 6b.

[6] Untraced pamphlet.

[7] E. Waugh, *Lancashire sketches* (1869).

[8] Of condolence, 14 May, Add MS 44213, f. 356.

He was a man unsurpassed, so far as my knowledge goes, in purity of character, or in soundness of judgment; and my love for him grew from year to year. Nor are tributes from your side of politics inappropriate: for such men purify the atmosphere of politics, and are of value to opponents as well as friends.

16. Tu.

Wrote to The Queen 1.1.—Ld Granville 1.1.—Mr Gurdon MP.—Dean of Windsor—Bp of Durham—Sir W. Harcourt—L. Cavendish—and minutes. Saw Mr G— Ld RG—Mr Chamberlain 1.1.—Lady Derby—Mr Onslow Ford (Sculptor). H of C. 2-5. Spoke on the sus[pect]s.[1] Dined with the W.H.G.s. Read Βιο-γραφία and Sir John Eliot's Letters.[2]

To Sir W. V. HARCOURT, home secretary, 16 May 1882.   MS Harcourt dep. Adds 10.

Chamberlain has kindly shown me the Healy amendments on the Bill against Crime, and he will now carry them to you.

I have not passed judgment on any in detail but I am agreeably surprised by their *fairness & mildness* as a whole.

To one I have a natural leaning, as I pressed it in the Cabinet (not successfully) viz. letting in the County Court Judge as more competent than the two resident Magistrates.

Evidently the mildness of the Tories has had an excellent effect on Healy & Co.

Tomorrow I conclude that Trevelyan and the Law Officers (Ireland) will see these amendments and I should like to consider with you whether the Cabinet should see them on Thursday.

[P.S.] You will see from the inclosed[3] that you have no choice in relation to the Lords Address

17. Wed.

Wrote to The Queen 1.1.—Sir W. Harcourt—Earl of Fife—Mr Fawcett—Helen Gladstone—Lady Derby—Crown Prince of Denmark[4]—and minutes. We dined with dear Lucy. Saw Mrs Bolton [R]. Calls—Mr G—Lord RG—Ld Granville—Mr Chamberlain—Sir Thos G.—Herbert J.G. Wrote a few verses on F.C's noble end.[5] Read War of Irish Confederation.[6]

To LADY DERBY, 17 May 1882.'*Private*'.   Add MS 44475, f. 156.

It is a horrid blow! Let me take the good side first. I do not mean that it looks like a political severance; for his letter[7] is all that we could desire, & is kindness itself.

Moreover, as I said yesterday, the ship is labouring in the waves, and though I have strong faith, and I hope an entire determination, I fully admit that an overture under such

[1] Replied to Balfour's strong attack; *H* 269. 837; see next day.
[2] Sir J. Eliot, *De jure maiestatis... and the Letter-Book*, ed. P. B. Grosart, 2v. (1882).
[3] Enclosed note from Selborne: either House has power to stop confirmation of statutes made by the commissioners.
[4] Comments on the Danish constitution; Add MS 44475, f. 157.
[5] Add MS 44766, ff. 83-95.   [6] See 11 Jan. 82.
[7] To Granville, this day, declining 'the very flattering offer' of a place in the Cabinet for 'purely private and personal' reasons; 'my confidence in the government is entire and unshaken'; Add MS 44141, f. 55.

circumstances is more like a request than an offer. And such a request there is a perfect title to decline, without either dispute or expostulation.

But it is a great public loss. His character, his powers, his influence, are comparatively neutralised where he is now, instead of telling, as they would have told in a measure proportioned to the stress & pressure of the times, that is to say a measure unusually full.

Besides and behind all this, I have two personal griefs: English griefs, not French *griefs*; first, it takes away my last hope of sitting in Cabinet with your husband. My hour-glass is all but run out. He will appear, when I disappear. My second grief is yet meaner & more personal. I was exulting in the notion of quitting my second office, the Chancellorship of the Exchequer, and thus becoming a little less unequal to the load on me, by an excellent arrangement. *Now*, I fear my other mode of change would dislocate without marked public advantage, & I must go straining & struggling on. The only comfort I can suggest is that you are not likely to see me too often at tea.

To HELEN GLADSTONE, 17 May 1882.   Hawarden MSS.

I cannot refrain from writing a line to tell you how vexed, I might also say cut to the heart, I am about Mr. Balfour's exhibition yesterday: the speech in which he charged the Government with infamy and falsehood, (in terms almost absolutely unveiled) and ended with the obstructive and most inadequate motion to adjourn the House.[1]

Do not suppose I am either personally wounded, or sorry for the Government. Such charges are advantageous to the objects of them.

But I am concerned, and also perplexed, for him—are his notions of conduct & social laws turned inside out, since the days when I knew him, enjoyed his hospitality, viewed him with esteem and regard, nay was wont to mate him with the incomparable F. Cavendish, now lost to our eyes but not our hearts, as the flower of rising manhood in the land? To see a man *like this* given over to the almost raving licence of an unbridled tongue does grieve me, and I cannot make light of it & do not wish I could, any more than I should if I saw someone rend the Madonna di San Sisto from top to bottom.

You may ask me what is the use of this. It is simply that I would ask you to say as much (or as little) of this as you can, & think proper, either to his sister,[2] or to Mr. Sidgwick—they will at least know that it cannot possibly be insincere.

We are going to dine with the dear Lucy at her special request.

Matters are not unhopeful in Ireland; except as to the non-discovery.

[P.S.] I was (so far) glad to hear that it was unpremeditated, and solicited by his friends.

To Sir W. V. HARCOURT, home secretary, 17 May 1882.   MS Harcourt dep. 8, f. 135.

There is only one matter in your forcible letter[3] on which I differ, and that is comparatively unimportant I believe in its bearing on the Crime Bill—your estimate of the Resident Magistrates,[4] whom however we ought not to damage, but about whom I think my means of forming a judgment have during the last two years been not inconsiderable. I feel certain that your estimate is very different from that of Spencer who believes no very small proportion of them to be decidedly below the mark. Forster is I think of the same mind.

---

[1] Balfour claimed the govt. 'stood alone in its infamy', had 'degraded' the executive & had 'negotiated with treason'; Gladstone claimed the charges 'disgraceful only to those who make them'; *H* 269. 837.

[2] i.e. Eleanor Sidgwick, Helen's Principal at Newnham, Cambridge.

[3] Of this day, Add MS 44197, f. 54, on the Crimes Bill.

[4] 'Excellent men . . . the backbone of order'; ibid.

As to your arguments I adopt them pretty much in the lump. What I am anxious for—and you will admit that my responsibility in the matter is considerable—is

1. The speedy passing of the Bill in its general lines unaltered.

2. That whatever we accept or refuse it should be done in a kindly tone towards the Irish members, until, by a new start in offending, through obstruction or otherwise, they force us to adopt a different course.

3. That their amendment(s) should be judged on their merits & not on the ground that any concession is bad *ipso facto* if made to them.

4. That in cases where their suggestions are inadmissible, we should not be prevented from considering whether there is any other form of amendment. For example I adopt your argument against the *press* amendment. But I do not like the caution money, and when it was passed in the Cabinet I had no idea that the forfeiture would be a merely executive & discretionary act. I quite agree with you on the intimidation amendment. But I suppose you have well considered a point which it would be hard for me to pronounce upon—is *any* new definition of intimidation necessary, or might intimidation be dealt with like fair rent?

It would be a good thing if we could find any point which the Irish thought to be of *great* importance, and we thought to be of *small* importance on which we might meet them.

[P.S.] Please to consider with me on your return from Windsor whether there need be a Cabinet tomorrow.

18. *Th. Ascension Day.*[1]

St Margaret's m. service & H.C. Ten to breakfast. Saw Mr G—Ld R.G.—Herbert J.G.—Mr A. Morley—William H.G.—Mr Knowles. H. of C. $4\frac{1}{2}$–$8\frac{1}{4}$ and $9\frac{1}{2}$–1.[2] Read War of the Confederation: Æneid. Wrote to Dean of Windsor—Ld M[ayor] of London—The Queen 1.1.1.

19. *Fr.*

Wrote to Bp of Durham—Mr E.A. Budge—Ld Bath—A.G. for Ireland—Ld Rosebery—L. Cavendish—The Queen 1.1.—Sir J. Holker[3]—& minutes. H. of C. 2–5, 6–7, $9\frac{1}{2}$–$1\frac{1}{4}$. Spoke on Crime Prevention Bill.[4] Saw Mr G—Ld RG—Mr Courtney *cum* Mr Trevelyan—Lord Granville—Mr Errington. Read War of the Confederation—Henry VI. Part 1.

20. *Sat.* [*Dollis Hill*]

Wrote to Ld Halifax—Bp of Moosonnee[5]—Ld Kimberley—Sir Thos G.—Sir R. Lingen—Ld Spencer—Mrs Heywood—Mr Forster—Rev. E. Wilberforce—and minutes. At 4 to Dollis Hill[6] for Sunday. Saw Mr G—Ld RG—Mr Onslow Ford—Ld Granville—Lucy Cavendish—Miss Talbot—Mrs Th. Read Häckel on

[1] For Catherine Gladstone's mem. of her meeting with Lady Derby on Derby's joining the govt., see *Autobiographica*, iv. 60.

[2] Questions; Crimes Bill; *H* 269. 956.

[3] Sir John Holker, b. 1828; resigned this day as lord justice of appeal and d. 24 May.

[4] *H* 269. 1116.

[5] In Canada: John Horden; see Add MS 44475, f. 181.

[6] Aberdeen's Regency villa by Willesden, used frequently by the Gladstones, the telephone exchange for this area being later named GLAdstone.

Creation[1]—B. Jerrold on Egypt[2]—and Jebb's Bentley.[3] Worked a little on F.C. Verses.

To LORD HALIFAX, 20 May 1882.					Halifax MSS A/4/88.

I have to thank you for both your kind notes:[4] and some day I hope we may have the pleasure of talking about the noble companion & friend so early lost.

I also thank you for your comforting assurances. That we, & that I, have nothing to conceal, I hope to find an opportunity of showing in an emphatic way. In our opinion Forster has made a grievous mistake: & may even unconsciously have been influenced by the change in his position. When once the evidence was put before us, we had not a shadow of *right* to keep Parnell in prison.

The Parliamentary atmosphere is clearing, and Spencer is working admirably. I should have difficulty in naming another man, all things considered, so fit for the manifold exigencies of the place.

Parnell has given us as yet no reason to complain. His speech yesterday was the very best he could have made. There is fear of a cave against him.

To LORD SPENCER, Viceroy of Ireland, 20 May 1882.					Althorp MSS K5.

Please to consider this letter of Selborne's with reference to the Irish part. According to my recollection Fitzgerald would as *Peer* be far less presentable and efficient than Sullivan.

For the first time the Irish answered to the call yesterday, wisely alarmed about the effect a mistake might have on the Arrears Bill. Parnell made the very best speech he could. Mitchell Henry abused him for his mild language about the Bill! The Parliamentary sky is clearer. I continue to watch all your sayings & doings with pleasure. If you are not the right man in the right place, there is none. On Monday we shall see the Amendments to the Crime Bill. In considering what may be admissible or otherwise pray remember that facilities for speedy passage now *may* be a most important element as compared with time to be spent on renewal years hence.[5]

21. S. aft. Ascn.

Willesden Ch St Mary's mg, & H.C.—Admirable Sermon, Mr Wharton.[6] Worked on F.C. Verses. Read Häckel on Creation—Gostwick on Germ. Culture—Gaume on the Good Robber.[7]

22. M. [London]

Off to London 10.30. Wrote to Mr E.G. Salisbury—Ld Spencer—The Queen— and minutes. Saw Mr G—Ld RG—Mr Chamberlain—Ld Carlingford[8]—Irish Law Officers. H. of C. $4\frac{1}{2}$–8 and $10\frac{1}{2}$–$3\frac{1}{4}$. Spoke on arrears; & in the night wrangle.[9] Read War of the Confederation. No (?) sleep till 6 A.M. of

---

[1] E. H. P. A. Haeckel, *The history of creation*, 2v. (1876).
[2] W. B. Jerrold, *Egypt under Ishmael Pasha* (1879).					[3] R. C. Jebb, *Richard Bentley* (1876).
[4] Of 10 and 19 May, Add MS 44183, f. 187, on Cavendish.
[5] Spencer urged a stiff attitude to amndts. to the bill; *Spencer*, i. 200.
[6] Joseph Crane Wharton, vicar of Willesden.
[7] J. J. Gaume, *Life of the good thief* (1882).
[8] Conclave and decision to persuade Gladstone not to second Northcote if he moved for a cttee. on Kilmainham; Carlingford diary, Add MS 63690.					[9] *H* 269. 1268.

23. Tues.

Wrote to Mr Ayrton—The Queen 1.1.1.—Mr Vernon—Mr Barclay—Mr Aylmer—The Speaker—Mrs O'Shea—and minutes. H of C. 2-7 (Procedure & arrears) & 9½-12¼ Crime Bill.[1] Cabinet 12-2. Saw Mr Whitbread *cum* Ld Tavistock. Saw Mr G—Ld RG—Mr Gibson—Ld Kimberley—Ld Granville. Read Bentley's Life.

Cabinet. Tues. May 23. 82. Noon.[2]

1. 8 Sub commissioners invited to attend Lords Committee.[3] Application from Commissioners.

   If commissioners think fit to represent the great inconvenience & interference with statutory duties, & to say they must recommend their Sub Commissioners to decline any voluntary attendance while [blank].
2. Wolff's question.[4] No production of letter. No Committee—challenge of every kind to be made.
3. Lowther's letter. Extract read.
4. Arrears Bill. Is tenant right to be an asset or is inability to be irrespective of it. What shall Childers say? a. That the object is to keep the tenant in his farm. b. as a going farm. c. Judge will have power to consider whether the tenant right shd. be charged.
5. Davitt's speech.[5] Question to Harcourt. No step to be taken. (Same under late Govt.)
6. Under Reserve Act, no provision for calling Parlt. if not sitting. To be proposed that same condition shd apply as in the case of the Militia—i.e. call Parlt. in ten days.
7. Select Comm. on Arrears Bill. (Hartington) *No.*

To Mrs O'SHEA, 23 May 1882.   Add MS 44269, f. 79.

I thank you for your very frank letter,[6] and I will be equally frank in reply, nor will I be less secret than you ask of me—no one being aware of your letter but myself.

I have no prejudice, and no recollection which should hinder my seeing Mr Parnell for a public object. I have thought it my duty, ever since arriving at the conclusion that there was no longer any warrant for detaining him within prison doors, carefully to avoid any act or word that could injure his position or weaken his hands in doing good. But, applying this criterion to your request, I am clearly of opinion, as at present advised, that a private interview between him & myself would have this very effect. It might also impair my means of action, but of this I see less cause to think at the present moment.

On this ground only, and because I can see no countervailing advantage to compensate for a serious mischief, I do not think I ought to see him in the manner you have described.

[1] *H* 269. 1448.
[2] Add MS 44643, f. 113.
[3] i.e. on the workings of the Land Act.
[4] Asking for publication of Gladstone's letter to Forster on the Kilmainham affair. 'Mr G. brought on his idea of offering to appear before a Select Committee to disprove the "compact" with Parnell. Cabinet all agst. it, & he gave it up'; Carlingford's diary, 23 May 1882, Add MS 63690.
[5] In Manchester, on 20 May, on expropriation of landlords.
[6] Of this day, Add MS 44269, f. 75, offering to arrange a meeting between Gladstone and Parnell at Eltham or elsewhere, the letter not to be mentioned 'to *anyone.* I have not, and shall not even to Captain O'Shea'.

24. Wed

Wrote to The Queen 1.1.—Mr Justice Fitzgerald—Mr Justice Bowen—Ld Granville Tel.—Ld Spencer—& minutes. Saw Mr G—Ld RG—Sir C. Dilke—Mr
Marum—Mr Courtney—Capt Lyttelton—The Speaker. Dined with Lucy Cavendish. Read B. Jerrold on Egypt. H of C. 12¼-3 and 3½-5. Spoke on Dillon &
Illegality.[1] Saw Lady Derby & wrote Mem.[2]

To LORD SPENCER, Viceroy of Ireland, 24 May 1882.   Althorp MSS K5.

The plot thickens in Parliament about the Crime Bill. On the one hand various
speeches, especially legal ones, and among them not Russell only but Mr. Cohen, a
closely attached supporter and perhaps typical man, fostered pretty sharp criticism &
demand for a good deal of change in Committee.[3] On the other hand, Dillon, in I think
the worst Irish speech I ever heard, lifted the barrier at once of illegality and of revolt
from Parnell. This outrageous speech which I followed at once in the debate, has rallied
to the Bill a considerable mass of opinion on one side, and increased I hope & think the
fulness of determination to pass it. I mean to pass it unimpaired in essence; but this may
admit of much questioning & even objection on particulars.

Your own remarks are conceived I think in a temper entirely reasonable & considerate,
and I do not apprehend any *great* difficulty except that of time which grows rather
rapidly. I read Mr. Naish's paper with pleasure.[4]

How good of you to find time to apologise for your writing; but you should do this to
men who write copper-plate, not to me. The wonder is how you write at all, and how you
compass your immense work without ever losing balance. May your strength continue.

Parnell has thus far run quite true but it seems doubtful whether he can hold his ground.
The Tories, & I am sorry to add Forster, have done much to increase his difficulties.

25. Th.

Wrote to The Queen 1.1.—Ch. Justice Morris—E. Wilberforce (Tel.)—Mr M.
Hussy MP.—Mrs O'Shea—Mr Peel—Mr Caird—Mr Childers—Mr Vernon—and
minutes. H of C. 4½-8¼ and 9½-1¼.[5] Eight to breakfast. Saw Mr G—Ld RG—Ld
Granville—Sir J. Lacaita. Read Shakesp. Henry VI—B. Jerrold on Egypt.

26. Fr.

Wrote to The Queen 1.1.—Dean of Windsor—Mrs Th.—and minutes. H of C.
2¼-6½. Spoke on Egypt.[6] Saw Mr G—Lord R.G—Ld Granville *cum* Sir C. Dilke—
do alone. Saw Mrs Bolton [R]. Read Henry VI (finished II)—B. Jerrold's Egypt
(finished)—Life of Bentley.

[1] Dillon claimed the bill was 'calculated to drive the oppressed poor in Ireland into secret combination and into crime'; Gladstone called his speech 'heartbreaking'; *H* 269. 1548.
[2] Further attempt, unsuccessful for the time being, to reconstruct the ministry *via* Derby's accession; *Autobiographica*, iv. 60. See 16–17 May 82.
[3] See 18 Mar. 58 and *H* 269. 1575.
[4] John Naish, Dublin Castle's legal adviser; worked on the bill, see *Spencer*, i. 191.
[5] Crimes Bill; *H* 269. 1617.
[6] When questioned by Lawson, whom Gladstone assured there was not 'the slightest belief in my
own mind that there is any probability of an occasion arising for the employment of force';
H 269. 1714.

27. *Sat.* [*The Durdans*]

Off at 9.50 to the Durdans. Saw Mr Godley. Drive & conversation with Ld R[osebery]. Wrote to The Queen—Mr Welby—Ld Kimberley—& minutes. Read Jebbs Bentley—Froude's Carlyle—A.B. Wildered Parishioner.[1]

To LORD KIMBERLEY, colonial secretary, 27 May 1882.   Add MS 44545, f. 145.

I agree with everything, I think that is contained in your private letter to Bulwer.[2]

The refusal of responsible Government in Natal, though not in itself a good, seems to be a godsend for the moment, as it leaves us freedom of action. The only thing which makes me uneasy is the question of time. I may have got into confusion about dates, & may mis-measure possibilities, but I was in hopes that by or about this time we should have received Bulwer's opinion on the return of Cetewayo. Instead of that is opened a prospect of his visiting Zululand.

And after all he is the judge of what is necessary to provide him with adequate materials and grounds for a report. But the 'sliding' of affairs for so considerable a time is as you intimate a great evil & danger—and there is another point—which weighs upon my mind. The burden of proof lies upon that side of the argument, which is against Cetewayo, not on that in his favour. What right have we to detain him? for if we set him free I take it for granted that, quite apart from any question of our being the agents in restoring him, he would go into the country at once, & fight his own way.

My answer to the question I have put would be, we have no right at all, unless we have solid reason to believe that the interest of Zululand requires it. If the interest of Zululand does not require it, if its condition is not better now, but worse,—as I rather suppose?—than it was under Cetewayo—I can hardly suppose that we have engagements towards the present batch of chiefs which justify our detaining him.

As we cannot act without Bulwer's definitive report, which his interesting dispatch does not give, I should rather recommend your telegraphing to say we hope that when he does report, he will report not only on the abstract question whether he should be restored, (or allowed to act for himself) or not, but likewise on the question what *modus operandi* is to be adopted by us in the event of our effecting, aiding, or allowing, his restoration.

And yet, he does not even feel able to reach the point of saying whether the party for, or the party against, is the stronger.

28. *Whits.*

Ch. & H.C. 11 A.M: and no more. Saw Granville early & long on Egypt. Wrote to Ld Granville—Ld Kimberley—Mrs Macarthur—Mr Dodson—& minutes. Party small, & pleasant: Mr Smalley, Mr Trafford.[3] Read A.B. Wildered (finished)—Gostwick, German Culture—Ld Grey on Ireland(!)[4]

29. *M.*

Wrote to Ld Spencer—Ld Granville Tel. 1.1.1. & 1.1.1.—Mr Sidgwick—Mr Salisbury & minutes. Drive to the noble view at Betchworth. Conversation with R &

[1] 'The Ritualist's Progress . . . by A. B. Wildered, parishioner' (1875).

[2] Sent on 26 May, Add MS 44227, f. 166, but not found; cf. Kimberley's wire of 3 June requesting Bulwer's report and proposing Cetewayo's restoration; Bulwer prevaricated until 29 July, then accepted restoration in part of Zululand only, with provisos; *PP* 1883 xlix. 513.

[3] G. W. Smalley, American journalist (see 15 Feb. 72); Trafford unidentified.

[4] In *N.C.*, xi. 977 (June 1882).

the pleasant guests. Read Froude's Carlyle—Jebb's Bentley. Touched the verses a little: but they require much care & slow handling.[1]

30. Tu.

Wrote to D of Argyll—Bp of Durham—Mr Woolner—Sir W. Harcourt—Ld Coleridge—Ld Chancellor Tel.—Sir G. Prevost—C.S. Palmer—Dr Taylor—Ld Granville Tel. & l.—and minutes. Read Froude's Carlyle—O'Grady's Cuculain.[2] Went to Mr Dixon's & saw his solemn wood of yews (Cherkley).[3] Much conversation.

To Sir G. PREVOST, canon of Gloucester, 30 May 1882.   Add MS 44545, f. 146.

I thank you for your letter and inclosure[4] and I am very glad to see such signs of healthful interest, over a wide circle, in the important question of the Ecclesiastical Courts. For my own part I am much more anxious to see what is bad, in this matter, put down or paralysed, than what is good, or in theory correct, established and put in operation.

This sounds paradoxical: but I have long felt that, in the time to come, religion and religious bodies must rely much more upon moral authority and suasion, than upon penal, coercive, or strictly judicial proceedings. A Lord Penzance turned against the Church Association and its abettors would I think be a misfortune.[5] It is better that they should quietly die out, and die out probably they will. Their hold on the religious intelligence of the country grows weaker from day to day. Without the provocation given by the Roman secessions I doubt whether they could ever have existed: and that plague I trust has ceased, whatever other plagues may still be active.

I have paid no attention, for a good while, to the [Deceased] Wife's Sister Bill: but I presume it is still framed on the old lines and prohibits ecclesiastical marriages. I am not sure that more can be done. What you say of E. Wilberforce pleases me much. The appointment was one not to be filled at hap-hazard. Pray recollect how happy we should be to see you either at Hawarden or at a Thursday breakfast in London.

31. Wed.

Wrote to The Queen—Mr A. Arnold—Sir C. Dilke—Bp of Winchester—Dean of Windsor—Ld Spencer—& minutes. 1–5¼. To London for Cabinet on Egypt. H[artingto]n stiff & difficult. Saw Mr G.—Ld Granville—Ld Rosebery—Ld Tenterden—Ld G. cum Ld T. & Sir C. Dilke. Read Froude's Carlyle—Dr Taylor Covenanters.[6]

Cabinet. Wed. May 31. 82. 2 PM.[7]
1. Egypt. Shall we agree to the French proposal?[8] Much discussion Hartington opposing.

[1] On Cavendish; see 17 May 82n.
[2] S. J. O'Grady in *Early bardic literature, Ireland* (1879).
[3] Abraham Dixon, 1815–1907, of Cherkley Court, Surrey.
[4] Printed memorial to abp. of Canterbury requesting repeal of the Public Worship Regulation Act; Add MS 44475, f. 196.
[5] James Plaisted *Wilde, 1816–99; cr. Baron Penzance 1869; as judge and Dean of Arches administered Public Worship Act, being blamed for its ineffectiveness. The evangelical Church Association encouraged litigation against ritualists.
[6] J. Taylor, *Scottish covenanters* (1881).
[7] Add MS 44643, f. 117. Gladstone noted as absent Spencer, Harcourt, Carlingford, Childers.
[8] For a Conference at Constantinople; Britain participated; Ramm II, i. 376ff.

2. Spain. Measures may be taken by F.O. in concert with C.O. as to wine. Profess readiness to modify Tariff when revenue permits, perhaps more largely than the mere 28° v. 26°.

3. Cetewayo. Telegram with a view to settlement approved.[1]

4. Scotch Entails. Bill may go on.

Justice to the public, even more than to myself, convinces me that I ought to make an effort to obtain an efficient Chancellor of the Exchequer.

Derby is off.

Childers remains for C. of E. ship: W.O. might be offered to Goschen.

I am disposed to say a few words of intimation here. May 31. 82. [Gladstone]

I agree. H[artington].[2]

To Sir C. W. DILKE, foreign undersecretary, 31 May 1882.   Add MS 43875, f. 102.

I have spoken to Lord Granville on the Spanish matter, and have read (in Lord G.s temporary absence) your memorandum[3] to the Cabinet.

The Cabinet think that it will be proper to take all reasonable measures for dealing with the question of Gibraltar smuggling, particularly as to Tobacco: and Lord Kimberley will be ready to concert with you the proper terms in which the F.O. can make known this intention to Spain.

We cannot at this moment disturb the Wine Duties even to the extent of £60,000 per annum: for we are actually increasing the Carriage Duties to meet the absolute wants of the Treasury for the year. But you are quite at liberty to say that, so soon as financial circumstances will allow, we are disposed to modify our system of Wine Duties in a manner favourable to Spain which would probably include, or perhaps go beyond, the modification demanded. This if it is understood, that upon the basis now described, by reciprocal voluntary arrangement, we shall have extended to us the m.f.n. Clause. Of course there is no admission that Spain has a *grievance* under our present scale of Wine Duties.

Thurs. June One. 1882. [*London*]

Wrote to Mr Barclay M.P.—Mr Goschen—Ld Ripon—Rev. Dr Grant—and minutes. Read Froude's Carlyle—Jebb's Bentley. Left before 3 after this pleasant holiday, even to the last moment. Saw Mr G—Ld RG—Ld Granville—Ld Reay—Mr F. Leveson. H. of C. 4–8½ and 9½–1¼. Crime Bill. In wh we have asked rather overmuch.[4]

To G. J. GOSCHEN, M.P., 1 June 1882. '*Secret*'.   Add MS 44161, f. 282.

I am now in a condition to submit your name to the Queen for the War Secretaryship of State; if as I hope the difficulty which kept us apart at a former period is now removed, and if as I also hope your will consents to my request.

I refer, of course, to the question of the County Suffrage: as to which I have understood but I cannot say authoritatively, that your vote on the adjournment of Mr A. Arnold's motion or rather debate, signified that you thought the time had come, when the principle might properly be admitted.

[1] See 27 May 82.
[2] Holograph note passed to Hartington; Add MS 44643, f. 120.
[3] Of this day, on smuggling at Gibraltar; Add MS 44149, f. 77.
[4] *H* 269. 1924.

Undoubtedly the position of the Government upon this question is unchanged: and I think it is our decided opinion that it should be settled during and by the present Parliament. This means, that it should be taken in hand not later than the year after next, so as to have a year to spare in case of accidents. *Next* year I hope will be devoted to effectual dealing with the question of Local Government. I will not excuse myself for writing to you on the strength of information not demonstrative; because I am sure you will ascribe the act to its true cause, my desire (and I am certain that of my Colleagues) again to reckon you among those confidentially associated with the Government in the discharge of public duty at this important crisis.[1]

To LORD RIPON, Viceroy of India, 1 June 1882.   Add MS 43515, f. 11.

I cannot sufficiently thank you for the most kind & acceptable letter with which you have followed up your telegram[2] on the subject of the deplorable massacre of May 6 in Phoenix Park.

The black act brought indeed a great personal grief to my wife & me; but we are bound to merge our own sorrow in the larger & deeper affliction of the widow & the father, in the sense of the public loss of a life so valuable to the nation, & in the consideration of the great & varied effects it may have on immediate & vital interests.

Since the death of this dearly loved son, we have heard much good of the Duke, whom indeed we saw at Chatsworth after the funeral & we have seen much of Lucy his wife, which has been good éven beyond what we could have hoped.

I have no doubt you have heard in India the echo of words spoken by Spencer from a letter of his in which she said she could give even him, if his death were to work good to his fellow-men, which indeed was the whole object of his life.

These words have had a tender effect, as remarkable as the horizon excited by the slaughter. Spencer wrote to me that a priest in Connemara read them from the altar: when the whole congregation spontaneously fell down upon their knees.

In England, the national attitude has been admirable. The general strain of language has been 'do not let this terrible and flagitious crime deter you from persevering with the work of justice['].

On the whole, I am hopeful of the immediate future of Ireland in the main point, that is bringing all her desires & all her controversies upon the safe ground of peace & legality. So far as our limited experience has gone, outrage has been visibly diminishing in quantity & in flagrancy. The hold of the Land Act on the country grows stronger, & its execution more sensibly rapid & efficient.

Forster's judgment, had we followed it, would have led us into indescribable error & mischief.

Again let me thank you heartily for all the good & salutary words of your letter, & as heartily I return them. Also with Lady Ripon accept my best thanks for your kindness to my son Harry, who I hope is not undeserving of it.

[P.S.] I am so glad to hear of no further interruptions to your health & the excellent work for which you employ it.

2. Fr.

Wrote to Lady Derby—Mr S. Gladstone—Prof. Jebb—Mr A. Mitchell—The Queen—Sir H. Verney—& minutes. Saw Mr G—Ld RG—Ld Granville l.l.—Mrs

---

[1] Goschen replied next day, Add MS 44161, f. 284, his views on the suffrage unchanged, thus unable to accept office.

[2] Letter untraced; telegram at Add MS 44286, f. 270.

O'Shea[1]—Ld Hartington—Mr Bright. H of C. $4\frac{1}{4}$-$8\frac{1}{4}$ & $9\frac{1}{4}$-1.[2] Read Jebb's Bentley finished—Froude's Carlyle (II).

3. Sat. [The Durdans]

Wrote to Earl of Cork—Dean of Windsor—The Queen l.l.—Mr Whitbread—Lucy Cavendish—& minutes. Went to the Costa Exhibition.[3] Saw Mr C.—Mr Watts. To the Durdans at midnight. Saw Mr G—Ld R.G.—Ld Granville—Mr Childers—Christies. Entertained my [Queen's] Birthday Company at dinner, & both parties afterwards. The Prince kind & sociable as ever. Read Froude's Carlyle—Recollections of Emerson.[4]

If Carlyle was vain, it was not with a vulgar vanity. If he was selfish, if intolerant, or whatever faults there were, they were always idiosyncratic: so powerful an individuality overspread them all. It is this individuality which attracts, even more than genius. It is, more profoundly and intimately than genius, what we are. Why is it that Johnson attracts and interests more than almost any other person in our literary history: than almost any, for I am not sure if there be any exception unless it be Shakespeare, more for example than Scott or Dryden or Coleridge or Spenser or Pope: not because his treasure of genius was greater but because he presented a more powerful and more deeply cut individuality. Hence I find Carlyle to exercise a great attractive force upon me while I cannot recognise him as just or wise though he shows me, in lucid or lurid light as the case may be, fragments both of justice and of wisdom.

Though ever sensible of weakness, conflict, or depression in himself, he was as towards the outer world and the public, wonderfully αὐτάρκης.[5]

4. Trin. S.

The church at 11 AM with HC and $6\frac{1}{2}$ P.M. Read Gostwick. Long Church & Theol. conversation with Mr MacColl. Conversation with Sir W. Harcourt.

5. M. [London]

Wrote to Ld Chancellor—Abp of Canterby—The Queen l.l.—Ld Chancr Law—Mrs Bolton—and minutes. H of C. $4\frac{3}{4}$-$8\frac{1}{2}$ and 10-$12\frac{3}{4}$.[6] Drive with C. Back to London at noon. Saw Mr G—Ld R.G.—Ld Granville cum Ld Northbrook—Mr West—Mr Whitbread[7]—Mr Bright. Read Gostwick (finished)—G. Smith on Cobden & Peel[8]—Mitchell on Dalkeith.[9]

6. Tu.

Wrote to Miss de Lisle—Ld Bessborough—Mr Trevelyan—Ld Granville—The Queen—Lucy C.—and minutes. Wrote out & sent to Lucy [Cavendish] my

---

[1] Her first interview with Gladstone; see O'Shea, Parnell, i. 269-70.   [2] Crimes Bill; H 269. 1941.
[3] Exhibition of paintings by 'Signor Costa' at the Fine Art Society; T.T., 5 June 1882, 1e.
[4] Probably M. D. Conway, Emerson at home and abroad (1882).
[5] 'sufficient in himself'; holograph dated 3 June 1882; Add MS 44766, f. 82.
[6] Crimes Bill: H 270. 83.
[7] Failing to persuade him to join the cabinet; Bahlman, Hamilton, i. 284.
[8] N.C., xi. 869 (June 1882).
[9] A. Mitchell, Political and social movements in Dalkeith from 1831 to 1882 (privately printed, 1882).

verses on May 6, 1882. Saw Mr G—Ld RG—Ld Granville—Mr Hine—Mrs Bolton (better news)—Ld Hartington 1.1.—Scotts—Mr Arthur Peel—Mr Bright—Mr Childers. Read Emerson's Remains.—Froude's Carlyle.

7. Wed.

Wrote to The Queen 1.1.—Mr Chamberlain—and minutes. H of C. $12\frac{1}{4}$-6. Spoke on Intimidation.[1] Saw Mr G—Ld RG—Sig. Morelli[2]—Mr Bright—Ld Mount Temple—Mr K. Mackenzie—Mr Burne Jones. Dined at Mr Grahams. Finished Emerson—Read Froude's Carlyle.

8. Th.

Wrote to Sir W. Harcourt—Ld Kimberley—Mr Shaw MP—Lord C.J. May—Mr Mitchell—Mr Chamberlain—The Queen—Lucy Cavendish—& minutes. Read Froude's Carlyle—Mitchell's Dalkeith. Saw Mr H—Lord R.G.—Lord Granville—Mr Shaw—Mr Chamberlain—W.H.G.—Att. General. Saw our baby grandchild Evelyn: & was charmed with her. H of C. $4\frac{3}{4}$-$8\frac{1}{2}$ and $9\frac{1}{2}$-$1\frac{1}{4}$.[3]

To J. CHAMBERLAIN, president of the board of trade,   Chamberlain MSS 5/34/12.
8 June 1882. '*Private*'.

There are one or two things which, if you have a convenient opportunity of time and place, I think you might usefully say to Mr Parnell, as your own opinions, if they are your own opinions, and if you think proper so to do.[4]

1. It seems to me plain that any covenant as to policy on Irish affairs with Irish members is inadmissible as it would act prejudicially in respect to its own purpose: and even that intentions are to be more safely observed and defined, as a general rule, than indicated.

2. I am *very anxious* it should be borne in mind by those whom it concerns that the greatest mischief will arise from any undue, or even any very great prolongation of the proceedings in committee on the Crime Prevention Bill. Yesterday made it quite obvious, if it was doubtful before, that a certain number of Irish members (following a practice at present by no means confined to small minorities) intend not merely to protest and argue, which would be quite fair and right, but in the event of not obtaining their way to punish the House of Commons for differing from them by the consumption of its greatest treasure, its time.

Ordinarily this is a punishment safe to those who inflict it, as well as most severe to those who suffer it and to the country at large.

But in this instance it will react powerfully on the Arrears Bill and upon all other legislation possible for Ireland.

Upon the Arrears Bill first and specially.

The time is very near at hand when we *must* return to the consideration of supply. Our first duty is to finish the present Committee if we can. I begin to fear, from the excessive time consumed at every step, that when this is done we shall be compelled to take

[1] In dispute with Dillon; *H* 270. 391.
[2] Perhaps Charles Francis Morelli, 1800–82; a director of Covent Garden.
[3] Questions; Crimes Bill; *H* 270. 490.
[4] Chamberlain explained a press cutting on a 'conference of some length' with Parnell in the lobby as the result of an accidental meeting; Parnell anxious for a concession on report stage of the Crimes Bill; Add MS 44125, f. 145.

Supply. The Tories when they have got the Crime Bill may not openly oppose the Arrears Bill but *through the medium* of *Supply* they can postpone it *ad libitum*, and with it whatever else lies behind it.

Thus the delay and defeat of Irish legislation will be the work of those who are now beginning to obstruct the Crimes Bill.

All this I was writing when your letter came in, inclosing one from Labouchere.

It is not for me to take any notice of what some would call the threat that things may revert to what they were under the Forster *régime*. My duty is only to examine what Justice requires us to do towards promoting harmony and forwarding business.

Sir W. Harcourt stated yesterday with the utmost clearness that we must and will ask for the fourth Clause in such a form as to put down boycotting. I wish Mr L. had heard Mr Davey's excellent speech yesterday. I think Mr Synan's was in the same sense.

The Home Secretary stated not less clearly our disposition to consider without prejudice any amendment compatible with the full attainment of this object.

I believe that in the matter of what is called *coercion* my appetite is decidedly less keen than the average appetite even of English Liberals, and even of pretty stout ones. But nothing would induce me to assent to a Clause doing less as to boycotting than what I have now said.

I quite agree that we ought to come as promptly as we can to our conclusions as to any amendment of the Clause that may be proposed. But how can this be done while we are compelled by Biggar & Co. to waste our precious hours on a preliminary and now perfectly barren debate?[1]

To Sir W. V. HARCOURT, home secretary, 8 June 1882.   MS Harcourt dep. 8, f. 141.

I send herewith for your perusal.

1. A note of this morning from Chamberlain[2] with copy of a letter of Labouchere's which it inclosed.

2. A letter from me to C. partly conceived & written before his note arrived, partly in answer to it—I have read this. Our first obligation is to keep the body & substance of our enactment intact: our next to do simply & promptly as far as may be whatever is allowable to be done at all in meeting views like those of Davey.

The 'situation' is very complex and difficult & I am desirous you should know what occurs to me upon it.

9. *Fr.*

Wrote to Sir W. Gregory—Ld Granville—Ld Spencer—Mr Childers—Mrs Th—Mr Chamberlain—The Queen—and minutes. Saw Messrs Davidson—Mr H—Ld R.G. (2)—Ld Granville—Sol. General—Mr Chamberlain *cum* Sol. Gen.—Sir W. Harcourt: with whom there was a short breeze, on the Bill. H of C. $4\frac{1}{4}$-$8\frac{1}{4}$ & $9\frac{1}{4}$-$12\frac{1}{2}$.[3] Read Mitchell's Dalkeith Life—Froude's Carlyle.

1. Except that I do not see how the Queen's Government can be assenting parties to those few words of Col. Brackenbury's p. 7[4] that sanction shall be given to illegal acts

---

[1] In Chamberlain, *Political memoir*, 67.

[2] Dated this day, MS Harcourt dep. 8, f. 143, on negotiations with Parnell.

[3] Crimes Bill; *H* 270. 666. Harcourt felt 'the Party were beginning to say that he [Gladstone] was lukewarm on the Bill'; Gardiner, i. 445.

[4] Copy of Brackenbury's mem. in Spencer MSS (see *Spencer*, i. 205-6).

short of felony, I do not think the confidence he asks can be refused. The words which I have noticed appear to be in conflict with words near the bottom of p. 6. 2. With the exception of a perfectly trifling matter when I was Sec. of State for the Colonies 36 years ago, I am absolutely ignorant of the machinery by which Secret Service is worked *in either of its branches*, and I am unaware whether there are any reserves which can be made available. 3. The object which Col. Brackenbury has in view is paramount but he writes as if all he had to do was to appeal to the Executive Government. 4. It is to be observed that he does not limit himself to 20 m[ille] for a given time, but seems to ask a pledge without limit for more when the 20 m have been spent. 5. He ought certainly if he can to state his maximum for the year if a pledge is to be taken from the Govt. in regard to it, because the rules are *absolute* which controul the public Issues. 6. When it is known what the figure is to be, the subject should I think be referred to those officers of the Govt. who are conversant with the rules & practice of Secret Service, not as to the *purpose* or policy, but as to the modus operandi, to see what can be found from funds now at command & what must be asked from Parliament. 7. I have reason to believe that Parnell has, after a struggle, stopped the Fenian supplies from Paris.[1]

10. Sat. [*Dollis Hill*]

Wrote to Rev. E. Wilberforce—Dean of Windsor—Mr R. Duff—The Queen—and minutes. Gaietés Th. to see Hernani.[2] Cabinet 12–2¼. Saw Mr H—Ld R.G. 11.— Ld Granville—Ld Carlingford. Walk 1½ hour. Drove to Dollis Hill after the play. Read Arnold's Eton Boy[3]—Froude's Carlyle.

Cabinet. Sat. June 10. Noon.[4]
1. Egypt. recited by Ld Granville.
2. Question as to release of men suspected of murder (Dyke). Answer to be general. Harcourt to see Trevelyan.
3. Procedure on the [Crime Prevention] Bill. W.E.G. stated preference for continuous sitting over urgency.
4. Discussion on principle of amendments. Spencer's amendments considered & (except as to proclaiming for Clause 1). Saving *clause* for political agitation to be drawn in line of Mr Healy's Proviso.

[5]Amendments. Urgency. Continuous sitting: say on Thursday if need be.
Chamberlain on Parnell. Harcourt imputes to Chamberlain 'To regard Parnell as a beneficent influence whose hands are to be strengthened by concessions on our part'. 'Either he has influence, or he has not'. *Proposals to be regarded on their own merits.* Rumours abroad.
 Chamberlain: has sacrificed his own opinions. Is quite willing to retire from Govt. Harcourt deduced reluctance.

To Sir W. V. HARCOURT, home secretary, 10 June 1882. MS Harcourt dep. Adds 10.

 R. Grosvenor says *Labouchere* tells him you agreed last night *privately* to some amendment of Healy's which is to have a great healing effect. Is he rightly informed?

---

[1] Initialled and dated 9 June 1882; Add MS 44766, f. 98.
[2] With Bernhardt and Guitry. [3] M. Arnold, 'An Eton boy', *F.R.*, xxxvii. 683 (June 1882).
[4] Add MS 44643, f. 121. Cabinet demanded by Hartington for Egyptian discussion; *Africa and the Victorians*, 105–6.
[5] Undated holograph; Add MS 44643, f. 123.

It will be very useful if you refer to the 'negotiations' as Chamberlain alone can say how the matter stands.

As to the amendments I do not understand that *much* of Labouchere's letter still exists for practical purposes.[1]

11. *St Barn. & 1 S. Trin.*[2]

Willesden Ch. 11, & 6.30 PM. Wrote to The Queen—Mr Hamilton. Saw Ld Rosebery—W.H.G.—Lady Stepney. Read Spectre of the Vatican[3]—Geikie, Hours with the Bible[4]—Mozley, Reminiscences.[5]

12. *M. [London]*

Wrote to Rev G. Butler—Dean of Windsor—Ld Derby—Ld Granville—The Queen 1.1.—Ld Spencer & minutes. H of C. $4\frac{3}{4}$–$8\frac{1}{2}$ & $9\frac{1}{4}$–$12\frac{3}{4}$: Crime Bill.[6] Saw Mr H—Ld R.G.—Mr Welby—Mrs Th—Mrs O'Shea—Ld Granville—Miss Ponsonby—Mr Childers. Read Mozley Reminisc.—Carlyle's Froude. Mrs O'Shea's account[7] of Parnell represents him as in the same mind & as hopeful of putting down outrages.

To LORD SPENCER, Viceroy of Ireland, 12 June 1882.   Althorp MSS K5.

Many thanks for your letter of yesterday:[8] I need not trouble you with a long reply.

1. As to expedition with the Bill you will remember that there was some delay in printing it. Without doubt it has been unduly retarded, but not more than, perhaps not so much as, the Tories retarded our other business from & since the Address in all matters they did not like. I have hope we may now move more rapidly. If not, we think of asking for *continuous sitting.*

2. As to the recent crimes I with less means of judgment had come to your conclusion that the hand of Secret Societies, notably of Fenians is visible in them.

3. To these I believe Parnell to be at present as much opposed as we are. I believe also he has laid an embargo on the [Land] League Funds in Paris: further that he still has good hope of stopping outrage.

4. Practically a great unity prevailed in the Cabinet on Saty. as to the amendments & nothing I believe will be proposed except what you have suggested or are certain to approve. I am extremely glad of them.

5. I did not delay Colonel B[rackenbury]'s papers for an hour—my main suggestions were that he should state his outside limit (for getting the money is really difficult) & that those Civil Servants who are practically conversant with the rules & methods of S[ecret] S[ervice] should meet to consider & recommend as to the *modus operandi.* Harcourt seemed fearful, and a little sceptical, as to the plan.

[1] Harcourt's guarded reply stressed the need for the Cabinet to be told of the negotiations, but gave no details; Add MS 44197, f. 60.

[2] Riots this day in Alexandria, *ca.* 50 Europeans dead; see M. E. Chamberlain, 'The Alexandrian massacre', *Middle Eastern Studies*, xiii.

[3] [J. Wyse], *The spectre of the Vatican* (1875).   [4] See 18 Dec. 81.

[5] T. Mozley, *Reminiscences, chiefly of Oriel college and the Oxford Movement*, 2v. (1882); see to de Lisle, 18 June 82.

[6] *H* 270. 841.   [7] i.e. during their conversation.

[8] Add MS 44309, f. 18 on progress of the Bill, and Brackenbury's plans for curtailing secret societies.

However discouraging these recent events I cannot think there is any new & permanent cause for depression.

13. Tu.

Wrote to The Speaker—Ld Kimberley—The Queen—Ld Greville—& minutes. H. of C. $2\frac{1}{4}$–$6\frac{3}{4}$ and $9\frac{3}{4}$–$2\frac{1}{2}$.[1] Read Froude's Carlyle—Mozley Reminiscences. Saw Mr G—Ld R.G—Mr Whitbread—Baron Malortie—Mr Dillwyn—Lord Granville—Mr Onslow—Conclave on Arrears Bill (at H of C.)—The Speaker. Twelve to dinner.

14. Wed.

Wrote to the P.M.G.[2]—Bp of Winchester—Mary G.—The Queen l. & tel.—and minutes. H of C. $12\frac{1}{4}$–$5\frac{3}{4}$. Spoke on Egypt.[3] Dined with Lucy Cavendish still in a frame most sound, Christian, & heroic. Saw Mr G—Ld R.G—Ld Granville. Read Mozley.

15. Th.

Wrote to Mr Childers—Ld Advocate—Mr Lefevre—Sir W. Harcourt—Mr West—Ld Spencer—The Queen l.l.—and minutes. Saw Mr G—Ld R.G.—Mr Fawcett—Ld Granville—Mr Welby—Sir W. Harcourt—Mr Lefevre—Mr Bright—Sir C. Dilke. Quasi-Cabinet at H. of C.[4] Read Froude's Carlyle—Mozley's Reminiscences. Eight to breakfast. Conversation with Sir W. Gregory—Mr C. Field—Mr E. Balfour. H of C. $4\frac{3}{4}$–$8\frac{1}{4}$ & $9\frac{1}{4}$–$12\frac{3}{4}$.[5]

To J. B. BALFOUR, M.P., Lord Advocate, 15 June 1882.   Add MS 44545, f. 152.

Please to look at Sir J. Hay's question for today.[6]

I am strongly in favour of the principle of delegating many Bills to great Committees so as to save the Committee Stage in the House: & of giving *large* scope to the principle of local or class representation in local or class Bills. But this question is one which, as to *local* Bills (i.e. Bills not for the U.K.) has not yet been disposed of by the Cabinet.

Hay's suggestion is impracticable. But I would ask you to *consider* whether it would be advisable to call the Scotch members together, or to ask any other means of eliciting their opinion on the question whether they generally & strongly desire any special measure to be adopted, in anticipation of & without prejudice to what may be settled as to Procedure generally, for the purpose of putting forward Scotch business.

The assent of the Cabinet would be necessary before any *step* could be actually taken.

---

[1] Crimes Bill; *H* 270. 988.

[2] Not found published.

[3] *H* 270. 1143: Egypt: need to keep liberty of action, and hold a Conference.

[4] 'a sudden Cabinet in Mr G's room at the H. of C. Dufferin is instructed today to require the Sultan to consent to meeting of the Conference at once, & to send troops to Egypt. The question of sending troops of our own with or without France, in case of the Sultan refusing (wh I cannot expect), long discussed & treated as a possible necessity. Childers & Northbrook were to prepare for it': Carlingford's diary, 15 June 1882.

[5] Crimes Bill; *H* 270. 1280.

[6] Requesting suspension of the Half-past Twelve Rule to allow extra time for Scottish business; *H* 270. 1272.

16. Fr.

Wrote to Lady F. Cavendish—Sir W. Harcourt—Govr of Bank—Mr Armitage—
Mr Forster—Sir H. Ponsonby—Mrs Bolton—Rev. T. Mozley—The Queen—and
minutes. H of C. 2½–7 and 9½–1.[1] Saw Mr G—Ld R.G (2)—Ld Granville *cum* Ld
Northbrook—Mr Leahy[2]—Mr Childers—Ld Advocate. Read Froude's Carlyle—
Mozley's Reminiscences. Dined with Phillimore. He gets weak in body & begins
to contemplate resignation.[3]

To Sir W. V. HARCOURT, home secretary, 16 June 1882.   MS Harcourt dep. Adds 10.

Your note presents an undeniable difficulty but one without a perceptible remedy.[4] A
proposal of continuous sitting is inapplicable until the matter remaining to be handled
can in our judgment be brought within one sitting, and in urgency, at present, I can see
nothing but present and prospective embarrassment more complicated than what we
now have to deal with.

One thing I would suggest for your serious consideration, which may do good & can
hardly do harm. It is unquestionably a general rule & practice that a Government shall
give notice as far as possible of the amendments it may mean to make in its own Bill. I
think the rule has not yet been much followed in the present case: & I would suggest that
the time has come when the important, & chiefly conciliatory amendments you have to
make on the Search, press, & other clauses should as far as possible be put upon the
paper.

They *might* have a softening, & quickening, effect.

To Mrs O'SHEA, 16 June 1882. '*Private*'.[5]   Add MS 44269, f. 86.

Any paper transmitted to me by you will have my early & best attention. Tomorrow I
leave town, perhaps early in the afternoon, to remain away from D. Street until Mond.
forenoon.

When I saw you I directed your attention to some Clauses (especially Search & Press
together with the Magisterial Tribunal) on which it was proposed to make amendments
of a mitigating character: & to a clause of reservation to protect political & constitutional
discussion or as it is popularly termed agitation. The point on which declarations already
made peculiarly tie the hand of the Govt. is the duration of the Act.

[1] Spoke on Egypt; Crimes Bill; *H* 270. 1419.

[2] James Leahy, 1822–?; home rule M.P. Kildare 1880–92.

[3] 'Gs dined here. He wonderfully vigorous & well. We had a very long conversation on past
present & future politics, & the Church. He told me his general health was stronger than it had been
for some years & he could only ascribe it to the prayers of his friends.

(Quite secret). There will be an autumn session, the object of wh. will be to pass the measure as to
procedure in Parlt. having done wh. he will resign. Of the 25 Irish members, he sd. 12 at least were
men of great ability. He was anxious I should read Mozley's memoirs just published. He sd he felt his
eye sight failing him & deafness slightly increasing. In every other respect he was stronger than he
was 2 or 3 years ago. Nothing could exceed his expressions of affection towards myself. . . . The
Police have insisted upon G's being attended by a policeman in plain clothes'; Phillimore's diary, the
last surviving entry.

[4] The temper of the Liberal party 'thoroughly roused'; Add MS 44197, f. 66.

[5] Holograph copy. Mrs O'Shea this day, Add MS 44269, f. 84, requested a meeting next day 'to
submit (privately) a written proposal'. She sent Parnell's mem. next day; ibid., f. 87. See Hammond,
297.

17. Sat. [*Dollis Hill*]

Wrote to Ld Granville 1.1.—Mrs O'Shea—Sir W. Harcourt—The Queen—Ld Kimberley—Mr Lawson—& minutes. Attended the Levee. Finished Froude's Carlyle. Read Mozley Reminiscences. Saw Mr G—Ld R.G.—Ld Granville—Mr Welby—Musurus Pasha. Off to Dollis Hill at 4.30.

To Sir W. V. HARCOURT, home secretary, 17 June 1882.   MS Harcourt dep. Adds 10. '*Private*'.

It was I think understood in the Cabinet that the Law Officers were to look into [and] state for us the exact value of the words 'treason-felony' in the Bill, & what we should lose by omitting them on report.[1]

I am of course an *ignoramus* on the matter; but I am very desirous to be informed, not because I have formed an opinion adverse to the words but simply to know whether or not it would be worthwhile ιo keep them at a heavy cost—or in other words desirable to part with them *if* parting with them were to be productive of great advantages.

I will tell you on Monday my reason for asking.

18. 2 S. Trin.

Willesden Ch. 11 A.M. (with HC.) & 6.30 P.M. Read Mozley—Geikie—Milligan on Greek Religion.[2] Wrote to Miss de Lisle—Ld Spencer—Mr Godley—& minutes.

To Miss M. DE LISLE, 18 June 1882.   Add MS 44545, f. 154.

When Père Hyacinthe or M. Loyson was here previously I had personal intercourse with him.[3] It is now a relief to me that official cases keep me outside the precinct of religious controversies by filling my hands more than enough with other duties and by the sense they always bring to my mind that one in Government superadds in a certain measure to his own individuality a character representative of his nation which though it cannot change his convictions or authorize his contravening them yet modifies his sphere & conditions of action.

I am much concerned at the charges to which you think him to be liable—he had always seemed to me a sincere and loyal soul and I had never heard him utter a word of violence or rancour. I suppose you would not wish me to make inquiry about them; & as I have no practical or external duties towards him perhaps it is as well that I should not.

A *most* interesting book has lately been published which I am reading; the reminiscences of Mr. T. Mozley the brother in law of Cardinal Newman, and one of his early followers and affectionate admirers from the first, who became a most distinguished writer in the Times but now shows that he has retained all his interest in those deep matters of religion and the Church which have been agitated among us now for half a century with such important results not only to England but to Christendom. The hand of the Almighty has directed all the currents but has been itself unseen. The next half century may bear yet larger witness on the same subjects. Though Mozley came to different con-

---

[1] i.e. on the night-search clause, Gladstone siding with Spencer against Harcourt (already ready to apply the Aliens Act to England); Gardiner, i. 448.

[2] W. Milligan, *Religion of ancient Greece* (1882).

[3] See 28 Nov. 70, 24 Mar., 20 May 76, 19 Oct. 79; Loyson's case raised by Miss de Lisle in letters of 2 and 8 June, Add MS 44475, ff. 226, 249.

clusions from his friend & leader, his affection & admiration remain quite unimpaired & there is much in this book about Cardinal Newman which I think has never come out before.

To LORD SPENCER, Viceroy of Ireland, 18 June 1882. '*Secret*'.   Althorp MSS K5.

I do not think it is within my personal competence to give a pledge to Colonel Brackenbury in the terms you mention,[1] for the question is not one of mere expedition but a political question of the utmost delicacy and I think it should be introduced to the Cabinet—probably by Harcourt as your natural organ in your absence. At the same time I *agree* in your opinion that by one means or another the money ought to be found. You may think my assent to the £5000 at variance with what I have said but the application was urgent and I understand that this amount can if necessary be scraped out of Secret Service funds already existing.

I have never been conversant with the administration of those funds and am very sceptical about the system now established. Nothing can be more mischievous in such a matter than to be obliged to draw attention & give room for criticism & even obstruction in Parliament when difficult times come & a special call is made.

But I need not go further into this matter. I have another to mention—which please not to name to any third person without my knowledge.

P[arnell] has now altered his proposal about the duration of the Act & asks that *if there be a new Parliament within three years* the Act shall then expire within 3 months after its assembling. Apart from the exact number three which appears too small, I think there is much to be said for this proposal. The Parliamentary case for it would be doubtless this— that the nation may have changed its mind & that in this contingency it is not unfair to provide for a *new trial.* But I do not doubt that underneath there lies another considera- tion which may be roughly described as the fear of Jim Lowther[2] & the desire to make him consult a little Irish wishes & opinions. It is I believe likely that this change might *greatly* assist in facilitating progress—but the main question is whether it be allowable? I think it to be so, but then I have never been inclined to stand stiffly on the mere question of duration—I should have thought it good economy to make a sure gain of (say) a fort- night now at the risk of bringing a longer battle a twelve-month nearer—but I think you have taken a more rigid view. But if you have anything to say by a short ciphered tele- gram on receipt pray let me have it. Incidentally I consider that we cannot make a change of this kind without your assent.

19. M. [London]

Wrote to Ld Kimberley—Mr Chamberlain—Ld Aberdare—Sir W. Harcourt—Mr Rickards—The Queen 1.1.—Ld Spencer Tel.—and minutes. At 10½ we left for London: & I went to be examined by Commn on the Connah's Quay &c. R[ail] R[oad] Bill.[3] Saw Mr G—Ld RG—Ld Granville—Mr [C.M.] Norwood—Mr Trevelyan—and many others. Read Mozley's Reminisc. Cabinet 2–4¼. House 5¼–8¼ & 9½–1.[4] Dined at Sir C. Forster's. Conversation with Mr Rogers—Mr Curteis—Mr Ainger.

[1] On 17 June, Add MS 44309, f. 38: Spencer thinks Brackenbury must have access to more than £5000.   [2] Irish secretary 1878–80.
[3] Expanding the connection between Deeside and Liverpool.
[4] Egyptian questions; Crimes Bill; *H* 270. 1608.

Cabinet. D. St. June 19. 2 PM.[1]

1. Course of business in H of C. Autumn meeting for procedure projected—provisionally well received. No new Bills of importance unless urgent to be introduced. Agricultural Bills: glance at 'Grand Committees'
2. Cartwright in Egypt to act as Consul while Malet is ill: with Malet's advice.[2]
3. Course to be taken in the Conference.[3] Hn. wished to announce to Conference *now* that we & the French, or *we*, shd. interfere if the Sultan does not. Cabinet thought this premature. Most opinions on *sole* interference were *contra*[?].
4. Extension of Alien Act to England.[4]
5. Cabinet to decide to give Brackenbury's demand.[5]
6. Search Clause—to settle on Bench.

20. Tu.

Wrote to Sir Thos G.—Sir W. Harcourt 1 1.1.—Mr Douglas—Mr Duncan—The Queen. H of C. & quasi-Cabinet 2¼–7¼. Close encounter with Harcourt: & a still deeper embroglio about Egypt & the Suez Canal. Saw Mr G—Ld RG—Ld Granville—Sir W. Harcourt—Mrs Bolton. Read Mozley—finished Mitchell's Dalkeith. Dined with Lucy. H of C. (2°) 9¼–1¼.[6]

Quasi-Cabinet. June 20. 1882.[7]

1. Shall we print Reports of Lords' Committee for H of C? (Dillon). (Stands for tomorrow).
2. Search Clause. Harcourt did not raise the point. (Old decision stands).
3. Conversation on Egypt & Suez Canal. Various projects discussed but not with a view to immediate decision. to meet tomorrow for instructions to Dufferin.

To Sir W. V. HARCOURT, home   MS Harcourt dep. 8, ff. 147–9 and dep Adds 10.
secretary, 20 June 1882.[8]

[First letter:]   I have just sent round according to your wish. Spencer's original recommendation was contained I think in a letter to me. I have had no further communication from him on the subject. If there has been a correspondence with him upon the subject, perhaps we could see it. I understand Trevelyan to say that an amendment giving effect to the suggestion was drawn.

The regular course I need hardly say would have been that on the decision of the Cabinet the amendment should have been drawn and put on the notice papers. Perhaps the pressure of business prevented this. If there be technical difficulty is postponement until the Report out of the question? Of course I am ready to take any personal part but I should be sorry to do it in a way to make any difference of opinion noticeable.

---

[1] Add MS 44643, f. 124; holograph note reads: 'Questions on Egypt not to be answered without notice except as to occurrences known or alleged to have happened—as to concurring questions—quicken Conference—restrict basis'; ibid., f. 125.

[2] i.e. (Sir William) Chauncy Cartwright, 1853–1933; acting 2nd sec. in Egypt May 1882; acting Consul there 17 June–23 Aug. 1882; witnessed bombardment of Alexandria.

[3] See 31 May 82.   [4] See 20 June 82.

[5] i.e. £5000 forthwith and up to £50,000 (the sum demanded by Brackenbury) if necessary over two years; see also Bahlman, *Hamilton*, i. 290 and to Welby, 22 June 82.

[6] Egypt; business of the House; *H* 270. 1762.

[7] Add MS 44643, f. 126; marked 'Not reported', i.e. to the Queen.

[8] Part in Gardiner, i. 448.

[Second letter:]   Now that we have discovered Mr. Power's mistake, it seems that the question of search has reverted to the exact position which it held when the Cabinet resolved to amend the Clause: and I hope I may assume that this is your view.

Should you think it necessary, I could ask our colleagues to meet at the H. of C. on this subject: but it would only be, so far as I am concerned, to state reasons which are for me binding and absolute. I do not conceal the fact that, as I abandoned the line of legislation which I had preferred last year in deference to the Cabinet and the Irish Government of that day, so this year I have consented to a good deal that I would not have chosen in deference to the Cabinet, and still more to Spencer, in his arduous position, and after his admirable conduct. But it is quite another matter to pass into law any power, and especially one so invidious, which Spencer is willing to forego. I think you will see it is not strange or unreasonable, from my point of view, that this should stand with me as a principle of action.

At the same time I am most sorry to trouble you, amidst your very severe work, on a matter where our respective views have not been quite the same. But what I say tends to shorten, as I hope, not to lengthen, labour.

[Third letter:]   I received your letter[1] while Granville was with me a few minutes ago & told him the contents. 1. On Search I have already said my last words. 2. On Alien Bill— Granville feels the subject to be of much delicacy & requiring examination which requires time—I join him in recommending that the question stand over to the report and be kept open.

21. Wed.

Wrote to Ld Granville—The Queen 1.1.—Miss Terry—and minutes. Nineteen to dinner. Read Mozley. Drive with C. Saw Mr G—Ld RG—Musurus P.—Ly de Vesci—Lady Cowper—D. of Argyll. Cabinet 2-4. Scots Agric. Deputn at Noon.[2] H of C. 2-6.[3]

Cabinet. (H of C). June 21. 1882. 2 PM.[4]
1. Agree to Dillon's having the Report of the Lords' Committee [on the Land Act].
2. Instructions to Dufferin read. In principle approved. Mem. within agreed to as the groundwork for dealing with the question of intervention in Egypt.
3. Communicate with France upon, & consider in the Depts, means whereby to protect the Suez Canal from interruption—in case a necessity should arise.
4. Bulwer to be moved in the sense of allowing Cetewayo to visit England unless he can allege very strong reasons otherwise.[5]
5. W.E.G.'s answer to Smith tomorrow considered & agreed on.[6]

[Memorandum on Egypt][7]
1. Propose in Conference that Sultan should send troops.
2. Support proposal with reasons.

---

[1] Add MS 44197, f. 74; Harcourt was 'not unwilling' to apply the Aliens Act to England.
[2] Farmers Alliance of Scotland, requesting changes in the land laws; *T.T.*, 22 June 1882, 6c, 9b.
[3] Crimes Bill; *H* 270. 1888.
[4] Add MS 44643, f. 129.
[5] See 9 Aug. 82.
[6] On Egypt; Gladstone promised papers to 31 May; *H* 271. 69.
[7] Holograph note dated 21 June 1882, fair copy sent to Granville, see Ramm II, i. 381.

3. Intimate that if Conference decline, or if Sultan decline, we shall invite Conference to concert effectual means for the re-establishment of legality and security in Egypt.
4. So far as we can at present judge, the form of this invitation will be to ask the Powers to provide for or sanction a military intervention other than Turkish under their authority.

1. The precedent of Admiral Hornby's iron-clad in 1877[1] is in principle applicable to the circumstances of the moment.
2. The Sultan should be informed that we throw upon him the responsibility for the safety of the Canal.
3. If the Conference meet & frame or sanction *an arrangement for the internal peace & security of Egypt, this will include the security of the Canal.*
4. If the Conference does not meet, or does not arrive at any such arrangement, we shall be free to act without it for the purpose of keeping open the Canal.
5. During the present uncertainty & absence of arrangement[?] it is permissible to have means at hand (as in 77) for dealing with any obstruction should it occur, but not to propose or frame a plan for occupying the Canal or landing on Egyptian territory without any sanction from or reference to Europe.
W.E.G. Ju. 21. 82.[2]

To Miss ELLEN TERRY, 21 June 1882.   Add MS 44545, f. 155.

I am equally obliged and sorry.[3] It would have given me very great pleasure to accept your kind proposal, but that I have been for some time bound by a particular engagement at Eton on Saturday evening.

22. Th.

Wrote to Sir S. Northcote—Sir H. Ponsonby—Mr Welby—Duc d'Aumale—Mr West—Sir G. Birdwood—The Queen—and minutes. H. of C. 4¾–8¼ and 9½–1¼. Various speaking.[4] Eight to breakfast. incl. Mr T. Mozley & H. Spencer. Very interesting. Saw Mr G—Ld RG—Ld Granville. Read Mozley Reminisc.—Democracy.[5]

To R. E. WELBY, assistant financial secretary, 22 June 1882.   Add MS 44545, f. 155.

The Cabinet, impressed with the weight and urgency of Lord Spencer's recommendation offered in the present circumstances of Ireland as to Secret Societies, have agreed 1. That Colonel Brackenbury shall be supplied with the sum of £5 m[ille] forthwith for purposes of Secret Societies. 2. That in case of need further sums for Secret Societies may be supplied which in two years might possibly reach the maximum of £50 m[ille].
It will be requisite that consultation should be held as soon as may be convenient among those habitually entrusted with regulating the finance of the Fund to consider

---

[1] Derby's Note of 6 May 1877 recognised 'the necessity of keeping open' the canal route, blockade being 'a menace to India and a grave injury to the commerce of the world'; Hornby's flagship was off Port Said by 16 May 1877; Seton-Watson, 173; *T.T.*, 17 May 1877, 5f. See 3 July 82.
[2] Add MS 44643, f. 131; marked 'Private'.
[3] Letter from Miss Terry, 20 June, Add MS 44475, f. 305, asking Gladstone to attend her benefit at the Lyceum on 24 June, '*the* event of the season'.
[4] Egypt; public business; education; Crimes Bill; *H* 271. 51.
[5] H. Adams, *Democracy; an American novel* (1880).

what will be the best method of proceeding, & of preparation, for giving effect to the decision of the Cabinet.[1]

23. Fr.

Wrote to Duc d'Aumale—Ld Kimberley—Mrs O'Shea—Sir Thos Acland—J.G. Talbot—The Queen—& minutes. Saw Mr G—Ld R.G.—Mr Mundella—Sir T. Acland—Mr Newdigate—Sir H. Parkes—Scotts. Read Democracy—Mozley's Reminisc. (Finished). H of C. $2\frac{1}{4}$-7 & 9-$12\frac{1}{2}$.[2]

To H. N. GLADSTONE, 23 June 1882.   Hawarden MSS.

I have rather been expecting to have from you some requisition for money, on behalf of Herbert MP or Rev. Stephen, for the Jute Mill or some other mode of investment. How does this matter stand? I am not like one of your great merchants with masses of money always going backwards and forwards but I am rather flush just now in a small way at my Bankers so that if you want to get any thing you had better 'take me while I am in the humour for it'.

Politics are in a singular state. I do not see that the Government is weakened or in danger. But the House of Commons is fearfully crippled by the excessive, nay unmeasured use, of the privilege of speech among its own members. Nay not among the whole of them. For of the majority, who sit on the Govt. side, the greater part remain, with wonderful self denial, almost wholly silent. A lot of unruly Tories who won't answer to Northcote's orders, and of unruly Irishmen who outrun Parnell, are the main causes of the mischief. But while the sands of 1882 are not yet run out we must make a great effort to emancipate the House from its unworthy and rebellious children.

At present we are obliged in the main to give up our hopes for the Session. A strong Bill for the repression of crime, a liberal Bill for getting rid of the mass of arrears in Ireland, and a Corrupt Practices Bill, appear likely to be its principal achievements.

In Ireland there is yet much to do, especially as to getting within the circle of the secret societies & breaking them up. But the power of the Land Act is effectually proved, and the resistance to rent is in the main broken down. Agrarian outrage is likewise upon the whole diminishing. The massacre in Phoenix Park remains like a black cloud upon the rearward sky: and the loss of F. Cavendish will ever be to us all as an unhealed wound.

In Egypt the embarrassments have been extreme. But the Conference has gone to work and this is of itself a considerable fact; a bulwark against precipitate follies.

At home we are thank God well and happy. Mama wears wonderfully: and as to myself though sight & hearing fail a little, and I feel the heart a little weaker, I am astonished at the measure in which under much pressure health & strength are continued to me, & very thankful to know that the prayers of many constantly ascend on my behalf. I earnestly hope however that this fiftieth year of public life may bring at least my official existence to a close.

It is a great delight dearest Harry to think that we are now within the twelvemonth which should bring you back among us. It is a delight to hear of you & will be a greater

---

[1] Welby replied this day, Add MS 44338, f. 192, that the two ministers 'who receive Secret Service money of any amount (except the Parliamentary Secy. of the Treasury)' are the foreign secretary (£15,000) and the Irish secretary (£6000); these two will husband their fund to permit £8000 for Brackenbury, plus £8000 from 'civil contingencies', till March; no 'formal record in the Treasury' to be made of the cabinet decision.

[2] Questioned on Egypt; Crimes Bill; *H* 271. 198.

delight again to see you. Meantime & always may the smile of the Almighty be upon you & His arm sustain & guide you. Ever your afft. Father, WE Gladstone.

To Mrs. O'SHEA, 23 June 1882. '*Early*'.   Add MS 44545, f. 156.

I have received your note,[1] and I return the inclosure. Reflecting on the subject, I have come to the conclusion that there would be no advantage in my calling on you again with reference to the Crime Prevention Bill. I have had much at heart the purpose of expediting proceedings on this Bill, in order that we might go forward with the Arrears Bill, and with other business, of which also part is Irish: but I have failed: and the loss of time on the Crime Bill will be I fear repeated and cumulated by a similar loss on the Bill which follows it, and which appears to be menaced with obstinate resistance. All that remains to me is to work for the best on each case as it arises, with a steady aim at the good of all classes of the community. When the present strain is relaxed, there may be greater freedom of communication, with less suspicion. Whatever else happens I have an unshaken faith in this; that, if we can get well planted on the basis of *legality*, the publicity and free discussion guaranteed by our institutions, and by the spirit of the nation, will allow and enable all other questions, with a little time, to work themselves out in a manner fairly healthy and satisfactory.

I am sure you will not set down to discourtesy the conclusion at which I have arrived.

24. Sat St Joh. Bapt. [Eton]

Wrote to Mr Osborne Morgan—Ld Spencer—Mr H. Spencer—Ld Granville—Sir H. Ponsonby—Mr A.E. West—Mr S. Lawley—Saw Mr G—Ld R.G—Ld Granville. Went to Christie's early to see the Hamilton furniture &c: the very top of luxe and splendour.[2] Off to Eton before 3.30. Saw a match in the U.S. Fields with good play. We slept in Coleridge's House now lent to E. Lyttelton & a friend. Much pleasant conversation: an Homeric discourse with Curzon.[3] In the College precincts, the ideal & the actual seem very widely severed! Read Democracy—Brother Lawrence.[4]

To Sir H. PONSONBY, the Queen's secretary, 24 June 1882.   Add MS 45724, f. 122.

From what Lord Granville reports of his visit to Windsor, I am afraid lest I should have deviated from my rule as to expressing the view of or conclusion of the Cabinet on matters in which there is actual or usual communication with the Queen. I thought I had been pretty careful in this matter, but if you have observed or should observe any case in which I have deviated from my rule I shall [be] much obliged by your noticing it. *Unless* there is anything to say on this head, pray do not take the trouble of reply.[5]

To LORD SPENCER, Viceroy of Ireland, 24 June 1882.   Althorp MSS K5.

I have often thought of your isolation as regards the proceedings of the Cabinet: but I concluded that you had an arrangement with some humane & less occupied colleague.[6]

---

[1] Of 22 June, Add MS 44269, f. 90, proposing another meeting in Thomas's Hotel on Parnell's proposals (see 16 June 82). See Hammond, 305.

[2] Sale of family effects, including the Beckford library, by 12th duke of Hamilton; see 16 Aug. 82n.

[3] Francis Nathaniel Curzon, 1865-1941; Eton and Balliol; later a stockbroker.

[4] Untraced.   [5] Docketed 'no answer'.

[6] Spencer had requested copies of Gladstone's 'communications to the Queen after Cabinet'; Add MS 44309, f. 49; none of the copies sent survives; *Spencer*, i. 211.

I will send you copies of my reports as you desire. But

1. As there ought not to be any duplicates of these letters, which are entirely between the Queen and me, & for which the Cabinet has no responsibility, I rely entirely on the regular destruction of the copies.

2. These reports are, as between colleagues, very imperfect. What the Queen cares to hear, & ought to hear, embraces of course a very large field & the most important subjects; but there is much business transacted piecemeal so to speak, but without interest or importance, which does not require to be, & hardly could be, reported to her.

The Bill drags slowly along. There is obstruction, but not more than is now habitual, on contested matters, with *both* the Oppositions. The volume of subjects in the Bill is so great and formidable, that it evidently could not pass without a very large expenditure of time.

To A. E. WEST, Chairman of the Inland Revenue,   Add MS 44545, f. 157.
24 June 1882. '*Private*'.

I observe that Northcote & others of his friends on the front Bench have observed a temperate and Parliamentary course in questions about Egypt: while many of the supporters have been unruly, & their unruliness appears to have received distinct countenance from the speech of Salisbury last night in the House of Lords.

I do not like to offer public acknowledgements to Northcote on this ground, as I am afraid I might increase the difficulties of his position; which it is one of my primary duties to avoid. If you had an opportunity of letting his son[1] know informally that these are my ideas I should be obliged to you.

25. 3 S. Trin.

Eton Chapel mg: St George's aftn. Breakf. at Miss Evans's. Luncheon at Dr Hornby's. Saw Dean Wellesley respecting Mrs Butler:[2] Canon Anson[3] respecting Egypt. Saw Hartington—Messenger from London. Saw Mr Durnford:[4] & the young Duke of Newcastle: he is weakly but an interesting youth, reputed excellent. Wrote to The Queen—Mr Hamilton. Read Robertson on Prophets[5]—Shorthouse Introd. to Herbert[6]—Thackeray on the Library. Much conversation in evg with these good & pleasant fellows.

26. M. [London]

To the Castle to make a duty-call: then off to town. Wrote to Sir W. Harcourt—Dean of Windsor—The Queen—Dean of St Paul's—& minutes. Saw Mr G—Ld RG—Ld Granville—Mr Childers—Depn of Chambers of Commerce[7]—Dr Milligan—Rev. Mr [blank]—Principal Tulloch—Ld Balfour. Read Democracy. Dined at Ld Aberdare's. H of C. $4\frac{1}{4}$–8 & $10\frac{1}{2}$–$12\frac{3}{4}$.[8]

---

[1] Walter Stafford Northcote, 1845–1927; on the I.R.B. with West 1877–92; 2nd Earl of Iddesleigh 1887.

[2] See to Wellesley, 26 June 82.

[3] See 15 June 39 and above, ii. 653; no particular Egyptian connection found.

[4] Walter Durnford, taught at Eton 1870–99.

[5] W. Robertson Smith, *The prophets of Israel* (1882).

[6] J. H. Shorthouse, *The Temple, with an introductory essay* (1882).

[7] No account found.

[8] Ireland; *H* 271. 434.

To G. V. WELLESLEY, dean of Windsor, 26 June 1882.   Add MS 44545, f. 157.

I am sorry to hear that the Queen has been troubled in mind about Mrs. [Josephine] Butler on account of her activity in respect of the Contagious Diseases Acts; and the form of her activity.[1] Since that time I have no recollection of having been made aware of it. It lay therefore in the distance for me—and it never occurred to me to name this repulsive subject to the Queen.

At the time named, I was Prime Minister, and went to Liverpool for some function at Mr. Butler's College.[2] She, through Mr. Stansfeld, then my colleague, asked leave to converse with me on the Acts. I begged to be excused. But, at the entertainment which followed the function, I sat by her for the best part of two hours, and passed the bulk of the time in conversation with her. She never came near the forbidden ground. But I am not sure that ever during my life I was so impressed, in a single conversation, with the fine mind, and the noble, pure, and lofty character of a woman. She seemed to me one who, wherever she goes, must win her way & carry all before her. I never saw her before or since; though I had seen, long before, the singularly beautiful medallions of her head, executed I think by Munro.

I can understand differences of opinion as to the soundness of her judgment in the line she had taken. At the same time it is indubitable that she was pursuing a purpose which she believed to be one of high morality. In that view she is sustained by some very great authorities. A Royal Commission, selected (as I well remember) with extraordinary care, after a laborious investigation reported by a majority against the Acts: and the Government of 1868–74 determined on bringing in a Bill which swept away nine tenths of what they contained. But it was intended to retain one or two regulations which were thought useful. These the adversaries of the Acts would not tolerate: and thus it was that the measure fell to the ground.

This however is not the question before us. Had I submitted the name ten years ago, I should certainly (at the very least) have consulted you as to bringing it before the Queen. On this occasion as I have said it did not occur to me, only dwelling in my mind as a thing of the past.[3]

27. Tu.

Wrote to Lady Sydney—Sir J.F. Stephen—Mrs Hope—Ld Granville—The Queen—Lady Gladstone—& minutes. H of C. $2\frac{1}{2}$–7 and $9\frac{3}{4}$–$12\frac{3}{4}$.[4] Saw Mr G—Ld R.G—Mr J. Talbot—Mr Morley—Mr Rathbone—Mr Morgan. Dined with the Wests. Read A Faithful Lover[5]—Democracy (finished).

To Sir J. F. STEPHEN, 27 June 1882.[6]   C.U.L. Add 7349/15/68.

Nothing can be clearer than your title to put the question which you have addressed to me;[7] and, I am happy to add, my recollection is clear and my answer will be simple.

---

[1] Gladstone proposed G. Butler (Josephine Butler's husband), eventually successfully, for a canonry at Winchester.

[2] For this, and his report to Stansfeld, see 21 Dec. 72.

[3] Wellesley showed this letter to the Queen, Add MS 44340, f. 210.

[4] Crimes Bill; *H* 271. 547.

[5] K. S. Macquoid, *A faithful lover*, 3v. (1882).

[6] Secretary's copy, signed by Gladstone.

[7] On 26 June, Add MS 44475, f. 337: was Mozley right in stating that Gladstone appointed Rogers to the colonial office as 'a lawyer was wanted in the department. Sir James resented the imputation . . .'? T. Mozley, *Reminiscences* (1882), i. 111; the para. was omitted in the 2nd ed. (1882).

Mr. Mozley must have been misinformed as to the purpose with which Mr. Rogers, now Lord Blachford, was added, in 1846, to the staff of the Colonial Office. I see that he does not profess to speak with positive knowledge. But as for the account which he gives of my intent in making the appointment, I can only say it is an entire mistake. No motive of the kind was present to my mind.

I ought perhaps to stop here, and not to pretend to speak of your Father's reputation either legal or civil, as I am not on the first of these points a competent witness, and as the two are closely bound together. But I may observe that, long before 1846, Sir James Stephen had guided the Colonial Office through the mass of difficult and tangled questions raised by the West Indian controversy. This was a task far more arduous, and requiring I should think far more of legal skill, than anything that lay before the Office in 1846. It is inconceivable that, after his great achievements in prior years, he should have been thought to require other aid at this time to bring the department up to a due standard of legal competency.

All my recollections of your Father are of one among the most brilliant, if not actually the most brilliant, of the civil servants of his day. I was Under-Secretary of State for the Colonies in 1835 when I had Lord Aberdeen for a chief. There was no man of the time who had a higher faculty of appreciation. I distinctly remember his telling me that the masterly drafts of his Assistant Under Secretary, instead of adding to his cares, gave him a lively pleasure in their perusal. This is in some degree beside the point, but I thought you might like to hear it.

At the opening of his highly interesting and really important work, Mr. Mozley describes the failure of his eyesight. The impression I received at several points of the work has been that this cause may have interfered in some instances with careful revision, and with resort to verifying sources. I feel certain it has been as far as possible from his intention either to do injustice or to give pain.[1]

28. Wed.

Wrote to Duc d'Aumale—Mr J. Talbot—Mr Rathbone—Sir D. Corrie—The Queen—& minutes. H of C. 2–6.[2] Read Blackie on the Sutherland Clearings[3]—Evenings with a Reviewer.[4] Saw Mr G—Ld R.G—Ld Granville. Quasi-Cabinet at H. of C. on Egypt. Dined at Sir N. Rothschild's—conversation with him—Lady R—Mrs Sands.

Quasi-Cabinet at H. of C. on Egypt. June 28. 82. 6½–7½ PM.[5]
See my letter to H.M.[6]   All present.

To Sir H. D. C. WOLFF, M.P., 28 June 1882. '*Private*'.   Add MS 44545, f. 159.

I should have wished to make an explicit answer to the question of which you have given notice for tomorrow.[7] But circumstances which have come to my knowledge today lead me to believe that, at the present moment, any ministerial answer touching on the

---

[1] Stephen replied this day, ibid., f. 343, touched and 'deeply gratified by what you say of my father'.
[2] Crimes Bill; *H* 271. 675.
[3] J. S. Blackie, probably 'Gaelic societies, Highland depopulation and land tenure reform' (1880).
[4] J. Spedding, *Evenings with a reviewer, or Macaulay and Bacon*, 2v. (1881).
[5] Add MS 44643, f. 132.
[6] Not found in Royal Archives or in Gladstone's copies in B.L.
[7] Wolff postponed his question but threatened a motion; *H* 271. 775.

question of reforms in Egypt might be productive of mischief or hindrance to public interests.

I therefore have to request of you the favour that you will kindly postpone your question for the present. It is needless to say there is no change in our position as to the subject matter of it.

29. Th. St Peter.

Wrote to Viceroy of Ireland—Mrs O'Shea—The Queen—and minutes. Attended Council at Windsor. Gracious audience: of little meaning. Saw Mr G—Ld R.G—Ld Granville—Dean of St Paul's—Mr Irving—Sir H. Ponsonby—Ld Fitzgerald—Ld Kimberley—Ld Justice Bowen—Mr Welby—Mr Leeman MP. Dined with Lucy Cavendish. H of C. 4½-8 and 9-1.[1] Read A Faithful Lover. Thirteen to breakfast.

To Mrs. O'SHEA, 29 June 1882.   Add MS 44545, f. 159.

I thank you for your letter[2] & I return the inclosure. Your injunction respecting it has been observed.

The news of another double murder in Galway again darkens the horizon.[3] This exacerbation of the Fenian passion is terrible.

I do not doubt that your friend does all he can, & I observe that what we may call ordinary outrage declines.

May 1-27 compared with June 1-27 show offences against the person, June *increase* from 10 to 18. Other offences except letters June decrease from 130 to 98. Letters June *decrease* from 226 to 140. But these savage murders exhibit an open unstaunched source of mischief which goes far to destroy all confidence. I am afraid the Irish World party are not without complicity.

Time too slips away. 'When is the Arrears Bill to become law?' I ask myself in vain.

30. Frid. St P[aul]

Wrote to Ld Kimberley—Mr Courtney—Macmillans—Mr Welby—Murrays—The Queen—& minutes. Read The Churkiss case.[4] H of C. 2½-7 and 9-3: in the continuous sitting.[5] Dined with the Wolvertons, to meet the bridal pair.

1 July[6] Sat. [Dollis Hill]

Wrote to Ld Monck—Ld Granville—The Queen—& minutes. Rose at 10 & went to H of C. forthwith. Left at 7¼ after the second suspension. My share of the

[1] Crimes Bill; *H* 271. 780.
[2] Of 26 June, Add MS 44269, f. 93, regretting absence of meeting ('I beg that you will not "Boycott" me altogether'), and enclosing a letter to be returned; Gladstone's undated note reads 'Inclosure [name & date effaced] is a letter to Parnell condemning Ford (Irish World) for setting up Davitt to be leader of the agitation leaving the Parlt. party to Parnell ...'; enclosed letter is in O'Shea, *Parnell*, ii. 3.
[3] John H. Blake, Clanricarde's Steward, and Mr Kane shot this day near Loughrea.
[4] *Sic*; probably the title of an untraced novel.
[5] Continuous sitting, on the 'General Powers' clauses of the Crimes Bill, until 8 p.m. on Saturday, 25 Irish M.P.s being suspended in two bouts, F. H. O'Donnell accusing the chair (Playfair) of 'infamy'; *H* 271. 938.
[6] Wrongly dated '30' by Gladstone.

sitting I take at nineteen hours. Anxious Cabinet on Egypt behind the Chair 4–5.[1] Consultations with the Speaker—Childers—R.G.—& others. Saw Mr G. Off to Dollis Hill 7.20. Read Paul on Aberdeenshire.[2]

2. *S 4 Trin.*

Ch. (and H.C.) 11 A.M. Read Paul's Aberdeen—Geikie's Half Hours[3]—Contemp Rev on Creeds in U.S.[4] Wrote to Ld Kimberley—Ld Granville—The Queen—Mr E.J. Rickards.[5] Saw Ld Granville—Ld Tweedmouth. Conversation with Ly Tavistock.

3. *M. [London]*

Back to D. St at 11.30. Wrote to Ld Kimberley—The Speaker (2)—The Queen (2)—and minutes. Dined at D. of Cleveland's. Saw Mr G—Ld RG—Ld Granville. Cabinet 2–4. H of C. 4$\frac{3}{4}$–9 and 11–1$\frac{1}{2}$.[6] Read Paul's Aberdeenshire—A faithful lover.

Cabinet. Monday July 3. 1882. 2 PM.[7]
1. Conference at Constantinople. Answer to Lyons dissenting from Freycinet's change of front agreed on.[8]
2. Instruction to Admiral in the event of resumption of work on fortifications to warn & then destroy: or in the event of attempt to stop the port.[9]
3. Answer to Menabrea. What is his plan for the Canal? Cannot have the question raised while the main question of the Egyptian situation remains undecided by the Conference.
4. No ship to Port Said at present.
5. Case of O'Donnell considered.

Mem. In Cabinet.[10] If O'Donnell, without a satisfactory apology, leaves the matter where it was, a reprimand preferred. If he aggravate the offence, either in his first explanation, or after the reprimand, then suspension for a term longer or shorter according to circumstances but not less than 14 days.

To H. B. W. BRAND, the Speaker, 3 July 1882.   Brand MSS 297.

1. I quite agree that one day's suspension [of O'Donnell], not having the effect of a second suspension under the Standing Order of Northcote, is too little. 2. I confess however to being impressed with Playfair's suggestion of a reprimand from the Speaker. This

[1] See Ramm II, i. 383.
[2] W. Paul, *Past and present of Aberdeenshire* (1881).
[3] See 11 June 82.
[4] *C.R.*, xlii. 130 (July 1882).
[5] Edward James Rickards, solicitor, on arrangements for duke of Newcastle's education; Hawn P.
[6] Spoke on behaviour of O'Donnell, eventually suspended for a fortnight; *H* 271. 1274.
[7] Add MS 44643, f. 133.
[8] Freycinet suggested separate terms with Arabi; Granville proposed expression of surprise at his change of front; Ramm II, i. 384.
[9] Seymour on 6 July warned British subjects to leave Egypt; on 9 July he threatened bombardment unless fortification works stopped; he bombarded Alexandria 11 July.
[10] Undated holograph; Add MS 44643, f. 134; further note on procedure for F. H. O'Donnell, ibid., f. 136.

was the penalty inflicted by the house upon O'Connell when some 40 or 45 years back he (I think) charged a Committee with perjury. This seems a precedent. Speaker Abercrombie discharged the duty with an excessive leniency which destroyed the effect but this is an avoidable fault.[1] 3. It seems to me that as suspension was a disused punishment, & was re-introduced by the Standing Order very advisedly & within certain limits, a haphazard or piece-meal extension of it may not be desirable. 4. The fact that it is Playfair's suggestion weighs with me. 5. I quite agree as to the duty of supporting him to the utmost practicable degree. His office is so burdensome that I often wonder how any human being can bear it. 6. I have referred to May. [*Parliamentary Practice*] Ed. 8. p. 117. [P.S.] I have referred about O'Connell. It is p. 93.[2]

4 Tu.

Wrote to Ld Kimberley—Ld Granville—The Queen. Visited Christie's. Saw Mr G—Ld RG—Ld Granville—M. Lesseps—M. Sinadino[3]—Mr Bright (2)—Ld Hartington *cum* Mr Childers—Sir W. Harcourt. Twelve to dinner. H of C. 2¾–7 and 10–12¼.[4] Read A faithful Lover—Mr V. Stuart's Egypt.[5]

5. Wed.

Wrote to The Queen (2)—Ld Northbrook—Sir D. Wolff—M. Sinadino—Ld Granville—and minutes. H. of C. 12–6 (Arrears Bill) including Cabinet 3–5.[6] Drive with C. afr & walk. Saw Mr G—Ld RG—Ld Houghton—Sir W. Harcourt—Mr Bright—The Speaker—M. Donat.[7] Dined at Ld Reay's. Read 'The faithful Lover'. My brain is *very* weary.

To LORD NORTHBROOK, first lord of the admiralty,   Add MS 44545, f. 161.
5 July 1882.

1. I think the telegram[8] you have sent was quite within the bounds of your discretion: but it strikes me the impression was that the vessel sent was to be substituted for a smaller one now there. 2. I am not a very good judge as to the terms of a warning, but undoubtedly in case of a bombardment of the fortifications I should think the British authorities at Port Said or elsewhere should make the commanders of ships intending to

---

[1] On 26 February 1838 O'Connell 'was reprimanded in his place by the Speaker' after making 'a foul charge of perjury'; May, *Parliamentary Practice*, 8th ed., 93.

[2] Brand replied this day, Add MS 44195, f. 110: 'as between suspension and admonition, I leave the matter to your better judgment'.

[3] Alexandrian Greek banker representing the Khedive; Gladstone wrote him next day 'not surprised but only pleased' to be able to contradict a rumour 'so injurious to the Khedive'; Add MS 44545, f. 161.

[4] Moved in 401:19 the Crimes Bill as 'urgent'; the Speaker then laid the Rules for urgency; *H* 271. 1392.

[5] H. W. V. Stuart, probably *The funeral tent of an Egyptian Queen* (1882).

[6] No notes found; on Egypt: 'The instructions to Sir Beauchamp Seymour appeared to require no addition. The Cabinet however were disposed to concur with Mr Childers who gave his opinion as Minister of War that it would be well to strengthen the garrisons in the Mediterranean by the addition of two battalions'; CAB 14/16/34. See also Ramm II, i. 385–6.

[7] Unidentified; could read 'Douit'.

[8] PRO ADM 1/6632, f. 14: 'Send immediately any vessel you can conveniently spare to Port Said to protect British subjects. Acquaint French admiral, but no hostile action should be taken in the Canal without orders from home. . . .'

enter the Canal, *or* move about the Egyptian coast, fully aware of what had occurred.
3. Northcote asked me if there was ground for the apprehension which seemed to have
reached him, that some of the smaller British vessels might suffer seriously from the fortification. I told him I had heard of no such apprehension from the naval authorities & that
we relied upon them in such a matter.

6. *Th.*

Wrote to Sir T.E. May—Mr Wilberforce—Ld Granville—Mr Trevelyan—Mr S.
Lawley—Ld Kimberley—Mr Childers—The Queen—& minutes. Read Evenings
with a Reviewer.[1] Saw Mr G—Ld RG—Ld Granville—Mrs Th. Nine to breakfast.
H of C. $4\frac{1}{2}$–$8\frac{1}{4}$ and 9–$2\frac{3}{4}$. Voted in 283:208 for Arrears Bill: a seriously diminished
majority.[2]

To R. G. WILBERFORCE, 6 July 1882. '*Private*'.   Add MS 44545, f. 162.

I do not feel that you need be under any difficulty or pressure with respect to the letters
which you have sent me.[3] My memory does not record any single instance in which your
Father's advancement to Winchester was associated even by the most censorious of men
with political subserviency. It was a very small acknowledgement of his best services to
the Church of England, given when greater ones had been (as I think) unhappily withheld.

Undoubtedly he gave me a warm personal support, and probably he suffered for it, but
with his politics generally I was far from satisfied and more than once I think I had a
friendly expostulation with him about them.

To show you how small a space, *relatively* to other matters connected with his name &
action, politics occupied in my mind, I remain under the impression, perhaps erroneous,
that he offered some opposition to the Bill for the Disestablishment of the Irish Church.[4]
This did not I think much surprise me. A Bishop is apt to get a twist in these matters. A
still older and nearer friend of mine Bishop Hamilton objected to the same Bill though as
I reminded him he had when a young clergyman and Fellow of Merton said to me 'Why
will they not give us the Churches, and let us *go*'.

I have no recollection of Lord Lyttelton's having written 'in my name'[5] but it is perfectly possible that I may have said to him what I had said to the Bishop, and if he asked
my opinion about *his* also conveying it may have encouraged the idea.

7. *Fr.*

Wrote to Ld Granville—Mr F. Harrison—Mr Richard—Mrs O'Shea—The
Queen—and minutes. H. of C. 2–7 and 9–$12\frac{1}{2}$.[6] Read a Faithful Lover. Saw Mr G—
Ld R.G.—Ld Granville (settled a serious matter)[7]—Mr Bright—Mr Chamberlain.
We were beaten today on the Search Clause through Whig defections & Irish

[1] See 28 June 82.
[2] *H* 271. 1718.
[3] Exchange of letters between S. Wilberforce and Lyttelton; Add MS 44476, f. 5.
[4] See Gladstone's sharp letters of 21 Jan., 12 June 69.
[5] Probably Wilberforce's unpublished pamphlet on disestablishment; *Wilberforce*, iii. 282.
[6] Govt. attempt to soften the search clause of the Crimes Bill defeated in 194:207, 25 liberals voting with the Opposition and the Irish not attending; Hammond, 294; *H* 271. 1790.
[7] Probably Granville's overcoming Gladstone's reluctance to summon the cabinet; see Ramm, II,
i. 386.

abstentions. A blow to me, very welcome if it displaced me; but from the nature of the case it will not. I conversed largely on the matter with Bright.

8. Sat [Dollis Hill]

Wrote to Mr Trevelyan—The Queen—& minutes. Went at night to Dollis Hill. Cabinet 12-3½: very stiff, on Egyptian & Suez questions. Saw Mr G—Lord R.G.—Ld Granville—Herbert G.—A.G. for Ireland. Went to Romeo & Juliet. Saw Mr Irving, & then Miss Terry, 'behind'.[1] She acted beautifully. Read Lords Report on Irish Land[2]—Belmore on do in 19th Cent.[3]

Cabinet. July 8. 1882. Noon.[4]
3. Arrears Bill. Language to be held upon occasion as to standing or falling, in given contingencies. We treat it as *necessary.*
2. Land Bill—amendments. Announce impossibility of proceedings this year—?—& adjournment for procedure?
Course of business on assumption that Crime & Arrears Bill become Laws.
1. The situation. See mem. of July 8 herewith. Words added, at Harcourt's instance, with general approval.[5]
4. Arrears Bill. Amendment *as to tenant right.* Draft proposed—W.E.G. to see Trevelyan.
5. Granville proposed a draft respecting Suez Canal & communication with France. Withdrawn.[6]
6. Letter of Childers to Indian Department respecting preliminary steps—qualified & approved.
7. Telegrams of Beauchamp Seymour read. His answer to the Consuls approved. Guns on Fort Ajenni: not to be a *casu belli* i.e. not to authorise operations.

The occurrence of Friday was so far as I know without precedent, and I entertained personally views with regard to it on which it is unnecessary to dwell but which I fear are out of date. However this may be I have endeavoured to weigh what has happened with reference to its practical bearings & to the peculiar responsibilities of the Government at the present time.

The House has placed in the hands of the Government a power of restriction of liberty and of domestic security, which the Government deems to be unnecessary. But the powers of the Bill generally are discretionary powers. The duty of the Government will be to put into action only such of them as it may find to be necessary. With regard to this power I cherish the hope that no such necessity may arise. If the necessity should arise the Government would of course be under the same obligation with respect to this power as with regard to the other powers given by the Bill.

9. 5 S. Trin.

Willesden Ch. 11 A.M. and 6½ P.M. Wrote to Ld Granville (2). Read Princeton Review on New England Divorces—Robn Smith, Prophets of Israel—Geikie,

---

[1] i.e. behind the scenes at the Lyceum.
[2] Lords select cttee. on Land Law (Ireland); *PP* 1882 xi.
[3] *N.C.*, xii. 120 (July 1882).
[4] Add MS 44643, f. 137; another draft at ibid., f. 146.
[5] See below; the added phrase is 'to its practical bearings &'.
[6] Gladstone dissatisfied with Granville's shift towards intervention; but despatch sent on 10 July; Ramm II, i. 387-8.

Half Hours with the Bible. Conversation with Ld Wolverton—Ld Balfour—Lady Balfour.

10. M. [London]

Back to London at 11¼. Wrote to Sir W. Harcourt—Mr Heneage—Rev. Mr Wood—Dr Kinnear—Mr Bright—Mr Otway—Ld Spencer—Ld Kimberley—The Queen—Ld Granville—& minutes. Read A Faithful Lover (at night). Saw Mr G—Ld R.G.—Ld Granville l.l.—Do *cum* Ld Northbrook—Mr Welby—Mr Trevelyan. H. of C. 4¾–8½ & 9½–1½. Engaged in various operations.[1]

To J. BRIGHT, chancellor of the duchy, 10 July 1882. '*Private*'.   Add MS 44545, f. 163.

If news from Alexandria should unhappily arrive which (according to the tenor of a recent conversation you held with me in the House of Commons) might lead you to contemplate a serious step, I would venture to urge upon you not to take such a step without a little time for reflection.

I say a little time, for a long time would abridge such freedom of judgment as you may at present enjoy, but a very little time, even 12 or 24 hours, might throw very great lights upon the question whether, if Seymour is driven to bombard, his action will tend to further disturbance or to peace.[2]

You will have seen with some satisfaction that in order to avoid extremities, when after receiving one lying promise he could not ask for another, he has notwithstanding devised a humane appointment.

[P.S.] A third letter from Otway within, for your approval.

To Sir W. V. HARCOURT, home secretary, 10 July 1882.   MS Harcourt dep. Adds 10.

Many thanks for the books.[3] I do not like to be the sole depository of your letter[4] of yesterday and unless I hear from you to the contrary I will circulate it among our colleagues.

11. Tu.[5]

Wrote to Ld Spencer—Ld Kimberley—Mr MacColl—Sir H. Ponsonby—Mr Leake—Lord Mayor—Ld Granville—The Queen—and minutes. Saw Mr G—Ld RG—Ld Granville—Sir R. Wilson. H of C. 2¼–7 and 9¾–1: Arrears Bill.[6] Short drive with C. A very stiff day. Fourteen to dinner. Read Molly Maguire.[7]

Jul. 11. Sketch for the Session.[8]
Presuppose: passing of Crime Bill, Arrears Bill.
Then: 1. We abandon all the Speech Bills except the Corrupt Practices. 2. Cannot amend

[1] Questions on Egypt; announced autumn session; Arrears Bill; *H* 271. 1965.
[2] Bright replied, resigning, on 12 July; Trevelyan, *Bright*, 433.
[3] *The Molly Maguires* and *The American Irish* (see 21 July 82).
[4] Irish situation 'growing progressively & rapidly worse', according to Errington; Harcourt was reluctant for it to be circulated; Add MS 44197, f. 80 and Gardiner, i. 451.
[5] The British fleet this day bombarded Alexandria.   [6] *H* 272. 35.
[7] F. P. Dewees, *The Molly Maguires. The origin, growth and character of the organization* (Philadelphia, 1877); sent by Harcourt; see 21 July 82, also 5 Dec. 82.
[8] Add MS 44766, f. 103.

Land Act. a. Purchase; b. Judicial Rent; c. Emigration; d. Leases; e. *date* of Judicial Rent; f. Labourers. 3. Pass financial necessary business—(& such secondary Bills as we can). 4. Adjourn, probably to day *in the latter half of October.* 5. For procedure: to wh we should propose to *give precedence daily* as far as possible.

12. Wed.

Wrote to The Queen—Ld Granville (2)—Mr Bright—Rev. N. Hall—Musurus Pacha: & minutes. Saw Mr G—Ld RG—Ld Northbrook. H of C. 12¼-6.[1] Read Molly Maguire. Visited the Breadalbanes at six & went over their interesting house or palace. Dined with Musurus Pacha. Had an interesting conversation with him on the grave event of yesterday: we were really agreed on prospective issues, and very harmonious. Saw likewise Italian Ambassador & Spanish & Greek Ministers: all spoke in tones of congratulation & peace.[2]

To J. BRIGHT, chancellor of the duchy, 12 July 1882.　　　　Add MS 43385, f. 303.
'*Immediate*'.[3]

I write these few lines, not with any intention of bringing a battery to bear upon you, but simply to tell you that the view I expressed in my last note has I think acquired some degree of confirmation by the course of events since I wrote it & since the action of yesterday.

My view was that the particular use of force, which was in contemplation *might* be found effectually to serve the ends of peace.

It is much too soon to say that this has been, or will be, the case; but things look towards such a result. A flag of truce, which can hardly mean anything but some sort of surrender, has actually been sent to the fleet. We have no reason to anticipate any disapproval from any of the Powers. Any protest from Turkey will be a protest fired in the air to save appearances, & will, as a show, be irresistibly attractive to the Sultan; all whose acts, or words at any rate, are shams. We have not got peace in Egypt, but we are I do believe nearer by a good deal to peace than we were 48 hours ago. I rely on your wisdom, on your friendship, & on the prospects before you of being eminently useful on behalf of peace, to do nothing abruptly. I am glad to find a spirit of calm dwelling, today, on some ruffled surfaces.

To LORD KIMBERLEY, colonial secretary, 12 July 1882.　　　　Add MS 44545, f. 165.

I cannot withhold my assent from your proposal as I see nothing better than Sir H. Robinson's suggestion.[4] I would however make the *Imperial* part of the action as little prominent as possible.

One or two members of the Cabinet have given very special attention to these South African matters—would you not do well to consult them.

[P.S.] Please however to read Courtney's man:—he has a double point of view. His policy may be *ultimately* right.

---

[1] *H* 272. 173; on the bombardment; Egypt 'without any law whatever'.
[2] Report in Ramm II, i. 393.
[3] Gladstone's letter presumably crossed with Bright's resigning; see 10 July 82n.
[4] Telegrams of 9 and 11 July, proposing a 'middle course' for Bechuanaland, i.e. short of a protectorate, imposing order by a joint force of local men; Add MS 44227, ff. 206–10.

13. Th.

Wrote to Ld Granville—Musurus Pacha—Mr Bright—Ld Northbrook—The
Queen l.l.—and minutes. Saw Mr G—Ld RG—Ld Northbrook—and others.
Cabinet 12-1½. Conclave on Arrears' Bill 2½-3¾. H. of C. 4½-8½ and 9½-1.[1] Read
Molly Maguire.

Cabinet. 13 July 82.[2]
1. Telegrams to Alexandria as to the Fleet and the state of the city. Avoid further
   destruction.
   Communicate with Khedive for order. Naval reliefs: no action in Canal without further orders. Marines &c. may be landed on invitation or on concurrence. Invite European ships if any to cooperate.
2. Arrears Bill amendments to be considered in W.E.G.'s room.
3. Take up transport in India.

To J. BRIGHT, chancellor of the duchy, 13 July 1882.   Rochdale MSS F/5/1/BRI/1.

The kindness of your letter[3] is beyond even what I expected; & yet I am not satisfied
with it; considering it, to the best of my power from your point of view.
   I do not think it fair to ask you to see me as it would seem hardly consistent with
proper respect after what you have said. Yet I should like you to know the view that is
taken of the recent act.
   I dined last night with Musurus & had a pretty full conversation with him: it ended
with his saying how completely we were agreed & that we two could settle it at a sitting.
   Not only with him but with the Italian Spanish & Greek Ministers I had conversations
& all the four were united with me in believing that the action at Alexandria had brought
us materially nearer to peace order & legality in the East.
   Pray consider the immense force of such a fact, if it be one.

To LORD NORTHBROOK, first lord of the admiralty,   Add MS 44266, f. 135.
13 July 1882.[4]

I have jotted down such ideas as occur to me on these important matters.
Alexandria: 1. Work of reconstruction—Carry as far as is important from a military point
of view—but no further. 2. Govt of town if abdicated by Arabi—encourage Dervisch to
assume it, with the concurrence & on behalf of the Khedive. 3. Shall he be assisted say by
marines, *at his request*, for purposes of police. 4. Should France be invited to concur.

14. Fr.

Wrote to Ld Granville l.l.—Dr Wilberforce—Mr Bright—Mr Herbert RA—The
Queen—Mrs Bolton—Mr Godley—Lord Spencer—& minutes. Dined with the
Jameses. Read Evenings with Reviewer. Saw Mr G—Ld RG—Mr Courtennay
[*sic*]—Mr Welby—Mr Mundella—Mr Ashley—Ld Granville *cum* Ld North-
brook—Mr Bright, I fear in vain—Scotts—Sir J. St Aubyn. Conclave at night on
G's dispatch to Paris.[5] H of C. 2¼-6¾ and 9½-1½.[6]

---

[1] Questions on Egypt; Arrears Bill; *H* 272. 284.
[2] Add MS 44643, f. 148.   [3] See 10 July 82n.
[4] Holograph.   [5] See Ramm II, i. 394n.
[6] Egypt; Arrears Bill; *H* 272. 458.

To J. BRIGHT, chancellor of the duchy, 14 July 1882.[1]   Rochdale MSS F/5/1/BRI/1.
'*Most private*'.

At this critical moment, I desire to put on paper, without enlargement, the substance of the remarks which you allowed me to address you in conversation today. I merely change them into the form of a letter.

The act of Tuesday was a solemn & painful one, for which I feel myself to be highly responsible, & it is my earnest desire that we should all view it now as we shall wish, at the last, that we had viewed it.

Subject to this testing rule, I address you as one whom I suppose not to believe all use whatever of military force to be unlawful: as one who detests war in general & believes most wars to have been sad errors (in which I greatly agree with you), but who in regard to any particular use of force would look upon it for a justifying cause, & after it would endeavour to appreciate its actual effect.

The general situation in Egypt had latterly become one in which everything was governed by sheer military violence. Every legitimate authority—the Khedive, the Sultan, the Notables, & best men of the country such as Cherif & Sultan Pachas had been put down, and a situation of *force* had been created, which could only be met by force.

This being so we had laboured to the uttermost, almost alone but not without success, to secure that, if force were employed against the violence of Arabi, it should be force armed with the highest sanction of law: that it should be the force of the Sovereign, authorised & restrained by the United Powers of Europe, who in such a case represent the civilised world.

While this is going on, a bye-question arises. The British fleet, lawfully present in the waters of Alexandria, had the right & duty of self defence. It demanded the discontinuance of attempts made to strengthen the armament of the fortifications, to which attempts no limit of degree could be made to attach. Met by fraud & falsehood in its demand, it required surrender with a view to immediate dismantling: and, this being refused, it proceeded to destroy.

By this proceeding we have become responsible for the slaughter of many persons, defenders of the works, & probably for a few casualties in the town.

The conflagration which followed, the pillage & any other outrages effected by the released convicts, these are not due to us, but to the seemingly wanton wickedness of Arabi, who must have known perfectly well that the Admiral had no force for an invasion of the country, even if he (Arabi) was authorised to disbelieve every word of our professions on the subject.

Such being the amount of our act, what has been its reception, & its effect?

As to its reception, we have not received or heard of a word of disapproval from any Power great or small, or from any source having the slightest authority.

As to its effect it has taught many lessons, struck a heavy perhaps a deadly blow at the reign of violence, brought again into the light the beginnings of legitimate rule, shown the fanaticism of the East that massacre of Europeans is not likely to be perpetrated with impunity, & greatly advanced the Egyptian question towards a permanent & peaceable solution.

I feel that in being party to this work, I have been a labourer in the cause of peace.

Your cooperation in that cause, with reference to preceding & collateral points, has been of the utmost value, & has enabled me to hold my ground, when without you it might have been difficult.

---

[1] Bright replied, 15 July, Add MS 44113, f. 181: 'Your letter & arguments do not help me in the least in your direction—they are so at variance with my views that they show my attempting to go with the Govt. is impossible.'

It will be a great blow, not only to feeling, but to public principles & purposes, not alone to these generally, but especially in relation to peace as against war, & law as against violence & arbitrary will, should that cooperation be withdrawn.

15. Sat. [*Windsor*]

Wrote to Mr Maclaren—Musurus P.—The Queen l.l.—Ld Granville l. & Tel.—Mr Childers—& minutes. Off to Windsor (Deanery) 3.50 PM. Saw Mr G—Ld R.G— W.H.G.—Ld Northbrook—Sir H. Ponsonby. Read G. Smith, & Tuke, in 19th Cent.[1]—Ann. Reg. 1816 on Algiers[2]—Seeley on Natural Religion[3]—Evenings with a Reviewer.

To H. C. E. CHILDERS, war secretary, 15 July 1882.[4]   Add MS 44130, f. 50.

I hope you will not present any professional objection to interfere with the urgent proposal of Gr[anville] Northbr[ook] & myself to supply Seymour with the aid of troops for purposes of police in Alexandria.

The case is most peculiar. It is not a mere question of the inconvenience of a dual command for practical purposes though that is serious enough. But in my opinion the political reason for stamping the operation with the character of a police operation under Seymour in continuation of what is already done is imperative. We must not be suspected of invasion & to introduce a military force as such under military command wd I fear place us under hopeless suspicion in this respect & might entail grave complications. I therefore rely on your tact & wisdom to settle the matter.

You have allowed soldiers as I understand to be used under civil authority in Ireland for purposes of order—and this is a case, & a very high case, of the order of the world.[5]

16. 6 S. Trin.

St Georges mg (with H.C.) and evg. Migrated to the Castle. Long audience of the Queen: she was most frank, & kind. Dined with H.M. Walk with the Dean, & much conversation. Wrote to Sir H. Ponsonby—Ld Granville—Mr Childers Tel. Read Natural Religion—Halfhours with the Bible.

17. M. [*London*]

Wrote to Sir D. Currie—The Queen l.l.—Mr Bright—Abp of Canterb.—Dean of Windsor—Bp of Winchester—& minutes. Dined at Sir C. Forster's. Saw Mr G— Ld R.G—Ld Granville—Mr Trevelyan—Ld Northbrook—Mr Welby. H of C. 4½– 8½ and 10–1.[6] Read Evgs with a Reviewer. Returned to London 11.30.

---

[1] *N.C.*, xii. 1, 134 (July 1882).
[2] Ch. ix of *Annual Register* (1816) on the punitive bombardment of Algiers, leading to emancipation of Christian slaves and prisoners: 'with the generosity, characteristic of Great Britain, she has performed this great public service entirely at her own expense'.
[3] J. R. Seeley, *Natural religion* (1882); see 13 Aug. 82.
[4] Holograph copy.
[5] Childers replied that by law soldiers must be commanded by officers and that such had been the case in Ireland; Add MS 44130, f. 52.
[6] Questions; Bright's resignation; Arrears Bill; *H* 272. 718.

18. Tu.

Wrote to The Queen 1.1.—Card. MacCabe[1]—Mr Blunt—Ld Granville—&
minutes. H of C. 4½-7 and 9-1.[2] Saw Mr G—Ld RG—Ld Northbrook—Mr
Trevelyan—Mr Childers—Mr Go[schen?] [sic]. Cabinet 1-2¾. Read Molly
Maguire—Hist. Dispatch on Egypt.[3] Drive with C.

Cabinet. July 18. 82. 1 P.M.[4]
1. Ld Mayor's Dinner. To be Wed. Aug. 7.
2. Emigration Clauses of I[rish] G[overnment] Division.[5] Majority for.
3. Division on 3 R. Arrears Bill. Egypt. Shall the party meet?
4. Spanish Treaty question. Chamberlain wishes retaliation. All against it.
5. 1300[6] men to be sent from Malta for the defence of Alexandria.

19. Wed.

Wrote to Mr Ashley—Mr Spurgeon—Ld Spencer—The Queen 1.—Mr Forster—
and minutes. Conclave on Egypt 11½-12½. H. of C. 12½-4. Arrears Bill got out of
Committee.[7] Drive with C. Saw Mr G—Ld RG.—Mr Goschen—Mr V. Stuart—
Rev Dr [blank]—Mr Escott—Lady Coke. Dined at Ld Aberdeen's. Read Molly
Maguire.

To LORD SPENCER, Viceroy of Ireland, 19 July 1882.   Althorp MSS K5.

I am obliged to write to you with succinctness almost abrupt, for the Egyptian question
and the Arrears Bill added on to the course of ordinary business render it necessary not to
waste a word. The demands of Egypt, in the various phases of the question, are most
urgent, and almost incessant.

As regards the Search Clause,[8] rest assured that, so far as I know, there is no cause for
further correspondence; and so I have told Granville. I believe that any difficulty or
apprehension you have felt has been caused by peculiarity of opinion much more on my
side than on yours. In my eyes, as Liberty, especially in the form of domestic security (and
in this you would agree) is a very sacred thing, and as the House of Commons is the
special guardian of liberty, while the Government is the special guardian of order, it is a
great offence, or as I should call it an outrage, for the House of Commons, while it has
confidence in the Government, to force upon it provisions restrictive of liberty, which it
does not think necessary for the fulfilment of its proper duty, the maintenance of order. It
was the enabling character of the Clause which permitted me to acquiesce in this outrage; and as I have not given in any adhesion to the proposal except in the case of necessity, I also expressed my conviction that the case of necessity if it arose would be duly
examined, and that I should have through your kindness due warning about it. Again I say

[1] Edward *MacCabe, 1816–85; abp. of Dublin 1879; cardinal 1882; denounced agrarian agitation.
[2] Egypt; Arrears Bill; *H* 272. 902.
[3] Not found.
[4] Add MS 44643, f. 150.
[5] Clauses of the Arrears Bill to sponsor emigration; Gladstone noted as voting 'Aye': Granville,
Dodson, Hartington, Chamberlain, Northbrook, Carlingford; 'No': Kimberley, Harcourt, Childers,
W.E.G.; ibid. f. 151.
[6] '14' written above this figure.
[7] *H* 272. 1017.
[8] Spencer's letters of 15 and 17 July discussed the search clause and the P.P.P. Act; *Spencer*, i. 215.

my opinions are probably in a great degree peculiar to myself but this does not absolve me from the duty of acting upon them, although it imposes a special obligation to respect the prevailing sentiment.

On this matter I have not been so very succinct after all: and I have still to add that I have heard from Johnson what you propose to do, and I believe it is all the case admits of since you are unfortunately precluded from reserving the case to yourself as to the first initiation of a search by night otherwise than conformably to the terms of our Proviso.

2. I am very glad you have been able to come to the conclusion that you need not ask for a renewal of the L.P.P. Act [i.e. P.P.P. Act]. For I think that both the House and even the Cabinet have now for a good while regarded it as practically dead, and have viewed the Crime Prevention Act as taking its place. Indeed it is hard to state what would be the amount of a renewal of the L.P.P. Act in its old terms. Were it strictly limited to the members of secret or Fenian i.e. murderous societies, the case might be very difficult indeed. I am now speaking only my own opinions, and those first opinions.

3. The Arrears Bill, as far as it is an Arrears Bill, has now come virtually to the close of the discussions on its particulars, except as to the question of a Fourth Commissioner. But the question of Emigration is also to be introduced, and clauses suggested by you are to be adopted by the Government. There was much difference of opinion in the Cabinet, not on your plan in particular, but on the adoption of any plan involving a grant of public money. Your clauses will be conformable to the views of the greater part of your colleagues. I am one of those who entertain insurmountable objections to any plan of the kind on its merits. But I have not sought to raise the question above its proper level, and grave as my apprehensions are, I give way, not only out of general deference, but from feeling that a man, who is looking for the very first legitimate opportunity of retirement from office, ought not to press unduly on his colleagues his views on a question essentially prospective, and one in which their share and concern must be very far beyond his own.

4. I have viewed with satisfaction the progressive though variable diminution in Ireland of Agrarian outrages generally, which I connect with the growing influence of the Land Act, and the more & more widely felt failure of the No-Rent Crusade. Looking to the more atrocious murders of this year as due to secret organisations separate from mere agrarian discontent, we have concurred freely in your plans for getting at the interior of the Secret Societies, as was done with reference to the Molly Maguires in Africa [*sic*; *sc.* America]: I hope, notwithstanding the late incident, so repulsive in itself, of Col. Brackenbury's proceedings,[1] these plans may succeed, and relieve Ireland from the darkest of its stains and the chief remaining unmitigated cause of insecurity and alarm.

I hope that in this long story I have given you no occasion for the labour of reply.

20. Th.

Wrote to Sir J. Pease—Mr Marum MP—Ld Granville 1.1.—The Queen 1.1.—and minutes. Cabinet $2\frac{1}{2}$-$4\frac{1}{4}$. Read Molly Maguire. Saw Mr G—Ld RG—Mr Childers *cum* Ld Northbrook—Ld Granville—Mr Courtney—Fisheries Deputn[2]—Sir R. Cross. Dined at Lucy's. H of C. $4\frac{1}{4}$-8 and $9\frac{3}{4}$-$12\frac{1}{2}$.[3]

---

[1] Brackenbury had written a mem. urging 'the immediate renewal of the Act', i.e. suspension of habeas corpus; Brackenbury was also trying to take part in the Egyptian expedition, a lack of commitment deplored by Spencer; Add MS 44309, f. 71.

[2] No account found.

[3] Arrears Bill; *H* 272. 1104.

Cabinet. July 20. 2½ PM. D. St.[1]
Egypt.
a. Water supply of Alexandria. Admiral authorised to act for the best.
b. dispatch of ½ Corps d'Armée to the Mediterranean agreed to
c. Sir G. Wolseley to command & Adye Chief of the Staff.
d. To keep out for a month certain militia regiments. W.E.G. dissents.
e. Notice to Parlt. Vote of credit.[2]
f. Not to take up transport in India yet.
g. Whether to sound Italy-Postponed.
Chancellorship of the Duchy.[3]

'Sultan has signified his assent to be represented in the conference but has given no answer as to sending troops to Egypt.'
Notice for Monday. a. Vote of Credit. b. Provision for charge. Strong appeal about questions: except as to what are in the strict sense matters of fact.

21. Fr.

Wrote to Mr Bright—Sir S Loyd Lindsay[4]—Ld Granville—Ld Spencer—Sir W. Harcourt—The Queen—and minutes. Dined at Houghton's. H of C. 2½-7 and 10½-12¾. Spoke briefly on Arrears Bill.[5] Saw Mr G—Ld RG—Ld Granville—Ld Hartington—Mrs Bolton—Mr Trevelyan—Sir C. Dilke—Mrs Barton—Mrs Fitzgerald. Finished Molly Maguire. Read The American Irish.[6]

To Sir W. V. HARCOURT, home secretary, 21 July 1882.   MS Harcourt dep. 8, f. 157.

I return this very curious & valuable work on the Molly Maguire organisation.[7] I do hope you will have it turned to account by reprint in this country (though as a work it is very ill done) or by sending it to the Spectator or some other journal with special commendation to notice. On the whole it throws more light on the case of Ireland than almost anything I have ever read.[8]
I venture to keep the other book yet a little while. Thanks.

To LORD SPENCER, Viceroy of Ireland, 21 July 1882.[9]   Althorp MSS K5.

After the break-down of Brackenbury I am tempted to write a few lines.
It seems to me no very natural mode of action to seek for the head of any detective agency in the ranks of the military profession. All its habits and traditions appear

---

[1] Add MS 44643, f. 154.
[2] Note summoning Northbrook and Childers 'for a preliminary conversation on *finance* & its effect on procedure' at ibid., f. 158.
[3] Bright succeeded by Kimberley; see to Kimberley, 22 July 82.
[4] Asking Sir R. Loyd Lindsay not to put his question on Egypt; Add MS 44545, p. 170.
[5] New emigration clause; *H* 272. 1226.
[6] P. H. Bagenal, *The American Irish and their influence in Irish politics* (1882); a well-documented account, especially of the Fenian press.
[7] See 11, 22 July 82.
[8] On 25 August 1882, MS Harcourt dep. Adds 10, Gladstone urged 'pray do not forget . . . the republication of Molly Maguire. If only money is wanted, I can manage.'
[9] Part in *Spencer*, i. 217.

anything but calculated to mature this accomplishment. A soldier may be a consummate head of detectives but I think it must be in spite of his being a soldier. Neither am I well satisfied, though here the case is not so strong, why it is that for a purpose of this kind there seems to be an inclination among to turn to the Indian Services [*sic*]. No service with the habit of command seems especially calculated to form the qualities that are wanted. Had I the matter in my hands I certainly should be disposed to seek for advice & suggestions among solicitors practised in the investigation of crime: *possibly* even for instruments.

I have been reading with great interest and profit the astonishing account contained in the American work 'Molly Maguire' of the murderous organisation in the mining districts of Pennsylvania, and of its detection in a great degree through the superintending energy of Mr. Gowan, head of the Philadelphia & Reading Railway Company. It would seem to me, after reading that book, which presents a case of Ireland over again & even something more, all worked by the Irish, worthwhile to inquire through the Foreign Office Agency what advice or suggestions might be obtained from a man like Mr. Gowan if disposed to give aid. Do not reply.

22. Sat. [*Dollis Hill*]

Wrote to Mr Childers—Ld Kimberley (2)—Mr Magniac—The Queen Tel. 1.1.— Mr Bright—Mrs Th.—Mr Bartlett—Mr Courtney—Sir Thos G.—Sir C. Dilke—Mr Mudie—& minutes. Saw Mr G—Ld RG—Ld Granville *cum* Sir C. Dilke—Ld Northbrook—Mr Childers—Mr Welby. Went off at four to the Dollis. Read Letter to Cowen[1]—Mudies Stray Leaves[2]—Blunt on Islam[3]—The American Irish.

To LORD KIMBERLEY, colonial secretary, 22 July 1882.   Add MS 44545, ff. 170–1.

[First letter:]   I have heard this morning that you are looking for a home for Cetywayo.

You are most welcome to appropriate my house in Harley Street for his use without any charge.

The only condition I should make is its being delivered up clean, in rooms & furniture, to my agents Messrs. Grogan & Boyd, Piccadilly, on his departure.

There are seven bedrooms, besides servants' bedrooms; three sitting rooms, besides one very small one. Four stalls in the stables.[4]

[Second letter:]   Will you allow me to propose your name to the Queen as provisional successor to Bright in the Duchy. The business is slight, & with your knowledge of land you will I believe find it scarcely sensible.[5]

23. 7 S. Trin.

Willesden Ch mg and evg. Wrote to Ld Granville 1.1.—Sir Thos G.—The Queen—E. Hamilton. Read Life of Molinos[6]—Seeley, Natural Religion. Translated Cowper's most beautiful Hymn 'Hark my soul, it is the Lord', which we had in the Morning Service, into Italian: a daring act, but I could not help it.[7]

---

[1] *A plain letter to Joseph Cowen, esq., by a Gladstonian radical* (1882).
[2] By C. E. Mudie (1872).   [3] W. S. Blunt, *The future of Islam* (1882).
[4] Cetewayo was given lodgings in Melbury Road, Kensington.
[5] Kimberley thus held the colonial office and the chancellorship of the duchy jointly.
[6] J. Bigelow, *Molinos the Quietist* (1882).
[7] Tr. as 'Senti, senti, anima mia'; various versions made; Add MS 44766, ff. 107–114; published in *N.C.*, xiv. 357 (September 1883).

To Sir T. GLADSTONE, 23 July 1882.   Add MS 44545, f. 171.

Though I cannot definitely judge, and though I think there is now little expectation of any useful help from the Sultan (who is wholly untrustworthy) yet I think it is quite uncertain as yet whether the whole British force that is now under orders for the Mediterranean will have to land in Egypt. What I expect is that Alexandria will be our base of operations: & most probably that Arabi will be crushed with little fighting. He has I think within the last 10 days shown himself to be one of the greatest villains alive.

24. M. [London]

Back to London before eleven. Corrected my hymn. Wrote to Ld Hartington—The Queen 1.1.1.—and minutes. Cabinet 12½-2. Worked on Egyptian question. Saw Mr G—Ld R.G—Ld Granville 1.1.1. (Conclave)—Sir Thos G. H of C. 4¾-9 & 9¾-12. Spoke an hour or more in stating the Egyptian case.[1] Read Life of Molinos.

Cabinet. July 24. 1882. 12.30.[2]
1. Language of message respecting Reserves. determined.
2. Indian troops to be ordered: Hartington to ask for assent of Parlt.
3. Invitation to other Powers—Terms of a letter to France agreed on: 'we shall think ourselves entitled to accept the cooperation of any Power willing to give it.'

25. Tu.

Wrote to Watsons—The Queen Tel. & L.—Ld Granville 1.1.—Sir Thomas G.—& minutes. Again amending Hymn. H of C. 2¼-5½ and 9-1.[3] Saw Mr G—Ld RG—Ld Granville—Ld Northbrook—Mr Welby—Sir Thos G.—Mr Courtney. Drive with C. Read Life of Molinos (finished)—A faithful Lover.

To Sir T. GLADSTONE, 25 July 1882. '*Private*'.   Hawarden MSS.

I send you my hearty congratulations on the return of your birthday, and I cannot add a more brotherly wish than that when it again returns it may please God that with continuing health and strength you may have been relieved from your present anxiety about your son.

I proceed to give you all the news I can about our prospects of action but in *strict reliance* upon your absolute secrecy.

1. The French Ministry is in danger from a coalition between those who think it has gone too far & those who want it to go further. It is uncertain whether the effect of a change would be that France would take a more forward position—but this is possible. 2. The Turks seem today more anxious to participate, & this may come to pass, but the amount of advantage from it is uncertain. 3. It is not impossible that Italy may cooperate. Probably all these points will be cleared up in the course of the week.

26. Wed.

Wrote to The Queen—Ld Granville 1.1.—Sir Thos G.—Mr Hamilton—Ld Hartington—& minutes. Saw Mr G—Ld RG—Ld Granville—Mr Knowles. H of C.

[1] Moving a Vote of Credit of £2,300,000; *H* 272. 1574.
[2] Add MS 44643, f. 160.
[3] Spoke on Elcho's Resolution (withdrawn) on Egypt; *H* 272. 1690.

$12\frac{1}{4}$–$5\frac{3}{4}$.[1] Dined with the Mount Temples. Read Lecky's Hist Engl. Vol 3.[2]—A faithful Lover (finished). Insufficient.

27. Th.

Wrote to Freshfields—Sir R. Cunliffe—Watsons—Mr Chamberlain—Ld Granville—Ld Hartington—The Queen 1.1.—Sir H. Ponsonby Tel.—& minutes. Eleven to breakfast. Saw Mr G—Ld R.G—Ld Granville—Scotts. Read Lecky—American Irish. Fugitive Cabinet at 6. Went with Helen to the new Courts to receive cheques: and saw the fine Hall and parts of the vast buildings. H of C. $4\frac{3}{4}$–$8\frac{1}{2}$ & $9\frac{1}{2}$–$2\frac{1}{4}$. Spoke (40 m) in winding up at Hartington's request, who was to have done the work.[3] Debate favourable.

28. Fr.

Wrote to Mr Dodson—Mr Hutton—The Queen 1.1.—Sir C. Dilke—and minutes. H. of C. $2\frac{1}{4}$–7. Spoke on Finance & explained on Egypt.[4] Also 10–$10\frac{1}{2}$. Read Lecky's History. Saw Mr G—Ld R.G—Ld Granville—Ld Northbrook—Sir Thos G.—on Egypt & H.J.G.s affairs.

29. Sat. [Farnham Castle]

Wrote to Sir Thos G.—The Queen—Mr Lefevre—Mr Whitbread—Mrs Pringle—Major Cesnola—and minutes. Saw Mr G—Ld RG—Ld Granville. Cabinet 12–$2\frac{1}{4}$. Off at 4 to Farnham Castle[5]—a very fine thing. Saw the Bp, Bp of Ely, Ld Coleridge. Read Ewart Conroy[6]—Tracts.

Cabinet, Sat. July 29. 82. Noon.[7]
1. Clearing the decks of business. Park plan? Same principle.
2. Adjourn to what date? (probable) (can be called together during adjournment)
3. Gibson's amendment—All but Hn. incline to refuse.[8]
4. Committee to frame plan of Devolution—& invite Whitbread.[9]
5. Plan not to be announced until we meet for Procedure.
6. Arrears Bill Amendments. Conversation.

1. Ld Granville read note of Davidoff's communication: actual dissolution of Conference. Not considered unfriendly.
2. Instruction to Dufferin as within[10] agreed on.
3. Obtain authority of Khedive for Adm. Hoskins to act in the Canal as he may find it necessary. Action postponed till we hear what takes place in Paris.

---

[1] Spoke on army reserve; *H* 272. 1823.
[2] Vols. iii and iv of W. E. H. Lecky, *History of England in the eighteenth century* (1882); see 17 Apr. 78.
[3] Credit voted in 275: 19; *H* 272. 2106.   [4] *H* 273. 34, 66.
[5] Palace of bp. of Winchester (E. H. *Browne) by Farnham, Surrey; bp. of Ely (J. R. Woodford) also present; both appt. by Gladstone.
[6] H. Powell, *Ewart Conroy* (1882).
[7] Add MS 44643, f. 162.
[8] Gibson's amndt. for $\frac{2}{3}$ Commons vote in case of closure.
[9] i.e. Whitbread to be asked to help plan procedure; he declined.
[10] Not found with cabinet notes; see PRO 30/29/143; probably the draft at Add MS 44766, f. 115.

4. Proposal of Cartwright to cut telegraphic line at Kantona—postponed.
5. (Arrear Clause) I have never contemplated any other than changes of secondary importance in the Tenure Clauses.
6. Prince of Wales—Cabinet against his going to Egypt.
7. Channel Tunnel—Papers to be circulated.

30. 8 S. Trinity.

Farnham Ch. mg. with H.C.—Chapel Service evg. Walk round the Park with the two Bps. Conversation with Coleridge on the ideas of the Future Life. Read Clem. Alex. V.[1]—Life of Macmillan[2]—Seeley, Nat. Religion.

31. M. [London]

Wrote to Sir F. Doyle—Ld Granville—Mr Lefevre—The Queen Tel. & 1.1.1.— Rev. Mr Eyre—& minutes. Cabinet 2-4. H. of C. $4\frac{1}{2}$-$8\frac{3}{4}$ and $10\frac{1}{2}$-$12\frac{1}{2}$.[3] Saw Mr G—Ld R.G.—Mr Carnegie[4]—& others. Came up from beautiful Farnham 10-11$\frac{3}{4}$. Read Macmillan's Life.

Cabinet. Monday Jul. 31. 82. 2 PM[5]
1. Egypt. Information. Turkish deal of 28 Jul. Answer agreed on.
2. Canal. But to avoid action (except under necessity) until we are prepared for complete action (Ismailia).
3. Instructions to Wolseley; Put down Arabi & establish Khedive's power. Alison to pass under Wolseley's authority when he arrives. & other points.
4. Kimberley read Telegram for a qualified restoration of Cetewayo from Bulwer. His reply disclaims annexation—accepts qualified restoration—inquires about Protectorate.[6]

Tues. Aug. One 1882.

Wrote to Mayor of Denbigh—The Queen Tel. & l.l.l.—Sir D. Wedderburn— Count Cadorna—Ld Houghton—& minutes. H of C. at $4\frac{1}{4}$: 6-7$\frac{3}{4}$, & again.[7] Read Life of Macmillan—Doyle's Yorkshire Heiress.[8] Saw Mr G—Ld RG—Ld Granville—The Speaker—Mr Mundella *cum* Mr Courtney—Ld Rosebery—Mr C.[P.] Villiers (a marvel)[9]—Mr J.R. Herbert—Sir J. Lacaita. Luncheon at Mrs Th.s. Ten to dinner.

[1] i.e. the 5th book of Clement of Alexandria's *Stromateis.*
[2] T. Hughes, *Memoir of Daniel Macmillan* (1882).
[3] Egyptian expenses; *H* 273. 267.
[4] Andrew *Carnegie, 1835-1919; manufacturer, philanthropist and enthusiastic Gladstonian; their first meeting, earlier this month, was arranged by Rosebery, see B.J. Hendrick, *Andrew Carnegie* (1932), i. 256-9.
[5] Add MS 44643, f. 165.
[6] Not in PRO CO 179/141.
[7] Questions; *H* 273. 374.
[8] Early version of Sir F. H. C. Doyle, *The Yorkshire heiress, a comedy* (1885?).
[9] See 11 July 42n.; M.P. for Wolverhampton 1835-98; a close friend of Mrs Thistlethwayte.

2. Wed.

Wrote to Mr Barker—Ld Granville l.l.—Mr Trevelyan—Messrs Barker & Hignett *draft*—Archdn Brown—and minutes. H. of C. at one.[1] Saw Mr G—Ld RG—Ld Granville—Mr [R.H.] Hutton—Sir W. Harcourt—Scotts—Mr Cashel Hoey. Dined with Mr Hutton at the Devonshire. Then carried off to the House-dinner where I made a short speech.[2] Read 19th Cent. on Ireland—On Mohametans of India[3]—Swinburne's Memoirs.[4]

3. Th.

Wrote to The Queen 1.1. and Tel.—and minutes. H. of C. $4\frac{1}{2}$–$8\frac{1}{2}$ & $9\frac{1}{2}$–$11\frac{3}{4}$.[5] Read Macmillan's Life—American Irish (finished)—Carnegie.[6] Saw Mr G—Ld R.G—The O'Conor Don—Bp of London—Mr Macmillan—Sir E. Malet—Sir John Adye—N. Lyttelton—Sir W. Harcourt. Cabinet 2–4.

Cabinet. Thurs. Aug. 3. 82. 2 PM.[7]
1. Arrears Bill.·Amendments of Lords. Considered provisionally: to be resumed on Sat.
2. Procedure. Reject Gibson's amt? Decision postponed.
3. Business (Lefevre's plan?) Indian budget? after Supply & Arrears Amendments.
5. Dufferin on the Italian proposition respecting the Canal, to take part only *quoad* temporary arrangements.
6. Dilke to say in H of C. today as to Turkish Bills: we regard these bills as unauthorised & without any value. advise Khedive accordingly.
7. Beauchamp Seymour to cut Telegraph from Cairo to Syria—wh. Kh. has asked
8. Granville to let Turk understand that we cannot indefinitely prolong negotiations with him about our allied intervention.
9. Authorise D[ilke] to say that Turkish troops cannot be allowed to land until satisfactory arrangements have been made on the two points—& that Seymour has been so instructed.
10. Admiral not to allow present landing.
11. Shall G. sound Bismarck through Herbert B. as to mode of stating our case respecting sole action. *No.*

4. Fr.

Wrote to The Speaker—Mrs Bolton—Mrs Th.—Sir W. Harcourt—The Queen—Mr Playfair—Ld Spencer—and minutes. Saw Mr G—Ld RG—Ld Granville—Mr S. Gladstone—The Speaker. Read Macmillan's Life. H of C. $4\frac{1}{4}$–$8\frac{1}{2}$ & 10–$12\frac{3}{4}$.[8]

---

[1] Grosvenor apologised for his late arrival; *H* 273. 505.
[2] No report found.
[3] *N.C.*, xii. 175, 193 (August 1882).
[4] Perhaps H. Swinburne, *Travels in the Two Sicilies*, 2v. (1783–5).
[5] Questions; Dilke dealing with some Egyptian points; *H* 273. 614.
[6] A. Carnegie's travel journal, privately published (1882); Hendrick, *Carnegie*, i. 236.
[7] Add MS 44643, f. 166.
[8] Macfarlane's unsuccessful motion for Royal Commission on Scottish crofters; *H* 273. 766.

To Sir W. V. HARCOURT, home secretary,   MS Harcourt dep. 8, f. 159.
4 August 1882. '*Private*'.

I thought it not difficult yesterday to see what the Cabinet would probably decide to-morrow. Then comes the question what next? and next?

Taking the worst alternatives all the way through we may have before us 1. Rejection of the Bill; 2. Prorogation; 3. Reintroduction; 4. Second rejection—and then? Here comes up your suggestion.

And it really would be an advantage if either alone or with the Law Officers you would reckon the *dates* within which on the basis of your plan a Dissolution might take place and a new Parliament might for the third time take up an Arrears Bill.

To L. PLAYFAIR, M.P., chairman of ways and means,   Playfair MSS.
4 August 1882. '*Private & Confidential*'.

I receive your letter with much regret. When you come to act upon the intention you describe as formed, it will not be an easy matter to fill your place. There is certainly a point at which domestic calls must begin to assert themselves against Parliamentary engagements.

I am very glad however that you do not contemplate any early step,[1] and that you propose to keep your determination secret until the time for acting upon it shall come near. It would be disastrous were either the act, or the promulgation, to be so timed as to stand in any apparent connection with the bare[?] struggle to maintain the authority of the Chair. Unquestionably the burdens of your office have been beyond all common measure: but it is (as they say) upon the cards that they may be prospectively lightened by an effective measure of Devolution if the House can muster sufficient courage to adopt one. Should such a thing happen, there will be nothing so far as I am concerned to hinder your reconsideration of the subject of your letter.

5. *Sat.* [*Dollis Hill*]

Wrote to The Queen—Ld Hartington—Mr Trevelyan—Ld Spencer—Sir C. Dilke—and minutes. Cabinet 12–2¼. Off to Dollis in afternoon. Calls. Saw Mr G—Ld R.G—Ld Granville. Read Macmillan's Life—Harwood on Democracy[2] —Letter of De Blignières.[3] Discussed the Hymn & Ital. Version with Lacaita. The difficulties are very great.[4]

Cabinet. Sat. Aug. 5. 82. Noon.[5]
1. Military Convention with Turkey.[6] (a Plan of landing to be agreed in the Convention). Terms to be considered between W.O. & F.O.
2. Lords Amendments to the Arrears Bill considered & determined—except the 'hanging gale' amt.[7] which stands over.
3. Channel Tunnel. Conversation, stands to next Cabinet.

---

[1] Playfair's retiral was announced in April 1883; for this letter and his account of his waning position, see T. W. Reid, *Memoirs of Lyon Playfair* (1900), 290ff., 308. See 9 Aug. 82.

[2] G. Harwood, *The coming democracy* (1882).

[3] E. G. de Blignières, *Le contrôle anglo-français en Egypt* (1882); commented on in Ramm II, i. 409.

[4] See 23 July 82.   [5] Add MS 44643, f. 168.

[6] See 13 Sept. 82.

[7] Also known as Waterford's amndt., it appeared ambiguously to provide extra compensation for the landlord; *H* 273. 1158–9.

6. *9 S. Trin.*

Willesden Church & H.C. mg. Tried various amendments of the Hymn. Saw Ld Abn—Ld Tweedmouth. Read Ch. Quarterly on Kyriakos—on Darwin—on Shairp—on the Census[1]—&c.—Seeley's Natural Religion.

7. *M.* [*London*]

Back to London at 11. Wrote to Mr Weld Blundell—The Speaker—Ld Carlingford 1.1.—Ld Spencer—Ld Granville—Mr Forster—Sir T. Acland—Ld Elcho—Ld Chancellor—The Queen—& minutes. Saw Mr G—Ld RG—Mr Trevelyan—Mr Childers—Mr Forster—A.G. Ireland and S.G. Ireland on Amts. 2-3½. Conclave in C. room on Ld Waterford's Amendt. H. of C. 4½-7¼ and 9¾-12¾.[2] Read Carnegie's Journey—Arnold (19th Cent) on Letters & Science: valuable.[3]

To Sir T. D. ACLAND, M.P., 7 August 1882.   Add MS 44545, f. 177.

I will only for a few moments contravene your kind injunction not to reply to your letter.[4] I was glad & sorry to receive it; glad you well know why, sorry because I fear it was one act of disobedience, and am sure you cannot be the better for it.

If I was a prize-ox at a former date, I am now something better (as I flatter myself) namely a model patient & when on my back I neither do nor leave undone, neither lie nor stir nor breathe, except according to the Doctor's orders. In this I pray you to imitate me—and, I ought to add, in very little else.

You have longest served me for a reference as the model of a man young in spite of years; and I hope you will again stand me in good stead for the like purpose: but then you must behave properly! It is not for *me* to deny your title to retire before the close of this Parliament, as I hope to lodge a similar claim. But I hope it will be the natural not the forced or premature close—and of these last-named I have no *great* apprehension at present.

Ireland is calming down and unless the Lords stir it up again I hope the process will continue. If general anticipation be a test we ought to come pretty well through the present Irish row.

To LORD CARLINGFORD, lord privy seal, 7 August 1882.   Add MS 44545, f. 176.
'*Immediate*'.

I have seen your Memorandum,[5] but you will perhaps let me say it does not in my view *begin at the beginning.* Surely the first thing to be done is to show what objection can be taken to *our words as they stood* when the Bill went to the Lords. This I have not yet heard done.

Our desire was that the rent of 1881 should be paid or acquitted: and we wished to take care lest money really paid for 1881 and out of its crops should by a vicious custom of arrear-laden Estates be put down in the books and receipted as rent for a previous year, the oldest of those in arrear.

These objects are right? If so do *our* words attain them? Do they go beyond them?

---

[1] *Church Quarterly Review*, xiv. 309 (July 1882).
[2] Egypt; *H* 273. 973.
[3] *N.C.*, xii. 216 (August 1882).
[4] Acland's letter in Acland, 345, on his deafness etc.; also: 'don't forget that if there is a *Dissolution before the county franchise is settled the farmers will vote blue*'.
[5] Not found, but on the role of the court; Carlingford and Bessborough both cautious about giving 'the court a more imperative direction'; Add MS 44123, f. 116.

8. *Tu.*

Wrote to Ld Hartington—Sir G. Young—B. de Ferrières—Mr Anderson—Mr Elliot—Ld Carlingford—The Queen 1.1.—and minutes. Read Carnegie's Tour. Twelve to dinner. Saw Mr G—Ld R.G—Sir T.G.—The Irish Law Officers. H of C. $4\frac{1}{2}$-$8\frac{1}{2}$ and $9\frac{1}{4}$-$10\frac{1}{2}$. Again 11-$12\frac{1}{2}$. Spoke on the Lords Amendments.[1] All went well.

9. *Wed.*

Wrote to The Queen—Reay—& minutes. Interview with Cetewayo at noon for half an hour.[2] I was much interested & pleased. H of C. $12\frac{1}{2}$-6. Spoke on the Play-fair motion.[3] $6\frac{3}{4}$-11. Dined at the Mansion House: & returned thanks for Ministers. The audience favourable.[4] Saw Mr G—Ld RG—Sir J. Lacaita—Mr Whitbread.

10. *Th.*

Wrote to Ld Granville—Sol. Gen. Irel.—Mr Sullivan—The Queen—& minutes. Read Lecky's Hist. Saw Mr G.—Ld R.G—Ld Granville—Mr Childers—Mrs Bolton—Lord Acton—Mr Courtney—Mr H. Fowler. H. of C. $4\frac{1}{2}$-$8\frac{1}{4}$ and $9\frac{1}{4}$-$12\frac{1}{2}$.[5] Lucy came to us.

11. *Fr.*

Wrote to Ld Granville—Ld Rosebery—Mr Bancroft[6]—Archbishop of Canterbury—The Queen—and minutes. Saw Mr G—Ld RG—Mr Leake MP & others. Saw Hunter, Howard, & another [R]. H of C. $4\frac{1}{2}$-$8\frac{1}{4}$ and 9-$10\frac{1}{2}$.[7] Read Bancroft U. S. Constn—Lecky's Hist. England.

To Sir S. H. NORTHCOTE, M.P., 11 August 1882.   Add MS 44545, f. 178.

I can at once accede to your suggestion.[8] Had there been a general concurrence of opinion, there would have been some convenience in arranging so that members might know pretty exactly the arrangements under which they might have to return in October. But it is plain as you observe that the House is not now in a state to debate with advantage any question of this kind, should there be a disposition to do so. Please therefore to consider the matter as one standing over until our re-assembling.

[1] Arrears Bill: Lords amndts.; *H* 273. 1151.

[2] No account found.

[3] Cowen's motion criticizing Playfair's handling, as chairman of cttees., of Irish suspensions; *H* 273. 1307.

[4] *T.T.*, 10 August 1882, 6a.

[5] Supply; *H* 273. 1414.

[6] George Bancroft, 1800-91; had sent his *History of the formation of the constitution of the United States of America*, 2v. (1882), with a quotation from Gladstone as its epigraph; Bancroft told Gladstone, 24 July 1882, Add MS 44476, f. 71: 'as all the reviewers in our Journals have caught them [Gladstone's words] up, your name has been carried very widely through the land as the friend of America, where it was already cherished as the foremost defender of liberty in Europe'.

[7] Arrears Bill amndts.; *H* 273. 1512.

[8] This day, Add MS 44217, f. 207; motion of precedence for procedure ought not to be made before October.

To G. BANCROFT, historian, 11 August 1882.　　　　　Add MS 44545, f. 178.

Pray accept my best thanks for the present of your work which I have just received, and have begun to examine, with peculiar pleasure.

In itself a valuable possession, I prize it much more as coming from yourself. Further, I think it a great wonder that you should have thought those words of mine, which you have attached to the work, to be worthy of going forth to your great nation, as at least an independent and sincere testimony to the Constitution; which I first learned intelligently to admire on reading Marshall's Life of Washington,[1] soon after the beginning of that half century of public life which is now within a few months of its close.

12. Sat.

Wrote to The Queen—The Speaker—& minutes. Cabinet 12–2¾. Saw Mr G—Ld RG. Dined with Jane Wortley at the Ranger's, Blackheath. Conversation with her, the MP. & Lady Wentworth. Saw Howard, & books which supply a Chapter of human knowledge [R].

Cabinet. Sat. Aug. 12. 82. Noon.[2]
1. Course of business. a. Announce on Monday. b. Adjourn to Tues. Oct. 24. c. Move adjournment Thursday next. d. Then move precedence for Procedure. e. Take it de diem in diem.
2. Plan of procedure. a. Gibson—provisional compromise abandoned. b. Withdraw No. 12.[3] c. Amend Resolutions? reserve liberty.
3. Channel Tunnel. Childers' proposal—that the approvals of 72 and 74–5 shd. not be recalled but conditions laid down by scientific Committee shd. be enforced.[4] Any Bill not to be objected to on 2 R on condition of being referred to a strong & probably a Joint Committee.
　　Not adopted. The Bills are disposed of. A Joint Committee (or two Committees[ )] next year.
4. Indian Estimate 1880m[ille]. Reference to be made, as mild as possible, not excluding recons[ideratio]n of proportions of expence.
5. Cetewayo. Ld K. submitted draft Telegram. Partial restoration: provision for other interests: against delay.[5]

To H. B. W. BRAND, the Speaker, 12 August 1882.　　　　　Brand MSS 303.

The Cabinet have conversed pretty largely on the subject of procedure and I should be glad if you would allow me to see you on Monday before the House meets. Will you name an hour when I might call upon you? Perhaps you would ask Sir Erskine May to come? P.S. Your letter received.[6] On Rule 2 I suggest that 20 or 10 members should demand the vote of the House. I like Mr. Salt. Mr. James would be got rid of by Dodson's plan.

---

[1] See 15 Sept. 48.
[2] Add MS 44643, f. 171.
[3] Resolution on the Monday rule for cttee. of Supply.
[4] Gladstone's note reads: 'We are fighting on your side. The other alternative is *recalling* the proceedings of 72 & 74–5'; ibid., f. 173.
[5] Promised to Cetewayo in talks at the C.O., 15 and 17 August; *PP* 1883 xlix. 527.
[6] Of 11 August, Add MS 44195, f. 111, on standing cttees.

13. 10 S. Trin.

Marylebone Ch mg & Chapel Royal aft. Read Preventive Work.[1]—Half Hours
with the Bible—Seeley, Nat. Religion, finished. I like not the book.

14. M.

Wrote to Mr Bryant—Ld Granville—Sir D. Currie—Mr Warwick Brookes—Mr
Lefevre—Mrs Bolton—Mrs Th.—Mrs Hunter—Mr Heneage—The Queen—&
minutes. Began upon arrangements for escape.[2] Dined with Mr Knowles at
Reform Club. Much interesting conversation. Saw Mr G—Ld RG—Sir Thos G.—
Mr Vivian MP.—Scotts. Work at London Library. Read Lecky's Hist. England.
H of C. $4\frac{1}{2}$–$7\frac{3}{4}$ and 11–1.[3]

Pol[*itics*].[4]
Causes tending to help the Conservative party & give it at least an occasional preponderance though a minority of the nation.
1. Greater wealth available for the expences of elections.
2. Greater unity from the comparative scantiness of such explosive matter within the party,
    as is supplied by the activity of thought and opinion in the Liberal party, not always suffi-
    ciently balanced: with which activity self-seeking is apt to mix.
3. The existence of powerful professional classes more or less sustained by privilege or by
    artfully constructed monopoly: the Army, the Law, the Clergy.
4. The powerful influence attached to the possession of land, & its distribution in few hands
    not merely from legal arrangements but from economic causes.
5. The impossibility of keeping the *public* in mind always lively and intent upon great
    national interests, while the opposite sentiment of class never slumbers.
6. The concentration of the higher and social influences, thus associated with Toryism, at
    the fixed seat of government, and their ready & immediate influence from day to day on
    the action of the legislature through the different forms of social organisation used by
    the wealthy & leisured class.

Th. I too have my 'Grammar of Assent.'[5] The frame & constitution of things wherein we live
teach me to believe in an Author of unbound intelligence who works towards justice
truth and mercy.
    Thus, seeing the sin & pain that are in the world, without being able to account for them,
my grammar of assent teaches me that this derangement of the natural order for evil may
probably & reasonably be accompanied by exceptional provisions for good, meant to supply
the defect of nature, in her efforts made insufficient for their end. In a word I find the idea of
a revelation wholly conformable to the reason of the case, estimated upon the facts with
which experience supplies us, & according to the rules which in the common business of life
are deemed the rules of common sense.
    Next if there is nothing unreasonable in the opening of a special model of knowledge &
guidance to meet a special need, it is not less agreeable to sound sense that towards the
maintenance of this special knowledge there should be a written & more definite record, as

---

[1] Not found.
[2] i.e. from London; see 19 Aug. 82.
[3] Statement on procedure, Gibson's amdt., and autumn session; *H* 273. 1695.
[4] Holograph dated 14 August 1882, Add MS 44766, f. 117; in *Autobiographica*, iv. 103.
[5] i.e. as well as Newman; see 27 Mar. 70, 25 Aug. 78.

well as a living though more variable[?] tradition. And further for the conservation of the record, & for organising & guiding the tradition I am not surprised (but should rather have been surprised had it been otherwise) that for the conservation of the record, & for organising and guiding the tradition there should have been founded in the world by Christ our Lord a Society for perpetual though not perfect life, which we term the Church.[1]

15. Tu.

Wrote to Mr Thorold Rogers—Mr Lefevre—The Queen—and minutes. H. of C. 4¼–7 & 8¾–12¾.[2] Saw Mr H[3]—Ld RG—The Prince of Wales & the two Princes who came at two[4]—Ld Granville—Ld Northbrook—Mr Childers—Ld Hartington—Mrs Bolton. Read Leckie's England—Sullivan's Ireland[5]—D. of Devonshire (in Ld Rochester).[6]

To J. E. THOROLD ROGERS, M.P., 15 August 1882.   Add MS 44545, f. 179.

I apprehend that the part which the Viceroy designs to play with respect to Irish emigration is auxiliary, & if so it may be difficult for him to avail himself of your public-spirited offer.[7] I will however send him your letter & in the meantime I thank you for it. I trust you will make a careful study of social America, about which we know so little & ought to know so much.

16. Wed.

Wrote to Sir J. Lacaita—Sir H. Ponsonby—Sir W. Harcourt—Abp. of Canterbury—The Queen—Ld Chancr—and minutes. H. of C. 12–2½. Spoke on Egypt.[8] Drive with C. and walk. Went to the Fish Dinner in evening. A great enthusiasm shown towards me: which I could only meet with a bantering speech.[9] Saw Mr H—Ld RG—Ld Chancellor—Ld Advocate. Read Lecky's Hist.

To Sir H. PONSONBY, the Queen's secretary,   Add MS 44545, f. 179.
16 August 1882.

I hope to see you on Friday but in the meantime I write to say that I paid due attention to your note about the Hamilton Library,[10] but that I have heard nothing on the subject from the Trustees of the Museum.

It is sometimes said that in this country the State is illiberal to purchases connected with

[1] Holograph dated 14 August 1882; Add MS 44766, f. 118.
[2] Misc. business; *H* 273. 1808.
[3] 'Mr H.' (E. W. Hamilton) had just taken over as senior secretary from 'Mr G.' (J. A. Godley), thus bypassing Horace Seymour, 1843–1902, who stayed in post until December 1884; Bahlman, *Hamilton*, i. xix–xx.
[4] i.e. the Princes Albert Edward and George, later George V; see 10 Mar. 64, 20 Mar. 65.
[5] See 3 Nov. 77.
[6] J. Wilmot, Lord Rochester, *The works of the Earls of Rochester, Dorset, the Duke of Devonshire* (1721).
[7] No letter found.
[8] On Lawson's motion; *H* 273. 1940.
[9] No report found.
[10] William Alexander Louis Stephen Douglas-Hamilton, 1845–95; 12th duke of Hamilton 1863; race-horse owner and sportsman; sold off family MSS, books and paintings in various lots, many being bought by German museums and libraries; the Beckford library was sold in four sales, June 1882–November 1883.

art & libraries. My impression is that we spend far more upon them than any other country, and that there is no library in the world—and in particular not the Bibliotheque Nationale though it is the first library in the world—which is endowed like that of the Museum.

The Botticelli Dante is I believe an affair of many thousand pounds. But it derives its value I imagine almost entirely from its being in fact a collection of paintings by Botticelli; a great artist without doubt; but I can conceive a question whether in this view it is altogether an appropriate purchase for a National Library. At the same time, I do not venture to form that opinion. In truth it is difficult for any one connected with the Treasury to touch the initiative of these questions, there being another Department, namely the Museum Trust, of which it is the business to bring them before us when occasion arises.

To LORD SELBORNE, lord chancellor, 16 August 1882.   Selborne MS 1868, f. 56.

I have just received the inclosed note from the Archbishop of Canterbury. Please to send it to Sir W. Harcourt. I do not think I have any clear or positive province of personal duty in respect to it: but I certainly hope that an end will now be put to the imprisonment of Mr. Green by the Crown: though it would have pleased me better if it could have been done by a law, & by far the best of all, if it could have been by a law reforming & limiting our present law of contempt *generally*, which I own appears to me to deserve very strong reprobation. I speak of contempt generally, as distinct from merely ecclesiastical contempt, and I also speak under the supposition that there is not any limit to the imprisonment which a person may suffer if only his obstinacy continues.[1]

On receiving your letter this morning I at once referred it to Sir W. Harcourt.

[P.S.] I venture to say I did not see the occasion for adding a week to Mr. Green's imprisonment in order to let the opposite party act if so disposed, for they must I presume have been prepared for the deprivation beforehand, & therefore for the opportunity of acting. I send also a copy of my reply to the Archbishop.

17. Th.

Wrote to The Queen—Abp of Canterbury—Mr Gray MP.—Ld Chancellor—Mr J. Morley—Sir J.P. Hennessy—Mrs O'Shea—Agnes Wickham—& minutes. Read Lecky's Hist. Saw Mr Bancroft Denis—Mr H—Ld R.G.—Sir C. Dilke—Sir A. Colvin—Sir Thos G.—The Speaker *cum* Ld R.G.—Conclave on the Gray affair, a very bad one.[2] Saw Ld Granville. H. of C. 2–7 and again at 9, from the middle of Harcourt's dinner through Biggar's spite agt the House.[3]

To J. MORLEY, editor of the *Pall Mall Gazette*, 17 August 1882. Add MS 44545, f. 181.

I am very glad to receive Mr. Cobden's letters[4] & I sincerely thank you for sending them. Also I thank you very sincerely for your kind words about the Government & myself. In the matter of the Arrears Bill the Tories have certainly played into our hands. We have before us in Egypt warlike operations which we have found unavoidable but which I hope is effectually localized. I wish I could feel quite satisfied about the little home campaign to come in October. I trust you will enjoy your well-earned holiday.

---

[1] See 6 Sept. 81n.

[2] Imprisonment of E. D. Gray in Dublin for 3 months for contempt of court; see 23, 29 Aug., 20 Oct. 82.   [3] The Gray affair; *H* 273. 1978. See 20 Oct. 82.

[4] On 16 August, Add MS 44255, f. 37, Morley returned 'the whole of your letters to Mr. Cobden' (see also 24 Oct. 81n.) and sent congratulations 'upon this issue of the session, as it now stands. The Government is in a more excellent position in the country than even its best friends could have hoped. . . .'

To LORD SELBORNE, lord chancellor, 17 August 1882.   Selborne MS 1868, f. 60.

With reference to the suggestion that a new Royal Commission should be appointed on the subject of Marriages of Affinity,[1] I am not quite sure whether you put it forward with the weight of your own decided assent, or mainly as a project approved by other persons of weight. To me it does not much commend itself, as it looks rather like an agitation for further change, beyond the issues of the Wife's Sister Bill. Yet I hardly think that from that point of view you would approve it.

I do not know again in what sense you would appoint an inquiry by Commission into the Law of Divorce. For my part, I should hardly feel myself able, even were I so inclined, to take any step in a forward direction with respect to that law, & on the other hand I hardly suppose it is meant that a Commission should inquire whether legislation ought to recede.

The main point that strikes me is this: some particular purpose, or *animus*, some presumable practical intention, seems to be involved in the notion of a Royal Commission on any of these great & delicate subjects. What is it, & which way does it look, & why? In any case I think that evidently this is not the *moment* for practical steps, as no Commission goes to work in August or September & you would probably agree with me that the Cabinet would have to consider any suggestion of this class before it could be acted on.

[P.S.] I forgot to mention this last evening in the boat. I much wish it had been possible to get your fully formed opinion on the proceedings for contempt in Dublin.

18. Fr. [Osborne House]

Wrote to Scotts—Ld Spencer 1.1—W.H.G.—Ld Granville Tel.—Mr Whitbread—Mr Hamilton—Messrs Barker & Hignett (from draft already written & submitted to WHG)—and minutes. Off at nine to Osborne. The harvest along the road, pleasant to see. Saw Mr Hamilton—Ld Carlingford—Sir H. Ponsonby. Saw H.M. twice, and dined with her. Most gracious. Council at 1.30. Went with Sir H.P. to see Norris Castle. Read Rev. Mercer's Tract[2]—Lecky's Hist—and [blank.]

19. Sat. [Cruising on the Palatine]

Wrote to Ld Rosebery—Mrs Wellesly—Mrs Bolton—and minutes. Saw Sir H. P[onsonby] & Sir J. Cowell. Off at 10¾ to the Palatine.[3] We sailed to Portland: four hours with much motion, which I did not stand well, being fresh from hard brain work, which makes a great difference in the power of resisting sea-sickness. However I rallied in Portland Harbour, and fed. Began the Old Curiosity Shop:[4] but was not fit for much.

To LORD ROSEBERY, home undersecretary, 19 August 1882.   N.L.S. 10022, f. 122.

A line in haste to say that I feel that it *is* incumbent upon me to visit my constituents before the close of the year.[5] They have been as patient as they were zealous. In accordance with your view I will not carry the question further now—except to say that I am a little shocked at the possibility of imposing a further burden upon your hospitality, which however is very strongly-backed.

---

[1] Raised by Selborne, 16 August, Add MS 44297, f. 268, recognising possibility of its leading to inquiry into divorce.   [2] Perhaps L. P. Mercer, 'The little ones' (1882).
[3] Wolverton's yacht.   [4] Dickens (1841).
[5] Rosebery wrote, 18 August, Add MS 44288, f. 108, proposing a visit in late November/early December.

20. 11 S. Trin.

Wrote to Sir W. Harcourt—Ld Spencer—Mr Hamilton—& minutes. Went ashore at 9½ & drove up to the height: seeing the pretty Military Chapel and the curious fossil specimens on the way to the Convict Church. Then we went over the prison & had luncheon with the Governor.[1] The service was deeply interesting & the whole that we saw most remarkable.

Read Scrimgeour on Xt Crucified[2]—Robertson on O.T. Prophets.[3]

To Sir W. V. HARCOURT, home secretary, 20 August   MS Harcourt dep. Adds 10. 1882.

Will you kindly send back to Downing Street or send direct to Spencer, the letter[4] from the American Detective ⟨Pilkington⟩ Pinkerton which I sent you some time ago?

I write from Portland where in a luxurious & hospitable yacht we wait smooth water outside.

21 M.

Wrote to Mr Hamilton l. & then Tel.—Dr W. Phillimore—W.H.G.—Sir W. Harcourt—The Queen—Ld Granville Tel. Went to the Chesil Bank & over part of the hill back. Saw the tiny fishing boats launched: & heard the men's grievance. Saw Deputation from Weymouth. Read Lecky—Old Curiosity Shop.

22. Tu. [Iwerne Minster]

Wrote to Sir H. Verney—Sir H. Bruce—Sir C. Dilke—Ld Spencer—Sir W. Harcourt—Mr Courtney—Mr Fawcett—and minutes.

The wind last night wilder than ever. Happy are the land-locked. And the place is interesting. In the afternoon we went off to Weymouth & Iwerne minster:[5] where I was astonished by the operations, as to house and place, which Wolverton has effected in less than four years. Read Lecky's Hist.—Ludlow on Zululand[6]— Old Curiosity Shop.

23 Wed.

Wrote to Ld Kimberley—Mr Hamilton l. & Tel.—Ld Spencer—& minutes. Forenoon Survey of the garden grounds stables kennels &c. Afternoon drove to Bryanstone & saw Ld Portman. Conversation on P. of Wales's affairs. At 84 Ld P. is fresh & active. Read Ludlow—Leckie—O.C. Shop.

To LORD KIMBERLEY, colonial secretary, 23 August 1882.   Add MS 44545, f. 183.

I send you a book by Captain Ludlow on Zululand, recently sent to me, together with the commendatory letter which accompanied it. It is violently miso-Cetywayo & philo-Dunn.[7]

---

[1] Portland prison, where Parnell and Dillon had been imprisoned.   [2] See 14 May 82.
[3] One of F. W. Robertson's many works.   [4] Not found.
[5] Wolverton's house near Weymouth. The party generally was much disturbed by seasickness; see *Mary Gladstone*, 262.
[6] W. R. Ludlow, *Zululand and Cetewayo* (1882).
[7] See 22 Aug. 82; depicts Cetewayo as a cruel savage, and 'Chief' John Dunn, who lived in Zululand, as an English squire. Kimberley returned it on 25 August, Add MS 44227, f. 224, commenting 'Dunn

Will not the Queen rather spoil our 'fat friend', as Beau Brummel called George IV. to his face after quarrelling with him.

To LORD SPENCER, Viceroy of Ireland, 23 August 1882.   Add MS 44545, f. 183.

1. I have received with much pleasure your letter of the 21st.[1] Will not Lawson however himself expose himself to the risk of a rebuff if he asks Gray for any engagement: & on the other hand is it not an anomalous proceeding to require a Sheriff to enter into recognisances? Is it quite impossible to obtain from him a spontaneous assurance suggested by some friend? I know not what the man is but when I went to Ireland five years ago he voluntarily expressed to me a great desire for the reunion of his friends with the Liberal party, & he then took up & carried through the business of giving me the freedom of the City of Dublin.[2]
2. Still more satisfactory is it to have the likelihood of tracing home the horrible quintuple murder.[3] If the gang be so large there may be hope of an opening to get within the Fenian circle.
3. We have much reason to be thankful thus far for the progress of affairs in Egypt.
[P.S.] I write from Iwerne, Dorset.

24. Th.

Wrote to Mr Sellar MP—Ld Spencer—Rev. S.E.G.—Mr Welby—C.G.—Mr Hamilton l. & tel.—and minutes. Read Lecky—O.C. Shop. Drove to Eastbury, & walked in the place. Conversation with Ld W. on the future.

To Mrs GLADSTONE, 24 August 1882.   Hawarden MSS.

I inclose a letter to Stephy. If you think it unwise you are to keep it back. But the motive with which I have written the last half is to prevent his going into the C.W. affair with a fixed *arrière pensée* to act at once upon the other in case of failure.[4]

I suppose his natural time will be Oct–Nov when we are in town for the H of C. & procedure.

Finding that Sanders my dentist leaves down in the middle of Saturday for the continent, I think I ought to go up tomorrow as my chewing machinery is unsatisfactory. There is no promise of yachting weather I fear for days at any rate. This day has gone to the bad since you left. Mary offers herself for Salisbury. Tomorrow I hope to write to you from London. I will not say the yacht is impossible, but Wolverton I think is not sanguine though wishful, & the chance is but poor.

In the case of Egypt the evidence is still but partial but undeniably all the signs are good. It would not surprise me if next week were to see the crisis.

The Doctor from London has come down and gives a favourable account of Lady W.

I think I ought to send Clifton more than my photograph: what do you say—who frames the print tidily & moderately?

has feathered his nest but the stories put about by the Cetewayo party against him are ... mostly untrue or exaggerated.'

    [1] Add MS 44309, f. 102; Judge James Anthony Lawson, 1817–87, imprisoned E. D. Gray, M.P., Sheriff of Dublin & proprietor of the *Freeman's Journal* for 3 months for doubting the jury's sobriety in the trial of F. Hynes.
    [2] See 7 Nov. 77.
    [3] The murder of the Joyce family at Maamstrasna on 8 Aug., the motive complex and obscure; Gladstone may have been wrong in assuming Fenian responsibility; see Hammond, 315ff.
    [4] See 10 Sept. 82.

I have a vision of Hawarden next week as probable. Viewing the shortness of the recess we ought to make the most of it. Ever your afft WEG

25. Fr. [London][1]

Wrote to Sir H. Ponsonby—Mr Pringle—Mr Sheridan—Ld Spencer—Ld Granville—Sir W. Harcourt—C.G.—Mrs Bolton—& minutes. Off at 10.30: D. St 2.45. Saw Mr Hamilton—Ld Northbrook *cum* Mr Childers 4–5½.—Ld Granville. Saw Ricardo [R]. Read Lecky—O.C. Shop.

To Mrs GLADSTONE, 25 August 1882.   Hawarden MSS.

I left Iwerne at 10.30 and arrived here 2.45.

Another evil night has further postponed, and much impaired, any hope of yachting. The rain has also been copious. But there is no note of it in the colour of the harvest which is bright and wholesome.

I have seen Northbrook and Childers who are well satisfied about Egypt particularly the former. It is thought that by Monday there will probably be important news from Wolseley and light thrown on the future. This being so I reckon at present at staying over Sunday but with great hopes of getting down to you on Monday evening should there be no revival of the yachting plans.

Mary was received with open arms at Salisbury.

I am afraid that yesterday and today will, coming together, be very fatiguing for you but I hope change of air will help to give you good sleep and bring it sound.

Last night I had a round O at Iwerne: an event!

Lady W. is said still to have the remains of the fever hanging about her—She did not come to dinner yesterday, or show this morning: still they hold by the doctor's decidedly good account.

I am afraid I shall not be able to get hold of Sanders today and can only have one visit tomorrow as he goes off to the Continent in the afternoon. I have asked Mrs Hampton for a *fish* dinner today as being more agreeable to the state of my grinding apparatus.

It will give me very lively pleasure if Burlingham[2] is chosen doctor today. Ever your afft WEG

There was no truth in the Standard story yesterday of the 2000 prisoners &c; it was wholly premature.

26. Sat.

Wrote to Ld Spencer—W. Phillimore—C.G.—Dean of Windsor—Sir H. Ponsonby—& minutes. Conclave on Egyptian affairs at 10.15.—All much pleased. Saw Mrs Bolton X—Wade X. Saw Mr H.—Sir R. Lingen—Nieces A. & Mary. Went to Saunders.[3] Read Lecky—O.C. Shop.

To Mrs GLADSTONE, 26 August 1882.[4]   Hawarden MSS.

Certainly you have done well and gallantly: I hope you are not too tired. Inclosed is the report from the Times.

I have seen Saunders who postpones his journey abroad on account of the *weather & me*:

[1] Egyptian camps at Tel-el-Mahuta and Mahsameh occupied this day with minimal British losses.
[2] The Hawarden physician; see 15 Aug. 78n.
[3] The dentist.
[4] Part in Bassett, 237.

very kindly anyway. I am promised freedom from him by four on Monday. Unless I stay on account of Egypt, I hope therefore to get down by the 5 PM train reaching Chester 9.23.

We are all much pleased & very thankful for the news of Sir Garnet Wolseley's engagement. It seems to show that the Egyptians will not stand for any thing like a pitched battle in the open field, and it still further improves the military prospect.

The Sultan continues his tricks and perfidy but we are in no way dependent on him.

I am dining quietly at home but I dine with Northbrook on Monday if I stay. No improvement in yachting prospects. The storm signal was put up yesterday at Portland.

The Archbishop of Canterbury's illness looks formidable, & comes on the back of a weak state of health. There have, it seems, been rumours of his resignation lately. An account at Lambeth is that this forenoon he was 'the same'. Nothing since then. The succession to him would be difficult to supply.

I missed the T.G.s in Eaton Place but have seen A & M here. They report better of Louey, & are very thankful for the Egyptian news.

Good accounts of Sir R.P. from his son. Hoping to meet soon. Ever Yours afft WEG

To G. V. WELLESLEY, dean of Windsor, 26 August 1882.   Add MS 44545, f. 184.

The announced illness of the Archbishop [Tait] leads me to recall your attention to a letter of mine in which I gave names as fit to be considered for the succession.[1]

The claims of the Bishop of Winchester [Browne] are perhaps the highest, with his long experience of the Bench. But he has fulfilled the three score years & ten. Born apparently in 1811. How high should this be considered as an objection. Is the Bishop of Durham [Lightfoot] the next in order. Pray think over the matter. At Lambeth the answer to inquiries (from Addington) is 'the same' at 9.30 this morning.

The news from Egypt excellent thus far. I hope you find Westgate suit your purpose [*sic*] [P.S.] Bishop of Winchester is very fresh & well.

27. 12 S. Trin.

Red Lion Squ. Ch. mg & St Paul's Knightsbr. Evg. Saw Lady James—Mrs Bolton—Mrs Church—Wade [R]. Wrote to C.G.—Dean of Windsor. Read Abp Hamilton's Catm[2]—Townsend on Schoolmen[3]—Contemp. Rev. on Seeley's Nat. Religion—& on Salvation Army.[4]

To G. V. WELLESLEY, dean of Windsor, 27 August 1882.   Add MS 44545, f. 185.

No special account of the Archbishop is to be had at Lambeth today, which is thought good. But the illness is a heavy blow at best. Further reflection leads me to prefer the older of the two I named yesterday, in case there is a vacancy. The Episcopal experience in the other case, & this after a student's life, is very short.

28. M.

Wrote to C.G. l. & Tel.—Ld Wolverton Tel. & l.—Ld Carlingford—Mrs Burton—Sir H. Ponsonby—Sir Thos G.—Ld Hartington—The Queen—Sir C. Dilke—&

[1] Not found.
[2] J. Hamilton, *The catechism set forth by Bishop Hamilton* (1882 ed.); Gladstone encouraged T. G. Law to edit a new ed. and wrote the preface to it; see 27 Sept. 84.
[3] W. J. Townsend, *The great schoolmen of the middle ages* (1881).
[4] *C.R.*, xliii. 175, 442 (August–September 1882).

minutes. Read Lecky—Finished O.C. Shop. Saw Mr H—Ld Granville—Scotts—
Dean of St Pauls—Conclave on Egypt 4-5.—Mr Saunders [the dentist] under
whose hands, although the gentlest, I was sadly reminded how, perhaps owing to
severe brainwork, I have lost the power of bearing firmly any sharp pain in the
head. Saw Adm. Cooper Key. Dined at the Admiralty.

To Mrs GLADSTONE, 28 August 1882.   Hawarden MSS.

I have been much perplexed about movements. It is a little like the Egyptian question:
Wolverton is the Khedive: you & Mary are the Powers: the weather is—the Sultan, & it is
impossible to say any thing worse of it. I tried the Meteorological Society: but can get no
forecast extending beyond tomorrow forenoon. It certainly has not a settled appearance. A
second failure would be almost ridiculous. And there is certainly *more* objection on Egyptian grounds to my being ever so little out of the reach of at least the Telegraph.

I think your estimate of Lady Waterford's condition can hardly be correct, or she would
not be so loath to visit *any* one as she appears to be: but I am really sorry about Mary. Try
more seriously to get her to Hawarden.

Now I am off to the dentist.

Back from him at 4, after a *mauvaise demi-heure*, for in truth I have, I am sorry to say, probably as the consequence of severe brain-work, lost all power of bearing pain in the head, & it
made me perspire profusely. But he is most careful & really gives wonderfully little pain.

Wolseley has fought no more but telegraphs to say that the effect of his actions of 24th &
25th has been much more than he expected: the 10000 of the enemy completely broken &
dispersed—& the chief military adviser of Arabi a prisoner.

I now write at 6.15 to say that after infinite distraction of mind & purpose—having regard
to your wish & Wolverton's—I now feel obliged to give up the notion of the sea—The
weather is not promising and so (unless some *great* change takes place I mean to take the
2.45 with Zadok tomorrow for Chester (due 7.20) where I daresay you will kindly send for
us. I write to Wolverton & in hope of meeting. Remain ever, Yours afft WEG

To LORD HARTINGTON, Indian secretary, 28 August 1882.   Add MS 44545, f. 185.

I return Ripon's letter[1] with only two adverse remarks, first that the argument is a little
clouded by warmth, & secondly that I wish he had turned his mind in some measure to the
monstrous amount of the charge, & not exclusively to the question who should pay it. I
agree in your view of Ripon's argument but as it is avowedly supplemental to the coming
dispatch we must I suppose wait to see what that may contain.

No doubt consultation might have been very desirable but we all but broke down
altogether from the multitude of priests we had to consult as it was, & there are periods
when the House of Commons with its tempest of questions from day to day appeared to be
likely to be quite uncontroulable. How could we do less, under the circumstances, than
announce some intention, subject as the announcement was to further consideration in
respect of what the Indian Government might say.

No doubt our calculations are thrown out by the enormous amount of the Indian Charge,
& this may entail a reconsideration should the proportions at the close appear to stand anything like what they do now.

[1] Not in Chatsworth MSS.

29. *Tues.* [*Hawarden*]

Wrote to Ld Spencer l.l.—Dean of Windsor—Ld R. Grosvenor—Mr Trevelyan—
Mr Courtney—and minutes. 2¼–8 to Hawarden by Chester. Saw Mr H.—Mr
Welby—Sir R. Lingen—Mrs Bolton—Mrs O'Shea. Read acct of Rochdale—Lecky's
Hist. England.

To LORD R. GROSVENOR, chief whip, 29 August 1882.   Add MS 44545, f. 185.

1. Wolverton, *a propos* of making Otway a Privy Councillor, observes that he is a great
stag.

2. Mrs. O'Shea, on the part of her husband puts in a plea for Mr. Hamilton's place should
it be vacant.[1]

3. The weather is hopeless, & I am off today for Hawarden. Wishing you a pleasant holiday & complete banishment of all inconveniences in the throat.

To LORD SPENCER, Viceroy of Ireland, 29 August 1882.   Althorp MSS K5.

[First letter:]   1. You will find the letter of the Treasury very severe. There may be occasions when it is necessary to act under fear & pressure. I can hardly judge whether this is to
be one of them. But the reasoning in the official letter from Dublin appeared to us, & certainly to me, to be so very far short of the mark that it was hardly possible to make it the
ground of an assent. The first duty therefore was to work this out. The question of an
Executive necessity & a compliance with authority in derogation of ordinary administrative
rules, is another matter.[2]

2. In truth I am afraid that this is the wing of a larger question; that we have foolishly
chosen to make our Constabulary force in Ireland a local army or something too like it, &
that we are in some danger of having the question of the Indian local army over again.
[P.S.] I am not sure that I know what has been done about a commission to examine complaints; but I fear any commission for such a purpose apart from the Executive is a very
formidable affair; I believe however that the Resolution to appoint one was authorised in
your time.

[Second letter:]   Last night Mrs. O'Shea sent me a note desiring to see me & she has been
here this forenoon. Parts of her conversation were for you: other parts you will I think like to
know.

1. She spoke of Hynes.[3] I told her that I felt certain you would, with good advice,
thoroughly satisfy *yourself* upon the question whether any of the matters touching which
the jurymen were impressed, ought in any way to affect the verdict. But that in no case could
I interfere.

2. She put in a plea for her husband to succeed Mr. Hamilton[4] in the event of a change. I
said that any wish proceeding from her husband (N.B. to whom we are certainly under some
obligation) was entitled to attention & respect; but that the matter rested with you, & I gave
her no further encouragement.

---

[1] i.e. at this day's meeting. Grosvenor replied, 3 September, Add MS 44315, f. 86, that Otway's
'speculations compare favourably with the Rt. Hon. C. Raikes, though that may not be saying much'
and that he discounted Wolverton's advice; he doubted 'O'Shea's qualifications for any place of trust',
especially for the Irish undersecretaryship: his participation in the affair was 'to make the foundation of
a claim for a berth under Govt.—*every* Irishman, without a single exception, always jobs'. See to Mrs.
O'Shea, 1 Nov. 82.

[2] Dublin police about to strike for extra pay; *Spencer*, i. 221.

[3] See 23 Aug. 82.   [4] i.e. Robert Hamilton, acting under-secretary at Dublin Castle.

3. She tells me that the expenditure of the Ladies Land League has been as high as from £7000 to £10000 per week; but badly administered & with much waste.

4. That Parnell has now broken up the Ladies' Land League for all practical purposes, & has stopped the supplies, which until some weeks back were furnished partly from America & partly through Egan, this latter I imagine the chief part: from America very little comes now.

5. Parnell has, in despite of Egan, locked up the invested monies of the League, near £60,000. He has no power over American supplies.

6. Davitt & Dillon are both in great dudgeon with Parnell by reason of his restricted action on the land & national questions. She speaks of him as thoroughly bent on legality (which I tell her is the whole question), & does not say they are otherwise; but she impeaches Davitt for vanity & Dillon for being a *tête montée.*

7. She feels strongly the improved state of Ireland, in this I presume, as in most else, reflecting Parnell.

[P.S.] I am off to Hawarden this afternoon. I feel strongly all you say about interference with the Judges. But I hope Lawson will interfere with himself. Otherwise I fear he will have a very disagreeable time when Parliament meets; few to defend his excess of power & some who would gladly keep silent perhaps compelled more or less to speak.

To G. V. WELLESLEY, dean of Windsor, 29 August 1882.   Add MS 44545, f. 185.

Without doubt 'the man' when you can get him is much beyond what they now term 'his environment'.[1] But while I have seen in the Bishop of Durham [Lightfoot] everything that is good, I have not seen in him anything that is great. In governing force & manhood, I should not think of comparing him with the present archbishop whose life I think we ought all to desire. As between the two named, I have seen no note of any great difference in governing force—have you? Both have shown themselves men of love and peace, & good Diocesan Governors, the one for 18 years, the other for three. This I think not an unfair statement of the case?

As regards learning, the Bishop of Durham has I suppose the first exegetical place in this country: the Bishop of Winchester [Browne] has supplied the church with one of its classical books—that on the articles.

Do I understand you to mean that the Bishop of Winchester is disparaged by his communications or cooperation with Dr. Döllinger, the first theologian of his generation?

I shall thankfully accept your offer of preliminary action should the occasion unhappily arise.

30. *Wed.*

Ch. 8½ AM. Wrote to Padre Tosti, & minutes. Worked on papers, now packing, & affairs. Drive with E. & walk with E. Wickham & E. Talbot viewing the glorious harvest, all cut. Read Lecky—Ross's Poems[2]—Wood's Ancient Astronomy.[3]

To LORD WOLVERTON, 30 August 1882.   Add MS 44545, f. 186.

On referring to the Daily Telegraph[4] I found a thoroughly contemptible article which must have been written by the same author—I know him not—that composed the 'apology'

---

[1] Wellesley had reported Lightfoot a man of resolve, 'not to be governed'; Add MS 44340, f. 217.
[2] W. T. Ross, *Poems* (1881).
[3] J. Wood, *Ancient astronomy, modern science and sacred cosmology* (1882).
[4] *D.T.*, 30 August 1882, 4f.; the leader.

to me some years ago. It was very ambiguous about the correspondent who it said had been misinformed, & only said he was on his way home. However, this might carry the meaning you had charitably put upon it, and, as it is of the essence of justice not to depend upon reciprocity, I wrote a note to Lawson[1] accordingly, though not without difficulty, so much was I disgusted with the grovelling character of the production as a whole.

A fine day here, not uncloudy but fair & with a good corn-drying wind, quite enough to disable me on board a yacht. So it is well I gave way to a clear necessity. The crops between this house & Chester are by far the finest I have seen in 400 miles of country recently traversed—in places it seems as if the fields were *covered* all over with shocks. Every straw cut—carrying began today—a little sprouting talked of. I hope Lady Wolverton is better & perhaps I ought to hope you are or soon will be with her.

31. Th.

Ch. 8½ A.M. Wrote to Mr Hamilton Tel.—Ld Granville Tel.—The Queen Tel.—Mr Childers—Mrs Bolton—W.L. Gladstone—Mrs Th.—Sir W. Harcourt—Mr Richard—D. of Leinster—Rev. Mr Eyre. Walk with W.H.G. Conversation with E. Talbot, who went. An admirable man. Read Lecky's Hist.

To H. C. E. CHILDERS, war secretary, 31 August 1882.   Childers MS 5/145.

I have the reply from you & Northbrook[2] to my telegram & though my leaning is unchanged I certainly have no such knowledge or confidence as might tempt me to press further my opinion. I proceeded upon the idea that Dufferin's *pro* weighs more than the Khedive's *con*: that the Turks might be exasperated by having to land at a point of extreme disadvantage, & that if you let them land at Alexandria you could march them off in parties regularly to the point where they would have come to shore at Aboukir.

As to the Sultan's 'confidence' I am not sure that such a commodity can be said to exist.[3]

In this district there is a splendid harvest on the ground, all cut, but the rain today is much against it.

To Sir W. V. HARCOURT, home secretary, 31 August   MS Harcourt dep. Adds 10.
1882.

I agree with you in accepting, & indeed warmly welcoming the Chancellor's plan as to the law of contempt which appears to be little less than the abatement of a public scandal.[4]

I concur in your observation as to Judges[5] and would suggest whether it would be enough to send to Law in Ireland and to Inglis and Moncrieff in Scotland, and whether it is necessary to do more than take the opinion of the *heads* in England.

It is really an almost angelic height of virtue in the Chancellor to set to work, in the first week of the vacation, with his productive powers.

---

[1] See Add MS 44545, f. 186. For the 'apology' for the Negropontis affair see above, ix. xliv n. 4. Wolverton replied, 2 September, Add MS 44349, f. 146: 'you have given Lawson *quite* as much as he deserved'.

[2] Not found.

[3] Childers replied next day, Add MS 44130, f. 66, that he had taken up Wolseley's suggestion of 3000 Turkish troops at the canal under Wolseley's command.

[4] Harcourt, 28 August, Add MS 44197, f. 95, sent Selborne's sketch of a Contempt of Court Bill.

[5] Judges 'raise any possible objection to any measure of Law Reform especially such as touch their own personal dignity'; ibid.

To H. RICHARD, M.P., 31 August 1882.   Add MS 44545, f. 187.

I thank you for sending me the Herald of Peace, and I have carefully read the contents. I will only hazard ⟨two⟩ a single observation⟨s⟩.

⟨The first is that⟩ I am not conscious of any change in my own standard of action, or in that of my colleagues, since the day when, after three military miscarriages, we tried severely the temper of this nation by declining to shed the blood of the Boers of the Transvaal & offered them peace.[1]

⟨The second is, that it is difficult for those who have not followed the acts described in the correspondence, to understand to what a degree we were bound by actual covenants, some of them not known to the world, & how our field of action has been narrowed. We have felt ourselves bound in honour to the lawful ruler of the country to assist him, in the honourable & faultless discharge of his duties, against a military despotism established by one who as we have lately had the best means of knowing has not only been labouring hard to defeat the international engagements by which Egypt was bound but to *sell* to the Sultan, in return for his support, the acquired liberties of that country, and to replace it under the Turkish yoke.⟩

Fr. Sept. One 1882.

Ch. 8½ A.M. Wrote to The Queen l. & Tel l.l.—Sir W. Harcourt—Mr Hamilton Tel. l.l.—Ld Spencer Tel.—Sir R. Wilson—Dr Dollinger—Mr Howell—& minutes. Worked on private papers. Read 19th Cent. Egypt[2]—Paris Newspapers—Carver on Ireland:[3] and Lecky's Hist.

To Sir W. V. HARCOURT, home secretary,   MS Harcourt dep. 8, f. 161.
1 September 1882.

The original purpose of this note was to say I had heard from my daughter of the case of Dr. Orange. She thinks you have managed to allow him £100. I am not rich in the Royal Bounty Fund (on account of the Leopold marriage) but *if you think* there is a case for it I will gladly try to find him £100 more, or upwards.

Just as I was going to write this I heard of Spencer's bold measure in dismissing 200 of the Dublin Police. It does honour to his manliness & as far as I can judge his prudence. I am sure that in case of need you will see what *you* can do to support him.

I do not venture *to dogmatise* without knowledge, but I *think* that were I in your place I should be inclined to offer him a small batch of picked London policemen whose advent would strike terror.[4]

It was only a few days ago that I wrote to Spencer that we (for half a century) had been building up the Irish police as a local army, & that in contemplating it I often thought of the local Army of India.

[P.S.] do you think the rate-payers of Flintshire might now be relieved in respect of me? It is hardly possible in the country to regulate corporal movements so as to make the supervision effectual.

---

[1] The letter this far sent to Richard in Hamilton's fair copy, dated 3 September (National Library of Wales); the rest copied by Hamilton though deleted on the draft. See Bahlman, *Hamilton*, i. 332.

[2] *N.C.*, xii. 324 (September 1882).

[3] Not found.

[4] Harcourt replied, 3 September, he had no power, despite the police strike in Dublin, to *order* Metropolitan Police to Ireland, and was cautious about volunteers; nor could he be responsible for lifting the police guard at Hawarden; Add MS 44197, f. 100.

To LORD SPENCER, Viceroy of Ireland, 1 September 1882.   Althorp MSS K5.

I need say little on the copious letter of yesterday which you too modestly describe as uninteresting, but I will just observe
1. That I think O'Shea's name should be borne in mind with a view to any *suitable* opportunity, as he has conferred favour on the Government.[1] 2. That I think we quite understand one another on the subject of the grant to the Dublin police. 3. That I hope Lawson is not going to sleep upon his laurels, for I think that unless he mends his position he will when the House of Commons resumes work be firmly & also strongly attacked, & weakly defended, inasmuch as his conduct is indefensible from its extravagance. We cannot swear black is white even to defend a judge.

I am sorry to say we have a day of warm moisture which I fear is threatening to a grand harvest in this district all cut & hardly any got.

2. Sat.

Ch. 8½ A.M. Wrote to Sir H. Ponsonby—Mr H.W. Gladstone[2]—Ld Granville—Mr Welby—Mr Childers Tel.—Viceroy Tel.—& minutes. Read Wood on Cosmology—Ross's Poems—Lecky finished Vol III—Cowper's Life.[3] Walk with SEG & E.W.

3. 13 S. Trin.

Ch. mg & evg (H.C.). Wrote to Mr Hamilton 1. & Tel.—Ld Granville—The Queen Tel.—Mr Oxenham—& minutes. Read Newman, Days of Grace in India[4]—Life of Ralegh (Dr)—Dante Paradiso I. Saw Willy's baby a fresh, a most dear & charming child.[5]

To G. V. WELLESLEY, dean of Windsor, 3 September   Add MS 44340, f. 219.
1882.[6]

For some days I hoped and thought the Archbishop might recover. But this vision has passed away. The Queen has already I think made as many Archbishops as Geo. III, namely three, and now she will have to make a fourth.

Ruminating much upon the subject, I find my mind goes back upon a third name of the five I first mentioned to you, although I should think Bishop Winchester's claim paramount but for his age. It is a grave objection. Bishop Benson can enter into no competition with Bishop Lightfoot in his character as a writer, though I believe he is a man of respectable theological attainments knowing more, for example, than the present Archbishop. In standing, as to age they may be considered the same: as to episcopal standing, Bishop Benson has two years more. Both are excellent and liberal-minded men. I incline to think Bishop Benson has superior recommendations 1. In *dignity*; 2. In the *proof* given

---

[1] Spencer, 31 August, Add MS 44309, f. 128, 'could not for a moment conceive' of O'Shea succeeding Hamilton.
[2] Hugh Williamson Gladstone, 1851–83, cousin, s. of Rev. J. M. (see 4 Jan. 26); convert to Rome 1871; sought 'five minutes conversation' to resolve family dispute on whether Helen died a Roman Catholic; correspondence and visits ensued; Hawn P.
[3] R. Southey, *The works of William Cowper . . . with a life of the author* (1835).
[4] H. S. Newman, *Days of grace in India; a record of visits to Indian missions* (1882).
[5] i.e. Evelyn; see 5 Jan. 82.
[6] Holograph, marked 'Not sent on' perhaps because Tait rallied briefly; he d. 3 December.

of organising power; 3. In the probability of hearty acceptance by all 'schools' in the Church. I likewise *conceive* him to be a man of higher spiritual fervour, so to speak.

I cannot think, as an expression of yours implies that you may, that Bishop Browne would be regarded as the man of a particular party. He has never lain under this reproach. But I am obliged to admit to myself that it is much to expect at 71 a vigorous start in the duties of a new and great office.

In the particulars I have stated, I have as usual turned my mind inside out while writing to you. I have been swayed in some degree by what you said as to the man. Only one point more. Bishop Lightfoot was certainly a great leader of men at Cambridge. But this was the work of a teacher, and very distinguishable indeed from that of an Archbishop, who cannot except in the rarest possible circumstances (none that I know of since Archbishop Laud) be expected to govern the *thought* of the Church.

How I wish you would come here. But know it is no use dunning you.

4. M.

Ch. 8½ A.M. Wrote to The Queen L. & tel—Ld Kimberley—Sir W. Harcourt—Ld Granville—Ld Spencer—Mr Errington—& minutes—W.L. Gladstone. Walk & drive: watching the corn anxiously. Read Lecky—Southey's Cowper.

To Sir H. PONSONBY, the Queen's secretary, 4 September   Add MS 45724, f. 124.
1882.

I hope & think we are well out of the Alexandria–Aboukir business through the expressed desire of Wolseley to have the force upon the Canal. For though the perfidy of the Sultan (insincerity is really too weak a word) leaves him not a shred of claim, yet something may be due to the feelings of his men & the danger of irritating them, & we are also loath to have a row with him, not so much (at least in my mind) from any fear as to Egypt as from a disinclination to reopen the whole Eastern Question & give an opening to the land-hunger of some, if not all, of the Powers.

5. Tu.

Ch. 8½ A.M. Wrote to Sir H. Ponsonby—Sir W. Harcourt—& minutes. Visited the Roberts' farm. Walk & conversation with A. Lyttelton. Read Lecky's Hist.— Account of Hamilton—Southey's Cowper.

6. Wed.

Ch. 8½ A.M. Wrote to Mrs Bolton—Ld Ripon—Ld Spencer—The Queen—Mr Collings MP.—Mr Salkeld—Mr Sexton MP. Read Southey's Cowper—Lecky's Hist. Engl.—Hamilton's Parl. Logic.[1] Walk with A.L. & the party.

To LORD RIPON, Viceroy of India, 6 September 1882.   Add MS 43515, f. 15.

It is of course a matter of much regret that your personal view of the question of Indian charge for the hostilities in Egypt should be so different from that of the Cabinet, to whom the matter of principle did not appear to be at all doubtful; but I for one am very glad that you should have stated broadly & fully the grounds of your opinion. In your letter to Hartington you refer to the coming dispatch, & we have taken our resolution from the first subject to any representations from you & your Government. I do not now

[1] See 25 Apr. 45.

carry the matter at all further. Our reservation is a real one, & we should have no feeling of shame or reluctance in acting upon it if cause be shown. There are many in the House of Commons (including members of the late Government, anxious I suppose to atone at our expence for their offences) who have every disposition to give India fair play, or more. It does not appear to me that the citation from a speech of mine made in June is in any way relevant to the question what should be the incidence of the military charge. If I remember right, it did not contemplate war, & had reference to our diplomatic objects. Whether this be so or not, it made no more reference to English than to Indian interests. It simply described (as we then viewed them) the actual things which we sought to do.

There is no doubt that we are discharging single-handed an European duty: & the consideration is also to be weighed that India is not consulted, & that her reputation & influence are not directly in question, but *only* her material interests. All these reasons have I think weighed with us, I will not say in fixing, for we have not fixed, but in estimating the sort of proportion in which as we think India ought to be charged.

When we were dealing with this subject, although we might well expect that sea transport would be more expensive in India, yet taking all things together we did not anticipate any *great* excess in the cost of the Indian expedition, man for man, as compared with the English. It was therefore only in our minds to put upon India a moderate percentage of the total charge.

What we were not prepared for was the *enormous* figure of the Indian estimate, which we are totally at a loss to understand, & which certainly seems to suggest that the question of amount as well as of incidence, demands the attention of your Government. It will probably be better, as the matter now stands, that neither we, nor the House of Commons, should resume the subject of repartition until the operations are complete, & until we know more about the real total of the charge. Hartington has already signified that, if the vast excess in India *cost* be really unavoidable, that fact of itself may have to be taken into account by us. But, as I now understand, you object to our calling for any payment whatever from India, & this is what, as at present advised, I cannot understand. I suppose we must proceed upon the principle that this maintenance of the connection with this country is an Indian as well as a British interest. The material interest both for Britain & for India is the interest in the Canal. That interest is very specially Indian. Other trades gain by the Canal as well as the Indian, but none (of any consequence) in anything like the same degree. In India it is an unmixed & an enormous benefit; to England great but mixed; it has actually *taken away* from this country branches, I believe considerable, of what used to be our entrepôt trade, in carrying Indian & Chinese produce to the Mediterranean.

Apart from attempts to fix minutely the quantity of our several interests, the quality is the same both military & commercial. Apart from the Canal, we have no interest in Egypt itself which could warrant intervention (in my opinion). But the safety of the Canal will not coexist[?] with illegality & military violence in Egypt: & I doubt whether Parliament & the nation would have sanctioned, as they almost unanimously sanctioned, our proceeding, except for the Canal. It seems to me that the exclusion of India from charge on this occasion cannot be affirmed on any ground except the assertion that the entire business of maintaining the communications is British & that (as appears to be the just inference) India has no interest in maintaining the connection. Enough of this. I have written, as you wrote, frankly & without misgiving.

We have a good harvest on the ground this year, in this district a very good one, & a steady glass gives us after some apprehensions a fair prospect, please God, of seeing it well got in. Ireland improves; & Spencer has met a bad moment in the Dublin Police with courage, prudence, & success. In Egypt all has thus far gone well. We have procedure to deal with in October–November: a most grave subject. Should things continue to run in

smooth channels, I trust that ere the close of the year I may be enabled to effect my
personal retirement & leave behind me a vigorous & prosperous Government.[1]

7. Th.

Ch. 8½ A.M. Wrote to Mr Hamilton Tel.—Sir R. Lingen—Mr Trevelyan—The
Queen Tel.—Mr Welby—Ld Granville l.l. and Tel.—Ld Nelson—Mr Childers
l.l.—Sir J. Pauncefoot—& minutes. Late work at night: a messenger from London. Read Lecky—Southey's Cowper—Molesworth's Ch. History[2]—G. Hamilton
Parl. Logic. Cut the dead Deodara, with Willy.

To H. C. E. CHILDERS, war secretary, 7 September 1882.   Add MS 44545, f. 192.

One principal subject of apprehension with us as I conceive is lest the city of Cairo
should be subjected to the same fate as that of Alexandria. Is there any precaution which
we can take.[3] It seems to me worth consideration whether instruction, or a suggestion
should be sent to Wolseley, with a view to his proclaiming that every one, of whatever
rank, who should take part in incendiarism or other criminal destruction of life or property, would be put to death without fail.[4] If this is announced it would come in combination with a formal assurance of kind and clement treatment to the people?
    Please to consider the matter.
[P.S.] I was perfectly satisfied with your Telegrams on 1. Landing of Turks. 2. Terms for
the enemy.

8. Fr.

Ch. 8½ A.M. Wrote to The Queen Tel. l.l.—Ld Granville Tel & l.—Mr Hamilton
Tel.—Ld Spencer—Mr Oxenham—Mrs Bolton—& minutes. Walk with Lucy.
Began cutting a dead oak. Read Lecky—Southey's Cowper—Hamilton—Orkney
Trials for Witchcraft.[5]

9. Sat.

Ch. 8½ A.M. Wrote to Messrs Barker & Co.—The Queen l. & tel.—Ld Rosebery—Ld Granville—Mr Childers—Mr Trevelyan (substituted)—Mr Hullah—Mr
Hamilton Tel.—Sir H. Ponsonby—Mrs Th.—and minutes. Saw Mr Carrington[6]
and settled with him the basis of the deed for transferring the fee simple of my
land to my son William. Walk with Lucy: and felled the dead oak with W.H.G.
Ten to dinner. Read Lecky—Southey's Cowper—Hamilton (P. Logic &
Speeches, finished)—and [blank.]

---

[1] Ripon's first protest untraced (see 28 Aug. 82); he replied, 6 October, Add MS 44286, f. 273: 'we
do not deny that India has *an* interest in Egypt; what we contend is that that interest is not such',
compared to England's, to justify her bearing 'so large a proportion of the total cost'; the row will
again raise the cotton duties controversy; Ripon dismayed at Gladstone's hint of retirement.
[2] See 27 Dec. 81.
[3] Childers agreed to reinforce existing instructions on this; Add MS 44200, f. 75.
[4] Childers did not comment on this suggestion.
[5] *Trials for witchcraft, sorcery and superstition, in Orkney* (1837).
[6] Alfred Carrington of Barkett, Hignett and Carrington, Chester solicitors.

To LORD ROSEBERY, home undersecretary, 9 September   N.L.S. 10022, f. 124.
1882.

Your projected Italian tour makes me wish I were in your pocket, though you might
have a counterwish in that case for relief by means of the 'light fingered gentry'.[1]

There is no possibility of working off a political visit to Midlothian before the re-
assembling of Parliament. The natural time so to speak would seem to me to lie in the
first few days of December. There is however an uncertainty that remains. The settlement of procedure ought not to require more than a fortnight or three weeks; but who
shall say how far faction may prolong the time? I must be in town on Wednesday for a
Cabinet.

(14 S. Trin.) S. 10.

Ch mg and aft. Conversation with Stephen on his critical matter.[2] Wrote to Ld
Granville—Mr Childers—Mr Welby—The Queen l. & tel.—Mr Trevelyan—&
minutes. Read Smyth on the Govt of God[3]—Anal. of Newman's Apologia[4]—and
various Tracts.

To H. C. E. CHILDERS, war secretary, 10 September 1882.   Add MS 44545, f. 194.

I am a little startled at your letter[5] as I think you will probably have expected. Perhaps
explanation may throw light on the subject of the anticipated increase of charge. Meantime I put these two questions. 1. What is the increase of force beyond that included in
the original estimate which warrants an addition of £74,000 to an estimate of £900,000
in respect of a) this increase, b) an addition of one month to three months. 2. Has not the
progress made been as good as could have been reasonably expected? & if so does not the
addition of one month now bring into question the justness of the estimate of *three*
months originally submitted? However the case may stand, we must I apprehend wait for
further experience before it can be the subject of practical consideration either for me or
for the Chancellor of the Exchequer who may have to make the next Budget.
P.S. I receive from Welby today a disagreeable account of the actual progress of the
expenditure. After all we have said on the wars of our opponents this is a ticklish subject
& I think the Treasury may have to call upon the spending Departments for explanations,
so that Parliament may see where & how any calculation may have broken down.

11. M.

Ch. 8½ A.M. Wrote to Hugh W. Gladstone—Ld Granville—Mrs Bolton—Mr
Hamilton—H.C. Jones—and minutes. Saw Stephen further—Lucy—and C.G.—on
Stephen's matters. He went off pliantly. Walk with E. Wickham & A. Lyttelton.

---

[1] Rosebery wrote on 7 September, Add MS 44288, f. 110, to check Gladstone did not intend a
Midlothian visit before the Session.
[2] In two long letters (23 June, 17 August, Hawn P), S. E. Gladstone told his parents of his failure
to become engaged (suitor unnamed), his dissatisfaction with work in the Hawarden parish ('too
closely related to what may be called the "temporal power" or the ruling family of the place'), and his
intention (unfulfilled) to join the Oxford Mission in Calcutta.
[3] W. W. Smyth, *The government of God* (1882).
[4] J. N. D[arby], *Analysis of Dr. Newman's 'Apologia pro Vita Sua'* (1886).
[5] Not found; on 11 September Childers described it as an '*outside* Estimate, constructed
cautiously'; Add MS 44130, f. 82.

Tea at Miss Rigby's. Read Southey's Cowper—Lecky—Piers Ploughman[1]—
Popular Ballads[2]—Hogg's Poems[3]—Lecky's Hist.

12. Tu.

Ch. 8½ AM. Wrote to Ld Kimberley—Sir R. Wilson—Mr Dodson—Mr Childers
—and minutes. Woodcraft with W.H.G. Worked upon papers. Read Southey's
Cowper—Lecky's Hist. (Finished IV)—Hogg's Poems—and [blank.]

To H. C. E. CHILDERS, war secretary, 12 September 1882.   Add MS 44545, f. 194.

I think that it would be well to let Parliament know when or soon after it reassembles
the best estimate of Egyptian war charge we can then make. The Cabinet will then also
have to consider 1) whether the vote of credit should be enlarged—which I assume as
pretty certain 2) whether we shall ask a further provision of means. But we may be sure of
factious effects to use war-charge as a means of obstructing procedure & we must if possible steer clear of this work by carrying procedure first.

An urgent official letter from the War Department has been sent to me today stating that
there will be an extra charge on account of the detention in troops in Natal on which the
Secretary of State for the Colonies it is said 'has now decided'. This I suppose has relation to
Cetewayo's restoration. I will ascertain without delay & then reply to your letter.

13. Wed. [London]

Off at 8. D St 2¾. Wrote to Mr Trevelyan—Ld Granville—Mr Hutton—Mr
Childers—The Queen—C.G. 1. and 2 Tel.—Sir T.G. 2 Tel.—Mrs Bolton [R].
Cabinet 3–5. Dined at Mr Childers. Saw Ld Granville—Mr Childers—Ld Chan-
cellor—Ld Northbrook—Mr Hamilton. Read Amours de Henri IV[4]—Fortnightly
Rev. on Austria—Political History—the House of Lords—Chronicle.[5]

Cabinet. Wed. Sept. 13. 82. 3 PM.[6]
1. To sign the [Military] Convention if all the terms of the Proclamation are amended
   according to our demands. Memorandum appended to Convention, limiting Turkish
   force to between 2000 & 3000.[7]
2. Question of the Canal discussed, in connection with the Acts of the Company to us as
   the Khedive's Agents. Chancellor to communicate[?] with Pauncefoot [*sic*].
3. Cabinet to consider this & other points tomorrow.
4. Ripon's dispatch on the question of charge: without any positive conclusion.

14. Th.

Wrote to Mr Childers—Mr Lefevre—C.G.—Sir Thos G.—Scotts—D. of Newcastle—Ld Spencer—Ld Lyttelton—Mrs O'Shea. Saw The King of Greece—

---

[1] Probably in T. Wright's ed. (1842).
[2] First v. of F. J. Child, *English and Scottish popular ballads*, 5v. (1882–98).
[3] See 25 May 26.
[4] P. Colan, *La belle Gabrielle, ou les amours de Henri IV* (1814).
[5] In fact a mixture of *F.R*, xxxvii. 620 (May 1882) and *C.R*, xlii. 383 (September 1882).
[6] Add MS 44643, f. 175. Wolseley this day captured Arabi's camp in the battle of Tel-el-Kebir, Arabi
escaping.
[7] Never signed; fruitless negotiations ended with the Constantinople conference.

Mr Welby—Mrs Bolton—Sir Thos G. Conclave on Egyptian affairs which are by the great mercy of God rapidly moving towards the conclusion of the war. We sat 2-4 P.M.[1] Dined with Welby at the Garrick *en quatre* & went to the Savoy Theatre.[2] Read Sir R. Temple's Chapter on Canning.[3]

15. Fr.

Wrote to O'Gorman Mahon—Ld Granville—The Queen Tel & 2[4]—Mr Trevelyan—Sir T.G. Tel.—C.G. l. & Tel.—H.N.G.—Mad. Novikoff—Ld Cardwell—Gen. Wolseley—Mr Childers—Adm. Seymour—and minutes. Conclave on Egypt $12\frac{1}{2}$-$2\frac{1}{2}$. Another flood of good news. No more blood I hope. Wolseley in Cairo: Arabi a prisoner: God be praised. Saw Mr Hamilton. Saw Mrs Bolton—aftn & evg. A sad case but of much interest [R]. Read Macaulay's Lays[5]—Temple's India.

THE SETTLEMENT OF EGYPT[6]

Preliminary Paper

When armed resistance in Egypt has altogether ceased, the settlement of the country will have to be considered at once, and it will have to be 1. *Military*; 2. *Political*

Of these the first is of necessity immediate; the second though requiring prompt treatment will be subsequent.

There is also the great question of the Suez Canal.

I. *Military* Settlement

In regard to the military settlement of Egypt, among its heads will be

1. The total disbandment of the rebel force—trial of criminals—disposal (by banishment?) of officers or others now constituting a dangerous class.

2. The organisation of a force under the Khedive to maintain order and to secure his throne.

This force to be a. Military—as far as is requisite to defend the territory especially in the direction of the Soudan, and the person of the Khedive. This force should be fixed at a minimum. b. Police for the maintenance of order.

It will have to be considered from what source other than indigenous the military force can be supplied:—especially with reference to Mahometans or others from India.

3. The withdrawal of the foreign occupation as early as possible. This will be regulated exclusively, and from point to point, by the consideration of security for life and property.

No charge will be imposed upon Egypt in respect of the military operations now concluded. But it will have to be considered whether, in respect of such force as may have to remain, while the new force for the Khedive is in preparation, Egypt should bear the charge or a portion of it. Also after the country is so to speak handed over, a small British force may be retained, at the desire of the Khedive and at the cost of Egypt, until the new state of things shall have been adequately considered.

Such force ought if possible not to exceed two, or from two to three, thousand men.

---

[1] Not a formal cabinet; no report to the Queen. British troops this day entered Cairo.

[2] Gilbert and Sullivan's *Patience.*

[3] 'Canning the Just' in Sir R. Temple, *Men and events of my time in India* (1882).

[4] Recommending baronies for Wolseley and Seymour, thus ending the vexed question of the Wolseley peerage; Guedalla, *Q*, ii. 210.

[5] See 3 Nov. 42.

[6] Initialled and dated 15 September 1882, PRO 30/29/126; printed for cabinet as CAB 37/9/83 and in P. Knaplund, *Gladstone's foreign policy* (1935), 280.

4. As in the political settlement of the country, its neutralization will be provided for, so also the seaward fortifications of Egypt should be dismantled and destroyed.

Would it be right however to allow certain defensive works at the entrance and issue of the Canal?

5. Provision has already been made for the due trial of offenders especially those accused of *crime* (other than rebellion) and against the use of barbarous methods of punishment.

6. It is assumed that the military settlement of Egypt will naturally, as to the first three heads, remain in the hands of England as a consequence of the war and to avoid the inconvenience and delays of a reference to the Powers, in a case where Society has not only been disturbed by war but disorganised through the total overthrow of civil authority by the very instrument appointed to maintain it.

II. *Political Settlement*

In regard to the *political* settlement of Egypt, the following heads will have to be considered: 1. The Sovereignty; 2. The local institutions; 3. The Canal; 4. The international engagements. Here, & especially as to the two last, the agency of the Powers will properly come in. But it seems needful, at least in regard to the two first that England should have a well defined basis on which to proceed, in the use of the initiative which will naturally fall to her and otherwise; and that all the preliminary steps she may have to take before the Powers are in action should be taken in view of this basis.

I. *The Sovereignty*

The Sovereignty of the Sultan has wholly failed to fulfil its purposes, and the re-establishment of orderly Government against lawlessness and anarchy has been left to foreign intervention. The commission of Dervish Pasha produced no result for good while it gave time for organizing the rebel power. When its failure was obvious, and when the Powers desired the armed interference of the Sultan as Sovereign it could not be had. The movements of the Sultan towards armed interference have been subsequent to the decision of England and to her proceeding to act upon that decision, and have taken no effect. Finally, the work has been accomplished not by the Proclamation of the Sultan but by the victory at Tel-el-kebir.

The former basis of the Sultan's power in Egypt has therefore failed both *de jure* and *de facto.*

The Sultan may justly claim a) The continuance of the tribute; b) The homage of the Khedive; c) But the title to demand the aid of Egyptian forces must go to the ground when Egypt will not, in the proper sense, possess an army; d) So will the title of the Sultan to appoint local sovereigns whom he is unable or unwilling to maintain.

Would it not be well if the Committee hereinafter mentioned were, besides the question of the Canal, to examine into the conditions of the Balkan and Rouman Suzerainties, in order to clear the question as to 1. Any further rights which it may be desirable to reserve to the Sultan; 2. A law of succession to the local throne in case the present law should be deemed insufficient; 3. The conduct of the foreign relations of Egypt.

II. *The Local Institutions*

1./ It appears absolutely necessary that the privileges heretofore accorded to Egypt by firman, and all that may be found requisite for the future well being and order of that country in the course of the impending arrangements, should be made irrevocable as between Turkey and Egypt.

2./ And further that the Egyptian territory should be neutralized.

3./ Subject to all due provisions for the fulfilment of international engagements, it is presumed that England will make a firm stand for the reasonable development of self governing institutions in Egypt. These if successful would form the best security against any attempts of the Sultan to re-establish the former state of things. Would it not be well if this part of the subject were treated promptly with the Khedive, whose authority is presumed to be adequate for the purpose; and on whom the consideration of the matter seems almost to be forced in connection with the recent organic law? Little sympathy could be expected from the Powers in promoting the development of securities for liberty; while in England they will be demanded, and will be hailed with satisfaction.

4./ All it is assumed will agree that the exemptions from taxation now enjoyed by foreigners as such ought not to continue.

III. *The Control*

Under this head I would suggest that the Khedive should signify in a formal manner his intention to use the aid of foreign officers with a view to the maintenance of Egyptian credit and the faithful discharge of obligations. But that the tenure of office by these functionaries should no longer be dependent on the consent of the respective Governments. The subject of international obligations would it is presumed be matter for consideration of the Powers.

———

There remains still for consideration the question of the Suez Canal under the two main heads of

1./ The recent conduct and the powers of the Company in the face of the Khedive—this branch of the subject has been far advanced by the valuable memorandum of the Lord Chancellor.[1] It now appears that the rights of the Khedive may have to be enlarged, and in any case will have to be backed by executory provisions which at present seem to be wanting.

2./ There is also the great question whether for the general interest and for our own the Canal should be neutralised.

It is proposed that a preliminary examination of the whole subject of the Canal should be undertaken, to aid the Cabinet in forming its conclusions, by a Committee composed of representatives of: The Foreign Office; The Law; The Naval and Military Departments, with the addition of individuals whose aid may be desirable—under the presidency of a Cabinet Minister.

This division of the subject, though it calls for early treatment, seems to be less urgent than those which have been previously sketched.

To H. C. E. CHILDERS, war secretary, 15 September 1882.   Childers MS 5/147.

Why were not the guns fired on Telelkebir?[2] Why should they not, still better, be fired tomorrow on that + Kafr Dowar + Cairo.

[P.S.] I fired them (as sham War Minister) in 1846 for Indian victories.[3]

To LORD CARDWELL, 15 September 1882.   Add MS 44545, f. 196.

I write a hearty line to congratulate *you* on the spirit-stirring intelligence from Egypt, which has overflowed us like the waves of a rising tide for three successive days, and which amounts, according to every appearance, to a termination alike rapid and successful of the war in Egypt.

———

[1] Of 14 September; CAB 37/9/82 and Selborne II ii. 67.
[2] i.e. guns fired in the London parks to mark the victory.
[3] See 23 Feb. 46.

In his noble song on the Battle of the Baltic, Campbell, our Tyrtaeus,[1] says
> 'Let us think of those who sleep
> Full many a fathom deep
> By thy wild and stormy steep, Elsinore.'[2]

Happily there are but few of our countrymen, contributors in the field to this great work, of whom we have now to think with these mournful associations.

But we must and do think of one, who, far at this moment from the tumult of our labours and our joys, laid in other years the foundations of this great success, by his enlightened, courageous, and indefatigable work in the reorganisation of the British Army.

I rejoice at this important juncture to render to you the testimony at once, I hope, of an old friend, and of an impartial witness.

To Madame O. NOVIKOV, 15 September 1882.   Add MS 44545, f. 195.[3]

I write to thank you very sincerely for your kind congratulations[4] on the successes in Egypt. We and the whole country are in a state of rejoicing, and I hope of thankfulness to God Almighty, who has prospered us in what I feel & know to be an honest undertaking. Mindful perhaps of what occurred in 1878, after the heroic sacrifices & efforts of your great & difficult war, some in Russia have looked upon us with a jealous eye. Whether the England of 1882 deserves to be so regarded by any, or whether we too have been labouring in the common interests of justice & of civilisation, a little time will show. It is pleasant to find that you do not wait to see us tested by this 'little time', but believe in us & congratulate us.

We certainly ought to be in good humour, for we are pleased with our army, our navy, our admirals, our Generals, & our organisation! Matters were not so conducted in the days of the Crimea. We have paid much, since then, to improve our little army; and as it now appears not without fruit. It is hardly more than 9 weeks since we determined to send some 35,000 men to a distance of say 3000 miles—and it has pleased God to give a quick result.

I thank you again for your kind words. Let me return them by words of a sincere condolence on the death of your heroic Skobeleff.[5] Under the heavy pressure of my office & of the Session I watched with a warm & cordial interest the sad tidings that concerned him. The departure of a hero from this world is for all mankind an object of true sympathy: he was a hero: may peace be with him & may your country have many more.

To Sir G. J. WOLSELEY, 15 September 1882.   Add MS 44545, f. 196.

I have not in the course of a long public life discharged a more agreeable duty than today has fallen to my lot in proposing to you by Telegraph you should receive a Barony in acknowledgement of your splendid services.

I will not, while the flush of the accumulated good news is still upon me, trust myself to describe either the interest or the confidence with which I have followed your movements or the admiration which your masterly conduct awakens in my mind or the joy with which I contemplate the brilliant success it has pleased Providence to award you as the crown of your efforts.

---

[1] Exhortatory Spartan poet of 7th century B.C.
[2] A fairly accurate rendering; see J. L. Robertson, *The complete poetical works of Thomas Campbell* (1907), 191.
[3] In Stead, *M.P. for Russia*, ii. 130.   [4] Telegram this day, Add MS 44168, f. 277.
[5] General Skobelev, hero of Plevna, d. 9 July.

There are a multitude of points which I could mass together in illustration of what I have now said but I will not waste your precious time with the eulogies of an ignorant man.

16. Sat. [Hawarden]

Wrote to Bp of London—Ld Granville—Abp of York Tel.—Mr Childers (2)—Rev. Mr Davidson—Mr Fawcett—Sir Jas Lacaita—and minutes. Saw Mr Hamilton—The O'Gorman Mahon. Packing books & arranging papers. Off at 2.15. reached Hawarden 8.15. Conversation with Mr Oxenham. Read Hist. Univ. St Andrews[1]—Life of Cowper.

To H. C. E. CHILDERS, war secretary, 16 September 1882.   Childers MS 5/148.

As the guilty man I should like to say that I have assured Parliament there was no legal state of war, as we were not at war with any recognised state or Power. This was the case in the U.S. all through the Secession war.

I hope the guns will crash all the windows.

To H. FAWCETT, postmaster general, 16 September 1882.   Add MS 44545, f. 197. *'Private & Confidential'*.

I can say at once, & without reserve, that such a declaration as the one supposed at the end of your letter[2] would not be consistent with your position in the Government, as it would (not in intention but in effect) be a heavy blow aimed from within at the view which the ministers have announced as being, subject to correction, their own view; and for which it is their duty to secure that, in case they adhere to it, it shall have whatever authority may belong to a decision of the Government.

What I should think quite open to you, & ample for the purpose of reserving your liberty of action, would be to say that at the present moment all the facts are not before us, that you bear fully in mind all declarations you have previously made, and that when the proper time comes it will be for you to consider in what relation they stand to the case about to be raised.

It is evident that you are at present wholly uncommitted; & so I think you are entitled to stand. I do not however follow your argument about escape from the control of Parliament (which I was myself the immediate instrument of establishing), as Parliament will certainly control the decision in the present case.

As you have had access to the dispatch of the Indian Government, so you will I hope, think it right to ask for the reply which I believe Lord Hartington proposes to make to it. You will doubtless bear in mind his reference to the subject in the Budget speech.

The enormous estimate, I am tempted to call it monstrous, which came from India undoubtedly took us by surprise. We had considered the matter with different anticipations. It is our duty to bear in mind the preposterous charges of the Abyssinian War, and to be on our guard against the danger of authorising other people beyond our effective control, to spend our money. I shall be much mistaken if the course we have pursued does not produce some comparative economy.

The proper course for us is, as we think, now to wait for the facts which cannot be long in coming sufficiently to our knowledge & to see how far they differ from our original

[1] J. M. Anderson, *The University of St Andrews* (1878).
[2] Of 15 September, Add MS 44156, f. 139; could he be allowed to say that he 'could not support a proposal to throw the whole expenses upon India'?

anticipations, *to which alone our decision has had reference.* You will not be sorry to hear that we shall, I hope forthwith, proceed to discharge a very costly portion of the Indian duty, by carrying the force back to India with our own means & at our cost. And on the whole I hope that what I have said may meet your concurrence sufficiently for the present moment.

To J. JACKSON, bishop of London, 16 September 1882.   Tait MS 100, f. 160.
'*Immediate*'.

Viewing the illness of the Archbishop of Canterbury, I know not exactly what can now be done to recommend some brief and simple thanks-giving in the Churches tomorrow for the very signal and as I hope beneficial success which has been bestowed upon the British arms in Egypt. But I take it upon me to assure you if anything of this nature could be accomplished the Government would view it with great satisfaction. I expect that the Guns will be fired in the Park today.
[P.S.] I telegraph to the Archbishop of York to acquaint him that I have addressed this note to Your Lordship.

17. 15 S. Trin.

Ch mg. A cold prevented me in evg. Walk with Mr Oxenham. Wrote to Sir W. Harcourt—Sir H. Ponsonby Tel.—Dean of ChCh—Dr Abbott—Messrs Grogan —& minutes. Read Southey's Life of Cowper—Church & State in England; a poor affair.[1]

To Rev. Dr. E. A. ABBOTT, 17 September 1882.   Add MS 44545, f. 198.

You address yourself to all subjects with such force and clearness that I should be glad to enter with you fully on the Egyptian question,[2] were it in my power, which unhappily it is not. I must be very brief & must trust to your indulgence.

It is the fact that our interference with the strong hand in Egyptian affairs came to us *de facto* as a question of honourable obligation, in a position made not for us but by us. We had I believe I may say no communication with the Bondholders, and the Chairman was also Chairman of the Stafford House Meeting called to discredit us. The rights of the Bondholders, through anterior circumstances, have I believe acquired the sanction of international law and I am not sure that we have any power to interfere with them. To the burden of the debt, the wickedness of Arabi or his friends have added by the burning of Alexandria a sum approaching six millions, and I know not how much more by his military expenditure and his creation of officers by *thousands.* But I hope that we shall be enabled to effect a large military economy and I do not at all despair of the financial future.

I do not think that any fresh utterance is due from me on the subject of the spirit in which we shall use any power we have acquired. In the last sentence of a speech made a few days before the adjournment I said enough to cover me with disgrace in case we should be found to employ that strength for selfish aims or otherwise than for the welfare of the Egyptian people.[3]

---

[1] T. W. Mossman, *The relations which at present exist between church and state in England: a letter to . . . Gladstone* (1882); on erastianism.
[2] No letter or article found.   [3] See 16 Aug. 82.

To Sir W. V. HARCOURT, home secretary,   MS Harcourt dep. 8, f. 165.
17 September 1882.[1]

I am glad to learn that not only the sky but all the skies are bright with you at Balmoral. Were we not pleased and thankful now, what would make us so?

No doubt great difficulties remain: and we have great questions to consider. The first of these is whether Egypt is to be hereafter, and whether we are now to lay the ground for her being, for the Egyptian people, or for something else? I say for the Egyptian people, just as Bulgaria for the Bulgarian people, although Egypt cannot at the moment undertake so large a share of self-government, and is also hampered with definite external obligations which she cannot set aside.

The Queen expressed to me at Osborne a desire that Egypt should be independent. There was not then as much temptation, as there is now, to say otherwise.

The great question of British interest is the canal, and this turns on neutralisation, aye or no. Pray turn your mind to it. There is much difference of opinion: and we must endeavour to expiscate the matter thoroughly (you are a Scot for the time being).

I am sorry to say we have arranged, as it now stands, to go hence to Penmaenmawr, where Lady F. Cavendish is, on Thursday or Friday. But if it would secure our seeing you here, we could, & gladly would, put off our engagement to the following Monday. Please let me know by telegraph if you can.

I entirely agree with you about Childers & Northbrook.[2]

[P.S.] The hand of the London police is now off me: but in Flintshire (where they are considerate beyond any thing) I still, to my serious regret, weigh heavily on the rates.

I inclose, for H.M., Sir G. Wolseley's grateful acceptance. How splendidly he has made[?] his character as a general.

18. M.

In bed till near noon: having a cold. Wrote to Ld Granville tel & l.—Dean of ChCh—Mr Lee—Mrs Bolton—Mr Behrens—Ld Shaftesbury—Sir J. Lacaita—The Queen—& minutes. I spent the afternoon with Mr Hugh W. Gladstone, discussing his case and that of the Roman Church. He made a very favourable impression upon me. The news of Dean Wellesley's death made this a very death day to me. A small clergy dinner. Read Bells Poems[3]—D. MacCarthy's do[4]—Southey's Cowper.

19. Tu.

Fought my cold (a mild one). Ch. 8½ AM. Wrote to Sir W. Harcourt—Mr Hamilton Tel—Duke of Cambridge—Ld Granville—Ld Spencer—Canon Anson—Mr Fawcett—Abp of York—& minutes. Walk with C.G. Mr Oxenham went. Read Southey's Cowper—Letters of Elis. & James I.[5]

---

[1] Part in Gardiner, i. 459.

[2] Harcourt's letter of 15 September; Add MS 44197, f. 105: 'they have organised victory as completely as Wolseley has achieved it'.

[3] Perhaps R. Bell, *Early ballads* (1864).

[4] D. F. MacCarthy, *Poems* (1882).

[5] *Letters of Queen Elizabeth and James VI*, the Camden Society (1849).

To F. ANSON, canon of Windsor, 19 September 1882.   Add MS 44546, f. 1.

I thank you for the very interesting account you have given me of the illness of our dear friend [G. V. Wellesley].[1] Not a word of it had reached me before. I had letters from him when he was at Westgate but no ill report.

It is a great blow, a blow so great that I know not how to describe it; his loss to me is irreparable. With few even of my colleagues have I taken as much personal counsel as with him during the last 14 years; & never have I taken it with any man in greater harmony, or more to my advantage.

He was a man as remarkable, as he was unpretending, pure as gold, true as steel. I reckoned his life the most precious in the Church of England, and I had, especially this year, looked forward confidently, perhaps audaciously, to its prolongation. But we have nothing to lament on his account; he has passed to his rest & his reward.

[P.S.] I cannot but regret his not being buried at Windsor with which he is so closely & so variously associated.

To LORD SPENCER, Viceroy of Ireland, 19 September 1882.   Althorp MSS K5.

I will only say on your letter of yesterday[2] that I for one cannot take exception to your view of Parnell (you are aware that Mrs. O'Shea's communications are wholly uninvited).

My own opinion is pretty distinct to the effect

That he fomented outrage under the No Rent manifesto for a considerable time, perhaps not with direct knowledge about the Secret Societies

That when he made up his mind that the Land Act would win the day, he determined to bow his neck to facts and no longer encourage crimes which would not attain the desired end

That since his liberation he has acted on this basis with as much consistency as he could, and had endeavoured to influence his friends in the same sense.

It would have been perhaps hardly worth while to put this on paper but that it gives me the opportunity to congratulate you on your tour & its results, and to express the pleasure with which I see the confluence of praise from all quarters upon your government.

20. *Wed.*

Ch. 8½ AM. Wrote to Supt GWR Tel.—Mr Hamilton l. & Tel.—Dr Acland Tel.— Mr Childers—Sir W. Harcourt—Sir R. Cross—Sir R. Phillimore—Sir R. Lingen— Warden of Keble—Messrs Ogilvy—Mr Rutherford—H.J.G.—Duke of Newcastle—Mrs B.—Ld Granville—Mrs Th.—Adm. Sir Cooper Key—and minutes. Read Southey's Cowper Vol III—and [blank.] To bed early.

21. *Th.* [*The Coppice, Henley*]

Up at 6: off at 6.30. Reached Oxford at 12: attended the funeral at one: the assembly not what it ought to have been in the case of such a man as Dr Pusey.[3] Saw The Dean of Ch.Ch.—Warden of Keble—Dean of St Paul's—Mrs Brine[4]—

---

[1] Add MS 44476, f. 159. Wellesley was buried at Stratfieldsaye.

[2] In *Spencer*, i. 221, with this reply.

[3] Pusey d. 16 September at Ascot; he was buried in the nave of Christ Church cathedral, Gladstone being one of the pall-bearers. The regius chair of Hebrew was thus vacant; see 4, 23 Oct. 82.

[4] Pusey's nurse, wife of Rev. J. E. B. Brine.

Rev W. Pusey—Dr Acland—Walter Phillimore—Ch. Wood. Walk with Lavinia. Off to the Coppice at 5.30.[1] Found Sir R.P. stronger: kind as ever. Wrote to Ld Granville—Bp of B. & Wells—Mr Hamilton Tel.—and minutes. Read Southey's Cowper.

22. Fr.

Wrote to Ld Spencer—The Queen l.l. & Tel—Ld Granville l.l. & Tel—Ld Hartington—Sir Thos G.—Mr Childers—C.G.—Dean of ChCh—Mrs Bolton—Rev. E. Wickham—Mr Hamilton Tel.—Miss Montague Tel.—and minutes. Drive & walks with Sir RP. Finished Cowper's Life: a noteworthy book, & none other would have done any justice to such a man. Read Miss Marjoribanks.[2]

To H. C. E. CHILDERS, war secretary, 22 September 1882.   Childers MS 5/150.

Your letter of yesterday[3] set out most clearly the state of the case as to the return of the troops.

I think the Queen may have some natural apprehension lest we, or lest I, should have some inclination to press against or upon the Generals a premature return of troops. I cannot think she will feel any difficulty when she is assured that this is not the case.

We may consider the force in Egypt at three several stages: 1. The full army, as now. 2. The army to be retained while the Khedive's defensive arrangements are in course of incubation. 3. The small contingent which may remain in Egypt, at the charge of Egypt, until his authority is well consolidated.

As to the first, it seems almost that, we having the command of the sea, we cannot have reason to keep in Egypt after some 60,000 (I suppose) will have been disarmed, the same force which was necessary to carry their works, conquer & disarm them. And, within the limits of moderation, I think promptitude in returns would tend even to enhance the admiration justly created by promptitude of dispatch.

Therefore I think it is no part of our business to discourage the General in making arrangements to send home as soon as he deems it safe the men whom he believes that he can spare. There would I think be something almost ludicrous in our slackening his operations while they are confined within these bounds. And this is the only question of the moment. I send Granville a copy of what I write to you.

You speak of the beginning of October; but I am in hopes that he will make a commencement at least before that date. Also that he will get rid of the Indian force, if possible, among the first.

On your second question there seems to be nothing unreasonable in assuming the figure of 12,000, which you think is Wolseley's, for the intermediate stage.

With respect to the question of charge on Egypt at this stage, there would certainly be an advantage, beyond any economy to our Exchequer, in calling on Egypt to pay something. For otherwise, feeling himself, as he will feel, perfectly secure in our hands & without any jealousy, he [the Khedive] might unduly press for the prolongation of our period of occupation, if it brought him a *large* saving. He might I should think properly be charged, & as to the particulars I have no doubt you with Granville will arrange them rightly.

[1] Sir R. Phillimore's house. Gladstone was thus in Oxford during the meeting which founded Pusey House, but it is not clear if he attended it; Liddon, *Pusey*, iv. 391.
[2] M. O. W. Oliphant, *Miss Marjoribanks*, 3v. (1866).
[3] Add MS 44130, f. 98: reduction of troops in Egypt to about 12,000 to start probably at the beginning of October; Khedive should pay a capitation rate 'for a certain force' from date of his disbanding of his army.

23. Sat. [Hawarden]

Wrote to Ld Granville—& minutes. Off at eleven to Reading & Mortimer, then the funeral at Strathfieldsaye.[1] It was all reverent and touching. Saw The Prince of Wales—Sir H. Ponsonby—Ld Sydney—Dr Rowsell—Col. Ellis—Edw. Wickham & Agnes—Ld R. Gower. Left at 3.30. Reached Hawarden at ten. Read Cowper's Letters—Miss Marjoribanks.

24. 16 S. Trin.

Ch mg & evg. Wrote to Sir H. Ponsonby—Duchess of Wellington—Ld Spencer—Mr Bright—Archdn Harrison—Messrs Parry—and minutes. Conversation with S.E.G. Read Cox's Presbn Classis[2]—Estcourt on Engl. Orders.[3]

25. M.

Ch. 8½ A.M. Wrote to Canon Farrar[4]—Ld Granville—Ld Sydney—Dean of St Pauls—Mr Hugh Gladstone—Mr Luttrell—and minutes. Worked 3 hours on arranging (& deranging) books. Walk with W.H.G. Read Cheyney's [sic] Sermon—Commentary on Is. LIII[5]—Bride of Lammermoor[6]—and Seneca Consolatio.

26. Tu.

Ch. 8½ A.M. Wrote to Archdn Denison—Ld Granville (2)—Ld Spencer—Ld Aberdeen—Sir J. Lacaita—Mrs Bolton—Mr Marum MP—Mr Pease MP—Mr Morley—and minutes. The Eaton party came over. Conversation with the Duke [of Westminster]. The Duchess very natural & pleasing. Mary L[yttelton] a *trump.* Worked 1½ h. on books. Read Mrs Yelverton's Martyrs of Circumstance[7]—Seneca, Consolatio.

To J. MORLEY, editor of the *Pall Mall Gazette*,   Add MS 44255, f. 39.
26 September 1882.

A paragraph in the Pall Mall Gazette of yesterday refers to an expression of mine at the time of the Election which has been repeatedly remarked on. The phrase used was 'hands off'. It was applied by me, in conversation with a newspaper correspondent to Austria. But the gentleman now states that it was applied to Austria in Bosnia and Herzogovinia. This is an entire mistake. I had stated in Parliament that this part of the arrangements made at Berlin was in my view tolerable, considering the great difficulty of the case. But in 1880 the Jingo papers were confidently preaching the advance of Austria along the Balkan Peninsula, and *down to Salonica.* This scheme I attacked to the best of my ability.

---

[1] Of G. V. Wellesley.
[2] J. C. Cox, *Wirksworth presbyterian classis* (1880).
[3] E. E. Estcourt, *The question of Anglican ordination discussed* (1873).
[4] Frederick William *Farrar, 1831–1903; headmaster of Marlborough 1871–6; rector of St Margaret's, Westminster and canon of Westminster 1876–95; preacher and author; see above, ix. xxviii.
[5] T. K. Cheyne, 'Life through Christ and for Christ' (1880) and *The prophecies of Isaiah* (1882 ed.); a candidate for the Hebrew chair.
[6] Scott (1819); see 8 Aug. 26.
[7] M. T. Yelverton, i.e. M. T. Longworth, *Martyrs to circumstance*, 2v. (1861).

Count Karolyi, as I stated in Parliament, disclaimed it in terms the most unequivocal, and I then withdrew all I had said. But it referred only to a forward movement, and I believed the correspondent to understand it at the time. I should be obliged by your stating positively that he is in error on this one point, as it is not without public importance.[1]

I hope you have enjoyed your vacation.

To LORD SPENCER, Viceroy of Ireland, 26 September 1882.   Althorp MSS K5.

We shall be delighted if you can come here. We have no early absence in view, except a few days at Penmaenmawr. No man has better earned his vacation—if such it can be called. I rejoice in your being able to take it.

Some time ago I signified to Mrs O'Shea that we had better not meet again.[2] Her letters I cannot controul but do not encourage. I think she has been of some use in keeping Parnell on the lines of moderation, and I imagine he prefers the wife to the husband as an organ.

We must have one or more Cabinets just before the 24th. But except procedure, it is difficult to say what business may be ready for them. Egypt is a long evil running itself out but slowly.

[P.S.] We expect the Northbrooks on the 9th—possibly the Derbys, but no answer yet.

27. Wed.

Ch. 8½ AM. Wrote to Mr Seymour Tel.—The Queen l.l.—Ld Spencer—Ld Granville l.l.—Mr Millais—Mr Russell MP.—Sir G. Bowyer—Bp of Liverpool—Lady Phillimore—& minutes. Walk with Mr Tuke & Mr Hughes. Read Memoir of Warwick Brookes (& distributed copies)[3]—Seneca, *Consolatio*—Mrs Yelverton.

28. Th. [Penmaenmawr]

Ch. 8¼ AM. Wrote to Bp of Salisbury—Ld Houghton—Mr MacColl—Mr Seymour Tel. l.l.—The Queen—Ld Spencer Tel.—Rev. Mr Harvey—Sir H. Ponsonby Tel.—Mrs Bolton—Ld Morley l. & tel.—Mrs Th.—and minutes. 11¾–2¼. To Penmaenmawr where Lucy [Cavendish] hospitably entertains us. Read Life of Collier[4]—Bride of Lammermoor. The people recognise us and are beyond anything kind.

29. Fr. St M. & all Angels.

Penmr. Church 10 a.m. Wrote to Sir H. Ponsonby—Ld Chancellor—Ld Granville—Dean of Ch.Ch.—Morley—Mr A. Robinson—Mr B. Price—Mr Seymour Tel. and minutes. Sea walk mg: went up Penmaenbach aftn. Saw Mr Gibson MP—Geo Talbot. Read Cheyne's Essays on Isaiah—Bride of Lammermoor—Contemp. Rev., Temple on Egypt.[5]

---

[1] Morley promised to 'put the matter right'; Add MS 44255, f. 41. Para. of correction in *P.M.G.*, 28 September 1882, 3. See also to Karolyi, 4 May 80.
[2] See 23 June 82; 'I quite dread the fact of her communications leaking out' wrote Spencer on 25 September, prompted by E. W. Hamilton; *Spencer*, i. 223.
[3] Untraced memoir of Warwick Brookes, Manchester artist, d. August 1882; details of his life printed in *Manchester City News*, 26 August 1882 *et seq.* (see Boase, i. 419).
[4] Perhaps J. P. Collier, *An old man's diary*, 4v. (1871–2).
[5] R. Temple on Egypt in *C.R.*, xlii. 495 (October 1882).

30. Sat

Ch 8.30 a.m. Slight diarrhoea from change to cold: but walked: 'farmyard pay'. Wrote to The Queen 2 & Tel—Bp of Winchester 1 & Tel—Sir H. Ponsonby 1 & Tel.—Ld Granville—Mr Dodson—Sir J. Lacaita—Mr Courtney and minutes. Read Bride of Lammermoor—Contemp. Rev. Muhall on Egypt—Powell on Procedure[1]—Life of Collier. Walk in afternoon—with the Ladies.

17 S. Trin. Oct. One 82.

Reluctantly kept my bed till late in the evening: a little Castor Oil. Wrote to The Queen & copy—Mr Seymour Tel—and minutes. Read Collier (finished)— Cheyne on Isaiah—Modern Rev. Religion in France & other Articles[2]—Bp of Salisbury's Charge.[3]

2. M.

Rose at 1. Drive in aft: to see Aber Vale &c.&c. Wrote to Ld Hartington—Ld Granville l.l.—Mr Seymour Tel—Ld Morley Tel—The Queen—Ld Kimberley— Ld Rosebery and minutes. Read The Bride—wonderful! Cheyne's Essays.

To LORD KIMBERLEY, colonial secretary, 2 October 1882.   Add MS 44546, f. 12.

I do not feel very easy about the question of Zululand under the terms of Bulwer's report,[4] or at all sure that you can proceed to specialise the conditions of a plan without the Cabinet.

The situation is a very delicate one for we are called upon to adjust the conditions according to the views of a man who tells us plainly that there are conclusive objections (329) to the basis of your plan, which is the partial restoration of Cetewayo: and further, while we have mainly contemplated, as to the districts not embraced in the restoration, placing them under other Chiefs, and binding them as we shall bind Cetewayo to govern in a certain way, Bulwer says we must take this position of the country under our direct 'protection authority & rule' (332), 'direct authority or rule' (323), 'direct government & administration'. And this is to be under the Natal Government, so that if I understand it right we may have responsibility without effective controul.

You treat 'Natal Government' as meaning the Governor of Natal, but is this Bulwer's meaning? Are there conclusive reasons why the non-restored part of the country should be treated *very* differently from the restored? Will not our responsibility for this part, under Bulwer's plan, be as great as if it were directly annexed? Does the Cabinet know the ground it is invited to tread, and is it safe to proceed if this be in doubt? Is not Bulwer looking mainly to the convenience of reserving part of Zululand as a receptacle for the surplus native population of Natal, and is he not too much viewing the Zululand question through Natal spectacles? Do we know the opinion of Sir H. Robinson and must not he be taken into account?

I have put down many notes of interrogation but they are really summed up in *one* saying that I doubt whether we have not reached a stage at which [the] question grows too

---

[1] M. C. Mulhall on Egyptian finance, Baden-Powell on the clôture, *C.R.*, xlii. 525 (October 1882).
[2] *Modern Review*, iii. 474 (July 1882).
[3] By G. Moberly (1882).
[4] Bulwer's report of 25 August (377 pp. in MS, Schreuder, 301) proposed Natal's control over non-Cetewayo Zululand (see 27 May 82n.); *PP* 1883 xlix. 557.

big to be treated by you & me, and whether you will not have to print this report (unless parts can be omitted) & let the Cabinet deal with it.

[P.S.] I must own I think (after hasty examination) the tone of this Report is rather needlessly antagonistic, & not cooperative—he assumes too much *authority* for the settlement of 1879, and takes no account of the change brought in by breach of continuity. You have put a bit in his mouth by your paragraph about the charge of governing the non-restored district.[1]

To LORD ROSEBERY, home undersecretary, 2 October 1882.   N.L.S. 10022, f. 126.

It is beyond even your usual kindness—and that is saying a great deal—to write to me from Florence[2] on the death of the Dean of Windsor. A most sad loss to me in two ways; and in one way to any one who may stand in my place. He was a most sagacious as well as warm-hearted man. People would I *suppose* have called him a Tory, but we always talked politics with the utmost freedom and without the smallest discord. Singularly modest & retiring, he was, in this [and] many other ways, a great Christian. He might, if he had lived, have been on the road to the Archbishopric.

On this & many matters I should like to talk. You I know always travel by telegraph, and I address this to Lansdowne House. Are you going to Scotland? Can you, and if Lady R. so much the better, come to Hn.? We expect Northbrook on Monday—Spencers on Saturday week.

Again let me say I am grateful for your kindness.

3. Tu. [*Hawarden*]

Ch 8½ a.m. Wrote to Bp of Winchester—Ld Morley—Grogan & Boyd—Sir A. Gordon—Ld Granville—Ld Spencer—Mr Villiers Stuart and minutes. Luncheon at Mr Kneeshaws[3] and walk. Farewells—and speech to a large gathering at the Station.—Off at 5. Hawarden at 7.30. Read Bride of L.—Fortnightly on Skobeleff & Valedictory.[4]

To LORD SPENCER, Viceroy of Ireland, 3 October 1882.   Althorp MSS K5.

1. I am glad to conclude with you for the 14th.

2. As to the Judgeships, do I understand from you that it is necessary to fill up *both* the Irish Judgeships? Perhaps I am too fidgetty in my desire to do something towards reducing the enormous charge of Government in Ireland. I am not quite sure whether you have intended to imply this necessity in your letter,[5] or not.

3. As far as I am able to judge, we shall now be in a condition to defend Lawson[6] effectively, and I am extremely glad of it.

What an equinoctial you had to encounter.

4. Wed.

Ch 8½ a.m. Saw S.E.G.—C.G. on house affairs—1½ hour on books. Wrote to Ld

[1] Kimberley replied, 4 October, Add MS 44228, f. 1, 'not at all disposed to controvert your observations about the Zulu question'; Bulwer 'too much under the influence of Natal local opinion'; Robinson's view to be sought.
[2] On 27 September, Add MS 44288, f. 111.
[3] Henry Kneeshaw of Penmaenmawr, J.P. and D.L.; a tory.
[4] On General Skobelev, and Morley's 'Valedictory' as ed., *F.R.*, xxxviii. 405, 511 (October 1882).
[5] Of 2 October, Add MS 44309, f. 175.   [6] See 23 Aug. 82.

Hartington—Mr G. Saunders[1]—Mr Parker—Ly F. Cavendish—Mr Banks—Herbert J.G.—Mr Hutton—Mrs Bennett—Ld Powis—Dean of Ch.Ch.—Mr Palgrave—Archdn Palmer—Ld Gr. Tel—Dean of St Paul's and minutes. Read Saunders on Constantine &c.—Bride of Lammermoor finished. On perusing after a long interval this extraordinary work seems to me even greater than my recollection figured it. And K. Blind on Parties.[2]

To LORD HARTINGTON, Indian secretary,   Chatsworth MSS 340. 1274.
4 October 1882. '*Private*'.

I must own that I think the Queen's resolute attempts to disturb & impede the reduction of the army in Egypt, are (to use a plain word) intolerable. It is my firm intention not to give in, so far as I am personally concerned, for a moment to proceedings almost as unconstitutional as they are irrational; though the unreasonableness of her ideas is indeed such that it is entitled to the palm in comparison with their other characteristics.

It is unfortunate that Childers is out of the way but [Lord] Morley [undersecretary for war] I think acquits himself like a man.

[P.S.] The few figures you send me about Trade of & with India[3] quite suffice for my purpose. As to the figures of expenditure I have according to your suggestion sent at once to London.

To H. G. LIDDELL, dean of Christ Church, 4 October   Add MS 44545, f. 15.
1882.

I am *glad* to say the Hebrew Chair has given me a great deal of trouble. This means that, instead of finding it difficult to get a really good Oxford Hebraist, I find that after putting aside several possible names on various grounds (e.g. Archdeacon Palmer as put aside by himself) there are at least the four men of whom you first mentioned to me, Oxford men proper, all of whom stand *high* in Hebrew Scholarship and are qualified thus far to sustain the honour of the Chair. I have had counsel—spontaneous or solicited—from the following advisers among others—besides yourself: Mr G. Wickham; Dean of St. Paul's [R. W. Church]; Dean of Wells [Plumptre]; Archdeacon Harrison; Mr. A. Robinson (*full*); Bishop of Salisbury [Moberly]; Dr. Farrar (of Durham); E. Talbot; Dr. Bright—and I feel only sorry that do what I may I must pass by very good and very considerable men.

Out of those four three have remained entirely silent and Mr Cheyne has certainly not passed the bounds of modesty.

I have set before me as the main points to be ascertained 1) Hebrew Scholarship, as to extent, soundness, & originality; 2) Teaching aptitude; 3) Capacity to work the Chair in its due relation to Theology at large; 4) General attainments. I need not speak of high personal character as that comes out in all. It will hardly be possible to get a man best in all the points, but there need I am sure be no dishonour done to the Chair. The aggregate of *marks* so to speak runs at present in the direction of Driver[4] but I have not the *whole* evidence before me yet, though I am getting near it.

[1] George Saunders, 1859-1922, of Glasgow university and Balliol, had sent his Rectorial prize essay on Constantine the Great; later a foreign correspondent.
[2] K. Blind on European revolutionary parties, *C.R.*, xlii. 455, 603 (September–October 1882).
[3] Sent on 2 October; Add MS 44146, f. 66.
[4] Samuel Rolles *Driver, 1846-1914; offered the regius chair of Hebrew on 23 Oct.; an exceptionally successful appointment. Liddell had written, 24 September, proposing him for his scholarship, with some reservations about his teaching; Add MS 44236, f. 373.

To LORD POWIS, 4 October 1882.   Add MS 44546, f. 14.

You certainly hit a blot.[1] There is a great difficulty about military Peerages. But I am not satisfied with your remedy. Mere precedence would not be worth taking. I think a better remedy would be found in Life Peerages. I am less anxious however to see the House of Lords set about useful changes, because I am very ill satisfied with the one change it did make. I always thought they ought to have regulated proxies, not (virtually) extinguished them. It is questionable whether, in condemning them outright, they did not strike a blow at their own Constitution. Receive I pray you with indulgence my very conservative complaint.

5. *Th*

Ch 8½ a.m. Wrote to Ld Morley Tel.–Ld Granville–Mrs Bolton–Lady Derby–Scotts–Messrs Leeman–Mr R. Connyer–Mr Hugh Gladstone–and minutes. Calls, drive & walk with C. Three hours on books. Read Defoe on Hoadly[2]–Wiclif on the Eucharist[3]–Legend of Montrose (began)[4]–Memoir of Bp Geste.[5]

To LORD KIMBERLEY, colonial secretary, 5 October 1882.   Add MS 44546, f. 16.

I hate sending to a colleague, and not least to you who present everything in so clear a way, any reply of an obstructive character but your answer relieves me & shows me that my difficulties were not pure shadows. I do indeed think that Bulwer's report[6] *reeks* with Natal, Natal, Natal, from beginning to end: and my hasty examination has given me a certain mistrust which may I hope in later stages of the affair be dispelled. Robinson's opinion will be of great value. I must say that next to propitiating Natal, Bulwer's paper seems to contemplate hedging for himself in case of miscarriage. In every line it breathes 'mind it was not I'.

6. *Fr.*

Ch 8½ a.m. Wrote to Ld Kimberley–Ld Granville–Ld Rosebery–Messrs Grogan–Queen 1 & Tel–Rev. W. Connor–Mr [blank] (respecting Brooks and minutes). Worked 4½ hours on books. Read Legend of Montrose–Memoirs (?) of Geste–Geste on the Eucharist[7]–Lang's Helen of Troy.[8]

7. *Sat.*

Ch 8½ a.m. Wrote to Ld Granville–Princ. Librarian Museum Tel–Rev. T.G. Law–Mrs O'Shea[9]–Mr Seymour Tel–Mr West–Sir Thos G.–Archdn Palmer & minutes. Worked 2½ hours on Library. Phillimores & Hugh W. Gladstone came. Conversation on business & Theology. Read Helen of Troy. Geste on Holy Eucharist.

[1] Letter untraced; Powis often spoke on military affairs, though no speech on military peerages found.
[2] D. Defoe, *A friendly rebuke to one Parson Benjamin* [i.e. B. Hoadly] (1719).
[3] J. Wiclif, *Christ's real body not in the Eucharist* (1857 ed.).
[4] By Scott (1819); see 12 Aug. 26.
[5] H. G. Dugdale, *The life and character of Edmund Geste* (1840).
[6] See 2 Oct. 82.
[7] W. Goode, *A supplement... on the Eucharist* (1858); with Geste's letters.
[8] A. Lang, *Helen of Troy* (1882).
[9] See 10 Oct. 82.

8. *18 S. Trin.*

Ch 11 a.m. & 6½ P.M. Lessons as usual. Wrote to Mr Seymour Tel.—Lord Sydney—Mr Hutton—The Queen l.l. and minutes. Read Bp Geste's works (finished) and Life of Dupont.[1] Much conversation with Mr H. Gladstone, as we were setting out for evening Church he was seized with a fit at the front door, & put to bed.

9. *M.*

Ch 8½ a.m. Wrote to Ld Hartington—Ld Granville—Mr Hubbard—Ld Kimberley Tel.—Messrs Ogilvy & Co and minutes. The Northbrooks & Lady Grosvenor[2] came. Walk with Mr [W.G.F.] Phillimore. Read Helen of Troy and [blank.] Mr Hugh G. better, sat with him.

To LORD HARTINGTON, Indian secretary,   Chatsworth MSS 340. 1275.
9 October 1882.[3]

I do not think the length of your letter requires any apology. It is useful to have all the points raised in a difficult matter. I had better say at once that it contains much in which I cannot follow you, but there would be little advantage in my enumerating the points one by one, and arguing upon them. The more so, as the matters in which we are agreed are fundamental; and especially there is the fact that we both take a very serious view of the matter.

Indeed I go beyond you in this that I think there is one very grave element in the case which you do not mention. It is this, that a large part, probably the majority, of the Conservative party are not agreed with us as to our aim. We want a drastic reform of procedure, with a view both to a diminution of the aggregate labours of the House of Commons and especially to a more rapid and extensive transaction of legislative business. This is exactly what they do *not* want. The noble function which they assign to the House of Lords, of retarding the hasty proceedings of the House of Commons is at present more conveniently and safely for them, performed by the state of procedure in the House of Commons itself: and this advantage I do not think they will lightly surrender.

I was, as you know, originally of the opinion that the closing power was not worth all the squabbling it would cost; but I gave way to you and to the Cabinet generally. I still hold the same opinion: but I have now to consider together, with the *plus* quantity of value in the closing power, the *minus* quantity on the other side of the equation, which is practically the same thing, namely, the difficulty and discredit of retirement from a ground which we have actually taken up—which we have fought for many nights—and to which I believe the large majority of our friends attach, like our foes, a vast, though as I think, an exaggerated importance.

However, we are agreed in thinking that under the circumstances we ought if possible to 'do something' as it is called for the purpose of easing the situation. Your 'something' is to accept Gibson. There is to my mind one argument in favour of this, namely our temporary and qualified acceptance of it in the beginning of May. The case is indeed a very different one, but many might not see the difference.

---

[1] Perhaps Mrs P. Aubin, *The life of C. Du Pont* (1739).
[2] Sibell Mary, *née* Lumley, m. 1874 Lord Grosvenor, who d. 1884; she m. 1887 George Wyndham.
[3] Partly printed in Holland, i. 376, with Hartington's letter of 7 October explaining his extreme anxiety about the autumn session and his alarm at any revival of 'the intensity and bitterness of party spirit'. For Gibson's ⅔ amndt., see 1 Apr. 82.

The arguments *against* it are in my view overwhelming: 1. The Speaker, having examined, declared that he could not see his way to working it. 2. It is a complete recession from the announcement most deliberately made before the adjournment. That announcement was itself a recession, but upon cause, and cause of a very definite kind. We cannot without very great discredit go on heaping one recession upon another. 3. The principle of it is utterly bad. The best that can be said for it is that it would never work except in a very rare case like that of Jan. or Feb. 1881. The normal attitude of a Government is that of putting business forward. On contested matters, the normal attitude of the Opposition is that of keeping it back. Gibson's motion simply hands over to the Opposition by a solemn decision, and upon system, the power to say whether the closing power shall or shall not be used in aid of business. It is the adoption of a false principle with a futile and negative result.

I think I have already shown my disposition to concur with others in this important matter, which can only be settled in my opinion by a concurrence impossible except through a temper of that description. But, this notwithstanding, I need not after what I have said pursue the argument on Gibson's motion farther. The plan which I have proposed is to keep our scheme as a whole, but only to take it by Resolution to be in force down to the close of next Session (1883). I am content for the present to rest it on these considerations: 1. It involves no change of front. 2. Either its acceptance, or its refusal would materially mend our position. 3. The principle of it has been approved, indeed was suggested by the Speaker.

The objection to this plan cannot be put more strongly than by you. But I do not think you have rightly apprehended the proposition which you are answering. My meaning is this: that there is a very good hope that, upon a short trial, all parties would come to see that a closing power, such as we propose, could not *possibly* be used with effect in an unjust or harsh manner against a large minority i.e. a regular opposition.

There is yet another plan; dropping the subject for the present, while reserving our title to bring it forward in the event of our finding the Reform we propose insufficient without it.

In this there would no doubt be something of recession; but, speaking as the person who would probably have to execute the operation, I do not say that this must be *such* a recession as to be absolutely inadmissible. I just hope however for a favourable consideration of the plan I have put forward, though, all circumstances considered, I feel under no obligation to push it with an extreme of tenacity.

I will send your letter round [the Cabinet] with copy of this reply.

10.

Ch 8½ a.m. Wrote to Mrs O'Shea (new Edn)—The Queen—Ld Granville—King of the Belgians—The Speaker—Ld Sherbrook—Mr Forster—Sir H. Ponsonby—Mrs Cunningham—Sir J. Pauncefoot and minutes. Walk & conversation with Northbrook. Mr Hugh Gladstone went; conversation with him & MP. A grand tea at the Coffee-house for 8! Showed them the woods. Read Helen of Troy (finished)—Davidson's Last Things.[1] Ecl. 1 & Etd. & Translation—Life of Goodwin.[2] We are beyond anything pleased with Lady Grosvenor—

[1] S. Davidson, *The doctrine of last things* (1882).
[2] Perhaps T. Jackson, *The life of J. Goodwin* (1872).

To W. E. FORSTER, M.P., 10 October 1882.   Add MS 44546, f. 20.

It pleases me to take up my pen to write to you. I thank you for your letter and return the inclosure which is very satisfactory.[1] It is strikingly confirmed in the papers of this morning which announce that the American contributions [to the Fenians] are now to cease.

Let me thank you also for your congratulations about Egypt. We have only to desire that Granville may be as happy in what is now to come as Childers & Northbrook have been in the fighting part.

I am extremely glad you are interested so warmly in *John Inglesant*, which laid hold on me as it has done on you. Without doubt it is open to various criticisms. But it is a remarkable effort both of mind and heart, with the very highest aim: the aim of learning and of showing how the inner life of man, the life with God, can best be nourished amidst the difficult conditions imposed [by] the outer world and its affairs.

Like you I have been told he was a member of the Society of Friends.[2] And his family have been busy, I understand, for four generations in manufacturing oil of vitriol!

To Mrs. O'SHEA, 10 October 1882. '*Private*'.[3]   Add MS 44269. f. 134.

I will make known the purport of your communication[4] and its enclosure to one or two of my colleagues, without waiting for the assembling of the Cabinet which may not be for a fortnight. I do not think that the Government would consent to mix together the questions of Irish Land and Procedure. Were they however to do so, the fact of such a *tack* would injure, in the view of Parliament & the country generally, any proposals which they might make on either subject.

As respects the points still remaining open under the Land Act, I think those interested in them should for the moment estimate our probable future conduct by what is known of the past, whether for evil or for good.

As regards procedure, it is certainly my personal opinion, that, in any plan of Devolution, if the plan is to have any pretention to completeness, which Parliament ought or is likely to adopt, regard ⟨should⟩ may be had to the local principle, and a reasonable scope may be given to it. One of the powerful arguments in favour of such plans is their tendency to promote the passing of measures in which particular parts of the United Kingdom are particularly interested and beyond the rest.

⟨In sending you this limited reply, I allow myself the satisfaction of acknowledging the spirit and intent of the memorandum which, in the exercise of his right as a Member of Parliament, Mr. Parnell has framed and transmitted.⟩

I am doubtful whether the circuitous mode of communication which you have so kindly favoured, may not lead, if it were to become known, to suspicion & misapprehension. And I am inclined to think that, if Mr. Parnell in the exercise of his discretion is disposed at any time to make a communication to the Government, the best channel would be that which is the most usual, viz. the channel supplied by the intervention of my friend Lord R. Grosvenor.

[1] Account of his experiences by Mr O'Shaughnessy, an Irish sub-commissioner, sent from Brussels by Forster, 1 October, Add MS 44160, f. 205.
[2] J. H. Shorthouse was reared a Quaker, but 'stood notably for cultured Anglicanism' (*D.N.B.*).
[3] Holograph draft; for the complex composition of this letter, begun on 7 October, see Hammond, 309–11.
[4] Of 6 October, with a mem. by Parnell on procedure and a proposed Land Bill; Add MS 44269, f. 124.

11. *Wed.*

Ch 8½ a.m. Wrote to Mr Seymour Tel—Ld De Tabley—Mr Hutton—Mr Wilberforce—Mr A. Lang—Ld Mayor of Dublin—Ld Chancellor—Ld Granville Tel—
and minutes. Expedition to Eaton 1–5.[1] We went over everything: a marvel.
Read Miss Marjoribanks[2]—Cadorna, Questione d'Egitto.[3] Conversation with
Northbrook.

To C. DAWSON, M.P., Lord Mayor of Dublin,   Add MS 44546, f. 21.
11 October 1882.

I am obliged by your Lordship's comments on procedure,[4] and on public affairs generally. I will communicate on your Lordship's suggestion as to procedure with one of my
colleagues who has gathered much information on the subject.

With respect to the franchise in Ireland, I am not in a condition to announce at this
moment what may be the first legislative proposal of the Government, but I conceive it to
be the desire of my colleagues to see the Irish franchise extended.

12. *Th.*

Ch. 8½ AM. Wrote to Count Cadorna—Ld Granville—Mr Childers—D. of
Sutherland—Seymour L. & Tel.—Mr Sparrow[5]—Mrs Bolton—Messrs Barker l. &
Tel.—Mrs Th.—Mr Sharp l. & Tel.—Ld Sydney—Bishop Strossmayer[6]—and
minutes. Walk with C. Read Miss Marjoribanks—Cadorna on Egypt—Wilson,
War of 1870[7]—Davidson, Last Things. Worked 2 h on books.

To the DUKE OF SUTHERLAND, 12 October 1882.   Add MS 44546, f. 22.

I am a little staggered at your proposal[8] that we should purchase the Egyptian Railways: and I am afraid Europe would take the act as a flat negative of our protocol of disin-
terestedness and the like. I will however certainly lay it before Granville, from whom you
will perhaps anticipate a more favourable consideration.

I daresay you have wound up the harvest on your beautiful coast farms, and I hope it is
a good one. Here, the highest authorities give an excellent report.

13. *Fr.*

Ch. 8½ AM. Wrote to Ld Granville Tel.—Mr Childers Tel.—Sir Thos G.—Grogan
& Boyd—The Queen—Sir H. Ponsonby—Mr Godley—Rev. Mr Barrett—Ld Kin-
naird—& minutes. Read 'Last Things' (finished)—Wilson, War of 1870—Barrett,
Sermon on Pusey[9]—Miss Marjoribanks. Worked on books.

---

[1] The Grosvenors' great house across the Cheshire border.
[2] See 22 Sept. 82.
[3] C. Cadorna, *Le Relazioni internazionali dell'Italia e la questione dell'Egitto* (1882).
[4] Not found.
[5] J. W. Sparrow; had sent pears; Add MS 44546, f. 22.
[6] In R. W. Seton Watson, *The Southern Slav question* (1911), 443.
[7] R. Wilson, *The Franco-German war* (1881).
[8] Letter sent on to Granville; see Ramm II. i. 446 and 20 Oct. 82.
[9] G. S. Barrett, 'The influence of the late Dr. Pusey' (1882).

14. Sat.

Ch. 8½ AM. Wrote to Mr Seymour Tel.—Ld Granville—The Queen—Mr Court-
ney—Mrs Murrell—Scotts—and minutes. Also Circular to Members.[1] Read Mon
Oisiveté (1787)[2]—Wardle's Address.[3] Company came.[4] Walk with Palgrave. Saw
Count Münster—Lord Spencer. Saw Mr Smethwick. Ten to dinner.

15. 19 S. Trin.

Ch. 11 AM and 6.30 P.M. Wrote to Ld Hartington—Mr Seymour—Mr Dodson—
Dr Greenhill—Mr Childers—& minutes. Saw Count Münster—Lord Spencer.
Walk with the party. Conversation with Houghton. Read Abbot on the visibility
of the Church[5]—Horne on Roger Bacon[6]—Butler (Geo.) Sermons.[7]

To LORD HARTINGTON, Indian secretary,   Chatsworth MSS 340. 1276.
15 October 1882.

The reply to Mrs. O'Shea[8] is gone, with modifications, and with a Paragraph proposing
that any further communication, should there be such, should come through another
channel.

My recollection about the Cabinet is that there was informal conversation about it, but
not any decision of any kind; much less that no communication should at any time be
held with Parnell except across the table.[9]

In my opinion, as a general rule, every member of Parliament is entitled to make communications to the Government, at any time, & even though he be in avowed opposition
to it: the exceptions to this rule, if any, would I think have to be founded on very definite
grounds. I hold advisedly that this is a *right* of a member of Parliament as such, & not a
mere matter of policy. I cannot help thinking you may be inclined to allow some force to
the consideration of the character with which a member of Parliament as such is
invested.

I think with you it would be very advantageous if Parliament could let Irish land lie
fallow for a season—I should be glad, however, if circumstances were to allow of the
passing of a good measure for local government in Ireland next year.

16. M.

Ch. 8½ AM. Houghton, C. Münster and the Spencers after a long conversation
went. Walk with N. Lyttelton, fresh from Egypt,—and Lacaita. Wrote to Grogan
& Boyd—Granville Tel. l.l.—Sir T. Acland—and minutes. Also the very long
letter to Spencer on the subject of my retirement, to be pondered both before it

[1] Summons for the autumn session.
[2] C. Remi, *Mon Oisiveté* (1779); the 1787 ed. was entitled *Considerations philosophiques sur les moeurs. . . .*
[3] Sir T. Wardle, 'An address on art culture' (1882).
[4] Houghton, the Spencers, Münster, Lacaita, sundry Lytteltons.
[5] G. Abbot, *A treatise on the perpetual visibilitie and succession of the true Church* (1624).
[6] Not found.
[7] G. Butler, *Sermons preached in Cheltenham College chapel* (1862).
[8] See 10 Oct. 82. Hartington's comments on the O'Shea correspondence were sent to Granville (Add MS 44146, f. 87); he deplored sending the reply.
[9] Probably at one of the August cabinets, but not minuted.

goes, and after.[1] Read Legend of Montrose—Persecution of Dr Welton[2]—Catholic Presbyterian, on Egypt, & divers Articles.[3]

17. Tu.

Ch. 8½ A.M. Wrote to Ld Hartington—Ld Granville—The Queen—Mr Seymour—Mr Childers—The Speaker—& minutes. Worked 2 h on Library. Walk with C. Read Mrs Butler on Shakespeare[4]—Legend of Montrose.

To H. B. W. BRAND, the Speaker, 17 October 1882.   Brand MSS 307.

I will with your leave communicate further with you on Saturday: meantime I thank you for your letter.[5]

I have understood you to say you shrank from the responsibility of working our first rule with Gibson's amendment, as not seeing your way to it. Plainly the Opposition mean that if we get our first rule it shall be at the expence of much delay, suffering, & embarrassment to public business. I do not know what the Cabinet will say but some certainly appear to shrink from paying this heavy price.

I incline to think this is one of the cases, like those of Bradlaugh & Parnell's release, in which, if an Opposition means not to be scrupulous they have a good opening for making political capital.

The weakness of Liberal knees in some cases on our own side is an indication in this sense.

18. Wed.

Ch. 8½ AM. Wrote to Sir J. Lacaita—Ld Granville Tel. l.l.—Rev. M. M'Coll—Ld Sydney—Mrs Wickham—The Queen—Mr Hayward—Sir S. Hayes—Mr Bentley—Mr Childers—& minutes. Walk with Herbert & long political & Estate conversation. Called on Mr Brown: severe.[6] Worked on Library 1½ h. Read Legend of Montrose—Mrs Butler on Shakespeare (finished).

19. Th.

Ch. 8½ AM & 7 PM Harvest festival; full congr. hearty service excellent sermon. Wrote to Mr Gladstone Lingham[7]—Dr Dollinger—Mr Wood—Warden of Keble—Mrs Th.—Ld Granville l.l.—Mr Seymour—Mr Chamberlain—& minutes. Worked 2 h on Library. Read (all) The Hour of Death—Legend of Montrose (finished). Mrs Hamilton came & daughr.[8] Conversation with Herbert for his speech.

[1] See 24 Oct. 82.
[2] *The church distinguished from a conventicle: in a narrative of the persecution of Dr. Welton and his family* (1718?).
[3] *Catholic Presbyterian*, viii. 241 (October 1882).
[4] Not found; presumably privately printed work by Josephine Butler.
[5] Of 15 October, Add MS 44195, f. 121: 'rules' should be made Standing Orders.
[6] His bodyguard; see 20 Oct. 82.
[7] Unidentified.
[8] Isabel and Constance Hamilton, E.W.'s mother and sister.

To J. CHAMBERLAIN, president of the board of trade,   Chamberlain MSS 5/34/15.
19 October 1882.

Thank you for your memorandum:[1] which I have read & certainly hope that whatever happens we shall keep faith about promoting within safe limits Egyptian liberties. You should I think show it to Granville.

To J. J. I. VON DÖLLINGER, 19 October 1882.   Add MS 44140, f. 445.

I thank you sincerely for your letter,[2] & I answer it promptly as I am about to plunge into a sea of business in Cabinet & the House of Commons, & if I did not write now I might delay unduly. I shall however touch lightly & briefly on the several topics.

I begin with your last. We must not take Egypt, either formally or virtually, for these among other reasons; 1. We have too much to do already; 2. It would be a bad example, as Cyprus was; 3. It would not improbably accelerate a great crisis in the East for which we are not prepared.

Next on the question of Establishment, as to which you are uneasy. I have not the same amount or kind of fear on this question, as you & many others. But in some way I have conveyed to you an erroneous impression. When I saw you in 1874, the new law,[3] & internal troubles connected with it, produced a state of things which might rapidly have brought a crisis. But the authors of that law are now weary if not ashamed of it. And though the crisis may be in the womb of the future, & probably is there, I do not think it near, & do not expect to see it. My hope is that the English Church will after it have a greater career; but she wants much preparation for it, & this she is gradually getting.

Now as to Palmer.[4] I have sent at once to Mr. McColl your very important & interesting statement, in an extract from your letter *verbum verbo.* I have often spoken of the great weight attaching to this work however far it may be from perfection: & it greatly sustains me when I read a judgment on it carrying such authority as yours.

I may perhaps be able to make known to Dr. Liddon what you have said of Pusey whose life I am told he is about to write.

There is one very important personage connected with the working of the Anglican Reformation who remains too much in the shade, & who is not mentioned I believe by Palmer. This is Geste, Bishop of Salisbury, the *principal* actor in the measures taken on the accession of Elizabeth.

What noble sentiments Bishop Strossmayer has put into the Dedication of his great Cathedral!

P.S. I have not yet read the Archbishop's Article on Mozley;[5] but I dissent from the proposition you have drawn from it. There is indeed, in certain classes, a wide disintegration of belief: but those of the educated laity, who go as far as Arnoldism go a great deal farther. Farther even than [A. P.] Stanley, but it would be a mistake to confound Arnold as to opinions with his pupil & biographer.

---

[1] Of 18 October, in Chamberlain, *Political Memoir*, 74: objections to a 'sole and individual guarantee to Egypt'.

[2] Not found; no letters from Döllinger after 1880 in Add MS 44140; presumably returned to author: Gladstone's letters ibid. are typed copies.

[3] i.e. the Public Worship Regulation Act, passed just before Gladstone's visit to Munich which led to the Vatican pamphlets; see 8–21 Sept. 74 and vii. cxii.

[4] Proposed new ed., never completed, of W. Palmer, *Treatise on the Church of Christ*, 2v. (1838); see 20, 27 Mar. 81.

[5] See 21 Oct. 82.

20. Fr. [London]

Wrote to Mrs Bolton—The Queen—C.G.—Mr Dwyer Gray—M.G.—and minutes. 9¼-3½. To London. In Chester I signed the Deeds which divest me of my landed property and transfer it to Willy. Conversation with Mr Brown of the Flintshire Constabulary: who I hope has now done with me. They have all been most kind. Cabinet 3½-6½. Dined at Mrs Th.s. Mr [C.P.] Villiers there, in surprising freshness. Read Miss Marjoribanks.

Cabinet. Oct. 20. 82. 3 PM.[1]
1. Khedive's offer of an offer of residence. Safer to decline.
2. Harcourt. Convict Prison. Postponed.
3. Arabi. His fate should depend on proof of *crimes.* Malet to report at once important proof or disproof.
4. Purchase of Egyptian Railways. (Duke of Sutherland) by supporting a Company. Malet not to mix himself up in it.[2]
5. Conversation on the Controul. Various opinions.
6. Conversation on procedure—the three courses. (Apparent leaning against Gibson).[3]
7. Vote of thanks—notices on Tuesday for Thursday.
8. Committee on Gray's case at any rate NOT to be given.[4]

21. Sat.

Wrote to Mr Gray MP—Mr Chamberlain—The Queen—Mr Whitbread—C.G.—Attorney General—& minutes. Cabinet 1-6. Very difficult: but all right. Saw Mrs Bolton—Mr S.—Lord R.G—Ld Granville—The Speaker. Dined at Granville's & saw Ld Lyons: Lady de Vesci. Read Miss Marjoribanks—Abp of Cant. on Mozley.[5]

Cabinet. Oct. 21. 1 PM.[6]
1. Procedure. Gray's Case—move comm[itt]ee; Thanks—Thursday; Course to be taken on the Procedure—simply Persevere.
2. Many Grants. Partially discussed.
3. Granville's Draft D.[7] Baker's plan too large. Egypt to be neutralised by act of the Powers if possible. Sultan to make a firman which will limit his powers, which must be reduced. Neutralisation. Reconsideration of right to ask Egyptian troops. No further firmans. Commit us to generality.
4. Draft on Controul read and amended.

[1] Add MS 44643, f. 176. Papers on trial of Arabi in FO 78/3618.
[2] See to Sutherland, 12 Oct. 82.
[3] See 2 Nov. 82.
[4] E. D. Gray, M.P., imprisoned for contempt (see 17 Aug. 82); on 24 October, after next day's change of plan, Gladstone moved for a select cttee. on privilege; *H* 274. 34.
[5] A. C. Tait, 'Thoughts suggested by Mr Mozley's *Oxford reminiscences*', *Macmillan's Magazine*, xlvi. 417 (October 1882).
[6] Add MS 44643, f. 177.
[7] Draft of dispatch to Lyons, in terms as stated here; see Ramm II, i. 449n. Notion of a '*sole* guarantee' by Britain abandoned, see C. Howard, *Britain and the Casus Belli 1882-1902* (1974), 114.

Abolition of the Controul. Substitution of a financial adviser who may at the desire of the Khedive attend Councils and exercise the rights of inquiry and advice upon finance, without any power of active interference in administration. This financial adviser to be probably the head of the direction of the Caisse [de la Dette]. Again he may be an Egyptian Minister & an Englishman as proposed by Egypt[,] then the French to have the Presidency. Basic—no compulsion.

1. Equality of taxation between Egyptians & foreigners. 2. Reduction of European personel in number & charge. 3. Receivership of Caisse de la Dette Publique—To remain. 4. President to advise Khedive (as friend not officially on behalf of the Govt. of his nation) when called upon & also at his invitation from time to time to attend Council of ministers. His advice may cover the whole province of the late Controul. 5. Management of domains—to remain. Work to be expedited.[1]

To J. CHAMBERLAIN, president of the board of trade,   Chamberlain MSS 5/34/16.
21 October 1882.

I am truly sorry for your absence from today's Cabinet for besides dealing with Procedure (in which we simply *persevere*) we have spent much time on Egyptian matters and especially on the very delicate and difficult questions connected with the abolition of the controul. I cannot attempt to report particulars and nothing is fixed as to form but I was greatly pleased with the general spirit of the discussion which might be summed up in the words 'NO compulsion' i.e. as to matters not already sealed by international compact and private right. On Monday at two we meet to bring Devolution into shape. I *hope* your gout may by that time have relaxed its hold.[2]

To Sir H. JAMES, attorney general, 21 October 1882.   James MS M45. 31.

The Cabinet thinks that upon the whole, considering that the Irish will make the motion for a Committee on Gray's case if we do not make it, & the time will thus be taken from us, we had better make it ourselves.[3] By precedent this motion ought apparently to be made by me: but I hope you will be prepared kindly to produce if needful the precedents & to argue the case. Perhaps you will kindly consult with R. Grosvenor on the nomination of the Committee.

To Mrs GLADSTONE, 21 October 1882.[4]   Hawarden MSS.

I will not leave you letterless for this post but I have been very busy and am rather tired. A stiff but good Cabinet on very difficult matters—first as to procedure and secondly Egypt, on which the points were debated with great ability, especially by Northbrook, Hartington, and Harcourt—who avowed he had completely changed his mind on the most important of them, since last night, when, dining at Granville's, he had argued also with great ability the other way. But the questions are very delicate & difficult.

Agnes sends me an unreproachful little note and incloses one from William of Wykeham.[5]

Last night, at Thistlethwayte Hall, i.e. in G. Square, I was really amazed at the

¹ Memoranda at Add MS 44643, ff. 178–80.
² Chamberlain replied, 22 October, Add MS 44125, f. 173, again opposing 'single control'.
³ See 20, 24 Oct. 82. Whitbread and Goschen refused to chair the cttee. so Gladstone fell back on Northcote; James MS M45. 32.
⁴ Part in Bassett, 239; letter headed 'My dearest Love'.
⁵ i.e. William G. Wickham, his grandson.

freshness, nimbleness, and force of [C. P.] Villiers, past eighty but perfectly young & extremely shrewd.

No news on household matters: I got to bed at an hour as good [as] at Hawarden & hope to do the same tonight. Ever your afft.[1]

22. 20 S. Trin.

Chapel Royal mg. St Margaret's evening. Saw Ld Wolverton—Mr M'Coll on [Archdeacon W.] Palmer's Work. Wrote to The Queen—C.G.—& the substance of a letter to W.H.G. on the occasion of transferring the lands.[2] Read Hales's Remains[3]—Carlyle on Spirits—Cantab. on Apostolic Succession[4]—Elijah—Revised Version. Viewed the return of the Life Guards [from Egypt] from Lady Ailesbury's Balcony: a singularly touching spectacle.

23. M.

Wrote to The Queen Tel—Bp of Salisbury—Rev. Mr Driver[5]—Mr Loverdo—Mr Bryce MP—Mr MacColl. Worked a little on arranging and examining books. Saw Mr H.—Ld R.G.—Quasi Cabinet on Resolution, with Co-adjutors: & then discussion on Egypt 1–6$\frac{1}{4}$.[6] C.G. came. Reviewed and sent letter to W.H.G. Read Miss Marjoribanks.

To J. BRYCE, M.P., 23 October 1882.   Bryce MS 10, f. 36.

I am not favourable, personally, to raising the wide question of Church Endowments on and for the removal of a few hundreds a year from the Canonry which endows the Hebrew Chair. In all else I strongly agree.[7]

I determined from the first to reserve the rights of Parliament. I should very gladly see a purely philological and historical Hebrew Chair in Oxford—and you may even find that your recommendation of Mr. Driver has not been thrown away. I have, in a laborious examination, been agreeably surprised at the number of distinguished or creditable scholars available for the Chair.

24. Tu.

Wrote to The Queen 1.1.—Rev. Mr Spurgeon—Ld Spencer—Rev. Mr MacColl—The Speaker—H.H. Dhuleep Singh—Mr Monro—Lady Brownlow and minutes. Saw Mr H.—Ld R.G.—Lady Holker—Sir R. Blennerhassett—Mr Mowbray.[8] Cabinet 2–3$\frac{3}{4}$. H of C. 3$\frac{3}{4}$–9.[9] Had much speaking. We made a good opening. Read QR (Burgon) on Pusey[10]—Miss Marjoribanks. Visit to No 73.[11]

[1] No signature.   [2] Hawn P.; see 9 Sept. 82.
[3] J. Hales, *Golden remains*, 3v. (1659).
[4] *Apostolical succession not a doctrine of the Church of England . . . by Cantab* (1870).
[5] See 4 Oct. 82n.   [6] Despatch in light of decision of 21 Oct. agreed.
[7] Bryce to S. G. Lyttelton, passed on to Gladstone, 16 October 1882, Bryce MS 11, f. 64: intended last Session to introduce a bill secularising the chair for 'Oriental Semitic languages', *via* the endowed Canonry, as 'a reasonable corollary of what has been done for the Professorship of Greek at Cambridge': given the chair's unchanged status, Bryce urged Cheyne's or Driver's appointment.
[8] Perhaps (Sir) Robert G. C. Mowbray, 1850–1916; barrister; active in tory circles; tory M.P. 1886–95.   [9] Arguing with Churchill; procedure; E. D. Gray; *H* 274. 11.
[10] *Q.R.*, cliv. 515 (October 1882).   [11] i.e. his Harley Street house.

Cabinet. Tues. Oct. 24. 1882. 2 PM.[1]
1. Committee for Cabinet on divers bye questions: the Sheikh: Congo: Madagascar:[2] Ld Kimberley, Ld Hartington, Mr Childers, Ld Northbrook.
2. Procedure Resolutions Amdts: read & approved.
3. Persia: Malcolm Khan has credentials as ambassador. Communication to be held with Foreign Powers as to acknowledging.
4. Answer for Dilke as to Errington when Wolfe asks.
5. Granville & I to meet Northbrook & Childers tomorrow at 3 in my room.
6. Granville's Draft Ac[count] on expenditure in Egypt. To be amended in Para. 3 by softening.
7. Kimberley mentioned the position of the Zulu question.
8. Chamberlain criticised the dispatch agreed on yesterday out of Cabinet by most of the Ministers, & sent.

To LORD SPENCER, Viceroy of Ireland, 24 October 1882.   Add MS 44546, f. 29.

[First letter:]   The inclosed letter, sent for custody rather than reply, though dated today was written just after you left Hawarden, and sums up as well as expounds some part of my conversation with you. I shall send a copy of it to Granville and perhaps Hartington: to no others for the present.

'*Private & Confidential*'.[3]   Althorp MSS K5.

[Second letter:]   As the stream of our conversation led us, half unawares, into personal & prospective matter touching myself, I wish that you should have before you a clear outline of what I think to be, in modern phrase, the situation.

In 1874, I desired to retire from the Leadership of the Liberal party. There was then a kind of provisional compromise, & I took but little part in general business during the Session, after the start of the new Government.

At the beginning of 1875 in spite of much friendly remonstrance, I effected my retirement; & Hartington took the lead in the House of Commons, Granville acting as the head of the party. Hartington was new to the work: but he held the office through five anxious years, with acknowledged, and constantly growing, credit and efficiency.

During 1875 and 1876, I doubt if I ever made a speech, except on comparatively rare occasions, & in the character of a hearty ⟨but⟩ independent follower.

At the end of 1876 there was a debate on the Eastern Question. The Government had pursued a policy of abstention. This had reached a point at which I thought it to be ⟨wholly⟩ at variance with the obligations entailed by the Crimean War & the Peace of Paris. As the only Ex-Minister in the House of Commons who had been responsible for that war, I was compelled to make my protest.

On the authentication of the news respecting the massacres in Bulgaria, I followed this up in September with a pamphlet & a speech as my contribution to a general movement intended to draw the Government into action.

This movement brought about the Constantinopolitan Conference of 1876–7. It happened that in that recess I moved much about the country, but I used great care to avoid agitation against the Government. The meeting at St James's Hall[4] was a meeting to

---

[1] Add MS 44643, f. 181.
[2] F.O. mem. on French claims to Madagascar, 24 Oct. 1882; Add MS 44628, f. 134.
[3] Copy sent on 27 October 'to Lord Granville & Lord Hartington only, as a secret letter'; docketed by Hartington 'seen'; Add MS 44309, f. 191.
[4] See 8 Dec. 76.

strengthen the hands of Lord Salisbury, even more than to protest against the language of Lord Beaconsfield.

The subsequent period, from 1876 until the Dissolution, was, I admit, a period of great & latterly of incessant personal activity. But, even in those years, so far was I from seeking to widen my field of action, that I did not speak against the Government on the South African questions, & I was silent upon Egypt, as well as upon much home policy which I disapproved.

About 1878 it was arranged that I was to sit in this Parlt. for Edinburgh, a seat considered to be one of the quietest in the country. But, about the beginning (I think) of 1879, it was pressed upon me to attack the Midlothian seat, then held by the Tories. It at once appeared to me that this was a very serious affair, & might prove larger than the simple wresting of even a difficult seat from the adversary. I declined to move in it without Granville's express sanction, which was given. I had then no choice; for there was no effort which it was not in my eyes a duty to make for the purpose of putting an end to the scheme of Government then in action.

When the Election was over, I considered myself bound to take office, if I were called upon by the Queen, & if no Liberal Government were formed by the leaders without me. I made up my mind that I could only do this as head of the Government: & that it could only be for the special purpose of meeting the state of facts on which the Election turned, & that, with the ending of that state of facts my mission would end also; & the lead would naturally revert to those who, apart from circumstances altogether special, were by every possible title its legitimate possessors.

According to this definition, I consider that the time for my retirement had arrived a full twelvemonth ago. But other special circumstances had then arisen, of such a nature as to make it impossible for me to decline facing them. These were—

a. The state of Ireland
b. The entanglements in Egypt
c. The state of the House of Commons.

In the first, there was required a reversal of the disintegrating movement. In the second, a definitive solution. In the third, a serious effort to enable the House to liberate itself from an unworthy servitude.

Under the two first heads, the advance has been such that for me, I think, the special & detaining force has nearly passed away.

When the third has been disposed of by the serious effort I have named (& I mean no more than an effort), then, unless the basis of all my views and acts since 1873 is to be changed, the season for my retirement will have arrived.

The principal reasons, then, for accomplishing it, say before the close of the year, will be

1. To restore the natural and normal state of things, which existed up to 1880.

2. To allow a man of seventy three years (next December) old, & fifty of public service, to relieve himself from a life of contention which has been unusually sharp, & to devote whatever time may still be allotted him, in the main at least, to employments more appropriate, & less violently imperious than those of his present public life.

These reasons, each of which ought to suffice, are backed by another yet more commanding: namely that increase of disinclination to my work, and disposition (in homely phrase) to scamp it, which I think & know to be a sign of diminished power, I mean of power diminished below the point at which it ought to stand, in order to master in any tolerable degree the most difficult parts of that work. This I consider to be the supervision, and often the construction, of weighty legislative measures, which are duties I fear inseparable from my present place in the House of Commons & in the Government.

The work of that kind, which is to come on as soon as the House recovers its liberty, is great & formidable. There is, in the Government & the party, plenty of energy, fresh and yet mature, to cope with it. I cannot & dare not face it as I have been accustomed to do. It would be of no good to anyone, that I should remain on the stage like a half-exhausted singer, whose notes are flat, & everyone perceives it except himself. Such a condition of things ought to be met by prevention, & not by remedy; & kind nature, if we give her fair play, helps us with premonitory signs, of which the person concerned should always be the first interpreter. I do not contemplate immediate Parliamentary extinction. A part may yet remain, the part of independent cooperation upon occasion, which may be sought when it is desired, & which can be, & has been, safely & usefully discharged by many public men after they have bid a final adieu to office. Another issue, that of passing at once from the tumult & absorption of the present position either to dotage or the grave, presents a picture for which no man should (I think) wish to supply the subject. The coming time is marked by all the notes of an opportunity, & my conviction is that if neglected it can hardly recur.

Such is the outlook before me. But action, which is in its nature final, should be tested by reflection; & it is for this purpose that I have given my ideas so much of shape, as to enable me carefully & repeatedly to test them by a quiet survey.

Before closing I would add that there are several lessons of a more secondary & personal kind, all of them inclining me in the same direction as these main ones, which I have given, but which, though they are far from insignificant, might not of themselves suffice to warrant my conclusion.

This letter traverses much ground, & gives but an incomplete explanation after all, so that I must ask pardon both for its length & in one sense for its brevity.[1]

25. *Wed.*

Wrote to The Queen—Sir B. Seymour (2)—and minutes. Conclave on material for Vote of thanks 4–5. H. of C. 12¼–6: on Procedure.[2] Saw Mr H.—Ld R.G. We went to the Lyceum & saw Much Ado about Nothing: admirable. We saw Mr I. & Miss Terry afterwards. Read M.A. about Nothing—Miss Marjoribanks.

26. *Th.*

Wrote to Sir C. Ducane—Mr Hubbard—The Queen—and minutes. Saw Mr H.—Ld R.G—Sir J. Lubbock. Visited No. 73. Got up the Egyptian case. H. of C. 4¼–8¼ & 10¼–1. Spoke (very long) on Thanks.[3]—A good night on the whole. Dined at Sir T. May's. Read Miss Marjoribanks. Conversation with Lady Goldsmid.[4]

27. *Fr.*

Wrote to Ld Kimberley—The Queen l.l.l.—Agnes W.—Mrs Th.—and minutes. Saw Mr H—Ld R.G.—Mr Trevelyan—Mr Courtney—Mr Forster—Mr Carrington. H. of C. 4¼–8½ & 9¼–12¾.[5] Read Miss Marjoribanks.

---

[1] Spencer's reply, 29 Oct., 44309, f. 198, argued Gladstone had not 'sufficiently considered the Public results of your retirement'. See also Ramm II, i. 450 and to Hartington, 13 Nov. 82 and n.

[2] *H* 274. 78.

[3] *H* 274. 179; radical amdt. to the vote of thanks to the forces defeated in 25:230.

[4] Virginia, wife of Sir J. Goldsmid (see 28 June 66).

[5] Procedure; *H* 274. 289.

To LORD KIMBERLEY, colonial secretary, 27 October 1882.   Add MS 44546, f. 29.

Bulwer is indeed an awkward customer[1] & I do not at the moment recollect a case in which so difficult a question has been worked through so adverse an instrument.

What would you think of sending, or letting me send, this letter to Gurdon, one of my old private Secretaries, an able & thoroughly upright man, not *Colensian*, who has been twice in South Africa, & is I think an annexationist, but who would not I think be governed by his own leanings & would conform to the actual situation.[2]

28. Sat.

Wrote to Rev. Mr Driver—Att. General—Dean of Ch.Ch.—Ld Spencer—The Queen—Sir H.D. Wolff—Sir S. Northcote—Ld Hartington—Mr Maciver—& minutes. Worked in Harley St. Met Sir G. Wolseley at the RR.[3] Delighted with his simple unselfconscious manner. Saw Mr G—Ld R.G—Mrs Birks. Read Miss Marjoribanks. Dinner of 12 at home.

To Sir H. D. C. WOLFF, M.P., 28 October 1882. *'Private'*.   Add MS 44546, f. 30.

I thank you both for the tone and the matter of your letter.[4] I think myself safe in saying that if the case of Arabi prove to be like those of Kossuth or Garibaldi, his head is as safe on his shoulders as yours or mine. It has been from the first our desire, and we have taken steps for giving effect to the desire, that no man should on this occasion lose his life merely for having shared in the rebellion. But these are matters of great gravity with which Arabi stands in more or less presumable connection. Our business is to see, as well as we can, that the presumption is tested by proof. It will be the question of crime or no crime, which I believe will decide his fate: and, as in duty bound, I shall be glad if the result be 'no crime'.

29. 21 S. Trin.

Savoy mg (SEG) & Chapel Royal aft. Wrote to Lady Goldsmid. Read Cantab. (finished)—Life of Jarrow[5]—Aitken on Grace[6]—and ... Saw Granville—Quasi-Cabinet $2\frac{1}{2}$-$4\frac{1}{2}$. P.M.

30. M.

Wrote to Dr Liddon—Ld E. Fitzmaurice—Mr M'Coll—Mr Courtney MP—The Queen—Mr Woolner—Mrs Bolton—& minutes. Saw Mr H.—Ld RG—Makolem Khan[7]—Mrs Th—Mr Woolner. Worked in Harley St. H of C. (& Gray Committee) $3\frac{1}{2}$-$8\frac{1}{2}$ and $9\frac{1}{4}$-$12\frac{1}{4}$: working Procedure.[8] Read Miss Marjoribanks.

[1] Kimberley, 26 October, Add MS 44228, f. 12, reported 'a most unsatisfactory letter from Bulwer. He has but one idea, namely, that the present state of affairs' is the fault of 'the Bishop', i.e. Colenso.
[2] No answer found; Gladstone told Kimberley, 1 November, Add MS 44546, f. 31 that this approach had proved 'rather barren'.
[3] Gladstone and Childers were cheered at the railway station as well as Wolseley; *T.T.*, 30 October 1882, 8a.
[4] Not found.
[5] Perhaps *The inventories of... Jarrow*, ed. J. Raine (1855).
[6] W. H. M. H. Aitken, *The school of grace* (1880).
[7] Persian minister in London 1873–89.
[8] *H* 274. 386.

31. Tu.

Wrote to The Speaker—Mr Gray MP—The Queen—Mr Westell—and minutes.
Read Miss Marjoribanks. Nine to dinner. H of C. $4\frac{1}{4}$–$8\frac{1}{4}$ and 10–$12\frac{1}{4}$. Spoke 1
hour in reply to Gibson.[1] Worked in Harley St. Visited Donaldsons & Fontana's
fearful Club.[2]

Wed. Nov. One 1882.

Wrote to Ld Kimberley—Ld Granville—Abp of York—Mr Goalen—Mrs
O'Shea—and minutes. Saw Mr H—Ld RG—Ld Granville—Gray Committee &
H. of C. $12\frac{1}{2}$–$5\frac{3}{4}$.[3] Dined at Mr Roundell's. Saw Sir G. Wolseley—Lady W.—Mr
Lowell—Duchess of Teck—Lady Stanley Ald. Read Miss Marjoribanks.

To Mrs. O'SHEA, 1 November 1882.   Add MS 44546, f. 31.

You have in your hands my former letter on the wish of your husband to succeed Mr.
Hamilton.[4] In regard to the particular office, I can add nothing to that former letter, for
the Viceroy is, & I am not, primarily responsible for the appointment. I may say generally,
what indeed I may probably have stated before, that I am very sensible of the public
service rendered by Captain O'Shea, that I shall always be ready to hear testimony to it
where such testimony can be useful, and that it would give me much pleasure to see it
acknowledged by any suitable appointment which Captain O'Shea might desire.

2. Th.

Wrote to Mr Bond (Museum)[5]—Mr Childers—Ld Spencer—Dr Liddon—Mr
Fort MP[6]—The Queen l.l.—& minutes. Saw Mr H.—Ld RG—Mr Courtney—Sir
R. Cross (Eccl. Courts)—Mr West—Madame Novikoff—Ld C. Beresford—
Liberal Deputation.[7] Ten to breakfast. Dined with the Wests. Read Miss Mar-
joribanks. H of C. $4\frac{3}{4}$–8 and 10–$1\frac{1}{4}$. Majority of 84 agt $\frac{2}{3}$.[8]

To H. C. E. CHILDERS, war secretary, 2 November 1882.   Add MS 44546, f. 31.
'Early'.

R. Grosvenor says there will certainly be opposition to the Military Grants—and wishes
them postponed until the regular Session. If we do this we must make the annuities run
from the date of the Peerages.
May I tell the House that we do not *at present* anticipate any necessity for a money
Vote? Please send this to Northbrook and let me have if possible a joint reply.[9]
[P.S.] On your note about the Egyptian Army I would say tomorrow's Cabinet will give
you the opportunity.

---

[1] Gibson's amndt. for $\frac{2}{3}$ rather than a simple majority; *H* 274. 488.
[2] Rescue work? Not surprisingly, the club not found listed.   [3] *H* 274. 564.
[4] See 29 Aug. 82; Gladstone may have confused that meeting with writing a letter. See to Grosvenor, 29 Aug. 82. Mrs O'Shea again urged the appt. on 30 October; Add MS 44269, f. 143.
[5] (Sir) Edward Augustus *Bond, 1815–98; librarian of the British Museum 1878–88.
[6] Richard Fort, jnr., 1856–1918; liberal M.P. Clitheroe 1880–5.
[7] London liberals supporting the procedure resolutions; *T.T.*, 3 November 1882, 8f.; Gladstone
told them: 'I have had 184 addresses of different kinds . . . and there has not been the slightest varia-
tion of opinion among them.'   [8] i.e. Gibson's amndt. defeated in 238:322; *H* 274. 749.
[9] Childers agreed; Add MS 44130, f. 141.

3. Fr.

Wrote to Sir H. Ponsonby—Mr Lefevre—Mr Dodson—The Queen l.l.—& minutes. H. of C. 4¼–8¼ and 9–1.[1] Cabinet 2–4¼. Saw Mr H—Ld RG—Ld Granville. Read half Il[iad] III—Fortnightly on Falkland & on Conserv. Party.[2]

Cabinet Nov. 3. 82. 2 PM. Friday.[3]
3. Draft refusal submitted. Approved. [Not?][4] to serve processes on Ld Macdonald's Tenants in Skye.[5]
2. Lord Mayor's Dinner. WEG to go.
1. Aylmer's Motion for a Commission to inquire into Industrial Resources of Ireland. No.[6]
4. General view as to Arabi. Discussion.
5. Instructions to Dufferin. Draft read and accepted.[7]
6. Draft answer to Musurus on the mission of Dufferin, declining to delay it. Accepted.
7. Ditto on Slave Trade & Slavery. To be most urgently pressed, but with a direction [?] to Ld D. in point of time.
8. Egyptian Army. (Southern Army separate, paid from Soudan revenues).[8]

WEG's motion. Nov. 3. 82.[9]
    Not to discourage Egyptian Govt. from adopting any form of arrangement wh it may deliberately judge to be conducive to the security of the Khedive's Govt. & the contentment & tranquility of the country. We assume as a matter not open to doubt that such an arrangement would be consonant to justice.
    To suggest to that Govt. to consider carefully whether there is not great public inconvenience in any serious prolongation of the proceedings connected with the trial.

I wish to represent to those of my Colleagues, who have any considerable amount of civil patronage at their disposal, that Mr O'Shea has rendered spontaneously considerable service to the Government, and to the country, by finding a way out of the very embarrassing predicament in which we found ourselves past spring through the imprisonment (necessary as it had been) of three members of Parliament.
    His desire is or has been to succeed Mr Hamilton in Ireland as Under Secretary. This appears to be out of the question. But the debt is real; and so is the desire to have it acknowledged. WEG Nov. 3. 82.
Please initial this as an acknowledgment of receipt.[10]

---

[1] Questions; spoke on procedure; *H* 274. 769.   [2] *F.R.*, xxxviii. 548, 668 (November 1882).
[3] Add MS 44643, f. 181.   [4] Illegible phrase.
[5] The crofters' movement in Skye. The cabinet was reluctant to approve the use of troops and urged an increased force of police; CAB 41/16/51.
[6] John Evans Freke-Aylmer (1838–1907; tory M.P. 1880–5) had presented a memorial from 59 M.P.s; Gladstone apparently conveyed this decision, but he persevered unsuccessfully; *H* 274. 493, 276. 299.
[7] For Dufferin's mission to Egypt (from 7 Nov.) see Cromer, i ch. 18 and *PP* 1883 lxxxiii. 15.
[8] British serving officers were prevented from serving in this army, but William *Hicks, 1830–83, retired Indian army, was not.
[9] Add MS 44643, f. 182.
[10] Holograph, initialled by Granville, Kimberley, Harcourt and Spencer; Add MS 44766, f. 134. Hamilton noted 'Mr G. will not get much sympathy on this account from his colleagues'; Bahlman, *Hamilton*, i. 357; nothing seems to have come of this circular. See 29 Aug., 1 Nov. 82.

4. Sat.

Wrote to V. Prov. Monro[1]—Sir H Ponsonby—Mr Blackie—and minutes. Dined at Sir C. Dilke's. Saw Mr H—Ld Granville—Mrs Bolton—Dean of Westmr—Sir W.C. James—Mr Bywater—Russian Ambr. Worked on books & papers—from Harley St & otherwise. Read Ed. Review.

5. 22 S. Trin.

Chapel Royal at noon (H.C.) and evg. Saw S. Lyttelton (in charge). Dined with the Phillimores: *he* approved of my plan of withdrawal. Read Westmr Rev. on Qu. Caroline Matilda[2]—Ch Quarty on Revised Text[3] and on [blank]—Tracts on Wm Duke of Devonshire[4]—Whiston & Henley[5]—Young Dissenter[6]—& Life of Perinchief.[7]

6. M.

Wrote to The Queen—and minutes. H of C. $4\frac{1}{2}$-$8\frac{1}{4}$ and $9\frac{3}{4}$-12.[8] Dined at Sir C. Forster's. Saw Mr H—Ld RG—Mr Westell—Ld Granville—The Speaker—Conclave on Egypt—Gray Committee $12\frac{1}{2}$-$2\frac{1}{2}$. Nat. Portr Gall. Trust $2\frac{3}{4}$-$3\frac{1}{2}$. Read The Amber Witch.[9]

7. Tu.

Wrote to Mr Trevelyan—The Queen—Sir T.E. May—Sir R. Wilson—Sir J. Lambert—& minutes. Nine to dinner. Saw Mr H—Ld RG—Mr Seymour—Visited 73 Harley St—& said Goodbye.[10] Luncheon with Mrs Birks. H of C. $4\frac{1}{2}$-$8\frac{1}{4}$ and 10-$12\frac{1}{4}$.[11] Read The Amber Witch.

To G. O. TREVELYAN, Irish secretary, 7 November 1882.   Add MS 44546, f. 32.

Please to consult with the Irish Law Officers as to the best course to be taken with respect to any difficulties which have arisen, or may arise, under the Arrears Act in connection with the limitation to November 30. My impression is that it may be the best course to let the Act take its course and deal with any difficulties, which may have been found insurmountable, at the beginning of the Session? The nicer points are not now in my recollection & I cannot undertake at present to recover them.[12]

[1] D. B. Monro (see 13 Nov. 78), vice-provost of Oriel college.
[2] *Westminster Review*, lxii. 336 (October 1882).
[3] *Church Quarterly Review*, xv. 127 (October 1882).
[4] i.e. on William, 1st duke of Devonshire; perhaps J. Grove, *The lives of all the earls and dukes of Devonshire* (1764).
[5] J. Henley, *Mr Henley's letters... which concern Mr Whiston* (1727).
[6] Not found.
[7] Probably R. Perrinchief, *The royal martyr* (1676).
[8] Procedure; *H* 274. 867.
[9] See 10 Aug. 44.
[10] Let to W. H. H. Jessop; see 1 Apr. 82n.
[11] Procedure; *H* 274. 958.
[12] Trevelyan replied, 9 November, Add MS 44335, f. 62: Land Commissioners could be used more effectively in getting information from petty session clerks.

8. *Wed.*

Wrote to The Queen l.l.—Lord Brabourne—Mr Playfair—The Prince of Wales—& minutes. H of C. & Cabinet 12¾–5½.[1] Saw Mr G—Ld R.G.—Ld Granville—Sir E. Wood—Musurus Pacha—Lady Derby—Adm. Hoskins[2]—The Speaker—Sir G. Wolseley. Spoke once more on closure. Sixteen to dinner and large evening party. An entertainment to the commanders on the return from Egypt. A singular communication from Mrs O'Shea: Ld R.G. replied.[3] Read The Amber Witch.

Cabinet. Wed. Nov. 8. 1882. 2½ PM[4]

1. Trusteeship &c. of Civil Officers. Decline Mr Mitford's request. Lay paper before H. of C.[5]
0 (2. Entering on the Journals the Speaker's words as to evident sense.)
3. Northcote—day for Egypt? Not to interrupt debates on Procedure.
4. Ld Granville's draft to Ld Lyons on the Controul considered & agreed to—i.e. we decide to adhere. Also agreed to announce our views as to the use of Suez Canal in peace & war.

9. *Th.*

Wrote to Mr Trevelyan—Cardinal Newman—The Speaker—Mr Mitford—Mr Childers—Sir H. Ponsonby—The Queen l.l.—Ld Folkestone—Dr Quinn—and minutes. Saw Mr H—Ld R.G.—Ld Kimberley—Ld Granville—The Speaker—Sir C. Dilke—Sir W. Harcourt. H of C. 4½–6¼ and 10–11¾.[6] Attended the Guildhall feast: spoke for Ministers. Audience the best I have known there.[7]

To CARDINAL NEWMAN, 9 November 1882.   Add MS 44546, f. 33.

Let me thank your Eminence most warmly for sending me Palmer's visit to the Russian Church.[8] It is I am certain full of interest in itself, & it is most valuable as a gift from you.

I have stolen a short time from business today to read your Preface, for the temptation was irresistible. It leaves upon me an impression, which agrees with the impression left by seeing him in 1866 at Rome,[9] that in the course of his life both character & mind had been considerably modified. I cling to the hope of yet seeing you some day or other, by some happy turn of fortune, & I could then readily explain my meaning.

[1] Procedure, 17th night; *H* 274. 1077.
[2] Sir Anthony Hiley *Hoskins, 1828–1900; lord commissioner of admiralty 1880–2; sent to Alexandria after the bombardment; 1889–91 c. in c. Mediterranean.
[3] Further request for a post for W. H. O'Shea; Bahlman, *Hamilton*, i. 357.
[4] Add MS 44643, f. 183.
[5] A. B. Mitford (1837–1916, 1st Baron Redesdale 1902), sec. to commissioners of works, was denied permission while a Crown servant to be a remunerated governor of the Borneo Co.; Add MS 44546, f. 33. See 14 Feb. 85.
[6] Questions; procedure; *H* 274. 1126.
[7] *T.T.*, 10 November 1882, 8a.
[8] W. Palmer of Magdalen, *Notes of a visit to the Russian Church in the years 1840, 1841*, ed. J. H. Newman (1882).
[9] Palmer of Magdalen was a convert to Rome; see 27 Mar. 33, 19 and 21 Nov. 66.

10. Fri.

Wrote to Mr J. Leslie—Mr Childers (2)—Mr A. Kelso—Mr Courtney—The Queen—D. of Cambridge—& minutes. H of C. $4\frac{1}{2}$–$8\frac{1}{2}$ & $9\frac{3}{4}$–$1\frac{1}{4}$. Voted in 304 agt 260 on Res. I. *good*.[1] Saw Mr H—Ld RG—Count Münster—Mrs Bolton. Conclave on Res. 2: saw the Speaker, also Sir T. May, on it. Saw Mr Childers—C. Münster—Mr Goschen. Dined at Lucy's. Read Palmer & Russia—Coles on Buddhism[2]—Amber Witch (finished): a noteworthy book.

11. Sat.

Wrote to D. of Argyll—Sir H. Ponsonby—Mr Grenfell—Mrs Crawfurd[3]—Mr Dodson—Ld Granville and Ld Spencer on *the* subject[4]—and minutes. Saw Mr H—Ld Granville—Mr Froude—Mr Kinglake—Mad. Novikoff—with whom we had tea. Read Palmer & Russia—Marie Antoinette.[5] In the evening we witnessed the first performance of Tennyson's new play: with pain for the reception was not good & we were somewhat puzzled.[6]

12. 23 S. Trin.

Ch. Royal mg & aft. Trouble about Meech.[7] Wrote to Mrs Wellesley—Mr Carrington (Tel). Read Palmer & Russia—Jenkins on Romanism—Brown on Atheism.[8] Saw Sir W. James—Mr Seymour.

13. M.

Wrote to Ld Hartington—Mr Bywater—Mr Holt—Mr Dodson—The Queen—and minutes. Court of Exchequer for [pricking the] List of Sheriffs 2–3 P.M. Cabinet 3–$4\frac{1}{4}$. House $4\frac{1}{4}$–$8\frac{1}{4}$ and $8\frac{3}{4}$–$12\frac{1}{2}$.[9] Saw Mr H—Duke of Argyll—Mr Thorold Rogers. Saw the Indian Officers at noon: most interesting. In the forenoon we discussed Tennyson's play & I read the *Critiques*. Read Warren on Ancient Cosmology.[10]

Cabinet. N. 13. 82. Monday. 2. 45 PM.[11]
1. Northcote's question (41) on Bourke's motion.[12]
2. Hays (42) postpone.[13]

[1] *H* 274. 1283.
[2] Untraced.
[3] Probably Frances, wife of E. H. J. Crawfurd, former liberal M.P. (see 12 May 54).
[4] i.e. Gladstone's retirement; see to Spencer, 24 Oct. 82.
[5] Perhaps *La Dauphine Marie Antoinette en Champagne, 1770, par le comte de Barthélemy* (1882).
[6] Tennyson's last play and only prose work, *The promise of May*, a melodrama in Lincolnshire dialect; a failure at the Globe. See 14 Nov. 82.
[7] Probably a domestic matter; see 11 Dec. 82.
[8] R. Jenkins, *Romanism* (1882).
[9] Procedure, 2nd rule, and goaded by Churchill and Yorke into challenging tories to move for a cttee. on Kilmainham; *H* 274. 1329, 1370; see 16 Nov. 82.
[10] W. F. Warren, *The true key to ancient cosmology* (1882).
[11] Add MS 44643, f. 184.
[12] i.e. on Egypt; this led to Gladstone's statement on 14 Nov.; *H* 274. 1406.
[13] On gratuities for the troops; *H* 274. 1549.

3. Mr Bradlaugh's letter. Day.
4. Shd. our Ambassador's stop diplomatic relations with the Porte if Sultan sends a Commission.

If we had claimed to deal with Arabi we could only dismiss him—or take him out of Egypt.

To J. G. DODSON, president of the local government board,   Monk Bretton 57.
13 November 1882.

I assent with perfect confidence to your proposed appointment of Mr. Owen.

Have you considered whether it would be an improvement in the organisation of your Department to appoint two Permanent Secretaries, one for Poor Law and one for Local Government, getting rid of your Assistant Secretaries and to provide for the work as far as might be necessary by an increase not on the staff. I have heard this suggested, and it looks as if it might be worth inquiry but I do not venture to give an opinion.[1]

To LORD HARTINGTON, Indian secretary,   Chatsworth MSS 340. 1279.
13 November 1882.[2]

I thank you very much for your letter. There is no hurry. In no case should I do anything in a hurry: there is much to consider. I am bound to visit Midlothian: this must of course be after the prorogation. I look to a preliminary conversation with Granville; and I will then communicate with you further. My idea generally is that there is no *great* question immediately or soon to come on, probably none for this Parliament, on which Whigs and Radicals could not put up their horses together. I think Ireland is the sorest place, but this is not markedly a question of division between our sections.

14. Tu.

Wrote to Mr Dickson MP—Mrs L. Tennyson—Ld Granville—The Queen l.l.—& minutes. H of C. $4\frac{1}{2}$-$8\frac{1}{4}$ & 9-1 on Procedure, & Egypt.[3] Saw Mr H—Ld RG—Mr Bryce—and others. Read Palmer & Russia. Not a scrap of walk.

To Mrs. Lionel TENNYSON, 14 November 1882.   Add MS 44546, f. 35.

During & after our dubious experience on [Saturday] night I fear that I may have seemed indifferent, but I was only stupid & therefore puzzled.[4] I never had any taste of a first night before & of the pains & accidents with which plays come into the world. I rather come now amidst my uncertainties to this conclusion that the theatre requires a

---

[1] Hamilton wrote to Dodson on Gladstone's behalf on 15 November, Monk Bretton 57: 'He hopes from what you say that Mr. Owen will not be found averse to developing as well as supporting proposals in the direction of decentralisation, when the question of local government comes to be dealt with,—a principle to which Mr Gladstone was given to understand that Sir John Lambert, with all his excellent qualities, did not readily lend himself.' (Sir) Hugh Owen, 1835-1916; secretary of L.G.B. 1882-98.

[2] In Holland, i. 379, together with Hartington's of 12 November opposing Gladstone's retirement at this time: 'I think the leadership of the House of Commons, in its present temper, an impossibility for any one but yourself.'

[3] And Parnell, objecting to 'Kilmainham treaty' appearing in reference terms for proposed select cttee.; H 274. 1411.

[4] See 11 Nov. 82. Mrs Tennyson replied, 15 November, Add MS 44477, f. 256: 'what you say exactly expresses our own feeling about the Play—and about the dear Play-wright'.

playwright as well as a poet—& that, if the two characters are to be contained in one, the poet, instead of walking out has to stoop a good deal. Like the Corinthians in religion, a London gallery requires to be fed with milk rather than strong meat, or the strong meat must be greatly boiled down. My own profession, & act, if I may call it so, teaches me a lesson—*we* are obliged to throw aside all idea of abstract excellence or beauty, take our audience for our standard, & deliberately work by it for its immediate results. There is nothing, so far as my experience goes, which the great divinity we thus worship more resents, than an attempt to speak above his head. Most of all would this be the case if our subject seemed to perceive that everything should be absolutely on his level. Among the higher order of makers, who are called makers by preference, Shakespeare as an actor had that felicity that he had the stage as it were for his starting point, & was fastened to it by necessity, while on the other hand he was able to bring down to it unimpaired, in most things, his marvellous inspirations. Homer was happier still, in singing to a people who, without anything conventional either to guide or fetter them, seem to have given them in their pure infancy a truly perfect gift of appreciation. The whole question of the theatrical 'gods' & their inexorable & irresponsible proceedings, is a most curious one, & suggestive of many things. Every human being should find lessons in every turn of accidents; in this case however it seems that the author's bigness has prevented him from passing through the little wicket which a smaller man would have entered without difficulty & which was the appointed road to acceptance in the gallery. Perhaps things may mend: I hope so, though the mending blows my speculations into air.

15. Wed.

Wrote to Ld Granville—Mr Agnew—The Queen—and minutes. Saw Mr H—Ld RG—Mr Godley—Mr Solomon—The Crown Princess. Dined at Dr Phillimore's. German Embassy after. Read Palmer in Russia—and Tracts. H of $12\frac{1}{4}$-6 on Procedure.[1]

16. Th.

Wrote to Mr Childers—Mr Dodson—Mr Walpole—Mr Lefevre—The Queen l.l.l.—and minutes. H. of C. $4\frac{3}{4}$-$8\frac{1}{4}$ and 9-1.[2] Saw Mr H—Ld R.G—Musurus Pasha. Cabinet $12\frac{1}{2}$-$2\frac{1}{4}$. Mr Agnew on the Miniatures. Read Palmer in Russia.

Cabinet. Nov. 16. 82. 12 $\frac{1}{2}$ PM.[3]
1. Inquiry into Parnell's release.
   Resolved a. to make no objection on the part of the Govt. to the form of words last handed to Ld R. G[rosvenor] (within)[4] b. to intimate that we cannot break off the proceedings or [? on] procedure—and that the Committee shd. be small and chosen mainly by the Committee of Selection.[5]
2. Trial of Arabi. Private to Ld D[ufferin]. See Ld Granville's Tel. No. 6 of Nov. 15—agreed thus: unless it can be regularly proved by clear evidence that he is guilty of crime meriting a severe punishment, (in which case there may be further communica-

---

[1]　*H* 274. 1492.
[2]　Procedure; *H* 274. 1559.
[3]　Add MS 44643, f. 187.
[4]　Draft of wording, ibid., f. 190. See 14 Nov. 82n.
[5]　'Gladstone expressed his regret to his colleagues that he had been carried away by his temper'; Gwynn, i. 489.

tion required) suggest to Khedive whether he wd banish him from Egypt under proper conditions—& dwell on the importance of expedition in any case.[1]
3. Agreed to support France in consolidating the Debt & Daira arrangements under her Presidency.[2]

17. Fr.

Wrote to Mr Childers—Mr Lefevre—The Queen—Mrs Wellesley—Ld Shaftesbury—Mr Bywater—& minutes. H. of C. 4½-8¼ and 9-12½. Conclave on Yorke's motion.[3] Luncheon at 15 G. Square: & a walk. Saw Mr H—Lord R.G—Cornish Members of H of C.[4]—Mr Dickson MP—Sol. Gen. Ireland. Read Palmer in Russia.

18. Sat.

Wrote to Mr Lucy—Mr Whitbread—Mr Welby—Ld Northbrook—Ld Spencer—The Crown Princess—Sir W. Harcourt—Mrs Bolton—Mr L. Tennyson. At 12½ we had the Review on the Parade ground.[5] Admirably seen. We had a large party & luncheon afterwards. It was deeply interesting and full of suggestion. I was amazed at the high quality of the Line Regiments. The Household Troops were always splendid. Read Marie Antoinette[6]—Palmer's Visit to Russia—Ashton's Queen Anne.[7] Dined with Mr MacColl—Conversation with him (on Sir W.P.'s book)[8]—Mr Escott—Bp of Peterborough. Saw Mr H—Ld R.G.

To Sir W. V. HARCOURT, home secretary,   MS Harcourt dep. Adds 10.
18 November 1882. '*Private*'.

  F. Stanley is both moderate and gentlemanlike, but he is I fear thoroughly weak, and no better than a conduit in these matters.[9]
  With regard to Devolution my own personal declarations are such as to leave me no power of receding. To postpone it would be either to abandon it or again to involve the business of the Session in hopeless confusion. It appears to me, on the merits, to be *the* battlefield which is immediately advantageous for us, and as thoroughly bad for the Conservatives. Natheless [*sic*] I do not say they will not obstruct for my view has all along been the reverse of sanguine on this head.

19. 24 S. Trin.

Chapel Royal mg. Whitehall aftn. Wrote to Ld Granville. Saw Mr H.—Mrs Stonor—Mr Denman. Dined at Mrs Heywoods. Read Wodrow's Life[10]—Jenkins on Romanism—Palmer's Visit to Russia.

---

  [1] Dufferin arranged that Arabi plead guilty to rebellion and be sentenced to death with subsequent commutation to exile; Arabi left for Ceylon on 26 December; Cromer, i. 336.
  [2] In fact France declined the presidency and 'resumed its liberty of action'; Cromer, i. 340.
  [3] On the 'Kilmainham' select cttee.; *H* 274. 1639.   [4] No account found.
  [5] Parade of returning troops on Horse Guards.   [6] See 11 Nov. 82.
  [7] J. Ashton, *Social life in the reign of Queen Anne*, 2v. (1882).
  [8] i.e. on republishing *The treatise of Christ* by the other Palmer, W. Palmer of Worcester; see 19 Oct. 82.
  [9] Reported by Harcourt, 17 November, Add MS 44197, f. 133, as claiming procedural changes would go through *if* Grand Cttees. postponed.
  [10] R. Wodrow, *The life of James Wodrow* (1828).

20. M.

Wrote to The Queen l.l.—Ld Granville l.l.—Ld Portarlington—and minutes. H. of C. 4½–8 & 8¾–1, on Procedure.[1] Read M. Antoinette (finished). Saw Mr H—Ld R.G—Ld Northbrook—Mr Welby—Mr Trevelyan—Sir F. Doyle—Mr Childers—H.J.G.—Dean Wellesley's Memorial Committee 3 P.M. at Marlb. House.

21. Tu.

Wrote to Mrs Bolton—Mr Cowen MP—Ld Hartington—Mr Gray MP—Ld Kimberley—The Queen—Ld Granville—& minutes. Read Palmer in Russia. Gray Commee 12–1. Saw Mr H—Ld RG—H.J.G. (on new Club)[2]—Sir A. Gordon—Mr Dodson—The Speaker (Procedure)—Sir T. May. H of C. 4½–8¼ and 9¼–12¾.[3]

To H. C. E. CHILDERS, war secretary, 21 November 1882.   Add MS 44546, f. 38.

I have before me your two letters of the 15th inst.,[4] one giving your estimate of the excess which the Egyptian expedition will entail upon Army Votes beyond the Vote of Credit already taken; the other asking a decision as to the maximum monthly charge to be imposed upon Egyptian revenues from a date to be named, but which you assume at 1 October.

Upon the first point, viz. the excess beyond the Vote of Credit, I assume it is so stated as to include extra charge, so that as far as you can judge, Parliament is to hear no more of the extra charge in connection with Egypt. May I, for instance, understand it to include the gratuity to the men? It is most important that the statement should be complete, & when this is made clear between us, an official letter should, as you suggested, be addressed to the Treasury.

As regards the second point, I think that so far as, from the best information & judgments on the spot, Egyptian revenues will bear it, all charge that would otherwise appear on the Votes in respect of the occupying force should be defrayed by these Revenues. I mean of course all charge in excess of sums provided in the original army estimates for the men constituting the occupying force.

It will perhaps be best that your office with its Departmental knowledge should submit a carefully drawn estimate of the charge for that force, & should propose the outlines of a plan for partitioning the charge, taking for its basis all the available Egyptian Army Fund. When that plan is before us we will lend our best assistance in supplementing your information & we will consider together the amount which Egypt may fairly be called upon to provide.

22. Wed.

Wrote to E. Talbot—Ld Shaftesbury—Mr Childers—Archdn Grant—The Queen—and minutes. Read Palmer in Russia. Saw Mr H—Ld R.G—Mr Villiers Stuart—Sir C. Dilke—Dean Church. H of C. 12¼–5¾.[5] Dined at Lady M. Alford's.

---

[1] H 274. 1744.
[2] The National Liberal Club, of which Gladstone became President, established at a meeting this month; *The National Liberal Club; a description* (1888).
[3] Questions; procedure; H 274. 1798.
[4] Add MS 44130, ff. 156–9; an extra £40,000 per month.   [5] Procedure; H 274. 1859.

23. Th.

Wrote to Sir S. Northcote—Ld Hartington—The Queen—Col. Kingscote—Mr Monk—Ld Northbrook—Ld Morley—Mr Childers—Mayor of Chester—and minutes. Saw Mr H—Ld RG—Ld Granville—Mrs Bolton—The Speaker. Read Vice Versâ,[1] breakdown—Palmer in Russia: a most interesting & valuable work. (finished). H of C. $4\frac{3}{4}$–$8\frac{1}{2}$ and $9\frac{1}{4}$–1.[2] Wrote rudiments of a Queens Prorogation Speech.

24. Fr.

Wrote to Mr Childers—Mr Dodson—Mr Bryce MP—Sir S. Scott & Co.—The Queen—Ld Granville—Ld Kimberley—Sir H. Ponsonby—Ld Hartington—Sir C. Dilke—& minutes. H of C. $4\frac{1}{2}$–9 and 10–1.[3] Saw Mr H—Ld RG—Mr Knowles—Scotts—Ld Halifax—Mr Agnew. Read Q.R.[4] Drive with C.

To LORD KIMBERLEY, colonial secretary, 24 November 1882.   Add MS 44546, f. 40.

So far as I can judge, I adopt your general view as to the Zulu country.[5] What do you say to consulting Chamberlain, & possibly Courtney, before going to the Cabinet? I retain your letter *in case.* Will Gaozi[6] be an effective wall of partition, or will he be a clay pot between two iron pots? You adhere I presume to your principle of self-support for the protected territory, & trust to the balance which Bulwer shows. It will be for him with the Resident to make both ends meet.
[P.S.] Dispatch is evidently most desirable. There is *now* hope of a Speech Cabinet on Monday, & this matter might be taken immediately after Tuesday when there is a council.[7]

25. Sat.

Wrote to Sir W. Harcourt—The Speaker—Mr Blake MP—Sir T.E. May—The Queen—Sir H. Ponsonby Tel.—Dr A. Clark—& minutes. Dined with Lucy Cavendish: conversation with her. Saw Mr H—Ld R.G—Mad. Novikoff. Read Contemp. Rev. on Egypt—& on French peasant Proprietary.[8] $10\frac{1}{2}$–12. Long conversation with Granville, much of it on my personal position & needs.

To Sir W. V. HARCOURT, home secretary, 25 November 1882.   MS Harcourt dep. 8, f. 169.

A Commission on Highland Crofters seems to be the small end of a very large question, and it evidently can only be determined by the Cabinet which meets on Monday.
The notice for Dec. 5 by Sir W. Ffolkes appears to block out Macfarlane.

[1] F. Anstey, *Vice Versa; or, a lesson to fathers* (1882).
[2] Questions; arrears; *H* 274. 1935.
[3] Questions; Kilmainham; procedure; *H* 275. 57.
[4] *Q.R.*, cliv. 295 (October 1882).
[5] Kimberley, 23 November, Add MS 44228, f. 25, forwarding Bulwer's 'very clear and able' report; Kimberley believed 'he makes out his case for the separation of Usibebe's country from Cetewayo's'.
[6] The minor chief ruling between Cetewayo and John Dunn.
[7] See 27 Nov. 82.
[8] *C.R.*, xlii. 659, 764 (November 1882).

Doubtless you will look back to the arguments (such as they appeared at the time) of the Lord Advocate against the Commission in the Summer.

I return your inclosure which affords no ray of light.[1]

26. 25 S. Trin.

Chapel Royal mg and evg. Wrote to Ld Granville.[2] Saw Mr H. Conversation with Dr Clark on my intention of retirement 3-4. Read Abbey & Overton's Hist. of Ch. of England.[3] Dined with the Phillimores: much conversation with Sir R.

27. M.

Wrote to Ld Granville—Mad. Novikoff—The Queen l.l.—Mr Courtney—Ld Spencer—Ald. Macarthur—& minutes. Saw Mr H—Ld RG—The Speaker. Cabinet 12½-3½. H of C. 4½-8¼ and 9½-12¾.[4] Read Abbey & Overton's Hist.— Reinach on Egyptn Question.[5]

Cabinet. Monday N. 27. 82. 12½ PM.[6]

✓ 1. Prorogation Speech. Read amended & approved.
✓ 2. Prorogue to what day. Early in Jan.?, & finally Feb. 15. Thurs.[7]
✓ 3. Cost of the War. Started [discussion]. Charge on India—to stand over. Charge on Egypt: from Oct. 1. *in the main.*
✓ 5. Commission on Highland Crofters, stated by Harcourt—announce intention to employ[?] the law for service of summons. If military force required there *may* arise a case for the Commission.[8]
✓ 6. Khedive to be Commander in Chief. It is not a military office, so he may take it— tho' he cannot appoint any officer above a Colonel.
✓ 7. Ld. Granville's deputation tomorrow on Abyssinia.[9] General opinion that intervention will be ultimately unavailable [*sic*]: but not to discourage deputn.
8. Ld Kimberley's Telegram on Cetewayo & Zululand read and approved.

To L. H. COURTNEY, secretary to the Treasury,　　　　Add MS 44546, f. 40.
27 November 1882.

The Cabinet will meet on *Friday at two*, and will take into consideration the question of the Zanzibar Contract, which in some powerful quarters it will be recommended to

---

[1] Harcourt's letter this day, argued a Royal Commission was unavoidable and enclosed a letter from a free church minister on Raasay; Add MS 44197, f. 144.

[2] A *résumé* of their discussion on the 25th: 'I feel myself incapable of grappling with the hard constructive work that is coming on. It need not however, if I judge rightly, come on until after Easter 1883'; at the least, 'a chancellor of the Exchequer ought to be appointed at once ...'; if Hartington declined, then Childers; Ramm II, i. 458.

[3] C. J. Abbey and J. H. Overton, *The English Church in the eighteenth century*, 2v. (1878).

[4] Procedure; *H* 275. 142.

[5] J. Reinach on Egypt and France, *N.C.*, xii. 821 (December 1882).

[6] Add MS 44643, f. 191.

[7] E. W. Hamilton, Gladstone's secretary, attended for this item; Bahlman, *Hamilton*, i. 367.

[8] Napier Royal Commission on crofters appt. March 1883.

[9] *Sic*; slip of the pen for Madagascar, see CAB 41/16/57. Malagasy envoys were trying to prevent a French protectorate; see F. W. Chesson, 'The Malagasy mission' in S. P. Oliver, *The true story of the French dispute in Madagascar* (1885).

continue on grounds other than Postal, or even Commercial. Will you kindly be on the ground to give your view.

28. Tu.

Wrote to Ld Granville—The Queen Tel. & l.l.—Mr Bright—Mrs Wellesley—& minutes. Read Abbey & Overton. Saw Mr H.—Ld R.G—Mr Jenkinson[1]—Ld Granville—Mr Welby. H of C. $4\frac{1}{2}$-$8\frac{1}{2}$ & $9\frac{1}{2}$ to after midnight. We got over our First Resolution on Delegation by a good majority.[2]

29. Wed.

Wrote to Ld Spencer—Sir H. Ponsonby—Sir R. Wilson—& minutes. Read Abbey & Overton—Archbishop of Tuam. H of C. $12\frac{1}{4}$-$5\frac{3}{4}$.[3] Some diarrhoea came on & I had to lie up in my room. Saw Mr H—Ld RG—Mr Whitbread. Having got quiet again, dined at Mr Ralli's.

30. Th.

Wrote to Ld Granville—Ld Hartington—The Queen l.l. A laborious day. Saw Mr H—Ld RG—Ld Granville. Off to Windsor 11.45. Audience, & Council. On return, called to see Ld Derby & finally settled that he takes the Indian Office.[4] We took a slight survey of public affairs. It was altogether hearty & satisfactory. H of C. $4\frac{3}{4}$-$8\frac{1}{4}$ & $9\frac{1}{2}$-$6\frac{1}{4}$ working Devolution. The progress good (at the end); the end comes in view.[5] Read Abbey & Overton—Hyndman's Pamphlet.[6] Dined at Lucy's.

To LORD HARTINGTON, Indian secretary, 30 November 1882. Add MS 44546, f. 42.

The Indian Charge £1140 m[ille] is more than a fourth of the total charge; the Indian force 2/11ths of the total force. The view of the Cabinet originally was, in the rough, that India should pay a share of the charge in proportion to her share of the force. 2/11ths of the charge would be £820,000; and we should have to pay India £320 m[ille] in cash.[7] Childers approves as you will see within. He writes me another note to express a fear that Fawcett will kick. I am not aware that this is so; nor that the Cabinet ought wholly to change its view if it were so.

If you approve of this plan we may mention it in Cabinet tomorrow & correspond with Ripon & the Indian Government upon it.

---

[1] (Sir) Edward Jenkinson, 1835-1919; Spencer's private secretary 1882-4 and successor to Brackenbury. See 1 Dec. 82, 12 Dec. 85.
[2] i.e. delegation to standing cttees.; *H* 275. 312.
[3] Questions on Egypt; procedure; *H* 275. 318.
[4] Negotiated by Granville; Bahlman, *Hamilton*, i. 367. But see 11 Dec. 82n., 12, 15 Dec. 82.
[5] *H* 275. 411.
[6] H. M. Hyndman, probably *The textbook of democracy. England for all* (1881).
[7] Hartington replied this day that this was inadequate; Add MS 44146, f. 120.

Fr. Dec. 1. 1882.

Wrote to Mr Childers—Ld Spencer—Ld Ripon—Sir W. Harcourt—The Queen—& minutes. Saw Mr H—Ld RG—Ld Hartington. Cabinet 2-4½ in my C. of E. room: I was on the sofa. Skipped the House: when all was successfully wound up in my absence.[1] A great day, as I think, for the House of Commons itself.

Cabinet. 2 PM Friday Dec. 1. 82[2]
1. Official Changes. Announced: actual & contingent. Most secret.[3]
2. Indian Charge. repay India £448000.[4]
3. Relief of distress. Ireland. General approval of Spencer. Carl[ingford], Kimb[erley] & Dodson will make special remarks to Spencer.
4. Zanzibar Contract. Provisional prolongation for—months. Treasury, Admiralty, F.O. & Dodson to consider[?]. FO. consider a) Service[?] by tender b) Sultan of Z's proceeding. Northbrook agreed there wd. be[?] serious unease[?] in the Admiralty.
5. Evelyn Wood to be commander under the Khedive of the Egyptian force.
6. French answer on the controul, asking for an expert. Ans. yes when you have accepted the plan in principle.
7. Prorogue to Feb. 15.

To H. C. E. CHILDERS, war secretary, 1 December 1882.   Add MS 44130, f. 190.

I am now about to tell you what I hope you will keep for a while as more secret than the grave. Derby is coming in as Indian Secretary. Hartington is willing to take the War Office, which I know you would gladly quit for the Exchequer, & *you* know how desirous I am to be rid of this office. But both in my mind & in Hartington's arose the question about your health, as we are now about new arrangements & a new start; I may add that in my private opinion he would like to have the choice of the Exchequer open to him, were it not for your wish to take it and mine to make it over to you as the man who would work it most efficiently. I am extremely glad therefore to learn from my wife that you intend to obtain the very best opinion you can, & most earnestly do I hope, which I am also sanguine in believing, that the report will be such as to enable you to take to the new office without fear.

You will have a great advantage and a great lightening of labour, in your knowledge & experience, as well as in your thorough & accomplished aptitude.

The basis of my action is not so *much* a desire to be relieved of labour, as an anxiety to give the country a much better finance Minister than myself; whose eyes will be always ranging freely & vigilantly over the whole area of the great establishments, the public service, & the laws connected with his office, for the purposes of improvement & of good husbandry.

I have a question to ask you still: when do you come to get the medical advice you have

[1] The four Resolutions on procedure accepted as Standing Orders after 34 nights of debate; *H* 275. 518.
[2] Add MS 44643, f. 193.
[3] Granville's note reads: 'By mentioning Childers for the Exchequer you have planted a blow, of which you are not aware. W.H!!!; ibid., f. 194. It is unclear how far beyond this, and, presumably, the accession of Derby, Gladstone's announcement went.
[4] India was to pay about £600,000, with the British Treasury contributing this amount; Bahlman, *Hamilton*, i. 369.

decided on asking? The matter does not press for a day or two, but if possible the delay should be short.[1]

[P.S.] Excuse bad writing; I am on my back with slight indisposition.

To LORD RIPON, Viceroy of India, 1 December 1882.   Add MS 43515, f. 21.
'*Private & confidential*'.

I had hoped to write to you a real letter in answer to your last[2] which opened points of the greatest importance and interest. But I am a little laid up today, after rather long and severe labour in the House of Commons, where our Resolutions on Procedure and Devolution are now all but carried: a task which we never could have accomplished except by means of autumn sittings and a command virtually exclusive of the whole time of the House.

I hope you will be satisfied that in regard to the question of Indian charge we have done our best, when I tell you that we propose to make a repayment to India of a considerable part of the sum which she has disbursed or is disbursing on account of the Egyptian operations. We, the two Governments, respectively stand very far apart in our convictions as to the relative interests of England & India in the war. In such circumstances instead of remaining 'poles asunder', and each maintaining stiffly an extreme view, the duty of men who are friends seems to be to try and approach. This we have done, & have made a great step towards you, encouraged by observing that in your despatch, towards the close, while you hold out the Abyssinian precedent as the proper model you confine your actual contention to this that India should not pay the whole charge of her contingent. When I tell you that we have agreed to repay you £500 m[ille] out of the £1140 m[ille], which by last estimate you have paid or are about to pay, as a final quittance of the whole matter, I think you will feel that we have determined on proposing an essentially equitable, as well as from our point of view a liberal arrangement.[3]

I must forbear from touching any of the other points in your letter for want of time; except that I must express my cordial sympathy with your generous views as to local Government in India.

[P.S.] Vilely written: but I am on my back with momentary indisposition.

To LORD SPENCER, Viceroy of Ireland, 1 December 1882.[4]   Althorp MSS K5.

Having now read your papers[5] on coming Distress, I write to confirm my acceptance of your plan. I presume that you will not make known until it becomes absolutely necessary your intention to fall back in case of extreme need on other than local funds: but will hold it in reserve. Further it seems to me quite plain that the public fund to which we should resort is the Church Surplus as it may now be deemed certain that the charge of the Arrears Act will press upon it but slightly. All this we shall speak of in the Cabinet of today; which is not likely I think to fall short of what I have said.

[P.S.] I had a conversation with Mr. Jenkinson & was much pleased with him.

[1] Childers, 2 December, Add MS 44130, f. 191, asked if Gladstone was sure about Hartington's 'claims & feelings', and expected to answer about his health '*early* in next week'. On 6 December, he reported a need for 'some weeks' absolute rest'; Gladstone clinched the new arrangements by return; ibid., ff. 194–8.
[2] See 6 Sept. 82n.
[3] Ripon replied, 26 December, Add MS 44286, f. 298, that he had already wired Kimberley accepting; he continued personally to think India overburdened, but accepted the bargain.
[4] In *Spencer*, i. 227.
[5] Add MS 44628, f. 162: rely as much as possible on locally financed indoor relief.

I write on my back, having now at last given way under the heavy work.

After Cabinet. Your colleagues heartily agree with your general policy of working through the Poor Law & Workhouse test—nor do they reject the notion of an ultimate resort to public aid, the form open to your consideration, but the source we thought might be the Church Fund if sufficient.

2. Sat.

Wrote to Mr Sidgwick—and minutes. Saw Mr H—Ld RG. Off to Windsor at 11.45. Conversation with Ld Carlingford—Mr Chamberlain—Sir H. Ponsonby. Audience at Windsor, with a free & kindly conversation on the See of Canterbury:[1] & Council. Then to Mr Hamerton's Organ[2]—and the Prorogation. Saw the Speaker—Ld Granville. Read Abbey & Overton—Arabi's impudent self-defence.[3]

3. Advent S.

Ch. Royal at noon—Burdon St Ch in evg. Wrote to Ld Granville—Lord Chancellor—The Queen. Saw Mr H—Ld Houghton—D of Westmr. Read Scottish Review[4]—Abbey & Overton—Coster's Poems.[5]

4. M.

Wrote to Ld Granville—Sir W. Harcourt—Mr Mitford—The Queen l.l.—Att. General—and minutes. Cabinet $2\frac{1}{2}$-$4\frac{1}{2}$. Saw Mr H.—Dean of St Paul's—Master of the Rolls—Ld Rosebery—Ld Granville. Read Abbey & Overton's Hist. Dined at Ld Granville's: & went to Iolanthe:[6] a perfect piece of scenic representation—with much fun. Attended the opening of the New Law Courts: a splendid ceremonial.[7] Luncheon at Middle Temple afterwards.

Cabinet. Mond. Dec. 4. 82. $2\frac{1}{2}$ PM.[8]
1. Arabi & Ceylon.[9]
2. French reply to Controul.
3. Malagasy Embassy: Granville's reply.[10]
4. Measures for first section of the Session.[11]
5. Sir E. Wood (4 m[ille] p.a) & Egypt. See letter to H.M.[12]

---

[1] Tait's illness. He d. next day. See 9 Dec. 82.
[2] On display in Harrow.
[3] Ahmed Arabi, 'Instructions to my counsel', *N.C.*, xii. 969 (December 1882).
[4] First number of the *Scottish Review.*
[5] G. T. Coster, *Poems and hymns* (1882).
[6] By Gilbert and Sullivan (1882), at the Savoy; see 6 Dec. 82.
[7] Street's new courts in the Strand, on whose financing Gladstone had spent much time as Chancellor in the 1860s.
[8] Add MS 44643, f. 195; Carlingford, Childers, and 'others from *part*', noted absent.
[9] Exile there, see 16 Nov. 82n.
[10] Granville was to prevent 'precipitate action' on Madagascar; *L.Q.V.*, 2nd series, iii. 367.
[11] Bankruptcy, patent laws, criminal code, corrupt practices, in the early part of the Session, the first three *via* the new cttees.; Bahlman, *Hamilton*, i. 370.
[12] Granville to arrange details; part in *L.Q.V.*, 2nd series, iii. 367.

To Sir H. JAMES, attorney general, 4 December 1882. '*Private*'.   Add MS 44546, f. 43.

The Cabinet think that the section of time before Easter 1883 should so far as legisla-tion is concerned, be occupied as follows: 1. Criminal code, 2. Bankruptcy, 3. Patents, to be introduced forthwith & referred to Standing Committees in prosecution of our announcements & of the understanding now established. 4. Corrupt Practices; to take any other evenings which may be available for legislation in the early part of the session.

They request you to consider, & I think virtually to decide, whether to include in your Corrupt Practices Bill the provisions needful to accompany the renewal of the Ballot Act. [P.S.] I hope you did not starve today in consequence of all your kindness & attention.

5. *Tu.* [*Cuffnell's, Lyndhurst*]

Wrote to Dean of St Pauls—Mad. Novikoff—Scotts—Pr. of Wales—The Queen—Mr Mitford—Ld Kimberley—Mr Trevelyan—Sir T. Acland—Professor [F.W.] Newman—Lord R. Grosvenor—and minutes. Saw Mr H.—Ld Granville—Ld Bath—Ld Rosebery. Off at 2 to Sir W. Harcourt's at Cuffnalls.[1] Read Pamphlets —Monod on Maclay & N. Guinea[2]—Lucy on the Molly Maguires.[3]

To LORD R. GROSVENOR, chief whip, 5 December 1882.   Add MS 44546, f. 43.

1. The questions of Cabinet may be soon settled & there may be two or even three to take in. Among moderates E. Fitzmaurice & Brand seem foremost—who among Radicals? Chamberlain strongly recommends Illingworth.

2. The Wigan Election is not pleasant; but I suppose it was to be expected. It makes the question of a petition at Salisbury more important.[4] How does this stand? Is there a diffi-culty about money? Could there be a subscription if this be so? I for one should be quite ready to subscribe.
[P.S.] I am off to Cuffnells.

To G. O. TREVELYAN, Irish secretary, 5 December 1882.   Add MS 44546, f. 44.

I thank you much for your letter and I rejoice in the spirit of cordiality which pervades it.[5] But I deserve no thanks, for truly it is not matter of boast to avoid sometimes one of the most stupid, inexcusable, and suicidal of all errors, namely that of not knowing good help and good public service when one gets it.

I was about to write to you on the subject of an Irish Local Government Bill. By the Land Acts we have I hope laid a foundation for social order in Ireland. But we ought to have a political system also for that country, as we have for this, so that it might at length begin to feel that its government was a thing of its own and not alien, nor foreign. I do not know whether such a Bill can be passed next Session but in any case I hope it will be pre-pared, and pass it will if my convictions are shared by others. Such a Bill, especially if founded on Lord Russell's (alleged) basis, viz., working by the four Provinces, may be

[1] Harcourt rented this house in the New Forest from Mrs Hargreaves, da. of Dean Liddell and original of *Alice*; Gardiner, i. 461–2.
[2] Author *sic*; untraced.
[3] E. W. Lucy, *The Molly Maguires of Pennsylvania* (1882), sent by Sidgwick; cf. 11 July 82n.
[4] Liberals failed to capture one of the Wigan seats at a by-election following a petition, but they had not held it since 1868; they lost Salisbury at a by-election in November, the subsequent petition being dismissed.
[5] Of 3 December, Add MS 44335, f. 74, thanking Gladstone for the confidence he has shown in Trevelyan and Spencer.

regarded by the Home Rulers as a concession, but if it be a means of winning their favour, which I do not expect, it is far more important in my view as providing us with some bulwark against those attacks which they carry on by charging the Empire & the Exchequer with all the local wants of Ireland for want of those local powers by which they might be dealt with.

I hope that Spencer & you will turn with a will to preparing a measure of this kind, which would require not to be a timid one if it is to be of any, or at least of effectual use.[1]

6. *Wed.*

Wrote to Ld Granville—Rev. Davison—Mrs Baker—U.S. Minister—Mr Sullivan —& minutes. Here we were received with extreme kindness. Much pleasant conversation. Drive of 14 miles in the Forest. Read Lucy's Molly Maguires— Rose's Diary[2] and [blank].

To ARTHUR S. SULLIVAN, 6 December 1882. '*Private*'.   Add MS 44546, f. 45.

Though I am very sorry that your kind wish to bring me to the Savoy Theatre on Monday should have entailed on you so much trouble, I must thankfully acknowledge the great pleasure which the entertainment gave me. Nothing, I thought, could be happier than the manner in which the comic strain of the piece was blended with its harmonies of sight & sound, so good in taste and so admirable in execution from beginning to end.[3]

7. *Th.*

Wrote to Sir F. Doyle—Ld Granville l. & Tel.—Mr Blackwood Tel.—Mr Childers—Ld Rosebery—Mad. Novikoff—Professor Stuart—Mr Courtney—Sir C. Trevelyan—Mr Ramsay—Ld Maclaren[4]—& minutes. The Harcourts went to Windsor but we staid with the Sandys guests, acc. to order. Another drive in the Park—all snow-clad. Much American conversation. Read Rose's Diary—finished Molly Maguires.

To LORD ROSEBERY, home undersecretary, 7 December   N.L.S. 10022, f. 132. 1882.

I should not like to interpose in any way calculated to impede the freedom of your private communications, to which in important matters affecting yourself personally you have I think a right under the seal of secrecy without referring to me.[5]

Beyond this I do not think that I can go at this moment for I do not have any new facts that have arisen. The words of the paragraph you quote appear to me altogether suitable to what I said on Tuesday, and I do not see the signs of conflict between the two indications which present themselves to your mind. The 'further manipulations' then antici-

[1] Trevelyan replied, 5 December, Add MS 44335, f. 76, having seen Spencer: 'very serious considerations indeed come in' *re* a bill to be ready for next session; see 30 Dec. 82.

[2] See 14 Jan. 60.

[3] Sullivan replied, 10 December, Add MS 44478, f. 55, 'gratified at your valued praise of "Iolanthe"'.

[4] John McLaren, 1831–1910, s. of the Edinburgh M.P.; liberal M.P. Wigtown 1880–1; lord of session from 1881.

[5] Rosebery's letter of 6 December, Add MS 44288, f. 113, reminded Gladstone of his letter of 30 July 81 and protested at Gladstone's 'frank intimation of yesterday', i.e. that he could not be moved for the time being. See 12 Dec. 82n.

pated are now about to take place. The likelihood of development still remains, and if it is such as I hope to make it it will not be unimportant: but you will agree that I cannot make my own place, to which I looked in part, full and empty at once. Perhaps if I understand your meaning more clearly I may be able to meet it better than in this imperfect note.

8. Fr.

Wrote to Ld Granville—Sir H. Ponsonby Tel.—Mr Seymour Tel.—Mr Court-ney—Dean of Rochester—& minutes. Lyndhurst Ch (a beautiful structure of Butterfield's) at 11 A.M. service. Also went over Mr Lascelles's House.[1] Drive & walk in the forest. Read Malortie's Egypt[2]—Rose's Diary. 11–12. P.M. Discussed the near future with Sir W. Harcourt. Sir W.H. pleased me much by his vivid impressions & high estimate of James Hope.[3]

9. Sat. [London]

Off at 11 to London. Wrote to Mr Courtney Tel.—Mr . . . Tel.—Mr Cowan—Mr Herbert—Mr Noble—Mr Dodson—The Queen (to recommend the Bp of Truro[4] for the See of Canterbury) and minutes. We came up with Mr & Mrs Sandys. Saw Sir W. Harcourt—Mr Childers—Sir R. Lingen—Count Menabrea—Sir C. Dilke—Ld Wolverton—Mr Hamilton. Read through Laura di Bulzo[5] and Abbey & Overton.

10. 2 S. Adv.

Chapel Royal mg and [blank.] Wrote to Ld Granville Tel.—The Queen Tel. & l.—Ld E. Clinton—Ld Hartington—Sir H. Ponsonby—Lady S. Opdebeeck. Luncheon at Ld Wolverton's & a long & comforting conversation with him on my plans for retirement. Saw Mr Hamilton on Office arrangements. Dined at Sir R. Phillimore's: we conversed upon the two retirements. He encourages me. Read Abbey & Overton—Contemp. on Xty & Paganism[6]—Phillimore's Review of A. & O.[7]

11. M.

A day of cares. Conversation with Herbert on the Meech case.[8] Wrote to Sir W. Harcourt—Dr Clark—Ld Hartington Tel.—Ld R. Grosvenor Tel.—Ld Kimberley Tel.—Bishop of Chester. Saw Mr H.—Ld Granville mg & evg. Off at 12.45 to Windsor in the frost fog. Saw Ld Dalhousie—Sir H. Ponsonby. Audience of H.M. at 3. Most difficult ground: but, aided by the beautiful manners, we got over it

---

[1] The Queen's House, Lyndhurst; Gerald William Lascelles, deputy-surveyor of the New Forest.
[2] C. von Malortie, *Egypt: native rulers and foreign interference* (1882).
[3] Gladstone's confidant in the 1830s and 1840s; see above, iii. xxxiii. The catholic convert Hope was an improbable object of estimation for the archprotestant Harcourt.
[4] i.e. E. W. Benson; the Queen objected, Gladstone prevailing.
[5] Untraced.
[6] *C.R.*, xlii. 916 (December 1882).
[7] Untraced review of Abbey and Overton.
[8] See 12 Nov. 82.

better than might have been expected.¹ Returned to D. St at 5.30. Took my measures in concert with Lord G. Read Abbey & Overton. Dined with the Lytteltons.

To W. JACOBSON, bishop of Chester, 11 December 1882.   Add MS 44546, f. 48.
'*Secret*'.

I write you these few secret lines to obtain your advice on a point connected with the succession to the See of Canterbury. Many who might well have been thought of, you among them, have passed the limit of age for assuming such a charge. To waive details, this point has been reached, that the two Prelates most eligible are the Bishops of Winchester and Truro,² the first somewhat old, and the second somewhat young for the office.

My question relates to the latter of the two. There is in some quarters an apprehension that the leading Clergy—and especially the Bishops—would resent having a Bishop of no more than (I believe) 53 put over them. It seems clear that he possesses in a remarkable degree every other primary qualification, but the question is whether this of age below the usual age for such an appointment would entail a serious disability.

On this, though you are not in the Province, I want to beg your candid opinion. This is my principal point. But if you know anything of the Bishop of Winchester as to probable disability of health and energy, I shall be glad to profit by that knowledge also.³

12. Tu.

Wrote to Sir M. Montefiore⁴—Mr Childers—Mr Holt—Earl of Derby—Mrs Th— Earl Spencer—Mr Morley—The Queen—Ld Rosebery—Ld Granville—Mrs Bolton—Ld Thurlow—& minutes. Saw Mr H—Ld R.G—Ld Houghton—Sir C. Dilke—W. Phillimore—Mrs Th.—Mr Blackwood. Conclave at Ld Granville's 12– 1¾ on the official block. Luncheon in G. Square. Dined at A. West's. Saw Mr A. West—Mr [R.] Temple West—Mr Courtney—Mr Robinson. Read Abbey & Overton.

Tues. Dec. 12. 82. WEG, Gr., Hn., Ld R.G.
We decided 1. Appt. & announcement of Childers to go forward *at once.* 2. Postpone the others. 3. Adopt for D. alternative of C.O. 4. WEG to invite Derby to town on Thursday. 5. Ld R.G. to sound Stansfield [*sic*] on Chairmanship of W. & M.⁵

To R. D. HOLT, 12 December 1882.   Add MS 44546, f. 47.

I cannot allow the occasion of your extraordinary success in Liverpool to pass by without a word of congratulation which I desire to offer to Mr. Smith, your victorious candidate, to the Liberal Association, and to yourself, who have so long, in days of protracted gloom and under so many rebuffs, stood without flinching in the front of the battle.⁶

---

¹ His proposal of Benson as abp., Derby for the India Office, Dilke for the Duchy; the last two were objected to by Victoria, agreement being reached on Benson; Add MS 44766, f. 150; Bahlman, *Hamilton*, i. 375; *Autobiographica*, iv. 62.
² i.e. E. H. Browne and E. W. Benson.   ³ No reply in Add MS 44218.
⁴ Sir Moses Haim *Montefiore, 1784–1885; stockbroker and philanthropist.
⁵ Holograph note, Add MS 44766.
⁶ Samuel *Smith (1836–1906, Liverpool cotton merchant and philanthropist) won Liverpool at a by-election, defeating A. B. Forwood; 'the result was an astonishment to us all' (S. Smith, *My Life-*

It is well to have grounds for believing that, in whatever way the honour of the victory is to be apportioned—and doubtless large shares are due to the character and ability of the Candidate, and to the skill which shaped the tactics—it is not due to the 'Irish vote', for that under present circumstances is of all foundations the most 'giddy and unsure'.

May you be enabled to consolidate effectually the fortunes which you have thus, for the first time after a long period, brought into a position of prosperity.

To LORD ROSEBERY, home undersecretary, 12 December   N.L.S. 10022, f. 138.
1882, '*Private*'.

I am so much pressed by other matters and from *other quarters*, that I must be very brief in answering your letter.[1] Quickness of perception has many advantages, but has this drawback that it sometimes supplies in a speech what has not been present to the mind of the speaker. I think you will remember 1. That I spoke of seniority only in connection with good service. 2. That I said and implied no more than that it was an element in the case—there are many others. 3. That I introduced the subject for the purpose of pointing out that I understood the claim whatever it might be would probably be put out of the way by the desire of the individual named to move upon other lines.

Certainly *good and hard* work in an office is an element in these cases, though not the only one. I hope you may be disposed to agree with me that there is no great cause for uneasiness in these disclosures.

Rearrangements of departments are among the most difficult questions that I know: and even the large fund of leisure that I have enjoyed during the present year has not enabled me fully to see my way, or the way of the Govt., as to the best arrangement for Scotch business, nor have I been able to fix in my own mind the time, though I regard it as a practical question, standing for early settlement.

Your prospects are brilliant as well as wide, but even you cannot dispense with much faith and patience.[2]

To LORD SPENCER, Viceroy of Ireland, 12 December 1882.   Althorp MSS K5.

On yours of the 8th,[3]

(1) I have recommended Johnson.[4] (2) I entirely enter into & accept your plan of succession. (3) In speaking of the meditated changes as to remuneration of Law Officers in Ireland, doubtless you mean the same basis, not the same figures. I quite agree—it will be a real improvement. Also I thankfully accept the assurances you give me, which I well know, like every thing else that comes from you, are genuine.

[P.S.] '*Secret*' I am truly sorry that want of time prevents me from entering fully on the question of official modifications here: but *1.* an *immediate* change as to your office is very uncertain,[5] *2.* I think the end will be Derby and Dilke in the Cabinet.

Work (1902), 138). Smith 'won because of more Tory than Irish abstentions'; P. Waller, *Democracy and sectarianism* (1981), 39. This letter in *T.T.*, 19 December 1882, 4f.

[1] Hamilton held back Rosebery's letter of 10 December complaining at his want of promotion to the cabinet, but on Rosebery's instruction gave it to Gladstone this day; *Rosebery*, 137.
[2] Rosebery replied, 16 December, that he could not remain a party to an arrangement so derogatory to Scotland; N.L.S. 10022, f. 140.
[3] Add MS 44309, f. 223.
[4] William Moore Johnson, 1828–1918, liberal M.P. Mallow and Irish attorney general, to be a judge.
[5] i.e. the lord presidency which Spencer held in addition to the viceroyalty until March 1883.

13. Wed.[1]

Wrote to Ld Granville—The Queen l.l.—Ld E. Clinton—Sir P. Braila—Ld Derby—Greek Govt Tel.—Ld Kimberley—Sig. Mareschalchi—Ld Lorne—Patriarch Alexa[2]—Mr White—Archbp Cyprus[3]—Sir Thos G.—W.H. Gladstone—Mr Tallents[4]—Rev. D. Robertson—Mrs Th.—Khedive of Egypt,[5] & others, Tel.—Sir T.E. May—Mrs Watkins—and minutes. Saw Mrs Anson: Winens [R]. Saw Mr H—Mr Godley—Mr Seymour—Mr Godley—Ld Granville—Mr Welby *bis.* Dined with the Godleys. Saw Ld Chancellor. Read Abbey & Overton.

14. Th.

Wrote to Mrs Winens—The Queen l.l.l. (also minute for E.W.H. to Sir H.P.)—King of the Belgians—Mr Chamberlain—Ld Granville l.l.—Duke of Devonshire—Miss de Lisle—Ld Mayor—Sir H. Verney—Sir W.C. James—Dr Clark (U)—Sir J. Lubbock—& minutes. Dined at F. Leveson's. Conversation with Lady Blennerhassett—Mr Hayward. Read Abbey & Overton. Saw Mr H.—Ld Granville—Sir C. Dilke—Mr Childers. Luncheon in G. Square to meet Ld Strathnairn:[6] *passé.* A laborious day.

To J. CHAMBERLAIN, president of the board of trade,   Chamberlain MSS 5/34/17.
14 December 1882.

Dilke has shown me, & deposited with me, your letter.[7] I shall be glad, if I can, to avoid acting upon it. But I cannot refrain from at once writing a hasty line to acknowledge the selfsacrificing spirit in which it is written, & which I am sure you will never see cause to repent or change.

15. Fr.

Wrote to Ld Derby—Ld Granville—The Queen l.l.l. Tel l.l.—Ld Aberdare—Mr Rathbone—Mr Ralli—Mr Chamberlain—Ld Sydney—Mr Mavrocordato—Ld Kimberley Tel. Saw Mr H—Ld R. Grosvenor—Ld Granville—Ld Derby—Sir H. Ponsonby. Conclave at 5 on return from Ld Derby's. He had agreed to accept the Colonial Office.[8] Corresp. with Windsor afterwards ended in a settlement *talquale.* Dined at Lucy's. Read Abbey & Overton. Preparations for departure.

---

[1] *The Times* this day (pp. 3–4) carried, as its contribution to the Gladstone parliamentary jubilee celebrations, a long and rather favourable 'political retrospect' of his career. He was presented with addresses from about 240 liberal associations (*T.T.*, 14 December 1882, 7a). See 13 Dec. 32.
[2] Letter untraced.
[3] Ibid.
[4] Thanking him for congratulations from Newark town council; *T.T.*, 15 December 1882, 7f.
[5] Letter untraced.
[6] Hugh Henry *Rose, Lord Strathnairn, 1803–95, an old soldier; suppressed Fenians 1865–70.
[7] Of 13 December, to Dilke, agreeing to accept the duchy of Lancaster if Dilke thereby gained a place in the cabinet; Garvin, i. 381.
[8] Thus Derby took the Colonial Office, Kimberley moving to the India Office, and Hartington to the War Office.

To J. CHAMBERLAIN, president of the board of trade,   Chamberlain MSS 5/34/18.
15 December 1882.

I thank you most sincerely for your kind & friendly letter.[1] As regards the prospective part of it, I can assure you that I should be slow to plead the mere title to retirement which long labour is supposed to earn. But I have always watched, & worked according to, what I felt to be the measure of my own mental force. A monitor from within tells me that though I may still be equal to some portions of my duties, or as little unequal as heretofore, there are others which I cannot face. I fear therefore I must keep in view an issue which cannot be evaded.

16. Sat [Hawarden]

Wrote to Ld Aberdare—Count Menabrea—Bp of Truro—Bp of Bangor—Mr Tyrrell—Ld Rosebery—Sir C. Dilke—Mr Thomson Hankey—and minutes. Preparations for departure. To Windsor at 11.45. Audience of H.M.—very smooth. Saw Sir H. Ponsonby—Ld Hartington—Ld Derby. On to Hn at 10¼ P.M. Read [blank.]

17. 3 S. Adv.

Hawarden Church 11 a.m. 6 P.M. Wrote to Mr Hamilton l & Tel—Ld Coleridge—Sir C. Dilke—Sir W. Harcourt—Ld Granville and minutes. Read Burke's Hist. Portraits[2]—Foreign Review—Life of Martin Boos (orig.)[3]—Life of Bp Wilberforce Vol. III.[4]

To Sir W. V. HARCOURT, home secretary,   MS Harcourt dep. 8, f. 170.
17 December 1882.

Dilke tells me that you favour the idea of asking Dodson to take the Duchy. No doubt the exchange between Chamberlain & Dilke is in some respects awkward. But it is willing on both sides, and is arranged between them. I am afraid that Dodson would be very unwilling indeed—that it would be very like turning him down—that people would say *aut hic aut nusquam*, if he is not fit for the Local Board, what is he fit for? and finally that Chamberlain would leave a place he fills extremely well for one he has not any previous preparation for. Moreover it does not get over the difficulty of making more shifts but increases it. I write this to show you the matter has not been overlooked though things may have escaped me which have met your sharper vision.
[P.S.] Should Fawcett's case unhappily take an evil turn, the G.P.O. would be the best resort.

18. M.

Ch 8½ a.m: and at Bellis (under gardener)'s funeral. Wrote to Mr Hamilton Tel l.l.l.—Lady Derby—The Queen—Mr Jerningham—Ld Spencer l.l.—Mr Ollivant—Mrs Bower[5]—Sir W. Harcourt—Ld Rosebery—Mr Tupper—Mr West—Ld

[1] Of 13 December; sending congratulations on Gladstone's parliamentary jubilee and stressing his importance 'at the head of affairs'; Garvin, i. 379.
[2] See 28 July 80.
[3] C. Bridges, *The life of Martin Boos, Roman Catholic priest in Bavaria* (1855).
[4] See 22 Nov. 80.
[5] Had sent a sketch by her fa., George Lance; Add MS 44546, f. 53.

Granville and minutes. Read Burke's Portraits—Life of Wilberforce. Walk with W.H.G. Saw S.E.G. on the vacancy at Llandaff.[1]

To Sir W. V. HARCOURT, home secretary,   MS Harcourt dep. 8, f. 172.
18 December 1882.

My letter of yesterday has anticipated the chief part of yours.[2] I am sure you will see that I have at any rate done my best to consider the matter. The rubs and anxieties have been incessant: if you remain in town perhaps you will communicate with Dilke on whom they now turn. You will understand that it is physically impossible for me to keep my colleagues informed as I could wish. *How* to get through, I do not quite see: but I must go through somehow.

Bryce is a rising man, & well worth considering. It appears (to my surprise) that he is as old as Raikes. If you see Dodson or any colleague please to talk over the matter. If he is to be proposed he ought to have notice.

[P.S.] I return Chamberlain's letter: of course I shall save him *if* I can.

To LORD ROSEBERY, home undersecretary, 18 December   N.L.S. 10022, f. 142.
1882. '*Private*'.

Ever since I got rid of the almost daily pressure of Procedure in the House of Commons, I have been engaged from day to day in most anxious & trying communications, which still continue.

These may have blunted my apprehension in other directions, & may have prevented me from gathering distinctly from your recent letters—to speak plainly, which I think is the best way in which I can show my sense of your innumerable kind acts—either what you intend, or, especially, why you intend it.

When we came into office, the Daily Telegraph referred to a list of 32 great subjects in arrear, & said, of course these will be disposed of immediately! I thought this rather unreasonable. The case before us is not parallel: except as to this; that when men are working as hard as they can, they cannot work harder. I am not however sure that you think I am working as hard as I can: indeed the inference from your letters would seem to be the reverse.

At the present moment a special arrangement has for the first time been adopted with a view to the better dispatch of Scotch business: & of the working of this arrangement no account is before me such as to enable me to form a judgment upon it. I hardly think the time & circs., thus viewed, to be appropriate for a complaint of what you seem to regard & treat as contumacious inattention. If you will lay before me your views of existing wants, & of the proper mode of supplying them, so that they may be considered by me, & by the Cabinet, this shall not be neglected. At present I hardly know that I have any materials before me.

In any case it is not probable that any plan involving reconstruction of any kind could be published until near the time when it could be discussed on the Estimates.[3]

[P.S.] I have been so glad to hear good accounts of Lady Rosebery.

---

[1] On d. of bp. Ollivant; Richard Lewis, 1821–1905, archdeacon of St. David's, was appt.

[2] Of 17 December, on Chamberlain's 'generosity & self sacrifice'; Add MS 44197, f. 154.

[3] Rosebery replied demanding either a new arrangement for Scottish business at once, or acceptance of his resignation; both sides of the correspondence were sent to Granville, who calmed both men; *Rosebery*, 140–5.

19. Tu.

Ch 8½ a.m. Wrote to Bp of Winchester—Ld Granville—Bp of Chester—Mr E. Arnold—Dean of St Pauls—Mr Trevor—Ld Hartington—Mr Hamilton Tel—Ld Granville Tel—Sir R. Blennerhassett—Sir C. Dilke—Ld Aberdare—Duke of Grafton and minutes. Woodcraft—on the fallen fir. Read Wilberforce Vol. III.—Marbeau, Slaves et Teutons[1]—Arnold, Pearls of the Faith.[2]

To LORD HARTINGTON, Indian secretary,   Chatsworth MSS 340. 1294.
19 December 1882.

Nothing can be kinder than your note;[3] and I would on no account close any door, considering the pressure & tension of the existing situation, but I cannot see any likely combination, other than those already proposed. I am however very willing to avail myself of the eye-sight of others. From letters which Granville will today send you at my request, you will see my actual position with the Queen. My first aim is to bring her back to Dilke: my second, that she shall put her horses up with Chamberlain. If both decline, I think you, G. & I shall have to meet in London. I do not say an exchange between Dodson & Dilke (as Duchy) should be declined if the first D. were willing. But I fear Dilke would carry no knowledge whatever to the Local Board, though I can well *believe* in his aptitude without actually knowing it. If you have a mind to feel Dodson's pulse, this might be done at once, for without doubt this would be a great relief to the Queen, and I do not suppose Dilke would object. Dodson would I imagine leave the Cabinet with satisfaction, with a hope of the Speakership: but could we open *that* perspective? Your writing to the Queen, should you see an opening, could in my opinion do nothing but good to any public interest.

20. Wed.

Ch 8½ a.m. Wrote to Bp of Bangor Tel—Ld Hartington Tel—Rev. Mr M'Coll—Mr A. Arnold—Sir H. Vivian—The Queen—Ld Aberdare—Sig. G. Giulani[4]—Bp of St Andrews and minutes. Read Teutons et Slaves—Bp Wilberforce's Life—Pearls of Faith—Burke's Characters. Walk with W.H.G.

21. Th. St Thos.

Ch. 8½ a.m. with H.C. Wrote to Sir H. Ponsonby—The Queen 1 & Tel—Ld Rosebery—Ld Enfield—Mr Hamilton—Mr R. Hardy—Ld Granville l.l.—Mr E. Macivor[5]—Prince Rodokanakis—Lady Llanover—Mr Bywater—Mr W. Fowler & minutes. Walk with W. & fatiguing Estate talk; not his fault. Read Wilberforces Life—Burke's Hist Portraits—Slaves et Teutons.

[1] E. Marbeau, *Slaves et Teutons* (1882).
[2] E. Arnold, *Pearls of the faith, or Islam's rosary* (1883); sent by the author.
[3] Of 18 December, Add MS 44146, f. 132: 'the Dilke hitch is not removed'; Hartington ready to act as broker with Dodson.
[4] Letter extolling virtues of Dante, placed in 1884 in Dante's house in Florence by Mariotti; *T.T.*, 21 January 1884, 5d.
[5] E. McIvor of Lairg sent a miniature; Add MS 44477, f. 112.

22. Fr.

Church 8½ a.m. Wrote to Mr S. Hazzopulo[1]—The Queen l.l.l.—Ld Aberdare—Ld Granville l.l.—Sir C. Dilke—Mr Courtney and minutes. Saw Bp of Bangor at great length on the perplexed question of the vacant See of Llandaff. (Took him over the old Castle). He was most kind & fair. Saw S.E.G. on the same subject. Worked on a large Ash with W. & H. Read Wilberforce's Life—Teutons et Slaves.

23. Sat.

Wrote to Mrs Stoner l.l.—Mr Seymour Tel—Ld Rosebery—Ld Hartington Tel— Sir G. Bowyer—Sir H. Ponsonby Tel—Mr West—Mr Macgregor Tel—Mr Dodson—Bp of St Asaph—Mr Seymour—Lord Derby and minutes. We finished felling the ash. Saw Lady Ormonde. Lucy C. came. Read Burke Vol. III.—Life of Wilberforce—Slaves et Teutons.

To J. G. DODSON, president of the local government board,   Monk Bretton 60.
23 December 1882. '*Private*'.

I write a line of hearty thanks for the permission you have given me to propose Dilke for your office, and yourself for the Duchy, which, though of higher rank, and of agreeable incidents, has not in nearly the same degree what I have no doubt you regard as the capital recommendation of work. When we meet I will give you the detail of all that has occurred. For the present, and on paper, I will only say that the difficulties have been great and that your kindness will supply a solution for them.

24. 4 S. Adv.

Ch 11 a.m. and 6½ P.M. Wrote to Ld Granville Tel—Sir H. Ponsonby l.l. & Tel— Mr Seymour Tel—Sir G. Ady—Messrs Farrar—Mrs Bolton—Bp of St Andrew's— Ld Spencer—The Queen & minutes. Read Life of Wilberforce—Life of Martin Boos—Rawlinson on the Age of Man.[2] Conversation with S.E.G. on the Welsh Bishopric.

To LORD SPENCER, Viceroy of Ireland, 24 December 1882.   Althorp MSS K6.

All good Christmas greetings. From which I pass to the other end of the scale—Biggar's speech.[3] It was I thought perhaps the most loathsome that even that reptile has ever delivered. I have not it before me, and my memory may err. I remember that he attacks you most foully—and thus attacks the Government at its strong point, not any weak one. But I do not recollect what he says of Judges & Juries. Do you think it would be prudent to bring into Court anything aimed only at the Executive?
This is a grave question which I am sure you will sift, or have sifted, thoroughly. I remember once the Times charged me with acting treason as a servant of the Crown. I wanted to prosecute them (as an individual, not by the power of the Crown): but every-

[1] S. Hazzopulo had written on Greece in Greek, from Higher Broughton, sending a casket; Hawn P.
[2] G. Rawlinson, *The antiquity of man historically considered* (1883).
[3] On 18 December at Waterford, attacking Spencer for executing death sentences on Joyce, Walsh and Hynes; he was committed for trial, Spencer dropping the prosecution in March 1883; *Spencer*, i. 233.

one dissuaded me, and I gave it up. You will see what my leanings are: but leanings are not a final judgment. I need not refer to any other point touched in your letter.

25. Xm. Day.

Ch 11 a.m. with H.C. and 7 P.M. Wrote to Bp of Truro—Bp of Bangor—The Queen—Sir C. Dilke—Ld Rosebery—Mr Seymour—Ld Granville & minutes. Read Life of Martin Boos—finished Life of the great Bishop Wilberforce.

26. St Stephen.

Ch 8½ a.m. Wrote to Mr Seymour Tel & l—Sir H. Ponsonby Tel & l.—Ld Rosebery Tel.—The Queen—Sir A. Gordon—Sir T.G.—Sir W. Harcourt—Sir F. Doyle—Ld R. Grosvenor—Scotts—Ld Chancellor—Bp of Bangor—Ld Granville and minutes. Kibbling with W. & H. Read Slaves et Teutons—Burke's Tudor Portr. (finished III.) Banks's Fall of Troy.[1]

27. St John.

Lumbago, due to want of care yesterday kept me in bed. Wrote to Mr Seymour Tel—Bp of St Asaph—l & Tel—Ld Granville Tel—Ld Sudeley—Ld Bessborough —Mr E. Arnold—Ld Hartington—Rev. Mr Sinclair & minutes. Read Life of M. Boos. Also finished Banks, Fall of Troy—Arnold's 'Pearls' finished. Arranged for giving H. 4m[ille] of his portion: to be lent to WHG.

28. Th. H. Inn.

Confined most of the day. Wrote to Bp of St Davids—The Queen Tel.—Bp of Durham—Mr Puller Tel.—Bp of Bangor—Pr. L. Napoleon—Abp of Dublin—Sir W. Harcourt—Sir C. Dilke—Ld Granville—Mr Courtney—Mr Seymour—Dr A. Clark—and minutes.

To Sir C. W. DILKE, president of the local government board,   Add MS 43875, f. 122. 28 December 1882. '*Secret*'.

Many thanks for your letter.[2] Messages are sometimes sent to the Queen about honours, and some kinds of appointment, but not I think as to political office.

However, I ought to mention that I have just had a telegram from her showing that she looks with some interest or even keenness to the words of explanation as to the distant past which you propose to use. They were not in any way a matter of bargain; but, as a free tender on your own part, I make no doubt you will redeem liberally and handsomely the words of promise which I reported to the Queen, and read to you.

Notwithstanding the rubs of the past, I am sanguine as to your future relations with the Queen. There are undoubtedly many difficulties in that quarter: but they are in the main confined to three or four Departments. Your office will not touch them: while you will have in common with all your colleagues the benefit of two great modifying circumstances which never fail, the first her high good manners, and the second her love of truth. I am the more desirous to do her justice, because, while she conducts all

[1] J. Banks, *The destruction of Troy, a tragedy* (1679).
[2] Of 26 December, Add MS 44149, f. 114; accepts Gladstone's offer of the local govt. board; understands it not to be usual to send the Prime Minister letters to be forwarded to the Queen.

intercourse with me in absolute and perfect courtesy, I am convinced, from an hundred tokens, that she looks forward to the day of my retirement as a day, if not of jubilee yet of relief.

I have entered on these explanations, because it is my fervent desire, on every ground, to reduce difficulties, in such high and difficult matters, to their minimum; and because with the long years which I hope you have before you, I also earnestly desire that your start should be favourable in your relations with the Sovereign.[1]

To Sir W. V. HARCOURT, home secretary,   MS Harcourt dep. 8, f. 181.
28 December 1882.

1. Rosebery will be most welcome here.[2] It is a most singular case of strong self-delusion: a vein of foreign matter which runs straight across a clear & vigorous intellect, and a high-toned character.
2. Cross was put forward some time ago by Grosvenor: I have proposed him to Kimberley.
3. I am glad to say Derby declares himself better pleased with the C.O. than with the plan originally contemplated.
4. I agree with you as to the honours of Cambridge: but you have omitted the chief trophy of all—the return of Raikes.
5. When we meet I will endeavour to run a tilt with you on behalf of Bishop Wilberforce:[3] and I hope you will tell me, now or then, what was Beaconsfield's version of a most curious affair.

I am truly sorry you were not able to prolong your term at Cuffnells which you made so pleasant to your friends.

To J. B. LIGHTFOOT, bishop of Durham, 28 December 1882.   Add MS 44478, f. 271.

I welcome cordially your intervention in the matter of the Llandaff see.[4] Indeed I was just about to write to you to ask the following question. 1. Does Archdeacon Watkins know Welsh: & if so is it as a native or as an acquired language? 2. What does your Lordship think of his general qualifications for the See?

A vacancy in a Welsh see costs me more trouble than six English vacancies. I feel it my duty to ascertain if possible by a process of exhaustion whether there is any completely fit person to be had among men of Welsh mother tongue. In the main it is a business of constantly examining likely or plausible cases & finding they break down. The Welsh are to be got at through the pulpit: & yet here is a special danger, for among the more stirring Welsh clergy there is as much wordy & windy preaching as among the Irish.

I have not yet finally abandoned the notion of a Welshman, having certain cases still under examination. In the mean time I have been reminded of Archdeacon Watkins: hence my queries to your Lordship. I want to know whether he will do as a pure Welshman; & if not, then whether as semi Welshman he is the best man available.

But what of Mr Wilkinson? My reply—at present very private—is that it seems to me as if beyond all others he was made for Truro & Truro for him. And I *think* that Bishop Benson fervently desires, on this ground, that Mr Wilkinson should succeed him.[5]

---

[1] Part in Gwynn misdated, i. 497, with Dilke's oblique apology for his republicanism.
[2] Harcourt's letter of 24 December on Rosebery, 'bent on a Cabinet place'; Add MS 44197, f. 158.
[3] Harcourt thought Wilberforce 'the most self seeking false & malignant of human beings'; 27 December, Add MS 44197, f. 166 and Gardiner, i. 467.
[4] Lightfoot had written on behalf of G. H. Wilkinson; Add MS 44478, f. 197.
[5] Lightfoot replied that 'Watkins may be called half a Welshman', but questioned whether he could preach in Welsh without training; ibid., f. 289.

29. Fr.

Another year of mercy and forbearance. Why encumbereth it the ground?

Got out to Church 8¼ A.M. Resolutely stole two hours from the public & made the annual sketch of my property: also a note of those transactions of the year, which form part of my relieving and unwinding plan.

Wrote to Prince of Wales Tel.—Ld Hartington Tel l.l.—Mr Seymour Tel.—Ld Aberdare—Bp of St Asaph—Ld Granville—Mr Parker MP—Rev. D. Williams[1]—Mr R. Davies MP[2]—and minutes. Read Slaves et Teutons (finished)—Naville on Atheism[3]—Cadorna on Egypt.[4] Wrote paragraphs proposed for dispatch to France about Egypt.[5]

And here I close a personal year of great mercies. This Christmas time has indeed been darkened by my being engaged in controversies at Osborne and with Rosebery. But there is or ought to be no room in my breast for anything but wonder & thankfulness to God. Perhaps on the 31st I may have a more free moment for retrospect and prospect.

30. Sat.

Ch 8½ a.m. Wrote to Ld Aberdeen Tel—Mr Seymour Tel and l—Sir W. Harcourt—Sir P. Braila—Ld Granville—A. Otway—Mr Trevelyan—Mr Richard—Bp of Bangor—Ld Hartington—Ld Kimberley & minutes. Saw Mr MacColl—Rev. S.E.G.—Llandaff &c. Began survey of my Midlothian Speeches—alas Two Vols!—for the coming visit.[6] Read Life of Boos—De Bale's Hygiene and Tracts.[7]

To H. RICHARD, M.P., 30 December 1882.   National Library of Wales.

I send an answer to the Memorial[8] you have addressed to me. It is, from the unusual nature of the case, restrained in its expressions.

In writing to you however I may say that I do not feel quite sure how far you think the claim of Nonconformists *as such* can be pressed, for example in a case like that of the Headship of Trinity College, Cambridge. Would you say in that case more than it was the duty of the Prime Minister to search for the best man, & to take care that no religious profession was allowed to bias his choice?

At the same time I do not doubt with you that, as the facilities of Education are enlarged, & are more & more turned to account by Nonconformists, their share in the 'administrative & official life' of the country will be enlarged. It can hardly be said as yet to be sufficient. I may however say that Nonconformity was more largely represented in the two Cabinets it has been my duty to form, than in the Parliaments out of which they were formed.

I am again involved in the cares of a vacant Welsh See, & grave cares they are. Any suggestion you may be kind enough to offer will be received by me with attention, & with the confidence in your impartiality which you are well entitled to claim.

[1] David Williams, priest in Llandaff; Add MS 44546, f. 62.
[2] Richard Davies, 1818–96; liberal M.P. Anglesey 1868–86.
[3] E. Naville, *The Heavenly Father. Lectures on modern atheism*, tr. H. Downton (1865).
[4] See 11 Oct. 82.
[5] Probably the basis for Granville's despatch of 3 Jan. 1883; *PP* 1883 lxxxiii. 38.
[6] But see to Rosebery, 8 Jan. 83; see *T.T.*, 20 Dec. 1882, 8a.
[7] Perhaps H. Dobell, *On diet and regimen* (1882).
[8] Not found.

To G. O. TREVELYAN, Irish secretary, 30 December 1882.   Add MS 44546, f. 63.

I have today for the first time been able to read & consider your interesting letter on Irish business for the Session.[1] Such has been *my* Christmas holiday. I think you will find it necessary to make a selection from your selection: though all might more easily be managed if the House were now prepared to use the method of Grand Committees for portions of the United Kingdom. Perhaps some independent member if a suitable one can be found, might be encouraged to take up certain of the Irish subjects, which we may be unable to include in our Budget. The subject of Local Government eclipses all the rest in importance. As long as the portentous centralization of the present system continues, Government will be to the common Irishman, I am afraid, an exotic, a foreign thing, & he may for long look upon it with a consequent aversion, which will extend even to its simplest & most needful & beneficial acts. I hope it will be founded upon the four Provinces, were it for no other reason than that the Irish counties afford (I speak as one seeing something of Wales) areas too narrow. I see no reason why you should wait for, or depend upon, an English measure. Such Provincial bodies would I hope be capable of rendering far greater service than any weaker bodies could.

The many questions connected with Irish Land & Public works are most dangerous & can only be rendered innocuous by our having really responsible & rather weighty bodies to deal with.

I should regard the door as wholly closed against giving them something to do in (1) Primary Education, (2) Local Police. I have no objection to take to any of your suggestions. Thanks too for the notice about the Ulster Appeals.

31. S. aft Xm.[2]

Ch 11 a.m. and 6½ P.M. Wrote to Sir Ch. Dilke—Card. Newman—Mr Holms[3]— Ld Hartington—Mr Rowsell and minutes. Read Mozley, Essays[4]—S.s admirable sermon at Barrow[5]—Macalister on Development.[6]

To Sir C. W. DILKE, president of the local government board,   Add MS 43875, f. 125. 31 December 1882.

As Cabinets are liable to be called at 24 hours notice, possibly even less, you cannot have any guarantee against them;[7] but there is no plan or foreseen occasion for any Cabinet during January.

The St. James Gazette is pretty certain to be read at Osborne and its opening comments on your speech may be useful.

Let me add a sentence to *integrate* our past correspondence.[8] I passed over the suggestion about clearing the Admiralty a) from reluctance to start Northbrook's removal to

---

[1] Of 23 December, Add MS 44335, f. 80: Irish business for next session: 1. local govt.; 2. Registration Bill; 3. fisheries; 4. Police Bill; 5. denominational training colleges assistance.

[2] Space left at the end of this entry for the usual retrospect, but never written.

[3] Probably William Holms, liberal M.P. Paisley 1874, resigned 1883.

[4] See 12 Feb. 79.

[5] In MS.

[6] A. Macalister, 'Evolution in church history' (1882).

[7] Dilke was considering holidaying in France; Add MS 44149, f. 119.

[8] The Prince of Wales and Dilke both canvassed Northbrook for the India Office, Dilke for the Admiralty; Gwynn, i. 494.

any less efficient place, b) on account of Parliamentary displacements: not at all because it was too big a place to vacate and offer.

I am afraid I differ from you on one point: your refusal to shorten my political future.

It rejoices me that you speak against centralisation, which it seems many now charge on the Liberals as a distinctive point of practise if not creed.

[P.S.] Let me wish you a good New Year.

Mon. Jan. 1. Circumcision.

Wrote to Pr. of Wales Tel.—King of the Belgians Tel—Mr Seymour Tel l.l.—Ld Rosebery Tel—Mr Courtney—Bp of Chester—Miss de Lisle—Bp of Bangor l.l.— Miss L. Walsh[1]—Ld Aberdare—Sir Thos G.—Mr Duckham MP—Mr Godley— Rev. Mr Suffield—Sir G. Wood—Sir Geo. Provost—Mrs Th. and minutes. Walk with Lucy. Saw S.E.G. on the See of Llandaff; also Mr M'Coll. Read Question Egyptienne (Martens)[2]—Home Rule in Scotland 19th Cent.[3]—Midlothian Speeches.

To L. H. COURTNEY, financial secretary, 1 January 1883.   Add MS 44546, f. 65.

I do not quite understand why these papers, belonging to the letter of the Irish Government dated December 13, and reaching me January 1, have not been to Mr. Childers, to whom they strictly belong & whose opinion must be the principal one in dealing with them (P.S. I have found the explanation).

My own opinion is that resort to the Consolidated Fund in this case is inadmissible, & I accept no part of the argument in the Irish letter which bears upon this point. I am not sure that I fully understand the distinctions they make between rate in aid for England, & rate in aid for Ireland. I agree with your views in regard to that principle & I think it of very great importance that no precedent should be made now for meeting *local* Irish distress out of the Consolidated Fund.

As between the *first* & *second* of the three forms of ultimate resort, I see no reason why the Treasury should rule the question absolutely, but I dissent from the argument of the Irish Government against resort to the Church Surplus, and have no faith in the doctrine of wholesale emigration through the agency of the Imperial Government.

As regards the mode of proceeding, I would suggest that the views of the Treasury as at present advised might for the present be embodied in a draft and this draft in the first instance sent to the Irish Government. It might also be sent to Mr. Childers and confirmed or modified according to his opinion in its ultimate form as an official letter: also according to any impression which the Irish Government might make by its arguments put in like form. The field of controversy between the departments might thus be narrowed to the points which in the view of each respectively were thought essential.

To J. A. GODLEY, 1 January 1883.   Add MS 44546, f. 65.

On reference to my journals I find you are as usual careful & accurate; yet that I am not wrong.[4] I *was* made President of the Board of Trade on June 10, 1843;[5] but I attended my first Cabinet on May 15. I take that old Duke of Newcastle as a measure of the possible, or the maximum attained, 1. In Cabinet Office, 2 (perhaps) in total duration of official life.

I am glad you have put in Granville. Argyll is very close on my heels in Cabinet Office. I was appointed Vice President of the Board of Trade on September 3, 1841.

---

[1] Thanking her for a gift; *T.T.*, 10 January 1883, 6e.
[2] F. de Martens, *La question égyptienne et le droit international* (1882).
[3] W. S. Dalgleish in *N.C.*, xiii. 14 (January 1883).
[4] Godley sent 'by way of a "Christmas card"' a table he had made of relative lengths of office-holding; Add MS 44222, f. 265.
[5] i.e. the formal Council meeting; see 13, 15 May, 10 June 43.

[P.S.] There is yet another point. Ought my service in the Ionian Islands, unpaid but strictly official, to be reckoned to my credit? I think it was about 4 months. I return your inclosures for final consideration.[1]

To Canon Sir G. PREVOST, 1 January 1883.   Add MS 44546, f. 65.

I thank you for *all* your good words[2] but I would (such is the pressure of business upon me) have availed myself of your kind permission to be silent had I not thought I might offer a consolatory suggestion as to the operation of the [Deceased] Wife's Sister Bill, supposing it to pass in the form which I have stipulated it should take & which I believe it will bear. In that form it leaves untouched all the ecclesiastical prohibitions: I therefore can hardly suppose that any clergyman could be held personally liable for treating as an offence what the law of his church proscribed. This is of course but my poor conjecture. What may be the prospects of the Bill I cannot say.[3]

2. Tu.

Ch. 8½ a.m. Last night my sleep was further cut down to 3 . . . 4 hours. Hardly enough oil for my lamp I fear. More wearing personalities today. Wrote to Seymour Tel l.l.–Sir H. Ponsonby l & Tel–Palace (St David's)–Bp of Bangor– Ld Granville l & Tel. Charades at the Orphanage. Ld E. Fitzmaurice l & Tel–Sir C. Dilke–Ld Rosebery–Sir P. Heywood[4] and minutes. Read Mitchell on Past and Present[5]–Dunckley on Conservatism[6]–Plumptre on Dante.[7] Saw Mr M'Coll & S.E.G. on the testimonies respecting the See.

3. Wed.

Sleep improved from 3½–4½ hours: too little for me, though it has served for greater & better men. Wrote to Bp of Bangor tel & l–The Speaker–Mr L. Play-fair–Sir T.[E.] May–Rev. A. Duncan–Ld E. Fitzmaurice Tel–Ld Granville–Dr Mitchell–Bp Strossmayer & minutes. Read The Antiquary (in the night)[8]– Froude on the Oxford movement[9]–Strutt on Xtn Inquiry.[10]

4. Th.

Ch 8½ a.m. A much more successful night–up to six hours. Wrote to Bp of Bangor Tel–Ld Granville Tel–Mr Playfair–Ld Rosebery Tel–Sir C. Dilke–C. Rosenborg–Mr Seymour–Ld Aberdare–Hn Postmaster & minutes. Walk to

---

[1] Godley thought this should not be included; 3 January, Add MS 44223, f. 1.
[2] Undated letter, Add MS 44478, f. 236, approving of Benson's appt., and hoping that if Deceased Wife's Sister Bill is carried, Gladstone will protect clergy declining communion to its beneficiaries.
[3] Rejected by the Lords in June.
[4] Sir (Thomas) Percival Heywood, 1823–97; 2nd bart. 1865; on presentation to Miles Platting (i.e. the Green affair), Add MS 44546, f. 67.
[5] Sir A. Mitchell, *The past in the present* (1880).
[6] H. Dunckley, 'The conservative dilemma', *C.R.*, xliii. 141 (January 1883).
[7] E. H. Plumptre, *The Divina Commedia* (1883).
[8] Scott (1816); see 15 Dec. 48.
[9] J. A. Froude, 'The Oxford Counter-reformation', reprinted in his *Short studies* (1883), iv. 163.
[10] P. Strutt, *The inductive method of Christian inquiry* (1877).

Buckley & saw Mr Torr:[1] in preparation for the night. Read The Antiquary—Strutt's Christn Inquiry—Froude's Oxford movement. Saw Mr MacColl—Mr E. Wickham.

5. Fr.

Ch 8½ a.m. Sleep say 5–5½ hours. Wrote to Mr Hamilton Tel—Mr Seymour Tel—Mr Forster—Bp of Bangor—Herbert J.G.—Ld Granville—Mr Cross M.P.—Ld Kimberley—Sir C. Dilke Tel. Two walks with Rosebery. Drive & conversation with C. Rather puzzled as to resuming my preparations for Midlothian. Read The Antiquary (night & day)—Mitchell's P & P. In the Psalms this day, as so often in the straiter[?] passages of my life, God's love supplied me with a touching telling word. 'Mine eyes are ever looking unto the Lord: for he shall pluck my feet out of the net.'[2] Can it be that He is backing, & thus taking, my side in the controversy about my early retirement? But what it may be, all glory be His.

To LORD KIMBERLEY, Indian secretary, 5 January 1883.   Add MS 44546, f. 68.

My work has been so severe that I have been ill able to keep up that moderate acquaintance with the tone of the press on current affairs which is almost a necessity, but the little that I see gives me the impression that our measures respecting Zululand are seriously misapprehended & are treated as leaning much more in principle a permanence [sic] to annexation in part & in part to protection than is really the case. If this is not so I dare say you will kindly set me at ease in a few words. But if it is so may there not be grounds for inspiring some newspaper a little with a view to correction. But see below. I write to you rather than to Derby because this has happened (if it has happened at all) at a moment of transition. My own visit to Midlothian might afford an opportunity but I am not yet absolutely certain it will come off, for the long uninterrupted pressure of work has somewhat deranged me & some days may pass before I can be assured as to undertaking the journey. Perhaps it may be as well to wait until this is decided. And as it would be needful to communicate with Derby if anything is to be done through the Peers, time might not be lost. But I rely on hearing from you some intimation of your idea as to the true character of our measures.[3]
[P.S.] I write to Cross.

6. Sat. Epiph.

Ch 8½–9¾, with H.C.—Dearest C's birthday. Clark telegraphed that he would come. Last night I had but two hours. Wrote to Bp of Bangor Tel—Ld Granville—Sir H. Ponsonby l.l.—Ld Hartington—Sir C. Dilke—Bp of Carlisle & minutes. Much conversation with F. Leveson [Gower]—also with Rosebery: who went.[4] Hamilton on the ground helped me much. We had a party in the house: but Mary played me to sleep in the evening: ten hours in bed & strange to say 8 hours sleep.

---

[1] i.e. W. F. W. Torre, the vicar.   [2] Psalm xxv. 14; the set psalm for the 5th day.
[3] Kimberley replied, 7 January, Add MS 44228, f. 42, rehearsing at length the govt.'s case on Cetewayo and suggesting Gladstone explain it when in Midlothian, 'or, if not, through a friendly newspaper'.
[4] Without discussing the Scottish Office or his position; *Rosebery*, 145.

7. 1 S. Epiph.

Ch 11 a.m. with H.C. and 6½ P.M. Wrote to Ld Kimberley—Ld Rosebery Tel—
The Queen—Ld Granville—Bp of Bangor and minutes. Read a few Tracts. Conversation with F. Leveson—Mr Holland—Mr Stuart. Dr Clark came in the
afternoon and I had two conversations with him. After examining & hearing
carefully, he stopped Midlothian, and prescribed *rest* as far as possible until the
meeting of Parliament.[1] Last night, almost strangely, out of eleven hours in bed
I slept full nine.

1. My practice of regulating action by brain.
2. Single sign of brain-resentment heretofore—neuralgia now & then, at the close of the
   Session.
3. Slight indication of breach in sleep during the autumn sittings.
4. Aggravated since come here. No notice taken until this week.
5. This week much further aggravation; best night 6 hours, worst (Friday) 2 hours.
6. Some neuralgia in the last three days but not bad.
7. I do not perceive bodily health and functions to be affected, except the brain, which
   has slight confusion and great sense of weakness all through the day: increase of it
   today. Beguiled in conversation, but returns. No sleepiness in the daytime or evening.
8. During the week I have reduced my transaction of business to the necessary, and given
   up reading and preparing for my visit to Midlothian. But matters have not improved,
   indeed the contrary. Light reading however continues to be agreeable to me.[2]

8. M.

Ch 8½ a.m. Wrote to Duchess of Roxburgh[3]—The Queen—Ld Rosebery—Rev.
S.E.G. (Llandaff) and minutes. Read Antiquary—Mothers & Daughters—finished Past & Present. Further conversation with Clark. he went off at 11; over-
flowing with kindness. Walk with the party: visited St Johns [Pentrobin].

To LORD ROSEBERY, home undersecretary, 8 January 1883.   N.L.S. 10022, f. 187.

I much regret that I have to confirm by letter the intimation, made to you yesterday by
telegraph,[4] that Dr. Clark, who had kindly come from London to visit me, had directed in
an unequivocal manner the abandonment of my projected visit to Midlothian in the
present month. The disturbance of sleep, which led Dr. Clark to this conclusion, is in his
view temporary; due only to too great and too prolonged a strain of work, and to be cured
by a short period of abstinence as nearly complete as may be, possibly accompanied with
change of place for the moment.

To pay this visit to Midlothian, and to give my generous constituents the opportunity
of comparing fully & in detail my declarations before the election of 1880 with my
conduct since, has all along been regarded by me as matter of high obligation. I was much
concerned to postpone the fulfilment of this duty on account of the Autumn sittings, and

---

[1] Postponement announced in *T.T.*, 10 January 1883, 6e.
[2] Add MS 44766, f. 6 (misplaced). Docketed: 'Communicated to Dr Clark on his visit Hn. Sunday
Jan. 7. 83.'
[3] Successfully offering her the mistress-ship of the robes; Add MS 44479, f. 97.
[4] And foreshadowed in a letter to Rosebery of 2 January; N.L.S. 10022, f. 185.

I lament still more the present necessity for a further postponement: but I look with un-diminished confidence to paying my visit at a future and I hope not very distant day.

9. Tu.

7 hours sleep: following 6½ D.G. Ch 8½ a.m. Conversation with S.E.G. (Llan-daff)—Mr Holland—Mr Stewart—W.H.G. Conclave on Contagious Diseases Act: Malsano.[1] Wrote to the Queen (on the two Sees—with all my little stock of art)[2]—Ld Kimberley—Sir C. Dilke—Herbert J.G.—Sir T. Brassey—Mr A. Reader & minutes. Read Sc. Rev. on Dr Smith's Poems[3]—Antiquary—Mother & Daugh-ters[4]—Life of Oberlin.[5] Walk & drive.

To LORD KIMBERLEY, Indian secretary, 9 January 1883.   Add MS 44546, f. 70.

I have only to say that I concur in all you write about Zululand.[6] I was a party to your whole plan. When I saw the stir among those bland 'correspondents' I began to think, can it have been twisted by local agency[7] (you will understand me) in the application. You quite satisfy me. I think I had better leave it to you to settle the matter with Derby as to any publication.

My head has been, not unnaturally under the circumstances, playing tricks for once. Already I feel the benefit of partial relief. Midlothian is gone overboard. If you send Derby your letter you will let him understand why I opened the subject with you—i.e. because I wanted to be assured there was no deviation overseas from the exact thing I had known & you had ordered.

10. Wed.

Ch 8½ a.m. Wrote to Ld Granville l.l.—Mr Macivor & minutes. Read The Anti-quary—Schomberg's Odyssey with original[8]—Life of Oberlin—Coaching days, half a Vol.[9] Sleep continues better: but went to bed for a cold: some other secondary indications. The visitors went. Cath. went off to work, really on my account, in Scotland.[10]

11. Th.

Kept my bed. A good night, full six hours. Wrote to Dr A. Clark—Mr Wilkinson (offering Truro)—minutes *viva voci.*[11] Saw W.H.G. *bis.* Read The Antiquary (it is indeed delightful)—Old Coaching Days—and other smatterings.

[1] 'in an unhealthy state'.
[2] G. H. Wilkinson (not liked by the Queen) for Truro, R. Lewis for Llandaff; not printed, but see *L.Q.V.*, 2nd series, iii. 398.
[3] *Scottish Review*, i. 52 (November 1882).
[4] [C. F. Gore], *Mothers and daughters; a tale of the year 1830*, 3v. (1831).
[5] J. E. Butler, *The life of Jean Frederic Oberlin, pastor of the Ban de la Roche* (1882).
[6] See 5 Jan. 83n.
[7] i.e. by Bulwer.
[8] Tr. G. A. Schomberg (1879).
[9] S. Harris, *Old coaching days* (1882).
[10] Not very successfully; her visit led to a row with Lady Rosebery; *Rosebery*, 145.
[11] i.e. dictating rather than drafting.

12. Fr.

A great night & over-sleep: nine hours. The secondary indications cleared off rapidly. Wrote to Archdeacon Lewis—Ld Granville—The Queen—Mr Forster—Mr Brand and minutes. Finished the Antiquary—read Coaching Days. Saw Mr H: *viva voce* minutes. Saw S.E.G. on Llandaff.

13. Sat.

Rose at 10½. Wrote to Ld Granville—Mr Brinsley Richards[1]—Ld Wolverton Tel—Mr Cross MP—Professor Robertson[2]—and minutes. Read Bickersteth's Evangelical Churchmanship[3]—Old Coaching Days (finished)—Life of Oberlin—Mr Isaacs.[4] Yesterday the secondary symptoms all disappeared: but restlessness reappeared at night. I had about 5 hours.

14. 2 S. Epiph.

More restlessness last night: about 4 hour but of good sleep (as usual) Ch 11 a.m. They would not let me go in evening. Saw S.E.G. Wrote to Ld Kimberley—The Queen—Mrs Bolton—Sir S. Scott & Co. Saw Mr H.: correspondence disposed of by *viva voce* instructions. Read the blessed Psalms—Hore's 18 Cent. Ch of England[5]—Life of Oberlin finished—Faber's Hymns (some gems).[6]

15. M.

4½ hours last night. Wrote to Messrs Rivington—Lady Grosvenor—Scotts—Ld Hartington—Bp of St David's—Rev. Mr Wilkinson—Herbert J.G.—Ld Granville. Read Tuckwell on Canning[7]—Warden on Theatre Fires[8]—Mackay on Scottish Tongue[9]—OConnor Hist. Irish people.[10] Forenoon conversations with W.H.G. on Estate affairs—HJG on the Meech business.[11]

To LORD HARTINGTON, war secretary, 15 January 1883.   Add MS 44546, f. 72.

Cross has accepted,[12] upon a letter of mine, which did not in any way reopen the question of the Indian charge but absolved him from any special duty of defence. I am not able to send it as my copy of it is gone to Kimberley for his information.

I do not quite concur in your recollection as to what the Cabinet did. I think that in unison with Childers I proposed a contribution of a sum like £440,000 or £450,000, & in

[1] James Brinsley Richards, 1846–92 ('an assumed name', Boase); newspaper correspondent living in France; on diarist's life at Eton: 'I played football a little, not hockey: and sculled incessantly in summer'; Add MS 44546, f. 71. See 12 May 83.
[2] J. Roberton, professor of conveyancing at Glasgow.
[3] E. H. Bickersteth, *Evangelical churchmanship and evangelical eclecticism* (1883).
[4] E. M. Crawford, *Mr Isaacs: a tale of modern India* (1883).
[5] A. H. Hore, *Eighteen centuries of the Church in England* (1881).
[6] By F. W. Faber, many eds.
[7] Untraced.
[8] H. F. Warden, 'The theatre's unrehearsed tragedy', "Fire and Life"' (1882).
[9] C. Mackay, *Poetry and humour of the Scottish language* (1882).
[10] R. O'Connor, *Chronicles of Eri; being the history of the Irish people*, 2v. (1822).
[11] Obscure, probably more domestic business.
[12] J. K. Cross to be Indian undersecretary, despite his views on the Indian charge.

compliance with the wish of the Cabinet, & that all might agree it was moved up to £500,000.[1] Since that time I know of no new fact but the *acceptance* of the plan by Ripon, as well as by Baring.

I have mentioned Cross to the Queen & they can tell you in Downing Street when her acceptance of him comes. It is one of the offices not formally submitted.

It is a matter of regret that Brand should think an office less than his due which has been relinquished by Adye & which was held by Stocks: although of course he cannot work it with all their authority, however well he may do his work. Perhaps the feeling may rub off.

I am due in town tomorrow to start on Wednesday for the South of France.

[P.S.] Here is just come a singularly nice note from Brand: the matter seems to stand quite well.

16. Tu. [London]

Ch. 8¼ AM: farewell to the moment to those holy and happy walls. I have to report my worst night: sleep not one hour. And dear C. but little better. We shall see what change of air with God's blessings may effect. Perhaps much. Easy & rapid journey to London in about 5 hours. Repose but no sleep. Wrote to Mrs Wellesley—The Queen Tel.—& minutes. Saw Mr H.—Mr S.—Mrs Godley—Mr Wilkinson: a very interesting conversation. Dr Clark came at seven: firm & encouraging in all his views: including the ulterior doctrine which I cannot admit. We dined with Lucy: & went early to bed.

17. Wed. [On train]

Up at 6.30: At Charing Cross 7.25. Many friends. Conversation with Harcourt. Dover at 9.30. Conversation with Granville. Passage 1¼ hour. Paris 6.30 and travelled all night in a fauteuil coupée:[2] for wh. the fine was I think £11. Read 1½ Book of the Odyssey.

18. Th. [Château Scott, Cannes]

We breakfasted at Marseilles, after a night from which much could not be expected. Splendid line of scenery from M. to Cannes. Arrived at 3.30. Besides our friends Wolverton & Acton, many English had gathered at the station & gave me a very kind reception. We were driven immediately to the Château Scott[3] nobly situated, admirably planned: and the kindness even exceeded the beauty and the comfort. Read another 1½ book of Odyssey. Records of the English Catholics.[4] To bed early.

[1] See 1 Dec. 82; Hartington thought the cabinet had not 'finally disposed' of the point; Add MS 44146, ff. 159.

[2] i.e. an armchair in a compartment with one row of seats, effectively a Pullman ('fauteuil d'un Pullman', 1873).

[3] Wolverton's villa, 'one of the finest houses in Cannes, beautifully situated in ten acres of grounds, well laid out, and commanding extensive views over the Gulf ... with an excellent water supply, well-drained, and elaborately decorated'; *T.T.*, 22 January 1883, 5d.

[4] *Records of the English Catholics under the penal laws*, 2v. (1878–82).

19. Fr.

Woke at 7¾ after 8½ hours of sleep D.G. Here we fall into the foreign hours: the *snack* early, déjeuner a la fourchette at noon, dinner at 7, break up at 10. Saw Ld Acton. Drove up the Boulevard Leader. I am stunned by this wonderful place & so vast a change at a moments notice in the conditions of life. Read Hom Od IV (and wrote on do)—Dixon's Hist Ch. of Engl.[1]

20. Sat.

I had seven hours to score.[2] Wrote to Ld R. Grosvenor—Dr A. Clark—Mr W. Miller and minutes. Saw Ld Acton—Sir C. Dilke—Duke of Argyll & made calls. Read Odyssey—Max Müller on India[3]—Dixon's Hist Ch of Engl.—S. gave us prayers at 6.30.

To Dr. A. CLARK, 20 January 1883.   Add MS 44546, f. 72.

You will I think like to have a line from me, & I am thankful to assure you that whatever the future may have to say I seem to have made a decidedly good start. We got through the journey by the aid of special arrangements, though without much sleep: *I* never have been a good sleeper in a train. But my first night here gave me 8½ hours & my second 7; moreover I feel invigorated & have less sense of weakness in the brain, enjoying thoroughly this variety in my life & the absence of business.

What I am inclined to feel is a desire to do full justice to this experiment by prolonging my stay as much as I may. I need not ask you to write, nor wish it, unless you have any monition or instruction to convey, in which case I am sure you will do it without my asking. We are at the Chateau Scott & the immense kindness of our hosts & their excellent provisions for me ought to do us almost as much good as the climate.

To LORD R. GROSVENOR, chief whip, 20 January 1883.   Add MS 44546, f. 72.

After 48 hours here, what with the place & the infinite kindness of my hosts, I am thankful to say that I have made at any rate a good start. A few days more will suffice to show whether the ground can be held & improved. The invigorating air agrees with us all and business is now for once kept at arm's length.

My present disposition naturally is to profit as much as I can by the distance interposed between me and my work: & that I may not cause unnecessary inconvenience I write (1). To ask you to admonish me when I ought to send out the circular for the opening. I suppose it must be dated from hence. (2). To put in your hands the business of choosing a mover and seconder if you like to ask Hartington in my name to undertake the selection.

The Liverpool man ought to be thought of?[4] Since I wrote this Wolverton has made the same suggestion.

[P.S.] This is a wonderful place to me, who had only seen it in flying through, 16 years ago.

---

[1] R. W. Dixon, *History of the Church of England* (1878).
[2] Notes kept of hours slept; *Autobiographica*, iv. 63.
[3] F. Max Müller, *India, what can it teach us?* (1883).
[4] i.e. S. Smith, victor in the by-election (see 12 Dec. 82); in fact C. T. D. Acland and T. R. Buchanan moved and seconded the Address; *H* 276. 99.

21. Septa S.

St Paul's Ch mg: aftn service at house by S. Wrote to Prof. Max Müller and minutes. Read Dixon's Hist—Manning on Act of 1870[1]—Franciosi on Dante.[2] Visited M. Dognins wonderful garden, a fairy land indeed.

22. M.

Wrote to Ld Granville a long letter & a ciph. Tel. on Hns. Speech about local Government in Ireland.[3] Visited the Vallances depôt & drove all over the Antibes peninsula. Wrote on the Odyssey.—Read Dixon's History—Odyssey Bb. V. VI.—Schmidt, Ethik des Griechen[4]—Vinet, Lettres[5]—Miller, the Riviera.[6] Conversation with Ld Wolverton—D. of Argyll—Mr Wollaston[7]—Ld Acton.

23. Tu.

Wrote to W.H.G.—Messrs Cook. Saw Sir C. Murray—Count Pahlen: aged 93.[8] Suggestive of many thoughts. Read Odyssey—Dixon's Hist—Miller Riviera— Scherer on Religion. Wrote on Homer's *Ethik.* Whist in evg.

24. Wed.

Prayers 6.30 P.M. Wrote to Ld Chancellor—Sir G. Provost—Ld Spencer—Ld Aberdare—Mr Hamilton. Read Odyssey—Dixon's Hist. Ch. of England— Account of the Nevada Foot Prints[9]—Fitzgerald Family of Geo III.[10] Mr Vincent dined.[11]

To LORD SPENCER, Viceroy of Ireland, 24 January 1883.   Althorp MSS K6.

I must send you a word of congratulation on your present prospects as well as of thanks for the threefold intimation, good in each point, of your letter.[12]

I most earnestly hope that you are making real progress in the great enterprise of discovery as to the assassination societies, while I feel perfectly assured that you are on the right road.

I am also delighted to receive your confirmation of the good reports of the agrarian condition of the country, and hardly less so to know that you are so soon to emerge from the minor conflict with the speechmakers.

This is a most noteworthy place & climate & has thus far answered right well—with the aid of the immense kindness & hospitality of our hosts.

[P.S.] We were delighted to fall in with your sister coming out of Church on Sunday.

[1] *F.R.*, xii. 958 (December 1882).
[2] G. Franciosi, probably his *Dante e Raffaello* (1882).
[3] Supporting an Irish Local Govt. Bill against Hartington's cautions; Ramm II, ii. 9.
[4] L. V. Schmidt, *Die Ethik der alten Griechen*, 2v. (1882).
[5] A. Vinet, *Lettres*, 2v. (1882).
[6] W. Miller, *Wintering in the Riviera* (1879, 2nd ed. 1880).
[7] William Munro Wollaston, chaplain of St. Paul's, Cannes.
[8] Count Nicholas Pahlen, a Russian liberal *émigré.*
[9] Untraced.
[10] P. H. Fitzgerald, *The royal dukes and duchesses of the family of George III*, 2v. (1882).
[11] C. Howard Vincent, vice-consul in Cannes.
[12] Of 21 January, Add MS 44310, f. 5: evidence being gathered against secret societies.

25. *Th. Conv. St. P.*

St Paul's 11 a.m. Wrote to Ld Granville Tel. Walk with Ld Acton. Visit from the Prefet & the Mayor. Tea party: saw divers guests. Read Odyssey—Dixon's Ch. Hist.—Miller on Riviera—Family of George III. Wrote on the Reformation Crisis.[1] Whist in evg.

26. *Fr.*

Prayers 6.30 P.M. Wrote Parl. Circular—also to Ld R. Grosvenor. Read as yesterday respecting Miller & Murray's Handbook. Wrote Homeric notes. Saw Ld Acton.

27. *Sat.*

Prayers at 6.30 PM. Wrote to [blank] Finished Dixon Vol II—Read Odyssey— Family of George III—Life of Clerk Maxwell[2]—Max Müller on India. Drive to Mougins.[3] Whist in evg.

28. *Sexa S.*

St Paul's mg and service by S.E.G. evg. Read Scherer's Melanges de Critique Religieuse[4]—Life of Clerk Maxwell. Saw Prince of Wales—Count de Paris: to whom I spoke freely on the Floquet &c proposals.[5] Wrote to Dr Clark—Ld Granville. Conversation with Ld W[olverton] on the ideas afloat in the Cabinet.

29. *M.*

Prayers 6.30 P.M. Wrote to Ld Granville Tel—Mr Hamilton Tel. Read Odyssey—Scherer—Max Müller on India. Steamed to St Marguérite (Lerins).[6] Conversation with Ld Acton. Whist in evg.

30. *Tu.*

Wrote to E. Hamilton—Lady S. Opdebeeck—Rev. Mr Wilkinson. Read Od.— Scherer—Max Müller—Life of Clerk Maxwell—Carden Costituzione Inglese.[7] Prince of Wales came to [*sc.* from] Mentone—Conversation with him—D. of Vallombrosa—Mrs Viner.[8] Whist in evg. Studied on suggestions for the Queen's Speech.

---

[1] On Elizabeth and Laud, 'humanly speaking the creators in one sum [? sense] of Anglicanism'; Add MS 44767, f. 50 (misplaced).

[2] L. Campbell and W. Garnett, *The life of James Clerk Maxwell* (1882).

[3] Inland from Cannes.

[4] By E. H. A. Scherer (1860).

[5] Charles Thomas Floquet's bill to expell Bourbons and Bonapartist princes, though eventually rejected, began crisis which led to the Ferry ministry of 21 February.

[6] Island off Cannes.

[7] R. Cardon, *Svolgimento storico della costituzione inglese*, 2v. (1883).

[8] Eleanor, wife of Robert Charles de Grey Vyner of York (relative of Ripon); established quite a close relationship with the Gladstones.

31. Wed.

Prayers 6½ P.M. Wrote to Ld Granville (2)—Ld Ripon Tel—Bp of St Davids. Drove to Antibes. Read Od—Scherer—Cardon. Whist in evg. Saw D. of Argyll & took him to M. Dognins Garden. My letters of today to G. with some notes for a Q. Speech define my attitude in regard to the present retention of office.[1]

Feb. One (Thurs) 1883

Prayers 5.30 P.M. Wrote to Ld Granville Tel—Mr Hamilton Tel—Ld Chancellor—Dean of Ch.Ch. and minutes. Read Od.—Scherer—Clerk Maxwell. Drive to Esterelles.[2] Long evening's conversation with Argyll.

2. Fr.

Prayers 6.30 P.M. Read as yesterday. Wrote to Granville Tel and others. Cabinet on the important letters from London.[3] Walk with Acton: calls: saw Sir J. Macneile and Lady E.[4]

3. Sat.

Prayers 6.30 P.M. Wrote to Ld Granville l.l.—Ld Hartington—Mad. Loyson—Ld Spencer. Read Od—Scherer—Max Müller's India. Whist in evg. Drive to the Estrelles. Saw Italian Consul (Nice): conversation on Cyprus and Sinobombaci.[5]

To LORD HARTINGTON, war secretary,   Chatsworth MSS 340. 1320.
3 February 1883.[6] 'Secret'.

I have read your letter to Granville in which your view on the formidable difference lately developed is exhibited with your usual force and frankness.

Formidable it is, in my mind, for your contention cuts deep down into my elementary and fixed ideas; it seems to me to revive in principle the opposition offered in 1836-8 to the establishment of elective municipalities in Ireland, and indeed to be hard to reconcile with the policy as a whole which has been pursued towards Ireland in and since 1829.

However, I hope the suggestion I have made for the speech may be thought suitable to give us time, and time, which is a great teacher, may disclose much and alter much between this date and Easter.

You do not deal with the considerations stated by me in my letter to Granville of Jan. 22, and I need not now refer to them, but I will notice one or two matters suggested by your letter to him.

It is highly probable that there was no discussion in the Cabinet on the paragraph of Jan. 1881 but this could only be because all were agreed.

It was only when the Session of that year was considerably advanced that Forster abandoned the idea of bringing in his Bill.

[1] i.e. if either local govt. generally or 'Franchise and Redistribution' forms the chief measure of the Queen's Speech, he would probably have to retire at Easter because of their complexity; London govt. 'might' suffice for the present year' if combined with Irish local govt.; Ramm II, ii. 14.
[2] Mountains between Cannes and Fréjus.
[3] Queen's suggestion via Granville that he take a peerage; declined next day; Ramm II, ii. 16.
[4] i.e. Argyll's sister and her husband; see 11 Dec. 59n.
[5] Probably sic; obscure.
[6] Printed in Holland, i. 390 together with part of Hartington to Granville, 30 January 1883.

We did not omit the subject in 1882 but while announcing positively a measure for England and Wales we announced that it would apply financially to Scotland but that the case of Ireland (and this was essential in regard to finance) would be reserved for a separate consideration.

This fell short of an absolute promise for the session of 1882, but neither was it, nor was it taken to be, a retreat from the ground taken in 1881, and it seems hardly compatible with the policy recently announced by you, at least it would have been pushing reticence very far, if we had used such words with such a policy in our minds. Nor was such a policy, I believe, even mooted in the Cabinet.

Accordingly, when challenged on the subject in the course of the Session, I, without doubt or question, referred to the state of business as the reason why we had not redeemed the pledge of 1881, and expressed my hopes of its early redemption. I have no words before me, but I believe I have not overstated the general effect.

Owing probably to the circumstances of the time preceding my departure, I do not know the precise point up to which Chamberlain may have gone in a recent speech. But I looked at my son Herbert's words and I do not think he used any words which went beyond his just liberty or, viewing his position, could tend to commit or hamper the Government.

If, however, I understand rightly Forster's language, he contemplates as impending a measure of local Government for Ireland; and his voice is an important one in the matter.

I had a long conversation with Argyll last night. His general tone is unaltered: but not only did he seem to have no idea of withholding local government from Ireland, but he even glanced quite spontaneously at the idea of some kind of Irish legislature as a thing which might have to be entertained.

Lorne is a person sufficiently conservative, but a short time ago he wrote me a remarkable letter, in which, from his Canadian experience, he recommended a *large* allowance of local government to Ireland.[1]

In my opinion one of the most vitally important objects we have attained since we took office has been splitting the Home Rule party and reducing it for all practical purposes from (say) 65 to 40. What will the section now with us say if we make such an announcement as you seemed to shadow forth? Indeed, I am not very sure what our Ulster men would say.

I admit that the pledges of the Government have touched County Government only, and that my leaning to Provincial Assemblies (or some combination of counties) is an ulterior development. I am told that this was Lord Russell's plan. I can readily believe it, for, regarding the scheme as Conservative, I incline to consider this form of it the most Conservative. Whether any special power of control ought to be reserved is a matter open, I think, to consideration, on which I could not at once say aye or no.

These remarks are made by way of clearing the ground; but what I hope for is a breathing time, during which none of us should in any respect commit himself in advance of what has been said or done.

To LORD SPENCER, Viceroy of Ireland, 3 February 1883.　　　　　　Althorp MSS K6.
'*Secret*'.[2]

1. Ingenuousness on your side, and confidence on mine, cause us I think to correspond together with a total absence of reserve, and I ask you therefore to believe that in what I said to you, or to Granville, about your dealings with the M.P.s I had *neither* the slightest idea that it was your duty to consult with me beforehand (the difficulty or practical

[1] See 17 May 83 for Lorne's later contribution.
[2] First part in *Spencer*, i. 240.

responsibility of which I can well conceive), nor had I come to any conclusion that the steps were wrong, though I had misgivings. Argyll, who was here last night, referred to the Biggar case and thought it imprudent. I only replied that your position was difficult, but you believed this measure had done good. I must add that he most *warmly* praised your work in Ireland.

2. As regards local Government while I am grieved to find your view has been modified in a sense adverse to mine, yet I hope I have sent to Granville a suggestion which will give us time; and, apart from this, it is a real pleasure to read a statement so candid, and so clear, as that which you have written. Nor need I, as I feel confident, give you any fresh assurance of my disposition to give due weight to your authority.

Further my difference with you is less wide than it *may* (or may not) prove to be with Hartington for it is a question of the year only, whereas were we to say we would give no more franchise or local powers to Ireland until we were satisfied that they were to be used in a different manner, I think the consequences of this would be what has so often happened. We should go in like a lion, and come out like a lamb, and the end would be a highly inconvenient if not perilous triumph of Irish Nationalism at a very early date, on a rather large scale.

Still I must own that the question, even when narrowed to one of a comparatively short time, is grave enough—(a) on account of our pledges, (b) on account of the probable sentiments of our Irish Liberals, including those whom we have detached from the extreme party, (c) on account of the urgent need on imperial grounds, of beginning to give an Irish character to Irish authority in local matters, (d) and of the yet more urgent, if perhaps not greater, necessity of setting up in Ireland bodies which can deal with us on behalf of Ireland, & with a real Irish responsibility, in regard to the pressing & even menacing questions of public works, peasant proprietary, loans to cultivators, emigration, & the like. These are matters which it will be most difficult to deal with by mere postponement. You look ⟨upon⟩ at this question from a point of view set in Dublin; I from the floor of the H. of Commons. Yet I must add that I have little faith in the expectation that the country wd. be helped to settle down by our abstinence from legislation which we have promised, & have admitted to be needful & perhaps urgent. I should look to the proposing of a good scheme of local Govt. as a much more composing treatment, independent of my desire to get a good Irish buffer placed between the Imperial authority & those numerous wants of Ireland which have always pressed hard upon us, & for which we are in danger of becoming more & more responsible.

I send you herewith a copy of a letter which I have written to Hartington. Waiting an intimation from Granville as to the time when I am to return. . . .

4. *Quinqua S.*

St Pauls mg & aft—H.C.—& good preaching. Between Churches, luncheon with Mrs Vyner, met Lady Queensberry,[1] whose gentle sorrow is so deeply interesting. Then to the Argylls. After service saw Mad. Loyson. Wrote to Ld Hartington—Mr Hamilton—W.H.G. Read Scherer—Ritschl, Rechtfertigung[2]—Scott Hollands Sermon[3]—Kennedy's do.[4]

---

[1] Sybil, wife of 8th marquis of Queensberry (known for boxing, adultery and pursuit of O. Wilde); she divorced him in 1887.
[2] A. Ritschl, *Die Christliche Lehre von der Rechtfertigung und Versöhnung*, 3v. (1870-4).
[3] H. S. Holland, 'In memoriam' (1883); on Pusey.
[4] B. H. Kennedy, 'The divinity of Christ' (1883).

5. M.

Off at eleven to Grasse & Gourdon,[1] under the auspices of Mr Cross.[2] The first sight is wonderful; but the precipices were too sharp for my poor head[3] & I turned back: Ld Acton would kindly come with me. Much conversation with him & with Mr Cross. Back at 7.30. Whist in evg. Read Od.—Scherer—Life of Knox[4]—Rev. 2 Mondes on Bosnia &c.[5]

6. Tu.

Wrote to Sir J. Stephen—Ld Granville Tel—Professor Jebb. The whole after-noon was devoted to the Carnival at Nice, a strange, fantastic, but wondrous sight. Was pelted largely. Great attention from the Prefet, The Consul & others. The Prefet drove us through & round the town, which is really splendid. Read Od.—Scherer—Memoirs of Knox—Life of C. Maxwell—Max Müller—De Rongé (France).[6] Whist in evg.

To Professor R. C. JEBB, 6 February 1883.   Add MS 44546, f. 77.

The paper you have sent me is most interesting.[7] My opinions on the various points would be of no value were I rash enough to conclude with confidence upon them, but when the proper time comes I shall be happy to subscribe.

The only point on which I am tempted to remark is the relation of the scheme to the Government and to the Universities. The great endowments existing in England create a broad difference between our case and that of France or Germany. This you have frankly recognised in contemplating public subscription as your main resource. But I should have thought more might be expected, than your paper contemplates, from the official action, so to call it, of the Universities, in respect both of authority, and of funds. This only by the way.

I hope for a meeting with you in London later in the year.

To Sir J. F. STEPHEN, 6 February 1883.   Add MS 44546, f. 77.

I thank you very much for your kindness in sending what must be an important as well as interesting work, the History you have just published of Criminal Law and I hope to derive much advantage from it.[8]

With regard to the interference of the State for the protection of Religion against offence, I remember a *dictum* of O'Connell's in 1833[9] which made a deep and operative impression upon me at the time though my prejudices against him were strong and irrational. It was to this effect, spoken of course from the point of view appropriate to a man who believed in full: that when the State, in a Christian country, had by law allowed

---

[1] Village in the mountains N. of Cannes.
[2] John Walter Cross, widower and biographer of George Eliot; see *Mary Gladstone*, 279.
[3] For Gladstone's vertigo, see above, v. lvi.
[4] Unclear which; probably J. J. Hornby, *Remains of Alexander Knox*, 4v. (1834–7).
[5] *Revue des Deux Mondes*, lv. 535 (February 1883).
[6] Possibly P. Deroulède, *Chants patriotiques* (1882).
[7] On the proposed 'English' School in Athens, Add MS 44479, f. 178; see 18 May, 25 June 83.
[8] Sent with a letter pointing out chapters of particular interest, 1 February, Add MS 44479, f. 190.
[9] In fact on 18 Feb. 1834, quoted by Gladstone in the Bradlaugh deb. on 26 April; *H* 278. 1190.

the Divinity of our Saviour to be denied, it was on religious as well as non-religious grounds an error to impose any other limitation.

[P.S.] I am not sure which of your pre-names you commonly used, but I am pleased to address you by that which belonged to your father [i.e. Sir James].

7. Ash Wed.

Trinity Ch 11 a.m. Wrote to Ld Granville Tel—and 1. Luncheon at Ld Acton's. Drive and long conversation with him—personal & political & religious. Read Od—Life of Clerk Maxwell—Max Müller—Pinkerton on Spy System in Amn War.[1]

8. Th.

Prayers 6½ P.M. Wrote to Ld Granville l.l. & Tel: after much thought & consultation.[2] Also E. Hamilton—Dean of Westminster—Chancr of Exr—Mad. Loyson and minutes. Took a party to the Dognin Garden. Saw M. Dognin—Ld Acton—Duke of Argyll—Mrs Crawford[3]—M. Clemenceau.[4] Read Od.—Clerk Maxwell—Pinkerton. Lady W[olverton']s party—Whist in evg.

9. Fr.

St Paul's [chapel] 3 P.M. Wrote to Sec. [Archbishop] Tait Memorial. Wrote on Phoenicianism in Ithaca.[5] Saw Comte de Paris—Duke of Argyll—M. Clemenceau. Read Odyssey—Clerk Maxwell (finished)—Argyll on the Highlands[6]—The Month—divers articles.

10. Sat.

Prayers 6½ P.M. Wrote to Prince of Wales—Ld Hartington—Comte de Paris l.l.—E. Hamilton 1 & Tel.—Mr Childers—Sig. Mancini. Read Odyss—Scherer—Life of A. Nasmyth.[7] Drive to Piguemas.[8] Dinner party.[9] Whist in evg. Made notes for Clerk Maxwell's life.[10] Saw Pere Hyacinthe.

---

[1] A. Pinkerton, *The spy of the rebellion* (1883).

[2] Responding amiably but cautiously to Granville's assurance that there was no plot to keep him in Cannes till Easter so as to shelve Irish local govt.; Ramm II, ii. 20.

[3] Emily Crawford, Paris correspondent of the *Daily News*, who reported the conversation on France, Ireland and decentralization with Clemenceau in *D.N.*, 12 February 1883, 5c; Hamilton told Harcourt, 17 February 1883, MS Harcourt dep. Adds 10: 'Mrs Crawford was, as you rightly supposed, the culprit'; pressing herself on Gladstone *via* Wolverton despite Acton's warning, she 'overheard inaccurately part of the conversation'.

[4] Georges Clemenceau, 1841-1929; then leader of the Radical Republicans against Ferry's 'opportunism'.

[5] Not found.

[6] Argyll, 'On the economic condition of the Highlands', *N.C.*, xiii. 173 (February 1883).

[7] *James Nasmyth. An autobiography*, ed. S. Smiles (1883).

[8] Sc. Pégomas, N.W. of Cannes.

[9] Probably that reported (chiefly Clemenceau's remarks on France) in *D.N.*, 12 February 1883, 5c.

[10] Add MS 44767, f. 8.

To LORD HARTINGTON, war secretary, 10 February 1883.   Add MS 44546, f. 77.

I have telegraphed this day a reference to my letter of Thursday to Granville which conveys my idea of the decided reticence with which any pressing inquiry about local institutions in Ireland may & should be met.[1]

I am almost disposed, though it is hazardous, to generalise & say that in regard to measures which are of a rank to come into the Speech, but are not named or promised in it, one should never, at the opening of the Session, go beyond the speech itself, in one direction or another. Indeed it is commonly unsafe to give explanations about those measures which are promised.

With regard to the dinner on Wednesday, Hamilton will attend to any directions you may give & convey them to our Housekeeper, who, having been with us for 40 years, knows pretty well what to do, although there is not a man-servant on the ground except a Butler & a boy; to be aided by some ex-Butlers, now married, & messengers.

You will I have no doubt give the proper intimations to your mover & seconder. I should say the rule is to tie them pretty tightly to the speech in all which they will seem to say by inspiration and for the Government, but to leave them a reasonable liberty in what they may desire to say for & from themselves.

Pray do not think yourself bound to answer my letters, unless it be upon points which you may consider to require it with reference to some present or necessary object.

[P.S.] You will I daresay hear more about Healy's Bill[2] which may or may not be important.

To P. S. MANCINI, 10 February 1883.   Add MS 44546, f. 78.

I am very sensible of the kindness which has prompted the letter you have written to me on the part of the Italian Government as well as your own, and I hardly know how to thank sufficiently His Majesty the King for having been pleased to express an interest in my health.[3]

Through my long political life sleep has been to me a mainstay, and the failure of it, for the first time between November and January last led me [to] take what is rather a violent measure for one holding my office, and to place myself here for some weeks. The air of the place, and exemption from business carried as far as it could be, have done me great good.

I need hardly assure you, Sir, of the pleasure with which I contemplate the progress of Italy, and the consolidation of the Kingdom and the nationality. These sentiments are deeply rooted in my heart and I feel confident that the chill of old age will not affect the real fervour with which I entertain them.

To the COMTE DE PARIS, 10 February 1883.   Add MS 44479, f. 206.

I take the liberty of informing Your Royal Highness that I saw M. Clemenceau yester-day evening, & had some conversation with him. It turned principally upon Egypt but it also touched the Bill now before the Senate.[4] He expressed to me a perfect confidence that the rejection would not be followed by a dissolution. He stated that it was as positively known that M. Grevy was annoyed, & even angry about the statements of Press

---

[1] Ramm II, i. 22: statement in the Speech not to be expanded for the present.

[2] For Irish County Councils; see 7 Apr. 83.

[3] Mancini (see 8 Sept. 51) was now foreign minister; for his good wishes, see Add MS 44479, f. 169.

[4] See 28 Jan. 83.

Reporters that he intended to dissolve. I asked him whether then, in his opinion, there would be no result from the late proceedings & the Bill. He answered none, unless that it would quicken the movement for the revision of the Constitution. Then I said as to the Bill itself & the affair connected with it, will it be *tombé par terre?*[1] He said yes, repeating the phrase.

11. 1 S. Lent.

St Paul's mg & aft. Luncheon at Mrs Vyner's. Saw The Prince of Wales—Mrs Praed Campbell & much conversation with Mrs V. whom I much like. Read Scherer Crit. Relig—Geraud, Unithéisme[2]—Bp Sandford Past. Letter[3]—Winn on Darwinism &c.[4] Wrote to D. of Argyll—Sir W. Harcourt.

To Sir W. V. HARCOURT, home secretary,					MS Harcourt dep. Adds 10.
11 February 1883.

I have not yet read the article in the Times to which you refer:[5] but I can assure you that I should have inferred, and probably believed, what you tell me, if you had not so thoroughly taken the trouble to assure me of it.

I am deeply indebted to you, as well as to all my colleagues, for the solicitude you have shown on my behalf, and I much regret that it should entail on them labour and inconvenience beyond the usual measure.

We have here floods of rain. If you have the same in England, I fear it will be to the great detriment of the farmers and the land at a critical season.

12. M.

Prayers 6½ P.M. Wrote to Ld Colchester—Mr Childers Tel and minutes. Dejeuner with Comte de Paris: they seem all so domestic & unworldly. Walk with Ld Acton: a most satisfactory mind. Wrote on Odyssey. Read Od.—Scherer (finished)—Falloux, Discours et Melanges[6]—Pinkerton on U.S. War—Hatch on Canonical Obedience.[7] Acton dined: much conversation.

13. Tu.

Prayers 6½ P.M. Wrote to Professor de Marzo[8]—Nice Postmaster—Mr Sands[9]—Dean of St Paul's—Mr Hamilton—Sir J. Lacaita. Walk with the Wolvertons, discussing sites. Whist in evg. Read Odyss—Falloux (much)—Lady Bloomfield[10]—Gneist, Verfassungsgeschichte[11]—Glasson, Hist. du Droit. [12]

---

[1] 'entombed'.
[2] P. Géraud, *L'Unitéisme, religion universelle* (1882).
[3] By C. W. Sandford (1882).
[4] J. M. Winn, *Darwin* (1883).
[5] Letter of 9 February, Add MS 44198, f. 1, on *T.T.* article on London govt.
[6] F. A. P. de Falloux, *Discours et Mélanges politiques*, 2v. (1882).
[7] E. Hatch, 'Canonical obedience', *C.R.*, xliii. 289 (February 1883).
[8] Antonio Gualberto de Marzo, professor in Florence; published extensively on Dante.
[9] M. Sands of Jamaica, on land there; Add MS 44546, f. 79.
[10] G. Bloomfield, *Reminiscences of court and diplomatic life*, 2v. (1883).
[11] H. R. von Gneist, *Englische Verfassungsgeschichte* (1882).
[12] E. D. Glasson, *Histoire du Droit . . . de l'Angleterre*, 6v. (1881-3).

14. Wed.

Prayers 6½ P.M. Today I feel dual—I am at Cannes & in D. St at my dinner.[1] Wrote to Prefet des Alpes Mar[itimes][2]—Ld Granville—Mr Childers—Mr Hamilton—Welldon [*sic*]—Rev. Mr Wilkinson—Sir W. Harcourt and minutes. Read Odyssey (finished)—Scherer's Alex. Vinet[3]—Do. Falloux Mélanges—Lady Bloomfield. Long walk with Acton. Whist in evg.

15 Th.

Prayers 6½ P.M. There is a noise at Westminster, & I hear it not![4] Wrote to Mr Childers l. & Tel.—Ld Granville—Ld Wolseley—Mr Hamilton Tel.—Notes on Mrs Crawford.[5] Calls: saw the Brougham Villa:[6] Lady Wolverton's party. Read Scherer's Vinet—Fortnightly on Affairs—on HL of Lords—Wilberforce— Wilberforce & Westbury[7]—Ly Bloomfield, Reminiscences. Whist in evg.

To H. C. E. CHILDERS, chancellor of the exchequer,   Add MS 44546, f. 80.
15 February 1883.

1. Since my message of today,[8] reflection has given me a little more light on the Healy matter. I seem to see why (probably) I refused Parnell. It was to reserve intact to the power of the House of Commons, which might have chosen to deal itself with its own member legally convicted of a great criminal *offence*. Unless it is thought (which I should hardly think) that in this instance a similar desire might be felt, I should think it difficult to refuse Healy's application; while it would of course be best that the question should not arise.

2. I am sorry to find you could not avoid a further augmentation of the regular estimates. Of course the 12000 tons[9] must have been sanctioned on the merits, & not because they were deemed a fit rate in 1869 (in comparing with large reductions). 3. I by no means press, or can adhere to, the opinion that the 500 m.[10] should be charged against the outstanding increment of Income Tax 1883–4; under the circumstances which you mention.

16. Fr.

Prayers 6½ PM. Read Vlasto's deeply interesting Derniers Jours[11]—Ly Bloomfield's Rem. Whist in evg. 9½–4¼. Trip in steamer: weather middling. We went among the French Ironclads. Then at St Honorat saw the Church, old cloister 8th Cent, & convent of 11th Cent. strikingly situated. Over the cell doors in the modern convent were names of special saints with special virtues: the last was

---

[1] i.e. the eve of session dinner.
[2] Sending his Midlothian speeches; Add MS 44546, f. 80.
[3] E. H. A. Scherer, *Alexandre Vinet* (1853).
[4] Parliament met this day.   [5] Not found; see 8 Feb. 83.
[6] Villa Eléonore-Louise; Brougham popularised Cannes, wintering there from 1834.
[7] All in *F.R.*, xxxix (February 1883).
[8] Not found.
[9] Of Ironclads, agreed as the annual amount in 1869; Add MS 44130, f. 208.
[10] Include 'the £500,000 in the Suppl. Estimate for this year (1882–3) and start fair next year'; ibid.
[11] E. A. Vlasto, *Les derniers jours de Constantinople* (1883); sent through Madame Loyson; Add MS 44479, f. 200.

Les SS. Anges
Vertu
La Chasteté.

Strange! in every way. Then we looked at Napoule & returned. Walk with Ld Acton. Wrote to [blank.]

17. Sat.

Prayers 6½ P.M. Wrote to W.H.G.—Bp of St David's—Ld Granville. Shopping & visited Savile Villa with its magnificent view. Read Iliad—Derniers Jours, finished. Visited Sir G. Elliot—[read] Lady Bloomfield—Encycl. Sciences Religieuses. Dinner party.

18 2 S. Lent.

St Paul's Ch. 11 AM (H.C.) & 3 P.M. Luncheon at Mrs Vyner's: a person to be much liked. Wrote to Mr Smith. Read Lilly on the Religion of the Future[1]—Huet, Scepticisme[2]—Scherer's Vinet.

19. M.

Prayers 6½ P.M. Dinner party. Whist in evg. Long walk with Ld Acton in the rain. Read Lady Bloomfield—Knox Introdn to Historical papers[3]—Iliad—Huet et le Scepticisme. Wrote to. . . .

20. Tu.

Prayers 6½ PM. Wrote to Ld Granville Tel.—and minutes. Visited Villa Clementieu. Whist in evg. Read Iliad—Huet &c—Knox—Ly Bloomfield—Worked on Iliad. Read also the long and harrowing particulars of the Saturday illuminations at Kilmainham.[4]

21. Wed.

Prayers 6½ PM. Wrote to Ld Lyons—Ld Granville l. & tel.—Mr Hamilton—Duke of Argyll—& minutes. Drive to Mrs Holland's—and to Auribeau:[5] such a dreary solitude. One old beggar in the street with downward gaze: & a class of boys through the windows of the school. Conversation with Lord Acton. Read Iliad—Huet, et le Scept. (finished)—Knox's Introduction—Lady Bloomfield. Dinner party: whist.

22. Th.

Prayers 6½ P.M. Wrote to W.H.G., MP.—H.J.G., M.P.—Mr Wilkinson—Rev. N. Pococke[6]—Mr W. Egerton Tatton—& minutes. Saw Lady Galloway—Gen.

---

[1] In C.R., xliii. 204 (February 1883).
[2] Perhaps C. Bartholmess, *Huet, ou le scepticisme théologique* (1850).
[3] T. F. Knox, *The letters . . . of William Cardinal Allen, with an historical introduction* (1882).
[4] Opening of the Phoenix Park murder trial; James Carey, in 'a startling surprise', turned Queen's evidence; *T.T.*, 19 February 1883, 6d.   [5] Inland, N.W. of Cannes.
[6] See 29 Jan. 49; his many works 'not remunerative'; Gladstone sent him £250 'from a small public fund at my command'; Add MS 44546, f. 83.

Tchetchaieff?—Sig. Rignawic?[1]—Duchess of Vallombrosa—Sir J. Keatinge—& others at the afternoon gathering. Read Iliad—Scherer's Vinet (finished)—Knox's Introduction—Lady Bloomfield. Walk with Ld Acton. Calls. Saw Ld Cardwell—a sad spectacle, monitory of our lot.[2]

23. Fr.

Wrote to Bp of Ripon—The Queen—Mr Hamilton—Mrs Th.—& minutes. Read Iliad—Lady Bloomfield—Knox's Introdn (finished). Expedition to Grasse and St Cessaire: of much interest & much beauty. NB dogtooth ornament on the Church. We were out seven hours, or more.

24. Sat.

Wrote to Ld. G. (Tel.)—Lucy Cavendish—Chef de Gare at Nice. Read Iliad—Lady Bloomfield (finished). Went to Nice, then in Col. Farquharson's[3] [yacht] Titania all along the coast to La Colla near San Remo, examining the points as we went along, especially that wicked San [sc. Monte] Carlo,[4] and its new Church. The sea & sky were all we could desire. Out 8½ hours. Saw Duke of Argyll—Lord Acton.

25. 3 S. Lent.

St Paul's mg & Ch.Ch. aftn. Luncheon at Mrs Vyner's & many farewells. Called on Count Pahlen. Visited the old Church. Saw Ld Acton. Read Scottish Review on Abp Tait—Scottish Theology—Celtic Hymns (Ld Bute)[5]—De Cornelia, La Religione[6]—Small's Versions in Verse.[7]

26. M. [On train]

I part from Cannes with a heavy heart. Wrote to M. Dognin—and minutes. Saw M. Dollfuss—Ed. Petit Marseillais. Read The Iliad—copiously. Off by the 12.30 train. We exchanged bright sun, splendid views, & a little dust, at the beginning of our journey, for frost & fog, which however hid no scenery, at the end.

27. Tu. [British Embassy, Paris]

Reached Paris at 8, & drove to the Embassy, where we had a most kind reception. Wrote to Ld Granville Tel. & l.—Ld Spencer—Sir W. Harcourt. Went with Ld L[yons] to see M. Grevy: also Challemel Lacour[8] in his most palatial abode.

[1] *Sic*; neither identified.
[2] He d. 1886 after 'a very lingering illness' (*D.N.B.*), having lost his mind.
[3] Probably James Ross Farquarson of Invercauld; see 3 Sept. 84n.
[4] Aristocratic gambling at Monte Carlo was a concern of both Gladstone and the Queen; see, e.g. Guedalla, *Q*, ii. 168.
[5] *Scottish Review*, i. 236 (February 1883).
[6] Perhaps G. V. Pilati de Cornelio, *La rincarnazione* (1882).
[7] J. Small, *The Monarche and other poems of Sir D. Lindesay* (1883).
[8] François-Paul-Jules Grévy, 1813–91; president of the republic 1879–87; Paul-Armand Challemel-Lacour, 1827–96; ambassador in London 1880–2; foreign minister 1883. Neither interview was rewarding, see Ramm II, ii. 33.

Looked about, among the shops: & at the sad face of the Tuileries. An Embassy party to dinner: excellent company. Read Iliad—2½ B[ooks]—M'Kenzie, Highland Clearances.[1]

To Sir W. V. HARCOURT, home secretary,   MS Harcourt dep. 9, f. 2.
27 February 1883.

I thank you for your letter[2] and though what I have written to Granville has certainly been the expression of an opinion which I hold not doubtfully, I shall be most desirous to know your views and reasons in full, which I think have not yet been before me. I propose also on my return to revert to your paper, which I remember as a very able one, and to the reply I made with respect to which as I have such ready means of reference I had better not trust my recollection.

The prolongation of proceedings on the Address is provoking. It makes me doubt whether I had not better postpone my arrival until Friday; as I have the notion that my coming before the Address and Report are out of the way might have a tendency to stir up the embers.

[P.S.] I make no doubt you have borne in mind Sir George Grey's failure to absorb the City Police when he made the effort.

To LORD SPENCER, Viceroy of Ireland, 27 February 1883.   Althorp MSS K6.

Many thanks for your letter.[3] I was desirous you should know how strongly and clearly I was with you about Carey. The question is something like that of Parnell's release: there could not be any doubt (in our view) as to the right thing, but it was not quite pleasant to do.[4]

The wanton consumption of all this time in retrospective debate on the Address has materially cut into the available time of the Session, and abridging our means of action has given force to the dilatory argument on every difficult measure.

It is a happy circumstance that Lucy finds comfort (as I *hoped* she would) in the idea that her husband's life was not deliberately aimed at. She sees Providence where others see accident, and strange indeed was the series of such accidents, if they are so to be called, that brought about the loss of a life which every day I feel to have been more and more precious to the country.

Your observation on Sheridan is full of force. Naturally I have things in me to say on the recent Debates, but they are better unsaid, and therefore am better away until the House is clear of the subject.

Though I feel it rather presumptuous to differ, I cannot help hoping that we need *not* look for reprisals in consequence of the Kilmainham revelations.

I go as a good deal by the Molly Maguire case in Pennsylvania, and also by what seems to me the reason of the thing.

Jenkinson seems to have rendered splendid service. After my conversation in London[5] I am not at all surprised. He made on me the most decided as well as most favourable impression.

[P.S.] Your brother seemed to need some change: I hope Cannes will do for him what it has done for me.

---

[1] A. Mackenzie, *History of the Highland clearances . . . and verbatim report of the trial of the brave crofters* (1883).
[2] Of 24 February, on the metropolitan police; Add MS 44198, f. 3.
[3] Of 22 February, Add MS 44310, f. 10.
[4] See 20 Feb. 83n.   [5] See 28 Nov. 82.

28. *Wed.*

Wrote to Ld Granville l. & Tel.—Ld Wolverton—Canon Rawlinson—Dean of St Paul's & minutes. Saw M. Leon Say—M. Waddington—M. Jules Ferry[1]—Mr Challemel Lacour—Mr Plunkett. Parties at luncheon and dinner. Read Homer Il.—Mackenzie's Narrative—De Lisle on Libri frauds.[2]

Th. Mch One 1883.

Wrote to Ld Hartington—Ld Granville—M. De Lisle—Ld Mount-temple—Mr Childers Tel.—Mr Miles—& minutes. Visited the Louvre—St. Clotilde. Bought at Justin's. Saw Prince Orloff—Ld Lyons—Mrs Craven. Read Iliad (Largely)—Mackenzie on Highlands. The Cravens & others dined.

2. *Fr.* [*London*]

At nine (or after) we bad farewell to our most kind host and by six we were safely landed in D. St. A bright day & rapid passage. Read the Iliad: & the Correspondant on Bismarck.[3] Saw Ld Granville—Ld Hartington—W.H.G.—Mr Childers—H.J.G.

3. *Sat.*

Wrote to The Queen l.l.—Mr Childers—Abp of Canty—Mrs Gardiner—Ld Kimberley—Mrs Craven—Ld Blachford—Sir S. Northcote—& minutes. Saw Ld Chancellor—Ld Granville—Ld Carlingford—Ld E. Clinton—Sir H. Ponsonby—Ld R. Grosvenor—Mr Hamilton—Mr Westell. 11¾-3½. To Windsor for the Council, & Audience of H.M. Read Iliad—Mrs Craven on Salvation Army—Sir R. Temple on Indian Local Govt.[4]

To Mrs. P. M. A. A. CRAVEN,[5] 3 March 1883.   Add MS 44546, f. 85.

Your article,[6] for which many thanks, is most interesting: your appreciation of the Salvation Army, like Cardinal Manning's, is I think, fair & just, notwithstanding the heavy slap you could not help administering in the last sentences: & about the poor *ministres anglicans*, & what they ought to have done for so susceptible a people, I will say nothing at all, except that no church on earth has had grosser abuses than the English, or has more gallantly rallied itself against them, in this last half century, through the action mainly of its clergy.

The citation from the Archbishop of Capua is strikingly eloquent. But this would be a flattering & not a truthful epistle, were it to close here. My controversial words however shall not be for the Church to which I belong. I find the Archbishop's eloquent & pious peroration a fatal, & too common, defect. It handles the controversy between the Church

---

[1] Jules Ferry, 1832–93; had on 17 Feb. formed an 'opportunist' ministry which lasted till 1885.
[2] On the Ashburnham collection; 'I have had the advantage of conversing with M. Jules Ferry & M. Waddington on the subject'; to Miss De Lisle, 1 March 1882, Add MS 44546, f. 85.
[3] No copy found.
[4] *C.R.*, xliii. 373 (March 1883).
[5] See 30 Sept. 45n.
[6] In *Le Correspondant*, 25 February 1883; see *Life of Mrs. Augustus Craven* (1894), ii. 134 and Manning in *C.R.*, lxii. 335 (September 1882).

& the Age as if all the right were on one side & all the wrong on the other. Doubtless he believes it is so that right & wrong are in this world partitioned. Life & thought have taught me another lesson: & I fear that for much of what is dangerous, & may prove ruinous, in the spirit & tendencies of our time, not Christians only but only, & not Churches only, but the rulers of Churches, are largely if not mainly responsible. I am a traditionist. But tradition is history. *Somebody* has said that to appeal to history is treason. In my opinion it *is* treason; all but the *t*.[1]

4. 4 S. Lent.

Chapel Royal noon (with H.C.) & aftn. Dined with the Phillimore's. Saw Sir R.P.—Walter P.—the Farquhars—Mr M'Coll (on Palmer's work). Read Dean Bradley's Three Lectures on Stanley[2]—Quaker Anecdotes.[3]

5. M.

Wrote to Messrs Miles—The Queen l.l.—& minutes. Cabinet 2–4. H. of C. $4\frac{3}{4}-7\frac{1}{2}$ and $9-12\frac{1}{2}$.[4] Resumed work with heavy mind. Saw Mr Hamilton—Ld RG—Rev Mr Wilkinson—The Speaker—Mr Childers. Read Contemp. Rev. (Rae) on Highland Crofters.[5]

Cabinet. Mch 5. 1883. 2 PM[6]

✓   1. Order of business. H of C.

ansr. for	a. Supply
today	
anxious to	
go forward	b. 2nd Readings of Grand Committee Bills
in the C.	
but do not expect	
to read 2° before Easter	c. Affirmation

2. Bright Clauses. H of L. see my mem.
   Commission?   agreed with
   Committee   Granville.[7]

3. Indian Guard. Difficulties cropped up.[8]

✓   4. Layard's Case. Cabinet generally of opinion that under the circs. he shd not be appointed to Rome.[9]

5. Commercial Treaties. (E. Fitzmaurice is to manage Commercial Dept.) No

---

[1] Mrs. Craven replied, 6 March, Add MS 44479, f. 300, largely agreeing, but defending the abp.: 'truth abides, as *we* think, only complete in the Church [i.e. the Roman catholic church] ... how much I enjoyed that hour's conversation with you the other day, reminding me of those of 45 years ago!!!'

[2] G. G. Bradley, *Recollections of A. P. Stanley* (1883).

[3] By R. Pike (3rd ed. 1881).

[4] Spoke on Egypt, Transvaal; *H* 276. 1448, 1552.

[5] *C.R.*, xliii. 357 (March 1883).

[6] Add MS 44644, f. 2; attached note by Hamilton: 'I have reason to think that a caution to Sir C. Dilke as to absolute secrecy of Cabinet proceedings would be desirable.'

[7] Not found, though see note at end of this Cabinet.

[8] Wanted by the Queen; an Act of Parliament was needed; see Guedalla, Q, ii. 230.

[9] Eventual failure of Layard's long campaign for the Rome embassy; see G. Waterfield, *Layard of Nineveh* (1963), 456–63.

decl[aratio]n agt. Comml. Tariff. Treaties to be made but F.O. not to commit itself without authority.

6. Demand of Russia on Persia for a strip of territory, (wh wd place Russia in contact with Afghan frontier inhabited[?] by Turkomans). No objection can be taken.
7. Dodson started Zanzibar arrangements: he is to prepare a paper.[1]

[*Gladstone*:] Ld. Gr[anville]: It seems that the re-appointment of the Committee on the Bright Clauses—for which we shd. have no responsibility—is much less dangerous than a [Royal] Commission & that Lansdowne might carry his plan before the Committee? [*Granville*:] Spencer has written strongly to Carlingford against the Commission.[2]

6. Tu.

Wrote to The Queen l.l.—Rev. Mr MacColl—Mr West—Mr Herb. Mason—and minutes. H. of C. 5-8¼.[3] Saw Mr H.—Ld RG—Mr Trevelyan—Scotts—Ld Lyttelton. Read Iliad—Contemp. Rev. on Govt of Paris[4]—Mr Isaacs.[5] Attended the Drawingroom, at which the representation of so many new countries is to me most interesting.

7. Wed.

Wrote to Mr M. Fenton—Sir R. Phillimore—Ld Lyons—D. of Westminster—The Queen—Messrs Deighton[6]—Bp of Exeter—Rev. Mr Edmonds—Chancr of Exr— and minutes. Dined with the Wests: whist. Saw Mr H—Mr S—Ld RG—Ld Granville—Mr N. Hunt—Sir C. Ducane—Mr Villiers—Count Münster—Mr Godley—Mr Scoones[7]—Mr Murray. Luncheon at 15 G.S. Visited the Acad. Exhibition (Rossetti pictures incl.)[8] Read Iliad—Mr Isaacs—Ld Blachford on Ch Courts.[9]

To H. C. E. CHILDERS, chancellor of the exchequer,   Add MS 44546, f. 86.
7 March 1883.

I am sorry that some words in your paper on Irish distress[10] seem to treat the question as placed *by us* before the Cabinet. I advise your writing at once to Spencer & saying that we adhere to our objectives: it will be for him to put his case in what form he likes, &,

[1] See 20 Apr. 83.
[2] Undated holograph note; Add MS 44644, f. 5.
[3] Misc. business; *H* 276. 1587.
[4] *C.R.*, xliii. 439 (March 1883).
[5] See 13 Jan. 83.
[6] Correction of errors in *Versus Tennysonienses*; Add MS 44546, f. 86.
[7] W. Baptiste Scoones had sent his *Four centuries of English letters* (1880, 3rd ed. 1883); Hawn P.
[8] At Burlington House.
[9] F. Rogers, Lord Blachford, *Some account of the legal development of the colonial episcopate* (1883).
[10] Not found; Childers told Spencer this day that he and Gladstone 'adhere to our objection to have any recourse to the Consolidated Fund' and that reservation of Church Funds for emigration was 'inadmissable'; Althorp MSS.

probably either by a written paper or through Trevelyan orally or both, to place the matter before the Cabinet. I think better of the merits (or demerits) of resort to the Church Fund under the circumstances than you do.[1] To reserve it for a 'large measure of emigration' to which the Government has never given a word of encouragement, & on this ground to change forthwith the consolidated Fund, is in my opinion a course absolutely inadmissible.

8. Th.

Wrote to The Queen—Ld Granville—Mr Childers—Ld Provost of Edinburgh[2]— Sir A. Layard—Ld Blachford—Col. Carrington—& minutes. H. of C. 5–8¼ and 9½–12¼.[3] W.C.J. & T.G. Party dined. Saw Mr H—Ld RG—Japanese Minister[4]— Rev. Mr Wilkinson—Ld Granville—Mr Childers—W.H.G. Read Iliad—Scoones, English Letters.

To Sir A. H. LAYARD, 8 March 1883.   Add MS 44546, f. 87.

Since I received your note this morning, Granville has mentioned to me the assurances he had given you on my behalf. I desire to report, and even to enlarge them. Nothing that has passed between you and me remains on my mind as a cause in any degree for resentment, and my desire is that all such matters should be entirely excluded from the consideration of any question which may at any time arise with reference to your being employed in Her Majesty's service.[5]

As this was the only practical issue which I believe you contemplated raising at a personal interview—and indeed there is no other on which I am competent to enter—I hope you may consider your purpose as already gained.[6]

9. Fr.

Wrote to Mr Childers—Pres. St Ed. Hall—Mr Leatham—Ld Rosebery—Mr Scoones—The Queen—& minutes. H. of C. 4¾–8¼ and 9–12¾.[7] Read Iliad— Scoones Book of letters—and Mr Isaacs. Saw Mr H—Ld RG—Ld Granville—Sir R. Wilson—Chancr of Exr—Mr Bright—Conclave on [Scottish] Seeds Bill—& on Scotch business.

To LORD ROSEBERY, home undersecretary, 9 March 1883   N.L.S. 10022, f. 191.

With reference to the National Liberal Club, my reluctance is sore, but the occasion is strong & special, & I think a refusal would be wrong.[8] I should prefer an afternoon gathering to either the body of a banquet or the tail of one, which are anti-Clarkian.
[P.S.] I hope we may meet soon, though my head is hardly above water.

[1] See 1 Dec. 82.
[2] Thanking him for a memorial on a Scottish office, and assuring him of its 'careful consideration'; *T.T.*, 12 March 1883, 6e.
[3] Questions; supply; *H* 276. 1759.
[4] Mori Arinori; no account found; probably on arrangements for visit of the statesman Ito Hirobumi to study the constitution.
[5] See 5 Mar. 82; Layard believed the Negropontis affair still rankled with Gladstone, causing his exclusion from the embassy; Waterfield, op. cit., 462.
[6] Layard accepted the explanation, but still complained; Add MS 44480, f. 11.
[7] Spoke on Jamaica; *H* 276. 1962.
[8] See 2 May 83.

10. Sat.

Wrote to The Queen l.l.—Ld Granville—Mr Trevelyan—Ld Spencer—Dean of St Paul's—and minutes. Cabinet 2-5 PM. Sat to Bassano, Photographer.[1] Saw Mr H—Ld R.G—Rev. Mr Wilkinson (who is indeed admirable)—and others. H of C. 2-5½ & 8-10½.[2] Read Iliad (finished)—Mr Isaacs—Watts on Rossetti.[3]

Cabinet. Sat. Mch. 10. 2 PM.[4]

1. Ireland. Spencer's proposals.[5] Determined on the whole not to entertain: & to decline supporting Bills for the Amendment of the Land Act.
2. Transvaal. (Mapok War: no *locus standi* for interference).[6]
Bechuana Land. War beyond the Borders. Transvaal Govt. Proposedly neutral. Individuals have in numbers interfered & occupied. We might punish the marauders by an expedition of 1000 men & establish a virtual Protectorate.
   To recognise the obligations to the two chiefs Mankowane & Montsioa.
   To compensate them.
   A case has arisen in wh we are not prepared to use the means of force wh we are entitled to use. Question will arise as to maintaining the obligation & apparent responsibility.
3. Madagascar. We cannot interfere. No title—or interest—to justify interference.
4. Ld Derby mentioned proposal from Queensland to take at their own charge the unappropriated part of New Guinea.
5. Marjoribanks motion.[7] To be reduced [sc. referred] to a Committee: no public grant desired. Childers few words to be added.
6. Indian Body Guard. Kimberley requested answer. *Indian Army sum not available* by law.

Notes.

Plan the border how you will, the difficulty will always arise *on the border*. We had always remonstrated[?] *de facto.* Attempt by the Keate Award[8] to settle an old trouble. Obligations to Chiefs do not arise out of the Transvaal War.

To G. O. TREVELYAN, Irish secretary, 10 March 1883.   Add MS 44546, f. 87.

We must try to get you to come to the Cabinet in my room today for a short time in order to help in considering the course we are to take in regard to Parnell's bill on Wednesday. Probably you concur in Spencer's opinion: & the questions are (1) shall we depart from the course taken last year (when support was declined) (2) if we are to oppose Parnell's 2nd Reading, in what form shall it be done.
[P.S.] Perhaps the Attorney General might come, *also*, or *instead.*

11. 5 S. Lent.

Chapel Royal Noon & 5.30. Saw Ld E. Fitzmaurice—Sir C. Forster—Gerty & her baby. Read Blunt, Hist. Refn I[9]—Quaker Anecdotes—Ch Quart on Eccl.

---

[1] Of Old Bond Street: 'the photographs leave but little to be desired'; *T.T.*, 11 April 1883, 12a. The frontispiece to this volume.
[2] Supply; *H* 277. 3.   [3] T. Watts, 'The truth about Rossetti', *N.C.*, xiii. 404 (March 1883).
[4] Add MS 44644, f. 9.   [5] On amending the Land Act; Add MS 44310, f. 24.
[6] Energetic Transvaal defeat and dispersal of the Mapoch tribe, despite British Resident's protests; Schreuder, 372.   [7] On harbours, accepted by the govt.; *H* 277. 377.
[8] The border line of 1871; Schreuder, 171.
[9] J. H. Blunt, *The reformation of the Church of England 1514-1662*, 2 v. (1882).

Courts—Carlyle: & other articles.[1] Lucy Cavendish dined. What an edifying picture in all her words & works.

12. M.

Wrote to Ld Spencer l.l.—The Khedive—The Queen—Ld Carrington—Sir H. Ponsonby—& minutes. Attended Levee: much royal congratulation. Saw Mr H—Ld R.G—Mr Ashley—Count Münster—Russian Ambr—Italian Ambr. British Museum 3-4$\frac{1}{4}$ to see Ashburnham Coll[ectio]n.[2] Also saw Mr Newton. H of C. 6-8$\frac{1}{4}$ and 10-12$\frac{1}{2}$.[3] Read Mr Isaacs.

13. Tu.

Wrote to Ld Granville—The Queen—and minutes. H. of C. 4$\frac{3}{4}$-8$\frac{1}{4}$ and 9-12$\frac{1}{2}$.[4] Finished Mr Isaacs: mi spiace.[5] Saw Mr H—Ld RG—Ld Granville—Ld Derby—Sir H. Layard—Conclave on Regent's Park inclosure[6]—C of E. & Mr Lefevre on Cathedral monies & E[cclesiastical] C[ommissioners].

14. Wed.

Wrote to The Queen—Ld Spencer—Mr Duckham—Mr Ramsay—Sir Jas Hogg—Mrs Bolton—and minutes. H of C. 12$\frac{1}{2}$-2$\frac{3}{4}$. Spoke on Parnell's Irish Land Bill.[7] Saw Mr H—Ld R.G—Canon Fremantle—Ld Alcester—Lady Derby—Mr Villiers—Ld Kinnaird. Read Blunt, Hist. Reformn—Quaker Anecdotes.

15. Th.

A little upset by the return of cold, I kept the House. Wrote to The Lord Chancellor—Ld Carlingford—Scotts—The Speaker—Mr Dawson MP—Ld Chancr Law—Mr Cowan—Mr Richard MP—Sir W. Harcourt—Archbp of Canterbury—and minutes. Saw Mr H—Ld R.G—Ld Granville—Ld Bath—Chancr of Exr—Dr A. Clark—Mr Rathbone. Ten to dinner. Read Blunt's Hist.—Quaker Anecdotes—Firth on Municipal Govt of London.[8]

To LORD CARLINGFORD, lord privy seal,   Carlingford MSS CP1/209.
15 March 1883. '*Secret*'.

I have to propose to you that, in connection with the new arrangement for the conduct of affairs with regard to Agriculture, I should submit your name to the Queen to succeed Lord Spencer in the office of President of the Council.[9]

[1] *C.Q.R.*, xv. 301, 368 (January 1883).
[2] See 14 Apr., 26 May 83.
[3] Questions; *H* 277. 214.
[4] Questions; *H* 277. 371.
[5] 'I don't like it' (though this could also mean 'with much regret').
[6] Extra 20 acres added to the Park, 1883.
[7] Opposing any attempt to 'disturb the main provisions' of the Land Act; *H* 277. 476.
[8] J. F. B. Firth, *London government and how to reform it* (1882).
[9] Carlingford became lord president on 19 March, retaining the privy seal; on 18 July, Carlingford MSS CP1/216, Gladstone pointed out to him that he could only, as customary, draw one salary; 'there would be *no* chance of carrying the vote for a double Salary'. For agriculture, see 17 Mar., 17 Apr. 83.

There is however one point in which I think the peculiar features of the case require a preliminary notice. The great business of superintending Education is driven by the force of circumstances mainly into the hands of the Vice President, who thus obtains a large knowledge both of the work to be done and of the persons who do it, among whom arise many questions of promotion in addition to the questions of new appointments. Appointments and promotions must be made on the responsibility of the Head, who must therefore reserve in all cases the freedom of his final judgment. But the circumstances seem to recommend that, in regard to those descriptions of business which fall mainly to the Vice President, the President should take him into council and hear what he has to say in matters of appointment to office and especially of promotion, subject of course to the statement I have made as to his responsibility and his freedom, which are inseparably united. I think I may look for your concurrence in these views.

[P.S.] You will remember the ideas of last year about agricultural affairs. I suppose the natural upshot would be that if the agricultural man were a Commoner, the President of the Council would answer for them in the House of Lords: not otherwise.

To Sir W. V. HARCOURT, home secretary, 15 March 1883. MS Harcourt dep. 9, f. 4.

I have now examined a paper drawn by Sir R. Lingen[1] during my absence on the Continent, with reference to a *portion* of the paper recently drawn by Rosebery on the management of Scotch business, which was sent to him for perusal & comment. His paper brings very succinctly into view some part of the history of the question. I send herewith copies for you and Rosebery: and one also which I recommend your sending to the Lord Advocate, whose opinion ought of course to be asked. I have also a report by Lord Advocate Maclaren on the subject, which is probably in your possession. I send these papers to promote the sifting of the question & without prejudice to any particular mode of proceeding it may be thought fit to adopt.

16. Fr.

Wrote to Ld Kinnaird—Ld Chancellor—Mr Gibson—The Queen—& minutes. H of C. 2½-7. Spoke on Transvaal.[2] Saw Mr H—Ld RG—Mr Wilkinson—Pr. of Wales—Mr Chamberlain—Ld Alcester—Ld Granville, walk & long conversation. Dined at Ld Northbrook's. Visited the scene of smash caused by last night's explosion.[3] Read Blunt's Hist—Quaker Anecdotes. Mr Rathbone's appeal of last night was of a character to move me much.[4]

17. Sat.

Wrote to The Speaker—Ld Chancellor—Sir W. Harcourt—W. Phillimore—The Queen l.l.—Rev. Dr Butler—Ld Spencer—Dean of Winchester. Saw Mr H—Ld RG.—Mrs Bolton—do *cum* Mr Bolton—W. Lyttelton. Dined with Lucy Cavendish. Cabinet 2-5. Read Blunt—Quaker Anecdotes.

[1] Not found.
[2] Moving amndt. on Bechuanaland; *H* 277. 734.
[3] Dynamite near the local govt. office; extensive damage but no deaths.
[4] Probably a foretaste of Rathbone's impassioned plea for caution about being drawn into South African racial politics; but also condemnation of the Boers, 'degrading themselves below the level of the savages they despised'; *H* 277. 755.

Cabinet. Sat. Mch. 17. 83. 2 PM.[1]
1. Amendment on Transvaal motion. Insert 'and others'.[2]
2. Order of business as to Bills etc.: Thurs. Supply, Civil, 29th Mch; Friday week Transvaal Apr 6.; Bills. 1. Grand Committee Bills (or Affirmation).
3. New provision for Agricultural Affairs.[3] Harcourt proposed transfer to L.G.B. of Mines, Factories.
4. Scotch business. Project of a Committee discussed with favour: final decision postponed until after circulation of papers.
5. Harcourt detailed his measures in consequence of the explosion—has called in 300 Policemen from the outskirts.[4]
6. Resolved to prepare materials of a communication to U.S. upon the language of O Don[ovan] Rossa and Sheridan, telegraphing to West to send over instantly by telegraph passage in proof.[5]

18. Palm S.

Chapel Royal mg (Abp of Canterbury) & Evg. Saw Prince of Wales—Sir R. & Walter Phillimore—W.H.G.—Mr Hamilton. Wrote to Ld Granville—Mrs Bolton. Dined with Sir R. Phillimore. Read Life of Ld Hatherley[6]—Finding of Christ[7]—Blunt's Hist. Reformn.

19. M.

Wrote to Rev. Dr Allon—The Queen l.l.—Mr Dodson—Ld Chancellor—Ld Bath—Archbishop of Canterbury—Bp of Lincoln—W. Phillimore—and minutes. Saw Mr H—Ld RG.l.l.—Mrs Bolton—Chancr of Exr—Mr Chamberlain—Rev. Mr Wilkinson—The Speaker. H of C. 5-8¼ and 9½-1¾.[8] Read Mathieson, Visit to America[9]—Blunt Hist. Ref.

To E. W. BENSON, Archbishop of Canterbury,   Benson MS 3/6/28.
19 March 1883.

I am sorry to have given endless trouble: but Lord Derby is already a family Trustee of the Museum. I think I have another good name to present in Lord Rosebery, a lover of books, and of the contents of books. The Speaker approves of this selection.[10]

20. Tu.

Wrote to The Queen l.l.—Sir W. Harcourt—Ld Rosebery—Ld C. Campbell—and minutes. Read Donovan.[11] H of C. 2¼-6 & afr: spoke on Procedure.[12] Saw Mr H—Ld RG—Sir H. Elliot—Sir Thos G.—Lady Spencer. Dined at Sir Thos G.s.

[1] Add MS 44644, f. 12.   [2] Deb. of previous evening not resumed.
[3] Committee of Council for Agriculture, with Chancellor of the Duchy (Dodson) as Vice-President; Add MS 44644, f. 14.
[4] See 16 Mar. 83.   [5] See 28 Apr. 83.
[6] W. R. W. Stephens, *A memoir of Baron Hatherley* (1883).
[7] *The perfect way; or, the finding of Christ* (1882).
[8] Questions; Bankruptcy Bill; *H* 277. 816.   [9] Not found.
[10] See 27 Mar. 83.   [11] By A. E. Bayly; see 27 Apr. 83.
[12] For the Transvaal deb., *H* 277. 942.

To Sir W. V. HARCOURT, home secretary,   MS Harcourt dep. 9, f. 8.
20 March 1883.

I received your Memorandum yesterday[1] & have not yet been able to read it with the attention it requires: but without doubt it should be circulated.

Would you kindly cause the passages in Fortnightly & Contemp. articles to be marked in pencil in the margin, which you rely on as proving that there can be no combination of police authorities? The gravity of the question can hardly be exaggerated in my view of it.

Could you send me a Map or refer me to one showing the area of the Metropolitan Police District as *existing*, and as *proposed*, with the areas of the Parliamentary Boroughs marked?

To LORD ROSEBERY, home undersecretary, 20 March 1883.   N.L.S. 10022, f. 193.

Hamilton has shewn me your notes of the 17 & 18.[2] I fully appreciate your motive for not writing to me; but I have remained ignorant till today of what I now learn, & I own it seems to me that the proceeding is premature.

The Cabinet is considering what they can best do in what I think, & perhaps they think a difficult question; & although you may think it an easy one, & it is not for me to set up my own opinion dogmatically, yet is it a convenient course to anticipate their decision by the announcement you propose to make in Scotland? & to anticipate it in the sense of assuming that it cannot be satisfactory?[3]

21. Wed.

Wrote to Ld Rosebery—The Speaker—Ld Stair—Mr Marum MP.—Mr Wells RA.[4]—Lady Phillimore—Ld Chancr—Rev. Mr Holland—and minutes. At 10.15 I went to be present at R. Phillimore's farewell to the Bar.[5] Both he & the Attorney General did their parts excellently well. Saw Mr H—Ld Carlingford—Ld E. Fitzmaurice. Dined with Lucy C. Read Donovan—Blunt. 12½–5. Went to Windsor for luncheon and audience, with C. The Queen had only a stool for her foot.

22. Th.

Chapel Royal 11 AM. Wrote to Lady Phillimore—Ld Strafford—Bp of Lincoln— M. Leon Say—Ld Granville—and minutes. Read Blunt—Donovan. Saw Mr H—Mr & Mrs Th.—Mr Wilkinson. Worked on books &c.

To J. B. L. SAY, 22 March 1883.   Add MS 44546, f. 92.

Thank you for your courtesy in sending me a copy of the French report on the Channel Tunnel.[6] I will not attempt to remark on it, or on the subject to which it refers, beyond

[1] See Add MS 44198, f. 15; on police authorities for London.
[2] Copy docketed: 'His position at H.O.', Add MS 44546, f. 91; Rosebery was now declining any special responsibility for Scottish affairs; Hamilton persuaded him to destroy his first reply to this letter; *Rosebery*, 146.
[3] Rosebery replied, 21 March, Add MS 44288, f. 157, that his announcement was in no way connected with any Cabinet decision 'present, future, or possible'.
[4] Henry Tanworth Wells, 1828–1903; artist; had sent sketch of new law courts for the Queen; Add MS 44480, f. 61.
[5] The doorman, not recognizing him, at first refused him entry; *T.T.*, 22 March 1883, 7e.
[6] 'Chemin de Fer Sous-Marin. Extrait du Procès-Verbal'; Add MS 44480, f. 48.

repeating the acknowledgement, made to you in conversation, of the high discretion with which you spoke, & the assurance that no word will proceed from my mouth to aggravate the difficulties, be they small or great, with which the question may at present be surrounded.

23. *Good Friday.*

Chapel Royal mg: St Peter's Eaton Square afterwards, Passion Services. Saw Ld Sydney—Ld Halifax—Mr H. In evg went to the Messiah at A[lbert] Hall, rather reluctantly. Wrote to Ld Chancellor—Ld Granville—Mr Salkeld—Mrs Th.—& minutes. Read Blunt's Hist. Refn.

24. *Easter Eve.* [*Holmbury*][1]

Westminster Abbey at 10 A.M. One of the few sublime Churches. Wrote to The Queen—Sir W. Harcourt—Mr Hamilton—Ld Northbrook—and minutes. Off at one to Holmbury. Walk with F. Leveson [Gower]. Read Donovan—Weingarten's Pascal.[2] Saw Mr H—Lucy Cavendish—Mr Lowell.

To Sir W. V. HARCOURT, home secretary,   MS Harcourt dep. 9, f. 10.
24 March 1883.

I thank you for your most kind letter of yesterday;[3] and I shall best show my thankfulness I believe by looking at the question which it opens on the nearest and most practical side.

We meet on 29th, which is given to Supply (i.e. to Preliminary Notices). Our first business after Supply is to read a second time the Bills which are to go to Standing Committees. For these three second readings I allow the Monday and Thursday of the following week, April 2 & 5. I take it for granted that on April 9 we must move the second reading of the Affirmation Bill. There will then be nine or possibly ten nights available before Whitsuntide. Let us suppose three (a moderate estimate) are given to Supply. The Affirmation Bill must of course be pressed with none but necessary intervals: it *may* allow a night or two for other business before Whitsuntide, or it may not. If it does, the competition will lie between: Corrupt Practices 2R; Tenants' Compensation Introd.; Municipal Govt. Introd. No day is likely to be available for any of these before April 11th at the earliest. Unless the Municipal Bill is brought in then or *soon* after, you I think believe, and I should say rightly, it cannot go on this year.

At an early Cabinet perhaps about Saturday Ap. 7 I think will be the time for looking in the face this competition of Bills, and considering what is to be done. It may be that postponement may be expedient on account of the difficulty as to the Police: or it may be that postponement is required by the state of business; but in any case it will give much scandal & cause some discredit.

Derby is plainly right I think in saying that the three cannot go forward. Postponing any of them is all the more serious because it is *difficult* to see how to postpone the question of suffrage beyond next year; though I will not say this cannot be done.

[1] Lord E. F. Leveson-Gower's house in Surrey; see 19 July 73.
[2] H. Weingarten, *Pascal als Apologet des Christenthums* (1863).
[3] Add MS 44198, f. 19 and Gardiner, i. 483: 'uncomfortable' about the London Bill as uncertain about demand for it.

25. *Easter Day & Annunc.*

Ch mg H.C. good & aft. Read Weingarten Pascal—do Revolutionskirchen[1]—Religieuse excommuniée[2]—Life of Hatherley.

26. *E. Monday.*

Ch 11 A.M. Read and worked on London Muncipality. Read Donovan—Weingarten's Pascal—Life of Hatherley. Wrote to C.G.—Mrs Bolton—Sir W. Harcourt. Much conversation Whist in evg.

To Mrs GLADSTONE, 26 March 1883.   Hawarden MSS.

I think I ought to have written yesterday to wish you a happy Easter but we were for some time at the very satisfactory little church, and the post went out at 3.30.

There was a rather blessed change in the weather on Saturday afternoon and I am in hopes it may have served you in good stead, and may enable you to send us thoroughly satisfactory accounts of a conquered cold. Indeed it seems hardly too much to cherish not a certainty but a hope that your 'shingles' may have been the settlement of a long account & that after this clearance you are again to have a really good state of health, both sleeping and waking.

The party here has been as usual well chosen. The Brodricks who have been very good company are just gone & the Blennerhassetts arrive. All the rooms in the House are full. Our friend the *chef*, who is considered to be the double of Mr Evarts, has presented me with a walking stick of his own cutting and making. And I have been put in requisition this afternoon to cut down a cherry tree, a task which I have executed with great moderation.

Masie has brought in a notice of an early post which obliges me to close quickly.

Pray tell Stephy, who has been interviewed and exhibited in the newspapers that I think he 'The Rev. Gentleman' spoke with great discretion and as far as I can judge was not far from the mark.[3] I must however knock off, & am your ever afft WEG

To Sir W. V. HARCOURT, home secretary,   MS Harcourt dep. 9, f. 12.
26 March 1883.

You have very naturally referred, in writing to me to the letter which I addressed to you in December 1881[4] on your most able Memorandum of that date and you are disappointed at my having spoken of the question of the Police in the Metropolis as one lifted above the region of detail, whereas I had classed it differently when I wrote to you before.[5] I think you will find on consideration that firstly I then described my letter as a letter of '*first thoughts*' and said I *thought* the points on which my mind was not then satisfied were below the rank of principles: but also secondly and mainly that what I said of Police was quite different from the tone of your recent paper. You objected to handing over the Police 'at the present moment' and thought the public would view the 'immediate transfer with alarm' but you saw 'the arguments which might be urged for the transfer' and thought 'it might be' that 'later the Corporation, when it had established its claim

---

[1] H. Weingarten, see 26 Feb. 76.
[2] Not found.
[3] Probability but not certainty of retirement; *P.M.G.*, 24 March 1883, 7.
[4] See 19 Dec. 81.
[5] i.e. on 16 Dec. 81.

to public confidence, would acquire the Police authority'. Thus, though this did not come up to my mark there really did not seem to be a difference of principle between us, for I was not then, nor am I now, disposed to stand for an instantaneous transfer.

I own that I have read your paper of *this* year with some dismay, because it seems to treat all Municipal authority over police as a relative evil only to be tolerated, because unavoidable (which I do not *think* it is), and if I understand it aright it claims the authority for the Sec. of State as a standing & permanent institution.

As yet I have written nothing in the way of argument upon the subject: and I am desirous to avoid it for non sum qualis eram bonae sub regno Cynarae.[1] You I am sorry to say are as far as possible from having converted me (not that I deny the great force of some of your points but I think the conclusion lies in another direction) and probably I should be not less far from converting you. I would rather look to the most practical issues, and see whether there is no possibility of marking out a ground which we may occupy in common.

I have sent some queries on the subject to Hamilton, and told him not to refrain from referring to you or your office for information if necessary.[2]

27. E. Tues.

Ch. 10½ AM. Wrote to Dean of Westminster—Mr Hamilton L.l.l.Tel.l.l.—Sir Jas Watson—Ld Rosebery—Mr Hayward—Ld Granville—Ld Chancellor—Att. General—Ld R. Grosvenor—C.G.—and minutes. Walk with F. Leveson. Read Life of Hatherley—Weingarten on Pascal. Much conversation with the Blennerhassetts, especially Lady B. Their religious position is peculiar, & full of interest.[3]

To LORD R. GROSVENOR, chief whip, 27 March 1883.[4]   Add MS 44315, f. 115.

Your letting me off on Friday is more than I had expected: but as you have been so merciful, I think of going to Sandringham on that day and remaining until Monday. Please to make out, hypothetically, such a Committee as you think *might* be appointed on the question of Scottish business; to give an idea how it would work. Harcourt is I think unduly apprehensive that it would recommend the creation of a Secretary of State.

Weather an alternation of sun & snow. Glass capricious but low.

To Sir W. V. HARCOURT, home secretary,   MS Harcourt dep. Adds 10.
27 March 1883.

I have sent the papers (with a preliminary query) on the plan for aiding Crofters' Emigration to Childers, to whom it belongs to consider them in conjunction with you.

The plan requires much consn. as we could not embark in public aid for emigration without considering the procedure & the limits. I have before this time given Royal Bounty for Emigration but unhappily I am much crippled by having undertaken to find money in aid of the Prince's journey in Ireland so that I could find but little.

---

[1] Horace, *Odes*, 4. 1. 3: 'I am not what I was in the reign of the good Cynara'.
[2] Harcourt's lengthy reply of 29 March stressed the need for the Home Secretary to control the Metropolitan Police: 'the advance of democracy make[s] a popular body altogether unfit to conduct such a machinery'; Add MS 44198, f. 25.
[3] Both liberal Catholics, friends of Acton and Döllinger; see 17 Dec. 70, 12 Oct. 79.
[4] Holograph.

To R. McG. HAYWARD, 27 March 1883.   Add MS 44545, f. 94.

I am exceedingly pleased to hear that a dinner is to be given to the remaining sixteen of the Scot & Lot Voters who were on the register when I had my first electoral campaign in Newark over 50 years ago.

Had I had any hope of being free to attend, I would certainly have begged the favour of an invitation for myself. As this cannot be, I ask that I may be allowed to direct my cook to supply a plum pudding for the occasion, and I beg to be informed of the day so that it may not arrive too soon or too late.[1]

To LORD ROSEBERY, home undersecretary, 27 March 1883.   N.L.S. 10022, f. 202.

I thank you with and from my whole heart for your letter.[2]

Concidunt venti, fugiuntque nubes.[3] There was a good deal of meaning in the words I used to you, and I could more easily & clearly state the ulterior parts of it to you in speech than in writing. I will now only say that what I expected in 'six months' was a manipulation with a view to the fulfilment of our pledge to make a new provision with respect to Agriculture, or to Agriculture & Trade. It was Spencer's removal to Ireland which unexpectedly postponed this first part of the operation until a date quite recent. *Behind* it lay in my mind several matters, Scotch affairs among them, and a hope of some better defined arrangement about them, but not more than a hope, although there were other elements which all taken together seemed to me to involve a certainty of fact, not of time. Since then, especially from the state of affairs in Ireland, and in the House of Commons, there has been little but delay, affecting almost all operations alike, and if you have most naturally suffered vexation, I can assure you that I have profoundly shared it.

I am writing from memory on the spur of the moment but I think what I have stated is strictly accurate as far as it goes, and I need only, for the present, and until we meet (I hope soon), repeat my thanks for your kind & generous words.

As to the Museum, I think you are quite right to consider: but please to bear in mind that the calls of the Trusteeship are very slight indeed: what is more like a pledge of serious action is election to the Standing Committee, a perfectly independent & ulterior affair.[4]

To Sir James WATSON, 27 [March] 1883.   NLS 741, f. 50.

I thank you very much for your letter and inclosure:[5] & I rejoice in the homage done to Bright, though had I been in Glasgow he would have shut me out, as an 'Episcopal', from witnessing his triumph on Good Friday. Let me also use the opportunity thus afforded me for conveying to you once more my best wishes & warm regard.

28. *Wed.*

Wrote to [blank] and minutes. Drive to Losely: a gem.[6] Then to Mr Ralli's.[7] Whist in evg. Read Milligan's Address[8]—Donovan—finished Weingarten's Pascal.

---

[1] Add MS 44480, f. 69; the 1832 Reform Act ended the scot and lot franchise save for those already voters, by 1883 a small band. Hayward was a Newark architect and Overseer.

[2] His second, more temperate, reply, apologising; see 20 Mar. 83n., *Rosebery*, 146 and Add MS 44288, f. 161.

[3] Horace, *Odes*, 1. 12. 30: 'the winds drop and the clouds flee.'

[4] Rosebery accepted the Trusteeship after, to Gladstone's irritation, much prevarication; *Rosebery*, 147-8.   [5] Not found.

[6] Elizabethan house near Guildford.   [7] P. Ralli (see 8 May 71) at Alderbrook, Cranleigh.

[8] W. Milligan, 'The present position and duty of the Church of Scotland' (1882).

29. Th. [London]

Started at 10.35 and bid goodbye to the Blennerhassetts at the station. D St at 1.30. Wrote to The Queen l.l.—Mrs Bolton—Mr Butt (MP)[1]—E. Hamilton—W.H.G.—Mr Chamberlain—& minutes. H. of C. 4½–8 and 9½–12¼.[2] Read Donovan (finished). Saw Mr H.—Ld RG—Sol. Gen.—Head of Surrey Constabulary—Chancr of Exr—Mr Fowler—Do *cum* R. Grosvenor on Irish Contract.

30. Frid. [Sandringham]

Of at 11.30 to Sandringham. Reception kinder if possible even than heretofore. Wrote to Ld Justice Brett[3]—Ld Chancellor—Mr Playfair—Sir W. Harcourt—Lady Jessell—The Queen—& minutes. Read Life of Hatherley—Mad. de Stael.[4] Aretin Moderne.

To Sir W. V. HARCOURT, home secretary,   MS Harcourt dep. 9, f. 15.
30 March 1883. '*Private*'.

You must have been hard pressed of late with letter writing, and I am desirous to spare you, therefore, in the matter of letter reading. Also while I quite agree with you in thinking that the Police question ought to be soon settled, and have therefore suggested Saturday Ap. 7 as a time when it might be mentioned, I am desirous not to be precipitate, and to take what time I can without putting others to inconvenience, before indicating by what means in my view we can all of us best work together. In no case that I can foresee ought the author of the Bill to founder, but I trust that the Bill will not split upon any rock of internal differences.

I also hold to my pledge & wholly waive the argument with which I feel myself rather full; only observing in your ingenious simile of the angle and the produced lines that mine is not produced for I really am just where I was.

Though a staunch Unitarian in my general view of the question yet looking forward to the continuous extension which the Metropolis is likely within the next century to undergo, I ask myself whether it is certain that it would be inexpedient to take the river for a dividing line, and proceed on the lines of dualism. I do not however go beyond saying that this point seems to me to deserve examination.

There is another point, not of argument on the merits but of tactic that I should like to mention. I have some fear of an awkward combination between men (perhaps not numerous) who take my sorry view of municipal rights and privileges and the far larger body of Tories, with Liberals who are infected with Tory fears, against the idea of a gigantic municipality. Were we to found ourselves in principle upon centralised Police as a permanent institution, I fear it would be used with some effect as an argument against an Unitarian Bill that it obliged us to deprive the Municipality of the first among its ordinary functions. However what I hope is that this may be parried.

---

[1] Making Charles Parker Butt (d. 1892, liberal M.P. Southampton 1880-3) a judge.
[2] Spoke on forests; *H* 277. 1027.
[3] Making William Baliol *Brett (1815-99, tory M.P. and solicitor-general 1868, judge 1875) master of the rolls on d. of Jessell.
[4] A. L. G. de Staël-Holstein, *A treatise on ancient and modern literature*, 2v. (1803); doubtless read encouraged by Lady Blennerhassett, then writing on de Staël; see Figgis and Laurence, *Acton's Correspondence*, i. 268.

31. Sat.

Wrote to W.H.G. l. & tel.—& minutes. Root-cut a small tree in the forenoon: then measured oaks in the Park: one of 30 feet. In the afternoon we drove to Houghton, a stately house and place, but woe-begone.[1] Conversation with Abp of Canterbury—Prince of Wales: & others. Read L'Aretin Moderne—Life of Hatherley—Law's Account of Craig.[2]

1 S.E. [1 April]

Sandringham Ch. mg West Newton evg. Good services & Sermons from the Abp. The Prince bid me read the Lessons. Much conversation with the Abp. also D. of Cambridge—Rosebery—Mr Cockerell. Read 19th Cent.on Revised Version—Manning on Education[3]—Life of Hatherley—Craig's Catechism. Wrote to D of Edinb. (Tel.)—Mr Carrington (copy l. to WHG.)[4]

2. M. [London]

Off at 11. D. St at 3.15. Wrote to The Queen l.l.l.—Ld Portarlington—Mr Tupper—Ld Granville—& minutes. Long conversations with the Archbishop in the train. Saw Mr H—Lord R.G—W.H.G.—Chancellor of the Exchr—Lord E. Fitzmaurice—Mr Cross—Mr Goschen—Mr Forster—Mr Holland. Dined at Grillions. H of C. 5–8 and 10–12½.[5] Read Mad. de Stael's Life[6]—Life of Hatherley.

To M. F. TUPPER, 2 April 1883.   Bodley MS Eng. lett. e. 1., f. 181.

I thank you for your note[7] and I can assure you that I believe the promoters of the Affirmation Bill to be already on the side you wish me to take, and the opponents to be engaged in doing (unwittingly) serious injury to religious belief. You may be interested in looking at an article by Lord Aberdeen in the new Number of the Fortnightly Review.[8]

3. Tu.

Wrote to D. of Argyll—Sir W. Harcourt—Mr Hutton—Watson & Smith—The Queen l.l.l.—& minutes. Read Mrs Carlyle's Letters.[9] H of C. 4¾–8½ and 10–1¼. Spoke on Congo & Channel Tunnel.[10] Saw Mr H—Ld RG—Ld Gr.—Mr Courtney. Visited Christie's. Cabinet 2–4¼.

[1] Once Sir R. Walpole's; in decline since the sales in the late 18th century.
[2] T. G. Law, *Introductory memoir of [John Craig] including a reprint of his catechism* (1883).
[3] *N.C.*, xiii. 314 (February 1883).
[4] Hawarden mortgages; see 20 Sept. 80.
[5] Questions, on Kilmainham; *H* 277. 1173.
[6] Unclear which; perhaps that by M. Norris (1853).
[7] On 31 March, Tupper, 'urged by friends', sent his broadsheet verses denouncing Bradlaugh, 'So help me, God'; Add MS 44336, f. 329.
[8] Docketed by Tupper: 'Gladstone's Jesuitical reply to my exhortation that he would not support the Atheist'. Lord Aberdeen, 'The Affirmation Bill', *F.R.*, xxxix. 475 (April 1883).
[9] *Letters and memorials of Jane Welsh Carlyle*, ed. J. A. Froude, 3v. (1883).
[10] *H* 277. 1321, 1372.

Cabinet. Tues. [*3*] *Ap. 83. 2 PM.*[1]
1. Budget. Childers stated his proposals.
   6d. Telegrams.
   Railway duty remitted on 1d a mile fares, subject to conditions.
   0.2. ⟨Transvaal⟩
[The following items are deleted:] 3. Congo. 4. Agriculture—official arrangement for.
5. Privy Seal. 6. Scotch affairs. 7. Opium Treaty.

4. Wed.

Wrote to Ld R.G.—Mr Justice Fry[2]—Ld Granville—Me M. Roze Mapleson[3]—
Lady Sydney—Ld Rosebery—The Queen. Saw Mr H—Ld RG—Mr Wilkinson—
Scotts—W.H.G. *cum* Mr Carrington on the Aston mines, a very tough job[4]—Ld
Granville—Mr Buxton M.P.

To Sir W. V. HARCOURT, home secretary,   MS Harcourt dep. 9, f. 19.
4 April 1883. '*Private*'.

Ever since the discovery that we stood so far apart on the Government of the Municipal Police, I have thought that a way out of the difficulty was to be found, quite compatible with your principle and mine, in postponement, with a maintenance of things as they
are in the interval, and without any prejudice to the future at the close of the specified
term, when it would be for Parliament to consider whether the new Municipality had
shown its capacity, or whether an Imperial authority was still to rule.

Knowing that Granville has leaned to your way of thinking, I addressed a letter to him,[5]
of which I send you a copy herewith: and doing this as soon as I think I could gain no
fresh light from further reflection.

To LORD ROSEBERY, home undersecretary, 4 April 1883.   N.L.S. 10022, f. 204.

I do not know whether you feel yourself barred by anything you have since resolved or
done, but if you are not so barred I think you might assist the Cabinet in considering the
question of Scotch business if you were to develop and reduce to form the plan you mentioned to me last night with reference to some of the Scotch Boards.
[P.S.] As far as I have read, I value the Mrs. Carlyle's letters lower than the modest rate at
which you estimate the life of Lord Hatherley.

5. Th.

Wrote to The Speaker—Ld C. Hamilton—The Queen—Sir R. Collier—Ly
Aberdeen—Sir A. Hobhouse—Ld Portman—Sir W. Harcourt—D. of Devonshire—Rev. Mr Eyton—and minutes. Saw Mr H—Ld R.G.—W.H.G. *cum* Mr Carrington—Sir H. Ponsonby—Sir W. Harcourt—Russian Ambassador—Danish
Minister. We dined at Clarence House. I am delighted with the frank & simple
character of the Duchess [of Edinburgh].[6] Read Ld Hatherley (finished)—Ld

---

[1] Add MS 44644, f. 20.
[2] Making Sir Edward *Fry, 1827–1918, an appeal court judge; Add MS 44546, f. 97.
[3] Inviting Captain and Marie Roze Mapleson of Finchley New Road to breakfast.
[4] The estate near Hawarden, bought in 1873, which brought Gladstone into conflict with the
miners; see above, viii. cviii–cx.
[5] See Ramm II, ii. 41.
[6] See 16 July 73. Clarence House was the Edinburghs' London residence.

Abn on Affirmn Bill.[1] H of C. (took William W.)[2] $4\frac{3}{4}$-$7\frac{3}{4}$ and $10\frac{3}{4}$-$12\frac{1}{2}$. Childers made an admirable but rather combative Budget Speech.[3]

To LADY ABERDEEN, 5 April 1883.   Add MS 44546, f. 97.

I will refer to the Lord Advocate the representation you have forwarded[4] respecting the higher education of women, assuring you that it is a question in which I feel a cordial interest.

I am much concerned to hear of Mr. Wharton's mishap (I hope it is not more) and I have certainly a high opinion of his pastoral capacity, but I am so pressed by other real and meritorious claims that I fear I cannot say more.[5]

Dollis has lost none of its charms in my eyes and I thank you sincerely for again opening a prospect in that direction.

[P.S.] Your husband has been very brave about the Affirmation Bill: I feel sure that in the long run he will not suffer for it.[6]

To Sir W. V. HARCOURT, home secretary,   MS Harcourt dep. 9, f. 29.
5 April 1883. '*Secret*'.

I would ask you to devote a few more moments to consider whether you have rightly apprehended the effect of my letter.[7]

The general principle is this: that while we ask Parliament to legislate on a Municipality for London generally during the present year, we likewise ask it to postpone for a term the consideration of the question of Police, as the immediate transfer to the new Municipality is inadmissible, while it might in your own original language, acquire the Police authority, when it had established its claim to public confidence.

I am truly sorry if you now think that such a proposal does not 'tend in any degree' to produce a solution of our difficulties, for it seems to me to be in its essence your own first plan.

I admit that you always contemplated an immediate transfer of the City Police, & that I recommend postponement *en bloc*, but I have done this as mainly a question of tactic, but I am not absolutely wedded to an opinion upon it so as to set myself against the view of my colleagues.

Your saying that I propose to postpone the *transfer* for a definite period encourages me to write this note for what I propose to postpone is not the transfer but the consideration of the subject.

[P.S.] Need I say that the acceptance of your offer to efface yourself *by me* is impossible; were it only because a man with one foot in the political grave ought not to slay another man who has both feet on *terra firma.*

6. *Fr.*

Wrote to Sir W. Harcourt—Ld Granville—The Queen l.l.—Att. General—& minutes. H. of C. $4\frac{3}{4}$-$8\frac{1}{4}$ & 9-$1\frac{1}{4}$. Spoke on Expenditure Committee.[8] Saw Mr

---

[1] See 2 Apr. 83n.   [2] W. Wickham, his grand-son.
[3] Gladstone immediately followed Northcote's reply to Childers, not entirely defending the Chancellor against Northcote's charge of 'one of the most controversial and partizan' of Budget speeches; *H* 277. 1538.
[4] Not found; she replied with thanks, 6 April, Add MS 44090, f. 130.
[5] Pressed for preferment by Lady Aberdeen; see 21 May 82.
[6] See 2 Apr. 83.   [7] See 4 Apr. 83.
[8] Accepting Rylands' motion for reduction in expenditure consistent with efficiency; *H* 277. 1663.

H—Ld RG—HJG—Sir R. Cross—Ld Northbrook—Att. General—Sir R. Welby—
and . . . Read Lubbock on Balance Sheet[1]—Quaker Anecdotes.

To Sir H. JAMES, attorney general, 6 April 1883.　　　　　James MS M45. 49.

Before acknowledging this Memorial of 13600 Clergy on the Affirmation Bill I would
ask you to look at the point marked 1. Is the name of God mentioned in the present Affirmation? I apprehend not: then what do they mean. With regard to retrospective action I
am doubtful as to our case on the merits: perhaps you will let me have a few words with
you on this point.
The Memorial is more restrained & moderate than I had expected.[2]

7. Sat.

Wrote to Ld Egerton—Mr Trevelyan—The Queen—Att. General—Ld Rose-
bery—Ld Sydney—& minutes. Saw Mr Hamilton—Ld Sydney—Ld Granville—
Sir R. Temple—Lady Stanley—Sir H. Rawlinson. Cabinet 2-5. Dined at Sir J.
Lubbock's. 1.30. Meeting of Trustees B.M. to elect (Rosebery).[3]

Cabinet, Sat. Ap. 7. 1883. 2 PM.[4]
1. Explosives. Clauses considered. Action to be retrospective. Move on Monday as far as
   possible with the stages.
2. Affirmation Bill. This to be Retrospective Operation.[5]
3. ⟨Agric. Committee⟩ Queen's birthday.
0 4. Privy Seal.
5. O'Connor Powers plan.[6] Trevelyan to oppose.
6. Elective Councils Bill. Subject must remain with the Govt. which cannot move this
   year.[7]

To Sir H. JAMES, attorney general, 7 April 1883.　　　　　James MS M45. 50.
'*Secret*'.

The Cabinet have considered the retrospective operation of the Affirmation Bill, &
arrived at the conclusion that we ought not to persist with it. I shall be happy to converse
with you as to the *modus operandi.*

To LORD ROSEBERY, home undersecretary,　　　　　N.L.S. 10022, f. 210.
7 April 1883.

I have to acknowledge your letter[8] & we will try our hand at ascertaining whether your
plan can be further formulated, and exhibited in connection with figures.
The Lord Advocate has sent Harcourt a paper, which I have not yet seen but hope to
see soon.

---

[1] J. Lubbock, 'Our national balance sheet', *N.C.*, xiii. 561 (April 1883).
[2] In all, there were 710298/174667 signatures against/for the 1883 bill; Arnstein, 183.
[3] See 19, 27 Mar. 83.　　　　　　　　　　　　　[4] Add MS 44644, f. 25.
[5] But see this day's letter to James.
[6] Statutory Commission to promote Irish migration; *H* 277. 1984.
[7] Healy's bill moved for him on 11 April by Barry; Trevelyan accepted the principle but rejected
the measure; *H* 278. 3.
[8] Rosebery sent in a detailed plan, warning that detail must not be an excuse for delay; Add MS
44288, f. 162.

I have not yet asked the Cabinet to look further into the matter but I still lean to the opinion that a Committee of the House of Commons may afford the best means of putting the question forward.[1]

Probably you have observed Mr. Dalrymple's rather hostile question addressed to me.[2]

Your own personal position has come to be mixed up with the matter we have lately been discussing.

I am afraid you do not much like the general business of the Home Office; but I am sure you will take no step without weighing all points carefully. You are certainly outside the line of Peers holding high office, but the office which you do hold gives you a certain position, not in the world or the country, but in regard to advancement; & I do not hesitate to say that, as matters now stand, among those Peers who do not hold high office your claim for consideration would in my estimation stand as the first, upon the occurrence of a suitable opportunity.

To G. O. TREVELYAN, Irish secretary, 7 April 1883.   Add MS 44546, f. 98.
'*Secret*'.

The Cabinet, as you have expected, authorise you to oppose O'Connor Power's motion on Tuesday; and of course without prejudice to the general questions he touches, but in objection to his proposal.[3]

The Cabinet also think that on the Elective Councils Bill we should say that the subject is one with respect to which the responsibility must remain with the Govrnment which has already declared that it cannot proceed with the matter during the present session.

8. 2 S.E.

Chapel Royal mg & evg. Visited Gertrude, awaiting her near confinement. Dined at Sir R. Phillimore's. Read De Lisle on the Oath—[blank] on Bp Wilberforce—Blunt's Hist—Renan Eglise Catholique[4]—Brown's Evidences.[5]

9. M.

Wrote to Mr R. Brown jun.—M. de Laveleye—Mr Webster MP—The Queen—Ld Rosebery—and minutes. H of C. 4½-8¼ and 9-12½.[6] Saw Mrs Bolton—Mr H—Ld R.G.—Mr Moon (LNW)—Sir C. Dilke—Mr Trevelyan. Read The Priest's Blessing[7]—Blunt's Hist—Nicolaides on Iliad.[8]

10. Tu.

Wrote to Duchess of Sutherland—Mrs Th.—Sir H. Vivian—Miss Swan[9]—The Queen—& minutes. Read Reid on Currency[10]—Blunt's Hist. finished Vol 1. Saw

[1] Rosebery's reply next day protested at this delay; ibid., f. 164.
[2] On 5 April Gladstone put off answering Dalrymple's question on Scottish affairs; *H* 277. 1504.
[3] See 10 Apr. 83.
[4] Probably vol. vi of E. Renan, *Histoire des origines du Christianisme* (1863-83).
[5] Robert Brown had sent his paper on the evidences; Add MS 44546, f. 98.
[6] Questions; *H* 277. 1840.
[7] See 8 Sept. 81.   [8] See 26 Jan. 67.
[9] Annie Shepherd Swan, 1860-1943, Edinburgh novelist; had sent her *Aldersyde* (1883); see 16 Apr. 83.
[10] W. R. Reid, *The enhancing value of gold and the industrial crisis* (1883).

Mr H—Ld R.G.—Ld Granville—Mrs Bolton—Mr Wilkinson—Conclave on Mail
Contract 12-1—Ld Kimberley—Att. General. H of C. $4\frac{3}{4}$-8 and $9\frac{1}{2}$-$1\frac{3}{4}$. We got
safe out of a dangerous discussion.[1]

11. Wed.

Wrote to Sir C. Dilke—Att. General—Mr J. A. Acton—Dean of Wells—Mr Child-
ers—and minutes. Worked on arranging books & papers. Saw Mr H—Ld RG—
The Speaker—Mr Morley. Dined at Ld Reay's. Worked on financial papers.
Read Church Furniture in Berkshire[2]—and [blank]

To Sir C. W. DILKE, president of the local government board,   Add MS 43875, f. 136.
11 April 1883.

I quite agree in the opinion[3] that the withdrawal of the announcement of a Bill for local
Government in the Metropolis would be a serious mischief, and a blow to the Government: but I am not sure whether your memorandum means that in your opinion we
ought (as I understand Chamberlain to recommend) to adventure such a Bill (if time permits) including a provision to extinguish Municipal controul of the Police in the City, and
not including any provision for suspending and holding over the judgement of Parliament
on the general question between Municipal and State Police.

12. Th.

Wrote to Atty General—Ld Devon—Mr Firth MP.—The Queen—Ld Rosebery—
and minutes. Read Aldersyde. Seven to breakfast. Saw Mr H—Ld RG—Mr
MacColl—Mr Knowles—Ld Granville—Ld Derby—Sir C. Dilke—Att. General—
C. of E. *cum* Mr Courtney. H of C. $4\frac{3}{4}$-7 and $11\frac{3}{4}$-$12\frac{3}{4}$.[4] Went to the Opera to see
& hear Colomba: much pleased.[5]

13. Fr.

Wrote to Ld Northbrook—Ld Hartington—Mr Lefevre—The Queen l.l.—&
minutes. H of C. $2\frac{1}{4}$-7 and at nine.[6] Dined at Sir C. Forster's. Saw Mr H.—Ld
RG—Mr Wilkinson—Chancr of Exr—Mr Courtney—Depn on Irish Mail 12-1.—
Dean of Peterborough—Mr Hayward—Mr Dodson—Sir C. Dilke. Read Aldersyde &c.

14. Sat.

Wrote to The Queen—Ld Granville l.l.—Sir W. Harcourt—Bp of St Albans—Mr
Murray—and minutes. Dined with the Hardys & saw the amateur play. May
[Hardy] is really charming. Cabinet 2-5. Saw Mr H—Ld RG—Ld Kimberley—Ld
Derby—Mr Wilkinson—Dean of Durham. Read Aldersyde—Fortnightly Review.

[1] O'Connor Power's motion (see 7 Apr. 83) withdrawn; *H* 277. 2011.
[2] Perhaps *Parish goods in Berkshire... with an introduction by W. Money* (1879).
[3] Dilke's docket, on a letter of Seymour, on preventing by compromise 'the calamity of the loss of
the Bill'; Add MS 44149, f. 135.
[4] Questions; *H* 278. 88.
[5] A. C. Mackenzie's opera produced by Carl Rosa at Drury Lane.
[6] Gorst's motion on Transvaal; *H* 278. 202.

Cabinet. Sat. Ap. 14. 83. 2 PM.[1]

1. Contagious Diseases—open question? YES. R. Grosvenor to make this known. Wait issue of debate for further consideration. Minimise our intervention in the debate.
2. ⟨Affirmation Bill.⟩ Ashburnham Collection.[2] Decline purchase en bloc but say we might consider parts of the collection.
3. Pell. Local Rating. Support A. Grey's amendment.[3]
4. Criminal Code Bill. As to Brady's execution until after the criminal appeal. Not to reserve.
5. Transvaal procedure. Business till Whits after next week.—Estimates—Affirmation— Possibly Transvaal, & conditionally
6. Vote for Petersburgh coronation—(Hereafter)[4]
7. Contagious Diseases Animals. Govt. will not prohibit importation of live animals.

15. 3 S.E.

Chapel Royal mg & aft. Wrote to Mr Godley. Reviewed papers & notes on Church Preferments. Saw Ld Granville—E. Lyttelton—Mr Ottley—W. Lyttelton: a noble picture of a sufferer—W.H.G. Read Berkshire Church furniture (finished)—Renan Eglise Catholique—Aldersyde (finished)

16. M.

Wrote to the Queen l.l.—Archdn Browne—Mr Hopwood—The Viceroy Tel.—Sir C. Dilke—Princess of Wales—Dean of Wells—Miss Swan—D. of Richmond—Mr Firth MP[5]—Mr R. Brown jun.—& minutes. H. of C. 5–8¼ and 9½–1.[6] Saw Mr H— Ld RG—Bp Elect [R. Lewis] of Llandaff—Mr Godley—Chancr of Exchr l.l.—Sir C. Dilke—Mr Trevelyan—Mr Courtney—Mr Dodson. Read Scoones, Engl. Letters[7]—Moncure Conways Carlyle.[8]

To Archdeacon R. W. BROWNE, 16 April 1883.   Add MS 44546, f. 100.

The circumstances to which you refer[9] in connection with the Affirmation Bill are of a most painful character & may constitute an impediment to an act of justice.

I do not know if you are aware that the Bill, as we shall propose to shape it, will be detached from the case of Mr Bradlaugh as it will have no retrospective operation.

To take cognisance of moral conduct in any *Law* regulation admission to Parliament would be mischievous even if it were not impossible: to allege immorality in connection with atheism & as its fruit would be open to the answer that there are many atheists of irreproachable life.

But I must add that in my opinion to maintain on principle a religious test which *catches* the atheist in the name of the Deity, & admits *ex proprio* Deists, Pantheists,

[1] Add MS 44644, f. 28.
[2] Vast library of Bertram Ashburnham, 1797–1878, 4th earl of Ashburnham; the govt. bought the Stowe part of the collection; notes on it at ibid., f. 29.
[3] To A. Pell's motion for relief of local rates in respect of national services; *H* 278. 454.
[4] See 28 Apr. 83.
[5] Acknowledging his urgent appeal, circulated to the Cabinet, for a London Municipal Govt. Bill; Add MS 44480, f. 157.
[6] Questioned on Bradlaugh; *H* 278. 320.
[7] See 7 Mar. 83.
[8] M. D. Conway, *Thomas Carlyle* (1881).
[9] Browne's letter untraced.

Positivists, Secularists, & I know not how many more, is a course highly & in many ways injurious to religion.

To J. A. GODLEY, 16 April 1883.   Add MS 44546, f. 100.

There is great force in what you say about Low Churchmen for *Deaneries*.[1] I give up Mr. Cadman. What do you think of: Mr. Perceval—Mr. Webb in Decanal duties first rate but they want a Liberal; Mr. Curteis of Lichfield; Mr. Medd, a man very high commended by Dean Church; Mr. Creighton has been named & has points numerous & excellent but under 40 is rather young for a Dean.[2]

To Annie S. SWAN, 16 April 1883.   N.L.S. Acc. 6003.

I have now read the work[3] which you did me the honour to present to me with a very kind inscription, and I feel obliged to add a line to my formal acknowledgements already sent. I think it beautiful as a work of art and it must be the fault of a reader if he does not profit by the perusal. Miss Nesbit and Marget will I hope long hold their places among the truly living sketches of Scottish character.

17. Tu.

Wrote to The Queen l.l.—Ld Chancellor—Att. General—Mr Wilkinson—Mr Rathbone—Sir A. Hobhouse[4]—Mr Vernon—Ld Carlingford—Ld Ripon—and minutes. Saw Mr H—Ld RG—Ld Granville—Mr Hopwood. H of C. $4\frac{3}{4}$-$8\frac{1}{4}$ and $9\frac{1}{2}$-2. Spoke on local taxation.[5] Read Scoones, English Letters—M. Conway's Carlisle [*sic*].

To LORD CARLINGFORD, lord president and   Carlingford MSS CP1/212.
lord privy seal, 17 April 1883.

I suppose there will be an Order in Council on the arrangement for Agricultural affairs. Can we dispense with the title of Vice President altogether in this case, & say during our pleasure the Chr. of the Duchy shall *act as* the Vice President of the said Committee. Men might be selected from the Govt. on the formation of an Adminn. to form the Committee, as was done in the case of Education—with harmony and advantage.

Please try to bring this matter to a head.[6]

---

[1] *Re* the Winchester deanery: 'I like Low Churchmen to be made Bishops and Canons, but not Deans'; Add MS 44223, f. 7.

[2] W. Cadman, see 3 June 76; unclear which Perceval; B. Webb, see 4 July 57; G. H. Curteis, see 7 Mar. 56; P. G. Medd, see 2 Dec. 67; M. Creighton, see 14 May 78. G. W. Kitchin, see 12 June 62, was appt.

[3] See 10 Apr. 83; this letter is tipped in to the author's copy. She replied, 19 April, Add MS 44480, f. 209, that her publishers wished to publish Gladstone's letter, but she felt it 'too sacred'; letter docketed 'Letter *is* now published'; it was included in the second impression. Facsimile in A. S. Swan, *My Life* (1934), 42.

[4] Unable to appt. as a Charity Commissioner Sir Arthur *Hobhouse, 1819–1904; see L. T. Hobhouse and J. L. Hammond, *Lord Hobhouse* (1905), 137.

[5] Grey's amdt. to Pell's motion on local taxation only carried by 14; *H* 278. 516.

[6] Further short mem. by Gladstone, 19 April, Carlingford MSS CP1/214, pressing for action; on 20 April, Add MS 44123, f. 161, Carlingford reported he had written to relevant persons. Dodson wished to be styled 'President of the Council of Agriculture'; Bahlman, *Hamilton*, ii. 412.

To LORD RIPON, Viceroy of India, 17 April 1883.   Add MS 43515, f. 23.

I thank you for your most considerate letter of March 24[1] which has just arrived, and I hasten to set you at ease with reference to your friendly anxiety on our behalf. There was an attempt to fret and fume in the House of Commons about the Ilbert Bill,[2] but it was short-lived and futile. In principle I have been and am strongly with you, and as to tactics my own judgment has never gone beyond keeping the question open. After reading what you very candidly say, I feel that an error may have been committed, but I am by no means sure that it has been committed. My son Harry, whose judgment is I think very sound, takes exactly your view. No doubt it is generally true that a Government is not only bound to act according to reason, but also is responsible for provoking unreason. Yet unreason must and ought sometimes to be braved, and the only question is was the occasion such as to render it worth while. This I have not knowledge enough to decide: the chief point against you, in my eyes, is your own judgment.

At the same time I feel the question not to be so easy of solution, as it probably would be in an homogeneous community. There is a question to be answered; where, in a country like India, lies the ultimate power, and if it lies for the present on one side but for the future on the other, a problem has to be solved as to preparation for that future, and it may become right and needful to chasten the saucy pride so apt to grow in the English mind towards foreigners, and especially towards foreigners whose position has been subordinate.

The uprising of native opinion on your side is a circumstance full of interest.

Turning to other matters, I have made light of ominous paragraphs in the newspapers about your having determined on immediate return to England. It has been a great satisfaction to us that you have not acted upon the right, which I conceive that you carried away with you from home, to dismiss yourself from office after a very short term, provided certain questions should have been disposed of. India has come back under your guidance to what may be rudely termed the normal state, and though we must all for her sake wish you to stay, our wish must not count for more than it is worth, especially if it be true that the effect of the climate & country on Lady Ripon is not all that we could desire.

Here we have no Parliamentary crisis in immediate view, and the situation has its brighter and its darker features. In Ireland rents are paid, the law is generally obeyed, the Land Commission is becoming master of its work. The war with secret societies continues but I cannot think otherwise than that Right has got the upper hand. As to the business of the Session, we shall be obliged I think to drop one or more of our measures. But the Grand Committees are working thoroughly well. This may turn out to be a circumstance of vast importance, and in any case it is full of hope for the future.

My wife received Lady Ripon's message with much interest and returns her love. The Cannes escapade was a perfect novelty in my official life, but the change operated in a manner beyond all my expectations, and at once brought back my sleep.

18. Wed.

Wrote to Mr Dodson—Mr A. Arnold—Rev. Mr Pale—and minutes. Dined at Bp of Ely's. Saw Mr H—Ld RG.—Mrs Bolton X—Bp of Ely—Bp of Winchester—Lady Derby—Dean of St Pauls—Mr Wood. Read Q.R. on France in 1783 and on [blank].[3]

---

[1] See Wolf, *Ripon*, 136, 146 with part of this reply; see also Add MS 44287, f. 1.

[2] C. P. Ilbert's Criminal Procedure Amdt. Bill allowed certain Indians jurisdiction over Europeans; the European community protested violently throughout 1883; Ripon regretted the timing of the bill and its drafting; a compromise bill passed in Jan. 1884; Gopal, *Ripon*, ch. 9.

[3] *Q.R.*, clv. 459 (April 1883).

19. Th.

Wrote to Ld Kimberley—Mr Stewart—Ld Spencer—Mr Th. Rogers—Ld Chancellor—Card. Manning—Mr Buchanan—Mrs Ogilvy—Ld Granville—Ld Carlingford—Mr Rathbone—The Queen l.l.—& minutes. Nine to breakfast. Saw Mr H—Ld RG—Mr Wilkinson—Mr Mapleson—Mad. Rose Mapleson. H of C. 5–8¼ and 9–1½: on the Annuity Bills.[1] Read Scoones, Br. letters—Moncure Conway's Carlyle.

To CARDINAL MANNING, 19 April 1883.[2]   Add MS 44250, f. 197.

I thank you much for your kind note[3] though I am sorry to have given you the trouble of writing it.

Both of us have much to be thankful for in the way of health, but I should have hoped that your extremely spare living would have saved you from the action of anything like gouty tendencies.

As for myself I can in no way understand how it is that for a full half century I have been permitted & enabled to resist a pressure of special liabilities attaching to my path of life, to which so many have given way. I am left as a solitary surviving all his compeers. But I trust it may not be long ere I escape into some position better suited to declining years.

20. Fr.

Wrote to Mr Duckham—Mr Wilkinson—Mr Sp. Wells[4]—Ld Spencer—The Queen—and minutes. Read Scoones—Conway's Carlyle. Saw Mr H—Ld RG—HJG—Chancr of Exr—Mr Lefevre—Ld Hartington—Sir R. Welby. H of C. 4¾ & 9½–11½. *Paired* for Mr Stansfeld.[5]

21. Sat.

Wrote to The Queen—Ld Wolseley—Archd. Denison—Bp of Oxford l.l.—M. Sachs—and minutes. Cabinet 2–5½. Saw Mr H—Ld RG—Rev. Mr Wilkinson—Russian Ambassador—Mr Irving—Mrs Chaplin—Abp of Canterb.—Duchess of Edinburgh—and others. Large dinner party. D. & Dss of Edinb. & Abp of Canterbury. Evening party after.

Cabinet. Ap. 20. [sc. *21*] 83. *2 PM.*[6]
1. Alcester and Wolseley Annuities. Learn from W. (& A.) whether it wd. be agreeable to him that provided we find it offers an easier prospect in Parlt. we shd. substitute a grant of 25 m[ille]
0 2. Tenants' Compensation Bill. Discussed. Will be retained.

---

[1] For Wolseley and Alcester; *H* 278. 633.
[2] Holograph draft.
[3] Of this day, Add MS 44250, f. 195: note of thanks (for a gift?), and a comment on his health.
[4] Baronetcy for Thomas Spencer *Wells, 1818–97, the Queen's surgeon.
[5] On Stansfeld's motion opposing compulsory examination of women under the Contagious Diseases Acts; *H* 278. 749; see next day.
[6] Add MS 44644, f. 33.

3. Contagious Diseases. Agreed that we must move. Hn. to ans. on Monday that we have taken the Res. into imm. consn. & will in due time announce result.[1]
4. Queensland & New Guinea.
Zanzibar Contract.[2]

22. 4 S.E.

Chapel Royal mg & aft. Dined with Lucy C.—Saw Gertrude G., waiting patiently. Worked on Oaths. Read L'Eglise Chrétienne—Life of Sands[3]—Quaker Anecdotes—Sermons & Tracts, various.

23. M.

The Govt. is three years old today?[4] Wrote to Ld Chancellor—Prince of Wales—The Queen l.l.—Princess of Wales—& minutes. Read Marcy Argenteau Corresp. (Introduction).[5] Levee at 2. P.M. Saw Mr H—Ld RG—Attorney General—Ld Sherbrooke—Ld Hartington. Dined at Sir C. Forsters. H of C. $4\frac{3}{4}$–8 and $9\frac{3}{4}$–12.[6]

To LORD SELBORNE, lord chancellor, 23 April 1883.   Selborne MS 1868, f. 196.

I sent your letter[7] *re* New Guinea on to Lord Derby; having read it with much sympathy & concurrence. It will take a great deal to convince me of the necessity or propriety of any annexation at all upon that island-continent.

24. Tu.

On Monday night a gap of 3 h. in my sleep was rather ominous; but it was not repeated. Wrote to Chancr of Exchr—Sir A. Gordon—Mr Heneage—Ld Wolseley—Mr Duckham—Ld Granville—The Queen l.l.l.l.l.—& minutes. Saw Archbp of Canterbury with whom I had a very long conversation on the Affirmation Bill & on 'Church & State' Policy generally, as well as on special subjects. Saw Mr H—Ld RG—Ld Gr.—Two ladies Corry (luncheon)[8]—Mr O'Shaughnessy. Read Marcy Argenteau—Trial of Asgell[9]—Quaker Anecdotes. Globe Theatre in evg: excellent female acting.[10]

[Derby:] There are more South African troubles in prospect. But we cannot, and need not, deal with them yet. D. Ap. 24.

---

[1] Govt. surprised by large majority (70) for Stansfeld's resolution for repeal; Hartington answered on 23 April; *H* 278. 910.
[2] Note from Dodson requesting its discussion; Add MS 44644, f. 36.
[3] *Journal of . . . David Sands* (1848).
[4] Precisely; see 23 Apr. 80.
[5] F. C. de Mercy-Argenteau, *Correspondance secrète entre Marie-Thérèse et le Cte. de M-A* (1874); author often mis-spelt by Gladstone.
[6] Affirmation Bill 2°R; *H* 278. 915.
[7] Of 22 April, copy in Selborne MS 1868, f. 192, disliking annexation of any part of New Guinea.
[8] Not further identified.
[9] Perhaps J. Asgill, *Defence upon his expulsion from the . . . Commons in 1707* (1712).
[10] 'Lady Clare' by R. W. Buchanan, with Ada Cavendish, Lydia Cowell; his attendance in the royal box was solicited 'as early as possible' by Buchanan; Add MS 44480, f. 152.

[Gladstone:] Ought not all parties to be made aware that they ought not to count upon the assumption of any new responsibilities in regard to Basutoland by the Imperial Govt., on the probable or possible retirement of the Colonial Govt.? Q[uer]y Circulate? WEG Ap 25.

[Derby:] This will not be an easy or a simple matter. We may refuse to take back the Basutos, but in that case there is sure to be a fight between them and their neighbours of the Orange Free State. Or we may give them 'Home Rule' under a kind of protectorate, controlling their external relations, but leaving them free in regard of internal affairs. This I believe is all they want. But the question does not press, and we shall have Sir H. Robinson home soon. Meantime I will circulate the letter. D. Ap. 25.[1]

To T. DUCKHAM, M.P., 24 April 1883. *'Private'*.   Add MS 44546, f. 104.

I have given to the memorandum[2] you have sent me the most respectful consideration.

I am afraid not only that a demand for urgency would be powerfully opposed; but that if obtained it would do nothing effectual towards legislation on Local Government & a solid adjustment of the question of Local Taxation.

Most gladly would I promote the settlement of such a question by handing over my office to some more capable & younger man, could I see that such a course would promote the attainment of the important end in view.

But you do not conceal from yourself that the great difficulty lies in the state of business in the House of Commons—& the impediments offered to its transaction.

To sweep away every other legislative engagement, & to reverse the finance of the year as well as reconstruct it, would be I fear the only measures which could give anything like a clear stage for dealing with this one among the great measures, the urgency of which is I fear indisputable.

During the first 40 years of my life, Governments had an instrument ready to perform any work to which it might be applied. *Now*, the business has been to refashion the instruments; and though this refashioning may when fully accomplished restore the efficiency of the legislative Chamber, it has thus far been from the necessity of the case little but a deduction from our available time.

I trust that better days are coming.

P.S. The word inscribed on this letter is not intended to prevent your showing it to any of those gentlemen on whose behalf you have written.

25. *Wed. (St Mark)*

Wrote to Sir H. Ponsonby—Ld Derby—Mr O'Shaughnessy—Ld Kimberley—Murrays—Sir W. Harcourt—Sir R. Cross—Sir F. Doyle—Mr Buchanan—Attorney General—and minutes. Read Marcy Dargenteau & Tyler on Oaths.[3] Saw Mr H—Ld RG—Ld Granville—Sir E. Scott—Ld Wolseley—Ld Sydney—Duke of Cambridge—D. of Bedford—Ld Chancellor. Worked on Oaths Question.

[1] Add MS 44141, f. 73.
[2] Not found; see 17 Apr. 83n. Thomas Duckham, 1845-1902; liberal M.P. Herefordshire 1880-6, with special interest in local taxation.
[3] Not found.

To LORD DERBY, colonial secretary, 25 April 1883.   Add MS 44546, f. 104.

1. I entirely agree about Lansdowne[1] & about the prudence of sounding him privately before a recommendation is submitted. On account of Granville's personal affection for the family, I ascertained his view, & it is altogether favourable.

2. I remember to have recommended a Governor of United Canada when I was Secretary of State for the Colonies;[2] and I find no trace of my having recommended Dufferin as First Lord for the dominion. I therefore think the recommendation when the time comes should probably proceed from you, but the point can be made certain by finding whether the Secretary of State recommended Dufferin.

3. The second Jorissen[3] conversation is less pleasant than the first. It rather strengthens my impression in favour of a very temperate statement through the President I suppose of our ostensible grounds of complaint against the Transvaal Government, that we may complete the evidence in the case before coming to a judgment.

I do not think that we the Government of 1881 have any self-love to bias us in the matter. We took to the Convention as the best, perhaps the only feasible, expedient in a critical situation.

To Sir W. V. HARCOURT, home secretary,   MS Harcourt dep. Adds 10.
25 April 1883.

I cannot at the moment say what will be subjects for Saturday besides Landlord & Tenant Bill—but *may* it not perhaps become necessary by that day to decide our course about London Municipal Bill. You have given me your opinion, but you would wish to be present if that matter is ripe.

To LORD KIMBERLEY, Indian secretary, 25 April 1883.   Add MS 44546, f. 104.

We must try on Saturday to settle the *Scotch* as well as the English Bill.[4]

I have lived long in Scotland, and not heard much then, if at all, of working out the farms in the last years of the lease, but my evidence is merely negative & I have had personally nothing to do with landed property in Scotland. R. Grosvenor thinks they have covenants in their leases entitling the tenant to reimbursement. If so it helps the matter very much—the point is easily ascertained.

It has occurred to me as worth consideration whether this Bill might be introduced in the Lords. Please do think of this.[5]

26. Th.

Wrote to Sir R. Cross—Ld Lawrence—Sir A. Layard—Dean of St Pauls—The Queen l.l.—& minutes. Read Quaker Anecdotes. Eleven to breakfast. Saw Mr H—Ld RG—Sir A. Gordon—Mr Carl Rosa[6]—Sir W. Harcourt. H of C. 5¼-8½ and 9½-11¾. Made a long and *begeistert*[7] speech on the Affirmation Bill: taking the bull by the horns.[8]

---

[1] As replacement for Lorne in Canada; he accepted on 7 May; see Add MS 44141, ff. 70, 77.

[2] Cathcart in 1846.

[3] Edward J. P. Jorissen, 1829-1912; on a deputation from Kruger to Derby; for his two talks, on 6 and 18 April, on native and boundary questions, see Schreuder, 344.

[4] Kimberley replied this day that this would be impossible; Add MS 44228, f. 65.

[5] Both Agricultural Holdings Bills were introduced in the Commons.

[6] Carl Augustus Nicholas *Rosa, 1842–89; his opera company was at Drury Lane 1883-7; see 12 Apr. 83.   [7] 'animated'.

[8] *H* 278. 1177 and Bassett, *Speeches*, 581; published as a pamphlet.

27. Fr.

Wrote to Rev. W.H. Harvey—Sir W. Harcourt l.l.—The Queen l.l.—Miss Lyall—
Rev. Dr Smith—Mr Murray—Mr Pennington—Mr Storrs—Bp of Truro—Mr
Kitchin—Mr Davidson—and minutes. Saw Mr H—Ld R.G—Mrs Hardy. Dined at
Ld Sydney's. Went at 2.20 to the Gaiety Th. to see Mr Pennington in Ingomar:[1]
excellent acting. Saw Mr H—Ld R.G—Sir W. Harcourt—Ld Sydney—Sir C.
Dilke. H of C. 5–7¾ and 10½–1.[2] Read Quaker Anecdotes.

To Miss A. E. BAYLY, 'E. Lyall', 27 April 1883.   Add MS 44546, f. 106.

When you did me the honour to send me the copy of your lately published novel
'Donovan' I returned my formal thanks. I have since employed my scraps of time in reading it through,[3] & wish now to make an acknowledgement relative not only to your
courtesy but to the work itself. I cannot but admire the fidelity with which, while it avoids
being didactic, it conveys true & deep knowledge: & combines a thorough equity & clarity
towards an atheist with a not less thorough homage to the authority of truth. Let me presume to add my poor tribute especially to the first volume as a very delicate & refined
work of art.

To Sir W. V. HARCOURT, home secretary,   MS Harcourt dep. Adds 10.
27 April 1883.

In few words, after seeing R. Grosvenor & hearing his report from Hartington, I *accept*
your argument & general view for the Debate on Local Option tonight:[4] relying entirely
on you to make it indisputably clear that we remain altogether severed from any pledge
on behalf of the Permissive Bill, the essence whereof (or the *differentia*), lies I conceive in
the idea of Plebiscite.

To Rev. G. W. KITCHIN, 27 April 1883.   Add MS 44546;, f. 107.

I have the pleasure of proposing to you with the sanction of Her Majesty that you
should succeed Dean Bramston in the Deanery of Winchester. There has been I understand a dilapidation on the revenues from agricultural distress, which I trust is temporary,
but you will of course make any inquiries you may think proper.

I hope it will be agreeable to you to accept this preferment, which I propose to you as a
recognition of your great services in Oxford to the cause of education.[5]

28. Sat.

Wrote to Ld Northbrook—Rev. Dr Allon—The Queen l.l.—and minutes.
Cabinet 2–6½. Saw Mr G—Ld R.G—Ld Kimberley—Portuguese Minister. Visited
the two Water Colour Exhibitions:[6] they are really as a whole astonishing.

[1] 'Under the special patronage of the Prime Minister and Mrs Gladstone'; Pennington, a survivor
of the Light Brigade's charge, recited Sir F. H. Doyle's poem; *T.T.*, 27 April 1883, 12e.
[2] Spoke and voted (thus changing his vote) for Lawson's resolution on local option; *H* 278. 1364.
[3] 'E. Lyall' (pseud. of Ada Ellen Bayly, 1857–1903), author of *Donovan*, 3v. (1882); she replied
with thanks, 4 May, Add MS 44480, f. 284. See 20 Mar. 83.
[4] As in his letter of 26 April, Add MS 44198, f. 48: local option 'simply a chapter in the volume of
Local Government'.
[5] Accepted on 30 April; Add MS 44480, f. 266.
[6] In Hine's Gallery, King Street and the Royal Society of Watercolour Painters in E. Pall Mall.

Eighteen to dinner, and evening party afterwards. The Prince of Wales light in hand as usual. They staid until close on midnight. Finished Quaker Anecdotes.

Cabinet. Sat. Ap. 28. 83. 2 PM.[1]
1. Landlord & Tenant Bill. Ld Kimberley reported on Scotch conference that existing leases should be included. Particulars various settled. Distress limited to one year.
2. Annuities: Wolseley & Alcester. 1. to be a lump sum. 2. Alcester 25 m[ille]. 3. Wolseley 30m.
3. ⟨Scottish business⟩ Postpone definitives. London Bill—& whether to struggle for Tuesday for Affirmation Bill.
4. St. Petersburgh Coronation. Vote: F.O. & C. of E. to try to arrange the charge so as not to include the name of the C. of E. who should receive no money. France gives 15m. Nicholas. D of Dev. 10m. Granville 10m. 1861 Clarendon £6200 (coronation K. of Prussia); 1881 P. of Wales £2000.
5. American Govt. & representation respecting the assassination literature. Freylingham's dispatch read. Dispatch to be prepared.[2]
6. Hartington mentioned the conclusions as to Contagious Diseases Act. They were approved: Metrop. Police withdrawn.
7. Arrangements for Scotch business. (Postponed at 5.30).[3]

29. 5 S.E.

Chapel Royal mg & St Margaret's aftn. Saw A. Tennyson—Lucy Cavendish & the nobly beautiful engraving of F.—Young Sarah Lyttelton—Canon W.L. a living monument of Christian patience. Wrote a few corrections of speech. Read Wright, Song of Solomon—Weill, Mystères de la Creation[4]—Brown, Fire Baptism[5]—Life of Sands—H. Moncreiff on Freeth. Controv.[6]

30. M.

Wrote to Sir H. Ponsonby—Ld Granville—Ld Northbrook—Ld Wolseley—Dean of Worcester—Mr Dodson—Lady G. Peel—Lady Jessel—The Queen & minutes. Dined with the James's. Saw Mr H—Ld RG—Ld Advocate—Sir R. Welby—Ld Granville—Sir A. Pease & Mr Bolton—Mr Lefevre—Mrs Pell. H of C. 5–8¼ and 10–1.[7] Read Huxley's Egypt, Bryce on Mr [J.R.] Green: M'Millan.[8] Wrote on Homer's Geotypy.

Tues May One SS. Phil. & J.

Wrote to The Lord Advocate—Ld Moncreiff—Ld Clifton—Sir H. Ponsonby l.l.— Ld Sydney—Dean of Worcester Tel.—Canon Furse—Ld Northbrook—Prince

---

[1] Add MS 44644, f. 43.
[2] Reviewing British protests at U.S.A.-planned Fenian plots; Ramm II, ii. 46.
[3] Granville's note, Add MS 44644, f. 46: 'Rosebery considers his fate in the balance today & I don't know if he can last till another Cabinet?'; Gladstone: 'I was not aware of this—do you consider that we must take it *on his account?*'
[4] A. Weill, *Mystères de la creation* (1856).
[5] S. B. Brown, *The fire-baptism of all flesh* (1882).
[6] H. W. Moncrieff, *The Free Church principle* (1883).
[7] Affirmation Bill; *H* 278. 1439.
[8] *Macmillan's Magazine*, xlviii. 26, 59 (May 1883).

L.L. Bonaparte—and minutes. H of C. $4\frac{3}{4}$–8 and $10\frac{1}{2}$–$11\frac{1}{2}$.[1] Saw Mr H—Ld RG—
Dr Milligan—Ld Granville—Chr of Exchr—Sir R. Welby. Dined at the Dean of
Westminster's, to meet Tennyson, who read me his Tiresias,[2] & talked of the
Channel Tunnel. Read Ld Cowper on Whigs[3]—Renan Souvenirs &c.[4]—Scoones,
English Letters.

2. Wed.

Wrote to Lady Cowper—and minutes. Worked on financial papers. H of C. at
one to move Adjournment for tomorrow.[5] Read Palmer on Oxf. movemt[6]—
Marcy Dargenteau Corr.—O.Donnell in Contemp. Review.[7] Attended Liberal
Club dinner and spoke for nearly an hour, a considerable physical effort, wh
much restrains mental action.[8] Saw Mr H—Ld RG—Mr Huskisson—Ld Granville.

3. Th. Ascension Day.

Chapel Royal 11 AM with H.C. Wrote to Mr Chamberlain—Mr Hamilton—Mr
Grove—Rev. Mr Villiers—Mr Sullivan—W.L. Gladstone—Mr Macfanen—Mrs
Bolton—Mrs Th.—The Queen—and minutes. Began Carlyle & Emerson Corr.[9]
Saw Mr H—Ld RG—Mrs Ellice. H of C. at 5 P.M., 7–$8\frac{1}{4}$ & 10–$1\frac{3}{4}$. Defeated by
295:289 on the Affirmation Bill.[10]

4. Fr.

Wrote to Bishop of Ripon—Ld Spencer—The Speaker—The Queen—& minutes.
H. of C. 5–$8\frac{1}{2}$ and $9\frac{1}{2}$–$1\frac{1}{4}$.[11] Read Carlyle Emerson Corr. Royal Academy $10\frac{1}{2}$–12.
In half the rooms saw some most beautiful pictures. Saw Mr G—Ld RG—Mr
Agnew—Mr Cross MP—Mr Stephenson.

5. Sat.

Wrote to Sir W. Harcourt—Ld Granville—The Queen—& minutes. Cabinet 12–
$2\frac{1}{2}$. Royal Academy $2\frac{1}{4}$–$4\frac{1}{2}$. Visited Mr Woolner's Studio to see sketch-model for
F.C.[12] Saw Mr H—Ld RG—Lady Holker 5–6—Mr L. Stanley—Lady Stanley—
Miss. . . . Read Carlyle Emerson Corr.—Mrs Oliphant on Froude.[13]

---

[1] Questions; Affirmation Bill and its timetable; *H* 278. 1579.
[2] Then under revision, published 1885; see C. Ricks, *The poems of Tennyson* (1987), i. 623.
[3] *N.C.*, xiii. 729 (May 1883).
[4] J. E. Renan, *Souvenirs d'Enfance et de Jeunesse* (1883).
[5] No sitting on Ascension Day; on this occasion only achieved by a division; *H* 278. 1871.
[6] By W. Palmer, *C.R.*, xliii. 636 (May 1883).
[7] F. H. O'Donnell, 'Fenianism, past and present', ibid., 747.
[8] Inaugural banquet of the National Liberal Club; *T.T.*, 3 May 1883, 12b.
[9] *The correspondence of Thomas Carlyle and R. W. Emerson 1834–1872*, ed. C. E. Norton, 2v. (1883).
[10] Hartington concluded for the govt.; *H* 278. 1821.
[11] Bradlaugh; *H* 278. 1143.
[12] Recumbent figure for Cartmel Priory church.
[13] Mrs Oliphant, 'Mrs Carlyle', *C.R.*, xliii. 609 (May 1883); review of Froude.

Cabinet. Sat. May 5. 83. 12 (noon).[1]
1. Scotch business. Arrangements for.
    WEGs note: I cannot recommend legislation—this year especially: Backwardness of Supply—Customs Bill—Vote of Credit—Want of case—Tenants Bill—Corrupt Practices—Irish Bills. Can we carry it: the Opposition, the Irish, the Economists.
Alternatives. 1. Committee. 2. Legislation. U. Sec. H.O. New Dept. 3. *Now* or *next year.* Harcourt made the Rosebery argument. 1. Committee; (2) Bill now: to take chance; 3. Bill now with Committee; 4. Bill next year. *(2) adopted.*
2. [Westminster] Abbey and Peterborough Cathedral. Letter to be addressed to Abp. of Cant. to know what the Ecc. Commissioners wd. advise as to option now existing of taking estates[?] & as to care of fabrics.
3. Irish Emigration Scheme.[2] Childers's mem. adopted: with much misgiving in minds of W.E.G. and others as to any *public* aid. Unsatisfactory[?] ideas.
                         (In Semi-Cabinet)
3a. (South African Debate. To adhere to ground.) Decline giving a night for *Bechuana* Debate.
4. Abandonment of London Municipal Bill. Raise the point: state urgency of Supply.
5. Stanhope's motion.[3] Accept, adding 'in every branch when economy is practicable'.

To Sir W. V. HARCOURT, home secretary,   MS Harcourt dep. Adds 10.
5 May 1883. '*Immediate*'.

There is a point not mentioned in your letter of last night[4] about Scotch affairs—the point of legislation.

Do I understand you to recommend that the Govt. should introduce a Bill to establish a Scotch Department & should add this Bill, which will be gravely contested, to the work of the Session? Would you or would Childers take charge of such a Bill? (Could such a Bill be referred after the second reading to a Select Committee?)

6. *S. aft Asc.*

Ch. Royal mg with H.C.—Guards Chapel evg: Knox Little preached—there was much to be said. Read V. Lee on Disbelief—Haweis on J.R. Green[5]—Life of Bp Gleig[6]—Life of Sir C. Reed[7]—Zincke Plough & Dollar[8]—Divers Sermons.

7. *M.*

Wrote to Ld St Leonard's—Rev. Mr MacColl—Mr Bright—Mr Rathbone MP— Ld Rosebery—Sir H. Ponsonby—The Queen—and minutes. 12–1. Opening of the Musical College by the Pr. of Wales.[9] Saw Abp of Canterbury—Mr H— Mr S.—Ld RG—Mr Dodson—Att. General. H of C. $5\frac{1}{4}$–$8\frac{1}{2}$ & $9\frac{1}{2}$–$11\frac{3}{4}$.[10] Read Carlyle Emerson Corr. Cabinet 2–4.

[1] Add MS 44644, f. 49.
[2] Spencer's mem. of 4 May, Add MS 44629, f. 34; Childers' mem. not found.
[3] For a cttee. on reduction of expenditure of India; J. K. Cross moved the amndt.; *H* 279. 277. See 8 May 83.   [4] Add MS 44198, f. 53.
[5] *C.R.*, xliii. 685, 732 (May 1883).
[6] W. Walker, *Life of G. Gleig, Bishop of Brechin* (1878).
[7] C. E. B. Reed, *Memoir of Sir Charles Reed* (1883).
[8] F. B. Zincke, *The plough and the dollar, or the Englishry of a century hence* (1883).
[9] The Royal College of Music; *T.T.*, 8 May 1883, 10c.
[10] Statement on business, including Scotland; *H* 279. 45.

Cabinet. Monday May 7. 1883. 2 PM.[1]
1. Draft Dispatch to US—amended & approved.
2. Firth's question.[2] W.E.G. sketched his statement of business.
3. Extra demanded for Secret Service 3⟨10⟩m[ille] at least.[3]
4. Opening of Red River desired by Emperor of Annam approved by China. Want us to speak to the French. *No.*[4]

To LORD ROSEBERY, home undersecretary,   N.L.S. 10022, f. 220.
7 May 1883.

I would have written to you on Saturday but I was so busy that I could not even get off my letter to the Queen by post, and I also felt sure Harcourt would write.

It will I hope be a relief to your mind to know that the Cabinet decided that Harcourt should introduce on an early day after Whitsuntide a Bill to make better provision or further provision for the transaction of business relating to Scotland.

You will I am sure give your best aid in considering what branches of business should be attached to the new office & placed under its chief.

I am to mention the intention of the Cabinet today.

8. *Tu.*

Wrote to Ld Kimberley (2)—Mr Saunders—Mr Fawcett—The Queen l.l.—Ld Derby—and minutes. Seven to dinner. H of C. 4.45–8½ and 10¼–12¾.[5] Saw Mr H—Ld RG—H.J.G.—Duchess of Sutherland—Ld Moncreiff—Mr Fawcett—Ld Carlingford. Attended the entertainment given by the Winchester boys at Stafford House: & proposed the thanks. Attended Cattle Disease Deputn.[6] Read Scoones, Letters—Emerson & Carlyle Corr.

To H. FAWCETT, postmaster-general, 8 May 1883.   Add MS 44546, f. 111.

It has been agreed by the Cabinet that Mr. Cross shall propose to amend Stanhope by limiting his motion to branches of expenditure in which economy may be practicable: this ought to remove all difficulty as to the particular subject of Stanhope's motion.

There is much to be said in favour of a Committee on the Act of 1858. But Stanhope has started this subject at the last moment & we must consult as well as we can in the House. My own impression is that the subject of the Committee ought perhaps at this juncture to be dissociated from that of economy.

Mr. Onslow has given to his declaration of opinion on the Indian contribution the form of a distinct vote of censure which of course the Government must resist *à outrance.*
[P.S.] The reservation in accepting Stanhope on economy will I believe be fully explained by Mr. Cross.

---

[1] Add MS 44644, f. 53.
[2] On Commons' business; *H* 279. 45.
[3] Note from Childers stating Welby's concern for an immediate Cabinet decision, Harcourt and Spencer each wanting £5000; Gladstone's gloss: 'May they not a short time hence demand more?'; Add MS 44644, f. 57.
[4] Independence of emperor of Annam recognized by France 1874, but area placed under French protectorate, Aug. 1883.
[5] Deb. on Indian expenditure adjourned; eventually negatived on 27 July; *H* 279. 264.
[6] Dpn. on foot and mouth disease; *T.T.*, 9 May 1883, 5b.

To LORD KIMBERLEY, Indian secretary, 8 May 1883.   Add MS 44546, f. 111.

1. I am sorry to see no notice of the amendment which I think it was settled that Mr. Cross was to move on Stanhope's motion. I think he should communicate with the Speaker to see whether he can be called. Mr. Onslow has a notice down but it is for an addition. Peel once said to me when I was going to speak officially 'don't be short'. So I should say to your Under Secretary today. He has an excellent faculty of exposition in economical matters & I have no doubt a lucid statement from him will be of great use.

2. I think there is no objection to your making your proposed offer to Courtney whenever you like to do it.

[P.S.] I refer (about Mr. Cross) to the main question raised by Stanhope—not to Onslow's vote of censure.[1]

9. Wed.

Wrote to W.H.G.—Mr J. Bright—Mr Dodson—S[elina] Lady Milton—Mr Tennant—Sir H. Ponsonby—Rev. R. Davidson[2]—& minutes. Read Palestine Channel Syndicate[3]—Carlyle & Em. Corresp. Dined with the Miss Monks. Saw Mr H—Ld RG—Mr S—H.J.G.—Ld Carlingford—Sir F. Doyle—Mrs Th.

10. Th.

Wrote to Mr MacColl—Bp of London—The Queen l.l.l.—Mr Chambers—Lord Bath—and minutes. Conclave on Cattle Importation.[4] Ten to breakfast. Saw Mr H—Ld RG—Mr Hutton—Mr Bright—Rev Mr Stanton. H of C. $5\frac{1}{4}$-$8\frac{1}{2}$ & $9\frac{1}{2}$-$1\frac{1}{4}$.[5] Read Marcy d'Argenteau—Emerson Carlyle Corr.—Scoones, English letters.

11. Fr.

Wrote to Mr L. Stanley—Princess Christian—Mr Warren—The Queen—& minutes. H of C. 2-7.[6] Dined at Lady Ashburton's. Conclave on Suez Canal. Do on Leopold Candidature for Canada.[7] Saw Mr H—Ld RG—Ld Granville—Mr Lowell—Lady Ashburton—Sybella [Lyttelton]. Read Carlyle Emerson. Packing books.

London Municipal Bill, and Police[8]

In the Cabinet of Saturday last, there was a short conversation about the London Municipal Bill, and a reference was made to differences of opinion between Ministers as a reason for the abandonment of the Bill.

---

[1] Second letter to Kimberley this day, Add MS 44228, f. 72, designates Onslow's motion as 'a distinct Vote of Censure'. Cross moved his amndt. this day; *H* 279. 277.

[2] Offering deanery of Windsor to Randall Thomas *Davidson, 1848-1930; Tait's chaplain 1877-82; dean of Windsor 1883-95; bp. of Winchester 1895-1903; abp. of Canterbury 1903. As abp. took custody of the Gladstone diaries at Lambeth 1928 (see above, i. xxxv).

[3] Meeting held on 10 May on proposed new canal across the Suez isthmus to outflank Lesseps' monopoly; *T.T.*, 11 May 1883, 10b.

[4] Foot and mouth disease in S. of England throughout the summer. See 10 July 83.

[5] Questions; govt. defeated on income tax collection; *H* 279. 412.

[6] Moved adjournment of the House; *H* 279. 535.

[7] Jottings of objections to Leopold at Add MS 44767, f. 37. Lansdowne was eventually appt. *vice* Lorne. See to Derby, 19 May 83.

[8] Add MS 44198, f. 60.

It is still open to the Cabinet to determine either way about the Bill. But various circumstances, some of them recent, have contributed to enhance the importance of the question. On this & on all grounds I am desirous that the Cabinet should fully comprehend the difference of opinion now subsisting, so far as I can throw light upon it.

There is certainly a difference of opinion between Sir W. Harcourt and myself, which I am sure we both regret.

His views as to the controul of the Municipal Police have been fully set forth in a paper circulated among members of the Cabinet some weeks ago.

I will only state my views with regard to the point immediately at issue, and will avoid all general argument. 1. I regard the superintendence of the Police, for all the ordinary purposes of security to life and property, as an essential, and as perhaps the most appropriate valuable and important function of our Local Governments; and in towns of the Municipalities. 2. I am not prepared to admit that the vast and growing population of the Metropolis permanently place it beyond the application of this principle. 3. I admit, however, that the time has not arrived when Parliament can advantageously consider whether the power now exercised by the Secretary of State can be transferred to the new Metropolitan Municipality; and if so whether it should be under any & what reserves. 4. My proposal, therefore, is that the present state of things generally should be continued in the Bill for a term of say five years; so that the next Parliament may reconsider and determine the question in the full light of experience. 5. I think that the controul of the City Police should, during the five years, remain as now: I am also persuaded that, *if* we propose to give it at once to the Secretary of State we shall probably, and perhaps rather disastrously fail. 6. Nevertheless, having regard to all the circumstances of the case & my own position, I have made known my willingness to be responsible even for the proposal I have last described.

In these sentences I think I have supplied my colleagues with exact means of estimating the difference of opinion now existing between Sir W. Harcourt & myself.

W.E.G. May 11. 83

12. Sat. [Hawarden]

Wrote to Mr Leigh (Rev.)—Mr Richardson—Mr Maginnis—Ld Granville l.l.—H. Seymour—S. Lady Lyttelton—& minutes. Saw Mr Symons. Off at 11.30. Hawarden at 6. Read Archd. Browne's Charge—Richards on W.E.Gs Oxford days[1]—Le Bourgeois Gentilhomme[2]—The truth about Opium Smoking[3]—Rossetti's Vita Nuova.[4]

13. Whits.

Parish Ch mg with H.C. & Evg. Wrote to Ld Granville—Rev. Mr Bevan—and minutes. Read Bevan on Welsh Church—Wordsworth on New Bishoprics[5]—Bate on Mind & Body[6]—Pelliccia.[7]

[1] Ch. xxxiv, 'Mr Gladstone's schooldays', in J. Brinsley-Richards, *Seven Years at Eton 1857–1864* (1883); see 13 Jan. 83n.
[2] By Molière (1670); see 3 Oct. 25.
[3] Anon. tract (1882).
[4] D. G. Rossetti, *Notes on the Vita Nuova and minor poems of Dante* (1866).
[5] Untraced.
[6] J. Bate, *Influence of mind on mind* (1883).
[7] A. A. Pelliccia, *The polity of the Christian Church* (1883).

To Rev. W. L. BEVAN, 13 May 1883.   Add MS 44546, f. 113.

I thank you very much for your interesting work on the history of the Church in Wales. As respects the statements which are attributed to me, they certainly assert more than I can prove, and must I think have been conjectural, rather than assertions of fact.[1]

There yet remains an interesting and important problem which has not been solved. During the great struggle under Charles I Wales was a great stronghold of the Church: so says Mr. Hallam.[2] And I apprehend that it is also true that Puritanism struck there but small and feeble roots.

Two centuries pass and the Welsh are a non-conforming nation. How & why did this great change come about? The plunder of the Church had been wrought in the 16th century. If she had had nothing she would have been in the same condition with our non-conforming brethren. Some say that before the Welsh people became non-conforming Christians, they were godless. Until better informed, I do not believe a word of it. Of the facts I certainly know very little, but I one day examined some diocesan records at St. Asaphs of (about) 1740 or 1750, they represented a good not a bad state of things. In the small, very small, rural town of Abergele, there were I think between 450 and 500 communicants at Easter.

14. Whitm.

Ch. 8½ AM & H.C. Wrote to Rev. Orby Shipley—Sir W. Harcourt—Ld Granville—& minutes. Conversation with Mr Ottley—The Rector. Read Fortnightly Rev. on Green—Carlyle—Italy—Elijah's Mantle (very cleverly *written*, but a sad moral bathos).[3] Finished Bourgeois Gentilhomme.

To Sir W. V. HARCOURT, home secretary,   MS Harcourt dep. 9, f. 42.
14 May 1883.

I am very desirous that the Cabinet should finally take its line on the London Bill freely, if possible, and without being driven to a negative conclusion by differences about Police. With this view I wish to point out the form into which I could agree to cast my proposal about the five years term. It *might* be made to run thus: the present powers to be prolonged for five years and until Parliament shall otherwise provide. I do not remember the exact words, but the model form would be that of the Bank Charter Act of 1844.

I beg you not summarily to dispose of this and I cannot but think you will be led to accept it.[4]

At this moment I believe very few of the Cabinet are aware of the exact form of the difference between your & my opinion: or rather they are now for the first time learning it through my Memorandum.

[1] W. L. Bevan, 'Historical note on the episcopate in Wales' (1879), 21–2; disagrees with diarist's argument in 1870 that William III, not the Hanoverians, first followed a hostile religious policy towards Wales.

[2] H. Hallam, *The constitutional history of England*, ii. 230 (2nd ed. 1839): 'most of Wales, where the prevailing sentiment was royalist'.

[3] Churchill's anon. attack on tory leadership since Beaconsfield, *F.R.*, xxxix. 613 (May 1883).

[4] Harcourt did not accept, but emphasised the substantial difference between control 'vested in the Municipality & any contention that it ought now and always to be in the Executive'; 16 May, Add MS 44198, f. 66.

To Rev. ORBY SHIPLEY,[1] 14 May 1883.   Add MS 44546, f. 114.

Allow me to thank you for your kindness in sending me your papers on the *Dies Irae.*[2] I have not leisure to give them at this moment the attention they deserve. But I do not doubt that your searching minuteness of comparison will be useful to the difficult art of translation generally.

Trusting to your indulgence I venture to take exception to your treating Sir Walter Scott's most noble verses in the 'Lay' as a translation of the *Dies Irae.*[3] You are not illiberal to them: and in what I think an error you follow a train of predecessors. My contention is that the *Dies Irae* supplied Scott with a suggestion, not an original; and that, setting out from that suggestion, he composed what is not only an original but very decidedly the grandest piece of sacred poetry in the English language; such a piece as would have compelled Johnson, could he have read it, to alter his doctrine respecting that kind of composition.[4]

15. Tu.

Ch. 8½ A.M. Wrote to Mr Hamilton—Sir H. Taylor—Mr Westell—Duke of Albany—Earl of Derby—The Queen—and minutes. Read Taylor's Autobiography[5]—Fennell, Introd. to Pindar[6]—Pindar—a little: Froissart—Les Femmes Savantes.[7] Drive with C. & W. Also an exhausting walk & salutations among 2000 visitors to the Park; who were most hearty and kind. Received an Address.

16. Wed.

Ch. 8½ AM. Wrote to Mr Wilson (Birmm)—Ld Granville—Mr MacColl—and minutes. Read Les Femmes Savantes—Picton, Municipal Records[8]—Pindar. Ol.—Cardon Costituz. Inglese.[9] Drove with C.

To Rev. M. MacCOLL, 16 May 1883.   Add MS 44546, f. 115.

I feel the force of what you say as the prospects of *Theology* in the Church of England though I doubt whether it is at this moment declining. The currents which have been allowed to run so strongly against it at the Universities have been I think a main cause of the mischief.[10]

But though I rarely disagree with you I am afraid I cannot properly treat Epworth in the manner you propose and intrust so large a parochial work to a person whose mind is to entertain it only as a secondary object.

---

[1] Orby Shipley, 1832-1916; anglican priest, converted to Rome 1878; author and antiquarian.
[2] Sent on 11 May; Hawn P.
[3] Scott, 'The Lay of the last Minstrel', c. vi. xxxi; the verses take the *Dies Irae* as a starting point.
[4] 'The ideas of Christian Theology are too simple for eloquence, too sacred for fiction, and too majestic for ornament'; S. Johnson, 'Waller' in *The lives of the English poets, Works* (1816 ed.), ix. 276.
[5] H. Taylor, *Autobiography 1800-1875*, 2v. (privately printed 1874-7); see to Taylor, 24 Mar. 85.
[6] C. A. M. Fennell, *Pindar* (1879).
[7] By Molière (1672); see 17 Apr. 26.
[8] Sir J. A. Picton, *The city of Liverpool. Selections from the municipal archives and records*, 2v. (1883-6).
[9] See 30 Jan. 83.
[10] MacColl wrote on 8 May, Add MS 44244, f. 148, on the difficulties of revising Palmer (see 20, 27 Mar. 81), and suggested Greig for Ewelme.

Ewelme would have done very well for Mr. Greig but for the statutory restriction.[1] I must wait another opportunity. I am going to look up the case of Lord Mulgrave[2] as a possible man for Epworth.

17. *Th.*

Ch. 8½ A.M. Wrote to Marquis of Lorne—The Queen—Ld Granville—Mr Bright—Mme. Soldane—Bp of Ely—& minutes. Read Pindar Ol.—Cardon, La Costituz. Inglese—Les Femmes Savantes finished—Le Malade Imaginaire.[3] Saw Mr Bevington.

To the MARQUIS OF LORNE, governor-general of Canada,   Add MS 44546, f. 115.
17 May 1883.

I shall be very glad to receive any further communications which you may kindly address to me with respect to local self-government in Ireland.[4]

Nothing has happened which in my view ought to slacken the desire for measures of that kind: but the block of business still continuing in the House of Commons, even after the mitigations effected by the new rules, smites with paralysis a multitude of good wishes and intentions.

I found your Father at Cannes well and full of force. But I am afraid he has suffered sharply since I left the place.

18. *Fr.*

Ch. 8½ A. M. Wrote to Lady Phillimore—Bp of Carlisle—Ld Granville—Sir W. Harcourt—E.W. Hamilton l. & Tel.—and minutes. Conversation with WHG on Hawarden affairs. Saw Mr Ottley. Woodcraft—more gently. Read Pindar Olymp.—Cardon, Costituz. Inglese—Le Malade Imaginaire (finished). Arranged with Bailey for new Book accommodation: say 1400 volumes.

To E. W. HAMILTON, 18 May 1883.   Add MS 48607B, f. 163.

1. Any thing about the Cannes Photographs?

2. Any thing from Sir J. A. Picton of Liverpool about his 'Municipal Records'[5]

3 Please look at *questions* for Monday & see how to clear them off. I do not come up till Wedy.

4. I return the 'National' & have read Austin (not too good-natured, not accurate, but with much truth), and Pembroke:[6] I am glad that he continues to think. In principle, perhaps my Coalwhippers Act of 1843 was the most Socialistic measure of the last half century.

5 WHG. says there is a very shameful print of me with Bradlaugh & Besant in a St James's Street window—I should like to have a copy.

---

[1] Living to be held by an Oxford M.A.; Gladstone had burnt his fingers on the W. W. Harvey case, see 12 July 71.

[2] Offered the living of Epworth on 20 May, Add MS 44546, f. 116, which he declined.

[3] By Molière (1673); see 30 Sept. 25.

[4] Lorne wrote on 1 May, Add MS 44480, f. 274, sending material on Canadian opinion on Ireland; he supported provincial assemblies, see the duke of Argyll, *Passages from the past* (1907), ii. 476.

[5] See 16 May 83.

[6] A. Austin, 'The prime minister's dilemma' [i.e. retirement]; Lord Pembroke, 'Liberty and socialism', *National Review*, i. 321, 336 (May 1883).

6. I read Jebb, & take a sincere interest in the plan:[1] but am not well enough *up* in it to offer suggestions. I hope however some College or permanent authority will assume the chief responsibility.

7. Fisheries Exhibition. I have not I think been invited, & thought this kind of the P. of W.—I do not think that at my time of life I cd. fairly have been expected to attend even if it had not been in the holidays.

To Sir W. V. HARCOURT, home secretary,   MS Harcourt dep. 9, f. 44.
18 May 1883. '*Private*'.

I am truly sorry that you find all the propositions that I have made with a view to narrowing the distance between our opinions necessary to be rejected on the instant. The correspondence between us is singularly one-sided. You have argued largely for your view of the subject of the Metropolitan Police on the merits (as you were entitled to do). On my side of this question I have been almost entirely silent.

Nor will I now trouble you with any such argument. Your Memorandum of last year, in explanation of your Bill, treated the question 'in whose hands shall be the superintendence of the Metropolitan Police?' *as one open to further consideration.* All that I ask is to stand upon the principle of that Memorandum.

But I understand you now to require that as far as it can be done by any present decision, this future consideration shall be excluded *from the Bill and the debate*: for so high, you think, is the principle involved that it is necessary the whole Cabinet should be of one mind, not only on what is now to be done, but upon what is to be held of permanent as well as present necessity; and should be prepared to argue this 'very high'.

There are three matters, apart from the argument upon the merit (as to which I take it we are both 'past praying for') which bear upon this subject; political expediency, Parliamentary practicability; and the general rules and methods, under which the cooperation of independent minds in Cabinet may become practicable.

On the last of these three questions I have a considerable advantage over you in an experience which began just forty years back. And I must say that I think the conditions you lay down as to unity of opinion are such as would go far to render the cooperation of independent minds in Cabinet impracticable. It has always, in my experience, been found sufficient for the preparation and enactment of laws that the Ministers should be agreed on what was there and then to be done. It is surely too much to require that all should be prepared to bind themselves for all time where they entertain the greatest doubts and scruples, merely because some may be ready to proceed to this length.

It seems to me that this rigid exaction is peculiarly inappropriate in a case where the reasons on the side of the exactor are administrative—which I take to be your case—and the reasons against him, or the 'doubts and scruples' have regard to high and permanent principles of civil liberty: for such are in my view, the principles of local self-government.

In your mind, I admit, State-police for the Metropolis is a permanent necessity. Let me then quote a precedent. No man could have a deeper conviction on any matter, as to its permanent necessity, than Sir Robert Peel had on the principle of his [Bank] Act of 1844: every one who knew him knew that this was a kind of Baptismal Creed with him. Yet he voluntarily proposed and carried its enactment in the very same terms as to liberty of future re-consideration, as I have been now proposing. He thought the judgment of the future would confirm, with the aid of more experience, the judgment of the present. Was he not right?

I think I have shown in my own case that I accept those rules of concession as a condition of cooperation, which I now try to press upon you. To quote an instance. In 1880 I

---

[1] See 6 Feb., 25 June 83.

was averse to the suspension of the *Habeas Corpus* Act; and I recommended in a Memorandum a different plan: but not obtaining from Forster, or any other Minister with whom I happened to confer, much encouragement, I accepted Forster's plan as fit under all the circumstances, and supported it. I am not sure that I should have been able to support it, had he required of me more than that concurrence for the present & under all the circumstances, which I ask you to be content with.

Difference of opinion on future contingencies germain to the present matter has often been known as well as tolerated, in very high regions of principle: as for example when the Government of Lord Grey agreed to carry the Irish Church Bill of 1833 though utterly at variance among themselves on the application of the property of the Irish Church.

I will promise not to detain you so long on the two other topics.

Parliamentary practicability. It is my opinion (*valeat quantum*) that no amount of high arguing by the Cabinet will avail to carry through the present House of Commons a plan of Municipal Reform for London which shall *unite* the three conditions of a. One Municipality for the whole. b. Permanent State Police for the ⟨whole⟩ Municipality generally. c. Extinction of the Municipal Controul over the City Police.

There remains the point of political expediency. I cannot do otherwise than place rather high the political expediency, or necessity, of going forward with the London Bill during the present year. I think circumstances have made it higher than it was a few weeks ago. The Liberal party as a rule draws its vital breath from great Liberal measures. Sometimes it cannot. It so happens that at present we have many good Bills in hand; but they are not understood as distinctly Liberal Bills. The country is set upon our holding in the main to our programme: it would be serious to drop out the central piece. I admit that the burden upon you would be heavy. But you would have some very efficient aid from within and also from without the Cabinet. I do not wish to push the argument too far: but thus far I go, that it will be a *serious responsibility* to set up a difference of opinion such as to preclude the Cabinet from discussing freely the question whether to drop the Bill or to proceed with it.

I should be delighted to see Spencer at any or all Cabinets. But I do not admit that Irish considerations bear upon the specific question now under discussion between you and me: or that the Fenian plots, at which he has dealt such a deadly blow, are a permanent institution of the country. Nor do I think that the matter is one easily to be settled by arguing in the Cabinet. I propose that the Cabinet should read the series of letters which have passed between you and me on this subject. Have you quite realised to yourself this fact that you, with the memorandum of last year as your starting point, have greatly *receded* from me & my standing-ground; while I at any rate have carried concession to such a point that I have offered for the sake of union to concur in so framing the Bill that instead of the purer *status quo* it may include a proposal to suppress the existing Municipal controul: although I think we might possibly or probably fail to carry the provision.

What I would venture to suggest to you, and I hope you will favourably consider the suggestion, is that you should *yourself* lay all the facts, perhaps best of all the letters, before some few of our colleagues, choosing those whom for any reason you may think most available under the circumstances for consultation.

Forgive this long letter. Of its dimensions it is the first, and I hope will be the last, with which I need assail you.

19. Sat.

Wrote to W.H.G.—Sir H. Ponsonby Tel and l.—Mr Hamilton Tel.—Sig. Cardon[1]—Scotts—Mr Fennell[2]—The Queen—Earl of Derby—& minutes. Tea at E. Dumaresques. Woodcraft with W. & S. Read Pindar Ol.—George Dandin[3]—Froissart's Chron.—and Pope Hennessy on Ireland.[4] Saw Dr Waters.

To LORD DERBY, colonial secretary, 19 May 1883. *'Private'.*   Add MS 44546, f. 116.

It is perhaps as well that the Leopold affair should have come rapidly to a conclusion, for it could only end I think one way.[5] I am afraid he is not only disappointed but sore & angry.

It would probably be well to know the opinions of the other colleagues whom you consulted about Canada before opening any glimpse of Victoria. The difficulties there are greatly simplified if not removed. Indeed as to the climate I should not be surprised to find that it was deemed positively beneficial to a person affected as he is. Long ago I contemplated sending Sir W. Denison to Tasmania,[6] but as he was liable to epileptic fits, medical opinions were taken, & they were to the effect that he would probably be better in that climate. He lived long there & elsewhere; & I *think* he came back cured.

We shall I suppose soon have the New Guinea case regularly before us. I hope we may find ourselves in a condition utterly to quash this annexation effected by Queensland on her own sole authority, for I suppose her to be untrustworthy as well as unauthorised. If the Australian colonies would combine into some kind of Colonial Union, we should at all events have much better means of approaching the question. They would present to us some substantial responsibility for whatever they might undertake. I am sorry to find, only a recent discovery with me, that we have already made annexations of some of the circumjacent islands.

[P.S.] The simple fact of making one of the Queen's sons the subordinate of the Secretary of State is such a novelty that it requires to be turned round & round & well looked over on all sides.

20. Trin S.

Ch 8 AM H.C. 11 A.M. 6½ P.M. (S.E.G. on H. Trin—excellent). Read Valdez Minor Works[7]—Bp of Carlisle, Science & Faith[8]—Brahmo Somaj 1881 & 2.[9]—Rev. Mr [blank] on Affn Bill—and other Tracts. Wrote to Mr Hamilton—Ld Mulgrave—Mr MacColl—and minutes.

21. M.

Ch. 8½ A.M. Wrote to Mr Hamilton Tel.—Mr A. Reader—Mr Coleridge—Miss Collet—Mr Holt—& minutes. Worked on papers & books. Read Pindar Pyth.—Life of Valdes[10]—Molière, L'Avare. Woodcraft.

---

[1] Thanking R. Cardon, Italian legal historian, for his book; Add MS 44546, f. 116.
[2] Note of thanks to Charles Augustus Maude Fennell for his *Pindar.*
[3] By Molière (1668); see 16 Feb. 26.
[4] Sir J. Pope Hennessy, *Sir Walter Raleigh in Ireland* (1883).
[5] Leopold hoped to succeed Lorne as governor general of Canada, but Victoria vetoed the suggestion; nothing came of the antipodean alternative, suggested by Derby on 17 May. See 25 Apr. 83.
[6] See 20 June 46.   [7] Probably J. de Valdès, *XVII Opuscules*, ed. J. T. Betts (1882).
[8] H. Goodwin, *Walks in the regions of science and faith* (1883).
[9] Sent by Miss S. Collet; see 25 Dec. 76.
[10] E. Boehmer, *Lives of . . . J. and A. de Valdès* (1883).

22. Tu.

Ch. 8$\frac{1}{2}$ AM. Wrote to Mr Hamilton—C.G.—Mr Childers—Ld Spencer—Ld Kimberley—& minutes. Read Pindar (largely)—Molière, L'Avare (finished). Revelled in the woods, with Willy. Worked on books & papers.

To LORD KIMBERLEY, Indian secretary, 22 May 1883.   Add MS 44546, f. 117.

If by chance the first of these two letters[1] has not met your eye, I advise your reading it.

Some day I suppose the Ilbert Bill will be named in Cabinet. My feelings are strongly with Ripon but my information is not perfect. He will probably send home his full case for our consideration?

To LORD SPENCER, Viceroy of Ireland, 22 May 1883.   Althorp MSS K6.

I think the best thing I can do to procure the unbiased consideration of your proposal about further operations for material development in Ireland is to print Mr. Hamilton's memorandum & your covering letter.[2]

There was much scruple & hesitation in the Cabinet[3] about the Stephens plan, which (plan) however I rather helped onwards than otherwise.

We have been & are moving at a great pace on this dangerous ground & I feel very doubtful whether we ought now to quicken it. Sound & strong local institutions for Ireland are in my opinion the proper pre-condition. I do not write under the influence of Treasury motives only. I would almost say that every new loan to a farmer is a new danger. Your argument for guarantees *versus* loans is one not to be dismissed in a moment.

23. Wed. [London]

8$\frac{1}{2}$-3$\frac{1}{4}$. To Windsor: had audience of the Queen. On to London at six. Wrote to Mr Birkbeck[4]—Bp of London—Ld Derby—Mr Dodson—& minutes. Dined at Bp of Winchesters. Saw Mr Aplin—Mr Mitchell—Sir H. Ponsonby—Sir T. Acland—Mr Hamilton. Read Pindar—and [blank].

To LORD DERBY, colonial secretary, 23 May 1883.   Add MS 44546, f. 117.

I have read with great interest the account of your interview with Sir H. Robinson.[5] He appears to have stated his views with great force & to be admirably reported.

I go with him on one question where he appears still to suspend his judgment: namely against the retention of a Resident in the Transvaal if we give up the Convention.

The statement on Basutoland appears to be excellent all through.

Has the Convention with the Transvaal done no good whatever, checked no evil whatever? This is a vital question. I think Sir H. R. seems prepared to answer in plain terms 'no, none whatever'. But ought we not to hear the opinion & report of the Resident on this? Query whether also of Bulwer? And if so, should it not be at once asked by telegraph? It is a distinct question, in some measure, from that of our complaints for infraction.

---

[1] Not found; Kimberley replied, 23 May, Add MS 44228, f. 73, that he was in constant communication with Ripon on the Ilbert Bill and would be glad to explain it in Cabinet.

[2] Letter and mem. on need for 'new ground for Government intervention in Ireland', e.g. agricultural and transport improvements; printed for cabinet; Add MS 44310, ff. 93-5.

[3] See 5 May 83.

[4] Probably (Sir) Edward Birkbeck, 1838-1907; tory M.P. Norfolk 1879-92; cr. bart. 1886.

[5] On 16 May on the future of the 1881 Pretoria Convention which Robinson wanted supported or dismantled; Schreuder, 348.

There is another question, about the Bechuanas, on which I should be glad of an answer. In the memorandum it seems to be assumed that if a force were sent we should only have to deal with squatting freebooters. But is it not practically certain that if we are to help the 2 M.s[1] we should be involved in a quarrel with their native, as well as their squatting, enemies.

Forgive this scrawl written on the rail.

To Sir W. V. HARCOURT, home secretary,   MS Harcourt dep. 9, f. 50.
23 May 1883.

I thank you very much for your note.[2] Granville tells me you are troubled, as indeed who must not be? in the question of time. It has occurred to me as worth consideration whether if we are able virtually or mainly to put aside the police question and if we get the principle of our Unitarian Bill decided on the second reading, it would be possible to refer the detail of the Clauses to a General Committee.

I feel that if the London Bill cannot go forward now, it will be very difficult to secure precedence for it in the future sessions of *this* Parliament. Without doubt its going on means either an extreme protraction of the present sittings, or meeting in October to finish off. But there are some independent arguments in favour of that most disagreeable course. On the question of *indefinite* postponement I cannot but feel, besids [*sic*] the public objection to the measure, that *you* have conceived a great plan, and you ought to receive the reward in fame which the successful prosecution of it cannot fail to bring. I write on the rail Windsor-wards.

[P.S.] Six policemen on my back all the time I have been at Hawarden. Yet I have survived: each of them I am bound to say more civil than can be told.

24. *Th.*

Wrote to Att. General—Mr Naylor—Mr P. Brown—S. Lyttelton (sen)—Ld E. Fitzmaurice—Sir W. Harcourt—Duchess of Sutherland—The Queen—& minutes. H. of C. 5–7 and 9½–12¾.[3] Saw Mr H—Ld R.G. Saw Sir W. Harcourt, Sir C. Dilke, Mr Childers: all on London Mun. Bill. Read Scoones's Letters[4]—Carlyle & Emerson Corr.[5]

To Sir W. V. HARCOURT, home secretary,   MS Harcourt dep. 9, f. 52.
24 May 1883. '*Immediate*'.

I thank you for your letter though it sorely disappoints me. You do not say whether the ministers you assembled[6] have read my letter to you from Hawarden? or heard it?[7] If not, I will send it them.

25. *Fr.*

Wrote to Lady Holker—Lucy Cavendish—Mr Dodson—Att. General—Ld Houghton—The Queen l.l.—Mr Reader—and minutes. H. of C. 5–8½. Spoke on

[1] i.e. Montshiwa and Mankurwane, Bechuana chiefs.
[2] Not found.
[3] Questions; supply; *H* 279. 761.
[4] See 7 Mar. 83n.   [5] See 3 May 83.
[6] Meeting of Cabinet ministers held by Harcourt, which recommended introduction and 2°R of the London Bill; Add MS 44198, f. 77.
[7] Harcourt replied that '*all the correspondence*' was circulated 'to the whole Cabinet'; ibid., f. 79.

Armenia.[1] Saw Mr H—Ld RG—HJG—Messrs Norchi[2]—Mrs Th.—Ld Granville. Read Mercy d'Argenteau Corresp.[3]

26. Sat.

Wrote to Ld Spencer—Mr Borlase—Mr Trevelyan—Prince L.L. Bonaparte—Mr Childers—Hobart Pacha[4]—The Queen—& minutes. Cabinet 2–5¾: stiff. Saw Mr H.—Ld RG—Ld Granville & conclave—P. of Wales (Canada & Duke of A[lbany]). [Queen's] Birthday dinner to 36. Nearly stifled with smoke. Neuralgia began, & was sharp at night. Read Carlyle—Emerson II.

Cabinet. Sat. May 26. 83.[5]
0 ⟨1. Bright Banquet June 14. Will a Peer attend? What Peer?⟩[6]
2. State of business. Days demanded. 52 or 54 *without London Bill.* Govt. days down to about Aug. 20: 24. what more time shall we ask? What shall be the programme? Shall we announce it at a meeting of the party? & obtain their adhesion *with intent to carry it?* On ⟨Thursday⟩? Tuesday—see letter to H.M.[7]
3. Trawling, Scotch—Chamberlain proposed a Commission of Inquiry. He is to discuss & settle the matter with C. of E.[8]
4. Basutos. Ld D[erby] stated the case & certainty of a renunciation. Basutos shd. not be repudiated. Nor shd. they be coerced. Cabinet agreed that if they are reasonable we shd. renounce.
   'not to decide on refusing the proposal to take over Basuto territory. To make conditions with the Cape as to their sharing the expense. &c. To obtain the assent of the Chiefs & people as far as can be done. Unless these conditions are complied with to accept no responsibility in the matter'. Words of Ld D—adopted.[9]
5. Ashburnham collection.[10] Ld A. demands 90 m[ille]. Cabinet advise
6. D. of Wellington Statue removal for £4700. To be tested.
7. Ilbert's Bill—Ld Ripon studying means of amending. Bill cannot be given up.
8. Sunday Closing Bill for Durham. will support: not binding the Govt.
9. Privy Seal. To await inquiry as to signatures necessary for validity of documents.
10. Congo plan. Whydah: there is to be a right reserved to ask Portugal to waive her right.[11]

27. 1 S. Trin.

Better but kept the house till drive at 3½, Chapel Royal 5.30. Saw Gerty and her dear little baby.[12] Wrote to Ld Derby. Read Fabers Hymns—Essex Rector on the Age of Man[13]—Renan, Souvenirs.[14]

[1] On Bryce's resolution; the house was counted during his speech; *H* 279. 923.
[2] Importers of sculpture. [3] See 23 Apr. 83.
[4] Declining to see him; Add MS 44546, f. 119. [5] Add MS 44644, f. 58.
[6] This entry scored out. [7] CAB 41/17/9, which adds little.
[8] The Dalhousie Royal Commission on trawling, PP 1884–5 xvi. 471.
[9] Basutoland subsequently became a crown colony; Schreuder, 342–3.
[10] See 14 Apr. 83. Ashburnham had declined an offer of £70,000 for part of the collection, demanding £90,000; CAB 41/17/9.
[11] i.e. Portugal not to be required, as originally proposed, to cede Fort Whydah in Dahomey, but British permission needed before its cession to another power; see Granville to d'Antas, 1 June, with draft treaty; F.O.C.P. 4865.
[12] Constance Gertrude Gladstone, grand-da., b. 2 May 1883.
[13] Untraced. [14] E. Renan, see 1 May 83.

28. M.

Wrote to The Queen l.l.l.—Ld Kimberley—Sir T. Acland—Mr Forster—& minutes. H of C. 5¼-8½ & 9½-12.[1] Read Carlyle Emerson Corr. Saw Mr H.—Ld R.G—Ld Granville—Ld Bray[2]—Mr Childers—Dr Clark—Mr Whitbread—Mr Bright—Mr Goschen—Att. General. A good night & quinine are helping me on.

To W. E. FORSTER, M.P., 28 May 1883. '*Private*'.   Add MS 44546, f. 120.

A little while after I had passed you in the Division Lobby, I looked about for you but you had left the House. My object was to mention to you generally the purpose of the meeting which is to be held tomorrow. We have felt that the time has arrived when the Government ought to announce to the House its views with respect to the business of the session. In consequence of events which have happened since the Queen's Speech, we think we cannot now ask the House to go through with all the larger Bills we had projected; & making the best choice we can, we keep to the Agricultural Holdings & the Corrupt Practices, & drop the London Bill for the year. To work *through* the design thus reduced, including of course all such Bills as may return from the Grand Committees, will require serious effort from us & from the House. Our object in asking for the meeting is to announce our intention to spare no effort for the purpose, & to appeal to our friends for that resolute & harmonious support in this decision, which alone can make it effective for the purpose in view.

I hope you will not disapprove this plan.[3]

29. Tu.

Wrote to Ld Granville—Ld Kimberley—The Queen—and minutes. 11-12¼ Party meeting on the state of business. Very good.[4] Saw Mr H—Ld RG—Mr Seymour—Conclave on course of business. H of C. 4¾-8¼ and 9½-11½.[5] Read Carlyle Emerson II (finished)—Hull on Suez Canal.[6] Dined at Sir W. James's.

30. Wed.

Wrote to Ld Derby—Ld Granville—Sir J. Picton—Baron Ferrières—Mr Mason—Ld Carlingford—& minutes. Dined at home to go to the notable Homeric play at Sir C. Freake's: difficult, & highly successful.[7] Saw Mr H—Ld RG—Ld Granville—B. Museum Depn *cum* C of E.[8]—Lady Holker. Read Mercy d'Argenteau and Richards on W.E.G.[9]

To LORD DERBY, colonial secretary, 30 May 1883.   Add MS 44546, f. 120.

You may have seen what I said yesterday in answer to Hicks Beach.

By the end of June or early in July we may have to arrange for a discussion.

[1] Questions; Ireland; *H* 279. 963, 975.
[2] Alfred T. T. Verney-Cave, 1849-1928; 5th Baron Bray 1879.
[3] No reply found.
[4] 'There was no appreciable difference of opinion'; *T.T.*, 30 May 1883, 11a.
[5] Statement on business announcing abandonment of the London govt. bill; *H* 279. 1105.
[6] E. C. P. Hull, *England and the Suez Canal* (1883).
[7] At Cromwell House, with Mrs Bram Stoker 'the beauty'; *Mary Gladstone*, 291.
[8] See 2 June 83.
[9] See 12 May 83.

We ought to prepare ourselves, so far as it can be done by any action of our own, to say 1. What is our attitude with respect to the Convention. 2. Whether we think there is any case for rendering aid to any Bechuana Chiefs. 3. What is our information about the troubles in Zululand & the conduct of Cetewayo. 4. What course we shall take as to the Cape & Basuto question. I therefore think you may be quite right in asking the Transvaal Government to state their case on the Convention: but probably as it is a distinct measure, it would be well to name it in Cabinet.[1]

31. Th.

Wrote to The Queen l.l.—Mr Bullen—Ld Bath—and minutes. H. of C. $4\frac{1}{2}$–$6\frac{1}{2}$ and $9\frac{1}{2}$–1: calm weather now.[2] Saw Mr H—Ld R.G—Sir A. Gordon—Chr of Exr—and others. Read Vie de Talleyrand.[3] Saw The Speaker & Conclave on the O'Kelly case.[4]

Frid. June One 1883.

Wrote to The Queen l.l.l.l.—Ld Dufferin—Mr Trevelyan—Lord Ripon—H.N.G.— and minutes. Saw Mr H—Ld RG—D. of Argyll—Ld Granville—Mr Bond—Cav. di Giovanni[5]—Mr West. Visited Br. Museum to examine Italian Versions of the Threefold question to St Peter.[6] H. of C. $4\frac{3}{4}$–$8\frac{1}{4}$ and $11\frac{3}{4}$–$12\frac{3}{4}$.[7] Read Vie de Talleyrand—Hobhouse on Ilbert Bill.[8] [9]June 1. Mr Rally's Theatrical. Saw M. Coquelin.

To H. N. GLADSTONE, 1 June 1883.   Hawarden MSS.

The woefully scanty list of my letters to you will receive in these few lines little more than a nominal addition: but I cannot resist sending to you, inclosed herewith, an admirable article, by Sir Arthur Hobhouse, on the Ilbert Bill, published today in the Contemporary Review.

Though not exactly informed on all the details of the case my feeling for the Bill is strong and unequivocal; it would take much to convince me that it is not in substance just & right: and as to its opportuneness, I do not think that is disproved by the mere fact that there has been an adverse excitement among the English Residents. I read your words about the Bill with much satisfaction.

God bless you dearest Harry. Be assured you are never for a day out of my innermost thoughts. Things are not at present going badly for us here: & thank God my health holds wonderfully, though my desire to escape has been in no respect abated.

---

[1] Derby, 29 May, Add MS 44141, f. 96 suggested the Transvaal be asked officially their wishes as to a modification of the 1881 Convention. See 13 June 83.

[2] Questions; supply; *H* 279. 1331.

[3] Perhaps that by L. Bastide (1838).

[4] J. C. McCoan, M.P., had been challenged to a duel by J. O'Kelly, M.P.; the Speaker next day asked O'Kelly for an assurance of peaceful behaviour.

[5] Michele di Giovanni, Italian advocate; see Add MS 44234, f. 77 and 6 Mar. 75.

[6] Set out for him by E. A. Bond of the Museum; particular purpose of this search unknown; Add MS 44481, f. 92.

[7] O'Kelly; inland revenue, accusing Churchill of 'worthless trash' in his accusations against A. West; *H* 279. 1489, 1516.

[8] Sir A. Hobhouse, 'Native Indian judges: Mr Ilbert's Bill', *C.R.*, xliii. 795; see this day's letters.

[9] Rest of entry added later up the side of the page.

To LORD RIPON, Viceroy of India, 1 June 1883.   Add MS 43515, f. 26.

Primrose has sent me on your suggestion & report on the meeting of natives at Bombay about the Ilbert Bill; which I shall carefully read.[1]

My information is not yet full or exact, but my interest in the question is great, and my prejudice, or conviction as to principles, is wholly and warmly with you: wholly, as to my understanding of the general view; warmly because in that general view great interests of the future seem to me to be at stake.

I do not admit that the simple fact of the excitement in the Anglo-Indian community *of itself* impeaches effectually the prudence or opportuneness of your act; and on that subject, while bearing in mind what you have said, I reserve your judgment.

Sir A. Hobhouse has written a very strong article in the Contemporary for June, which pleases me extremely. I do not send it as it is sure to reach you otherwise. But I send it to my son Harry in Calcutta, who is staunch, and who reports that he does not know above three Anglo-Indians or English residents in Calcutta who agree with him in approving the Bill.

The House of Commons is tolerably calm and business makes some progress. This may readily change. But I do not attach weight to the Tory vaticinations of a speedy re-advent to power.

2. Sat.

Wrote to Mr Hornby—The Queen. Cabinet 2–5. Attended Garibaldian Commemn at Stafford House: & spoke on request.[2] Saw Mr G—Ld R.G—Cav. di Giovanni—Mrs Watkins—Archbp of York—Mrs Watkins. Saw four [R]. Dined at Sir A. Hayter's. Read Talleyrand—Reviews.

Cabinet. Sat. June 2. 83. 2 PM.[3]

[1] Fawcett. Demands 1 ₥ for Parcels & P.O. Development. C. of E. to impress upon the PMG the necessity of letting Treasury know at the outside expense[?] of the whole matter. ½ ₥

2. *South Africa.* Transvaal. Ld D[erby] asked authority to initiate. Notion of a Comm[issione]r. started. (Ld Reay possibly).[4] (a)
     Basuto—Dispatch agreed to.
     Bechuana. (q[uer]y send trustworthy person to the scene?) included in (a) as to Comm[issione]r.

3. British Museum Deputation. Cabinet adhered to its proposition.[5]

4. Mr Errington.

3. 2 S. Trin.

Guards Chapel mg, & H.C.—Ch. Royal aft. Read [A.V.] Dicey on Disestabl.—MacColl on Lawlessness[6]—Essex Rector, Age of Man—... Duntriensis[7]—Orator

---

[1] Public meeting on 28 April; see Gopal, *Ripon*, 147. See 17 Apr. 83.
[2] Reminisced on Garibaldi's visit (see 12–25 Apr. 64) and his 'seductive simplicity of manner'; *T.T.*, 4 June 1883, 10a.
[3] Add MS 44644, f. 62.
[4] Harcourt suggested Rosebery, and there was an inconclusive discussion; Schreuder, 356.
[5] Not to increase its grant for the Ashburnham collection; CAB 41/17/10.
[6] A. V. Dicey, 'Legal aspects of disestablishment', M. MacColl, 'Clergy and the law', *F.R.*, xl. 822, 841 (June 1883).   [7] Obscure.

Horsley Tracts[1]—Cobbe on Agnostic Morality.[2] Wrote to U.S. Minister—Earl of Derby.

4. M.

Wrote to Prince of Wales—Mr M'Coll—The Queen l.l.—and minutes. Saw Mr H.—Ld R.G—Ld Granville—Conclave on Rosebery—Ld Hartington on do. H of C. $4\frac{3}{4}$–$8\frac{1}{4}$ & $9\frac{1}{2}$–[blank].[3] Saw Henley [R]. Read Life of Talleyrand—Scoone's Letters—Mercy d'Argenteau.

To Rev. M. MacCOLL, 4 June 1883.   Add MS 44546, f. 122.

I think the eulogy passed in the Spectator[4] on your paper in the Fortnightly Review is thoroughly deserved. It was hardly possible to make the case weak, but you have turned its strength to the utmost account.

There is not I think quite so much force on the appeal to a class of persons at the close, as in the general argument.

Mr. Dicey's[5] paper, which precedes yours, pointedly shows how a man may be a lawyer, probably a good lawyer, but a careless observer & a bad historian. His account of the very curious question of the Dissenters' Chapels Bill (1844) is utterly slipshod.

Upon an appeal to the Bishop of Salisbury for further information, I am glad to have found I should be quite justified in proposing Sir J. Philipps for Epworth. This is *Private.*

5.

Wrote to Mr G. Russell—Bp of Durham—The Queen—Sir W. Harcourt—Rev. S.E.G.—Sir C. Dilke—Chr of Exr—Sir Thos Acland—Mr Godley—Dean of Westminster—and minutes. Saw Mr H—Ld RG—Sir W. Harcourt—Ld Rosebery—Sir C. Dilke—Mr Godley—Mr Hibbert—Chr of Exr. Drive with M. Read Mercy d'Argenteau—R. Gower's Reminiscences[6]—Vie de Talleyrand. H of C. $2\frac{1}{2}$–$3\frac{3}{4}$.[7]

6. Wed.

Wrote to The Queen—Sir R. Phillimore Tel.—Sir Jas Philipps (Rev.)—Prof. Donaldson—Sir W. Muir. Saw Mr H—Ld R.G.—Mr Chamberlain—Sir C. Dilke—Sir W. Harcourt—Ld Derby—Ld Bath—Lady Pembroke (with whom I had an interesting conversation at dinner)—C. Corti. Read Talleyrand—Mercy d'Argenteau—Ronald Gower Vol 1. Drive with C. Dined with the Baths. Lady Salisbury's party afterwards.

---

[1] S. Horsley, *Tracts in controversy with Dr. Priestley* (1789).
[2] F. P. Cobbe, 'Agnostic morality', *C.R.*, xxxiii. 783 (June 1883).
[3] Questions on South Africa; *H* 279. 1644. Rosebery's resignation received this day.
[4] *The Spectator*, 2 June 1883, 695.
[5] Albert Venn *Dicey, 1835–1922; professor of English law, Oxford, 1882–1909; became an ardent Unionist; see 12 Nov. 86.
[6] Lord R. C. S. Leveson Gower, *My Reminiscences*, 2v. (1883), with sundry Gladstoniana.
[7] Attending questions; *H* 279. 1740.

To Professor JAMES DONALDSON,[1] 6 June 1883.   Add MS 44546, f. 123.

You will readily understand that I thought it best to delay acknowledging your very interesting letter[2] until the immediate question raised by the discussion in the House of Commons last Thursday was disposed of. It has been disposed of in a way which for many reasons I would have deprecated. But if unhappily Lord Rosebery *was* to resign, the resignation has been effected in the best manner. It is placed on a defined & insulated ground, from which references cannot readily be drawn; & it is accompanied with a clear understanding which goes as far as possible towards placing any resumption of office a short time hence on a footing nearly approaching that of continuance.

With regard to the immediate object of your letter, my answer will be short.

The Cabinet is a subtle & delicate piece of mechanism, which has been forming itself mainly within the last hundred years, & which is at once one of the most important & I think absolutely the least intelligible of the institutions of the country.

From an exterior point of view it appears simply even to the most intelligent observer (*videlicet* to yourself) to meet a case of high personal distinction, & of strong Scotch feeling & desire, by an addition to the Cabinet.

But even the best class of opinion or pressure from without will not excuse those within for doing what from their point of view they see to be inadmissible. A *host* of questions surround every admission into a Cabinet which is other than a mere substitution; & more than one of these questions have had such a bearing as to prevent action in the sense you desire.   .

There is however as I believe in the minds of my colleagues as there undoubtedly is in my own, a cordial desire for the political advancement of Lord Rosebery, & if to the Cabinet so much the better. There is perhaps no man of his age in either House whose political future is so assured; & this consideration will I hope qualify any regret you may naturally feel on the present occasion.

I must not conclude without thanking you sincerely for those parts of your letter in which I am directly concerned.

[P.S.] If you are in town on any Thursday during the remainder of the season, would you do me the favour of announcing yourself to breakfast with me (at ten)?

7. *Th.*

Wrote to Bp of Oxford—Ld Granville—Mr Forewood—Mr Stephenson—Ld Derby—The Queen—& minutes. H of C. $4\frac{3}{4}$-$8\frac{1}{2}$ & $9\frac{3}{4}$-$1\frac{1}{4}$.[3] Eleven to breakfast. Saw Mr H—Ld R.G—C.G. respecting Knox Little—Mr Gifford Palgrave[4]—Mr Browning. Read Mercy d'Argenteau—Vie de Talleyrand.

8. *Fr.*

Wrote to Sir G. Balfour—Mr D. Grant—The Queen—and minutes. H. of C. 2-7 and 9-2 AM.[5] Read Vie de Talleyrand. Morning walk. Missed Mrs B [R]. Saw Mr H—Ld RG—Cav. de' Giovanni—Servian Minister.

---

[1] See 4 July 79.

[2] Of 31 May, Add MS 44481, f. 103: Rosebery said to have saved Scotland from revolution; should be in the cabinet.

[3] Spoke on Corrupt Practices Bill; *H* 279. 1932.

[4] William Gifford Palgrave, 1826–88; consul in Bulgaria 1878, in Siam 1879, in Uruguay 1884. Presumably home on leave.

[5] Spoke on Alcester's grant, and Egypt; *H* 280. 38, 134.

9. Sat. [Berkhampstead]

Wrote to Mrs Th.—and minutes. Off at 12 to Lady S[arah] Spencer's charming Villeggiatura.[1] In aft. to Ashridge & its glorious drive, perhaps unequalled: now in its greatest beauty. Saw Mr H—Ld RG—Ld C. Bruce—Ld Lyttelton. Read Vie de Talleyrand—Barrett on the Temptation[2]—Mrs Delany.[3]

10. 3 S. Trin.

Great Berkhampstead (noble) Church 11 A.M. & Ashridge evg. The people in G.B. very enthusiastic. Read Renan Souvenirs—Vie de Talleyrand—Denison's (wild) Charge[4]—Divers Sermons. Wrote to E. Hamilton Tel.—Miss de Lisle—Sir Thos G.—and minutes.

11. M. [London]

Back to London at 11. Wrote to Countess Bothmer[5]—Mrs Wellesley—Mr Bullen—Chancr of Exr—The Queen—and minutes. Saw Mr H—Ld R.G—The Speaker—Ld Granville—Mrs Bolton. Conclave (Bis) on Egypt. H of C. $4\frac{3}{4}$–$8\frac{1}{2}$ & $10\frac{1}{2}$–$2\frac{1}{4}$.[6] Dined at Sir C. Forsters: saw Deans of Durham & Llandaff. Read Vie de Talleyrand.

12. Tu.

Wrote to The Queen—The Speaker—& minutes. Drive with C.G. & walk. H of C. $4\frac{1}{4}$–7 and 9–1.[7] Saw Mr H—Ld RG—Archbp of Canterbury—Ld Advocate—Sir N. Rothschild. Read Talleyrand—Hermann Agha[8]—M'Combe[?] on Irish Taxn.[9]

13. Wed.

Wrote to Mr Forster—Ld Granville l.l.—The Queen—Att. General for Ireland—Mr Downing—& minutes. Cabinet 2–5. Dined at Mr Lowell's. Saw Mr H—Ld RG. Read Vie de Talleyrand—Mercy d'Argenteau.

Cabinet. Wed. June 13. 83. 2 PM.[10]
1. Transvaal Commissioner. Commissioner to be sent—for revision of the Convention which *wd. of necessity involve* his examining the questions connected with the state of Bechuana Land in conjunction with the High Commissr.[11]

---

[1] 'Country seat', at Berkhampstead; Lady Sarah Isabella Spencer, 1838–99; da. of 4th Earl Spencer.
[2] By J. T. Barrett (1821).
[3] M. Delany, *Autobiography and correspondence*, 3v. (1861).
[4] G. A. Denison, 'The Church and the world' (1883); attack on disestablishment and democracy.
[5] Countess Mary von Bothmer had sent her *Aut Caesar aut nihil*, 3v. (1883); on the assassination of Alexander II.
[6] Spoke on Wolseley's grant; *H* 280. 288.
[7] Spoke on Irish land; *H* 280. 446.
[8] W. G. Palgrave, *Hermann Agha: an eastern narrative*, 2v. (1872 and later eds.); see 7 June 83.
[9] Name scrawled; possibly an article in *McComb's Presbyterian Almanac* (1840–73).
[10] Add MS 44644, f. 69.
[11] Reay was agreed on as Commissioner; Schreuder, 358–9.

2. New Guinea. See separate Mem.
3. Basuto draft. Par. released as to Cape contribution *over & above* Customs Duties.[1]
4. Ashburnham collection. C. of E. may buy the Stowe.[2]
5. Ld Ripon's displeasure: soothing dispatch will go. Nothing to report to the Queen?[3]
6. Reduction of army in Egypt.

June 13. [New Guinea]. Ld D. to prepare Draft on this basis:
1. Act of annexation null. 2. Annexation to Queensland appears inadmissable. 3. No facts before us at the present moment wh. wd. justify any measure of or tending towards annexation. (4. Admiralty to instruct Commodore Erskine to visit the coast & inform us). 5. Door to be left open to the Colonies to make case for it. (6. F.O. & Admiralty to apprise C.O. of their views (wh are adverse).[4]

New Guinea. Sketch for consideration.[5]
1. That we cannot advise H.M. to confirm or recognise the late so-called annexation. 2. That in consequence of the steps taken in Queensland, we inquire from the several Australian Colonies whether & on what grounds they deem it important for their own interests respectively that such an annexation, or any part or form thereof, should take effect. 3. whether they propose to make any provision, jointly or otherwise, for the pecuniary charge arising in consequence, or for the performance of the duties entailed in exercion of the powers to be assumed. 4. If not, what they contemplate or recommend in regard to these several points or any others belonging to the subject. 5. Reports when received from the Colonies to be considered by H.M. Govt.

14. Th.

Wrote to Ld Northbrook—Sir H. Ponsonby—Bp of Lincoln—Abp of Armagh—The Queen—Mr Hamilton—Mr Bass—P.M. General—& minutes. Nine to breakfast. Conversation with Count Corti—Sir W. Muir—Mr Knowles. Saw Mr H—Ld R.G—Mr Whitbread—Mr West. Dined at Mr Wests. H of C. 5–7¾ and 10¼–12½.[6] Read Vie de Talleyrand—Hermann Agha.

To Sir H. PONSONBY, the Queen's secretary, 14 June 1883.   Add MS 44546, f. 125.

Hamilton showed me your letter of June 11 from which it appears that the Queen thinks my recommendations for Church appointments have been all from the side of the High Church. This was so very widely different from my own recollections that I have made lists of the appointments to Bishoprics, Deaneries, & the most important parishes, as to which my memory is not clear & the recollections are sometimes made simply under the guidance of Bishops & principal incumbents.

The results are as follows.

There have been 30 important appointments. Out of them I have recommended 11 who would probably be called High Churchmen (*not one* of them, so far as I know, unsympathetic towards other portions of the Clergy), & 19 who are not.

On further examination it will appear that the High Churchmen whom I take to be a

---

[1] Gladstone's draft at Add MS 44644, f. 72.   [2] See 14 Apr. 83.
[3] Nothing reported to the Queen; CAB 41/17/11.
[4] Add MS 44644, f. 73. Decision to disallow Queensland's annexation, though with proviso for reconsideration, announced by Derby on 2 July; *H* 281. 16 and R. C. Thompson, *Australian imperialism in the Pacific* (1980), 66.
[5] Add MS 44644, f. 74.   [6] Questions; corrupt practices; *H* 280. 557.

decided majority of the Clergy as well as a decided minority of my recommendations—have gone as a rule to the places of hard work & little pay.

For example they have got 5 out of 10 *parochial* recommendations; but, out of 16 appointments to Deaneries & Canonries, they have received 4, & those, with the exception of Mr. Furse, the worst. I could supply you with the lists in detail.

One admission I must make: the evidently Broad Churchmen are too large a proportion of the non-High, & the Low Churchmen rather too small, a disproportion which I should hope to remove, but undoubtedly the Low Churchmen of the present day has [*sic*] a poorer share than half a century ago of the working energy of the Church.

All these terms High, Low & Broad are rather repugnant to me, but I use them as a currency of tokens with which it is difficult to dispense.

[P.S.] As to my classification of the men I will only say I think it is one which Dean Wellesley would have been ready to countersign.

I am concerned to hear that the Queen does not make very rapid progress at Balmoral.

15. *Fr.*

Wrote to Ld Granville—Ld Dufferin—Ld Hartington—Mr Jas Patten—The Queen—Mr R. Lawley—Mr Heneage MP—& minutes. Saw Mr H—Ld RG—Att. General—Sir W. James. Read Renan Souvenirs—Hermann Agha—Vie de Talleyrand. H of C. 2¼-7.[1] Dined at Sir W. James's.

To Mrs. O'SHEA, 15 June 1883., '*Private*'.[2]   Add MS 44546, f. 126.

I hope you will indulgently let me ask you to substitute tomorrow a letter for an interview.[3]

I have not great faith in my power of carrying accurately in my memory points perhaps of nicety, in which others with myself are interested and have a joint responsibility, though if it were a matter known to be within my own discretion I would not interfere with your choice of a medium for communication.

16. *Sat.* [*Dollis Hill*]

Wrote to Mr Robinson—Ld R. Churchill—Ld Lansdowne—Ld Kimberley—& minutes. Off at four to Dollis Hill, & most kind friends there. Saw Mr H—Ld RG—Ld Granville—Do *cum* Ld Derby. Calls. Missed Hunter (12) [R?]. Read Mercy d'Argenteau—Vie de Talleyrand.

To LORD RANDOLPH CHURCHILL, M.P., 16 June 1883.   Churchill MSS 121.

On Lord Granville's return from Warwickshire, I have at once consulted with him on the subject of your letter of the 12th. I do not think that I can make any substantial addition to the statement which you have cited from a report of my speech in the House of Commons, unless it be that in any step the Government may take they will have due regard to the position of the Khedive as the Ruler of Egypt, and to the

[1] Statement on business; *H* 280. 694.
[2] In Hammond, 365. Mrs. O'Shea this day requested a meeting: 'I can assure you I do not desire to ask for the Viceroyalty! or any favour'; Add MS 44269, f. 179.
[3] Mrs. O'Shea replied, 18 June, ibid., f. 182, that she had wished to relate Parnell's proposals for this Session on registration, Labourers Bill, Poor Law Bill.

responsibilities under which they lie with reference to the peace & welfare of that country.[1]

17. 4 S. Trin.

Willesden Ch mg (with H.C.) & evg. Read Essex Rector (finished) on Age of Mankind—Renan, Souvenirs—Mrs Booth on the Salvation Army.[2]

18. M. [London]

Back to London. Wrote to Att. General—Ld Advocate—Mr Bright—Ld Kimberley—The Queen—and minutes. Read Vie de Talleyrand II & III. Saw Mr H—Ld R.G. l.l.l.—The Speaker—Mr Robinson—Ld Granville—Mr Escott—Mr Morley MP. H of C. $4\frac{3}{4}$–$8\frac{1}{2}$ and $9\frac{1}{2}$–$12\frac{1}{2}$. Difficult speech on Bright's case.[3]

To Sir H. JAMES, attorney general, 18 June 1883.   James MS M45. 59.

I do not know whether you have solved the riddle of undue spiritual influence, & I beg you in no case to answer this note, which I write for the chance, however remote, of its being useful.[4]

It occurred to me as worth consideration whether undue spiritual influence, or the use of spiritual menaces, could be dealt with in your *legislation*, on the principle on which as I understand the law deals with anti-Christian or anti-religious reasonings—i.e. that as long as the language is serious, decent, argumentative it is allowed—but not when it disregards decency and common feeling and becomes an appeal to the passions, whether of fear or any other.

The one endeavouring to enlighten the action of the understanding, the other to supersede it.

19. Tu.

Wrote to Ly Ailesbury—Ld Sydney—Mr Hutton—Mrs O'Shea[5]—The Queen l.l.— H.H. The Khedive of Egypt (dft)[6]—and minutes. H of C. $2\frac{1}{2}$–$3\frac{1}{2}$, $5\frac{1}{2}$–7 & 12–$12\frac{3}{4}$.[7] Saw Mr H—Ld R.G.—Chancr of Exr—Lady Reay—Mad. Neruda—Count H. Bismarck—Prince Cantacuzene[8] & others. Dinner party, and evening party afterwards. Read Vie de Talleyrand—Mercy d'Argenteau.

20. Wed.

Wrote to Ld Derby—and minutes. Dined at Ld Cowper's: a choice & charming party. Saw Mr H—Ld RG—Count Menabrea—Mr Hutton—Sir S. Northcote.

---

[1] Churchill wrote this day at great length, using materials supplied by W. S. Blunt, offering evidence for his charge that the Khedive was 'the real author' of the massacres in Alexandria in June 1882; Add MS 44481, f. 246. See 26 June 82, *PP* 1884 lxxxviii. 263 and FO 78/3617.

[2] C. Booth, *The Salvation Army in relation to Church and State* (1883).

[3] Northcote's motion that Bright's Birmingham speech on the conservative party was a breach of privilege, defeated; *H* 280. 819.

[4] James this day amended his Corrupt Practices Bill, in the light of Parnell's proposal on 15 June, to include 'spiritual injury' as a forbidden threat; *H* 280. 843.

[5] Harmony achieved on the 'spiritual injury' amndt. (see 18 June 83n.); Add MS 44546, f. 128.

[6] Granville excised references to Churchill; Add MS 44481, f. 283 and Ramm II, ii. 55–7.

[7] Corrupt practices; *H* 280. 929.   [8] See 18 June 84.

Read Vie de Talleyrand (III)—Mercy d'Argenteau. Drove down to the Crystal Palace for the second act of today's Handel celebration. A marvellous piece of organisation, but in its musical results mixed.

To LORD DERBY, colonial secretary, 20 June 1883.   Add MS 44546, f. 128.

It was most unfortunate that your note arrived at the very moment when I was fastened to an engagement which I could not break.

The subject was not wholly new to me, as Lady Mary told me last night the substance of the Telegram from the Transvaal.

Subject to correction, I am rather averse to working the subject here. First I do not see how we can deal with the Bechuana question here, as the High Commission & the Cape are concerned. Secondly I think that if men come here from the Transvaal they will come closely tied up with instructions leaving them little or no elbow room so that they would continually refer & make very slow work indeed. Thirdly it is awkward in this matter which has become so polemical again to shift our ground.

There may be prejudicing reasons the other way but I send you my notions uncorrected.

Could we meet tomorrow before rather than after luncheon. I want to go & inquire in the afternoon for J. Manners of whom Northcote gives a bad account.

21. Th.

Wrote to Duc d'Aumale—Count Bylandt—Mr Cross MP—The Speaker—The Queen—and minutes. H of C. 5–8 and $10\frac{3}{4}$–$12\frac{1}{2}$.[1] Dined at Sir T. May's. Saw Mr H—Ld RG—Ld Granville—Sir A. Otway—Do *cum* Ld Derby—The Speaker—Ld Reay—Sir T.E. May (on H. of C. prospects)—Chr of Exchr. Read Vie de Talleyrand—Mercy d'Argenteau.

22. Fr.

Wrote to Rev. Mr Overton—Sir H. Ponsonby—Ld Lorne—Mr Dodson—The Queen—and minutes. Dined with Lucy. Saw Mr H—Ld R.G. l.l.—Ld Granville—Mr Mitchell Henry. H of C. $3\frac{3}{4}$–7 and 9–$12\frac{1}{2}$.[2] Read Mercy d'Argenteau—Vie de Talleyrand—Hermann Agha (finished).

Memorandum to LORD DERBY, colonial secretary.   Add MS 44141, f. 116.
22 June 1883.

Not knowing the opinion of Lord Derby on these papers, or of Lord Kimberley who made the arrangement with Cetywayo, I only observe for the present 1. That while the case is made to turn on the conduct of Cetewayo, we have no report or information on that conduct from the Resident with Cetewayo, who ought I presume to be the principal witness; 2. The paper suggests various doubts as to the wisdom of retaining a Reserve. It was done I think very much to meet the views of Sir H. Bulwer who always seems to me to treat the Zulu question with a paramount regard to the interests of Natal.

WEG June 22. 83.

---

[1] Questions, corrupt practices; *H* 280. 1145.
[2] Corrupt practices, Ireland; *H* 280. 1274.

To Sir H. PONSONBY, the Queen's secretary, 22 June 1883.[1]   Add MS 44546, f. 128.
'*Private*'.

Re Chamberlain's speech; I am sorry to say I had not read the report until I was
warned by your letters to Granville & to Hamilton; for my sight does not now allow me to
read largely the small type of newspapers. I have now read it, & I must at once say with
deep regret. We had done our best to keep the Bright celebration in harmony with the
general tone of opinion by the mission which Granville kindly undertook.

I am the more sorry about this speech, because Chamberlain has, this year in particular, shown both tact & talent in the management of questions not polemical such as the
Bankruptcy Bill.

The speech is open to exception from three points of view, as I think: first in relation to
Bright, secondly in relation to the Cabinet, thirdly, & most especially, in relation to the
Crown, to which the speech did not indicate the consciousness of his holding any special
relation. I am considering, & I have consulted with one or two of my colleagues, what best
to do in the matter, either by & through Mr. Chamberlain himself, or otherwise.

23. Sat. [*Coombe Hurst*]

Wrote to Ld Granville—Bp of Carlisle—The Queen—Sir W. Harcourt—Sir R.
Cross, & minutes. Read Mercy d'Argenteau—Vie de Talleyrand. Off at 4 to
Combe Hurst.[2] Cabinet 12–3. Saw Mr H—Ld RG.

Cabinet. Sat. June 23. 83. Noon.[3]
1. Ashburnham Collection. Accept Stowe division for *45 m[ille]*.
2. Transvaal Convention. New facts: a. Offer of Transvaal to send. b. Desire of Cape
Govt. not to be the scene. WEG to announce acceptance of offer of Transvaal to send a
person with full powers (subject to Volksraad) as sent (before Monday).[4] Inquire further
as to views of Cape respecting Bechuana Land.
3. Notice to be given on *Monday* that we will ask the House to give us the 9 PM sitting
on Tuesdays.
4. Suez Canal. Terms of Childers as to drop of rates in 29 v. 5 to be maintained.[5] Question for Monday. Comparison of views largely entered upon. Harmony of views on
many points. Questions of great moment still in review including the revenue[?] &
amount of reduction of rates. Not advantageous to make any statement now. Before a
binding agreement is arrived at, public announcement will be made.[6]
5. Irish Tramways. C. of E. merely to guarantee a minimum rate of interest on examined
& sound undertakings. 3 years experiment.
6. Irish Land Commn. & Land Committee. Commn. be advised not to send in any reply
to the Committee. (But to the Govt. later if needful).

---

[1] Printed in Morley, iii. 112. For Chamberlain's speech at the Bright jubilee on 13 June, see
Garvin, i. 393–5.
[2] Near Kingston; one of the seats of Mrs Vyner, whom he met in Cannes (see 30 Jan. 83).
[3] Add MS 44644, f. 77. Note from Gladstone: 'Is New Guinea ready today?'; Derby replied: 'No.
We settled the general principle. I will send you the draft . . .'; ibid., f. 79. See 13 June 83.
[4] i.e. that the Transvaal should send an 'ambassador' to Britain to discuss the Convention, rather
than Britain send a Commissioner to South Africa.
[5] i.e. in the negotiations for the Provisional Agreement on the development of the Canal, involving a) a second canal and b) a reduction of rates.
[6] Notes for answer given by Gladstone to W. M. Torrens on 25 June; *H* 280. 1430.

24. 5 S. Trin.

Ch. mg & evg—Much interesting conversation aft. and evg. Lady M. Vyner,[1] Mrs Vyner, H. Cowper. Read Renan, Souvenirs—Kn. Little on the Passion[2]—Adams, Bible Scientific.[3]

25. M. [London]

Wrote to D. of Norfolk—Mr Stewart MP—The Queen—Mr Woodall MP.—& minutes. Read English Letters—Vie de Talleyrand (finished III). Meeting at Marlborough House on School of studies at Athens. 18 speeches in an hour.[4] Saw Mr H—Ld R.G—Ld Granville—Sir C. Dilke—Ld Hartington—Chancr of Exr—Mr Lefevre. H. of C. 5-8½ & 9½-12½.[5]

26. Tu.

Wrote to Sir Jas Paget—Ld Carlingford—Ld Spencer—Ld R. Churchill—Rev. S.E.G.—Sir H. Ponsonby—The Queen—Ld Granville—& minutes. Twelve to dinner, & large evening party. I used the aid of a stick. Saw Mr H—Ld R.G—Sir W. Harcourt—Count Karolyi—Mr Richard MP—Mr Norwood MP. & others. Conversation with Duc d'Aumale. Read Mercy d'Argenteau—Scoones, Engl. Letters.[6] Began Lady Cowper's Diary.[7] H of C. 2¼-6½.[8]

To LORD CARLINGFORD, lord president and lord privy seal, 26 June 1883.   Add MS 44546, f. 129.

Please to look at the motions of Lubbock and Geo. Hamilton for Friday evening in relation to a new Department of Education.[9] Mundella is I believe not producible at a late hour in the evening[10] & I shall have to look to them. Please to put down what you think the strongest heads of objection. I am assuming that you do object, and I think the assumption is pretty safe.[11]

To LORD RANDOLPH CHURCHILL, M.P., 26 June 1883.   Churchill MSS 129.

I have to acknowledge your letter of this day.[12]

We have taken steps to make sure the fulfilment of our pledges with respect to the trial of Ahmed Khandeel and we have no reason to suppose there will be any deviation from

[1] Lady Mary Vyner, 1809-92; da. of 2nd earl de Grey and R. C. de G. Vyner's mother.
[2] W. J. Knox Little, *The mystery of the passion* (1881).
[3] C. C. Adams, *The Bible: a scientific revelation* (1882).
[4] Meeting from which sprang the British School though govt. declined funds; see H. Waterhouse, *The British School at Athens* (1986), 7, and 6 Feb. 83.
[5] Questions, corrupt practices; *H* 280. 1428.   [6] See 7 Mar. 83n.
[7] M. Cowper, *Diary of Mary, Countess Cowper* (1864).
[8] Questions, corrupt practices; *H* 280. 1555.   [9] See 29 June 83.
[10] Mundella's illness, convenient to Gladstone, as Mundella rather sympathised with the proposals; see Armytage, 219-20.
[11] Carlingford replied, 28 June, Add MS 44123, f. 173, sending 'rough notes' on the motions, hostile to them: 'the notion of a great extension of State control over all education from top to bottom is very distasteful & alarming to many people'; the duke of Richmond also opposed.
[12] Add MS 44481, f. 308: is delay in execution possible if Ahmed Khandeel found guilty? Churchill sent further papers on 30 June; ibid., f. 313 and Churchill MSS 131, 134.

the course of justice in regard to him, while we have agents on the spot who would at once notice such deviation.

Were it accidentally to occur we believe it would be corrected, but to anticipate it would not in our view be either just or politic, and we cannot make a demand which would imply alike the title and the necessity to review the trial.

To Sir H. PONSONBY, the Queen's secretary, 26 June 1883.[1]   Add MS 45724, f. 142.

It appeared to me in considering the case of Mr. Chamberlain's speech that by far the best correction would be found, if a natural opportunity should offer, in a speech differently coloured from himself. I found also that he was engaged to preside on Saturday next at the dinner of the Cobden Club. I addressed myself therefore to this point, and Mr. Chamberlain will revert, on that occasion, to the same line of thought. On seeing the report I shall be in a condition to form my opinion how far the object in view has been attained.

27. Wed.

Wrote to Ld Granville—Mr Chamberlain—Ld Coleridge—Sir F. Doyle—Sir A. Gordon—Sir W. Jenner—& minutes. Read Mercy d'Argenteau. Dined at Sir J. Goldsmid's. Saw Mr H—Ld RG—Sir Jas Paget—Lady Goldsmid. 4–7. Expedition to the Tower, guided by Mr Lefevre. Of deep but in the main very mournful interest.

28. Th.

Wrote to Ld Albemarle—Mr Johnston—The Queen—Lady Breadalbane—Ld Lyons—& minutes. H of C. $4\frac{3}{4}$–8 and after midn.[2] Saw Mr H—Ld RG—Ld Granville—Mr Fagan—Ld Houghton—Mr Hutton—Sir J. Lubbock—O'Gorman Mahon. Read Scoones, Letters—Mercy d'Argenteau (finished I.) Dined with the Brownlows: much pleasant conversation with her & with Lady Ampthill.

29. Fr.

Wrote to Lady Lyndhurst—Lady S. Milton—Ld Coleridge—Ld Spencer—Mr Talbot MP—Mr Vivian MP—Mr Playfair MP—Mr Carbutt MP—The Queen—and minutes. Dined at Sir W. James's. Saw Mr H—Ld RG—Sir C. Dilke—Chancr of Exr—Sir W. Jenner—Ld E. Clinton. H of C. 2–$6\frac{1}{4}$ and 9–1. Spoke at some length on Educn Dept.[3] Read Mercy d'Argenteau—Scoones, English Letters. Drive with C.G.

To LORD SPENCER, Viceroy of Ireland, 29 June 1883.   Althorp MSS K6.

I hope we shall be able to weather the Education storm,[4] with your & other aid. The atmosphere of the House of Commons is now calm, & the horizon for the time clear.

---

[1] Printed in Morley, iii. 112, which conflates this with a later letter.
[2] Questions; supply; *H* 280. 1708.·
[3] Opposing motions on a ministry of education, chiefly on constitutional rather than educational grounds; *H* 280. 1945.
[4] Spencer wrote, 28 June, Add MS 44310, f.109, opposing change in the education dept., and reporting generally improved climate of Ireland.

I am rejoiced at your account of Ireland. My doctrine always is, let us have legality (which you under God have given us) & I have no fear of any thing that is worked compatibly with that condition.

It is also to be borne in mind that, though Parnell is a Sphinx, the most probable reading of him is that he works for & with the law as far as he dare. I have even doubt whether he hates the Government. And I am persuaded that there is a good deal of underground gratitude in the mind of the Irish people; though I will not say it may not be prevented by other considerations from coming much to the surface for practical purposes.

We look forward with pleasure to the 10th when you & Lady Spencer dine here.

To C. R. TALBOT, M.P., 29 June 1883.   Add MS 44546, f. 131.

The memorial from Cardiff which you have forwarded to me[1] has had my serious attention, and I will bring it under the notice of Sir W. Harcourt.

I believe we have been right in allowing a local principle to prevail as to Sunday Closing but there are obvious inconveniences in diversity of practice and the way of escape from them is not at present plain.

30. Sat. [*The Durdans, Epsom*]

Wrote to The Queen l.l.—Sir H. Ponsonby—Ld Lyons—Mr Johnson—Mrs Th.— Mr Forster—& minutes. Saw Mr H—Ld RG—Ld Granville—do *cum* Mr Childers—Mr Doulton & Mr Tinworth at Lady James's Tea. Read Mercy d'Argenteau—Account of Sadlers Wells—Blessington Correspondence.[2] Speaker's great dinner.[3] Conversation with Abp of Canterbury—Mrs Benson— Lady Salisbury. Off to the Durdans at 11.55.

To LORD LYONS, ambassador to France, 30 June 1883.   Add MS 44546, f. 132.

A Bargain! and there is an end of it, till the 25th.[4]

I have just been discussing with Granville & the Chancellor of the Exchequer the next stop in the Canal business. We think it will be well in many ways to get Charles Lesseps over here (with his father or otherwise I am not quite sure) to prosecute the matter. We can offer pecuniary assistance of some real value: & we are very anxious to conclude if we can do it with a fair regard to the views & interests of the mercantile community, who in this case represent the *consumer*, that is to say the world.[5]

---

[1] Not found.

[2] Probably R. R. Madden, *The literary life and correspondence of the Countess of Blessington* (1855).

[3] Social function; Prince of Wales etc.; *T.T.*, 2 July 1883, 9f.

[4] Proposed day for meeting: 25 July; Add MS 44481, f. 310.

[5] For the Provisional Agreement, see 7 July 83; for the subsequent row leading to its withdrawal, see 13, 19-23 July 83.

WHERE WAS HE?
January 1881–June 1883

The following list shows where the diarist was each night; he continued at each place named until he moved on to the next. Names of the owners or occupiers of great houses have been given in brackets on the first mention of the house.

1 January 1881	London	13 August	Mentmore, Leighton Buzzard (Rosebery)
5 February	High Elms, Farnborough (Sir J. Lubbock)	15 August	London
		24 August	The Castle, Deal (Sydney)
7 February	London		
19 February	Brighton	3 September	Walmer Castle (Granville)
21 February	London		
5 March	St George's Hill (Sir F. Egerton)	7 September	London
		10 September	Hawarden
7 March	London	6 October	Spring Bank, Headingley, Leeds (J. Kitson)
19 March	The Durdans, Epsom (Rosebery)		
		11 October	London
21 March	London	14 October	Hawarden
9 April	Hawarden	26 October	Knowsley Park (Derby)
25 April	London	29 October	Hawarden
7 May	The Durdans	8 November	London
9 May	London	14 November	Hawarden
21 May	Pembroke Lodge (Lady Russell)	30 November	Windsor
		3 December	Hawarden
23 May	London		
3 June	The Durdans	5 January 1882	London
18 June	Windsor	10 January	Hawarden
20 June	London	24 January	London
25 June	Littleburys, Mill Hill (Aberdeen)	8 March	Windsor
		9 March	London
27 June	London	1 April	The Durdans
2 July	Littlebury's	4 April	Hawarden
4 July	London	17 April	London
9 July	York Lodge (Grant Duff)	22 April	The Durdans
		24 April	London
11 July	London	26 April	Windsor
16 July	Windsor	28 April	London
18 July	London	29 April	St. George's Hill
23 July	Littlebury's	1 May	London
25 July	London	11 May	Chatsworth (Devonshire)
30 July	Littlebury's		
1 August	London	12 May	London
6 August	Littlebury's	20 May	Dollis Hill (Aberdeen)
8 August	London	22 May	London

27 May	The Durdans	23 September	Hawarden
1 June	London	28 September	Penmaenmawr
3 June	The Durdans	3 October	Hawarden
5 June	London	20 October	London
10 June	Dollis Hill	5 December	Cuffnell's, Lyndhurst
12 June	London		(Harcourt)
17 June	Dollis Hill	9 December	London
19 June	London	16 December	Hawarden
24 June	Eton College		
26 June	London		
1 July	Dollis Hill	16 January 1883	London
3 July	London	17 January	On train
8 July	Dollis Hill	18 January	Château Scott, Cannes
10 July	London		(Wolverton)
15 July	Windsor	26 February	On train
17 July	London	27 February	British Embassy, Paris
22 July	Dollis Hill	2 March	London
24 July	London	24 March	Holmbury (Leveson-
29 July	Farnham Castle (Bishop		Gower)
	of Winchester)	29 March	London
31 July	London	30 March	Sandringham (Prince of
5 August	Dollis Hill		Wales)
7 August	London	2 April	London
18 August	Osborne House (The	12 May	Hawarden
	Queen)	23 May	London
19 August	On ship	9 June	Berkhampstead (Lady S.
22 August	Iwerne Minster (Wol-		Spencer)
	verton)	11 June	London
25 August	London	16 June	Dollis Hill
29 August	Hawarden	18 June	London
13 September	London	23 June	Coombe Hurst (Mrs.
16 September	Hawarden		Vyner)
21 September	The Coppice, Henley	25 June	London
	(Phillimore)	30 June	The Durdans

LIST OF LETTERS BY CORRESPONDENT, PUBLISHED IN VOLUME X

A note on the editing of these letters will be found with the equivalent list in Volume VII.

Abbot, Rev. Dr. E. A.
  17 September 1882
Aberdeen, Lady, see Gordon
Acland, Dr. H. W.
  2 August 1881
Acland, Sir T. D., *M.P.*
  13 January 1882
  28 March 1882
  7 August 1882
Acton, J. E. E. D., 1st Baron Acton
  14 December 1881
  26 December 1881
Allon, Rev. H.
  28 March 1881
Anson, Canon F.
  19 September 1882
Argyll, Duke of, see Campbell
Arnold, Matthew
  8 July 1881
  5 April 1882

Bagehot, Mrs.
  25 April 1881
Balfour, J. B., *M.P.*
  15 June 1882
Bancroft, Professor G., *historian*
  11 August 1882
Bankes, J. S.
  7 April 1882
Baring, T. G., 1st Earl of Northbrook
  3 May 1882
  5 July 1882
  13 July 1882
Bayly, Miss A. E., *novelist*
  27 April 1883
Bedford, duke of, see Russell
Benson, Archbishop E. W.
  19 March 1883
Bessborough, Lord, see Ponsonby
Bevan, Rev. W. L.
  13 May 1883

Blennerhassett, Sir R., *M.P.*
  17 September 1881
Blunt, W. S.
  20 January 1882
Bond, E. A.
  2 May 1881
Bradlaugh, C., *M.P.*
  20 June 1881
  2 July 1881
  18 February 1882
Brand, H. B. W., *M.P.*, 1st Viscount Hampden
  20 January 1881
  7 June 1881
  3 July 1881
  23 August 1881
  18 January 1882
  31 January 1882
  1 April 1882
  7 May 1882
  3 July 1882
  12 August 1882
  17 October 1882
Bright, John, *M.P.*
  29 September 1881
  22 October 1881
  10 July 1882
  12 July 1882
  13 July 1882
  14 July 1882
Broadhurst, H., *M.P.*
  8 January 1881
  4 January 1882
  7 April 1882
Brodrick, W., 8th Viscount Midleton
  27 September 1881
Browne, Archdeacon R. W.
  16 April 1883
Bryce, J., *M.P.*
  23 October 1882

Colhurst, D. La Touche, *M.P.*
20 January 1881
Corry, M. W. L., 1st Baron Rowton
19 April 1881
Courtney, L. H., *M.P.*
27 November 1882
1 January 1883
Cowan, J., *chairman Midlothian Liberal Association*
30 May 1881
Cowper, F. T. De G., 7th Earl Cowper
4 June 1881
22 August 1881
1 September 1881
5 September 1881
9 September 1881
21 April 1882
26 April 1882
1 May 1882
2 May 1882
3 May 1882
Craven, Mrs. P. M. A. A., *author*
3 March 1883

Damer, H. J. R. Dawson-, 3rd Earl of Portarlington
2 September 1881
Darwin, C. R.
30 April 1881
Dawson, C., *Lord Mayor of Dublin*
11 October 1882
De Lisle, Miss M.,
18 June 1882
Derby, Earl of, see Stanley
Dilke, Sir C. W., 2nd Bart., *M.P.*
1 January 1881
28 July 1881
2 November 1881
1 January 1882
4 January 1882
31 May 1882
28 December 1882
31 December 1882
11 April 1883
Dodson, J. G., *M.P.*, 1st Baron Monk Bretton
19 January 1881
4 November 1881
21 November 1881
24 November 1881
10 January 1882
30 January 1882

11 March 1882
14 March 1882
13 November 1882
23 December 1882
Döllinger, J. J. I. von
19 October 1882
Donaldson, Professor J.
6 June 1883
Donnelly, I., *author*
11 March 1882
Douglas, F. R. Wemyss-Charteris-, Lord Elcho
31 January 1881
Douglas, J. S., 8th Marquis of Queensberry
18 April 1881
Doyle, Sir F. H. C.
22 October 1881
Duckham, T., *M.P.*
24 April 1883
Dufferin, 1st Earl of, see Hamilton

Elcho, Lord, see Wemyss-Charteris-Douglas

Fawcett, H., *M.P.*
28 March 1881
16 September 1882
8 May 1883
Fitzgerald, C. W., 4th Duke of Leinster
5 October 1881
Forster, W. E., *M.P.*
1 January 1881
10 January 1881
5 March 1881
6 March 1881
29 March 1881
4 April 1881
22 April 1881
15 May 1881
17 May 1881
31 May 1881
6 June 1881
27 August 1881
5 September 1881
8 September 1881
21 September 1881
27 September 1881
3 October 1881
4 October 1881
5 October 1881
9 October 1881
13 October 1881

6 March 1881
17 March 1881
22 March 1881
29 March 1881
14 April 1881
18 April 1881
15 May 1881
17 May 1881
25 May 1881
3 June 1881
4 June 1881
9 June 1881
12 June 1881
18 June 1881
24 June 1881
7 July 1881
29 July 1881
29 August 1881
26 September 1881
28 September 1881
29 September 1881
2 October 1881
4 October 1881
6 October 1881
19 October 1881
30 October 1881
3 November 1881
10 December 1881
3 January 1882
26 January 1882

16 April 1882
27 May 1882
12 July 1882
22 July 1882
23 August 1882
2 October 1882
5 October 1882
27 October 1882
24 November 1882
5 January 1883
9 January 1883
25 April 1883
8 May 1883
22 May 1883
Wolff, Sir H. D. C., *M.P.*
28 June 1882
28 October 1882
Wolseley, Sir G. J., *soldier*
15 September 1882
Wolverton, Lord, see Glyn
Wood, Sir C., 1st Viscount Halifax
9 February 1881
18 September 1881
20 May 1882
Woolner, T., *sculptor*
22 December 1881
29 December 1881

Zankof, D. K.
26 May 1881